The Heritage of World Civilizations

D0564998

The Heritage of
WORLD
CIVILIZATIONS

THIRD EDITION

Albert M. Craig HARVARD UNIVERSITY

William A. Graham HARVARD UNIVERSITY

Donald Kagan YALE UNIVERSITY

Steven Ozment HARVARD UNIVERSITY

Frank M. Turner YALE UNIVERSITY

VOLUME I
To 1600

Macmillan College Publishing Company

NEW YORK

A portion of this book previously appeared in *The Western
Heritage* by Donald Kagan, Steven Ozment, and Frank M.
Turner.

Earlier editions copyright © 1986 and 1990 by Macmillan
Publishing Company

Macmillan College Publishing Company
866 Third Avenue, New York, New York 10022

Macmillan College Publishing Company is part of
the Maxwell Communication Group of Companies.

Maxwell Macmillan Canada, Inc.
1200 Eglinton Avenue East
Suite 200
Don Mills, Ontario M3C 3N1

Library of Congress Cataloging-in-Publication Data

The Heritage of world civilizations / Albert M. Craig . . . [et al.].—
  3rd ed.
     p.   cm.
   Includes index.
   ISBN 0-02-325507-2
    1. Civilization—History.   I. Craig, Albert M.
  CB69.H45   1994   93-26716
  909—dc20   CIP

Printing 1 2 3 4 5 6 7 8   Year: 0 1 2 3 4 5 6 7 8 9

Acquisitions Editor: Robert Miller
Developmental Editor: David Chodoff
Production Supervisor: Sharon Lee
Production Manager: Nick Sklitsis
Text Designer: Pat Smythe
Cover Designer: Pat Smythe/Leslie Baker
Photo Researchers: Diana Gongora/Bob Shatz
Photo Editor: Chris Migdol

This book was set in Cheltenham Light typeface by York Graphic Services,
Inc., and was printed and bound by Rand McNally and Company.
The cover was printed by New England Book Components.

Preface

The interaction and interdependence of the nations and peoples of the world are greater today than in any previous era of history. People with differing cultural heritages and religious outlooks are being drawn into ever closer contact with one another. Economic, political, and military developments in one part of the world quickly affect millions of people in other parts. The vast expansion of markets for products as diverse as oil, electronics, and fast food have changed the standard of living virtually everywhere. And the problems that attend these changes—environmental pollution, overpopulation, and urban sprawl—affect every continent.

This situation is itself the result of a major historical development—the close of the European era of world history. Between approximately 1500 and the middle of the twentieth century, Europeans and their colonists in North America and elsewhere dominated the world through the strength of their political organization, economic productivity, and military might. That era came to an end during the third quarter of the twentieth century as the nations of Asia, the Near East, and Africa achieved new positions on the world scene. Their new political independence, their control over strategic natural resources (especially oil), the expansion of their economies (particularly those of the nations on the Pacific rim of Asia), and, in some cases, their access to nuclear weapons have changed the shape of world affairs.

All of us confront political and economic relationships unimagined even half a century ago. On this transformed world stage the students who read this book will spend their lives. These changing conditions demand that we approach history from a global perspective. This volume provides just that perspective. It is our hope that the study of world civilizations, by showing students the processes that have brought them and their neighbors together, will help them better understand and appreciate one another. Through the exploration of the diverse civilizations of the world, students should enter it better informed and more culturally sensitive.

We have aimed not merely to describe the world's civilizations, but also to convey an inner sense of what each civilization meant to those who lived in it. For that reason we have paid special attention to the emergence of the major religious traditions. These link present-day civilizations to their most ancient roots and continue to exert a powerful influence worldwide. We have also endeavored to bring a comparative perspective to our survey and to trace the threads of interaction that have linked civilizations throughout history.

Historians have recently brought a vast array of new tools and concepts to bear on the study of history. Our coverage has attempted to introduce students to various aspects of social and intellectual history as well as to the more traditional political and diplomatic coverage. We firmly believe that only through an appreciation of all pathways to understanding of the past can the real heritage of world civilizations be claimed.

Changes in the Third Edition

The third edition of *The Heritage of World Civilizations* includes several major revisions designed to enhance the book's global and comparative perspective.

- Five "Comparative Perspectives" essays have been added. Each of these essays, which are spread through the book and fall between chapters, looks at a particular topic from a comparative perspective. The five topics are: (1) Writing, Literacy, and Orality; (2) Ancient Slavery; (3) Family Life West and East in the Premodern Era; (4) Technology and History; and (5) Global Democratization.

- Coverage of Africa has been greatly expanded. Two chapters—8 and 19—devoted to that continent have been added, and the material on Africa in Chapters 33 and 39 has been revised and updated.
- Substantial new material has been added in Chapters 1 and 23 on native civilizations of the Americas.
- The material on Latin America in Chapters 23, 27, 32, and 39 has been extensively revised.
- Coverage of the Middle Ages in Europe has been revised with new sections on the Byzantine Empire (Chapter 14), medieval Russia (Chapter 15), Pope Innocent III (Chapter 15), slavery in the Renaissance (Chapter 17), and the social history of the Reformation (Chapter 18).
- Chapters 38 and 39 on the world since World War II have been substantially rewritten to reflect the dramatic events of the past decade.
- New material on social history has been added throughout the text.
- A cross-reference feature has been added to selected primary source documents to call attention to documents elsewhere in the book dealing with similar issues from other times and cultures.
- Many new maps have been added, and all maps have been redrafted in two colors for this edition.

Readers familiar with earlier editions will also notice that this edition has been completely redesigned in a handsome, two-color format.

Pedagogical Elements

Many features of the text make it accessible to students and reinforce key concepts.

- *Part essays* open each of the seven major sections of the book. These serve to preview the coverage in the subsequent chapters and highlight major trends and movements.
- *Part timelines* show the major events in five regions—Europe, the Near East and India, East Asia, Africa, and the Americas—side by side.
- *Comparative Perspectives* essays examine important topics from a cross-cultural perspective.
- *Chapter outlines* on the opening page of each chapter help students organize the content of the chapter before reading and serve for review after reading.
- *Primary source documents* include selections from sacred books, poems, philosophy, political manifestos, letters, and travel accounts. These acquaint students with the raw material of history and pro-

vide an intimate contact with the people of the past and their concerns. Selected documents have a *cross reference* feature alerting students to documents elsewhere in the text that treat similar issues.

- *In World Perspective* sections conclude each chapter and place important developments in the chapter in the context of contemporary developments in the rest of the world.
- *Color portfolios* with photographs and interpretive essays treat the major world religions—Judaism, Hinduism, Buddhism, Christianity, Islam—and contemporary religion.

We should note that most scholarship on China uses the Wade-Giles system of romanization for Chinese names and terms. In order that students may be able to move easily from the present text to advanced works of scholarship in Chinese history, we have used the Wade-Giles system throughout. China today, however, uses another system known as *pinyin.* Virtually all Western newspapers have adopted it. Therefore, for Chinese history since 1949 we have included the *pinyin* spellings in parentheses after the Wade-Giles.

Also, we have followed the most accurate currently accepted English transliterations of Arabic words. For example, today *Koran* is being replaced by the more accurate *Qur'an;* similarly *Muhammad* is preferable to *Mohammed* and *Muslim* to *Moslem.* We have not tried to distinguish the letters *'ayn* and *hamza;* both are rendered by a simple apostrophe ('), as in *Shi'ite.*

With regard to Sanskritic transliteration, we have not distinguished linguals and dentals, and both palatal and lingual "s" are rendered "sh," as in *Shiva* and *Upanishad.*

Teaching Supplements

To help ease the burden of teaching such a comprehensive course as world civilization, we have made available several very useful supplements.

- An *Instructor's Manual* prepared by Perry Rogers, Ph.D., Ohio State University, provides summary and multiple-choice questions for each part essay; chapter summaries; outlines of key points and concepts; identification questions; multiple-choice and essay questions to be used for tests; and a suggested list of relevant films and videos.
- A *Study Guide,* also prepared by Perry Rogers, includes chapter summaries, key concepts, identification questions, short-answer exercises, and essay questions.

- A *Test Bank* and *Computerized Test Bank* provide thousands of test items. The computerized version allows instructors to choose various test configurations and add their own questions.
- *Map transparencies* of maps from the text provide strong visual support for lectures.
- A *Computerized Study Guide* presents students with review questions that help them assess their understanding of the material in the text.

Acknowledgments

We are grateful to the many scholars and teachers whose thoughtful and often detailed comments helped shape this revision:

Wayne Ackerson, *Salisbury State University*
Jack Martin Balcer, *Ohio State University*
Charmarie J. Blaisdell, *Northeastern University*
Chun-shu Chang, *University of Michigan, Ann Arbor*
William J. Courteney, *University of Wisconsin*
James B. Crowley, *Yale University*
Bruce Cummings, *University of Chicago*
Stephen F. Dale, *Ohio State University, Columbus*
Raymond Van Dam, *University of Michigan, Ann Arbor*
Bill Donovan, *Loyola College of Maryland*
Suzanne Gay, *Oberlin College*
Katheryn L. Green, *University of Wisconsin, Madison*
David Griffiths, *University of North Carolina, Chapel Hill*
David Kieft, *University of Minnesota*
David Lelyveld, *Columbia University*
Jan Lewis, *Rutgers University, Newark*
James C. Livingston, *College of William and Mary*
Richard L. Moore, Jr., *St. Augustine's College*
Robin S. Oggins, *Binghamton University*
Louis A. Perez, Jr., *University of South Florida*
Cora Ann Presley, *Tulane University*
Norman Ravitch, *University of California, Riverside*
Philip F. Riley, *James Madison University*
Thomas Robisheaux, *Duke University*
Dankwart A. Rustow, *City University of New York*
James J. Sack, *University of Illinois at Chicago*
Daniel Scavone, *University of Southern Indiana*
Charles C. Stewart, *University of Illinois*
Harry L. Watson, *Loyola College of Maryland*
Paul Varley, *Columbia University*

Finally, we would like to thank the dedicated people at Macmillan who helped produce this revision: our acquisitions editor, Robert Miller; our development editor, David Chodoff; our photo researchers, Diana Gongora, Robert Schatz, and Chris Migdol; Pat Smythe, who was responsible for the new design of this edition; Sharon Lee, production supervisor; and Nick Sklitsis, production manager.

About the Authors

Albert M. Craig is the Harvard-Yenching Professor of History at Harvard University, where he has taught since 1959. A graduate of Northwestern University, he took his Ph.D. at Harvard University. He has studied at Strasbourg University, and at Kyoto, Keio, and Tokyo universities in Japan. He is the author of *Chóshú in the Meiji Restoration* (1961), and, with others, of *East Asia, Tradition and Transformation* (1978). He is the editor of *Japan, A Comparative View* (1973) and co-editor of *Personality in Japanese History* (1970). At present he is engaged in research on the thought of Fukuzawa Yukichi. For eleven years (1976–1987) he was the director of the Harvard-Yenching Institute. In 1988 he was awarded the Order of the Rising Sun by the Japanese government.

William A. Graham is professor of the History of Religion and Islamic Studies, director of the Center for Middle Eastern Studies, and master of Currier House at Harvard University. He has taught there for twenty years in the Department of Near Eastern Languages and Civilizations. He is the author of *Divine Word and Prophetic Word in Early Islam* (1977), which was awarded an American Council of Learned Societies prize in the History of Religions in 1977–1978. His most recent book is *Beyond the Written Word: Oral Aspects of Scripture in the History of Religion* (1987). He studied for his B.A. in comparative literature (Classics, German, French) as a Morehead Scholar at the University of North Carolina in Chapel Hill, and for the A.M. and Ph.D. degrees in the comparative study of religion as a Woodrow Wilson and Danforth Graduate Fellow at Harvard University. He is the recipient of John Simon Guggenheim (1981) and Alexander von Humboldt (1982) research fellowships.

Donald Kagan is Bass Professor of History and Classics and Western Civilization at Yale University, where

he has taught since 1969. He received the A.B. degree in history from Brooklyn College, the M.A. in classics from Brown University, and the Ph.D. in history from Ohio State University. During 1958–1959 he studied at the American School of Classical Studies as a Fulbright Scholar. He has received three awards for undergraduate teaching at Cornell and Yale. He is the author of a history of Greek political thought, *The Great Dialogue* (1965); a four-volume history of the Peloponnesian War, *The Origins of the Peloponnesian War* (1969); *The Archidamian War* (1974); *The Peace of Nicias and the Sicilian Expedition* (1981); *The Fall of the Athenian Empire* (1987); and a biography of Pericles, *Pericles of Athens and the Birth of Democracy* (1991). With Brian Tierney and L. Pearce Williams, he is the editor of *Great Issues in Western Civilization*, a collection of readings.

Steven Ozment is McLean Professor of Ancient and Modern History at Harvard University. He has taught Western Civilization at Yale, Stanford, and Harvard. He is the author of eight books. *The Age of Reform, 1250–1550* (1980) won the Schaff Prize and was nominated for the 1981 American Book Award. *Magdalena and Balthasar: An Intimate Portrait of Life in Sixteenth Century Europe* (1986) and *Three Behaim Boys: Growing Up in Early Modern Germany* (1990) were selections of the History Book Club, as is also his most recent book, *Protestants: The Birth of a Revolution*, an interpretation of the German Reformation.

Frank M. Turner is John Hay Whitney Professor of History at Yale University, where he served as University Provost from 1988 to 1992. He received his B.A. degree at the College of William and Mary and his Ph.D. from Yale. He has received the Yale College Award for Distinguished Undergraduate Teaching. He has directed a National Endowment for the Humanities Summer Institute. His scholarly research has received the support of fellowships from the National Endowment for the Humanities and the Guggenheim Foundation. He is the author of *Between Science and Religion: The Reaction to Scientific Naturalism in Late Victorian England* (1974), *The Greek Heritage in Victorian Britain* (1981), which received the British Council Prize of the Conference on British Studies and the Yale Press Governors Award, and *Contesting Cultural Authority: Essays in Victorian Intellectual Life* (1993). He has also contributed numerous articles to journals and has served on the editorial advisory boards of *The Journal of Modern History, Isis,* and *Victorian Studies.*

Brief Contents

Detailed Contents

Part I: The Coming of Civilization 1

Part II: Empires and Cultures of the Ancient World 82

Part III: Consolidation and Interaction of World Civilization

Part IV: The World in Transition 472

Part V: Enlightenment and Revolution in the West 744

Part VI: Into the Modern World 840

Documents

Maps

Color Plates

The Coming of Civilization

The way of life of prehistoric cave dwellers differed immensely from that of today's civilized world. Yet the few millennia in which we have been civilized are but a tiny fraction of the long span of human existence. Especially during the recent millennia, changes in our culture have far outpaced changes in our bodies. We live a highly organized and often sedentary life but still retain the emotional makeup and motor reflexes of primitive men and women.

Homo sapiens—modern humans—first appeared about one hundred thousand years ago. Since then, the pace of human control over the environment has constantly accelerated. It took us tens of thousands of years to learn to use fire and to make stone tools, to domesticate the dog, and to master the rudiments of agriculture. It took us another seven to nine thousand years to develop cities, systems of writing, then bronze and iron. Several hundred years later occurred the great religious and philosophical revolutions of the ancient world, followed by the empires of China, India, Iran, and Rome that straddled the B.C.–A.D. divide.

Now, two thousand years later, humans have unlocked the power of the atom, walked on the moon, and broken the genetic code. The pace of new discoveries continues to quicken, but the earliest advances are no less impressive than more recent ones. The invention of writing late in the fourth millennium B.C., for example, may have been a less complex task than the breaking of the genetic code in the twentieth century A.D., but it was probably more difficult.

The timetable for the development of river-valley civilizations varied. The Near Eastern cultures began earlier, followed by India and China. But the parallelism in stages of development is remarkable. First came agriculture and pottery; then cities, writing, and bronze; and, finally, iron and empire. In the Americas, the civilizations of Mesoamerica and the Andes followed a similar sequence. Does the logic of nature dictate that once agriculture develops, cities will arise in alluvial river valleys favorable to intensive cultivation? Was it inevitable that the firing of clay to produce pots would reduce metallic oxides and lead to the discovery of smelting? Did the formation of the aristocratic and priestly classes, who controlled the resources of cities, automatically lead to record keeping and writing?

That is to say, did agriculture set in motion a train of similar events in widely separated regions? Or, is diffusion a more likely cause? At least in Eurasia and Africa, if not between those continents and the Americas, is it not conceivable that contacts between the early civilizations were more numerous than we now imagine? The earliest written languages—the Sumerian cuneiform, the Egyptian hieroglyphs, and the Chinese ideographs—probably had independent origins. They are too dissimilar to be the result of diffusion. But what of seeds, bronze, and iron? Might not migrating peoples or wandering merchants have carried these items over long distances? Both hypotheses—diffusion and independent origins—are plausible. However, in the absence of evidence, a definitive answer cannot be given. Little remains even of the material culture of the men and women of these earliest civilizations. Understanding their lives is like reconstructing a dinosaur from a broken tooth and a fragment of jawbone.

In or near the same Eurasian and African river valleys that saw the birth of civilization occurred the religious and philosophical revolutions that permanently marked the world thereafter: monotheistic Judaism, from which would later develop the world religions of Christianity and Islam; Hinduism and Buddhism in southern Asia; and the philosophies of China and Greece. The simultaneity of their appearance was striking. The Hebrew prophets, Buddha, Confucius, and Socrates, if not all contemporaries, were grouped within a few hundred years of each other in the first millennium B.C. Most founders of the great religions based their teachings on intensely personal religious experiences, on experiences that cannot be analyzed in historical terms. Yet, we can examine their historical contexts and note certain similarities.

The coming of the bronze and iron ages—and we speak of bronze and iron partly as a shorthand for many complex developments—led to a series of political and spiritual crises of the early civilizations across the world. The founders of the great religions and philosophies responded to these crises with new visions of humanity's place in the universe, and with new and more universal ethics. It is their greater universalism that distinguishes the world religions from those centered more narrowly on a particular tribe or people. Of course, all religions spring from a common human impulse and treat the questions of how to live and what life means in the face of death. But Buddhism, Christianity, and Islam differed from the Shinto of Japan, the religions of the Egyptians or Mayas, or even the Zoroastrianism of ancient Iran in contending that their answers were true for all peoples and times. It was this universalism that made them missionary religions.

Similarly, the philosophies of China and Greece were more universal than previous systems of thought. Confucianism eventually spread to Korea, Japan, and Vietnam, countries whose customs were quite different from those of China. It became the basis for laws in these countries because its ethics transcended particular Chinese institutions.

Greek ideas played an equivalent role in the West. They joined Judaic concepts to form Christianity. The gospel according to Saint John starts: "In the beginning was the Word *(logos)*, and the Word was with God, and the Word was God." In Greek, *logos* means something like "universal principle" or "reason." Universal Greek conceptions also lay at the base of the Roman law code *(ius gentium)* used to govern provinces with different peoples and widely varying customs. This last example says something about the transition from the older civilizations to the empires of the ancient world. These empires, to be sure, were built by armies, not philosophies. But for their leaders to govern and their bureaucracies to function, they had to have philosophies and laws.

This Egyptian artist's painting from about 1350 B.C. portrays a young royal couple walking in a garden. [Bildarchiv Preussischer Kulturbesitz]

Birth of Civilization

1

Prehistory: Early Human Beings and Their Culture

Scientists estimate that the earth may be as much as six billion years old, that creatures very much like humans may have appeared three to five million years ago, and that our own species of human beings goes back at least one hundred thousand years. Humans are different from other animals in that they are capable of producing and passing on a culture. *Culture* may be defined as the ways of living built up by a group and passed on from one generation to another. It may include behavior, material things, ideas, institutions, and religious faith. The source of human creativity is our large and convoluted brain. We create ideas and institutions. We formulate our thoughts in speech, allowing us to transmit our culture to future generations. We also can bring together our fingers and thumb, enabling us to make and hold tools, The combination of speech and material invention was necessary for the development of human culture.

The anthropologist designates early human cultures by their tools. The earliest period is the Paleolithic (from Greek, "old stone") Age. In this immensely long period (from perhaps 600,000 to 10,000 B.C.), people were hunters, fishers, and gatherers, but not producers, of food. They learned to make and use tools of stone and of perishable materials like wood, to make and control fire, and to pass on what they learned in language. In the regions where civilization ultimately was born, people depended on nature for their food and were very vulnerable to attacks from wild beasts and to natural disasters. Their responses to troubles may have been rooted in fear of the unknown—of the uncertainties of human life or the overpowering forces of nature. Such fear is often one element in human recourse to magic as an effort

3

These paintings from the Paleolithic period are found on the roof of the Altamira cave in northern Spain. The upper animal, a bison, and the lower animal, a boar, were both targets of early hunters. [Bettmann Archive]

to coerce—or to religion to propitiate—superhuman forces often thought to animate or direct the natural world.

But preliterate human beings are, and were, also much closer to nature than more civilized peoples. This closeness to nature seems to be another primary reason for the evidence of religious faith and practice, as well as magic, that goes as far back as archaeology can take us. Fear or awe, exultation, gratitude, and empathy with the natural world must all have figured in the cave art and in the ritual practices, such as burial, that we find evidenced at Paleolithic sites around the globe. Human life itself is a kind of miracle. The concern in all known societies with life's major transitions—birth, puberty, marriage, and death—was probably a source of "rites of passage" among the earliest human beings as well. For example, the many figurines of pregnant women (or goddesses?) that have been found at prehistoric sites might have been used in rites aimed at ensuring fertility or successful childbirth. However, given the sparse evidence, all we can say is that the sense that there is more to the world than meets the eye—in other words, the religious response to the world—seems to be as old as humankind.

The style of life and the level of technology of the Paleolithic period could support only a sparsely settled society. If the hunters were too numerous, the available game would not suffice. In Paleolithic times, people were subject to the same natural and ecological constraints that today maintain a balance between wolves and deer in Alaska.

During this period and most probably relatively near its close, humans from the Eurasian landmass crossed the Bering Sea and began to populate the American continent. We are not sure why they undertook this migration, which would ultimately separate them from other human groups for many thousands of years, but it is likely that the pursuit of a more certain food supply was one of the reasons.

Human life in the Paleolithic Age was likely characterized by a division of labor by gender. The men engaged in hunting; fishing; making tools and weapons; and fighting against other families, clans, and tribes. The women, less mobile because of frequent childbearing, smaller in stature, and less strong and swift than the men, gathered nuts, berries, and wild grains; wove baskets; and made clothing. Women gathering food probably discovered how to plant and care for seeds. This knowledge eventually made possible the coming of the Age of Agriculture—the Neolithic revolution.

Only a few Paleolithic societies made the initial revolutionary shift to agriculture—indeed in many areas, right into our own time, some isolated peoples have been content to continue to depend on hunting and gathering—and anthropologists and archaeologists disagree on the reasons for the shift. In the past, some scientists thought that climatic change—a drop in temperature and rainfall—forced people to be inventive and to seek new ways of acquiring food. But newer evidence suggests that there was little climatic variation in Neolithic times. Other theories focus on the human element: a possible growth in population, an increased sense of territoriality, and a resulting interference with the pursuit of herds for hunting.

However it happened, some ten thousand years ago parts of what we now call the Near East began to shift from a hunter-gatherer culture to a settled agricultural one. Because the shift to agriculture coincided with advances in stone tool technology—the development of precise carving and grinding—this period is called the Neolithic (from Greek, "new stone") Age. Animals as well as food crops were domesticated. The important invention of pottery made it possible to store surplus liquids, just as the invention of baskets had earlier made it possible to store dry foods. Cloth came to be made from flax and wool. Crops required constant care from planting to harvest, so the Neolithic people built permanent buildings, usually in clusters near the best fields. These same changes occurred among the peoples on the American continents but approximately four thousand years later.

The agricultural revolution may not, however, have produced an immediate population explosion anywhere that it occurred. Anthropologists suggest that village living produced a much greater incidence of disease because early village dwellers had no provisions for the disposal of human and animal waste. The Neolithic villages also provided attractive targets for raiders.

Still, agriculture provided a steadier source of food and a greater production of food in a given area. It thus provided the basis for a denser population over time. It was a major step in the human control of nature, and it was a vital precondition for the emergence of civilization. The earliest Neolithic societies appeared in the Near East about 8000 B.C., in China about 4000 B.C., in India by at least 3600 B.C., and in Mesoamerica (modern Mexico and Central America) about 4000 B.C. The Neolithic revolution in the Near East and India was based on wheat, in China on millet and rice, and in Mesoamerica on maize.

Neolithic villages and their culture, as they gradually grew from and replaced the Paleolithic way of life, could be found on almost any kind of terrain. But beginning about four thousand years before the Christian era, people began to settle in substantive numbers in the river-watered lowlands of Mesopotamia, Egypt, northern China, and northwestern India. Here a new style of life evolved: an urban society and civilization. The shift was accompanied by the gradual introduction of new technologies and by the invention of writing. The major Neolithic settlements in the Americas were in Mesoamerica and in the Andean region of South America.

Again, we do not know why people first chose to live in cities, with their inherent disadvantages: overcrowding, epidemics, wide separation from sources of food and raw materials, and the concentration of wealth that permitted organized warfare. Perhaps cities were created because, to quote the Greek philoso-pher Aristotle, "Man is by nature a political animal." Perhaps they arose merely because they offered more possibilities for amusement, occupational choice, and enrichment than had the Neolithic villages. In any event, by about 3000 B.C., when the invention of writing gave birth to history, urban life was established in the valleys of the Tigris and Euphrates rivers in Mesopotamia (modern Iraq) and of the Nile in Egypt. Somewhat later, urban life arose in the Indus Valley of India and the Yellow River basin of China (see Map 1-1 on p. 6). The greatest early city in America, Teotihuacán, emerged during the second century B.C. The development of urban centers by no means meant the disappearance of numerous outlying peasant agricultural villages. Nevertheless, with the coming of cities, writing, and metals, humankind had attained civilization.

Early Civilizations in the Near East

Civilization, then, is a form of human culture in which many people live in urban centers, have mastered the art of smelting metals, and have developed a method of writing. The rich alluvial plains where civilization began made possible the production of unprecedented surpluses of food, but only if there was an intelligent management of the water supply. Proper flood control and irrigation called for the control of the river by some strong authority capable of managing the distribution of water. This control and management required careful observation and record keeping. The first use of writing may have been to record the behavior of the river and the astronomical events that gave clues about it. It was also used by the powerful individuals (the kings) who dominated the life of the river valleys to record their possessions; by priests to record omens and religious texts; by merchants and artisans to record business transactions; and by others to record acts of government, laws, and different kinds of literature.

This widely varied use of writing reflects the complex culture of the urban centers in the river valleys. Commerce was important enough to support a merchant class. Someone discovered how to smelt tin and copper to make a stronger and more useful material—bronze—which replaced stone in the making of tools and weapons: The importance of this technological development is reflected in the term *Bronze Age.* The great need for record keeping created a class of scribes, because the picture writing and compli-

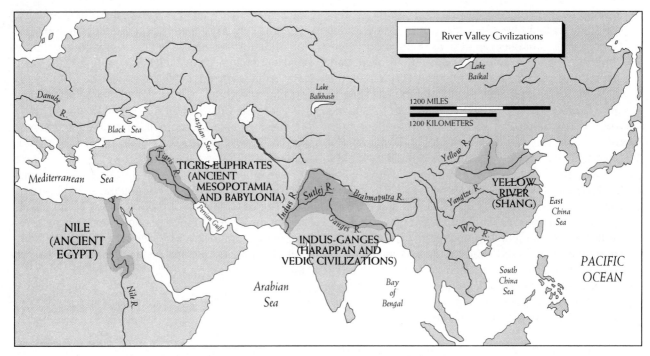

MAP 1-1 THE FOUR GREAT RIVER VALLEY CIVILIZATIONS TO CA. 1000 B.C. *By ca. 2000* B.C.
urban life was established along the Tigris and Euphrates rivers in Mesopotamia,
the Nile River in Egypt, the Indus and Ganges rivers in India, and the Yellow River in
China.

cated scripts of these cultures took many years to learn and could not be mastered by many. To deal with the gods, temples were built, and many priests attended and administered them. The collection of all these people into cities gave the settlements an entirely new character. Unlike Neolithic villages, they were communities established for purposes other than agriculture. The city was an administrative, religious, manufacturing, entertainment, and commercial center.

The logic of nature pointed in the direction of the unification of an entire river valley. As a result, these civilizations in time produced unified kingdoms under powerful monarchs who often came to be identified with divinity. The typical king in a river-valley civilization was regarded either as a god or as the delegate of a god. Around him developed a rigid class structure. Beneath the monarch was a class of hereditary military aristocrats and a powerful priesthood. Below them were freemen, mostly peasants, and at the bottom were serfs or slaves. Most of the land was owned or controlled by the king, the nobility, and the priests. These were conservative cultures of numerous peasant villages and a few urban centers. Such cultural patterns took form early and changed only slowly and grudgingly.

The Fertile Crescent: Mesopotamian Civilization

The first civilization appears to have arisen in the valley of the Tigris and Euphrates rivers: Mesopotamia (the term means land "between the rivers" in Greek). Its founders seem to have been a people called Sumerians, who controlled the southern part of the valley (Sumer) close to the head of the Persian Gulf by the dawn of history, around 3000 B.C. (see Map 1-2). At first, city-states about one hundred square miles in size dotted the landscape. Ur, Erech, Lagash, and Eridu are examples of such cities that archaeologists have revealed to us. Quarrels over water rights and frontiers led to incessant fighting, and in time, stronger towns conquered weaker ones and expanded to form larger units, usually kingdoms.

While the Sumerians were fighting with their neighbors and among themselves for supremacy in the south, a people called Semites from the Arabian Desert on the west had been moving into Mesopotamia north of Sumer. Their language and society were different from those of the Sumerians, but they soon absorbed Sumerian culture and established their own kingdom, with its capital at Akkad, near a later city known to us as Babylon. The most famous Akkadian

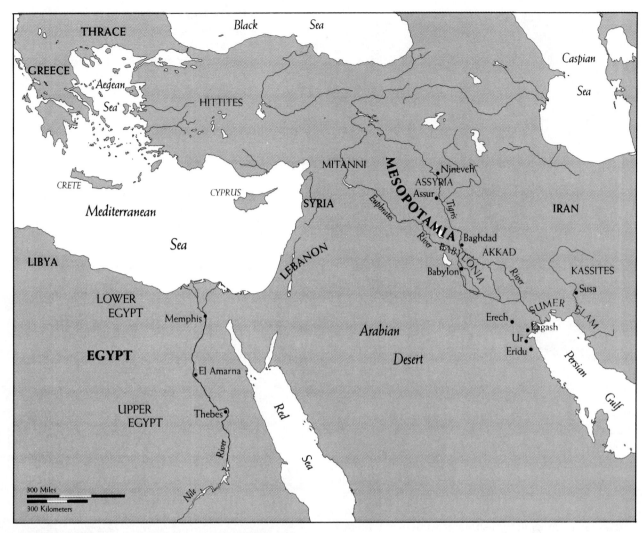

MAP 1-2   THE ANCIENT NEAR EAST   *Egypt was early united into a single state. Mesopotamia, in contrast, was long divided into a number of city-states.*

king was Sargon, who conquered Sumer and extended his empire in every direction. Legends grew up around his name, and he is said to have conquered the "cedar forests" of Lebanon, far to the west near the coast of the Mediterranean Sea. He ruled about 2340 B.C. and established a family, or dynasty, of Semitic kings who ruled Sumer and Akkad for two centuries.

External attack and internal weakness destroyed Akkad. About 2125 B.C., the city of Ur in Sumer revolted and became the dominant power, and this Third Dynasty of Ur established a large empire of its own. About 2000 B.C., however, it was swept aside by another Semitic invasion that ended Sumerian rule forever. Thereafter, Semites ruled Mesopotamia, but the foundations of their culture were Sumerian. The

Semites changed much of what they inherited; but in law, government, religion, art, science, and all other areas of culture, their debt to the Sumerians was enormous.

The fall of the Third Dynasty of Ur (ca. 2100–2000 B.C.) put an end to the Sumerians as an identifiable group. The Sumerian language survived only in writing, as a kind of sacred language known only to priests and scribes, preserving the cultural heritage of Sumer. For about a century after the fall of Ur, dynastic chaos reigned, but about 1900 B.C., a Semitic people called the Amorites gained control of the region, establishing their capital at Babylon. The high point of this Amorite, or Old Babylonian, dynasty came more than a hundred years later under its most famous king, Hammurabi (ca. 1792–1750 B.C.)

This carving in low relief known as the Stele of the Vultures shows the Sumerian king Eannatum of Lagash conquering the neighboring city of Umma. It belongs to the early years of Sumerian dynastic history, perhaps about 2500 B.C. [Hirmer Fotoarchiv, Munich]

King Hammurabi receiving the law from the sun god. This is the upper part of a cast of the stele on which the law code issued by the Babylonian king Hammurabi (ca. 1792–1750 B.C.) is inscribed in cuneiform characters. The original stele is in the Louvre in Paris. [Bildarchiv Preussischer Kulturbesitz]

Hammurabi is best known for the law code connected with his name. Codes of law existed as early as the Sumerian period, and Hammurabi's plainly owed much to earlier models, but it is the fullest and best preserved legal code we have from ancient Mesopotamia or, indeed, from anywhere. The code reveals a society strictly divided in class: nobles, commoners, and slaves, whom the law did not treat equally. In general, punishments were harsh, literally applying the principle "an eye for an eye, a tooth for a tooth." The prologue to the code makes it clear that law and justice came from the gods through the king.

About 1600 B.C., the Babylonian kingdom fell apart under the impact of invasions from the north and east by the Hittites and the Kassites. The Hittites were a raiding party who plundered what they could and then withdrew to their home in Asia Minor. The Kassites, a people from the Iranian plateau, stayed and ruled Mesopotamia for five centuries.

GOVERNMENT.   From the earliest historical records, it is clear that the Sumerians were ruled by monarchs in some form. Some scholars have thought that they could detect a "primitive democracy" in early Sumer, but the evidence, which is poetic and hard to interpret, shows no more than a limited check on royal power even in early times. The first historical city-states had kings or priest-kings who led the army,

Hammurabi Creates a Code of Law in Mesopotamia

Hammurabi's Babylonian empire stretched from the Persian Gulf to the Mediterranean Sea. Building on earlier laws, Hammurabi compiled one of the great ancient codes. It was discovered about seventy-five years ago in what is now Iran. Hammurabi, like other rulers before and after him, represented himself and his laws as under the protection and sponsorship of all the right gods. Property was at least as sacred as persons, and the eye-for-an-eye approach characterizes the code. Here are a few examples from it.

▶ *For other perspectives on law, leadership, and government, see the following document boxes: "Legalism" (Ch. 2), "Thucydides Reports Pericles on Athenian Democracy" (Ch. 4), "Polybius Summarizes the Roman Constitution" (Ch. 5), "The Edicts of Ashoka" (Ch. 7), "Machiavelli Discusses the Most Important Trait for a Ruler" (Ch. 17), and "Some Reforms of Akbar" (Ch. 24).*

LAWS

If a son has struck his father, they shall cut off his hand.

If a seignior has destroyed the eye of a member of the aristocracy, they shall destroy his eye.

If he has broken another seignior's bone, they shall break his bone.

If he has destroyed the eye of a commoner or broken the bone of a commoner, he shall pay one mina of silver.

If he has destroyed the eye of a seignior's slave or broken the bone of a seignior's slave, he shall pay one-half his value.

If a seignior has knocked out a tooth of a seignior of his own rank, they shall knock out his tooth.

If he has knocked out a commoner's tooth, he shall pay one-third mina of silver. . . .

EPILOGUE

I, Hammurabi, the perfect king,
was not careless (or) neglectful of the black-headed (people),
whom Enlil had presented to me,
(and)whose shepherding Marduk had committed to me;
I sought out peaceful regions for them;
I overcame grievous difficulties; . . .
With the mighty weapon which Zababa and Inanna entrusted to me,
with the insight that Enki allotted to me,
with the ability that Marduk gave me,
I rooted out the enemy above and below;
I made an end of war;
I promoted the welfare of the land;
I made the peoples rest in friendly habitations; . . .
The great gods called me,
so I became the beneficent shepherd whose scepter is righteous. . . .

James B. Pritchard, *Ancient Near Eastern Texts,* 3rd ed. (Princeton: Princeton University Press, 1969), pp. 164–180.

administered the economy, and served as judges and as intermediaries between their people and the gods. At first, the kings were thought of as favorites and representatives of the gods; later, on some occasions and for relatively short periods, they instituted cults that worshiped them as divine. This union of Church and State (to use modern terminology) in the person of the king reflected the centralization of power typical of Mesopotamian life. The economy was managed from the center by priests and kings and was planned very carefully. Each year, the land was surveyed, fields were assigned to specific farmers, and the amount of seed to be used was designated. The government estimated the size of the crop and planned its distribution even before it was planted.

This process required a large and competent staff; the ability to observe and record natural phenomena; a good knowledge of mathematics; and, for all of this, a system of writing. The Sumerians invented the writing system known as *cuneiform* (from the Latin *cuneus,* "wedge"). The name comes from the wedge-shaped stylus with which they wrote on clay tablets; the writing also came to be used in beautifully cut characters in stone. Sumerians also began the development of a sophisticated system of mathematics. The calendar they invented had twelve lunar months. To make it agree with the solar year and to make possible accurate designation of the seasons, they introduced a thirteenth month about every three years.

RELIGION.   The Sumerians and their Semitic successors believed in gods in the shape of humans who were usually identified with some natural phenomenon. They were pictured as frivolous, quarrelsome, selfish, and often childish, differing from humans only in their greater power and their immortality. Each appears to have begun as a local deity. The people of Mesopotamia had a negative and gloomy picture of the afterworld as a "land of no return." Their religion dealt with problems of this world, and they employed prayer, sacrifice, and magic to achieve their ends. Expert knowledge was required to reach the perfection in wisdom and ritual needed to influence the gods, so the priesthood flourished. A high percentage of the cuneiform writing that we now have is devoted to religious texts: prayers, incantations, curses, and omens.

It was important to discover the will and intentions of the gods, and the Sumerians sought hints in several places. The movements of the heavenly bodies were an obvious evidence of divine action, so astrology was born. They also sought to discover the divine will by examining the entrails of sacrificial animals for symbolic signs in their particular features. All of this

Sumerian statuettes from Tell Asmar. The group, dating from 3000–2500 B.C., *was found buried beside the altar of a temple at a site near modern Baghdad. The tallest figure in this collection of gods, priests, and worshippers is the god Abu, the "lord of vegetation." [Courtesy of the Oriental Institute, University of Chicago]*

A clay model of a liver inscribed with omens and magical texts. Such model livers were used to help predict events and determine the will of the gods. [Courtesy of the Trustees of the British Museum]

religious activity required numerous scribes to keep records, as well as learned priests to interpret them.

Religious thought, in the form of myth, played a large part in the literature and art of Mesopotamia. A *myth* (from the Greek, "story" or "plot") is a narrative that deals with truths about relationships between the human and the transcendent. In the poetic language of myth, the Sumerians and their successors told tales of the creation of the world, of a great flood that almost destroyed human life, of an island paradise from which the god Enki was expelled for eating forbidden plants, or a hero named Gilgamesh who tried to gain immortality, and many more.

Religion was also the inspiration for the most interesting architectural achievement in Mesopotamia: the ziggurat. The ziggurat was an artificial stepped mound surmounted by a temple. It may have been a symbolic representation of the cosmic mountain that many cultures have thought lies at the center of the world. Neighbors and successors of the Sumerians adopted the style, and the eroded remains of many of these monumental structures, some partly restored, still dot the Iraqi landscape.

SOCIETY. We have a very full and detailed picture of the way people in ancient Mesopotamia conducted their lives and of the social conditions in which they lived during the reign of Hammurabi. More than fifty royal letters, many business contracts, and especially the Code of Hammurabi are the sources of our knowledge. We find that society was legally divided into three classes: nobles, commoners, and slaves. Punishment for crimes committed against freemen was harsher than for crimes against slaves, and crimes committed against nobles were considered more serious than those against commoners.

Slaves were chiefly captives from wars, although some native Babylonians were enslaved for committing certain crimes, such as kicking one's mother or striking an elder brother. Parents could sell their children into slavery or pledge themselves and their entire family as surety for a debt. In case of default, they would all become slaves of the creditor for a stated period of time. Some slaves worked for the king and the state, others for the temple and the priests, and still others for private citizens. Their tasks varied accordingly. Most of the temple slaves appear to have been women, who were probably used to spin and weave and grind flour. The royal slaves did the heavy work of building palaces, canals, and fortifications. Private owners used their slaves chiefly as domestic servants. Some female slaves were used as concubines.

Laws against fugitive slaves or slaves who denied their masters were harsh, but in some respects, Mesopotamian slavery appears enlightened compared to other slave systems in history. Slaves could engage in business and, with certain restrictions, hold property. They could marry free men or women, and the resulting children would be free. A slave who acquired the necessary wealth could buy his or her own freedom. Children of a slave by the master might be allowed to share in his property after his death.

The Nile Valley: Egyptian Civilization

While a great civilization arose in the valley of the Tigris and Euphrates, another, no less important, emerged in Egypt. The center of Egyptian civilization was the Nile River. From its source in central Africa, the Nile runs north some four thousand miles to the Mediterranean, with long navigable stretches broken by several cataracts. Ancient Egypt included the 750 miles of the valley from the First Cataract northward to the sea and was shaped like a long-necked funnel with two distinct parts. Upper (southern) Egypt was the stem, consisting of the narrow valley of the Nile. The broad, triangular delta, which branches out about 150 miles from the sea, formed the mouth of the funnel, or Lower Egypt (see Map 1-1). The Nile alone made life possible in the almost rainless desert that surrounded it. Each year, the river flooded and covered the land, and when it receded, it left a fertile mud that could produce two crops a year. The construction and maintenance of irrigation ditches to preserve the river's water, with careful planning and organization of planting and harvesting, produced an agricultural prosperity unmatched in the ancient world.

The Nile also served as a highway connecting the long, narrow country and encouraging its unification. Upper and Lower Egypt were, in fact, already united into a single kingdom at the beginning of our historical record, about 3100 B.C. Nature helped protect and isolate the ancient Egyptians from outsiders. The cataracts, the sea, and the desert made reaching Egypt difficult for foreigners with friendly or hostile purposes. Egypt knew far more peace and security than Mesopotamia. This security, along with the sunny, predictable climate, gave Egyptian civilization a more optimistic outlook than the civilizations of the Tigris–Euphrates, which were always in fear of assault from storm, flood, earthquake, and hostile neighbors.

The more than three-thousand-year span of ancient Egyptian history is traditionally divided into thirty-one royal dynasties. They range from the first, founded by Menes, the unifier of Upper and Lower Egypt, to the last, established by Alexander the Great, who conquered Egypt in 322 B.C. The dynasties are conventionally arranged into periods (see timeline on page 17). The unification of Egypt was vital, for even

more than in Mesopotamia, the entire river valley required the central control of irrigation. By the time of the Third Dynasty, the king had achieved full supremacy and had imposed internal peace and order; his kingdom enjoyed great prosperity. The capital was at Memphis in Lower Egypt, just above the delta. The king was no mere representative of the gods but a god himself. The land was his own personal possession, and the people were his servants.

Nothing better illustrates the extent of royal power than the three great pyramids built as tombs by the kings of the Fourth Dynasty. The largest, that of Khufu, was originally 481 feet high and 756 feet long on each side; it was made up of 2.3 million stone blocks averaging 2.5 tons each. It was said by the much later Greek historian Herodotus to have taken one hundred thousand men twenty years to build. The pyramids are remarkable not only for the technical skill that was needed to build them but even more for what they tell us of the royal power. They give evidence that the Egyptian kings had enormous wealth, the power to concentrate so much effort on personal projects, and the confidence for undertakings of such long duration. There were earlier pyramids and many were built later, but those of the Fourth Dynasty were never surpassed.

THE OLD KINGDOM. In the Old Kingdom, royal power was absolute. The pharaoh, as he was later called (the term originally meant "great house" or "palace"), governed his kingdom through his family and appointed officials removable at his pleasure. The peasants were carefully regulated; their movement was limited; and they were taxed heavily, perhaps as much as one-fifth of what they produced. Luxury accompanied the king in life and death, and he was raised to a remote and exalted level by his people. Such power and eminence could not be sustained by force alone. The Egyptians worked for the king and obeyed him because he was a living god on whom their life, safety, and prosperity depended. He was the direct source of law and justice, so no law codes were needed.

In such a world, government was merely one aspect of religion, and religion dominated Egyptian life. The gods of Egypt had many forms: animals, humans, and natural forces. In time, Re, the sun god, came to have a special dominant place, but for centuries there seems to have been little clarity or order in the Egyptian pantheon. Unlike the Mesopotamians, the Egyptians had a rather precise idea of an afterlife. They took great care to bury their dead according to their

The Egyptians believed in the possibility of life after death through the god Osiris. The character of each person's life had to be tested by forty-two assessor gods before the person could be presented to Osiris. In this scene from an illustration of the Book of the Dead, *the decreased and his wife (on the left) watch the scales of justice weighing his heart (on the left side of the scales) against the feather of truth. The jackal-faced god Anubis also watches the scales, while the ibis-headed god Thoth keeps the record.* [Courtesy of the Trustees of the British Museum]

custom and supplied the grave with things that the departed would need for a pleasant life after death. The king and some nobles had their bodies preserved as mummies. Their tombs were beautifully decorated with paintings and religious texts useful in the next life; food and furnishings were provided at burial and even afterward. Some royal tombs were equipped with full-sized ships for the voyage to heaven. At first only kings were thought to achieve eternal life; then nobles were included; finally, all Egyptians could hope for immortality. The dead had to be properly embalmed, and the proper spells had to be written and spoken.

The Egyptians developed a system of writing not much later than the Sumerians. Although the idea may have come from Mesopotamia, the form of their script was independent. It began as picture writing and later combined pictographs with sound signs to produce a difficult and complicated script that the Greeks called *hieroglyphics* ("sacred carvings"). A great deal of surviving hieroglyphics are preserved on wall paintings and carvings, but most Egyptian writing was done with pen and ink on a fine paper made from the papyrus reed found in the delta. Egyptian literature was more limited in depth and imagination than the Mesopotamian writings. Hymns; myths; magical formulas; tales of travel; and "wisdom literature," or bits of advice to help one get on well in the world, have been preserved. But nothing as serious and probing as the story of Gilgamesh was produced in the more optimistic world of Egypt.

THE MIDDLE KINGDOM. The power of the kings of the Old Kingdom waned as priests and nobles gained more independence and influence. The governors of the regions of Egypt, called *nomes,* gained hereditary claim to their offices, and their families acquired large estates. About 2200 B.C., the Old Kingdom collapsed and gave way to the decentralization and disorder of the First Intermediate period (ca. 2200–2052 B.C.). Finally, the nomarchs (governors) of Thebes in Upper Egypt gained control of the country and established the Middle Kingdom in about 2052 B.C.

The rulers of the Twelfth Dynasty restored the pharaoh's power over the whole of Egypt, although they could not completely control the nobles who ruled the nomes. Still, they brought order, peace, and pros-

The Sphinx. Located at Giza, near modern Cairo, the great Sphinx seems to have been associated with the pyramid of Khafre, a king who ruled Egypt some time after 2600 B.C. The origin of the colossal lion with the head of a man is not known, but the face is thought to be a likeness of the pharaoh himself. [Hirmer Fotoarchiv, München]

perity to a troubled land. They encouraged trade and extended Egyptian power and influence northward toward Palestine and southward toward Ethiopia. Although they moved the capital back to the more defensible site at Memphis, they gave great prominence to Amon, a god especially connected with Thebes. He became identified with Re, emerging as Amon-Re, the main god of Egypt.

The kings of this period seem to have emphasized their role in doing justice. In their states, they are often shown as burdened with care, presumably concern for their people. Tales of the period place great emphasis on the king as interested in right and in the welfare of his people. Much later, in the New Kingdom, ethical concerns appeared, as they had in the law codes of Mesopotamia, but the divine status of the kings gave them a strong religious tinge.

THE NEW KINGDOM (THE EMPIRE). The Middle Kingdom disintegrated in the Thirteenth Dynasty with the resurgence of the power of the local nobility. About 1700 B.C., Egypt suffered an invasion. Tradition speaks of a people called the Hyksos who came from the east and conquered the Nile Delta. They seem to have been a collection of Semitic peoples from the area of Palestine and Syria at the eastern end of the Mediterranean. Egyptian nationalism reasserted itself in about 1575 B.C., when a dynasty from Thebes drove out the Hyksos and reunited the kingdom. In reaction to the humiliation of the Second Intermediate period, the pharaohs of the Eighteenth Dynasty, the most prominent of whom was Thutmose III (1490–1436 B.C.), created an absolute government based on a powerful army and an Egyptian empire extending far beyond the Nile valley.

From the Hyksos, the Egyptians learned new military techniques and obtained new weapons. To them they added determination, a fighting spirit, and an increasingly military society. They pushed the southern frontier back a long way and extended Egyptian power farther into Palestine and Syria and beyond to the upper Euphrates River. They were not checked until they came into conflict with the powerful Hittite empire of Asia Minor. Both powers were weakened by the struggle, and although Egypt survived, it again became the victim of foreign invasion and rule, as one foreign empire after another took possession of the ancient kingdom.

Akhnaton worshipping Aton. The scene carved into this stone stele shows eighteenth-dynasty Pharaoh Akhnaton (1367–1350 B.C.) paying homage to the newly enthroned god Aton, the disk of the sun. [Library of the Egyptian Museum, Cairo]

The Eighteenth Dynasty, however, witnessed an interesting religious change. One of the results of the successful imperial ventures of the Egyptian pharaohs was the growth in power of the priests of Amon and the threat it posed to the position of the king. When young Amenhotep IV (r. 1367–1350 B.C.) came to the throne before the middle of the fourteenth century B.C., he was apparently determined to resist the priesthood of Amon. He was supported by his family and advisers and ultimately made a clean break with the worship of Amon-Re. He moved his capital from Thebes, the center of Amon worship, and built an entirely new city about three hundred miles to the north at a place now called El Amarna. Its god was Aton, the physical disk of the sun, and the new city was called Akhtaton. The king changed his own name to Akhnaton, "It pleases Aton." The new god was different from any that had come before him, for he was believed to be universal, not merely Egyptian. Unlike the other gods, he had no cult statue but was represented in painting and relief sculpture by the symbol of the sun disk.

The universal claims for Aton led to religious intolerance of the worshipers of the other gods. Their temples were shut down, and the name of Amon-Re was chiseled from the monuments on which it was carved. The old priests, of course, were deprived of their posts and privileges, and the people who served the pharaoh and his god were new, sometimes even foreign. The new religion, moreover, was more remote than the old. Only the pharaoh and his family worshiped Aton directly, and the people worshiped the pharaoh. Akhnaton's interest in religious reform apparently led him to ignore foreign affairs, which proved disastrous. The Asian possessions of Egypt fell away. This imperial decline and its economic consequences presumably caused further hostility to the new religion. When the king died, a strong counterrevolution swept away the work of his lifetime.

His chosen successor was soon put aside and replaced by Tutankhamon (r. 1347–1339 B.C.), the young husband of one of the daughters of Akhnaton, the beautiful Nefertiti. The new pharaoh restored the old religion and wiped out as much as he could of the memory of the worship of Aton. He restored Amon to the center of the Egyptian pantheon, abandoned El Amarna, and returned the capital to Thebes. There, he and his successors built his magnificent tomb, which remained remarkably intact until its discovery in 1922. The end of the El Amarna age restored power to the priests of Amon and to the military officers. A general named Horemhab became king (r. 1335–

?1308 B.C.), restored order, and recovered much of the lost empire. He referred to Akhnaton as "the criminal of Akhtaton" and erased his name from the records. Akhnaton's city and memory disappeared for over three thousand years, to be rediscovered only by chance about a century ago.

Akhnaton Intones New Hymns to Aton, the One God

These hymns were composed during the reign of Amenhotep IV (1367–1350 B.C.), or Akhnaton, as he called himself after instituting a religious revolution in Egypt.

Thou makest the Nile in the Nether World,
Thou bringest it as thou desirest,
To preserve alive the people of Egypt
For thou hast made them for thyself,
Thou lord of them all, who weariest thyself for them;
Thou lord of every land, who risest for them.
Thou Sun of day, great in glory,
All the distant highland countries,
Thou makest also their life,
Thou didst set a Nile in the sky.
When it falleth for them,
It maketh waves upon the mountains,
Like the great green sea,
Watering their fields in their towns.

How benevolent are thy designs, O lord of eternity!
There is a Nile in the sky for the strangers
And for the antelopes of all the highlands that go
    about upon their feet.
But the Nile, it cometh from the Nether World for
    Egypt.

Thou didst make the distant sky in order to rise
    therein,
In order to behold all that thou hast made,
While thou wast yet alone
Shining in thy form as living Aton,
Dawning, glittering, going afar and returning.
Thou makest millions of forms
Through thyself alone;
Cities, villages, and field, highways and rivers,
All eyes see thee before them,
For thou art Aton of the day over the earth,
When thou has gone away,
And all men, whose faces thou hast fashioned
In order that thou mightest no longer see thyself
    alone;

[Have fallen asleep, so that not] one [seeth] that
    which thou has made,
Yet art thou still in my heart.

REVELATION TO THE KING

There is no other that knoweth thee
Save thy son Akhnaton.
Thou hast made him wise
In thy designs and in thy might.

UNIVERSAL MAINTENANCE

The world subsists in thy hand,
Even as thou hast made them
When thou hast risen they live,
When thou settest they die;
For thou art length of life of thyself,
Men live through thee.

The eyes of men see beauty
Until thou settest.
All labour is put away
When thou settest in the west.
When thou risest again
[Thou] makest [every hand] to flourish for the king
And [prosperity] is in every foot,
Since thou didst establish the world,
And raise them up for thy son,
Who came forth from thy flesh,
The king of Upper and Lower Egypt,
Living in Truth, Lord of the Two Lands,
Nefer-khepru-Re, Wan-Re [Akhnaton],
Son of Re, living in Truth, lord of diadems,
Akhnaton, whose life is long;
[And for] the chief royal wife, his beloved,
Mistress of the Two Lands, Nefer-nefru-Aton,
    Nofretete,
Living and flourishing for ever and ever.

James H. Breasted, *The Dawn of Conscience* (New York: Charles Scribners' Sons, 1933, 1961), p. 137.

PERIODS IN ANCIENT EGYPTIAN HISTORY (DYNASTIES IN ROMAN NUMERALS)	
ca. 3100–2700 B.C.	Early Dynastic period (I–II)
ca. 2700–2200 B.C.	Old Kingdom (III–VI)
ca. 2200–2052 B.C.	First Intermediate period (VII–X)
ca. 2052–1786 B.C.	Middle Kingdom (XI–XII)
ca. 1786–1575 B.C.	Second Intermediate period (XIII–XVII)
ca. 1700 B.C.	Hyksos invasion
ca. 1575–1087 B.C.	New Kingdom (or Empire) (XVIII–XX)
ca. 1087–30 B.C.	Post-Empire (XXI–XXXI)

For the rest of its independent history, Egypt returned to its traditional culture, but its mood was more pessimistic. The *Book of the Dead,* a product of this late period, was a collection of spells whereby the dead could get safely to the next world without being destroyed by a hideous monster. Egypt itself would soon be devoured by powerful empires, and the Pharaonic civilization would pass from history forever.

Ancient Near Eastern Empires

During the time of the Eighteenth Dynasty in Egypt, new groups of peoples had established themselves in the Near East: the Kassites in Babylonia, the Hittites in Asia Minor, and the Mitannians in northern Mesopotamia. They all spoke languages in the Indo-European group, which includes Greek, Latin, Sanskrit, Persian, Celtic, and the Germanic languages and are thought to have originated in the Ukraine or to the east of it. The Kassites and the Mitannians were warrior peoples who ruled as a minority over more civilized folk and absorbed their culture without changing it.

HITTITES.   The Hittites arrived in Asia Minor about 2000 B.C., and by about 1500 B.C., they had established a strong, centralized government with a capital at Hattusas (near Ankara, the capital of modern Turkey). Between 1400 and 1200 B.C., the Hittites contested Egypt's control of Palestine and Syria. They were strong enough to achieve a dynastic marriage with the daughter of the powerful Nineteenth Dynasty

pharaoh Ramses II, in about 1265 B.C. By 1200 B.C., the Hittite kingdom was gone, swept away by the arrival of new, mysterious Indo-Europeans. However, Neo-Hittite centers flourished in Asia Minor and Mesopotamia for a few centuries longer.

In most respects, the Hittites reflected the influence of the dominant Mesopotamian culture of the region, but their government resembled more closely what we know of other Indo-European cultures. Their kings did not claim to be divine or even to be the chosen representatives of the gods. In the early period, the king's power was checked by a council of nobles, and the assembled army had to ratify his succession to the throne. The Hittites appear to have been responsible for a great technological advance, the smelting of iron. They also played an important role in transmitting the ancient cultures of Mesopotamia and Egypt to the Greeks, who lived on their frontiers.

ASSYRIANS.   The fall of the Hittites was followed shortly by the formation of empires that dominated the Near East's ancient civilizations and even extended them to new areas. The first of these empires was established by the Assyrians, whose homeland was in the valleys and hills of northern Mesopotamia along, and to the east of, the Tigris River. They had a series of capitals, of which the great city of Nineveh is perhaps best known (modern Mosul, Iraq). They spoke a Semitic language and, from early times, were a part of the culture of Mesopotamia. Akkadians, Sumerians, Amorites, and Mitannians had dominated Assyria in turn.

The Hittites' defeat of Mitanni liberated the Assyrians and prepared the way for their greatness from earlier than 1000 B.C. By 665 B.C., they had come to control everything from the southern frontier of Egypt, through Palestine, Syria, and much of Asia Minor, down to the Persian Gulf in the southeast. They succeeded in part because they made use of iron weapons. Because iron was more common than copper and tin, it was possible for them to arm more men cheaply. The Assyrians were also fierce, well disciplined, and cruel. Their cruelty was calculated, at least in part, to terrorize real and potential enemies, for the Assyrians boasted of their brutality.

Unlike earlier empires, the Assyrian Empire systematically and profitably exploited the area it held. The Assyrians employed different methods of control, ranging from the mere collection of tribute, to the stationing of garrisons in conquered territory, to removing entire populations from their homelands and scattering them elsewhere, as they did to the people of the kingdom of Israel. As a result of their military and administrative skills, they were able to hold vast areas even as they absorbed the teachings of the older cultures under their sway.

In addition to maintaining their own empire, the Assyrians had to serve as a buffer of the civilized Middle East against the barbarians on its frontiers. In the seventh century B.C., the task of fighting off the barbarians so drained the overextended Assyrians that the empire fell because of internal revolution. A new dynasty in Babylon joined with the rising kingdom of Media to the east (in modern Iran) to defeat the Assyrians and destroy Nineveh in 612 B.C. The successor kingdoms, the Chaldean or Neo-Babylonian and the Median, did not last long; they were swallowed, by 539 B.C., by yet another great eastern empire, that of the Persians.

Early Indian Civilization

To the east of Mesopotamia, beyond the Iranian plateau and the mountains of Baluchistan, the Asian continent bends sharply southward into the southern oceans. This great triangular projection of Asia south of the massive mountain barrier of the Himalaya is known today as the *Indian subcontinent.* From sites well north in modern Pakistan and Afghanistan to the southern tip of India and Sri Lanka (Ceylon), archaeologists have unearthed evidence of diverse Paleolithic cultures. The latest of them probably existed side by side with the many Neolithic and Bronze Age sites also found on the subcontinent.

The earliest Neolithic pottery and agricultural hunting tools, together with evidence of settled life,

As these reliefs from royal palaces show, the Assyrians boasted about their cruelty. The Assyrian kings used a policy of calculated terror to hold their empire together and to discourage revolt by subject peoples and attack by foes. Above, the decapitated heads of enemies are counted by royal scribes as part of the spoils of victory. Below, the army of Ashurbanipal sacks the city of Hamanu in Syria. [Werner Forman]

have been dated as early as about 5500 B.C. They are in present-day Pakistan, in the foothills of Sind and Baluchistan. The Neolithic revolution thus came to the subcontinent somewhat later than to the Near East. Some used to believe that it was imported from the west, but today scholars think that it was of independent origin in much, if not all, of the subcontinent.

The beginning of identifiable civilization in India was unusual, in that the initial breakthrough to literate, urban culture in the Indus Valley lasted only a few hundred years. The Aryan culture that replaced the Indus civilization was foreign and bore little relation or resemblance to it. It centered on a different part of northern India, first the extreme northwest (Gandhara, the Panjab), then the plains west of the upper Ganges, and then along the Ganges itself. Although this Aryan culture provided the base for all later Indian civilization, it existed for nearly a millennium without taking up writing or building large cities. Because of the different character of these two cultures, we shall look at each separately.

Harappan Civilization on the Indus River

The first breakthrough to civilization in the subcontinent came in the region of modern Pakistan, where a culture emerged boasting Bronze Age tools, developed cities, a writing system, and diversified social and economic organization. As one might expect, this civilization flourished on the fertile floodplains of one of the two largest river systems of the subcontinent, the Indus and its tributaries (see Map 1-3 on p. 20). Several sizable rivers flow west and south out of the Himalaya in Kashmir and the Punjab (Panjab, "five rivers") to merge into the single stream of the Indus as it crosses Sind to empty into the Indian Ocean. (The second great river system of the subcontinent, the Ganges and its tributaries, also rises in the Himalaya but flows south and east to the Bay of Bengal on the opposite side of the subcontinent.) The Indus culture is sometimes also called *Harappan*, from the name of the site, Harappa, where archaeologists first discovered it. Until the excavations began in the 1920s, no one knew of its existence. Today, two cities, Harappa and Mohenjo-Daro, and numerous lesser towns of this culture have been unearthed and studied.

Of the four great river-valley civilizations that mark the beginnings of literate, urban culture, the Indus is the one about which we know the least. Our relative ignorance is due to two factors.

First, this civilization disappeared as a living cultural tradition sometime before the middle of the second millennium B.C. It was once commonly assumed that this culture was destroyed by invading steppe peoples from the northwest, the Indo-European-speaking tribes who migrated in the second millennium B.C. from the Eurasian steppelands west, south, and eastward into new territories. (The groups that entered India and, at about the same time, Iran, are known as Aryans.) Now scholars recognize that there is no firm evidence to support this hypothesis, and without new evidence, the true cause of the passing of Indus civilization must remain one of history's unsolved mysteries.

Second, although we have many Indus inscriptions (mostly small stamp seals cut into soapstone), no one has been able to decipher them. Many scholars think that the Indus language was a Dravidian tongue, which would place it in the same family as some languages still spoken in the subcontinent, the most important of which is Tamil in southern India. Until it can be read, we have no self-testimony of the Indus peoples to guide us. Without the patient, still-unfolding work of modern archaeologists, this once great and widely dispersed civilization would have remained a wholly "vanished" culture. Now, however, we know that it flourished for at least five hundred years, and perhaps longer, before it passed from history's stage forever. Although material remains do not give us access to the history of the rise and fall of the Indus society, or to its precise institutions, they do yield indisputable evidence of a high culture. We can make some educated guesses about the Indus civilization, based on archaeological data and inferences from later Indian life and culture.

GENERAL CHARACTER. The Indus or Harappan civilization covered an area many times larger than either of its contemporaries, Middle Kingdom Egypt and Third Dynasty Ur. Yet this vast territory was united in a culture of remarkable homogeneity, as the archaeological finds tell us. The similarities in city layouts, building construction, weights and measures, seal inscriptions, artifacts, and even the size of the burnt brick used in all the Indus towns for buildings and floodwalls point to the unusual uniformity of this civilization. Such uniformity suggests a strong, perhaps centralized, government, an integrated economic system, and good internal communications.

The Indus culture is thought to have remained

MAP 1-3 INDUS AND VEDIC ARYAN CULTURES *The probable contours of the heartlands of the two oldest civilizations of southern Asia suggest only that Indus culture is likely to have influenced the Vedic Aryans, even if the influence cannot be proved. Some scholars surmise, for example, that the fortified Aryan city of Hariyupiya, mentioned in later texts, may have been the same site as the older Indus city of Harappa.*

strikingly unchanged over the centuries that it endured (probably from about 2250 to 1750 B.C., although some scholars argue for 2500–1500 B.C.). Change does not seem to have been prized. Because the main cities and towns lay in river lowlands subject to periodic flooding, they had to be rebuilt numerous times in Indus history. The excavations show that each new level of construction closely followed the pattern of the previous one. Similarly, we find no evidence of any development in the Indus pictographic script in the more than two thousand stamp seals thus far uncovered. Stability, regularity, and traditionalism seem to have been hallmarks of this society. Such unusual continuity has led scholars to speculate that Indus civilization may have flourished under a single conservative, theocratic, priestly state rather than a more unstable, secular state or states dominated by a royal court.

CITIES.   The major sites at Harappa and Mohenjo-Daro appear to have been two centers of Indus cul-

ture. Each probably had a population of at least thirty-five thousand and was meticulously laid out on a similar plan. On the western side of the city stood a large, walled citadel on a raised rectangular platform about eight hundred by fourteen hundred feet in size; east of this platform lay the town proper, which was laid out on a careful north-south-east-west grid of main avenues, some of which were thirty feet wide. The citadel apparently contained the main public buildings. An impressively large bath, with a brick-lined pool and columned porticos, has been excavated at Mohenjo-Daro, and both sites have buildings tentatively identified as temples.

Each city boasted a large granary for food storage. Cemeteries were laid out on the periphery of each. The town "blocks" formed by the main avenues were crisscrossed by small, less rigidly planned lanes, off which opened private houses of various sizes, sometimes more than one story. The typical house was built around a central courtyard and presented only blank walls to the outside lanes. This arrangement is

Ancient Mohenjo-Daro, like most cities of the Indus Valley civilization, was built principally of mud brick. The structures are laid on straight lines; streets cross each other at right angles. The impression is one of order, prosperity, and civic discipline.

recalled by present-day houses in many Near Eastern and Indian cities.

Perhaps the most striking feature of these cities, however, was a complex system of covered drains and sewers. Private houses were serviced by wells, bathrooms, and latrines, and the great bath at Mohenjo-Daro was filled from its own large well. The drainage system that served these facilities in the Indus towns was an engineering feat unrivaled in the ancient world until the time of the Romans, nearly two thousand years later.

ECONOMIC LIFE. The Indus state had an economy based on a thriving agriculture. Wheat and barley were the main crops; peas, lentils, sesame, and cotton were also important. Whether artificial irrigation or only flood control was used is not known, but indications are that the whole Indus region was more densely vegetated and productive than it is today. Cattle, dogs, goats, sheep, and fowl were raised, and elephants and water buffalo were known and possibly tamed for work as well. Cotton weaving, metal working, and wheel-driven pottery making were practiced. Trade contacts abroad are indicated by Indus stamp seals found in Mesopotamia; the "Melukka" region mentioned in ancient Akkadian texts as a source of ivory, precious stones, and other wares may have been the Indus basin.

Excavations in the Persian Gulf indicate that the island of Bahrain may have been a staging point for Indus-Mesopotamian sea trade. Metals and semiprecious stones were apparently imported from present-day Iran and Afghanistan, as well as from Central Asia, modern Rajasthan, and Mysore in peninsular India, and perhaps from Arabia. There are also indications from shared drawing motifs that these trade contacts resulted in cultural borrowings.

MATERIAL CULTURE. Without literary remains, we must look to pottery, tools, sculpture, ornaments, and other objects unearthed at Indus sites to glean some idea of arts, crafts, and technology. The chief evidence of creative art is found in the fine bronze and stone statues that have been recovered. We find also an accomplished mastery of design and production techniques in various artifacts: copper and bronze tools and vessels, impressive black-on-red painted pottery, dressed stonework, stone and terra-cotta figurines and toys, silver vessels and ornaments, gold jewelry, and dyed woven fabric. The numerous flat stamp seals of stone are our major source, along with some pottery painting and small copper-tablet en-

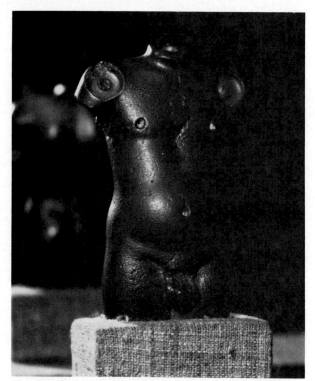

Stone torso from Mohenjo-Daro. [Borromeo/Art Resource]

gravings, for both the Indus script and the portrayals of animals, humans, and what are thought to be divine or semidivine beings.

Such handiwork shows the Indus capabilities at their best. Unfortunately, no monumental or wall art, beyond some decorative brickwork, has been found in the excavations. There are no friezes, mosaics, or large-scale sculpture. In general, the range of art and artifacts seems limited by comparison with that of ancient Egypt or Mesopotamia.

RELIGION. The Indus remains give us somewhat more to speculate about in the religious realm. The elaborate bath facilities suggest practices like the ritual bathing and water purification rites that are so important in Indian life even in the present day. Later Hindu (and possibly even elements of Indo-Aryan) polytheism and image worship may also have historical links with Indus ideas and practices. This possibility is suggested by the stone images from the so-called "temples" of Mohenjo-Daro and the far more common terra-cotta figurines found at many sites. Later symbols important to Hindus, such as the pipal tree or the swastika sign, are also found on Indus artifacts.

Indus stone stamp seals. Note the familiar humped bull of India. [Borromeo/EPA]

Among the most common images, the large number of male animals—above all, the humped bull—might be symbols of power and fertility or may conceivably indicate some kind of animal worship. Other depicted animals are the tiger, the snake, and a unicornlike animal. The recurring figure of a male with a leafy headdress and horns, often seated in a posture associated later in India with yogic meditation, has been likened to the Aryan "Lord of All Creatures." This figure merges with the major god Shiva in Hindu piety. Such a comparison is strengthened by some pictures in which the seated figure has three faces and an erect phallus, both common elements of Shiva iconography.

The many terra-cotta figurines of females, often pregnant or carrying a child, could be a prefiguration of the goddess (Devi, Durga, and so on) who, as the consort of Shiva, is widely worshiped in India today. Similar female images have been found in other prehistoric cultures, but their actual significance is purely conjectural. If goddess worship did exist in the Indus culture, it may be one of the elements of pre-Aryan religion that survived in folk tradition; it re-emerged over a millennium later, after 500 B.C., as a prominent feature of Hindu culture. Other aspects of Indus religion—the burial customs, for example—do not seem to have later Hindu analogies. However, they remind us that the Indus peoples, like all others, had their own ways of coming to terms with the mysteries of birth, life, and death, even if we can only guess at what these were.

THE PASSING OF INDUS CIVILIZATION. This distant culture has thus far kept more secrets than it has revealed. Its ruins tell us that sometime in the early second millennium B.C., it went into decline. Some think that it was destroyed by abnormal flooding or changes in the course of the Indus even before the first Aryan invaders arrived. These warlike peoples probably first appeared in the upper Indus area about 1800 B.C. They later swept with their horse-drawn chariots in successive waves across the northern plains of the subcontinent as far as the Ganges valley. As we have indicated, the culture that they established across much of northern India exhibits little trace of clear Indus survivals. The sacred texts of this culture, the Vedas, refer only occasionally either to enemies whose strongholds were destroyed with the help of the gods or to "dark," "snub-nosed," small and ugly "slaves" brought under subjection by the conquerors.

The Indus civilization remains too much in the shadows of prehistory for its full influence to be seen. Even the common theory that India's Dravidian-speaking people are descendants of the Indus peoples remains to be proved. Still, these forgotten predecessors of the Aryans probably made significant contributions to later life in the subcontinent in ways yet to be discovered.

Vedic Aryan Civilization of Northern India

By comparison with the Indus civilization, we know much more about the Aryan culture that effectively "refounded" Indian civilization. Unlike the Indus culture, that of the Indo-Aryans was not an urban civilization. It left behind neither city ruins nor substantial artifacts beyond tools, weapons, and pottery. But the Vedas did survive, and we give the name *Vedic* to the early Aryan culture of northern India because the Vedic texts are virtually the exclusive source of our

Hymn to a Rigvedic Goddess

Here we see the personification of a natural phenomenon, the night, as a goddess whom worshipers can petition. Such hymns make up the Rigveda collection and mirror the close relationship of nature and the transcendent world in the Vedic Aryan world view.

TO NIGHT

With all her eyes the goddess Night looks forth approaching many a spot:
She hath put all her glories on.

Immortal, she hath filled the waste, the goddess hath filled height and depth:
She conquers darkness with her light.

The goddess as she comes hath set the Dawn her sister in her place:
And then the darkness vanishes.

So favour us this night, O thou whose pathways we have visited
As birds their nest upon the tree.

The villagers have sought their homes, and all that walks and all that flies,
Even the falcons fain for prey.

Keep off the she-wolf and the wolf; O Night, keep the thief away:
Easy be thou for us to pass.

Clearly hath she come nigh to me who decks the dark with richest hues:
O morning, cancel it like debts.

These have I brought to thee like kine. O Night, thou child of heaven, accept
This laud as for a conqueror.

—Rig Veda (10.127)

From *Hinduism,* ed. by L. Renou (New York: George Braziller, 1962), p. 71.

---

knowledge of it. Although the latest portions of the Vedas date from perhaps 500 B.C., the oldest may go back to 1700 B.C. Because these texts are not historical, but ritual, priestly, and speculative works, they tell us little about specific events. But the Vedas do offer evidence for some general inferences about religion, society, values, and thought in early Aryan India.

Veda, which means "knowledge," is the collective term for the texts still recognized today by most Indians as the holiest sources of their tradition. In Hindu perspective, Veda is the eternal wisdom realized by the most ancient seers and preserved over thousands of years by generations of professional reciters in unbroken oral transmission. We speak of "the Vedas" in the plural to refer to the four major compilations of Vedic ritual texts and the explanatory and speculative texts associated with each. The most significant of the four main collections for the history of the early Aryans is the collection of 1,028 religious hymns known as the Rig Veda, which contains the oldest materials. The latest Rigvedic hymns date from ca. 1000 B.C., the oldest from perhaps 1700–1200 B.C.,

when the Aryans spread across the northern Indian plains as far as the upper reaches of the Ganges.

Aryan is a different kind of term. The second-millennium invaders of northern India called themselves *Aryas* to distinguish themselves from the peoples that they conquered. Vedic Sanskrit, the language of the invaders, gave this word to later Sanskrit as a term for "noble," or "free-born" *(arya).* The word is found also in old Iranian texts *(Iran* is itself a name derived from the Old Persian equivalent of *Arya).* It seems to have been the original name of peoples who migrated out of the steppeland between Eastern Europe and Central Asia into Europe, Greece, Anatolia, the Iranian plateau, and India during the second and first millennia B.C. Those who moved into India can thus be more precisely designated *Vedic Aryans,* or *Indo-Aryans.*

In the nineteenth century, *Aryan* was the term applied to the widespread language group known more commonly today as *Indo-European.* To this widely distributed family belong Greek, Latin, and the Romance languages, the Germanic languages, the Slavic tongues, and the Indo-Iranian languages of Persian and Sanskrit and their derivatives. The common basis of all these Indo-European tongues is evident in similar names for both family relations (*father, mother,* and so on) and divine beings (for example, Latin *deus,* and Sanskrit *deva,* "god"). The perverse misuse of *Aryan* in Nazi Germany referred to a white "master race." This term is now usually restricted to linguistic use for the Indo-Iranian branch of the Indo-European family (Sanskrit, Persian, and so on), or to historical use for the particular peoples who invaded northern India and the Iranian plateau in the second millennium B.C.

"ARYANIZING" OF NORTH INDIA. The Vedic Aryans were seminomadic warriors who reached India via the mountain passes of the Hindu Kush, in modern Afghanistan. Theirs was probably a gradual migration of rather small tribal groups. These Aryans were horsemen and cattle herders rather than farmers and city builders. They, like their Iranian relatives, left their mark not in their material culture but in the changes that their conquest of new territory brought to existing society: a new language, a new social organization, new techniques of warfare, and new religious forms and ideas.

Hymn to Indra

This hymn celebrates especially the greatest deed ascribed to Indra, the slaying of the dragon Vritra to release the waters needed by people and livestock. Whether these waters are the rain or the dammed-up rivers is difficult to say. This victory also symbolizes the victory of the Aryans over the dark-skinned Dasas and the very creation of the world from the dragon's body. Note the sexual and rain imagery. The kadrukas *may be the bowls used for soma in the sacrifice. The* vajra *is Indra's thunderbolt; the name Dasa for the lord of the waters is also that used for the peoples defeated by the Aryans and for all enemies of Indra, of whom the* Pani *tribe is one.*

Indra's heroic deeds, indeed, will I proclaim, the first ones which the wielder of the vajra accomplished. He killed the dragon, released the waters, and split open the sides of the mountains.

He killed the dragon lying spread out on the mountain; for him Tvashtar fashioned the roaring vajra. Like bellowing cows, the waters, gliding, have gone down straightway to the ocean.

Showing off his virile power he chose soma; from the three *kadrukas* he drank of the extracted soma. The bounteous god took up the missile, the vajra; he killed the first-born among the dragons.

When you, O Indra, killed first-born among the dragons and further overpowered the wily tricks (māyā) of the tricksters, bringing forth, at that very moment, the sun, the heaven and the dawn—since then, indeed, have you not come across another enemy.

Indra killed Vritra, the greater enemy, the shoulderless one, with his mighty and fatal weapon, the vajra. Like branches of a tree lopped off with an axe,

the dragon lies prostrate upon the earth. . . .

Over him, who lay in that manner like a shattered reed flowed the waters for the sake of man. At the feet of the very waters, which Vritra had [once] enclosed with his might, the dragon [now] lay [prostrate]. . . .

With the Dasa as their lord and with the dragon as their warder, the waters remained imprisoned, like cows held by the Pani. Having killed Vritra, [Indra] threw open the cleft of waters which had been closed.

You became the hair of a horse's tail, O Indra, when he [Vritra] struck at your sharp-pointed vajra—the one god *eka deva* though you were. You won the cows, O brave one, you won soma; you released the seven rivers, so that they should flow. . . .

Indra, who wields the vajra in his hand, is the lord of what moves and what remains rested, of what is peaceful and what is horned. He alone rules over the tribes as their king; he encloses them as does a rim the spokes.

—Rig Veda 1.32

Wm. Theodore de Bary et al., *Sources of Indian Tradition* (New York: Columbia University Press, 1963).

Without documentation, we can piece together only the broad outlines of the early Aryans' gradual subjugation of northern India and their equally gradual shift from pastoral nomadism to settled agriculture and animal husbandry. We know that they penetrated first into the area of the Panjab and the Indus

Hymn to the Lord of Creatures

Here we have the creation of the world depicted as a Vedic sacrifice in which the primeval male principle, Purusha, is sacrificed by the gods as priests, apparently as an offering to himself. This paradox can occur in part because the figure Purusha is a blend of aspects of the male principle (Virāj in the text was originally a female principle of creative power), the god Agni, and the power of the sacrifice itself. The hymn is a late one, and its reference to the creation of the four social classes of humankind is the first such mention in an Indian text (Brahmans *formed the priestly class;* Rajanyas, *the warriors;* Vaishyas, *the merchant or commoner groups; and* Shudras, *the serf or servant class). These divisions became and remained in later India the four major categories of the social order (note that the warriors were later called* Kshatriyas).
▶ *Compare this account of the origins of the world with that of the Greek atomists in "The Atomists' Account of the Origin of the World Order" (Ch. 2, p. 74).*

Thousand-headed Purusha, thousand-eyed, thousand-footed—he, having pervaded the earth on all sides, still extends ten fingers beyond it.

Purusha alone is all this—whatever has been and whatever is going to be. Further, he is the lord of immortality and also of what grows on account of food.

Such is his greatness; greater, indeed, than this is Purusha. All creatures constitute but one quarter of him, his three quarters are the immortal in the heaven.

With his three quarters did Purusha rise up; one quarter of him again remains here. With it did he variously spread out on all sides over what eats and what eats not.

From him was Virāj born, from Virāj there evolved Purusha. He, being born, projected himself behind the earth as also before it.

When the gods performed the sacrifice with Purusha as the oblation, then the spring was its clarified butter, the summer the sacrificial fuel, and the autumn the oblation.

The sacrificial victim, namely, Purusha, born at the very beginning, they sprinkled with sacred water upon the sacrificial grass. With him as oblation the gods performed the sacrifice, and also the Sādhyas [a class of semidivine beings] and the rishis [ancient seers].

From that wholly offered sacrificial oblation were born the verses [rc] and the sacred chants; from it were born the meters *(chandas);* the sacrificial formula was born from it.

From it horses were born and also those animals who have double rows [i.e., upper and lower] of teeth; cows were born from it, from it were born goats and sheep.

When they divided Purusha, in how many different portions did they arrange him? What became of his mouth, what of his two arms? What were his two thighs and his two feet called?

His mouth became the brāhman; his two arms were made into the rājanya; his two thighs the vaishyas; from his two feet the shūdra was born.

The moon was born from the mind; from the eye the sun was born; from the mouth Indra and Agni; from the breath (prāna) the wind (vāyu) was born.

From the navel was the atmosphere created, from the head the heaven issued forth; from the two feet was born the earth and the quarters (the cardinal directions) from the ear. Thus did they fashion the worlds.

Seven were the enclosing sticks in this sacrifice, thrice seven were the fire-sticks made, when the gods, performing the sacrifice, bound down Purusha, the sacrificial victim.

With this sacrificial oblation did the gods offer the sacrifice. These were the first norms (dharma) of sacrifice. These greatnesses reached to the sky wherein live the ancient Sādhyas and gods.

—Rig Veda 19.90

Wm. Theodore de Bary et al., *Sources of Indian Tradition* (New York: Columbia University Press, 1963).

Valley (ca. 1800–1500 B.C.), presumably in search of grazing lands for their cattle and other livestock. They would have exploited their military superiority (based on the use of horses, chariots, and copper-bronze weaponry) to overcome the Indus peoples or their successors in these regions.

Echoes of such conflict seem to occur in some Rigvedic hymns; for example, those in which the god Indra is hailed as the warrior who smashes the fortifications of enemies (possibly the conquest of the Indus citadels?) and slays the great serpent who had blocked the rivers (possibly the destruction of the dams used to control the rivers of the Indus area for agriculture?). Where some later Rigvedic hymns speak of human rather than divine warriors, actual historical events may lie behind the legends. An example is the late hymn that praises the king of a tribe called the *Bharatas*—whence the modern name of India, *Bharat,* "land of the Bharatas."

In what may be called the Rigvedic period (ca. 1700–1000 B.C.), the newcomers settled in the Panjab and beyond, where they took up agriculture as well as stock breeding. The Thar desert blocked any southward expansion, so their subsequent movement was to the east. How far they penetrated before 1000 B.C. is not clear, but their main locus remained the Panjab and the plains west of the Yamuna River (northwest of modern Delhi). Then, between about 1000 and 500 B.C., these Aryan Indians (for no longer can we speak of them as a foreign people) spread across the Doab, the "two-rivers" plain formed between the Yamuna and the Ganges, and beyond. They cleared (probably by burning) the heavy forests that covered this area at that time and settled there. They also moved further northeast to the Himalayan foothills and southeast along the Ganges, in what was to be the cradle of subsequent Indian civilization. During this age, the importance of the Panjab receded sharply.

This later Vedic period (ca. 1000–500 B.C.) is often referred to as the Brahmanic age because of the dominance of the priestly religion of the Brahman class attested in later Vedic commentaries called the *Brahmanas* (ca. 1000–800 or 600 B.C.). This age is sometimes also called the *epic age,* because it provided the setting for the two classical Indian epics, the *Mahabharata* and the *Ramayana.* Both were composed much later, probably only in the period ca. 400 B.C.–A.D. 200, but they contain older materials and refer to dimly remembered events of earlier times. The *Mahabharata,* the longest epic poem in the world, centers on the power struggle of two Aryan

clans in the area to the north and west of modern Delhi, perhaps around 900 B.C. The *Ramayana* tells of the legendary and dramatic adventures of King Rama, whose travels may at one level recall the movement of northern Indian culture into southern India about the end of the Brahmanic period. Both epics evidence the complex cultural mixing of Aryan, Indus, and other earlier subcontinent peoples.

By about A.D. 200, this mixing would give rise to a distinguishable "Indian" civilization over most of the subcontinent. Its basis was clearly Aryan, but its language, society, and religion had assimilated much that was non-Aryan. Harappan culture vanished, but elements of it and other regional cultures played their part in the formation of Indian culture as we know it.

VEDIC ARYAN SOCIETY. The Aryans brought with them a society apparently characterized by patrilineal family descent and inheritance. The masculine orientation of the society was reflected in its overwhelmingly male gods. The patriarchal family was the basic unit of society. Marriage seems to have been monogamous, and widows could remarry.

Related families formed larger kin groups. The largest social grouping was the tribe, which was ruled by a tribal leader, or *raja* ("king" in Sanskrit, and a cognate of the latin *rex*), whose power was shared with a tribal council. In early Vedic days, the ruler was chosen for his prowess and was never a priest-king. His chief function was to lead in battle; he had originally no sacred authority. Alongside him was a chief priest, who looked after the often elaborate sacrifices on which religious life centered. We do not know if the king originally acted as the judge in legal matters, although by late Vedic, or Brahmanic, times he performed this function with the help of the priests. In the Brahmanic period, the power of the priestly class increased along with that of the king, who was now a hereditary ruler claiming divine qualities sanctioned by the priestly establishment.

Although there were probably identifiable groups of warriors and priests, Aryan society seems originally to have distinguished only two basic grades of society: the noble and the common. The *Dasas,* the darker, conquered peoples, came to form a third group (together with those who intermarried with them) of the socially excluded. Over time, a more rigid set of social classes, four in number, evolved. By the late Rigvedic period, these four divisions, or *varnas*, had become so basic as to be sanctioned explicitly in religious theory. These four classes (excluding the non-Aryan *Dasas*) were the priestly *(brahman),* the warrior/noble *(Kshatriya)*, the peasant/tradesman *(Vaishya),* and the servant *(Shudra)* groups, a division that has continued in theory into the present as a general way of organizing the far more numerous subgroups known as *castes* (see Chapter 7). It was, of course, only the members of the three upper classes who were full participants in the various spheres of social, political, and religious life. This isolation of the lowest groups foreshadowed the rigidity of caste distinctions that would later become a basic element in Indian life.

MATERIAL CULTURE.   The early, seminomadic Aryans had little in the way of impressive material culture. They did not build cities or even monuments as far as we know. A gray-painted pottery is one of the few physical remains of their culture. They lived simply in wood and thatch or, later, mud-walled dwellings; measured wealth in cattle (presaging the later importance of the cow in Hindu India?), and had developed craftsmanship in carpentry and bronze metal working. Iron probably was not known in India before 1000 B.C. Gold was used for ornamentation. Wool provided the basic textiles, and alongside stock breeding, some cultivation, especially of grains, was practiced. Intoxicating drink was well known, both the *soma* used in religious rites and a kind of mead.

Music seems to have been a highly developed art and pastime; singing and dancing are mentioned in the texts, as are various musical instruments. Gambling appears to have been a popular and frequent vice. Betting on chariot racing may have attracted the more affluent, but it is dicing above all that we hear of in Vedic and epic texts. One of the few secular pieces among the Vedic hymns is a "Gambler's Lament," which closes with a plea to the dice: "Take pity on us. Do not bewitch us with your fierce magic. Let no one be trapped by the brown dice!"

The Brahmanic age has left us only a few more material remains. It was still not a time of developed urban culture, even in the mud-brick towns that were growing up as new lands were burned clear for cultivation and village settlements. There were now established kingdoms with fixed capitals, and trade was growing, especially along the Ganges, although we have no mention of a true coinage system. Specialized groups of craftsmen—goldsmiths, basketmakers, weavers, potters, and entertainers—are mentioned in the later texts.

We do not know when writing was introduced or developed. To judge from references to its common use by around 500 B.C., it may have been about 700 B.C. The evidence shows that Indian goods were again finding their way to Mesopotamia during this period, which suggests that writing may have been reintroduced in the subcontinent through this trade connection. Yet so highly developed was the oral tradition of Veda transmission among the Brahman class, that writing continued to be scorned as an unworthy medium for the sacred texts of the Veda.

RELIGION.   The most important contributions of Vedic India to later history were religious. In the Vedas, we can glimpse the broad outlines and development of Vedic-Brahmanic religion over the thousand years following the arrival of the first Aryans in the subcontinent. However, they tell us only about the public cult and domestic rituals of the Aryan upper classes, not about popular traditions of the masses. We can surmise that among the latter, many Harappan and other non-Aryan practices and ideas continued to flourish. Apparently non-Aryan elements are visible occasionally even in the Vedic texts themselves, especially later ones such as the Upanishads (after ca. 800 B.C.), in their emphasis on fertility and female deities, ritual pollution and ablutions, and the transmigration of the soul after death.

The central Vedic cult, which was controlled by priests serving a military aristocracy, was dominant until the middle of the first millennium B.C. By this time other, perhaps older, religious forms were evidently asserting themselves among the populace.

The increasing ritual formalism of Brahmanic religion generated challenges in both religious practice and speculative thought. It culminated in the rise and spread of the Buddhist, Jain, and Hindu traditions (see Chapter 2).

The earliest Indo-Aryans seem to have worshiped numerous gods, who most often embodied or were associated with powers of nature. We see vestiges of this association in the Rigvedic hymns, which are addressed to anthropomorphic gods. Despite their human form, these gods are commonly linked to one or more natural phenomena: the sky, the clouds, or the sun. Whether the human aspect of what may once have been deified natural forces was due to a gradual deification or mythologizing of the ancient human heroes, we cannot say. But the deities we encounter in the Rig Veda are comparable to those of Greek religion. They are also probably distantly related to the latter; note, for example, the similar names of the Aryan father-god Dyaus and the Greek father-god Zeus, which point to a common Indo-European source. In Vedic India, however, unlike in Greece, the father-god had receded in importance before the rising cult of his children. Chief among them was Indra, god of war and the storm. A rowdy god not unlike the old Norse Thor, he led his heavenly warriors across the sky to slay dragons or other enemies with his thunderbolt in his hand.

Also of major importance was Varuna, who may have connections with the later Iranian god Ahura Mazda and Uranus, Greek god of the heavens. Varuna was more remote from human affairs than Indra. He was depicted as an imperial or regal figure who sat on his heavenly throne and guarded the cosmic order, *Rta*, which is both the law of nature and the universal moral law or truth. As the god whose great holiness commanded awe and demanded righteous behavior, Varuna had characteristics of a supreme, omnipresent divinity.

Another god whose central place in the Vedas stands out is Agni, the god of fire (his name, which is the word for "fire" in Sanskrit, is related to Latin *ignis*, "fire," and thus to our *ignite*). He had diverse roles. He was the god who mediated between earth and heaven through the offering of the fire sacrifice; thus, he was the god of the sacrifice and the priests; and he was also the god of the hearth and hence the home. Like the elusive flame, he was a mysterious deity about whose form and presence in all earthly fires there is much speculation in the Rig Veda.

Many other gods could be mentioned: Soma, the god of the hallucinogenic soma plant and drink; Ushas, the goddess of dawn (one of very few feminine deities); Yama, god of the dead; Rudra, the archer and storm god; Vishnu, a solar deity; and the sun god Surya. A major characteristic of the Vedic hymns is that when any single god is addressed, he or she is praised as possessing a wide variety of powers. Many of these powers may normally have been associated with other deities, but this did not bar attributing them also to the god the worshiper was addressing.

The focus of Vedic religious life was sacrifice to the gods. In the sacrificial ritual, the sacrificers seem to have experienced the presence of the gods to whom they made their offering.

The drinking of soma juice was a prominent sacrificial ritual that greatly enhanced the subjective experience of the participants. There seems to have been no emphasis on thanksgiving or expiation of guilt through sacrifice. The recurring theme was the desire for the good things of this life: prosperity, health, victory, and the like. Fire sacrifices were particularly important on a large, both public and private, domestic scale. There were also exclusively royal rituals,

ANCIENT INDIA	
ca. 2250–1750 B.C. (2500–1500?)	Indus (Harappan) civilization
ca. 1800–1500 B.C.	Aryan peoples invade northwestern India
ca. 1500–1000 B.C.	Rigvedic period: composition of Rigvedic hymns; Panjab as center of Indo-Aryan civilization
ca. 1000–500 B.C.	Later Vedic period: Doab as center of Indo-Aryan civilization
ca. 1000–800/600 B.C.	Composition of *Brahmanas* and other Vedic texts
ca. 800–500 B.C.	Composition of major Upanishads
ca. 700–500 B.C.	Probable introduction of writing
ca. 400 B.C.–A.D. 200	Composition of great epics, the *Mahabharata* and *Ramayana*

such as that of the elaborate and seldom performed horse sacrifice.

By Brahmanic times, there had emerged considerable mystical and speculative interpretation of the sacrifice in which sacrificer, sacrificial animal, and god were all identified with one another. Even the creation of the world is described in one Rigvedic hymn as the sacrifice of a primordial being to himself by the lesser gods. The late Vedic texts also emphasize magical and cosmic aspects of ritual and sacrifice. Indeed, some of the *Brahmanas* indicate that only through the exact performance of the sacrifice is the world order maintained.

The word *Brahman* was originally used to designate the ritual utterance, and it came to refer also to the generalized divine power present in the sacrifice. In the Upanishads, some of the latest Vedic texts and the ones most concerned with speculation about the universe, *Brahman* was extended to refer to the Absolute, the transcendent principle of reality. As the guardian of ritual and the master of the sacred word, the priest was known throughout the Vedic Aryan period by a related word, *Brahmana*, for which the English is *Brahman*. Echoes of these associations were to lend force in later Hindu tradition to the special status of the Brahman caste groups as the highest class of

MAP 1-4 BRONZE AGE CHINA DURING THE SHANG DYNASTY, 1766–1050 B.C. *An Yang was a capital toward the end of the Shang dynasty. Loyang was the capital of the Eastern Chou.*

society. We shall see this in Chapter 7 when we take up the Indian story once more.

Early Chinese Civilization

Neolithic Origins in the Yellow River Valley

Agriculture began in China about 4000 B.C. in the basin of the southern bend of the Yellow River. This is the northernmost of East Asia's four great river systems. The others are the Yangtze in central China, the West River in southern China, and the Red River in what is today northern Vietnam. All drain eastward into the Pacific Ocean. In recent millennia, the Yellow River has flowed through a deforested plain, cold in winter and subject to periodic droughts. But in 4000 B.C., its climate was warmer, with forested highlands in the west and swampy marshes to the east. The bamboo rat that today can be found only in semitropical Southeast Asia lived along the Yellow River.

The chief crop of China's agricultural revolution was millet. A second agricultural development focusing on rice may have occurred on the Huai River between the Yellow River and the Yangtze near the coast. In time, wheat entered China from the west. The early Chinese cleared land and burned its cover to plant millet and cabbage and, later, rice and soybeans. When the soil became exhausted, the fields were abandoned, and sometimes early villages were abandoned, too. The tools were of stone: axes, hoes, spades, and sickle-shaped knives. The early Chinese domesticated pigs, sheep, cattle, dogs, and chickens. Game was also plentiful, and hunting continued to be important to the village economy. In excavated village garbage heaps of ancient China are found the bones of deer, wild cattle, antelopes, rhinoceros, hares, and marmots. Grain was stored in pottery painted in bold, geometric designs of red and black. This pottery gave way to a harder, thin black pottery, made on a potter's wheel, whose use spread west along the Yellow River and south to the Yangtze. The tripodal shapes of Neolithic pots prefigure later Chinese bronzes.

The earliest cultivators lived in wattle-and-daub pit-dwellings with wooden support-posts and sunken, plastered floors. Their villages were located in isolated clearings along the slopes of river valleys. Archaeological finds of weapons and the remains of earthen walls suggest tribal warfare between villages. Of the religion of these people, little is known, although some evidence indicates the worship of ancestral spirits. They practiced divination by applying heat to a hole drilled in the shoulder bone of a steer or the undershell of a tortoise, and then interpreting the resulting cracks in the bone. They buried their dead in cemeteries with jars of food. Tribal leaders wore rings and beads of jade.

Early Bronze Age: The Shang

The traditional history of China tells of three ancient dynasties:

2205–1766 B.C.	Hsia
1766–1050 B.C.	Shang
1050–256 B.C.	Chou

Until early in this century, modern historians saw the first two as legendary. Then, in the 1920s, archaeological excavations at "the wastes of Yin" near present-day An Yang uncovered the ruins of a walled city that had been a late Shang capital (see Map 1-4). Other Shang cities have been discovered more recently. The ruins contained the archives of the department of divination of the Shang court, with thousands on thousands of "oracle bones" incised with archaic Chinese writing. The names of kings on the bones fit almost perfectly those of the traditional historical record. The recognition that the Shang actually existed has led historians to suggest that the Hsia may also have been an actual dynasty. Perhaps the Hsia was a late

Neolithic black-pottery kingdom; perhaps it already had bronze and represents the earliest, still missing stage of Chinese writing.

The characteristic political institution of Bronze Age China was the city-state. The largest was the Shang capital, which, frequently moved, lacked the monumental architecture of Egypt or Mesopotamia. The walled city contained public buildings, altars, and the residences of the aristocracy and was surrounded by a sea of Neolithic tribal villages. By late Shang times, several such cities were spotted across the north China plain. The Shang kings possessed political, economic, social, and religious authority. When they died, they were sometimes succeeded by younger brothers and sometimes by sons. The rulers of other city-states acknowledged their authority.

The military aristocracy went to war in chariots, supported by levies of foot soldiers. Their weapons were spears and powerful compound bows. Accounts tell of armies of three or four thousand troops and of a battle involving thirteen thousand. The Shang fought against barbarian tribes and, occasionally, against other city-states in rebellion against Shang rule. Captured prisoners were enslaved.

Inscribed oracle bone from the Shang Dynasty city of An Yang. [Columbia University]

Chinese Writing

The Chinese system of writing dates back at least to the Shang dynasty (1766–1050 B.C.), when animal bones and tortoise shells (the so-called oracle bones) were incised for the purpose of divination. About half of the three thousand characters used in Shang times have been deciphered. They evolved over the centuries into the fifty thousand characters found in the largest dictionaries. But even today only about three or four thousand are in common use. A scholar may know twice that number.

Characters developed from little pictures. Note the progressive stylization. By 200 B.C., the writing had become standardized and close to the modern form of the printed character.

	Shang (1400 B.C.)	Chou (600 B.C.)	Seal Script (200 B.C.)	Modern
Sun				
Moon				
Tree				
Bird				
Mouth				
Horse				

Other characters combined two pictures to express an idea. The following examples use modern characters:

Sun 日 + moon 月 = bright 明

Mouth 口 + bird 鳥 = to chirp 鳴

Woman 女 + child 子 = good 好

Tree 木 + sun 日 = east 東

It was a matter of convention that the sun behind a tree meant the rising sun in the east and not the setting sun in the west.

Characters were formed several other ways. In one, a sound element was combined with a meaning element. Chinese has many homonyms, or words with the same sound. The character 台, for example, is read *tai* and means "elevation" or "to raise up." But in spoken Chinese, there are other words with the same sound that mean "moss," "trample," a "nag," and "idle." Thus

Tai 台 + grass 艹 = moss 苔

Tai 台 + foot 足 = trample 踏

Tai 台 + horse 馬 = a nag 駘

Tai 台 + heart 心 = idle 怠

In each case the sound comes from the 台, and the meaning from the other element. Note that the 台 may be at the bottom, the top, or the right. This positioning, too, is a matter of convention.

Tables by A. Craig; calligraphy by Teruko Craig.

One feature of Shang civilization was its system of writing. Scribes at the Shang court kept records on strips of bamboo, which have not survived. But there are inscriptions on bronzes as well as on the oracle bones. Some bones contain the question put to the oracle, the answer, and the outcome of the matter. Representative questions were: Which ancestor is causing the king's earache? If the king goes hunting at Ch'i, will there be a disaster? Will the king's child be a son? If the king sends his army to attack an enemy, will the deity help him? Was a sacrifice acceptable to ancestral deities? What we know of Shang religion is based on the bones.

The Shang Chinese believed in a supreme "Deity Above," who had authority over the human world. There were also lesser natural deities—the sun, moon, earth, rain, wind, and the six clouds—who served at the court of the Deity Above. Even the Shang king sacrificed not to the Deity Above but to his ancestors, who interceded with the Deity Above on the king's behalf. Kings, while alive at least, were not divine but were the high priests of the state. In Shang times, as later, religion in China was closely associated with cosmology. The Shang people observed the movements of the planets and stars and reported eclipses. Celestial happenings were seen as omens from the gods above. The chief cosmologists also recorded events at the court. The Shang calendar had a month of 30 days and a year of 360 days. Adjustments were made periodically by adding an extra month. The calendar was used by the king to tell his people when to sow and when to reap.

A second mark of Shang civilization was the mastery of bronze technology. Bronze appeared in China about 2000 B.C., a thousand years behind Mesopotamia and five hundred years after India. Because Shang methods of casting were more advanced than those of Mesopotamia, and because the designs emerge directly from the preceding black-pottery culture, an independent origin is likely. Bronze was used for weapons, armor, and chariot fittings, and for a variety of ceremonial vessels of amazing fineness and beauty.

A third feature of Shang society, and indeed of all

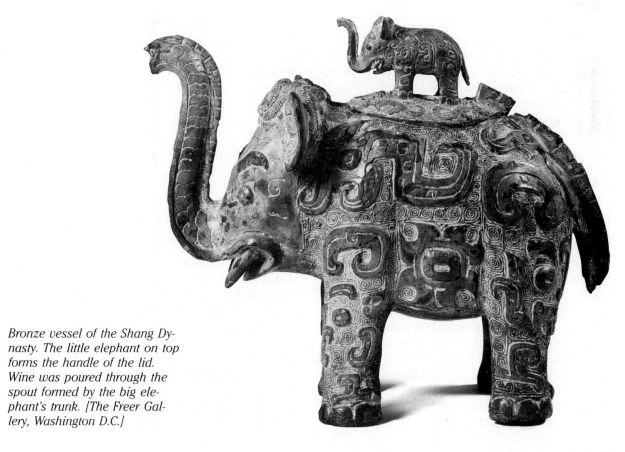

Bronze vessel of the Shang Dynasty. The little elephant on top forms the handle of the lid. Wine was poured through the spout formed by the big elephant's trunk. [The Freer Gallery, Washington D.C.]

Human Sacrifice During the Shang

By the seventh century B.C., *human sacrifices were less frequent, but they still happened. A poem composed when Duke Mu of the state of Ch'in died in 631 casts doubt on whether religious belief or the honor of it all made the victims go gladly to the grave. Were human feelings different, Professor K. C. Chang has asked, a thousand years earlier during the Shang? Note the identification of Heaven with "that blue one," the sky.*

"Kio" sings the oriole
As it lights on the thorn-bush.
Who went with Duke Mu to the grave?
Yen-hsi of the clan Tsu-chu.
Now this Yen-hsi
Was the pick of all our men;
But as he drew near the tomb-hole
His limbs shook with dread.
That blue one, Heaven,
Takes all our good men.
Could we but ransom him
There are a hundred would give their lives.

"Kio" sings the oriole
As it lights on the mulberry-tree.
Who went with Duke Mu to the grave?
Chung-hang of the clan Tsu-chu.
Now this Chung-hang
Was the sturdiest of all our men;
But as he drew near the tomb-hole
His limbs shook with dread.
That blue one, Heaven,
Takes all our good men.
Could we but ransom him
There are a hundred would give their lives.

The Book of Songs, trans. by Arthur Waley (New York: Grove Press, 1960), p. 311.

---

early river-valley civilizations, was that as humans gained freedom from nature through agriculture and bronze technology, they abandoned the rough equality of primitive society and used their new powers to create a rigidly stratified society in which the many were compelled to serve the few. A monopoly of bronze weapons enabled aristocrats to exploit other groups. A hierarchy of class defined life in the Chinese city-state. The king and the officials of his court lived within the walled city. Their houses were spacious, built above the ground with roofs supported by rows of wooden pillars, resting on foundation stones. Their life-style was, for ancient times, opulent. They wore fine clothes, feasted at banquets, and drank wine from bronze vessels. In contrast, a far larger population of agricultural workers lived outside the city in cramped pit dwellings. Their life was meager and hard. Archaeological excavations of their underground hovels have uncovered only pottery pots.

Nowhere was the gulf between the royal lineage and the baseborn more apparent than it was in the Shang institution of human sacrifice. One Shang tomb 39 feet long, 26 feet wide, and 26 feet deep contained the decapitated bodies of humans, horses, and dogs, as well as ornaments of bone, stone, and jade.

When a king died, hundreds of slaves or prisoners of war, sometimes together with those who had served the king during his lifetime, might be buried with him. Sacrifices also were made when a palace or an altar was built.

Later Bronze Age: The Western Chou

To the west of the area of Shang rule, in the Wei valley near the present-day city of Sian, lived the Chou people. The Wei River is a tributary of the Yellow River.

They were less civilized, closer to the Neolithic black-pottery culture, but more warlike than the Shang. According to the oracle bones, they had relations with the Shang, sometimes friendly, sometimes hostile. In 1050 B.C., the Shang were weakened by campaigns against nomads in the north and rebellious tribes in the east. According to the traditional historical record, the last Shang kings had become weak, cruel, and tyrannical. The Chou seized the opportunity, made alliances with disaffected city-states, and swept in, conquering the Shang.

In most respects, the Chou continued the Shang

pattern of life and rule. The agrarian-based city-state continued to be the basic unit of society. It is estimated that there were about two hundred in the eighth century B.C. The hierarchy of classes was not unlike that of the Shang: kings and lords, officials and warriors, peasants, and slaves. Slaves were used primarily as domestic servants. Because the Chou were culturally backward, they assimilated the culture of the Shang. Ideographic writing developed without interruption. Bronze ceremonial vessels continued to be cast, although Chou vessels lack the fineness that set the Shang above the rest of the Bronze Age world.

The Chou kept their capital in the west but set up a secondary capital at Loyang, along the southern bend of the Yellow River. They appointed their kinsmen or other aristocratic allies to rule in other city-states. Blood or lineage ties were essential to the Chou pattern of rule. The Chou king was the head of the senior branch of the family. He performed the sacrifices to the Deity Above for the entire family. The rankings of the lords of other princely states—which, for want of better terms, are usually translated into the titles of English feudal nobility: duke, marquis, earl, viscount, and baron—reflected their degree of closeness to the senior line of Chou kings.

One difference between the Shang and the Chou was in the nature of political legitimacy. The Shang kings, descended from shamanistic rulers, had an inbuilt religious authority and needed no theory to justify their rule. But the Chou, having conquered the Shang, needed a rationale for why they, and not the Shang, were the rightful rulers. Their argument was that Heaven (the name for the supreme being that gradually replaced the "Deity Above" during the early Chou), appalled by the wickedness of the last Shang king, had withdrawn its mandate to rule, awarding the mandate, instead, to the Chou. This concept of the mandate of Heaven was subsequently invoked by every dynasty in China down to the twentieth century. In the beginning, Heaven was both cosmological and anthropomorphic. The ideograph for Heaven 天 is related to that for man 人. In the later Chou, although Heaven continued to have a moral will, it became less anthropomorphic and more a metaphysical force.

Iron Age: The Eastern Chou

In 771 B.C., the Wei valley capital of the Western Chou was overrun by barbarians. In Chinese tradition, the event provided the equivalent of "crying wolf." The last Western Chou king was so infatuated with a favor-

ite concubine that he repeatedly lit the bonfires that signaled a barbarian attack. His concubine would clap her hands in delight at the sight of the army assembled in martial splendor. But the army tired of the charade, and when invaders actually came, the king's beacons were ignored. The king was killed and the Chou capital sacked. The heir to the throne, with some members of the court, escaped to the secondary capital at Loyang, two hundred miles to the east and just south of the bend in the Yellow River.

The first phase of the Eastern Chou is sometimes called the Spring and Autumn period after the classic history by that name that treats the 772- to 481-year span. After their flight to Loyang, the Chou kings were never able to reestablish their old authority. Loyang remained a center of culture and ritual observances. But by the early seventh century B.C., its political power was nominal: Kinship and religious ties to the Chou house had worn thin, and it no longer had the military strength to reimpose its rule. During the seventh and sixth centuries B.C. in China, the political configuration was an equilibrium of many little principalities on the north-central plain surrounded by larger, wholly autonomous territorial states along the borders of northern China (see Map 1-5). The larger states consolidated the areas within their borders,

MAP 1-5 EARLY IRON AGE TERRITORIAL STATES IN CHINA DURING THE SIXTH CENTURY B.C. *After the fall of the Western Chou in 771 B.C., northern China divided into territorial states that became increasingly independent of the later Chou kings.*

absorbed tribal peoples, and expanded, conquering states on their periphery.

To defend themselves against the more aggressive territorial states, and in the absence of effective Chou authority, the smaller states entered defensive alliances. The earliest alliance, of 681 B.C., was directed against the half-barbarian state of Ch'u (pronounced "chew"), which straddled the Yangtze in the south. Princes and lords of smaller states elected as their hegemon (or military overlord) the lord of a northern territorial state and pledged him their support. At the formal ceremony that established the alliance, a bull was sacrificed. The hegemon and then the other lords smeared its blood on their mouths and before the gods swore oaths to uphold the alliance. That the oaths were not always upheld can be surmised from the Chinese expression "to break an oath while the blood is still wet on one's lips."

During the next two centuries, alliances shifted and hegemons changed. At best, the alliances only slowed down the pace of military aggrandizement.

The second phase of the Eastern Chou is known as the Warring States period after a chronicle of the same name treating the years from 401 to 256 B.C. By the fifth century B.C., all defensive alliances had collapsed. Strong states swallowed their weaker neighbors. The border states grew in size and power. Interstate stability disappeared. By the fourth century B.C., only eight or nine great territorial states remained as contenders. The only question was which one would defeat the others and go on to unify China.

Three basic changes in Chinese society contributed to the rise of large territorial states. One was the expansion of population and agricultural lands. The walled cities of the Shang and Western Chou had been like oases in the wilds, bounded by plains, marshes, and forests. Game was plentiful; thus, hunting, along with sheep and cattle breeding, supplemented agriculture. But in the Eastern Chou as the population grew, the wilds began to disappear, the economy became almost entirely agricultural, and hunting became an aristocratic pastime. Friction arose over boundaries as states began to abut. These changes accelerated in the late sixth century B.C. after the start of the Iron Age. Iron tools cleared new lands and plowed deeper, raising yields and increasing agricultural surpluses. Irrigation and drainage canals became important for the first time. Serfs gave way to farmers, who bought and sold land. By the third century B.C., China had about twenty million people, making it the most populous country in the world, a distinction that it has never lost.

EARLY CHINA	
4000 B.C.	Neolithic agricultural villages
1766 B.C.	Bronze Age city-states, aristocratic charioteers, pictographic writing
771 B.C.	Iron Age territorial states
500 B.C.	Age of philosophers
221 B.C.	China is unified

A second development was the rise of commerce. The roads built for war were used by merchants. Goods were transported by horses; oxcarts; riverboats; and the camel, which entered China in the third century B.C. The products of one region were traded for those of another. Copper coins joined bolts of silk and precious metals as media of exchange. Rich merchants rivaled in life-style the landowning lower nobility. New outer walls were added to cities to provide for expanded merchant quarters. The bronze bells and mirrors, clay figurines, lacquer boxes, and musical instruments found in late Chou tombs give ample evidence that the material and artistic culture of China leaped ahead during this period, despite its endemic wars.

A third change that doomed the city-state was the rise of a new kind of army. The war chariots of the old aristocracy, practical only on level terrain, gave way to cavalry armed with crossbows. Most of the fighting was done by conscript foot soldiers. The armies of the territorial states numbered in the hundreds of thousands. The old nobility gave way to professional commanders. The old aristocratic etiquette, which governed behavior even in battle, gave way to military tactics that were bloody and ruthless. Prisoners were often massacred.

Change also affected government. The lords of the new territorial states began to style themselves as kings, taking the title that previously only the Chou royalty had enjoyed. At some courts, the hereditary nobility began to decline, supplanted by ministers appointed for their knowledge of statecraft. To survive, the new states had to transform their agricultural and commercial wealth into military strength. To collect taxes, conscript soldiers, and administer the affairs of state required records and literate officials. Academies were established to fill the need. Beneath the ministers, a literate bureaucracy developed. Its members were referred to as *shih*, a term that had once meant "warrior" but gradually came to mean "scholar-bureaucrat." The *shih* were of mixed social origins, including the petty nobility, literate members of the old warrior class, landlords, merchants, and rising commoners. From this class came the philosophers who created the "one hundred schools" and transformed the culture of China.

Civilization in the Americas

Still other areas of human civilization arose on the two American continents. It is generally believed that peoples from Asia crossed the Bering Sea at least twenty thousand years ago. There were probably several such migrations. Over the course of centuries, these Asian immigrants to the Americas continued to move south and east from what is now Alaska until they eventually crossed the more than eleven thousand miles to the tip of South America and the more than four thousand miles to the eastern regions of North America. In light of the vast distances and imposing geographic barriers involved, these ancient migrations must have been as heroic as any in human history. From them a wide variety of original American cultures and many hundreds of languages arose.

The earliest immigrants to the Americas, like all other Paleolithic peoples, lived from hunting, fishing, and gathering. At the time of the initial migrations, there were herds of mammoths to be hunted, but mammoths and many other forms of game had become extinct in the Americas by the end of the ice age. A distinct shortage of sources of animal protein developed in many parts of the two continents, including the North American Southwest, Mesoamerica, and much of South America. Neither horses nor cattle populated the American continents by the time of the European contact. Where fishing or small game were not sufficiently plentiful, people had to rely on protein from vegetable sources. One result was that the original Americas participated in the Neolithic revolution in a quite remarkable manner. American production of agricultural foodstuffs providing protein far outpaced that of European agriculture. In this regard one of the most important early developments was the cultivation of maize. Wherever maize could be extensively grown, a major ingredient in the food supply was secured. The cultivation of maize appears to have been in place in Mexico by approximately 4000 B.C. and to have developed further south somewhat later. Other important foods were potatoes (developed in the Andes), manioc, squash, beans, peppers, and tomatoes. Many of these foods entered the diet of Europeans, Asians, and other peoples after the European conquest of the Americas in the sixteenth century A.D.

Eventually four areas of relatively dense settlement emerged in the Americas. One of these, in the Pacific Northwest in the area around Puget Sound, depended on the extraordinary abundance of fish in the region rather than on agriculture and did not develop urbanized states. Another was the Mississippi valley, where, based on maize agriculture, the inhabitants developed a high level of social and political integration that had, however, collapsed several centuries before European contact. The other two, Mesoamerica and the Andean region of South America, saw the emergence of strong and long-lasting states. In other regions with maize agriculture and settled village life—notably the North American Southwest—food sup-

Olmec Head. This colossal head, now in the Museo Nacional de Antropología in Mexico City, was excavated at San Lorenzo. Carved of basalt, it may be a portrait of an Olmec ruler. Olmec civilization thrived between 1500 and 800 B.C. [Government of Mexico]

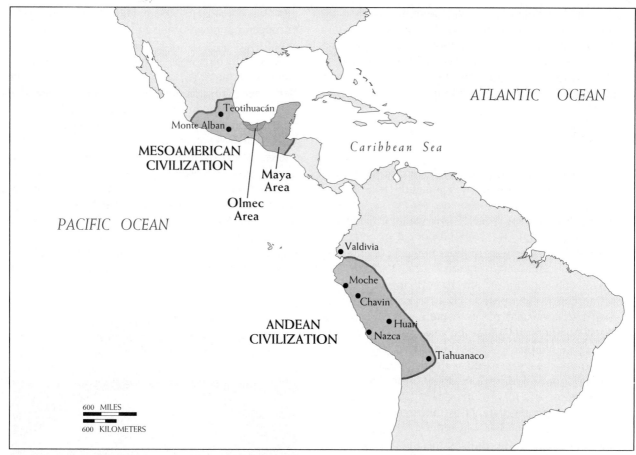

MAP 1-6 CIVILIZATION IN MESOAMERICA AND THE ANDEAN REGION *Both Mesoamerica and the Andean region of South America saw the development of a series of civilizations beginning between 1500 and 1000 B.C.*

plies might have been too insecure to support the development of states.

A series of civilizations arose in Mesoamerica, starting approximately in 1500 B.C., on the Gulf coast in the region of modern Veracruz, with that of the Olmecs, best known today for the monumental stone faces they created (see Map 1-6). Succeeding civilizations in Central Mexico (the Classic period civilization of Teotihuacán and the Post-Classic civilizations of the Toltecs and Aztecs), the Oaxaca area (Monte Alban), and the Yucatán and Guatemala (the Classic and Post-Classic Maya) built extensive cities, developed writing and sophisticated calendar systems, and were organized in complex social and political structures.

Civilization in the Andes—in present-day Ecuador, Peru, Bolivia, and northern Chile—was characterized by alternating periods of integration and independent regional development. The first great regional tradition—called Chavín after the archaeological site at Chavín de Huantar in the highlands of Peru—developed around 900 B.C. and ended by about 200 B.C. Artifacts in the distinctive Chavín style can be found over a large area dating to this period, which

EARLY CIVILIZATIONS OF MESOAMERICA	
1500–800 B.C.	The Olmec
A.D. 200–750	The Classic period in Central Mexico. Dominance of Teotihuacán in the Valley of Mexico and Monte Alban in the Valley of Oaxaca.
A.D. 300–900	The Classic period of Maya civilization in the Yucatán and Guatemala

archaeologists call the Early Horizon. Too little is known, however, to say whether the spread of the style represents actual political integration or perhaps only the influence of a strong religious center. The period following the decline of Chavín, which archaeologists call the Early Intermediate period, saw the development of regional cultures. Notable among them are the Moche culture on the northern coast of Peru and the Nazca culture on the southern coast. A second period of integration—called the Middle Horizon—occurred around 600 A.D., this time probably associated with an empire (or perhaps two empires) centered on the highland sites of Huari and Tiahuanaco. A second period of regional independence—the Late Intermediate period—was dominated on the northern coast of Peru by the Chimu successors of the Moche state. This period ended

EARLY CIVILIZATION OF THE ANDES	
900–200 B.C.	Chavín (Early) Horizon
A.D. 100–600	Early Intermediate period (Moche on the northern coast of Peru, Nazca on the southern coast)
A.D. 600–1000	Middle (Huari/Tiahuanaco) Horizon

with the founding of the vast, tightly controlled empire of the Incas in the fourteenth and fifteenth centuries A.D.

The achievements of these native American civilizations (some of which we will discuss in greater de-

A ceramic vessel in feline form of the Chavín culture of ancient Peru. Both the feline motif and the stirrup-shaped form of the spout were enduring elements in Andean art. This piece comes from the site of Tembladera in Peru. The Chavín culture flourished from about 900 to 200 B.C. [The Metropolitan Museum of Art, The Michael C. Rockefeller Memorial Collection of Primitive Art, Purchase, Nelson A. Rockefeller Gift 1968. (1978.412.217)]

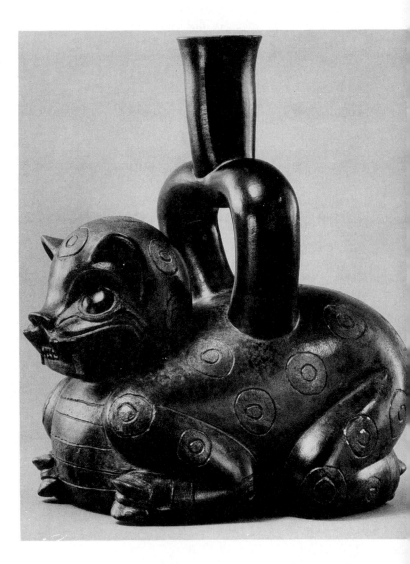

tail in Chapter 23) are all the more remarkable in light of technologies that they lacked. They did not use the wheel for transportation, nor did they make extensive use of metallurgy. They had not invented the plow. They did not know about gunpowder. They did not have oceangoing ships. They did achieve remarkable skills in pottery and weaving and constructed some of the most impressive sculptural and architectural monuments in the world. The level of technology that the original Americans possessed when the Europeans arrived, however, was probably not much different from that of a thousand years earlier. That technological disparity was the single most important element in the success of the European conquest.

The original Americans also stood virtually isolated for thousands of years from other human civilizations that were developing on the Eurasian land mass and Africa. They appear to have come into significant contact with the rest of the world only with the European voyages of discovery that started in 1492. That vast era of separation meant that there were numerous diseases against which Europeans had developed immunities but from which the original Americans remained unprotected. Their vulnerability to these diseases cost the lives of hundreds of thousands during the sixteenth century after European contact.

The geographic and cultural isolation of the Americas and the devastation of so many native American societies in the wake of the conquest have limited the information available to us about their development. Their languages were often unwritten, and the historical accounts that were written were often revised as one group conquered another. In turn the later Europeans interpreted the lives and history of these peoples from a distinctly European standpoint. Consequently many mysteries about the original peoples of America remain.

Suggested Readings

GENERAL PREHISTORY

V. GORDON CHILDE, *What Happened in History* (1946). A pioneering study of human prehistory and history before the Greeks from an anthropological point of view.

M. EHRENBERG, *Women in Prehistory* (1989). An account of the role of women in early times.

D. C. JOHNSON and M. R. EDEY, *Lucy: The Beginning of Mankind* (1981). An account of the African origins of humans.

CHARLES L. REDMAN, *The Rise of Civilization* (1978). An attempt to use the evidence provided by anthropology, archaeology, and the physical sciences to illuminate the development of early urban society.

NEAR EAST

HENRI FRANKFORT, *Ancient Egyptian Religion: An Interpretation* (1948). A brief but masterful attempt to explore the religious conceptual world of ancient Egyptians in intelligible and interesting terms.

HENRI FRANKFORT et al., *Before Philosophy* (1949). A brilliant examination of the mind of the ancients from the Stone Age to the Greeks.

ALAN GARDINER, *Egypt of the Pharaohs* (1961). A sound narrative history.

O. R. GURNEY, *The Hittites* (1954). A good general survey.

W. W. HALLO and W. K. SIMPSON, *The Ancient Near East: A History* (1971). A fine survey of Egyptian and Mesopotamian history.

THORKILD JACOBSEN, *The Treasures of Darkness: A History of Mesopotamian Religion* (1976). A superb and sensitive re-creation of the spiritual life of Mesopotamian peoples from the fourth to the first millennium B.C.

SAMUEL N. KRAMER, *The Sumerians: Their History, Culture and Character* (1963). A readable general account of Sumerian history.

A. T. OLMSTEAD, *History of Assyria* (1923). A good narrative account.

JAMES B. PRITCHARD, ed., *Ancient Near Eastern Texts Relating to the Old Testament* (1969). A good collection of documents in translation with useful introductory material.

D. B. REDFORD, *Akhenaten* (1987). A new study of the controversial religious reformer.

G. ROUX, *Ancient Iraq* (1964). A good recent account of ancient Mesopotamia.

W. F. SAGGS, *Everyday Life in Babylonia and Assyria*, rev. ed. (1987). A new edition of a classic work.

W. F. SAGGS, *The Greatness That Was Babylon* (1962). An excellent narrative account of Mesopotamian history.

K. C. SEELE, *When Egypt Ruled the East* (1965). A study of Egypt in its imperial period.

B. G. TRIGGER et al., *Ancient Egypt: A Social History* (1982).

JOHN A. WILSON, *Culture of Ancient Egypt* (1956). A fascinating interpretation of the civilization of ancient Egypt.

INDIA

D. P. AGRAWAL, *The Archaeology of India* (1982). A fine survey of the problems and data. Detailed, but with excellent summaries and brief general discussions of major issues.

B. and R. ALLCHIN, *The Birth of Indian Civilization: India and Pakistan Before 500* B.C. (1968). A one-volume summary of prehistoric India from an archaeological perspective.

W. T. DE BARY et al., comp., *Sources of Indian Tradition* (1958; 2nd rev. ed., 2 vols., New York, 1988). A fine anthology of original texts in translation from all periods of Indian civilization.

A. L. BASHAM, *The Wonder That Was India,* 2nd rev. ed. (1963). Chapters 1 and 2 provide a readable and carefully done introduction to ancient India through the Aryan culture. Still the classic general work.

E. C. L. DURING CASPERS, "Summer, Coastal Arabia and the Indus Valley in Protoliterate and Early Dynastic Eras," *JESHO* 22, 2 (1979): 121–135.

C. CHAKRABORTY, *Common Life in the Rigveda and Atharvaveda—An Account of the Folklore in the Vedic Period* (1977). An interesting attempt to reconstruct everyday life in the Vedic period from the principal Vedic texts.

D. D. KOSAMBI, *Ancient India: A History of Its Culture and Civilization* (1965). The most readable survey history of India to the fourth century A.D. See Chapters 2–4 on prehistoric, Indus, and Aryan culture.

W. D. O'FLAHERTY, *The Rig Veda: An Anthology* (1981). An excellent selection of vedic texts of different kinds in prosaic but very careful translation with helpful notes on the texts.

G. L. POSSEHL, ed., *Harappan Civilization: A Contemporary Perspective* (1982). Many helpful articles on recent developments in Indus research, including urbanization, the Indus script, trade relations, decline, and demise of this culture.

J. E. SCHWARTZBERG, ed., *A Historical Atlas of South Asia* (1978). The definitive reference work for matters of historical geography. Includes chronological tables and substantive essays.

R. L. SINGH, ed., *India: A Regional Geography* (1971). An excellent reference source for each of the major regions of the subcontinent.

CHINA

K. C. CHANG, *The Archeology of Ancient China,* 4th ed. (1986). The standard work on the subject.

K. C. CHANG, *Art, Myth, and Ritual, The Path to Political Authority in Ancient China* (1984). A study of the relation between shamans, gods, agricultural production, and political authority during the Shang and Chou dynasties.

K. C. CHANG, *Shang Civilization* (1980).

D. HAWKES, *Ch'u Tz'u, The Songs of the South* (1985). Chou poems from the southern state of Ch'u, superbly translated.

C. Y. HSU, *Ancient China in Transition: An Analysis of Social Mobility 722–222* B.C. (1965). A study of the Eastern Chou dynasty.

C. Y. HSU, *Western Chou Civilization* (1988).

X. Q. LI, *Eastern Zhou and Qin Civilizations* (1986). This work includes fresh interpretations based on new archaeological finds.

AMERICAS

M. D. COE, *America's First Civilization* (1968). Examines the earliest civilizations of Mesoamerica.

L. S. CRESSMAN, *Prehistory of the Far West: Homes of Vanished Peoples* (1977). Examines the earliest history of native Americans in the Pacific Northwest.

V. W. FITZHUGH and A. CROWELL, *Crossroads of Continents: Cultures of Siberia and Alaska* (1988). Covers the area where the immigration from Eurasia to the Americas began.

R. FORD, ed., *Prehistoric Food Production in North America* (1985). Examines the origins of agriculture in the Americas.

D. HEYDEN and P. GENDREP. *Precolumbian Architecture of Mesoamerica* (1975). A discussion of the architecture of Mesoamerica.

P. D. HUNT, *Indian Agriculture in America: Prehistory to the Present* (1987). Includes a discussion of preconquest agriculture.

J. D. JENNINGS, ed., *Ancient South Americans* (1983). Articles on Andean prehistory.

S. MASUDA, I. SHIMADA, and C. MORRIS, *Andean Ecology and Civilization* (1985). Includes coverage of the earliest civilizations in the Andes.

M. MOSELEY, *The Incas and Their Ancestors: The Archaeology of Ancient Peru* (1992). A recent overview of Peruvian archaeology by a prominent Andeanist.

J. A. SABLOFF, *The New Archaeology and the Ancient Maya* (1990). A lively account of recent research in Maya archaeology.

Writing, Literacy, and Orality

In the modern world, writing is easily taken for granted. It surrounds us—in books, magazines, newspapers, and pamphlets; on instructions, forms, labels, and signs. Literacy, the ability to read and write, has become almost a basic survival skill. People who cannot read and write are at an increasingly severe disadvantage throughout the world. Yet writing is no more than about five thousand years old. Its invention, one of the greatest of human accomplishments, was linked to the emergence of complex societies in various places around the globe.

DEVELOPMENT OF WRITING Writing is a system for translating words into visual symbols that can be preserved indefinitely on a medium such as paper, clay, or stone. Its precursors include pictograms and ideograms that represented objects and concepts directly. True writing, although it may employ pictographic or ideographic elements, represents not only objects or ideas but also the spoken words or sounds of human speech. The earliest true writing systems appeared in various parts of the Mediterranean and wider Asian world before the first millennium B.C. Some seven ancient scripts survive: Sumerian (from ca. 3100 B.C.), Egyptian (from ca. 3000 B.C.), proto-Elamite (from ca. 3000 B.C.), Indus Valley (from ca. 2200 B.C.), Cretan (from ca. 2000 B.C.), Hittite (from ca. 1500 B.C.), and Chinese (from ca. 1300 B.C.; see the box on Chinese writing in Chapter 1). The Sumerian, Egyptian, Hittite, and Chinese scripts have been deciphered; indeed, modern Chinese writing evolved directly and continuously out of its ancient form. The proto-Elamite, Indus Valley, and Cretan scripts have not yet been deciphered. Outside of Eurasia, in the Americas, the Maya developed a system of writing in the early centuries of the first millennium A.D.

The first writing systems were *logographic*—they used a separate sign for each word in a language. Later systems were *syllabic*—with separate signs for the individual syllables of a language—and *alphabetic*—having separate signs for individual consonant and vowel sounds. Alphabetic systems require the fewest separate signs; logographic systems the most.

Historians have traditionally viewed writing as one of the defining elements of civilization. Indeed, in a literal sense—to the extent that it is based on the study of written documents—history begins with writing. Many present-day scholars, however, would argue that civilization, broadly defined, does not depend on writing (see Chapter 8). Likewise, history, broadly defined, draws on many sources—evidence from art and archeology, for example—and not just written documents.

Some have argued that when a previously nonliterate society acquires literacy, its collective "mentality"—the postulated patterns of thought of the people it comprises—undergoes a fundamental change. Specifically, according to this argument, literacy makes rational and abstract thinking possible, which, in turn, permits a level of political, economic, and social complexity unavailable to nonliterate societies. Although writing certainly correlates with certain kinds of political and economic complexity, this theory places too much confidence in dubious ideas about group mentalities and attaches too much importance to the effect of literacy on thought. As anthropologists have shown, non-literate "oral" societies exhibit every bit as much social complexity and intricate thought as literate societies and are equally capable of change.

The invention of writing, then, may not have altered human nature, but it did have a dramatic effect on human society. As the anthropologist Jack Goody puts it, "Writing . . . made it possible to scrutinize discourse in a different kind of way by giving oral communication a semi-permanent form; this scrutiny favored the increase in scope of critical activity . . ."[1] Literate culture made possible the development of historical and scientific inquiry, fostered technological advance, and contributed to the building of ever more complex social and economic systems.

GROWTH OF LITERACY Today we tend to view literacy as a measure of development: A high literacy rate, we believe, is a basic characteristic of an "advanced" society. A high esteem for literacy, however, is not unique to the modern age; virtually every culture that has mastered the art of writing or has come into contact with literate culture has assigned immense prestige to the written word. Where only a small priestly or other elite has been literate—the case, for example, in many of the earliest civilizations and in Europe for

[1] *The Domestication of the Savage Mind* (Cambridge, U.K.: Cambridge University Press, 1977), p. 37.

much of the Middle Ages—mystery and reverence have typically surrounded books. Where literacy has been more widespread—for example, in the modern world and, to a lesser extent, in the premodern Islamic world and in ancient Greece and Rome—its prestige has been associated with the economic or social advantage it confers.

The invention of the movable-type printing press by Johann Gutenberg in fifteenth-century Europe, according to some scholars, may have had an even more revolutionary impact on human communication than the invention of writing. This argument, however, like arguments about the importance of writing to begin with, can be taken too far. The invention of movable-type printing certainly does not demonstrate the superiority of the post-Renaissance Western world, nor was it by itself the central cause of the eventual political, scientific, and material dominance of the West in the nineteenth and most of the twentieth centuries. Nonetheless, most historians would want to give the invention of movable-type printing a solid place among the factors in the extraordinary period of productivity, expansion, and development experienced by Western Europe from the sixteenth through the twentieth centuries.

All the technological elements required for the printing press had been developed in East Asia well before Gutenberg's time. Paper was invented in China as early as 100 A.D.; wood block printing goes back at least to the second century A.D.; individual Chinese characters, or ideographs, were being made of earthenware at least by 1041; and by 1300, Koreans were casting characters in bronze. The Chinese, Koreans, and other Asian peoples had thus long been using methods and mechanisms not substantially different from the fifteenth-century European block presses. Why then did a mass market for printed works appear in Europe and not in Asia? One important reason appears to be that all European languages were written in alphabetic scripts, with only 20 to 30 individual symbols, whereas Chinese was written in an ideographic script with thousands of individual characters (see the box on Chinese writing in Chapter 1). Alphabetic writing proved a substantial advantage for print technology; one that the ancient Chinese, for example, had not enjoyed when they developed the basic techniques of relief printing. To produce a reasonable-sized publication, a European printing press required the casting of only about twenty alphabetic letters plus

A New Kingdom Scribe. *Throughout ancient Egypt's long history, the honor and status bestowed on the professional scribe were great. Writing was understood to be something special in the transmission of learning and culture. In the words of one New Kingdom text, those who wrote things down might perish, but not their books: "Writing lets [a human being] live on in the mouth of the reader. . . . [Wise men] have gone, their names have been forgotten, but writings keep their memory alive." [Bildarchiv Preussischer Kulturbesitz]*

numbers and punctuation marks; a Chinese press would have required the casting of thousands of characters.

Be that as it may, the printing press made printed material readily available, which, combined with other factors,

A European Printshop. *This 1568 woodcut by Hans Sachs shows typesetting (rear) and printing (front) underway in an early printshop. Printing made it possible to reproduce exactly and in quantity both text and illustrations, leading to the distribution of scientific and technical information on a scale unimaginable in the pre-print world. [Houghton Library, Harvard University]*

helped expand the literate population. Subsequent to the spread of print technology in Europe and its colonial offshoots from the sixteenth century onward, the West moved toward mass literacy earlier than any other part of the world. Some characteristics of Protestant Christianity—its use of vernacular languages rather than Latin for Bible reading and liturgy, for example, and its emphasis on widespread education as a means to give individuals direct access to scripture, prayerbooks, and hymnals—contributed to this process. Another factor was that the practical demands of everyday life in the increasingly complex world that developed in Europe after the sixteenth century came more and more to require literacy. This period, which saw the Industrial Revolution and the development of massive imperialism and colonial expansion, also saw the advent of

state-sponsored education in many countries. Literacy statistics in two countries where Protestant educational efforts were particularly strong vividly illustrate the result of these combined forces. In Sweden the overall adult literacy rate was between 20 and 50 percent in 1680; by 1750 it was between 65 and 98 percent. In Scotland, the overall adult literacy rate was 15 percent in 1600, 33 percent in 1675, and 75 percent in 1750.

Sweden and Scotland, however, are best-case examples, and as even they show, the transition to high literacy was a gradual and often irregular process, although they had the printing press and a strong emphasis on education. In other countries, the results were not always as dramatic. In France, for example, literacy appears to have risen among adult males by up to 62 percent between 1690 and 1790, but the 1690 level was only about 29 percent and the 1790 level only about 47 percent. In England, adult male literacy rose from 45 percent in 1675 to 56 percent in 1775, a gain of only 11 percent. Adult female literacy in both cases would have been much lower. Because social expectations were different for men than for women and because women had much more limited access to schooling than men, female literacy throughout Europe was lower, often much lower, than male literacy until recently.

Although the increases in literacy in prenineteenth-century Europe were significant, the greatest increases came after the middle of the nineteenth century. It is estimated that by 1930, no less than 90 percent of all European adults were literate, whereas even as late as 1850 the figure was at most 50 percent (and that figure excludes Russia, where overall adult literacy is estimated to have been only 5–10 percent). In the 1840s in England as a whole, only about 70 percent of males and 50 percent of females could sign their names; in France, the estimated overall adult literacy in 1851 was only 55–60 percent. As late as 1871, overall adult literacy in highly rural Italy is reckoned to have been no more than about 31 percent, and only about 52 percent in 1901.

Worldwide literacy has similarly increased dramatically since the nineteenth century, especially since 1945. Although accurate statistics are difficult to come by, the most recent United Nations Educational, Scientific, and Cultural Organization (UNESCO) estimates (1990) give some measure of the degree of progress. Alongside those countries with greater than 90 percent adult literacy, such as the United States, Canada, Chile, Argentina, Uruguay, South Korea, Thailand, Israel, the nations of the former U.S.S.R., and the nations of Europe, there remain many countries with less than 60 percent literacy levels. These are primarily the poorest, most overpopulated, and least urbanized nations. Thus the literacy rate in Afghanistan is 29 percent, in

Bangladesh 35 percent, Cambodia 35 percent, India 48 percent, Iran 46 percent, Nepal 26 percent, Pakistan 35 percent, and Yemen 39 percent. In most African states the rate is less than 50 percent, although Kenya (69 percent), Tunisia (65 percent), and Zimbabwe (67 percent) are exceptions. Other countries have moved faster toward high literacy: Adult literacy in China is estimated at 73 percent, in Indonesia 77 percent, Malaysia 78 percent, Venezuela 88 percent, Brazil 81 percent, and Mexico 87 percent.

LITERACY AND ORALITY When thinking about writing and literacy in any period, it is important to remember how differently societies have used and valued both written and oral communication. The high value modern society puts on literacy can lead us to overlook the abiding importance of a far more ancient method for transmitting knowledge over generations—the oral tradition. Before writing, all knowledge was transmitted orally, and for most of history since the invention of writing, oral transmission in many societies retained high esteem. This is particularly true in regard to sacred religious texts. In the culture of Brahmanic and classical India, for example (see Chapter 1), oral transmission was held to be far superior to written communication, and the holy Vedas could be transmitted only orally—with the aid of incredibly rigorous mnemonic techniques—even long after the advent of writing. The only valid means of transmitting the Muslims' sacred scripture, the Qur'an (which means "the Recitation"), is still today, as it always has been, through oral transmission. Highly learned and literate specialists still memorize the text and several sets of variant readings. Memorization of the Torah by Jews and of the Lotus Sutra in some Buddhist traditions are additional examples of the strong preference, even today, for internalizing sacred texts rather than simply reading them in silent study.

A book was for long more an oral than a written reality. So few people were able to read until recently that virtually all reading was with full voice; publication involved public reading rather than distribution of written copies of a text; a document was something one heard, not something one read in silence. Memorization and rote repetition were for many centuries the basic forms of learning, and in places they remain so even today.

Our current high rates of literacy and our increasing reliance on print may be mixed blessings. These advances have been accompanied by the loss of the habits as well as the advanced techniques of memorization, recitation, and declamation, and with them, possibly, an impoverishment of language and a decline in our ability to enjoy language as art. When books were still "speaking pages" rather than merely black and white, silent documents, our relationship with words and linguistic expression may have been richer.

REFERENCES

CARLO M. CIPOLLA, *Literacy and Development in the West* (1969).
ELIZABETH L. EISENSTEIN, *The Printing Press as an Agent of Change: Communications and Cultural Transformations in Early Modern Europe* (1979). 2 vols.
I. J. GELB, *A Study of Writing,* rev. ed. (1963).
JACK GOODY, *The Domestication of the Savage Mind* (1977).
JACK GOODY, *The Logic of Writing and the Organization of Society* (1986).
WILLIAM A. GRAHAM, *Beyond the Written Word: Oral Aspects of Scripture in the History of Religion* (1987).
ERIC A. HAVELOCK, *The Literate Revolution in Greece and Its Cultural Consequences* (1982).
MARSHALL MCLUHAN, *The Gutenberg Galaxy: The Making of Typographic Man* (1962).
JAMES MORAN, *Printing Presses: History and Development from the Fifteenth Century to Modern Times* (1973).
UNESCO, *Statistical Yearbook 1990* (1990).

A Torah scroll. Such a scroll is used in the synagogue and symbolizes the Judaic commitment to the life of the Law. [Jewish Museum, Frank J. Darmstaedter]

2

The Four Great Revolutions in Thought and Religion

Between 800 B.C. and 300 B.C., four philosophical or religious revolutions occurred that shaped the subsequent history of the world. The names of many involved in these revolutions are world famous; for example, Socrates, Plato, Aristotle, the Buddha, Isaiah, and Confucius. All occurred in or near the four heartland areas in which the river valley civilizations (described in Chapter 1) had appeared one-and-a-half or more millennia earlier. The transition from the early river-valley civilizations to the intellectual and spiritual breakthroughs of the middle of the first millennium B.C. is schematized in the chart below.

The most straightforward case is that of China. Both geographically and culturally, its philosophical breakthrough grew directly out of the earlier river-valley civilization. There was no such continuity anywhere else in the world. The natural barriers of the central Asian steppes, mountain ranges, and deserts

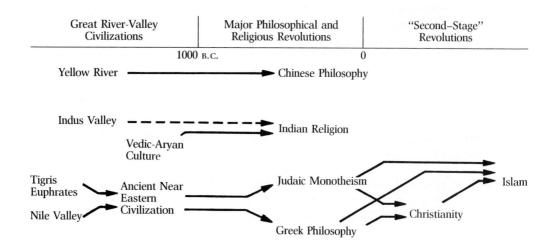

Great River-Valley Civilizations	Major Philosophical and Religious Revolutions	"Second–Stage" Revolutions

1000 B.C.   0

Yellow River ⟶ Chinese Philosophy

Indus Valley ⟶ Indian Religion
Vedic-Aryan Culture

Tigris Euphrates ⟶ Ancient Near Eastern Civilization ⟶ Judaic Monotheism ⟶ Islam
Nile Valley ⟶ Greek Philosophy ⟶ Christianity

allowed China to develop its own unique culture relatively undisturbed and uninfluenced by outside forces.

The sharpest contrast with China is the Indian subcontinent, where there was neither geographic nor cultural continuity. By the middle of the second millennium B.C., the Indus civilization had collapsed. It was replaced by the culture of the Indo-Aryan warriors who swept in from the northwest. Absorbing many particulars from the earlier tradition, they built a new civilization on the plains further east along the mighty Ganges. The great tradition of Indian thought and religion emerged after 600 B.C. from this Ganges civilization.

In Southwest Asia and along the shores of the Mediterranean, the transition was more complex than that in either China or India. No direct line of development can be traced from the Nile civilization of ancient Egypt or the civilization of the Tigris–Euphrates river valley to Greek philosophy or Judaic monotheism. Rather, the ancient river-valley civilizations evolved into a complex amalgam that we call ancient Near Eastern civilization. This cosmopolitan culture included diverse older religious, mythical, and cosmological traditions, as well as newer mystery cults. The Greeks and the ancient Hebrews were two among many outside peoples who invaded this region, settled down, and both absorbed and contributed to the composite civilization.

Judaic monotheism and Greek philosophy—representing very different outgrowths of this amalgam—were important in their own right. They have continued as vital elements in Western and Near Eastern civilizations. But their greatest influence occurred some centuries later when they joined to help shape, first, Christianity and, then, Islam. When we talk of the major cultural zones in world history since the mid-first millennium A.D., they are the Chinese, the Indian, the Western-Christian, and the Islamic. But the latter two were formed much later than the Chinese and the Indian. They represent a second-stage formation of which the first stage was the Judaic and the Greek.

Before turning to a brief consideration of each of the original breakthroughs that occurred between 800 and 300 B.C., we might ask whether they have anything in common.

1. It is not accidental that all of the philosophical or religious revolutions occurred in the areas of the original river-valley civilizations. These areas contained the most advanced cultures of the ancient world. They had sophisticated agriculture, cities, literacy, and specialized trades and professions. The material preconditions for breakthroughs in religion and thought were present.

2. Each of the revolutions in thought and ethos was born of a crisis in the ancient world. The appearance of iron meant better tools and weapons and, by extension, greater riches and more powerful armies. Old societies began to change and then to disintegrate. Old aristocratic and priestly codes of behavior broke down, producing a demand for more universalized rules of behavior, that is to say, for ethics. The very relation of humans to nature or to the universe seemed to be changing. This predicament led to new visions of social and political order. There is more than an accidental similarity between the Jewish Messiah, the Chinese sage-king, and Plato's philosopher-king. Each was a response to a crisis in a society of the ancient world. Each would rejoin ethics to history and restore order to a troubled society.

3. The small number of philosophical and religious revolutions is notable. They can be counted on the fingers of one hand. The reason is not that humans' creativity dried up after 300 B.C. but that subsequent breakthroughs and advances tended to occur within the original traditions, which, absorbing new energies, continued to evolve.

4. After the first- and second-stage transformations, much of the cultural history of the world is of the spread of cultures derived from these original heartlands to ever wider spheres. Christianity spread to northern and eastern Europe, the Americas, and parts of Asia; Buddhism to central, southeastern, and eastern Asia; Confucianism to Korea, Vietnam, and Japan; and Islam to Africa, southeastern Europe, and southern, central, and southeastern Asia. Sometimes the spread occurred by movements of people; in other cases, some areas were like dry grasslands needing only the spark of the new ideas to ignite them.

5. Once a cultural pattern was set, it usually endured. Each major culture was resistant to the others, and only rarely was one displaced. Even in modern times, although the culture of modern science, and the learning associated with it, has penetrated every cultural zone, it has reshaped—and is reshaping, rather than displacing—the major cultures. Only Confucianism, the most secular of the traditional cultures, crumbled at the touch of science, and even its ethos remains a potent force in East Asian societies. One reason for the endurance of these major cultures is that they were not only responses to particular cri-

ses, but also attempts to answer universal questions concerning the human condition: What are human beings? What is our relation to the universe? How should we relate to others?

Philosophy in China

The beauty of Shang bronzes is breathtaking, but they also have an archaic strangeness. Like Mayan stone sculpture, they are products of a culture so far removed from our own as to be almost incomprehensible. By contrast, in Confucian writings and poetry of the Eastern Chou (771–256 B.C.), we encounter a humanism that speaks to us directly. However much the philosophies of these centuries grew out of the earlier matrix of archaic culture, they mark a break with it and the beginning of what we think of today as the Chinese tradition.

The background of the philosophical revolution in China was the disintegration of the old Chou society (see Chapter 1 for details) New territorial states took the place of the many Chou city-states. Ruthless, upstart, peasant armies, augmented by an early Iron Age cavalry, began to replace the old nobles, who had gone to war in chariots. A rising merchant class disrupted the formerly stable agricultural economy. As the old etiquette crumbled—as the old rituals lost their force—a search began for new principles by which to recreate a peaceful society and new rules by which to live.

Of the four great revolutions in thought of the first millennium B.C., the Chinese was more akin, perhaps, to the Greek than to the Indian religious transformations or to Judaic monotheism. Just as Greece had a gamut of philosophies, so in China there were the "one hundred schools." (When Mao Tse-tung said in 1956, "Let the one hundred flowers bloom"—encouraging a momentary easing of intellectual repression—he was referring to the creative era of Chou philosophy.) Whereas Greek thought was speculative and more concerned with the world of nature, Chinese thought was sociopolitical and more practical. Even the Taoist sages, who were inherently apolitical, found it necessary to offer a political philosophy. Chinese thought also had far greater staying power than Greek thought. Only a few centuries after the glory of Athens, Greek thought was submerged by Christianity. It became the handmaiden of theology and did not reemerge as an independent force until the Renaissance. In contrast, Chinese philosophy, although challenged for a time by Buddhism, remained

The Temple of Heaven. The three-storied "Temple of Prayer for a Good Harvest" is part of the "Temple of Heaven" to the south of Peking. [The Bettmann Archive]

dominant down to the early twentieth century. How were these early philosophies able to maintain such a grip on China when the cultures of every other part of the world fell under the sway of religions?

Part of the answer is that most Chinese philosophy was not without a religious dimension. But it was another kind of religion, having assumptions quite different from those of the West. In the Christian or Islamic worldview, there is a God who, however concerned with humankind, is not of this world. This worldview leads to dualism, the distinction between an otherworld, which is supernatural, and this world, which is natural.

In the Chinese worldview, the two spheres are not separate: The cosmos is seen as a single, continuous sphere that includes heaven, earth, and man. Heaven is above. Earth is below. Man, ideally guided by a wise and virtuous ruler, stands in between and regulates or harmonizes the cosmological forces of heaven and earth by the power of his virtue and by performing the sacrifices. The forms that this cosmology took under the last Manchu dynasty can be seen today in the city of Peking: The Temple of Heaven is in the south; the Temple of Earth is in the northeast; and the Imperial Palace is, symbolically at least, in between. To say that the emperor's sacrifices at the Temple of Heaven were secular (and, therefore, not religious) or religious (and not secular) misses the point. It projects our own dualistic assumptions onto China. Similarly, when we speak of the Taoist sage becoming one with nature, it is not the nature of a twentieth-century natural scientist; it is a nature that contains metaphysical and cosmological forces of a kind that our worldview might label as religious.

Most of the one hundred schools—if, in fact, there were that many—are unknown today. Many works disappeared in the book burning of the Ch'in dynasty (256–221 B.C.). But apart from the three major schools of Confucianism, Taoism, and Legalism, enough have survived to convey a sense of the vitality and creativity of Chou thought:

1. *Rhetoricians.* This school taught the arts of persuasion to be used in diplomatic negotiations. Its principal work instructed the rulers of territorial states by using historical anecdote. A practical work, it was popular for its humor and lively style.

2. *Logicians.* This school taught logic and relativity. For example, one proposition was "The south has no limit and has a limit." Another was "A white horse is not a horse": The concept of *horse* is not the same as the concept of *white horse.*

3. *Strategists. The Art of War* by Sun-tzu became the classic of military science in China and is studied today by guerrillas and in military academies around the world. It praises the general who wins victories without battles but also talks of organizing states for war, of supply, of spies, and of propaganda.

4. *Cosmologists.* This school described the functions of the cosmos in terms of *yin* and *yang,* the complementary negative and positive forces of nature, and in terms of the five elements (metal, wood, earth, fire, and water). Its ideas were later absorbed by other schools.

5. *Mohists.* Mo-tzu (470–391 B.C.) was an early critic of Confucius. His goals were peace, wealth, and the increase of population. He taught an ethic of universal love—to overcome a selfish human nature. He preached discipline and austerity and was critical of whatever lacked utility, including music, other arts, elaborate funerals, wasteful rites, and, above all, war. To achieve his goals, Mo-tzu argued for a strong state: Subjects must obey their rulers, who, in turn, must obey Heaven. Heaven would punish evil and reward good. To promote peace, Mo-tzu organized his followers into military units to aid states that were attacked.

Confucianism

Confucius was born in 551 B.C. in a minor state in northeastern China. As he received an education in writing, music, and rituals, he probably belonged to

Confucius, depicted wearing the robes of a scholar of a later age. [National Palace Museum, Taipei, Taiwan, Republic of China]

the lower nobility or the knightly class. His father died when Confucius was young, so he may have known privation. He made his living by teaching. He traveled with his disciples from state to state, seeking a ruler who would put his ideas into practice. His ideas, however, were rejected as impractical, although he may once have held a minor position. He died in 479 B.C., having failed to find a ruler to advise but honored as a teacher and scholar. The name *Confucius* is the Latinized form of K'ung Fu-tzu, or Master K'ung, as he is known in China.

We know of Confucius only through the *Analects,* his sayings collected by his disciples, or perhaps by their disciples. They are mostly in the form of "The Master said," followed by his words. The picture that emerges is of a man of moderation, propriety, optimism, good sense, and wisdom. In an age of cruelty and superstition, he was humane and rational. He was upright. He demanded much of others and more of himself. Asked about death, he replied, "You do not understand even life. How can you understand

Confucius Defines the Gentleman

For over two thousand years in China, the cultural ideal was the gentleman, who combined knowledge of the ancient sages with an inner morality and outer propriety.

▶ *Compare the ideals suggested here with those of the ancient Greeks presented in the box titled "Theognis of Megara Gives Advice to a Young Aristocrat" (Ch. 3).*

The Master said, "I never enlighten anyone who has not been driven to distraction by trying to understand a difficulty or who has not got into a frenzy trying to put his ideas into words.

"When I have pointed out one corner of a square to anyone and he does not come back with the other three, I will not point it out to him a second time."

The Master said, "Yu, shall I tell you what it is to know. To say you know when you know, and to say you do not when you do not, that is knowledge."

The Master said, "Is it not a pleasure, having learned something, to try it out at due intervals? Is it not a joy to have friends come from afar? Is it not gentlemanly not to take offence when others fail to appreciate your abilities?"

Someone said, "Repay an injury with a good turn. What do you think of this saying?" The Master said, "What, then, do you repay a good turn with? You repay an injury with straightness, but you repay a good turn with a good turn."

Lin Fang asked about the basis of the rites. The Master said, "A noble question indeed! With the rites, it is better to err on the side of frugality than on the side of extravagance; in mourning, it is better to err on the side of grief than on the side of formality."

The Master said, "I suppose I should give up hope. I have yet to meet the man who is as fond of virtue as he is of beauty in women."

The Master said, "The gentleman agrees with others without being an echo. The small man echoes without being in agreement."

The Master said, "The gentleman is at ease without being arrogant; the small man is arrogant without being at ease."

The Master said, "There is no point in seeking the views of a gentleman who, though he sets his heart on the Way, is ashamed of poor food and poor clothes."

Confucius, *The Analects,* trans. by D. C. Lau (New York: Penguin Books, 1979), pp. 86, 65, 59, 129, 67, 134, 122, 123, 73, respectively.

---

death?"[1] Asked about how to serve the spirits and the gods, in which he did not disbelieve, he answered, "You are not able even to serve man. How can you serve the spirits?"

Confucius described himself as a transmitter and a conservator of tradition, not an innovator. He idealized the early Shang and Chou kings as paragons of virtue and particularly saw the early Chou society as a golden age. He sought the secrets of this golden age in its writings. Some of these writings, along with later texts, became the Confucian classics, which through most of subsequent Chinese history had an authority

not unlike Scripture in the West. Five of the thirteen classics were the following:

1. *The Book of Changes* (also known as the *Classic of Divination*). A handbook for diviners, this book was later seen as containing metaphysical truths about the universe.

2. *The Book of History.* This book contains documents and speeches from the early Chou, some authentic. Chinese tradition holds that it was edited by Confucius. It was interpreted as the record of sage-kings.

3. *The Book of Poetry.* This book contains some three hundred poems from the early Chou. Representing a sophisticated literary tradition, it includes love songs as well as poems of friendship, ritual, and poli-

[1] This quotation and all quotations from Confucius in this passage are from Confucius, *The Analects,* trans. by D. C. Lau (Penguin Books, 1979).

tics. Many were given political and moral interpretations in later times.

4. *The Book of Rites.* This book includes both rituals and rules of etiquette. Rites were important to Confucians, both as a support for proper behavior and because they were seen as corresponding to the forces of nature.

5. *The Spring and Autumn Annals.* A brief record of the major occurrences from 722 to 481 B.C. in the state where Confucius was born, this book, according to Chinese tradition, was edited by Confucius and reflected his moral judgments on past historical figures.

Basing his teachings on these writings, Confucius proposed to solve the turmoil of his own age by a return to the good old ways of the early Chou. When asked about government, he said, "Let the ruler be a ruler, the subject a subject, the father a father, the son a son." (The other three of the five Confucian relationships were husband–wife, older brother–younger brother, and friend–friend.) If everyone fulfilled the duties of his or her status, then harmony would prevail. Confucius understood the fundamental truth that the well-being of a society depends on the morality of its members. His vision was of an unbroken social harmony extending from the individual family member below to the monarch above.

But a return to the early Chou was impossible. China was undergoing a dynamic transition from hundreds of small city-states to a few large territorial states. New, specialized classes were appearing (see pages 35–37). Old rituals no longer worked. In this situation, it was not enough to stress basic human relationships. The genius of Confucius was to transform the old aristocratic code into a new ethic that could be practiced by any educated Chinese. His reinterpretation of the early Chou tradition can be seen in the concept of the *chun-tzu.* This term literally meant the son of the ruler or the aristocrat. Confucius redefined it to mean a person of noble behavior, a person with the inner virtues of humanity, integrity, righteousness, altruism, and loyalty, and an outward demeanor and propriety to match.

This redefinition was not unlike the change in the meaning of *gentleman* in England from one who is gentle-born to one who is gentle-behaved. But whereas *gentleman* remained a fairly superficial category in the West, in China it went deeper. Confucius saw ethics as grounded in nature. The true gentleman was in touch with his own basic nature, which, in turn, was a part of the cosmic order. Confucius ex-

This Western Chou bronze bell was hung from the ring at the top and rung with a wooden mallet. The pre-Confucian inscription commemorating a ruler's victory expresses many ideas—about the relation of the ruler to Heaven, the military basis of state power, the barbaric character of border peoples, and the nature of the family—that were later incorporated into Chinese philosophy and social thought. [National Palace Museum, Taipei, Taiwan, Republic of China]

pressed this saying: "Heaven is the author of the virtue that is in me." Confucius's description of his own passage through life goes far beyond the question of good manners: "At fifteen I set my heart on learning; at thirty I took my stand; at forty I came to be free from doubts; at fifty I understood the Decree of Heaven; at sixty my ear was attuned; at seventy I followed my heart's desire without overstepping the line."

Confucius often contrasted the gentleman with the small or common person. The gentleman, educated in the classics and cultivating the Way, understands moral action. The common people, in contrast, "can be made to follow a path but not to understand it." Good government for Confucius depended on the appointment to office of good men, who would serve as examples for the multitude: "Just desire the good yourself and the common people will be good. The virtue of the gentleman is like wind; the virtue of the small man is like grass. Let the wind blow over the grass and it is sure to bend." Beyond the gentleman was the sage-king, who possessed an almost mystical virtue and power. For Confucius, the early Chou kings were clearly sages. But Confucius wrote, "I have no hopes of meeting a sage. I would be content if I met someone who is a gentleman."

Confucianism was not adopted as the official philosophy of China until the second century B.C., during the Han dynasty. But two other important Confucian philosophers had appeared in the meantime. Mencius (370–290 B.C.) represents the idealistic extension of Confucius's thought. His interpretation was accepted during most of subsequent history. He is famous for his argument that humans tend toward the good just as water runs downward. The role of education, therefore, is to uncover and cultivate that innate goodness. Moreover, just as humans tend toward the good, so does Heaven possess a moral will. The will of Heaven is that a government should see to the education and the well-being of its people. The rebellion of a people against its government is the primary evidence that Heaven has withdrawn its mandate. At times in Chinese history, only lip service was paid to a concern for the people. In fact, rebellions occurred more often against weak governments than against harsh ones. But the idea that government ought to care for the people became a permanent part of the Confucian tradition.

The other influential Confucian philosopher was Hsun-tzu (300–237 B.C.), who represents a tough-minded extension of Confucius's thought. Hsun-tzu felt Heaven was amoral, indifferent to whether China was ruled by a tyrant or a sage. He believed human nature was bad or, at least, that desires and emotions, if unchecked and unrefined, led to social conflict. So he placed a great emphasis on etiquette and education as restraints on an unruly human nature. He emphasized good institutions, including punish-ments and rewards, as a means for shaping behavior. These ideas exerted a powerful influence on thinkers of the Legalist school.

Taoism

It is often said that the Chinese have been Confucian while in office and Taoist (pronounced "Dah-oh-ist") in their private lives. Taoism offered a refuge from the burden of social responsibilities. The classics of the school are the *Lao-tzu,* dating from the fourth century B.C., and the *Chuang-tzu,* dating from about a century later.

The central concept is the *Tao,* or way. It is mysterious and cannot be named. It is the creator of the universe, the sustainer of the universe, and the process or flux of the universe. The *Tao* functions on a cosmic, not a human, scale. As the *Lao-tzu* put it, "Heaven and Earth are ruthless, and treat the myriad creatures as straw dogs; the sage (in accord with the *Tao*) is ruthless, and treats the people as straw dogs."[2]

What does it mean to be a sage? How does a human join the rhythms of nature? The answer given by the *Lao-tzu* is by regaining or returning to an original simplicity. Various similes are used to describe this state: "to return to the infinite," "to return to being a babe," or "to return to being the uncarved block." To attain this state, one must "learn to be without learning." Knowledge is bad because it creates distinctions, because it leads to the succession of ideas and images that interfere with participation in the *Tao.* One must also learn to be without desires beyond the immediate and simple needs of nature: "The nameless uncarved block is but freedom from desire."

If the sage treats the people as straw dogs, it would appear that he is beyond good and evil. But elsewhere in the *Lao-tzu,* the sage is described as one who "excels in saving people." If not a contradiction, this is at least a paradox. The resolution is that the sage is clearly beyond morality but is not immoral or even amoral. Quite to the contrary, by being in harmony with the *Tao* the sage is impeccably moral—as one who clings to the forms of morality or makes morality a goal could never be. So in the *Lao-tzu,* it is written, "Exterminate benevolence, discard rectitude, and the people will again be filial; exterminate ingenuity, discard profit, and there will be no more

[2] All quotations from the *Lao-tzu* are from Lao-Tzu, *Tao Te Ching,* trans. by D. C. Lau (Penguin Books, 1963).

Taoism

LAO-TZU TELLS OF THE WAY OF THE SAGE

The way that can be spoken of
Is not the constant way;
The name that can be named
Is not the constant name.
The nameless was the beginning of heaven and earth;
The named was the mother of the myriad creatures.

The spirit of the valley never dies
This is called the mysterious female.
The gateway of the mysterious female
Is called the root of heaven and earth.
Dimly visible, it seems as if it were there,
Yet use will never drain it.

There is a thing confusedly formed,
Born before heaven and earth.
Silent and void
It stands alone and does not change,
Goes round and does not weary.
It is capable of being the mother of the world.
I know not its name
So I style it "the way."

When the way prevails in the empire, fleetfooted
horses are relegated to ploughing the fields; when the
way does not prevail in the empire, war-horses breed
on the border.

One who knows does not speak; one who speaks
does not know.

Therefore the sage puts his person last and it comes
first,
Treats it as extraneous to himself and it is preserved.
Is it not because he is without thought of self that he
is able to accomplish his private ends?

CHUANG-TZU COMPARES GOVERNMENTAL OFFICE TO A DEAD RAT

When Hui Tzu was prime minister of Liang, Chuang
Tzu set off to visit him. Someone said to Hui Tzu,
"Chuang Tzu is coming because he wants to replace
you as prime minister!" With this Hui Tzu was filled
with alarm and searched all over the state for three
days and three nights trying to find Chuang Tzu.
Chuang Tzu then came to see him and said, "In the
south there is a bird called the Yuan-ch'u—I wonder
if you've ever heard of it? The Yuan-ch'u rises up from
the South Sea and flies to the North Sea, and it will
rest on nothing but the Wu-t'ung tree, eat nothing but
the fruit of the Lien, and drink only from springs of
sweet water. Once there was an owl who had gotten
hold of a half-rotten old rat, and as the Yuan-ch'u
passed by, it raised its head, looked up at the Yuan-
ch'u, and said, 'Shoo!' Now that you have this Liang
state of yours, are you trying to shoo me?"

Lao-tzu selection from Lao-tzu, *Tao Te Ching*, trans. by D. C. Lau (New York: Penguin Books, 1963).
Chuang-tzu selection from *The Complete Works of Chuang-tzu*, trans. by B. Watson (New York: Columbia
University Press, 1968), p. 188.

thieves and bandits." In this formulation, we also see
the basis for the political philosophy of Taoism,
which can be summed up as "not doing" *(wu wei)*.
What this means is something between "doing nothing" and "being, but not acting." In this concept,
there is some overlap with Confucianism. The Confucian sage-king exerts a moral force by dint of his internal accord with nature. If a Confucian sage were
perfect, he could rule without doing. Confucius said,
"If there was a ruler who achieved order without taking any action, it was, perhaps, Shun [the sage em-
peror]. There was nothing for him to do but to hold
himself in a respectful posture and to face due
south." In Taoism, all true sages had this Shun-like
power to rule without action: "The way never acts yet

nothing is left undone. Should lords and princes be
able to hold fast to it, the myriad creatures will be
transformed of their own accord." Or, says the *Lao-
tzu*, "I am free from desire and the people of themselves become simple like the uncarved block." The
sage acts without acting, and "when his task is accomplished and his work is done, the people will say,
'It happened to us naturally.'"

Along with the basic Taoist prescription of becoming one with the Tao are two other assumptions or
principles. One is that any action pushed to an extreme will initiate a countervailing reaction in the direction of the opposite extreme. The other is that too
much government, even good government, can become oppressive by its very weight. As the *Lao-tzu*

Lao-tzu, the founder of Taoism, as imagined by a later artist. [Freer Gallery of Art, Washington D.C.]

put it, "The people are hungry; it is because those in authority eat up too much in taxes that the people are hungry. The people are difficult to govern; it is because those in authority are too fond of action that the people are difficult to govern." Elsewhere, the same idea was expressed in even homelier terms: "Govern a large state as you would cook small fish," that is, without too much stirring.

Legalism

The third great current in classical Chinese thought, and by far the most influential in its own age, was Legalism. Like the philosophers of other schools, the Legalists were anxious to end the wars that plagued China. True peace, they felt, required a united country, and to this end they advocated a strong state. They favored conscription and looked on war as a means of extending state power.

The Legalists did not seek a model in the distant past. In ancient times, said one, there were fewer people and more food, so it was easier to rule; different conditions require new principles of government. Nor did the Legalists model their state on a heavenly order of values. Human nature is selfish, argued both of the leading Legalists, Han Fei-tzu (d. 233 B.C.) and Li Ssu (d. 208 B.C.). It is human to like rewards or pleasure and to dislike punishments or pain. If laws are severe and impartial, if what strengthens the state is rewarded and what weakens the state is punished, then a strong state and a good society will ensue.

Laws, therefore, should contain incentives for loyalty and bravery in battle, and for obedience, diligence, and frugality in everyday life. The Legalists despised merchants as parasites and approved of productive farmers. They particularly despised the purveyors of doctrines different from their own and were critical of rulers who honored the philosophers while ignoring their philosophies.

Legalism was the philosophy of the state of Ch'in, which destroyed the Chou in 256 B.C. and unified China in 221 B.C. Because Ch'in laws were cruel and severe, and because Legalism put human laws above an ethic modeled on Heaven, later generations of Chinese have execrated its doctrines. They saw it, not without justification, as a philosophy that consumed its founders: Han Fei-tzu became an official of the

Ch'in state but was eventually poisoned in a prison cell by Li Ssu, who was jealous of his growing influence. Li Ssu, although he became prime minister of Ch'in, was killed in 208 B.C. in a political struggle with a court eunuch. Yet, for all of the abuse heaped on the Legalist doctrines, their legacy of administrative and criminal laws became a vital part of subsequent dynastic China.

Legalism

▶ *For other perspectives on law, leadership, and government, see the following document boxes: "Hammurabi Creates a Code of Law in Mesopotamia" (Ch. 1), "Thucydides Reports Pericles on Athenian Democracy" (Ch. 4), "Polybius Summarizes the Roman Constitution" (Ch. 5), "The Edicts of Ashoka" (Ch. 7), "Machiavelli Discusses the Most Important Trait for a Ruler" (Ch. 17), and "Some Reforms of Akbar" (Ch. 24).*

HAN FEI-TZU ARGUES FOR THE EFFICACY OF PUNISHMENTS

Now take a young fellow who is a bad character. His parents may get angry at him, but he never makes any change. The villagers may reprove him, but he is not moved. His teachers and elders may admonish him but he never reforms. The love of his parents, the efforts of the villagers, and the wisdom of his teachers and elders—all the three excellent disciplines are applied to him, and yet not even a hair on his shins is altered. It is only after the district magistrate sends out his soldiers and in the name of the law searches for wicked individuals that the young man becomes afraid and changes his ways and alters his deeds. So while the love of parents is not sufficient to discipline the children, the severe penalties of the district magistrate are. This is because men became naturally spoiled by love, but are submissive to authority. . . .

That being so, rewards should be rich and certain so that the people will be attracted by them; punishments should be severe and definite so that the people will fear them; and laws should be uniform and steadfast so that the people will be familiar with them. Consequently, the sovereign should show no wavering in bestowing rewards and grant no pardon in administering punishments, and he should add honor to rewards and disgrace to punishments—when this is done, then both the worthy and the unworthy will want to exert themselves. . . .

HAN FEI-TZU ATTACKS CONFUCIANISM

There was once a man of Sung who tilled his field. In the midst of his field stood the stump of a tree, and one day a hare, running at full speed, bumped into the stump, broke its neck, and died. Thereupon the man left his plow and kept watch at the stump, hoping that he would get another hare. But he never caught another hare, and was only ridiculed by the people of Sung. Now those who try to rule the people of the present age with the conduct of government of the early kings are all doing exactly the same thing as that fellow who kept watch by the stump. . . .

Those who are ignorant about government insistently say: "Win the hearts of the people." If order could be procured by winning the hearts of the people, then even the wise ministers Yi Yin and Kuan Chung would be of no use. For all that the ruler would need to do would be just to listen to the people. Actually, the intelligence of the people is not to be relied upon any more than the mind of a baby. If the baby does not have his head shaved, his sores will recur; if he does not have his boil cut open, his illness will go from bad to worse. However, in order to shave his head or open the boil someone has to hold the baby while the affectionate mother is performing the work, and yet he keeps crying and yelling incessantly. The baby does not understand that suffering a small pain is the way to obtain a great benefit.

Now, the sovereign urges the tillage of land and the cultivation of pastures for the purpose of increasing production for the people, but they think the sovereign is cruel. The sovereign regulates penalties and increases punishments for the purpose of repressing the wicked, but the people think the sovereign is severe. Again he levies taxes in cash and in grain to fill up the granaries and treasuries in order to relieve famine and provide for the army, but they think the sovereign is greedy. Finally, he insists upon universal military training without personal favoritism, and urges his forces to fight hard in order to take the enemy captive, but the people think the sovereign is violent. These four measures are methods for attaining order and maintaining peace, but the people are too ignorant to appreciate them.

From W. T. de Bary et al., *Sources of Chinese Tradition* (New York: Columbia University Press, 1960), pp. 146–147, 144, 142, 143.

Religion in India

By the mid-first millennium B.C., new social and religious forms took shape in the Indian subcontinent. A tradition was created that drew both on the older traditions of the Aryan ruling and priestly elites, and on non-Aryan ideas and practices. This tradition took its "classical" shape only much later, sometime in the early Christian era. We can call it *Indian,* as distinct from the earlier Vedic-Brahmanic culture (described in Chapter 1), in that its fundamental institutions and ideas came to prevail at all levels of society in virtually every part of the subcontinent. Despite staggering internal diversity and divisions, and long periods of foreign rule, this Indian culture has survived for at least two thousand years as a coherent tradition of historical heritage, social organization, and religious worldview.

"Indian" and "Hindu"

Indian culture and tradition include more than is commonly implied by the word *Hindu* today. Earlier, *Hindu* was simply a word for *Indian.* It came from the Indo-Iranian name for the Indus and was originally the term used by outsiders, like the ancient Persians and the Greeks, to refer to the people or the land of the subcontinent. Even invading Muslims, and then invading Western Christians, used *Hindu* to characterize the most prominent religious and social institutions of India as a whole. The concept of *transmigration,* the sacredness of the Vedas and of the cow, the worship of Shiva or Vishnu, and the caste system head the list of such "Hindu" institutions. Yet not all Indians in the past twenty-five hundred years have accepted all of these and other related institutions. Most obviously, Indian Buddhists, Jains, Muslims, Sikhs, and Christians have rejected at least some of them.

We cannot say exactly when the typical aspects of Hindu society and religious life as we know it today were "in place." Some argue that it was only after A.D. 200 (or even 400), rather than sometime in the latter half of the first millennium B.C. However we date the beginning of "Hindu" religion and culture, we must remember that such usage lumps together an immense diversity of social, racial, linguistic, and religious groups. It is totally inaccurate to think of *Hindu* as a term for any single or uniform religious community.

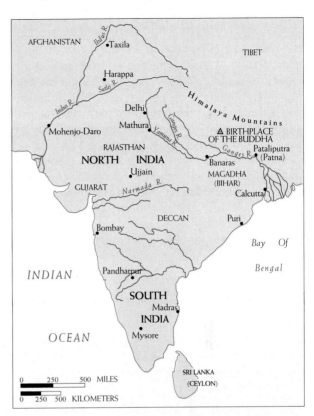

MAP 2-1 HEARTLANDS OF INDIAN CULTURE *Major ancient and modern cities of the subcontinent and their locations relative to major rivers are shown. Note that while North India is thought of as the cradle of Vedic and classical Indian religion and culture, the south was the locus, especially in the post-Gupta period but also earlier, of important, long-lived regional dynasties, major religious movements, and brilliant artistic traditions.*

Indian, on the other hand, commonly refers today to all native inhabitants of the subcontinent, including Muslims, Sikhs, and Christians (who belong to traditions considerably younger than the Buddhist, Jain, or Hindu). In this book, we shall on occasion use the term *Indian* in this inclusive sense when referring to the subcontinent as a geographic or political whole, or to its peoples. However, for the period before the arrival of Muslim culture (ca. A.D. 1000), *Indian* will be used to refer to the distinctively Indian tradition of thought and culture that began with the flowering of Upanishadic speculation and Buddhist and Jain thought around the middle of the first millennium B.C. This "Indian" tradition achieved its classical formulation in the Hindu society and religion of the first millennium A.D. However, the Jains of India and the Buddhists of wider Asia were also its legitimate heirs.

Historical Background

We saw in Chapter 1 how, in the later Vedic or Brahmanic period, a priest-centered cult dominated the upper classes of Aryanized northern Indian society. Apparently, by the sixth century B.C., this ritualistic cult had grown so extreme in its basically magical approach to ritual and piety that it became an elite, esoteric cult to which most people had little or no access. The elaborate animal sacrifices on behalf of Aryan rulers were an economic burden on the peasants of the countryside, whose livestock provided the victims. Such sacrifices were also largely irrelevant to the religious concerns of peasant and town-dweller alike. New, ascetic tendencies placed in question the basic values and practices of the older Aryan religion.

Hindus have traditionally viewed the Absolute (Brahman) *to be manifested in this world in a vast array of gods and goddesses. This statue (which dates to ca. A.D. 1100) shows Vishnu, Lakshmi, and Garuda. [University of Michigan, Dr. Spink]*

Skepticism in religious matters accompanied social and political upheavals during the seventh and sixth centuries B.C.

The latest Vedic texts themselves reflected a reaction against excessive emphasis on the power of sacrifice and ritual formulas, accumulation of worldly wealth and power, and hope for an afterlife in some kind of paradise. The treatises of the *Brahmanas* (ca. 1000–800 B.C.) dealt with the ritual application of the old Vedic texts, the explanation of Vedic rites and mythology, and the theory of the sacrifice. They had focused earlier on control of the sacred power *(Brahman)* present in sacrificial ritual, but now they gave ever greater attention to acquiring this power through knowledge instead of ritual acts.

This tendency became central in the Upanishadic (ca. 800–500 B.C.) treatises, which proposed meditations on the meaning of ritual and the nature of *Brahman.* These texts carried to new levels of subtlety previous Vedic theories about the origin and nature of reality and the relation of thought and action to ultimate truth. The principal ideas that would guide all later Indian tradition are first clearly visible in the Upanishads, and in the thought and institutions of the early Jain and Buddhist movements (fifth century B.C.). The Upanishadic thinkers represent the culmination of the Vedic-Brahmanic tradition in many ways. The Jain and Buddhist traditions, on the other hand, were but the most enduring of a series of sixth- and fifth-century-B.C. religious movements that explicitly rejected much of the Vedic-Brahmanic tradition of sacrificial ritualism and class distinction.

Both the Upanishadic sages and the early Jains and Buddhists shared a number of ideas and concerns that signaled the "coming of age" of Indian thought. Their thinking and piety influenced not only all later Indian intellectual thought, but, through the spread of the Buddhist tradition, much of the intellectual and religious life of East and Southeast Asia as well. Thus, the middle centuries of the first millennium B.C. in India began a religious and philosophical revolution that ranks alongside those of Chinese philosophy and religion, Judaic monotheism, and Greek philosophy as a turning point in the history of civilization.

The Upanishadic Worldview

In the Upanishads, we see two new emphases. These were already evident in two sentences from the prayer of one of the earliest Upanishadic thinkers, who said, "From the unreal lead me to the Real. . . . From

These sunnyasis, *or "renouncers," in the city of Benares have given up homes and families for a life of poverty, discipline, and meditation. [Diana L. Eck]*

death lead me to immortality." The first request points to the Upanishadic focus on speculation about the nature of things, the quest for ultimate truth. Here ritual takes a back seat to meditation; knowledge, not the sacred word or act, has become the ultimate source of power.

The second new emphasis reflects a new concern with life after death. The old Vedic ideal of living a full and upright life so as to attain an afterlife in some kind of heaven of the fathers, among the gods, is no longer seen as an adequate ideal or goal. Immortality is now interpreted in terms not of afterlife but of escape from all existence—earthly, or heavenly, or any other. These two Upanishadic emphases gave birth to a series of ideas that were to change the shape of Indian thought forever. Together they provide the key to its basic worldview.

THE NATURE OF REALITY. The quest for knowledge by the sages of the Upanishads concentrated on the nature of the individual self *(atman)* and its relation to ultimate reality, or *Brahman.* The gods now take a lesser place as only one part of the total scheme of things. They are themselves subject to the laws of existence and not to be put on the same plane with the transcendent Absolute. Prayer and sacrifice to particular gods for their help are one thing; realization of

Brahman is something altogether different. The latter is possible only through the action of the mind, not the bodily acts of ritual.

The culmination of the Upanishadic speculation is the recognition that the way to the Absolute is through the self. Through contemplation, *Atman-Brahman* is recognized not as some divine being that can be addressed as a deity, but as the very principle of reality itself: the unborn, unmade, unchanging infinite. Of this reality, all that can be said is that it is "neither this nor that," because the ultimate cannot be conceived of or described in finite terms. Beneath or behind the impermanence of ordinary reality is the changeless *Brahman,* to which the immortal self of every being belongs. The difficulty is recognizing this self, and with it the Absolute, while one is caught in the realm of normal existence.

A second, related focus of Upanishadic inquiry was into the nature of "normal" existence. The realm of life is seen to be ultimately impermanent, ever in change. What seem to be "solid" things—the physical world, our bodies and personalities, worldly success—are revealed in the Upanishads to be finally insubstantial, impermanent, and ephemeral. Even happiness is passing. Existence is neither satisfying nor lasting in any fundamental sense. Only *Brahman* is enduring, eternal, unchanging—the unmoved

Discussions of *Brahman* and *Atman* from the Upanishads

A REPORT OF THE SAGE SANDILYA'S STATEMENT ABOUT THE IDENTITY OF ATMAN AND BRAHMAN

"Verily, this whole world is Brahman. Tranquil, let one worship it as that from which he came forth, as that into which he will be dissolved, as that in which he breathes. Now, verily, a person consists of purpose. According to the purpose which a person has in this world, thus does he become on departing hence. So let him form for himself a purpose. He who consists of mind, whose body is life, whose form is light, whose conception is truth, whose soul [atman] is space, containing all odors, containing all tastes, encompassing this whole world, the unspeaking, the unconcerned—this Soul of mine within the heart is smaller than a grain of rice, or a barley-corn, or a mustard-seed, or a grain of millet; or the kernel of a grain of millet; this Soul of mine within the heart is greater than the earth, greater than the atmosphere, greater than the sky, greater than these worlds. Containing all works, containing all desires, containing all odors, containing all tastes, encompassing this whole world, the unspeaking, the unconcerned—this

Soul of mine within the heart, this is Brahman. Into him I shall enter on departing hence. If one would believe this, he would have no more doubt."—Thus used Sandilya to say . . . .

—Chandogya Upanishad 3.14

THE YOUNG BRAHMAN, SHVETAKETU, IS INSTRUCTED IN THE IDENTITY OF ATMAN AND BRAHMAN BY HIS FATHER

"These rivers, my dear, flow, the eastern toward the east, the western toward the west. They go just from the ocean to the ocean. They become the ocean itself. As there they know not 'I am this one,' 'I am that one'—even so, indeed, my dear, all creatures here, though they have come forth from Being, know not 'We have come forth from Being.' Whatever they are in this world, whether tiger, or lion, or wolf, or boar, or worm, or fly, or gnat, or mosquito, that they become. That which is the finest essence—this whole world has that as its soul. That is Reality. That is Atman. That art thou, Shvetaketu."

—Chandogya Upanishad 6.10

Selections taken with minor changes from Robert Ernest Hume (trans.), *The Thirteen Principal Upanishads*, 2nd ed. rev. (London: Oxford University Press, 1931), pp. 209–210, 246–247.

---

ground of existence. This perception already shows a marked tendency toward the eventual emphasis of the Buddhists on impermanence and suffering as the fundamental facts of existence as we know it.

LIFE AFTER DEATH.   The new understanding of immortality that emerges in the Upanishads is related to these basic perceptions about the self, the Absolute, and the world of existence. It runs, as we noted, counter to the older Vedic-Aryan concept of an immortal existence either in heaven or in hell after this life is finished. The Upanishadic sages developed the concept of existence as a ceaseless cycle of existence, a never-ending alternation between life and death. This idea was not only to have major implications for Indian speculative thought; it was also to become the basic assumption of all Indian thought and religious life.

The idea of the endless cycle of renewed existence, which Indians refer to as *samsara,* is only superficially to be compared to or translated as our idea of "transmigration" of souls. For Indians, it is the key to the nature of reality as we can know it. Furthermore, it is a fact that is not promising or liberating, but suffocating or burdensome. In the Indian context, *samsara* refers to the terrifying prospect of endless "redeath" as the normal lot of all beings in this world, whether animals, plants, humans, or gods. This is the fundamental problem posed for all later Indian thought. It is the problem to which the great Indian thinkers of the mid-first millennium B.C., from the sages of the Upanishads to the Buddha, addressed themselves most centrally.

KARMA.   The key to the solution of the dilemma of *samsara* lies in the concept of *karma,* which in Sanskrit literally means "work" or "action." At base, it is the concept that every action has its inevitable effects, sooner or later, and that as long as there is action of mind or body, there is continued effect, and hence continued existence. Good deeds bring good results, perhaps even rebirth in a heaven or as a god, and evil ones bring evil consequences, whether in this life or in rebirth in the next, whether in the everyday world or in the lower worlds of hell. Because of the fundamental impermanence of everything in existence (heavens and hells included), the good as well as the evil is temporary. The flux of existence knows only movement, change, endless cause and effect far transcending a mere human life span, or even a mere world eon.

SOLUTIONS.   Working from the ruthless analysis of existence posed in the Upanishads and taken as the starting point of all later Indian thought, the solution to the problem of *samsara* that was worked out in the Indian tradition is of two kinds. The first alternative or strategy involves maximizing good actions and minimizing bad actions, in order to achieve the best possible rebirth in one's next round of existence. The second is different; it involves "release" *(moksha)* from existence: escaping all karmic effects by escaping action itself.

The first strategy has been followed by the great masses of Hindus, Buddhists, and Jains over the centuries. It has been characterized by Franklin Edgerton as the "ordinary norm," as opposed to the "extraordinary norm," the path of only the select elite, the greatest seekers of Upanishadic truth, Jain asceticism, or the Buddhist "middle path." Essentially, the ordinary norm involves a life lived according to some code of social responsibility. The most significant codes for Indian history are those recognized by most Hindus, Buddhists, and Jains over the centuries. On the other hand, the seekers of the extraordinary norm are usually involved in some kind of ascetic discipline aimed at withdrawal from the karmic cycle altogether and the consequent release *(moksha)* from cause and effect, good and evil, birth and rebirth. These two characteristic Indian responses to the problem posed by *samsara* show how the fundamental forms of Indian thought and piety took shape in the middle and later first millennium B.C.

SOCIAL RESPONSIBILITY: *DHARMA* AS IDEAL.   The ordinary norm, or ideal of life in the various traditions of Indian religiousness, can be summarized as life lived according to *dharma.* Although *dharma* has many meanings in Indian usage, its most common is similar to that of the Vedic-Aryan concept of *Rta* (see Chapter 1). In this sense, *dharma* means "the right (order of things)," "moral law," "right conduct," or even "duty." It includes the cosmic order (compare the Chinese *Tao*) as well as the right conduct of political, commercial, social, and religious affairs and individual moral responsibility. For most people—those we might call the laity, as distinguished from monks and ascetics—life according to *dharma* is the life of moral action that will lead to a better birth in the next round of existence.

Life according to *dharma* has several implications. First, it accepts action in the world of *samsara* as necessary and legitimate. Second, it demands acceptance of the responsibilities appropriate to one's sex, one's class and caste group, one's stage in life, and one's other particular circumstances. Third, it allows for legitimate self-interest: One's duty is to do things that acquire merit for one's eternal *atman* and to avoid those that involve demerit, or evil consequences. Fourth, rebirth in heaven, in paradise, is the highest goal attainable through the life of *dharma.* However (fifth), all achievement in the world of *dharma* (which is also the world of *samsara*), even the attainment of heaven, is ultimately impermanent and is subject to change.

ASCETIC DISCIPLINE: *MOKSHA* AS IDEAL.   For those who have the mental and physical capacity to abandon the world of ordinary life and to find freedom from *samsara,* the implications for living are in direct contrast to those of the ordinary norm. First, action is viewed as negative, whether it is good or bad, for action produces only more action, more *karma,* more rebirth. Second, nonaction is achieved only by withdrawal from "normal" existence. The person seeking release *(moksha)* from *samsara* has to move beyond the usual responsibilities of family and society. Most often, this removal involves becoming some kind of "renouncer"—whether a homeless Hindu hermit, yogi, or wanderer, or a Jain or Buddhist monk. Third, this renunciation of the world and its goals demands selflessness, or absence of ego. One must give up the desires and attachments that the self normally needs to function in the world. Fourth, the highest goal is not rebirth in heaven at all, but *moksha,* release from all rebirth and redeath. Finally, *moksha* is lasting, permanent. Its realization means no more becoming, no more existence, no more suffering in the realm of *samsara.* Permanence, eternity, transcendence, and freedom from suffering are its attributes.

SEEKERS OF THE EXTRAORDINARY NORM. The ideas that led individuals to seek the extraordinary norm appeared fully elaborated for the first time in the Upanishads. These ideas were particularly congenial to an increasing number of people who abandoned both the ritualistic religious practices and the society of class distinctions and material concerns around them. It is noteworthy that many of these seekers were of warrior-noble *(Kshatriya)*, not *Brahman*, birth. They took up the wandering or hermit existence of the ascetic, seeking in yogic meditation and self-denial or even self-torture to gain spiritual powers. The higher seekers tried to transcend the body and bodily existence in order to realize the Absolute.

In the sixth century B.C., a number of teachers of new ideas appeared, especially in the lower Ganges basin, in the area of Magadha (modern Bihar). Most of them rejected traditional forms of religiousness as well as the authority of the Vedas in favor of one or another kind of ascetic discipline as the true spiritual path. Two of these teachers acquired sufficient followings that their ideas and practices became the foundations of new and lasting traditions of piety and faith, those of the Jains and the Buddhists.

Mahavira and the Jain Tradition

The Jains trace their tradition to Vardhamana, known as Mahavira ("the great hero"), who lived about 540 to 468 B.C. Mahavira is held by his followers to have been the final *Jina* ("victor" over *samsara*) or *Tirthankara* ("ford maker," one who finds the way across the waters of existence), in a line of twenty-four great teachers who have appeared in the latter, degenerative half of the present-world time cycle. The Jains (or *Jainas*, "adherents of the *Jina*") see in Mahavira a human teacher, not a god. He found and taught the way to extricate the self, or soul, from the bonds of the material world and its accumulations of *karma*.

In the Jain view, there is no beginning or end to phenomenal existence, only innumerable, ceaseless cycles of generation and degeneration. The universe is alive from end to end with an infinite number of souls, all of which are immortal, omniscient, and pure in their essence. But all are caught in the web of *samsara*, whether as animals, gods, humans, plants, or even inanimate stones or fire. *Karma* here takes on a quasi-material form: Any thought, word, or deed attracts karmic matter that clings to and encumbers the soul. The greatest amounts come from evil acts, espe-

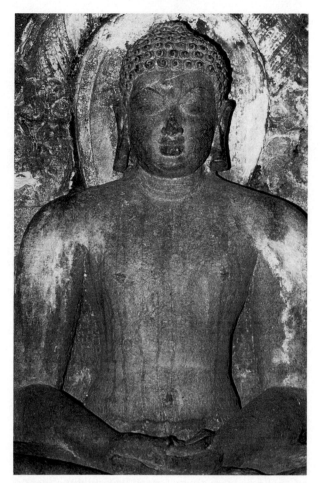

A statue of Mahavira. In this portrayal, the founder of the Jain path of purification and release exhibits the serenity of the Jina *who has "conquered" samsara. [Robert Radin]*

cially those done out of hate, greed, or cruelty to any other being.

Mahavira's path to release focused on the elimination of evil thoughts and acts, especially those harmful to others. His radical ascetic practice aimed at destroying one's karmic defilements and, ultimately, all actions leading to further karmic bondage. At the age of thirty, Mahavira entered the radical self-denial of a wandering ascetic and eventually gave up even clothing altogether (the latter a practice followed today by a relatively small sect of Jain mendicants). After a dozen years of self-deprivation and yogic meditative discipline, he attained enlightenment. Then, for some thirty years, he went about teaching his discipline to others. At the age of seventy-two, he chose to fast to death in order to burn out the last karmic residues, an action that has been emulated by some

Jain Comments on *Samsara* and the Monastic Virtues

The following two selections from a later Jain writing give some idea of how vividly the suffering of the self in the many forms of existence it undergoes is conceived of (Selection 1) and how totally Jain ascetics should fight all selfishness and self-pity as they undertake the stern discipline that will rid them of karmic accretions (Selection 2).

From clubs and knives, stakes and maces, breaking my limbs,
An infinite number of times I have suffered without hope.
By keen-edged razors, by knives and shears,
Many times I have been drawn and quartered, torn apart and skinned.
Helpless in snares and traps, a deer,
I have been caught and bound and fastened, and often I have been killed. . . .
A tree, with axes and adzes by the carpenters
An infinite number of times I have been felled, stripped of my bark, cut up, and sawn into planks. . . .
Ever afraid, trembling, in pain and suffering,
I have felt the utmost sorrow and agony. . . .
In every kind of existence I have suffered
Pains which have scarcely known reprieve for a moment.

—*Uttaradhyayana* 19.61–64, 71, 74

If another insult him, a monk should not lose his temper,
For that is mere childishness—a monk should never be angry.
If he hears words harsh and cruel, vulgar and painful,
He should silently disregard them, and not take them to heart.
Even if beaten he should not be angry, or even think sinfully,
But should know that patience is best, and follow the Law.

. . . .

When his limbs are running with sweat, and grimed with dust and dirt
In the heat of summer, the wise monk will not lament his lost comfort.
He must bear it all to wear out his karma, and follow the noble, the supreme Law.
Until his body breaks up, he should bear the filth upon it.

—*Uttaradhyayana* 2.24–37

From W. T. de Bary et al., *Sources of Indian Tradition* (New York: Columbia University Press, 1958), pp. 59–60, 64–65.

of the most advanced of Jain ascetics down to the present day.

It would, however, be very wrong to think of the entire Jain tradition in terms only of the extreme ascetic practices of some Jain mendicants. (Such practices can involve the attempt to avoid hurting even the tiniest organisms by wearing cloth masks and drinking only strained water.) Monks are bound basically by the five great vows that they share with other monastic traditions like the Buddhist and the Christian: not to kill, steal, lie, engage in sexual activity, or own anything.

Most Jains are not monks. Today, as in earlier centuries, there is a thriving lay community of perhaps three million Jains, most in western India (Gujarat and Rajasthan). Laypersons of both sexes have close ties to the monks (also of both sexes), whom they support with gifts and food. Many Jain laypersons spend some time during their lives in retreat with monks.

Jains tend to be merchants because of their aversion to farming and other occupations that involve harming plants or animals. They are vegetarians and regard *ahimsa,* "noninjury" to any being, as the paramount rule. In this latter emphasis, they have had great influence on Indian values. For example, Mahatma Gandhi, who came from a Jain area, seems to have been influenced by them in his adoption of *ahimsa* as a central tenet of his thought. Jains are known, in addition, for their hospitals—not only for humans, but also for animals. Compassion is for them, as for Buddhists, the great virtue. The merit of

Jain lay worshippers of the digambara *sect in the Puja Temple at Indore. The often lavish Jain temples, built with lay donations, are centers for lay participation in the Jain tradition. [Robert Radin]*

serving the extraordinary-norm seekers who adopt the mendicant life and of living a life according to the high standards of the community provides a goal even for those who as laypersons are following the ordinary norm.

The Buddha

It can be argued that India's greatest contribution to world civilization was precisely the tradition of faith that eventually withered away in the subcontinent itself. The Buddhist tradition remains one of the greatest universalist forms of faith in the world today, but numbers only small minorities in India proper. Yet that is where it was born, where it received its fundamental shape, and where it left its mark on Hindu and Jain religion and culture. Like the two other great universalist traditions, Christianity and Islam, it traces

its origins to a single figure who has loomed larger than life in the community of the faithful over the centuries.

This figure is Siddhartha Gautama, known as the "sage of the Shakya tribe" and, above all, as the Buddha, or the "enlightened/awakened one." A contemporary of Mahavira, Gautama was also born of a *Kshatriya* family (ca. 566 B.C.) in apparently comfortable if not, as the legend has it, royal circumstances. His people lived near the border of modern Nepal in the Himalayan foothills. The traditional story of how Gautama came to be the teacher of the "middle path" to release from *samsara* begins with his sheltered life of ease as a young married prince.

At the age of twenty-nine, Gautama suddenly realized the reality of aging, sickness, and death as the human lot. Revolted at his previous delight in sensual pleasures and even his wife and child, he abandoned his home and family to seek an answer to the dilemma of the endless cycle of mortal existence. After this "Great Renunciation," he studied first with renowned teachers and then took up extreme ascetic disciplines of penance and self-mortification. Still finding no answer, Gautama turned finally to intense yogic meditation under a pipal tree in the place near Varanasi (Banaras) known as Gaya. In one historic night, he moved through different levels of trance, during which he realized all of his past lives, the reality of the cycle of existence of all beings, and how to stop the karmic outflows that fuel suffering existence. At this point, he became the Buddha; that is, he achieved full enlightenment—the omniscient consciousness of reality as it is. Having realized the truth of suffering existence, he committed himself to the goal of gaining release for all beings.

From the time of the experience under the Bodh Tree, or "enlightenment tree," Gautama devoted the last of his earthly lives before his final release to teaching others his "middle path" between asceticism and sensual indulgence. This path has been the core of Buddhist faith and practice ever since. It begins with realizing the "four noble truths"—(1) all life is *dukkha,* or suffering; (2) the source of suffering is desiring; (3) the cessation of desiring is the way to end suffering; and (4) the path to this end is eightfold: right understanding, thought, speech, action, livelihood, effort, mindfulness, and concentration. The key idea of the Buddhist teaching, or *dharma,* is that everything in the world of existence is causally linked. The essential fact of existence is *dukkha:* All existing is suffering, for no pleasure, however great, is

The "Turning of the Wheel of the Dharma": Basic Teachings of the Buddha

The following are selections from the sermon said to have been the first preached by the Buddha. It was directed at five of his former companions, with whom he had practiced extreme austerities. When he abandoned asceticism to mediate under the Bodh Tree, they had left him. This sermon is said to have made them the first to follow him. Because it set in motion the Buddha's teaching, or dharma, *on earth, it is usually described as "setting in motion the wheel of* dharma.*" The text is from the* Dhammacakkappavattana-sutta.

Thus have I heard. The Blessed One was once living in the Deer Park at Isipatana (the Resort of Seers) near Baranasi (Benares). There he addressed the group of five bhikkhus.

"Bhikkhus, these two extremes ought not to be practiced by one who has gone forth from the household life. What are the two? There is devotion to the indulgence of sense-pleasures, which is low, common, the way of ordinary people, unworthy and unprofitable; and there is devotion to self-mortification, which is painful, unworthy and unprofitable.

"Avoiding both these extremes, the Tathagata has realized the Middle Path: it gives vision, it gives knowledge, and it leads to calm, to insight, to enlightenment, to Nibbana. And what is that Middle Path? It is simply the Noble Eight-fold Path, namely, right view, right thought, right speech, right action, right livelihood, right effort, right mindfulness, right concentration. This is the Middle Path realized by the Tathagata, which gives vision, which gives knowledge, and which leads to calm, to insight, to enlightenment, to Nibbana. . . .

"The Noble Truth of suffering *(Dukkha)* is this: Birth is suffering; aging is suffering; sickness is suffering; death is suffering; sorrow and lamentation, pain, grief and despair are suffering; association with the unpleasant is suffering; dissociation from the pleasant is suffering; not to get what one wants is suffering—in brief, the five aggregates of attachment are suffering.

"The Noble Truth of the origin of suffering is this: It is this thirst (craving) which produces re-existence and re-becoming, bound up with passionate greed. It finds fresh delight now here and now there, namely, thirst for non-existence (self-annihilation).

"The Noble Truth of the Cessation of suffering is this: It is the complete cessation of that very thirst, giving it up, renouncing it, emancipating oneself from it, detaching oneself from it.

"The Noble Truth of the Path leading to the Cessation of suffering is this: It is simply the Noble Eight-fold Path. . . .

"'This is the Noble Truth of Suffering *(Dukkha)*': such was the vision, the knowledge, the wisdom, the science, the light, that arose in me with regard to things not heard before. 'This suffering, as a noble truth, should be fully understood.'

"'This is the Noble Truth of the Cessation of suffering': such was the vision 'This Cessation of suffering, as a noble truth, should be realized.'

"'This is the Noble Truth of the Path leading to the Cessation of suffering': such was the vision, 'This Path leading to the Cessation of suffering, as a noble truth, has been followed (cultivated).'

"As long as my vision of true knowledge was not fully clear regarding the Four Noble Truths, I did not claim to have realized the perfect Enlightenment that is supreme in the world with its gods, in this world with its recluses and brahmanas, with its princes and men. But when my vision of true knowledge was fully clear regarding the Four Noble Truths, then I claimed to have realized the perfect Enlightenment that is supreme in the world with its gods, in this world with its recluses and brahmanas, with its princes and men. And a vision of true knowledge arose in me thus: My heart's deliverance is unassailable. This is the last birth. Now there is no more rebecoming (rebirth)."

This the Blessed One said. The group of five bhikkhus was glad, and they rejoiced at his words.

—*Samyutta-nikaya*, LVI, II

From Walpola Rahula, *What the Buddha Taught* (New York: Grove Press, 1974), pp. 92–94.

An early carving showing the chakra, *or wheel of* dharma, *the Buddha's teaching, adored by humans and gods. The tree is the Bodh-tree under which Gautama attained enlightenment and became the Buddha. [Diana L. Eck]*

permanent (here we see the Buddhist variation on the central Indian theme of *samsara*). *Dukkha* comes from desire, from craving, from attachment to self.

Thus, Buddhist discipline focuses on the moral "eightfold path" and the cardinal virtue of compassion for all beings, with the intent of eliminating the selfish desiring that is literally the root of *samsara* and its unavoidable suffering. The Buddha himself had attained this goal. When he died (ca. 486 B.C.) after a life of teaching others how to eliminate desire, he passed from the round of existence forever. In Buddhist terminology, he attained *nirvana,* the extinguishing of continued karmic bondage. This attainment was to become the starting point for the growth and eventual spread of the Buddhist *dharma,* which was to take on diverse and far different forms in its long history.

Like the Jain movement, the Buddhist movement involved not only followers who were willing to renounce marriage and normal occupations to become part of the Buddha's communities of monks or nuns, but also laypersons who would strive to live by the high moral standards of the tradition and support those who were willing and able to strive as mendicants to realize full release. Like the Jain tradition, the Buddhist tradition encompassed from the start seekers of both the extraordinary and the ordinary norms in their present lives. This dual community has remained characteristic of all forms of Buddhism wherever it is practiced. Certainly, we shall have occasion later to see how varied these forms have been historically. But however much the essentially a-theistic, a-ritualistic, and pragmatic basic tradition was later modified and expanded, so that popular Buddhism would encompass even theistic devotion to a divinized Buddha and other enlightened beings, the fundamental vision of a humanly attainable wisdom that leads to compassion and release remained.

The varying visions of Upanishadic, Jain, and Buddhist thought have proved durable, albeit in very different ways and degree in India itself, as we have noted. The emergence of "Hindu" tradition was to draw on all three of these revolutionary strands in Indian thought and to integrate their fundamental ideas about the universe, human life, morality, and society into the cultic and mythic strands of Brahmanic and popular Indian practice.

The Religion of the Jews

The world of the ancient Near East, both in Egypt and in the lands east of the Mediterranean across to the Iranian plateau, was a polytheistic world. Everywhere people worshiped local or regional gods and goddesses. Some of these deities were associated with natural places and phenomena such as mountains or animals, the sky or the earth. For example, Shamash in Mesopotamia and Re in Egypt were both sun gods. Others were tribal or local deities, such as Marduk in Babylonia or Atum, the patron god of the Egyptian city of On (Heliopolis). Still others represented elemental powers of this world or the next, as was the case with Baal, the ancient fertility god of the Canaanite peoples, and Ishtar, whom the Sumerians worshiped as a goddess of love and the Assyrians as a goddess of war. Furthermore, from our perspective, the gods were represented, by and large, as arbitrary and amoral beings who were often no more affected by the actions of human beings than were the natural forces that some of them represented.

If the gods were many and diverse, so too were the religious traditions of the ancient Near Eastern world. Even the major traditions of religious thought in Egypt and Mesopotamia did not offer comprehensive interpretations of human life that linked history and human destiny to a transcendent or eternal realm of meaning beyond this world—or at least no one interpretation was able to spread and become dominant in this highly pluralistic, religiously fragmented world.

Out of this polytheistic and pluralistic world came the great tradition of monotheistic faith represented historically in the Jewish, Christian, and Islamic communities. This tradition traces its origin not to any of the great imperial cultures of the ancient Near Eastern world, but to the small nation of the Israelites. Although they were only a tiny tribal people whose external fortunes were at the mercy of the ebb and flow of the great dynasties and empires of the first millennium B.C., their impact on the global history of civilization was far greater than that of their giant neighbors. For all the glories of the great civilizations of the Fertile Crescent and the Nile valley, it was the Israelites, not the Babylonians or the Egyptians, who founded a tradition that significantly affected later history. This tradition was ethical monotheism.

Monotheism, faith in a single, all-powerful God who is the sole creator, sustainer, and ruler of the universe, may well be older than the Hebrews, but it made its first clear appearance with them. It was with the Hebrews that emphasis on the moral demands and ethical responsibilities placed on the individual and the community by the one God was first definitively linked to human history itself (and the divine plan for that history). This historically based ethical and monotheistic tradition culminated later in the Jewish, Christian, and Islamic religions, but its direction had been set much earlier.

The beginnings of the tradition lie far back in the early history of an obscure tribal people whom later history knows as the Hebrews. The path from the appearance of this group as nomadic tribes in the northern Arabian peninsula, sometime after 2000 B.C., to the full flowering of Judaic monotheism in the mid-first millennium B.C. was a long one. Before we turn to the monotheistic revolution itself, we need to look briefly at the history of the Hebrews.

From Hebrew Nomads to the Israelite Nation

The history of the Hebrew people, later known as Israelites, must be pieced together from various sources. They are mentioned only rarely in the records of their ancient Near Eastern neighbors, so we must rely chiefly on their own accounts as compiled in the Hebrew Bible (or Old Testament, in Christian terminology). It was not intended as a history in our sense; rather, it is a complicated collection of historical narrative, wisdom, literature, poetry, law, and religious witness. Scholars of an earlier day in the West tended to discard the Bible as a source for historians, but the most recent trend is to take it seriously while using it cautiously and critically. Although its earliest written portions go back at most only to the ninth century B.C. (it came to be fixed in the form in which it is known today only in the second century A.D.), it contains much older oral materials in its earliest parts. These allow us at least some glimpses of the earliest history of the Hebrew tribe.

We need not reject the tradition that the patriarch Abraham came from Ur in Mesopotamia and wandered west with his Hebrew clan to tend his flocks in the land along the eastern shore of the Mediterranean that became known to later history as Palestine. Such a movement would be in accord with what we know of a general migration of seminomadic tribes from Mesopotamia westward after about 1950 B.C. Any precise dating of the arrival of the Hebrews in the region of Palestine is impossible, but it might have been as early as 1900 B.C. or as late as 1600 B.C.

It is, however, with the patriarchal figure of Moses, at about the beginning of the thirteenth century B.C., that the Hebrews come onto the stage of history with greater clarity. Some of Abraham's people had settled down in the Palestinian area, but others apparently had wandered farther westward, into Egypt, perhaps with the Hyksos invaders (see Chapter 1). As the biblical narrative tells it, they had, by about 1400 B.C., become a settled but subject and even enslaved people there. Under the leadership of Moses, a segment of the Egyptian Israelites left the land of Egypt in search of a new homeland in the region to the east from which Abraham's descendants had come. The Children of Israel may then have wandered in the Sinai Desert and elsewhere for several decades before reaching Canaan, the province of Palestine that is described in the Bible as their promised homeland. The Bible presents this experience as the key event in

"Moses Breaking the Tablets of the Law," by Rembrandt van Rijn. The breaking of the tablets is one of the major symbols from biblical history and an important theme in Western literature and art. [Royal Palaces, Berlin]

Israel's history: the forging of the covenant, or mutual pact, between God, or *Yahweh,* and his people. We interpret the events of this Exodus period as the time that the Israelites emerged as a nation, a people with a sense of community and common purpose.

By about 1200 B.C., they had carved out a new Pal-

THE ISRAELITES	
CA. 1000–961 B.C.	Reign of King David
CA. 961–922 B.C.	Reign of King Solomon
722 B.C.	Assyrian conquest of Israel (northern kingdom)
586 B.C.	Destruction of Jerusalem; fall of Judah (southern kingdom); Babylonian captivity
539 B.C.	Restoration of temple; return of exiles

estinian homeland for themselves at the expense of the Canaanite inhabitants of the area. After perhaps two centuries of consolidation and an existence as a loose federation of tribes, the now settled nation reached its peak as a monarchy under kings David and Solomon in the tenth century B.C. But the sons of Solomon could not maintain the unity of the kingdom, and it split into two parts in the ninth century B.C.: Israel in the north of Palestine and Judah, with its capital at Jerusalem, in the south (see Map 2-2).

The rise of the great empires around them brought disaster to the Israelites. The northern kingdom fell to the Assyrians in 722 B.C.; its people were scattered and, according to tradition, lost forever, the so-called ten lost tribes. Only the kingdom of Judah, with its seat at Jerusalem, remained, and hereafter we may call the Israelites Jews. In 586 B.C., Judah was defeated by the Neo-Babylonian king Nebuchadnezzar II. He destroyed the center of the Jewish cult, the great temple built by Solomon, and carried off the cream of the Jewish nation as exiles to be resettled in Babylon. There, in the "Babylonian captivity" of the Exile, without a temple, the Jews managed still to cling to their traditions and faith. After the new Persian dynasty of the Achaemenids defeated the Babylonians in 539 B.C., they were allowed to return and resettle in their homeland. Many, but not all, of the exiles did return, and by about 516 B.C., a second temple was erected in a restored Jerusalem after the Exile.

The new Judaic state continued to be dominated by foreign peoples in the following centuries, but it was able to maintain its religious and national identity and occasionally to assert itself. However, it was again destroyed and its people dispersed after the destruction of Jerusalem by the Romans, in A.D. 70 and again in A.D. 132. By this time, however, the Jews had developed a religious worldview that would far exceed and long outlive that of any Judaic national state.

The Monotheistic Revolution

The fate of this small nation would be of little interest were it not for its unique religious achievement. It developed a tradition of faith that amounted to a revolution in ways of thinking about the human condition, the meaning of life and history, and the nature of the divine. It was not the overt history of the Judaic state down to its catastrophic end in A.D. 132 that was to have lasting historical importance, but what the Jews

MAP 2-2 ANCIENT PALESTINE *The Hebrews established a unified kingdom under Kings David and Solomon in the tenth century* B.C. *After Solomon the kingdom was divided into Israel in the north and Judah, with its capital, Jerusalem, in the south. North of Israel were the great commercial cities of Phoenicia.*

made of that history and how they interpreted it. The revolutionary character of this interpretation lay in its uniquely moralistic understanding of human life and history and the uncompromising monotheism on which this understanding was based.

At the root of this monotheistic tradition stands the figure of Abraham. Not only Jews but also Christians and Muslims look to him as the symbolic founder of their monotheistic faith. It is likely that the Hebrews in Abraham's time were much like other primitive tribal peoples in their religious attitudes. For them, the world must have been alive with many supernatural or divine powers: ancestral spirits, personifications or masters of the forces of nature, and divinities associated with particular places. Abraham probably conceived of his Lord simply as the most powerful of many divinities whom people might worship. But for the strength of his faith in God, the later biblical account recognizes him as the "Father of the Faithful," the first of the Hebrew patriarchs to enter into a covenant, or mutual pact, with God. In this covenant, Abraham promised to serve only this God, and this God promised in turn to bless Abraham's descendants and guide them as his special people.

The Temple Mount, seen from the west. The traditional site of the Jerusalem Temple (the Herodian western "wailing" wall, is in the center), the Temple Mount is a holy site especially to Muslims, as well as to Jews and Christians. The dome at the left is the Muslim Dome of the Rock sanctuary (A.D. 692); at the far right is the Al-Aqsa mosque, built only a few years later. [David H. Wells, 1990]

God's Purpose with Israel

In the first selection here, God, speaking through the prophet Jeremiah (fl. 626–586 B.C.), says that Jerusalem will be given over to the Babylonians. But he goes on to assure the Jews that he will also "gather them" together again and restore the "everlasting covenant" when he brings them again to Palestine. Such words provided the exiles in Babylon with an interpretation of their fate that helped them hold to their faith even in a foreign land. In the second selection, we hear the unknown prophetic voice of the so-called Second Isaiah, which dates from about 540 B.C. Here God addresses Israel as his suffering servant and promises to comfort and restore the Israelites as "a light to the nations." Such prophetic promises reflect the self-understanding of Israel with regard both to the tragedies of their history and to their special role as God's chosen instrument in his larger plan of salvation for all the nations of the earth.

The word of the Lord came to Jeremiah: "Behold, I am the Lord, the God of all flesh; is anything too hard for me? Therefore, thus says the Lord: Behold, I am giving this city into the hand of the Chalde'ans and into the hand of Nebuchadnez'zar king of Babylon, and he shall take it. . . . For the sons of Israel and the sons of Judah have done nothing but evil in my sight from their youth; the sons of Israel have done nothing but provoke me to anger by the work of their hands, says the Lord. . . .

"Now therefore thus says the Lord, the God of Israel, concerning this city of which you say, 'It is given into the hand of the king of Babylon by sword, by famine, and by pestilence': Behold, I will gather them from all the countries to which I drove them in my anger and my wrath and in great indignation; I will bring them back to this place, and I will make them dwell in safety. And they shall be my people, and I will be their God. I will give them one heart and one way, that they may fear me for ever, for their own good and the good of their children after them. I will

make with them an everlasting covenant, that I will not turn away from doing good to them; and I will put the fear of me in their hearts, that they may not turn from me. I will rejoice in doing them good, and I will plant them in this land in faithfulness, with all my heart and all my soul."

—Jeremiah 32:26–28, 30, 36–41

Behold my servant, whom I uphold,
my chosen, in whom my soul delights;
I have put my spirit upon him,
  he will bring forth justice to the nations.
He will not cry or lift up his voice, or make it
heard in the street;
a bruised reed he will not break,
  and a dimly burning wick he will not quench;
  he will faithfully bring forth justice.
He will not fail or be discouraged
  till he has established justice in the earth;
  and the coastlands wait for his law.

—Isaiah 42:1–4

From H. G. May and B. M. Metzger, eds., *The Oxford Annotated Bible with the Apocrypha: Revised Standard Version* (New York: Oxford University Press, 1965).

As is the case with the faith of Abraham, it is difficult to say how much the Mosaic covenant at Sinai actually represented the achievement of an exclusively monotheistic faith. A notion of the supremacy of Yahweh is reflected in the biblical emphasis on the Israelites' rejection of all other gods at this time—and on their subsequent victory, through Yahweh's might, over the Canaanites. Certainly, the covenant event was decisive in making the Israelites a people united and identified by their special relationship to God. At Sinai, they received both God's holy Law (the Torah)

and his promise of protection and guidance as long as they kept the law. This covenant was the necessary first step in the monotheistic revolution that came to full fruition several hundred years later. From Sinai forward, the Israelites looked on themselves as God's chosen people among the nations, and on their history as the history of the mighty acts of God.

The monotheistic revolution might thus be said to have begun with Abraham or Moses. Historically, we can trace it primarily from the division of the Israelite kingdom into two parts in 922 B.C. After this event men and women arose who were known as the *prophets*. Inspired messengers of God, prophets were sent to call people back from the worship of false gods to the worship of the one true God, and from increasing immorality and injustice to obedience to God's commandments.

Here we cannot trace the colorful history of the great and lesser prophets of Israel. The important point is that their activity was directly tied to the crucial events of Israelite history in the middle centuries of the first millennium B.C. In the biblical interpretation of these events, we can see the consolidation of the Judaic religious tradition in process. This consolidation, even amidst the political disintegration of the Israelite kingdom, was largely the result of the activities of the prophets. Their concern with purifying the faith and the morality of their people focused in particular on two ideas that proved central to Judaic monotheism.

The first was the significance of history in the divine plan. Calling on the Jews' awareness of the covenant made at Sinai, the prophets saw in Israel's past and present troubles the hand of God punishing them for failing in their covenant duties. Their prophecies of coming disaster at the hands of enemies were based on the conviction that unless Israel changed its ways, more punishment would follow. But they were not only prophets of doom. When the predicted disasters came, their vision extended to seeing Israel the "suffering servant" among the nations, the people who, by their trials, would purify other nations and bring them also eventually to God. Here the nationalistic, particularistic focus of previous Israelite religion gave way to a universal, and therefore more complete, monotheism: Yahweh was God of all, even the Babylonians or Assyrians.

The second idea, or set of ideas, centered on the nature of Yahweh. The prophets saw in him the transcendent ideal of justice and goodness. From this view followed naturally the demand for justice and goodness in his worshipers, both individually and collectively. God was a righteous God who expected righteousness from human beings. No longer could he be understood only as the object of a sacrificial cult: He was a moral God who demanded fairness and goodness, not blood offerings and empty prayers. A corollary of God's goodness was his love for his people, as especially the prophet Hosea (late eighth century B.C.) emphasized. However much he might have to punish them for their sins, God would eventually lead them back to him and his favor.

In the linking of the Lord of the Universe to history and to morality lay the heart of the breakthrough to true ethical monotheism. The Almighty Creator was seen as actively concerned with the actions and fates of his human creatures as exemplified in Israel. This concern was reflected in his involvement in history; history took on transcendent meaning. God had created humankind for an ultimately good purpose: They were called on to be just and good like their Creator, for they were involved in the fulfillment of his divine purpose. Most concretely, this fulfillment would come in the restoration of Israel as a people purified of their sins: "I will put my law within them, and I will write it upon their hearts; and I will be their God, and they shall be my people" (Jeremiah 31:33).

However, even after the Exile, the full realization of the prophecied days of peace and blessedness under God's rule clearly still had not come. The Jews were scattered from Egypt to Babylonia, and their homeland remained in the control of stronger powers. Out of this context developed the late prophetic concept that the culmination of history would come in a future Messianic age. Faith and morality became tied to human destiny, even without the still later Jewish idea that a day of judgment would end the golden age of the Messiah. The significance of these ideas, some of which might have come from the Jews' encounter with Zoroastrian traditions during the Exile, did not stop with Judaic religion. They went on to play a key role in similar Christian and Muslim ideas of a Messianic deliverer, resurrection of the body, and a life after death.

Alongside the prophets, the other key element in the monotheistic revolution of the Jews was the Law itself. The Law is embodied in the five books of Torah (the Pentateuch, or "five books" of Genesis, Exodus, Leviticus, Numbers, and Deuteronomy). The central place of the Law in Jewish life was reestablished, after a period of decline, by King Josiah of Judah shortly before the fall of Jerusalem and the Exile. Its presence and importance in Judaic faith enabled the Jews to survive the loss of the Temple and its priestly cult even in exile, thereby fixing the Torah even over Jerusalem as the ultimate earthly focus of faith in God. Its centrality for the Jewish nation was reaffirmed after the reestablishment of the Temple, by Ezra and Nehemiah, in the fifth century B.C.

In the second century B.C., the enduring role of the Torah was ensured by its physical compilation, together with the books of the prophets and other writings, into the Holy Scriptures, or the Bible. In the Bible we have the record of the Jews' long road to the recognition of God's law for his people, as well as the actual Law of the Torah itself. A holy, authoritative, divinely revealed scripture as an element of Judaic monotheism had revolutionary consequences, not only for Jews, but also for Christians and Muslims. In many ways, it put the seal on the monotheistic revolution that had made the sovereignty and righteousness of God the focal point of faith. It thereby affirmed the meaning of human action and human history for the faithful through the tangible historical record of God's law and Israel's historical experience.

In the evolution of Judaic monotheistic faith, we see the beginning of one of the major traditions of world civilization. For the first time, in the Jews we find a nation defined not primarily by dynastic, linguistic, or geographic considerations, but above all by shared religious faith and practice. This was something new in human history. It was to have still greater effects in later times when not only Judaic but also Christian and Muslim tradition would change the face of major portions of the world.

Greek Philosophy

Different approaches and answers to many of the same concerns as those of the original monotheists were offered by ancient Greek thought. Calling attention, even this early, to some of those differences will help to point up the distinctive outlook of the Greeks and of the later cultures of Western civilization that have drawn heavily on it.

Greek ideas had much in common with the ideas of earlier peoples. The gods of the Greeks had most of the characteristics of the Mesopotamian deities, magic and incantations played a part in Greek lives, and their law was usually connected with divinity. Many, if not most, Greeks in the ancient world must have lived their lives with notions not very different from those held by other peoples. But, surprisingly, some Greeks developed ideas that were strikingly different and, in so doing, set a part of humankind on an entirely new path. As early as the sixth century B.C., some Greeks living in the Ionian cities of Asia Minor raised questions and suggested answers about nature that produced an intellectual revolution. In speculating about the nature of the world and its origin, they made guesses that were completely naturalistic and included no reference to supernatural powers. One historian of Greek thought put the case particularly well:

In one of the Babylonian legends it says: "All the lands were sea. Marduk bound a rush mat upon the face of the waters, he made dirt and piled it beside the rush mat." What Thales did was to leave Marduk out. He, too, said that everything was once water. But he thought that earth and everything else had been formed out of water by a natural process, like the silting up of the Delta of the Nile. It is an admirable beginning, the whole point of which is that it gathers together into a coherent picture a number of observed facts without letting Marduk in.[3]

Thales was the first Greek philosopher. His stating the question of the world's origin in a naturalistic form as early as the sixth century B.C. might have been the beginning of the unreservedly rational investigation of the universe, and so the beginning of both Western philosophy and Western science.

The same relentlessly rational approach was used even in regard to the gods themselves. In the same century as Thales, Xenophanes of Colophon expressed the opinion that humans thought that the gods were born and had clothes, voices, and bodies like themselves. If oxen, horses, and lions had hands and could paint like human beings, they would paint gods in their own image; the oxen would draw gods like oxen and the horses like horses. Thus black people believed in flat-nosed, black-faced gods, and the Thracians in gods with blue eyes and red hair.[4] In the fifth century B.C., Protagoras of Abdera went so far in the direction of agnosticism as to day, "About the gods I can have no knowledge either that they are or that they are not or what is their nature."[5]

This rationalistic, skeptical way of thinking carried over into practical matters as well. The school of medicine led by Hippocrates of Cos (about 400 B.C.) attempted to understand, diagnose, and cure disease without any attention to supernatural forces or beings. One of the Hippocratics wrote of the mysterious disease epilepsy: "It seems to me that the disease is no more divine than any other. It has a natural cause, just as other diseases have. Men think it divine merely because they do not understand it. But if they called everything divine which they do not understand, why, there would be no end of divine things."[6] By the fifth century B.C., it was possible for the historian Thucydides to analyze and explain the behavior of humans in society completely in terms of human nature and

---

[3]Benjamin Farrington, *Greek Science* (London: Penguin Books, 1953), p. 37.

[4]Frankfort et al., *Before Philosophy* (1949), pp. 14–16.

[5]Hermann Diels, *Fragmente der Vorsokratiker*, 5th ed., by Walther Kranz (Berlin: Weidmann, 1934–1938), Frg. 4.

[6]Ibid., Frgs. 14–16.

chance, leaving no place for the gods or supernatural forces.

The relative unimportance of divine or supernatural forces also characterized Greek views of law and justice. Most Greeks, of course, liked to think in a vague way that law came ultimately from the gods. In practice, however, and especially in the democratic states, they knew very well that laws were made by humans and should be obeyed because they represented the expressed consent of the citizens. Law, according to the fourth century B.C. statesman Demosthenes, was "a general covenant of the whole State, in accordance with which all men in that State ought to regulate their lives."[7]

The statement of these ideas, so different from any that came before the Greeks, opens the discussion of most of the issues that appear in the long history of civilization and that remain major concerns in the modern world: What is the nature of the universe and how can it be controlled? Are there divine powers, and if so, what is humanity's relationship to them? Are law and justice human, divine, or both? What is the place in human society of freedom, obedience, and reverence? These and many other problems were confronted and intensified by the Greeks.

Reason and the Scientific Spirit

The rational spirit characteristic of Greek geometric pottery and even of many Greek myths blossomed in the sixth century B.C. into the intellectual examination of the physical world and the place of humankind in it that we call philosophy. It is not surprising that the first steps along this path were taken in Ionia, which was on the fringe of the Greek world and therefore in touch with foreign ideas and the learning of the East. The Ionians were among the first to realize that the Greek account of how the world was created and maintained and of the place of humans in it was not universally accepted. Perhaps this realization helped spark the first attempts at disciplined philosophical inquiry.

We have already met Thales of Miletus, who lived early in the sixth century B.C. He believed that the earth floated on water and that water was the primary substance. This was not a new idea; what was new was the absence of any magical or mythical elements in the explanation. Thales observed, as any person can, that water has many forms: liquid, solid, and gaseous. He saw that it could "create" land by alluvial

[7] *Against Aristogeiton*, p. 16.

Thales of Miletus, the first Greek philosopher. His explanation for the origin of the world was based on reason and the observation of nature without any need for the supernatural. [Bettmann Archive]

deposit and that it was necessary for all life. These observations he organized by reason into a single explanation that accounted for many phenomena without any need for the supernatural. The first philosopher thus set the tone for future investigations. Greek philosophers assumed that the world was knowable, rational, and simple.

The search for fundamental rational explanations of phenomena was carried forward by another Milesian, Anaximander. He imagined that the basic element was something undefined, "unlimited." The world emerged from this basic element as the result of an interaction of opposite forces—wet and dry, hot and cold. Anaximander pictured the universe in eternal motion, with all sensible things emerging from the "unlimited," then decaying and returning to it. He also argued that human beings originated in water and had evolved to the present state through several stages, including that of a fish.

Anaximenes, another Milesian who flourished about 546 B.C., believed air to be primary. It took different forms as a result of the purely physical processes of rarefaction and condensation.

Heraclitus of Ephesus, who lived near the end of the sixth century B.C., carried the dialogue further. His famous saying, "All is motion," raised important problems. If all is constantly in motion, it would appear that nothing ever really exists. Yet Heraclitus believed that the world order was governed by a guiding

The Atomists' Account of the Origin of the World Order

Leucippus and Democritus were Greek thinkers of the fifth century B.C. *who originated the theory that the world is entirely material, made up of atoms and the void, moving through space without external guidance. They provided a fundamental explanation of things that was purely natural, without divine or mythical intervention. Their view was passed on and later influenced such Renaissance scientists as Galileo.*

▶ *Compare this explanation of the origins of the world with that presented in the box titled "Hymn to the Lord of Creatures" in Chapter 1.*

The world-orders arise in this way. Many bodies of all sorts of shapes "split off" from the infinite into a great void where, being gathered together, they give rise to a single vortex, in which, colliding and circling in all sorts of ways, they begin to separate apart, like to like. Being unable to circle in equilibrium any longer because of their congestion, the light bodies go off into the outer void like chaff, while the rest "remain together" and, becoming entangled, unite their motions and produce first a spherical structure.

This stands apart like a "membrane," containing in itself all sorts of bodies; and, because of the resistance of the middle, as these revolve the surrounding membrane becomes thin as contiguous bodies continually flow together because of contact with the vortex. And in this way the earth arose, the bodies which were carried to the middle remaining together. Again, the surrounding membrane increases because of the acquisition of bodies from without; and as it moves with the vortex, whatever it touches it adds to itself.

Certain of these, becoming entangled, form a structure at first very watery and muddy; but afterward they dry out, being carried about with the rotation of the whole, and ignite to form the substance of the heavenly bodies.

Certainly the atoms did not arrange themselves in order by design or intelligence, nor did they propound what movements each should make. But rather myriad atoms, swept along through infinite time or myriad paths by blows and their own weight, have come together in every possible way and tried out every combination that they could possibly create. So it happens that, after roaming the world for aeons of time in making trial of every combination and movement, at length they come together—those atoms whose sudden coincidence often becomes the origin of mighty things: of earth and sea and sky and the species of living things.

The first selection is from Diogenes Laertius 9.31; the second is from Lucretius, *De Rerum Naturae* 5.419–431. Both are cited in and translated by J. M. Robinson, *An Introduction to Early Greek Philosophy* (Boston: Houghton Mifflin, 1968), pp. 206, 208–209.

principle, the *logos,* and that though phenomena changed, the *logos* did not. *Logos* has several meanings, among them "word," "language," "speech," and "reason." So when Heraclitus said that the physical world was governed by Logos, he implied that it could be explained by reason. In this way, speculations about the physical world, what we would call natural science, soon led the way toward even more difficult philosophical speculations about language, about the manner of human thought, and about knowledge itself.

In opposition to Heraclitus, Parmenides of Elea and his pupil Zeno argued that change was only an illusion of the senses. Reason and reflection showed that reality was fixed and unchanging because it

seemed evident that nothing could be created out of nothingness. Such fundamental speculations were carried forward by Empedocles of Acragas, who spoke of four basic elements: fire, water, earth, and air. Like Parmenides, he thought that reality was permanent but not immobile, for the four elements were moved by two primary forces, Love and Strife, or, as we might be inclined to say, attraction and repulsion.

This theory was clearly a step on the road to the atomic theory of Leucippus of Miletus and Democritus of Abdera. They believed that the world consisted of innumerable tiny, solid particles that could not be divided or modified and that moved about in the void. The size of the atoms and the arrangement in which they were joined with others produced the secondary qualities that the senses could perceive, such as color and shape. These qualities—unlike the atoms themselves, which were natural—were merely conventional. Anaxagoras of Clazomenae, an older contemporary and a friend of Pericles, had previously spoken of tiny fundamental particles called *seeds,* which were put together on a rational basis by a force called *nous,* or "mind." Thus, Anaxagoras suggested a distinction between matter and mind. The atomists, however, regarded "soul," or "mind," as material and believed that everything was guided by purely physical laws. In the arguments of Anaxagoras and the atomists, we have the beginning of the philosophical debate between materialism and idealism that has continued through the ages.

These discussions interested very few, and, in fact, most Greeks were suspicious of such speculations. A far more influential debate was begun by a group of professional teachers who emerged in the mid-fifth century B.C. and whom the Greeks called *Sophists.* They traveled about and received pay for teaching practical techniques such as rhetoric, a valuable skill in democracies like Athens. Others claimed to teach wisdom and even virtue. They did not speculate about the physical universe but applied reasoned analysis to human beliefs and institutions. This

The Sophists: From Rational Inquiry to Skepticism

The rational spirit inherent in Greek thought was carried to remarkable and dangerous extremes by the Sophists in the fifth century B.C. They questioned even the nature, the existence, and the origin of the gods, subjecting these matters to rational analysis.

Concerning the gods, I do not know whether they exist or not. For many are the obstacles to knowledge: the obscurity of the subject and the brevity of human life.

Prodicus says that the ancients worshiped as gods the sun, the moon, rivers, springs, and all things useful to human life, simply because of their usefulness—just as the Egyptians deify the Nile. For this reason bread is worshiped as Demeter, wine as Dionysus, water as Poseidon, fire as Hephaestus, and so on for each of the things that are useful to men.

There was a time when the life of man was disorderly and bestial and subject to brute force; when there was no reward for the good and no punishment for the bad. At that time, I think, men enacted laws in order that justice might be absolute ruler and have arrogance as its slave; and if anyone did wrong he was punished. Then, when the laws prohibited them from doing deeds of violence, they began to do them secretly. Then, I think, some shrewd and wise man invented fear of the gods for mortals, so that there might be some deterrent to the wicked even if they did or said or thought something in secret. Therefore

he introduced the divine, saying that there is a god, flourishing with immortal life, hearing and seeing with his mind, thinking of all things and watching over them and having a divine nature; who will hear everything that is said among mortals and will be able to see all that is done. And if you plan any evil in secret it will not escape the notice of the gods, for they are of surpassing intelligence. In speaking thus he introduced the prettiest of teachings, concealing the truth under a false account. And in order that he might better strike fear into the hearts of men he told them that the gods dwell in that place which he knew to be a source of fears to mortals—and of benefits too—namely, the upper periphery where they saw lightnings and heard the dreaded rumblings of thunder and saw the starry body of the heaven, the beauteous embroidery of that wise craftsman Time, where the bright glowing mass of the sun moves and whence dark rains descend to earth. With such fears did he surround men, and by means of them he established the deity securely in a place befitting his dignity, and quenched lawlessness. Thus, I think, did some man first persuade mortals to believe in a race of gods.

The first selection is from Diogenes Laertius 9.51; the next two are from Sextus Empiricus, *Against the Schoolmasters* 9.18, 9.54. All are cited in and translated by J. M. Robinson, *An Introduction to Early Greek Philosophy* (Boston: Houghton Mifflin, 1968), pp. 269–270.

human focus was characteristic of fifth-century-B.C. thought, as was the central problem that the Sophists considered: They discovered the tension and even the contradiction between nature and custom, or law. The more traditional among them argued that law itself was in accord with nature, and this view fortified the traditional beliefs of the *polis,* the Greek city-state.

Others argued, however, that laws were merely conventional and not in accord with nature. The law was not of divine origin but merely the result of an agreement among people. It could not pretend to be a positive moral force, but merely had the negative function of preventing people from harming each other. The most extreme Sophists argued that law was contrary to nature, a trick whereby the weak controlled the strong. Critias went so far as to say that the gods themselves had been invented by some clever man to deter people from doing what they wished. Such ideas attacked the theoretical foundations of the *polis* and helped provoke the philosophical responses of Plato and Aristotle in the next century.

Political and Moral Philosophy

Like thinkers in other parts of the world around the middle of the first millennium B.C., some Greeks were vitally concerned with the formulation of moral principles for the governance of the state and the regulation of individual life, as well as more abstract problems of the nature of existence and transcendence. Nowhere is the Greek concern with ethical, political, and religious issues clearer than in the philosophical tradition that began with Socrates in the latter half of the fifth century B.C. That tradition continued with Socrates' pupil Plato and Plato's pupil Aristotle. Aristotle also had great interest in and made great contributions to the scientific understanding of the physical world, but he is perhaps more important for his impact on later Western and Islamic metaphysics.

The starting point for all three of the philosophical giants of Hellenic political and moral philosophy was the social and political reality of the Greek city-state,

MAJOR PHILOSOPHERS	
469–399 B.C.	Socrates
429–347 B.C.	Plato
384–322 B.C.	Aristotle

or *polis.* The greatest crisis for the *polis* was the Great Peloponnesian War (435–404 B.C.), which is discussed in Chapter 4. Probably the most complicated response to this crisis may be found in the life and teachings of Socrates (469–399 B.C.). Because he wrote nothing, our knowledge of him comes chiefly from his disciples Plato and Xenophon and from later tradition. Although as a young man he was interested in speculations about the physical world, Socrates later turned to the investigation of ethics and morality. As Cicero put it, he brought philosophy down from the heavens.

Socrates was committed to the search for truth and for the knowledge about human affairs that he believed could be discovered by reason. His method was to go among men, particularly those reputed to know something, like craftsmen, poets, and politicians, to question and cross-examine them. The result was always the same: Those he questioned might have technical information and skills but seldom had any knowledge of the fundamental principles of human behavior. It is understandable that Athenians so exposed should be angry with their examiner, and it is not surprising that they thought Socrates was undermining the beliefs and values of the *polis.* Socrates' unconcealed contempt for democracy, which seemingly relied on ignorant amateurs to make important political decisions without any certain knowledge, created further hostility. Moreover, his insistence on the primacy of his own individualism and his determination to pursue philosophy even against the wishes of his fellow citizens reinforced this hostility and the prejudice that went with it.

But Socrates, unlike the Sophists, did not accept pay for his teaching; he professed ignorance and denied that he taught at all. His individualism, moreover, was unlike the worldly hedonism of some of the Sophists. It was not wealth or pleasure or power that he urged people to seek, but "the greatest improvement of the soul." He differed also from the more radical Sophists in that he denied that the *polis* and its laws were merely conventional. He thought, on the contrary, that they had a legitimate claim on the citizen, and he proved it in the most convincing fashion. In 399 B.C., he was condemned to death by an Athenian jury on the charges of bringing new gods into the city and of corrupting the youth. His dialectical inquiries had angered many important people, and his criticism of democracy must have been viewed with suspicion. He was given a chance to escape, but in Plato's *Crito* we are told of his refusal because of his veneration of the laws.

Socrates' career set the stage for later responses to the travail of the *polis;* he recognized its difficulties and criticized its shortcomings. Although he turned away from an active political life, he did not abandon the idea of the *polis.* He fought as a soldier in its defense, obeyed its laws, and sought to put its values on a sound foundation by reason.

THE CYNICS.   One branch of Socratic thought—the concern with personal morality and one's own soul, the disdain of worldly pleasure and wealth, and the withdrawal from political life—was developed and then distorted almost beyond recognition by the Cynic school. Antisthenes (ca. 455–ca. 360 B.C.), a follower of Socrates, is said to have been its founder, but its most famous exemplar was Diogenes of Sinope (ca. 400–ca. 325 B.C.). Socrates disparaged wealth and worldly comfort, so Diogenes wore rags and lived in a tub. He performed shameful acts in public and made his living by begging, in order to show his rejection of convention. He believed that happiness lay in satisfying natural needs in the simplest and most direct way. Because actions to this end, being natural, could not be indecent, they could and should be done publicly.

Socrates questioned the theoretical basis for popular religious beliefs; the Cynics ridiculed all religious observances. As Plato said, Diogenes was Socrates gone mad. Beyond that, the way of the Cynics contradicted important Socratic beliefs. Socrates, unlike traditional aristocrats such as Theognis, believed that virtue was not a matter of birth but of knowledge and that people did wrong only through ignorance of what is virtuous. The Cynics, on the contrary, believed that virtue was an affair of deeds and did not need a store of words and learning. Wisdom and happiness came from pursuing the proper style of life, not from philosophy. The Cynics moved even further from Socrates by abandoning the concept of the *polis* entirely. When Diogenes was asked about his citizenship, he answered that he was *kosmopolites,* a citizen of the world. The Cynics plainly had turned away from the past, and their views anticipated those of the Hellenistic Age.

PLATO.   Plato (429–347 B.C.) was by far the most important of Socrates' associates and is a perfect example of the pupil who becomes greater than his master. He was the first systematic philosopher and therefore the first to place political ideas in their full philosophical context. He was also a writer of genius, leaving us twenty-six philosophical discussions.

Almost all are in the form of dialogues, which somehow make the examination of difficult and complicated philosophical problems seem dramatic and entertaining.

Born of a noble Athenian family, Plato looked forward to an active political career until he was discouraged by the excesses of the Thirty Tyrants and the execution of Socrates by the restored democracy. Twice he made trips to Sicily in the hope of producing a model state at Syracuse under the tyrants Dionysius I and II, but without success. In 386 B.C., Plato founded the Academy, a center of philosophical investigation and a school for training statesmen and citizens that had a powerful impact on Greek thought and lasted until it was closed by the Emperor Justinian in the sixth century A.D.

Like Socrates, Plato firmly believed in the *polis* and its values. Its virtues were order, harmony, and justice, and one of its main objects was to produce good people. Like his master, and unlike the radical Sophists, Plato thought that the *polis* was in accord with nature. He accepted Socrates' doctrine of the identity of virtue and knowledge and made it plain what that knowledge was: *episteme,* science, a body of true and unchanging wisdom open to only a few philosophers, whose training, character, and intellect allowed them to see reality. Only such people were qualified to rule; they themselves would prefer the life of pure contemplation but would accept their responsibility and take their turn as philosopher-kings. The training of such men required a specialization of function and a subordination of the individual to the community. This specialization would lead to Plato's definition of justice: that each man should do only that one thing to which his nature was best suited.

Plato saw quite well that the *polis* of his day suffered from terrible internal stress, class struggle, and factional divisions. His solution, however, was not that of some Greeks, that is, conquest and resulting economic prosperity. For Plato, the answer was in moral and political reform. The way to harmony was to destroy the causes of strife: private property, the family—anything, in short, that stood between the individual citizen and devotion to the *polis.*

The concern for the redemption of the *polis* was at the heart of Plato's system of philosophy. He began by asking the traditional questions: What is a good man, and how is he made? The goodness of a human being was a theme that belonged to moral philosophy, and when it became a function of the state, the question became part of political philosophy. Because goodness depended on knowledge of the

Plato Reports the Claims of the Sophist Protagoras

Plato (ca. 429–347 B.C.) remains to many the greatest of the ancient philosophers. Protagoras, the famous Sophist from Leontini in Sicily, came to Athens in 427 B.C. and created great excitement. In the following passage from the dialogue Protagoras, *Plato's spokesman, Socrates, introduces a young man who wishes to benefit from Protagoras's skills.*

When we were all seated, Protagoras said: Now that the company are assembled, Socrates, tell me about the young man of whom you were just now speaking.

I replied: I will begin again at the same point, Protagoras, and tell you once more the purport of my visit: this is my friend Hippocrates, who is desirous of making your acquaintance; he would like to know what will happen to him if he associates with you. I have no more to say.

Protagoras answered: Young man, if you associate with me, on the very first day you will return home a better man than you came and better on the second day than on the first, and better every day than you were on the day before.

When I heard this, I said: Protagoras, I do not at all wonder at hearing you say this; even at your age, and with all your wisdom, if any one were to teach you what you did not know before, you would become better no doubt: but please to answer in a different way—I will explain how by an example. Let me suppose that Hippocrates, instead of desiring your acquaintance, wished to become acquainted with the young man Zeuxippus of Heraclea, who has lately been in Athens, and he had come to him as he has come to you, and had heard him say, as he heard you say, that every day he would grow and become better if he associated with him: and then suppose that he were to ask him, "In what shall I become better, and in what shall I grow?"—Zeuxippus would answer, "In painting." And suppose that he went to Orthagoas the Theban, and heard him say the same thing, and asked him, "In what shall I become better day by day?" he would reply, "In flute-playing." Now I want you to make the same sort of answer to this young man and to me, who am asking questions on his account. When you say that on the first day on which he associated with you he will return home a better man, and on every day will grow in like manner,—in what, Protagoras, will he be better? and about what?

When Protagoras heard me say this, he replied: You ask questions fairly, and I like to answer a question which is fairly put. If Hippocrates comes to me he will not experience the sort of drudgery with which other Sophists are in the habit of insulting their pupils; who, when they have just escaped from the arts, are taken and driven back into them by these teachers, and made to learn calculation, and astronomy, and geometry, and music (he gave a look at Hippias as he said this); but if he comes to me, he will learn that which he comes to learn. And this is prudence in affairs private as well as public; he will learn to order his own house in the best manner, and he will be able to speak and act for the best in the affairs of the state.

Plato, *Protagoras*, trans. by Benjamin Jowett in *The Dialogues of Plato*, Vol. 1 (New York: Random House, 1937), pp. 88–89.

good, it required a theory of knowledge and an investigation of what the knowledge was that was required for goodness. The answer must be metaphysical and so required a full examination of metaphysics. Even when the philosopher knew the good, however, the question remained of how the state could bring its citizens to the necessary comprehension of that knowledge. The answer required a theory of education. Even purely logical and metaphysical questions, therefore, were subordinate to the overriding political questions. In this way, Plato's need to find a satisfactory foundation for the beleaguered *polis* contributed to the birth of systematic philosophy.

ARISTOTLE. Aristotle (384–322 B.C.) was a pupil of Plato who owed much to the thought of his master, but his very different experience and cast of mind led him in some new directions. He was born in northern Greece, the son of the court doctor of neighboring Macedon. As a young man, he came to study at the

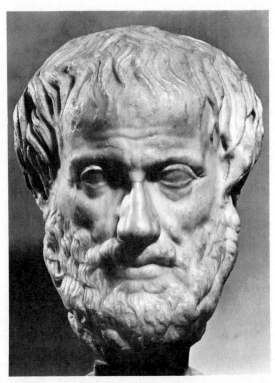

This is believed to be an ancient copy of an actual portrait of the philosopher Aristotle (383–322 B.C.). [Kunsthistorisches Museum, Vienna]

Academy, where he stayed until Plato's death. Then he joined a Platonic colony at Assos in Asia Minor, and from there, he moved to Mytilene. In both places, he carried on research in marine biology, and biological interests played a large part in all his thoughts. In 342 B.C., Philip, the king of Macedon, appointed him tutor to his son, the young Alexander (see Chapter 4). In 336, he returned to Athens, where he founded his own school, the Lyceum, or the Peripatos, as it was also called based on the covered walk within it. In later years, its members were called *Peripatetics.* On the death of Alexander in 323 B.C., the Athenians rebelled from Macedonian rule, and Aristotle found it wise to leave. He died at Chalcis in Euboea in the following year.

The Lyceum was a very different place from the Academy. Its members took little interest in mathematics and were concerned with gathering, ordering, and analyzing all human knowledge. Aristotle wrote dialogues on the Platonic model, but none survived. He and his students also prepared many collections of information to serve as the basis for scientific works, but of them only the *Constitution of the Athenians,* one of 158 constitutional treatises, remains. Al-

most all of what we possess is in the form of philosophical and scientific studies, whose loose organization and style suggest that they were lecture notes. The range of treated subjects is astonishing, including logic, physics, astronomy, biology, ethics, rhetoric, literary criticism, and politics.

In each field, the method was the same. Aristotle began with observation of the empirical evidence, which in some cases was physical and in others was common opinion. To this body of information he applied reason and discovered inconsistencies or difficulties. To deal with these, he introduced metaphysical principles to explain the problems or to reconcile the inconsistencies. His view on all subjects, like Plato's, was teleological; that he, both Plato and Aristotle recognized purposes apart from and greater than the will of the individual human being. Plato's purposes, however, were contained in the Ideas, or Forms—transcendental concepts outside the experience of most people. For Aristotle, the purposes of most things were easily inferred by observation of their behavior in the world.

Aristotle's most striking characteristics are his moderation and common sense. His epistemology finds room for both reason and experience; his metaphysics gives meaning and reality to both mind and body; his ethics aims at the good life, which is the contemplative life, but recognizes the necessity for moderate wealth, comfort, and pleasure.

All these qualities are evident in Aristotle's political thought. Like Plato, he opposed the Sophists' assertion that the *polis* was contrary to nature and the result of mere convention. His response was to apply the teleology that he saw in all nature to politics as well. In his view, matter existed to achieve an end, and it developed until it achieved its form, which was its end. There was constant development from matter to form, from potential to actual. Therefore, human primitive instincts could be seen as the matter out of which the human's potential was a political being could be realized. The *polis* made individuals self-sufficient and allowed the full realization of their potentiality. It was therefore natural. It was also the highest point in the evolution of the social institutions that serve the human need to continue the species: marriage, household, village, and finally, *polis.* For Aristotle, the purpose of the *polis* was neither economic nor military but moral: "The end of the state is the good life," the life lived "for the sake of noble actions," a life of virtue and morality.[8]

---

[8] Aristotle, *Politics,* 1280b, 1281a.

Characteristically, Aristotle was less interested in the best state—the utopia that required philosophers to rule it—than in the best state practically possible, one that would combine justice with stability. The constitution for that state he called *politeia*, not the best constitution, but the next best, the one most suited to and most possible for most states. Its quality was moderation, and it naturally gave power to neither the rich nor the poor but to the middle class, which also had to be the most numerous. The middle class possessed many virtues: Because of its moderate wealth, it was free of the arrogance of the rich and the malice of the poor. For this reason, it was the most stable class. The stability of the constitution also came from being a mixed constitution, blending in some way the laws of democracy and those of oligarchy. Aristotle's scheme was unique because of its realism and the breadth of its vision.

All the political thinkers of the fourth century B.C recognized that the *polis* was in danger, and all hoped to save it. All recognized the economic and social troubles that threatened it. Isocrates, a contemporary of Plato and Aristotle, urged a program of imperial conquest as a cure for poverty and revolution. Plato saw the folly of solving a political and moral problem by purely economic means and resorted to the creation of utopias. Aristotle combined the practical analysis of political and economic realities with the moral and political purposes of the traditional defenders of the *polis*. The result was a passionate confidence in the virtues of moderation and of the middle class and the proposal of a constitution that would give it power. It is ironic that the ablest defense of the *polis* came soon before its demise.

The concern with an understanding of nature in a purely rational, scientific way remained strong through the fifth century B.C., culminating in the work of the formulators of the atomic theory, Democritus and Leucippus, and in that of the medical school founded by Hippocrates of Cos. In the mid-fifth century B.C., however, men like the Sophists and Socrates turned their attention to humankind and to ethical, political, and religious questions. This latter tradition of inquiry led, by way of Plato, Aristotle (in his metaphysical thought), and the Stoics, to Christianity and had, as well, a substantial impact on Judaic and Islamic thought. The former tradition of thought, following a line from the natural philosophers, the Sophists, Aristotle (in his scientific thought), and the Epicureans, had to wait until the Renaissance in Western Europe to exert an influence. Since the eighteenth century, this line of Greek thought has been the more influential force in Western civilization. It may not be too much to say that since the Enlightenment of that century, the Western world has been engaged in a debate between the two strands of the Greek intellectual tradition. As Western influence has spread over the world in recent times, that debate has become of universal importance, for other societies have not seen cause to separate the religious and philosophical from the scientific and physical realms as radically as has the modern West.

Suggested Readings

CHINA

H. G. CREEL, *What Is Taoism? And Other Studies in Chinese Cultural History* (1970).

W.T. DE BARY et al. *Sources of Chinese Tradition* (1960). A reader in China's philosophical and historical literature. It should be consulted for the later periods as well as for the Chou.

Y. L. FUNG, *A Short History of Chinese Philosophy*, ed. D. Bodde (1948). A survey of Chinese philosophy from its origins down to recent times.

D. C. LAU, trans., *Lao-Tzu, Tao Te Ching* (1963).

D. C. LAU, trans., *Confucius, The Analects* (1979).

F. W. MOTE, *Intellectual Foundations of China* (1971).

B. I. SCHWARTZ, *The World of Thought in Ancient China* (1985).

A. WALEY, *The Book of Songs* (1960).

A. WALEY, *Three Ways of Thought in Ancient China* (1956). An easy yet sound introduction to Confucianism, Taoism, and Legalism.

B. WATSON, trans., *Basic Writings of Mo Tzu, Hsun Tzu, and Han Fei Tzu* (1963).

B. WATSON, trans., *The Complete Works of Chuang Tzu* (1968).

H. WELCH, *Taoism, The Parting of the Way* (1967).

INDIA

A. L. BASHAM, ed., *A Cultural History of India* (1975). A fine collection of historical-survey essays by a variety of scholars. Relevant here is Part I, "The Ancient Heritage" (chaps. 2–16).

A. L. BASHAM, *The Wonder That Was India*, rev. ed. (1963). Chap. VII, "Religion," is a superb introduction to the Vedic-Aryan, Brahmanic, Hindu, Jain, and Buddhist traditions of thought.

W. N. BROWN, *Man in the Universe: Some Continuities in Indian Thought* (1970). A superb and brief reflective summary of major patterns in Indian thinking.

W. T. DE BARY et al., *Sources of Indian Tradition* (1958). 2 vols. Vol. I, *From the Beginning to 1800*, ed.

Judaism

Monotheism, the belief in one unique God who is the creator of the universe and its all-powerful ruler, first became a central and lasting element in religion among the Hebrews, later called Israelites and also Jews. Their religion, unlike many forms of polytheistic worship that characterized the ancient world, demanded moral rectitude and placed ethical responsibilities both on individuals and on the community as a whole. Their God had a divine plan for human history, and the behavior of his chosen people was linked to it. This vision of the exclusive worship of the true God, obedience to the laws governing the community that derive from Him, and a strong ethical responsibility was connected to humanity's historical experience in this world. Ultimately it gave rise to three great religions: Judaism, Christianity, and Islam.

At the beginning of this tradition stands Abraham, recognized as the founder of their faith by all three of its branches. According to the story recorded in the Torah, this first of the Hebrew patriarchs entered into a Covenant with God in which Abraham promised to worship only this God, who in turn promised to make Abraham's descendants His own chosen people— chosen to worship Him, to obey His laws, and to undertake a special set of moral responsibilities. The Covenant was renewed with Moses at Mount Sinai. God freed the Israelites from bondage; promised them the land of Canaan (later called Palestine, part of which is now Israel); and gave them the Law (the Torah), including the Ten Commandments, by which they were to guide their lives. As long as they lived by His law he would give them his guidance and protection.

In time the Israelites formed themselves into a kingdom that remained unified from about 1000 to 922 B.C. In the period after its division, men and women called prophets emerged. These people, thought to be inspired by God, recalled the Israelites from their lapses into idolatry and immorality. Even as the kingdom was disintegrating and the Israelites falling under the control of alien empires, the prophets preached social reform and a return to more Godly ways. At the center of their vision was their place in history, in the fulfillment of God's plan for humankind. The prophets saw Israel's misfortune as punishment for failing to keep the Covenant, and predicted disaster if the Israelites did not change their ways. When disasters came, the Jewish kingdoms were captured, and the people were enslaved and exiled, they interpreted Israel's status as a chosen people to mean their sufferings were part of a process whereby they would become "a light unto the nations," leading other nations to the true worship of God. By this time, at the latest, the God of the Israelites was understood not only as the single God worshiped by the Jews but also as the universal God for all humanity.

It also was the prophets who gave full expression to the Jews' belief that God was righteous and demanded righteousness from his people. At the same time, he was also a God of love; although he might need to punish his people for their sins, he would one day reward them with divine favor. Traditional Jewish belief expects that the Messiah, or "Anointed One," will someday come and establish God's kingdom on earth. He will be a descendant of King David who will restore the kingdom of Israel and rebuild the sanctuary in Jerusalem destroyed, finally, by the Romans. He will introduce an age of universal brotherhood in which all nations will acknowledge the true God and the righteous of past generations will be restored to life.

The Jews are very much "the people of the Book," and the foremost of their sacred writings is the Bible, consisting of the five books of Moses (the Torah), the books of the prophets, and other writings. Its heart is the Torah, the source of Jewish law. Over the centuries new experiences required the interpretation of the Law to fit new circumstances, which was accomplished by the oral Law, no less sacred than the written Law. Compilations of interpretation and commentary by wise and learned teachers were brought together to form the Talmud.

The destruction of their temple by the Romans in A.D. 70 hastened the scattering of the Jews throughout the empire. Thereafter almost all Jews lived in the Diaspora (dispersion), without a homeland, a political community, or a national or religious center, until the establishment of the Jewish state of Israel in 1948. However, most Jews still live in other countries. A dominant experience for modern Judaism was the Holocaust, the culmination of centuries of persecution, during which Hitler and the Nazis killed some six million Jews in a deliberate attempt to destroy the entire people in Europe. Despite that massacre, the Jewish people and their religion live on in Israel and in many other countries.

The adherents of Judaism are divided into several groups who hold significantly different views about the place of tradition and the traditional Law in the modern world. Perhaps all of them, however, would give assent to the saying of Hillel, the great Talmudic teacher of the first century B.C.: "What is distasteful to you do not to your fellow man. This is the Law, all the rest is commentary. Now go and study."

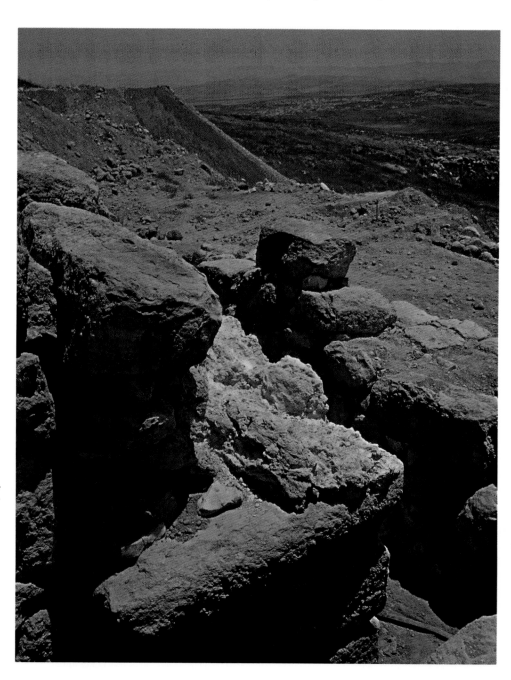

I-1   The Ruins of Masada. *Masada, a fortress overlooking the Dead Sea in Israel, was the last holdout of the Jews in their rebellion against Roman rule. Jewish zealots—one thousand men, women, and children—endured in this stronghold for almost two years before it was finally captured in* A.D *73. [Erich Lessing/Magnum]*

I-2   Israel's Bondage in Egypt. *The biblical story of the Israelites' slavery in Egypt, their liberation by Moses, and the renewal of Israel's covenant with God is a critical part of the history of the Jews and their religion. This scene—painted in Thebes ca. 1450 B.C. on a wall of the tomb of Rechmire, the vizier, or minister, of the pharaohs Thutmose III and Amenophis II—shows an overseer directing a construction gang of slaves doing the kind of work the Israelites were compelled to perform. [Erich Lessing/ Magnum]*

I-3   Exile of the Israelites. *In 722 B.C. the northern part of Jewish Palestine, the kingdom of Israel, was conquered by the Assyrians. Its people were driven from their homeland and exiled all over the vast Assyrian Empire. This wall carving in low relief comes from the palace of the Assyrian king Sennacherib at Nineveh. It shows the Jews with their cattle and baggage going into exile. [Erich Lessing/ Magnum]*

I-4   Reconstruction of the Temple of Jerusalem. *This is a model of a reconstruction of the Temple at Jerusalem. It was originally erected by King Solomon in the tenth century* B.C. *as the kingdom's religious center and the symbol of Jewish unity. It was finally destroyed by Titus, the son of the Roman emperor Vespasian in* A.D. *70 as part of the crushing of a Jewish rebellion. (Masada, shown in photo I-1, was the last holdout of this rebellion.) [Art Resource]*

I-5   The Jews under Islam. *This painting from an Ottoman Turkish manuscript of the late-sixteenth century shows the founder of Islam, the prophet Muhammad, ordering the execution of Jews refusing to embrace Islam. Through much of the history of the Islamic world, however, Jews (and Christians), although usually denied rights equal to Muslims, were tolerated as "people of the book" (the Bible). [Chester Beatty Library, Dublin, Ireland]*

I-6   The Prato Haggadah, a Spanish Illuminated Passover Haggadah, ca. 1300 (above). *The Sephardic Jews developed a rich and distinctive culture in Spain. In 1492, however, they were forcibly expelled from Spain after Ferdinand and Isabella drove out the last Islamic rulers and imposed Christianity throughout the country. The Passover ceremony celebrates the escape of the Israelites from bondage in Egypt. These pages begin the story of the four sons, each of whom requires a different explanation of the Passover story. The simpleton son sits atop the Hebrew word tam ("simple") at the top of the right page, while the son "who does not know how to ask" sits with his arms crossed at the bottom. [Courtesy of the Library of the Jewish Theological Seminary of America]*

I-7   Jews in Medieval France. *This French miniature painting from the mid-thirteenth century shows a debate between Jews and Christians, probably before the French king Louis IX (Saint Louis), who presided over such a debate. [Bibliothèque Nationale, Paris]*

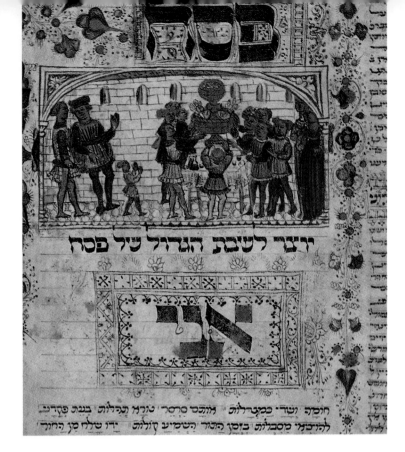

I-8   Passover in Renaissance Italy. *The Jews were scattered all over Europe by the end of the Middle Ages. This illumination from a 1466 Hebrew manuscript in Italy is from a Passover Haggadah. [Reproduced by courtesy of the Board of the British Library]*

I-9   Jews in Fifteenth-Century Germany. *This illumination from a Hebrew manuscript in the State and University Library of Hamburg shows the houses in the Jewish quarter of the city. They are crowded together in the lower part of town near the defensive walls. [Staats- und Universitätsbibliothek, Hamburg]*

I-10   A Rabbi in Seventeenth-
Century Holland. *Jews persecuted
in and driven from other European countries in the seventeenth
century found a haven in The
Netherlands. This painting of a
rabbi is by the great Dutch
painter Rembrandt van Rijn. [Bild-
archiv Preussischer Kulturbesitz]*

I-11   A Viennese Synagogue
*(painting by Richard Moser, 1922).
Despite considerable anti-Semitism,
many Jews found Vienna to be an
attractive and hospitable city in the
nineteenth century and flourished
in this capital of the Habsburg
Empire. Hitler's occupation of Austria in 1938, however, virtually
ended Jewish life in the city. Most
Viennese Jews were victims of the
Holocaust in World War II. [Bild-
archiv Preussischer Kulturbesitz]*

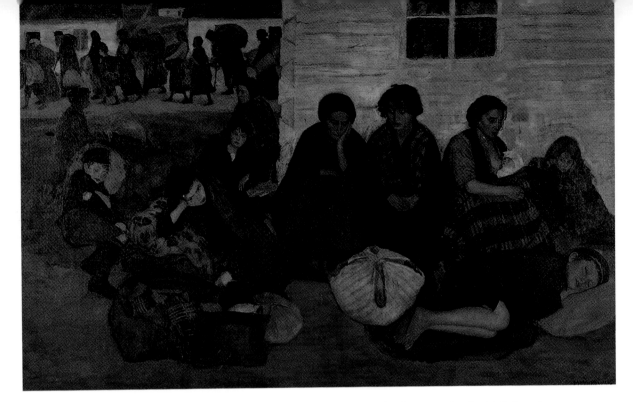

I-12   Russian Persecution of the Jews. *This 1910 painting,* After the Pogrom *by the Polish painter Maurycy Minkowski, shows a group of Jews in the aftermath of a pogrom, an organized persecution of Jews that often became a massacre. Often encouraged by the Russian government, pogroms were especially frightful in the late nineteenth and early twentieth centuries. [Jewish Museum/Art Resource]*

I-13   Nazi Anti-Jewish Propaganda. *Virulent racist hostility towards the Jews was a fundamental doctrine of Hitler's Nazi movement in Germany. This propaganda poster printed during World War II shows the emblems of Great Britain, the United States, and the Soviet Union, the allied coalition fighting Germany and its Axis partners. Behind them is a crude caricature of a Jew. The legend on the poster reads: "Behind the enemy the Jew." Hitler's hatred of the Jews led to the Holocaust in which some six million Jews were murdered. [Bildarchiv Preussischer Kulturbesitz]*

and rev. Ainslie T. Embree. (1988). Excellent selections from a wide variety of Indian texts, with good introductions to chapters and individual selections.

T. J. HOPKINS, *The Hindu Religious Tradition* (1971). A first-rate, thoughtful introduction to Hindu religious ideas and practice.

W. RAHULA, *What the Buddha Taught,* 2nd ed. (1974). A clear, concise, and readable introduction to Buddhist thought from a traditionalist Theravadin viewpoint, with primary-source selections.

R. H. ROBINSON and W. L. JOHNSON, *The Buddhist Religion: A Historical Introduction,* 3rd ed. (1982). An excellent first text on the Buddhist tradition, its thought, development, and diffusion.

R. C. ZAEHNER, *Hinduism* (1966). One of the best general introductions to central Indian religious and philosophical ideas.

ISRAEL

J. BRIGHT, *A History of Israel* (1968), 2nd ed. (1972). One of the standard scholarly introductions to biblical history and literature.

W. D. DAVIES and L. FINKELSTEIN, eds., *The Cambridge History of Judaism.* Vol. I, *Introduction: The Persian Period* (1984). Excellent essays on diverse aspects of the exilic period and later.

J. NEUSNER, *The Way of Torah: An Introduction to Judaism* (1979). A sensitive introduction to the Judaic tradition and faith.

L. W. SCHWARZ, ed., *Great Ages and Ideas of the Jewish People* (1956). Especially interesting is the first section, "The Biblical Age," by Yehezkel Kaufmann.

GREECE

J. BURNET, *Early Greek Philosophy* (1963). Stresses the rational aspect of Greek thought and its sharp break with mythology.

F. M. CORNFORD, *From Religion to Philosophy* (1912). Emphasizes the elements of continuity between myth and religion on the one hand and Greek philosophy on the other.

B. FARRINGTON, *Greek Science* (1953). A lively interpretation of the origins and character of Greek scientific thought.

G. B. KERFERD, *The Sophistic Movement* (1981). An excellent description and analysis.

J. LEAR, *Aristotle: The Desire to Understand* (1988). A brilliant yet comprehensible introduction to the work of the philosopher.

J. M. ROBINSON, *An Introduction to Early Greek Philosophy* (1968). A valuable collection of the main fragments and ancient testimony to the works of the early philosophers, with excellent commentary.

G. VLASTOS, *The Philosophy of Socrates* (1971). A splendid collection of essays illuminating the problems presented by this remarkable man.

G. VLASTOS, *Platonic Studies,* 2nd ed. (1981). A similar collection on the philosophy of Plato.

Empires and Cultures of the Ancient World

The last five hundred years before the beginning of the Christian era and the two centuries that followed saw the appearance of great empires in Iran, India, and China, and of the Roman Empire in the Mediterranean. Although each arose in response to local conditions, they had common features. Each replaced a confusion of local sovereign units, whether aristocratic family domains, smaller territorial states, tribal confederacies, or city-states, with vast centralized monarchies. Each had the large, efficient armies needed to conquer and control new lands. They all created well-organized bureaucracies to regulate their widespread empires and built extensive roads to ease communication and transportation. They all systematically imposed and collected taxes to pay for the armies and bureaucracies, for the construction of roads and defenses, and for the splendor of their imperial courts and palaces.

The military, political, and economic unification of vast territories produced considerable periods of relative peace and prosperity. There is evidence of communication and trade even between the Romans and the distant empires of India and China. Imperial unification also had cultural consequences. The imposition of a single rule over different peoples in a far-flung empire encouraged the use of a common tongue, at least as a second language, which assisted the formation of a common culture. The Greeks, the Romans, the Hindus, and the Chinese produced great works in a variety of literary genres, such as epic poetry, history, and philosophy, which set a stamp on their own societies and served as the bases for later cultural developments. In all four areas, the wealth and patronage of the monarchs, the general prosperity of their empires, and the desire for splendor gave great impetus to such arts as painting, sculpture, and architecture.

The rise of these empires also brought important developments in religion. The Iranian conquests under the Achaemenid dynasty spread the religion of Zarathushtra (Zoroaster) throughout the Persian Empire, and the quasi-monotheistic faith had a powerful and broad influence before the tide of Islam swept over it in the seventh century A.D. In India in the third century B.C., under the Mauryan king Ashoka, Buddhism took on a missionary character and spread across Asia to the east and west. In the first century B.C., it came to China, where it competed not only with Confucianism but also with a new form of Taoism that had taken on a more mysterious and otherworldly character during the Later Han period. In Greece, as the city-states gave way to the great empires of Philip and Alexander of Macedon and their Hellenistic successors, a largely amoral paganism gave way to such quasi-religious philosophies as Stoicism. In the Roman Empire that succeeded the Hellenistic kingdoms, Christianity ultimately overcame all competitors to become the official religion by the end of the fourth century A.D. These religious movements stressed morality, and most of them were more otherworldly than their predecessors, placing greater emphasis on escape from the pain and troubles of this world and the search for personal immortality.

Such developments seem to have had some connection with the loss of prosperity; the increase of warfare, both internal and external; and the collapse of stability. None of the great empires could avoid a cycle of growth and decline. There was never enough wealth to sustain the cost of empire beyond a limited period of time. Taxes rose beyond the citizens' capacity to pay, and bureaucracies became bloated and ineffective. More and more depended on the central government, but talented leadership was not always available. The attractions of civilization drew the envy of vigorous barbarians outside the empires, at the same time as internal problems and diminished willingness to fight reduced the capacity of the empires to resist. The Achaemenids fell victim to Alexander the Great, but the rule of his Hellenistic successors was brief. The Parthians, who succeeded to the old Persian Empire, were never able to impose the same imperial and cultural unity. In India, the Mauryan Empire did not long survive the death of its gentle king Ashoka, giving way to local uprisings and barbarian assaults from central Asia. Both China and Rome, weakened by internal struggles, gave way to barbarian assaults and saw the collapse of central authority. In both cases, the conquering tribes were themselves conquered by the religions of their victims, Buddhism and Confucianism in China and Christianity in Rome. In India, China, and Rome, moreover, the cultural achievements of the great empires would later serve as the bases for new advances in civilization.

	EUROPE	NEAR EAST/INDIA
3000 B.C.	*ca. 2500–1100* Minoan civilization on Crete *ca. 1600–1100* Mycenaean civilization on Greek mainland	*ca. 3000* Emergence of civilization along the Nile River *ca. 2300* Emergence of Harappan civilization in Indus Valley *2276–2221* Sargon of Akkad creates the first Mesopotamian Empire *ca. 2000* Epic of Gilgamesh *1750* Hammurabi's Code
1500 B.C.	*ca. 1100–800* Greek "Dark Ages" *800* Etruscan civilization begins in Italy *ca. 750–550* Rise of the *polis* *594* Solon's legislation at Athens *509* Foundation of the Roman Republic *508* Democracy established in Athens	*ca. 1500* Aryan peoples migrate into northwestern India *960–933* Rule of Hebrew king Solomon *ca. 628–551* Traditional dates of Zarathushtra *ca. 537–486* Siddhartha Gautama *559–529* Cyrus the Great creates the Persian Empire
500 B.C.	*480–479* Persian invasion of Greece *478* Foundation of Delian League/Athenian Empire *431–404* Peloponnesian Wars *338* Battle of Chaeronia; Macedonian conquest of Greece *336–323* Career of Alexander the Great	*ca. 540–468* Vardhamana Mahavira, founder of Jain tradition *334* Alexander begins conquest of the Near East; invades India in 327 *321–181* Mauryan Empire in India *ca. 300* Foundation of Seleucid dynasty in Anatolia, Syria, and Mesopotamia; Ptolemaic dynasty in Egypt
300 B.C.	*264* Rome rules all of Italy *146* Rome destroys Carthage; rules all of western Mediterranean *44–31* Civil wars destroy Republic *31* Rome rules Mediterranean *31* B.C.–A.D. *14* Principate of Augustus	*269–232* Mauryan Emperor, Ashoka, patronizes Buddhism *247* B.C.–A.D. *224* Parthian dynasty controls Persia *180* B.C.–A.D. *320* India politically divided
A.D. 1	*96–180* The Good Emperors rule Rome *180–284* Breakdown of the *Pax Romana* *306–337* Constantine reigns *313* Edict of Milan *325* Council of Nicaea *391* Theodosius makes Christianity the official imperial religion *ca. 400–500* The Germanic invasions *426 The City of God,* by Augustine *476* The last Western emperor is deposed	*30* Crucifixion of Jesus *70* Romans destroy the Temple at Jerusalem *ca. 224* Fall of Parthians, rise of Sasanids, in Persia *ca. 320–500* Gupta Dynasty in India *ca. 400* Chandra Gupta (r. 375–415) conquers western India; increases trade with Near East and China *ca. 450* The Huns invade India

EAST ASIA	AFRICA	THE AMERICAS
ca. 3000 Neolithic cultures in China *ca. 3000* Jōmon culture in Japan *1766* Bronze Age city-states and writing in China *ca. 1600–1050* Shang civilization in China	*ca. 3000* Practice of agriculture spreads from Nile River Valley to the Sudan *ca. 2000* Ivory and gold trade between Kush (Nubia) and Egypt *ca. 1500* Practice of agriculture spreads from the Sudan to Abyssinia and the savannah region	*ca. 4000* Maize already domesticated in Mexico
1027–771 Western Chou Dynasty, China *ca. 771* Iron Age territorial states in China *771–256* Chou dynasty in China *ca. 551–479* Confucius in China	*750* Kushite king Kashta conquers Upper Egypt; founds 25th Egyptian dynasty *ca. 720* Kushite king Piankhy completes conquest of Egypt and reigns as king of Kush and Egypt *ca. 600* Meroitic period of Kushan civilization begins	*ca. 1500–800* Olmec civilization in Mesoamerica *ca. 900–200* Chavín (Early) Horizon in Andean South America
ca. 500–200 Rise of Mohist, Taoist, and Legalist schools of thought in China *403–321* Period of the Warring States in China *ca. 300* Jōmon Neolithic culture in Japan replaced by Yayoi culture		
221 Ch'in emperor unites all of China *207* End of Ch'in dynasty *206* B.C.–A.D. *8* Former Han Dynasty in China *ca. 179–104* Han philosopher, Tung Chung-shu *ca. 145–90* Han historian, Ssu-ma Chien *141–187* Emperor Wu Ti of China reigns	*25* Romans sack Kushite capital of Napata *100* B.C.–A.D. *1* Probable first Indonesian migrations to East African coast	*ca. 200* B.C.–A.D. *750* Classic period in central Mexico; dominance of Teotihuacán
9–25 Interregnum of Wang Mang in China *25–220* The Later Han Dynasty, China *ca. 220–590* Spread of Buddhism in China *221–280* Three Kingdoms Era in China *ca. 300–500* Barbarian invasions of China *ca. 300–680* Archaic Yamato state in Japan	*ca. 200* Camel first used for trans-Saharan transport *ca. 200–900* Expansion of Bantu people *ca. 250* Aksum (Ethiopia) controls the Red Sea trade *ca. 300–400* Rise of kingdom of Ghana *ca. 350* Kush ceases to exist	*ca. 100–600* Early Intermediate period in Andean South America; Moche and Nazca cultures *ca. 300–900* Classic period Maya in the Yucatan and Guatemala

This golden death mask was found by Heinrich Schliemann in the shaft graves at Mycenae. It is dated to the period 1550–1500 B.C. Schliemann thought he had found the mask of Agamemnon, leader of the Achaeans' expedition to Troy in Homer's epics. [National Archaeological Museum of Greece]

The Rise of Greek Civilization

About 2000 B.C., Greek-speaking peoples settled the lands surrounding the Aegean Sea and established a style of life and formed a set of ideas, values, and institutions that spread far beyond the Aegean corner of the Mediterranean Sea. Preserved and adapted by the Romans, Greek culture powerfully influenced the society of Western Europe in the Middle Ages and dominated the Byzantine Empire in the same period. The civilization emerging from the Greek and Roman experience spread across Europe and in time crossed the Atlantic to the Western Hemisphere.

At some time in their history, the Greeks of the ancient world founded cities on the shores of the Mediterranean Sea, and pushing on through the Dardanelles, they placed many settlements on the coasts of the Black Sea in southern Russia and as far east as the approaches to the Caucasus Mountains. The center of Greek life, however, has always been the Aegean Sea and the lands in and around it. This location at the eastern end of the Mediterranean very early put the Greeks in touch with the more advanced and earlier civilizations of the Near East: Egypt, Asia Minor, Syria-Palestine, and the rich culture of Mesopotamia. A character in one of Plato's dialogues says, "Whatever the Greeks have acquired from foreigners they have, in the end, turned into something finer."[1] This proud statement indicates that the Greeks were at least aware of how much they had learned from other civilizations.

[1] *Epinomis,* 987 d.

Bronze Age on Crete and on the Mainland to ca. 1150 B.C.

One source of Greek civilization was the culture of the large island of Crete in the Mediterranean. With Greece to the north, Egypt to the south, and Asia to the east, Crete was a cultural bridge between the older civilizations and the new one of the Greeks.

The Minoans

The Bronze Age came to Crete not long after 3000 B.C. In the third and second millennia B.C., a civilization arose that powerfully influenced the islands of the Aegean and the mainland of Greece. This civilization has been given the name *Minoan,* after Minos, the legendary king of Crete.

Scholars have established links between stratigraphic layers at archaeological sites and specific styles of pottery and other artifacts found in the layers. On this basis they have divided the Bronze Age on Crete into three major divisions with some subdivisions. Dates for Bronze Age settlements on the Greek mainland, for which the term *Helladic* is used, are derived from the same chronological scheme.

During the Middle and Late Minoan periods in the cities of eastern and central Crete, a civilization developed that was new and unique in its character and in the beauty of its art and architecture. Its most striking creations were the palaces uncovered at such sites as Phaestus; Haghia Triada; and, most important, Cnossus. The palace design and paintings show the influence of Syria, Asia Minor, and Egypt, but the style and quality are unique to Crete. The absence of strong defensive walls suggests that the Minoan cities were not built with defense in mind.

Along with palaces, paintings, pottery, jewelry, and other valuable objects, clay writing tablets like those found in Mesopotamia have been excavated. The tablets, which were preserved accidentally when they were hardened in a great fire that destroyed the royal palace at Cnossus, have three distinct kinds of writing on them. One has proved to be an early form of Greek. The contents of the tablets, primarily inventories, reveal an organization centered on the palace and ruled by a king who was supported by an extensive bureaucracy that kept remarkably detailed records. This sort of organization is typical of early civilizations in the Near East but, as we shall see, is nothing like that of the Greeks after the bronze age.

Yet the inventories were written in a form of Greek. Why should Minoans, who were not Greek, write in a language not their own? This question raises the larger one of what the relationship was between Crete and the Greek mainland during the Bronze Age. It leads us to an examination of mainland, or Helladic, culture.

The Mycenaeans

In the third millennium B.C., most of the Greek mainland, including many of the sites of later Greek cities, was settled by people who used metal, built some impressive houses, and traded with Crete and the islands of the Aegean. The names they gave to places—names that were sometimes preserved by later invaders—make it clear that they were not Greeks and that they spoke a language that was not Indo-European.

Not long after 2000 B.C., many of the Early Helladic sites were destroyed by fire, some were abandoned, and still others appear to have yielded peacefully to an invading people. These signs of invasion probably signal the arrival of the Greeks.

The invaders succeeded in establishing control of the entire mainland. All over Greece, there was a smooth transition between the Middle and Late Helladic periods. The shaft graves cut into the rock at the royal palace–fortress of Mycenae show that these conquerors prospered and sometimes became very rich. At Mycenae, the richest finds come from the period after 1600 B.C. The city's wealth and power had reached their peak during this time, and the culture of the whole mainland during the Late Helladic period goes by the name *Mycenaean.* Greek invaders also established themselves in a still flourishing Crete, and there is good reason to believe that at the height of Mycenaean power (1400–1200 B.C.), Crete was part of the Mycenaean world.

The excavation of Mycenae, Pylos, and other Mycenaean sites reveals a culture influenced by, but very different from, the Minoan culture. Mycenae and Pylos, like Cnossus, were built some distance from the sea. It is plain, however, that defense against attack was foremost in the minds of the founders of the Mycenaean cities. Both cities were built on hills in a position commanding the neighboring territory. The Mycenaean people were warriors, as their art, architecture, and weapons reveal. The success of their campaigns and the defense of their territory required strong central authority, and all available evidence shows that the kings provided it. Their palaces, in which the royal family and its retainers lived, were located within the walls; most of the population lived outside the walls. The palace walls were usually covered with paintings, like those on Crete, but instead of peaceful scenery and games, the Mycenaean murals depicted scenes of war and boar hunting.

About 1500 B.C., the already impressive shaft graves were abandoned in favor of *tholos* tombs. These were large, beehivelike chambers cut into the hillside; built of enormous, well-cut, fitted stones; and approached by an unroofed passage *(dromos)* cut horizontally into the side of the hill. The lintel block alone of one of these tombs weighs over a hundred tons. Only a strong king whose wealth was great, whose power was unquestioned, and who commanded the labor of many could undertake such a project. His wealth probably came from plundering raids, piracy, and trade. Some of this trade went westward to Italy and Sicily, but most of it was with the islands of the Aegean; the coastal towns of Asia Minor; and the cities of Syria, Egypt, and Crete. The Mycenaeans sent pottery, olive oil, and animal hides in exchange for jewels and other luxuries.

Tablets containing Mycenaean writing have been found all over the mainland; the largest and most useful collection was found at Pylos. The tablets revealed a world very similar to the one shown by the records at Cnossus. The king, whose title was *wanax,* held a royal domain, appointed officials, commanded servants, and kept a close record of what he owned and what was owed to him. This evidence confirms that the Mycenaean world was made up of a number of independent, powerful, and well-organized monarchies.

These were prosperous and active years for the Mycenaeans. Their cities were enlarged, their trade grew, and they even established commercial colonies in the East. They are mentioned in the archives of the Hittite kings of Asia Minor. They are also named as marauders of the Nile Delta in the Egyptian records, and sometime about 1250 B.C. they probably sacked the city of Troy on the coast of northwestern Asia Minor, giving rise to the epic poems of Homer, the *Iliad* and the *Odyssey* (see Map 3-1). Around the year 1200 B.C., however, the Mycenaean world showed signs of great trouble, and by 1100 B.C., it was gone: Its palaces were destroyed; many of its cities abandoned; and its art, its pattern of life, its system of writing buried and forgotten.

What happened? The Greeks themselves believed in a legend that told of an invasian of Dorians, a rude people from the north who spoke a different Greek

CHRONOLOGY OF THE RISE OF GREECE	
ca. 2900–1150 B.C.	Minoan period
ca. 1900 B.C.	Probable date of the arrival of the Greeks on the mainland
ca. 1600–1150 B.C.	Mycenaean period
ca. 1250 B.C.	Sack of Troy (?)
ca. 1200–1150 B.C.	Destruction of Mycenaean centers in Greece
ca. 1100–750 B.C.	Dark Ages
ca. 750–500 B.C.	Major period of Greek colonization
ca. 725 B.C.	Probable date of Homer
ca. 700 B.C.	Probable date of Hesiod
ca. 700–500 B.C.	Major period of Greek tyranny

dialect from that of the Mycenaean peoples. According to the legend, the Dorians joined one of the Greek tribes, the Heraclidae, in an attack on the southern Greek peninsula of Peloponnesus, which was repulsed. One hundred years later they returned and gained full control. This legend of "the return of the Heraclidae" has been identified by some modern historians with the Dorian invasion, the incursion from the north into Greece of a less civilized Greek people speaking the Dorian dialect. It is an interpretation not currently fashionable, but none better has been offered.

Greek "Middle Ages" to ca. 750 B.C.

The immediate effects of the Dorian invasion were disastrous for the inhabitants of the Mycenaean world. The palaces and the kings and bureaucrats who managed them were destroyed. The wealth and organization that had supported the artists and the merchants were likewise swept away by a barbarous people who did not have the knowledge or social organization to maintain them. Many villages were abandoned and never resettled. Some of their inhabitants probably turned to a nomadic life, and many perished.

Another result of the invasion was the spread of the Greek people eastward from the mainland to the Aegean islands and the coast of Asia Minor. The Dori-

MAP 3-1   THE AEGEAN AREA IN THE BRONZE AGE   *The Bronze Age in the Aegean area
lasted from about 1900 to about 1100* B.C. *Its culture on Crete is called Minoan and
was at its height about 1900–1400* B.C. *Bronze Age Helladic culture on the mainland
flourished from about 1600–1200* B.C.

ans themselves, after occupying most of the Peloponnesus, swept across the Aegean to occupy the southern islands and the southern part of the Anatolian coast.

Although these migrations made the Aegean a Greek lake, the fall of the advanced Minoan and Mycenaean civilizations virtually ended trade with the old civilizations of the Near East. Nor was there much trade within Greece. Each community was left largely to its own devices, forcing the Greeks to turn inward. This happened at a time when the Near East was also in disarray, and no great power arose to impose its ways and its will on the helpless people who lived about the Aegean. These circumstances allowed the

Greeks time to recover from their disaster and to create their unique style of life.

Age of Homer

For a picture of society in these "dark ages," many scholars believe that the best source is Homer. His epic poems, the *Iliad* and the *Odyssey,* tell of the heroes who captured Troy, men of the Mycenaean age, but the world described in those poems clearly is a different one. Homer's heroes are not buried in *tholos* tombs but are cremated; they worship gods in temples, whereas the Mycenaeans had no temples; they have chariots but do not know their proper use in warfare. The poems of Homer are the result of an oral tradition that went back into the Mycenaean age. Through the centuries, bards sang tales of the heroes who fought at Troy, using verse arranged in rhythmic formulas to aid the memory. In this way, some very old material was preserved until the poems were finally written, no sooner than the eighth century B.C., but the society these old oral poems describe seems to be that of the tenth and ninth centuries B.C.

In the Homeric poems, the power of the kings was much less than that of the Mycenaean rulers. The ability of the kings to make important decisions was limited by the need to consult the council of nobles. The nobles felt free to discuss matters in vigorous language and in opposition to the king's wishes. In the *Iliad,* Achilles does not hesitate to address Agamemnon, the "most kingly" commander of the Trojan expedition, in these words: "thou with face of dog and heart of deerfolk devouring king." Such language might have been impolite, but it was not treasonous. Although the king was free to ignore the council's advice, it was risky for him to do so.

The right to speak in council was limited to male noblemen, but the common people could not be ignored. If a king planned a war or a major change of policy during a campaign, he would not fail to call the common soldiers to an assembly, where they could listen and express their feelings by acclamation, even though they could not take part in the debate. The evidence of Homer shows that even in these early times, the Greeks, unlike their predecessors and contemporaries, practiced some forms of limited constitutional government.

Homeric society, nevertheless, was sharply divided into classes, the most important division being between nobles and commoners. We do not know the

---

Odysseus Addresses Nobles and Commoners: Homeric Society

The Iliad *was probably composed about 750* B.C. *In this passage, Odysseus is trying to stop the Greeks at Troy from fleeing to their ships and returning to their homes. The difference in his treatment of nobles and commoners is striking.*

When he came upon anyone of royal birth or high rank, he went up to him and made courteous attempts to restrain him. "I should not think it right," he said, "to threaten you, sir, as I should a common man. But I do beg you to stand fast yourself and to make your followers do the same. You do not really know what King Agamemnon has in mind. This is only an experiment with them; they will soon feel his fist. Did we not all of us hear what he said at the Council? I am afraid that he might be angry with the troops and punish them for this. Kings are divine and they have their pride, upheld and favoured as they are by the Counsellor Zeus."

With the rank and file he had a different way. When he caught any of them giving tongue he struck the offender with his staff and rated him severely. "You there," he said, "sit still and wait for orders from your officers, who are better men than you, coward and weakling that you are, counting for nothing in battle or debate. We cannot all be kings here; and mob rule is a bad thing. Let there be one commander only, one King, set over us by Zeus the Son of Cronos of the Crooked Ways."

Homer, *The Iliad*, trans. by E. V. Rieu (New York: Viking Penguin, 1950), p. 45.

origin of this division, but we cannot doubt that at this time Greek society was aristocratic. Birth determined noble status, and wealth usually accompanied it. Below the nobles were peasants, landless laborers, and slaves. We cannot tell whether peasants owned the land they worked outright and so were free to sell it or if they worked a hereditary plot that belonged to their clan and was therefore not theirs to dispose of as they chose. It is clear, however, that peasants worked hard to make a living.

Far worse was the condition of hired agricultural laborers. Slaves, at least, were attached to family households and so were protected and fed. In a world where membership in a settled group gave the only security, free laborers were desperately vulnerable. Slaves were few in number and were mostly women who served as maids and concubines. Some male slaves worked as shepherds. Few, if any, worked in agriculture, which depended chiefly on free labor throughout Greek history.

The Homeric poems hold up a mirror to this society, and they reflect an aristocratic code of values that powerfully influenced all future Greek thought. In classical times, Homer was the schoolbook of the Greeks. They memorized his text, settled diplomatic disputes by citing passages in it, and emulated the behavior and cherished the values they found in it. Those values were physical prowess, courage; fierce protection of one's family, friends, and property; and above all, one's personal honor and reputation. Returning home after his wanderings, Odysseus ruthlessly kills all the suitors of his wife because they have used up all his wealth, wooed his wife, scorned his son, and so dishonored him. Speed of foot, strength, and, most of all, excellence at fighting in battle are what make a man great, yet Achilles leaves the battle and allows his fellow Greeks to be slain and almost defeated because Agamemnon has wounded his honor by taking away his battle prize. He returns not out of a sense of duty to the army but because his dear friend Patroclus has been killed. In each case, the hero seeks to display the highest virtue of Homeric society, *arete*—manliness, courage in the most general sense, and the excellence proper to a hero.

This quality is best revealed in a contest, or *agon*. Homeric battles are not primarily group combats but a series of individual contests between great champions. One of the prime forms of entertainment is the athletic contest, and the funeral of Patroclus is celebrated by such a contest. The central ethical idea in Homer can be found in the instructions that the father of Achilles gives to his son when he sends him off to

This painting by an artist called the Menelaus Painter appears on a vase from the seventh century B.C. *found at Eleusis, the site of the mystery cult in northwest Attica. It illustrates the scene in Homer's* Odyssey *where the hero blinds the one-eyed monster Polyphemus so that he and his companions can escape from the Cyclops' cave. [Hirmer Fotoarchiv, Munich]*

fight at Troy: "Always be the best and distinguished above others." The father of another Homeric hero has given his son exactly the same orders and has added to them the injunction "do not bring shame on the family of your fathers who were by far the best in Ephyre and in wide Lycia." Here in a nutshell we have the chief values of the aristocrats of Homer's world: to vie for individual supremacy in *arete* and to defend and increase the honor of the family. They would remain prominent aristocratic values long after Homeric society was only a memory.

The *Polis*

The characteristic Greek institution was the *polis*. The common translation of that word as "city-state" is misleading, for it says both too much and too little. All Greek *poleis* began as little more than agricultural villages or towns, and many stayed that way, so the word *city* is inappropriate. All of them were states, in the sense of being independent political units, but they were much more than that. The *polis* was thought of as a community of relatives; all its citizens, who were theoretically descended from a common ancestor, belonged to subgroups such as fighting brotherhoods *(phratries)*, clans, and tribes. They worshiped the gods in common ceremonies.

Aristotle argued that the *polis* was a natural growth and that man (explicitly male; Greek women were not full participants in the life of the *polis*) was by his nature "an animal who lives in a *polis.*" Man alone had the power of speech and from it derived the ability to distinguish good from bad and right from wrong, "and the sharing of these things is what makes a household and a *polis.*" A man who was incapable of sharing these things or who was so self-sufficient that he had no need of them was not a man at all, but either a wild beast or a god. Without law and justice, man was the worst and most dangerous of the animals. With them he could be the best, and justice existed only in the *polis.* These high claims were made in the fourth century B.C., hundreds of years after the *polis* had come into existence, but they accurately reflected an attitude that was present from the first.

Development of the Polis

Originally the word *polis* referred only to a citadel—an elevated, defensible rock to which the farmers of the neighboring area could retreat in case of attack. The Acropolis in Athens and the hill called Acrocorinth in Corinth are examples. For some time, such high places and the adjacent farms comprised the *polis.* The towns grew gradually and without planning, as the narrowness and the winding, disorderly character of their streets show. For centuries, they had no city walls. Unlike the city-states of the Near East, they were not placed for commercial convenience on rivers or the sea, nor did they grow up around a temple to serve the needs of priests and to benefit from the needs of worshipers. The availability of farmland and of a natural fortress determined their location. They were placed either well inland or far enough away from the sea to avoid piratical raids. Only later and gradually did the *agora* appear within the *polis.* It was not only a marketplace but also a civic center and the heart of the Greeks' remarkable social life, which was distinguished by conversation and argument carried on in the open air.

Some *poleis* probably came into existence early in the eighth century B.C. The institution was certainly common by the middle of that century, for all the colonies that were established by the Greeks in the years after 750 B.C. took the form of the *polis.* Once the new institution had been fully established, true monarchy disappeared. Vestigial kings survived in some places, but they were almost always only ceremonial figures without power. The original form of the *polis* was an aristocratic republic dominated by the nobility through its council of nobles and its monopoly of the magistracies.

The Hoplite Phalanx

A new military technique was crucial to the development of the *polis.* In earlier times, the brunt of the fighting had been carried on by small troops of cavalry and individual "champions" who first threw their spears and then came to close quarters with swords.

The hoplite phalanx. This vase painting from the so-called "Chigi" vase is the earliest surviving picture of the new style of close-order, heavily armed infantry adopted by the Greeks toward the end of the eighth century B.C. Notice the large circular shields, helmets, greaves, body armor, raised spears, and the close order of the soldiers. The flute player provides music to help keep the soldiers in step. [Hirmer Fotoarchiv, Munich]

Toward the end of the eighth century B.C., however, the hoplite phalanx came into being. It remained the basis of Greek warfare thereafter.

The hoplite was a heavily armed infantryman who fought with a sword and a pike seven to nine feet long. These soldiers were formed into a phalanx (massed arrangement) in close order, usually at least eight ranks deep. As long as the hoplites fought bravely and held their ground, there would be few casualties and no defeat, but if they gave way, the result was usually a rout. All depended on the discipline, strength, and courage of the individual soldier. At its best, the phalanx could withstand cavalry charges and defeat infantries not as well protected or disciplined. Until defeated by the Roman legion, it was the dominant military force in the eastern Mediterranean.

The usual hoplite battle in Greece was between the armies of two *poleis* quarreling over a piece of land. One army invaded the territory of the other at a time when the crops were almost ready for harvest. The defending army had no choice but to protect its fields. If the army was beaten, its fields were captured or destroyed and its people might starve. In every way, the phalanx was a communal effort that relied not on the extraordinary actions of the individual but on the courage of a considerable portion of the citizens.

The phalanx and the *polis* arose together, and both heralded the decline of the kings. The phalanx, however, was not made up only of aristocrats. Most of the hoplites were farmers working relatively small holdings. The immediate beneficiaries of the royal decline were the aristocrats, but because the existence of the *polis* depended on the small farmers, the farmers' wishes could not for long be wholly ignored. The rise of the hoplite phalanx created a bond between the aristocrats and the peasants who fought in it, and this bond helps to explain why class conflicts were muted for some time. It also guaranteed, however, that the aristocrats, who dominated at first, would not always be unchallenged.

Expansion of the Greek World

From the middle of the eighth century B.C. until well into the sixth, the Greeks vastly expanded the territory they controlled, their wealth, and their contacts with other peoples in a burst of colonizing activity that placed *poleis* from Spain to the Black Sea. A century earlier, a few Greeks had established trading posts in Syria. There they had learned new techniques in art and crafts and much more from the older civilizations of the Near East. About 750 B.C., they borrowed a writing system from one of the Semitic scripts and added vowels to create the first true alphabet. The new Greek alphabet was easier to learn than any earlier writing system and made possible the widely literate society of classical Greece.

Greek Colonies

Syria and its neighboring territory were too strong to penetrate, so the Greeks settled the southern coast of Macedonia and the Chalcidic peninsula (see Map 3-2). These regions were sparsely settled, and the natives were not well enough organized to resist the Greek colonists. Southern Italy and eastern Sicily were even more inviting areas. Before long, there were so many Greek colonies in Italy and Sicily that the Romans called the whole region *Magna Graecia* ("Great Greece"). The Greeks also put colonies in Spain and southern France. In the seventh century B.C., Greek colonists settled the coasts of the northeastern Mediterranean, the Black Sea, and the straits connecting them. About the same time, they established settlements on the eastern part of the northern African coast. The Greeks now had outposts throughout the Mediterranean world.

Most colonies, although independent, were friendly with their mother cities. Each might ask the other for aid in time of trouble and expect to receive a friendly hearing, although neither was obliged to help.

Colonization had a powerful influence on Greek life. By relieving the pressure and land hunger of a growing population, it provided a safety valve that allowed the *poleis* to escape civil wars. By confronting the Greeks with the differences between themselves and the new peoples they met, colonization gave them a sense of cultural identity and fostered a Pan-

MAP 3-2 PHOENICIAN AND GREEK COLONIZATION *Most of the coast line of the Mediterranean and Black seas was populated by Greek or Phoenician colonies, as shown on the map on the opposite page. The Phoenicians were a commercial people who planted their colonies in North Africa, Spain, Sicily, and Sardinia, chiefly in the ninth century B.C. The height of Greek colonization came later, between about 750 and 550 B.C.*

hellenic ("all-Greek") spirit that led to the establishment of a number of common religious festivals. The most important ones were at Olympia, Delphi, Corinth, and Nemea.

Colonization also encouraged trade and industry. The influx of new wealth from abroad and the increased demand for goods from the homeland stimulated a more intensive use of the land and an emphasis on crops for export, chiefly the olive and the wine grape. The manufacture of pottery, tools, weapons, and fine artistic metalwork as well as perfumed oil, the soap of the ancient Mediterranean world, was likewise encouraged. New opportunities allowed some men, sometimes outside the nobility, to become wealthy and important. These newly enriched men became a troublesome element in the aristocratic *poleis,* for they had an increasingly important part in the life of their states but were barred from political power, religious privileges, and social acceptance by the ruling aristocrats. These conditions soon created a crisis in many states.

The Tyrants (ca. 700–500 B.C.)

The crisis produced by the new economic and social conditions usually led to or intensified factional divisions within the ruling aristocracy, sometimes to civil war. In the years between 700 and 550 B.C., the result was often the establishment of a tyranny.

The founding tyrant was usually a member of the ruling aristocracy who either had a personal grievance or led one of the competing factions. He often rose to power as a result of his military ability and support of the politically powerless group of the newly wealthy, and of the poor peasants as well. When he took power, he often expelled many of his aristocratic opponents and divided at least some of their land among his supporters. He pleased his commercial and industrial supporters by destroying the privileges of the old aristocracy and by fostering trade and colonization.

The tyrants presided over a period of population growth that saw an increase especially in the number of city dwellers. They responded with programs of public works that included improvement of the drainage systems, care for the water supply, the construction and organization of marketplaces, the building and strengthening of city walls, and the erection of temples. They introduced new local festivals and elaborated the old ones. They were active in the patronage of the arts, supporting poets and artisans with gratifying results. All this activity contributed to the

tyrants' popularity, to the prosperity of their cities, and to their self-esteem.

In most cases, the tyrant's rule was secured by a personal bodyguard and by mercenary soldiers. An armed citizenry, necessary for an aggressive foreign policy, would have been dangerous, so the tyrants usually pursued a program of peaceful alliances with other tyrants abroad and avoided war.

By the end of the sixth century B.C., tyranny had disappeared from the Greek states, replaced in most cities by relatively broad oligarchies. Forced to repress continued and growing opposition, the last tyrants were universally hated for the cruelty and repression they employed. They left bitter memories in their own states and became objects of fear and hatred everywhere.

From a more distant perspective, however, it is clear that the tyrants made important contributions to the development of Greek civilization. They put an end, for a time, to the crippling civil wars that threatened the survival of the aristocratic *poleis.* In general, they reduced the warfare between the states. They encouraged the economic changes that were necessary for the future prosperity of Greece. They increased Greece's degree of communication with the rest of the Mediterranean world and made an enormous contribution to the cultivation of crafts and technology, as well as of the arts and literature. Most important of all, they broke the grip of the aristocrats and put the productive powers of the most active and talented of its citizens fully at the service of the *polis.*

Society and Culture in Archaic Greece

Styles of Life

As the dark ages came to an end, the features that would distinguish Greek society thereafter took shape. The role of the artisan and the merchant grew more important as contact with the non-Hellenic world became easier, but the great majority of people continued to make their living from the land. Wealthy aristocrats with large estates, powerful households, families, and clans, however, led very different lives from those of the poorer peasants and the independent farmers who had smaller and less fertile fields.

PEASANTS.   Peasants rarely leave a record of their thoughts or activities, and we have no such record from ancient Greece. The poet Hesiod (ca. 700 B.C.),

Hesiod's Farmer's Almanac

Hesiod was a farmer and poet who lived in a village in Greece about 700 B.C. His poem Works and Days *contains wisdom on several subjects, but its final section amounts to a farmer's almanac, taking readers through the year and advising them on just when each activity is demanded. Hesiod painted a picture of a very hard life for Greek farmers. In the following passage he talks about one of the few times when the farmer is free from toil, during the hottest part of summer.*

But when House-on-Back, the snail, crawls from
the ground up
the plants, escaping the Pleiades, it's no longer time
for vine-digging;
time rather to put an edge to your sickles, and rout
out your helpers.
Keep away from sitting in the shade or lying in bed till
the sun's up
in the time of the harvest, when the sunshine
scorches your skin dry.
This is the season to push work and bring home your
harvest;
get up with the first light so you'll have enough to live
on.
Dawn takes away from work a third part of the work's
measure.
Dawn sets a man well along on his journey, in his
work also,
dawn, who when she shows, has numerous people
going their ways; dawn who puts the yoke upon
many oxen.
But when the artichoke is in flower, and the
clamorous cricket
sitting in his tree lets go his vociferous singing, that
issues
from the beating of his wings, in the exhausting season of summer,

then is when goats are at their fattest, when the wine
tastes best,
women are most lascivious, but the men's strength
fails them
most, for the star Seirios shrivels them, knees and
heads alike,
and the skin is all dried out in the heat; then, at that
season,
one might have the shadow under the rock, and the
wine of Biblis,
a curd cake, and all the milk that the goats can give
you,
the meat of a heifer, bred in the woods, who has
never borne a calf,
and of baby kids also. Then, too, one can sit in the
shadow
and drink the bright-shining wine, his heart satiated
with eating
and face turned in the direction where Zephyros
blows briskly,
make three libations of water from a spring that keeps
running forever
and has no mud in it; and pour wine for the fourth
libation.

Hesiod, *Works and Days,* trans. by Richmond Lattimore (Ann Arbor: University of Michigan Press, 1959), pp. 87, 89.

however, who presented himself as a small farmer, was certainly no aristocrat. From his *Works and Days* we get some idea of the life of such a farmer. The crops included grain, chiefly barley but also wheat; grapes for wine; olives for food, but chiefly for oil, used for cooking, lighting, and washing; green vegetables, especially the bean; and some fruit. Sheep and goats provided milk and cheese. The Homeric heroes had great herds of cattle and ate lots of meat, but by Hesiod's time land fertile enough to provide fodder for cattle was needed to grow grain. He and small farmers like him tasted meat chiefly from sacrificial animals at festivals.

These farmers worked hard to make their living. Although Hesiod had the help of oxen and mules and one or two hired helpers for occasional labor, his life was one of continuous toil. The hardest work came in October, at the start of the rainy season, the time for the first plowing. The plow was light and easily broken, and the work of forcing the iron tip into the earth was back-breaking, although Hesiod had a team of oxen to pull his plow. Not every farmer was so fortunate, and the cry of the crane that announced the time of year to plow "bites the heart of the man without oxen."

Autumn and winter were the time for cutting wood, building wagons, and making tools. Late winter was the time to tend to the vines, May the time to harvest the grain, July to winnow and store it. Only at the height of summer's heat did Hesiod allow for rest, but when September came, it was time to harvest the grapes. No sooner was that task done than the cycle started again. The work went on under the burning sun and in the freezing cold.

Hesiod wrote nothing of pleasure or entertainment. Less austere farmers than Hesiod gathered at the blacksmith's shop for warmth and companionship in winter, and even he must have taken part in religious rites and festivals that were accompanied by some kind of entertainment, but the life of the peasant farmers was hard and their pleasures few.

ARISTOCRATS. Most aristocrats were rich enough to employ many hired laborers, sometimes sharecroppers and sometimes even slaves, to work their extensive lands and were therefore able to enjoy leisure for other activities. The center of aristocratic social life was the drinking party, or *symposion*. This activity was not a mere drinking bout, meant to remove inhibitions and produce oblivion. The Greeks, in fact, almost always mixed their wine with water, and one of the goals of the participants was to drink as much as the others without becoming drunk.

The *symposion* was a carefully organized occasion, with a "king" chosen to set the order of events and to determine that night's mixture of wine and water. Only men took part, and they ate and drank as they reclined on couches along the walls of the room. The sessions began with prayers and libations to the gods. Usually there were games, such as dice or *kottabos*, in which wine was flicked from the cups at

Theognis of Megara Gives Advice to a Young Aristocrat

Theognis was born about 500 B.C. and lived to see his native city Megara torn by social upheaval and civil war. His poems present the political and ethical ideas of the Greek aristocracy. The "sons of Asclepius" mentioned below are physicians.

▶ *Compare Theognis' advice to the Confucian ideals of gentlemanly behavior presented in the box titled "Confucius Defines the Gentleman" in Chapter 2.*

Do not consort with bad men, but always hold to the good. Eat and drink with them, whose power is great, sit with them and please them. You will learn good from good men, but if you mingle with the bad you will lose such wisdom as you already have. Therefore consort with the good and one day you will say that I give good advice to my friends.

We seek thoroughbred rams, asses, and horses, Cyrnus, and a man wants offspring of good breeding. But in marriage a good man does not decline to marry the bad daughter of a bad father, if he gives him much wealth. Nor does the wife of a bad man refuse to be his bedfellow if he be rich, preferring wealth to goodness. For they value possessions and a good man marries a woman of bad stock and the bad a woman of good. Wealth mixes the breed. So do not wonder, son of Polypaus, that the race of your citizens is obscured since bad things are mixed with good.

It is easier to beget and rear a man than to put good sense into him. No one has ever discovered a way to make a fool wise or a bad man good. If God had given the sons of Asclepius the knowledge to heal the evil nature and mischievous mind of man, great and frequent would be their pay. If thought could be made and put into a man, the son of a good man would never become bad, since he would obey good counsel. But you will never make the bad man good by teaching.

The best thing the gods give to men, Cyrnus, is judgment; judgment contains the ends of everything. O happy is the man who has it in his mind; it is much greater than destructive insolence and grievous satiety. There are no evils among mortals worse than these—for every evil, Cyrnus, comes out of them.

Donald Kagan, ed., *Sources in Greek Political Thought*, ed. by D. Kagan (New York: Free Press, 1965), pp. 39–40.

This scene showing a battle between the Olympian gods and attacking giants is part of the sculpture decorating the treasury of the Siphnians constructed at Delphi ca. 530 B.C. Because the island of Siphnos was very wealthy in the sixth century, its people could afford to erect a find building to hold their offerings to Apollo at his major shrine. [Delphi Museum]

different targets. Sometimes dancing girls or flute girls offered entertainment. Frequently, the aristocratic participants provided their own amusements with songs, poetry, or even philosophical disputes. Characteristically, these took the form of contests, with some kind of prize for the winner, for aristocratic values continued to emphasize competition and the need to excel, whatever the arena.

This aspect of aristocratic life appears in the athletic contests that became widespread early in the sixth century B.C. The games included running events; the long jump; the discus and javelin throws; the *pentathlon,* which included all of these; boxing; wrestling; and the chariot race. Only the rich could afford to raise, train, and race horses, so the chariot race was a special preserve of aristocracy. Wrestling, however, was also especially favored by the nobility, and the *palaestra* where they practiced became an important social center for the aristocracy. The contrast between the hard, drab life of the peasants and the leisured and lively one of the aristocrats could hardly be greater.

Culture

RELIGION. Like most ancient peoples, the Greeks were polytheists, and religion played an important part in their lives. A great part of Greek art and literature was closely connected with religion, as was the life of the *polis* in general. The Greek pantheon consisted of the twelve gods who lived on Mount Olympus: Zeus, the father of the gods; his wife, Hera; his brother, Poseidon, god of the seas and earthquakes; his sisters, Hestia, goddess of the hearth, and Demeter, goddess of agriculture and marriage; and his children—Aphrodite, goddess of love and beauty; Apollo, god of the sun, music, poetry, and prophecy; Ares, god of war; Artemis, goddess of the moon and the hunt; Athena, goddess of wisdom and the arts; Hephaestus, god of fire and metallurgy; and Hermes, messenger of the gods, who was connected with commerce and cunning.

On the one hand, these gods were seen as behaving very much like mortals, with all the human foibles, except that theirs were superhuman, as were their strength and immortality. On the other hand, Zeus, at least, was seen as being a source of human justice, and even the Olympians were understood to be subordinate to the Fates. Each *polis* had one of the Olympians as its guardian deity and worshiped the god in its own special way, but all the gods were Panhellenic. In the eighth and seventh centuries B.C., common shrines were established at Olympia for the worship of Zeus, at Delphi for Apollo, at the Isthmus of Corinth for Poseidon, and at Nemea once again for Zeus. Each held athletic contests in honor of its god, to which all Greeks were invited and for which a sacred truce was declared.

The worship of these deities did not involve great emotion. It was a matter of offering prayer, libations, and gifts in return for protection and favors from the god during the lifetime of the worshiper. There was no hope of immortality for the average human and little moral teaching. Most Greeks seem to have held to the commonsense notion that justice lay in paying one's debts; that civic virtue consisted of worshiping the state deities in the traditional way, performing the required public services, and fighting in defense of the state; and that private morality meant to do good to one's friends and harm to one's enemies.

In the sixth century B.C., the influence of the cult of Apollo at Delphi and of his oracle there became very great. The oracle was the most important of several that helped satisfy human craving for a clue to the future. The priests of Apollo preached moderation; their advice was exemplified in the two famous sayings identified with Apollo: "Know thyself" and "Nothing in excess." Humans need self-control *(sophrosyne)*. Its opposite is arrogance *(hybris)*, which is brought on by excessive wealth or good fortune. *Hybris* leads to moral blindness and finally to divine vengeance. This theme of moderation and the dire consequences of its absence was central to Greek popular morality and appears frequently in Greek literature.

The somewhat cold religion of the Olympian gods and of the cult of Apollo did little to attend to human fears, hopes, and passions. For these needs, the Greeks turned to other deities and rites. Of them, the most popular was Dionysus, a god of nature and fertility, of the grapevine and drunkenness and sexual abandon. In some of his rites, the god was followed by maenads, female devotees who cavorted by night, ate raw flesh, and were reputed to tear to pieces any creature they came across.

POETRY.   The great changes sweeping through the Greek world were also reflected in the poetry of the sixth century B.C. The lyric style, whether sung by a chorus or sung by one singer, predominated. Sappho of Lesbos, Anacreon of Teos, and Simonides of Cous composed personal poetry, often speaking of the pleasure and agony of love. Alcaeus of Mytilene, an aristocrat driven from his city by a tyrant, wrote bitter invective.

Perhaps the most interesting poet of the century from a political point of view was Theognis of Megara. An aristocrat who lived through a tyranny, an unusually chaotic and violent democracy, and an oligarchy that restored order but that ended the rule of the old aristocracy, Theognis was the spokesman for the old, defeated aristocracy of birth. He divided everyone into two classes, the noble and the base; the former were good, the latter bad. Those nobly born had to associate only with others like themselves if they were to preserve their virtue; if they mingled with the base, they became base. Those born base, on the other hand, could never become noble. Only nobles could aspire to virtue, and only nobles possessed the critical moral and intellectual qualities, respect or

The god Dionysus dancing with two maenads, his female followers. The vase decoration is by a painter who worked between about 559 and 525 B.C. [Bibliothèque Nationale, Paris]

honor, and judgment. These qualities could not be taught; they were innate. Even so, nobles had to be carefully guarded against corruption by wealth or by mingling with the base. Intermarriage between the noble and the base was especially condemned. These were the ideas of the unreconstructed nobility, whose power had been destroyed or reduced in most Greek states by this time. These ideas remained alive in aristocratic hearts throughout the next century and greatly influenced later thinkers, Plato among them.

Major City-States

Generalization about the *polis* becomes difficult not long after its appearance, for although the states had much in common, some of them developed in unique ways. Sparta and Athens, which became the two most powerful Greek states, had especially unusual histories (see Maps 3-3 and 3-4).

MAP 3-3 ATTICA AND VICINITY *Citizens of all towns in Attica were also citizens of Athens.*

MAP 3-4 THE PELOPONNESUS *Sparta's region, Laconia, was in the Peloponnesus. Nearby states were members of the Peloponnesian League under Sparta's leadership.*

Tyrtaeus Describes Excellence:
Code of the Citizen Soldier

The military organization of citizen soldiers for the defense of the polis *and the idea of the* polis *itself, which permeated Greek political thought, found echoes in Greek lyric poetry. A major example is this poem by Tyrtaeus, a Spartan poet who wrote about 625* B.C. *It gives important evidence on the nature of warfare in the phalanx and the values taught by the* polis.

I would not say anything for a man nor take account
of him
   for any speed of his feet or wrestling skill we might
   have
not if he had the size of a Cyclops and strength to go
with it,
   not if he could outrun Bóreas, the North Wind of
   Thrace,
not if he were more handsome and gracefully formed
than Tithónos,
   or had more riches than Midas had, or Kinyras too,
not if he were more of a king than Tantalid Pelops,
   or had the power of speech and persuasion
   Adrastos had,
not if he had all splendors except for a fighting spirit.
   For no man ever proves himself a good man in war
     unless he can endure to face the blood and the
     slaughter,
   go close against the enemy and fight with his
   hands.
Here is courage, mankind's finest possession, here is
   the noblest prize that a young man can endeavor to
   win,
and it is a good thing his city and all the people share
with him
   when a man plants his feet and stands in the foremost spears
relentlessly, all thought of foul flight completely forgotten,
   and has well trained his heart to be steadfast and to
   endure,
and with words encourages the man who is stationed
beside him.
   Here is a man who proves himself to be valiant in
   war.
With a sudden rush he turns to flight the rugged battalions
   of the enemy, and sustains the bearing waves of
   assault.
And he who so falls among the champions and loses
his sweet life,

so blessing with honor his city, his father, and all
his people,
   with wounds in his chest, where the spear that he
   was facing has transfixed
that massive guard of his shield, and gone through
his breastplate as well,
why, such a man is lamented alike by the young and
the elders,
   and all his city goes into mourning and grieves for
   his loss.
His tomb is pointed out with pride, and so are his
children,
   and his children's children, and afterward all the
   race that is his.
His shining glory is never forgotten, his name is remembered,
   and he becomes an immortal, though he lies under
   the ground,
when one who was a brave man has been killed by
the furious War
   God
   standing his ground and fighting hard for his children and land.
But if he escapes the doom of death, the destroyer of
bodies,
   and wins his battle, and bright renown for the work
   of his spear,
all men give place to him alike, the youth and the
elders,
   and much joy comes his way before he goes down
   to the dead.
Aging he has reputation among his citizens. No one
tries to interfere with his honors or all he deserves;
all men withdraw before his presence, and yield their
seats to him,
   and youth, and the men of his age, and even those
   older than he.
Thus a man should endeavor to reach this high place
of courage
   with all his heart, and, so trying, never be backward in war.

Greek Lyrics, trans. by Richmond Lattimore (Chicago: University of Chicago Press, 1949, 1950, 1955), pp. 14–15.

Sparta

At first, Sparta seems not to have been strikingly different from other *poleis,* but about 725 B.C., the pressure of population and land hunger led the Spartans to launch a war of conquest against their western neighbor, Messenia. This First Messenian War gave the Spartans as much land as they would ever need. The reduction of the Messenians to the status of serfs, or Helots, after the war meant that the Spartans did not even have to work the land that supported them.

The turning point in Spartan history came with the Second Messenian War, a rebellion of the Helots, assisted by Argos and some other Peloponnesian cities, about 650 B.C. The war was long and bitter and at one point threatened the existence of Sparta. After the revolt had been put down, the Spartans were forced to reconsider their way of life. They could not expect to keep down the Helots, who outnumbered them perhaps ten to one, and still maintain the old free-and-easy habits typical of most Greeks. Faced with the choice of making drastic changes and sacrifices or abandoning their control of Messenia, the Spartans chose to introduce fundamental reforms that turned their city forever after into a military academy and camp.

SOCIETY.   The new system that emerged late in the sixth century B.C. exerted control over each Spartan from birth, when officials of the state decided which infants were physically fit to survive. At the age of seven, the Spartan boy was taken from his mother and turned over to young instructors who trained him in athletics and the military arts and taught him to endure privation, to bear physical pain, and to live off the country, by theft if necessary. At twenty the Spartan youth was enrolled in the army and lived in barracks with his companions until the age of thirty. Marriage was permitted, but a strange sort of marriage it was, for the Spartan male could visit his wife only infrequently and by stealth. At thirty, he became a full citizen, an "equal," and was allowed to live in his own house with his wife, although he took his meals at a public mess in the company of fifteen comrades. His food, a simple diet without much meat or wine, was provided by his own plot of land, which was worked by Helots. Military service was required until the age of sixty; only then could the Spartan retire at last to his home and family.

This educational program extended to the women, too. They were not given military training, but female infants were examined for fitness to survive in the same way as males. Girls were given gymnastic training, were permitted greater freedom of movement than among other Greeks, and were equally indoctrinated with the idea of service to Sparta. The entire system was designed to change the natural feelings of devotion to family into a more powerful commitment to the *polis.* Privacy, luxury, and even comfort were sacrificed to the purpose of producing soldiers whose physical prowess, training, and discipline made them the best in the world. Nothing that might turn the mind away from duty was permitted. The very use of coins was forbidden lest it corrupt the desires of Spartans. Neither family nor money was allowed to interfere with the only ambition permitted to a Spartan male: to win glory and peer respect by bravery in war.

GOVERNMENT.   The Spartan constitution was mixed, containing elements of monarchy, oligarchy, and democracy. There were two kings, whose power was limited by law and also by the rivalry that usually existed between the two royal houses.

The oligarchic element was represented by a council of elders consisting of twenty-eight men over sixty, who were elected for life. These elders had important judicial functions, sitting as a court in cases involving the kings. They also were consulted before any proposal was put before the assembly of Spartan citizens. In a traditional society like Sparta's, they must have had considerable influence.

The Spartan assembly consisted of all males over thirty. Theoretically, they were the final authority, but because, in practice, debate was carried on by magistrates, elders, and kings alone, and because voting was usually by acclamation, the assembly's real function was to ratify decisions already taken or to decide between positions favored by the leading figures. In addition, Sparta had a unique institution, the board of ephors. This consisted of five men elected annually by the assembly. Originally they appear to have been intended to check the power of the kings, but gradually they acquired other important functions: They controlled foreign policy, oversaw the generalship of the kings on campaign, presided at the assembly, and guarded against rebellion by the Helots.

By about 550 B.C., the Spartan system was well established, and its limitations had been made plain. Suppression of the Helots required all the effort and energy that Sparta had. The Spartans could expand no further, but they could not allow unruly independent neighbors to cause unrest that might inflame the Helots.

When the Spartans defeated Tegea, their northern

neighbor, they imposed an unusual peace. Instead of taking away land and subjecting the defeated state, Sparta left the Tegeans their land and their freedom. In exchange, they required the Tegeans to follow the Spartan lead in foreign affairs and to supply a fixed number of soldiers to Sparta on demand. This became the model for Spartan relations with the other states in the Peloponnesus, and soon Sparta was the leader of an alliance that included every Peloponnesian state but Argos; modern scholars have named this alliance the Peloponnesian League. It provided the Spartans with the security they needed, and it also made Sparta the most powerful *polis* in Hellenic history. By 500 B.C., Sparta and the league had given the Greeks a force capable of facing mighty threats from abroad.

Athens

In the seventh century B.C., Athens was a typical aristocratic *polis.* The aristocrats held the most and best land and dominated religious and political life. There was no written law, and decisions were rendered by powerful nobles on the basis of tradition and, most likely, self-interest. The state was governed by the Areopagus, a council of nobles deriving its name from the hill where it held its sessions. Annually, the council elected nine magistrates called archons, who themselves joined the Areopagus after their year in office. Because the archons served for only a year, were checked by their colleagues, and looked for-

ward to a lifetime as members of the Areopagus after their terms were ended, it is plain that the Areopagus, not the archons, was the true master of the state.

In the seventh century B.C., the peaceful life of Athens experienced some disturbances that were caused in part by quarrels within the nobility and in part by the beginnings of an agrarian crisis. Many Athenians worked family farms, from which they obtained most of their living. It appears that they planted wheat, the staple crop, year after year without rotating fields or using sufficient fertilizer. In time, this procedure exhausted the soil and led to bad crops. To survive, some farmers had to borrow from wealthy neighbors to get through the year. In return, they promised one-sixth of the next year's crop. The arrangement was marked by the deposit of an inscribed stone on the entailed farms. As bad harvests persisted, debtors had to pledge their wives, their children, and themselves as surety for new loans. Inevitably, many Athenians defaulted and were enslaved. Some were even sold abroad. Revolutionary pressures grew among the poor, who began to demand the abolition of debt and a redistribution of the land.

SOLON AND REFORM.   The circumstances might easily have brought about class warfare and tyranny, but the remarkable conciliatory spirit of Athens intervened. In the year 594 B.C., as tradition has it, the Athenians elected Solon, a successful general and talented poet, and gave him extraordinary powers to legislate and revise the constitution. Immediately, he attacked the agrarian problem by canceling current debts and forbidding future loans secured by the person of the borrower. He helped bring back many Athenians enslaved abroad and freed those in Athens enslaved for debt. This program was called the "shaking off of burdens." It did not, however, solve the fundamental economic problem, and Solon did not redistribute the land. In the short run, therefore, he did not put an end to the economic crisis, but his other economic actions had profound success in the long run. He forbade the export of wheat and encouraged that of olive oil. This policy had the effect of making wheat more available in Attica and encouraging the cultivation of olive oil and wine as cash crops. By the fifth century B.C., this form of agriculture had become so profitable that much Athenian land was diverted from grain production to the cultivation of cash crops, and Athens became dependent on imported wheat.

Solon also changed the Athenian standards of weights and measures to conform with those of Corinth and Euboea and the cities of the East. This change also encouraged commerce and turned Athens in the direction that would lead to great prosperity in the fifth century B.C. He also encouraged industry by offering citizenship to foreign artisans, and his success is reflected in the development of the outstanding Attic pottery of the sixth century.

Solon also significantly changed the constitution. Athenian citizenship had been confined only to those who had an Athenian father. Solon made it possible for useful immigrants to acquire citizenship, too. Then all Athenian citizens were divided into four classes on the basis of wealth, measured by annual agricultural production.

Men whose property produced five hundred measures were called five-hundred-measure men, and those producing three hundred measures were called cavalry; these two classes alone could hold office and sit on the Areopagus.

Producers of two hundred measures were called owners of a team of oxen; they were allowed to serve as hoplites. They could be elected to the council of four hundred chosen by all the citizens, one hundred from each tribe. Solon seems to have meant this council to serve as a check on the Areopagus and to prepare any business that needed to be put before the assembly.

The last class, producing fewer than two hundred measures, were the *thetes.* They voted in the popular assembly for the magistrates and the council members and on any other business brought before them by the magistrates. They also sat on a new popular court established by Solon. At first, this court must have had little power, for most cases continued to be heard in the country by local barons and in Athens by the aristocratic Areopagus. But the new court was recognized as a court of appeal, and by the fifth century B.C., almost all cases came before the popular courts.

PISISTRATUS THE TYRANT.   Solon's efforts to avoid factional strife failed. Within a few years of his reforms, contention reached such a degree that no magistrates could be chosen. Out of this turmoil emerged the first Athenian tyranny. Pisistratus, a nobleman, faction leader, and military hero, seized power firmly. His rule rested on the force provided by mercenary soldiers. He engaged in great programs of public works, urban improvement, and religious piety. Temples were built and religious centers expanded and improved. New religious festivals were introduced, such as the one dedicated to Dionysus, the god of fertility, wine, and ecstatic religious worship imported from

Phrygia in Asia Minor. Old ones, like the Great Panathenaic festival, were amplified and given greater public appeal. Poets and artists were supported to add cultural luster to the court of the tyrant.

Pisistratus aimed at increasing the power of the central government at the expense of the nobles. The festival of Dionysus and the Great Panathenaic festival helped fix attention on the capital city, as did the new temples and the reconstruction of the Agora as the center of public life. Circuit judges were sent out into the country to hear cases, another feature that weakened the power of the local barons. All this time, Pisistratus made no formal change in the Solonian constitution. Assembly, councils, and courts met; magistrates and councils were elected; Pisistratus merely saw to it that his supporters were chosen. The intended effect was to blunt the sharp edge of tyranny with the appearance of constitutional government, and it worked. The rule of Pisistratus was remembered as popular and mild. The unintended effect was to give the Athenians more experience in the procedures of self-government and a growing taste for it.

INVASION BY SPARTA.   Pisistratus was succeeded by his oldest son, Hippias, who followed his father's ways at first. In 514 B.C., however, his brother Hipparchus was murdered as a result of a private quarrel. Hippias became nervous, suspicious, and harsh. At last, one of the noble clans exiled by the sons of Pisistratus, the Alcmaeonids, won favor with the influential oracle at Delphi and used its support to persuade Sparta to attack the Athenian tyranny. Led by their ambitious king, Cleomenes I, the Spartans marched into Attica in 510 B.C. and deposed Hippias, who went into exile to the Persian court. The tyranny was over.

The Spartans must have hoped to leave Athens in friendly hands, and indeed Cleomenes' friend Isagoras, a rival of the Alcmaeonids, held the leading position in Athens after the withdrawal of the Spartan army. Isagoras, however, faced competitors, chief among them Clisthenes of the restored Alcmaeonid clan. Clisthenes lost out in the initial political struggle among the noble factions. Isagoras seems then to have tried to restore a version of the pre-Solonian aristocratic state. As part of his plan, he carried through a purification of the citizen lists, removing those who had been enfranchised by Solon or Pisistratus and any others thought to have a doubtful claim. Clisthenes then took an unprecedented action—he turned to the people for political support and won it with a program of great popular appeal. In response, Isagoras called in the Spartans again; Cleomenes arrived and allowed Isagoras to expel Clisthenes and a large number of his supporters. But the fire of Athenian political consciousness, ignited by Solon and kept alive under Pisistratus, had been fanned into flames by the popular appear of Clisthenes. The people refused to tolerate an aristocratic restoration and drove out the Spartans and Isagoras with them. Clisthenes and his allies returned, ready to put their program into effect.

CLISTHENES, THE FOUNDER OF DEMOCRACY. A central aim of Clisthenes' reforms was to diminish the influ-

Aristogeiton and Harmodius were Athenian aristocrats who were slain while assassinating Hipparchos, brother of the tyrant Hippias. After the overthrow of the Pisistratids, the Athenians erected a famous statue to honor their memory. This is a Roman copy. [Art Resource/Alinari/SCALA]

ence of traditional localities and regions in Athenian life, for they were an important source of power for the nobility and of factions in the state. Clisthenes immediately enrolled the disenfranchised who had supported him in the struggle with Isagoras. Ten new tribes replaced the traditional four. The composition of each tribe guaranteed that no region would dominate any of them. Because the tribes had common religious activities and fought as regimental units, the new organization would also increase devotion to the *polis* and diminish regional divisions and personal loyalty to local barons.

A new council of five hundred was invented to replace the Solonian council of four hundred. Final authority in all things rested with the assembly, composed of all adult male Athenian citizens. Debate was free and open; any Athenian could submit legislation, offer amendments, or argue the merits of any question. It is fair to call Clisthenes the father of Athenian democracy. He did not alter the property qualifications of Solon, but his enlargement of the citizen rolls; his diminution of the power of the aristocrats; and his elevation of the role of the assembly, with its effective and manageable council, all give him a firm claim to that title.

As a result of the work of Solon, Pisistratus, and Clisthenes, Athens entered the fifth century B.C. well on the way to prosperity and democracy. It was much more centralized and united than it had been and was ready to take its place among the major states that would lead the defense of Greece against the dangers that lay ahead.

The Persian Wars

The Greeks' period of fortunate isolation and freedom at last came to an end. In the middle of the sixth century B.C., these Greek cities of Asia Minor came under the control of Lydia and its king, Croesus (ca. 560–546 B.C.). The Lydian rule seems not to have been very harsh, but the Persian conquest of Lydia in 546 B.C. brought a subjugation that was less pleasant.

The Persians required their subjects to pay tribute and to serve in the Persian army. They ruled the Greek cities through local individuals, who governed their cities as tyrants. The Ionians had been moving in the direction of democracy and were not pleased with monarchical rule, yet the Persian tribute was not excessive, and there was general prosperity.

Ionian Rebellion

The Ionian Greeks, nevertheless, preferred to be free, and when an opportunity for liberty came they seized it. The private troubles of the ambitious tyrant of Miletus, Aristagoras, started the Ionian rebellion of 499 B.C. He had urged a Persian expedition against the island of Naxos; when it failed, he feared the consequences and organized the rebellion. To gain support, he overthrew the tyrannies and proclaimed democratic constitutions. Then he turned to the mainland states for help, first petitioning Sparta, the most powerful Greek state. The Spartans, however, would have none of Aristagoras's promises of easy victory and great wealth.

Aristagoras next sought help from the Athenians, who were related to the Ionians and had close ties of religion and tradition with them. The Athenian assembly agreed to send a fleet of twenty ships to help the rebels. This expedition was strengthened by five ships from Eretria in Euboea, which participated out of gratitude for past favors.

In 498 B.C., the Athenians and their allies made a swift march and a surprise attack on Sardis, the old capital of Lydia and now the seat of the Persian governor, and burned it. The revolt spread throughout the Greek cities of Asia Minor outside Ionia, but the Athenians withdrew and took no further part, and gradually the Persians reimposed their will. In 495 B.C., they defeated the Ionian fleet at Lade, and in the next year they wiped out Miletus. Many men were killed; others were transported to the Persian Gulf, and the women and children were enslaved. The Ionian rebellion was over.

The War in Greece

In 490 B.C., the Persians launched an expedition directly across the Aegean to punish Athens, to restore Hippias, and to gain control of the Aegean Sea. The resistance was led by Miltiades, an Athenian and an outstanding soldier who had fled from Persian service after earning the anger of Darius (r. 521–486 B.C.). His knowledge of the Persian army and his distaste for submission to Persia made him an ideal leader. He led the army to Marathon in Attica and won a decisive victory. The battle at Marathon (490 B.C.) was of enormous importance to the future of Greek civilization. A Persian victory would have destroyed Athenian freedom, and the conquest of all the mainland Greeks would have followed. The greatest achievements of

Greek Wars Against Persia	
ca. 560–546 B.C.	Greek cities of Asia Minor conquered by Croesus of Lydia
546 B.C.	Cyrus of Persia conquers Lydia and gains control of Greek cities
499–494 B.C.	Greek cities rebel (Ionian rebellion)
490 B.C.	Battle of Marathon
480–479 B.C.	Xerxes' invasion of Greece
480 B.C.	Battles of Thermopylae, Artemisium, and Salamis
479 B.C.	Battles of Plataea and Mycale

with the fleet for supplies. If the Greeks could defeat the Persian navy, the army could not remain in Greece long. Themistocles knew that the Aegean was subject to sudden devastating storms that might damage or destroy the enemy fleet. His strategy was to

Greek hoplite attacking a Persian soldier. The contrast between the Greek's heavy metal body armor, large shield, and long spear and the cloth and leather garments of the Persian gives some indication of the reason for the ultimate Greek victory. This Attic red-figure vase is said to be from the island of Rhodes and was made about 475 B.C. [Metropolitan Museum of Art; Rogers Fund, 1906]

Greek culture, most of which lay in the future, would have been impossible under Persian rule. The Athenian victory, on the other hand, made a positive contribution to those achievements. It instilled in the Athenians a sense of confidence and pride in their *polis,* and themselves.

For the Persians, Marathon was only a small and temporary defeat, but it was annoying. Internal troubles, however, prevented swift revenge. It was not until 481 B.C., that Darius's successor, Xerxes (r. 486–465 B.C.), gathered an army of at least one hundred fifty thousand men and a navy of more than six hundred ships for the conquest of Greece. The Greeks in general had not made good use of the delay, but Athens was an exception. Themistocles had become its leading politician, and he had always wanted to turn Athens into a naval power. His first step was to build a fortified port at Piraeus during his archonship in 493 B.C. A decade later, the Athenians discovered a rich vein of silver in the state mines, and Themistocles persuaded them to use the profits to increase their fleet. By 480 B.C., Athens had over two hundred ships, the backbone of the navy that defeated the Persians.

As the Persian army gathered south of the Hellespont, only thirty-one Greek states out of hundreds were willing to fight. They were led by Sparta, Athens, Corinth, and Aegina. In the spring of 480 B.C., Xerxes launched his invasion. The Persian strategy was to march into Greece, destroy Athens, defeat the Greek army, and make Persian subjects of the Greeks. The huge Persian army, however, needed to keep in touch delay the Persian army and then to bring on the kind of naval battle he might hope to win.

The Greek League, founded specifically to resist this Persian invasion, met at Corinth as the Persians were ready to cross the Hellespont. The league chose Sparta as leader on land and sea and sent a force to Tempe to try to defend Thessaly. Tempe proved to be indefensible, so the Greeks retreated and took up new positions at Thermopylae (the "hot gates") on land and off Artemisium at sea. The opening between the mountains and the sea at Thermopylae was so narrow that it might be held by a smaller army against a much larger one. The Spartans sent their king, Leonidas, with three hundred of their own citizens and enough allies to make a total of about nine thousand. The Greeks may have intended to hold only long enough to permit the Athenians to evacuate Athens or to force a sea battle, or they may have hoped to hold Thermopylae until the Persians were discouraged enough to withdraw. Perhaps they thought of all these possibilities, for they were not mutually contradictory.

Severe storms wrecked a large number of Persian ships while the Greek fleet waited safely in its protected harbor at Chalcis in Euboea. Then Xerxes attacked Thermopylae, and for two days the Greeks butchered his best troops without serious loss to themselves. On the third day, however, a traitor showed the Persians a mountain trail that permitted them to attack the Greeks from behind. Many allies escaped, but Leonidas and his three hundred Spartans all died. At about the same time, the Greek and Persian fleets fought an indecisive battle at nearby Artemisium, and the fall of Thermopylae forced the Greek navy to withdraw.

If an inscription discovered in 1959 is authentic, Themistocles had foreseen this possibility, and the Athenians had begun to evacuate their homeland before sending their fleet north. The fate of Greece was decided in a sea battle in the narrow waters to the east of the island of Salamis to which the Greek fleet withdrew after the battle of Artemisium. Themistocles persuaded the reluctant Peloponnesians to stay by threatening to remove all the Athenians from Greece and settle them anew in Italy. The Spartans knew that they and the other Greeks could not hope to win without the aid of the Athenians. Because the Greek ships were fewer, slower, and less maneuverable than those of the Persians, the Greeks put soldiers on their ships and relied chiefly on hand-to-hand combat. In the ensuring battle the Persians lost more than half their ships and retreated to Asia with a good part of their army, but the danger was not over yet.

The Persian general Mardonius spent the winter in central Greece, and in the spring, he unsuccessfully tried to win the Athenians away from the Greek League. The Spartan regent, Pausanias, then led the largest Greek army up to that time to confront Mardonius in Boeotia. At Plataea, in the summer of 479 B.C., Mardonius died in battle, and his army fled toward home. Meanwhile, the Ionian Greeks urged King Leotychidas, the Spartan commander of the fleet, to fight the Persian fleet at Samos. At Mycale, on the nearby coast, Leotychidas destroyed the Persian camp and its fleet offshore. The Persians fled the Aegean and Ionia. For the moment, at least, the Persian threat was gone.

Rise of Greek Civilization in World Perspective

Hellenic civilization, a unique cultural experience, is at the root of Western civilization. It has powerfully influenced the peoples of the modern world. Itself influenced by the great Bronze Age civilization of Crete, it emerged from the collapse of the Bronze Age civilization on the Greek mainland that we call Mycenaean. These earlier civilizations resembled others in Egypt, Mesopotamia, Palestine–Syria, China, India, and elsewhere more than they did the Hellenic version that sprang from them. They had highly developed urban lives; a system of writing; strong, centralized monarchical system of government ruling over tightly organized, large bureaucracies; hierarchical social systems; professional-standing armies—and a regular system of taxation to support it all. To a greater or lesser degree (more in Egypt, less in China), these early civilizations tended toward cultural stability and uniformity. The striking fact about the emergence of Hellenic civilization was its sharp departure from this pattern of development. The collapse of the Mycenaean world produced a harsh drop in the level of material well-being for the Greeks. It also caused a decline in the cultural level. Cities were swept away and replaced by small farm villages. Trade was all but ended, and communications not only between the Greeks and other peoples but even among the Greeks themselves were sharply curtailed. The art of writing was lost for more than three centuries. The matrix of Hellenic civilization was a dark age in which a small number of poor, isolated, illiterate people were ignored by the rest of the world and left alone to develop their own kind of society.

During the three-and-a-half centuries from about 1100 to 750 B.C., the Greeks set the foundations for their great achievements. The crucial unit in the new Greek way of life was the *polis,* the Hellenic city-state. There were hundreds of them, ranging in size from a few thousand inhabitants to hundreds of thousands. Each city-state evoked a kind of loyalty and attachment by its citizens that made the idea of dissolving one's own *polis* into a larger unit unthinkable. The result was a dynamic, many-faceted, competitive, sometimes chaotic society in which rivalry for excellence and victory had the highest value.

This competitive quality marked Greek life throughout its history. Its negative aspect was constant warfare among the states. Its positive side was its extraordinary achievement in literature and art, where competition, sometimes formal and organized, spurred poets and artists.

The *poleis* were republics. Class distinctions were less marked and less important than those in other civilizations, partly because the Greeks were so poor and the differences in wealth among them were relatively small. The introduction of a new mode of fighting, the hoplite phalanx, had further leveling effects on a class system, for it placed the safety of the state in the hands of the average farmer. Armies were made up of unpaid citizen-soldiers, who returned to their farms after a campaign. As a result, political control was shared with a relatively large portion of the people, and participation in political life was highly valued.

Even when the art of writing was newly acquired from western Semites (perhaps the Phoenicians), there was no bureaucracy, for there were no kings and not much economic surplus to support them. Most states imposed no regular taxation. There was no separate caste of priests and little concern with any life after death. In this varied, dynamic, secular, and remarkably free context there arose a speculative natural philosophy based on observation and reason. Greek ideas formed the root of modern natural science and philosophy.

Expanded contact and trade with the rest of the world increased the wealth of many Greek cities and brought in valuable new information and ideas. Greek art was powerfully shaped by Egyptian and Near Eastern models that were always adapted and changed rather than copied. The growth of trade often produced social and economic strain, leading to the overthrow of traditional aristocratic regimes by tyrants. Because monarchic rule was anathema to the Greeks, these regimes were temporary. They were usually replaced by oligarchies of greater or lesser breadth, but in Athens the destruction of the tyranny brought the world's first democracy. Sparta, on the other hand, developed a uniquely stable government that avoided tyranny over its citizens and impressed the other Greeks.

The Greeks' time of independent development, untroubled by external forces, came to an end in the sixth century B.C., when Iran's powerful Achaemenid dynasty conquered the Greek cities of Asia Minor. When the Persian kings tried to conquer the Greek mainland, however, the leading *poleis*—Sparta, Athens, Corinth, and Thebes—managed to put their quarrels aside and unite against the common enemy. Their determination to preserve their freedom carried them to victory over tremendous odds.

Suggested Readings

A. ANDREWES, *Greek Tyrants* (1963). A clear and concise account of tyranny in early Greece.

A. ANDREWES, *The Greeks* (1967). A thoughtful general survey.

JOHN BOARDMAN, *The Greeks Overseas* (1964). A study of the relations between the Greeks and other peoples.

A. R. BURN, *The Lyric Age of Greece* (1960). A discussion of early Greece that uses the evidence of poetry and archaeology to fill out the sparse historical record.

A. R. BURN, *Persia and the Greeks,* 2nd ed. (1984). A thorough narrative and analysis of the conflict between the Persians and the Greeks down to 479 B.C.

J. B. BURY and R. MEIGGS, *A History of Greece,* 4th ed., (1975). A thorough and detailed one-volume narrative history.

P. CARTLEDGE, *Sparta and Lakonia* (1979).

J. CHADWICK, *The Mycenaean World* (1976). A readable account by a man who helped decipher Mycenaean writing.

E. R. DODDS, *The Greeks and the Irrational* (1955). An excellent account of the role of the supernatural in Greek life and thought.

R. DREWS, *The Coming of the Greeks* (1988). A fine discussion of the Greeks' arrival as part of the movements of the Indo-European peoples.

V. EHRENBERG, *From Solon to Socrates* (1968). An interpretive history that makes good use of Greek literature to illuminate politics.

V. EHRENBERG, *The Greek State* (1964). A good handbook of constitutional history.

J. V. Fine, *The Ancient Greeks* (1983). An excellent survey that discusses historical problems and the evidence that gives rise to them.

M. I. Finley, *Early Greece* (1970). A succinct interpretive study.

M. I. Finley, *World of Odysseus,* rev. ed. (1965). A fascinating attempt to reconstruct Homeric society.

W. G. Forrest, *The Emergence of Greek Democracy* (1966). A lively interpretation of Greek social and political developments in the archaic period.

P. Green, *Xerxes at Salamis* (1970). A lively and stimulating history of the Persian War.

C. Hignett, *A History of the Athenian Constitution* (1952). A scholarly account, somewhat too skeptical of the ancient sources.

C. Hignett, *Xerxes' Invasion of Greece* (1963). A valuable account, but too critical of all sources other than Herodotus.

S. Hood, *The Minoans* (1971). A sketch of Bronze Age civilization on Crete.

D. Kagan, *The Great Dialogue: A History of Greek Political Thought from Homer to Polybius* (1965). A discussion of the relationship between the Greek historical experience and political theory.

G. S. Kirk, *The Songs of Homer* (1962). A discussion of the Homeric epics as oral poetry.

H. D. F. Kitto, *The Greeks* (1951). A personal and illuminating interpretation of Greek culture.

W. K. Lacey, *The Family in Ancient Greece* (1984).

H. L. Lorimer, *Homer and the Monuments* (1950). A study of the relationship between the Homeric poems and the evidence of archaeology.

O. Murray, *Early Greece* (1980). A lively and imaginative account of the early history of Greece to the end of the Persian War.

D. L. Page, *History and the Homeric Iliad,* 2nd ed. (1966). A well-written and interesting, if debatable, attempt to place the Trojan War in a historical setting.

G. M. A. Richter, *Archaic Greek Art* (1949).

C. Roebuck, *Economy and Society in the Early Greek World* (1984). A valuable study.

B. Snell, *Discovery of the Mind* (1960). An important study of Greek intellectual development.

A. M. Snodgrass, *The Dark Age of Greece* (1972). A good examination of the archaeological evidence.

C. G. Starr, *The Economic and Social Growth of Early Greece, 800–500* B.C. (1977).

C. G. Starr, *Origins of Greek Civilization, 1100–650* B.C. (1961). An interesting interpretation based largely on archaeology and especially on pottery styles.

Emily Vermeule, *Greece in the Bronze Age* (1972). A study of the Mycenaean period.

A. G. Woodhead, *Greeks in the West* (1962). An account of the Greek settlements in Italy and Sicily.

W. J. Woodhouse, *Solon the Liberator* (1965). A discussion of the great Athenian reformer.

D. C. Young, *The Olympic Myth of Greek Athletics* (1984). A lively challenge to the orthodox view that Greek athletes were amateurs.

The striding god from Artemisium. This bronze statue dating about 460 B.C. was found in the sea near Artemisium, the northern tip of the large Greek island of Euboea. Exactly whom he represents is not known. Some have thought him to be Poseidon holding a trident; others believe that he is Zeus hurling a thunderbolt. In either case, he is a splendid representative of the early classical period of Greek sculpture and now lives at the Athens archaeological museum. [Bettmann Archive]

Classical and Hellenistic Greece

4

Classical Greece

The Greeks' remarkable victory over the Persians in 480–479 B.C. won them another period of freedom and autonomy, a time when they carried their political and cultural achievement to its height. In Athens, especially, the victory produced a great sense of confidence and ambition. Spartan withdrawal from active leadership against the Persians left a vacuum that was filled by the Delian League, which soon turned into the Athenian Empire.

At the same time as it tightened its hold over the Greek cities in and around the Aegean Sea, Athens developed an extraordinarily democratic constitution at home. Fears and jealousies of this new kind of state and empire created a split in the Greek world that led to a series of major wars. These wars impoverished Greece and left it vulnerable to conquest. In 338 B.C. Philip of Macedon conquered the Greek states, putting an end to the age of the *polis*.

The Delian League

The unity of the Greeks had shown strain even in the life-and-death struggle against the Persians. Within two years of the Persian retreat, the unity yielded almost completely to a division of the Greek world into two spheres of influence, dominated by Sparta and Athens. The need of the Ionian Greeks to obtain and defend their freedom from Persia and the desire of many Greeks to gain revenge and financial reparation for the Persian attack brought on the split.

Sparta had led the Greeks to victory, and it was natural to look to the Spartans to continue the campaign. But Sparta was ill-suited to the task, which re-

113

quired a long-term commitment and continuous naval action far from the Peloponnesus.

The emergence of Athens as the leader of a Greek coalition against Persia was a natural development. Athens had become the leading naval power in Greece, and the same motives that had led Athens to support the Ionian revolt moved it to try to drive the Persians from the Aegean and the Hellespont. The Ionians were at least as eager for the Athenians to take the helm as the Athenians were to accept the responsibility and opportunity.

In the winter of 478–477 B.C., the islanders, the Greeks from the coast of Asia Minor, and some from other Greek cities on the Aegean met with the Athenians on the sacred island of Delos. Here, they swore oaths of alliance. As a symbol that the alliance was meant to be permanent, they dropped lumps of iron into the sea; the alliance was to hold until these rose to the surface.

The aims of this new Delian League were to free those Greeks who were under Persian rule, to protect all against a Persian return, and to obtain compensation from the Persians by attacking their lands and taking booty. League policy was determined by a vote of the assembly in which each state, including Athens, had one vote. Athens, however, was clearly designated leader.

These potsherds from fifth-century B.C. Athens were used as ballots in the process by which citizens were banished from Athens. They are inscribed with the names of two famous Athenian statesmen, Themistocles, son of Neocles, and Aristides, son of Lysimachus. At different times each man was banished from Athens for ten years. [Agora Excavations, American School of Classical Studies at Athens]

KEY EVENTS IN ATHENIAN HISTORY BETWEEN THE PERSIAN WAR AND THE GREAT PELOPONNESIAN WAR

478–477 B.C.	Delian League founded
ca. 474–462 B.C.	Cimon leading politician
467 B.C.	Victory over Persians at Eurymedon River
465–463 B.C.	Rebellion of Thasos
462 B.C.	Ephialtes murdered; Pericles rises to leadership
461 B.C.	Cimon ostracized
461 B.C.	Reform of Areopagus
ca. 460 B.C.	First Peloponnesian War begins
454 B.C.	Athens defeated in Egypt; crisis in the Delian League
449 B.C.	Peace with Persia
445 B.C.	Thirty Years' Peace ends First Peloponnesian War

From the first, the league was remarkably successful. The Persians were driven from Europe and the Hellespont, and the Aegean was cleared of pirates. Some states were forced into the league or were prevented from leaving. The members approved coercion because they believed it was necessary for the common safety. In 467 B.C., a great victory over the Persians at the Eurymedon River in Asia Minor routed the Persians and added a number of cities to the league.

Cimon, son of Miltiades, the hero of Marathon, became the leading Athenian soldier and statesman soon after the Persian War. Themistocles appears to have been driven from power by a coalition of his enemies. Ironically, the author of the Greek victory over Persia of 480 B.C. was ostracized and ended his days at the court of the Persian king. Cimon, who was to dominate Athenian politics for almost two decades, pursued a policy of aggressive attacks on Persia and friendly relations with Sparta. In domestic affairs, Cimon was conservative. He accepted the democratic constitution of Clisthenes, which appears to have become somewhat more limited after the Persian War. Defending this constitution and this foreign policy, Cimon led the Athenians and the Delian League to victory after victory. His own popularity grew with success.

The First Peloponnesian War

In 465 B.C., the island of Thasos rebelled against the league. After a siege of more than two years, Cimon forced an end to the rebellion. The revolt of Thasos had an important influence on the development of the Delian League, on Athenian politics, and on relations between Athens and Sparta. It was the first recorded instance in which Athenian interests alone seem to have determined league policy, a significant step in the evolution of the Delian League into the Athenian Empire. When Cimon returned to Athens from Thasos, he was charged with taking bribes not to conquer Macedonia, although that was not part of his assignment. He was acquitted, and the trial was proved to be only a device by which his political opponents had tried to reduce his influence.

The democratic opposition's program at home was to undo the gains made by the conservative council, called the Areopagus, and to bring about further changes in the direction of democracy. Abroad, the enemies of Cimon wanted to break with Sparta and contest its claim to leadership over the Greeks. They intended at least to establish the independence of Athens and its alliance. The head of this faction was Ephialtes. His supporter, and the man chosen to be the public prosecutor of Cimon, was Pericles, a member of a distinguished Athenian family.

When the Thasians began their rebellion, they asked Sparta to invade Athens the next spring. The ephors agreed, but an earthquake, accompanied by a rebellion of the Helots that threatened the survival of Sparta, prevented the invasion. The Spartans asked their allies, the Athenians among them, for help. In Athens, Ephialtes urged the Athenians "not to help or restore a city that was a rival to Athens but to let Sparta lie low and be trampled underfoot," but Cimon persuaded them to send help. The results were disastrous. The Spartans sent the Athenian troops home, fearing "the boldness and revolutionary spirit of the Athenians." While Cimon was in the Peloponnesus helping the Spartans, Ephialtes stripped the Areopagus of almost all its power. In the spring of 461 B.C., Cimon was exiled, and Athens made an alliance with Argos, Sparta's traditional enemy. Almost overnight, Cimon's domestic and foreign policies had been overturned.

The new regime at Athens was confident and ambitious. When Megara, getting the worst of a border dispute with Corinth, withdrew from the Peloponnesian League, the Athenians accepted the Megarians as allies. This alliance gave Athens a great strategic advantage, for Megara barred the way from the Peloponnesus to Athens. The alliance also brought on the First Peloponnesian War, for Sparta resented the defection of Megara to Athens. The early years of the war brought Athens great success. The Athenians conquered Aegina and gained control of Boeotia. At one point, Athens was supreme and invulnerable, controlling the states on its borders and dominating the sea (see Map 4-1).

In 454 B.C., however, the tide turned. In that year, a disastrous defeat struck an Athenian fleet that had gone to aid an Egyptian rebellion against Persia. The great loss of men, ships, and prestige caused rebellions in the empire, forcing Athens to make a truce in Greece in order to subdue Athens' allies in the Aegean. In 449 B.C., the Athenians ended the war against Persia. In 446 B.C., the war on the Greek mainland broke out again. Rebellions in Boeotia and Megara removed Athens' land defenses and brought a Spartan invasion. Rather than fight, Pericles, the commander of the Athenian army, agreed to a peace of thirty years. By the terms of the agreement, he abandoned all Athenian possessions on the continent. In return, the Spartans gave formal recognition to the Athenian Empire. From then on, Greece was divided into two power blocs: Sparta and its alliance on the mainland and Athens ruling its empire in the Aegean.

The Athenian Empire

After the Egyptian disaster, the Athenians moved the Delian League's treasury to Athens and began to keep one-sixtieth of the annual revenues for themselves. As a result of the peace with Persia, there seemed no further reason for the allies to pay tribute. In spite of Athenian propaganda, nothing could cloak the fact that Athens was becoming the master and its allies mere subjects (see Map 4-2). By 445 B.C., only Chios, Lesbos, and Samos were autonomous and provided ships. All the other states paid tribute.

The change from alliance to empire came about because of the pressure of war and rebellion and in large measure because the allies were unwilling to see to their own defenses. The empire was not universally unpopular and had many friends among the lower classes and the democratic politicians. Nevertheless, it came to be seen more and more as a tyranny. But the Athenians had come to depend on the empire for prosperity and security. The Thirty Years' Peace of 445 B.C. had recognized the empire, and the Athenians were determined to defend it at any cost.

Black Sea

Heraclea

Astacus

Chalcedon

Byzantium

Cius

Dascylium

ASIA

MINOR

PISIDIA

PAMPHYLIA

LYCIA

Phaselis

Propontis

PHRYGIA

MYSIA

LYDIA

Magnesia

CARIA

Rhodes

Lampsacus

Cyzicus

RHODES

Cyme

Smyrna

Ephesus

Halicarnassus

THRACE

Abydos

TROAD

AEOLIS

Phocaea

Colophon

Notium

Priene

Miletus

CNIDUS

Sestos

Troy

Clazomenae

Elaeus

Methymna

Erythrae Teos

COS

Mytilene

Chios

SAMOS

Abdera

LESBOS

ICARIA

CARPATHOS

Philippi

SAMOTHRACE

Aegean

CHIOS

AMORGUS

Cretan

Amphipolis

IMBROS

ICARIA

Sea

Eion

Stagira

THASOS

Mt. Athos

Sea

ANDROS

NAXOS

Sea

Torone

LEMNOS

MYKONOS

Cnossus

PAEONIA

CHALCIDICE

Olynthus

SKYROS

TENOS

DELOS

CRETE

Pella

Thessalonica

Potidaea

Scione

PAROS

Cortyna

Tylissus

MACEDONIA

Methone

Pydna

SYROS

SERIPHOS

Mt. Olympus

CYNTHOS

SIPHNOS

MELOS

Carystus

Larisa

Mt. Pelium

Oropus

ANDROS

KEOS

EPIRUS

Pherae

ARTEMISIUM

EUBOEA

Chalcis

Eretria

Delium

Athens

ATTICA

Laureum

AEGINA

Epidaurus

Hermione

Dodona

THESSALY

LOCRIS

Elatea

BOEOTIA

Coronea

Decelea

Piraeus

SALAMIS

Ambracia

THERMOPYLAE

Mt.

Amphissa

Chaeronea

Plataea

Megara

CYTHERA

Parnassus

DELPHI

Thebes

Sicyon

Corinth

Nemea

Anactorium

AETOLIA

Naupactus

Leuctra

Argos

Cape

Malea

LEUCAS

ARCANANIA

Sollium

ACHAEA

ARCADIA

Tegea

Sparta

Cape

Taenarus

CEPHALLENIA

Mantinea

LACONIA

Gythium

ZACYNTHUS

Megalopolis

Mt. Taygetus

ELIS

Olympia

Messene

MESSENIA

Elis

Pylos

PELOPONNESUS

Ionian

Sea

Mediterranean Sea

Epidamnus

ILLYRIA

Apollonia

CORCYRA

MAP 4-1   CLASSICAL GREECE   *Greece in the classical period (ca. 480–338 B.C.) centered on the Aegean Sea. Although there were important Greek settlements in Italy, Sicily, and all around the Black Sea, the area shown in this general reference map (opposite page) embraced the vast majority of Greek states. The inset shows the location of the major monuments still visible on the Athenian Acropolis of the classical period.*

Athenian Democracy

Even as the Athenians were tightening their control over their allies at home, they were evolving the freest government the world had ever seen. This extension of the Athenian democracy took place chiefly under the guidance of Pericles, who succeeded to the lead-ership of the democratic faction after the assassination of Ephialtes in 462 B.C. Legislation was passed making the hoplite class eligible for the archonship. In theory, no adult male was thereafter prevented from serving on the basis of property class, although in practice almost all those elected to the highest offices came from aristocratic or wealthy families. Pericles himself proposed the law introducing pay for jury members, opening that important duty to the poor. Circuit judges were reintroduced, making swift impartial justice available even to the poorest residents in the countryside.

Finally, Pericles himself introduced a bill limiting citizenship to those who had two citizen parents. From a modern perspective, this measure might be seen as a step away from democracy, and, in fact, it

MAP 4-2   THE ATHENIAN EMPIRE ABOUT 450 B.C.   *The empire at its fullest extent. We see Athens and the independent states that provided manned ships for the imperial fleet but paid no tribute, dependent states that paid tribute, and states allied to but not actually in the empire.*

Thucydides Reports Pericles on Athenian Democracy

Pericles (ca. 495–429 B.C.) delivered this speech after the first campaigning season of the Great Peloponnesian War, probably late in the winter of 431 B.C. It is the most famous statement of the ideals of the Athenian imperial democracy.

▶ *For other perspectives on law, leadership, and government, see the following document boxes: "Hammurabi Creates a Code of Law in Mesopotamia" (Ch. 1), "Legalism" (Ch. 2), "Polybius Summarizes the Roman Constitution" (Ch. 5), "The Edicts of Ashoka" (Ch. 7), "Machiavelli Discusses the Most Important Trait for a Ruler" (Ch. 17), and "Some Reforms of Akbar" (Ch. 24).*

Our constitution does not copy the laws of neighbouring states; we are rather a pattern to others than imitators ourselves. Its administration favours the many instead of the few; this is why it is called a democracy. If we look to the laws, they afford equal justice to all in their private differences; if to social standing, advancement in public life falls to reputation for capacity, class considerations not being allowed to interfere with merit; nor again does poverty bar the way, if a man is able to serve the state, he is not hindered by the obscurity of his condition. The freedom which we enjoy in our government extends also to our ordinary life. There, far from exercising a jealous surveillance over each other, we do not feel called upon to be angry with our neighbour for doing what he likes, or even to indulge in those injurious looks which cannot fail to be offensive, although they inflict no positive penalty. But all this ease in our private relations does not make us lawless as citizens. . . . Our public men have, besides politics, their private affairs to attend to, and our ordinary citizens, though occupied with the pursuits of industry, are still fair judges of public matters; for, unlike any other nation, regarding him who takes no part in these duties not as unambitious but as useless, we Athenians are able to judge at all events if we cannot originate, and instead of looking on discussion as a stumbling-block in the way of action, we think it an indispensable preliminary to any wise action at all. . . .

In short, I say that as a city we are the school of Hellas; while I doubt if the world can produce a man, who where he has only himself to depend upon, is equal to so many emergencies, and graced by so happy a versatility as the Athenian.

Thucydides, *The Peloponnesian War,* trans. by Richard Crawley (New York: Random House, 1951), pp. 104–106.

would have barred Cimon and one of Pericles' ancestors. In Greek terms, however, it was quite natural. Democracy was defined in terms of those who held citizenship, and because citizenship had become a valuable commodity, the decision to limit it must have won a large majority. Participation in government in all the Greek states was denied to slaves, resident aliens, and women.

Within the citizen body, however, the extent of the democracy was remarkable. Every decision of the state had to be approved by the popular assembly—a collection of the people, not their representatives. Every judicial decision was subject to appeal to a popular court of not fewer than 51 and as many as 1,501 citizens, chosen from an annual panel of jurors widely representative of the Athenian male population. Most officials were selected by lot, without regard to class. The main elected officials, such as the generals and the imperial treasurers, were generally nobles and almost always rich men, but the people were free to choose others. All public officials were subject to scrutiny before taking office, could be called to account and removed from office during their tenure, and were held to a compulsory examination and accounting at the end of their terms. There was no standing army; no police force, open or secret; and no way to coerce the people.

If Pericles was elected to the generalship fifteen years in a row and thirty times in all, it was not because he was a dictator but because he was a persuasive speaker, a skillful politician, a respected general, an acknowledged patriot, and a man patently incorruptible. When he lost the people's confidence, they did not hesitate to depose him from office. In 443 B.C.,

A foundry is depicted on an Attic vase of the fifth century B.C. *Greek skill in metal work reached a high level by the fifth century. The major practical use was in weapons of war, but artistic applications, especially in bronze, were also important. Here we see an artisan stoking a furnace to maintain the high but carefully controlled temperature needed in his work.*

however, after the removal of his chief rival, he stood at the height of his power. He had been persuaded by the defeat of the Athenian fleet in the Egyptian campaign and the failure of Athens' continental campaigns that its future lay in a conservative policy of retaining the empire in the Aegean and living at peace with the Spartans. It was in this direction that he led Athens' imperial democracy in the years after the First Peloponnesian War.

Women of Athens

Greek society, like most cultures, was dominated by men. This was true of the democratic city of Athens in the great days of Pericles, in the fifth century B.C., no less than in other Greek cities. Nonetheless, the position of women in classical Athens has been the subject of much controversy. The bulk of the evidence—coming from the law, from philosophical and moral writings, and from information about the conditions of daily life and the organization of society—shows that women were excluded from most aspects of public life. They could not vote, take part in the political assemblies, hold public office, or take any direct part in politics. Male citizens of all classes had these public responsibilities and opportunities.

The same sources show that in the private aspects of life, women were always under the control of a male guardian: a father, a husband, or, failing these, an appropriate male relative. Women married young, usually between the ages of twelve and eighteen, whereas their husbands were typically over thirty; hence, they were always in a relationship like that of a daughter to a father. Marriages were arranged; the woman normally had no choice of husband, and her dowry was controlled by a male relative. Divorce was difficult for a woman to obtain, for she needed the approval of a male relative who was then willing to serve as her guardian after the dissolution of the marriage. In case of divorce, the dowry returned with the woman but was controlled by her father or the appropriate male relative.

The main function and responsibility of a respectable Athenian woman of a citizen family was to produce male heirs for the household *(oikos)* of her husband. If, however, her father's *oikos* lacked a male heir, the daughter became an *epikleros,* the "heiress" to the family property. In that case, she was required by law to marry the next of kin on her father's side in order to produce the desired male offspring. In the Athenian way of thinking, women were "lent" by one household to another for purposes of bearing and raising a male heir to continue the existence of the *oikos.*

Because the pure and legitimate lineage of the offspring was important, women were carefully segregated from men outside the family and were confined to the women's quarters in the house. Men might seek sexual gratification outside the house with prostitutes of high or low style, frequently recruited from abroad. But respectable women stayed home to raise the children, cook, weave cloth, and oversee the management of the household. The only public function of women was an important one in the various rituals and festivals of the state religion. Apart from these activities, Athenian women were expected to remain

Medea Bemoans the Condition of Women

In 431 B.C., Euripides (ca. 485–406 B.C.) presented his play Medea *at the Dionysiac festival in Athens. The heroine is a foreign woman who has unusual powers. In the speech that follows, she describes the fate of women in terms that appear to give an accurate account of the condition of women in fifth-century B.C. Athens.*

▶ *For comparative perspectives on the status of women at other times and places, see the following document boxes: "Chinese Women among the Nomads" (Ch. 9), "The Position of Women" (Ch. 9), "Women Industrial Workers Explain Their Economic Situation" (Ch. 27), "The Women of the Seneca Falls Convention Issue a Declaration of Female Independence" (Ch. 29), and "An English Feminist Defends the Right of the Female Franchise" (Ch. 30).*

Of all things which are living and can form a judgment
We women are the most unfortunate creatures.
Firstly, with an excess of wealth it is required
For us to buy a husband and take for our bodies
A master; for not to take one is even worse.
And now the question is serious whether we take
A good or bad one; for there is no easy escape
For a woman, nor can she say no to her marriage.
She arrives among new modes of behavior and manners,
And needs prophetic power, unless she has learned at home,
How best to manage him who shares the bed with her.

And if we work out all this well and carefully,
And the husband lives with us and lightly bears his yoke,
Then life is enviable. If not, I'd rather die.
A man, when he's tired of the company in his home,
Goes out of the house and puts an end to his boredom
And turns to a friend or companion of his own age.
But we are forced to keep our eyes on one alone.
What they say of us is that we have a peaceful time
Living at home, while they do the fighting in war.
How wrong they are! I would very much rather stand
Three times in the front of battle than bear one child.

Euripides, *Medea,* in *Four Tragedies,* trans. by Rex Warner (Chicago: University of Chicago Press, 1955), pp. 66–67.

---

home, quiet and unnoticed. Pericles told the widows and mothers of the Athenian men who died during the first year of the Peloponnesian War only this: "Your great glory is not to fall short of your natural character, and the greatest glory of women is to be least talked about by men, whether for good or bad."

This picture of women is largely accurate, but it does not fit well with what we learn from the evidence of the pictorial art, the tragedy and comedy, and the mythology of the Athenians. These sources often show women as central characters and powerful figures in both the public and the private spheres. Clytemnestra in Aeschylus's tragedy *Agamemnon* arranges the murder of her royal husband and establishes the tyranny of her lover, whom she dominates. The terrifying and powerful Medea negotiates with kings. We are left with an apparent contradiction clearly revealed by a famous speech in Euripides' tragedy *Medea.* (See the document on this page.)

The picture that Medea paints of women subjected to men accords well with much of the evidence, but we must take note of the fact that the woman who complains of women's lot is the powerful central figure in a tragedy bearing her name. This tragedy was produced at state expense before most of the Athenian population and was written by a man who was one of Athens' greatest poets and dramatists. Medea is a cause of terror to the audience and, at the same time, an object of their pity and sympathy as a victim of injustice. She is anything but the creature "least talked about by men, whether for good or for bad." There is reason to believe that the role played by Athenian women might have been more complex than their legal status might suggest.

The Great Peloponnesian War

In the decade after the Thirty Years' Peace of 445 B.C., the willingness of each side to respect the new arrangements was tested and not found wanting. About

435 B.C., however, a dispute arose in a remote and unimportant part of the Greek world, plunging the Greeks into a long and disastrous war that shook the foundations of their civilization. On one side stood Sparta and the Peloponnesian League; on the other Athens and its empire.

The Spartan strategy was traditional: to invade the enemy's country and threaten the crops, forcing the enemy to defend them in a hoplite battle. Such a battle the Spartans were sure to win, because they had the better army and they and their allies outnumbered the Athenians at least two to one. Any ordinary *polis* would have yielded or fought and lost, but Athens had an enormous navy, an annual income from the empire, a vast reserve fund, and long walls that connected the fortified city with the fortified port of Piraeus.

The Athenians' strategy was to allow devastation of the land to prove that Athens would not be defeated by the destruction of her crops, trees, and farmhouses. At the same time, the Athenians launched seaborne raids on the Peloponnesian coast to show that the allies of Sparta could be hurt. Pericles expected that within a year or two, three at most, the Peloponnesians would become discouraged and make peace, having learned their lesson. If the Peloponnesians held out, Athenian resources were inadequate to continue for more than four or five years without raising the tribute in the empire and running an unacceptable risk of rebellion. The plan required restraint and the leadership only Pericles could provide.

Ten years of war (431–421 B.C.) led to a stalemate concluded by the Peace of Nicias. The peace was for fifty years and guaranteed the status quo, with a few exceptions. Neither side carried out all its commitments, and several of Sparta's allies refused to ratify the peace.

In 415 B.C. Alcibiades, a young and ambitious leader, persuaded the Athenians to attack Sicily to bring it under their control. In 413 B.C., the entire expedition was destroyed. The Athenians lost some two hundred ships, about forty-five hundred of their own men, and almost ten times as many allies. It was a disaster perhaps greater than the defeat of the Athenian fleet in the Egyptian campaign some forty years earlier. It shook Athenian prestige, reduced the power of Athens, provoked rebellions, and brought the wealth and power of Persia into the war on Sparta's side.

It is remarkable that the Athenians were able to continue fighting in spite of the disaster. They sur-

THE GREAT PELOPONNESIAN WAR	
435 B.C.	Civil war at Epidamnus
432 B.C.	Sparta declares war on Athens
431 B.C.	Peloponnesian invasion of Athens
421 B.C.	Peace of Nicias
415–413 B.C.	Athenian invasion of Sicily
405 B.C.	Battle of Aegospotami
404 B.C.	Athens surrenders

vived a brief oligarchic coup in 411 B.C. and won several important victories at sea as the war shifted to the Aegean. As their allies rebelled, however, and were sustained by fleets paid for by Persia, the Athenians saw their financial resources shrink and finally disappear. When their fleet was caught napping at Aegospotami in 405 B.C., they could not build another. The Spartans—under Lysander, a clever and ambitious general who was responsible for obtaining Persian support—cut off the food supply through the Hellespont, and the Athenians were starved into submission. In 404 B.C., they surrendered unconditionally; the city walls were dismantled, Athens was permitted no fleet, and the empire was gone. The Great Peloponnesian War was over.

Struggle for Greek Leadership

THE HEGEMONY OF SPARTA. The collapse of the Athenian empire created a vacuum of power in the Aegean and opened the way for Spartan leadership, or hegemony. Fulfilling the contract that had brought them the funds to win the war, the Spartans handed the Greek cities of Asia Minor back to Persia. Under the leadership of Lysander, the Spartans went on to make a complete mockery of their promise to free the Greeks by stepping into the imperial role of Athens in the cities along the European coast and the islands of the Aegean. In most of the cities, Lysander installed a board of ten local oligarchs loyal to him and supported them with a Spartan garrison. Tribute brought in an annual revenue almost as great as that which the Athenians had collected.

Limited manpower, the Helot problem, and traditional conservatism all made Sparta less than an ideal state to rule a maritime empire. Some of Sparta's allies, especially Thebes and Corinth, were alienated by the increasing arrogance of Sparta's policies. In

404 B.C., Lysander installed an oligarchic government in Athens whose outrageous behavior earned them the title "Thirty Tyrants." Democratic exiles took refuge in Thebes and Corinth and created an army to challenge the oligarchy. Sparta's conservative king, Pausanias, replaced Lysander, arranging a peaceful settlement and ultimately the restoration of democracy. Thereafter, Athenian foreign policy remained under Spartan control, but otherwise Athens was free.

In 405 B.C., Darius II of Persia (r. 424–405 B.C.) died and was succeeded by Artaxerxes II. His younger brother, Cyrus, contested his rule and received Spartan help in recruiting a Greek mercenary army to help him win the throne. They marched inland as far as Mesopotamia, where they defeated the Persians at Cunaxa in 401 B.C., but Cyrus was killed. The Greeks were able to march back to the Black Sea and safety; their success revealed the potential weakness of the Persian Empire.

The Greeks of Asia Minor had supported Cyrus and were now afraid of Artaxerxes' revenge. The Spartans accepted their request for aid and sent an army into Asia, attracted by the prospect of prestige, power, and money. In 396 B.C., the command was given to Sparta's new king, Agesilaus (444–360 B.C.). His personality and policy dominated Sparta throughout its period of hegemony and until his death in 360 B.C. Hampered by his lameness and his disputed claim to the throne, he seems to have compensated for both by always advocating aggressive policies and providing himself with opportunities to display his bravery in battle.

SPARTAN AND THEBAN HEGEMONIES

404–403 B.C.	Thirty Tyrants rule at Athens
401 B.C.	Expedition of Cyrus, rebellious prince of Persia; Battle of Cunaxa
400–387 B.C.	Spartan War against Persia
398–360 B.C.	Reign of Agesilaus at Sparta
395–387 B.C.	Corinthian War
382 B.C.	Sparta seizes Thebes
378 B.C.	Second Athenian Confederation founded
371 B.C.	Thebans defeat Sparta at Leuctra; end of Spartan hegemony
362 B.C.	Battle of Mantinea; end of Theban hegemony

Agesilaus collected much booty and frightened the Persians. They sent a messenger with money and promises of further support to friendly factions in all the likely states. By 395 B.C., Thebes was able to organize an alliance that included Argos, Corinth, and a resurgent Athens. The result was the Corinthian War (395–387 B.C.), which put an end to Sparta's Asian adventure. In 394 B.C., the Persian fleet destroyed Sparta's maritime empire. Meanwhile the Athenians took advantage of events to rebuild their walls, enlarge their navy, and even to recover some of their lost empire in the Aegean. The war ended when the exhausted Greek states accepted a peace dictated by the Great King of Persia.

The Persians, frightened by the recovery of Athens, turned the management of Greece over to Sparta. Agesilaus broke up all alliances except the Peloponnesian League. He interfered with the autonomy of other *poleis* by using the Spartan army, or the threat of its use, to put friends in power within them. Sparta reached a new level of lawless arrogance in 382 B.C., when it seized Thebes during peacetime without warning or pretext. In 379 B.C., a Spartan army made a similar attempt on Athens. That action persuaded the Athenians to join with Thebes, which had rebelled from Sparta a few months earlier, to wage war on the Spartans. In 371 B.C., the Thebans, led by their great generals Pelopidas and Epaminondas, defeated the Spartans at Leuctra. The Thebans encouraged the Arcadian cities of the central Peloponnesus to form a federal league, freed the Helots, and helped them found a city of their own. They deprived Sparta of much of its farmland and of the men who worked it and hemmed it in with hostile neighbors. Sparta's population had shrunk, so it could put fewer than two thousand men into the field at Leuctra. Sparta's aggressive policies had led to ruin. The Theban victory brought the end of Sparta as a power of the first rank.

THEBAN HEGEMONY. Victorious Thebes had a democratic constitution, control over Boeotia, and two outstanding and popular generals, all of which formed the basis for Theban power after Leuctra. Pelopidas died in a successful attempt to gain control of Thessaly. Epaminondas consolidated his work, and Thebes was soon dominant over all Greece north of Athens and the Corinthian Gulf. The Thebans challenged the reborn Athenian empire in the Aegean.

All this activity provoked resistance, and by 362 B.C., Thebes faced a Peloponnesian coalition as well as Athens. Epaminondas once again led a victorious Boeotian army into the Peloponnesus at Mantinea but he died in the fight, and the loss of its two great leaders ended Thebes' dominance.

THE SECOND ATHENIAN EMPIRE. Athens had organized the Second Athenian Confederation in 378 B.C. It was aimed at resisting Spartan aggression in the Aegean, and its constitution was careful to avoid the abuses of the Delian League. But the Athenians soon began to repeat those abuses, although this time they did not have the power to put down resistance. When the collapse of Sparta and Thebes and the restraint of Persia removed any reason for voluntary membership, Athens' allies revolted. By 355 B.C., Athens had to abandon most of the empire. After two centuries of almost continuous warfare, the Greeks returned to the chaotic disorganization of the time before the founding of the Peloponnesian League.

Culture of Classical Greece

The repulse of the Persian invasion released a flood of creative activity in Greece rarely if ever matched anywhere at any time.

Fifth Century B.C.

The century-and-a-half between the Persian retreat and the conquest of Greece by Philip of Macedon (479–338 B.C.) produced achievements of such quality as to justify that era's designation as the Classical Period. Ironically, we often use the term *classical* to suggest calm and serenity, but the word that best describes the common element present in Greek life, thought, art, and literature in this period is *tension*. It was a time in which conflict among the *poleis* continued and intensified as Athens and Sparta gathered most of them into two competing and menacing blocs.

The victory over the Persians brought a sense of exultation in the capacity of humans to accomplish great things and a sense of confidence in the divine justice that brought arrogant pride low. But these feelings conflicted with a sense of unease as the Greeks recognized that the fate that had met Xerxes awaited all those who reached too far. Another source of tension was the conflict between the soaring hopes and achievements of individuals and the claims and limits put on them by their fellow citizens in the *polis*. These

forces were at work throughout Greece, but we know them best and they had the most spectacular results in Athens during its Golden Age, the time between the Persian and Peloponnesian wars.

ATTIC TRAGEDY. Nothing reflects these concerns better than the appearance of Attic tragedy as the major form of Greek poetry in the fifth century B.C. The tragedies were presented as part of public religious observations in honor of the god Dionysus.

The whole affair was very much a civic occasion. Each poet who wished to compete submitted his work to the archon. Each offered three tragedies, which might or might not have a common subject, and a satyr play (a comic choral dialogue with Dionysus) to close. The archon chose the best three competitors and awarded them each three actors and a chorus. The actors were paid by the state, and the chorus was provided by a wealthy citizen selected by the state to perform this service as *choregos,* for the Athenians had no direct taxation to support such activities. Most of the tragedies were performed in the theater of Dionysus on the south side of the Acropolis, and as many as thirty thousand Athenians could attend. Prizes and honors were awarded to the author, the actor, and the *choregos* voted best by a jury of Athenians chosen by lot. On rare occasions, the subject of the play might be a contemporary or historical event, but almost always it was chosen from mythology. Before Euripides, it always dealt solemnly with serious questions of religion, politics, ethics, morality, or some combination of these topics.

ARCHITECTURE AND SCULPTURE. The great architectural achievements of Periclean Athens, just as much as Athenian tragedy, illustrate the magnificent results of the union and tension between religious and civic responsibilities on the one hand and the transcendent genius of the individual artist on the other. Beginning in 448 B.C. and continuing until the outbreak of the Great Peloponnesian War, Pericles undertook a great building program on the Acropolis. The funds were provided by the income from the empire. The buildings were temples to honor the city's gods and a fitting gateway to the temples.

Pericles' main purpose seems to have been to represent visually the greatness and power of Athens, but in such a way as to emphasize intellectual and artistic achievement, civilization rather than military and naval power. It was as though these buildings were tangible proof of Pericles' claim that Athens was "the

The Acropolis was both the religious and civic center of Athens. In its final form it is the work of Pericles and his successors in the late fifth century B.C. This photograph shows the Parthenon and, to its left, the Erechtheum. [Greek National Tourist Office]

The porch of the maidens on the Erechtheum. This is a uniquely designed Ionic temple built on the Athenian Acropolis near the Parthenon between about 421 and 409 B.C. It housed the shrines of three different gods and presented special architectures in the porch facing the Parthenon. In place of the usual fluted columns, it uses statues of young girls taking part in a religious festival. Columns made from the draped female figure are called caryatids. *[Greek National Tourist Organization, New York]*

school of Hellas,"[1] that is, the intellectual center of all Greece.

HISTORY. The fifth century B.C. produced the first prose literature in the form of history. Herodotus, born shortly before the Persian War, deserves his title of the "father of history," for his account of the Persian War goes far beyond all previous chronicles, genealogies, and geographical studies. His history attempts to explain human actions and to draw instruction from them.

Herodotus accepted the evidence of legends and oracles, although not uncritically, and often explained human events in terms of divine intervention. Human arrogance and divine vengeance are key forces that help explain the defeat of Croesus by Cyrus as well as Xerxes' defeat by the Greeks. Yet the *History* is typical of its time in celebrating the crucial role of human intelligence as revealed by Miltiades at

[1]Thucydides, *The Peloponnesian War*, trans. by Richard Crawley (New York: Modern Library, 1982), p. 110.

The Theater at Epidaurus. This theater, built in the fourth century B.C., is one of the best preserved of ancient Greek theaters. Epidaurus, a city in the eastern Peloponnesus, was the site of the Sanctuary of Asclepius, the hero and god of healing. The sick and crippled came there, as to Lourdes in modern times, to be healed. The religious festivals included theatrical performances that drew large crowds. [Greek National Tourist Organization, New York]

Marathon and Themistocles at Salamis. Nor was Herodotus unaware of the importance of institutions. There is no mistaking his pride in the superiority of the Greek *polis* and the discipline it inspired in its citizen soldiers and his pride in the superiority of the Greeks' voluntary obedience to law over the Persians' fear of punishment.

Thucydides, the historian of the Peloponnesian War, was born about 460 B.C. and died a few years after the end of the Great Peloponnesian War. He was very much a product of the late fifth century B.C., reflecting the influence of the scientific attitude of the Hippocratic school of medicine as well as the secular, human-centered, skeptical rationalism of the Sophists. Hippocrates of Cos was a contemporary of Thucydides who was part of a school of medical writers and practitioners. They did important pioneer work in medicine and scientific theory, placing great emphasis on the need to combine careful and accurate observation with reason to make possible the understanding, prognosis, treatment, and cure of a disease.

In the same way, Thucydides took great pains to achieve factual accuracy and tried to use his evidence to discover meaningful patterns of human behavior. He believed that human nature was essentially unchanging, so that a wise person equipped with the understanding provided by history might accurately foresee events and thus help to guide them. He believed, however, that only a few had the ability to understand history and put its lessons to good use. He thought that even the wisest could be foiled by the

intervention of chance, which played a great role in human affairs. Thucydides focused his interest on politics, and in that area his assumptions about human nature do not seem unwarranted. His work has proved to be, as he had hoped, "a possession forever."[2] Its description of the terrible civil war between the two basic kinds of *poleis* is a final and fitting example of the tension that was the source of both the greatness and the decline of classical Greece.

Fourth Century B.C.

Historians often speak of the Great Peloponnesian War as the crisis of the *polis* and of the fourth century as the period of its decline. But the Greeks of the fourth century B.C. did not know that their traditional way of life was on the verge of destruction. Some looked to the past and tried to shore up the weakened structure of the *polis;* others tended toward despair and looked for new solutions; and still others averted their gaze from the public arena altogether. All of these responses are apparent in the literature, philosophy, and art of the period.

DRAMA. The tendency of some to avert their gaze from the life of the *polis* and to turn inward to everyday life, the family, and their own individuality is apparent in the poetry of the fourth century B.C. Tragedy

[2] Thucydides, *The Peloponnesian War,* Book 1, chap. 22, trans. by Donald Kagan (New York: Random House, 1982).

proved to be a form whose originality was confined to the fifth century B.C. No tragedies written in the fourth century B.C. have been preserved, and it was common to revive the great plays of the previous century. Some of the late plays of Euripides (ca. 484–406 B.C.), in fact, seem less like the tragedies of Aeschylus and Sophocles than forerunners of later forms such as the New Comedy (ca. 325–260 B.C.). Plays of Euripides like *Helena, Andromeda* and *Iphigenia in Tauris* are more like fairy tales, tales of adventure, or love stories than tragedies. Euripides was less interested in cosmic confrontations of conflicting principles than in the psychology and behavior of individual human beings. His plays, which rarely won first prize when first produced for Dionysian festival competitions, became increasingly popular during the fourth century B.C. and afterward.

Comedy was introduced into the Dionysian festival early in the fifth century B.C. Such poets as Cratinus, Eupolis, and the great master of the genre called Old Comedy, Aristophanes (ca. 450–ca. 385 B.C.), the only one from whom we have complete plays, wrote political comedies filled with scathing invective and satire against such contemporary figures as Pericles, Cleon, Socrates, and Euripides. The fourth century B.C., however, produced what is called Middle Comedy, which turned away from political subjects and personal invective toward a comic-realistic depiction of daily life, plots of intrigue, and mild satire of domestic situations. Significantly, the role of the chorus, which in some way represented the *polis,* was very much diminished. These trends all continued and were carried even further in the New Comedy, whose leading playwright, Menander (342–291 B.C.), completely abandoned mythological subjects in favor of domestic tragicomedy. His gentle satire of the foibles of ordinary people and his tales of lovers temporarily thwarted before a happy and proper ending would not be unfamiliar to viewers of modern situation comedies.

SCULPTURE. The same movement away from the grand, the ideal, and the general and toward the ordinary, the real, and the individual is apparent in the development of Greek sculpture. To see these developments, one has only to compare the statue of the *Striding God of Artemisium* (ca. 460 B.C.), thought to be either Zeus on the point of releasing a thunderbolt or Poseidon about to throw his trident, or the *Doryphoros* of Polycleitus (ca. 450–440 B.C.) to the *Hermes* of Praxiteles (ca. 340–330 B.C.) or the *Apoxyomenos* attributed to Lysippus (ca. 330 B.C.).

The Apoxyomenos, *attributed to the Greek sculptor Lysippus. Dating to ca. 330 B.C., it shows an athlete preparing for exercise. This is a Roman copy, in marble. The original was probably bronze. [Vatican Museum, xxv.19.33]*

Emergence of the Hellenistic World

The term *Hellenistic* was coined in the nineteenth century to describe the period of three centuries during which Greek culture spread far from its homeland to Egypt and far into Asia. The new civilization formed in this expansion was a mixture of Greek and Asian elements, although the degree of mixture varied from time to time and place to place. The Hellenistic world was larger than the world of classical Greece, and its major political units were much larger than the city-states, although they persisted in different forms. The new political and cultural order had its roots in the rise to power of a Macedonian dynasty that conquered Greece and the Persian Empire in the space of two generations.

Macedonian Conquest

The quarrels among the Greeks brought on defeat and conquest by a new power that suddenly rose to eminence in the fourth century B.C., the kingdom of Macedon. The Macedonians inhabited the land to the north of Thessaly, and through the centuries, they had unknowingly served the vital purpose of protecting the Greek states from barbarian tribes further to the north. By Greek standards, Macedon was a backward, semibarbaric land. It had no *poleis* and was ruled loosely by a king in a rather Homeric fashion. He was chosen partly on the basis of descent, but the acclamation of the army gathered in assembly was required to make him legitimate. Quarrels between pretenders to the throne and even murder to achieve it were not uncommon. A council of nobles checked the royal power and could reject a weak or incompetent king.

Hampered by constant wars with the barbarians, internal strife, loose organization, and lack of money, Macedon played no great part in Greek affairs up to the fourth century B.C. The Macedonians were of the same stock as the Greeks and spoke a Greek dialect, and the nobles, at least, thought of themselves as Greeks. The kings claimed descent from Heracles and the royal house of Argos. They tried to bring Greek culture into their court and won acceptance at the Olympic games. If a king could be found with the ability to unify this nation, it was bound to play a great part in Greek affairs.

PHILIP OF MACEDON. That king was Philip II (359–336 B.C.), who, while still under thirty, took advantage of his appointment as regent to overthrow his infant

RISE OF MACEDON	
359–336 B.C.	Reign of Philip II
338 B.C.	Battle of Chaeronea; Philip conquers Greece; founding of League of Corinth
336–323 B.C.	Reign of Alexander III, the Great
334 B.C.	Alexander invades Asia
333 B.C.	Battle of Issus
331 B.C.	Battle of Gaugamela
330 B.C.	Fall of Persepolis
327 B.C.	Alexander reaches Indus Valley
323 B.C.	Death of Alexander

nephew and make himself king. Like many of his predecessors, he admired Greek culture. Between 367 and 364 B.C., he had been a hostage in Thebes, where he learned much about Greek politics and warfare under the tutelage of Epaminondas. His natural talents for war and diplomacy and his boundless ambition made him the ablest king in Macedonian history. Using both diplomatic and military means, he was able to pacify the tribes on his frontiers and to make his own hold on the throne firmer.

Then he began to undermine Athenian control of the northern Aegean. He took Amphipolis, which gave him control of the Strymon valley and of the gold and silver mines of Mount Pangaeus. The income allowed him to found new cities, to bribe politicians in foreign towns, and to reorganize his army into the finest fighting force in the world.

INVASION OF GREECE. So armed, Philip turned south toward central Greece. His conquests threatened the vital interest of Athens, which still had a formidable fleet of three hundred ships.

Mosaic of a lion hunt from Pella, which became the royal capital of Macedon at the end of the fifth century B.C. The city developed rapidy under Philip II. [Bettmann Archive]

The Athens of 350 B.C. was not the Athens of Pericles. It had neither imperial revenue nor allies to share the burden of war on land or sea, and its own population was smaller than it had been in the fifth century B.C. The Athenians, therefore, were reluctant to go on expeditions themselves or even to send out mercenary armies under Athenian generals, for they had to be paid out of taxes or contributions from Athenian citizens.

The leading spokesman against these tendencies and the cautious foreign policy that went with them was Demosthenes (384–322 B.C.), one of the greatest orators in Greek history. He was convinced that Philip was a dangerous enemy to Athens and the other Greeks and spent most of his career urging the Athenians to resist Philip's encroachments. He was right, for beginning in 349 B.C., Philip attacked several cities in northern and central Greece and firmly planted Macedonian power in those regions. The king of "barbarian" Macedon was elected president of the Pythian Games at Delphi, and the Athenians were forced to concur in the election.

The years between 346 B.C. and 340 B.C. were spent in diplomatic maneuvering, each side trying to win strategically useful allies. At last, Philip attacked Perinthus and Byzantium, the lifeline of Athenian commerce, and in 340 B.C. he besieged both cities and declared war. The Athenian fleet saved both, so in the following year Philip marched into Greece. Demosthenes performed wonders in rallying the Athenians and winning Thebes over to the Athenian side, but in 338 B.C. Philip defeated the allied forces at Chaeronea in Boeotia in a great battle whose decisive blow was a cavalry charge led by the eighteen-year-old son of Philip, Alexander.

MACEDONIAN GOVERNMENT OF GREECE. The Macedonian settlement of Greek affairs was not as harsh as many had feared, although in some cities the friends of Macedon came to power and killed or exiled their enemies. Demosthenes continued to be free or engage in politics, and Athens was not attacked on the condition that it give up what was left of its empire and follow the lead of Macedon. The rest of Greece

Demosthenes Denounces Philip of Macedon

Demosthenes (384–322 B.C.) was an Athenian statesman who urged his fellow citizens and other Greeks to resist the advances of Philip of Macedon (ca. 359–336 B.C.). The following is from the speech we call the First Philippic, delivered probably in 351 B.C.

Do not imagine, that his empire is everlastingly secured to him as a god. There are those who hate and envy him, Athenians, even among those that are most friendly; and all feelings that are in other men belong, we may assume, to his confederates. But now they are cowed, having no refuge through your tardiness and indolence, which I say you must abandon forthwith. For you see, Athenians, the case, to what pitch of arrogance the man has advanced, who leaves you not even the choice of action or inaction, but threatens and uses (they say) outrageous language, and, unable to rest in possession of his conquests, continually widens their circle, and whilst we dally and delay, throws his net all around us. When then, Athe-

nians, when will ye act as becomes you? In what event? In that of necessity, I suppose. And how should we regard the events happening now? Methinks, to freemen the strongest necessity is the disgrace of their condition. Or tell me, do ye like walking about and asking one another:—is there any news? Why, could there be greater news than a man of Macedonia subduing Athenians, and directing the affairs of Greece? Is Philip dead? No, but he is sick. And what matters it to you? Should anything befall this man, you will soon create another Philip, if you attend to business thus. For even he has been exalted not so much by his own strength, as by our negligence.

Demosthenes, *The Olynthiac and Other Public Orations of Demosthenes*, trans. by C. R. Kennedy (London: George Bell and Sons, 1903), pp. 62–63.

Alexander on horseback. This is an equestrian statue believed to be of Alexander the Great (356–323 B.C.), the Macedonian king who conquered the Persian empire. The statue is cast in bronze and is thought to be a copy of an original by Lysippus. [National Museum, Naples]

was arranged in such a way as to remove all dangers to Philip's rule. To guarantee his security, Philip placed garrisons at Thebes, Chalcis, and Corinth; these garrisons came to be known as the "fetters of Greece." In 338 B.C., Philip called a meeting of the Greek states to form the Federal League of Corinth. The constitution provided for autonomy, freedom from tribute and garrisons, and suppression of piracy and civil war. The league delegates would make foreign policy, in theory without consulting their home governments or Philip. All this was a facade; not only was Philip of Macedon president of the league, but also he was its ruler. The defeat at Chaeronea meant the end of Greek freedom and autonomy. Although its form and internal life continued for some time, the *polis* had lost control of its own affairs and the special conditions that had made it unique.

Philip's choice of Corinth as the seat of his new confederacy was not made out of convenience or by accident. It was at Corinth that the Greeks had gathered to resist a Persian invasion almost 150 years earlier, and it was there in 337 B.C. that Philip announced his intention to invade Persia in a war of liberation and revenge as leader of the new league. In the spring

of 336 B.C., as he prepared to begin the campaign, Philip was assassinated.

In 1977, a mound was excavated at the Macedonian village of Vergina. The extraordinarily rich finds and associated buildings have led many scholars to conclude that this is the royal tomb of Philip II. If they are right, and the evidence seems persuasive, Philip richly deserved so distinguished a resting place. He found Macedon a disunited kingdom of semibarbarians, despised and exploited by the Greeks. At his death, Macedon was a united kingdom; master and leader of the Greeks; rich, powerful, and ready to undertake the invasion of Asia. The completion of this task was left to Philip's first son, Alexander III (356–323 B.C.), later called Alexander the Great, who came to the throne at the age of twenty.

Alexander the Great

Along with his throne, the young king Alexander inherited his father's plan to invade Persia. The idea was daring, for Persia's empire was vast and its resources enormous, but the usurper Cyrus and his Greek mercenaries had shown its vulnerability by penetrating deep into the Persian Empire at the beginning of the fourth century B.C.

THE CONQUEST OF PERSIA AND BEYOND. In 334 B.C., Alexander crossed the Hellespont into Asia. His army consisted of about thirty thousand infantry and five thousand cavalry; he had no navy and little money. These facts determined his early strategy: He aimed to seek quick and decisive battles to gain money and supplies from the conquered territory. He moved along the coast so as to neutralize the Persian navy by depriving it of ports.

Alexander met the Persian forces of Asia Minor at the Granicus River, where he won a smashing victory in characteristic style (see Map 4-3). He led a cavalry charge across the river into the teeth of the enemy on the opposite bank, almost losing his life in the process and winning the devotion of his soldiers. That victory left the coast of Asia Minor open, and Alexander captured the coastal cities, thus denying them to the Persian fleet.

In 333 B.C., Alexander marched inland to Syria, where he met the main Persian army under King Darius at Issus. Alexander himself led the cavalry charge that broke the Persian line and sent Darius fleeing to the east. He continued along the coast and captured previously impregnable Tyre after a long and ingenious siege, putting an end to the threat of the Persian navy. He took Egypt with little trouble and was greeted as liberator, pharaoh, and son of Re (the Egyptian god whose Greek equivalent was Zeus). At Tyre, Darius sent Alexander a peace offer, yielding his entire empire west of the Euphrates River and his daughter in exchange for an alliance and an end to the invasion. But Alexander aimed at conquering the whole empire and probably whatever lay beyond that.

MAP 4-3 ALEXANDER'S CAMPAIGNS *The route taken by Alexander the Great in his conquest of the Persian Empire, 334–323 B.C. Starting from the Macedonian capital at Pella, he reached the Indus valley before being turned back by his own restive troops. He died of fever in Mesopotamia.*

Arrian Describes Alexander's Actions at a Tragic Drinking Party

Arrian lived in the second century A.D., *almost five hundred years after Alexander the Great, but his* Anabasis *is the best ancient source of information about Alexander's career. In 328* B.C., *Alexander's expedition had reached Samarkand. By now he had adopted a number of Persian customs and had begun to reduce the distinction between Macedonians and Persians. The older Macedonians, in particular, were resentful, and the following passage describes a drinking bout in which a quarrel arose between Alexander and one of the most distinguished Macedonian veterans.*

When the drinking-party on this occasion had already gone on too long (for Alexander had now made innovations even in regard to drinking, by imitating too much the custom of foreigners), and in the midst of the carouse a discussion had arisen about the Dioscuri, how their procreation had been taken away from Tyndareus and ascribed to Zeus, some of those present, in order to flatter Alexander, maintained that Polyleuces and Castor were in no way worthy to compare with him and his exploits. Such men have always destroyed and will never cease to ruin the interests of those who happen to be reigning. In their carousal they did not even abstain from comparing him with Heracles, saying that envy stood in the way of the living receiving the honours due to them from their associates. It was well known that Clitus had long been vexed at Alexander for the change in his style of living in excessive imitation of foreign customs, and at those who flattered him with their speech. At that time also, being heated with wine, he would not permit them either to insult the deity or, by depreciating the deeds of the ancient heroes, to confer upon Alexander this gratification which deserved no thanks. He affirmed Alexander's deeds were neither in fact at all so great or marvellous as they represented in their laudation; nor had he achieved them by himself, but for the most part they were the deeds of the Macedonians. The delivery of this speech annoyed Alexander; and I do not commend it, for I think, in such a drunken bout, it would have been sufficient if, so far as he was personally concerned,

he had kept silence, and not committed the error of indulging in the same flattery as the others. But when some even mentioned Philip's actions without exercising a just judgment, declaring that he had performed nothing great or marvellous, they herein gratified Alexander; but Clitus being then no longer able to contain himself, began to put Philip's achievements in the first rank, and to depreciate Alexander and his performances. Clitus being now quite intoxicated, made other depreciatory remarks and even vehemently reviled him, because after all he had saved his life, when the cavalry battle had been fought with the Persians at the Granicus. Then indeed, arrogantly stretching out his right hand, he said, "This hand, O Alexander, preserved you on that occasion." Alexander could now no longer endure the drunken insolence of Clitus; but jumped up against him in a great rage. He was however restrained by his boon companions. As Clitus did not desist from his insulting remarks, Alexander shouted out a summons for his shield-bearing guards to attend him; but when no one obeyed him, he said that he was reduced to the same position as Darius, when he was led about under arrest by Bessus and his adherents, and that he now possessed the mere name of king. Then his companions were no longer able to restrain him; for according to some he leaped up and snatched a javelin from one of his confidential bodyguards; according to others, a long pike from one of his ordinary guards, with which he struck Clitus and killed him.

Arrian, *The Anabasis of Alexander*, trans. by E. J. Chinnock in *The Greek Historians*, ed. by F. R. B. Godolphin, Vol. 2 (New York: Random House, 1942), pp. 507–508.

In the spring of 331 B.C., Alexander marched into Mesopotamia. At Gaugamela, near the ancient Assyrian city of Nineveh, he met Darius, ready for a last stand. Once again, Alexander's tactical genius and

personal leadership carried the day. The Persians were broken and Darius fled once more. Alexander entered Babylon, again hailed as liberator and king. In January of 330 B.C., he came to Persepolis, the Per-

Alexander defeats Darius at the Battle of Issus, 333 B.C. *This Roman mosaic from Pompeii, dating to the first century* B.C., *depicts the important Macedonian victory. It shows Alexander the Great on horseback, his eyes meeting those of Darius, the Persian king, on his chariot. [National Museum, Naples]*

sian capital, which held splendid palaces and the royal treasury. This bonanza ended his financial troubles and put a vast sum of money into circulation, with economic consequences that lasted for centuries. After a stay of several months, Alexander burned Persepolis to dramatize the completion of Hellenic revenge for the Persian invasion and the destruction of the native Persian dynasty.

The new regime could not be secure while Darius lived, so Alexander pursued him eastward. Just south of the Caspian Sea, he came upon the corpse of Darius, killed by Darius's relative Bessus. The Persian nobles around Darius had lost faith in him and had joined in the plot. Although the murder removed Darius from Alexander's path, he now had to catch Bessus, who proclaimed himself successor to Darius. The pursuit of Bessus (who was soon caught), a great curiosity, and a longing to go as far as he could and see the most distant places took Alexander to the frontier of India.

Near Samarkand, in the land of the Scythians, he founded the city of Alexandria Eschate ("Furthest Alexandria"), one of the many cities bearing his name that he founded as he traveled. As a part of his grand scheme of amalgamation and conquest, he married the Bactrian princess Roxane and enrolled thirty thousand young Bactrians for his army. They were to be trained and sent back to the center of the empire for later use.

In 327 B.C., Alexander took his army through the Khyber Pass in an attempt to conquer the lands around the Indus River (modern Pakistan). He reduced its king, Porus, to vassalage but pushed on in the hope of reaching the river called Ocean that the Greeks believed encircled the world. Finally, his weary men refused to go on. By the spring of 324 B.C., the army was back at the Persian Gulf and celebrated in the Macedonian style, with a wild spree of drinking.

DEATH OF ALEXANDER. Alexander was filled with plans for the future; for the consolidation and organization of his empire; for geographic exploration; for building new cities, roads, and harbors; perhaps even for further conquests in the west. There is even some evidence that he asked to be deified and worshiped as a god, although we cannot be sure if he really did so or what he had in mind if he did. In June of 323 B.C., he was overcome by a fever and died in Babylon at the age of thirty-three. His memory has never faded, and he soon became the subject of myth, legend, and romance. From the beginning, estimates of him have varied. Some have seen in him a man of grand and noble vision who transcended the narrow limits of Greek and Macedonian ethnocentrism and aimed at the brotherhood of humankind in a great world state. Others have seen him as a calculating despot, given to drunken brawls, brutality, and murder. The truth is probably in between. Alexander was one of the greatest generals the world has seen; he never lost a battle or failed in a siege, and with a modest army, he conquered a vast empire. He had rare organizational talents, and his plan for creating a multinational empire was the only intelligent way of proceeding. He established many new cities—seventy, according to tradition—mostly along trade routes. These cities encouraged commerce and prosperity and introduced Hellenic civilization into new areas. It is hard to know if the vast new empire could have been held together, but Alexander's death proved that only he could have succeeded.

Nobody was prepared for Alexander's sudden death in 323 B.C., and affairs were further complicated by a weak succession: Roxane's unborn child and Alexander's weak-minded half-brother. His able and loyal Macedonian generals at first hoped to preserve the empire for the Macedonian royal house, and to this end, they appointed themselves governors of the various provinces of the empire. However, the conflicting ambitions of these strong-willed men led to prolonged warfare among various combinations of them, in which three of the original number were killed, and all of the direct members of the Macedonian royal house were either executed or murdered. With the murder of Roxane and her son in 310 B.C., there was no longer any focus for the enormous empire, and in 306 and 305 B.C. the surviving governors proclaimed themselves kings of their various holdings. Three of these generals—Ptolemy I, Seleucus I, and Antigonus I—founded dynasties of significance in the spread of Hellenistic culture.

For the first seventy-five years or so after the death of Alexander, the world ruled by his successors en-

---

HELLENISTIC DYNASTIES

Ptolemy I ?367–283 B.C.)	Founder of the Thirty-first Dynasty in Egypt, the Ptolemies, of whom Cleopatra, who died in 30 B.C., was the last
Seleucus I (?358–280 B.C.)	Founder of the Seleucid dynasty in Mesopotamia
Antigonus I (382–301 B.C.)	Founder of the Antigonid dynasty in Asia Minor and Macedon

---

joyed considerable prosperity. The vast sums of money he and they had put into circulation greatly increased the level of economic activity. The opportunities for service and profit in the east attracted many Greeks and relieved their native cities of some of the pressure of the poor. The opening of vast new territories to Greek trade, the increased demand for Greek products, and the new availability of things wanted by the Greeks, as well as the conscious policies of the Hellenistic kings, all helped the growth of commerce. The new prosperity, however, was not evenly distributed. The urban Greeks, the Macedonians, and the Hellenized natives who made up the upper and middle classes lived lives of comfort and even luxury, but the rural native peasants did not. During prosperous times, these distinctions were bearable, although even then there was tension between the two groups.

After a while, however, the costs of continuing wars, inflation, and a gradual lessening of the positive effects of the introduction of Persian wealth led to economic crisis. The kings bore down heavily on the middle classes, who, however, were skilled in avoiding their responsibilities. The pressure on the peasants and the city laborers became great, too, and they responded by slowing down their work and even by striking. In Greece, economic pressures brought clashes between rich and poor; demands for the abolition of debt and the redistribution of land; and even, on occasion, civil war.

These internal divisions, along with the international wars, weakened the capacity of the Hellenistic kingdoms to resist outside attack, and by the middle of the second century B.C. they were all gone, except for Egypt. The two centuries between Alexander and the Roman conquest, however, were of great and lasting importance. They saw the formation into a single political, economic, and cultural unit of the entire eastern Mediterranean coast and of Greece, Egypt, Mesopotamia, and the old Persian Empire. The period also saw the creation of a new culture that took root, at least in the urban portions of that vast area, one that deserves to be differentiated from the earlier one of the Greek city-states: Hellenistic culture.

Hellenistic Culture

The career of Alexander the Great marked a significant turning point in the thought of the Greeks as it was represented in literature, philosophy, religion, and art. His conquests and the establishment of the successor kingdoms put an end once and for all to the central role of the *polis* in Greek life and thought.

Deprived of control of their foreign affairs, their important internal arrangements determined by a foreign monarch, the postclassical cities lost the kind of political freedom that was basic to the old outlook. They were cities, perhaps—in a sense, even city-states—but not *poleis.* As time passed, they changed from sovereign states to municipal towns merged in military empires. Never again in antiquity would there be either a serious attack on or a defense of the *polis,* for its importance was gone. For the most part, the Greeks after Alexander turned away from political solutions for their problems and sought instead personal responses to their hopes and fears, particularly in religion, philosophy, and magic. The confident, sometimes arrogant, humanism of the fifth century B.C. gave way to a kind of resignation of fate, a recognition of helplessness before forces too great for humans to manage.

Philosophy

These developments are noticeable in the changes that overtook the established schools of philosophy as well as in the emergence of two new and influential groups of philosophers, the Epicureans and the Stoics. Athens' position as the center of philosophical studies was reinforced, for the Academy and the Lyceum continued in operation, and the new schools were also located in Athens. The Lyceum turned gradually away from the universal investigations of its

founder, Aristotle, even from his scientific interests, to become a center chiefly of literary and especially historical studies.

The Academy turned even further away from its tradition. It adopted the systematic Skepticism of Pyrrho of Elis, and under the leadership of Arcesilaus and Carneades, the Skeptics of the Academy became skilled at pointing out fallacies and weaknesses in the philosophies of the rival schools. They thought that nothing could be known and so consoled themselves and their followers by suggesting that nothing mattered. It was easy for them, therefore, to accept conventional morality and the world as it was. The Cynics, of course, continued to denounce convention and to advocate the crude life in accordance with nature, which some of them practiced publicly to the shock and outrage of respectable citizens. Neither of these views had much appeal to the middle-class city dweller of the third century B.C., who sought some basis for choosing a way of life now that the *polis* no longer provided one ready-made.

EPICUREANS. Epicurus of Athens (342–271 B.C.) formulated a new teaching that was embodied in the school he founded in his native city in 306 B.C. His philosophy conformed to the new mood in that its goal was not knowledge but human happiness, which he believed could be achieved if one followed a style of life based on reason. He took sense perception to be the basis of all human knowledge. The reality and reliability of sense perception rested on the acceptance of the physical universe described by the atomists, Democritus and Leucippus, in which atoms were continually falling through the void and giving off images that were in direct contact with the senses. These falling atoms could swerve in an arbitrary, unpredictable way to produce the combinations seen in the world; Epicurus thereby removed an element of determinism that existed in the Democritean system. When a person died, the atoms that composed the body dispersed so that the person had no further existence or perception and therefore nothing to fear after death. Epicurus believed that the gods existed but that they took no interest in human affairs. This belief amounted to a practical atheism, and Epicureans were often thought to be atheists.

The purpose of Epicurean physics was to liberate people from their fear of death, the gods, and all nonmaterial or supernatural powers. Epicurean ethics were hedonistic, that is, based on the acceptance of pleasure as true happiness. But Epicurus's definition of *pleasure* was chiefly negative: the absence of pain and trouble. The goal of the Epicureans was *ataraxia,* the condition of being undisturbed, without trouble, pain, or responsibility. Ideally, a man should have enough means to allow him to withdraw from the world and avoid business and public life; Epicurus even advised against marriage and children. He preached a life of genteel, restrained selfishness, which might appeal to intellectual men of means but was not calculated to be widely attractive.

STOICS.   Soon after Epicurus began teaching in his garden in Athens, Zeno of Citium in Cyprus (335–263 B.C.) established the Stoic school. Its name derived from the *Stoa Poikile,* or Painted Portico, in the Athenian Agora, where Zeno and his disciples walked and talked beginning about 300 B.C.

Like the Epicureans, the Stoics sought the happiness of the individual. Quite unlike them, the Stoics held a philosophy almost indistinguishable from religion. They believed that humans must live in harmony within themselves and in harmony with nature; for the Stoics, god and nature were the same. The guiding principle in nature was divine reason *(logos),* or fire. Every human had a spark of this divinity, and after death it returned to the eternal divine spirit. From time to time, the world was destroyed by fire, from the ashes of which a new world arose. The aim of humans, and the definition of human happiness, was the virtuous life, life lived in accordance with natural law, "when all actions promote the harmony of the spirit dwelling in the individual man with the will of him who orders the universe."[3] To live such a life required the knowledge possessed only by the wise, who knew what was good; what was evil; and what was neither, but "indifferent." Good and evil were dispositions of the mind or soul: Prudence, justice, courage, temperance, and so on were good, whereas folly, injustice, cowardice, and the like were evil. Life, health, pleasure, beauty, strength, wealth, and so on were neutral—morally indifferent—for they did not contribute either to happiness or to misery. Human misery came from an irrational mental contraction—from passion—which was a disease of the soul. The wise sought freedom from passion *(apatheia),* because passion arose from things that were morally indifferent.

Politically, the Stoics fit well into the new world. They thought of it as a single *polis* in which all human beings were children of god. Although they did not forbid political activity, and many Stoics took part in political life, withdrawal was obviously preferable because the usual subjects of political argument were indifferent. Because the Stoics aimed at inner harmony of the individual, because their aim was a life lived in accordance with the divine will, and because their attitude was fatalistic and their goal a form of apathy, they fit in well with the reality of post-Alexandrian life. In fact, the spread of Stoicism made simpler the task of creating a new political system that relied not on the active participation of the governed, but merely on their docile submission.

Literature

The literature of the Hellenistic period reflects the new intellectual currents and, even more, the new conditions of literary life and the new institutions created during that period. The center of literary production in the third and second centuries B.C. was the new city of Alexandria in Egypt. There the Ptolemies, the kings of Egypt during that time, founded the museum, a great research institute where scientists and scholars were supported by royal funds, and the library, which contained almost half a million volumes, or papyrus scrolls. In the library were the works making up the great body of past Greek literature of every kind, much of which has since been lost. The Alexandrian scholars saw to it that what they judged to be the best works were copied; they edited and criticized these works from the point of view of language, form, and content and wrote biographies of their authors. Much of their work was valuable and is responsible for the preservation of most of ancient literature. Some of it is dry, petty, quarrelsome, and simply foolish. At its best, however, it is full of learning and perception.

The scholarly atmosphere of Alexandria naturally gave rise to work in the field of history and its ancillary discipline, chronology. Eratosthenes (ca. 275–195 B.C.) established a chronology of important events dating from the Trojan War, and others undertook similar tasks. Contemporaries of Alexander, such as Ptolemy I, Aristobulus, and Nearchus, wrote what were apparently sober and essentially factual accounts of his career. Most of the work done by Hellenistic historians is known to us only in fragments cited by later writers, but it seems in general to have emphasized sensational and biographical detail rather than the rigorous impersonal analysis of a Thucydides.

[3] Diogenes Laertius, *Lives of Eminent Philosophers (Zeno)* (Cambridge, MA.: Harvard University Press, 1931–1938).

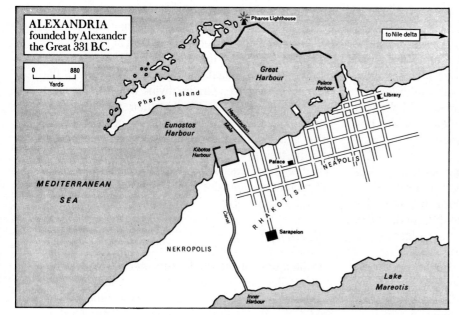

ALEXANDRIA
founded by Alexander
the Great 331 B.C.

0   880
Yards

Pharos Lighthouse

to Nile delta

Great
Harbour

Pharos   Island

Palace
Harbour

Library

Eunostos
Harbour

Hepstadion Mole

Kibotos
Harbour

Palace

NEAPOLIS

MEDITERRANEAN
SEA

R H A K O T I S

Canal

Sarapeion

NEKROPOLIS

Lake
Mareotis

Inner
Harbour

Map of Alexandria. Alexander the Great tended to build new cities along the major trade routes in his newly conquered provinces, several of which he allowed to be named for himself. Alexandria in Egypt was the only one to remain a place of consequence. His Macedonian successors, the Ptolemies, made it the capital of their Egyptian kingdom and a center of Hellenistic culture; its library and museum were famous centers of learning and scholarship, and its lighthouse, the Pharos, was a marvel of construction of the ancient world. [Michael Grant, Ancient History Atlas *(New York: Macmillan, 1971), p. 42]*

Architecture and Sculpture

The opportunities open to architects and sculptors were greatly increased by the advent of the Hellenistic monarchies. There were plenty of money, the royal need for conspicuous display, the need to build and beautify new cities, and a growing demand from the

well-to-do for objects of art. The new cities were usually laid out on the gridiron plan introduced in the fifth century B.C. by Hippodamus of Miletus. Temples were built on the classical model, and the covered portico or *stoa* became a very popular addition to the *agorai* of the Hellenistic towns.

Sculpture reflected the cosmopolitan nature of the Hellenistic world, for leading sculptors accepted commissions wherever they were attractive, and the result was a certain uniformity of style, although Alexandria, Rhodes, and the kingdom of Pergamum in Asia Minor developed their own characteristic styles. For the most part, Hellenistic sculpture carried forward the tendencies of the fourth century B.C., moving away from the balanced tension and idealism of the fifth century toward a sentimental, emotional, and realistic mode. These qualities are readily apparent in the statue of the *Dying Gaul,* dedicated by Attalus I, king of Pergamum, in about 23 B.C.

The mausoleum. This is a conjectural reconstruction of the tomb of King Mausolus of Caria in Asia Minor, which gave us the word "mausoleum." It was built at Halicarnassus in 353 B.C. by his widow, Queen Artemisia, and later made its way onto Hellenistic lists of wonders of the world. [Trewin Copplestone, general editor, World Architecture: An Illustrated History *(London: Hamlyn, 1963), p. 54]*

The Stoa of Attalus, Athens (left). Many Hellenistic kings sought to glorify their reigns by embellishing Athens in recognition of the city's intellectual fame. This two-story gallery of colonnaded shops was built by Attalus II, king of Pergamum (160–138 B.C.) in the Athenian Agora. It was reconstructed by American archaeologists and is now a museum. [American History Museum, Athens]

The Dying Gaul (right). This is a Roman copy of one of a group originally dedicated about 230 B.C. at the temple of Athena at Pergamum by Attalus I. It is now in the Museo Capitolino, Rome. [Bettmann Archive]

Mathematics and Science

Among the most spectacular and remarkable intellectual developments of the Hellenistic age were those that came in mathematics and science. It is not too much to say that the work done by the Alexandrians formed the greater part of the scientific knowledge available to the Western world until the scientific revolution of the sixteenth and seventeenth centuries A.D.

Euclid's *Elements* (written early in the third century B.C.) remained the textbook of plane and solid geometry until just recently. Archimedes of Syracuse (ca. 287–212 B.C.) made further progress in geometry, as well as establishing the theory of the lever in mechanics and inventing hydrostatics. The advances in mathematics, when added to the availability of Babylonian astronomical tables, allowed great progress in the field of astronomy. As early as the fourth century B.C., Heraclides of Pontus (ca. 390–310 B.C.) had argued that Mercury and Venus circulate around the sun and not the earth, and he appears to have made other suggestions leading in the direction of a heliocentric theory of the universe. Most scholars, however, give credit for that theory to Aristarchus of Samos (ca. 310–230 B.C.), who asserted that the sun,

Plutarch Cites Archimedes and Hellenistic Science

Archimedes (ca. 287–211 B.C.) was one of the great mathematicians and physicists of antiquity. He was a native of Syracuse in Sicily and a friend of its king. Plutarch discusses him in the following selection and reveals much about the ancient attitude toward applied science.

Archimedes, however, in writing to King Hiero, whose friend and near relation he was, had stated that given the force, any given weight might be moved, and even boasted, we are told, relying on the strength of demonstration, that if there were another earth, by going into it he could remove this. Hiero being struck with amazement at this, and entreating him to make good this problem by actual experiment, and show some great weight moved by a small engine, he fixed accordingly upon a ship of burden out of the king's arsenal, which could not be drawn out of the dock without great labour and many men; and, loading her with many passengers and a full freight, sitting himself the while far off, with no great endeav-our, but only holding the head of the pulley in his hand and drawing the cords by degrees. . . . Yet Archimedes possessed so high a spirit, so profound a soul, and such treasures of scientific knowledge, that though these inventions had now obtained him the renown of more than human sagacity, he yet would not deign to leave behind him any commentary or writing on such subjects; but, repudiating as sordid and ignoble the whole trade of engineering, and every sort of art that lends itself to mere use and profit, he placed his whole affection and ambition in those purer speculations where there can be no reference to the vulgar needs of life. . . .

Plutarch, "Marcellus," in *Lives of the Noble Grecians and Romans,* trans. by John Dryden, rev. by A. H. Clough (New York: Random House, n.d.), pp. 376–378.

---

along with the other fixed stars, did not move and that the earth revolved around the sun in a circular orbit and rotated on its axis while doing so.

The heliocentric theory ran contrary not only to the traditional view codified by Aristotle, but also to what seemed to be common sense. However, Hellenistic technology was not up to proving the theory, and, of course, the planetary orbits are not circular. The heliocentric theory did not, therefore, take hold. Hipparchus of Nicaea (b. ca. 190 B.C.) constructed a model of the universe on the geocentric theory, employing an ingenious and complicated design that did a very good job of accounting for the movements of the sun, the moon, and the planets. Ptolemy of Alexandria (second century A.D.) adopted Hipparchus's system with a few improvements, and it remained dominant until the work of Copernicus in the sixteenth century A.D.

Hellenistic scientists made progress in mapping the earth as well as the sky. Eratosthenes of Cyrene (ca. 275–195 B.C.) was able to calculate the circumference of the earth within about two hundred miles and wrote a treatise on geography based on mathematical and physical reasoning and the reports of travelers. In spite of the new data that were available to later geographers, Eratosthenes' map (see Map 4-4) was in many ways more accurate than the one constructed by Ptolemy that became standard during the Middle Ages.

Achievement of the Classical and Hellenistic Ages in World Perspective

The Classical Age of Greece was a period of unparalleled achievement. It carried forward the tradition of rational, secular speculation in natural philosophy and science, but turned its attention more to human questions in medicine and ethical and political philosophy. While the rest of the world continued to be characterized by monarchical, hierarchical, command societies, in Athens democracy was carried as

Devices of Hero of Alexandria. Hero lived late in the first century and was the author of a treatise on pneumatics. The two devices shown here have been reconstructed from his descriptions. The top device is for opening doors; the bottom device is a steam turbine. Both depended on the expansion of air or the vaporization of water when heated. The temple door appeared to open magically when a fire was lighted on the altar, illustrating one of Hero's goals for science, "producing bewilderment and awe." The turbine was treated as a mere toy. [H. Hodges, Technology in the Ancient World *(Harmondsworth: Penguin Books, 1959), p. 214]*

Map 4-4 The world according to Erastosthenes *Erastosthenes of Alexandria (ca. 275–195 B.C.) was a Hellenistic geographer. His map, reconstructed here, was remarkably accurate for its time. The world was divided by lines of "latitude" and "longitude," thus anticipating our global divisions.*

far as it would go before modern times. Although limited to adult males of native parentage, Athenian citizenship granted full and active participation in every decision of the state without regard to wealth or class. Democracy disappeared with the end of Greek autonomy late in the fourth century B.C. When it returned in the modern world more than two millennia later, it was broader but shallower. Democratic citizenship did not again imply the active direct participation of every citizen in the government of the state.

It was in this democratic imperial Athens that the greatest artistic, literary, and philosophical achievements took place. Many of the literary genres and forms that are vital in the modern world arose and were developed during this time. Analytical, secular history; tragedy and comedy; the philosophical dialogue; an organized system of logic; and logical philosophical treatise on almost every aspect open to human thought were among the achievements of the Classical Age. A naturalistic style of art evolved that placed human beings first as they ideally might look, and then as they really looked. This approach dominated Greek and Roman art until the fall of the Roman Empire, when it largely disappeared. It rose again to have a powerful effect on the Italian Renaissance and, through it, on the modern world.

These developments, it should be clear, diverge sharply from the experience of previous cultures and of contemporary ones in the rest of the world. To a great degree, they sprang from the unique political experience of the Greeks, which avoided monarchies and great, extended, land empires but was based on independent city-states. That unique experience came to an end with the Macedonian conquest, which ultimately made the Greeks subject to or part of some great national state or empire and brought an end to the Classical period.

The Hellenistic Age speaks to us less fully and vividly than that of classical Greece or of the Roman Republic and Empire, chiefly because it had no historian to compare with Herodotus and Thucydides or Livy and Tacitus. We lack a continuous, rich, lively, and meaningful narrative. This deficiency should not obscure the great importance of the achievements of the age. The literature, art, scholarship, and science of the period deserve attention in their own right. In addition, the Hellenistic Age performed a vital civilizing function. It spread the Greek culture over a remarkably wide area and made a significant and lasting impression on much of it.

Greek culture also adjusted to its new surroundings to a degree, unifying and simplifying its cultural

cargo so as to make it more accessible to outsiders. The various Greek dialects gave way to a version of the Attic tongue, the *koine,* or common language. In the same way, the scholarship of Alexandria established canons of literary excellence and the scholarly tools with which to make the great treasures of Greek culture understandable to later generations. The union of thought and belief introduced in this period also made understanding and accord more likely among peoples who were very different. When the Romans came into contact with Hellenism, they were powerfully impressed by it, and when they conquered the Hellenistic world, they became, as Horace said, captives of its culture.

The conquests of Alexander and the Hellenistic civilization that came with them greatly affected the conquered societies and their neighbors. The Seleucid successors of Alexander ruled some parts of the old Persian Empire for almost two centuries after his death, and Hellenistic culture continued to influence the urban upper classes for some time.

The Hellenistic influence reached even further under another group of Greeks who broke away from the Seleucids to form the Indo-Greek people of Bactria. By the second century B.C., they controlled parts of northern India. The legacy of Hellenism in the East is reflected in art as far away as China. In the West, of course, the legacy was more complete and influential, powerfully shaping the nature of the Roman culture that would ultimately dominate the entire Mediterranean world and make important contacts beyond it.

Suggested Readings

M. AUSTIN and P. VIDAL-NAQUET, *The Economic and Social History of Classical Greece* (1977). A combination of documents and explanation.

E. BARKER, *Political Philosophy of Plato and Aristotle* (1959). A sober and reliable account.

H. I. BELL, *Egypt from Alexander the Great to the Arab Conquest* (1948). A general history.

W. BURKERT, *Greek Religion* (1987). An excellent study by an outstanding student of the subject.

P. CARTLEDGE, *Agesilaus and the Crisis of Sparta* (1987). More than a biography of the Spartan king, it is a complex discussion of Spartan history and society.

G. CAWKWELL, *Philip of Macedon* (1978). A brief but learned account of Philip's career.

J. K. DAVIES, *Democracy and Classical Greece* (1978). Emphasizes archeological evidence and social history.

V. EHRENBERG, *The People of Aristophanes* (1962). A study of Athenian society as revealed by the comedies of Aristophanes.

J. R. ELLIS, *Philip II and Macedonian Imperialism* (1976). A study of the career of the founder of Macedonian power.

J. R. LANE FOX, *Alexander the Great* (1973). An imaginative account that does more than the usual justice to the Persian side of the problem.

PETER GREEN, *Alexander to Actium: The Historical Evolution of the Hellenistic Age* (1990). A remarkable synthesis of political and cultural history.

N. G. L. HAMMOND and G.T. GRIFFITH, *A History of Macedonia,* Vol. 2, *550–336* B.C. (1979). A thorough account of Macedonian history that focuses on the careers of Philip and Alexander.

W. JAEGER, *Demosthenes* (1938). A good biography of the Athenian statesman.

R. JUST, *Women in Athenian Law and Life* (1988). An account of women's place in Athenian society.

D. KAGAN, *The Archidamian War* (1974). A history of the first ten years of the Peloponnesian War.

D. KAGAN, *The Fall of the Athenian Empire* (1987). The last period of the war.

D. KAGAN, *The Outbreak of the Peloponnesian War* (1969). A study of the period from the foundation of the Delian League to the coming of the Peloponnesian War that argues that war could have been avoided.

D. KAGAN, *The Peace of Nicias and the Sicilian Expedition* (1981). A history of the middle period of the Peloponnesian War.

B. M. W. KNOX, *The Heroic Temper: Studies in Sophoclean Tragedy* (1964). A brilliant analysis of tragic heroism.

D. M. LEWIS, *Sparta and Persia* (1977). A valuable discussion of relations between Sparta and Persia in the fifth and fourth centuries B.C.

G. E. R. LLOYD, *Greek Science After Aristotle* (1974).

A. A. LONG, *Hellenistic Philosophy: Stoics, Epicureans, Sceptics* (1974). An account of Greek science in the Hellenistic and Roman periods.

R. MEIGGS, *The Athenian Empire* (1972). A fine study of the rise and fall of the empire, making excellent use of inscriptions.

H. W. PARKE, *Festivals of the Athenians* (1977). A fine discussion of the religious practices of the Athenians.

J. J. POLLITT, *Art and Experience in Classical Greece* (1972). A scholarly and entertaining study of the relationship between art and history in classical Greece, with excellent illustrations.

J. J. POLLITT, *Art in the Hellenistic Age* (1986). An extraordinary analysis that places the art in its historical and intellectual context.

M. I. ROSTOVTZEFF, *Social and Economic History of the Hellenistic World,* 3 vols. (1941). A masterpiece of synthesis by a great historian.

D. M. SCHAPS, *Economic Rights of Women in Ancient Greece* (1981).

B. S. STRAUSS, *Athens After the Peloponnesian War* (1987). An excellent discussion of Athens's recovery and of the nature of Athenian society and politics in the fourth century B.C.

W. W. TARN, *Alexander the Great,* 2 vols. (1948). The first volume is a narrative account, the second a series of detailed studies.

W. W. TARN and G.T. GRIFFITH, *Hellenistic Civilization* (1961). A survey of Hellenistic history and culture.

A. E. TAYLOR, *Socrates* (1953). A good, readable account.

V. TCHERIKOVER, *Hellenistic Civilization and the Jews* (1970). A fine study of the impact of Hellenism on the Jews.

F. W. WALBANK, *The Hellenistic World* (1981).

T. B. L. WEBSTER, *Hellenistic Poetry and Art* (1961). A clear survey.

A. E. ZIMMERN, *The Greek Commonwealth* (1961). A study of political, social, and economic conditions in fifth-century Athens.

A wall painting from a late Republican villa (first century B.C.) of a citharist and her attendant. This may be a Roman copy of a Hellenistic original, a reflection of the Roman emulation of Greek culture. [The Metropolitan Museum of Art, Rogers Fund, 1903]

Rome: From Republic to Empire

The achievement of the Romans was one of the most remarkable accomplishments in human history. The descendants of the inhabitants of a small village in central Italy ruled the entire Italian peninsula, then the entire Mediterranean coastline. They conquered most of the Near East and finally much of continental Europe. They ruled this vast empire under a single government that provided considerable peace and prosperity for centuries. At no time before the Romans or since has that area been united, and rarely, if ever, has it enjoyed a stable peace. But Rome's legacy was not merely military excellence and political organization. The Romans adopted and transformed the intellectual and cultural achievements of the Greeks and combined them with their own outlook and historical experience. They produced the Graeco-Roman tradition in literature, philosophy, and art that served as the core of learning for the Middle Ages and the inspiration for the new paths taken in the Renaissance. That tradition remains at the heart of Western civilization to this day.

Prehistoric Italy

The culture of Italy developed late. Paleolithic settlements gave way to the Neolithic mode of life only about 2500 B.C. The Bronze Age came about 1500 B.C., and about 1000 B.C., Italy began to be infiltrated by bands of new arrivals from across the Adriatic Sea and around its northern end. The invaders were warlike people who imposed their language and social organization on almost all of Italy. Their bronze work was better than their predecessors', and soon they made weapons, armor, and tools of iron. They cremated their dead and put the ashes in tombs stocked with weapons and armor. Before 800 B.C., people living in this style occupied the highland pastures of the Apennines. These tough mountain people—Umbrians, Sabines, Samnites, Latins, and others—spoke a set of closely related languages that we call *Italic.*

They soon began to challenge the earlier settlers for control of the tempting western plains. Other peoples lived in Italy in the ninth century B.C., but the Italic speakers and three peoples who had not yet arrived—the Etruscans, the Greeks, and the Celts—would shape its future.

The Etruscans

The Etruscans exerted the most powerful external influence on the Romans. Their civilization arose in

The Etruscan Apollo. The Etruscans had a powerful influence on Roman civilization and were themselves strongly influenced by Greek art and civilization. The Etruscans were thus one of the intermediaries through which Greek culture made its way to Rome. [Villa Giulia Museum, Rome/Art Resource]

MAP 5-1 ANCIENT ITALY *This map of the Italian peninsula and its neighbors in antiquity shows the major cities and towns, as well as a number of geographical regions and the locations of some of the Italic and non-Italic peoples of the area.*

Etruria (now Tuscany), west of the Apennines between the Arno and Tiber rivers, about 800 B.C. (see Map 5-1). Their origin is far from clear, but their tomb architecture, resembling that of Asia Minor, and their practice of divining the future by inspecting the livers of sacrificial animals point to an Eastern origin.

The Etruscans brought civilization with them. Their settlements were self-governing, fortified city-states, of which twelve formed a loose religious confederation. At first, these cities were ruled by kings, but they were replaced by an aristocracy of the agrarian nobles, who ruled by means of a council and elected annual magistrates. The Etruscans were a military ruling class that dominated and exploited the native Italians, who worked their land and mines and served as infantry in their armies. This aristocracy accumulated considerable wealth through agriculture, industry, piracy, and a growing commerce with the Carthaginians and the Greeks.

The Etruscans' influence on the Romans was greatest in religion. They imagined a world filled with gods and spirits, many of them evil. To deal with such demons, the Etruscans evolved complicated rituals and powerful priesthoods. Divination by sacrifice and omens in nature helped discover the divine will, and careful attention to precise rituals directed by priests helped please the gods. After a while, the Etruscans, influenced by the Greeks, worshiped gods in the shape of humans and built temples for them.

The Etruscan aristocracy remained aggressive and skillful in the use of horses and war chariots. In the seventh and sixth centuries B.C., they expanded their power in Italy and across the sea to Corsica and Elba. They conquered Latium (a region that included the small town of Rome) and Campania, where they became neighbors of the Greeks of Naples.

Royal Rome

In the sixth century B.C., Rome came under Etruscan control. Led by their Etruscan kings, the Roman army, equipped and organized like the Greek phalanx, gained control of most of Latium. They achieved this success under an effective political and social order that gave extraordinary power to the ruling figures in both public and private life.

Government

To their kings, the Romans gave the awesome power of *imperium,* the right to issue commands and to en-

force them by fines, arrests, and corporal or even capital punishment. The kingship was elective, and the office appears to have tended to remain in the same family. The Senate, however, had to approve the candidate, and the *imperium* was formally granted by a vote of the people in assembly. The basic character of Roman government was already clear: Great power was granted to executive officers, but it had to be approved by the Senate and was derived ultimately from the people. Ostensibly the Senate had neither executive nor legislative power; it met only when summoned by the king and then only to advise him. In reality, its authority was great, for the senators, like the king, served for life. The Senate, therefore, had continuity and experience, and as it was composed of the most powerful men in the state, it could not lightly be ignored.

In early Rome, citizenship required descent from Roman parents on both sides. All citizens were organized into the third branch of government, an assembly made up of thirty groups. It met only when summoned by the king; he determined the agenda, made proposals, and recognized other speakers, if any. For the most part, the assembly was called to listen and approve. Voting was not by head but by group; a majority within each group determined its vote, and the decisions were made by majority vote of the groups. Group voting was typical of all Roman assemblies in the future.

Family

The center of Roman life was the family. At its head stood the father, whose power and authority within the family resembled those of the king within the state. Over his children, he held broad powers analogous to *imperium* in the state, for he had the right to sell his children into slavery, and he even had the power of life and death over them. Over his wife he had less power; he could not sell or kill her. As the king's power was more limited in practice than in theory, so it was with the father. His power to dispose of his children was limited by consultation with the family; by public opinion; and, most of all, by tradition. The wife could not be divorced except for stated serious offenses, and even then she had to be convicted by a court made up of her male blood relatives. The Roman woman had a respected position and the main responsibility for managing the household. The father was the chief priest of the family. He led it in daily prayers to the dead that reflected the ancestor worship central to the Roman family and state.

The Tiber island at Rome. This island in the Tiber made the river fordable at its location and therefore helped determine the location of the city of Rome. Later bridges kept the crossing a popular one, as shown in this eighteenth-century etching by G. B. Piranesi.

Clientage

Clientage was one of Rome's most important institutions. The client was "an inferior entrusted, by custom or by himself, to the protection of a stranger more powerful than he, and rendering certain services and observances in return for this protection."[1] The Romans spoke of a client as being in the *fides,* or trust, of his patron, so that the relationship always had moral implications. The patron provided his client with protection, both physical and legal; he gave him economic assistance in the form of a land grant, the opportunity to work as a tenant farmer or a laborer on the patron's land, or simply handouts. In return, the client would fight for his patron, work his land, and support him politically. These mutual obligations were enforced by public opinion and tradition. When early custom was codified in the mid-fifth century

B.C., one of the twelve tablets of laws announced: "Let the patron who has defrauded his client be accursed."[2]

In the early history of Rome, patrons were rich and powerful, whereas clients were poor and weak. But as time passed, it was not uncommon for rich and powerful members of the upper classes to become clients of even more powerful men, chiefly for political purposes. Because the client–patron relationship was hereditary and sanctioned by religion and custom, it was to play a very important part in the life of the Roman Republic.

Patricians and Plebeians

In the royal period, Roman society was divided in two by a class distinction based on birth. The upper class

[1] E. Badian, *Foreign* Clientelae *(264–70* B.C.*)* (Oxford: Oxford University Press, 1958), p. 1.

[2] *Roman Civilization: Selected Readings,* Vol. 1, ed. by Naphtali Lewis and Meyer Reinhold (New York: Columbia University Press, 1963).

was composed of the patricians, the wealthy men who held a monopoly of power and influence. They alone could conduct the religious ceremonies in the state, sit in the Senate, or hold office, and they formed a closed caste by forbidding marriage outside their own group. The plebeians must originally have been the poor and dependent men who were small farmers, laborers, and artisans, the clients of the nobility.

As Rome and its population grew in various ways, families who were rich but outside the charmed circle gained citizenship. From very early times, therefore, there were rich plebeians, and incompetence and bad luck must have produced some poor patricians. The line between the classes and the monopoly of privileges remained firm, nevertheless, and the struggle of the plebeians to gain equality occupied more than two centuries of republican history.

The Republic

Roman tradition tells us that the republic replaced the monarchy at Rome suddenly in 509 B.C. as the result of a revolution sparked by the outrageous behavior of the last kings and led by the noble families.

Constitution

The Roman constitution was an unwritten accumulation of laws and customs that had won respect and the force of law over time. The Romans were a conservative people, so they were never willing to deprive their chief magistrates of the great powers exercised by the monarchs.

Polybius Summarizes the Roman Constitution

Polybius (ca. 203–120 B.C.) was a Greek from the city of Megalopolis, an important member of the Achaean League. As a hostage in Rome, he became a friend of influential Romans and later wrote a history of Rome's conquest of the Mediterranean lands. He praised the Roman constitution as an excellent example of a "mixed constitution" and as a major source of Roman success.

▶ *For other perspectives on law, leadership, and government, see the following document boxes: "Hammurabi Creates a Code of Law in Mesopotamia" (Ch. 1), "Legalism" (Ch. 2), "Thucydides Reports Pericles on Athenian Democracy" (Ch. 4), "The Edicts of Ashoka" (Ch. 7), "Machiavelli Discusses the Most Important Trait for a Ruler" (Ch. 17), and "Some Reforms of Akbar" (Ch. 24).*

As for the Roman constitution, it had three elements, each of them possessing sovereign powers: and their respective share of power in the whole state had been regulated with such a scrupulous regard to equality and equilibrium, that no one could say for certain, not even a native, whether the constitution as a whole were an aristocracy or democracy or despotism.

. . . .

The result of this power of the several estates for mutual help or harm is a union sufficiently firm for all emergencies, and a constitution than which it is impossible to find a better. For whenever any danger from without compels them to unite and work together, the strength which is developed by the State is so extraordinary, that everything required is unfailingly carried out by the eager rivalry shown by all classes to devote their whole minds to the need of the hour, and to secure that any determination come to should not fail for want of promptitude; while each individual works, privately and publicly alike, for the accomplishment of the business in hand. Accordingly, the peculiar constitution of the State makes it irresistible, and certain of obtaining whatever it determines to attempt. . . . For when any one of the three classes becomes puffed up, and manifests an inclination to be contentious and unduly encroaching, the mutual interdependency of all the three, and the possibility of the pretensions of any one being checked and thwarted by the others, must plainly check this tendency: and so the proper equilibrium is maintained by the impulsiveness of the one part being checked by its fear of the other. . . .

Polybius, *Histories*, Vol. 1, trans. by E. S. Shuckburgh (Bloomington: Indiana University Press, 1962), pp. 468, 473–474.

CONSULS. The Romans elected two patricians to the office of consul and endowed them with *imperium.* They were assisted by two financial officials called *quaestors,* whose number ultimately reached eight. Like the kings, the consuls led the army, had religious duties, and served as judges. They retained the visible symbols of royalty—the purple robe, the ivory chair, and the lictors (minor officials) bearing rods and axe who accompanied them—but their power was limited legally and institutionally as well as by custom.

The vast power of the consulship was granted not for life but only for a year. Each consul could prevent any action by his colleague by simply saying no to his proposal, and the religious powers of the consuls were shared with others. Even the *imperium* was limited, for although the consuls had full powers of life and death while leading an army, within the sacred boundary of the city of Rome the citizens had the right to appeal to the popular assembly all cases involving capital punishment. Besides, after their one year in office, the consuls would spend the rest of their lives as members of the Senate. It was a most reckless consul who failed to ask the advice of the Senate or who failed to follow it when there was general agreement.

The many checks on consular action tended to prevent initiative, swift action, and change, but this was just what a conservative, traditional, aristocratic republic wanted. Only in the military sphere did divided counsel and a short term of office create important problems. The Romans tried to get around the difficulties by sending only one consul into the field or, when this was impossible, allowing the consuls sole command on alternate days. In really serious crises, the consuls, with the advice of the Senate, could appoint a single man, the *dictator,* to the command and could retire in his favor. The dictator's term of office was limited to six months, but his own *imperium* was valid both inside and outside the city without appeal. These devices worked well enough in the early years of the republic, when Rome's battles were near home, but longer wars and more sophisticated opponents revealed the system's weaknesses and required significant changes.

Long campaigns prompted the invention of the proconsulship in 325 B.C., whereby the term of a consul serving in the field was extended. This innovation contained the seeds of many troubles for the constitution.

The introduction of the office of *praetor* also helped provide commanders for Rome's many campaigns. The basic function of the *praetors* was judi-cial, but they also had *imperium* and served as generals. By the end of the republic, there were eight *praetors,* whose annual terms, like the consuls', could be extended for military commands when necessary.

At first, the consuls classified the citizens according to age and property, the bases of citizenship and assignment in the army. After the middle of the fifth century B.C., two censors were elected to perform this duty. They conducted a census and drew up the citizen rolls, but this was no job for clerks. The classification fixed taxation and status, so that the censors had to be men of reputation, such as former consuls. The censors soon acquired additional powers. By the fourth century B.C., they compiled the roll of senators and could strike senators from that roll not only for financial reasons but for moral reasons as well. As the prestige of the office grew, becoming a censor came to be considered the ultimate prize of a Roman political career.

SENATE AND ASSEMBLY. The end of the monarchy increased the influence and power of the Senate. It became the single continuous deliberative body in the Roman state. Its members were leading patricians, often leaders of clans and patrons of many clients. The Senate soon gained control of finances and of foreign policy. Its formal advice was not lightly ignored either by magistrates or by popular assemblies.

The most important assembly in the early republic was the centuriate assembly. In a sense, it was the Roman army acting in a political capacity, and its basic unit was the century, theoretically one hundred fighting men classified according to their weapons, armor, and equipment. Because each man equipped himself, the organization was by classes according to wealth.

STRUGGLE OF THE ORDERS. The laws and constitution of the early republic clearly reflected the class structure of the Roman state, for they gave to the patricians almost a monopoly of power and privilege. The plebeians undertook a campaign to achieve political, legal, and social equality, and this attempt, which succeeded after two centuries of intermittent effort, is called the "struggle of the orders."

The most important source of plebeian success was the need for their military service. Rome was at war almost constantly, and the patricians were forced to call on the plebeians to defend the state. According to tradition, the plebeians, angered by patrician resistance to their demands, withdrew from the city and

RISE OF THE PLEBEIANS TO EQUALITY IN ROME	
509 B.C.	Kings expelled; Republic founded
450–449 B.C.	Laws of the Twelve Tables published
445 B.C.	Plebeians gain right of marriage with patricians
367 B.C.	Licinian-Sextian Laws open consulship to plebeians
300 B.C.	Plebeians attain chief priesthoods
287 B.C.	Laws passed by plebeian assembly made binding on all Romans

camped on the Sacred Mount. There they formed a plebeian tribal assembly and elected plebeian tribunes to protect them from the arbitrary power of the magistrates. They declared the tribune inviolate and sacrosanct, and anyone laying violent hands on him was accursed and liable to death without trial. By extension of his right to protect the plebeians, the tribune gained the power to veto any action of a magistrate or any bill in a Roman assembly or the Senate. The plebeian assembly voted by tribe, and a vote of the assembly was binding on plebeians. They tried to make their decisions binding on all Romans but could not do so until 287 B.C.

The next step was for the plebeians to obtain access to the laws, and by 450 B.C., the Twelve Tables codified early Roman custom in all its harshness and simplicity. In 445 B.C., plebeians gained the right to marry patricians. The main prize was consulship. The patricians did not yield easily, but at last, in 367 B.C., the Licinian-Sextian Laws provided that at least one consul could be a plebeian. Before long plebeians held other offices, even the dictatorship and the censorship. In 300 B.C., they were admitted to the most important priesthoods, the last religious barrier to equality. In 287 B.C., the plebeians completed their triumph. They once again withdrew from the city and secured the passage of a law whereby decisions of the plebeian assembly bound all Romans and did not require the approval of the Senate.

It might seem that the Roman aristocracy had given way under the pressure of the lower class, but the victory of the plebeians did not bring democracy. An aristocracy based strictly on birth had given way to an aristocracy more subtle, but no less restricted, based on a combination of wealth and birth. The significant distinction was not longer between the patricians and the plebeians but between the *nobiles*—a relatively small group of wealthy and powerful families, both patrician and plebeian, whose members attained the highest offices in the state—and everyone else.

These same families dominated the Senate, whose power became ever greater. It remained the only continuous deliberative body in the state, and the pressure of warfare gave it experience in handling public business. Rome's success brought the Senate prestige and increased its control of policy and confidence in its capacity to rule. The end of the struggle of the orders brought domestic peace under a republican constitution dominated by a capable, if narrow, senatorial aristocracy. This outcome satisfied most Romans outside the ruling group because Rome conquered Italy and brought many benefits to its citizens.

Conquest of Italy

Not long after the fall of the monarchy in 509 B.C., a coalition of Romans, Latins, and Italian Greeks defeated the Etruscans and drove them out of Latium for good.

GALLIC INVASION OF ITALY. At the beginning of the fourth century B.C., the Romans were the chief power in central Italy, but a disaster struck. In 387 B.C., the Gauls, barbaric Celtic tribes from across the Alps, defeated the Roman army and captured, looted, and burned Rome. The Gauls sought plunder, not conquest, so they extorted a ransom from the Romans and returned to their homes in the north. Rome's power appeared to have been wiped out. When the Gauls left, some of Rome's allies and old enemies tried to take advantage of its weakness, but by about 350 B.C., the Romans had recovered their leadership of central Italy and were more dominant than ever. Their success in turning back new Gallic raids added still more to their power and prestige. As the Romans tightened their grip on Latium, the Latins became resentful. In 340 B.C., they demanded independence from Rome or full equality, and when the Romans refused, they launched a war of independence that lasted until 338 B.C. The victorious Romans dissolved the Latin League, and their treatment of the defeated opponents provided a model for the settlement of Italy.

ROMAN POLICY TOWARD THE CONQUERED. The Romans did not destroy any of the Latin cities or their people, nor did they treat them all alike. Some in the vicinity of Rome received full Roman citizenship; others farther away gained municipal status, which gave them the private rights of intermarriage and commerce with Romans but not the public rights of voting and holding office in Rome. They retained the rights of local self-government and could obtain full Roman citizenship if they moved to Rome. They followed Rome in foreign policy and provided soldiers to serve in the Roman legions.

Still other states became allies of Rome on the basis of treaties, which differed from city to city. Some were given the private rights of intermarriage and commerce with Romans and some were not; the allied states were always forbidden to exercise these rights with one another. Some, but not all, were allowed local autonomy. Land was taken from some but not from others, and the percentage was not always the same. All the allies supplied troops to the army, in which they fought in auxiliary battalions under Roman officers, but they did not pay taxes to Rome.

On some of the conquered land, the Romans placed colonies, permanent settlements of veteran soldiers in the territory of recently defeated enemies. The colonists retained their Roman citizenship and

The Via Latina, here shown not far outside Rome, is one of the network of military roads that went from Rome into the Italian countryside. These roads enabled Roman legions to move swiftly to enforce their control of the peninsula and, conversely, also served as convenient avenues of invasion. The Via Latina is thought to be the earliest of these great roads, dating to the fourth century B.C. [Fototeca Unione]

The harbor of the ancient city of Carthage, near modern Tunis in North Africa, as reconstructed by an artist. [Radio Times Hulton Picture Library]

enjoyed home rule, and in return for the land they had been given, they served as a kind of permanent garrison to deter or suppress rebellion. These colonies were usually connected to Rome by a network of military roads built as straight as possible and so durable that some are used even today. They guaranteed that a Roman army could swiftly reinforce an embattled colony or put down an uprising in any weather.

The Roman settlement of Latium reveals even more clearly than before the principles by which Rome was able to conquer and dominate Italy for many centuries. The excellent army and the diplomatic skill that allowed Rome to separate its enemies help explain its conquests. However, the reputation for harsh punishment of rebels and the sure promise that such punishment would be delivered, made unmistakably clear by the presence of colonies and military roads, help account for the reluctance to revolt. But the positive side, represented by Rome's organization of the defeated states, is at least as important. The Romans did not regard the status given each newly conquered city as permanent. They held out to loyal allies the prospect of improving their status, even of achieving the ultimate prize, full Roman citizenship. In so doing, the Romans gave their allies a stake in Rome's future and success and a sense of being colleagues, although subordinate ones, rather than subjects. The result, in general, was that most of Rome's allies remained loyal even when put to the severest test.

DEFEAT OF THE SAMNITES. The next great challenge to Roman arms came in a series of wars with a tough mountain people of the southern Appenines, the Samnites. Some of Rome's allies rebelled, and soon the Etruscans and Gauls joined in the war against Rome. But most of the allies remained loyal. In 295 B.C., at Sentinum, the Romans defeated an Italian coalition, and by 280 B.C., they were masters of central Italy. Their power extended from the Po Valley south to Apulia and Lucania.

The victory over the Samnites brought the Romans into direct contact with the Greek cities of southern Italy, which they soon conquered. By 265 B.C., Rome ruled all Italy as far north as the Po River, an area of 47,200 square miles.

Rome and Carthage

Rome's acquisition of coastal territory and its expansion to the toe of the Italian boot brought it face to face with the great naval power of the western Mediterranean, Carthage (see Map 5-2). Late in the ninth century B.C., the Phoenician city of Tyre had planted a colony on the coast of northern Africa near modern Tunis, calling it the New City, or Carthage. In the sixth century B.C., the conquest of Phoenicia by the Assyrians and the Persians made Carthage independent and free to exploit its very advantageous situation.

The city was located on a defensible site and commanded an excellent harbor that encouraged com-

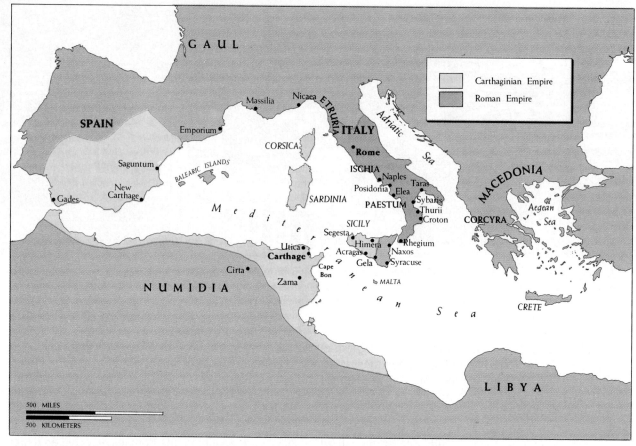

MAP 5-2 THE WESTERN MEDITERRANEAN AREA DURING THE RISE OF ROME *This map covers the theater of the conflicts between the growing Roman dominions and those of Carthage in the third century* B.C. *The Carthaginian empire stretched westward from the city (in modern Tunisia) along the North African coast and into southern Spain.*

merce. The coastal plain grew abundant grain, fruits, and vegetables. An inland plain allowed sheep herding. The Phoenician settlers conquered the native inhabitants and used them to work the land. Beginning in the sixth century B.C., the Carthaginians expanded their domain to include the coast of northern Africa west beyond the Straits of Gibraltar and eastward into Libya. Overseas, they came to control the southern part of Spain, Sardinia, Corsica, Malta, the Balearic Islands, and western Sicily. The people of these territories, although originally allies, were all reduced to subjection like the natives of the Carthaginian home territory, and they all served in the Carthaginian army or navy and paid tribute. Carthage also profited greatly from the mines of Spain and from the absolute monopoly of trade Carthage imposed on the western Mediterranean.

Early contacts between Rome and Carthage had been few but not unfriendly, but Rome's new proximity to Sicily brought conflict. Roman intervention in the Sicilian city of Messana in 264 B.C. produced the first Punic War (the Romans called the Carthaginians by their ancestral name, Phoenicians; in Latin the name is *Poeni* or *Puni*).

FIRST PUNIC WAR (264–241 B.C.). The war in Sicily soon settled into a stalemate. At last, the Romans built a fleet to cut off supplies to the besieged Carthaginian cities at the western end of Sicily. When Carthage sent its own fleet to raise the siege, the Romans destroyed it. In 241 B.C., Carthage signed a treaty giving up Sicily and the islands between Italy and Sicily and agreed to pay a war indemnity in ten annual installments, to keep its ships out of Italian waters, and not to recruit mercenaries in Italy. Neither side was to attack the allies of the other. Rome had earned Sicily, and Carthage could well afford the indemnity.

The treaty did not bring peace to Carthage, even for the moment. A rebellion broke out among the Carthaginian mercenaries, newly recruited from Sicily and demanding their pay. In 238 B.C., while Carthage was still in danger, Rome seized Sardinia and Corsica and demanded that Carthage pay an additional indemnity. This was a harsh and cynical action by the Romans; even the historian Polybius, a great champion of Rome, could find no justification for it. The Romans were moved, no doubt, by the fear of giving Carthage a base so near Italy, but their action was unwise. It undid the calming effects of the peace of 241 B.C. and angered the Carthaginians without preventing them from recovering their strength to seek vengeance in the future.

After the First Punic War, Carthage sent the general Hamilcar to Spain, where he built a strong and profitable colony. He befriended the local Iberians and enrolled their men in his army.

Hamilcar's successor, his son-in-law Hasdrubal, pursued the same policies. His success alarmed the Romans, and they imposed a treaty in which he promised not to take an army north across the Ebro River in Spain, although Punic expansion in Spain was well south of that river at the time of the treaty. Even though the agreement preserved the appearance of Rome's giving orders to an inferior, the treaty gave equal benefits to both sides. If the Carthaginians agreed to accept the limit of the Ebro to their expansion in Spain, the Romans would not interfere with that expansion.

SECOND PUNIC WAR (218–202 B.C.).   After 241 B.C., Carthage recovered strength by building a rich empire in Spain while Rome looked on with some concern. In 221 B.C. Hannibal (247–182 B.C.) took command of Carthaginian forces in Spain while still a young man of twenty-five. A few years before his accession, Rome had received an offer from the people of the Spanish town of Saguntum to become the friends of Rome. The Romans accepted, thereby taking on the responsibilities of friendship with a foreign state. At first, Hannibal was careful to avoid interfering with the friends of Rome, but the Saguntines, confident of Rome's protection, began to interfere with some of the Spanish tribes allied with Hannibal.

Finally, the Romans sent an embassy to Hannibal, warning him to let Saguntum alone and repeating the

THE PUNIC WARS	
264–241 B.C.	First Punic War
238 B.C.	Rome seizes Sardinia and Corsica
221 B.C.	Hannibal takes command of Punic army in Spain
218–202 B.C.	Second Punic War
216 B.C.	Battle of Cannae
209 B.C.	Scipio takes New Carthage
202 B.C.	Battle of Zama
149–146 B.C.	Third Punic War
146 B.C.	Destruction of Carthage

injunction not to cross the Ebro. The Romans probably expected Hannibal to yield as his predecessors had, but they misjudged their man. Hannibal ignored Rome's warning, besieged Saguntum, and took the town.

On hearing of Saguntum's fall, the Romans sent an ultimatum to Carthage demanding the surrender of Hannibal. Carthage refused, and Rome declared war in 218 B.C. Rome's policy between the wars had been the worst possible combination of approaches. Rome had insulted and injured Carthage by the annexation of Sardinia in 238 B.C. and had repeatedly provoked and insulted Carthage by interventions in Spain. But Roman policy took no measures to prevent the construction of a powerful and dangerous Punic Empire or even to build defenses against a Punic attack from Spain. Hannibal saw to it that the Romans paid the price for their blunders. By September of 218 B.C., he was across the Alps. His army was weary, bedraggled, and greatly reduced, but he was in Italy and among the friendly Gauls.

Hannibal defeated the Romans at the Ticinus River and crushed the joint consular armies at the Trebia River. In 217 B.C., he outmaneuvered and trapped another army at Lake Trasimene. Hannibal's first victory brought him reinforcements of fifty thousand Gauls, and his second confirmed that his superior generalship could defeat the Roman army. The key to success, however, would be defection by Rome's allies.

Sobered by their defeats, the Romans elected Quintus Fabius Maximus (ca. 275–203 B.C.) dictator. He understood that Hannibal could not be beaten by the usual tactics and that the Roman army, decimated and demoralized, needed time to recover. His strategy was to avoid battle while following and harassing Hannibal's army. When the Roman army had recovered and Fabius could fight Hannibal on favorable ground, only then would the Romans fight.

In 216 B.C., Hannibal marched to Cannae in Apulia to tempt the Romans into another open fight. The Romans could not allow him to ravage the country freely, so they sent off an army of some eighty thousand men to meet him. Almost the entire Roman army was killed or captured. It was the worst defeat in Roman history; Rome's prestige was shattered, and most of its allies in southern Italy, as well as Syracuse in Sicily, went over to Hannibal. In 215 B.C., Philip V, king of Macedon, made an alliance with Hannibal and launched a war to recover his influence on the Adriatic. For more than a decade, no Roman army would dare face Hannibal in the open field, and he was free to roam over all Italy and do as he pleased.

Hannibal had neither the numbers nor the supplies to besiege such walled cities as Rome and the major allies, nor did he have the equipment to take them by assault. To win the war in Spain, the Romans appointed Publius Cornelius Scipio (237–183 B.C.), later called Scipio Africanus, to the command in Spain with proconsular *imperium*. This was such a breach of tradition as to be almost unconstitutional, for Scipio was not yet twenty-five and had held no high office. But he was a general almost as talented as Hannibal. In 209 B.C., he captured the main Punic base in Spain, New Carthage. His skillful and tactful treatment of the native Iberians won them away from the enemy and over to his own army. Within a few years, young Scipio had conquered all Spain and had deprived Hannibal of hope of help from that region.

In 204 B.C., Scipio landed in Africa, defeated the Carthaginians, and forced them to accept a peace whose main clause was the withdrawal of Hannibal and his army from Italy. Hannibal had won every battle but lost the war, for he had not counted on the determination of Rome and the loyalty of its allies. Hannibal's return inspired Carthage to break the peace and to risk all in battle. In 202 B.C., Scipio and Hannibal faced each other at the battle of Zama. The generalship of Scipio and the desertion of Hannibal's mercenaries gave the victory to Rome. The new peace terms reduced Carthage to the status of a dependent ally of Rome. The Second Punic War ended the Carthaginian command of the western Mediterranean and Carthage's term as a great power. Rome ruled the seas and the entire Mediterranean coast from Italy westward.

Portrait of Hannibal (247–183 B.C.*), the great Carthaginian general, from a bust in the National Museum in Naples. [Erving Galloway]*

THE NEW IMPERIAL SYSTEM.   The Roman conquest of overseas territory presented a new problem. Instead of following the policy they had pursued in Italy, the Romans made Sicily a province and Sardinia and Corsica another. It became common to extend the term of the governors of these provinces beyond a year. The governors were unchecked by colleagues and exercised full *imperium*. New magistracies, in effect, were thus created free of the limits put on the power of officials in Rome. The new populations were neither Roman citizens nor allies; they were subjects who did not serve in the army but paid tribute instead. The old practice of extending citizenship and with it loyalty to Rome stopped at the borders of Italy. Rome collected the new taxes by "farming them out" at auction to the highest bidder. At first, the tax collectors were natives from the same province, later Roman allies, and finally Roman citizens below senatorial rank who became powerful and wealthy by squeezing the provincials hard. These innovations were the basis for Rome's imperial organization in the future;

in time they strained the constitution and traditions of Rome to such a degree as to threaten the existence of the republic.

The Republic's Conquest of the Hellenistic World

THE EAST. By the middle of the third century B.C., the eastern Mediterranean had reached a condition of stability. It was based on a balance of power among the three great kingdoms, and even lesser states had an established place. That equilibrium was threatened by the activities of two aggressive monarchs, Philip V of Macedon (221–179 B.C.), and Antiochus III of the Seleucid kingdom (223–187 B.C.). Philip and Antiochus moved swiftly, the latter against Syria and Palestine, the former against cities in the Aegean, in the Hellespontine region, and on the coast of Asia Minor.

The threat that a more powerful Macedon might pose to Rome's friends and, perhaps, even to Italy was enough to persuade the Romans to intervene. In 200 B.C., the Romans sent an ultimatum to Philip, ordering him not to attack any Greek city and to pay reparations to Pergamum. These orders were meant to provoke, not prevent, war, and Philip refused to obey. Two years later, the Romans sent out a talented young general, Flamininus, who demanded that Philip withdraw from Greece entirely. In 197 B.C., with Greek support, he defeated Philip in the hills of Cynoscephalae in Thessaly, bringing an end to the Second Macedonian War (the first had been fought while the Romans were still occupied with Carthage, from 215 to 205 B.C.). The Greek cities freed from Philip were made autonomous, and in 196 B.C., Flamininus proclaimed the freedom of the Greeks.

Soon after the Romans withdrew from Greece, they came into conflict with Antiochus, who was expanding his power in Asia and on the European side of the Hellespont. On the pretext of freeing the Greeks from Roman domination, he landed an army on the Greek mainland. The Romans routed Antiochus at Thermopylae and quickly drove him from Greece, and in 189 B.C., they crushed his army at Magnesia in Asia Minor. The peace of Apamia in the next year deprived Antiochus of his elephants and his navy and imposed a huge indemnity on him. Once again, the Romans took no territory for themselves and left a number of Greek cities in Asia free. They continued their policy of regarding Greece, and now Asia Minor, as a kind of

ROMAN OVERSEAS ENGAGEMENT	
215–205 B.C.	First Macedonian War
200–197 B.C.	Second Macedonian War
196 B.C.	Proclamation of Greek freedom by Flamininus at Corinth
189 B.C.	Battle of Magnesia; Antiochus defeated in Asia Minor
172–168 B.C.	Third Macedonian War
168 B.C.	Battle of Pydna
154–133 B.C.	Roman wars in Spain
134 B.C.	Numantia taken

protectorate in which they could intervene or not as they chose.

In 179 B.C., Perseus succeeded Philip V as king of Macedon. He tried to gain popularity in Greece by favoring the democratic and revolutionary forces in the cities. The Romans, troubled by this threat to stability, launched the Third Macedonian War (172–168 B.C.), and in 168 B.C., Aemilius Paullus defeated Perseus at Pydna. The peace imposed by the Romans reveals a change in policy and a growing harshness. It divided Macedon into four separate republics whose citizens were forbidden to intermarry or even to do business across the new national boundaries.

The new policy reflected a change in Rome from the previous relatively gentle one to the stern and businesslike approach favored by the conservative censor Cato (234–149 B.C.). The new harshness was applied to allies and bystanders as well as to defeated opponents. Leaders of anti-Roman factions in the Greek cities were punished severely. In 146 B.C., for instance, the ancient and wealthy commercial city of Corinth was plundered and then completely destroyed.

When Aemilius Paullus returned from his victory, he celebrated a triumph that lasted three days, during which the spoils of war, royal prisoners, and great wealth were paraded through the streets of Rome behind the proud general. The public treasury benefited to such a degree that the direct property tax on Roman citizens was abolished. Part of the booty went to the general and part to his soldiers. New motives were thereby introduced into Roman foreign policy, or, perhaps, old motives were given new prominence. Foreign campaigns could bring profit to the state, rewards to the army, and wealth, fame, honor, and political power to the general.

Plutarch Describes a Roman Triumph

In 168 B.C., *Lucius Aemilius Paullus defeated King Perseus in the battle of Pydna, bringing an end to the Third Macedonian War. For his great achievement, the Senate granted Paullus the right to celebrate a triumph, the great honorific procession granted only for extraordinary victories and eagerly sought by all Roman generals. Plutarch described the details of Paullus's triumph.*

The people erected scaffolds in the forum, in the circuses, as they call their buildings for horseraces, and in all other parts of the city where they could best behold the show. The spectators were clad in white garments; all the temples were open, and full of garlands and perfumes; the ways were cleared and kept open by numerous officers, who drove back all who crowded into or ran across the main avenue. This triumph lasted three days. On the first, which was scarcely long enough for the sight, were to be seen the statues, pictures, and colossal images which were taken from the enemy, drawn upon two hundred and fifty chariots. On the second was carried in a great many wagons the finest and richest armour of the Macedonians, both of brass and steel, all newly polished and glittering; the pieces of which were piled up and arranged purposely with the greatest art, so as to seem to be tumbled in heaps carelessly and by chance.

. . . .

On the third day, early in the morning, first came the trumpeters, who did not sound as they were wont in a procession or solemn entry, but such a charge as the Romans use when they encourage the soldiers to fight. Next followed young men wearing frocks with ornamented borders, who led to the sacrifice a hundred and twenty stalled oxen, with their horns gilded, and their heads adorned with ribbons and garlands; and with these were boys that carried basins for libation, of silver and gold.

. . . .

After his children and their attendants came Perseus himself, clad all in black, and wearing the boots of his country, and looking like one altogether stunned and deprived of reason, through the greatest of his misfortunes. Next followed a great company of his friends and familiars, whose countenances were disfigured with grief, and who let the spectators see, by their tears and their continual looking upon Perseus, that it was his fortune they so much lamented, and that they were regardless of their own.

. . . .

After these were carried four hundred crowns, all made of gold, sent from the cities by their respective deputations to Aemilius, in honour of his victory. Then he himself came, seated on a chariot magnificently adorned (a man well worthy to be looked at, even without these ensigns of power), dressed in a robe of purple, interwoven with gold, and holding a laurel branch in his right hand. All the army, in like manner, with boughs of laurel in their hands, divided into their bands and companies, followed the chariot of their commander; some singing verses, according to the usual custom, mingled with raillery; others, songs of triumph and the praise of Aemilius's deeds; who, indeed, was admired and accounted happy by all men, and unenvied by every one that was good; except so far as it seems the province of some god to lessen that happiness which is too great and inordinate, and so to mingle the affairs of human life that no one should be entirely free and exempt from calamities; but, as we read in Homer, that those should think themselves truly blessed whom fortune has given an equal share of good and evil.

Plutarch, "Aemilius Paullus," in *Lives of the Noble Grecians and Romans,* trans. by John Dryden, rev. by A. H. Clough (New York: Random House, n.d.), pp. 340–341.

THE WEST. Harsh as the Romans had become toward the Greeks, they were even worse in their treatment of the people of the Iberian Peninsula, whom they considered barbarians. The Romans committed dreadful atrocities, lied, cheated, and broke treaties in their effort to exploit and pacify the natives, who fought back fiercely in guerrilla style. From 154 to 133 B.C., the fighting waxed, and it became hard to recruit Roman soldiers to fight in the increasingly ugly war. At last, in 134 B.C., Scipio Aemilianus took the key city of Numantia by siege, burned it to the ground, and put an end to the war in Spain.

Roman treatment of Carthage was no better. Although Carthage lived up to its treaty with Rome faithfully and posed no threat, some Romans refused to abandon their hatred and fear of the traditional enemy. Cato is said to have ended all his speeches in the Senate with the same sentence, *"Ceterum censeo delendam esse Carthaginem"* ("Besides, I think that Carthage must be destroyed"). At last, the Romans took advantage of a technical breach of the peace to destroy Carthage. In 146 B.C., Scipio Aemilianus took the city, plowed up its land, and put salt in the furrows as a symbol of the permanent abandonment of the site. The Romans incorporated it as the province of Africa, one of six Roman provinces, including Sicily, Sardinia–Corsica, Macedonia, Hither Spain, and Further Spain.

Civilization in the Early Roman Republic: Greek Influence

Among the most important changes wrought by Roman expansion overseas were those in the Roman style of life and thought brought about by close and continued association with the Greeks of the Hellenistic world. Attitudes toward the Greeks themselves

ranged from admiration for their culture and history to contempt for their constant squabbling, their commercial practices, and their weakness. Such Roman aristocrats as the Scipios surrounded themselves with Greek intellectuals, like the historian Polybius and the philosopher Panaetius. Conservatives such as Cato might speak contemptuously of the Greeks as "Greeklings" *(Graeculi),* but even he learned Greek and absorbed Greek culture.

Before long, the education of the Roman upper classes was bilingual. In addition to the Twelve Tables, young Roman nobles studied Greek rhetoric, literature, and sometimes philosophy. These studies had an effect even on education and the Latin language. As early as the third century B.C., Livius Andronicus, a liberated Greek slave, translated the *Odyssey* into Latin. It became a primer for young Romans and put Latin on the road to becoming a literary language.

Religion

Roman religion was influenced by the Greeks almost from the beginning; the Romans identified their own gods with Greek equivalents and incorporated Greek mythology into their own. For the most part, however, Roman religious practice remained simple and Italian, until the third century B.C. brought important new influences from the east. In 205 B.C., the Senate approved the public worship of Cybele, the Great Mother goddess from Phrygia. Hers was a fertility cult accompanied by ecstatic, frenzied, and sensual rites that shocked and outraged conservative Romans to such a degree that they soon banned the cult to Romans. Similarly, the Senate banned the worship of Dionysus, or Bacchus, in 186 B.C. In the second century B.C., interest in Babylonian astrology also grew, and the Senate's attempt in 139 to expel the "Chaldaeans," as the astrologers were called, did not prevent the continued influence of their superstition.

Education

Human society depends on the transmission from generation to generation of the knowledge, skills, and values needed for life in any particular community. A

The temple of Vesta at Rome was built in the first century B.C. Vesta was the Roman goddess of the hearth. Her cult included an eternal flame, which was tended by the famous vestal virgins. [Art Resource]

system of education, whether formal or informal, is essential to each culture and reveals its character even as it tries to stamp that character on its children. The education provided in the early centuries of the Roman Republic reflected the limited, conservative, and practical nature of that community of plain farmers and soldiers.

Education was entirely the responsibility of the family, the father teaching his own son at home. It is not clear whether in early times girls received any education, although they certainly did later on. The boys learned to read, write, and calculate, and they learned the skills of farming. They memorized the laws of the Twelve Tables, Rome's earliest code of law; learned how to perform religious rites; heard stories of the great deeds of early Roman history and particularly those of their ancestors; and engaged in the physical training appropriate for potential soldiers. This course of study was practical, vocational, and moral. It aimed at making the boys moral, pious, patriotic, law-abiding, and respectful of tradition.

In the third century B.C., the Romans came into contact with the Greeks of southern Italy, and this contact produced momentous changes in Roman education. Greek teachers came to Rome and introduced the study of language, literature, and philosophy, as well as the idea of a liberal education, or what the Romans called *humanitas,* the root of our concept of the humanities. The aim of education changed from the practical, vocational goals of earlier times to an emphasis on broad intellectual training, critical thinking, an interest in ideas, and the development of a well-rounded person.

The first need was to learn Greek, for Rome did not yet have a literature of its own. For this purpose, schools were established in which the teacher, called a *grammaticus,* taught his students the Greek language and its literature, especially the poets and particularly Homer. Hereafter, educated Romans were expected to be bilingual. After the completion of this elementary education, Roman boys of the upper classes studied rhetoric—the art of speaking and writing well—with Greeks who were expert in those arts. For the Greeks, rhetoric was a subject of less importance than philosophy. But the more practical Romans took to it avidly, for it was of great use in legal disputes and was becoming ever more valuable in political life.

Cato Educates His Son

Marcus Porcius Cato (234–149 B.C.) was a remarkable Roman who rose from humble origins to the highest offices in the state. He stood as the firmest defender of the old Roman traditions at a time when Hellenic ideas were strongly influential. In the following passage, Plutarch tells how Cato attended to his son's education.

After the birth of his son, no business could be so urgent, unless it had a public character, as to prevent him from being present when his wife bathed and swaddled the babe. For the mother nursed it herself, and often gave suck also to the infants of her slaves, that so they might come to cherish a brotherly affection for her son. As soon as the boy showed signs of understanding, his father took him under his own charge and taught him to read, although he had an accomplished slave, Chilo by name, who was a schoolteacher, and taught many boys. Still, Cato thought it not right, as he tells us himself, that his son should be scolded by a slave, or have his ears tweaked when he was slow to learn, still less that he should be indebted to his slave for such a priceless thing as education. He was therefore himself not only the boys' reading-teacher, but his tutor in law, and his athletic trainer, and he taught his son not merely to hurl the javelin and fight in armour and ride the horse, but also to box, to endure heat and cold, and to swim lustily through the eddies and billows of the Tiber. His History of Rome, as he tells us himself, he wrote with his own hand and in large characters, that his son might have in his own home an aid to acquaintance with his country's ancient traditions.

Plutarch, *Cato Major,* Section 20, trans. by Bernadotte Perrin (London and New York: Loeb Classical Library, William Heinemann, 1914).

Some Romans, however, were powerfully attracted to Greek literature and philosophy. The Roman aristocrat Scipio Aemilianus, who finally defeated and destroyed Carthage, surrounded himself and his friends with such Greek thinkers as the historian Polybius and the philosopher Panaetius. Other Romans, such as Cato the Elder, were more conservative and opposed the new learning on the grounds that it would weaken Roman moral fiber. They were able on more than one occasion to pass laws expelling philosophers and teachers of rhetoric. But these attempts to go back to older ways failed. The new education suited the needs of the Romans of the second century B.C., who found themselves changing from a rural to an urban society and who were being thrust into the sophisticated world of the Hellenistic Greeks.

By the last century of the Roman Republic, the new Hellenized education had become dominant. Latin literature had come into being along with Latin translations of Greek poets, which formed part of the course of study, but Roman gentlemen were expected to be bilingual, and Greek language and literature were still central to the curriculum. Many schools were established, and the number of educated people grew, extending beyond the senatorial class to the equestrians and outside Rome to the cities of Italy.

Although the evidence is limited, we can be sure that girls of the upper classes were educated similarly to boys, at least through the earlier stages. They were probably taught by tutors at home rather than going to school, as was the increasing fashion among boys in the late Republic. Young women did not study with philosophers and rhetoricians, for they were usually married by the age the men were pursuing their higher education. Still, some women found ways to continue their education. Some became prose writers and others poets. By the first century A.D., there were apparently enough learned women to provoke the complaints of a crotchety and conservative satirist: Still more exasperating is the woman who begs as soon as she sits down to dinner, to discourse on poets and poetry, comparing Virgil with Homer; professors, critics, lawyers, auctioneers—even another woman—can't get a word in. She rattles on at such a rate that you'd think that all the pots and pans in the kitchen were crashing to the floor or that every bell in town was clanging. All by herself she makes as much noise as some primitive tribe chasing away an eclipse. She should learn the philosopher's lesson: "moderation is necessary even for intellectuals." And, if she still wants to appear educated and eloquent, let her dress as a man, sacrifice to men's gods and bathe in the men's baths. Wives shouldn't try to be public speakers; they shouldn't use rhetorical devices;

they shouldn't read all the classics—there should be some things women don't understand. I myself cannot understand a woman who can quote the rules of grammar and never make a mistake and cites obscure, long-forgotten poets—as if men cared about such things. If she has to correct somebody let her correct her girl friends and leave her husband alone.[3]

In the late republic, Roman education, although still entirely private, became more formal and organized. From the ages of seven to twelve, boys went to elementary school accompanied by a Greek slave called a *paedagogus* (whence our term *pedagogue*), who looked after his physical well-being and his manners and who improved his ability in Greek conversation. At school, the boy learned to read and write, using a wax tablet and a stylus, and to do simple arithmetic with the aid of an abacus and pebbles *(calculi)*. Discipline was harsh and corporal punishment frequent. From twelve to sixteen, boys went to a higher school, where the *grammaticus* undertook to provide a liberal education, using Greek and Latin literature as his subject matter. In addition, he taught dialectic, arithmetic, geometry, astronomy, and music. Sometimes he included the elements of rhetoric, especially for those boys who would not go on to a higher education.

At sixteen, some boys went on to advanced study in rhetoric. The instructors were usually Greek, and they trained their charges by requiring them to study models of fine speech of the past and by having them write, memorize, and declaim speeches suitable for different occasions. Sometimes the serious student attached himself to some famous public speaker and followed him about to learn what he could.

Sometimes a rich and ambitious Roman would support a Greek philosopher in his own home so that his son could converse with him and acquire the learning and polish thought necessary for the fully cultured gentleman. Some, like the great orator Cicero (106–43 B.C.), undertook what we might call postgraduate study by traveling abroad to study with great teachers of rhetoric and philosophy in the Greek world. One consequence of this whole style of education was to broaden the Romans' understanding through the careful study of a foreign language and culture. It made them a part of the older and wider culture of the Hellenistic world, a world that they had come to dominate and needed to understand.

[3] Juvenal, *Satires* 6.434–456, trans. by Roger Killian, Richard Lynch, Robert J. Rowland, and John Sims, cited by Sarah B. Pomeroy in *Goddesses, Whores, Wives, and Slaves* (New York: Schocken, 1975), p. 172.

Roman Imperialism

Rome's expansion in Italy and overseas was accomplished without a grand general plan. The new territories were acquired as a result of wars that the Romans believed were either defensive or preventive. Their foreign policy was aimed at providing security for Rome on Rome's terms, but these terms were often unacceptable to other nations and led to continued conflict. Whether intended or not, Rome's expansion brought the Romans an empire, and with it, power, wealth, and responsibilities (see Map 5-3).

The republican constitution, which had served Rome well during its years as a city-state and had been well adapted to the mastery of Italy, would be severely tested by the need to govern an empire beyond the seas. Roman society and the Roman charac-ter had maintained their integrity through the period of expansion in Italy. But they would be tested by the temptations and strains presented by the wealth and the complicated problems presented by an overseas empire.

Aftermath of Conquest

War and expansion changed the economic, social, and political life of Italy. Before the Punic Wars, most Italians owned their own farms, which provided most of the family's needs. Some families owned larger holdings, but their lands grew chiefly grain, and they used the labor of clients, tenants, and hired workers rather than slaves. Fourteen years of fighting in the Second Punic War did terrible damage to much Italian farmland. Many veterans returning from the wars found it impossible or unprofitable to go back to their

MAP 5-3 ROMAN DOMINIONS OF THE LATE REPUBLIC *The Roman Republic's conquest of Mediterranean lands—and beyond—until the death of Julius Caesar is shown here. Areas conquered before Tiberius Gracchus (ca. 133 B.C.) are distinguished from later ones and from client areas owing allegiance to Rome.*

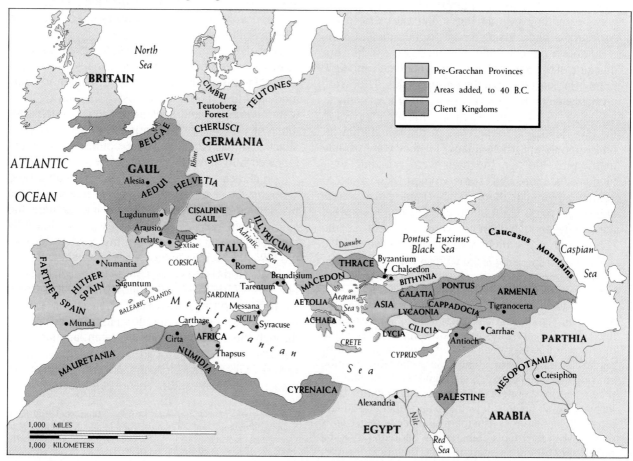

farms. Some moved to Rome, where they could find work as occasional laborers, but most stayed in the country to work as tenant farmers or hired hands. No longer landowners, they were also no longer eligible for the army. Often the land they abandoned was gathered into large parcels by the wealthy. They converted these large units, later called *latifundia,* into large plantations for growing cash crops—grain, olives, and grapes for wine—or into cattle ranches.

The upper classes had plenty of capital to stock and operate these estates as a result of profits from the war and from exploiting the provinces. Land was cheap, and slaves conquered in war provided cheap labor. By fair means and foul, large landholders obtained sizable quantities of public land and forced small farmers from it. These changes separated the people of Rome and Italy more sharply into rich and poor, landed and landless, privileged and deprived. The result was political, social, and ultimately constitutional conflict that threatened the existence of the republic.

The Gracchi

By the middle of the second century B.C., the problems caused by Rome's rapid expansion troubled perceptive Roman nobles. The fall in status of the peasant farmers made it harder to recruit soldiers and came to present a political threat as well. The patron's traditional control over his clients was weakened by their flight from their land. Even those former landowners who worked on the land of their patrons as tenants or hired hands were less reliable. The introduction of the secret ballot in the 130s B.C. made them even more independent.

In 133 B.C., Tiberius Gracchus tried to solve these problems. He became tribune for 133 B.C. on a program of land reform. The program aroused great hostility. When Tiberius put it before the tribal assembly, one of the tribunes interposed his veto. Unwilling to give up, he put his bill before the tribal assembly again. Again it was vetoed, so Tiberius, strongly supported by the people, had the offending tribune removed from office, thereby violating the constitution.

Tiberius then proposed a second bill, harsher than the first and more appealing to the people, for he had given up hope of conciliating the Senate. There could be no compromise: Either Tiberius or the Roman constitution must go under.

Tiberius understood the danger of prosecution that he would face if he stepped down from the tribunate, so he announced his candidacy for a second successive term, another blow at tradition. At the elections, a riot broke out, and a mob of senators and their clients killed Tiberius and some three hundred of his followers and threw their bodies into the Tiber River. The Senate had put down the threat to its rule, but at the price of the first internal bloodshed in Roman political history.

The tribunate of Tiberius Gracchus brought a permanent change to Roman politics. Heretofore, Roman political struggles had generally involved struggles for honor and reputation between great families or coalitions of such families. Fundamental issues were rarely at stake. The revolutionary proposals of Tiberius, however, and the senatorial resort to bloodshed created a new situation. Tiberius's use of the tribunate to challenge senatorial rule encouraged imitation in spite of his failure. From then on, Romans could pursue a political career that was not based solely on influence within the aristocracy; pressure from the people might be an effective substitute. In the last century of the Republic, such politicians were called *populares,* whereas those who supported the traditional role of the Senate were called *optimates* ("the best men").

The tribunate of Gaius Gracchus (brother of Tiberius) was much more dangerous than that of Tiberius because all the tribunes of 123 B.C. were Gaius's supporters, so there could be no veto, and a recent law permitted the reelection of tribunes. Gaius developed a program of such breadth as to appeal to a variety of groups. First, he revived the agrarian commission, which had been allowed to lapse. Because there was not enough good public land left to meet the demand, he proposed to establish new colonies: two in Italy and one on the old site of Carthage. Among other popular acts, he put through a law stabilizing the price of grain in Rome, which involved building granaries to guarantee an adequate supply.

Gaius broke new ground in appealing to the equestrian order in his struggle against the Senate. The equestrians (so called because they served in the Roman cavalry) were neither peasants nor senators. A highly visible minority of them were businessmen who supplied goods and services to the Roman state and collected its taxes. Almost continuous warfare and the need for tax collection in the provinces had made many of them rich. Most of the time, these wealthy men had the same outlook as the Senate; generally they used their profits to purchase land and to try to reach senatorial rank themselves. Still, they had a special interest in Roman expansion and in the exploitation of the provinces. Toward the latter part of

Appian Discusses Rome's Agrarian Crisis and the Proposal of Tiberius Gracchus

The changes that the second century B.C. had brought to Rome produced economic, social, political, and constitutional problems that demanded attention. The senatorial government was slow to move toward their solution, and the first major attempt at reform was undertaken in 133 B.C. by the tribune Tiberius Gracchus. Appian, a historian who lived in the second century A.D., described the situation.

The Romans, as they subdued the Italian nations successively in war, seized a part of their lands and built towns there, or established their own colonies in those already existing, and used them in place of garrisons. Of the land acquired by war they assigned the cultivated part forthwith to settlers, or leased or sold it. Since they had no leisure as yet to allot the part which then lay desolated by war (this was generally the greater part), they made proclamation that in the meantime those who were willing to work it might do so for a share of the yearly crops—a tenth of the grain and a fifth of the fruit. From those who kept flocks was required a share of the animals, both oxen and small cattle. They did these things in order to multiply the Italian race, which they considered the most laborious of peoples, so that they might have plenty of allies at home. But the very opposite thing happened; for the rich, getting possession of the greater part of the undistributed lands, and being emboldened by the lapse of time to believe that they would never be dispossessed, and adding to their holdings the small farms of their poor neighbors, partly by purchase and partly by force, came to cultivate vast tracts instead of single estates, using for this purpose slaves as laborers and herdsmen, lest free laborers should be drawn from agriculture into the army. The ownership of slaves itself brought them great gain from the multitude of their progeny, who increased because they were exempt from military service. Thus the powerful ones became enormously rich and the race of slaves multiplied throughout the country, while the Italian people dwindled in numbers and strength, being oppressed by penury, taxes, and military service. If they had any respite from these evils they passed their time in idleness, because the land was held by the rich, who employed slaves instead of freemen as cultivators.

. . . .

At length Tiberius Sempronius Gracchus, an illustrious man, eager for glory, a most powerful speaker, and for these reasons well known to all, delivered an eloquent discourse, while serving as tribune, concerning the Italian race, lamenting that a people so valiant in war, and blood relations to the Romans, were declining little by little in pauperism and paucity of numbers without any hope of remedy. He inveighed against the multitude of slaves as useless in war and never faithful to their masters, and adduced the recent calamity brought upon the masters by their slaves in Sicily, where the demands of agriculture had greatly increased the number of the latter; recalling also the war waged against them by the Romans, which was neither easy nor short, but long-protracted and full of vicissitudes and dangers. After speaking thus he again brought forward the law, providing that nobody should hold more than 500 jugera of the public domain. But he added a provision to the former law, that the sons of the present occupiers might each hold one-half that amount, and that the remainder should be divided among the poor by triumvirs, who should be changed annually.

Appian, *Roman History*, trans. by Horace White (London and New York: William Heinemann and the Macmillan Company, 1913), pp. 5–7.

the second century B.C., they came to have a clear sense of group interest and they began to exert political influence.

In 129 B.C., Pergamum became a new Roman province called Asia. Gaius put through a law turning over to the equestrian order the privilege of collecting its revenue. The equestrians were now given reality as a class, as a political unit that might be set against the Senate, and they might be formed into a coalition to serve Gaius's purposes.

Gaius easily won reelection as tribune for 122 B.C. He aimed at giving citizenship to the Italians, both to solve the problem that their dissatisfaction presented and to add them to his political coalition. But the common people did not want to share the advantages of Roman citizenship, and the Senate seized on this proposal as a way of driving a wedge between Gaius and his supporters.

The Romans did not reelect Gaius in 121 B.C., and he stood naked before his enemies. A hostile consul provoked an incident that led to violence. The Senate invented an extreme decree ordering the consuls to see to it that no harm came to the Republic; in effect, this decree established martial law. Gaius was hunted down and killed, and a senatorial court condemned and, without trial, put to death some three thousand of his followers.

Marius and Sulla

For the moment, the senatorial oligarchy had fought off the challenge to its traditional position. Before long, however, it faced more serious dangers arising from troubles abroad. The first grew out of a dispute over the succession to the throne of Numidia, a client kingdom of Rome near Carthage. The victory of Jugurtha (d. 104 B.C.), who became king of Numidia, and his massacre of Roman and Italian businessmen in Numidia gained Roman attention. Although the Senate was reluctant to become involved, pressure from the equestrians and the people forced the declaration of what became known as the Jugurthine War in 111 B.C.

As the war dragged on, the people, sometimes with good reason, suspected the Senate of taking bribes from Jugurtha. They elected Gaius Marius (157–86 B.C.) to the consulship for 107 B.C., and the assembly, usurping the role of the Senate, assigned him to the province of Numidia. This action was significant in several ways: Marius was a *novus homo,* a "new man," that is, the first in the history of his family to reach the consulship. Although a wealthy equestrian, he had been born in the town of Arpinum and was outside the closed circle of the old Roman aristocracy. His earlier career had won him a reputation as an outstanding soldier and something of a political maverick.

Marius quickly defeated Jugurtha, but Jugurtha escaped and guerrilla warfare continued. Finally, Marius's subordinate, Lucius Cornelius Sulla (138–78 B.C.), trapped Jugurtha and brought the war to an end. Marius celebrated the victory, but Sulla, an ambitious but impoverished descendant of an old Roman family, resented being cheated of the credit he

FALL OF THE ROMAN REPUBLIC	
133 B.C.	Tribunate of Tiberius Gracchus
123–122 B.C.	Tribunate of Gaius Gracchus
111–105 B.C.	Jugurthine War
104–100 B.C.	Consecutive consulships of Marius
90–88 B.C.	War against the Italian allies
70 B.C.	Consulship of Crassus and Pompey
60 B.C.	Formation of First Triumvirate
58–50 B.C.	Caesar in Gaul
53 B.C.	Crassus killed in Battle of Carrhae
49 B.C.	Caesar crosses Rubicon; civil war begins
46–44 B.C.	Caesar's dictatorship
45 B.C.	End of civil war
43 B.C.	Formation of Second Triumvirate
42 B.C.	Triumvirs defeat Brutus and Cassius at Philippi
31 B.C.	Octavian defeats Antony at Actium

thought he deserved. Soon rumors circulated crediting Sulla with the victory and diminishing Marius's role. Thus were the seeds planted for a personal rivalry and mutual hostility that would last until Marius's death.

While the Romans were fighting Jugurtha, a far greater danger threatened Rome from the north. In 105 B.C., two barbaric tribes, the Cimbri and the Teutones, had come down the Rhone Valley and crushed a Roman army at Arausio. To meet the danger, the Romans elected Marius to his second consulship when these tribes threatened again. From 104 B.C., he served five consecutive terms until 100 B.C., when the crisis was over.

While the barbarians were occupied elsewhere, Marius used the time to make important changes in the army. He began using volunteers for the army, mostly the dispossessed farmers and rural proletarians whose problems had not been solved by the Gracchi. They enlisted for a long term of service and looked on the army not as an unwelcome duty but as an opportunity and a career. They became semiprofessional clients of their general and sought guaranteed food, clothing, shelter, and booty from victories. They came to expect a piece of land as a form of mustering-out pay or veteran's bonus when they retired. Volunteers were most likely to enlist with a man who was a capable soldier and who was influential enough to obtain what he needed for them. They looked to him rather than to the state for their rewards. He, on the other hand, had to obtain these favors from the Senate if he was to maintain his power and reputation.

Marius's innovation created both the opportunity and the necessity for military leaders to gain enough power to challenge civilian authority. The promise of rewards won these leaders the personal loyalty of their troops, and that loyalty allowed them to frighten the Senate into granting their demands.

War Against the Italian Allies (90–88 B.C.)

For a decade, Rome took no action to deal with Italian discontent. In frustration, the Italians revolted and established a separate confederation with its own capital and its own coinage.

Employing the traditional device of divide and conquer, the Romans immediately offered citizenship to those cities that remained loyal and soon made the same offer to the rebels if they laid down their arms. Even then, hard fighting was needed to put down the uprising, and by 88 B.C., the war against the allies was over. All the Italians became Roman citizens with the protections that citizenship offered, but they retained local self-government and a dedication to their own municipalities that made Italy flourish. The passage of time blurred the distinction between Romans and Italians and forged them into a single nation.

Sulla's Dictatorship

During the war against the allies, Sulla had performed well, and he was elected consul for 88 B.C. A champion of senatorial control, he fought and won a civil war against Marius and his friends. He now held all power and had himself appointed dictator, not in the traditional sense, but for the express purpose of reconstituting the state. He had enough power and influence to make himself the permanent ruler of Rome. Yet he was traditional enough to want a restoration of senatorial government, reformed in such a way as to prevent the misfortunes of the past.

Sulla retired to a life of ease and luxury in 79 B.C. He could not, however, undo the effect of his own example: a general using the loyalty of his own troops to take power and to massacre his opponents, as well

Sculptured portrait of Sulla, the first Roman to seize control of the republic by force. [Staatliche Antikensammlungen und Glyptothek, Munich. Studio Koppermann]

as innocent people. These actions proved to be more significant than his constitutional arrangements.

Fall of the Republic

Pompey, Crassus, Caesar, and Cicero

Within a year of Sulla's death, his constitution came under assault. To deal with armed threats to its powers, the Senate violated the constitution by ignoring Sulla's rigid rules for holding office, which had been meant to guarantee experienced, loyal, and safe commanders.

Crassus and Pompey were ambitious men whom the Senate feared. Both demanded special honors and election to the consulship for the year 70 B.C.

They both won election and repealed most of Sulla's constitution. This opened the way for further attacks on senatorial control and for collaboration between ambitious generals and demagogic tribunes.

In 67 B.C., a special law gave Pompey *imperium* for three years over the entire Mediterranean and fifty miles in from the coast. He also was given the power to raise great quantities of troops and money to rid the area of pirates. His power was then extended to fight a war that had broken out in Asia Minor. When he returned to Rome in 62 B.C., he had more power, prestige, and popular support than any Roman in history. The Senate and his personal enemies had reason to fear that he might emulate Sulla and establish his own rule.

Rome had not been quiet in Pompey's absence. Crassus was the foremost among those who had reason to fear Pompey's return. Although rich and influential, he did not have the confidence of the Senate, a firm political base of his own, or the kind of military glory needed to rival Pompey. During the 60s B.C., therefore, he allied himself with various popular leaders. The ablest of these men was Gaius Julius Caesar (100–44 B.C.), a descendant of an old but politically obscure patrician family that claimed descent from the kings and even from the goddess Venus.

The chief opposition to Crassus' candidates for the consulship for 63 B.C. came from Cicero (106–43 B.C.), a "new man" from Marius's home town of Arpinum. He had made a spectacular name as the leading lawyer in Rome. He wanted to unite the stable elements of the state—the Senate and the equestrians—in a harmony of the orders. This program did not appeal to the senatorial oligarchy, but the Senate preferred him to Catiline, a dangerous popular politician thought to be linked with Crassus. Cicero and Antonius were elected consuls for 63 B.C., with Catiline running third.

Cicero soon learned of a plot hatched by Catiline. Catiline had run in the previous election on a platform of cancellation of debts, which appealed to discontented elements in general but especially to the heavily indebted nobles and their many clients. Made desperate by defeat, Catiline planned to stir up rebellions around Italy, to cause confusion in the city, and to take it by force. Quick action by Cicero defeated Catiline.

First Triumvirate

Toward the end of 62 B.C., Pompey landed at Brundisium and, to general surprise, disbanded his army, celebrated a great triumph, and returned to private life. He had achieved amazing things for Rome and simply wanted the Senate to approve his excellent arrangements in the east and to make land allotments to his veterans. But the Senate was jealous and fearful of overmighty individuals and refused his requests. In this way, Pompey was driven to an alliance with his natural enemies, Crassus and Caesar, because all three found the Senate standing in the way of what they wanted.

In 60 B.C. Caesar returned to Rome from his governorship of Spain. He wanted the privilege of celebrating a triumph, but the Senate refused. Caesar then performed a political miracle: He reconciled Crassus with Pompey and gained the support of both for his own ambitions. So was born the First Triumvirate, an

Portrait of Julius Caesar. The sculpture is in the Naples museum. [Art Resource/Alinari/SCALA]

informal agreement among three Roman politicians, each seeking his private goals, that further undermined the future of the Republic.

Dictatorship of Julius Caesar

Caesar's efforts were rewarded with election to the consulship for 59 B.C. The Triumvirate program was quickly enacted, and Caesar got the extraordinary command that would give him a chance to earn the glory and power with which to rival Pompey: the governorship of Illyricum and Gaul for five years.

Caesar was now free to seek the military success he craved. By 56 B.C., he had conquered most of Gaul, but he had not yet consolidated his victories firmly. He therefore sought an extension of his command, but quarrels between Crassus and Pompey so weakened the Triumvirate that the Senate was prepared to order Caesar's recall. To prevent the dissolution of his base of power, Caesar persuaded Crassus and Pompey to meet with him at Luca in northern Italy to renew the coalition. Having made allies of his rivals, Caesar was now free to return to Gaul and finish the job.

By the time he was ready to return from Gaul after his extended term, however, the Triumvirate had dissolved, and a crisis was at hand. At Carrhae in 53 B.C., Crassus died trying to conquer the Parthians, successors to the Persian Empire. Soon, Pompey broke with Caesar and joined the Senate in opposing him.

Early in January of 49 B.C., the more extreme faction in the Senate had its way and ordered Pompey to defend the state and Caesar to lay down his command by a specified day. For Caesar, this meant exile or death, so he ordered his legions to cross the Rubicon River, the boundary of his province. This action was the first act of the civil war.

In 45 B.C., Caesar defeated the last of the enemy forces under Pompey's sons at Munda in Spain. The war was over, and Caesar, in Shakespeare's words, bestrode "the narrow world like a Colossus."

Caesar's innovations generally sought to make rational and orderly what was traditional and chaotic. Another general tendency of his reforms in the political area was the elevation of the role of Italians and even provincials at the expense of the old Roman families, most of whom were his political enemies.

Caesar made few changes in the government of Rome, but his own monopoly of military power made the whole structure a sham. He treated the Senate as his creature, sometimes with disdain. His enemies were quick to accuse him of aiming at monarchy. A senatorial conspiracy gathered strength under the leadership of Gaius Cassius Longinus and Marcus Junius Brutus and included some sixty senators in all. On March 15, 44 B.C., Caesar entered the Senate, characteristically without a bodyguard, and was stabbed to death. The assassins regarded themselves as heroic "tyrannicides" and did not have a clear plan of action after the tyrant was dead. No doubt they simply expected the Republic to be restored in the old way, but things had gone too far for that. There followed instead thirteen years of more civil war, at the end of which the Republic received its final burial.

Second Triumvirate and the Emergence of Octavian

Caesar's heir was his grandnephew, Octavian, a youth of eighteen. He joined Marcus Antonius (Mark Antony) and Lepidus, two of Caesar's officers, in the Second Triumvirate to fight the assassins, who called themselves tyrannicides. The new triumvirs defeated the enemy in a great battle at Philippi in 42 B.C., but they soon quarreled among themselves. Octavian gained control of the western part of the empire. Antonius, together with Cleopatra, queen of Egypt, ruled the east. In 31 B.C., the forces of Octavian crushed the fleet and army of Antony and Cleopatra at Actium, putting an end to the conflict.

The civil wars were over, and at the age of thirty-two, Octavian was absolute master of the Mediterranean world. His power was enormous, but so too was the task before him. He had to restore peace, prosperity, and confidence, all of which required the establishment of a constitution that would reflect the new realities without offending unduly the traditional republican prejudices that still had so firm a grip on Rome and Italy.

Rome: From Republic to Empire in World Perspective

The history of the Roman Republic reflects almost as sharp a departure from the common experience of ancient civilizations as that of the Greek city-states. A monarchy in its earliest known form, Rome quite early expelled its king, abandoned the institution of monarchy, and established an aristocratic republic somewhat like the *poleis* of the Greek dark ages. Unlike the Greeks, however, the Romans continued to

Suetonius Describes Caesar's Dictatorship

Suetonius (ca. A.D. 69–ca. 140) wrote a series of biographies of the emperors, from Julius Caesar to Domitian. In the following selection, he described some of Caesar's actions during his dictatorship in the years 46–44 B.C.

His other words and actions, however, so far outweigh all his good qualities, that it is thought he abused his power, and was justly cut off. For he not only obtained excessive honours, such as the consulship every year, the dictatorship for life, and the censorship, but also the title of emperor, and the surname of Father of His Country, besides having his statue amongst the kings, and a lofty couch in the theatre. He even suffered some honours to be decreed to him, which were unbefitting the most exalted of mankind; such as a gilded chair of state in the senate-house and on his tribunal, a consecrated chariot, and banners in the Circensian procession, temples, altars, statues among the gods, a bed of state in the temples, a priest, and a college of priests dedicated to himself, like those of Pan; and that one of the months should be called by his name. There were, indeed, no honours which he did not either assume himself, or grant to others, at his will and pleasure. In his third and fourth consulship, he used only the title of the office, being content with the power of dictator, which was conferred upon him with the consulship; and in both years he substituted other consuls in his room, during the last three months; so that in the intervals he held no assemblies of the people, for the election of magistrates, excepting only tribunes and ediles of the people; and appointed officers, under the name of præfects, instead of the prætors, to administer the affairs of the city during his absence. The office of consul having become vacant, by the sudden death of one of the consuls the day before the calends of January [January 1], he conferred it on a person who requested it of him, for a few hours. Assuming the same license, and regardless of the customs of his country, he appointed magistrates to hold their offices for terms of years. He granted the insignia of the consular dignity to ten persons of prætorian rank. He admitted into the senate some men who had been made free of the city, and even natives of Gaul, who were semi-barbarians. He likewise appointed to the management of the mint, and the public revenue of the state, some servants of his own household; and entrusted the command of three legions, which he left at Alexandria, to an old catamite of his, the son of his freedman Rufinus.

He was guilty of the same extravagance in the language he publicly used, as Titus Ampius informs us; according to whom he said, "The republic is nothing but a name, without substance or reality. Sulla was an ignorant fellow to abdicate the dictatorship. Men ought to consider what is becoming when they talk with me, and look upon what I say as a law."

Suetonius, *The Lives of the Twelve Caesars*, trans. by Alexander Thompson, rev. by T. Forster (London: George Bell and Sons, 1903), pp. 45–47.

be in touch with foreign neighbors, including the far more civilized urban monarchies of the Etruscans, but they clung faithfully to their republican institutions. For a long time, the Romans remained a nation of farmers and herdsmen, to whom trade was relatively unimportant, especially outside Italy.

Over time, the caste distinctions between patricians and plebeians became unimportant, giving way to distinctions based on wealth. Distinctions led to an aristocracy of noble families, who held the highest elected offices in the state. The nobles enhanced their power by their military service. The Roman Republic from the first found itself engaged in almost continuous warfare with its neighbors. Wars were waged either in defense of its own territory, in fights over disputed territory, or in defense of other cities or states who were friends and allies of Rome.

In both their domestic and their foreign relations, the Romans were a very legalistic people who placed great importance on traditional behavior encoded into laws. Although backed by the powerful authority of the magistrates at home and the potent Roman army abroad, the laws were based on experience, common sense, and equity. Aimed at stability and fairness, Roman law succeeded well enough that few people who lived under it wanted to do away with it. Roman law grew during the imperial period and even beyond. During the European Middle Ages, it played an important part in the revival of the West and continued to exert an influence into modern times.

The force of Roman arms, the high quality of Roman roads and bridges, and the pragmatic character of Roman law helped create something unique: an empire ruled by a republic, first a large one including all of Italy, and later one that commanded the shores of the entire Mediterranean (and quite a distance inland in many places). Rome controlled an area comparable to some of the empires of the East with an effective power equal to those of the kings and emperors of China, India, and Iran. It acquired that territory, wealth, and power in a state managed by annual magistrates elected by the male Roman citizens and by an aristocratic Senate, which recognized popular assemblies and a published, impersonal code of law. Rome achieved its greatness with an army of citizens and allies, without a monarchy or a regular bureaucracy.

The temptations and responsibilities of governing a vast and rich empire, however, finally proved too much for the republican constitution. Trade grew, and with it a class of merchants and financiers called equestrians that was neither aristocratic nor agricultural but increasingly powerful. The influx of masses of slaves captured in war undermined the small farmers who had been the backbone of the Roman state and its army. As many of them were forced to leave their farms, they moved to the cities, chiefly to Rome, where they had no productive role.

Conscripted armies of farmers serving relatively short terms gave way to volunteer armies of landless men serving as professionals and expecting to be rewarded with gifts of land or money. The generals of these armies were not annual magistrates controlled by the Senate and the constitution but ambitious military leaders seeking glory and political advantage. The result was civil war and the destruction of the Republic. The conquest of a vast empire moved the Romans away from their unusual historical traditions toward the more familiar path of empire trodden by rulers in Egypt, Mesopotamia, China, India, and Iran.

Suggested Readings

F. E. Adcock, *The Roman Art of War Under the Republic* (1940). An analysis of Roman military procedures.

E. Badian, *Foreign Clientelae* (1958). A brilliant study of the Roman idea of a client–patron relationship extended to foreign affairs.

E. Badian, *Roman Imperialism in the Late Republic,* 2nd ed. (1968).

A. H. Bernstein, *Tiberius Sempronius Gracchus: Tradition and Apostacy* (1978). A new interpretation of Tiberius's place in Roman politics.

R. Bloch, *Origins of Rome* (1960). A good account of the most generally accepted point of view.

P. A. Brunt, *Social Conflicts in the Roman Republic* (1971).

B. Caven, *The Punic Wars* (1980).

T. Cornell and J. Matthews, *Atlas of the Roman World* (1982). Much more than the title indicates, this book presents a comprehensive view of the Roman world in its physical and cultural setting.

S. Dixon, *The Roman Mother* (1988). Describes the place of women within the Roman family.

D. C. Earl, *The Moral and Political Tradition of Rome* (1967).

R. M. Errington, *The Dawn of Empire: Rome's Rise to Power* (1972). An account of Rome's conquest of the Mediterranean.

M. Gelzer, *Caesar: Politician and Statesman,* trans. by P. Needham (1968). The best biography of Caesar.

E. S. Gruen, *The Hellenistic World and the Coming of Rome* (1984). A new interpretation of Rome's conquest of the eastern Mediterranean.

E. S. Gruen, *The Last Generation of the Roman Republic* (1973). An interesting but controversial interpretation of the fall of the Republic.

W. V. Harris, *War and Imperialism in Republican Rome, 327–70 B.C.* (1975). An analysis of Roman attitudes and intentions concerning imperial expansion and war.

L. P. Homo, *Primitive Italy and the Beginning of Roman Imperialism* (1967). A study of early Roman relations with the peoples of Italy.

A. Keaveney, *Rome and the Unification of Italy* (1988). The story of how Rome organized her defeated opponents.

J. F. Lazenby, *Hannibal's War: A Military History of the Second Punic War* (1978). A careful and thorough account.

F. B. Marsh, *A History of the Roman World from 146 to 30 B.C.,* 3rd ed., rev. by H.H. Scullard (1963). An excellent narrative account.

J. C. Meyer, *Pre-Republican Rome* (1983).

C. Nicolet, *The World of the Citizen in Republican Rome* (1980).

M. Pallottino, *The Etruscans,* 6th ed. (1974). Makes especially good use of archaeological evidence.

R. T. Ridley, *The History of Rome* (1989). A solid general history.

E. T. Salmon, *The Making of Roman Italy* (1982). The story of Roman expansion on the Italian peninsula.

E. T. Salmon, *Roman Colonization Under the Republic* (1970).

H. H. Scullard, *From the Gracchi to Nero,* 5th ed. (1982). A work of the same character and quality.

H. H. Scullard, *A History of the Roman World 753–146* B.C., 4th ed. (1980). An unusually fine narrative history with useful critical notes.

A. N. Sherwin-White, *Roman Citizenship* (1939). A useful study of the Roman franchise and its extension to other peoples.

R. E. Smith, *Cicero the Statesman* (1966). A sound biography.

D. Stockton, *Cicero: A Political Biography* (1971). A readable and interesting study.

D. Stockton, *The Gracchi* (1979). An interesting analytic narrative.

L. R. Taylor, *Party Politics in the Age of Caesar* (1949). A fascinating analysis of Roman political practices.

B. H. Warmington, *Carthage* (1960). A good survey.

G. Williams, *The Nature of Roman Poetry* (1970). An unusually graceful and perceptive literary study.

Soldiers of the elite Praetorian Guard, which was originally formed by Augustus into the personal bodyguard of the princeps. *They numbered nine thousand and earned twice the salary of legionary soldiers. [Musée du Louvre, Paris. Giraudon]*

Imperial Rome

6

The fall of the Roman Republic put an end to an unusual chapter in the history of civilization. Examples of nonmonarchical governments lasting for more than a relatively short time are few. And the experience of a republic lasting for almost five hundred years, as well as ruling a vast empire, has no parallel. The transition toward the more typical organization of vast territories into an imperial monarchy was difficult. The early generations of Romans after the collapse of the old order continued to think in republican terms; many of their members longed simply for a restoration of the Republic.

The years of Augustus's rule were crucial in making the transition, because he skillfully maintained the appearance of republican institutions that helped mask the monarchical reality. The passage of time made such deception less necessary. Hard times and chaos in the third century A.D. revealed more clearly the basic military foundations of the rule of the increasingly autocratic emperors. In the first century A.D., emperors began to be declared divine upon their deaths, and by the second century they were worshiped as gods during their lifetimes, just like the rulers of ancient Egypt, China, Japan, and most other early empires. The basis for this treatment, however, was established during the years in which Augustus ruled Rome.

The Augustan Principate

If the problems facing Octavian after the Battle of Actium were great, so too were his resources for addressing them. He was the master of a vast military force, the only one in the Roman world, and he had loyal and capable assistants. Yet the memory of Julius Caesar's fate was still clear in Octavian's mind, and its lesson was that it was dangerous to flaunt unprecedented powers and to disregard all republican traditions.

Octavian's constitutional solution proved to be successful and lasting, subtle and effective. Behind all the republican trappings and the apparent sharing of authority with the Senate, the government of Octavian, like that of his successors, was a monarchy. All real power, both civil and military, lay with the ruler, whether he was called by the unofficial title of "first citizen" *(princeps)*, like Octavian, who was the founder of the regime, or "emperor" *(imperator)*, like those who followed.

On January 13, 27 B.C., he put forward a new plan in dramatic style, coming before the Senate to give up all his powers and provinces. In what was surely a rehearsed response, the Senate begged him to reconsider, and at last he agreed to accept the provinces of Spain, Gaul, and Syria with proconsular power for military command and to retain the consulship in Rome. The other provinces would be governed by the Senate as before. Because his were the border provinces containing twenty of the twenty-six legions, his true power was undiminished, but the Senate responded with almost hysterical gratitude, voting him many honors. Among them was the semireligious title "Augustus," which carried implications of veneration, majesty, and holiness. From this time on, historians speak of Rome's first emperor as Augustus and of his regime as the Principate. This would have pleased him, for it helps conceal the novel, unrepublican nature of the regime and the naked power on which it rested.

Administration

Augustus made important changes in the government of Rome, Italy, and the provinces. Most of these changes had the effect of reducing inefficiency and corruption, eliminating the threat to peace and order by ambitious individuals, and reducing the distinction between Romans and Italians, senators and equestrians. Augustus controlled the elections and saw to it that promising young men, whatever their origin, served the state as administrators and provincial governors. In this way, equestrians and Italians who had no connection with the Roman aristocracy entered the Senate in great numbers. For all his power, Augustus was careful always to treat the Senate with respect and honor.

The Augustan period was one of great prosperity, based on the wealth that Augustus had brought in by the conquest of Egypt, on the great increase in com-

Emperor Augustus (r. 27 B.C.–A.D. 14). This statue, now in the Vatican, stood in the villa of Augustus's wife Livia. All the figures on the elaborate breastplate have symbolic significance. At the top, for example, Dawn in her chariot brings in a new day under the protective mantle of the sky god; in the center Tiberius, Augustus's future successor, accepts the return of captured Roman standards from a barbarian prince; and at the bottom is Mother Earth with a horn of plenty. [Copyright by Leonard von Matt]

merce and industry made possible by general peace and a vast program of public works, and on a strong return to successful small farming on the part of Augustus's resettled veterans.

The union of political and military power in the hands of the *princeps* enabled him to install rational, efficient, and stable government in the provinces for the first time.

The Emperor Augustus Writes His Testament

Emperor Augustus wrote a record of his achievements to be read, engraved, and placed outside his mausoleum after his death. The following selections are from that document.

13. The temple of Janus Quirinus, which our ancestors desired to be closed whenever peace with victory was secured by sea and by land throughout the entire empire of the Roman people, and which before I was born is recorded to have been closed only twice since the founding of the city, was during my principate three times ordered by the senate to be closed.

....

34. In my sixth and seventh consulships, after I had put an end to the civil wars, having attained supreme power by universal consent, I transferred the state from my own power to the control of the Roman senate and people. For this service of mine I received the title of Augustus by decree of the senate, and the doorposts of my house were publicly decked with laurels, the civic crown was affixed over my doorway, and a golden shield was set up in the Julian senate house, which, as the inscription on this shield testifies, the Roman senate and people gave me in recognition of my valor, clemency, justice, and devotion. After that time I excelled all in authority, but I possessed no more power than the others who were my colleagues in each magistracy.

35. When I held my thirteenth consulship, the senate, the equestrian order, and the entire Roman people gave me the title of "father of the country" and decreed that this title should be inscribed in the vestibule of my house, in the Julian senate house, and in the Augustan Forum on the pedestal of the chariot which was set up in my honor by decree of the senate. At the time I wrote this document I was in my seventy-sixth year.

Augustus, *Res Gestae*, trans. by N. Lewis and M. Reinhold, in *Roman Civilization*, Vol. 2 (New York: Columbia University Press, 1955), pp. 13, 19.

The Army and Defense

The main external problem facing Augustus—and one that haunted all his successors—was the northern frontier. In A.D. 9, a revolt broke out, led by the German tribal leader Herrmann, or Arminius, as the Romans called him. He ambushed and destroyed three Roman legions under the general Varus as they marched through the Teutoburg Forest. The aged Augustus abandoned the campaign, leaving a problem of border defense that caused great trouble for his successors.

Under Augustus, the armed forces achieved true professional status. Enlistment, chiefly by Italians, was for twenty years, but the pay was relatively good and there were occasional bonuses and the promise of a pension on retirement in the form of money or a plot of land. Together with the auxiliaries from the provinces, these forces formed a frontier army of about three hundred thousand men. In normal times, this number was barely enough to hold the line. The Roman army permanently based in the provinces played a vital role in bringing Roman culture to the natives. The soldiers spread their language and customs, often marrying local women and settling down in the area of their service. They attracted merchants, who often became the nuclei of new towns and cities that became centers of Roman civilization. As time passed, the provincials on the frontiers became Roman citizens and helped strengthen Rome's defenses against the barbarians outside.

Religion and Morality

A century of political strife and civil war had undermined many of the foundations of traditional Roman society. Because Augustus thought it desirable to try to repair the damage, he undertook a program aimed at preserving and restoring the traditional values of the family and religion in Rome and Italy. He intro-

RULERS OF THE EARLY EMPIRE

27 B.C.–A.D. 14	Augustus

THE JULIO-CLAUDIAN DYNASTY

A.D. 14–37	Tiberius
A.D. 37–41	Gaius (Caligula)
A.D. 41–54	Claudius
A.D. 54–68	Nero
A.D. 69	Year of the four emperors

THE FLAVIAN DYNASTY

A.D. 69–79	Vespasian
A.D. 79–81	Titus
A.D. 81–96	Domitian

THE "GOOD EMPERORS"

A.D. 96–98	Nerva
A.D. 98–117	Trajan
A.D. 117–138	Hadrian
A.D. 138–161	Antoninus Pius
A.D. 161–180	Marcus Aurelius

duced laws curbing adultery and divorce and encouraging early marriage and the procreation of legitimate children.

Augustus also worked at restoring the dignity of formal Roman religion, building many temples, reviving old cults, and reorganizing and invigorating the priestly colleges, and he banned the worship of newly introduced foreign gods. During his lifetime, he did not accept divine honors, although he was deified after his death, and as with Julius Caesar, a state cult was dedicated to his worship.

Civilization of the Ciceronian and Augustan Ages

The high point of Roman culture came in the last century of the Republic and during the Principate of Augustus. Both periods reflected the dominant influence of Greek culture, especially in its Hellenistic mode. The education of Romans of the upper classes was in Greek rhetoric, philosophy, and literature, which also served as the models for Roman writers and artists. Yet in spirit and sometimes in form, the art and writing of both periods show uniquely Roman qualities, each in different ways.

The Late Republic

CICERO. The towering literary figure of the late Republic was Cicero. He is most famous for his orations delivered in the law courts and in the Senate. Together with a considerable body of his private letters, these orations provide us with a clearer and fuller insight into his mind than the works of any other figure in antiquity. We see the political life of his period largely through his eyes. He also wrote treatises on rhetoric, ethics, and politics that put Greek philosophical ideas into Latin terminology and at the same time changed them to suit Roman conditions and values.

Cicero's own views combined the teachings of the Academy, the Stoa, and other Greek schools to provide support for his moderate and conservative practicality. He believed in the world governed by divine and natural law that human reason could perceive and human institutions reflect. He looked to law, custom, and tradition to produce both stability and liberty. His literary style, as well as his values and ideas, was an important legacy for the Middle Ages and, reinterpreted, for the Renaissance.

HISTORY. The last century of the Republic produced some historical writing, much of which is lost to us. Sallust (86–35 B.C.) wrote a history of the years 78–67 B.C., but only a few fragments remain to remind us of his reputation as the greatest of republican historians. His surviving work consists of two pamphlets on the Jugurthine War and on the Catilinarian conspiracy of 63 B.C. They reveal his Caesarean and antisenatorial prejudices and the stylistic influence of Thucydides.

Julius Caesar (100–44 B.C.) wrote important treatises on the Gallic and civil wars. They are not fully rounded historical accounts but chiefly military narratives written from Caesar's point of view and with propagandist intent. Their objective manner (Caesar always referred to himself in the third person) and their direct, simple, and vigorous style make them persuasive even today, and they must have been most effective with their immediate audience.

LAW. The period from the Gracchi to the fall of the Republic was important in the development of Roman law. Before that time, Roman law was essentially national and had developed chiefly by means of juridical decisions, case by case, but contact with foreign peoples and the influence of Greek ideas forced

A mosaic showing Vergil reading from the Aeneid *to the muses Epic Poetry and Tragedy. (Giraudon)*

a change. From the last century of the Republic on, the edicts of the *praetors,* which interpreted and even changed and added to existing law, had increasing importance in developing the Roman legal code. Quite early, the edicts of the magistrates who dealt with foreigners developed the idea of the *jus gentium,* or "law of peoples," as opposed to that arising strictly from the experience of the Romans. In the first century B.C., the influence of Greek thought made the idea of *jus gentium* identical to that of the *jus naturale,* or "natural law," taught by the Stoics. It was this view of a world ruled by divine reason that Cicero enshrined in his treatise on the laws, *De Legibus.*

POETRY. The time of Cicero was also the period of two of Rome's greatest poets, Lucretius and Catullus, each representing a different aspect of Rome's poetic tradition. The Hellenistic poets and literary theorists saw two functions for the poet, as entertainer and as teacher. They thought the best poet combined both roles, and the Romans adopted the same view. When Naevius and Ennius wrote epics on Roman history, they combined historical and moral instruction with pleasure. Lucretius (ca. 99–ca. 55 B.C.) pursued a similar path in his epic poem *De Rerum Natura (On the Nature of Things).* In it, he set forth the scientific and philosophical ideas of Epicurus and Democritus with the zeal of a missionary trying to save society

from fear and superstition. He knew that his doctrine might be bitter medicine to the reader: "That is why I have tried to administer it to you in the dulcet strains of poesy, coated with the sweet honey of the Muses."[1]

Catullus (ca. 84–ca. 54 B.C.) was a poet of a thoroughly different kind. He wrote poems that were personal, even autobiographical. In imitation of the Alexandrians, he wrote short poems filled with learned allusions to mythology, but he far surpassed his models in intensity of feeling. He wrote of the joys and pains of love, he hurled invective at important contemporaries like Julius Caesar, and he amused himself in witty poetic exchanges with others. He offered no moral lessons and was not interested in Rome's glorious history and in contemporary politics. In a sense, he is an example of the proud, independent, pleasure-seeking nobleman who characterized part of the aristocracy at the end of the Republic.

Age of Augustus

The spirit of the Augustan Age, the Golden Age of Roman literature, was quite different, reflecting the new conditions of society. The old aristocratic order, with its system of independent nobles following their own particular interests, was gone. So was the world of poets of the lower orders, receiving patronage from any of a number of individual aristocrats. Augustus replaced the complexity of republican patronage with a simple scheme in which all patronage flowed from the *princeps,* usually through his chief cultural adviser, Maecenas (d. 8 B.C.).

The major poets of this time, Vergil and Horace, had lost their property during the civil wars. The patronage of the *princeps* allowed them the leisure and the security to write poetry and at the same time made them dependent on him and limited their freedom of expression. They wrote on subjects that were useful for his policies and that glorified him and his family, but they were not mere propagandists. It seems evident that for the most part they were persuaded of the virtues of Augustus and his reign and sang its praises with some degree of sincerity. Because they were poets of genius, they were also able to maintain a measure of independence in their work.

VERGIL. Vergil (70–19 B.C.) was the most important of the Augustan poets. His first important works, the *Eclogues,* or *Bucolics,* are pastoral idylls in a

---

[1] Lucretius, *De Rerum Natura,* lines 931 ff (New York: Oxford University Press, 1922).

somewhat artificial mode. The subject of the *Georgics,* however, was suggested to Vergil by Maecenas. The model here was the early Greek poet Hesiod's *Works and Days,* but the mood and purpose of Vergil's poem are far different. It is, to be sure, a didactic account of the agricultural life, but it is also a paean to the beauties of nature and a hymn to the cults, traditions, and greatness of Italy. All this, of course, served the purpose of glorifying Augustus's resettlement of the veterans of the civil wars on Italian farms and his elevation of Italy to special status in the empire.

Vergil's greatest work is the *Aeneid,* a long national epic that succeeded in placing the history of Rome in the great tradition of the Greeks and the Trojan War. Its hero, the Trojan warrior Aeneas, personifies the ideal Roman qualities of duty, responsibility, serious purpose, and patriotism. As the Romans' equivalent of Homer, Vergil glorified not the personal honor and excellence of the Greek epic heroes but the civic greatness represented by Augustus and the peace and prosperity that he and the Julian family had given to imperial Rome.

HORACE. Horace (65–8 B.C.) was the son of a freed man and fought on the republican side until its defeat at Philippi. He was won over to the Augustan cause by the patronage of Maecenas and by the attractions of the Augustan reforms. His *Satires* are genial and humorous. His great skills as a lyric poet are best revealed in his *Odes,* which are ingenious in their adaptation of Greek meters to the requirements of Latin verse. Two of the *Odes* are directly in praise of Augustus, and many of them glorify the new Augustan order, the imperial family, and the empire.

OVID. The darker side of Augustan influence on the arts is revealed by the career of Ovid (43 B.C.–A.D. 18). He wrote light and entertaining love elegies that reveal the sophistication and the loose sexual code of a notorious sector of the Roman aristocracy. Their values and way of life were contrary to the seriousness and family-centered life that Augustus was trying to foster. Ovid's *Ars Amatoria,* a poetic textbook on the art of seduction, angered Augustus and was partly responsible for the poet's exile in A.D. 8 to Tomi on the Black Sea.

Ovid tried to recover favor, especially with his *Fasti,* a poetic treatment of Roman religious festivals, but to no avail. His most popular work is the *Metamorphoses,* a kind of mythological epic that turns Greek myths into charming stories in a graceful and lively style. Ovid's fame did not fade with his exile and death, but his fate was an effective warning to later poets.

HISTORY. The achievements of Augustus and his emphasis on tradition and on the continuity of his regime with the glorious history of Rome encouraged both historical and antiquarian prose works. A number of Augustan writers wrote scholarly treatises on history and geography in Greek. By far the most important and influential prose writer of the time, however, was Livy (59 B.C.–A.D. 17), an Italian from Padua. His *History of Rome* was written in Latin and treated the period from the legendary origins of Rome until 9 B.C. Only one-fourth of his work is extant; of the rest, we have only pitifully brief summaries. He based his history on earlier accounts, chiefly the Roman annalists, and made no effort at original research. His great achievement was in telling the story of Rome in a continuous and impressive narrative. Its purpose was moral—setting up historical models as examples of good and bad behavior—and, above all, patriotic. He glorified Rome's greatness and connected it with Rome's past, just as Augustus tried to do.

ARCHITECTURE AND SCULPTURE. The visual arts revealed the same tendencies as other aspects of Roman life under Augustus. Augustus was the great patron of the visual arts, as he was of literature. He embarked on a building program that beautified Rome, glorified his reign, and contributed to the general prosperity and his own popularity. He filled the Campus Martius with beautiful new buildings, theaters, baths, and basilicas; the Roman Forum was rebuilt; and Augustus built a forum of his own. At its heart was the temple of Mars the Avenger to commemorate Augustus's victory and the greatness of his ancestors. On Rome's Palatine Hill, he built a splendid temple to his patron god, Apollo. This was one of the many temples he constructed in pursuit of his religious policy.

Most of the building was influenced by the Greek classical style, which aimed at serenity and the ideal type. The same features were visible in the portrait sculpture of Augustus and his family. The greatest monument of the age is the Altar of Peace *(Ara Pacis),* dedicated in 9 B.C. Set originally in an open space in the Campus Martius, its walls still carry a relief. Part of it shows a procession in which Augustus and his family appear to move forward, followed in order by the magistrates, the Senate, and the people of Rome. There is no better symbol of the new order.

View of Pompeii (above), an Italian town on the Bay of Naples destroyed in A.D. 79 by the volcanic eruption of nearby Mt. Vesuvius. The eruption, which buried the town in volcanic ash, was witnessed by the younger Pliny and is described in his letters. The ash ironically had the effect of preserving for posterity a sample of the urban art and architecture of the early imperium. The ruins of Pompeii were accidentally discovered in the eighteenth century and have now been largely excavated, revealing a prosperous and pleasant town of moderate size with an active local political life. [Bildarchiv Preussischer Kulturbesitz]

This is a wall painting (left) from the town of Herculaneum outside Naples, which was destroyed and buried in the same eruption of Vesuvius that destroyed Pompeii in A.D. 79. The architectural forms it depicts appear to be related to the theatrical performances popular at the time. [National Museum, Naples]

Tacitus Gives a Provincial View of the Imperial Peace

Tacitus (A.D. 55–ca. 115) was a Roman senator. He is most famous as historian of Rome for the period A.D. 14–68, but the following selection comes from a eulogy for his father-in-law, Agricola (A.D. 40–93). It describes the defiance of Britons to Roman conquest, and in so doing provides a critical view of Roman policies.

The Britons, convinced at length that a common danger must be averted by union, had, by embassies and treaties, summoned forth the whole strength of all their states. More than 30,000 armed men were now to be seen, and still there were pressing in all the youth of the country, with all whose old age was yet hale and vigorous, men renowned in war and bearing each decorations of his own. Meanwhile, among the many leaders, one superior to the rest in valour and in birth, Galgacus by name, is said to have thus harangued the multitude gathered around him and clamouring for battle:—

"Whenever I consider the origin of this war and the necessities of our position, I have a sure confidence that this day, and this union of yours, will be the beginning of freedom to the whole of Britain. To all of us slavery is a thing unknown; there are no lands beyond us, and even the sea is not safe, menaced as we are by a Roman fleet. And thus in war and battle, in which the brave find glory, even the coward will find safety. Former contests, in which, with varying fortune, the Romans were resisted, still left in use a last hope of succour, inasmuch as being the most renowned nation of Britain, dwelling in the very heart of the country and out of sight of the shores of the conquered, we could keep even our eyes unpolluted by the contagion of slavery. To us who dwell on the uttermost confines of the earth and of freedom, this remote sanctuary of Britain's glory has up to this time been a defence. Now, however, the furthest limits of Britain are thrown open, and the unknown always passes for the marvellous. But there are no tribes beyond us, nothing indeed but waves and rocks, and the yet more terrible Romans, from whose oppression escape is vainly sought by obedience and submission. Robbers of the world, having by their universal plunder exhausted the land, they rifle the deep. If the enemy be rich, they are rapacious; if he be poor, they lust for dominion; neither the east nor the west has been able to satisfy them. Alone among men they covet with equal eagerness poverty and riches. To robbery, slaughter, plunder, they give the lying name of empire; they make a solitude and call it peace."

Tacitus, *Agricola*, in *Complete Works of Tacitus*, trans. by A. J. Church and W. Brodribb (New York: Random House, 1942), pp. 694–695.

Peace and Prosperity: Imperial Rome (A.D. 14–180)

The central problem for Augustus's successors was the position of the ruler and his relationship to the ruled. Augustus tried to cloak the monarchical nature of his government, but his successors soon abandoned all pretense. The rulers came to be called *imperator*—from which comes our word *emperor*—as well as *Caesar*. The latter title signified connection with the imperial house, and the former indicated the military power on which everything was based. Because Augustus was ostensibly only the "first citizen" of a restored republic and his powers were theoretically voted him by the Senate and the people, he could not legally name his successor. In fact, he plainly designated his heirs by favors lavished on them and by giving them a share in the imperial power and responsibility (see Map 6-1).

MAP 6-1   PROVINCES OF THE ROMAN EMPIRE TO A.D. 117
The growth of the Empire to its greatest extent is shown (on the opposite page) in three states—at the death of Augustus in 14 B.C., at the death of Nerva in A.D. 98, and at the death of Trajan in A.D. 117. The division into provinces is also indicated. The inset outlines the main roads that tied the far-flung empire together.

MAJOR ROADS
OF THE
ROMAN EMPIRE

Rome

Mediterranean Sea

500 MILES
500 KILOMETERS

PARTHIAN
EMPIRE

Persian Gulf

Caspian Sea

Tigris

Euphrates

ARMENIA

ASSYRIA

MESOPOTAMIA

CAPPADOCIA

PONTUS

BITHYNIA

GALATIA

PISIDIA

CILICIA

LYCIA

ASIA

ARABIA PETRAEA

A R A B I A

PALESTINE
Jerusalem

Red Sea

E G Y P T

CYPRUS

CRETE

Mediterranean Sea

LIBYA

CYRENAICA

Black Sea

Byzantium

MOESIA
(INF.)

THRACE

MACEDONIA

MOESIA
(SUP.)

ILLYRIA

GREECE

ACHAEA

DACIA

S A R M A T I A

PANNONIA
(INF.)

PANNONIA
(SUP.)

DALMATIA

NORICUM

RHAETIA

CISALPINE
GAUL

Danube

I T A L Y
Rome

SARDINIA

SICILY

CORSICA

Mediterranean Sea

BALEARIC ISLANDS

Carthage

AFRICA

NUMIDIA

A F R I C A

MAURETANIA

500 MILES
500 KILOMETERS

G E R M A N I A

Cologne
GERMANIA
(INF.)

GERMANIA
(SUP.)

GAUL
AQUITANIA

LUGDUNENSIS

NARBONENSIS

TARRACONENSIS

LUSITANIA

BAETICA

North Sea

BRITAIN

Wall of Antoninus
Wall of Hadrian

HIBERNIA

ATLANTIC
OCEAN

14 A.D. – Death of Augustus

14-98 A.D. Acquisitions,
Augustus to Trajan

98-117 A.D. Acquisitions During
the Reign of Trajan

This relief from Titus's arch of victory in the Roman Forum celebrates his capture of Jerusalem after a two-year siege. Spoils from the temple in Jerusalem were carried in triumphal procession by the Roman troops. The Jews found it difficult to reconcile their religion with Roman rule and frequently rebelled. [Art Resource]

Tiberius (emperor A.D. 14–37),[2] his immediate successor, was at first embarrassed by the ambiguity of his new role, but soon the monarchical and hereditary nature of the regime became patent. Gaius (Caligula, A.D. 37–41), Claudius (A.D. 41–54), and Nero (A.D. 54–68) were all descended from either Augustus or his wife, Livia, and all were elevated as a result of that fact. In A.D. 41, the naked military basis of imperial rule was revealed when the Praetorian Guard dragged the lame, stammering, and frightened Claudius from behind a curtain and made him emperor. In A.D. 68, the frontier legions learned what the historian Tacitus called the secret of empire: that an emperor could be made elsewhere than at Rome. Nero's incompetence and unpopularity, and especially his inability to control his armies, led to a serious rebellion in Gaul in A.D. 68. The year 69 saw four different emperors assume power in quick succession as different Roman armies took turns placing their commanders on the throne.

Vespasian (A.D. 69–79) emerged victorious from

the chaos, and his sons, Titus (A.D. 79–81) and Domitian (A.D. 81–96), carried forward his line, the Flavian dynasty. Vespasian was the first emperor who did not come from the old Roman nobility. He was a tough soldier who came from the Italian middle class. A good administrator and a hard-headed realist of rough wit, he resisted all attempts by flatterers to find noble ancestors for him. On his deathbed, he is said to have ridiculed the practice of deifying emperors by saying, "Alas, I think I am becoming a god."

The assassination of Domitian put an end to the Flavian dynasty. Because Domitian had no close relative who had been designated as successor, the Senate put Nerva (A.D. 96–98) on the throne to avoid chaos. He was the first of the five "good emperors," who included Trajan (A.D. 98–117), Hadrian (A.D. 117–138), Antoninus Pius (A.D. 138–161), and Marcus Aurelius (A.D. 161–180). Until Marcus Aurelius, none of these emperors had sons, so they each followed the example set by Nerva of adopting an able senator and establishing him as successor. This rare solution to the problem of monarchical succession was, therefore, only a historical accident. The result, nonethe-

[2]Dates for the emperors give the years of each reign.

less, was almost a century of peaceful succession and competent rule, which ended when Marcus Aurelius allowed his incompetent son, Commodus (A.D. 180–192), to succeed him, with unfortunate results.

There was, of course, some real opposition to the imperial rule. It sometimes took the form of plots against the life of the emperor. Plots and the suspicion of plots led to repression, the use of spies and paid informers, book burning, and executions. The opposition consisted chiefly of senators who looked back to republican liberty for their class and who found justification in the Greek and Roman traditions of tyrannicide as well as in the precepts of Stoicism. Plots and repression were most common under Nero and Domitian. From Nerva to Marcus Aurelius, however, the emperors, without yielding any power, again learned to enlist the cooperation of the upper class by courteous and modest deportment.

Administration of the Empire

From an administrative and cultural standpoint, the empire was a collection of cities and towns that had little to do with the countryside. Roman policy during the Principate was to raise urban centers to the status of Roman municipalities with the rights and privileges attached to them. The Romans enlisted the upper classes of the provinces in their own govern-

ment, spread Roman law and culture, and won the loyalty of the influential people.

As the efficiency of the bureaucracy grew, so did the number and scope of its functions and therefore its size. The importance and autonomy of the municipalities shrank as the central administration took a greater part in local affairs. The provincial aristocracy came to regard public service in their own cities as a burden rather than an opportunity; the price paid for the increased efficiency offered by centralized control was the loss of the vitality of the cities throughout the empire.

Augustus's successors, for the most part, accepted his conservative and defensive foreign policy. Trajan was the first emperor to take the offensive in a sustained way. Between A.D. 101 and 106, he crossed the Danube and, after hard fighting, established the new province of Dacia between the Danube and the Carpathian Mountains. He was tempted, no doubt, by its important gold mines, but he probably was also pursuing a new general strategy: to defend the empire more aggressively by driving wedges into the territory of threatening barbarians. The same strategy dictated the invasion of the Parthian Empire in the east (A.D. 113–117). Trajan's early success was astonishing, and he established three new provinces in Armenia, Assyria, and Mesopotamia, but his lines were overextended. Rebellions sprang up, and the campaign crumbled. Trajan was forced to retreat and died before getting back to Rome.

This is a detail from Trajan's column, which was erected at Rome ca. A.D. 110 to celebrate Emperor Trajan's (r. 98–117) victory over the Dacians beyond the Danube. Trajan pushed the boundaries of the Roman empire to their farthest limits, defeating the Parthians in the east, as well as the Dacians in the north. Carved in a spiraling relief, the column showed more than a thousand figures, accurately depicting people, buildings, flowers, animals, implements, and weapons. [Art Resource]

Hadrian returned to the traditional policy, keeping Dacia but abandoning the eastern provinces. Hadrians' reign marked an important shift in Rome's frontier policy. The Roman defense became rigid, and initiative passed to the barbarians. Marcus Aurelius was compelled to spend most of his reign resisting dangerous attacks in the east and on the Danube frontier, and these attacks put enormous pressure on the human and financial resources of the empire.

Culture of the Early Empire

LITERATURE. In Latin literature, the years between the death of Augustus and the time of Marcus Aurelius are known as the Silver Age, and as the name implies, work of high quality—although probably not of so high a quality as that of the Augustan era—was produced. In contrast to the hopeful, positive optimists of the Augustans, the writers of the Silver Age were gloomy, negative, and pessimistic. In the works of the former period, praise of the emperor, his achievements, and the world abound; in the latter, criticism and satire lurk everywhere.

Some of the most important writers of the Silver Age in the first century A.D. came from the Stoic opposition and reflected its hostility to the growing power and personal excesses of the emperors.

The writers of the second century A.D. appear to have turned away from contemporary affairs and even recent history. Historical writing was about remote periods, so there was less danger of irritating imperial sensibilities. Scholarship was encouraged, but we hear little of poetry, especially about any dealing with dangerous subjects.

During the third century A.D., romances written in

MAP 6-2 ANCIENT ROME *This is a sketch of the city of Rome during the late Empire. It indicates the seven hills on and around which the city was built, as well as the major walls, bridges, and other public sites and buildings. The Forum is between the Capitoline and Palatine hills.*

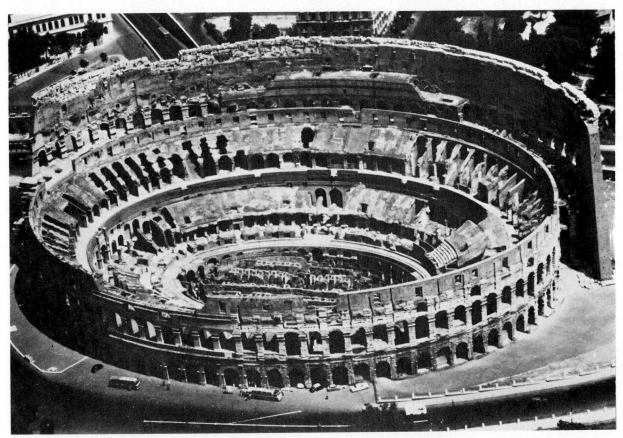

The Colosseum at Rome. The Romans called this building the Flavian Amphitheater because it was built by three successive emperors of the Flavian family—begun by Vespasian, dedicated in A.D. 80 by his son Titus, and finished by his younger son Domitian. How it acquired its present name is uncertain; it may derive either from its enormous size or from its proximity to a colossal statue of the emperor Nero. It is said to have been built by prisoners taken in the Jewish War and could seat fifty thousand spectators for the animal hunts, gladiatorial combats, mock sea battles, and other spectacles that took place in it. [Fototeca Unione]

Greek became popular and provide further evidence of the tendency of writers of the time to seek and provide escape from contemporary realities.

ARCHITECTURE. The prosperity and relative stability of the first two centuries of imperial Rome allowed the full development of the Roman contribution to architecture. To the fundamental styles of buildings developed by the Greeks, the Romans added little; the great public bath and a new, free-standing amphitheater were the main innovations (see Map 6-2).

The main contribution of the Romans lay in the great size of the structures they could build and in the advances in engineering that made these large structures possible. While keeping the basic post-and-lintel construction used by the Greeks, the Romans added to it the principle of the semicircular arch, borrowed from the Etruscans. They also made good use of concrete, a building material first used by the Hellenistic Greeks and fully developed by the Romans. The new principle, sometimes combined with the new material, allowed progress over the old style. The arch combined with the post and lintel produced the great Colosseum built by the Flavian emperors. When used internally in the form of vaults and domes, the arch permitted great buildings like the baths, of which the most famous and best preserved are those of the later emperors Caracalla and Diocletian.

One of Rome's most famous buildings, the Pantheon, begun by Augustus's friend Agrippa and rebuilt by Hadrian, is a good example of the combination of all these elements. Its portico of Corinthian columns

The Roman Baths: Two Views

Public baths played an important part in the lives of the Romans of the imperial period. The finest architects built them, beautifully and expensively, for the citizens not only of Rome, but also of most of the major cities in the empire. The baths served as vast community centers for social life and recreation. The first selection was written by Lucian, a writer of the second century A.D. *who described the magnificence of the baths. The second selection presents a more jaundiced view of the people who used them. It was written by Lucius Annaeus Seneca (ca. 4* B.C.–A.D. *65) who was Nero's tutor and a leading Roman representative of the Stoic school of philosophy.*

The building suits the magnitude of the site, accords well with the accepted idea of such an establishment, and shows regard for the principles of lighting. The entrance is high, with a flight of broad steps of which the tread is greater than the pitch, to make them easy to ascend. On entering, one is received into a public hall of good size, with ample accommodations for servants and attendants. On the left are the lounging rooms, also of just the right sort for a bath, attractive, brightly lighted retreats. Then, beside them, a hall, larger than need be for the purposes of a bath, but necessary for the reception of richer persons. Next, capacious locker rooms to undress in, on each side, with a very high and brilliantly lighted hall between them, in which are three swimming pools of cold water; it is finished in Laconian marble, and has two statues of white marble in the ancient style, one of Hygeia, the other of Aesculapius.

On leaving this hall, you come into another which is slightly warmed instead of meeting you at once with fierce heat; it is oblong, and has an apse on each side. Next to it, on the right, is a very bright hall, nicely fitted up for massage, which has on each side an entrance decorated with Phrygian marble, and receives those who come in from the exercising floor. Then near this is another hall, the most beautiful in the world, in which one can stand or sit with comfort, linger without danger, and stroll about with profit. It also is refulgent with Phrygian marble clear to the roof. Next comes the hot corridor, faced with Numidian marble. The hall beyond it is very beautiful, full of abundant light and aglow with color like that of purple hangings. It contains three hot tubs.

When you have bathed, you need not go back through the same rooms, but can go directly to the cold room through a slightly warmed chamber. Everywhere there is copious illumination and full indoor daylight. . . . Why should I go on to tell you of the exercising floor and of the cloak rooms? . . . Moreover, it is beautiful with all other marks of thoughtfulness—with two toilets, many exits, and two devices for telling time, a water clock that makes a bellowing sound and a sundial.

Lucian, "Hippias, or The Bath," in N. Lewis and M. Reinhold, *Roman Civilization*, Vol. 2 (New York: Columbia University Press, 1955), pp. 227–228.

I live over a bathing establishment. Picture to yourself now the assortment of voices, the sound of which is enough to sicken one. When the stronger fellows are exercising and swinging heavy leaden weights in their hands, when they are working hard or pretending to be working hard, I hear their groans; and whenever they release their pent-up breath, I hear their hissing and jarring breathing. When I have to do with a lazy fellow who is content with a cheap rubdown, I hear the slap of the hand pummeling his shoulders, changing its sound according as the hand is laid on flat or curved. If now a professional ball player comes along and begins to keep score, I am done for. Add to this the arrest of a brawler or a thief, and the fellow who always likes to hear his own voice in the bath, and those who jump into the pool with a mighty splash as they strike the water. In addition to those whose voices are, if nothing else, natural, imagine the hair plucker keeping up a constant chatter in his thin and strident voice, to attract more attention, and never silent except when he is plucking armpits and making the customer yell instead of yelling himself. It disgusts me to enumerate the varied cries of the sausage dealer and confectioner and of all the peddlers of the cook shops, hawking their wares, each with his own peculiar intonation.

Seneca, "Moral Epistles," in N. Lewis and M. Reinhold, *Roman Civilization*, Vol. 2 (New York: Columbia University Press, 1955), p. 228.

The Pantheon at Rome. A temple with baths and water gardens was built on this spot by Agrippa in 27–25 B.C. Destroyed by fire, it was rebuilt in its present form by Emperor Hadrian between A.D. 117 and 125 and then repaired by Septimus Severus ca. A.D. 200. [Italian Government Travel Office, New York]

is of Greek origin, but its rotunda of brick-faced concrete with its domed ceiling and relieving arches is thoroughly Roman. The new engineering also made possible the construction of more mundane but more useful structures like bridges and aqueducts.

SOCIETY. Seen from the harsh perspective of human history, the first two centuries of the Roman Empire deserve their reputation of a Golden Age, but by the second century A.D., troubles had arisen, troubles that foreshadowed the difficult times ahead. The literary efforts of the time reveal a flight from the present and from reality and the public realm to the past, to romance, and to private pursuits. Some of the same aspects may be seen in the more prosaic world of everyday life, especially in the decline of vitality in local government.

In the first century A.D., members of the upper classes vied with one another for election to municipal office and for the honor of doing service to their communities. By the second century, much of their zeal had disappeared, and it became necessary for the emperors to intervene to correct abuses in local affairs and even to force unwilling members of the ruling classes to accept public office. The reluctance to serve was caused largely by the imperial practice of holding magistrates and councilmen personally and collectively responsible for revenues that were due. There were even some instances of magistrates' fleeing to avoid their office, a practice that became widespread in later centuries.

All of these difficulties reflected the presence of more basic problems. The prosperity brought by the end of civil war and the influx of wealth from the east, especially Egypt, could not sustain itself beyond the first half of the second century A.D.. There also appears to have been a decline in population for reasons that remain mysterious. The cost of government kept rising as the emperors were required to maintain a costly standing army; to keep the people in Rome happy with "bread and circuses"; to pay for an increasingly numerous bureaucracy; and, especially in the reign of Marcus Aurelius, to wage expensive wars to defend the frontiers against dangerous and determined barbarian enemies.

The ever increasing need for money compelled the emperors to raise taxes, to press hard on their subjects, and to bring on inflation by debasing the coinage. These were the elements that were to bring on the desperate crises that ultimately destroyed the empire, but under the able emperors, from Trajan to Marcus Aurelius, the Romans met the challenge successfully.

Life in Imperial Rome: The Apartment House

The civilization of the Roman Empire depended on the vitality of its cities, of which no more than three or four had a population of more than seventy-five thousand, the typical city having about twenty thousand inhabitants. The population of Rome, however, was certainly greater than five hundred thousand, and some scholars think it was more than a million. People coming to it for the first time found it overwhelming and were either thrilled or horrified by its size, bustle, and noise.

The rich lived in elegant homes called *domus,* single-storied houses with plenty of space, an open central courtyard, and several rooms designed for specific and different purposes such as dining, sitting, or sleeping, in privacy and relative quiet. Although only a small portion of Rome's population lived in them, these houses took up as much as a third of the city's space. Public space for temples, markets, baths, gymnasiums, theaters, forums, and governmental buildings took up another quarter of Rome's territory.

This left less than half of Rome's area to house the mass of its inhabitants. Inevitably, as the population grew, it was squeezed into multiple dwellings that grew increasingly tall. Most Romans during the imperial period lived in apartment buildings called *insulae* ("islands") that rose to a height of five or six stories and sometimes even more. The most famous of them, the Insula of Febiala, seems to have "towered above the Rome of the Antonines like a skyscraper."[3]

These buildings were divided into separate apartments *(cenicula)* of undifferentiated rooms, the same plan on each floor. The apartments were cramped and uncomfortable. They had neither central heating nor an open fireplace; heat and fire for cooking came from small, portable stoves or braziers. The apartments were hot in summer, cold in winter, and stuffy and smoky when the stoves were lit. There was no plumbing, so tenants needed to go into the streets to wells or fountains for water and to public baths and latrines, or to less well-regulated places, to perform some natural functions. The higher up one lived, the more difficult these trips, so chamber pots and commodes were kept in the rooms. These receptacles were emptied into vats on the staircase landings or in the alley outside, or on occasion, the contents, and even the containers, were tossed out the window. Roman satirists complained of the discomforts and dangers of walking the streets beneath such windows, and Roman law tried to find ways to assign responsibility for the injuries done to dignity and person.

In spite of these difficulties, the attractions of the

city and the shortage of space caused rents to rise, making life in these buildings expensive as well as uncomfortable. Conditions were also dangerous. The houses were lightly built of concrete and brick, far too high for the limited area of their foundations, so they often collapsed. Laws limiting the height of buildings were not always obeyed and did not, in any case, always prevent disaster. The satirist Juvenal did not exaggerate much when he wrote, "We inhabit a city held up chiefly by slats, for that is how the landlord patches up the cracks in the old wall, telling the tenants to sleep peacefully under the ruin that hangs over their heads."

Even more serious was the threat of fire. The floors were supported by wooden beams, and the rooms were lit by torches, candles, and oil lamps. They were heated by braziers. Fires broke out easily but, without running water, were not easily put out; once started, they usually led to disaster.

When we consider the character of these apartments and compare them to the attractive public places in the city, we can easily understand why the people of Rome spent most of their time out of doors.

Rise of Christianity

The story of how Christianity emerged, spread, survived, and ultimately conquered the Roman Empire is one of the most remarkable in history. Its origin among poor people from an unimportant and remote province of the empire gave little promise of what was to come. Christianity faced the hostility of the established religious institutions of its native Judaea and had to compete not only against the official cults of Rome and the highly sophisticated philosophies of the educated classes but even against "mystery" religions like the cults of Mithra, Isis, and Osiris, and many others. The Christians also faced the opposition of the imperial government and suffered formal persecution, yet Christianity achieved toleration and finally exclusive command as the official religion of the empire.

Jesus of Nazareth

An attempt to understand this amazing outcome must begin with a discussion of Jesus of Nazareth, although there are many problems in arriving at a clear picture of His life and teachings. The most important evidence is in the Gospel accounts. The authors of the Gospels believed that Jesus was the son of God

[3] J. Carcopino, *Daily Life in Ancient Rome* (New Haven: Yale University Press, 1940), p. 26.

and that He came into the world to redeem humanity and to bring immortality to those who believed in Him and followed His way; to the Gospel writers, Jesus' resurrection was striking proof of His teachings. At the same time, the Gospels regard Jesus as a figure in history, and they recount events in His life as well as His sayings.

There is no reason to doubt that Jesus was born in the province of Judaea in the time of Augustus and that He was a most effective teacher in the tradition of the Jewish prophets. This tradition promised the coming of a Messiah (in Greek, *christos*—so *Jesus Christ* means "Jesus the Messiah"), the redeemer who would make Israel triumph over its enemies and establish the kingdom of God on earth. In fact, Jesus seems to have insisted that the Messiah would not establish an earthly kingdom but, at the Day of Judgment, would bring an end to the world as human beings knew it. On that day, God would reward the righteous with immortality and happiness in heaven and condemn the wicked to eternal suffering in hell. Until that day, which His followers believed would come very soon, Jesus taught the faithful to abandon sin and worldly concerns; to follow Him and His way; to follow the moral code described in the Sermon on the Mount, which preached love, charity, and humility; and to believe in Him and His divine mission.

Jesus had success and won a considerable following, especially among the poor. This success caused great suspicion among the upper classes. His novel

Mark Describes the Resurrection of Jesus

Belief that Jesus rose from the dead after his crucifixion (about A.D. 30) was and is central to traditional Christian doctrine. The record of the resurrection in the Gospel of Mark, written a generation later (toward A.D. 70), is the earliest we have. The significance to most Christian groups revolves about the assurance given them that death and the grave are not final and that, instead, salvation for a future life is possible. The appeal of these views was to be nearly universal in the West during the Middle Ages. The Church was commonly thought to be the means of implementing the promise of salvation; hence, the enormous importance of the Church's sacramental system, its rules, and its clergy.

▶ *Entering a cave and then reemerging signifies death and rebirth in the religions of many peoples. Compare this passage to "Darkness and the Cave of High Heaven" (Ch. 11).*

And when evening had come, since it was the day of Preparation, that is, the day before the sabbath, Joseph of Arimethea, a respected member of the council, who was also himself looking for the kingdom of God, took courage and went to Pilate, and asked for the body of Jesus. And Pilate wondered if he were already dead; and summoning the centurion, he asked him whether he was already dead. And when he learned from the centurion that he was dead, he granted the body to Joseph. And he bought a linen shroud, and taking him down, wrapped him in the linen shroud, and laid him in a tomb which had been hewn out of the rock; and he rolled a stone against the door of the tomb. Mary Magdalene and Mary the mother of Jesus saw where he was laid.

And when the sabbath was past, Mary Magdalene, and Mary the mother of James, and Salome, bought spices, so that they might go and anoint him. And very early on the first day of the week they went to the tomb when the sun had risen. And they were saying to one another, "Who will roll away the stone for us from the door of the tomb?" And looking up, they saw that the stone was rolled back; for it was very large. And entering the tomb, they saw a young man sitting on the right side, dressed in a white robe; and they were amazed. And he said to them, "Do not be amazed; you seek Jesus of Nazareth, who was crucified. He has risen, he is not here, see the place where they laid him. But go, tell his disciples and Peter that he is going before you to Galilee; there you will see him, as he told you." And they went out and fled from the tomb; for trembling and astonishment had come upon them; and they said nothing to any one, for they were afraid.

Gospel of Mark 15:42–47; 16:1–8 *Revised Standard Version of the Bible* (New York: Thomas Nelson and Sons, 1946 and 1952).

message and His criticism of the current religious practices connected with the temple at Jerusalem and its priests provoked the hostility of the religious establishment. A misunderstanding of the movement made it easy to convince the Roman governor that Jesus and His followers might be dangerous revolutionaries. He was put to death in Jerusalem by the cruel and degrading device of crucifixion, probably in A.D. 30. His followers believed that He was resurrected on the third day after his death, and that belief became a critical element in the religion that they propagated throughout the Roman Empire and beyond.

Although the new belief spread quickly to the Jewish communities of Syria and Asia Minor, there is reason to believe that it might have had only a short life as a despised Jewish heresy had it not been for the conversion and career of Saint Paul.

Paul of Tarsus

Paul (A.D. ?5–67) was born Saul, a citizen of the Cilician city of Tarsus in Asia Minor. Even though he was trained in Hellenistic culture and was a Roman citizen, he was a zealous member of the Jewish sect known as the Pharisees, the group that was most strict in its insistence on adherence to the Jewish law. He took a vigorous part in the persecution of the early Christians until his own conversion outside Damascus about A.D. 35. The great problem facing the early Christians was their relationship to Judaism. If the new faith was a version of Judaism, then it must adhere to the Jewish law and seek converts only among Jews. James, called the brother of Jesus, was a conservative who held to that view, whereas the Hellenist Jews tended to see it as a new and universal religion.

Paul, converted and with his new name, supported the position of the Hellenists and soon won many converts among the gentiles. Paul believed it important that the followers of Jesus be evangelists ("messengers"), to spread the gospel ("good news") of God's gracious gift. He taught that Jesus would soon return for the Day of Judgment, and it was important that all should believe in Him and accept His way. Faith in Jesus as the Christ was necessary but not sufficient for salvation, nor could good deeds alone achieve it. That final blessing of salvation was a gift of God's grace that would be granted to some but not to all.

Organization

Paul and the other apostles did their work well, and the new religion spread throughout the Roman Em-

pire and even beyond its borders. It had its greatest success in the cities and for the most part among the poor and uneducated. The rites of the early communities appear to have been simple and few. Baptism by water removed original sin and permitted participation in the community and its activities. The central ritual was a common meal called the *agape* ("love feast"), followed by the ceremony of the *eucharist* ("thanksgiving"), a celebration of the Lord's Supper in which unleavened bread was eaten and unfermented wine drunk. There were also prayers, hymns, and readings from the Gospels.

At first, the churches had little formal organization. Soon, it appears, affairs were placed in the hands of boards of *presbyters* ("elders") and *deacons* ("those who serve"). By the second century A.D., as their numbers grew, the Christians of each city tended to accept the authority and leadership of bishops (*episkopoi* or "overseers"), who were elected by the congregation to lead them in worship and supervise funds. As time passed, bishops extended their authority over the Christian communities in outlying towns and the countryside. The power and almost monarchical authority of the bishops was soon enhanced by the doctrine of Apostolic Succession, which asserted that the powers that Jesus had given His original disciples were passed on from bishop to bishop by the rite of ordination.

The bishops kept in touch with one another, maintained communications between different Christian communities, and prevented doctrinal and sectarian splintering, which would have destroyed Christian unity. They maintained internal discipline and dealt with the civil authorities. After a time, they began the practice of coming together in councils to settle difficult questions, to establish orthodox opinion, and even to expel as heretics those who would not accept it. It seems unlikely that Christianity could have survived the travails of its early years without such strong internal organization and government.

Persecution of Christians

The new faith soon incurred the distrust of the pagan world and of the imperial government. The Christians' refusal to worship the emperor was judged to be treason. The privacy and secrecy of Christian life and worship ran counter to a traditional Roman dislike of any private association, especially any of a religious nature, and the Christians thus earned the reputation of being "haters of humanity." Claudius expelled them from the city of Rome, and Nero tried to make

A Christian catacomb in Rome. The early Christians built miles of tunnels, called catacombs, in Rome. They were used as underground cemeteries and as refuges from persecution. [Archivi Alinari, 1991/Art Resource]

them scapegoats for the great fire that struck the city in A.D. 64. By the end of the first century, "the name alone"—that is, simple membership in the Christian community—was a crime.

Most persecutions during this period, however, were instituted not by the government but by mob action. But even this adversity had its benefits. It weeded out the weaklings among the Christians, brought greater unity to those who remained faithful, and provided the Church with martyrs around whom legends could grow that would inspire still greater devotion and dedication.

Emergence of Catholicism

The great majority of Christians never accepted complex, intellectualized opinions but held to what even then were traditional, simple, conservative beliefs. This body of majority opinion and the Church that enshrined it came to be called *Catholic,* which means "universal." Its doctrines were deemed orthodox, whereas those holding contrary opinions were heretics.

The need to combat heretics, however, compelled the orthodox to formulate their own views more clearly and firmly. By the end of the second century, an orthodox canon had been shaped that included the Old Testament, the Gospels, and the Epistles of Paul, among other writings. The process was not completed for at least two more centuries, but a vitally important start had been made. The orthodox declared the Church itself to be the depository of Christian teaching and the bishops to be its receivers. They also drew up creeds, brief statements of faith to which true Christians should adhere. In the first century, all that was required of one to be a Christian was to be baptized, to partake of the eucharist, and to call Jesus the Lord. By the end of the second century, an orthodox Christian—that is, a member of the Catholic church—was required to accept its creed, its canon of holy writings, and the authority of the bishops. The loose structure of the apostolic Church had given way to an organized body with recognized leaders able to define its faith and to exclude those who did not accept it.

Rome as a Center of the Early Church

During this same period, the church in the city of Rome came to have special prominence. Besides having the largest single congregation of Christians, Rome also benefited from the tradition that both Jesus' apostles Peter and Paul were martyred there. Peter, moreover, was thought to be the first bishop of Rome, and the Gospel of Matthew (16:18) reported Jesus' statement to Peter: "Thou art Peter [in Greek, *Petros*] and upon this rock [in Greek, *petra*] I will build my church." As a result of the city's early influence and of the Petrine doctrine derived from the Gospel of Matthew, later bishops of Rome claimed supremacy in the Catholic church, but as the era of the good emperors came to a close, this controversy was far in the future.

The Crisis of the Third Century

The pressure on Rome's frontiers, already serious in the time of Marcus Aurelius, reached massive proportions in the third century A.D. In the east, the frontiers

Emperor Valerian (r. A.D. 253–260) surrendering to Shapur I. This is a relief carved into a rock near the ancient Persian city of Persepolis. It commemorates the victory in 260 over the Romans by Shapur I of the Sassanid dynasty of Persian kings. Kneeling before Shapur is the chained Roman emperor, who quickly died in captivity. [American History Museum]

were threatened by a new power arising in the old Persian Empire. By A.D. 224, a new Iranian dynasty, the Sassanids, seized control from the Parthians and brought new vitality to Persia (see Chapter 12). They soon recovered Mesopotamia and made raids deep into Roman provinces.

Barbarian Invasions

On the western and northern frontiers, the pressure came not from a well-organized rival empire but from an ever increasing number of German tribes. These

REIGNS OF SELECTED LATE EMPIRE RULERS (ALL DATES ARE A.D.)	
180–192	Commodus
193–211	Septimius Severus
222–235	Alexander Severus
249–251	Decius
253–260	Valerian
253–268	Gallienus
268–270	Claudius II Gothicus
270–275	Aurelian
284–305	Diocletian
306–337	Constantine
324–337	Constantine sole emperor
337–361	Constantius II
361–363	Julian the Apostate
364–375	Valentinian
364–378	Valens
379–395	Theodosius

tough barbarians were always eager for plunder and were much attracted by the civilized delights they knew existed beyond the frontier of the Rhine and Danube rivers.

The most aggressive of the Germans in the third century A.D. were the Goths. Centuries earlier, they had wandered from their ancestral home near the Baltic Sea into the area of southern Russia. In the 220s and 230s they began to put pressure on the Danube frontier, and by about A.D. 250, they were able to penetrate into the empire and overrun the Balkan provinces. The need to meet this threat and the one posed by the Persian Sassanids in the east made the Romans weaken their western frontiers, and other Germanic peoples—the Franks and the Alemanni—broke through in those regions. There was a considerable danger that Rome would be unable to meet this challenge.

Rome's perils were caused, no doubt, by the unprecedentedly numerous and simultaneous attacks against it, but Rome's internal weakness encouraged these attacks. The pressure on the frontiers and epidemics of plague in the time of Marcus Aurelius forced the emperor to resort to the conscription of slaves, gladiators, barbarians, and brigands.

Septimius Severus (emperor A.D. 193–211) and his successors played a crucial role in the transformation of the character of the Roman army. Septimius was a military usurper who owed everything to the support of his soldiers. He meant to establish a family dynasty, in contrast to the policy of the good emperors of the second century A.D., and he was prepared to make Rome into an undisguised military monarchy. Septimius drew recruits for the army increasingly from peasants of the less civilized provinces, and the result was a barbarization of Rome's military forces.

Economic Difficulties

These changes were a response to the great financial needs caused by the barbarian attacks. Inflation had forced Commodus (r. A.D. 180–192) to raise the soldiers' pay, but the Severan emperors had to double it to keep up with prices, which increased the imperial budget by as much as 25 percent. The emperors resorted to inventing new taxes, debasing the coinage, and even selling the palace furniture to raise money. Even then, it was hard to recruit troops, and the new style of military life introduced by Septimius—with its laxer discipline, more pleasant duties, and greater opportunity for advancement, not only in the army but also in Roman society—was needed to attract men into the army. The policy proved effective for a short time but could not prevent the chaos of the late third century.

The same forces that caused problems for the army did great damage to society at large. The shortage of workers reduced agricultural production. As external threats distracted the emperors, they were less able to preserve domestic peace. Piracy, brigandage, and the neglect of roads and harbors hampered trade. So, too, did the debasement of the coinage and the inflation in general. Imperial exactions and confiscations of the property of the rich removed badly needed capital from productive use.

More and more, the government was required to demand services that had been given gladly in the past. Because the empire lived on a hand-to-mouth basis, with no significant reserve fund and no system of credit financing, the emperors were led to compel the people to provide food, supplies, money, and labor. The upper classes in the cities were made to serve as administrators without pay and to meet deficits in revenue out of their own pockets. Sometimes these demands caused provincial rebellions, as in Egypt and Gaul. More typically, they caused peasants and even town administrators to flee to escape their burdens. The result of all these difficulties was to weaken Rome's economic strength when it was most needed.

The Social Order

The new conditions caused important changes in the social order. The Senate and the traditional ruling class were decimated by direct attacks from hostile emperors and by economic losses. Their ranks were filled by men coming up through the army. The whole state began to take on an increasingly military appearance. Distinctions among the classes by dress had been traditional since the republic, but in the third and fourth centuries A.D. they developed to the point where the people's everyday clothing was a kind of uniform that precisely revealed their status. Titles were assigned to ranks in society as to ranks in the army. The most important distinction was the one formally established by Septimius Severus, which drew a sharp line between the *honestiores* (senators, equestrians, the municipal aristocracy, and the soldiers) and the lower classes, or *humiliores*. Septimius gave the *honestiores* a privileged position before the law. They were given lighter punishments, could not be tortured, and alone had the right of appeal to the emperor.

As time passed, it became more difficult to move from the lower order to the higher, another example of the growing rigidity of the late Roman Empire. Peasants were tied to their lands, artisans to their crafts, soldiers to the army, merchants and shipowners to the needs of the state, and citizens of the municipal upper class to the collection and payment of increasingly burdensome taxes. Freedom and private initiative gave way before the needs of the state and its every expanding control of its citizens.

Civil Disorder

Commodus was killed on the last day of A.D. 192, and the succeeding year was like the year A.D. 69: Three emperors ruled in swift succession, Septimius Severus emerging, as we have seen, to establish firm rule and a dynasty. The death of Alexander Severus, the last of the dynasty, in A.D. 235 brought on a half century of internal anarchy and foreign invasion.

The empire seemed on the point of collapse, but two able soldiers, Claudius II Gothicus (r. A.D. 268–270) and Aurelian (r. A.D. 270–275), drove back the barbarians and stamped out internal disorder. The soldiers who followed Aurelian on the throne were good fighters and made significant changes in Rome's system of defense. They built heavy walls around Rome, Athens, and other cities that could resist barbarian attack. They drew back their best troops from the frontiers, relying chiefly on a newly organized heavy cavalry and a mobile army near the emperor's own residence. Hereafter, the army was composed largely of mercenaries who came from among the Germans. The officers gave personal loyalty to the emperor rather than to the empire. These officers became a foreign, hereditary caste of aristocrats that increasingly supplied high administrators and even emperors. In effect, the Roman people hired an army of mercenaries, only technically Roman, to protect them.

The Late Empire

The Fourth Century and Imperial Reorganization

The period from Diocletian (r. A.D. 284–305) to Constantine (r. A.D. 306–337) was one of reconstruction

The Tetrarchs. This porphyry sculpture on the corner of the church of San Marco in Venice depicts Emperor Diocletian (r. A.D. 284–305) and his three imperial colleagues. They are in battle dress and clasp one another to express solidarity. This fourth-century sculpture was part of the booty brought back by the Venetians from their capture of Constantinople during the Fourth Crusade about nine hundred years later. [American History Museum]

and reorganization after a time of civil war and turmoil.

DIOCLETIAN. The emperor Diocletian was from Illyria (now Yugoslavia), a man of undistinguished birth who rose to the throne through the ranks of the army. He knew that he was not a great general and that the job of defending and governing the entire empire was too great for one man. He therefore decreed the introduction of the tetrarchy, the rule of the empire by four men with power divided on a territorial basis (see Map 6-3).

Diocletian was recognized as the senior Augustus, but each tetrarch was supreme in his own sphere. The Caesars were recognized as successors to each half of the empire, and their loyalty was enhanced by marriages to daughters of the Augusti. It was a return, in a way, to the happy precedent of the good emperors, who chose their successors from the ranks of the ablest men, and it seemed to promise orderly peaceful transitions instead of assassinations, chaos, and civil war.

CONSTANTINE. In 305, Diocletian retired and compelled his coemperor to do the same. But his plan for a smooth succession failed completely. In 310, there were five Augusti and no Caesars. Out of this chaos, Constantine, son of Constantius, produced order. In 324, he defeated his last opponent and made himself sole emperor, uniting the empire once again; he reigned until 337.

The emperor was a remote figure surrounded by carefully chosen high officials. He lived in a great palace and was almost unapproachable. Those admitted to his presence had to prostrate themselves before him and kiss the hem of his robe, which was purple and had golden threads going through it. The emperor was addressed as *dominus* ("lord"), and his right to rule was not derived from the Roman people but from God. All this remoteness and ceremony had a double purpose: to enhance the dignity of the emperor and to safeguard him against assassination.

Constantine erected the new city of Constantinople on the site of ancient Byzantium on the Bosporus,

MAP 6-3   DIVISIONS OF THE ROMAN EMPIRE UNDER DIOCLETIAN   *Diocletian divided the sprawling empire into four prefectures for more effective government and defense. The inset map shows their boundaries, and the large map gives some details of regions and provinces. The major division between east and west was along the line running from north to south between Pannonia and Moesia.*

which leads to both the Aegean and the Black seas, and made it the new capital of the empire. Its strategic location was excellent for protecting the eastern and Danubian frontiers, and, surrounded on three sides by water, it was easily defended. Until its fall to the Turks in 1453, it served as the bastion of civilization, the preserver of classical culture, a bulwark against barbarian attack, and the greatest city in Christendom.

ADMINISTRATION AND FINANCE.   The autocratic rule of the emperors was carried out by a civilian bureau-cracy, which was carefully separated from the military service to reduce the chances of rebellion by anyone combining the two kinds of power. The operation of the entire system was supervised by a vast network of spies and secret police, without whom the increasingly rigid totalitarian organization could not be trusted to perform. In spite of these efforts, the system was filled with corruption and inefficiency.

The cost of maintaining a four-hundred-thousand-man army as well as the vast civilian bureaucracy, the expensive imperial court, and the imperial taste for splendid buildings put a great strain on an already

Diocletian Attempts to Control Prices and Wages

Rome's troubles in the third century A.D. caused serious economic problems. Debased currency and vast government expenditures produced a runaway inflation. In an attempt to control it, Diocletian took the unprecedented step of issuing a decree that put ceilings on prices and wages throughout the empire in the year 301. In spite of the most drastic penalties prescribed by the decree, it was widely evaded. After a time, its failure was acknowledged, and the decree was at last revoked.

Who does not know that wherever the common safety requires our armies to be sent, the profiteers insolently and covertly attack the public welfare, not only in villages and towns, but on every road? They charge extortionate prices for merchandise, not just fourfold or eightfold, but on such a scale that human speech cannot find words to characterize their profit and their practices. Indeed, sometimes in a single retail sale a soldier is stripped of his donative and pay. Moreover, the contributions of the whole world for the support of the armies fall as profits into the hands of these plunderers, and our soldiers appear to bestow with their own hands the rewards of their military service and their veterans' bonuses upon the profiteers. The result is that the pillagers of the state itself seize day by day more than they know how to hold.

Aroused justly and rightfully by all the facts set forth above, and in response to the needs of mankind itself, which appears to be praying for release, we have decided that maximum prices of articles for sale must be established. We have not set down fixed prices, for we do not deem it just to do this, since many provinces occasionally enjoy the good fortune of welcome low prices and the privilege, as it were, of prosperity. Thus, when the pressure of high prices appears anywhere—may the gods avert such a calamity!—avarice will be checked by the limits fixed in our statute and by the restraining curbs of the law.

It is our pleasure, therefore, that the prices listed in the subjoined schedule be held in observance in the whole of our Empire. And every person shall take note that the liberty to exceed them at will has been ended, but that the blessing of low prices has in no way been impaired in those places where supplies actually abound. . . . Moreover, this universal edict will serve as a necessary check upon buyers and sellers whose practice it is to visit ports and other provinces. For when they too know that in the pinch of scarcity there is no possibility of exceeding the prices fixed for commodities, they will take into account in their calculations at the time of sale the localities, the transportation costs, and all other factors. In this way they will make apparent the justice of our decision that those who transport merchandise may not sell at higher prices anywhere.

It is agreed that even in the time of our ancestors it was the practice in passing laws to restrain offenses by prescribing a penalty. For rarely is a situation beneficial to humanity accepted spontaneously; experience teaches that fear is the most effective regulator and guide for the performance of duty. Therefore it is our pleasure that anyone who resists the measures of this statute shall be subject to a capital penalty for daring to do so. And let no one consider the statute harsh, since there is at hand a ready protection from danger in the observance of moderation. . . . We therefore exhort the loyalty of all, so that a regulation instituted for the public good may be observed with willing obedience and due scruple, especially as it is seen that by a statute of this kind provision has been made, not for single municipalities and peoples and provinces but for the whole world. . . .

"Diocletian's Edict on Maximum Prices," from the *Corpus Inscriptionum Latinarum*, Vol. 3, in N. Lewis and M. Reinhold, *Roman Civilization*, Vol. 2 (New York: Columbia University Press, 1955), pp. 465–466.

weak economy. Diocletian's attempts at establishing a uniform and reliable currency failed and led merely to increased inflation. To deal with it, he resorted to price control with his Edict of Maximum Prices in 301. For each product and each kind of labor, a maximum price was set, and violations were punishable by death. The edict failed, despite the harshness of its provisions.

Peasants unable to pay their taxes and officials unable to collect them tried to escape, and Diocletian resorted to stern regimentation to keep all in their places and at the service of the government. The terror of the third century had turned many peasants into *coloni*, tenant farmers who fled for protection to the *villas* ("country estates") of larger and powerful landowners. They were tied to the land, as were their descendants, as the caste system hardened.

DIVISION OF THE EMPIRE.   The peace and unity established by Constantine did not last long. His death was followed by a struggle for succession that was won by Constantius II (r. 337–361). His death left the empire to his young cousin Julian (r. 361–363), called by the Christians "the Apostate" as a result of his attempt to stamp out Christianity and restore paganism. Julian undertook a campaign against Persia, with the aim of putting a Roman on the throne of the Sassanids and ending the Persian menace once and for all. He penetrated deep into Persia but was killed in battle. His death put an end to the expedition and to the pagan revival.

The Germans in the west took advantage of the eastern campaign to attack along the Rhine River and the upper Danube River, but even greater trouble was

Arch of Constantine. The triumphal arch was a characteristic Roman imperial structure, and examples are found throughout the empire. This one at Rome was dedicated in 315 in celebration of Constantine's victory over Maxentius at the Milvian bridge. In the distance, through the center arch, note some remaining arches of a first-century aqueduct, the Aqua Claudia.

Such structures as this arch and the aqueduct illustrate a significant point: As an adjunct of the administration and maintenance of their far-flung empire and the need to provide for the citizens' safety and amusement, the Romans were immensely practical—almost compulsive—builders and engineers. Their bridges and aqueducts, temples and altars, triumphal arches and columns, theaters and arenas, palaces and villas, roads and government buildings, baths and public housing, harbor facilities, defensive walls, and fortresses were found all over the Mediterranean world and set standards that long challenged the West. [Alinari/Art Resource]

brewing along the middle and upper Danube (see Map 6-4). That territory was occupied by the eastern Goths, the Ostrogoths. They were being pushed hard by their western cousins, the Visigoths, who in turn had been driven from their home in the Ukraine by the fierce Huns, a nomadic people from central Asia. The Emperor Valentinian (r. 364–375) saw that he could not defend the empire alone and appointed his brother Valens (r. 364–378) as coruler. Valentinian made his own headquarters at Milan and spent the rest of his life fighting successfully against the Franks and the Alemanni in the west. Valens was given control of the east. The empire was once again divided in two. The two emperors maintained their own courts, and the two halves of the empire became increasingly separate and different. Latin was the language of the west and Greek of the east.

In 376, the hard-pressed Visigoths asked and re- ceived permission to enter the empire to escape the Huns. Contrary to the bargain, the Goths kept their weapons and began to plunder the Balkan provinces. Valens attacked the Goths and died, along with most of his army, at Adrianople in Thrace in 378. Theodosius (r. 379–395), an able and experienced general, was named coruler in the east. He tried to unify the empire again, but his death in 395 left it divided and weak.

For the future, the two parts of the empire went their separate and different ways. The west became increasingly rural as barbarian invasions continued and grew in intensity. The *villa*, a fortified country estate, became the basic unit of life. There, *coloni* gave their services to the local magnate in return for economic assistance and protection from both bar- barians and imperial officials. Many cities shrank to no more than tiny walled fortresses ruled by military

MAP 6-4   THE EMPIRE'S NEIGHBORS   *In the fourth century the Roman Empire was nearly surrounded by ever more threatening neighbors. The map shows who these so-called barbarians were and where they lived before their armed contact with the Romans.*

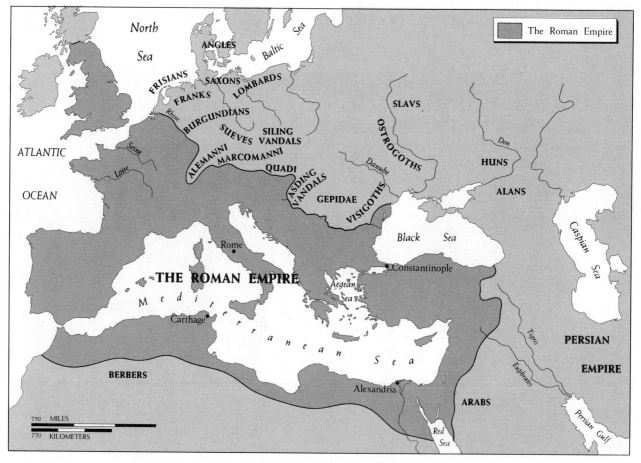

Ammianus Marcellinus Describes the People Called Huns

Ammianus Marcellinus was born about A.D. 330 in Syria, where Greek was the language of his well-to-do-family. After a military career and considerable travel, he lived in Rome and wrote an encyclopedic Latin history of the empire, covering the years A.D. 96–378 and giving special emphasis to the difficulties of the fourth century. Here he describes the Huns, one of the barbarous peoples pressing on the frontiers.

▶ *Compare this response to the Huns to that of Salvian in "Salvian the Priest Compares the Romans and the Barbarians" in Chapter 14. For another response to a clash of cultures, see "How the Hindus Differ from the Muslims" in Chapter 16.*

The people called Huns, barely mentioned in ancient records, live beyond the sea of Azof, on the border of the Frozen Ocean, and are a race savage beyond all parallel. At the very moment of birth the cheeks of their infant children are deeply marked by an iron, in order that the hair, instead of growing at the proper season on their faces, may be hindered by the scars; accordingly the Huns grow up without beards, and without any beauty. They all have closely knit and strong limbs and plump necks; they are of great size, and low legged, so that you might fancy them two-legged beasts or the stout figures which are hewn out in a rude manner with an ax on the posts at the end of bridges.

They are certainly in the shape of men, however uncouth, and are so hardy that they neither require fire nor well-flavored food, but live on the roots of such herbs as they get in the fields, or on the half-raw flesh of any animal, which they merely warm rapidly by placing it between their own thighs and the backs of their horses.

They never shelter themselves under roofed houses, but avoid them, as people ordinarily avoid sepulchers as things not fit for common use. Nor is there even to be found among them a cabin thatched with reeds; but they wander about, roaming over the mountains and the woods, and accustom themselves to bear frost and hunger and thirst from their very cradles. . . .

There is not a person in the whole nation who cannot remain on his horse day and night. On horseback they buy and sell, they take their meat and drink and there they recline on the narrow neck of their steed, and yield to sleep so deep as to indulge in every variety of dream.

And when any deliberation is to take place on any weighty matter, they all hold their common council on horseback. They are not under kingly authority, but are contented with the irregular government of their chiefs, and under their lead they force their way through all obstacles. . . . .

Ammianus Marcellinus, *Res Gestae*, trans. by C. D. Yonge (London: George Bell and Son, 1862), pp. 312–314.

commanders and bishops. The upper classes moved to the country and asserted ever greater independence of imperial authority. The failure of the central authority to maintain the roads and the constant danger from robber bands sharply curtailed trade and communications, forcing greater self-reliance and a more primitive style of life. The new world emerging in the west by the fifth century and afterward was increasingly made up of isolated units of rural aristocrats and their dependent laborers. The only institution providing a high degree of unity was the Christian Church. The pattern for the early Middle Ages in the west was already formed.

In the east, the situation was quite different. Constantinople became the center of a vital and flourishing culture that we call *Byzantine* and that lasted until the fifteenth century. Due to its defensible location, the skill of its emperors, and the firmness and strength of its base in Asia Minor, it was able to deflect and repulse barbarian attacks. A strong navy allowed commerce to flourish in the eastern Mediterranean and, in good times, far beyond it. Cities continued to prosper, and the emperors made their will good over the nobles in the countryside. The civilization of the Byzantine Empire was a unique combination of classical culture, the Christian religion,

Roman law, and eastern artistic influences. While the west was being overrun by barbarians, the Roman Empire, in altered form, persisted in the east. While Rome shrank to an insignificant ecclesiastical town, Constantinople flourished as the seat of empire, the "New Rome," and the Byzantines called themselves "Romans." When we contemplate the decline and fall of the Roman Empire in the fourth and fifth centuries, we are speaking only of the west. A form of classical culture persisted in the Byzantine east for a thousand years longer.

Triumph of Christianity

RELIGIOUS CURRENTS IN THE EMPIRE.   In the troubled times of the fourth and fifth centuries, people sought powerful, personal deities who would bring them safety and prosperity in this world and immortality in the next. Paganism was open and tolerant, and it was by no means unusual for people to worship new deities alongside the old and even to intertwine elements of several to form a new amalgam by the device called *syncretism.*

Christianity's success owed something to the same causes of the popularity of other cults, which are often spoken of as its rivals. None of them, however, attained Christianity's universality, and none appears to have given the early Christians and their leaders as much competition as the ancient philosophies or the state religion (see Map 6-5).

IMPERIAL PERSECUTION.   By the third century, Christianity had taken firm hold in the eastern provinces and in Italy. As times became bad and the Christians became more numerous and visible, popular opinion blamed disasters, natural and military, on the Christians. About 250, the Emperor Decius (r. 249–251) invoked the aid of the gods in his war against the Goths and required that all citizens worship the state gods publicly. True Christians could not obey, and Decius instituted a major persecution. Many Christians, even some bishops, yielded to threats and torture, but others held out and were killed. Valerian (r. 253–260) resumed the persecutions, partly in order to confiscate the wealth of rich Christians. His successors, however, found other matters more pressing, and the persecution lapsed until the end of the century.

Diocletian was not generous toward unorthodox intellectual or religious movements, and his own effort to bolster imperial power with the aura of divinity

(A)   200

(B)   200–400

(C)   400–600

MAP 6-5   THE SPREAD OF CHRISTIANITY   *Christianity grew swiftly in the third, fourth, fifth, and sixth centuries—especially after the conversion of the emperors in the fourth century. By 600, on the eve of the birth of Muhammad's new Muslim religion, Christianity was dominant throughout the Mediterranean world and most of Western Europe.*

boded ill for the Church, yet he did not attack the Christians for almost twenty years. In 303, however, he launched the most serious persecution inflicted on the Christians in the Roman Empire. The persecution horrified many pagans, and the plight and the demeanor of the martyrs often aroused pity and sympathy. For these reasons, as well as the incapacity of any large ancient state to carry out a program of terror with the thoroughness of modern totalitarian governments, the Christians and their Church survived to enjoy what they must have considered a miraculous change of fortune. In 311, Galerius, who had been one of the most vigorous persecutors, was influenced, perhaps by his Christian wife, to issue an edict of toleration permitting Christian worship.

The victory of Constantine and his emergence as sole ruler of the empire changed the condition of Christianity from a precariously tolerated sect to the religion favored by the emperor and put it on the path to becoming the official and only legal religion in the empire.

CHRISTIANITY BECOMES THE STATE RELIGION.   The sons of Constantine continued to favor the new religion, but the succession of Julian the Apostate posed a new threat. Although he refrained from persecution, he tried to undo the work of Constantine by withdrawing the privileges of the Church, removing Christians from high offices, and attempting to introduce a new form of pagan worship. His reign, however, was short, and his work did not last.

In 394, Theodosius forbade the celebration of pagan cults and abolished the pagan religious calendar. At the death of Theodosius, Christianity was the official religion of the Roman Empire.

The favored position of the Church attracted converts for the wrong reasons and diluted the moral excellence and spiritual fervor of its adherents. The problem of the relationship between church and state arose, presenting the possibility that religion would become subordinate to the state, as it had been in the classical world and in earlier civilizations. In the east, that is what happened to a considerable degree. In the west, the weakness of the emperors prevented such a development and permitted Church leaders to exercise remarkable independence. In 390, Ambrose, bishop of Milan, excommunicated Emperor Theodosius for a massacre he had carried out, and the emperor did humble penance. This act provided an important precedent for future assertions of the Church's autonomy and authority, but it did not put an end to secular interference and influence in the Church by any means.

ARIANISM AND THE COUNCIL OF NICEA.   Internal divisions proved to be even more troubling as new heresies emerged. The most important and the most

The Council at Nicea Creates the Test of Religious Orthodoxy

In 325, Emperor Constantine called a general council of leading Christians at Nicea in Asia Minor in an attempt to end the quarreling over the question of the Trinity. The Nicene Creed was the result. Adherence to it became a test of orthodoxy, and those rejecting it were declared heretics.

We believe in one God, the Father Almighty, maker of all things visible and invisible; and in one Lord Jesus Christ, the Son of God, the only-begotten of his Father, of the substance of the Father, God of God, Light of Light; very God of very God, begotten not made, being of one substance with the Father, by whom all things were made, both which be in heaven and in earth. Who for us men and for our salvation came down [from heaven] and was incarnate and was made man. He suffered and the third day he rose again, and ascended into heaven. And he shall come again to judge both the quick and the dead. And [we believe] in the Holy Ghost. And whosoever shall say that there was time when the Son of God was not, or that before he was begotten he was not, or that he was made of things that were not, or that he is of a different substance or essence [from the Father] or that he is a creature, or subject to change or conversion—all that so say, the Catholic and Apostolic Church anathematizes them.

"The Nicene Creed," from *The Seven Ecumenical Councils*, trans. by A. C. McGiffort and E. C. Richardson, 2nd series, Vol. 14 (New York: Library of the Nicene and Post-Nicene Fathers, 1900), p. 3.

threatening was Arianism, founded by a priest named Arius of Alexandria (ca. 280–336) in the fourth century. Arius's view did away with the mysterious concept of the Trinity, the difficult doctrine that holds that God is three persons (the Father, the Son, and the Holy Spirit) and at the same time one in substance and essence.

Athanasius (ca. 293–373), later bishop of Alexandria, saw the Arian view as an impediment to any acceptable theory of salvation, to him the most important religious question. He adhered to the old Greek idea of salvation as involving the change of sinful mortality into divine immortality through the gift of "life." Only if Jesus were both fully human and fully God could the transformation of humanity to divinity have taken place in Him and be transmitted by Him to his disciples. "Christ was made man," he said, "that we might be made divine."

To deal with the growing controversy, Constantine called a council of Christian bishops of Nicea, not far from Constantinople, in 325. For the emperor, the question was essentially political, but for the disputants, salvation was at stake. At Nicea, the view expounded by Athanasius won out, became orthodox, and was embodied in the Nicene Creed. But Arianism persisted and spread. Some later emperors were either Arians or sympathetic to that view. Some of the most successful missionaries to the barbarians were Arians, with the result that many of the German tribes who overran the empire were Arians. The Christian emperors hoped to bring unity to their increasingly decentralized realms by imposing the single religion, and over time, it did prove to be a unifying force, but it also introduced new divisions where none had previously existed.

Arts and Letters in the Late Empire

The art and literature of the late empire reflect the confluence of pagan and Christian ideas and traditions as well as the conflict between them. Much of the literature is polemical, and much of the art is propaganda.

The salvation of the empire from the chaos of the third century accomplished by a military revolution based on and led by provincials whose origins were in the lower classes. They brought with them the fresh winds of cultural change, which blew out not only the dust of classical culture but much of its substance as well. Yet the new ruling class was not interested in leveling society but wanted instead to establish itself as a new aristocracy. It thought of itself as effecting a great restoration rather than a revolution and sought to restore classical culture and absorb it. The confusion and uncertainty of the times were tempered in part, of course, by the comfort of Christianity, but the new ruling class sought order and stability—ethical, literary, and artistic—in the classical tradition as well.

Preservation of Classical Culture

One of the main needs and accomplishments of this period was the preservation of classical culture and the discovery of ways to make it available and useful to the newly arrived ruling class. The great classical authors were reproduced in many copies, and their works were transferred from perishable and inconvenient papyrus rolls to sturdier codices, bound volumes that were as easy to use as modern books. Scholars also digested long works like Livy's *History of Rome* into shorter versions and wrote learned commentaries and compiled grammars. Original works by pagan writers of the late empire were neither numerous nor especially distinguished.

Christian Writers

Of Christian writings, on the other hand, the late empire saw a great outpouring. There were many examples of Christian apologetics in poetry as well as in prose, and there were sermons, hymns, and biblical commentaries. Christianity could also boast important scholars. Jerome (348–420), thoroughly trained in both the east and the west in classical Latin literature and rhetoric, produced a revised version of the Bible in Latin, commonly called the Vulgate, which became the Bible used by the Catholic Church.

Probably the most important eastern scholar was Eusebius of Caesarea (ca. 260–ca. 340). He wrote apologetics, an idealized biography of Constantine, and a valuable reconstruction of the chronology of important events in the past. His most important contribution, however, was his *Ecclesiastical History*, an attempt to set forth the Christian view of history. He saw all of history as the working out of God's will. All of history, therefore, had a purpose and a direction, and Constantine's victory and the subsequent unity of empire and Church were its culmination.

The closeness and also the complexity of the relationship between classical pagan culture and that of the Christianity of the late empire are nowhere better displayed than in the career and writings of Augustine (354–430), bishop of Hippo in north Africa. He was born at Carthage and was trained as a teacher of rhetoric. His father was a pagan, but his mother was a Christian, and hers was ultimately the stronger influence. He passed through a number of intellectual way stations before his conversion to Christianity. His training and skill in pagan rhetoric and philosophy made him peerless among his contemporaries as a defender of Christianity and as a theologian. His greatest works are his *Confessions,* an autobiography describing the road to his conversion, and *The City of God.* The latter was a response to the pagan charge that Rome's sack by the Goths in 410 was caused by the abandonment of the old gods and the advent of Christianity. The optimistic view held by some Christians that God's will worked its way in history and was easily comprehensible needed further support in the face of this disaster.

Augustine sought to separate the fate of Christianity from that of the Roman Empire. He contrasted the secular world—the city of Man—with the spiritual—the City of God. The former was selfish, the latter unselfish; the former evil, the latter good. Augustine argued that history was moving forward, in the spiritual sense, to the Day of Judgment, but that there was no reason to expect improvement before then in the secular sphere. The fall of Rome was neither surprising nor important, for all states, even a Christian Rome, were part of the City of Man and therefore corrupt and mortal. Only the City of God was immortal, and it, consisting of all the saints on earth and in heaven, was untouched by earthly calamities.

Augustine believed that faith is essential and primary—a thoroughly Christian view—but that it is not a substitute for reason, the foundation of classical thought. Instead, faith is the starting point for the liberator of human reason, which continues to be the means by which people can understand what is revealed by faith. His writings constantly reveal the presence of both Christian faith and pagan reason—and the tension between them, a legacy he left to the Middle Ages.

The Problem of the Decline and Fall of the Empire in the West

Whether important to Augustine or not, the massive barbarian invasions of the fifth century put an end to effective imperial government in the West. For centuries, people have speculated about the causes of the collapse of the ancient world. Every kind of reason has been put forward, and some suggestions seem to have nothing to do with reason at all. Soil exhaustion, plague, climatic change, and even poisoning caused by lead water pipes have been suggested as reasons for Rome's decline in population, vigor, and the capacity to defend itself. Some blame the institution of slavery and the failure to make advances in science and technology that they believe resulted from it. Others blame excessive government interference in the economic life of the empire; others, the destruction of the urban middle class, the carrier of classical culture.

Perhaps a plausible explanation can be found that is more simple and obvious. It might begin with the observation that the growth of so mighty an empire as Rome's was by no means inevitable. Rome's greatness had come from conquests that provided the Romans with the means to expand still further, until there were not enough Romans to conquer and govern any more peoples and territory. When pressure from outsiders grew, the Romans lacked the resources to advance and defeat the enemy as in the past. The tenacity and success of their resistance for so long were remarkable. Without new conquests to provide the immense wealth needed for the defense and maintenance of internal prosperity, the Romans finally yielded to unprecedented onslaughts by fierce and numerous attackers.

To blame the ancients and the institution of slavery for the failure to produce an industrial and economic revolution like that of the later Western world, one capable of producing wealth without taking it from another, is to stand the problem on its head. No one yet has a satisfactory explanation for those revolutions, so it is improper to blame any institution or society for not achieving what has been achieved only once in human history, in what are still mysterious circumstances.

Imperial Rome in World Perspective

Perhaps we would do well to think of the decline of Rome as Gibbon did:

The decline of Rome was the natural and inevitable effect of immoderate greatness. Prosperity ripened the principle of decay; the cause of the destruction multi-

Imperial Rome. This is a model of a reconstruction of the city of Rome during the imperial period. At the left is the Circus Maximus, on the lower right is the Colosseum, and the Forum is just above the exact center of the picture. The Model is in the Museo della Civiltà Romana. [Bettmann Archive]

plied with the extent of conquest; and, as soon as time or accident had removed the artificial supports, the stupendous fabric yielded to the pressure of its own weight. The story of the ruin is simple and obvious; and instead of inquiring why the Roman Empire was destroyed, we should rather be surprised that it had subsisted so long.[4]

This explanation allows us to see the Roman Empire as one among several great empires around the world that had similar experiences.

Out of the civil wars and chaos that brought down the Republic, Augustus brought unity, peace, order, and prosperity. As a result, he was regarded with almost religious awe and attained more military and political power than any Roman before him. He ruled firmly but with moderation. He tried to limit military adventures and the costs they incurred. He supported public works that encouraged trade and communica-

tion in the empire. He tried to restore and invigorate the old civic pride, in which he had considerable success, and private morality based on family values. In this latter goal, he was less successful. He patronized the arts in such a way as to beautify Rome and glorify his reign. On his death, he was able to pass on the regime to his family, the Julio-Claudians.

For almost two hundred years, with a few brief interruptions, the empire was generally prosperous, peaceful, and well run, but problems were growing. Management of the many responsibilities assumed by the government required the growth of a large bureaucracy, which placed a heavy and increasing burden on the treasury, required higher taxes, and stifled both civic spirit and private enterprise. Pressure from barbarian tribes on the frontiers required a large standing army, which was also very costly and led to further rises in taxation.

In the late empire, Rome's rulers resorted to many devices for dealing with their problems, including

[4]Edward Gibbon, *Decline and Fall of the Roman Empire,* ed. by J. B. Bury, 2nd, ed., Vol. 4 (London: J. Murray, 1909), pp. 173–174.

putting down internal military rebellions led by generals from different parts of the empire. More and more, the emperors' rule and their safety depended on the loyalty of the army, so they courted the soldiers' favor with gifts of various kinds. This only increased the burden of taxes; the rich and powerful found ways to avoid their obligations, making the load on everyone else all the heavier. The government's control over the lives of its people became ever greater and the society more rigid as people tried to flee to escape the crushing load of taxes. Many measures were tried: inflating the currency, fixing farmers to the soil as serfs, building walls to keep the barbarians out, and bribing barbarian tribes to fight for Rome against other barbarians; but ultimately they all failed.

It is especially instructive to look at Rome from the perspective of the historians who discern a "dynastic cycle" in China (see Chapter 8). The development of the Roman Empire, although by no means the same as the Chinese, fits the same pattern fairly well. Like the Former Han Dynasty in China, the Roman Empire in the West fell, leaving disunity, insecurity, disorder, and poverty. Like similar empires in the ancient world, it had been unable to sustain its "immoderate greatness."

Suggested Readings

J. P. V. D. BALSDON, *Roman Women* (1962).

T. BARNES, *The New Empire of Diocletian and Constantine* (1982).

K. R. BRADLEY, *Slaves and Masters in the Roman Empire* (1989).

P. BROWN, *Augustine of Hippo* (1967). A splendid biography.

P. BROWN, *The World of Late Antiquity,* A.D. *150–750* (1971). A brilliant and readable essay.

J. BURCKHARDT, *The Age of Constantine the Great* (1956). A classic work by the Swiss cultural historian.

J. CARCOPINO, *Daily Life in Ancient Rome,* trans. by E. O. Lorimer (1940).

C. M. COCHRANE, *Christianity and Classical Culture* (1957). A study of intellectual change in the late empire.

E. R. DODDS, *Pagan and Christian in an Age of Anxiety* (1965). An original and perceptive study.

E. GIBBON, *The History of the Decline and Fall of the Roman Empire,* 2nd ed., 7 vols., ed. by J. B. Bury (1909–1914). One of the masterworks of the English language.

N. HANNESTAD, *Roman Art and Imperial Policy* (1988). An analysis of how the emperors used the arts to further their own and imperial interests.

A. H. M. JONES, *The Later Roman Empire,* 3 vols. (1964). A comprehensive study of the period.

D. KAGAN, ed., *The End of the Roman Empire: Decline or Transformation?* 3rd ed. (1992). A collection of essays discussing the problem of the decline and fall of the Roman Empire.

M. L. W. LAISTNER, *The Greater Roman Historians* (1963). Essays on the major Roman historical writers.

J. LEBRETON and J. ZEILLER, *History of the Primitive Church,* 3 vols. (1962). From the Catholic viewpoint.

H. LIETZMANN, *History of the Early Church,* 2 vols. (1961). From the Protestant viewpoint.

F. LOT, *The End of the Ancient World and the Beginnings of the Middle Ages* (1961). A study that emphasizes gradual transition rather than abrupt change.

E. N. LUTTWAK, *The Grand Strategy of the Roman Empire* (1976). An original and fascinating analysis by a keen student of modern strategy.

R. MACMULLEN, *Enemies of the Roman Order* (1966). An original and revealing examination of opposition to the emperors.

R. MACMULLEN, *Paganism in the Roman Empire* (1981).

R. MACMULLEN, *Roman Social Relations, 50* B.C. *to* A.D. *284* (1981).

F. B. MARSH, *The Founding of the Roman Empire* (1959).

F. MILLAR, *The Roman Empire and Its Neighbors,* 2nd ed. (1981).

A. MOMIGLIANO, ed., *The Conflict Between Paganism and Christianity* (1963). A valuable collection of essays.

H. M. D. PARKER, *A History of the Roman World from* A.D. *138 to 337* (1969). A good survey.

M. I. ROSTOVTZEFF, *Social and Economic History of the Roman Empire,* 2nd ed. (1957). A masterpiece whose main thesis has been much disputed.

E. T. SALMON, *A History of the Roman World, 30* B.C. *to* A.D. *138* (1968). A good survey.

C. G. STARR, *Civilization and the Caesars* (1965). A study of Roman culture in the Augustan period.

R. SYME, *The Augustan Aristocracy* (1985). An examination of the new ruling class shaped by Augustus.

R. SYME, *The Roman Revolution* (1960). A brilliant study of Augustus, his supporters, and their rise to power.

L. A. THOMPSON, *Romans and Blacks* (1989).

Stone relief (from ca. 475 B.C.) at Persepolis, the summer capital of the Achaemenids. The figures are Medes and Persians of the palace guard. They stand beside the east stairway to the great audience hall of the palace. [Bildarchiv Preussischer Kulturbesitz]

Iran, India, and Inner Asia to A.D. 200

From the Mediterranean to China, the period from about 600 B.C. to A.D. 200 saw the rise of centralized empires on a new and unprecedented scale. In this development, Iran and India preceded both China and the Roman west. Well before the Ch'in unification or the rise of the Han dynasty in China, and long before *imperium* replaced republic in Rome, the Achaemenids (ca. 539–330 B.C.), an Aryan dynasty from the southwestern part of the Iranian plateau, created an empire centered in Babylonia and Iran that was the greatest yet seen in world history. Two centuries later, in northeastern India, a local dynasty known as the Mauryans, centered in the state of Magadha in the Ganges basin, founded the first great Indian empire (ca. 321–ca. 185 B.C.). Both of these empires, like their later Chinese and Roman counterparts, developed sophisticated bureaucracies, professional armies, and strong communication systems. They also contributed to the development of distinctive cultural, political, and religious ideas and forms in the regions they influenced.

Another characteristic of the period 600 B.C. to A.D. 200 is increased contact and interaction among major civilizations. These centuries saw the first long-sustained contact among the major centers of culture from the Mediterranean to China. Although some links of trade and travel had already been established, the flourishing of the empires of Iran, India, China, and Rome increased and secured them. The large-scale empires created new markets for diverse goods, both material and human (such as slaves, soldiers, and artisans); new security along major trade routes; new impetus for both diplomacy and conquest abroad; and a generally wider interest in the world at large.

The conquests (334–323 B.C.) by Alexander the

Great of the Persian Empire and the regions of modern Afghanistan and northwestern India contributed dramatically to the growing contact among diverse cultures, races, and religious traditions. Although the empire they created was ephemeral, these conquests ended the Achaemenid dynasty and, in the east, allowed the rising Mauryan power to extend its control over all of North India. The Hellenes and steppe peoples of northeastern Iran and Central (Inner) Asia, who ruled first post-Alexandrine Iran and then post-Mauryan India down to the third century A.D., inherited a world with horizons irrevocably larger than those of their original homelands.

A third characteristic of this period is the rise, spread, and consolidation of major religious tradi-tions that would have considerable effect on later history from Africa to China. The evolution of Judaism in the Second Temple and Early Diaspora periods, as well as the rise and spread of Christianity and diverse Hellenistic cults were of considerable importance to the history of the Mediterranean and western Asia (see Chapters 2 and 6). In China, this period saw the rise of Han Confucianism and classical Taoist thought (see Chapters 2 and 9). In Iran it saw the origins and growth of Zoroastrian religious practice and thought. In India, it saw the gradual emergence of an identifiable Hindu tradition, the expansion of the Buddhist movement, and the spread of Buddhism abroad, especially into Southeast Asia and China.

IRAN

"Iran" is the name given to the huge expanse of southwest Asia that lies between the Caspian and the Arabian seas; it is bounded by Transoxiana to the northeast, the Indus Valley to the southeast, the Ti-gris–Euphrates basin to the southwest, and Armenia and the Caucasus to the northwest. The region is dominated by the vast expanse of the high central

A fifth-century B.C. *Achaemenid amphora from south-western Iran with double tube-handles. [Bildarchiv Preussischer Kulturbesitz]*

Iranian plateau at its center. It is cut off on all sides by mighty mountain ranges, principally the Hindu Kush, the Sulaiman chain, the Zagros, and the Elburz. In its central reaches, it contains two large, empty, and un-inhabitable salt deserts whose desolation is a more formidable barrier to travel than most of the great mountain chains themselves.

Early populations in Iran clustered in the plains, the lower mountain reaches, and the many fertile oases, wherever rainfall or ground water was plentiful and communication with outside areas easiest. Fore-most among these areas have been Persis, Media, Hyrcania, and Parthia. The great trade routes of Asian history have put Iran at the heart of east–west inter-change. But these routes and the subsequent location of major cities and towns have been determined more by the mountain passes and traversable stretches of the Iranian plateau than by the distances involved.

Ancient Background

The Iranians

The oldest texts in ancient Persian dialects show that the Aryan peoples who settled on the Iranian plateau itself, perhaps around 1100 B.C., were related to the Vedic or Indo-Aryans of North India. Presumably, both were pastoralists—horse-breeding peoples who had come originally from the Eurasian or Central Asian steppes. The most prominent of the ancient Iranian peoples were the Medes and the Persians. By the eighth century B.C., they had spread around the deserts to settle and control the western and southwestern areas of Iran, to which they gave their names, Media and Persis (later Fars), respectively.

The Medes developed a tribal confederacy in western Iran. By the end of the seventh century B.C., with the Neo-Babylonians, they were able to defeat the mighty Assyrians and break their hold on the Fertile Crescent. The rise of Persian power under the Achaemenid clan in the seventh and sixth centuries B.C. led to the replacement of Median supremacy on the Iranian plateau under the Achaemenid ruler Cyrus around 550 B.C. Many of the institutions that developed in the ensuing empire (such as the satrapy system of provincial administration) were likely continuations of Median practices, which had in turn been drawn from Babylonian and Assyrian models in many instances. Part of the genius of the Achaemenids' unparalleled imperial success lay in their ability to use existing institutions to build their own state and administer far-flung dominions well.

Ancient Iranian Religion

We know more about the religious tradition of ancient Iran than about other aspects of its culture, because our only pre-Achaemenid texts are religious. They suggest that the old Iranian culture and religion were similar to those of the Vedic Aryans. The importance of water and fire, the role of sacrifice, the centrality of the cow, and the names and traits of particular divine beings and religious concepts all have their counterparts in Vedic texts. The emphasis was on moral order, or the "Right"—that is, asha or arta (equivalent to the Vedic rta; see Chapter 1). The supreme heavenly deity was Ahura (the equivalent of the Vedic Varuna) Mazda, the "Wise Lord." These facts also reflect the kinship of Vedic and Iranian tradition. Still, the Iranian religion of the early second millennium was far from monolithic. Cultural variations in ancient Iran among the southeast (Sistan), the northeast (Parthia, Herat, and Bactria), the west (Media), and the southwest (Persis) were substantial.

Zoroaster and the Zoroastrian Tradition

The first person who stands out in Iranian history was not Cyrus, founder of the Achaemenid Empire, to whom we shall turn shortly, but the great prophet-reformer of Iranian religion, Zarathushtra, who is commonly known in the West by the Greek version of his name, Zoroaster. Although some scholars date his life to before 1000 B.C., according to the most common reckoning he lived from 628 to 551 B.C. in northeastern Iran. Not unlike the Hebrew prophets, the Buddha, and Confucius, Zoroaster preached a message of moral reform in an age when materialism, political opportunism, and ethical indifference were common. He found a royal protector in an eastern Iranian tribal leader said to have been converted to Zoroaster's ideas about 588 B.C.

In Zoroaster's hymns, we glimpse the values of a peasant-pastoralist society that was growing up along with early urban trade centers in northeastern Iran. These values contrasted with those of the nomadic warrior peoples of the steppes. For example, Zoroaster called for a reform of traditional animal sacrifices (especially those involving the particularly sacred cow and ox) to make them more humane to the victim.

Zoroaster himself was trained as a priest in the old Iranian tradition, but his hymns, or Gathas, reflect the new religious vision he championed. This vision stemmed from his passionate sense of personal encounter with Ahura Mazda as the most powerful of deities. He reinterpreted the old sacrificial fire as the symbol of the supreme Lord. He called on people to abandon worship of and sacrifice to all lesser deities, or daevas, whom he identified as demons rather than gods. He tried to reform the morality of his people by calling on them to turn from the "Lie" (druj) to the "Truth" (asha). He warned of a "final reckoning," when the good would be rewarded with "future glory" and the wicked punished with "long-lasting darkness, ill food, and wailing."

By the mid-fourth century B.C., the Zoroastrian reform had spread into western as well as eastern Iran. The quasi-monotheistic worship of Ahura Mazda, the Wise Lord, was rapidly accommodated to the veneration of older Iranian gods by the interpretation of these deities as secondary gods or even different manifestations of the wise Lord himself. What role the Iranian priestly clan known as the Magi played in these developments is not clear. They may have integrated Zoroastrian ideas and texts into their older, polytheistic tradition, becoming thereby architects of a reformed tradition. Certainly the name "magi" was later used for the priests of the tradition that we refer to as "Zoroastrian."

Zoroastrianism probably influenced not only the Jewish, Christian, and Muslim ideas of the messiah, angels, and devils, the last judgment, and an afterlife, but also certain important Buddhist concepts as well.

A Hymn of Zoroaster About the Twin Spirits of Good and Evil

The focus of Zoroaster's reform was the supremacy of Ahura Mazda (the "Wise Lord") over all the deities of the Iranian pantheon. He is pictured in the hymns, or Gathas, as the greatest of the ahuras, the divinities associated with the good. The world is seen in terms of a moral dualism of good and evil, which is represented on the divine plane in the twin spirits created by Ahura Mazda, both of whom are given the freedom to choose the Truth or the Lie. As the following selection shows, the "Most Holy Spirit" chose truth ("Righteousness"), and the "evil spirit" chose the evil of the Lie. Similarly, humans can choose with which side—the good spirit and the ahuras, or the evil spirit and the daevas ("the false gods")—they will ally themselves. The struggle on the divine level between the gods is mirrored in the struggle on the human level between the righteous and the evildoers, as the hymn here emphasizes. This selection is from Yasna ("Worship") section 30 of the main Zoroastrian holy book, the Avesta. It makes vivid the dualistic bent of Zoroastrianism.

YASNA 30

Now will I speak to those who will hear
Of the things which the initiate should remember:
The praises and prayer of the Good Mind to the Lord
And the joy which he shall see in the light who has
   remembered them well.

Hear with your ears that which is the sovereign good;
With a clear mind look upon the two sides
Between which each man must choose for himself,
Watchful beforehand that the great test may be ac-
   complished in our favour.

Now at the beginning the twin spirits have declared
   their nature,
The better and the evil,
In thought and word and deed. And between the two
The wise ones choose well, not so the foolish.

And when these two spirits came together,
In the beginning they established life and non-life,
And that at the last the worst existence should be for
   the wicked,
But for the righteous one the Best Mind.

Of these two spirits, the evil one chose to do the
   worst things;
But the Most Holy Spirit, clothed in the most steadfast
   heavens,
Joined himself unto Righteousness;
And thus did all those who delight to please the Wise
   Lord by honest deeds.

Between the two, the false gods also did not choose
   rightly,

For while they pondered they were beset by error,
So that they chose the Worst Mind.
Then did they hasten to join themselves unto Fury,
That they might by it deprave the existence of man.

And to him came Devotion, together with Dominion,
   Good Mind and Righteousness:
She gave endurance of body and the breath of life,
That he may be thine apart from them,
As the first by the retributions through the metal.

And when their punishment shall come to these
   sinners,
Then, O Wise One, shall thy Dominion, with the
   Good Mind,
Be granted to those who have delivered Evil into the
   hands of
Righteousness, O Lord!

And may we be those that renew this existence!
O Wise One, and you other Lords, and Righteous-
   ness, bring your alliance,
That thoughts may gather where wisdom is faint.

Then shall Evil cease to flourish,
While those who have acquired good fame
Shall reap the promised reward
In the blessed dwelling of the Good Mind, of the Wise
   One, and of Righteousness.

If you, O men, understand the commandments which
   the Wise One has given,
Well-being and suffering—long torment for the
   wicked and salvation for the righteous—
All shall hereafter be for the best.

From Jacques Duchesne-Guillemin, trans., *The Hymns of Zarathushtra*, trans. from the French by M. Henning (Boston: Beacon, 1963), pp. 103, 105, 107.

Hinduism

The term *Hinduism* is simply our modern word for the majority of the diverse religious traditions of India taken as a whole. Until the word was coined in the nineteenth century, it (like *Buddhism*) was not even a concept in the West, let alone in India itself. In contemporary usage, however, it has become a catchall term used for all the Indian religious communities that look upon the texts of the Vedas (see Chapter 1) as eternal, perfect truth.

The historical beginnings of the varied Hindu traditions can be traced to the ancient Aryan migrations into southern Asia in the second millenium before our common era. This was the age in which the Vedic hymns were composed. In them we find a pantheon of gods not unlike that found among the Greeks, the Romans, and other Indo-European peoples. Centered on a sacrificial cult of these gods, Vedic religion became more and more the preserve of the Brahman priestly class of early Indian society. The Brahmans gradually elaborated a cult characterized by complex rituals of sacrifice, involved purificatory rules, and increasingly fixed distinctions of birth on which the later caste system was based. These developments are mirrored in the later Vedic, or Brahmanical, texts (ca. 1000–500 B.C.) that provide commentary on and instructions for ritual use of the Vedic hymns.

After about 700 B.C., new developments set in. North India produced a series of religious reformers, most of whom championed knowledge and ascetic discipline rather than purity and ritual action. Some of these reformers broke with the Vedic tradition. Of these, Siddhartha Gautama (the Buddha; b. ca. 563) and Mahavira Vardhamana (founder of the Jain tradition; b. ca. 550) were the two most famous. Other thinkers reinterpreted the older sacrifice as an inner activity and deepened its spiritual dimensions. They further tried to link or to identify Transcendence, or Ultimate Being *(Brahman)*, with the inmost self *(atman)*. Their thinking is represented especially in the Upanishads, which many Hindus consider the most sublime philosophical texts in the Indian tradition.

Developed so long ago, such notions have been part of the complex but logically compelling vision of existence that lies behind the myriad forms of religious life known to us as Hinduism. In this vision, the immortal part of each human being, the *atman,* is enmeshed in existence, but not ultimately of it. The nature of existence is *samsara*—unending becoming and change, a ceaseless round of cause and effect determined by the inescapable consequences of *karma,* or "action." The doctrine of *karma* is a kind of moral as well as physical economy in which every act has unavoidable results; so long as mental or physical action occurs, becoming and life go on repeatedly. Birth determines one's place and duties in the traditional Indian caste system. Caste is the most visible and concrete reminder of the pervasiveness of the Hindu concept of absolute causality that keeps us enmeshed in existence. The final goal is to transcend at some point in this or another lifetime the endless round of rebirth, or *samsara,* in which we are all caught. Release, or *moksha,* is the only way out of this otherwise endless becoming and rebirth. *Moksha* may be gained through knowledge, action, or devotion.

On the popular level, the period after about 500 B.C. is most notable in Indian religious life for two developments. Both took place alongside the ever deeper entrenchment in society of caste distinctions and a supporting ethic of obligations and privileges. The first was the elaboration of ascetic traditions of inner quest and self-realization, such as that of yoga. The second was the rise of devotional worship of specific gods and goddesses who were seen by their worshipers as identical with the Ultimate—in other words, as supreme deities for those who served them. The latter development was of particular importance for popular religion in India. Evident in the famous and beloved Hindu devotional text, the *Bhagavad Gita,* it reached its highest level after A.D. 500 in the myriad movements of fervent, loving devotionalism, or *bhakti,* many of which remain important today. A striking aspect of Hindu piety has been its willingness to accommodate the focus on one "chosen deity" who is worshiped as supreme to a worldview that holds that the divine can and does take many forms. Thus most Hindus worship one deity, but they do so in the awareness that faith in other deities can also lead one to the Ultimate.

The period between about 500 B.C. and A.D. 1000 saw the rise of two gods, Vishnu and Shiva, to special prominence as the primary forms in which the supreme lord was worshiped. Along with the mother-goddess figure, who takes various names and forms (Kali and Durga, for example), Vishnu and Shiva have remained to the present day the most important manifestations of the divine in India. Their followers are known as Vaishnavas and Shaivas, respectively. Countless differing traditions of devotion are practiced among Vaishnavas and Shaivas, as well as other groups. However, a few recurring phenomena and ideas can suggest something of Indian religiousness in practice.

Hindu practice is characterized especially by temple worship *(puja)*, in which offerings of flowers, food, and the like are brought by the worshipers. The temple images are especially sought out by the faithful for the blessing that the sight of these images brings. Recitation of sacred texts, many of which are vernacular hymns of praise to a particular deity, are another important part of Hindu devotionalism. *Mantras,* or special recitative texts from the Vedas, are also used by many Hindus in their original Sanskrit form. These texts are thought to have extraordinary power. A prominent feature of Hindu life is preoccupation with purity and pollution, most evident in the food taboos associated with caste groupings.

The ascetic tendency in India is also highly developed. Although they are influential, only a tiny minority relative to the great masses of Indians take up a life of full renunciation. In this life, the ascetic worshiper does not settle in one place, take on possessions, or perform regular worship. He or she rather wanders about in search of teachers and devotes him- or herself to meditation and self-realization. Even though the majority of Hindus have families and work at their salvation through merit gained by *puja* and moral living, the ascetic ideal has an important place in the overall Indian worldview. This ideal is seen as valid and worthy of respect; it stands as a constant reminder of the deeper reality beyond the everyday world and any individual life.

II-1   The Birla Mandir Temple with Sacred Cows. *In India, cows are allowed to roam free. They are considered sacred because of their powerful symbolic associations, which include the virtue of generosity, the bounty of nature, and the sanctity of all forms of life. [Bernard Pierre Wolff/Magnum]*

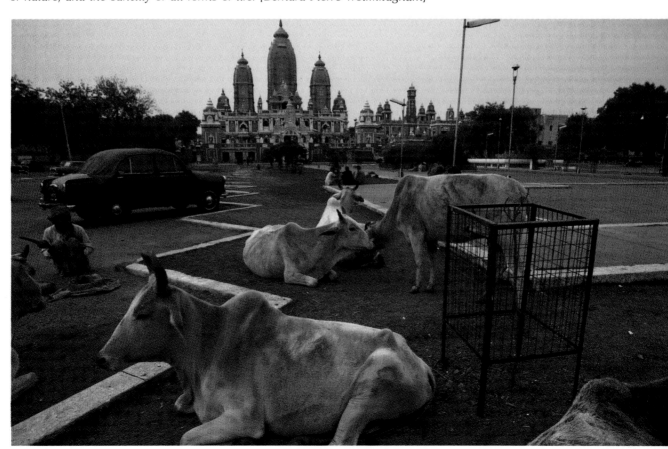

II-2   A Hindu Ascetic in Nepal. *The* sadhu, *or ascetic, shown here is a devotee of Shiva. He is meditating and fasting in observance of the annual celebration of Shivaratri, the holy night of Shiva. In his ascetic manifestation, Shiva is the model for the ascetic life of the* sadhu. *[Judith Aronson/Peter Arnold, Inc.]*

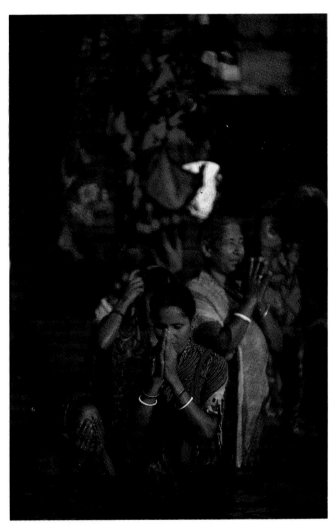

II-3   Purification Rituals in the Waters of the Holy Ganges. *Purification rituals are part of the obligatory daily rituals of all "twice-born" Hindus. The morning rituals performed by the women here in the Ganges include greeting the sun with recitation and prayer and purification by bathing. [Ian Berry/Magnum]*

II-4   Worshipers at a Small Hanuman Shrine in Varanasi *(Banaras). Hanuman, known as the "beautiful one," is a prominent figure in the great epic of the Ramayana. This monkey servant and friend of Lord Rama used his miraculous powers to help his master regain his abducted wife, Sita, from Sri Lanka, where she was held hostage by the demon king Ravana. Hanuman is worshipped as a folk deity for his magical powers, especially against evil spirits. He is also a model of devotion to Lord Rama. [Dale Williams]*

II-5   Krishna Holding Up Govardhana. *The beloved cycle of Krishna myths is popular not only among worshipers of Lord Krishna but also among most Indians. In this Bikaner painting from ca. 1690, Krishna uses the entire mountain of Govardhana as an umbrella to protect his homeland and sacred territory of Brindavan from the deluge sent down by the great god Indra. Indra appears on his elephant in the distance in the upper right of the painting. The women gathered around Lord Krishna are the cowherdesses, or gopis, famous from other tales of the Dark Lord. [Scala/Art Resource]*

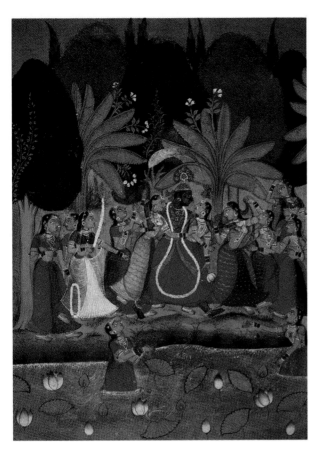

II-6   Krishna Dancing with the *Gopis. This seventeenth-century opaque watercolor with gold depicts one of the most frequent motifs of Indian art—the play and dancing of Lord Krishna with the cowherdesses of Brindavan. He lures them away from their homes to sport with him in the moonlight as his consorts. This sexual motif symbolizes the intense love between Krishna and his devotees and their consequent willingness to forsake all else for their lord. [Philadelphia Museum of Art, Gift of Mr. and Mrs. Lessing J. Rosenwald]*

II-7   Lord Vishnu Reclining on the Serpent of Eternity, Ananta. *Here Krishna, in his form as Lord Vishnu, is depicted in the act of creating the world, which emerges as the four-faced god Brahma from the lotus blossom that rises from Vishnu's navel. On the right, Krishna's consort, Radha (or Lakshmi), serves her lord. The serpent, Ananta (which means "without end" or eternal), rests upon the cosmic waters that existed before creation. [Dr. Walter Spink, University of Michigan]*

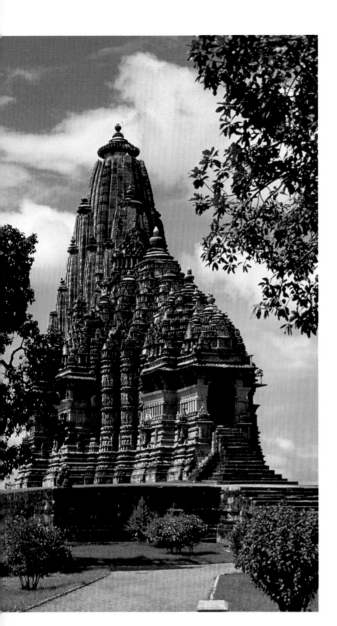

II-8 and II-9   Kajuraho, Temple of Kandariyo Mahadeva *(full view left, detail below). This famous eleventh-century Hindu temple sacred to the worship of Shiva as supreme Lord is built in the form of a mountain. All the way up to its main spire, or* shikara, *its exterior teems with subsidiary peaks or "spires" and is literally covered with images of mythical and royal figures, as seen in the detail photograph. The interior takes the form of a cave/womb sanctuary in which the image of Shiva is kept. [Front view: Dr. Walter Spink, University of Michigan; detail of facade: Scala/Art Resource]*

II-10   Shiva Nataraja, "Dancing Shiva." *This magnificent tenth-century Chola bronze statue from South India shows Shiva dancing on the body of a fallen demon. Bearing the emblems of creation and destruction that signify his mythic role, he dances the world in and out of existence, defeating death, and transcending time. [Borromeo, EPA/Art Resource]*

II-11   Kali Killing the Ashuras. *This eighteenth-century painting imaginatively portrays the goddess Kali riding her tiger as she destroys with her trident the larger of two demons, or ashuras. The depiction of Kali garlanded with bodies and in a hideous manifestation belies the fact that she is fervently worshiped by her devotees as a mother goddess. Like Shiva, her horrific form is part of her power to destroy demons and evil and hence can comfort as well as inspire fear and awe.* [Cleveland Museum of Art, Edward L. Whittemore Fund]

II-12   Devotional Painting of Worshiper and Ganesha. *Ganesh, or Ganesha, the elephant-headed "Lord of Categories," patron of learning and writing, and god of auspicious beginnings, is a ubiquitous figure in India; his image adorns the entrance of virtually every house and temple. His form symbolizes the unity of the microcosm (the human) and the macrocosm (the transcendent). Hindus view transcendence as taking many forms in the world of physical reality, reflecting a sensitivity to the presence of the divine in the transitory. They delight in a multiplicity of divine imagery, seeing in it an evocation of the deeper, incomprehensible nature of the transcendent reality that underlies and permeates all created things.* [Dr. Walter Spink, University of Michigan]

Zoroastrianism was wiped out as a major force by the spread of Islamic rule in the seventh and eighth centuries A.D. and later. However, its tradition continues in the faith and practice of the Parsis, a community today of perhaps one hundred thousand people, most of whom live in western India.

The First Iranian Empire (550–330 B.C.)

The Achaemenids

In October, A.D. 1971, the Iranian monarch Muhammad Reza Shah presided over a lavish pageant amid the ruins of the ancient Persian imperial city of Persepolis. This extravagant celebration commemorated the twenty-five-hundredth anniversary of the establishment under Cyrus the Great of "the imperial glory of Iran." The shah felt he had recreated this traditional Iranian ideal since the 1950s in his modern secularist regime. Although the Iranian revolution of 1978 thwarted his heavy-handed attempts to kindle a secular Iranian nationalism, modern Iran does have

an undeniably dual heritage: that of the rich Iranian Islamic culture of recent centuries and that of the far older, Indo-Iranian, Zoroastrian, and imperial culture of pre-Islamic Iran. The latter culture had its beginning with the Persian dynasty of the Achaemenids.

The rise of Iran as a world power and a major civilization is usually dated from the reign of Cyrus the Great (559–530 B.C.), the ruling prince of the Achaemenid clan. His regional power in southwestern Iran (Persis) went back at least to his grandfather, Cyrus I. The empire that he founded was anticipated in many ways by the sizable but loosely controlled empire of his predecessors, the Medes, in Anatolia and western Iran. According to Babylonian and Greek sources, Cyrus defeated the last Median king about 550 B.C. Then he moved swiftly westward, winning northern Assyria and Cilicia and subduing the Anatolian kingdom of Lydia, near the Aegean coast of Asia Minor. The Lydian capital, Sardis, became a provincial capital of the growing Persian state (and the base for diplomatic intrigue against the Hellenic *poleis*). Next, Cyrus turned to Babylon and, in less than three weeks, defeated the last Babylonian king.

This event, in 539 B.C., symbolically marks the beginning of the Achaemenid Empire, for it joined for

The ruins of the famous royal complex at Persepolis, begun about 518 B.C. The foundation of the treasury is in the foreground; part of the recently restored women's quarters is visible on the left; and the tall pillars of the main audience hall stand in the rear. [Bildarchiv Preussischer Kulturbesitz]

MAP 7-1   THE ACHAEMENID EMPIRE   *The empire created by Cyrus (shown on the map on the opposite page) had fullest extent under Darius when Persia attacked Greece in 490 B.C. It reached from India to the Aegean—and even into Europe—including the lands formerly ruled by Egyptians, Hittites, Babylonians, and Assyrians.*

the first time under one rule the Mesopotamian and Iranian spheres—a unity that would last for centuries (see Map 7-1). One of its immediate repercussions was the end of the Babylonian Exile of the Jews by the decree of Cyrus that the Jews be allowed to return to their Holy Land and rebuild their temple in Jerusalem (see Chapter 2). Babylon became for a time Cyrus's capital of choice, as Susa, Ecbatana, and Pasargadae also served at various points. Subsequently, Cyrus extended Achaemenid rule in the east before being killed in battle with steppe tribes there. His readiness to rule through local elites and institutions rather than to devastate and rebuild new infrastructures—as well as his ability to conquer—was perhaps the most notable legacy that he left to his heirs.

Early in his career, Cyrus had moved his capital from Susa to the old Median capital of Ecbatana (later Hamadan) for some time. He and his successors, in what was really a tribal confederation, adopted and continued Median administrative practice, and many Medes were highly placed in the new state. Thus, it is not surprising that the Achaemenid rulers are referred to in the Bible and other sources as the "Medes and Persians." What the Medes had set in motion, Cyrus and his heirs consolidated and expanded, so that the new Iranian Empire became the most extensive the world had ever seen.

The next ruler, Cambyses (r. 529–522 B.C.) added Egypt to the Achaemenid dominions. His brief reign was followed by a contest for succession that amounted to a virtual civil war extending from Babylonia to the Hindu Kush. The winner, Darius I, imposed stern measures even against the subject rulers of Egypt and Asia Minor. The reign of Darius (521–486 B.C.) was one of prosperity, in which the imperial borders reached their greatest extent—from Egypt in the west to southern Russia and Sogdiana (Transoxiana) in the north and the Indus Valley in the east. Susa and Persepolis served as Darius's principal capitals.

The next five rulers (486–359 B.C.) fared less well, and after 478 B.C., the Persians found themselves militarily inferior to the Greeks. Although they managed to keep the divided Greeks at bay by clever diplomacy, Greek cultural influence steadily grew in Anatolia. Repeated rebellions by Egypt, internal succession struggles, renewed conflict with Scythian tribes on the steppe borders, and less enlightened leader-

Darius on the throne. This relief from the treasury at Persepolis depicts Darius I granting audience to a Median nobleman. Note the incense burner before the king and the nobleman's gesture of respect. The scepter and lotus blossom held by Darius symbolize his kingship; his son and heir, Xerxes, stands behind him. [Bettmann Archive]

Inscription of Darius I: Building the Royal Palace at Susa

The Achaemenids, like other ancient rulers before them, used public inscriptions to underscore their victories and other accomplishments. Portions of an inscription of Darius, unearthed from the remains of Susa, the first of the two great palace-residences that he built (Persepolis being the second), tell of his building accomplishments there and show also the extent of Achaemenid power and dominion in its heyday.

. . . This is the palace which I built at Susa. From afar its ornamentation was brought. Downward the earth was dug, until I reached rock in the earth. When the excavation has been made, then rubble was packed down. . . . On that rubble the palace was constructed.

And that the earth was dug downward, and that the rubble was packed down, and that the sun dried brick was moulded, the Babylonian people, it did (these tasks). The cedar timber, this—a mountain by name Lebanon—from there was brought; the Assyrian people . . . brought it to Babylon; from Babylon the Carians and the Ionians brought it to Susa. The *yak* timber was brought from Gandara and from Carmania. The gold was brought from Sardis and from Bactria, which here was wrought. The precious stone lapis-lazuli and carnelian which was wrought here, this was brought from Sogdiana. The precious stone turquois, this was brought from Chorasmia, which was wrought here. The silver and the ebony were brought from Egypt. The ornamentation with which the wall was adorned, that from Ionia was brought. The ivory which was wrought here, was brought from Ethiopia and from Sind and from Arachosia. The stone columns which were here wrought—a village by name *Abiradus,* in Elam—from there were brought. The stone-cutters who wrought stone, these were Ionians and Sardians. The goldsmiths who wrought the gold, these were Medes and Egyptians. The men who wrought the wood, these were Sardians and Egyptians. The men who wrought the baked brick, these were Babylonians. The men who adorned the wall, these were Medes and Egyptians. Saith Darius the king: At Susa a very excellent [work] was [brought to completion]. Me may Ahuramazda protect, and Hystaspes, my father, and my country.

From R. G. Kent, *Old Persian Grammar, Texts, Lexicon* (New Haven, CT: American Oriental Society, 1950), as cited in R. Ghirshman, *Iran* (Harmondsworth, U. K.: Penguin Books, 1954), pp. 165–166.

ship plagued Achaemenid rule in this era. Much might have been recouped by the able, energetic Artaxerxes III (r. 359–338 B.C.), had he not been poisoned in a palace coup just as Philip of Macedon was unifying the Greeks. When Philip's son Alexander succeeded him, the days of the Achaemenid empire were numbered.

The Achaemenid State

Perhaps the greatest achievement of the Achaemenids was the relative stability of their rule. To justify their rule—and the title of *Shahanshah,* "king of kings"—they claimed that Ahura Mazda had entrusted them with universal sovereignty. An inscription of Darius makes this vivid: ". . . After Ahuramazdā saw "this earth" in turmoil he delivered it to me; he made me king; I am king by the will of Ahuramazdā."[1] Other inscriptions reflect the sense—underscored also through elaborate court ceremony and impressive architectural monuments—that the rulers earned Ahura Mazda's trust through justice and uprightness. The rulers acted as priests and sacrificers in the court rituals and symbolized their role as cosmic ruler by burning a special royal fire throughout each reign. The talents and evident charisma of the early leaders strengthened the force of their claim to special, divinely sanctioned royal status.

The Achaemenids were, however, tolerant of diversity in ways earlier empires had not been. In part, the sheer size of their realms demanded it, but the con-

---

[1] William W. Malandra, trans., *An Introduction to Ancient Iranian Religion* (Minneapolis: University of Minnesota Press, 1983), p. 50.

An Achaemenid seal depicting King Darius in his chariot on a lion hunt (from ca. 500 B.C.). The winged figure above the scene is a symbol for Ahura Mazda. [Bildarchiv Preussischer Kulturbesitz]

trast to later Roman imperial practice in this regard is striking. Even Darius's strong emphasis on Zoroastrian religious practice and theology did not bring forced conformity or conversion to the "state cult," as his lenient treatment of the Jews vividly shows.

The Achaemenids operated a powerful army, but their rule was not simply a military despotism. Much of their success lay in their administrative abilities and their willingness to learn and to borrow from predecessors like the Medes and conquered peoples like the Babylonians. Most of their leaders showed themselves adept at conciliation and sought to establish what has been termed a *pax Achaemenica*.[2] They were able to maintain continuity even while their state evolved from a relatively simple tribal confederation to a sophisticated monarchy. The state of Cyrus, with its largely Iranian troops and tribute system of revenue, was replaced by a monarchy supported by a noble class, professional armies (led by loyal Persian elite troops), an administrative system of provinces ruled by governors called satraps, and fixed-yield levies of revenue.

The excellence of the Achaemenids' administrative skills can also be seen in their communication and propaganda systems. A courier system linked the far-flung imperial outposts with the heartlands over a system of well-kept highways, which also served to move troops at maximum speed. The greatest of these highways, reaching from Sardis to Susa, was called "the King's Road" by Herodotus. A network of observers and royal inspectors kept the court abreast

of activities in diverse places. An efficient chancery with large archives and numerous scribes served many administrative needs. The bureaucratic adop-

IRAN TO THE THIRD CENTURY A.D.	
PEOPLES	
ca. 2000–1000 B.C.	Indo-Iranian (Aryan) tribes move south into the Panjab of India and the Iranian Plateau
835 B.C.	Assyrian text mentions kingdom of Medes and southwestern Iran
RELIGION	
ca. 628–551 B.C. (or before 1000 B.C.?)	Zoroaster (Zarathushtra), probably in eastern/northeastern Iran (perhaps originally in Herat?)
EMPIRES, RULERS	
559–530 B.C.	Reign of Cyrus the Great as Persian Achaemenid ruler
539–330 B.C.	Achaemenid Empire
331–330 B.C.	Alexander (d. 323) conquers Achaemenid empire
312–ca. 125 B.C.	Seleucid rule in part of old Achaemenid realm
ca. 248 B.C.–A.D. 224	Parthian empire of the Arsacids in Iran, Babylonia

[2] Richard N. Frye, *The Heritage of Persia* (New York: New American Library, 1966), p. 110.

tion of Aramaic, which had become the common language of the Near East under the Assyrians, helped link east and west. Royal proclamations were rapidly and widely distributed, often in multilingual form for different regions. Little is known of the actual judicial system, but Achaemenid inscriptions reflect a strong emphasis on universal justice and the rule of law throughout the empire.

The choice of strategically located capitals in western Iran, such as Ekbatana and Susa, was important to central control of the empire. In general, however, the Achaemenids moved the court as needed to one or another of their palaces, whether in Babylon or the Iranian highlands, and never had a single fixed capital. The satrapy divisions usually reflected the borders of the states that had been incorporated into the empire. The satraps were powerful princes in their own right. Although some of them revolted on occasion, the centralized power of the "king of kings" held together the diverse provinces and tribute-paying states.

The empire's overall stability for over two centuries testifies to the quality of the *pax Achaemenica*. Within this stable environment the cosmopolitan basis for the coming hellenization of western Asia in the wake of Alexander's conquests had already emerged.

INDIA

Imperial expansion on a large scale came to the South Asian or Indian subcontinent much later than it did to Iran. As we saw in Chapter 1, the subcontinent is a vast and highly diverse region. A cultural and religious heritage going back to the Aryan invaders of North India, and perhaps also to regional traditions stemming from the pre-Aryan Indus culture, has left its mark on the subsequent history of the subcontinent, despite the plethora of languages and regional traditions that have taken root there. Only rarely, however, has the whole area seen political unity even among a bare majority of its many inhabitants. Its current division—into India, Pakistan, and Bangladesh—is but its most recent. On only three previous occasions in its history has a really substantial part of the whole subcontinent been brought under the sway of a single state: during the Mauryan, Gupta, and Mughal periods of imperial rule. It is to the first of these that we now turn.

The First Indian Empire (321–185 B.C.)

It was only after the oriental campaigns of Alexander the Great, who conquered the Achaemenid Indian provinces of Gandhara and the Indus Valley in 327 B.C., that a regional kingdom became strong enough to unite much of North India under one ruler. Alexander himself made little or no impact on the subcontinent, except in the extreme northwestern area of Gandhara, where his passage opened the way for the increased Greek and Indian cultural interpenetration that developed under the Mauryan emperors of India. By contrast, the Mauryans themselves had a major impact on Indian history.

Political Background

The basis for empire in North India was the rise of regional states and commercial towns between the seventh and fourth centuries B.C. The most powerful of the states were the monarchies that clustered on the Ganges plains. North and northwest of the plains, in the Himalayan foothills and in the Panjab and beyond, tribal republics were more common. From two of these republics came the Buddha and Mahavira (see Chapter 2), although both spent much of their lives in the states of Kosala and Magadha, the two most powerful Ganges monarchies. In their lifetimes, Magadha emerged as the strongest state in India under Bimbisara (d. 493 B.C.).

Bimbisara was, as far as we know, the first king to build a centralized state (possibly on the Achaemenid model) strong enough for imperial expansion. He emphasized good roads, able administrators, and fair agricultural taxes. His son annexed Kosala, so that Magadha controlled the Ganges trade. Therefore, Magadha remained preeminent in the Ganges basin, even under several less competent successors. A new dynasty, the Nandas, replaced the last of these as rulers of Magadha in the mid-fourth century B.C.; their imperial hopes were soon dashed by the rise of the Mauryan clan.

The Mauryans

The first extensive Indian empire was established by Chandragupta Maurya (r. ca. 321–297 B.C.), a North Indian adventurer who seized Magadha and the Ganges basin in about 324 and made Pataliputra (the modern Patna) his capital (see Map 7-2). He next marched westward into the vacuum created by Alexander the Great's departure (326 B.C.) and brought the Indus region and much of west-central India under his control. A treaty with the invading Seleucus, Alexander's successor in Bactria, added Gandhara and Arachosia to his empire in the northwest. The Greek sources say that the treaty (303 B.C.) included a marriage alliance, possibly of a Seleucid woman to Chandragupta. Whether or not such a marriage occurred, there was much Seleucid-Mauryan contact thereafter.

Chandragupta's fame as the first great Indian empire builder is rivaled by that of his *Brahman* minister Kautilya. Known as the "Indian Machiavelli," Kautilya may have joined with Chandragupta, even before Chandragupta defeated the last Nanda ruler of Magadha, and thus may have become the real architect of Mauryan rule. However, he was probably not the real author of the most famous Indian treatise on the art of government, the *Arthashastra,* which is ascribed to him.

Chandragupta's son and successor, Bindusara (r. ca. 297–272 B.C.), was not long in taking up his father's imperial aspirations. He moved swiftly to conquer the Deccan, the great plateau that covers central

MAP 7-2   SOUTHWEST ASIA AND INDIA IN MAURYAN TIMES   *showing not only major cities and regions of greater Iran and the Indian subcontinent but also the neighboring eastern Mediterranean world. Although the Mediterranean was closely tied to Iran from Achaemenid times onward, its contacts with India in the wake of the conquests of Alexander the Great were many and varied.*

The Edicts of Ashoka

In the first of the two following excerpts from Ashokan edicts, we see the monarch's explanation of his change of heart and conversion to nonviolence after the Kalinga war and a statement of his determination to follow dharma. *"The Beloved of the Gods" was the common royal epithet used by Ashoka for himself. The second excerpt is from the end of Ashoka's reign and speaks of his efforts to better his and other people's lives by rule according to the dictates of* dharma.

▶ *For other perspectives on law, leadership, and government, see the following document boxes: "Hammurabi Creates a Code of Law in Mesopotamia" (Ch. 1), "Legalism" (Ch. 2), "Thucydides Reports Pericles on Athenian Democracy" (Ch. 4), "Polybius Summarizes the Roman Constitution" (Ch. 5), "Machiavelli Discusses the Most Important Trait for a Ruler" (Ch. 17), and "Some Reforms of Akbar" (Ch. 24).*

FROM THE THIRTEENTH ROCK EDICT

When the king, Beloved of the Gods and of Gracious Mien, had been consecrated eight years Kalinga was conquered, 150,000 people were deported, 100,000 were killed, and many times that number died. But after the conquest of Kalinga, the Beloved of the Gods began to follow Righteousness [*dharma*], to love Righteousness, and to give instruction in Righteousness. Now the Beloved of the Gods regrets the conquest of Kalinga, for when an independent country is conquered people are killed, they die, or are deported, and that the Beloved of the Gods finds very painful and grievous. . . . The Beloved of the Gods will forgive as far as he can, and he even conciliates the forest tribes of his dominions; but he warns them that there is power even in the remorse of the Beloved of the Gods, and he tells them to reform, lest they be killed.

For all beings the Beloved of the Gods desires security, self-control, calm of mind, and gentleness. The Beloved of the Gods considers that the greatest victory is the victory of Righteousness; and this he has won here [in India] and even five hundred leagues beyond his frontiers in the realm of the Greek king Antiochus, and beyond Antiochus among the four kings Ptolemy, Antigonus, Magas, and Alexander. Even where the envoys of the Beloved of the Gods have not been sent men hear of the way in which he follows and teaches Righteousness, and they too follow it and will follow it. Thus he achieves a universal conquest, and conquest always gives a feeling of pleasure; yet it is but a slight pleasure, for the Beloved of the Gods only looks on that which concerns the next life as of great importance. . . .

FROM THE SEVENTH PILLAR EDICT

In the past kings sought to make the people progress in Righteousness, but they did not progress. . . . And I asked myself how I might uplift them through progress in Righteousness. . . . Thus I decided to have them instructed in Righteousness, and to issue ordinances of Righteousness, so that by hearing them the people might conform, advance in the progress of Righteousness, and themselves make great progress. . . . For that purpose many officials are employed among the people to instruct them in Righteousness and to explain it to them. . . .

Moreover I have had banyan trees planted on the roads to give shade to man and beast; I have planted mango groves, and I have had ponds dug and shelters erected along the roads at every eight kos. Everywhere I have had wells dug for the benefit of man and beast. But this benefit is but small, for in many ways the kings of olden time have worked for the welfare of the world; but what I have done has been done that men may conform to Righteousness. . . .

I have enforced the law against killing certain animals and many others, but the greatest progress of Righteousness among men comes from exhortation in favor of noninjury to life and abstention from killing living beings.

I have done this that it may endure as long as the moon and sun, and that my sons and my great-grandsons may support it; for by supporting it they will gain both this world and the next.

From W. T. de Bary et al. (comps.), *Sources of Indian Tradition. Volume I: From the Beginning to 1800,* 2nd ed., ed. and rev. by Ainslee T. Embree (New York: Columbia University Press, 1988), pp. 142–143, 148–149.

India, dividing the far south (Tamilnad) from North India. Like his father, he had substantial contacts with the Seleucid Greeks, including Antiochus I of Syria, from whom he is said to have requested wine, figs, and a philosopher for his court.

ASHOKA. The third and greatest Mauryan emperor, Ashoka (r. ca. 272–232 B.C.), left numerous rock inscriptions. They are the first significant written sources in Indian history after those of the Indus culture. From Ashoka's edicts, we can piece together much of his reign and glimpse something of the man behind the royal name as well. In his first years as king, he continued the imperial tradition by conquering Kalinga, the last independent kingdom in North India and the Deccan. He thus extended Mauryan control over the whole subcontinent, except the far south.

Apparently revolted by the bloody Kalinga conquest, Ashoka underwent a religious conversion. Thereafter, he pursued the Buddhist "middle path" as the right course of conduct not only in personal but also in state relations. Accordingly, he forsook war, hunting, and animal flesh. Above all, he championed nonviolence *(ahimsa),* summing up his new course in the ideal of "conquest by righteousness" *(dharma).* This is not to say that the king abandoned all warfare, however much he may have abhorred bloodshed, but he did abandon further conquest. He also believed that by moral example he could win over others to humanitarian values. Within his realm, he looked on all his subjects as, in the words of one edict, his "children."

Ashoka's edicts show that he pursued the laity's norm of the Buddhist *dharma,* striving to attain heaven by the merit of good actions. He was not an exclusivist about his Buddhist faith, stressing tolerance for all traditions. However, he apparently sent out envoys to spread the Buddhist teaching, possibly even as far as Seleucid Macedonia in the west. Tradition has it that he was responsible for the more successful missionary work that brought the Buddhist *dharma* to Lanka (Sri Lanka, formerly Ceylon). Certainly the king of Lanka at the time was in friendly contact with Ashoka. Although Ashoka's edicts do not mention it, tradition also has it that a great Buddhist council was held at Pataliputra during Ashoka's reign (B.C. 250?). It is clear that he sought to raise standards of morality in all phases of life in his realm. For example, he appointed "*dharma* officials" under centralized control to investigate and promote public wel-

The Lion Capital of Sarnath. This famous Ashokan column capital was taken by India as its state seal after independence in 1947. It reflects both Persian and Greek influences. Originally the capital stood atop a mighty pillar some fifty feet high and the lions supported a huge stone wheel, the Buddhist "Wheel of the Dharma," the symbol of universal law. [Lauros/Giraudon]

fare and to foster just, moral government at the local level.

Ashoka evidently did ease some of the burdens that previous governments had imposed on their peoples, and he did institute many beneficial public works. However, by the end of his reign, the size of his empire had strained the limits of effective administration, and under his successors Mauryan rule fell apart. Neither Ashoka's Buddhism nor his rejection of military campaigns was, as some have suggested, what weakened imperial power; more likely factors in the decline and collapse of Mauryan rule were economic strains and increased bureaucratic corruption, as well as the inability of his heirs to claim the personal allegiances he had built up. After his death, local dynasties soon seized power from his successors in many areas.

Ashoka's enduring influence is hard to assess, but he did provide the model of the ideal king for later Hindu and Buddhist thought—the *chakravartin,* or universal monarch who rules with righteousness, justice, and wisdom. His name lives on as a symbol of enlightened, compassionate rule that has had few if any equals in the history of either the East or the West.

THE MAURYAN STATE. Mauryan bureaucracy was marked by centralization, standardization, and efficiency in long-distance communications, civil and military organization, tax collection, and information gathering (by a secret service). The fundamental unit of government, as before and ever after, was the village, with its headman and village council. Various numbers of villages formed districts within the larger provincial unit. The provinces were largely controlled through governors sent out from the capital. Some local rulers were confirmed in these positions also, much as with the Achaemenids (who very likely provided the model for much of Mauryan imperialism). The reputed pageantry and royal ceremonialism of the Mauryan court must also have enhanced royal authority.

The administration of the empire depended primarily on the king himself, who did, however, have an advisory council to assist him. Each of the three great Mauryan kings was associated with one of the "new" religious movements of the age: Chandragupta with the Jains (see Chapter 2), his son with the ascetic tradition of the group known as the Ajivikas, and Ashoka with the Buddhists. Such links must have strengthened the Mauryan, especially the Ashokan, claims to righteous leadership.

Revenues came primarily from taxing the produce of the land, which was regarded as the king's property. Urban trade and production were also taxed heavily. The Mauryan economic system also involved slavery, although most of it was domestic labor, often a kind of temporary indentured service.

THE MAURYAN LEGACY. An imperial ideal and a strengthened Buddhist movement were not the Mauryans' only gifts to Indian culture. They left behind new cosmopolitan traditions of external rela-

tions and internal communication that encouraged cultural development and discouraged provincialism. The many contacts of the Mauryans with the West reflect their international perspective, as do the Ashokan edicts, which were executed in various languages and scripts. Writing and reading must have been common by this time (perhaps as a result of Buddhist monastic schooling?), or the edicts themselves would have had no purpose. The Mauryans' excellent road system facilitated internal and external contacts on an unprecedented scale, above all west to Herat and northwest to Bactria. These roads would later be the routes for Buddhism's spread to Central Asia and China, as well as for successive invaders of the subcontinent moving in the opposite direction.

This era also saw the flourishing of cities across the empire: Pataliputra, Varanasi (Banaras), Ayodhya, Prayag (modern Allahabad), Ujjain, Taxila, and Qandahar. They remained centers for the arts, crafts, industry, literature, and education. The architecture of the Mauryan capital, Pataliputra, has not survived intact because of its wood and brick construction. But Greek travelers such as Megasthenes reported that its glories surpassed those of the Achaemenid palaces. Certainly the stone building and sculpture of the Ashokan period reflect sophisticated aesthetics and technique, as well as strong Persian and Greek influences.

Consolidation of Indian Civilization (ca. 200 B.C.–A.D. 300)

In the post-Mauryan period, the history of North India was dominated by the influx of a variety of foreign peoples whom we shall consider in the last section of this chapter. In the rest of the subcontinent, indigenous Indian dynasties held sway. These dynasties often controlled substantial regional empires that became centers for developing Indian cultural styles. In this period, a general pattern of regional and local political autonomy arose that would be broken only by the empire built much later by the Guptas (A.D. 320–ca. 550; see Chapter 12). Religiously and culturally, the centuries between the Mauryan and the Gupta eras saw the consolidation of patterns and styles that helped to shape Indian and, through the diffusion of Buddhism, Asian civilization ever after.

The Great Stupa at Sanchi, an outstanding example of early Buddhist relic mounds. The mound, seated on an Ashokan foundation, was added to over the centuries. Its most notable art work is the magnificent carvings on stone railings and gateways, one of which is shown in the left foreground. Sanchi is located in north-central India. [Dale Williams]

Economic Base

Although agriculture remained the basis of the economy, commerce flourished amid the post-Mauryan political fragmentation. India's merchant classes prospered, as their patronage of Buddhist and Jain buildings shows. The fine Mauryan road system facilitated trade across the length and breadth of India. Chinese and Roman demand for Indian luxury goods—jewels and semiprecious stones, sandalwood and teak, cotton and silk textiles, spices, and exotic animals—and for Indian slaves made India a center of world trade. Considerable wealth flowed in, as shown by archaeological discoveries of hoards of Roman gold coins and the remains of Roman trading communities in the Tamil south. Within India, guild organizations flourished and provided technical education in skilled crafts. Guilds were important targets of investment not only by the merchant class but by kings as well. Coin minting greatly increased after Mauryan times, and banking continued to thrive.[3]

High Culture

In the arts, the great achievements of these centuries were primarily Buddhist in inspiration. Northwestern India saw the rise of the Gandharan school of Buddhist art, named after the province that encompassed today's Pakistani Panjab and eastern Afghanistan. In Gandharan sculpture, Hellenistic naturalistic notions of form joined with the relatively recent Indian tradition of figural depiction of the Buddha and of *bodhisattva*s to produce relief and freestanding sculptural

[3] Romila Thapar, *A History of India*, vol. 1 (Harmondsworth, U. K.: Penguin Books, 1966), pp. 105–118.

figures characterized by flowing draped garments through which the muscular lines of the human body were readily discernible. In central India as early as the first century B.C., artists were producing stone-relief sculpture with the naturalistic, yet dynamic, flowing, plastic human and animal forms that would become earmarks of the "classical" style of Indian art. The finest surviving examples of this sculpture are the stone reliefs of the great Buddhist stupas (shrines) at Bharhut and Sañchi.

Language and literature during this period rested on the sophisticated Sanskrit grammar of Panini (ca. 300 B.C.?), which remains the present-day unsurpassed standard. Two masterpieces of Sanskrit culture, the epics of the *Mahabharata* and the *Ramayana,* had probably taken their general shape by A.D. 200. The first is a composite work concerned largely with the nature of *dharma* (the moral and cos-

The picture on the right shows the entrance to one of the many early Buddhist shrines, or chaitva-*halls, that were cut into rock-cliffs among the adjoining monasteries (*viharas*). Most of these rock-cut shrines—like the one in the picture below—are found in vertical cliffs not far from modern Bombay. [top photo: Bettmann Archives, bottom photo: Dale Williams]*

mic Law; see Chapter 2). Included in its earlier, narrative portions are systematic treatments of *dharma* such as the Bhagavad Gita, or "Song of the Blessed Lord," the most famous and influential of all Indian religious texts. Evidence of the rise of devotional cults is seen in the importance of Krishna in the *Mahabharata* (especially in the Gita) and Rama in the *Ramayana*. Both are major incarnations, or *avataras*, of Vishnu.

Religion and Society

The post-Mauryan period saw Buddhist monasticism and lay devotionalism thrive throughout the subcontinent. However, the dominance of the Brahmans in ritual matters and Vedic learning also continued. It was also a period of diffusion for popular devotional cults of particular gods, above all Shiva and Vishnu, which were to be the mainstays of all later "Hindu" religious life. The parallel development in Buddhist tradition was the rise, along with Mahayana thought (see Chapter 12), of a cult of the person of the Buddha. It focused on pilgrimages to sites where his relics were deposited or to places associated with his life. Toward the end of this age, Buddhism in its Mahayana form began to spread from India over the trade routes to Central Asia and eventually to China and Japan.

HINDU TRADITION. What we now call Hinduism emerged in this era. The major developments that were shaping a Hindu tradition were (1) the consolidation of the caste system, Brahman ascendancy, and the "high" culture of Sanskrit language and learning; (2) the increasing dominance of theistic devotionalism (especially the cults of Vishnu and Shiva); and (3) the intellectual reconciliation of these developments with the older ascetic and speculative traditions going back to the Upanishadic age. These social and religious developments would continue and solidify in the Gupta era and later times.

BUDDHIST TRADITION. Indian Buddhist monastic communities prospered during this period under mercantile and royal patronage—especially in or near urban centers—a trait they shared with the

INDIA FROM THE SIXTH CENTURY B.C. TO THE END OF MAURYAN RULE	
ca. 600–400 B.C.	Late Upanishadic age: local/regional kingdoms and tribal republics along the Ganges and in Himalayan foothills, the Panjab, and northwestern India
ca. 540–ca. 468 B.C.	Vardhamana Mahavira, Jain founder
ca. 537–ca. 486 B.C.	Siddhartha Gautama, the Buddha
ca. 550–324 B.C.	Regional empire of Maghadan kings
330–325 B.C.	Alexander campaigns in Indus Valley, Soghdiana, Bactria, and Panjab
324–ca. 185 B.C.	Mauryan empire controls most of northern India and the Deccan
ca. 272–232 B.C.	Reign of the Mauryan emperor Ashoka

Jains. Merchants found both traditions attractive and strongly supported Jain and Buddhist monasteries, presumably for the merit to be gained.

Buddhist lay devotion was a prominent part of Indian religious life, especially in the Ganges basin. However, it was a very different tradition from the Buddhism of the theological texts, which focuses on the quest for *nirvana* and the extraordinary norm (see Chapter 2). The Buddha and the Buddhist saints were naturally identified with popular Indian deities, and Buddhist worship was easily assimilated to common Indian patterns of theistic piety. Consequently, popular Buddhist practice was indistinguishable from countless other devotional cults that were coming to dominate the Indian scene. One reason that Buddhist tradition remained only one among many Indian religious paths was its absorption into the religious diversity that then and now typifies the Hindu religious scene.

Seleucids

We have seen that the successors of Alexander the Great in the Achaemenid lands, the Greek general Seleucus and his heirs, soon lost Arachosia and Gandhara to the Mauryans. They did, however, rule most of the former Achaemenid domains from about 312 to 246 B.C. and lesser portions until about 125 B.C. Alexander's policies of Greco-Persian fusion—the appointment of Iranians and Greeks as satraps, as well as large-scale Greek and Persian intermarriage—helped make the Seleucid rule of many eastern areas more viable. The new "cities"—or, more accurately, military colonies—that Alexander left behind provided bases for Seleucid control. As a foreign minority, the Seleucids had ultimately to maintain their power with mercenary troops. It was, however, the leaders of their own troops and satrapies whose imperial aspirations gradually whittled away at Seleucid rule. Always at war, neither Seleucus (r. 311–281 B.C.; see Chapter 4) nor the greatest of his successors, Antiochus the Great (r. 223–187 B.C.), ever secured lasting rule on the scale of the Achaemenids.

In the end, Alexander's policy of linking Hellenes with Iranians in political power, marriage, and culture bore fruit more lasting than empire. The Seleucid emphasis on the founding and cultivation of Greek-style cities stimulated the Hellenization process. During the third century B.C., Hellenistic culture and law became new ideals among the upper classes and intelligentsia of the Seleucid realms. The Seleucids did not encourage cultural mixing as had Alexander, but they did welcome into the ruling classes those non-Hellenes willing to become hellenized. Aramaic continued to be the common language from Syria to the Hindu Kush (although it was in decline in eastern Iran). Local social and cultural forms were by no means displaced, but Greek culture did penetrate.

Zoroastrian and related Iranian religious traditions declined with the loss of their imperial-cult status. The many syncretistic cults of the Mediterranean Hellenistic world made inroads even in the east in Seleucid and Parthian times. The later Parthians probably laid the groundwork for the still later revival of the Zoroastrian tradition. Mystery and savior cults were becoming more popular in the East and West. The new urban centers of the Hellenistic Age may have provided an environment in which the individual necessarily was less rooted in the established traditions of culture and religious life. This would have enhanced the attractiveness of the focus on individual salvation common to many lesser Hellenistic cults and to emerging traditions like the Christian, Mahayana Buddhist, Hindu devotionalist, and Manichaean that came to dominate Eurasia over the next few centuries.

Indo-Greeks

The extreme extent of Hellenization in the East was realized not by the Seleucids but by another line of Alexandrine successors, the Indo-Greeks of Bactria.[4] About 246 B.C., Bactria's Greek satrap broke away from the Seleucids. His successor, Euthydemus (r. ca. 235–ca. 200 B.C.), managed to extend his sway north and southwest; he withstood a Seleucid attempt at reconquest by Antiochus the Great in 208 B.C. His son Demetrius exploited the growing Mauryan weakness. By 175 B.C. he had crossed the Hindu Kush to conquer Arachosia; then he moved up the Indus Valley to take Gandhara. Demetrius and his successor, Menander, made Taxila their capital and were powerful enough to control other parts of northern India. Both were thoroughly "Indianized" in their orientation. Most of the Indo-Greeks were very Indian, even in language and religion, as their coins and inscriptions show.

Before their demise at the hands of invading steppe peoples (ca. 130–100 B.C.), these Indo-Greeks left their mark on civilization in all the areas around their Bactrian center. Bactria was a crucial area of transmission, if not a major source, of the later Greco-Buddhist art of Gandhara, one of history's remarkable examples of cross-cultural influence. The Indo-Greeks probably also played a role in the early spread of Buddhism from India to Central Asia. The most famous of the Bactrian rulers, Menander, or Milinda (r. ca. 155–130 B.C.?), is depicted as a Buddhist convert in a later Buddhist text, *The Questions of King Milinda*.

---

[4] In *The Indo-Greeks* (Oxford: Oxford University Press, 1957), A. K. Narian argues for *Indo-Greeks* as the appropriate term for these kings, who are usually called "Greco-Bactrians" or "Euthydemids."

Steppe Peoples

When we come to the Parthians, who succeeded the Seleucids in Iran, and to the steppe dynasties who succeeded the Indo-Greeks in Bactria and North India, separation of Iranian from Indian history is misleading. Both North India and the Iranian plateau were dominated from about 250 B.C. to A.D. 300 by Iranian tribal peoples originally from the Central Asian steppes. Although there is more tangible historical evidence for these incursions by steppe peoples into northeastern Iran and northwestern India than there is for any earlier Indo-Aryan migrations, they were not the first (or the last) such invasions. In fact, although commonly ignored, the nomadic steppe peoples, together with the great sedentary civilizations of the eastern Mediterranean, Mesopotamia, India, and China, have been one of the main forces in Eurasian history.

Parthians

The Parni, said to be related to the Scythians, were probably the major group of Iranian steppe peoples who had first settled in the area south of the Aral Sea and Oxus. In late Achaemenid times, they moved south into Parthia and gradually adopted its dialect. Thence forward, we can call them Parthians. The independent control of Parthia by its dynastic family (the Arsacids) dates from about 247 B.C. Shortly thereafter, the Parthians crossed the Elburz and began to extend their power onto the Iranian plateau. For decades only a regional power, the Parthians emerged under Mithradates I (ca. 171–138 B.C.) as a new imperial force in Eurasia. They were recognized as the true successors of the Achaemenids in Iran.

Facing weak Seleucid and Indo-Greek opposition, by ca. 140 B.C. Mithradates was able to secure a sizable empire. It covered the Iranian plateau and reached from Mesopotamia perhaps to Arachosia. Its center thereafter was his new winter capital at Ctesiphon, on the Tigris. The exact imperial borders and spheres of influence of the Parthians varied over time. But from their victory over the Romans at Carrhae in 53 B.C. (see Chapter 6) until their fall in A.D. 233, the Parthians were the major power of Eurasia alongside Rome. In the end, the pressure of the Kushan empire in the east and, above all, the constant Roman wars of their last century weakened the Parthians sufficiently for a new Persian dynasty to replace them.

Parthian marble bust of a woman. [Kawamei]

It is not easy to measure Parthian rule in Iran, despite its duration and successes, because of the scarcity and the bias of the available sources. For much of their long reign, the Parthians were under great pressure on all fronts—in Armenia, in Mesopotamia, and along their Indian and Central Asian frontiers. Yet during their rule, trade in and around their domains apparently increased. In particular, there is evidence of vigorous commerce north over the Caucasus, on the "silk road" to China, and along the Indian Ocean coast (the ancient Arabs' "monsoon route," used for the spice trade with the Indies).

Culturally, the Parthians were oriented toward the Hellenistic world of their Seleucid predecessors until the mid-first century A.D., after which they seem to have undergone a kind of Iranian revival. They then replaced Greek on their coins with Parthian and Aramaic, and they gave their cities their older Iranian names again. Their formerly Hellenic tastes in art turned to Iranian motifs like the hunt, the battle, and the feast. In late Parthian times, the Iranian national

INDO-GREEK, IRANIAN, INDIAN, AND STEPPE DYNASTIES AFTER ALEXANDER	
312–ca. 125 B.C.	Seleucid rule in part of old Achaemenid realm
312–246 B.C.	Height of Seleucid imperial strength
ca. 248 B.C.–A.D. 224	Parthian empire of the Arsacids in Iran, Babylonia
246–ca. 50 B.C.	Indo-Greek ("Graeco-Bactrian," "Euthydemid") rulers of region from modern Afghanistan to Oxus
ca. 155–130 B.C.?	Reign of Indo-Greek ruler Menander (Milinda)
247 B.C.–A.D. 223	Parthian Arsacid Empire
ca. 171–138 B.C.	Reign of Arsacid king Mithradates I
ca. 140 B.C.–ca. A.D. 100	Movements west and south of Yüeh Chih (including Kushans) and Sythians (Sakas) into Sogdiana, then Bactria, then northwestern India
ca. A.D. 50–ca. 250	Height of Kushan power in Oxus to Ganges region
ca. 78 (or 148?)	Accession of King Kanishka to Kushan throne in Taxila

Standing Buddha. This Gandharan-school statue of the Buddha from the second century A.D. reflects the marriage of Greco-Roman statuary styles with Indian Buddhist content. Although the head of this example has been recut in modern times, the elongated ears and the sign of wisdom on the forehead—both identifying marks of the Buddha—are typical of Gandharan sculptures. [Otto E. Nelson/The Asia Society]

epic took its lasting shape. Similarly, the worship of Ahura Mazda was preserved among the Magi, despite the success of other Eastern and Western cults and the common assimilation of Greek gods to Iranian ones. Yet the Parthians seem to have tolerated religious diversity. In their era, a huge variety of religious cults and cultural traditions rubbed shoulders with one another and vied for supremacy in different contexts.

Sakas and Kushans

The successors of the Indo-Greeks were steppe peoples even closer to their nomadic past then the Parthians. These peoples are often ignored by modern historians because they impinge on but do not figure centrally in Chinese, Iranian, or Indian history in our period. However, they played a major political and cultural role for several centuries, especially in the Indo-Iranian region. They reflect the cosmopolitan nature of the world of Central Asia, eastern Iran, and northwestern India at this time.

Beginning about 130 B.C., Scythian (Saka) tribes

The Buddha's Nirvana. This late second- or third-century A.D. *Gandharan-school relief has much in common with the style of contemporary Roman stone carvings. In this case, the Indian–Buddhist concept does not mesh well with the realistic Roman style and craftsmanship. Note the emotions of the bystanders at their loss of the Lord Buddha; such depictions of emotion would not appear in native Indian style. [Art Resource/Giraudon]*

from beyond the Jaxartes River (Syr Darya) overran northeastern Iran, taking Sogdiana's Hellenic cities and then Bactria. Thus ended the Indo-Greek heyday, although the last Greek petty ruler lasted in the upper Indus Valley until about 50 B.C. One group of Sakas soon extended their domain from Bactria into North India, as far as Mathura. Another went southwest into Herat and Sistan, where they encroached on the Parthians. In northwestern India, the Sakas were, in turn, defeated by invading Iranians known as the *Pahlavas*, who went on to rule in northwestern India in the first century A.D.[5] Pahlava rule did not, however, wipe out the Sakas, for we find Saka dynasties ruling in parts of northwestern and western India through the fourth century A.D.

[5] Tradition gives one of their rulers, Gondophares, the role of host to Saint Thomas, who is said to have brought Christianity to India. But because Gondophares probably ruled in the early to mid-first century A.D., it may be a confused report. Even if traditions of Thomas's mission to India are correct, some connect him instead with southern India.

The Sakas had been displaced earlier in Sogdiana by another steppe people, known from Chinese sources as the Yüeh Chih. They may have been driven from western China by the building of the Great Wall of China and/or drought in the steppes. These peoples, under the leadership of the Kushan tribe, next drove the Sakas out of Bactria. About a hundred years later, in the mid-first century A.D., they swept over the mountains into northwestern India. Here they ended Pahlava rule and founded a long-lived Indian Kushan dynasty that controlled a relatively stable empire from the upper Oxus regions over Bactria, Gandhara, and Arachosia, across the Panjab, and over the Ganges plains as far as Varanasi (Banaras). Their greatest ruler, Kanishka, reigned at either the end of the first century or the middle of the second A.D. He was the greatest patron of Buddhism since Ashoka. In their heyday (ca. the first to the third centuries A.D.), the power of the Kushans in Central Asia facilitated the missionary activity that carried Buddhism across the steppes and into China. A lasting Kushan contribution was the school of Greco-Buddhist art fostered in Gandhara by Kanishka and his successors and carried on by a later Kushan dynasty for another five hundred years.

Iran, India, and Inner Asia to the Third Century A.D. in World Perspective

By the second century A.D., we can see in the Indo-Iranian world the development of imperial governments whose power and influence far surpassed those of any before them. In and of themselves, such empires are not the measure of progress in what we call "civilization"—that is, citied, literate culture; technological sophistication; specialized division of labor; and complex social and political structures. Yet they are indices of the security and wealth necessary to progress in these areas. This was clearly the case in the empires of the Achaemenids and Mauryans. In this respect, developments in these Asian areas paralleled those in the wider world, where the Greek, Hellenistic, and Roman empires, like the Han empire of China, provided contexts in which civilization could flourish, grow, and spread.

In Asia, this was also an era in which widely influential, lasting religious traditions came of age. Some of them—the Christian, Buddhist, Confucian, and even Judaic and Hindu traditions—spread abroad and took root in cultures outside their places of origin. By contrast, the Zoroastrian tradition, like the Jain in India, never had great appeal outside its homeland, although its adherents would much later carry it with them to western India, where they continue today as the influential but small community of Parsees.

In this period, another important and portentous element for the history of civilization was an increase in cross-cultural contact, as epitomized by the Hellenizing conquests of Alexander the Great. The Central Asian reaches of Iran and India especially provided the great meeting ground of Iranian, Indian, Greek, and steppe-people's languages, customs, ideas, arts, and religious practices. In later centuries, the Iranian and Indian cultures continued to develop their own distinctive and largely independent forms, and Central Asia remained a fragmented but fertile cultural melting pot. Yet the age we have briefly surveyed here set in motion cross-cultural interchanges that would continue apace in later centuries. In this period, we see in Rome, Iran, and India, if less so in China, increased contacts with other cultures and increased influences from abroad. These contacts and influences were manifested in new peoples, governmental structures, technological innovations, specialized skills and arts, and ethico-religious ideas.

Suggested Readings

IRAN

M. BOYCE, *Zoroastrians: Their Religious Beliefs and Practices* (1979). The most recent survey, organized historically and based on extensive research and experience.

M. BOYCE, ed. and trans., *Textual Sources for the Study of Zoroastrianism* (1984). A fine collection of translated textual selections from a broad range of ancient Iranian materials.

J. M. COOK, *The Persian Empire* (1983). A recent, solid survey of the Achaemenid period.

JOHN CURTIS, *Ancient Persia* (1989). A small but excellent portfolio of photographs of artifacts and sites accompanied by a brief, clear historical survey and discussion of the arts and culture of ancient Iran as revealed in the art and archaeological record.

W. D. DAVIES and L. FINKELSTEIN, ed., *The Cambridge History of Judaism,* vol. 1 (Introduction; The Persian Period). Good articles on Iran and Iranian religion as well as on Judaism.

J. DUCHESNE-GUILLEMIN, trans., *The Hymns of Zarathushtra*, trans. M. Henning (1952, 1963). The best introduction to the original texts of the Zoroastrian hymns.

R. N. FRYE, *The Heritage of Persia* (1963, 1966). A first-rate survey of Iranian history to Islamic times that is readable but scholarly.

W. W. MALANDRA, trans. and ed., *An Introduction to Ancient Iranian Religion: Readings from the Avesta and Achaemenid Inscriptions* (1983). Helpful especially for texts of inscriptions relevant to religion.

INDIA

A. L. BASHAM, ed., *A Cultural History of India* (1975). A fine collection of historical-survey essays by a variety of scholars. See Part I, "The Ancient Heritage" (Chapters 2–16).

A. L. BASHAM, *The Wonder That Was India*, rev. ed. (1963). Excellent material on Mauryan religion, society, culture, and history.

N. N. BHATTACHARYYA, *Ancient Indian History and Civilization: Trends and Perspectives* (1988). Covers Mauryan and Gupta times as well as earlier periods, with chapters on political systems, cities and villages, idealogy and religion, and art.

W. T. DE BARY et al., comp., *Sources of Indian Tradition,* 2nd ed. (1958). Vol. I: *From the Beginning to 1800,* ed. and rev. Ainslie T. Embree (1988). Excellent selections from a wide variety of Indian texts, with good introductions to chapters and individual selections.

B. ROWLAND, *The Art and Architecture of India: Buddhist/Hindu/Jain,* 3rd rev. ed. (1970). The standard work, lucid and easy to read. Relevant here is Part Three, "Romano-Indian Art in North-West India and Central Asia."

V. A. SMITH, ed., *The Oxford History of India,* 4th rev. ed. by Percival Spear et al. (1981), pp. 71–163. A dry, occasionally dated survey history. Includes useful reference chronologies.

R. THAPAR, *Ashoka and the Decline of the Mauryans* (1973). The standard treatment of Ashoka's reign.

R. THAPAR, *A History of India,* Part I (1966), pp. 50–108. Contains three chapters on the period from ca. 600 B.C. to A.D. 200 that provide a basic survey.

STANLEY WOLPERT, *A New History of India,* 2nd ed. (1982). A basic survey history. Chapters 5 and 6 are on the Mauryans, Guptas, and Kushans.

GREEK AND ASIAN DYNASTIES

A. K. NARAIN, *The Indo-Greeks* (1957. Reprinted with corrections, 1962). The most comprehensive history of the complex history of the various kings and kingdoms.

F. E. PETERS, *The Harvest of Hellenism* (1970), pp. 222–308. Helpful chapters on the various Greek rulers of the eastern world, from Seleucus to the last Indo-Greeks.

J. W. SEDLAR, *India and the Greek World: A Study in the Transmission of Culture* (1980). A basic work that provides a good overview.

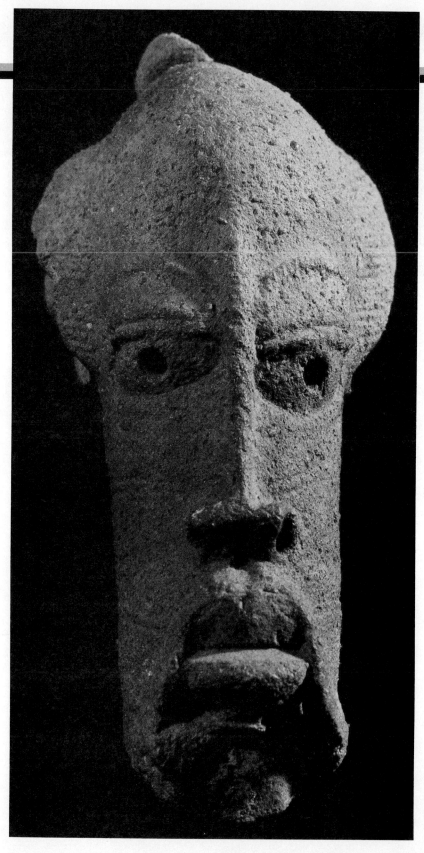

A terra-cotta head from the Iron-Age Nok culture, which occupied what is today northeastern Nigeria from about 900 B.C. to about A.D. 200. [Information Attaché of the Embassy of Nigeria, "Two Thousand Years of Nigerian Art," by Ekpo Exo, photograph by André and Ursula Held]

Africa: Early History to A.D. 1000

8

In this chapter, we shift our focus from the ancient societies that emerged on the northern shores of the Mediterranean—the Greek, Hellenistic, and Roman worlds—to the story of the world's second-largest continent, Africa, from the earliest glimpses provided by the archaeological record through the first millennium A.D. This is not a story of isolation. Africa is intimately linked with Eurasia—it forms the southern frontier of the Mediterranean world and connects to Asia through the Arabian peninsula. Good evidence suggests that the earliest humans emerged from Africa to populate the rest of the world, and the continent's subsequent history is one of ongoing interaction, both internal and with the rest of the world.

Problems of Perspective, Interpretation, and Sources

The Question of "Civilization"

In Chapter 1 we defined *civilization* in terms of a cluster of attributes—among them writing, urban life, and metallurgy—that relate to social complexity and technological development. Defined in this sense, the term usefully identifies some of the common characteristics of the ancient states that emerged in the Nile valley, Mesopotamia, the Indus and Ganges valleys, and China and that have been associated with larger, more complex societies since those ancient states. The term *civilization*, however, also has a broader meaning, associated with a people's cultural and artistic traditions and their general cultural sophistication. The two meanings are often confused, however, leading to the unfortunate assumption that societies that are not "civilizations" in the narrow sense—societies without writing, cities, or a state bureaucracy—are therefore "uncivilized" in the broader sense. Once we move outside the Nile valley and the Ethiopian highlands, most African societies down to recent times—indeed, most societies in the world for most of its history—may not have been civilizations in the narrow sense, but they were hardly uncivilized in the broader sense. African history includes many important states with writing, cities, and sophisticated technology; it also includes many societies with rich and varied traditions that did not happen to be organized into bureaucratic states with literate, urban populations and advanced technology.

The Source Problem

Interest in African history has increased greatly in recent decades, and scholars have given us glimpses of many formerly unknown or little-known African societies. Still there is much that we do not know. One reason for this is simply that research has not yet filled the gaps. Another, however, is that the sources available to historians for many regions and periods are sparse. This second problem is especially acute for the small, local societies without writing, centralized governmental bureaucracies, or large urban centers that characterize much of sub-Saharan African history. Even as late as 1880, for example, as many as 25 percent of all West Africans probably belonged to such "stateless" societies.

Stateless societies leave few historical records. Local oral traditions provide one valuable source of information about them. But even when combined with reports of outside observers, oral traditions can give us reliable access only to relatively recent history—no more than a few centuries.

Another source of information about the history and prehistory of both state and stateless African societies is archaeological research. The tropical climate that prevails in much of sub-Saharan Africa unfortunately destroys many types of artifacts that survive in drier regions. Nonetheless, the impressive work of archaeologists in many parts of Africa is giving us a far clearer picture of the outlines of its history than anything imaginable even a few decades ago. Recent archaeological and historical scholarship have brought to light, for example, many formerly unknown and little known cultures. Some of this work indicates that large and advanced societies and states may have existed in ancient Africa that are still unknown or little understood. The Nok or Zimbabwean cultures, for example, left impressive but so far hard-to-decipher remains.

A third important source consists of the reports of outside observers. It is only from about the end of the first millennium A.D., however, that we get, through the writings of Islamic historians, geographers, and travelers, and still later, those of Europeans, more than fleeting and geographically limited textual references to life and peoples in the vast reaches of Africa beyond Egypt, Ethiopia, and the African coast of the Mediterranean. Before this time, only a few brief accounts by Greek and Roman writers are available.

These outside written records are not of unmixed value. The Greek and Roman observers and, later, Islamic and European writers brought strong biases to their assessments of Africa and Africans, particularly sub-Saharan Africa; their commentaries have done much to form the preconceived notions and often negative stereotypes with which many outsiders still view this vast and diverse continent.

Because relatively little is known about small communities in Africa that left no written documents, monuments, or other decipherable artifacts of their history, a survey text like this tends to focus on the many larger societies, with known rulers, fighting forces, and towns or cities, that left their own records or that were noted and documented by outsiders. We shall try nonetheless to balance our presentation of those larger societies and states for which we have more adequate documentation with our discussions of those areas where smaller societies prevailed or where possibly very large states or societies have left us little in the way of source materials.

Physical Description of the Continent

Africa is huge and, in geological terms, massive (see Map 8-1). Its more than thirty million square kilometers compose one-fifth of the Earth's entire land mass. It is three-and-one-half times the size of the continental United States and second only to Asia in total area. Its geological massiveness is evident in its unusually high relief over virtually its entire expanse (the average continental elevation is 660 meters), which results in a lack of natural harbors and islands and produces the generally steep escarpments that surmount its narrow coasts. This high relief has made access to, as well as egress from, its interior difficult. All of Africa's major rivers (the Niger, Kongo [Zaïre], Nile, Zambezi, and Orange) lie largely in plateau basins and are

MAP 8-1 AFRICA: PHYSICAL FEATURES AND EARLY SITES *This map shows the major physical features of the continent, Iron Age sites of the western and central Sudan, and sites of the Napatan, Meroitic, and Aksumite empires.*

navigable in their inland reaches but not across the cataracts and falls that they traverse before they reach the coastlands. (Only the Nile has a relatively long, navigable reach below its cataracts in southern Egypt and Nubia.) The vast size and sharp physical variations, from high mountains to swamplands, tropical forest, and deserts, have also made rapid long-distance communication and movement difficult; consequently both were channeled along certain corridors (such as the Rift valley of East Africa, the coastal reaches of East or North Africa, the Sahelian savannah lands bordering the great equatorial forests, or the Niger or Zambezi river valley).

Africa is a continent that straddles the equator, and the special character of its various regions is due in considerable part to climatic considerations. As a whole, its climate is unusually hot. North and south of the equator, dense rain forests dominate a west-east band of tropical woodland territory from the southern coasts of West Africa across the Kongo or Zaïre basin nearly to the Kenyan highlands. (Note, however, that the tropical rain forests cover only about 5 percent of Africa's total surface area.) North and south of this band (and in the Kenyan highlands), the lush rain forests give way to open woodlands and broad grassy plains, or a mixture of the two, all of which are known as *savannah*. These in turn pass into the steppeland and semidesert region known as Sahel, and finally into true desert as one moves farther from the equator. Despite high rainfall and humidity in its western and central equatorial regions (except in the eastern highlands) and along its Indian Ocean coasts, Africa contains two of the world's greatest and driest desert regions. The Sahara ("the Desert": Arabic *al-Sahra*) is the world's largest desert and has historically been the major factor hindering contact between the Mediterranean world and sub-Saharan Africa. The Kalahari is its smaller but still vast counterpart in southwestern Africa. It partially cuts off the southern African plateau and coastal regions from much of central Africa.

Other natural factors are of importance to Africa's history. The soils of Africa are typically tropical in character, which means devoid of much humus, or vegetable mold, and generally easily leached of their mineral and nutrient contents. Thus, they are rapidly exhausted and not highly productive for extended periods. Water shortage is also a perennial problem for agriculture in most of Africa and a potent factor in its history past and recent. Crop pests and insects such as the tsetse fly, mosquito, and locust have also been enemies of both farming and pastoralism in Africa; the tseste fly specifically has blocked the spread of domesticated cattle and horse breeding to the forest regions of the continent. On the other hand, abundant animal life has made hunting or fishing an important way of survival in Africa, even in early times, one that continues in most regions.

The great mineral wealth of Africa has been very influential in shaping human activity throughout the continent. Salt was a very important trading commodity among some Africans for centuries. For example, it was an important focus of the trans-Saharan trade between the western Sudan and North Africa from as early as the first millennium A.D. Even earlier, iron was a major trading commodity between forest and savannah zones. Copper, mined in only limited areas on the continent, was also a much-sought-after and

traded commodity that played a major role in the very early development of an advanced civilization in Egypt. For centuries, gold was a significant trading commodity within the continent as well as an export. The ancient Egyptians sought the gold of Nubia; later, gold from West and central Africa was in demand in North Africa, the Mediterranean world, and the Indian Ocean.

Finally, we should note that by convention Africa is often discussed in terms of several major regions, and we shall on occasion make use of these designations, arbitrary and inexact though they may be: *North Africa*, including all the Mediterranean coastal regions from modern Morocco through modern Libya and the northern regions of the Sahara, including the Sahel, which marks the transition from mountains to true desert; *Nilotic Africa* (i.e., the lands of the Nile), roughly the area of the modern states of Egypt and Sudan; *the Sudan*, the broad belt of Sahel and savannah below the Sahara, which stretches from the Atlantic east across the entire continent, over the upper Nile to the Red Sea; *West Africa*, including the desert, Sahel, and savannah of the western Sudan as far east as the Lake Chad basin, and the woodland coastal regions from Cape Verde to Cameroon; *East Africa*, from the Ethiopian highlands (a high, fertile plateau cut off by steppe, Sahel, and desert to its north and south) and "the Horn of Africa" south along the coast over modern Kenya and Tanzania, an area split north to south by the Great Rift valley; *central Africa*, the region north of the Kalahari, stretching from the Chad basin in the north over the Zaïre basin southeast to Lakes Tanganyika and Malawi and down to the Zambezi River (or, sometimes, the Limpopo River) in the southeast; and *southern Africa*, from the Kalahari desert and Zambezi (or the Limpopo) south to the Cape of Good Hope.

African Peoples

Africa and Early Human Culture

Archaeological research of recent decades indicates that our hominid ancestors evolved in the Great Rift region of highland East Africa about 1.5 to 1.8 million years ago or perhaps even earlier. It was probably also here that, sometime before 100,000 B.C., modern humans—the species *homo sapiens (sapiens)*—appeared and from here that our ancestors moved to populate both the rest of Africa and the rest of the

The Hadar region of Ethiopia at the north end of the Great Rift valley has been a rich source of fossils of species probably ancestral to humans. At the bottom of the picture on the left is the campsite of paleontologists working in the region. On the right is "Lucy," one of the most famous fossils found in the region—the remains of one of the earliest creatures to walk upright. [left: David L. Brill, © National Geographic Society; right: Cleveland Museum of Natural History]

world over many thousands of ensuing years. In this sense, we are all Africans by descent.

The once popular view of Africa south of the Sahara as a vast region that was isolated from civilization until it was "discovered" by Europeans badly distorts reality. Although its interior and southern reaches were isolated from direct contact with Eurasian peoples and states until relatively recent centuries, African goods were for centuries in circulation in Indian-Ocean as well as Mediterranean trade, and Africa itself was hardly a vast empty continent peopled only by a few isolated tribal peoples. Archaeological research is documenting substantial and ancient internal movements of peoples—and with them languages, culture, and technologies—both north-south and east-west within the continent.

Commercial links between Africa and the outside

date to the beginning of antiquity. Egypt was always oriented to the Mediterranean, into which the Nile flowed, and to neighboring lands across the Red Sea, to which it had easy access. Well before the Christian era, the peoples of the upper Nile, the Abyssinian plateau (modern Ethiopia), and the coastal areas of East Africa below the Horn maintained contacts with Egypt, southern Arabia, and probably India and Indonesia by way of the Indian Ocean. Like Egypt, the rest of the North African coast was oriented to Mediterranean trade throughout antiquity. The Mediterranean littoral of Africa in particular was a place where Berber-speaking African peoples mixed with other Mediterraneans like the Phoenicians. Here the powerful Carthagenian Punic state arose in the mid-first millennium, only to fall prey to the imperialism of the upstart Roman state (see Chapter 5).

A Stone Age Saharan rock painting. One scholar believes this strikingly beautiful painting represents women gathering grain (represented by the dots, presumably). If so, it would have likely been wild grain unless cereal crops were cultivated very early here—something for which we have no evidence. Whether gathering grain or engaged in graceful dance, the figures here remind us of the ancient human presence in the once-green Saharan regions. [Erich Lessing/Magnum]

Diffusion of Languages and Peoples

Physical factors have played a major role in the regionalization of African history. Even so, both cultural and linguistic diffusion show that, despite natural barriers, Africa's peoples have not been as internally isolated or compartmentalized as was once thought. Language is a particularly interesting phenomenon in Africa. Between one and three thousand languages can be found there, depending on the way one distinguishes languages from dialects. However, all of them can be roughly divided into four major groups, plus two late arrivals, the Indo-European family brought in with European colonies and the much earlier Malayo-Polynesian group spoken only on Madagascar, the result of Southeast Asian colonialism in still earlier times.

The four major groupings are the Afro-Asiatic, the Nilo-Saharan, the Niger-Kongo, and the "Khoisan." The first originated either in southwestern Asia and Arabia or in Africa itself, but in any case near the Red Sea. It is represented in the Semitic languages (which include Arabic, Hebrew, Aramaic, and Syriac) of southwestern Asia, as well as the ancient Egyptian, Berber, Chadic, Kushitic, and Omotic languages, all of which belong basically to North and northeastern Africa. The Nilo-Saharan family is spread over an area generally to the southwest of the Afro-Asiatic group, from the upper Nile across the central Sahara into the Rift highlands. Niger-Kongo languages are found to the west and south of the Nilo-Saharan group, originally across the savannah and woodlands from west

of the Niger bend east and south to central and southern Africa. Finally, Khoisan is a collection of loosely related languages found today in various parts of southern Africa.[1]

Based on recent work in African linguistics and archaeology, one scholar, R. Oliver, has plausibly argued for the following scenario of movement and diffusion for these language groups. He links the development of language families with the growth in population that made larger communities and wider, long-term movements of peoples possible. According to his interpretation, by the latter part of the late Stone Age, during the Wet Holocene (after about 8000 B.C.; see p. 236), Afro-Asiatic languages had come out of the Jordan and Nile valleys and spread to Arabia and across North Africa. Two southward extensions of these languages, from central North Africa across the Sahara to the Chad basin, and from Egypt into the Ethiopian highlands and the Horn of Africa, likely occurred after 4000 B.C., in the latter part of the Wet Holocene, possibly through the movement of the pastoralists who also brought sheep and cattle herding to these regions.

The Nilo-Saharan languages may have originated among fishing and cereal-growing societies in the Nubian region of the Nile and spread before ca. 5000 B.C. west into the Sahara. They were later largely displaced there by the southward extension of Afro-

---

[1] For the entire discussion of language here and later in the chapter, we have followed the masterly summary and analysis of R. Oliver, *The African Experience* (1991), pp. 38–50.

Asiatic languages into the Sahara with their pastoralist carriers. Isolated Nilo-Saharan tongues such as Teda and Zaghawa in the Tibesti, or Songhay in the area above the Niger river, survived the Afro-Asiatic influx. Nilo-Saharan languages must also have spread southeastward with fishermen-farmers as far as the lakes region of the Great Rift valley, where at a later time they were partially displaced by Kushitic-speaking pastoralists or farmers.

The Niger-Kongo family had its homeland in the woodland savannah and equatorial forests of West and central Africa, perhaps in the area of the headwaters of the Niger and Senegal rivers west of the great bend of the Niger. Spoken by fisherfolk who may have begun to engage in farming also, this group spread to the Atlantic coast from the Senegal to the Cameroon mountains. Its largest subgroup, the Bantu speakers, later spread southward into the equatorial forestlands (largely as agriculturalists) and around the rain forests of central Africa (as herders as well as cultivators) until they entered finally the eastern and southern savannah regions.

The fourth language family, nowadays called Khoisan, apparently covered most of the southern half of the African continent by late Neolithic times but was largely displaced by the migration of Niger-Kongo Bantu speakers. The varied peoples who were the ancestors of today's Khoisan speakers apparently were still largely hunter-gatherers at this time. Over ensuing centuries, with the coming of the Bantu-speaking agriculturalists and pastoralists, most of them eventually adopted the settlers' languages, making Bantu tongues the most widely dispersed of African languages and confining the diverse Khoisan tongues to smaller areas than they had once covered.

The development of the complex language map of present-day Africa can thus be seen in terms of very ancient developments in food production and movement of peoples and ways of life in various directions within the continent. We shall have occasion to return to several of these developments in somewhat greater detail later in the chapter.

Racial Distinctions

Changes in African food production, the development of local settled cultures, and even larger patterns of civilization have been linked by some interpreters to the apparent differences in appearance of African populations. In more recent historical times, lighter skinned, Caucasoid African peoples have predomi-

nated in the Sahara, North Africa, and Egypt, whereas darker skinned, Negroid peoples have been the majority in the rest of Africa.[2] (The Greeks called all the black peoples they were aware of in Africa *Ethiopians*, "those with burnt skins." The Arabs termed all of Africa south of the Sahara and of Egypt *Bilad al-Sudan*, "the Land of the Blacks," and from this we get the term *Sudan*. Other, yellowish-brown peoples occur in smaller numbers in sub-Saharan, especially southern, Africa, largely as herding or hunter-gatherer groups. These peoples are known as the Khoikhoi and San—the "Hottentots" and "Bushmen" of unfortunate traditional European usage—or, collectively, the Khoisan; their greatest numbers are in the Kalahari and adjacent areas of present-day southern Africa.

Some theories have attempted to link differences of color or racial type to the development and spread of everything from language, agriculture, or cattle herding to iron working or state building in Africa. However, none of these theories is tenable, if only because the concept of race itself is a problematic one. As many scholars have pointed out, long periods of relative isolation of different human populations in prehistory led to differing common gene pools in different areas. Yet always, especially in more recent times, the mixing of different gene pools produced constant change. In Africa, the various populations were so mixed that most Africans might even best be considered to belong to one large race (or none), regardless of color or other physical attributes.[3] Thus, one should not make too much out of the obvious color differences in Africa. These differences have resulted from differing gene pools and, perhaps, some climatic adaptation. We do not know at what point in prehistory such factors led to differentiation between the Caucasoid peoples of North Africa, the Negroid peoples of the Sudan and regions further south, and the "brown" peoples of the more southern areas. All these types are found in an infinite variety of mixtures in most areas of Africa today, and categorizing them would not advance a reconstruction of the history of the continent.

[2] Note, however, that actual distribution of skin color in the past is very hard to determine; there is even sharp disagreement as to whether the ancient Egyptians were more "white" or more "black." See the discussions in G. Mokhtar, ed., *Ancient Civilizations of Africa*, Vol. 2 of *UNESCO General History of Africa* (London: Heinemann, 1981), pp. 27–83; and W. MacGaffey, "Who Owns Ancient Egypt?" *Journal of African History* 32 (1991): 515–519.

[3] See Philip Curtin et al., *African History* (London, 1978), pp. 14–16.

The Sahara and the Sudan to the Beginning of the Christian Era

Early Saharan Cultures

One of the most striking and imposing physical features of the African continent is the Sahara. Since the second millennium B.C., this vast arid wilderness has done much to separate the North African and Egyptian worlds from the massive band of the Sudan and, still further south, West and central Africa. Still, this desert barrier never fully hindered north-south contact and exchange. The Nile valley and the Great Rift plateau provided one corridor for movement of ideas and peoples south to north and vice versa. Similarly, the Red Sea, the Atlantic and Pacific coasts, and a few routes through the Sahara itself allowed considerable numbers of people and goods, not to mention ideas, to breach the great Saharan barrier as far back as our evidence can take us.

What is hard for us to imagine, however, is that at least until about 2500 B.C. the Sahara was not a vast desert but a land with lakes and rivers, trees, grasses, and a reasonable climate. We now know that during the so-called Wet Holocene period in Africa, from ca. 7500–2500 B.C., especially the southern half of the Sahara was positively well watered. In the earlier half of this period, Lake Chad was a sea larger than the present-day Caspian. The swamplands of the upper White Nile region were receiving water not only from Uganda but from the Kenya rift as well, where in some lakes the water level was as much as five hundred feet above today's. The increased animal, fowl, reptile, and fish populations in these periods would have allowed riparian (river- and lakeside) communities of considerable size to be supported with ease off the land, and excavations near Khartoum in the Sudan support the likelihood that this was the case. Here pottery was developed and used widely, as other excavations in the Aïr region of the Sahara have shown. Pastoralism and hunting as well as some domestication of food plants apparently developed in these regions.

However, when from ca. 2500 B.C. the Sahara underwent a relatively rapid dessication, the riverine and lakeside communities of this great expanse of territory gradually disappeared. The pastoralist and hunting culture that, as we can see from the cave paintings known today in the central Sahara, had de-veloped in these regions was forced farther south into the Sudanic regions, or, in some cases, possibly north toward the Mediterranean.[4]

By 1000 B.C., the dessication process was advanced enough to make the Sahara an immense east-west expanse of largely uninhabitable desert separating in substantial ways the greater part of the African continent from the Mediterranean coastal rim and the Near Eastern centers of early civilization. Even then, however, regular contacts between sub-Saharan Africa and the Mediterranean world in ancient times did not cease. We know, for example, that a number of north-south routes across the western and central Sahara were traversed by horses and carts or chariots, and most important, by migrating peoples long before the coming of the camel.

Neolithic Sudanic Cultures

Most interesting to speculate about are the repercussions of the Saharan dessication for later settled communities, especially those to the south in the Sahel and savannah belt of the Sudan. Evidence such as pottery remains from the first millennium B.C. points to the existence of preliterate but complex agricultural communities of Neolithic and early Iron Age culture that dotted the central and western reaches of the great belt of the sub-Saharan Sudan. We may surmise that these peoples, presumably speakers of Niger-Kongo languages, had once been spread farther north, in the formerly arable Saharan lands that they may have shared with the ancestors of the largely nomadic Berber-speaking peoples of contemporary west Saharan and North Africa.

This hypothesis has been bolstered by the excavation of settled cultures and towns from a more arable Saharan age in the desert regions of Mali, north of Timbuktu, and in the southwestern Sahara. These settlements date from the mid-fifth millennium B.C., when the Wet Holocene effects produced savannah conditions in this area (three to four thousand years later than in the central Sahara). Fishing settlements in Mali and coastal settlements in Mauritania date from this era. In inland Mauritania, remains of an ancient but later agricultural civilization with as many as two hundred towns have also been found. Here there is evidence of the transition from a hunting and fishing to a herding and rudimentary agricultural culture. One theory has it that the progressive dessication of the second millennium B.C. forced these peoples far-

[4]Oliver, pp. 31–37.

Evidence of prehistoric Saharan contact with the Sudan. The discovery of cave paintings such as this from the Tassili mountains in the western Sahara gives credence to Herodotus's report (ca. 450 B.C.) of a people called Garamantes (probably Berber), who lived in the desert oases and used horse chariots. Such drawings have been found from the Sahara south almost to the Niger River. [Douglas Mazonowica]

ther south. Pottery techniques found in the first-millennium settlements in places such as Jenne (in Mali) are clearly "offshoots of a Saharan pottery tradition."[5] The people making this move must have taken with them both their languages and the techniques of settled agriculture, especially those based on cereal grains, and of animal husbandry, because they kept to the savannah lands below the desert and Sahel. They also domesticated new crops using their old techniques. Assisted ultimately by the knowledge of iron working (probably passed on from North Africa or from the Nilotic kingdom of Kush), these people were able to effect an agricultural revolution. This led to considerable population growth in the more fertile of the Sudanic regions, especially those regions near the great river basins of the Niger and Senegal, and the Lake Chad basin. (A similar spread of agricultural techniques and cattle and sheep raising seems to have occurred down the Rift valley of the East African highlands.) This agricultural revolution, effected by some time in the first millennium B.C., provided the basis for the growth of new cultural centers in the sub-Saharan regions thereafter.

Whatever their earlier history, we know that in the first millennium B.C. the peoples of the Sudan developed and refined techniques for settled agriculture.

[5] S. J. and R. J. McIntosh, *Prehistoric Investigations at Jenne, Mali* (Oxford, U.K.: B.A.R., 1980), p. 436.

They must have carried these techniques along with their languages eastward through the savannahs of the Sudan and southward, largely along the rivers, into the tropical rain forests of West and central Africa. The result changed the face of sub-Saharan Africa, where previously small groups of hunter-gatherers had predominated. With the advent of early iron technology, these settled peoples were able to develop societies larger and more complex than those existing before them.

Early Iron Age and the Nok Culture

The unique common features of the oldest iron-smelting furnaces found in widely scattered sites across Africa over a span of nearly a millennium—from the seventh century B.C. to the fourth century A.D.—suggest that iron smelting in Africa was invented within the continent. The process appears to have originated in the northern half of the continent—the region with the earliest sites that show evidence of smelting—probably in Egypt and Nubia, or possibly in the central Saharan mountain highlands of the Tibesti, Hoggar, and Air. Thence it must have spread southward, most likely by different routes, into western, central, and eastern parts of the continent. The western route lay between the copper- and iron-rich area of southern Mauritania and both the seasonal flood area west of the great bend of the Niger River

Prehistoric West African sculpture from the Nok culture. Magnificent terra-cotta heads recovered from Nok sites reveal that the prehistoric civilization of western Sudan had highly developed artistic tastes and techniques. The style of terra-cotta castings like this one suggests that they may have had wooden prototypes. [National Museum of African Art, Smithsonian Institution]

(centered on the town of Jenne) and the region of the middle Senegal River further west. The central route, to which we will return, was from the Saharan mountains into northern Nigeria. In a route more to the east, iron appears to have spread indirectly from Meroe in Nubia (discussed later) through the Darfur or Ennedi highlands between the Chad basin and the Nile to the Bantu peoples in the savannah and forest regions on the northern side of the Kongo basin, and from there to the lakes regions of the East African Rift. The easternmost route of transmission was likely parallel to the East African coast, west of the Great Rift, from the Ethiopian highlands and ultimately Nubia down finally to the Zambezi and Limpopo.[6]

Some of the most significant Iron Age sites have been found in what is today northeastern Nigeria, on the Jos plateau. Here, near the village of Jos, archaeological digs have yielded evidence of an Iron Age people of what is called the Nok culture. Excavations at Nok sites have yielded stone tools, iron implements, and highly artistic terra cotta sculptures. The sites date between 900 B.C. and A.D. 200. Excavations at Taruga have recently isolated layers with iron tools from those below them without iron, allowing scholars to date the introduction of iron smelting to about the sixth century B.C. The Nok people combined agriculture with some cattle herding. They cleared substantial woodlands from the Jos plateau and built a strong agricultural base for themselves.

Two aspects of the Nok culture are of particular interest. The first is that the Nok people, who mastered the relatively difficult art of iron smelting by at least 500 B.C., had the earliest Iron Age culture of West Africa. That they likely acquired iron smelting by way of the Aïr mountains to the north is further evidence of early contact among African cultures.

The second important aspect of the Nok people is their extraordinary sculptural art, most vividly seen in the magnificent burial or ritual masks they produced. The apparent continuities of Nok sculptural traditions with those of other, later West African cultures to the south suggest that this culture had an important im-

[6] Oliver, pp. 64–76.

pact on later West and central African life. These continuities provide good indication that ancient communities of considerable sophistication laid a basis on which later, better-known Sudanic civilizations must have built.

Nilotic Africa and the Ethiopian Highlands

Moving east across the Sudan to the upper Nile basin, just above the first cataract, we come to the land of Kush, in lower Nubia. It was here that an Egyptianized segment of Negroid, Nilo-Saharan-speaking peoples of Nubia built the earliest known literate and politically unified civilization in Africa after that of pharaonic Egypt. As early as the fourth millennium B.C., the Old Kingdom pharaohs had subjugated and colonized Nubia. As early as the beginning of the second millennium B.C., however, an independent kingdom arose in Kush in the broad flat floodplain just above the third cataract of the Nile. The capital of this kingdom, Kerma, had been a major trading outpost for Middle Kingdom Egypt from as early as 2000 B.C. From it and other Sudanic settlements, a stream of building materials, ivory, slaves, mercenaries, and especially gold flowed north down the Nile.

The early Kushite kingdom reached its zenith during the period between the Middle and New kingdoms of Egypt, or about 1700–1500 B.C. The large, plundered tombs of eight rulers of Kush of this period survive at Kerma. All indications are that this was a wealthy and prosperous kingdom by any standard. Evidence in the ruins of the palace fortress as well as in the tombs suggests that these Nubian kings may have taken over the gold mines of lower Nubia from the weakened Egyptian state in the intermediate period. After the Hyksos invasions, with Egypt's recovery (from about 1500 B.C.) under the New Kingdom rulers, Kush was subjugated and came once more under Egyptian colonial rule, which meant also stronger Egyptian cultural influence. Then, sometime after 1000 B.C., as the New Kingdom floundered, a new Kushite state reasserted itself and by about 900 B.C. had conquered lower as well as upper Nubia, regaining independence and the wealth that flowed from the Nubian gold mines. This empire, centered first at Napata, just below the fourth Nile cataract, and then farther up the Nile at Meroe, proved a strong and lasting one. It survived from the tenth century B.C. until the fourth century A.D., when the Ethiopian Aksumites replaced Kush as the dominant power in northeastern Africa.

The Napatan Empire

Kerma remained an important trading center, whereas Kush was an Egyptian colony and continued

---

Kushite Conquest of Memphis

The following text is taken from a granite pillar that the Kushite king Piankhi had erected near Napata to commemorate his conquest of Egypt in the decade before 750 B.C. It describes the siege and capture of Memphis.

When day broke, at early morning, his majesty reached Memphis. When he had landed on the north of it, he found that the water had approached to the walls, the ships mooring at (the walls of) Memphis. Then his majesty saw that it was strong, and that the wall was raised by a new rampart, and battlements manned with mighty men. There was found no way of attacking it. Every man told his opinion among the army of his majesty, according to every rule of war. Every man said: "Let us besiege it—; lo, its troops are numerous." Others said: "Let a causeway be made against it; let us elevate the ground to its walls. Let us bind together a tower; let us erect masts and make the spars into a bridge to it. We will divide it on this (plan) on every side of it, on the high ground and———on the north of it, in order to elevate the ground at its walls, that we may find a way for our feet."

Then his majesty was enraged against it like a panther; he said: "I swear, as Re loves me, as my father, Amon (who fashioned me), favors me, this shall befall it, according to the command of Amon . . . I will take it like a flood of water. I have commanded . . . " Then he sent forth his fleet and his army to assault the harbor of Memphis; they brought to him every ferryboat, every (cargo) boat, every (transport), and the ships, as many as there were, which had moored in the harbor of Memphis, with the bow-rope fastened among its houses. (There was not) a citizen who wept, among all the soldiers of his majesty.

His majesty himself came to line up the ships, as many as there were. His majesty commanded his army: "Forward against it! Mount the walls! Penetrate the houses over the river. If one of you gets through upon the wall, let him not halt before it (so that) the (hostile) troops may not repulse you . . . "

Then Memphis was taken as (by) a flood of water, a multitude of people were slain therein, and brought as living captives to the place where his majesty was.

From J. H. Breasted, *Ancient Records of Egypt* (Chicago: University of Chicago Press, 1906), Vol. 4, pars. 861 ff. Reprinted in Basil Davidson, *The African Past* (New York: Grosset and Dunlap, 1967), pp. 51–52.

Ruins of the Great Amon Temple at Gebel (Mount) Barkal at the site of Napata, near Karima, Sudan. The Napatan kings were said to have been selected here by an oracle of the Egyptian god Amon, who was believed to reside inside the mountain. [Tim Kendall]

to be important after Kush regained its independence in the tenth century B.C. The leaders of the reestablished state, however, chose a site farther up the Nile than Kerma as their new capital. This town, Napata, was to become the center of a new Egyptianized Nubian state and culture that flourished for three centuries as the real successor to pharaonic Egypt. The royal line that ruled at Napata was culturally heavily Egyptianized; indeed, the rulers saw themselves as Egyptian. They practiced the Pharaohs' custom of marrying their own sisters, a practice known to many kingship institutions around the world. They buried their royalty embalmed in pyramids in traditional Egyptian style. They used Egyptian protocol and titles. In the eighth century B.C., they conquered Egypt proper and ruled it for about a century as the twenty-fifth pharaonic dynasty. This Kushite dynasty was driven out of Egypt proper only by the iron-equipped military might of Assyria around the middle of the seventh century B.C.

The Meroitic Empire

Forced back above the lower cataracts of the Nile by the Assyrians and kept there by the Persians, the Kushite kingdom became increasingly isolated from Egypt and the Mediterranean world and developed in its own distinctive ways. Invaded by an Egyptian army

in 591 B.C., Napata itself was sacked. This led to a relocation of the capital farther south in the prosperous city of Meroe, bringing the seat of rule closer to the geographic center of the Kushite domains. By this time, the Kushite kings had extended their sway westward into Kordofan, south above the confluence of the Blue and the White Nile, and southeast to the edges of the Abyssinian plateau. Meroe now became the kingdom's densely populated political and cultural capital. In the sixth century B.C., Meroe was the center of a flourishing iron industry, from which iron smelting may first have been dispersed west and south to the sub-Saharan world (although this is a much debated question). Certainly the Kushites traded widely to the west across the Sudan as well as with the Hellenistic world and beyond. It was a state built on a staggeringly wide network of internal African as well as external, intercontinental commercial relations. The Meroitic empire enjoyed a long and prosperous life before it began to decline, apparently about A.D. 100. It lasted, however, into the fourth century, when it was defeated and divided by Nuba peoples from west of the upper Nile and replaced as the dominant regional power by the rival trading state of Aksum on the Abyssinian plateau.

CULTURE AND ECONOMY.   The heyday of Meroitic culture was from about the middle of the third century

B.C. to the first century A.D. The kingdom was "middleman" for the varied African goods in demand in the Mediterranean and Near East: animal skins, ebony and ivory, gold, oils and perfumes, and slaves. The Kushites traded with the Hellenistic-Roman world, southern Arabia, and India, and in this regard were fully engaged in the larger international world. Economically, the Kushite lands between the Nile and the Red Sea were a major source of gold for Egypt and the ancient Mediterranean world. They also shipped quality iron to Aksum and the Red Sea. Cattle breeding and other forms of animal husbandry were of special importance, whereas agriculture along the banks of the Nile and more widely afield by irrigation was the other mainstay of the economy. Cotton cultivation in Kush preceded that of Egypt and may well have been an early export product of the kingdom.

This was an era of prosperity. Many monuments were built, including royal pyramids and the storied palace and walls of the capital. Fine pottery and jewelry were produced. Meroitic culture is especially renowned for its two kinds of pottery: The first, turned on wheels, was the product of an all-male industry attuned apparently to market demands, and the second, made exclusively by hand by women, was largely used domestically. This latter kind of pottery seems to have come out of an older tradition of African pottery craft that is found well outside the region of Kush—an indication of ancient traditions shared in varied regions of Africa and of the antiquity of substantial African internal trade.

RULE AND ADMINISTRATION. The political system of the Meroitic empire, like the pharaonic, was apparently traditionalist and stable over many centuries. The system did, however, have features that distinguished it from its Egyptian models. The king seems to have ruled strictly by customary law, presumably as interpreted by whatever priests or other religious professionals served the state's needs. According to some Greek accounts, his actions were limited by firm taboos, and violation of those taboos could lead to enforced royal suicide. There was also a royal election system, commented on by Herodotus and other Greek authors. Diodorus of Sicily says that the priests would present several outstanding candidates for king, and from this group the god would choose the new sacred king (by what oracular mechanism, we are not told). The priests apparently considered the king to be a living god, a practice known both in ancient Egypt and in many other African societies. A Kushite inscription on the coronation of a new king tells us, however, that King Aspelta (r. 593–568 B.C.) was elected to succeed his brother from among his other royal brothers by twenty-four high officials and military leaders.

From this inscription we see that royal succession was not from father to son, but within the royal family. Other inscriptions tell us that the succession was often through the maternal rather than the paternal line. The role of the queen mother in the election appears to have been crucial—another parallel, if not a direct link, to African practices elsewhere. Indeed,

The pyramids at Meroe, in a photograph taken in 1921 during an expedition by the Museum of Fine Arts, Boston. [Tim Kendall]

Herodotus Describes "the Ethiopians" of Meroitic Kush

[ca. 430 B.C.] I went as far as Elephantine [Aswan] to see what I could with my own eyes, but for the country still further south I had to be content with what I was told in answer to my questions. The most I could learn was that beyond Elephantine the country rises steeply; and in that part of the river boats have to be hauled along by the ropes—one rope on each side—much as one drags an ox. If the rope parts, the boat is gone in a moment, carried away by the force of the stream. These conditions last over a four days' journey, the river all the time winding greatly, like the Maeander, and the distance to be covered amounting to twelve *schoeni*. After this one reaches a level plain, where the river is divided by an island named Tachompso.

South of Elephantine the country is inhabited by Ethiopians who also possess half of Tachompso, the other half being occupied by Egyptians. Beyond the island is a great lake, and round its shores live nomadic tribes of Ethiopians. After crossing the lake one comes again to the stream of the Nile, which flows into it. At this point one must land and travel along the bank of the river for forty days, because sharp rocks, some showing above the water and many just awash, make the river impracticable for boats. After the forty days' journey on land one takes another boat and in twelve days reaches a big city named Meroë, said to be the capital city of the Ethiopians. The inhabitants worship Zeus and Dionysus alone of the Gods, holding them in great honor. There is an oracle of Zeus there, and they make war according to its pronouncements, taking from it both the occasion and the object of their various expeditions.

From the translation of *The Histories of Herodotus* by Aubrey de Selincourt (New York: Penguin, 1954), as cited by Basil Davidson, *The African Past* (New York: Grosset and Dunlap, 1967), pp. 52–53.

The Lion Temple and Kiosk at Naga in the Butana Desert, about sixty miles northeast of Khartoum. Naga, founded in the early first century A.D., was a Meroitic caravanserai on the Red Sea trade routes. Initially, Kushite religion appears to have followed Egyptian tradition. By the third century B.C., however, gods who were unknown to Egypt rose in importance. Judging by the presence of many temples like this, the lion-headed god Apedemak was one of the most important of these gods. [Tim Kendall]

the queen mother seems to have adopted formally her son's wife upon his succession. By the second century B.C., a woman had become sole monarch, initiating a long line of queens, or "Candaces" (*Kandake*, from the Meroitic word for queen mother).

We know very little of Meroitic administration. The empire seems to have been under the autocratic rule of the royal sovereign, perhaps on the Egyptian model. He or she presided over a central administration run by a number of high officials: chiefs of the treasury, seal bearers, chiefs of granaries, army commanders, and chiefs of scribes and archives. The various provinces had to be delegated to princes who must have functioned with considerable autonomy, given the likely slow communication over the vast and difficult terrain of the upper Nile and eastern Sudanic region.

SOCIETY AND RELIGION. As a result of the limited sources for Kushite history, we must largely speculate about the social structure outside the circle of the palace—the ruling class of monarch and relatives, priests, courtiers, and provincial nobility. We do find mention of slaves, most commonly female domestics, but also male laborers who were drawn largely from prisoners of war. We can presume that cattle breeders, farmers, traders, craftsmen, and minor government functionaries formed an intermediate class or classes between the slaves and the rulers.

In religious matters, we have no direct records of actual Kushite practices, but it is clear that they closely followed Egyptian traditions in their worship for a number of centuries. To judge from the great temples dedicated to him, Amon was the highest god for the earlier kings; and his priests had considerable influence. By the third century B.C., however, gods unknown to Egypt rose in importance alongside Amon and other Egyptian gods. Most notable was Apedemak, a warrior god with a lion's head. The many lion temples associated with him (as many as forty-six have been identified) reflect the great importance of this Kushite god. Such gods likely represented local deities who gradually rose to take their places alongside the highest Egyptian gods. However, some scholars have speculated about Iranian or Indian influences (via the Indian Ocean–Red Sea trade link) in the non-Egyptian elements of the Kushite cult.

The Aksumite Empire

A highland people who had developed their own commercially powerful trading state to the south of

EARLY AFRICAN CIVILIZATIONS	
ca. 7500–2500 B.C.	"Wet Holocene" period
ca. 2500 B.C.	Relatively rapid dessication of Saharan region begins
ca. 2000–1000 B.C.	Increasing Egyptian influence in Nubia
ca. 1000–900 B.C.	Kushite kingdom with capital at Napata becomes independent of Egypt
751–663 B.C.	Kushite kings Piankhi and Taharqa rule all Egypt
ca. 600–500 B.C.	Meroe becomes new Kushite capital
ca. 500 B.C.–A.D. 330	Meroitic kingdom of Kush (height of Meroitic Kushite power ca. 250 B.C.–A.D. 50)
ca. 500 B.C.–A.D. 500?	Nok culture flourishes on Jos plateau in western Sudan (modern central Nigeria)
First century A.D.	Rise of Aksum as trading power on Ethiopian (Abyssinian) plateau
ca. A.D. 330	Aksumite conquest of Kush

Kush delivered the *coup de grace* to the weakened Kushite empire, apparently about A.D. 330. This was the newly Christianized state of Aksum, which centered in the northern Ethiopian, or Abyssinian, highlands where the Blue Nile rises. With the ascendancy of the kingdom of Aksum, our sources lapse into relative silence concerning the Nubian regions of the Nile. Not until the rise of new Christian Nubian states in the mid-sixth century can we again pick up the historical threads of the inheritors of the land of Kush.

The new conquerors, the peoples of Aksum, were the product of a linguistic, cultural, and genetic mixing of African Kushitic speakers with Semitic speakers from Yemenite southern Arabia. This mixing occurred after southern Arabians infiltrated and settled on the Ethiopian plateau around 500 B.C. It gave to Aksum and later to Ethiopia their Semitic speech and script, which are closely related to South Arabian. Greek and Roman sources attest to the existence of an Aksumite kingdom from at least the first century

A giant stela at Aksum. Dating probably from the first century A.D., this giant carved monolith is the only one remaining of seven giant stelae—the tallest of which reached a height of 33 meters—that once stood in Aksum amidst numerous smaller monoliths. Although the exact purpose of the stelae is not known, the generally accepted explanation is that they were commemorative funerary monuments. Erecting them required engineering of great sophistication. [Picturepoint Ltd.]

A.D. By this time, the kingdom, through its chief port of Adulis, had already become the major ivory and elephant market of northeastern Africa. Adulis had been important in Ptolemaic times, when it was captured by Egypt and used as a conduit for Egyptian influence in the highlands. After Egypt fell to the Romans, Aksum and its major port became an important cosmopolitan commercial center.

In the first two centuries A.D., their location on the Red Sea gave the Aksumites a strategic seat astride the increasingly important Indian Ocean trade routes. These trade routes linked India and the East Indies, Iran, Arabia, and the East African coast with the Roman Mediterranean. A further basis of Aksum's power was its key location for controlling trade between the African interior and the extra-African world, from Rome to Southeast Asia—notably exports of ivory, but also of elephants, obsidian, slaves, gold dust, and other inland products.

By the third century A.D., Aksum was one of the most impressive states of its age in the African or western Asian world, as the remains of the imposing stone buildings and monuments of its major cities—Aksum, Adulis, and Matara—attest. A work attributed to the prophet Mani, ca. A.D. 216–277, describes Aksum as one of the four greatest empires in the world. From the late second century onward, the Aksumites often held tributory territories across the Red Sea in southern Arabia. They also gained control of all northern Ethiopia and conquered Meroitic Kush. Thus by the third and fourth centuries, they held sway over some of the most fertile cultivated regions of the ancient world: their own plateau, the rich Yemenite highlands of southern Arabia, and much of the eastern Sudan across the upper Nile as far as the Sahara.

The resulting empire was ruled by a king of kings in Aksum through tribute-paying vassal kings in the other subject states. By the sixth century, the Aksumite king was even appointing southern Arabian kings himself. The minting of its own coinage in gold, silver, and copper (it was the first tropical African state to do so) was an index and symbol of Aksum's political as well as economic power. As a state, it enjoyed a long-lived economic prosperity. Goods of the Roman-Byzantine world and India and Sri Lanka, as well as of neighboring Meroe, flowed into Aksum. In addition to trade, vast herds and good agricultural produce gave a firm base to Aksumite prosperity.

In religion, the pre-Christian paganism of Aksum resembled the pre-Islamic paganism of southern Arabia, with its various gods and goddesses who were closely tied to natural phenomena such as the sun, moon, and stars, and who were served with animal sacrifices. Evidence of Jewish, Meroitic, and even Buddhist minorities living in the major cities of Aksum has also been found—an index of the cosmopolitanism of the society and of its involvement with the larger Indian Ocean, western Asian, and South Asian worlds beyond the Red Sea.

In an inscription of the powerful fourth-century ruler, King Ezana, we read of his conversion to Christianity, which led to the Christianizing of the kingdom

Sixth-Century Account of Aksumite Trade

The following document is taken from a description of a trading voyage to Sri Lanka in A.D. 625 by a Greek-speaking monk and former merchant from Alexandria, known as Cosmas Indicopleustes. In the excerpt, he describes what he had heard of the area and its products and resources.

The region which produces frankincense is situated at the projecting parts of Ethiopia, and lies inland, but is washed by the ocean on the other side. Hence the inhabitants of Barbaria, being near at hand, go up into the interior and, engaging in traffic with the natives, bring back from them any kinds of spices, frankincense, cassia, calamus, and many other articles of merchandise, which they afterwards send by sea to Adule, to the country of the Homerites, to Further India, and to Persia. This very fact you will find mentioned in the Book of Kings, where it is recorded that the Queen of Sheba, that is, of the Homerite country, whom afterwards our Lord in the Gospels calls the Queen of the South, brought to Solomon spices from this very Barbaria, which lay near Sheba on the other side of the sea, together with bars of ebony, and apes and gold from Ethiopia, which, though separated from Sheba by the Arabian Gulf, lay in its vicinity. We can see again from the words of the Lord that he calls these places the ends of the earth, saying: *The Queen of the South shall rise up in judgment with this generation and shall condemn it, for she came from the ends of the earth to hear the wisdom of Solomon,* Matt. xii. 42. For the Homerites are not far distant from Barbaria, as the sea which lies between them can be crossed in a couple of days, and then beyond Barbaria is the ocean, which is there called Zingion. The country known as that of Sasu is itself near the ocean, just as the ocean is near the frankincense country, in which there are many gold mines. . . .

J. W. McCrindle, trans., *The Christian Topography of Cosmas, an Egyptian Monk* (London, 1897), as cited in G. S. P. Freeman-Grenville, ed., *The East African Coast,* 2nd ed. (London: Rex Collings, 1975), pp. 6–7.

NILOTIC AFRICA AND THE ETHIOPIAN HIGHLANDS

ca. 500 B.C.	Yemenites (southern Arabians) enter and settle on the Ethiopian plateau
30 B.C.	Egypt becomes part of Roman Empire of Octavian
ca. A.D. 1–100	Earliest mention (in Latin and Greek writers) of the kingdom of Aksum on Ethiopian plateau
ca. A.D. 330	Fall of Kushite empire to Elzana of Aksum
ca. A.D. 200–400	Heyday of Aksumite Ethiopia
ca. A.D. 500–600	Christianizing of the major Nubian states of Maqurra and Alwa
A.D. 652	Maqurra and Alwa make peace with Arab Muslim armies from Egypt

as a whole. The conversion of Ezana and his realm was the work of Frumentius, a Syrian bishop of Aksum who also served as secretary and treasurer to the king. Subsequently, under Alexandrian influence, the Ethiopian church became Monophysite in doctrine (that is, it adhered to the dogma of the single, unitary nature of Christ). This did not cut off Aksumite trading relations with Byzantium, however much Constantinople may have persecuted Monophysites at home. In the fifth century A.D., the native language of Ge'ez began to replace Greek in the liturgy, which proved to be a major step in the unique development of the Ethiopic or Abyssinian Christian church over the succeeding centuries.

Isolation of Christian Ethiopia

Aksumite trade continued to thrive through the sixth century, despite the decay of Rome. Strong enough at times to extend to the Yemen, Aksumite power was eclipsed in the end by the rise of Arab Islamic power. Nevertheless, the Aksumite state continued to exist long after its power had diminished. Having sheltered a refugee group of Muhammad's earliest Meccan converts, the Aksumites enjoyed relatively cordial relations with the new Muslim domains to the north in Egypt and across the Red Sea in the peninsula. But Aksum ceased to be a center of foreign trade and became more and more isolated. Its center of gravity shifted southward from the coast to the more rugged parts of the plateau. Here a Monophysite, Ge'ez-speaking culture emerged in the area of modern Ethiopia and lasted in relative isolation until modern times, surrounded largely by Muslim peoples and Islamic states.

Ethiopia's northern neighbors, the Christian states of Maqurra and Alwa, also survived for centuries in the former Meroitic lands of the Nilotic Sudan under treaty relations with Muslim Egypt. However, incursions of the Muslim Mamluk rulers of Egypt in the fourteenth and fifteenth centuries and Arab migration from about 1300 led ultimately to the Islamization and conversion of the whole Nubian region. Ethiopia was left as the sole predominantly Christian state in Africa.

The Western and Central Sudan

Agriculture, Trade, and the Rise of Urban Centers

Earlier we noted the presumed movements of Neolithic peoples southward from the Saharan regions into the western and central Sudan and ultimately into the forests of the African equatorial regions. The rain forests were inhospitable to cows and horses, largely because of the animals' inability to survive the sleeping sickness (*trypanosomiasis*) carried by the tsetse fly. But the agriculturalists who brought their cereal grains and stone tools south found particularly good conditions in the savannah just north of the West African forests. By the first or second century A.D., settled agriculture, now augmented by the use of iron tools, had become the way of life of most of the inhabitants of these western Sudanic lands. Agriculture had even made considerable progress in the forest regions farther south. The savannah areas seem to have experienced a substantial population explosion in the first few centuries A.D., especially in the areas close to the major water supplies: along the Senegal River, around the great northern bend in the Niger

River, and in the Lake Chad basin. Villages, and gradually some chiefdoms consisting of several villages, remained normally the largest political units during this period. As time went on, their growth provided the basis (and the need) for the eventual development of larger towns and political units in these areas of the western Sudan.

Trade was another element that eventually promoted or at least accompanied the rise of larger political units in the western and central Sudan. Regional and interregional trade networks in the western and central Sudan date to ancient times, and as we saw earlier, contacts between the Sudanic regions and the Mediterranean were maintained throughout the first millennium B.C. over trans-Saharan trading routes. Extensive east-west trade flourished in the Sahel, connecting the western Sahel to Egypt and the Nilotic

Excavations at Jenne-jeno (ancient Jenne), an early urban settlement in the western Sahel. Note the layer-cake stratification. This photograph shows work progressing in levels dating to the first centuries B.C. and the founding of the site by agriculturalists who came from the Saharan north. [R. J. Macintosh]

MAP 8-2   AFRICA: EARLY TRADE ROUTES AND EARLY STATES OF THE WESTERN AND CENTRAL SUDAN
This map shows some of the major routes of north-south trans-Saharan caravan trade and their links with Egypt and with sudanic and forest West Africa.

Sudan. From the western Sahel this trade connected to Saharan routes and sites to the north (see Map 8-2).

By the latter half of the first millennium B.C., a number of substantial urban settlements—among them Gao, Kumbi (also known as Kumbi Saleh), and Jenne—emerged in the western Sahel. Excavations at Jenne, in the upper Niger (the so-called Inland Delta) indicate that it dates from 250 B.C. and that it reached a population of more than ten thousand by the later part of the first millennium A.D.[7]

Even earlier evidence of urbanism has been found farther west and north, in the southern Mauritanian

[7] S. K. and R. J. McIntosh, pp. 41–59, 434–461; and R. Oliver, p. 90. The ensuing discussion of West African urban settlement is also taken primarily from Oliver's excellent summary discussion of current knowledge about this subject, id., pp. 90–101.

desert, where the remains of stone-walled towns of several thousand people have been dated into the second millennium B.C., a time when the area was one of lakes not yet dessicated by the climatic changes that followed the Wet Holocene. To the east, south of Lake Chad, in the lower reaches of the Chari and Lagone rivers that flow north to the great lake, as many as six hundred densely populated towns built by the Sao, a Chadic-speaking people, can be dated with reasonable certitude to the early first millennium A.D.

All of these early urbanized areas were characterized by an economy based on a mix of farming with fishing and hunting, and all developed in oasis or river regions rich enough to support dense populations and local and regional trade. The existence of relatively autonomous settlements in all of these cases made possible rather loose confederations or even widely dispersed imperial networks as time went on (and much earlier than scholars thought until very recently).

The introduction of the domesticated camel (the one-humped Arabian camel, or dromedary) from the east sometime around the beginning of the Christian era greatly increased the viability of trans-Saharan trade. By the early Christian centuries, the West African–settled communities were able to develop trading centers of considerable importance on their northern peripheries, in the Sahel near the edge of the true desert. The salt of the desert, so badly needed in the settled savannah, and the gold of West Africa, coveted in the north, were the prime commodities exchanged. However, many other items were also traded, including cola nuts, slaves, dates, and gum from West Africa, and horses, cattle, millet, leather, cloth, and weapons from the north.

Towns such as Awdaghast, Walata, Timbuktu, Gao, Tadmekka, and Agades have been the most famous southern terminals for this trade over the centuries. These centers allowed the largely Berber middlemen who plied the trade routes across the ever dangerous Sahara to traverse the desert via oasis stations between them and the North African coastal regions or even Egypt. Thus, some of the main routes ran as follows: (1) from the first three towns just mentioned to the major desert salt-producing center of Taghaza and thence to Morocco; (2) from Timbuktu, as from Gao, over the desert direct to Morocco; and (3) from Tadmekka and Agades to the desert market town of Ghat in the north-central Sahara and on to the coasts of Libyan North Africa. Other lines went north from the region of Lake Chad; one route stretched as far east as Egypt itself, passing through the mountain massifs of the central Sahara such as that of the Tassili and Ahaggar. As a typical full crossing could easily take two to three months, this was not an easy means of transporting goods.

Formation of Sudanic Kingdoms in the First Millennium

The first millennium A.D. saw the growth of settled agricultural populations and the development and expansion of trans-Saharan and other internal trade. These developments coincided with the rise of several sizable states in the western and central Sudan, significantly in the Sahel and savannah border region near the great sources of water below the Sahara. The most important states were located in the following regions: (1) Takrur on the Senegal River, from perhaps the fifth century, if not earlier; (2) Ghana, between the northern bends of the Senegal and the Niger, from the fifth or sixth century; (3) Gao, on the Niger southeast of the bend, from before the eighth century; and (4) Kanem, northeast of Lake Chad, from the eighth or ninth century. Although the origins and even the full extent of major states in these regions are shrouded in obscurity, each represents only the first of a series of large political entities in its region. All continued to figure prominently in subsequent West African history (see Chapter 19).

The states developed by the Fulbe people of Takrur and the Soninke people of Ghana depended early on their ability to draw gold for the Saharan trade with Morocco from the savannah region of Bambuhu (or Bambuk), west of the upper Senegal. Of all the sub-

THE WESTERN AND CENTRAL SUDAN: PROBABLE DATES FOR FOUNDING OF REGIONAL KINGDOMS	
ca. 400 A.D. or earlier	Takrur (Senegal River valley)
A.D. 400–600	Ghana (in Sahel between great northern bends of the Senegal and Niger rivers)
ca. A.D. 700–800 or before	Gao (on the Niger River southeast of great bend)
ca. A.D. 700–900	Kanem (northeast of Lake Chad)

Saharan kingdoms of the late first millennium, Ghana was the most famous outside of the region, largely owing to its substantial control over the gold trade. Its people built a large regional empire centered at its capital of Kumbi (also known as Kumbi Saleh). Inheriting his throne by matrilineal descent, the ruler was treated as a virtually semidivine personage whose interaction with his subjects was mediated by a hierarchy of government ministers. He is described in an eleventh-century Arabic chronicle as commanding a sizable army, including horsemen and archers, and being buried with his retainers under a dome of earth and wood. In contrast to the Soninke of Ghana, the Songhai rulers of Gao had no gold trade until the four-teenth century. Unlike its western neighbors, Gao was oriented in its forest trade toward the lower, not the upper, Niger basin and in its Saharan trade toward eastern Algeria, not Morocco.

All of these states were built on an agricultural base and settled populations. By contrast, the power of Kanem, on the northwestern side of Lake Chad, originated in the borderlands of the central Sudan and the southern Sahara. Here the first state formation was a nomadic federation of black tribal peoples that persisted long enough for the separate tribes to merge and form a single people, the Kanuri. They then moved south to take over the sedentary societies of Kanem proper, just east of Lake Chad, and, later,

The introduction of the camel to the Saharan regions sometime around the beginning of the Christian era greatly increased the efficiency of trans-Saharan trade and contributed to the growth of major trading centers such as Timbuktu, shown on the right. [Bettmann Archive; Photograph by Eliot Elisofon, National Museum of African Art, Eliot Elisofon Archives, Smithsonian Institution]

Bornu, west of Lake Chad. By the thirteenth century, the Kanuri had themselves become sedentary; their kingdom controlled the southern terminus of perhaps the best trans-Saharan route—that running north via good watering stations to the oasis region of Fezzan in modern central Libya and thence to the Mediterranean. We shall return to Kanem and the western Sudanic states and their later development in Chapter 19.

Central, Southern, and East Africa

The African subcontinent is that part of central, southern, and East Africa that lies south of a line from roughly the Niger delta and Cameroon across to southern Somalia on the east coast. Available sources have made it difficult to reconstruct the history of this region before A.D. 1000 in any detail. Some relatively certain facts and reasonable hypotheses have, however, emerged from a combination of linguistic, archaeological, and other research.

The Khoisan Peoples

In southern Africa, we find alongside the Bantu-speaking majority a minority who speak one of the varied languages belonging to either the Khoi or the San language groups that together are known as "Khoisan." The two groups that collectively constitute the Khoisan speakers are the San (long known in the west as the "Bushmen") and the Khoikhoi (the "Hottentots" of older European usage). Current thinking has it that these are two interrelated, nonhomogeneous groups whose members can be distinguished linguistically—but not physically—from the members of neighboring Bantu-speaking groups and other language groups of Africa.[8]

According to the conventional view, the Khoikhoi and San could be distinguished from each other largely by their livelihood. The Khoikhoi have generally been tagged as herdsmen and the San as hunter-

gatherers, but recent research has challenged this division. Both groups have also typically been seen as representing the survival of a "primitive" stage of cultural evolution, a view that many anthropologists and historians have sharply disputed recently. These scholars have argued that a great deal of the common wisdom about these peoples, who indeed do have very low social and economic status in the Namibia-Botswana-Zimbabwe-South Africa areas where their small communities still can be found, is the result of colonialist and post-colonialist prejudice against them.

The Khoisan are likely the descendants of the Neolithic and early Iron Age peoples—originally hunter-gatherers and later also pastoralists—who created the striking prehistoric rock paintings of southern Africa. They do not form a single cultural group but have developed linguistically and culturally diverse subgroups in different locales across southern Africa. Today they survive most prominently in the Kalahari region. The more homogeneous Khoikhoi were generally sheep- and cattle-herding pastoralists scattered across the south, yet speaking closely related Khoisan tongues. Their ancestors probably originated in northern Botswana. They were hunters who relatively late—probably between A.D. 700 and 1000—adopted animal herding from their Bantu-speaking southern African neighbors. Thus, they became primarily pastoralists and soon expanded over the best pasturelands of western southern Africa, as far south as the Cape of Good Hope. Here they flourished as pastoralist clans, sometimes united loosely as a tribe under a particularly strong chief, until their tragic encounter with the invading Dutch colonists in the mid-seventeenth century, which resulted in their demise as a distinct people.

Bantu Migrations and Diffusion

In the African subcontinent, the vast majority of the peoples speak one of more than four hundred languages that belong to a single language group known as *Bantu*. All of these languages are as closely related as are the Germanic or Romance tongues of Europe. Although the place of origin and routes of diffusion of Bantu tongues have long been debated, today there is increasing consensus that the location of the proto-Bantu language must have been in the region south of the Benue River, in eastern Nigeria and modern Cameroon. Thence, in the course of the later centuries B.C. and the first millennium A.D., migrations of Bantu-

---

[8]On the vexing problem of distinguishing San and Khoikhoi, see Richard Elphick, *Kraal and Castle: Khoikhoi and the Founding of White South Africa* (New Haven: Yale University Press, 1977), pp. xxi–xxii, 3–42; on the "construction" of their respective identities and for a summary of recent research on their antiquity and history, see E. N. Wilmsen, *Land Filled with Flies* (Chicago: University of Chicago Press, 1989).

speaking peoples must have taken their versions of this language in two basic directions: (1) south into the lower Zaïre (Kongo) basin and ultimately to the southern edge of the equatorial forest in present-day northern Katanga; and (2) east around the equatorial forests into the lakes of highland East Africa.

In all these regions, Bantu tongues developed and multiplied in contact with other languages. Likewise, Bantu speakers intermixed and adapted in diverse ways, as the wide variety of physical types among Bantu peoples today demonstrates. Further migrations, some as early as the fourth century A.D. and others as late as the twelfth or thirteenth century, dispersed Bantu peoples even more widely, into south-central Africa, coastal East Africa, and southern Africa. One result of this dispersion was the early civilization of "Great Zimbabwe" and Mapungubwe in the upper Limpopo region (treated in Chapter 19). The notion, however, that the Bantu or the Khoikhoi arrived in southern Africa at about the same time as the first European settlers is a recent fabrication used to justify apartheid.

How the Bantu peoples managed to impose their languages on the earlier cultures of these regions remains unexplained. The idea that they brought the knowledge of iron smelting with them and used it to dominate other peoples is not borne out by linguistic or other studies. The proto-Bantu had apparently been fishermen and hunters who also cultivated yams, date palms, and some cereals. They also raised goats and possibly sheep and some cattle, but they did not bring cattle with them in their migrations. Most of the migrating Bantu peoples seem to have been mainly cereal or grain agriculturists whose basic political and social unit was the village. Perhaps they had unusually strong social cohesion that allowed them to absorb other peoples; there is no evidence that they were military conquerors. Perhaps the Bantu simply had sufficient numbers to become dominant, or they may have brought diseases with them against which the aboriginals of the forests and the southern savannah had no immunities, much as later the European newcomers to the Cape brought the ravages of smallpox to the susceptible Khoikhoi.

In any case, their cultures became in time so fully interwoven with those of the peoples among whom they settled that the answers to these questions may never be known. For example, Bantu-Arab mixing on the eastern coasts produced the Swahili culture, which we shall encounter in Chapter 19. We find Bantu-speaking peoples as slash-and-burn farmers in the Zaïre River savannah, as cattle herders in the East African high plains, as perennial floodplain cultivators on the Zambezi River, and as terracing and irrigating farmers among the highland Kikuyu and Chagga peoples.

East Africa

The history of East Africa along the coast before Islam differed from that of the inland highlands. Long-distance travel was easy and common along the seashore but less so inland.

The coast had had maritime contact with India, Arabia, and the Mediterranean via the Indian Ocean and Red Sea trade routes from at least as early as the second century B.C. By contrast, we know very little about the long-distance contacts of the inland regions with the coastal areas until after A.D. 1000. Nonetheless, regional inland and regional coastal trade must also be very ancient. Both coastal and oversea trade remained important and interdependent over the centuries, because the Indian Ocean trade depended on the monsoon winds and could use only the northernmost coastal trading harbors of East Africa for round-trip voyages in the same year. The monsoon winds blow from the northeast from December to March and thus could carry sailing ships south from Iran, Arabia, and India only during those months; they blow from the southwest only from April to August, so ships could sail from Africa northeast during those months. Local coastal shipping thus had to haul cargoes from farther south than Zanzibar and then transfer them to other ships for the annual round-trip voyages to Arabia and beyond.

Long-distance trade came into its own in Islamic times—about the ninth century—as an Arab monopoly. However, long before the coming of Islam, trade was apparently largely in the hands of Arabs, many of whom had settled in the East African coastal towns and in Iran and India to handle this international commerce. We have documentation of Greco-Roman contact with these East African centers of the Red Sea and Indian Ocean trade from as early as the first century A.D. Most of the coastal trading towns were apparently independent, although Rhapta, the one town mentioned in the earliest Greek source, *The Periplus*, was a dependency of a southern Arabian state.

The overseas trade was, however, evidently even more international than the earliest surviving sources indicate. Today, Malagasy, the imported Malayo-Polynesian language of Madagascar, points graphically to the antiquity of substantial contact with the East Indies via the coastal trading routes of Asia's ancient southern rim. Evidence of an Indonesian migration even before the beginning of our era is seen in the fact that bananas, coconut palms, and other food crops indigenous to Southeast Asia spread across the entire African continent as staple foods. Further, as a result of the early regular commercial ties to distant lands of Asia, extra-African ethnic and cultural mixing has long been the rule for the East African coast; even today, its linguistic and cultural traditions are rich and varied (see Chapter 19).

Other African imports included such items as Persian Gulf pottery, Chinese porcelain, and cotton cloth. The major African export good around which the east coast trade revolved was ivory, which was in perennial demand from Greece to India and, from the tenth century, even China. The slave trade was another major business. Slaves were procured, often inland, in East Africa and exported to the Arab and Persian world, as well as to India or China. Gold, that perennial lure of outsiders to Africa, became important in external trade only in Islamic times, from about the tenth century onward, as we shall see in Chapter 19. Wood and food grains must also have been shipped abroad.

The history of inland East Africa south of Ethiopia is much more difficult to trace than that of the coast, again as a result of the absence of written sources and the immense difficulty of access until relatively recent times. We can, however, use linguistic clues and other evidence to note some key developments that underlay more recent history in the highlands. These regions had seen an early diffusion of peoples from the north, and changing conditions of subsistence over the centuries have continued to propel movements of small groups into new areas.

Of the early migrants from the north, first came peoples speaking Kushitic languages of the Afro-Asiatic family, likely cattle herders and grain cultivators. Perhaps as early as 2000 B.C., they pushed from their homeland on the Ethiopian plateau south down the Rift valley as far as the southern end of Lake Tanganyika. They apparently displaced Neolithic hunter-gatherers who may have been related to the Khoisan minorities of modern East and southern Africa. Although Kushitic languages are spoken from east of Lake Rudolph northward in abundance, farther south only isolated remnants of Kushitic speakers remain today, largely in the Rift valley in Tanzania.

Later, Nilotic-Saharan speakers moved from the

MOVEMENT AND CONTACT OF PEOPLES IN CENTRAL, SOUTHERN, AND EAST AFRICA	
ca. 1300–1000 B.C.	Kushitic-speaking peoples migrate from Ethiopian plateau south along Rift valley
ca. 400 B.C.–A.D. 1000	Probable era of major Bantu migrations into central, East, and southeastern Africa
200–100 B.C. or earlier	East African coast becomes involved in Indian Ocean trade
ca. 100 B.C.	Probable time of first Indonesian immigration to East African coast
ca. A.D. 100–1500	Nilotic-speaking peoples spread over upper Nile valley; Nilotic peoples spread over Rift valley region

southwestern side of the Ethiopian plateau west over the upper Nile valley by about A.D. 1000. Then they pushed east and south, following the older Kushite paths, to spread over the Rift valley area by the fifteenth century and subsequently much of the East African highlands of modern-day Uganda, Kenya, and Tanzania. Here they all but completely supplanted their Kushite predecessors. Two of these Nilotic peoples were the Lwo and Maasai. The Lwo spread far and wide over a nine-hundred-mile-long swath of modern Uganda and parts of the southern Sudan and western Kenya. They did so over a long period of time and mixed readily with various other peoples, absorbing new cultural elements and adapting to new situations wherever they went. The Maasai, on the other hand, were and still are cattle pastoralists fiercely proud of their separate language, way of life, and cultural traditions. These features have distinguished them sharply from the farming or hunting peoples whose settlements abutted their pasturages at the top of the southern Rift valley in Kenya and Tanzania. Here, southwest and west of both Mt. Kenya and Mt. Kilimanjaro, the Maasai have concentrated and remained.

These migrations from the north and those of the Bantu peoples, who also entered the eastern highlands over many centuries, from the west have made the highland regions a melting pot of Kushitic, Nilotic, Bantu, and Khoisan groups. Their characteristics are visible in today's populations, possessing an immense diversity of languages and cultures. As much as any part of Africa, here we see the radical diversity of peoples and cultures of the entire continent mirrored in the heritages of a single major region.

Africa to ca. 1000 A.D. in World Perspective

Pre-Islamic Africa is often viewed as a relatively isolated land mass that contributed little to political, cultural, and religious developments in the ancient world and was little engaged on the world scene. This perspective does not stand close scrutiny. To begin with, the human species probably originated in Africa. Pharaonic Egypt most notably, but also the Kushite kingdoms of Napata and Meroe and the Ethiopian state of Aksum, were all major political-military powers with highly developed cultures that were in regular interchange with other lands of the ancient world, from Rome to India and beyond.

Africa also made important contributions to other cultures. Nilotic African cultures had a strong influence on the Hellenistic world. The Greek scripture translation known as the Septuagint was produced by Jewish scholars in Egyptian Alexandria. Muhammad's fledgling community of Muslims was in part sustained by sanctuary offered by Christian Abyssinia. Augustine of Hippo was an African. Even Christian monasticism began in Egypt.

Thus, from a world perspective, Africa was engaged with neighbors far and near from at least the first millennium B.C.—in trading, in conflict and cooperation, in religious life, and in cultural life. An active internal trade brought goods from the interior of the continent to the centers of external exchange. In Africa, however, as in much of Eurasia, the imminent coming of the last major world religious and cultural tradition—that of Islam—would affect, redefine, or even eliminate the overt presence of many previous centers of civilization.

Suggested Readings

P. BOHANNAN and P. CURTIN, *Africa and Africans*, rev. ed. (1971). An enjoyable and enlightening discussion of African history and prehistory and of major African institutions (e.g., arts, family life, religion).

P. CURTIN, S. FEIERMANN, L. THOMPSON, and J. VANSINA, *African History* (1978). Probably the best survey history. The relevant portions are chaps. 1, 2, 4, 8, and 9.

T. R. H. DAVENPORT, *South Africa: A Modern History*, 3rd rev. ed. (1987). Chapter 1 gives excellent summary coverage of prehistoric southern Africa, the Khoisan peoples, and the Bantu migrations.

B. DAVIDSON, *The African Past* (1967). A combination of primary-source selections and brief secondary discussions trace sympathetically the history of the diverse parts of Africa.

J. D. FAGE, *A History of Africa* (1978). A fine general history. The relevant segment here is Part I, "The Internal Development of African Society" (chaps. 1–5).

P. GARLAKE, *The Kingdoms of Africa* (1978). A lavishly illustrated set of photographic essays that provide a helpful introduction to the various historically important areas of precolonial Africa.

R. W. JULY, *A History of the African People*, 3rd ed. (1980). Part I, "Ancient Africa" covers the precolonial centuries and offers a very readable historical introduction to African civilization.

R. W. JULY, *Precolonial Africa: An Economic and Social History* (1975). A very readable, topically arranged study. See especially "The Savannah Farmer," "The Bantu," "Cattlemen," and "The Traders" chapters.

J. KI-ZERBO, *Methodology and African Prehistory*. Vol. I of *UNESCO General History of Africa* (1981). Useful summary and interpretive articles (but of very uneven quality) treat diverse topics, including sources, languages, geography, and prehistory of the various regions.

G. MOKHTAR, *Ancient Civilizations of Africa*. Vol. II of *UNESCO General History of Africa* (1981). As in other volumes, the quality of articles varies greatly. Relevant chaps. are 8–16 on Nubia, Meroe, and Aksum; 17–20 on the Saharan region in ancient times; and 22–29 on the early history of the various regions of the African subcontinent.

R. OLIVER, *The African Experience* (1991). A masterly, balanced, and engaging sweep through African history. The chapters on prehistory and early history are outstanding summaries of the results and implications of recent research.

Tomb figure of standing attendant from the Former Han dynasty, second century B.C. *[Otto E. Nelson/The Asia Society]*

China's First Empire (221 B.C.–A.D. 220)

One hallmark of Chinese history is its striking continuity of culture, language, and geography. The Shang and Chou dynasties were centered in north China along the Yellow River or its tributary, the Wei. The capitals of China's first empire were in exactly the same areas, and north China would remain China's political center down through history to the present. If Western civilization had experienced similar continuity, it would have progressed from Thebes in the Valley of the Nile, to Athens on the Nile, Rome on the Nile, and then, in time, to Paris, London and Berlin on the Nile, and each of these centers of civilization would have spoken Egyptian and used a single writing system based on Egyptian hieroglyphics.

The many continuities in its history, however, did not mean that China was unchanging. One key turning point came in the third century B.C. when the old, quasi-feudal, multistate, Chou system gave way to a centralized bureaucratic government. The new centralized state built an empire stretching from the steppe in the north to Vietnam in the south.

The history of the first empire is composed of three segments:

256–206 B.C.	Ch'in dynasty
206 B.C.–A.D. 8	Former Han dynasty
A.D. 25–220	Later Han dynasty

The Ch'in dynasty is dated from 256 B.C., the year in which it overthrew the previous Chou dynasty. It went on to unify China in 221 B.C. The Western word *China* is derived from the name of this dynasty. In reshaping

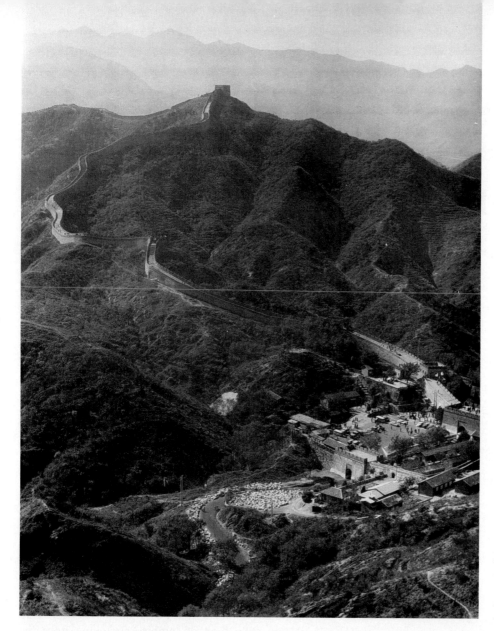

The Great Wall of China was originally built during the Ch'in dynasty (256–206 B.C.), but what we see today is the wall as it was completely rebuilt during the Ming dynasty (A.D. 1368–1644). [United Nations, 140806]

China, the Ch'in developed such momentum that it became overextended and collapsed a single generation after the unification. The Ch'in was followed by the two Han dynasties, each lasting about two hundred years. They both used the same dynastic name of Han because the Later Han was founded by a descendant of the Former Han. Historians usually treat each of the Han as a separate period of rule, although they were almost back to back and shared many institutions and cultural traits. So deep was the impression left by these two dynasties on the Chinese that even today they call themselves—in contrast to Mongols, Manchus, Tibetans, and other minorities—the "Han people," and their ideographs, "Han writing."

Ch'in Unification of China

Of the territorial states of the late Chou era, none was more innovative and ruthless than Ch'in. Its location on the Wei River in northwest China—the same area from which the Chou had launched their expansion a millennium earlier—gave it strategic advantages: It controlled the passes leading out onto the Yellow River plain and so was easy to defend and was a secure base from which to launch attacks on other states. From the late fourth century B.C., the Ch'in conquered a part of Szechwan and thus controlled two of the most fertile regions of ancient China. It welcomed

Legalist administrators, who developed policies for enriching the country and strengthening its military. Despite its harsh laws, farmers moved to Ch'in from other areas, attracted by the order and stability of its society. Its armies had been forged by centuries of warfare against the nomadic raiders by whose lands it was half encircled. To counter these raiders, Ch'in armies adopted nomadic skills, developing cavalry in the fourth century. Other states regarded the Ch'in as tough, crude, and brutal but recognized their formidable strengths.

In 246 B.C., the man who would unify China succeeded to the Ch'in throne at the age of thirteen. He grew to be vigorous, ambitious, intelligent, and decisive. He is famous as a Legalist autocrat; but he was also well liked by his ministers, whose advice he usually followed. (See Chapter 2 for a description of Legalism.) In 232 B.C., at the age of twenty-seven, he began the campaigns that destroyed the six remaining territorial states. On completing his conquests in 221 B.C., he adopted the glorious title we translate as "emperor"—a combination of ideographs hitherto used only for gods or mythic heroes—to raise himself above the kings of the former territorial states. Then, aided by officials of great talent, this First Ch'in Emperor set about applying to all of China the reforms that had been tried and found effective in his own realm. His accomplishments in the eleven years before his death in 210 B.C. were stupendous.

Having conquered the civilized world of north China and the Yangtze River basin, the First Emperor sent his armies to conquer new lands. They reached the northern edge of the Red River basin in what is now Vietnam. They occupied China's southeastern coast and the area about the present-day city of Canton (see Map 9-1). In the north and the northwest, the emperor's armies fought against the Hsiung Nu, Altaic-speaking Hunnish nomads organized in a tribal confederation. During the late Chou, northern border states had built long walls to protect settled lands from incursions by horse-riding raiders. The Ch'in emperor had them joined into a single Great Wall that extended fourteen hundred miles from the Pacific Ocean into central Asia. (By way of comparison, Hadrian's Wall in England was seventy-three miles long.) Its construction cost the lives of vast numbers of conscripted laborers—by some accounts, one hundred thousand; by others, as many as one million.

The most significant Ch'in reform, carried out by the Legalist minister, Li Ssu, extended the Ch'in system of bureaucratic government to the entire empire. Li Ssu divided China into forty prefectures, which

MAP 9-1 THE UNIFICATION OF CHINA BY THE CH'IN STATE
Between 221 and 206 B.C. the Ch'in state expanded and unified China.

were further subdivided into counties. The county heads were responsible to prefects, who, in turn, were responsible to the central government. Officials were chosen by ability. Bureaucratic administration was impersonal, based on laws to which all were subject. No one, for example, escaped Ch'in taxation. This kind of bureaucratic centralism broke sharply with the old Chou pattern of establishing dependent principalities for members of a ruler's family. Furthermore, to ensure the smooth functioning of local government offices, the former aristocracies of the territorial states were removed from their lands and resettled in the Ch'in capital, near present-day Sian. They were housed in mansions on one side of the river, from which they could gaze across at the enormous palace of the First Emperor.

Other reforms further unified the First Emperor's vast domain. Roads were built radiating out from the capital city. The emperor decreed a system of uniform weights and measures. He unified the Chinese writing system, establishing standard ideographs to replace the great variety that had hitherto prevailed. He established uniform axle lengths for carts. Even ideas did not escape the drive toward uniformity. Following the precepts of Legalism, the emperor and his advisers launched a campaign for which they subsequently

The army of life-size terra-cotta soldiers found in the tomb of the first emperor of the Ch'in dynasty (256–206 B.C.). [Liu Entai]

have been execrated throughout Chinese history. They collected and burned the books of other schools such as Confucianism and were said to have buried alive several hundred scholars opposed to the Legalist philosophy. Only useful books on agriculture, medicine, or Legalist teachings were spared.

But the Ch'in had changed too much too quickly to pay for the roads, canals, and the Great Wall. Taxes burdened the people. Commoners hated conscription and labor service and nobles resented their loss of status. Merchants were exploited, and scholars, except for Legalists, were oppressed. A Chinese historian wrote afterward: "The condemned were an innumerable multitude; those who had been tortured and mutilated formed a long procession on the roads. From the princes and ministers down to the humblest people everyone was terrified and in fear of their lives."[1] After the first Emperor died in 210 B.C., intrigues broke out at court and rebellions arose in the land. At the end, the Ch'in was destroyed by the domino effect of its own legal codes. When the generals sent to quell a rebellion were defeated, they joined

the rebellion rather than return to the capital and incur the severe punishment decreed for failure. The dynasty collapsed in 206 B.C.

In 1974, a farmer digging a well near Sian discovered the army of eight thousand life-sized terra-cotta horses and soldiers that guarded the tomb of the First Emperor. The historical record tells us that in the tomb itself, under a mountain of earth, are a replica of his capital; a relief model of the Chinese world with quicksilver rivers; other warriors with chariots of bronze; and the remains of horses, noblemen, and criminals sacrificed to accompany in death the emperor whose dynasty was to have lasted for ten thousand generations.

Former Han Dynasty (206 B.C.–A.D. 8)

The Dynastic Cycle

Confucian historians of China have seen a pattern in every dynasty of long duration. They call it the *dynastic cycle*. The stages of the cycle are interpreted in

[1]C. P. Fitzgerald, *China, A Short Cultural History* (New York: Praeger, 1935), p. 147.

Early Years of the Former Han Dynasty

The first sixty years of the Han may be thought of as the early phase of its dynastic cycle. Of the several rebel generals who emerged after the collapse of the Ch'in, one gained control of the Wei basin and went on to unify China. He became the first emperor of the Han dynasty and is known by his posthumous title of Kao Tsu. He rose from plebeian origins to become emperor, which would happen only once again in Chinese history. Kao Tsu built his capital at Ch'ang-an, not far from the former capitals of the Western Chou and the Ch'in. It took Kao Tsu and his immediate successors many years to consolidate their power because they consciously avoided actions that would remind the populace of the hated Ch'in despotism. They made punishments less severe and reduced taxes. Good government prevailed, the economy rebounded, granaries were filled, and vast cash reserves were accumulated. Later historians often singled out the early Han rulers as model sage emperors.

Han Wu Ti

The second phase of the dynastic cycle began with the rule of Wu Ti (the "martial emperor"), who came to the throne in 141 B.C. at the age of sixteen and remained there for fifty-four years, the second longest rule in all Chinese history. Wu Ti was daring, vigorous, and intelligent but also superstitious, suspicious, and vengeful. He wielded tremendous personal authority.

Building on the prosperity achieved by his predecessors, Wu Ti initiated new economic policies. A canal was built from the Yellow River to the capital in northwest China, linking the two major economic regions of north China. "Ever-level granaries" were established throughout the country so that the surplus from bumper crops could be bought and then resold in time of scarcity. To increase revenues, taxes were levied on merchants, the currency was debased, and some offices were sold. Wu Ti also moved against merchants who had built fortunes in untaxed commodities by reestablishing government monopolies—a practice of the Ch'in—on copper coins, salt, iron, and liquor. For fear of Wu Ti, no one spoke out against the monopolies, but a few years after his death, a famous debate was held at the court.

Known after the title of the chronicle as the "Salt and Iron Debate," it was frequently cited thereafter in China, and in Japan and Korea as well. On one side,

Chinese archaeologists restoring warriors from the tomb of the Ch'in emperor. [Liu Entai]

terms of the "mandate of heaven." The cycle begins with internal wars that eventually led to the military unification of China. The fact of unification is proof that heaven has given the unifier the mandate to rule. Strong and vigorous, the first ruler, in the process of consolidating his political power, restores peace and order to China. Economic growth follows, almost automatically. The peak of the cycle is marked by public works, further energetic reforms, and aggressive military expansion. During this phase, China appears invincible. But then the cycle turns downward. The costs of expansion, coupled with an increasing opulence at the court, place a heavy burden on tax revenues just as they are beginning to decline. The vigor of the monarchs wanes. Intrigues develop at the court. The central controls loosen, and provincial governors and military commanders gain autonomy. Finally, canals and other public works fall into disrepair, floods and pestilence occur, rebellions break out, and eventually the dynasty collapses. In the view of Confucian historians, the last emperors in a cycle are not only politically weak but morally culpable as well.

quasi-Legalist officials argued that the state should enjoy the profits from the sale of salt and iron. On the other side, Confucians argued that these resources should be left in private hands, for the moral purity of officials would be sullied by dealings with merchants. The Confucian scholars who compiled the chronicle made themselves the winner in the debate; but state monopolies became a regular part of Chinese government finance.

Wu Ti also aggressively expanded Chinese borders—a policy that would characterize every strong dynasty. His armies swept south into what is today northern Vietnam and northeast across Manchuria to establish a military outpost in northern Korea that would last until A.D. 313.

The principal threat to the Han was from the Hsiung Nu empire to the north. Their mounted archers could raid China and flee before an army could be sent against them. To combat them, Wu Ti employed the entire repertoire of policies that would become standard thereafter. When possible he "used the barbarian to control the barbarian," making allies of border nomads against those more distant. Allies were permitted to trade with Chinese merchants; they were awarded titles and honors; and their kings were sent Chinese princesses as brides. When this method did not work, he used force. Between 129 and 119 B.C., Wu Ti sent several armies of over one hundred thousand troops into the steppe, destroying Hsiung Nu power south of the Gobi Desert in southern Mongolia. To establish a strategic line of defense aimed at the heart of the Hsiung Nu empire further to the west, Wu Ti then sent seven hundred thousand Chinese colonists to the arid Kansu panhandle and extended the Great Wall to the Jade Gate outpost at the eastern end of the Tarim Basin. From this outpost, Chinese influence was extended over the rim oases of Central Asia, establishing the Silk Road that linked Ch'ang-an with Rome (see Map 9-2).

Government During the Former Han

To demonstrate their difference from the Ch'in emperor, the early Han emperors set up some Chou-like

---

Chinese Women Among the Nomads

About the year 105 B.C., Wu Ti sent a Chinese lady, Hsi-chun, to be the wife of a nomad king of the Wu-sun people of central Asia. When she got there, she found her husband to be old and decrepit. He saw her only once or twice a year, when they drank a cup of wine together. They could not converse, as they had no language in common.

My people have married me
In a far corner of Earth;
Sent me away to a strange land,
To the king of the Wu-sun.
A tent is my house,
Of felt are my walls;

Raw flesh my food
With mare's milk to drink.
Always thinking of my own country,
My heart sad within.
Would I were a yellow stork
And could fly to my old home!

Centuries later, the T'ang poet Tu Fu visited the village of another woman sent out to be the wife of a nomad king.

Ten thousand ranges and valleys approach the Ching Gate
And the village in which the Lady of Light was born and bred.
She went out from the purple palace into the desert-land;

She has now become a green grave in the yellow dusk.
Her face!—Can you picture a wind of the spring?
Her spirit by moonlight returns with a tinkling Song of the Tartars on her jade guitar,
Telling her eternal sorrow.

Arthur Waley, *Chinese Poems* (London: George Allen and Unwin, 1946), p. 43 (Selection 1); Witter Bynner and Kiang Kang-hsi, *The Jade Mountain* (New York, Alfred Knopf, 1929), p. 157 (Selection 2).

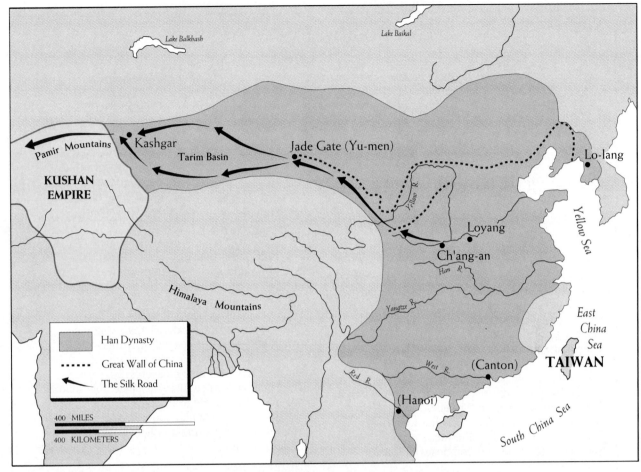

MAP 9-2 THE HAN EMPIRE 206 B.C.–A.D. 220 *At the peak of the Han expansion, the Han armies advanced far out into the steppe north of the Great Wall and west into Central Asia: The silk road to Rome passed through the Tarim Basin and the Kushan Empire.*

principalities: small, semiautonomous states with independent lords. This arrangement was, however, a token gesture. The principalities were closely superintended and then curtailed after several generations. Basically, despite its repudiation of the Ch'in and all its works, the Han continued the Ch'in form of centralized bureaucratic administration. Officials were organized by grades and were paid salaries in grain, plus cash or silk. They were recruited by sponsorship or recommendation: Provincial officials had the duty of recommending promising candidates. A school established at Ch'ang-an was said to have thirty thousand students by the Later Han. The bureaucracy grew until, by the first century B.C., there were more than one hundred thirty thousand officials—perhaps not too many for a population that, by that time, had reached sixty million.

During the course of the Han dynasty, this "Legalist" structure of government became partially Confucianized. It did not happen overnight. The first Han emperor, Kao Tsu, despised Confucians as bookish pedants—he once urinated in the hat of a scholar. But in time, Confucian ideas proved useful. The mandate of heaven provided an ethical justification for dynastic rule. A respect for old records and the written word fit in well with the vast bookkeeping the empire entailed. The Confucian classics gradually were accepted as the standard for education. Confucianism was seen as shaping moral men who would be upright officials, even in the absence of external constraints. For Confucius had taught the transformation of self through ethical cultivation and had presented a vision of benevolent government by men who were virtuous as well as talented. No one

The Position of Women

In the teachings of Confucius, a woman first obeyed her parents, then her husband, and finally her son—as the new family head. Descent was traced through the male line. A woman left her family and her ancestors at marriage to join those of her husband. A millennium before footbinding began in China, Fu Hsuan (A.D. 217–278) wrote this lament.

▶ *See also "Chinese Women Among the Nomads" in this chapter. For comparative perspectives on the status of women at other times and places, see the following document boxes: "Medea Bemoans the Condition of Women" (Ch. 4), "Women Industrial Workers Explain Their Economic Situation" (Ch. 27), "The Women of the Seneca Falls Convention Issue a Declaration of Female Independence" (Ch. 29), and "An English Feminist Defends the Right of the Female Franchise" (Ch. 30).*

WOMAN

How sad it is to be a woman!
Nothing on earth is held so cheap.
Boys stand leaning at the door
Like Gods fallen out of Heaven.
Their hearts brave the Four Oceans,
The wind and dust of a thousand miles.
No one is glad when a girl is born:
By *her* the family sets no store.
When she grows up, she hides in her room
Afraid to look a man in the face.
No one cries when she leaves her home—
Sudden as clouds when the rain stops.
She bows her head and composes her face,

Her teeth are pressed on her red lips:
She bows and kneels countless times.
She must humble herself even to the servants.
His love is distant as the stars in Heaven,
Yet the sunflower bends towards the sun.
Their hearts more sundered than water and fire—
A hundred evils are heaped upon her.
Her face will follow the year's changes:
Her lord will find new pleasures.
They that were once like substance and shadow
Are now as far as Hu from Ch'in [two distant places]
Yet Hu and Ch'in shall sooner meet
Than they whose parting is like Ts'an and
Ch'en [two stars].

Arthur Waley, *Translations from the Chinese* (1919, renewed 1947), pp. 84–85.

attempted to replace laws with a code of etiquette, but increasingly laws were interpreted and applied by men with a Confucian education.

The court during the Han dynasty exhibited features that would appear in later dynasties as well. All authority centered on the emperor, who was the all-powerful "son of heaven." The will of a strong adult emperor was paramount. When the emperor was weak, however, or ascended to the throne when still a child, others competed to rule in his name. Four contenders for this surrogate role appeared and reappeared through Chinese history: court officials, the empress dowager, court eunuchs, and military commanders.

Court officials were selected for their ability to govern: They staffed the apparatus of government and they advised the emperor directly. Apart from the emperor himself, they were usually the most powerful

men in China. Yet the position of court officials was often precarious. Few officials escaped being removed from office or banished once or twice during their careers. Of the seven prime ministers who served Wu Ti, five were executed by his order.

Of the emperor's many wives, the empress dowager was the one whose child had been named as the heir to the throne. Her influence sometimes continued even after her child became an adult emperor. But she was most powerful as a regent for a child emperor. On Kao Tsu's death in 195 B.C., for example, the Empress Lu became the regent for her child, the new emperor. Aided by members of her family, she seized control of the court and murdered a rival, and when her son was about to come of age, she had him killed and a younger son made the heir in order to continue her rule as regent. When she died in 180 B.C., loyal adherents of the imperial family who had opposed her rule massacred the members of her family.

Court eunuchs came mostly from families of low social status. They were brought to the court as boys, castrated, and assigned to work as servants in the emperor's harem. They were thus in contact with the future emperor from the day he was born, they became his childhood confidants, and they often continued to advise him after he had gained the throne. Emperors found eunuchs useful as counterweights to officials. But in the eyes of the scholars who wrote China's history, the eunuchs were greedy half men, given to evil intrigues.

Military leaders, whether generals or rebels, were the usual founders of dynasties. In the later phase of most dynasties, regional military commanders often became semi-independent rulers. A few even usurped the position of the emperor. Yet they were less powerful at the Chinese court than they were, for example, in imperial Rome, partly because the military constituted a separate category, lower in prestige than the better educated civil officials. It was also partly because the court took great pains to prevent its generals from establishing a base of personal power. An appointment to command a Han army was given only for a specific campaign, and commanders were appointed in pairs so that each would check the other.

Another characteristic of government during the Han and subsequent dynasties was that its functions were limited. It collected taxes, maintained military forces, administered laws, supported the imperial household, and carried out public works that were beyond the powers of local jurisdictions. But government in a district that remained orderly and paid its taxes was left largely in the hands of local notables and large landowners. This pattern was not, to be sure, unique to China. Most premodern governments, even those that were bureaucratic, floated on top of local society and lacked the means to reach down and interfere in the everyday lives of their subjects.

Decline and Usurpation

During the last decade of Wu Ti's rule in the early first century A.D., military expenses ran ahead of revenues. His successor cut back on military costs, eased economic controls, and reduced taxes. But over the next several generations, large landowners began to use their growing influence in provincial politics to avoid paying taxes. State revenues declined. The tax burden on smaller landowners and free peasants grew heavier. In 22 B.C., rebellions broke out in several parts of the empire. At the court, too, a decline set in. There was a succession of weak emperors. Intrigues, nepotism, and factional struggles grew apace. Even officials began to sense that the dynasty no longer had the approval of heaven. The dynastic cycle approached its end.

Many at the court urged Wang Mang, the regent for the infant emperor and the nephew of an empress, to become the emperor and begin a new dynasty. Wang Mang refused several times—to demonstrate his lack of eagerness—and then accepted in A.D. 8. He drew up a program of sweeping reforms based on ancient texts. He was a Confucian, yet he relied on new institutional arrangements, rather than moral reform, to produce a better society. He revived ancient titles, expanded state monopolies, abolished private slavery (about 1 percent of the population), made loans to poor peasants, and then moved to confiscate large private estates.

These reforms, however, alienated many. Merchants disliked the monopolies. Large landowners resisted the expropriation of their lands. Nature also conspired to bring down Wang Mang: The Yellow River overflowed its banks and changed its course, destroying the northern Chinese irrigation system. Several years of poor harvests produced famines. The Hsiung Nu overran China's northern borders. In A.D. 18, the Red Eyebrows, a peasant secret society, rose in rebellion. In A.D. 23, rebels attacked Ch'ang-an, and Wang Mang was killed and eaten by rebel troops. Wang Mang had tried to found a new dynasty from within a decrepit court without an independent military base. The attempt was futile. Internal wars continued in China for two more years until a large landowner, who had become the leader of a rebel army, emerged triumphant in A.D. 25. Because he was from a branch line of the imperial family, his new dynasty was viewed as a restoration of the Han.

Later Han (A.D. 25–220) and Its Aftermath

First Century

The founder of the Later Han moved his capital east to Loyang. Under the first emperor and his two successors, there was a return to strong central government and a laissez-faire economy. Agriculture and population recovered from the devastation caused by war. By the end of the first century A.D., China was as

A green glazed pottery model of a Later Han dynasty watchtower. Note the resemblance to later Chinese Buddhist pagodas. [W. R. Nelson Trust]

in the fifth century A.D., to Europe, where they were known as the Huns of Attila. In A.D. 97, a Chinese general led an army as far west as the shores of the Caspian Sea. The Chinese expansion in inner Asia, coupled with more lenient government policies toward merchants, facilitated the camel caravans that carried Chinese silk across the Tarim Basin to Iran, Palestine, and Rome.

Decline During the Second Century

Until A.D. 88, the emperors of the Later Han were vigorous; afterward they were ineffective and short lived. Empresses plotted to advance the fortunes of their families. Emperors turned for help to palace eunuchs, whose power at times surpassed that of officials. In A.D. 159, a conspiracy of eunuchs in the service of an emperor slaughtered the family of a scheming empress dowager and ruled at the court. When officials and students protested against the eunuch dictatorship, over a hundred were killed and over a thousand were tortured or imprisoned. In another incident in A.D. 190, a general deposed one emperor, installed another, killed the empress dowager, and massacred most of the eunuchs at the court.

In the countryside, large landowners who had been powerful from the start of the dynasty grew more so. They harbored private armies. Farmers on the estates of the mighty were reduced to serfs. The landowners used their influence to avoid taxes. Great numbers of free farmers fled south to avoid taxes. As a result, the remaining freeholders paid ever heavier taxes and labor services. Many peasants turned to neo-Taoist religious movements—the Yellow Turbans in the east and the Five Pecks of Rice Band in Szechwan—that provided the ideology and organization to channel their discontent into action. In A.D. 184, rebellions organized by members of the religious movements broke out against the government. Han generals suppressed the rebellions but stayed on to rule in the provinces they had pacified. In 220 A.D., they deposed the last Han emperor.

Aftermath of Empire

For more than three-and-a-half centuries after the fall of the Han, China was disunited. For several generations, it was divided into three kingdoms, whose heroic warriors and scheming statesmen were made famous by wandering storytellers. These figures later peopled the *Tales of the Three Kingdoms,* a great romantic epic of Chinese literature.

prosperous as it had been during the good years of the Former Han. The shift from pacification and recuperation to military expansion came earlier than it had during the previous dynasty. Even during the reign of the first emperor, south China and Vietnam were retaken. Dissension within the Hsiung Nu confederation enabled the Chinese to secure an alliance with some of the southern tribes in A.D. 50, and in A.D. 89 Chinese armies crossed the Gobi Desert and defeated the northern Hsiung Nu. This defeat sparked the migrations, some historians say, that brought the Hsiung Nu to the southern Russian steppes and then,

Chinese history during the post-Han centuries had two characteristics. The first was the dominant role played by the great aristocratic landowning families. With vast estates, huge numbers of serfs, fortified manor houses, and private armies, they were beyond the control of most governments. Because they took over many of the functions of local government, some historians describe post-Han China as having reverted to the quasi-feudalism of the Chou. The second characteristic of these centuries was that northern and southern China developed in quite different ways.

In the south, there followed a succession of ever weaker dynasties with capitals at Nanking. Although these six southern states were called dynasties—and the entire period of Chinese history from A.D. 220 to 589 is called the Six Dynasties era after them—they were in fact short-lived kingdoms, plagued by intrigues, usurpations, and coups d'état; frequently at war with northern states; and in constant fear of their own generals. The main developments in the south were (1) continuing economic growth and the emergence of Nanking as a thriving center of commerce; (2) the ongoing absorption of tribal peoples into Chinese society and culture; (3) large-scale immigrations of Chinese fleeing the north; and (4) the spread of Buddhism and its penetration to the heart of Chinese culture.

In the north, state formation depended on the interaction of nomads and Chinese. During the Han dynasty, Chinese invasions of the steppe had led to the incorporation of semi-Sinicized Hsiung Nu as the northernmost tier of the Chinese defense system—just as Germanic tribes had acted as the teeth and claws of the late Roman Empire. But as the Chinese state weakened, the highly mobile nomads broke loose, joined with other tribes, and began to invade China. The short-lived states that they formed are usually referred to as the "Sixteen Kingdoms." One kingdom was founded by invaders of Tibetan stock. Most spoke Altaic languages: the Hsien Pi (proto-Mongols), the Toba (proto-Turks), and the Juan Juan (who would later appear in eastern Europe as the Avars). But differences of language and stock were less important than these tribes' similarities:

1. All began as steppe nomads with a way of life different from that of agricultural China.
2. After forming states, all became at least partially Sinicized. Chinese from great families, which had preserved the Han traditions, served as their tutors and administrators.
3. All were involved in wars—among themselves, against southern dynasties, or against conservative steppe tribes that resisted Sinicization.
4. Buddhism was powerful in the north as in the south. As a universal religion, it acted as a bridge between "barbarians" and Chinese—just as Christianity was a unifying force in post-Roman Europe. The barbarian rulers of the north were especially attracted to its magical side. Usually Buddhism was made the state religion. Of the northern states, the most durable was the Northern Wei (A.D. 386–534), famed for its Buddhist sculpture.

Han Thought and Religion

Poems describe the splendor of Ch'ang-an and Loyang: broad boulevards, tiled gateways, open courtyards, watchtowers, and imposing walls. Most splendid of all were the palaces of the emperors, with their audience halls, vast chambers, harem quarters, and parks containing artificial lakes and rare animals and birds. But today little remains of the grandeur of the Han. Whereas Roman ruins abound in Italy and circle the Mediterranean, in China nothing remains above ground. Only from the pottery, bronzes, musical instruments, gold and silver jewelry, lacquerware, and clay figurines that were buried in tombs do we gain an inkling of the rich material culture of the Han period. And only from paintings on the walls of tombs do we know of its art.

But there is a wealth of written records that convey the sophistication and depth of Han culture. Perhaps the two most important areas were philosophy and history.

Han Confucianism

A major accomplishment of the early Han was the recovery of texts that had been lost during the Ch'in persecution of scholars. Some were retrieved from the walls of houses where they had been hidden; others were reproduced from memory by scholars. Debate arose regarding the relative authenticity of the old and new texts—a controversy that has continued until modern times. In 51 B.C. and again in A.D. 79, councils were held to determine the true meaning of the Confucian classics. In A.D. 175, an approved, official version of the texts was inscribed on stone tablets.

Court figures painted on ceramic tile in a Han dynasty tomb. [Museum of Fine Arts, Boston]

In about A.D. 100, the first dictionary was compiled. Containing about nine thousand characters, it helped promote a uniform system of writing. In Han times, as today, Chinese from the north could not converse with Chinese from the southeastern coast. But a common written language bridged differences of pronunciation, contributing to Chinese unity.

It was also in Han times that scholars began writing commentaries on the classics, a major activity for scholars throughout Chinese history. Scholars learned the classics by heart and used classical allusions in their writing.

Beyond the advances in scholarship, Han philosophers also extended Chou Confucianism by adding to it the teachings of cosmological naturalism. Chou Confucianists had assumed that the moral force of a virtuous emperor would not only order society but also harmonize nature. Han Confucianists explained why. Tung Chung-shu (ca. 179–104 B.C.), for example, held that all nature was a single, interrelated system. Just as summer always follows spring, so does one color, one virtue, one planet, one element, one number, and one officer of the court always take precedence over another. All reflect the systematic workings of *yang* and *yin* and the five elements. And just as one dresses appropriately to the season, so was it important for the emperor to choose policies appropriate to the sequences inherent in nature. If he was moral, if he acted in accord with Heaven's natural

system, then all would go well. But if he acted inappropriately, then Heaven would send a portent as a warning—a blue dog, a rat holding its tail in its mouth, an eclipse, or a comet. If the portent was not heeded, wonders and then misfortunes would follow. It was the Confucian scholars, of course, who claimed to understand nature's messages and advised the emperor.

It is easy to criticize Han philosophy as a pseudo-scientific or mechanistic view of nature. But it represented a new effort by the Chinese to encompass and comprehend the interrelationships of the natural world. Spurring an interest in nature, this effort led to inventions like the seismograph and to advances in astronomy, music, and medicine. It was also during the Han that the Chinese invented paper, the wheelbarrow, the stern-post rudder, and the compass (known as the "south-pointing chariot").

History

The Chinese were the greatest historians of the premodern world. They wrote more history than anyone else, and what they wrote was usually more accurate. Apart from the *Spring and Autumn Annals* and the scholarship of Confucius himself, history writing in China began during the Han dynasty. Why the Chinese were so history-minded has been variously ex-

A Chinese seismograph. The suspended weight swings in the direction of the earthquake. This moves a lever and a dragon drops a ball into the mouth of one of the four waiting ceramic frogs. [New York Public Library]

plained: because the Chinese tradition is this-worldly; because Confucianists were scholarly and their veneration for the classics carried over to the written word; because history was seen as a lesson book (the Chinese called it a mirror) for statesmen, and thus a necessity for the literate men who operated the centralized Chinese state.

The practice of using actual documents and firsthand accounts of events began with Ssu-ma Ch'ien (d. 85 B.C.), who set out to write a history of the known world from the most ancient times down to the age of the Emperor Wu Ti. His *Historical Records* consisted of 130 substantial chapters (with a total of over seven hundred thousand characters) divided into "Basic Annals"; "Chronological Tables"; "Treatises" on rites, music, astronomy, the calendar, and so on; "Hereditary Houses"; and seventy chapters of "Biographies," including descriptions of foreign peoples. A second great work, *The Book of the Han,* was written by Pan Ku (d. A.D. 92). It applied the analytical schema of Ssu-ma Ch'ien to a single dynasty, the Former Han, and established the pattern by which each dynasty wrote the history of its predecessor.

Neo-Taoism

As the Han dynasty waned, the effort to realize the Confucian ethic in the sociopolitical order became more and more difficult. Some scholars abandoned Confucianism altogether in favor of Neo-Taoism, or "mysterious learning," as it was called at the time. A few wrote commentaries on the classical Taoist texts that had been handed down from the Chou. The *Chuang Tzu* was especially popular. Other scholars, defining the natural as the pleasurable, withdrew from society to engage in witty "pure conversations." They discussed poetry and philosophy, played the lute, and drank wine. The most famous were the Seven Sages of the Bamboo Grove of the third century A.D. One sage was always accompanied by a servant carrying a jug of wine and a spade—the one for his pleasure, the other to dig his grave should he die. Another wore no clothes at home. When criticized, he replied that the cosmos was his home, and his house his clothes. "Why are you in my pants?" he asked a discomfited visitor. Still another took a boat to visit a friend on a snowy night, but on arriving at his friend's door, turned around and went home. When pressed for an explanation, he said that it had been his pleasure to go, and that when the impulse died, it was his pleasure to return. This story reveals a scorn for convention coupled with an admiration for an inner spontaneity, however eccentric.

Another concern of what is called Neo-Taoism was immortality. Some sought it in dietary restrictions and Yoga-like meditation; some, in sexual abstinence or orgies. Others, seeking elixirs to prolong life, dabbled in alchemy, and although no magical elixir was ever found, the schools of alchemy to which the search gave rise are credited with the discovery of medicines, dyes, glazes, and gunpowder.

Meanwhile among the common people, there arose popular religious cults that, because they included the Taoist classics among their sacred texts, are also called Neo-Taoist. Like most folk religions, they contained an amalgam of beliefs, practices, and superstitions. They had a pantheon of gods and im-

Ssu-ma Ch'ien on the Wealthy

More than half of the chapters in Ssu-ma Ch'ien's Historical Records *(early first century* B.C.*) were biographies of extraordinary men and women. He wrote of scholars, wandering knights, diviners, harsh officials and reasonable officials, wits and humorists, doctors, and money-makers. The following is his description of the vibrant economic life of Han cities and his judgments regarding the wealthy.*

Anyone who in the market towns or great cities manages in the course of a year to sell the following items: a thousand brewings of liquor; a thousand jars of pickles and sauces; a thousand jars of sirups; a thousand slaughtered cattle, sheep, and swine; a thousand *chung* of grain; a thousand cartloads or a thousand boat-lengths of firewood and stubble for fuel; a thousand logs of timber; ten thousand bamboo poles; a hundred horse carriages; a thousand two-wheeled ox carts; a thousand lacquered wooden vessels; brass utensils weighing thirty thousand catties; a thousand piculs of plain wooden vessels, iron vessels, or gardenia and madder dyes; two hundred horses; five hundred cattle; two thousand sheep or swine; a hundred male or female slaves; a thousand catties of tendons, horns, or cinnabar; thirty thousand catties of silken fabric, raw silk, or other fine fabrics; a thousand rolls of embroidered or patterned silk; a thousand piculs of fabrics made of vegetable fiber or raw or tanned hides; a thousand pecks of lacquer; a thousand jars of leaven or salted bean relish; a thousand catties of globefish or mullet; a thousand piculs of dried fish; thirty thousand catties of salted fish; three thousand piculs of jujubes or chestnuts; a thousand skins of fox or sable; a thousand piculs of lamb or sheep skins; a thousand felt mats; or a thousand *chung* of fruits or vegetables—such a man may live as well as the master of an estate of a thousand chariots. The same applies for anyone who has a thousand strings of cash [i.e., a million in cash] to lend out on interest. Such loans are made through a moneylender, but a greedy merchant who is too anxious for a quick return will only manage to revolve his working capital three times while a less avaricious merchant has revolved his five times. These are the principal ways of making money. There are various other occupations which bring in less than twenty percent profit, but they are not what I would call sources of wealth.

Thrift and hard work are without doubt the proper way to gain a livelihood. And yet it will be found that rich men have invariably employed some unusual scheme or method to get to the top. Plowing the fields is a rather crude way to make a living, and yet Ch'in Yang did so well at it that he became the richest man in his province. Robbing graves is a criminal offense, but T'ien Shu got his start by doing it. Gambling is a wicked pastime, but Huan Fa used it to acquire a fortune. Most fine young men would despise the thought of traveling around peddling goods, yet Yung Lo-ch'eng got rich that way. Many people would consider trading in fats a disgraceful line of business, but Yung Po made a thousand catties of gold at it. Vending sirups is a petty occupation, but the Chang family acquired ten million cash that way. It takes little skill to sharpen knives, but because the Chih family didn't mind doing it, they could eat the best of everything. Dealing in dried sheep stomachs seems like an insignificant enough trade, but thanks to it the Cho family went around with a mounted retinue. The calling of a horse doctor is a rather ignominious profession, but it enabled Chang Li to own a house so large that he had to strike a bell to summon the servants. All of these men got where they did because of their devotion and singleness of purpose.

From this we may see that there is no fixed road to wealth, and money has no permanent master. It finds its way to the man of ability like the spokes of a wheel converging upon the hub, and from the hands of the worthless it falls like shattered tiles. A family with a thousand catties of gold may stand side by side with the lord of a city; the man with a hundred million cash may enjoy the pleasures of a king. Rich men such as these deserve to be called the "untitled nobility," do they not?

Records of the Grand Historian of China, trans. from the *Shih chi* of Ssu-ma Ch'ien by Burton Watson (New York: Columbia University Press, 1961), pp. 494–495, 499.

The Castration of Ssu-ma Ch'ien

Why did the historian Ssu-ma Ch'ien let himself be castrated? When he incurred the wrath of the Emperor Wu Ti for defending a general defeated by the Hsiung Nu and was condemned to suffer this shame in 98 B.C., why did he not choose an honorable suicide? Read his explanation.

▶ *For a comparative perspective on victims of conscience, see "Thomas More Stands by His Conscience" (Ch. 18).*

A man has only one death. That death may be as weighty as Mount T'ai, or it may be as light as a goose feather. It all depends upon the way he uses it. It is the nature of every man to love life and hate death, to think of his relatives and look after his wife and children. Only when a man is moved by higher principles is this not so. Then there are things which he must do. The brave man does not always die for honor, while even the coward may fulfill his duty. Each takes a different way to exert himself. Though I might be weak and cowardly and seek shamefully to prolong my life, yet I know full well the difference between what ought to be followed and what rejected. How could I bring myself to sink into the shame of ropes and bonds? If even the lowest slave and scullery maid can bear to commit suicide, why should not one like myself be able to do what has to be done? But the reason I have not refused to bear these ills and have continued to live, dwelling among this filth, is that I grieve that I have things in my heart that I have not been able to express fully, and I am shamed to think that after I am gone my writings will not be known to posterity.

I too have ventured not to be modest but have entrusted myself to my useless writings. I have gathered up and brought together the old traditions of the world which were scattered and lost. I have examined the deeds and events of the past and investigated the principles behind their success and failure, their rise and decay, in one hundred and thirty chapters. I wished to examine into all that concerns heaven and man, to penetrate the changes of the past and present, completing all as the work of one family. But before I had finished my rough manuscript, I met with this calamity. It is because I regretted that it had not been completed that I submitted to the extreme penalty without rancor. When I have truly completed this work, I shall deposit it in some safe place. If it may be handed down to men who will appreciate it and penetrate to the villages and great cities, then though I should suffer a thousand mutilations, what regret would I have?

W. T. de Bary, W. T. Chan, and B. Watson, eds., *Sources of Chinese Tradition* (New York: Columbia University Press, 1960), pp. 272–273.

---

mortals and taught that the good or evil done in this life would be recompensed in the innumerable heavens or hells of an afterlife. These cults had priests, shamans who practiced faith healing, seers, and sorceresses. For a time, they also had hierarchical church organizations, but these were smashed when the Yellow Turbans and Five Pecks of Rice rebellions were suppressed at the end of the second century A.D. Local Taoist temples and monasteries, however, continued until modern times. With many Buddhist accretions, they furnished the religious beliefs of the bulk of the Chinese population. Even today, these sects continue in Taiwan and in Chinese communities in Southeast Asia.

Buddhism

Central Asian missionaries, following the trade routes east, brought Buddhism to China in the first century A.D. It was at first viewed as a new Taoist sect, which is not surprising because early translators used Taoist terms to render Buddhist concepts. *Nirvana,* for example, was translated as "not doing" *(wu-wei).* In the second century B.C., confusion of the two religions led to the very Chinese view that Lao-tzu had gone to India, where the Buddha had become his disciple, and that Buddhism was the Indian form of Taoism.

Then, as the Han sociopolitical order collapsed in the third century A.D., Buddhism spread rapidly. We

The Peach Blossom Spring

The poet Ta'o Ch'ien wrote in A.D. *380 of a lost village without taxes and untouched by the barbarian invasions and wars of the post-Han era. The simplicity and naturalness of his utopian vision were in accord, perhaps, with certain strains of Neo-Taoist thought. It struck a chord in the hearts of Chinese, and then Koreans and Japanese, inspiring a spate of paintings, poetry, and essays.*

During the T'ai-yuan period of the Ch'in dynasty a fisherman of Wuling once rowed upstream, unmindful of the distance he had gone, when he suddenly came to a grove of peach trees in bloom. For several hundred paces on both banks of the stream there was no other kind of tree. The wild flowers growing under them were fresh and lovely, and fallen petals covered the ground—it made a great impression on the fisherman. He went on for a way with the idea of finding out how far the grove extended. It came to an end at the foot of a mountain whence issued the spring that supplied the stream. There was a small opening in the mountain and it seemed as though light was coming through it. The fisherman left his boat and entered the cave, which at first was extremely narrow, barely admitting his body; after a few dozen steps it suddenly opened out onto a broad and level plain where well-built houses were surrounded by rich fields and pretty ponds. Mulberry, bamboo and other trees and plants grew there, and criss-cross paths skirted the fields. The sounds of cocks crowing and dogs barking could be heard from one courtyard to the next. Men and women were coming and going about their work in the fields. The clothes they wore were like those of ordinary people. Old men and boys were carefree and happy.

When they caught sight of the fisherman, they asked in surprise how he had got there. The fisherman told the whole story, and was invited to go to their house, where he was served wine while they killed a chicken for a feast. When the other villagers heard about the fisherman's arrival they all came to pay him a visit. They told him that their ancestors had fled the disorders of Ch'in times and, having taken refuge here with wives and children and neighbors, had never ventured out again; consequently they had lost all contact with the outside world. They asked what the present ruling dynasty was, for they had never heard of the Han, let alone the Wei and the Chin. They sighed unhappily as the fisherman enumerated the dynasties one by one and recounted the vicissitudes of each. The visitors all asked him to come to their houses in turn, and at every house he had wine and food. He stayed several days. As he was about to go away, the people said, "There's no need to mention our existence to outsiders."

After the fisherman had gone out and recovered his boat, he carefully marked the route. On reaching the city, he reported what he had found to the magistrate, who at once sent a man to follow him back to the place. They proceeded according to the marks he had made, but went astray and were unable to find the cave again.

J. R. Hightower, *The Poetry of Ta'o Ch'ien* (Oxford: Clarendon Press, 1970), pp. 254–255.

---

are reminded of the spread of Christianity at the end of the Roman Empire. Although an alien religion in China, Buddhism had some advantages over Taoism:

1. It was a doctrine of personal salvation, offering several routes to that goal.
2. It contained high standards of personal ethics.
3. It had systematic philosophies, and during its early centuries in China, it continued to receive inspiration from India.
4. It drew on the Indian tradition of meditative practices and psychologies, which were the most sophisticated in the world.

By the fifth century A.D., Buddhism had spread over all of China (see Map 9-3). Occasionally it was persecuted by Taoist emperors—in the north between A.D. 446 and 452, and again between A.D. 574 and 578. But most courts supported Buddhism. The "Bodhisattva Emperor" Wu of the southern Liang dynasty three times gave himself to a monastery and had to be ransomed back by his disgusted courtiers. Temples and monasteries abounded in both the north and the south. There were communities of women as well as of men. Chinese artists produced Buddhist painting and sculpture of surpassing beauty, and thousands of monk-scholars labored to translate sutras and philosophical treatises. Chinese monks went on pilgrimages to India. The record left by Fa Hsien, who traveled to India overland and back by sea between A.D. 399 and 413, became a prime source of Indian history. The T'ang monk Hsuan Tsang went to India from 629 until 645. Several centuries later, his pilgrimage was novelized as *Journey to the West* (later dubbed *Monkey* by Arthur Waley in his abridged English translation). The novel joins faith, magic, and adventure.

A comparison of Indian and Chinese Buddhism highlights some distinctive features of its spread. Buddhism in India had begun as a reform movement. Forget speculative philosophies and elaborate metaphysics, taught the Buddha, and concentrate on simple truths: Life is suffering, the cause of suffering is desire, death does not stop the endless cycle of birth

and rebirth; only the attainment of *nirvana* releases one from the "wheel of *karma*." Thus, in this most otherworldly of the world's religions, all of the cosmic drama of salvation was compressed into the single figure of the Buddha meditating under the Bodhi tree. Over the centuries, however, Indian Buddhism developed contending philosophies and conflicting sects and, having become virtually indistinguishable from Hinduism, was reabsorbed after A.D. 1000.

In China, there were a number of sects with different doctrinal positions. But the Chinese genius was more syncretic. It took in the sutras and meditative practices of early Buddhism. It took in the Mahayana philosophies that depicted a succession of Buddhas, cosmic and historical, past and future, all embodying a single ultimate reality. It also took in the sutras and practices of Buddhist devotional sects. Finally, in the T'ien-t'ai sect, the Chinese joined together these various elements as different levels of a single truth. Thus the monastic routine of a T'ien-tai monk would include reading sutras, sitting in meditation, and also practicing devotional exercises.

MAP 9-3   THE SPREAD OF BUDDHISM AND CHINESE STATES IN A.D. 500   *Buddhism originated in a Himalayan state in northwest India. It spread in one wave south in India and on to Southeast Asia as far as Java. But it also spread into northwest India, Afghanistan, Central Asia, and then to China, Korea, and Japan.*

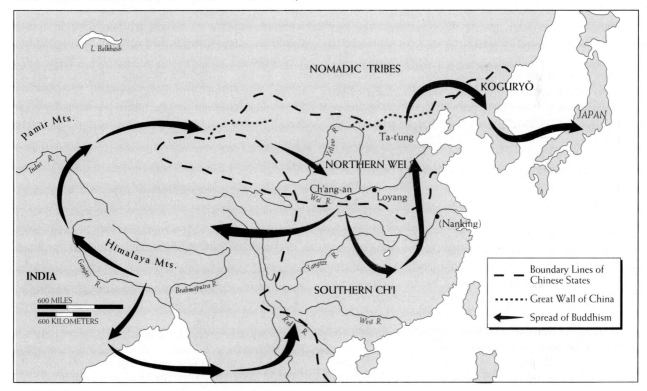

Socially, too, Buddhism adapted to China. Ancestor worship demanded that there be heirs to perform the sacrifices. In the absence of progeny, ancestors might become "hungry ghosts." Hence, the first son would be expected to marry and have children, whereas the second son, if he were so inclined, might become a monk. The practice also arose of holding Buddhist masses for dead ancestors. Still another difference between China and India was the more extensive regulation of Buddhism by the state in China. Just as Buddhism was not to injure the family, so Buddhism was not to reduce the taxes paid on land. As a result, limits were placed on the number of monasteries, nunneries, and monastic lands, and the requirement was made that the state must give its permission before men or women abandoned the world to enter a religious establishment. The regulations, to be sure, were not always enforced.

China's First Empire in World Perspective

Were there world-historical forces that produced at roughly the same time great empires in China, India, and the Mediterranean? Certainly there were similar features in these empires. All three came after revolutions in thought. The Han built on Chou thought (it would be hard to imagine the Han bureaucratic state without Legalism and Confucianism), just as Rome used Greek thought, and the Mauryan empire Buddhist thought. In each case, the conception of universal political authority sustaining the empire derived from earlier philosophies. All three were Iron Age empires, joining their respective technologies with new organizational techniques to create superb military forces.

The differences between the empires are also instructive. Contrast China and Rome. In China the pervasive culture—the only higher culture in the area—was Chinese—even before the first empire arose. This culture had been slowly spreading for centuries and in places outran the polity. Even the culture of the Ch'u peoples south of the Yangtse, although viewed as "semibarbarian" by northern Chinese, was only a variation of the higher culture. Thus cultural unity had paved the way for political unity.

In contrast, the polyglot empire of Rome encompassed quite different peoples, including older civilizations. The genius of Rome, in fact, was to fashion a government and a set of laws that could contain its cultural diversity. Geographically, however, Rome had an easier time of it, for the Mediterranean offered direct access to most parts of the empire and was a thoroughfare for commerce. China, in contrast, was largely landlocked. It was composed of several regional economic units, each of which, located in a segment of a river basin separated from the others by natural barriers, looked inward. It was the genius of Chinese administration, overcoming physical and spatial barriers, to integrate the country politically.

A second difference was that government in Han China was more orderly, more complex, and more competent than that of Rome. For example, civil officials controlled the Chinese military almost until the end, whereas in later Roman times, emperor after emperor was set on the throne by the army or the Praetorian Guard. The Roman empire was not a Chinese-type, single-family dynasty.

A third salient difference was in the military dynamics of the two empires. Roman power was built over centuries. Its history is the story of one state growing in power by steady increments, imposing its will on others, and gradually piecing together an empire. Not until the early centuries A.D. was the whole empire in place. China, in contrast, remained a multistate system right up to 232 B.C. and then, in a sudden surge, was unified by one state in eleven years. The greater dynamism of China during the first empire can be explained, perhaps, by the greater military challenge it faced across its northern border: an immense Hunnish nomadic empire. Because the threat was more serious than that posed to Rome by any European barbarian enemy, the Chinese response was correspondingly massive.

Suggested Readings

D. BODDE, *China's First Unifier* (1938). A study of the Ch'in unification of China, viewed through the Legalist philosopher and statesman Li Ssu.

T. T. CH'U, *Han Social Structure* (1972).

T. T. CH'U, *Law and Society in Traditional China* (1961). Treats the sweep of Chinese history from 202 B.C. to 1911.

A. COTTERELL, *The First Emperor of China* (1981).

R. COULBORN, *Feudalism in History* (1965). One chapter interestingly compares the quasi-feudalism of the Chou with that of the Six Dynasties period.

J. K. Fairbank, E. O. Reischauer, and A. M. Craig, *East Asia: Tradition and Transformation* (1989). A widely read single-volume history covering China, Japan, and other countries in East Asia from antiquity to recent times.

J. Gernet, *A History of Chinese Civilization* (1982). An excellent survey of Chinese history.

C. Y. Hsu, *Ancient China in Transition* (1965). On social mobility during the Eastern Chou era.

C. Y. Hsu, *Han Agriculture* (180). A study of the agrarian economy of China during the Han dynasty.

J. Levi, *The Chinese Emperor* (1987). A novel about the First Ch'in Emperor based on scholarly sources.

M. Loewe, *Everyday Life in Early Imperial China* (1968). A social history of the Han dynasty.

J. Needham, *The Shorter Science and Civilization in China* (1978). An abridgement of the multivolume work on the same subject with the same title—minus *Shorter*—by the same author.

C. Schirokauer, *A Brief History of Chinese and Japa-nese Civilizations* (1978). A standard text, especially good on literature and art.

M. Sullivan, *The Arts of China* (1967). An excellent survey history of Chinese art.

D. Twitchett and M. Loewe, eds., *The Ch'in and Han Empires, 221 B.C.–A.D. 220* (1986). (Vol. 1 of *The Cambridge History of China*.)

Z. S. Wang, *Han Civilization* (1982).

B. Watson, *The Columbia Book of Chinese Poetry* (1986).

B. Watson, *Records of the Grand Historian of China*, Vols. 1 and 2 (1961). Selections from the *Shih-chi* by Ssu-ma Ch'ien.

B. Watson, *Ssu-ma Ch'ien, Grand Historian of China* (1958). A study of China's premier historian.

A. Wright, *Buddhism in Chinese History* (1959).

Y. S. Yu, *Trade and Expansion in Han China* (1967). A study of economic relations between the Chinese and their neighbors.

Ancient Slavery

The institution of slavery is older than civilization, and it was present early in the histories of the ancient civilizations of Egypt, Mesopotamia, Greece, Rome, India, and China. The ancient world, like many parts of the later world, knew many forms of unfree labor—serfs and bondsmen called by various names—as well as outright slaves, so it is useful to attempt a definition. Slaves are property, fully under the domination of their master, and their labor is imposed by coercion. Unlike the relationship between serf and lord in medieval Europe, in which the serf retained some legal rights and the lord was bound by legal restraints and obligations (see Chapter 14), the relationship between master and slave was entirely one-sided. In many places and at many times in antiquity, however, the line between slavery and some forms of serfdom was indistinct, and the slave's position was not always the worse.

MESOPOTAMIA Slavery in the ancient world differed from one society to another and from time to time. In ancient Mesopotamia slaves owned by private individuals were few and were used chiefly as domestic servants, agricultural workers, or craftsmen. Because the average slave holder had no more than two or three slaves, he generally worked alongside them in the field or shop. In early Sumerian times slaves were chiefly captives in war but later came to include people who had defaulted on a debt or been sold as children into slavery by parents too poor to raise them. By the time of Hammurabi (ca. 1792–1750 B.C.), the chief source of slaves had become foreigners bought from slave traders.

In Mesopotamia, slaves were generally people of the same appearance and culture as their masters, they had been enslaved because of misfortunes to which their masters themselves were not immune, and they labored in their masters' homes or alongside them at their work. As a result, in many ways, slavery in Mesopotamia was milder than it might have been. Slaves could and did engage in business and acquire property. With their master's permission, slaves could use their profits to buy their own freedom. Male slaves could marry free women, and the children of such marriages were free. Still, Mesopotamian slavery was not easy. The slave was a piece of property bought, sold, leased, and exchanged, often tattooed or branded for identification and to deter escape. The Code of Hammurabi provided the death penalty for anyone who sheltered or helped

a fugitive slave to escape. Finally, there is little or no evidence that slaves were set free, except when they could purchase their own freedom.

EGYPT In Egypt, too, slavery existed from early times, but because agricultural labor was done by a vast class of serfs, slaves did not become numerous until the spread of Egyptian imperial power in the Middle Kingdom (2052–1786 B.C.). During that period black Africans from Nubia to the south and Asians from Palestine–Syria and beyond to the east who were captured in war were brought back to Egypt as slaves. The great period of Egyptian imperial expansion, the New Kingdom (1575–1087 B.C.), brought far greater numbers of captives into slavery in Egypt. Sometimes an entire people was enslaved, as the biblical tradition portrays the Hebrews about 1400 B.C. They were put to work in the fields alongside the serfs, in the shops as artisans, and in homes as domestic servants. Some were employed as policemen and soldiers. Many, however, labored to erect the great temples, obelisks, and other huge monuments that so impress all who see them. As in Mesopotamia, slaves were often branded for identification and to prevent escape, and freeing slaves was rare.

CHINA Fully developed Chinese slavery resembled the slave systems of the other complex ancient civilizations. The slave population included captives in war; victims of kidnapping and slave trading; and defaulted debtors and poor men who sold themselves, their wives, and their children into bondage. The range of the use of slaves was very wide:

> in farming, food and handicraft industries, commerce, and perhaps in mining; as business managers, bodyguards, fighters, tomb watchers, servants, grooms, singers, dancers, and acrobats; in concubinage, luxury and display, and in reinforcing the master's power. Government bondsmen worked as servants, retainers, clerks, accountants, and petty bureaucrats; in skilled crafts, game-keeping, ranching, and to some extent in heavy gang labor.[1]

---

[1]C. M. Wilbur, *Slavery in China During the Former Han Dynasty, 206* B.C.–A.D. *25* (New York: Kraus, 1943), p. 241.

Running slaves, from a detail of a statue of Ramses II at the entrance to the great temple of Abu Simbel (thirteenth century B.C.). In Egypt, as elsewhere in the ancient world, slaves were often captives taken in war. [UPI/Bettmann]

The evidence suggests that the primary form of slavery in the earliest dynasties was that of criminals to the government, so it is not surprising that the Chinese term for slaves carried the sense of "base" or "ignoble," whereas the rest of the population was called "good." Later, in the Han period (206 B.C.–A.D. 220) and afterward, the Chinese explained slavery as the result of the criminal acts of the slaves or their ancestors. A document from the Han period provided that "the wives and children of criminals shall be confiscated as slaves and tattooed on the face. . . . the genuine slaves of today are the descendants of criminal ancestors. Though a hundred generations pass by, they are still tattooed on the face and serve the government."[2] This sharp distinction between slaves and normal "good" people may help explain the connection that had arisen by the time of the T'ang dynasty (A.D. 618–907) between racial prejudice and slavery. The Chinese regarded foreigners, in general, as lesser beings, so they did not hesitate to enslave Turks, Koreans, Persians, and Indonesians, all of whom they referred to as "black." Their greatest contempt was reserved for the dark-skinned, uncivilized people of the islands off China's southern coast, many of whom were taken into slavery and brought to Canton in the seventh and eighth centuries. Because the Chinese feared pollution from mixture with inferior peoples, they forbade foreign slaves to have sexual intercourse with Chinese women.

INDIA Racial discrimination and prejudice also characterized slavery in India under its Aryan rulers as late as the Vedic period (ca. 1000–500 B.C.). These invaders from the north were contemptuous of the Dasas, the dark-skinned people whom they had subjected. The word *dasa,* in fact, came to mean slave as well as the name of the conquered people. It was only after centuries that the word lost its strictly ethnic meaning, and restrictions on mixture between groups were relaxed. Nevertheless, sexual relations between a slave and a free woman were punished by her mutilation and the death of both parties.

GREECE The Greeks had some form of slavery from the earliest times. The epic poems of Homer show us the women of conquered cities taken home by the victors to serve in their households as concubines. About 700 B.C. the Boeotian poet Hesiod takes the presence of agricultural slaves for granted. In early Greece, however, true chattel slavery appears to have been rare. The most common forms of bondage were different kinds of serfdom in relatively backward areas such as Crete, Thessaly, and Sparta. In Sparta, for instance, the ruling people conquered the natives of the region and reduced them to the status of helots, subjects who belonged to the Spartan state and worked the land for the benefit of their Spartan masters. Another form

[2]Cited in E. G. Pulleyblank, "The Origins and Nature of Chattel Slavery in China," *Journal of the Economic and Social History of the Orient* 1 (1958): 206.

of earlier bondage came about through default in debt. This condition involved a severe loss of freedom but usually stopped short of permanent loss. In Athens, however, about 600 B.C., such bondsmen, called *hektemoroi,* were sold outside their native land as true slaves, until the reforms of Solon put an end to debt-bondage entirely.

Chattel slavery proper began to increase about 500 B.C. and remained an important element in society. The main sources of slaves were war captives; the captives of pirates; and those people, at first enslaved through war, piracy, or other means, sold by slave traders. Like the Chinese, Egyptians, and many other peoples, the Greeks regarded foreigners as inferior, and most slaves working for the Greeks were foreigners. Greeks sometimes enslaved Greeks, but not to serve in their home territories.

The chief occupation of the Greeks, as of most of the world before our century, was agriculture. The great majority of Greek farmers worked small holdings too poor to support even one slave. Some were fortunate to have as many as one or two slaves to work alongside them. The upper classes had larger farms that were let out to free tenant farmers or worked by slaves, generally under an overseer who was himself a slave. Large landowners generally did not have a single great estate but several smaller farms scattered about the *polis.* This arrangement did not encourage the amassing of great hordes of agricultural slaves such as those later to work the cotton and sugar plantations of the New World.

Slaves were used in larger numbers in industry and especially mining. Nicias, a wealthy Athenian of the fifth century B.C., owned one thousand slaves whom he rented to a mining contractor for profit, but this is by far the largest number of which we know. In another instance of large slave holding in Athens, a family of resident aliens employed about 120 slaves in their shield factory. Most manufacturing, however, was on a very small scale, with shops using one, two, or a handful of slaves. Slaves worked as craftsmen in almost every trade, and, as was true for the agricultural slaves on small farms, they worked alongside their masters. A significant proportion of slaves were domestic servants, and many were shepherds. Publicly held slaves served as policemen, prison attendants, clerks, and secretaries.

The number of slaves in ancient Greece and their importance to Greek society are the subjects of controversy. We have no useful figures for the absolute number of slaves or their percentage of the free population in any city except Athens. There the evidence permits estimates for the slave population in the classical period (fifth and fourth centuries B.C.) that range from twenty thousand to one hundred thousand. Accepting the mean between the extremes, sixty thousand, and estimating the free population at its height at about forty thousand households would yield a figure of fewer than two slaves per family. It has been estimated that only a quarter to a third of free Athenians owned any slaves at all, so the distribution was unequal, with most families having no slaves and some having many.

Some historians have noted that in the American South during the period before the Civil War—where slaves made up less than one-third of the total population and three-quarters of free Southerners had no slaves—the proportion of slaves to free citizens was similar to that of ancient Athens. Because slavery was so important to the economy of the South, these historians suggest, it may have been equally important and similarly oppressive in ancient Athens. This argument has several problems.[3] For one thing, it is important to make a distinction between the cotton states of the American South before the Civil War, where a single cash crop, well suited for exploitation by large groups of slaves, dominated the economy and society, and Athens, where the economy was mixed, the crops varied, and the land and its distribution poorly suited to massive slavery.

Another major difference lay in the likelihood of a slave's achieving freedom. The freeing of American slaves was comparatively rare, but in Greece it was common. The most famous example is that of the Athenian slave Pasion, who began as a bank clerk, earned his freedom, became Athens's richest banker, and was awarded Athenian citizenship. Such cases were certainly rare, but the acquisition of freedom by slaves was not.

It is important also to distinguish the American South, where slaves differed from their masters by skin color and masters were increasingly hostile to freeing slaves and afraid of slave rebellions, from the very different society of classical Athens. There slaves walked the streets with such ease as to offend class-conscious Athenians. Plato, for example, complained about the Athenian democracy that "men and women who have been sold are no less free than their purchasers" (*Republic,* 563B).

Even more remarkable, the Athenians were on occasion willing to contemplate the liberation of all their slaves. In 406 B.C., their city facing defeat in the Peloponnesian War, they freed all slaves of military age and granted citizenship to those who rowed the ships that won the battle of Arginusae. Twice more at crucial moments, similar proposals were made, although without success. No such suggestion,

[3] M. I. Finley, "Was Greek Civilization Based on Slave Labor?" *Historia* 8 (1959): 151.

of course, would have been conceivable in the slave societies of the New World. (For more on American slavery and the Atlantic slave trade, see Chapters 19, 23, and 29.)

ROME Like most ancient peoples, the Romans had slaves from very early in their history, but among the shepherds and family-farmers of early Rome they were relatively few. Slavery became a fundamental element in the Roman economy and society only during the second century B.C., after the Romans had conquered most of the lands bordering the Mediterranean. In the time between the beginning of Rome's first war against Carthage (264 B.C.) and the conquest of Spain (133 B.C.), the Romans enslaved some two hundred fifty thousand prisoners of war, greatly increasing the availability of slave labor and reducing its price. Many were used as domestic servants to feed the growing appetite for luxury among the Roman upper classes, whereas at the other end of the spectrum, many were put to work in the mines of Spain and Sardinia. Some worked as artisans in small factories and shops or as public clerks. Slaves were permitted to marry, and they appear to have produced sizable families that increased the slave population. As in Greece, domestic slaves and those used in crafts and commerce were permitted to earn money; to keep it; and, in some cases, to use it to purchase their own freedom. Manumission (the freeing of slaves), in fact, was very common among the Romans, both upon the death of the master and during his lifetime. Rome's fire brigade at one point consisted of seven thousand former slaves; another example is one man who freed ten thousand of his slaves. After a time the Roman people included a considerable proportion of freedmen who had been slaves themselves or whose ancestors had been bondsmen. It was not uncommon to see the son or grandson of a slave become wealthy as a freedman and the slave himself or his son become a Roman citizen. Because Roman slaves came from all over the Mediterranean world, one result of the growth of slavery and the high rate of manumission was the transformation of the ethnic composition of the Roman population.

But the unique development in the Roman world was the emergence of an agricultural system that employed and depended on a vast number of slaves. By the time of Jesus there were between two and three million slaves in Italy,

about 35 to 40 percent of the total population, most of them part of great slave gangs that worked the vast plantations the Romans called *latifundia*. Turning from the grain that was the chief crop of the free Roman farmer, these large estates concentrated on such cash-producing products as wool, wine, and olive oil. The life of Rome's agricultural slaves appears to have been much harder than that of other Roman slaves and of slaves in other ancient societies, with the possible exception of slaves working in mines. The owners of the latifundia sought maximum profits and treated their slaves simply as means to that end. The slaves often worked in chains, oppressed by brutal foremen, and lived in underground prisons. The famous Roman statesman Cato was probably no different from his peers in feeding his slaves as cheaply as he could and treating them like machines, to be discarded when their usefulness ended.

Such harsh treatment led to a number of serious slave rebellions of a kind we do not hear of in other ancient societies. A rebellion in Sicily in 134 B.C. kept the island in turmoil for more than two years, and the rebellion of the gladiators led by Spartacus in 73 B.C. produced an army of seventy thousand slaves that repeatedly defeated the Roman legions and overran all of southern Italy before it was crushed. The Romans executed the survivors with exemplary brutality, lining the road from Capua to Rome with six thousand crucified slaves.

Slavery retained its economic and social importance in the first century of the imperial period, but its centrality began to decline in the second. The institution was never abolished nor did it disappear so long as the Roman Empire lasted, but over time it became less important. The reasons for this decline are rather obscure. A rise in the cost of slaves and a consequent reduction in their economic value seem to have been factors. More important, it appears, was a general economic decline that permitted increasing pressure on the free lower classes. More and more they were employed as *coloni*—tenant farmers—tied by imperial law to the land they worked, ostensibly free but bonded and obligated. Over centuries most agricultural slave labor was replaced by these increasingly serf-like *coloni*. Pockets of slave labor remained as late as the time of Charlemagne, but the system of ancient slavery had essentially been replaced by the time the Roman Empire fell in the West.

Consolidation and Interaction of World Civilizations

etween 500 and 1500, the major civilizations of the world shaped themselves politically and culturally in new and lasting ways.

China survived barbarian conquests and three centuries of political fragmentation to reestablish in 589 a united empire, the likes of which would never be known in Europe. In achieving this empire, the Chinese were aided by a universal philosophical system, Confucianism, which supported secular political power, and by a common written language and the technology to print it, which ensured cultural unity across China's vast regions. Even its dense population, close to fifty million in the year 750, encouraged unity and provided a base for communication, trade, and a stable empire. Chinese government evolved in this period from an imperial bureaucracy based on aristocratic families toward one based on a civil-service examination elite. In the transition, the emperor, at the head of the bureaucracy, became more powerful, more absolute. Mongol rule during the thirteenth century accelerated the development of absolutism that had begun in the previous Sung dynasty. Chinese culture, which had managed to absorb the foreign influence of Buddhism, became increasingly conservative and inward looking.

In Japan, regional tribal aristocracies gave way during the fifth and sixth centuries to the archaic Yamato kings. In Yamato society, Shinto, the indigenous religion, was part and parcel of daily life, family status, and political authority. From the seventh century, these early kings adopted the Chinese model of centralized government. During the Nara and Heian periods—roughly the eighth to twelfth centuries—court life was reshaped by Chinese culture and the Buddhist tradition that was also imported from China. Yet the Japanese preserved a separate identity, partly because their language was so different from Chinese and partly because Buddhism tolerated the indigenous Shinto religion in a way, for example, that Christianity in Europe did not tolerate Celtic and Germanic cults. During the early ninth century, samurai ("those who serve") warriors developed in local areas. Like knights in feudal Europe, they were responsible for maintaining the local order. During the Kamakura and Ashikaga periods—roughly the thirteenth to fifteenth centuries—confederations of samurai swept aside the Chinese-type court and established a distinctively Japanese form of government: military rule by feudal warriors under the shōgun, their military overlord. These same centuries were Japan's age of faith, centering on Pure Land and Zen Buddhism.

In Africa, this period witnessed the rise of regional empires. Outside of Islamic North Africa and Egypt, the most prominent were those in the western and central Sudan. Most notable was ancient Ghana, whose heyday was the late tenth and most of the eleventh centuries. However, the Kushite empire of Aksum, in the Ethiopian highlands, remained a major power even through the sixth century A.D.; it survived right through this age as the proud, culturally and religiously distinctive Christian state of Abyssinia, or Ethiopia. The remarkable regional culture of Great Zimbabwe, a southeastern African kingdom, held sway in the Zambezi–Limpopo area between about 1000 and 1500. In central and southern Africa, this age saw the slow but momentous diffusion of Bantu-speaking peoples from northwestern central Africa over most of the African subcontinent. In western and northern Africa, the centuries-old trans-Saharan trade routes saw increased commercial traffic, as well as new interchanges in people and ideas.

The gradual penetration of Islamic religion and culture across the Sahara into the Sudanic regions was one prominent feature of the period after 1000. In the same era, east Africa was undergoing even more pronounced Islamization in the development of Swahili civilization. It was also entering ever more prominently into the international trade network of the southern seas, which reached across the Indian Ocean all the way to Indonesia and China. By 1500, much of Africa was firmly caught up in the events and interrelations of the larger global community.

In Iran, a state religion of Zoroastrian orthodoxy and official use of the Middle Persian dialect assisted political centralization during the reign of the Sasanid kings (224–651). The Sasanids further strengthened their rule by international trade and government monopolies on industries like silk and glass. However, their centuries-long conflict with their chief rival, the Byzantine Empire, and the growth of regional nobles' strength so weakened the Sasanid rule that they proved easy prey to the Arab armies of Islam that finally destroyed them. The Persian language and culture developed and nourished under the Sasanids persisted, however, and ultimately greatly enriched the literature, art and architecture, and religious sensibilities of Islamic civilization.

In India, the incursions of Hun peoples in the first half of the sixth century ended the great classical era of Gupta culture and empire. The next millennium saw the caste system solidify, establishing hierarchical divisions within Indian society based on rules regulating the groups with whom one could eat, marry, and work. During these centuries, Hindu tradition gained the general shape it has today. Politically, the end of the Gupta empire led to the ascendancy of regional kingdoms. The arrival of Muslim Turks and Afghans after 1000 in northern India brought an Islamic political and cultural presence on a scale previously unknown. By 1500, Islam was an important part of the Indian scene, putting its architectural as well as its religious and political marks on Indian society.

In the seventh century, the new faith and culture of Islam emerged in Arabia. Muhammad, the proclaimed last in a line of monotheistic prophets, preached a fervent opposition to idolatry, immorality, and injustice in his homeland of western Arabia. Bound by a new supratribal allegiance, his Arab successors carried his crusade abroad, sweeping over most of the Byzantine realms, all of the Persian Empire, and into Spain, Central Asia, and the Indus Valley within a century. Muslim traders and mystical ("Sufi") brotherhoods spread Muslim faith and culture beyond the political boundaries of Islam. The influx of Turkish and Mongol peoples in later centuries expanded the political and military presence of Islam still further. Although split into factions, the Islamic community generally opted for unity over division and never experienced the regional and sectarian fragmentation that Christendom suffered. Only the Mongol invasions of the thirteenth and fourteenth centuries disrupted the political order in the Islamic heartlands.

Western Europe survived barbarian and Muslim invasions to create a Christian empire under Carolingian and Merovingian rulers, most notably during the reign of Charlemagne (768–814). Toward the end of this period, Western Europe became through the Crusades an aggressor itself in Byzantium and the Near East. From the start, there was competition between Western rulers and the Christian churches. In the West, the Christian Church never became the docile friend of kings and emperors that some Asian and Near Eastern religions were, and orthodox Christianity inclined also to be in the Byzantine Empire. In the West, emperor and pope struggled with each other repeatedly, occasionally to the death. During the twelfth and thirteenth centuries, "national" monarchies emerged in northern Europe, ending any possibility of a unified European empire. Europe henceforth developed as a collection of nation-states that remained politically and culturally diverse and highly competitive.

	EUROPE	NEAR EAST/INDIA
500 A.D.	*511* Death of Clovis, Frankish ruler of Gaul *529* Benedict of Nursia founds Benedictine Order *590–604* Pontificate of Gregory I, "the Great" *768–814* Charles the Great (Charlemagne)	*527–565* Justinian's reign *531–579* Reign of Chosroes Anosharvian in Iran *ca. 570–632* Muhammad *622* The Hijra *616–657* Reign of Harsha; neo-Gupta revival in India *651* Death of last Sasanid ruler *ca. 710* First Muslim invasion of India *661–750* Umayyad dynasty *680* Death of Al-Husayn at Karbala; second civil war begins *750–1258* Abbasid dynasty *786–809* Caliph Harun Al-Rashid reigns
800	*ca. 800–1000* Invasions of England and the Carolingian Empire (Vikings, Magyars, and Muslims) *843* Treaty of Verdun divides Carolingian Empire *910* Cluny Monastery founded *1019–1054* Yaroslav the Wise reigns; peak of Kievan Russia *1054* Schism between Latin and Greek churches *1066* Norman Conquest of England *1073–1085* Investiture controversy *1096–1270* The Crusades	*800–1200* Period of "feudal" over-lordship in India *900–1100* Golden Age of Muslim learning *945–1055* Buyid rule in Baghdad *994–1186* Ghaznavid rule in north-western India, Afghanistan, and Iran *1055–1194* Seljuk rule in Baghdad *1071* Seljuk Turks capture Jerusalem *1081–1118* Byzantine emperor Alexius Comnenus reigns *ca. 1000–1300* Turko-Afghan raids into India
1100	*1154–1158* Frederick Barbarosa invades Italy *1182–1226* St. Francis of Assisi *1198–1216* Pontificate of Innocent III *ca. 1100–1300* Growth of trade and towns *1215* Magna Carta granted *ca. 1225–1274* St. Thomas Aquinas *1265–1321* Dante Alighieri	*1174–1193* Saladin reigns *1192* Muslim conquerors end Buddhism in India *1206–1526* Delhi Sultanate in India; Indian culture divided into Hindu and Muslim *ca. 1220* Mongol invasions of Iran, Iraq, Syria, India *1258* Hulagu Khan, Mongol leader, conquers Baghdad *1260–1335* Il-Khans rule Iran
1500	*1337* Hundred Years' War begins *ca. 1340–1400* Geoffrey Chaucer *1347–1349* The Black Death *1375–1527* The Italian Renaissance *1485* Battle of Bosworth Field; accession of Henry Tudor to the throne of England *1492* Columbus's first voyage to the New World	*1366–1405* Timur (Tamerlame) reigns *1405–1494* Timurids rule in Transoxiana and Iran *1453* Byzantine Empire falls to the Ottoman Turks, with capture of Constantinople

EAST ASIA	AFRICA	THE AMERICAS
589–618 Sui dynasty reunifies China *607* Japan begins embassies to China *618–907* T'ang dynasty in China *701–762* Li Po, T'ang poet *710–784* Nara court, Japan's first permanent capital *712 Records of Ancient Matters,* in Japan *713–756* Emperor Hsuan Tsung reigns in China *755* An Lu-shan rebellion in China *794–1185* Heian (Kyoto) court in Japan	*ca. 500* States of Takrur and Ghana founded *ca. 500–700* Political and commercial ascendancy of Aksum (Ethiopia) *ca. 600–1500* Extensive slave trade from sub-Saharan Africa to Mediterranean *ca. 700–800* Ghanians begin to supply gold to Mediterranean *ca. 700–900* States of Gao and Kanem *ca. 800* Appearance of the Kanuri people around Lake Chad	*ca. 300–900* Classic period Maya in the Yucatan and Guatemala
856–1086 Fujiwara dominate Heian court *960–1279* Sung dynasty in China *ca. 1000 Pillow Book* by Sei Shōnagon and *Tale of Genji* by Murasaki Shikibu *1037–1101* Su Tung-p'o, Sung poet	*ca. 800–900* Decline of Aksum *ca. 900–1100* Kingdom of Ghana; capital city, Kumbi Saleh *ca. 1000–1100* Islam penetrates sub-Saharan Africa *1000–1500* "Great Zimbabwe" center of Bantu Kingdom in southeastern Africa	*ca. 600–1000* Middle (Huari/Tiahuanaco) Horizon in Andean South America
1130–1200 Chu Hsi, Sung philosopher *1165–1227* Genghis Khan begins Mongol Empire *1185–1333* Kamakura shogunate in Japan *1274, 1281* Mongol invasions of Japan *1279–1368* Mongol (Yuan) dynasty in China	*ca. 1100–1897* Kingdom of Benin in tropical rain forest region *1194–1221* Kanem Empire achieves greatest expansion *1203* Kingdom of Ghana falls to Sosso people *ca. 1230–1450* Kingdom of Mali *1230–1255* King Sundiata, first ruler of Mali Empire; Walata and Timbuktu become centers of trade and culture	*ca. 800–1400* Chimu Empire on north coast of Peru
1336–1467 Ashikaga shogunate in Kyoto *1368–1644* Ming dynasty in China *1405–1433* Voyages of Cheng Ho to India and Africa *1467–1568* Warring States era in Japan *1472–1529* Wang Yang-ming, Ming philosopher	*1307–1332* Mansa Musa, greatest king of Mali *1490s* Europeans establish trading posts on western African coast *mid-1400s* Decline of Mali Empire; creation of Songhai Empire *1468* Sonni Ali captures Timbuktu *1476–1507* Reign of King Mai Ali of Bornu in central Sudan *1493–1528* Songhai ruler, Askia Muhammed reigns; consolidates Songhai Empire	*1325* Founding of Aztec capital of Tenochtitlán *1428–1519* Period of Aztec expansion *1519* Cortes conquers Aztec Empire *ca. 1350–1533* Inca Empire in Peru *1533* Pizarro executes Inca ruler Atahualpa

A painting of irrigation methods on a farm south of the Yangtze. A farmer and his wife use their legs and feet to work the square-pallet chain pump. At left a boy drives a large water buffalo to turn a larger water-pumping device. The boy in the background fishes. [Photograph by Wan-go Weng/Collection of C. C. Wang]

Imperial China (589–1368)

10

If Chinese dynasties from the late sixth to the mid-fourteenth centuries were given numbers like those of ancient Egypt, the Sui and T'ang dynasties would be called the Second Empire; the Sung, the Third; and the Yuan, the Fourth. Numbers, however, would not convey the distinct personalities of these dynasties. The T'ang (618–907) is everyone's favorite dynasty: open, cosmopolitan, expansionist, exuberant, and creative. It was the example of T'ang China that decisively influenced the formation of states and high cultures in Japan, Korea, and Vietnam. Poetry during the T'ang attained a peak that has not been equaled since. The Sung (960–1279) rivaled the T'ang in the arts; it was China's great age of painting and was the most significant period for philosophy since the Chou, when Chinese philosophy began. Although not militarily strong, the Sung dynasty also witnessed an important commercial revolution. The Yuan (1279–1368) was a short dynasty of rule by Mongols during which China became the most important unit in the largest empire the world has yet seen.

Reestablishment of Empire: Sui (589–618) and T'ang (618–907) Dynasties

In the period corresponding to the European early Middle Ages, the most notable feature of Chinese history was the reunification of China, the recreation of a centralized bureaucratic empire consciously modeled on the earlier Han dynasty (206 B.C.–A.D. 220). The process of reunification, as usual, began in the north. The first steps were taken by the Northern Wei (386–534), the most enduring of the northern Sino-

Turkic states. It moved its court south to Loyang, made Chinese the language of the court, and adopted Chinese dress and surnames. It also used the leverage of its nomadic cavalry to impose a new land tax, mobilizing resources for state use. The Northern Wei was followed by several short-lived kingdoms. Because the emperors, the officials, and the military commanders of these kingdoms came from the same stratum of aristocratic families, the social distance between them was small, and the throne was often usurped.

A standing Buddha on a lotus pedestal from the early Sui dynasty (589–618). The work is carved from sandstone and has traces of pigment. [Asian Art Museum of San Francisco, The Avery Brundage Collection, B605360]

The Sui Dynasty

The general of mixed Chinese-Turkic ancestry, Sui Wen-ti, who came to power in 581 and began the Sui dynasty (589–618) was no exception to this rule. But he displayed great talent, unified the north, restored the tax base, reestablished a centralized bureaucratic government, and went on to conquer southern China and unify the country. During his reign, all went well. Huge palaces were built in his Wei valley capital. The Great Wall was rebuilt. The Grand Canal was constructed, linking the Yellow and Yangtze rivers. This canal enabled the northern conquerors to tap the wealth of central China. Peace was maintained with the Turkic tribes along China's northern borders. Eastern Turkic khans (chiefs) were sent Chinese princesses as brides.

The early years of the Second Sui emperor were also constructive, but then, Chinese attempts to meddle in steppe politics led to hostilities and wars. The hardships and loss of Chinese lives in campaigns against Korea and along China's northern border produced rising discontent. Natural disasters occurred. The court became bankrupt and demoralized. Rebellions broke out, and once again, there was a free-for-all among the armies of aristocratic military commanders. The winner, and the founder of the T'ang dynasty, was a relative of the Sui empress and a Sino-barbarian aristocrat of the same social background as those who had ruled before him.

Chinese historians often compare the short Sui dynasty with that of the Ch'in (256–206 B.C.). Each brought all of China under a single government after centuries of disunity. Each did too much, fell, and was replaced by a long dynasty. The T'ang built on the foundations that had been laid by the Sui, just as the Han had built on those of the Ch'in.

The T'ang Dynasty

The first T'ang emperor took over the Sui capital, renamed it Ch'ang-an, and made it his own. Within a decade or so, the T'ang dynasty had extended its authority over all of China; frugality was practiced in government; tax revenues were adequate to government needs; and Chinese armies had begun the campaigns that would push Chinese borders out further

MAP 10-1 THE T'ANG EMPIRE AT ITS PEAK DURING THE EIGHTH CENTURY *The T'ang expansion into Central Asia re-opened trade routes to the Middle East and Europe. Students from P'o-Hai, Silla (Korea), and Japan studied in the T'ang capital of Ch'ang-an, and then returned, carrying with them T'ang books and technology.*

than ever (see Map 10-1). Confucian scholars were employed at the court, Buddhist temples and monasteries flourished, and peace and order prevailed in the land. The years from 624 to 755 were the good years of the dynasty.

GOVERNMENT. The first T'ang emperor had been a provincial governor under the Sui before he became a rebel general. Many of those whom he appointed to posts in the new T'ang administration were former Sui officials who had served with him. In building the new administration, he and his successors had to reconcile two conflicting sets of interests. On the one hand, the emperor wanted a bureaucratic government in which authority was centralized in his own person. On the other hand, he had to make concessions to the aristocrats—the dominant elements in Chinese society since the late Han—who staffed his government and continued to dominate early T'ang society.

The degree to which political authority was centralized was apparent in the formal organization of the bureaucracy, at right.

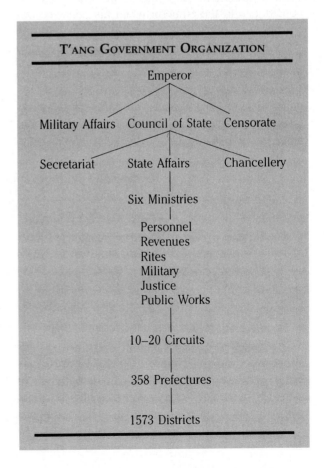

T'ANG GOVERNMENT ORGANIZATION

Emperor

Military Affairs   Council of State   Censorate

Secretariat   State Affairs   Chancellery

Six Ministries

Personnel
Revenues
Rites
Military
Justice
Public Works

10–20 Circuits

358 Prefectures

1573 Districts

A Petty Clerk Thinks About His Career

I'm not so poor at reports and decisions—
Why can't I get ahead in the government?
The rating officials are determined to make life hard.
All they do is try to expose my faults.
Everything, I guess, is a matter of Fate;
Still, I'll try the exam again this year.
A blind boy aiming at the eye of a sparrow.
Might just accidentally manage a hit.

In vain I slaved to understand the Three Histories;
Uselessly I pored over the Five Classics.
Until I'm old I'll go on checking census figures;
As in the past, a petty clerk scribbling in tax ledgers.
When I ask the Book of Changes it says there's trouble ahead;
All my life is ruled by evil stars.
If only I could be like the tree at the river's edge
Every year turning green again!

Cold Mountains: 100 Poems by Han-shan, trans. by B. Watson (New York, Grove Press, 1962), pp. 37, 48.

At the highest level were three organs: Military Affairs, the Censorate, and the Council of State. Military Affairs supervised the T'ang armies, with the emperor, in effect, the commander-in-chief. The Censorate had watchdog functions: It reported instances of misgovernment directly to the emperor and could also remonstrate with the emperor when his behavior was improper. The Council of State was the most important body. It met daily with the emperor and was made up of the heads of the Secretariat, which drafted policies; the Chancellery, which reviewed them; and State Affairs, which carried them out. Beneath State Affairs were the Six Ministries, which continued as the core of the central government down to the twentieth century; beneath them were the several levels of local administration.

Concessions to the interests of the aristocratic families were embodied in the tax system. All land was declared to be the property of the emperor and was then redistributed to able-bodied cultivators, who paid taxes in labor and grain. Because all able-bodied adult males received an equal allotment of land (women and children got less), the land tax system was called the "equal field system." But the system was not egalitarian. Aristocrats enjoyed special exemptions and grants of "rank" and "office" lands that, in effect, confirmed their estate holdings.

Aristocrats were also favored in the recruiting of officials. Most officials either were recommended for posts or received posts because their fathers had been high officials. They were drawn almost exclusively from the aristocracy, at first from the northwestern aristocratic families that had supported the dynasty from the start, and then, in time, from the aristocracies of other areas. Only a tiny percentage were recruited by examinations. Those who passed the examinations had the highest prestige and were more likely to have brilliant careers. But as only well-to-do families could afford the years of study needed to master the Confucian classics and pass the rigorous examinations, even the examination bureaucrats were usually the able among the noble. Entrance to government schools at Ch'ang-an and the secondary capital at Loyang was restricted to the sons of nobles and officials.

THE EMPRESS WU. Women of the inner court also continued to play a role in government. For example, Wu Chao (626–ca. 706), a young concubine of the strong second emperor, had so entranced his weak heir by her charms that when he succeeded to the throne, she was recalled from the nunnery to which all the former wives of deceased emperors were routinely consigned and was installed at the court. She poisoned or otherwise removed her rivals and became his empress. She also murdered or exiled the statesmen who opposed her growing influence. When the emperor suffered a stroke in 660, she completely dominated the court. After his death in 683, she ruled for seven years as regent and then, deposing her son, became emperor herself, the only woman in Chinese history to hold the title. She moved the court to Loyang in her native area and proclaimed a new dynasty. A fervent Buddhist with an interest in magic, she saw herself as the incarnation of the Buddha Maitreya and built temples throughout the land. She patronized the White Horse Monastery, appointing one of her favorites as its abbot. Her sexual appetites were said to have been prodigious. She ruled China until 705, when at the age of eighty she lost her hold and was deposed.

After Empress Wu, no woman would ever become emperor again; yet, remarkably enough, her machinations do not appear to have seriously weakened the court. So highly centralized was power during these early years of the dynasty that the ill effects of her intrigues could be absorbed without provinces breaking away or military commanders becoming autonomous. In fact, her struggle for power may have strengthened the central government, for, to overcome the old northwestern Chinese aristocrats, she turned not to members of her family but to the products of the examination system and to a group known as the Scholars of the North Gate. This policy broadened the base of government by bringing in aristocrats from other regions of China. The dynamism of a young dynasty may also explain why her rule coincided with the maximal geographical expansion of T'ang military power.

THE CH'ANG-AN OF EMPEROR HSUAN-TSUNG. Only a few years after Empress Wu was deposed—years filled with tawdry intrigues—Hsuan-tsung came to the throne. In reaction to Empress Wu, he appointed special government commissions headed by distinguished aristocrats to superintend the reform of government finances. Examination bureaucrats lost ground during his reign. The Grand Canal was repaired and extended. A new census extended the tax rolls. Wealth and prosperity returned to the court. Hsuan-tsung's reign (713–756) was also the most brilliant culturally. Years later, while in exile, Li Po wrote a poem in which memories of youthful exhilaration merged with the glory of the capital of Hsuan-tsung:

Long ago, among the flowers and willows,
We sat drinking together at Ch'ang-an.
The Five Barons and Seven Grandees were of our company,
But when some wild stroke was afoot
It was we who led it, yet boisterous through we were
In the arts and graces of life we could hold our own
With any dandy in the town—
In the days when there was youth in your cheeks
And I was still not old.
We galloped to the brothels, cracking our gilded whips,
We sent in our writings to the palace of the Unicorn,
Girls sang to us and danced hour by hour on tortoise-shell mats.
We thought, you and I, that it would be always like this.
How should we know the grasses would stir and dust rise on the wind?

Suddenly foreign horsemen were at the Hsien-ku Pass
Just when the blossom at the palace of Ch'in was opening on the sunny boughs. . . [1]

Ch'ang-an was an imperial city, an administrative city that lived on taxes. It was designed to exhibit the power of the emperor and the majesty of his court. At the far north of the city, the palace faced south. The placement was traditional: Confucius, speaking of Shun, said he had only "to hold himself in a respectful posture and to face due south." In front of the palace was a complex of government offices, from which an imposing five-hundred-foot-wide avenue led to the main southern gate. The city was laid out on a north–south, east–west grid, which one T'ang poet compared to a chessboard. Each block of the city was administered as a ward with interior streets and gates that were locked at night. Enclosed by great walls, the area of the city was thirty square miles. Its population was 1,960,186—half within the walls, the other half in suburbs—the largest city in the world. (The population of China in the year 750 was about fifty million—less than 5 percent of its present-day population.) Ch'ang-an was also a trade center from which caravans set out across Central Asia. Merchants from India, Iran, Syria, and Arabia hawked the wares of the Near East and all of Asia in its two government-controlled markets.

THE T'ANG EMPIRE. A Chinese dynasty is like an accordion, first expanding into the territories of its barbarian neighbors and then contracting back to its original, densely populated core area. The principal threats to the T'ang state were from Tibetans in the west, Turks in the northwest and north, and Khitan Mongols in Manchuria.

Toward these peoples, the T'ang employed a four-tier policy. When nothing else would work, the T'ang sent armies. But armies were expensive, and using them against nomads was like sweeping back an ocean tide with a broom. A victory might dissolve a confederation, but a decade or two later, it would reappear under a new tribal leader. For example, in 630, T'ang armies defeated the eastern Turks; in 648, they took the Tarim Basin, opening trade routes to western Asia for almost a century; and in 657, they defeated the western Turks and extended Chinese influence across the Pamir Mountains to petty states near Samarkand. By 698, however, the Turks were

[1] Arthur Waley, *The Poetry and Career of Li Po* (New York: Macmillan, 1950), pp. 87–88.

A bearded "barbarian" groom tends the charger of the second T'ang emperor (r. 626–649). This stone relief was found on the emperor's tomb. Note the stirrup, a Chinese invention of the fourth century A.D. *[University of Pennsylvania Museum]*

back invading northeastern China, and between 711 and 736, they were in control of all of the steppe from the Oxus River to China's northern frontier.

Chinese efforts against Tibet were much the same. From 670, Tibet expanded and threatened China. In 679, it was defeated. In 714, it rose again; wars were fought from 727 to 729; and a settlement was reached in 730. But wars broke out anew. In 752, Tibet entered an alliance with the state of Nan Chao in Yunnan. In 763, Tibetan forces captured and looted Ch'ang-an. They were driven out, but the point is that even during the good years of the T'ang, no final victory was possible.

The human costs of sending armies far afield was detailed in a poem by Li Po:

Last year we were fighting at the source of the Sang-kan;
This year we are fighting on the Onion River road.
We have washed our swords in the surf of Parthian seas;
We have pastured our horses among the snows of the T'ien Shan,
The King's armies have grown grey and old
Fighting ten thousand leagues away from home.
The Huns have no trade but battle and carnage;
They have no fields or ploughlands,
But only wastes where white bones lie among yellow sands.

Where the House of Ch'in built the great wall that was to
  keep away the Tartars.
There, in its turn, the House of Han lit beacons of war.
The beacons are always alight, fighting and marching
  never stop.
Men die in the field, slashing sword to sword;
The horses of the conquered neigh piteously to Heaven.
Crows and hawks peck for human guts,
Carry them in their beaks and hang them on the
  branches of withered trees.
Captains and soldiers are smeared on the bushes and
  grass;
The General schemed in vain.
Know therefore that the sword is a cursed thing
Which the wise man uses only if he must.[2]

The second tier of Chinese defenses was to use nomads against other nomads. The critical development for the T'ang was the rise to power of the Uighur Turks. From 744 to 840, the Uighurs controlled Central Asia and were staunch allies of the T'ang. Without their support, the T'ang dynasty would not have survived as long as it did.

A third tier was the defense along China's borders, including the Great Wall. At mid-dynasty, whole frontier provinces in the north and the northwest were put under military commanders who, in time, came to control the provinces' civil governments as well. The bulk of the T'ang military was in such frontier commands. At times, their autonomy and potential as rebels were as much a threat to the T'ang court as to the enemy.

Diplomacy is always cheaper than war. The fourth line of defense was to bring the potential enemy into the empire as a tributary. The T'ang defined the position of "tributary" with great elasticity. It included principalities truly dependent on China; Central Asian states conquered by China; enemy states such as Tibet or the Thai state of Nan Chao in Yunnan when they were not actually at war with China; the Korean state Silla, which had unified the peninsula with T'ang aid but had then fought T'ang armies to a standstill when they attempted to impose Chinese hegemony; and wholly independent states such as Japan. All sent embassies bearing gifts to the T'ang court, which housed and fed them and sent costly gifts in return.

For some countries, these embassies had a special significance. As the only "developed nation" in eastern Asia, China was a model for countries still in the throes of forming a state. An embassy gained access to the entire range of T'ang culture and technology: its philosophy and writing; governmental and land systems; Buddhism; and the arts, architecture, and medicine. In 640 there were eight thousand Koreans, mostly students, in Ch'ang-an. Never again would China exert such an influence, for never again would its neighbors be at that formative stage of development.

REBELLION AND DECLINE.   From the mid-eighth century, signs of decline began to appear. China's frontiers started to contract. Tribes in Manchuria became unruly. Tibetans threatened China's western border. In 751, an overextended T'ang army led by a Korean general was defeated by Arabs near Samarkand in western Asia, shutting down China's caravan trade with the West for more than five centuries. Furthermore, in 755, a Sogdian general, An Lu-shan, who commanded three Chinese provinces on the northeastern frontier, led his one hundred sixty thousand troops in a rebellion that swept across northern China, capturing Loyang and then Ch'ang-an. The emperor fled to Szechwan.

The event contained an element of romance. Ten years earlier, the emperor Hsuan-tsung had taken a young woman, Yang Kuei Fei, from the harem of his son (he gave his son another in exchange). So infatuated was he that he neglected not only the other "three thousand beauties of his inner chambers" but the business of government as well. For a while his neglect did not matter because he had an able chief minister, but when the minister died, he appointed his concubine's second cousin to the post, initiating a train of events that resulted in rebellion. En route to Szechwan, his soldiers, blaming Yang Kuei Fei for their plight, strangled her. The event was later immortalized in a poem that described her "snow-white skin," "flowery face," and "moth eyebrows," as well as the "eternal sorrow" of the emperor, who, in fact, was seventy-two at the time.

After a decade of wars and much devastation, a new emperor restored the dynasty with the help of the Uighur Turks, who looted Ch'ang-an as part of their reward. The recovery and the century of relative peace and prosperity that followed illustrate the resilience of T'ang institutions. China was smaller, but military governors maintained the diminished frontiers. Provincial governors were more autonomous, but taxes were still sent to the capital. Occasional rebellions were suppressed by imperial armies, sometimes led by eunuchs. Most of the emperors were weak, but three strong emperors appeared and

---

[2]Waley, pp. 34–35.

Pottery figures of court ladies playing polo, seventh century, T'ang dynasty. For over a millennium after the T'ang, participation in athletic contests was considered unfeminine. [W. R. Nelson Trust]

reforms were carried out. Edwin O. Reischauer, after translating the diary of a Japanese monk who studied in China during the early ninth century, commented that the "picture of government in operation" that emerges "is amazing for the ninth century, even in China":

The remarkable degree of centralized control still existing, the meticulous attention to written instructions from higher authorities, and the tremendous amount of paper work involved in even the smallest matters of administration are all the more striking just because this was a period of dynastic decline.[3]

Of the reforms of this era, none was more important than that of the land system. The official census,

[3]E. O. Reischauer, *Ennin's Travels in T'ang China* (New York: Ronald Press, 1955), p. 7.

on which land allotments and taxes were based, showed a drop in population from fifty-three million before the An Lu-shan rebellion to seventeen million afterward. Unable to put people back on the registers, the government abandoned the equal field system and replaced it with a tax collected twice a year. The new system, begun in 780, lasted until the sixteenth century. Under it, a fixed quota of taxes was levied on each province. After the An Lu-shan rebellion, government revenues from salt and iron surpassed those from land.

During the second half of the ninth century, the government weakened further. Most provinces were autonomous, often under military commanders, and resisted central control. Wars were fought with the state of Nan Chao in the southwest. Bandits appeared. Droughts led to peasant uprisings. By the 880s, warlords had carved all of China into indepen-

This pottery figurine from a mid-T'ang dynasty tomb depicts a Bactrian camel from west-central Asia. [Asian Art Museum of San Francisco]

dent kingdoms, and in 907, the T'ang dynasty fell. But within half a century, a new dynasty arose. The fall of the T'ang did not lead to centuries of division of the kind that had followed the Han. Something had changed within China.

T'ANG CULTURE.   The creativity of the T'ang period arose from the juxtaposition and interaction of cosmopolitan, medieval Buddhist and secular elements. The rise of each of these cultural spheres was rooted in the wealth and the social order of the recreated empire.

T'ang culture was cosmopolitan not just because of its broad contacts with other cultures and peoples but also because of its openness to them. Buddhist pilgrims to India and a flow of Indian art and philosophies to China were a part of it. The voluptuousness of Indian painting and sculpture, for example, helped shape the T'ang representation of the *bodhisattva*. Commercial contacts were widespread. Foreign goods were vended in Ch'ang-an marketplaces. Communities of central and western Asians were established in the capital, and Arab and Iranian quarters grew up in the seaports of southeastern China. Merchants brought their religions with them. Nestorian Christianity, Zoroastrianism, Manichaeism, Judaism, and Islam entered China at this time. Most would be swept away in the persecutions of the ninth century, but Islam and a few small pockets of Judaism survived until the twentieth century.

Central Asian music and musical instruments entered along the trade routes and became so popular as almost to displace the native tradition. T'ang ladies adopted foreign hairstyles. Foreign dramas and acrobatic performances by western Asians could be seen in the streets of the capital. Even among the pottery figurines customarily placed in tombs, there were representations of western Asian traders and central Asian grooms, along with those of horses, camels, and court ladies that today are so avidly sought by collectors and museums around the world. In T'ang poetry, too, what was foreign was not shunned but judged on its own merits or even presented as exotically attractive. Of a gallant of Ch'ang-an, Li Po wrote:

A young man of Five Barrows suburb east of the Golden Market,

Silver saddle and white horse cross through wind of
  spring.
When fallen flowers are trampled all under, where is it
  he will roam?
With a laugh he enters the tavern of a lovely Turkish
  wench.[4]

Later in the dynasty, another poet, Li Ho, wrote of
service on the frontier:

A Tartar horn tugs at the north wind,
Thistle Gate shines whiter than the stream.
The sky swallows the road to Kokonor.
On the Great Wall, a thousand miles of moonlight.[5]

The T'ang dynasty, although slightly less an age of
faith than the preceding Six Dynasties, was the golden
age of Buddhism in China nonetheless. Patronized by
emperors and aristocrats, the Buddhist establishment
acquired vast landholdings and great wealth. Temples and monasteries were constructed throughout
China. To gain even an inkling of the beauty and sophistication of the temple architecture, the wooden
sculpture, or the paintings on the temple walls, one
must see Hōryūji or the ancient temples of Nara in
Japan, for little of note has survived in China. The
single exception is the Caves of the Thousand Buddhas at Tunhuang in China's far northwest, which
were sealed during the eleventh century for protection from Tibetan raiders and were not rediscovered
until the start of the twentieth century. They were
found to contain stone sculptures, Buddhist frescoes,
and thousands of manuscripts in Chinese and Central
Asian languages.

Only during the T'ang did China have a "church"
establishment that was at all comparable to that of
medieval Europe, and even then it was subservient to
the far stronger T'ang state. Buddhist wealth and
learning brought with them secular functions. T'ang
temples served as schools, inns, or even bathhouses.
They lent money. Priests performed funerals and dispensed medicines. Occasionally, the state moved to
recapture the revenues monopolized by temples. The
severest persecution, which marked a turn in the fortunes of Buddhism in China, occurred from 841 to
845, when an ardent Taoist emperor confiscated millions of acres of tax-exempt lands, put back on the tax
registers 260,000 monks and nuns, and destroyed
4,600 monasteries and 40,000 shrines.

[4]S. Owen, *The Great Age of Chinese Poetry: The High T'ang* (New
Haven, CT: Yale University Press, 1980), p. 130.
[5]A. C. Graham, *Poems of the Late T'ang* (Baltimore: Penguin,
1965), p. 9.

Stone sculpture of bodhisattva *reflecting the full-
bodied, almost voluptuous T'ang ideal of Beauty.*
[Bettmann Archive]

During the early T'ang, the principal Buddhist sect
was the T'ien-t'ai, but after the mid-ninth century suppression, other sects came to the fore:

1. One devotional sect focused on Maitreya, a Buddha of the future, who will appear and create a paradise on earth. Maitreya (*Mi Lo* in Chinese and *Miroku*
in Japanese) was a cosmic messiah, not a human
figure. The messianic teachings of the sect often furnished the ideology for popular uprisings and rebellions like the White Lotus, which claimed that it
was renewing the world in anticipation of Maitreya's
coming.

2. Another devotional or faith sect worshiped the
Amitabha (*A Mi T'o* in Chinese, *Amida* in Japanese)
Buddha, the Lord of the Western Paradise or Pure
Land. This sect taught that in the early centuries after

the death of the historical Buddha, his teachings had been transmitted properly and people could obtain enlightenment by their own efforts, but that at present, the Buddha's teachings had become so distorted that only by reliance on Amitabha could humans obtain salvation. All who called on Amitabha with a pure heart and perfect faith would be saved. Developing a congregational form of worship, this sect became the largest in China and deeply influenced Chinese popular religion.

3. A third sect, and the most influential among the Chinese elites, was known in China, where it began, as *Ch'an* and is better known in the West by its Japanese name, *Zen*. Zen had no cosmic Buddhas. It taught that the historical Buddha was only a man and exhorted each person to attain enlightenment by his or her own efforts. Although its monks were often the most learned in China, Zen was anti-intellectual in its emphasis on direct intuition into one's own Buddha-nature. Enlightenment was to be obtained by a regimen of physical labor and meditation. To jolt the monk into enlightenment—after he had been readied by long hours of meditation—some Zen sects used little problems not answerable by normal ratiocination: "What was your face before you were conceived?" "If all things return to the One, what does the One return to?" "From the top of a hundred-foot pole, how do you step forward?" The psychological state of the adept attempting to deal with these problems is compared to that of "a rat pursued into a blocked pipe" or "a mosquito biting an iron ball." The discipline of meditation, combined with a Zen view of nature, profoundly influenced the arts in China and subsequently in Korea and Japan as well.

A third characteristic of T'ang culture was the reappearance within it of secular scholarship and letters. The reestablishment of centralized bureaucratic government stimulated the tradition of learning that had been partially interrupted after the fall of the Han dynasty in the third century A.D. There emerged a scholarly-bureaucratic complex. Most men of letters, whether historians, essayists, artists, or poets, were also officials, and most high-ranking officials painted or wrote poems. An anthology of T'ang poetry compiled during the Ming period contained 48,900 poems by almost 2,300 authors. This secular stream of T'ang culture was not ideologically anti-Buddhist. Officials were often privately sympathetic to Buddhism. But as men involved in the affairs of government, officials became increasingly this-worldly in their values.

Court historians of the T'ang revived the Han prac-tice of writing an official history of the previous dynasty. For the first time, scholars wrote comprehensive institutional histories and regional and local gazetteers. They compiled dictionaries and wrote commentaries on the Confucian classics. Other scholars wrote ghost stories or tales of adventure, using the literary language. (Buddhist sermons, in contrast, were often written in the vernacular.) More paintings were Buddhist than secular, but Chinese landscape painting had its origins during the T'ang. Nowhere, however, was the growth of a secular culture more evident than it was in poetry, the greatest achievement of T'ang letters.

Whether Li Po (701–762) can be called wholly sec-

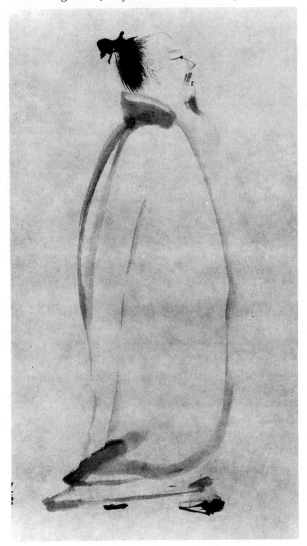

The T'ang poet Li Po, as imagined by the great Sung artist Liang K'ai. [Tokyo National Museum]

Poems by Li Po

THE RIVER MERCHANT'S WIFE: A LETTER

While my hair was still cut straight across my fore-
head
I played about the front gate, pulling flowers.
You came by on bamboo stilts, playing horse,
You walked about my seat, playing with blue plums.
And we went on living in the village of Chokan:
Two small people, without dislike or suspicion.

At fourteen I married My Lord you.
I never laughed, being bashful.
Lowering my head, I looked at the wall.
Called to, a thousand times, I never looked back.

At fifteen I stopped scowling,
I desired my dust to be mingled with yours
Forever and forever and forever.
Why should I climb the look out?

At sixteen you departed,
You went into far Ku-to-yen, by the river of swirling
eddies,
And you have been gone five months.
The monkeys make sorrowful noise overhead.

You dragged your feet when you went out.
By the gate now, the moss is grown, the different
mosses,
Too deep to clear them away!
The leaves fall early this autumn, in wind.
The paired butterflies are already yellow with August
Over the grass in the West garden;
They hurt me. I grow older.
If you are coming down through the narrows of the
river Kiang,
Please let me know beforehand,
And I will come out to meet you,
As far as Cho-fu-Sa.

Ezra Pound, *Personae* (New York: New Directions, 1926), pp. 130–131.

---

ular is questionable. He might better be called Taoist. But he clearly was not Buddhist. Born in Szechwan, he was exceptional among T'ang poets in never having sat for the civil service examinations, although he briefly held an official post at Ch'ang-an, given in recognition of his poetry. Large and muscular, he was a swordsman and a carouser. Of the twenty thousand poems he is said to have composed, eighteen hundred have survived, and a fair number have titles like "Bring on the Wine" or "Drinking Alone in the Moonlight." According to legend, he drowned while drunkenly attempting to embrace the reflection of the moon in a lake. His poetry is clear, powerful, passionate, and always sensitive to beauty. It also contains a sense of fantasy, as when he climbed a mountain and saw a star-goddess, "stepping in emptiness, pacing pure ether, her rainbow robes trailed broad sashes." Li Po, nearer to heaven than to earth, looked down below where

Far and wide Tartar troops were speeding,
And flowing blood mired the wild grasses
Where wolves and jackals all wore officials' caps.[6]

According to Li Po, life is brief and the universe is large, but this view did not lead him to renounce the world. His Taoism was not of the quietistic strain close to Buddhism. Rather, he exulted, identifying with the primal flux of *yin* and *yang*:

I'll wrap this Mighty Mudball of a world all up in a bag
And be wild and free like Chaos itself![7]

Tu Fu (712–770), an equally famous T'ang poet, was from a literary family. He failed the metropolitan examination at the age of twenty-three and spent years in wandering and poverty. At thirty-nine, he received an official appointment after presenting his poetry to the court. Four years later, he was appointed to a military post. He fell into rebel hands during the An Lu-shan rebellion, escaped, and was reappointed to a civil post. But he was then dismissed and suffered further hardships. His poetry is less lyrical and more allusive than Li Po's. It also reflects more compassion for human suffering: for the mother whose sons have been conscripted and sent to war; for brothers scattered by war; for his own family, to whom he returned after having been given up for

[6] Owen, p. 134.

[7] Owen, p. 125.

MAP 10-2 THE NORTHERN SUNG AND LIAO EMPIRES (top) AND
THE SOUTHERN SUNG AND CHIN EMPIRES (bottom) *During
the Northern Sung, the Mongol Liao dynasty ruled
only the extreme northern edge of China. During the
Southern Sung, in contrast, the Manchurian Chin dynasty ruled half of China.*

dead. Like Li Po, he felt that humans are short-lived
and that nature endures. Visiting the ruins of the palace of the second T'ang emperor, he saw "Grey rats
scuttling over ancient tiles" and "in its shadowed
chambers ghost fires green." "Its lovely ladies are the
brown soil" and only "tomb horses of stone remain."
But his response to this sad scene was to

Sing wildly, let the tears cover your open hands.
Then go ever onward and on the road of your travels,
Meet none who prolong their fated years.[8]

His response was unlike that of Li Po. It was close to
Stoicism but equally un-Buddhist.

Transition to Late Imperial China: The Sung Dynasty (960–1279)

Most traditional Chinese history was written in terms
of the dynastic cycle, and for good reason: The pattern of rise and fall, of expansion and contraction,
within each dynasty cannot be denied. Certainly, the
Sung can be viewed from this perspective. It reunified
China in 960, establishing its capital at Kaifeng on the
Yellow River (see Map 10-2). Mobilizing its resources
effectively, it ruled for 170 years. This period is called
the Northern Sung. Then it weakened. In 1127, it lost
the north but continued to rule the south for another
150 years from a new capital at Hangchow in east-
central China. The Southern Sung fell before the Mongol onslaught in 1279.

But there is more to Chinese history than the inner
logic of the dynastic cycle. Longer term changes that
cut across dynastic lines were ultimately more important. One such set of changes began during the late
T'ang period and continued on into the Sung period,
affecting its economy, society, state, and culture.
Taken together, these changes help to explain why
China after the T'ang did not relapse into centuries of
disunity as it had after the Han, and why China would
never again experience more than brief intervals of

disunity. In this section, we will skip over emperors
and empresses, eunuchs and generals, and focus instead on more fundamental transformations.

Agricultural Revolution of the Sung: From Serfs to Free Farmers

Local society in China during the Sui and the T'ang
periods had been dominated by landed aristocrats.

[8]Owen, pp. 223–224.

The tillers of their lands were little more than serfs. Labor service was the heaviest tax, and whether performed on the office or rank lands of aristocrats or on other government lands, it created conditions of social subordination.

The aristocracy weakened, however, over the course of the T'ang and after its fall. Estates became smaller as they were divided among male children at each change of generation. Drawn to the capital, the aristocracy became less a landed, and more a metropolitan, elite. After the fall of the T'ang, the aristocratic estates were often seized by warlords. As the aristocracy declined, the claims of those who worked the soil grew stronger, aided by changes in the land and tax systems. With the collapse of the equal field system (described earlier), farmers gained the right to buy and sell land. The ownership of land as private property gave the cultivators greater independence. They could now move about as they pleased. Taxes paid in grain gave way during the Sung to taxes in money. The commutation of the labor tax to a money tax gave the farmers more control over their own time. Conscription, the cruelest and heaviest labor tax of all, disappeared as the conscript armies of the early and middle T'ang gave way to professional armies.

Changes in technology also benefited the cultivator. New strains of an early-ripening rice permitted double cropping. In the Yangtze region, extensive water-control projects were carried out, and more fertilizers were used. New commercial crops were developed. Tea, which had been introduced during the Six Dynasties as a medicine and had been drunk by monks during the T'ang, became widely cultivated, and cotton also became a common crop. Because taxes paid in money tended to become fixed, much of the increased productivity accrued to the cultivator. Of course, not all benefited equally; there were landlords and landless tenants as well as independent small farmers.

The disappearance of the aristocrats also increased the authority of the district magistrate, who no longer had to contend with the aristocrats' interference in local affairs. The Sung magistrate became the sole representative of imperial authority in local society. But there were too many villages in his district for him to be involved regularly in their internal governance. As long as taxes were paid and order was maintained, the affairs of the village were left in the hands of the village elites. So the Sung farmer enjoyed not only a rising income and more freedom, but also a substantial measure of self-government.

One other development that began during the Sung—and became vastly more important later on—was the appearance of a scholar-gentry class. The typical gentry family contained at least one member who had passed the provincial civil-service examination and lived in the district seats or market towns. Socially and culturally, these gentry were closer to magistrates than to villagers. But they usually owned land in the villages and thus shared some interests with the local landholders. Although much less powerful than the former aristocrats, they took a hand in local affairs and at times functioned as a buffer between the village and the magistrate's office.

Commercial Revolution of the Sung

Stimulated by changes in the countryside, and contributing to them as well, were demographic shifts, innovative technologies, the growth of cities, the spread of money, and rising trade. These developments varied by region, but overall the Sung economy reached a new level of prosperity.

EMERGENCE OF THE YANGTZE BASIN. Until late in the T'ang, northern China had been the most populous and productive region. But from the late ninth century, the center of gravity of China's population, agricultural production, and culture shifted to the lower and eastern Yangtze region. Between 800 and 1100, the population of the region tripled as China's total population increased to about one hundred million. Its rice paddies yielded more per acre than the wheat or millet fields of the north, making rice the tax base of the empire. Its wealth led to the establishment of so many schools that regional quotas for the examination system were set by the government to prevent the Yangtze region from dominating all of China. The Northern Sung capital itself was kept in the north for strategic reasons, but it was situated at Kaifeng, further east than Loyang, at the point where the Grand Canal, which carried tax rice from the south, joined the Yellow River.

NEW TECHNOLOGY. During the Northern Sung, there developed in north China a coal and iron-smelting industry that provided China with better tools and weapons. Using coke and bellows to heat furnaces to the temperatures required for carbonized steel, it was the most advanced in the world.

Printing began in China with the use of carved seals. The earliest woodblock texts, mostly on Buddhist subjects, appeared in the seventh century. By the tenth century, a complete edition of the classics had been published, and by the mid-Sung, books printed with movable type were fairly common.

Other advances during the Sung were the abacus, the use of gunpowder in grenades and projectiles, and improvements in textiles and porcelains.

RISE OF A MONEY ECONOMY. Exchange during the T'ang had been based on silk. Coins had been issued, but their circulation was limited. During the Northern Sung, large amounts of copper cash were coined, but the demand rose more rapidly than the supply. Coins were made with holes in the center, and one thousand on a string constituted the usual unit for large transactions. Beginning in the Southern Sung, silver was minted to complement copper cash, ten times as much silver in the late twelfth century as in the early eleventh century. Letters of credit were used by merchants, and various kinds of paper money also were issued. The penetration of money into the village economy was such that by 1065, tax receipts paid in money had risen to thirty-eight million strings of cash—in comparison with a mere two million in mid-T'ang.

TRADE. The demand for money was spurred by the growth of trade. One may distinguish between trade within economic regions, trade between regions, and foreign trade. During the T'ang, most cities had been administrative, supported by taxes from the countryside. Official salaries and government expenditures created a demand for services and commercial products, making the cities into islands of commerce in a noncommercial hinterland. In most of China's seven or eight economic regions, this pattern continued during the Sung, but in the capital, and especially in the economically advanced regions along the Yangtze, cities became the hubs of regional commercial networks, with district seats or market towns serving as secondary centers for the local markets beneath them.

As this transition occurred, cities with more than one hundred thousand households almost quadrupled in number. The Northern Sung capital at Kaifeng is recorded as having had 260,000 households—probably more than one million inhabitants—and the Southern Sung capital at Hangchow had 391,000 households. Compare these capitals to those of backward Europe: London during the Northern Sung had a population of about 18,000; Rome during the South-

ern Sung had 35,000; and Paris even a century later had fewer than 60,000.

Furthermore, these Sung capitals, unlike Ch'ang-an with its walled wards that closed at night, were open within and spread beyond their outer walls. As in present-day Chinese cities, their main avenues were lined with shops. Merchant guilds replaced government officials as the managers of marketplaces. Growing wealth also led to a taste for luxury and an increasingly secular life-style. Restaurants, theaters, wine shops, and brothels abounded. Entertainment quarters with fortune tellers, jugglers, chess masters, acrobats, and puppeteers sprang up. Such activity had not been absent from Ch'ang-an, but the numbers increased, and now they catered to traders and rich merchants as well as to officials.

Trade between regions during the Sung was limited mainly to luxury goods like silk, lacquerware, medicinal herbs, and porcelains. Only where transport was cheap—along rivers, canals, or the coast—was interregional trade in bulk commodities economical, and even then, it was usually carried on only to make up for specific shortages.

Foreign trade also reached new heights during the Sung. In the north, Chinese traders bought horses from Tibetan, Turkic, and Mongol border states, and sold silks and tea. Along the coast, Chinese merchants took over the port trade that during the T'ang had been in the hands of Korean, Arab, and Irani merchants. The new hegemony of Chinese merchants was based on improved ships using both sail and oars and equipped with watertight compartments and better rudders. Chinese captains, navigating with the aid of the compass, came to dominate the sea routes from Japan in the north to Sumatra in the south. The content of the overseas trade reflected China's advanced economy: It imported raw materials and exported finished goods. Porcelains were sent to Southeast Asia and then were carried by Arab ships to medieval trading centers on the Persian Gulf and down the coast of East Africa as far south as Zanzibar.

Government: From Aristocracy to Autocracy

The millennium of late imperial China after the T'ang is often spoken of as the age of autocracy or as China's age of absolute monarchy. Earlier emperors, as we have noted, were often personally powerful, but beginning with the Sung, changes occurred that made it easier for emperors to be autocrats.

One change was that Sung emperors had direct personal control over more offices than their T'ang predecessors. For example, the Board of Academicians, an advisory office, presented the emperor with policy options separate from those presented by the Secretariat-Chancellery. The emperor could thus use the one against the other and prevent bureaucrats in the Secretariat-Chancellery from dominating the government.

A second change was that the central government was better funded than it had been previously. Revenues in 1100 were three times the peak revenues of the T'ang, partly as a result of the growth of population and agricultural wealth, and partly as a result of the establishment of government monopolies on salt, wine, and tea and various duties, fees, and taxes levied on domestic and foreign trade. During the Northern Sung, these commercial revenues rivaled the land tax; during the Southern Sung, they surpassed it. Confucian officials would continue to stress the primacy of land, but throughout late imperial China, commerce became a vital source of revenues.

A third change that strengthened the emperors was the disappearance of the aristocracy. During the T'ang, the emperor had come from the same Sino-Turkic aristocracy of northwestern China as most of his principal ministers, and he was, essentially, the organ of a state that ruled on behalf of this aristocracy. Aristocrats monopolized the high posts of government. They married among themselves and with the imperial family. They called the emperor the Son of Heaven, but they knew he was one of them. During the Sung, in contrast, government officials were commoners, mostly products of the examination system. They were separated from the emperor by an enormous social gulf and saw him as a person apart.

The Sung examination system was larger than that of the T'ang, if smaller than in later dynasties. Whereas only 10 percent of officials had been recruited by examination during the T'ang, the Sung figure rose to over 50 percent and included the most important officials. The first examination was given at regional centers. The applicant took the examination in a walled cubicle under close supervision. To ensure impartiality, his answers were recopied by clerks and his name was replaced by a number before his examination was sent to the officials who would grade it. Of those who sat for the examination, only a tiny percentage passed. The second hurdle was the metropolitan examination at the national capital, where the precautions were equally elaborate. Only one in five, or about two hundred a year, passed. The average successful applicant was in his mid-thirties. The final hurdle was the palace examination, which rejected a few and assigned a ranking to the others.

To pass the examinations, the candidate had to memorize the Confucian classics, interpret selected passages, write in the literary style, compose poems on themes given by the examiners, and propose solutions to contemporary problems in terms of Confucian philosophy. The quality of the officials produced by the Sung system was impressive. A parallel might be drawn with nineteenth-century Britain, where students in the classics at Oxford and Cambridge went on to become generalist bureaucrats. The Chinese examination system that flourished during the Sung continued, with some interruptions, into the twentieth century. The continuity of Chinese government during this millennium rested on the examination elite, with its common culture and values.

The social base for this examination meritocracy was triangular, consisting of land, education, and office. Without wealth, the years of study needed to pass the examinations could not be afforded. Such an education was far beyond the means of a poor peasant or city dweller. Without education, official position was out of reach. And without office, family wealth could not be preserved. The Chinese pattern of inheritance, as noted earlier, led to the division of property at each change of generation. Some families were successful in passing the civil service examinations for several generations running. More often, the sons of well-to-do officials did not study as hard as those with bare means. The adage "shirt sleeves to shirt sleeves in three generations" is not inappropriate to the Sung and later dynasties. As China had an extended-family or clan system, a wealthy official often provided education for the bright children of poor relations.

How the merchants related to this system is less clear. They had wealth but were despised by scholar-officials as grubby profit seekers and were barred from taking the examinations. Some merchants avoided the system altogether—a thorough education in the Confucian classics did little to fit a merchant's son for a career in commerce. Others bought land for status and security, and their sons or grandsons became eligible. Similarly, a small peasant might build up his holdings, become a landlord, and educate a son or grandson. The system was steeply hierarchical, but it was not closed nor did it produce a new, self-perpetuating aristocracy.

Sung Culture

As society and government changed during the T'ang-Sung transition, so too did culture. Sung culture retained some of the energy of the T'ang while becoming more intensely and perhaps more narrowly Chinese. The preconditions for the rich Sung culture were a rising economy, an increase in the number of schools and higher literacy, and the spread of printing. Sung culture was less aristocratic, less cosmopolitan, and more closely associated with the officials and the scholar-gentry, who were both its practitioners and its patrons. It also was less Buddhist than the T'ang had been. Only the Zen (Ch'an) sect kept its vitality, and many Confucians were outspokenly anti-Buddhist and anti-Taoist. In sum, the secular culture of officials that had been a sidestream in the T'ang broadened and became the mainstream during the Sung.

Chinese consider the Sung dynasty as the peak of their traditional culture. It was, for example, China's greatest age of pottery and porcelains. High-firing techniques were developed, and kilns were established in every area. There was a rich variety of beau-

The Sung dynasty philosopher Chu Hsi (1130–1200), whose Neo-Confucian ideas remained central down to the twentieth century. [National Palace Museum, Taiwan, R.O.C.]

An elegant Sung dynasty wine pot with green celadon glaze. [Asian Art Museum of San Francisco, The Avery Brundage Collection, B66P12]

tiful glazes. The shapes were restrained and harmonious. Sung pottery, like nothing produced in the world before it, made ceramics a major art form in East Asia. It was also an age of great historians. Ssu-ma Kuang (1019–1086) wrote *A Comprehensive Mirror for Aid in Government*, which treated not a single dynasty but all Chinese history. His work was more sophisticated than previous histories in that it included a discussion of documentary sources and an explanation of why he chose to rely on one source rather than another. The greatest achievements of the Sung, however, were in philosophy, poetry, and painting.

PHILOSOPHY. The Sung was second only to the Chou as a creative age in philosophy. A series of original thinkers culminated in the towering figure of Chu Hsi (1130–1200). Chu Hsi studied Taoism and Buddhism in his youth, along with Confucianism. A brilliant student, he passed the metropolitan examination at the age of eighteen. During his thirties, he focused his attention on Confucianism, deepening and making more systematic its social and political ethics by joining to it certain Buddhist and native metaphysical elements. As a consequence, the new Confucianism became a viable alternative to Buddhism for Chinese intellectuals. Chu Hsi became famous as a teacher at the White Deer Grotto Academy, and his writings were widely distributed. Before the end of the Sung, his Confucianism had become the standard interpretation used in the civil service examinations, and it remained so until the twentieth century.

If we search for comparable figures in other traditions, we might pick Saint Thomas Aquinas (1224–1274) of medieval Europe or the Islamic theologian al-Ghazali (1058–1111), each of whom produced a new synthesis or worldview that lasted for centuries. Aquinas joined Aristotle and Latin theology just as Chu Hsi joined Confucian philosophy and metaphysical notions from other sources. Because Chu Hsi used terms such as the *great ultimate* and because he emphasized a Zen-like meditation called "quiet sitting," some contemporary critics said his Neo-Confucian philosophy was a Buddhist wolf in the clothing of a Confucian sheep. This was unfair. Whereas Aquinas would make philosophy serve religion, Chu Hsi made religion or metaphysics serve philosophy. In his hands, the great ultimate (also known as principle or *li*) lost its otherworldly character and became a constituent of all things in the universe. Perhaps the Chu Hsi philosophy may be characterized as innerworldly.

Later critics often argued that Chu Hsi's teachings encouraged metaphysical speculation at the expense of practical ethics. Chu Hsi's followers replied that, on the contrary, his teachings gave practical ethics a systematic underpinning and positively contributed to individual moral responsibility. What was discovered within by Neo-Confucian quiet sitting was just those positive ethical truths enunciated by Confucius over a thousand years earlier. The new metaphysics did not change the Confucian social philosophy.

Chu Hsi himself advocated the selection of scholar-officials through schools, rather than by examinations. It is ironic that his teachings became a new orthodoxy that was maintained by the channelizing effect of the civil-service examinations. Historians argue, probably correctly, that Chu Hsi's teachings were one source of stability in late imperial China. Like the examination system, the imperial institution, the scholar-gentry class, and the land system, his interpretation of Confucianism contributed to continuity and impeded change. Some historians go further and say that the emergence of the Chu Hsi orthodoxy stifled intellectual creativity during later dynasties, which probably is an overstatement. There were always contending schools.

POETRY. Sung poets were in awe of those of the T'ang, yet Sung poets were also among China's best. A Japanese authority on Chinese literature wrote

T'ang poetry could be likened to wine, and Sung poetry to tea. Wine has great power to stimulate, but one cannot drink it constantly. Tea is less stimulating, bringing to the drinker a quieter pleasure, but one which can be enjoyed more continuously.[9]

The most famous poet of the Northern Sung was Su Tung-p'o (1037–1101), a man who participated in the full range of the culture of his age: He was a painter and calligrapher, particularly knowledgeable about inks; he practiced Zen and wrote commentaries on the Confucian classics; he superintended engineering projects; and he was a connoisseur of cooking and wine. His life was shaped by politics. He was a conservative, believing in a limited role for government and social control through morality. (The other faction in the Sung bureaucracy was the reformers, who stressed law and an expanded governmental role.)

Passing the metropolitan examination, Su rose through a succession of posts to become the governor of a province—a position of immense power. While considering death sentences, which could not be carried over into the new year, he wrote

New Year's Eve—you'd think I could go home early
But official business keeps me.
I hold the brush and face them with tears:
Pitiful convicts in chains,
Little men who tried to fill their bellies,
Fell into the law's net, don't understand disgrace.
And I? In love with a meager stipend
I hold on to my job and miss the chance to retire.
Do not ask who is foolish or wise;
All of us alike scheme for a meal.
The ancients would have freed them a while at New
    Year's—
Would I dare do likewise? I am silent with shame.[10]

Eight years later, when the reformers came to power, Su himself was arrested and spent one hundred days in prison, awaiting execution on a charge of slandering the emperor. Instead, he was released and sent into exile. He wrote, "Out the gate, I do a dance, wind blows in my face; our galloping horses race along as magpies cheer."[11] Arriving at his place of exile, he reflected

[9] Kojiro Yoshikawa, *An Introduction to Sung Poetry,* trans. by Burton Watson (Cambridge: Harvard University Press, Harvard-Yenching Institute Monograph Series, 1967), p. 37.

[10] Yoshikawa, p. 119.

[11] Yoshikawa, p. 117.

Su Tung-p'o Imagined on a Wet Day, Wearing a Rain Hat and Clogs

After Su's death, a disciple wrote:

When with tall hat and firm baton he stood in
council,
The crowds were awed at the dignity of the statesman in him.
But when in cloth cap he strolled with cane and
sandals,
He greeted little children with gentle smiles.

Kojiro Yoshikawa, *An Introduction to Sung Poetry,* trans. by Burton Watson (Cambridge, MA: Harvard
University Press, Harvard-Yenching Institute Monograph Series, 1967), p. 65, oppos., p. 122.

Between heaven and earth I live,
One ant on a giant grindstone,
Trying in my petty way to walk to the right
While the turning of the mill wheel takes me endlessly
   left.
Though I go the way of benevolence and duty,
I can't escape from hunger and cold.[12]

[12]Yoshikawa, p. 105.

But exile was soon turned to art. He farmed a plot
of land at the "eastern slope" from which he took his
literary name, Tung-p'o. Of his work there, he wrote

A good farmer hates to wear out the land;
I'm lucky this plot was ten years fallow.
It's too soon to count on mulberries;
My best bet is a crop of wheat.
I planted seed and within the month
Dirt on the rows was showing green.

An old farmer warned me,
Don't let seedlings shoot up too fast!
If you want plenty of dumpling flour
Turn a cow or sheep in here to graze.
Good advice—I bowed my thanks;
I won't forget you when my belly's full.[13]

After 1086, the conservatives regained control of the government, and Su resumed his official career. In 1094, another shift occurred and Su was again sent into exile on the distant southern island of Hainan. After still another shift, Su was on his way back to the capital when he died in 1101.

PAINTING. In the West, penmanship and painting are quite separate, one merely a skill and the other esteemed as an art. In China, calligraphy and painting were equally appreciated and were seen as related. A scholar spent his life with brush in hand. The same qualities of line, balance, and strength needed for calligraphy carried over to painting. Chinese calligraphy is immensely pleasing even to the untutored Western eye, and it is not difficult to distinguish between the elegant strokes of Hui-neng, the last emperor of the Northern Sung, and the powerful brushwork of the Zen monk Chang Chi-chih.

Sung painting was varied—of birds or flowers; of fish or insects; of horses, monkeys, or water buffalo; of scholars, emperors, Buddhas, or Taoist immortals. But its crowning achievement was landscapes. Sung landscapes are quite different from those of the West. Each stroke of the brush on silk or paper was final. Mistakes could not be covered up. Each element of a painting was presented in its most pleasing aspect; the painting was not constrained by single-point perspective. Paintings had no single source of illumination with light and shadow but an overall diffusion of light. Space was an integral part of the painting. A typical painting might have craggy rocks or twisted pine trees in the foreground, then mist or clouds or rain to create distance, and in the background the outlines of mountains or cliffs fading into space. If the painting contained human figures at all, they were small in a natural universe that was very large. Chinese painting thus reflected the same worldview as Chinese philosophy or poetry. The goal of the painter was to grasp the inner reality of the scene and not to be bound up in surface details.

In paintings by monks or masters of the Zen school, the presentation of an intuitive vision of an inner reality became even more pronounced. Paintings of Bodhidharma, the legendary founder of the

[13]Yoshikawa, pp. 119–120.

Is the enlightened man depicted in this painting meditating or dozing? Zen paintings often have a touch of humorous ambiguity. Note the broad calligraphic brushwork in this Southern Sung or Yuan dynasty painting done in the style of the Zen monk Shih K'o. [Tokyo National Museum]

Zen sect, are often dominated by a single powerful downstroke of the brush, defining the edge of his robe. Paintings of patriarchs tearing up sutras or sweeping dust with a broom from the mirror of the mind are almost as calligraphic as paintings of bamboo. A Yuan dynasty painting in the style of Shih K'o shows the figure of a monk or sage who is dozing or meditating. A Zen "broken ink" landscape might contain rocks, water, mountains, and clouds, each represented by a few explosive strokes of the brush.

China in the Mongol World Empire: The Yuan Dynasty (1279–1368)

The Mongols created the greatest empire in the history of the world. It extended from the Caspian Sea to the Pacific Ocean; from Russia, Siberia, and Korea in the north to Persia and Burma in the south. Invasion fleets were even sent to Java and Japan, although without success. Mongol rule in China is one chapter of this larger story.

Rise of the Mongol Empire

The Mongols, a nomadic people, lived to the north of China on grasslands where they raised horses and herded sheep. They lived in felt tents called yurts—they sometimes called themselves "the people of the felt-tents." Women performed much of the work and were freer and more easygoing than women in China. Families belonged to clans, and related clans to tribes. Tribes would gather during the annual migration from the summer plains to winter pasturage. Chiefs were elected, most often from noble lineages, for their courage, military prowess, judgment, and leadership. Like Manchu or Turkic, the Mongol tongue was Altaic.

The Mongols believed in nature deities and in the sky god above all others. Sky blue was their sacred color. They communicated with their gods through religious specialists called *shamans.* They traded and warred with settled peoples on the borders of their vast domain.

The founder of the Mongol Empire, Temujin, was born in 1167, the son of a tribal chief. While he was still a child, his father was poisoned. He fled and after wandering for some years, returned to the tribe, avenged his father, and in time became chief himself. Through his wife's tribe, he became part of an alliance with the Ch'in empire that ruled north China. By the time he was forty, he had united all Mongol tribes and had been elected their great khan, or ruler. It is by the title *Genghis* (also spelled *Jenghiz* or *Chinggis*) *Khan* that he is known to history. Genghis possessed

The world conqueror, Genghis Kahn (1167–1227). [National Palace Museum, Taiwan, R.O.C.]

an extraordinary charisma, and his sons and grandsons also became wise and talented leaders. Why the Mongol tribes, almost untouched by the higher civilizations of the world, should have produced such leaders at this point in history is difficult to explain.

A second conundrum is how the Mongols, who numbered only about a million and a half, created the army that conquered vastly denser populations. Part of the answer is institutional. Genghis organized his armies into "myriads" of ten thousand troops, with decimal subdivisions of one thousand, one hundred, and ten. Elaborate signals were devised so that, in battle, even large units could be manipulated like the fingers of a hand. Mongol tactics were superb: Units would retreat, turn, flank, and destroy their enemies. The historical record makes amply clear that Genghis's nomadic cavalry had a paralytic effect on all they encountered. Peerless horsemen, the Mongols fought with a compound bow, short enough to be used from the saddle yet more powerful than the English longbow.

They were astonishingly mobile. Each man carried his own supplies. Trailing remounts, they covered vast distances quickly. In 1241, for example, a Mongol army had reached Hungary, Poland, and the shore of the Adriatic and was poised for a further advance into Western Europe. But when word arrived of the death of the great khan, the army turned and galloped back to Mongolia to help choose his successor.

When this army encountered walled cities, it learned the use of siege weapons from the enemies it had conquered. Chinese engineers were used in campaigns in Persia. The Mongols also used terror as a weapon. Inhabitants of cities that refused to surrender in the Near East and China were put to the sword. Large areas in north China and Szechwan were devastated and depopulated in the process of conquest. Descriptions of the Mongols by those whom they conquered dwell on their physical toughness and pitiless cruelty.

But the Mongols had strengths that went beyond the strictly military. Genghis opened his armies to recruits from the Uighur Turks, the Manchus, and other nomadic peoples. As long as they complied with the military discipline demanded of his forces, they could participate in his triumphs. In 1206, Genghis promulgated laws designed to prevent the normal wrangling and warring between tribes that would undermine his empire. Genghis also obtained thousands of pledges of personal loyalty from his followers, and he appointed these "vassals" to command his armies and staff his government. This policy gave to his forces an

MAP 10-3 THE MONGOL EMPIRE IN THE LATE THIRTEENTH CENTURY *Note the four khanates: the Golden Horde in Russia, the Ilkhanate in Persia, Chagadai in Central Asia, and the Great Khanate extending from Mongolia to southern China.*

inner coherence that countered the divisive effect of tribal loyalties.

The Mongol conquests were all the more impressive in that, unlike the earlier Arab expansion, they lacked the unifying force of religious zeal. To be sure, at an assembly of chiefs in 1206, an influential shaman revealed that it was the sky god's will that Genghis conquer the world. Yet other unabashedly frank words attributed to Genghis may reveal a truer image of what lay behind the Mongol drive to conquest: "Man's highest joy is in victory: to conquer one's enemies, to pursue them, to deprive them of their possessions, to make their beloved weep, to ride on their horses, and to embrace their wives and daughters."[14]

Genghis divided his far-flung empire among his four sons. Trade and communications were maintained between the parts, but over several generations, each of the four khanates became independent. The khanate of Chagatai was in central Asia and remained purely nomadic. A second khanate of the Golden Horde ruled Russia from the lower Volga. The third was in Persia. The fourth, led by those who suc-

ceeded Genghis as great khans, centered first in Mongolia and then in China (see Map 10-3).

Mongol Rule in China

The standard theory used in explaining Chinese history is the dynastic cycle. A second theory explains Chinese history in terms of the interaction between the settled people of China and the nomads of the steppe. When strong states emerged in China, their wealth and population enabled them to expand militarily onto the steppe. But when China was weak, as was more often the case, the steppe peoples overran China. To review briefly:

1. During the Han dynasty (206 B.C.–A.D. 220), the most pressing problem in foreign relations was the Hsiung Nu empire to the north.

2. During the centuries that followed the Han, various nomadic peoples invaded and ruled northern China.

3. The energy and institutions of these Sino-Turkic rulers of the northern dynasties shaped China's reunification during the Sui (581–618) and T'ang (618–907) dynasties. The Uighur Turks also played a major role in T'ang defense policy.

[14] J. K. Fairbank, E. O. Reischauer, and A. M. Craig, *East Asia, Tradition and Transformation* (Boston: Houghton Mifflin, 1973), p. 164.

Kublai Khan, wearing ermine coat, with Mongol warriors at the hunt. Note the camel caravan in the hills at rear. [National Palace Museum, Taiwan, R.O.C.]

4. Northern border states became even more important during the Sung. The Northern Sung (960–1126) bought peace with payments of gold and silver to the Liao. The Southern Sung (1126–1279), for all of its cultural brilliance, was little more than a tributary state of the Chin dynasty, which had expanded into northern China.

From the very start of the Mongol pursuit of world hegemony, the riches of China were a target. But Genghis proceeded cautiously, determined to leave no enemy at his back. He first disposed of the Tibetan state to the northwest of China and then of the Manchu state of Chin that ruled north China. Mongol forces took Peking in 1227, the year Genghis died. They went on to take Loyang and the southern reaches of the Yellow River in 1234, and all of north China by 1241. During this time, the Mongols were interested mainly in loot. Only later did Chinese advisers persuade them that more wealth could be obtained by taxation.

Kublai, a grandson of Genghis, was chosen as the great khan in 1260. In 1264, he moved his capital from Karakorum in Mongolia to Peking. It was only in 1271 that he adopted a Chinese dynastic name, the Yuan, and, as a Chinese dynasty, went to war with the Southern Sung. Once the decision was made, the Mongols swept across southern China. The last Sung stronghold fell in 1279.

Kublai Khan's rule in Peking reflected the mixture of cultural elements in Mongol China. From Peking, Kublai could rule as a Chinese emperor, which would not have been possible in Karakorum. He adopted the Chinese custom of hereditary succession. He rebuilt Peking as a walled city in the Chinese style. But Peking was far to the north of any previous Chinese capital, away from centers of wealth and population; to provision it, the Grand Canal had to be extended. From Peking, Kublai could look out onto Manchuria and Mongolia and maintain ties with the other khanates. The city proper was for the Mongols. It was known to the West as *Cambulac,* "the city *(balya)* of the khan." Chinese were segregated in an adjoining walled city. The palace of the khan was designed by an Arab architect; its rooms were Central Asian in style. Kublai also maintained a summer palace at Shangtu (the "Xanadu" of Samuel Taylor Coleridge's poem) in Inner Mongolia, where he could hawk and ride and hunt in Mongol style.

Early Mongol rule in northern China was rapacious and exploitative, but it later shifted toward Chinese forms of government and taxation, especially in the south and at the local level. Because it was a foreign military occupation, civil administration was highly centralized. Under the emperor was a Central Secretariat, and beneath it were ten "Moving Secretariats," which became the provinces of later dynasties. These highly centralized institutions and the arbitrary style of Mongol decision making accelerated the trend toward absolutism that had started during the previous dynasty.

About four hundred thousand Mongols lived in China during the Yuan period. For such a tiny minority to control the Chinese majority, it had to stay separate. One measure was to make military service a monopoly of Mongols and their nomadic allies. Garrisons were established throughout China, with a strategic reserve on the steppe. Military officers were always regarded as more important than civil officials. A second measure was to use ethnic classifications in appointing civil officials. The highest category was the Mongols, who held the top civil and military posts. The second category included Persians, Turks, and other non-Chinese, who were given high civil posts. The third category was the northern Chinese, who included Manchus and other border peoples, and the fourth was the southern Chinese. Even when the examination system was sporadically revived after 1315, the Mongols and their allies took an easier examination; their quota was as large as that for Chinese; and they were appointed to the higher offices.

The net result was an uneasy symbiosis. Chinese officials directly governed the Chinese populace, collecting taxes, settling disputes, and maintaining the local order. Only a small number of these officials ever learned to speak Mongolian, yet without their positive cooperation, Mongol rule in China would have been impossible. The Mongols, concentrated in Peking, large cities, and in garrisons, spoke Mongolian among themselves and usually did not bother to learn Chinese. A few exceptions wrote poetry in Chinese and painted in the Chinese style. Communication was through interpreters. When a Chinese district magistrate sent a query to the court, the ruling was made in Mongolian. (The Mongols had borrowed the alphabet of the Uighurs to transcribe their tongue.) A word-for-word translation in Chinese was written below the Mongolian and passed back down to the magistrate. As the two languages are syntactically very different, the resulting Chinese was grotesque.

Foreign Contacts and Chinese Culture

Diplomacy and trade within the greater Mongol Empire brought China into contact with other higher

Marco Polo Describes the City of Hangchow

Marco Polo was a Venetian. In 1300, Venice had a population of more than one hundred thousand and was one of the wealthiest Mediterranean city-states. But Polo was nonetheless unprepared for what he saw in China. Commenting on Hangchow, China's capital during the Southern Sung, he first noted its size (ten or twelve times larger than Venice), then its many canals and bridges, its streets "paved with stones and bricks," and its location between "a lake of fresh and very clear water" and "a river of great magnitude." He spoke of "the prodigious concourse of people" frequenting its ten great marketplaces and of its "capacious warehouses built of stone for the accommodation of merchants who arrive from India and other parts." He then described the life of its people:

Each of the ten market-squares is surrounded with high dwelling-houses, in the lower part of which are shops, where every kind of manufacture is carried on, and every article of trade is sold; such, amongst others, as spices, drugs, trinkets, and pearls. In certain shops nothing is vended but the wine of the country, which they are continually brewing, and serve out fresh to their customers at a moderate price. The streets connected with the market-squares are numerous, and in some of them are many cold baths, attended by servants of both sexes, to perform the offices of ablution for the men and women who frequent them, and who from their childhood have been accustomed at all times to wash in cold water, which they reckon highly conducive to health. At these bathing places, however, they have apartments provided with warm water, for the use of strangers, who from not being habituated to it, cannot bear the shock of the cold. All are in the daily practice of washing their persons, and especially before their meals.

In other streets are the habitations of the courtesans, who are here in such numbers as I dare not venture to report; and not only near the squares, which is the situation usually appropriated for their residence, but in every part of the city they are to be found, adorned with much finery, highly perfumed, occupying well-furnished houses, and attended by many female domestics. These women are accomplished, and are perfect in the arts of blandishment and dalliance, which they accompany with expressions adapted to every description of person, insomuch that strangers who have once become so enchanted by their meretricious arts, that they can never divest themselves of the impression. Thus intoxicated with sensual pleasures, when they return to their homes they report that they have been in Kin-sai [Hangchow], or the celestial city, and pant for the time when they may be enabled to revisit paradise.

The inhabitants of the city are idolaters, and they use paper money as currency. The men as well as the women have fair complexions, and are handsome. The greater part of them are always clothed in silk, in consequence of the vast quantity of that material produced in the territory of Kin-sai, exclusively of what the merchants import from other provinces. Amongst the handicraft trades exercised in the place, there are twelve considered to be superior to the rest, as being more generally useful; for each of which there are a thousand workshops, and each shop furnishes employment for ten, fifteen, or twenty workmen, and in a few instances as many as forty, under their respective masters.

The natural disposition of the native inhabitants of Kin-sai is pacific, and by the example of their former kings, who were themselves unwarlike, they have been accustomed to habits of tranquility. The management of arms is unknown to them, nor do they keep any in their houses. Contentious broils are never heard among them. They conduct their mercantile and manufacturing concerns with perfect candour and probity. They are friendly towards each other, and persons who inhabit the same street, both men and women, from the mere circumstance of neighbourhood, appear like one family. In their domestic manners they are free from jealousy or suspicion of their wives, to whom great respect is shown, and any man would be accounted infamous who should presume to use indecent expressions to a married woman. To strangers also, who visit their city in the way of commerce, they give proofs of cordiality, inviting them freely to their houses, showing them hospitable attention, and furnishing them with the best advice and assistance in their mercantile transactions. On the other hand, they dislike the sight of soldiery, not excepting the guards of the grand khan, as they preserve the recollection that by them they were deprived of the government of their native kings and rulers.

▶ *For other travelers' reports, see "A Chinese Traveler's Report on the Gupta Realm" (Ch. 12), and "Ibn Battuta Visits Mogadishu and Kilwa (1331)" (Ch. 19).*

The Travels of Marco Polo (London: J. M. Dent, 1908), pp. 290–301.

civilizations for the first time since the T'ang period. Persia and the Arab world were especially important. Merchants, missionaries, and diplomats voyaged from the Persian Gulf and across the Indian Ocean to seaports in southeastern China. The Arab communities in Canton and other ports were larger than they had been during the Sung. Camel caravans carrying silks and ceramics left Peking to pass through the central Asian oases and on to Baghdad. Although the Mongols did not favor Chinese merchants and most trade was in other hands, Chinese trade also expanded. Chinese communities became established in Tabriz, the center of trading in western Asia, and in Moscow and Novgorod. It was during this period that knowledge of printing, gunpowder, and Chinese medicine spread to western Asia. Chinese ceramics influenced those of Persia as Chinese painting influenced Persian miniatures.

In Europe, first-hand knowledge of China was transmitted by the Venetian trader Marco Polo, who had served Kublai as an official between 1275 and 1292. His book, *A Description of the World,* was translated into most European languages. Many readers doubted that a land of such wealth and culture could exist so far from Europe, but the book excited an interest in geography. When Christopher Columbus set sail in 1492, his goal was to reach Polo's Zipangu (Japan).

Other cultural contacts were fostered by the Mongol toleration or encouragement of religion. Nestorian Christianity, spreading from Persia to Central Asia, reentered China during the Mongol era. Churches were built in the main cities. The mother of Kublai Khan was a Christian of this sect. Also, several papal missions were sent from Rome to the Mongol court. An archbishopric was established in Peking; a church was built, sermons were preached in Turkish or Mongolian, and choirboys sang hymns. Kublai sent the father and the uncle of Marco Polo with a letter to the pope asking for a hundred intelligent men acquainted with the seven arts.

Tibetan Buddhism with its magical doctrines and elaborate rites was the religion most favored by the Mongols. But Chinese Buddhism also flourished. Priests and monks of all religions were given tax exemptions. It is estimated that half a million Chinese became Buddhist monks during the Mongol century. The foreign religion that made the greatest gains was Islam, which became permanently established in Central Asia and western China. Mosques were built

in Peking, in the Islamic areas, and in southeastern port cities. Even Confucianism was regarded as a religion by the Mongols, its teachers being exempted from taxes. But as the scholar-gentry rarely obtained important offices, they saw the Mongol era as a time of hardship.

Despite these wide contacts with other peoples and religions, the high culture of China appears to have been influenced almost not at all—partly because China had little to learn from other areas, and partly because the centers of Chinese culture were in the south, the last area to be conquered and the area least affected by Mongol rule. Also, in reaction to the Mongol conquest, Chinese culture became conservative and turned in on itself. Scholars wrote poetry in the style of the Sung. New styles of painting developed, but the developments were from within the Chinese tradition, and the greatest Yuan paintings continued the style of the Sung. Yuan historians wrote the official history of the dynasties that preceded it. The head of the court bureau of historiography was a Mongol, but the histories produced by his Chinese staff were in the traditional mold. As the dynasty waned, unemployed scholars wrote essays expressing loyalty toward the Sung and satirizing the Mongols. Their writings were not censored: The Mongols either could not read them, did not read them, or did not care.

The major contribution to Chinese arts during the Yuan was by dramatists, who combined poetic arias with vaudeville theater to produce a new operatic drama. Performed by traveling troupes, the operas used few stage props. They relied for effect on makeup, costumes, pantomime, and stylized gestures. The women's roles were usually played by men. Except for the arias—the highlights of the performance—the dramas used vernacular Chinese, appealing to a popular audience. The unemployed scholars who wrote the scripts drew on the entire repertoire of the Sung storyteller. Among the stock figures in the operas were a Robin Hood-like bandit; a famous detective-judge; the T'ang monk who traveled to India; warriors and statesmen of the Three Kingdoms; and romantic heroes, villains, and ghosts. Justice always triumphed, and the dramas usually ended happily. In several famous plays, the hero gets the girl, despite objections by her parents and seemingly insurmountable obstacles, by passing the civil-service examinations in first place. As the examinations were not in effect during most of the Yuan, this resolution of the hero's predicament is one that looked back to the Sung pattern of government. Yuan drama continued almost unchanged in later dynasties, and during the nineteenth century, it merged with a form of southern Chinese theater to become today's Peking Opera.

Last Years of the Yuan

Despite the Mongol military domination of China and the highly centralized institutions of the Mongol court, the Yuan was the shortest of China's major dynasties. Little more than a century elapsed between Kublai's move to Peking in 1264 and the dynasty's collapse in 1368. The rule of Kublai and his successor had been effective, but a decline set in from the start of the fourteenth century. By then, the Mongol Empire as a whole no longer lent strength to its parts. The khanates became separated by religion and culture as well as by distance. Even tribesmen in Mongolia rebelled now and then against the great khans in Peking, who, in their eyes, had become too Chinese. The court at Peking, too, had never really gained legitimacy. Some Chinese officials served it loyally to the end, but most Chinese saw the government as carpetbaggers and saw Mongol rule as a military occupation. When succession disputes, bureaucratic factionalism, and pitched battles between Mongol generals broke out, the Chinese showed little inclination to rally in support of the dynasty.

Problems also arose in the countryside. Taxes were heavy and some local officials were corrupt. The government issued excessive paper money and then refused to accept it in payment for taxes. The Yellow River changed its course, flooding the canals that carried grain to the capital. At great cost and suffering, a labor force of one hundred fifty thousand workers and twenty thousand soldiers rerouted the river to the south of the Shantung peninsula. Further natural disasters during the 1350s led to popular uprisings. The White Lotus sect preached the coming of Maitreya. Regional military commanders, suppressing the rebellions, became independent of central control. Warlords arose. The warlord who ruled Szechwan was infamous for his cruelty. Important economic regions were devastated and in part depopulated by rebellions. At the end, a rebel army threatened Peking, and the last Mongol emperor and his court fled on horses to Shangtu. When that fell, they fled still deeper into the plains of Mongolia.

Imperial China in World Perspective

Rough parallels between China and Europe persisted until the sixth century A.D. Both saw the rise and fall of great empires. At first glance, the three-and-one-half centuries that followed the Han dynasty appear remarkably similar to the comparable period after the collapse of the Roman Empire: Central authority broke down, private armies arose, and aristocratic estates were established. Barbarian tribes, once allied to the empires, invaded and pillaged large areas. Otherworldly religions entered to challenge earlier official worldviews. In China, Neo-Taoism and then Buddhism challenged Confucianism, just as Christianity challenged Roman conceptions of the sociopolitical order.

But from the late sixth century A.D., a fundamental divergence occurred. Europe tailed off into centuries of feudal disunity and backwardness. A ghost of empire lingered in the European memory. But the reality, even after centuries had passed, was that tiny areas like France (one-seventeenth the size of China), Italy (one-thirty-second), or Germany (one-twenty-seventh) found it difficult to establish an internal unity, much less recreate a pan-European or pan-Mediterranean empire. This pattern of separate little states has persisted in Europe until today. In contrast, China, which is about the size of Europe and geographically no more natural a political unit, put a unified empire back together again, attaining a new level of wealth, power, and culture, and unified rule has continued until the present. What is the explanation?

One reason the empire was reconstituted in China was that the victory of Buddhism in China was less complete than that of Christianity in Europe. Confucianism survived within the aristocratic families and at the courts of the Six Dynasties, and the idea of a united empire was integral to it. It is difficult even to think of Confucianism apart from the idea of a universal ruler, aided by men of virtue and ability, ruling "all under Heaven" according to Heaven's mandate. In contrast, the Roman concept of political order was not maintained as an independent doctrine. Moreover, empire was not a vital element in Christian thought—except perhaps in Byzantium, where the empire lasted longer than it did in Western Europe. The notion of a "Christian king" did appear in the West, but basically, the kingdom sought by Jesus was not of this world.

A second consideration was China's greater cultural homogeneity. It had a common written language that was fairly close to all varieties of spoken Chinese. Minority peoples and even barbarian conquerors—apart from the Mongols—were rapidly Sinicized. In contrast, after Rome, the Mediterranean fell apart into its component cultures. Latin became the universal language of the Western church, but for most Christians it was a foreign language, a part of the mystery of the Mass, and even in Italy it became an artificial language, separate from the living tongue. The European languages and cultures were divisive forces.

A third factor was the combination in the post-Han northern Chinese states of economic strength based on Chinese agriculture with the military striking force of a nomadic cavalry. There was nothing like it in Europe. It was by such a northern state that China was reunified in A.D. 589.

A fourth and perhaps critical factor was China's greater population density. The province (called a *circuit* at the time) of Hopei had a registered population of 10,559,728 during the eighth century A.D. Hopei was about one-third the size of France, which in the eleventh century had a population of about two million. That is to say, even comparing China with France three centuries later, China's population density was fifteen times greater. (This comparison, it should be noted, is with a nonrice-producing area of China. Rice paddy areas were even more densely populated.) The far higher population density resulted in a different kind of history.

This explains why the Chinese could absorb barbarian conquerors so much more quickly than could Europe. It provided a larger agricultural surplus to the northern kingdoms than that enjoyed by comparable kingdoms in Europe. A denser population also meant better communications and a better base for commerce. To be sure, the centuries that followed the Han saw a decline in commerce and in cities. In some areas, money went out of use to be replaced by barter or the use of silk as currency. But the economic level remained higher than it was in early medieval Europe.

Several of the factors that explain the Sui-T'ang regeneration of a unified empire apply equally well or better to the Sung and subsequent dynasties. As schools were established and literacy rose, Confucianism and the ideal of a unified China became more widely accepted. Chinese culture was more homogeneous and less open to outside influences in the tenth century than it had been four centuries earlier. The population was denser, with the Yangtze basin emerging as a new center of gravity.

The same cyclic regeneration of centralized bureaucratic governments—even under outside conquerors—can also be analyzed in terms of the interests it served. For the military figure who established the dynasty, the bureaucratic state was a huge tax machine that supported his armies and bestowed on him revenues beyond the imaginings of contemporary European monarchs. Government by civilian officials also offered some promise for the security of his progeny by acting as a counterweight against other military figures. For the scholar-gentry class, service to the state was the means to maintain family wealth, power, and status. Nothing was better. For merchants, a strong state was not an unmixed blessing. It might tax their profits or establish monopolies on the commodities they traded, but it also provided order and stability. More often than not, commerce expanded during such periods. For farmers, the picture was also unclear. Taxation was often exploitative, but orderly exploitation was usually preferable to rapacious warlords, bandits, or marauding armies.

Comparisons across continents are difficult, but it seems likely that T'ang and Sung China had longer stretches of good government than any other part of the contemporary world. Not until the nineteenth century would comparable bureaucracies of talent and virtue begin to appear in the West.

Suggested Readings

GENERAL

J. CAHILL, *Chinese Painting* (1960). An excellent survey.

J. K. FAIRBANK, *China: A New History* (1992). The summation of a lifetime engagement with Chinese history.

F. A. KIERMAN, JR., and J. K. FAIRBANK, eds., *Chinese Ways in Warfare* (1974). Chapters by different authors on the Chinese military experience from the Chou to the Ming.

SUI AND T'ANG

P. B. EBREY, *The Aristocratic Families of Early Imperial China* (1978).

S. OWEN, *The Great Age of Chinese Poetry: The High T'ang* (1980).

E. G. PULLEYBLANK, *The Background of the Rebellion of An Lu-shan* (1955). A study of the 755 rebellion that weakened the central authority of the T'ang dynasty.

E. O. Reischauer, *Ennin's Travels in T'ang China* (1955). China as seen through the eyes of a ninth-century Japanese Marco Polo.

E. H. Schafer, *The Golden Peaches of Samarkand* (1963). A study of T'ang imagery.

D. Twitchett, ed., *Sui and T'ang China, 589–906,* Part 1 (1984). (Part 2, also in *The Cambridge History of China,* is forthcoming.)

G. W. Wang, *The Structure of Power in North China During the Five Dynasties* (1963). A study of the interim period between the T'ang and the Sung dynasties.

A. F. Wright, *The Sui Dynasty* (1978).

SUNG

C. S. Chang and J. Smythe, *South China in the Twelfth Century* (1981). China as seen through the eyes of a twelfth-century Chinese poet, historian, and statesman.

J. Gernet, *Daily Life in China on the Eve of the Mongol Invasion* (1962).

J. W. Haeger, ed., *Crisis and Prosperity in Sung China* (1975).

R. Hymes, *Statesmen and Gentlemen* (1987). On the transformation of officials into a local gentry elite during the twelfth and thirteenth centuries.

J. T. C. Liu and P. J. Golas, eds., *Change in Sung China: Innovation or Renovation?* (1969).

M. Rossabi, *China Among Equals* (1983). A study of the Liao, Ch'in, and Sung empires and their relations.

W. M. Tu, *Confucian Thought, Selfhood as Creative Transformation* (1985).

K. Yoshikawa, *An Introduction to Sung Poetry,* trans. by B. Watson (1967).

YUAN

T. T. Allsen, *Mongol Imperialism* (1987).

J. W. Dardess, *Conquerors and Confucians: Aspects of Political Change in Late Yuan China* (1973).

H. Franke and D. Twitchett, eds., *Alien Regimes and Border States, 710–1368* (to appear soon as Vol. 6 of *The Cambridge History of China*).

J. D. Langlois, *China Under Mongol Rule* (1981).

R. Latham, trans., *Travels of Marco Polo* (1958).

H. D. Martin, *The Rise of Chingis Khan and His Conquest of North China* (1981).

Unlike the full-bodied T'ang ideal, this bodhisattva *from the pre-Nara Hōryūji Temple reflects the artistic influence of the earlier Northern Wei dynasty. The T'ang style entered Japan during the Nara and early Heian periods. [Tokyo National Museum]*

11

Japan: Early History to 1467

J apanese history has three main turning points, each marked by a major influx of an outside culture and each followed by a massive restructuring of Japanese institutions. The first turning point was in the third century B.C., when an Old Stone Age Japan became an agricultural, metal-working society, similar to those on the Korean peninsula or in northeastern Asia. This era lasted until A.D. 600. The second turning point came during the seventh century, when whole complexes of Chinese culture entered Japan directly. Absorbing these, archaic Japan made the leap to a higher historical civilization, associated with the writing system, technologies, and philosophies of China, and with Chinese forms of Buddhism. Japan would remain a part of this civilization until the third turning point, in the nineteenth century, when it encountered the West.

Japanese Origins

The antiquity of humans in Japan is hotly debated in Japan today. A new archaeological find makes the front page of newspapers throughout Japan. Bookstores have rows of books, most of them popular works, asking the question: Who are we and where did we come from? During the ice ages, Japan was connected by land bridges to Asia. Woolly mammoths entered the northern island of Hokkaido, and elephants, sabre-toothed tigers, giant elks, and other continental fauna entered the lower islands. Did humans enter as well? Because Japan's acidic volcanic soil eats up bones, there are no early skeletal remains. The earliest evidence of human habitation is finely shaped stone tools dating from about 30,000 B.C. Then, from about 10,000 B.C., there is

Along with the cord-patterned pots, the hunting and gathering Jōmon people produced mysterious figurines. Is this a female deity? Why are the eyes slitted like snow goggles? [Otto E. Nelson/The Asia Society]

Jōmon or "cord-pattern" pottery, the oldest in the world. Archaeologists are baffled by its appearance in an Old Stone Age hunting, gathering, and fishing society—when in all other early societies pottery developed along with agriculture as an aspect of New Stone Age culture.

The Yayoi Revolution

After eight thousand years of Jōmon culture, the second phase of Japanese prehistory began about 300 B.C. It is called the Yayoi culture, after a place in Tokyo where its distinctive hard, white pottery was first unearthed. There is no greater break in the entire Japanese record than that between the Jōmon and the Yayoi. For at the beginning of the third century B.C., the agricultural revolution, the bronze revolution, and the iron revolution—which in the Near East, India, and China had been separated by thousands of years, and each of which singly had wrought profound transformations—burst into Japan simultaneously.

The new technologies were brought to Japan by peoples moving across the Tsushima Straits from the Korean peninsula. It is uncertain whether these immigrants came as a trickle and were absorbed—the predominant view in Japan—or whether they came in sufficient numbers to push back the indigenous Jōmon people. Physical anthropologists say that skulls from early Yayoi sites are quite different from those of the Jōmon. The early Yayoi migrants, using the same seacraft by which they had crossed from Korea, spread along the coasts of northern Kyushu and western Honshu. Yayoi culture rapidly replaced Jōmon culture as far east in Japan as the present-day city of Nagoya. After that, the Yayoi culture diffused overland into eastern Japan more slowly and with greater difficulty. Conditions were less favorable for agriculture, and a mixed agricultural-hunting economy lasted longer.

The early "frontier settlements" of the Yayoi people were located next to their fields. Their agriculture was primitive. By the first century A.D., the Yayoi population had expanded to the point at which wars were fought for the best land. Excavations reveal extensive stone-axe industries, and several skulls pierced by bronze and iron arrowheads have been found. An early Chinese chronicle describes Japan as made up of "more than one hundred countries" with wars and conflicts raging on all sides. During these wars, villages were relocated in defensible positions on low hills away from the fields. From these wars emerged a more peaceful order of regional states and a ruling class of aristocratic warriors. Late Yayoi excavations reveal villages once again located by fields and far fewer stone axes.

During the third century A.D., a temporary hegemony was achieved over a number of such regional states—or, more accurately, regional tribal confederations—by a queen named Pimiko. In the Chinese chronicle, Pimiko is described as a shaman who "occupied herself with magic and sorcery, bewitching the people." She was mature but unmarried. "After she became the ruler, there were few who saw her. She had one thousand women as attendants, but only one man. He served her food and drink and acted as a medium of communication. She resided in a palace surrounded by towers and stockades with armed guards in a state of constant vigilance."[1]

After Pimiko, references to Japan disappeared from the Chinese dynastic histories for a century and a half.

[1] L. C. Goodrich, ed., and R. Tsunoda, trans., *Japan in the Chinese Dynastic Histories* (South Pasadena, CA: Perkins Asiatic Monographs, 1951), p. 13.

Tomb Culture and the Yamato State

Emerging directly from the Yayoi culture was a period, A.D. 300–600, characterized by giant tomb mounds, which remain even today, dotting the landscape of the Nara–Osaka region. The early tombs—patterned on those in Korea—were circular mounds of earth built atop megalithic burial chambers. Later tombs were sometimes keyhole-shaped. The tombs were surrounded by moats and adorned with clay cylinders and statues of warriors, scribes, musicians, houses, boats, and the like. Early tombs, like the Yayoi graves that preceded them, contained mirrors, jewels, and other ceremonial objects. From the fifth century A.D., these objects were replaced by armor, swords, spears, and military trappings. The change reflected a new wave of continental influences. The flow of people and culture from the Korean peninsula into Japan that began with Yayoi was continuous into historical times.

Japan reappeared in the Chinese chronicles in the fifth century A.D. This period was also covered in the

CHRONOLOGY OF EARLY JAPANESE HISTORY	
8000–300 B.C.	Jōmon culture
EARLY CONTINENTAL INFLUENCES	
300 B.C.–A.D. 300	Yayoi culture
A.D. 300–680	Tomb culture and the Yamato state
A.D. 680–850	Chinese T'ang pattern in Nara and Early Heian Japan

earliest Japanese accounts of its own history, the *Records of Ancient Matters (Kojiki)* and the *Records of Japan (Nihongi)*, compiled in 712 and 720. These records dovetail with the evidence of the tombs. The picture that emerges is of regional aristocracies under the loose hegemony of the Yamato "'great kings." Historians use the geographic label "Yamato" because the courts of the great kings were located on the Yamato plain, near present-day Osaka, the richest ag-

Late Yayoi Japan as Presented in Chinese Histories

Weapons are spears, shields, swords, and wooden bows. The arrows are sometimes tipped with bone. The men all tattoo their faces and adorn their bodies with designs. The position and size of pattern indicate the difference of rank. The men's clothing is fastened breadth-wise and consists of one piece of cloth. The women tie their hair in bows, and their clothing, like our gown of one single piece of cloth, is put on by slipping it over the head. They use pink and scarlet to smear their bodies, as rice powder is used in China.

The women outnumber the men, and the men of importance have four or five spouses; the rest have two or three. The women are faithful and not jealous. There is no theft, and litigation is infrequent. When men break a law, their wives and children are confiscated; when the offense is serious, the offender's family is extirpated. At death mourning lasts for more than ten days, during which time members of the family weep and lament, without much drinking and eating; while their friends sing and dance.

When the lowly meet men of importance on the road, they stop and withdraw to the roadside. In conveying messages to them or addressing them, they either squat or kneel, with both hands on the ground. This is the way they show respect. When responding, they say "ah," which corresponds to the affirmative "yes."

When they go on voyages across the sea to visit China, they always select a man who does not arrange his hair, does not rid himself of fleas, lets his clothing [get as] dirty as it will, does not eat meat, and does not approach women. This man behaves like a mourner and is known as the fortune keeper. When the voyage turns out propitious, they all lavish on him slaves and other valuables. In case there is disease or mishap, they kill him, saying that he was not scrupulous in his duties.

L. C. Goodrich and R. Tsunoda, trans., *Japan in the Chinese Dynastic Histories* (South Pasadena, CA: Perkins Asiatic Monographs, 1951), pp. 1, 2, 13, 11, respectively.

A clay statue of a warrior in armor from an ancient tomb. [Tokyo National Museum]

ricultural region of ancient Japan. The Yamato rulers also held lands and granaries throughout Japan. The tomb of the great king Nintoku is 486 meters long and 36 meters high, with twice the volume of the Great Pyramid of Egypt. By the fifth century A.D., the great kings possessed sufficient authority to commandeer the labor for such a project.

The great kings awarded Korean-type titles to court and regional aristocrats, titles that implied a national hierarchy centering on the Yamato court. That these regional rulers had the same kind of political authority over their populations can be seen in the spread of tomb mounds throughout Japan.

The basic social unit of Yamato aristocratic society was the extended family *(uji)*, closer in size to a Scottish clan than to a modern household. Attached to

these aristocratic families were groups of specialist workers called *be.* This word was of Korean origin and was originally used to designate potters, scribes, or others with special skills who had immigrated from Korea. It was then extended to include similar groups of indigenous workers and groups of peasants. Yamato society had a small class of slaves, possibly captured in wars. There were also large numbers of peasants who were neither slaves nor members of aristocratic clans or specialized workers' groups.

What little is known of Yamato politics suggests that the court was the scene of incessant struggles for power between aristocratic families. There were also continuing efforts by the court to maintain control over outlying regions. Although marriage alliances were established and titles awarded, rebellions were not infrequent during the fifth and sixth centuries. Finally, there were constant wars with "barbarian tribes" in southern Kyushu and eastern Honshu on the frontiers of "civilized" Japan.

The Yamato Court and Korea

During the era of the Yamato court, a three-cornered military balance had emerged on the Korean peninsula between the states of Paekche in the southwest, Silla in the east, and Koguryo in the north (see Map 11-1). Japan was an ally of Paekche. Japan may also have maintained a trading base or military colony on the southern rim of Korea.

The Paekche connection was of vital importance to the Yamato court, enabling the court to expand its power within Japan. Imports of iron weapons and tools gave it military strength. The migration to Japan of Korean potters, weavers, scribes, metal workers, and other artisans increased its wealth and influence. The significance of the immigrants from Korea can be gauged by the fact that many became established as noble families. Paekche also served as a conduit for elements of Chinese culture. Chinese writing was adopted for the transcription of Japanese names during the fifth or sixth century. Confucianism entered in 513, when Paekche sent a "scholar of the Five Classics." Buddhism arrived in 538, when a Paekche king sent a Buddha image, sutras, and possibly a priest.

Eventually the political balance on the peninsula shifted against Japan. In 532, Paekche joined Silla in attacking Japan's southern rim colony, and by 562 Japan had been driven from Korea. But the severance of ties with Korea was less of a loss than it would have been earlier, for by this time Japan had succeeded in establishing direct relations with China.

MAP 11-1 YAMATO JAPAN AND KOREA (CA. 500 A.D.) *Paekche was Japan's ally on the Korean peninsula. Silla, Japan's enemy, was the state that would eventually unify Korea. (Note: Nara was founded in 710; Heian in 794.)*

Religion in Early Japan

The indigenous religion of Yamato Japan was an animistic worship of the forces of nature, later given the name of *Shinto,* or "the way of the gods," to distinguish it from Buddhism. In all likelihood, Shinto entered Japan from the continent as a part of Yayoi culture. The underlying forces of nature might be embodied in a waterfall, a twisted tree, a strangely shaped boulder, a mountain, or in a great leader who would be worshiped as a deity after his death. Mount

Fuji was holy not as the abode of a god but because the mountain itself was an upwelling of a vital natural force. Even today in Japan, a gnarled tree trunk may be circled with a straw rope and set aside as an object of veneration. The sensitivity to nature and natural beauty that pervades Japanese art and poetry owes much to Shinto. Throughout Japan's premodern history, most villages had shamans, or religious specialists who, by entering a trance, could contact directly the inner forces of nature and gain the power to foretell the future or heal sickness. The queen Pimiko was

Darkness and the Cave of High Heaven

The younger brother of the sun goddess was a mischief maker. Eventually the gods drove him out of heaven. On one occasion, he knocked a hole in the roof of a weaving hall and dropped in a dappled pony that he had skinned alive. One weaving maiden was so startled that she struck her genitals with the shuttle she was using and died.

▶ *Entering a cave and then reemerging signifies death and rebirth in the religions of many peoples. Compare this passage to "Mark Describes the Resurrection of Jesus" (Ch. 6).*

The Sun Goddess, terrified at the sight, opened the door of the heavenly rock cave, and hid herself inside. Then the Plain of High Heaven was shrouded in darkness, as was the Central Land of Reed Plains [Japan]. An endless night prevailed. The cries of the myriad gods were like the buzzing of summer flies, and myriad calamities arose.

The eight hundred myriad gods assembled in the bed of the Quiet River of Heaven. They asked one god to think of a plan. They assembled the long-singing birds of eternal night and made them sing. They took hard rocks from the bed of the river and iron from the Heavenly Metal Mountain and called in a smith to make a mirror. They asked the Jewel Ancestor God to make a string of 500 curved jewels eight feet long. They asked other gods to remove the shoulder blade of a male deer and to obtain cherry wood from Mount Kagu, and to perform a divination. They uprooted a sacred tree, attaching the string of curved jewels to its upper branches, hanging the large mirror from its middle branches, and suspending offerings of white and blue cloth from its lower branches.

One god held these objects as grand offerings and another intoned sacred words. The Heavenly Hand-Strong-Male God stood hidden beside the door. A goddess bound up her sleeves with clubmoss from Mount Kagu, made a herb band from the spindle-tree, and bound together leaves of bamboo-grass to hold in her hands. Then she placed a wooden box face-down before the rock cave, stamped on it until it re-sounded, and, as if possessed, she exposed her breasts and pushed her shirt-band down to her genitals. The Plain of High Heaven shook as the myriad gods broke into laughter.

The Sun Goddess, thinking this strange, opened slightly the rock-cave door and said from within: "Since I have hidden myself I thought that the Plain of Heaven and the Central Land of the Reed Plains would all be in darkness. Why is it that the goddess makes merry and the myriad gods all laugh?"

The goddess replied: "We rejoice and are glad because there is here a god greater than you." While she spoke two other gods brought out the mirror and held it up before the Sun Goddess.

The Sun Goddess, thinking this stranger and stranger, came out the door and peered into the mirror. Then the Hand-Strong-Male God seized her hand and pulled her out. Another god drew a rope behind her and said: "You may not go back further than this."

So when the Sun Goddess had come forth, the Plain of High Heaven and the Central Land of the Reed Plains once again naturally shone in brightness.

From the Records of Ancient Matters (Kojiki), translated by Albert Craig, with appreciation to Basil Hall Chamberlain and Donald L. Phillippi.

such a shaman. The sorceress is a stock figure in tales of ancient or medieval Japan. More often than not, women, receiving the command of a god, have founded the "new" religions in this tradition, even into the nineteenth and twentieth centuries.

A second aspect of early Shinto was its connection with the state and the ruling post-tribal aristocracy. The more potent forces of nature such as the sea, the sun, the moon, the wind, and thunder and lightning became personified as deities. Each clan, or extended family, had its own myth centering on a nature deity *(kami)* that it claimed as its original ancestor. Aristocratic families possessed genealogies tracing their descent from the deity. A genealogy was a patent of nobility and a claim to political authority. The head of a clan was also its chief priest, who made sacrifices to its deity. When Japan was unified by the Yamato court, the myths of several clans apparently were joined into a national composite myth. The deity of the Yamato great kings was the sun goddess, so she became the chief deity, while other gods assumed lesser positions appropriate to the status of their clan. Had another clan won the struggle, some other deity would have become paramount—perhaps a thunder god as in ancient Greece.

The *Records of Ancient Matters* and *Records of Japan* tell of the creation of Japan, of the deeds and misdeeds of gods on the "plain of high heaven," and of their occasional adventures on earth or in the underworld. In mid-volume, the stories of the gods, interspersed with the genealogies of noble families, give way to stories of early emperors and early Japanese history. The Japanese emperors, now the oldest royal family in the world, were viewed as the lineal descendants of the sun goddess and as "living gods." The Great Shrine of the Sun Goddess at Ise has always been the most important in Japan.

Nara and Heian Japan

The second major turning point in Japanese history was its adoption of the higher civilization of China. This is a prime example of the worldwide process (described in Chapter 2) by which the heartland civilizations spread into outlying areas. In Japan the process occurred between the seventh and twelfth centuries and can best be understood in terms of three stages. The first stage was learning about China. The second stage, mostly during the eighth and ninth centuries, saw the implantation in Japan of Chinese T'ang-type institutions. The third involved the further transformation of these institutions to better fit them to conditions in Japan. By the twelfth century, the creative reworking of Chinese elements had led to a distinctive Japanese culture, quite unlike that of China, yet equally different from that of the earlier Yamato court.

Seventh Century

The official embassies to China that began in A.D. 607 included traders, students, and Buddhist monks as well as representatives of the Yamato great kings. Like Third World students who study abroad today, Japanese who studied in China played key roles in their government when they returned. They brought back with them a quickening flow of technology, art, Buddhism, and knowledge of T'ang legal and governmental systems. But the difficulties of mastering Chinese and comprehending its philosophical culture were enormous for the Yamato Japanese. Large-scale institutional changes using the T'ang model actually began in the 680s with the Emperor Temmu and his successor, the Empress Jitō.

Prince Shōtoku (574–622) and two of his sons. Prince Shōtoku was a Buddhist and a reformer who began sending regular embassies to China in 607. [Bettmann Archive]

Temmu's life illustrates the interplay between court politics and the adoption of Chinese institutions. He came to the throne by leading an alliance of eastern clans in rebellion against the previous great king, his nephew. The *Records of Japan* describe Temmu as "walking like a tiger through the eastern lands." He then used Chinese systems to consolidate his power. He promulgated a Chinese-type law code, which greatly augmented the powers of the ruler. He styled himself as the "heavenly emperor" *(tennō)*, which thereafter replaced the earlier title of "great king." He rewarded his supporters with new court ranks and with positions in a new court government, both derived from the T'ang example. He extended the authority of the court and increased its revenues by a survey of agricultural lands and a census of their population. In short, although the admiration for Chinese things must have been enormous, much of the borrowing was dictated by specific, immediate, and practical Japanese concerns.

Nara and Early Heian Court Government

Until the eighth century, the capital was usually moved each time an emperor died. Then, in 710, a new capital, intended to be permanent, was established at Nara. It was laid out on a checkerboard grid like the Chinese capital at Ch'ang-an. But then it was moved again—some say to escape the meddling in politics of powerful Buddhist temples. A final move occurred in 794 to Heian (later Kyoto) on the plain north of Nara. This site remained the capital until the move to Tokyo in 1869. Even today, Kyoto's regular geometry reflects the Chinese concepts of city planning.

The superimposition of a Chinese-type capital on a still backward Japan produced as stark a contrast as any in history. In the villages, peasants—who worshiped the forces in mountains and trees—lived in pit dwellings and either planted in crude paddy fields or used slash-and-burn techniques of dry land farming. In the capital stood pillared palaces in which dwelt the emperor and nobles, descended from the gods on high. They drank wine, wore silk, and enjoyed the paintings, perfumes, and pottery of the T'ang. Clustered about the capital were Buddhist temples, more numerous than in Nara, with soaring pagodas and sweeping tile roofs. With what awe must a peasant have viewed the city and its inhabitants!

The emperors at the Nara and Heian courts were both Confucian rulers with the majesty accorded by Chinese law and Shinto rulers descended from the sun goddess. Protected by an aura of the sacred, their lineage was never usurped. All Japanese history constitutes a single dynasty, although not a few emperors were killed and replaced by other family members.

Beneath the emperor, the same modified Chinese pattern prevailed. Like the T'ang, Japan had a Council of State, but it was more powerful than that of China. It was the office from which leading clans manipulated the authority of an emperor, who usually reigned but did not rule. Beneath this council were eight ministries—two more than in China. One was a Secretariat and the other the Imperial Household Ministry. Size affected function: Where T'ang China had a population of sixty million, Nara Japan had only five million. There were fewer people to govern in Japan; there were no significant external enemies; and much of local rule, in the Yamato tradition, was in the hands of local clans. Consequently, more of the business of court government was with the court itself. Of the six thousand persons in the central ministries, more than four thousand were concerned in one way or another with the care of the imperial house. The Imperial Household Ministry, for example, had an official staff of 1,296, whereas the Treasury had only 305 and Military Affairs only 198.

Under the central court government were sixty-six provinces, which were further subdivided into districts and villages. In pre-Nara times, the regions had been governed by largely autonomous regional clans; but under the new system provincial governors were sent out from the capital. This change reduced the old regional aristocrats to the lesser posts of district magistrates. The new system substantially increased the power of the central aristocracy.

In other respects, Japanese court government was unlike that of China. There were no eunuchs. There was little tension between the emperor and the bureaucracy—the main struggles were between clans. The T'ang movement from aristocracy toward meritocracy also was absent in Japan. Apart from clerks and monastics, only aristocrats were educated, and only they were appointed to important official posts. Family counted for more than grades. A feeble attempt was made to establish an examination meritocracy on the Chinese model, but it failed completely.

Land and Taxes

The last Japanese embassy to China was in 839. By that time, the frenetic borrowing of Chinese culture had already slowed. The Japanese had taken in all they needed—or, perhaps, all they could handle— and were sufficiently self-confident to use Chinese ideas in innovative and flexible ways. The 350 years that followed until the end of the twelfth century were a time of assimilation and evolutionary change. Nowhere was this more evident than in the system of taxation.

The land system of Nara and early Heian Japan was the equal field system of the early T'ang. All land belonged to the emperor; it was redistributed every six years, and taxes were levied on people, not land. Those receiving land were liable for three taxes: a light tax in grain, a light tax in cloth, and a heavy labor tax. The system was complex, requiring land surveys, the redrawing of boundaries, and elaborate land and population registers. Even in China, with its sophisticated bureaucracy, this system broke down.

In the case of Japan, the marvel is that it could be carried out at all. The evidence of old registers and recent aerial photographs suggests that it was, at least in western Japan. Its implementation speaks of the immense energy and ability of the early Japanese, who so quickly absorbed much of Chinese administrative techniques.

Of course, as put into effect, the system was even less equal than in China. Imperial princes and high nobles received thousands or hundreds of units of rank lands, office lands, and merit lands, along with the labor to work them; local officials got less, and the cultivators did the work.

Whenever changes in a society are legislated or imposed from above, the results tend to be uniform. But when changes occur willy-nilly within a social system, the results are usually messy and difficult to comprehend. The evolution of the land system and taxation in late Heian Japan was of the second type.

One big change was from the equal field system to one of tax quotas payable in grain. First, the redistribution of land broke down and land holdings became hereditary. Officials discovered that peasants would not care for land they did not own, for land that would be redistributed every six years. Second, the main tax of labor service was converted to a grain tax. Officials found it more efficient to hire workers and pay them in grain than to use the labor of peasants who had no incentive to work. Third, the taxes levied on provinces and districts were made over into fixed quotas. Court officials, unable to maintain the elaborate records needed for the equal field system, gave each governor a quota, and the governor in turn gave one to each district magistrate. The governors kept any amount collected over the quota. The district magistrates, other local notables, and the military families associated with them, gradually used their part of the surplus to transform themselves into a new local ruling class.

Another big change, one that affected about half of the land in late Heian Japan, was the conversion of tax-paying lands to tax-free estates. Nobles and powerful temples in Kyoto did not want to pay taxes, so they used their influence at the court to obtain *immunities*—exemptions from taxation for their lands. From the ninth century, many cultivators began to commend their small holdings to such nobles, judging that they would be better off as serfs on tax-free estates than as free farmers subject to taxation. As a result of the random pattern of commendation, the typical estate in Japan was of scattered parcels of land, unlike the unified estates of Europe. The Japanese estates were managed by stewards, appointed from among the local notables. They took a share of the surplus grain for themselves, and forwarded the rest to the noble owner in Kyoto. The stewards, thus, were from the same stratum of local society as those who collected the tax quotas. Like district magistrates, they had a vital interest in upholding the local order.

Rise of the Samurai

During the Nara period, Japan experimented with a military system based on conscription. One-third of all able-bodied men between the ages of twenty-one and sixty were taken. Conscript armies, however, proved inefficient, so in 792 the court abolished conscription and began a new system relying on local mounted warriors. Some were stationed in the capital and some in the provinces. They were official troops whose taxes were remitted in exchange for military service. The Japanese verb "to serve" is *samurau,* so those who served became *samurai*—the noun form of the verb. Then, from the mid-Heian period, the officially recruited local warriors were replaced by nonofficial private bands of local warriors. They constituted the military of Japan for the next half millennium or so, until the foot-soldier revolution of the fifteenth and sixteenth centuries.

Being a samurai was expensive. Horses, armor, and weapons were costly, and if they were to be used effectively, long training was required. The primary weapon was the bow and arrow, used from the saddle. Most samurai were from well-to-do local families, such as those of district magistrates or notables, or were from military families supported by the local elites or by temples or shrines. Their initial function was to preserve local order and, possibly, to help with tax collection. But at times, even near the beginning, they contributed to disorder. From the second half of the ninth century, there are accounts of district magistrates leading local forces against provincial governors, doubtless in connection with tax disputes.

From the early tenth century, regional military coalitions or confederations began to form. They first broke into history in 939, when a regional military leader, a descendant of an emperor, became involved in a tax dispute. He captured several provinces, called himself the new emperor, and appointed a government of civil and military officials. The Kyoto court responded by recruiting another military band as its champion. The rebellion was quelled, and the rebel leader died in battle. That the Kyoto court could summon a military band points up the connections that enabled it to manipulate local military leaders and maintain its political control of Japan.

The rebellion of 939 was the first of a number of conflicts between regional military bands. Many wars were fought in eastern Japan—the "wild east" of those days. The east was more militarized because it was the headquarters for the periodic campaigns against the tribal peoples to the north. By the middle of the twelfth century, local and regional military bands were to be found in every part of Japan.

Late Heian Court Government

Even during the Nara period, much of the elaborate apparatus of Chinese government was of little use. By the early Heian period, the actual functions of government were taken over by three new offices outside the Chinese system:

1. *Audit officers.* A newly appointed provincial governor had to report on the accounts of his predecessor. Agreement was rare. So from the end of the Nara period, audit officers were sent to examine the books. By early Heian times, these auditors had come to superintend the collection of taxes and most other capital–province relationships. They tried to half the erosion of tax revenues. But as the quota and estate systems developed, this office had less and less to do.
2. *Bureau of archivists.* This bureau was established in 810 to record and preserve imperial decrees. Eventually it took over the executive function at the Heian court, drafting imperial decrees and attending to all aspects of the emperor's life.
3. *Police commissioners.* Established in the second decade of the ninth century to enforce laws and prosecute criminals, the commissioners eventually became responsible for all law and order in the capital. They absorbed military functions as well as those of the Ministry of Justice and the Bureau of Impeachment.

While new institutions were evolving, there also occurred shifts in the control of the court. The key figure remained the emperor, who had the power of appointments. Until the early Heian—say, the mid-ninth century—some emperors actually ruled or, more often, shared power with nobles of leading clans. From 856 the northern branch of the Fujiwara clan became preeminent, and from 986 to 1086 its stranglehold on the court was absolute. The administrative offices of the Fujiwara house were almost more

WHO WAS IN CHARGE AT THE NARA AND HEIAN COURTS	
710–856	Emperors or combinations of nobles
856–1086	Fujiwara nobles
1086–1160	Retired emperors
1160–1180	Military house of Taira

powerful than those of the central government, and all key government posts were monopolized by members of the Fujiwara family. The Fujiwara controlled the court by marrying their daughters to the emperor, forcing the emperor to retire after a son was born, and then ruling as regents in place of the new infant emperor. At times, they even ruled as regents for adult emperors. Fujiwara Michinaga's words were no empty boast when he said, "As for this world, I think it is mine, nor is there a flaw in the full moon."

Fujiwara rule gave way, during the second half of the eleventh century, to rule by retired emperors. The imperial family and lesser noble houses had long resented Fujiwara domination. Disputes within the Fujiwara house itself enabled an emperor to regain control. Imperial control of government was reasserted by Emperor Shirakawa, who reigned from 1072 to 1086 and, abdicating at the age of thirty-three, ruled for forty-three years as retired emperor. After his death, another retired emperor continued in the same pattern until 1156.

Ex-Emperor Shirakawa set up offices in his quarters not unlike the administrative offices of the Fujiwara family. He employed talented nobles of lesser families and sought to reduce the number of tax-free estates by confiscating those of the Fujiwara. He failed and ended, instead, by garnering huge estates for the imperial family. He developed strong ties to regional military leaders. His sense of his own power was reflected in his words—more a lament than a boast: "The only things that do not submit to my will are the waters of the Kamo River, the roll of the dice, and the soldier-monks [of the Tendai temple on Mount Hiei to the northeast of Kyoto]." But Shirakawa's powers were exercised in a capital city that was increasingly isolated from the changes in outlying regions, and even the city itself was plagued by fires, banditry, and a sense of impending catastrophe.

A momentous change occurred in 1160. The death of the ruling retired emperor precipitated a struggle

In the Heiji War of 1160, regional samurai bands became involved in Kyoto court politics. This is a scroll painting of the burning of the Sanjō Palace. [Museum of Fine Arts, Boston. Fenollosa-Weld Collection]

for power between another retired emperor and the reigning emperor. Each called in a military confederation for backing. The House of Taira defeated the armies of the Minamoto. Taira Kiyomori, the leader of the victorious confederation, had come to Kyoto to uphold an emperor, but finding himself in charge, he stayed to rule. His pattern of rule was quite Japanese: Court nobles kept their Chinese court offices; the reigning emperor, who had been supported by Kiyomori, retired and took control of the offices of the retired emperor and of the estates of the imperial family; the head of the Fujiwara family kept the post of regent, while Taira Kiyomori married his daughter to the new emperor, and when a son was born, Kiyomori forced the emperor to retire and ruled as the maternal grandfather of the infant emperor. That is to say, the Taira ruled as a new stratum atop the old social structure.

Aristocratic Culture and Buddhism in Nara and Heian Japan

If the parts of a culture could be put on a scale and weighed like sugar or flour, we would conclude that the culture of Nara and early Heian Japan was overwhelmingly one of Shinto religious practices and village folkways, an extension of the culture of the late Yamato period. The aristocracy was small and was encapsulated in the routine of court life, just as the Buddhist monks were contained within the rounds of their monastic life. The early Heian aristocracy comprised one-tenth of 1 percent of Japan's population. Most of the court culture had only recently been imported from China. There had not been time for the commoners to ape their betters or for the powerful force of the indigenous culture to reshape that of the elite.

The resulting cultural gap helps to explain why the aristocrats, insofar as we can tell from literature, found the commoners to be odd, incomprehensible, and, indeed, hardly human. The writings of the courtiers reflect little sympathy for the suffering and hardships of the people—except in Chinese-style poetry, where such feelings were expected. When the fictional Prince Genji stoops to an affair with an impoverished woman, she is inevitably a princess. Sei Shōnagon was not atypical as a writer: She was offended by the vulgarity of mendicant nuns; laughed at an illiterate old man whose house had burned down; and found lacking in charm the eating habits of carpenters, who wolfed down their food a bowl at a time.

Heian high culture resembled a hothouse plant. It was protected by the political influence of the court. It was nourished by the flow of tax revenues and income from estates. Under these conditions, the aristocrats of the never-never land of Prince Genji indulged in a unique way of life and created canons of elegance and taste that are striking even today. The speed with which T'ang culture was assimilated and reworked was amazing. A few centuries after Mediterranean culture had been introduced into northern Europe, there appeared nothing even remotely comparable to the *Tale of Genji* or the *Pillow Book*.

Chinese Tradition in Japan

Education at the Nara and Heian courts was largely a matter of reading Chinese books and acquiring the skills needed to compose poetry and prose in Chinese. These were enormous tasks, not only because there was no prior tradition of scholarship in Japan but also because the two languages were so dissimilar. To master written Chinese and use it for everyday written communications was as daunting a challenge for the Nara Japanese as it would have been for any European of the same century, but the challenge was successfully met. From the Nara period until the nineteenth century, most philosophical and legal writings, and most of the histories, essays, and religious texts in Japan, were written in Chinese. From a Chinese perspective, the writings may leave something to be desired. It would be astonishing if this were not the case, for the soul of language is the music of the spoken tongue. But the Japanese writers were competent, and the feelings and ideas they expressed were authentic—when not copybook exercises in the style of a Chinese master. In 883, when Sugawara Michizane wrote a poem on the death of his son, he quite naturally wrote it in Chinese. The poem began

Since Amaro died I cannot sleep at night;
if I do, I meet him in dreams and tears come coursing
down.
Last summer he was over three feet tall;
this year he would have been seven years old.
He was diligent and wanted to know how to be a good
son,
read his books and recited by heart the "Poem on the
Capital."[2]

The mentioned capital was Ch'ang-an, and the poem, one "used in Japan as a text for little boys learning to read Chinese."

Not only were Japanese writings in Chinese a vital part of the Japanese cultural tradition, but the original Chinese works themselves also became a part of the same tradition. The late T'ang poet Po Chu-i was early appreciated and widely read, and later, Tu Fu and Li Po were also read and admired. As in China itself, Chinese history was read, and its stock figures were among the heroes and villains of the Japanese historical consciousness. Chinese history became the mirror in which Japan saw itself, despite the differences in the two societies. Buddhist stories and the books of Confucianism also became Japanese classics, continuously accessible and consulted over the centuries for their wisdom and philosophy. The parallel might be the acceptance of "foreign books" such as the Bible, Plato, and Aristotle in England.

Birth of Japanese Literature

Stimulated by Chinese models, the Japanese began to compose poetry in their native tongue. The first major anthology was the *Collection of Ten Thousand Leaves (Man'yōshū)*, compiled in about 760. It contained 4,516 poems. The sentiments in the poems are fresh, sometimes simple and straightforward, but often sophisticated. They reveal a deep sensitivity to nature and strong human relationships between husband and wife, and parents and children. They also display a love for the land of Japan and links to a Shinto past.

An early obstacle to the development of a Japanese poetic tradition was the difficulty of transcribing Japanese sounds. In the *Ten Thousand Leaves*, Chinese characters were used as phonetic symbols. But there was no standardization, and the work soon became unintelligible. In 951, when an empress wished to read it, a committee of poets deciphered the work and put it into *kana*, the new syllabic script or alphabet that had developed during the ninth century. A second major anthology was the *Collection of Ancient and Modern Times*, compiled in 905. It was written entirely in *kana*.

The invention of *kana* opened the gate to the most brilliant developments of the Heian period. Most of the new works and certainly the greatest were by women, as most men were busy writing Chinese. One genre of writing was the diary or travel diary. An outstanding example of this genre was the *Izumi Shikibu Diary*, in which Izumi Shikibu reveals her tempestuous loves through a record of poetic exchanges.

The greatest works of the Heian period were by Sei Shōnagon and Murasaki Shikibu. Both were daughters of provincial officials serving at the Heian court. The *Pillow Book* of Sei Shōnagon contains sharp, satirical, amusing essays and literary jottings that reveal the demanding aristocratic taste of the early-eleventh-

---

[2]H. Sato and B. Watson, trans., *From the Country of Eight Islands* (Seattle: University of Washington Press, 1981), p. 121.

Development of Japanese Writing

No two languages could be more different than Chinese and Japanese. Chinese is nonsyllabic, uninflected, and tonal. Japanese is polysyllabic, highly inflected, and atonal. To adopt Chinese writing for use in Japanese was thus no easy task. What the Japanese did at first—when they were not simply learning to write in Chinese—was to use certain Chinese ideographs as a phonetic script. For example, in the Man'yōshū, the eighth-century poetic anthology, shira-nami *(white wave) was written with* 之 *for* shi, 良 *for* ra, 奈 *for* na, *and* 美 *for* mi. *Over several centuries, these phonetic ideographs evolved into a unique Japanese phonetic script:*

	ORIGINAL CHINESE IDEOGRAPH	SIMPLIFIED IDEOGRAPH	PHONETIC SCRIPT *(KANA)*
shi	之	之	し
ra	良	良	ら
na	奈	奈	な
mi	美	美	み

It is apparent in the above examples how the original ideograph was first simplified according to the rules of calligraphy and was then further simplified into a phonetic script. In modern Japanese, unmodified Chinese ideographs are used for nouns, verb stems, and adjectives, and the phonetic script is used for inflections and particles.

学生 は 図書館 へ 行きました.

Students/as for/library/to/went.
(The students went to the library.)

In the above sentence, the Chinese ideographs are the forms with many strokes, and the phonetic script is shown in the simpler, cursive forms.

---

century Heian court, for which, as Sir George Sansom said, "religion became an art and art a religion."[3]

The *Tale of Genji*, written by Murasaki Shikibu in about 1010, was the world's first novel. Emerging out of a short tradition of lesser works in which prose was a setting for poetry, *Genji* is a work of sensitivity, originality, and precise psychological delineation of character, for which there was no Chinese model. It tells of the life, loves, and sorrows of Prince Genji, the son of an imperial concubine, and, after his death, of his son Kaoru. The novel spans three-quarters of a century and is historical in nature, although the court society it describes is more emperor centered than the Fujiwara age in which Murasaki lived. The book may be seen as having had a "definite and serious

purpose." In one passage, Genji twits a court lady whom he finds reading an extravagant romance. She is "hardly able to lift her eyes from the book in front of her." But then Genji relents and says

I think far better of this art than I have led you to suppose. Even its practical value is immense. Without it what should we know of how people lived in the past, from the Age of the Gods down to the present day? For history books such as the *Chronicles of Japan* show us only one small corner of life; whereas these diaries and romances, which I see piled around you contain, I am sure, the most minute information about all sorts of people's private affairs.[4]

[3] G. Sansom, *Japan, A Short Cultural History* (New York: Appleton-Century-Crofts, 1962), p. 239.

[4] R. Tsunoda, W. T. deBary, and D. Keene, eds., *Sources of the Japanese Tradition* (New York: Columbia University Press, 1958), p. 181.

Aristocratic Taste at the Fujiwara Court:
Sei Shōnagon Records Her Likes and Dislikes

ELEGANT THINGS

A white coat worn over a violet waistcoat.

Duck eggs.

Shaved ice mixed with liana syrup and put in a new silver bowl.

A rosary of rock crystal.

Snow on wistaria or plum blossoms.

A pretty child eating strawberries.

FEATURES THAT I PARTICULARLY LIKE

Someone has torn up a letter and thrown it away. Picking up the pieces, one finds that many of them can be fitted together.

A person in whose company one feels awkward asks one to supply the opening or closing line of a poem. If one happens to recall it, one is very pleased. Yet often on such occasions one completely forgets something that one would normally know.

Entering the Empress's room and finding that ladies-in-waiting are crowded round her in a tight group, I go next to a pillar which is some distance from where she is sitting. What a delight it is when Her Majesty summons me to her side so that all the others have to make way!

HATEFUL THINGS

A lover who is leaving at dawn announces that he has to find his fan and his paper. "I know I put them somewhere last night," he says. Since it is pitch dark, he gropes about the room, bumping into the furniture and muttering, "Strange! Where on earth can they be?" Finally he discovers the objects. He thrusts the paper into the breast of his robe with a great rustling sound; then he snaps open his fan and busily fans away with it. Only now is he ready to take his leave. What charmless behavior! "Hateful" is an understatement.

A good lover will behave as elegantly at dawn as at any other time. He drags himself out of bed with a look of dismay on his face. The lady urges him on: "Come, my friend, it's getting light. You don't want anyone to find you here." He gives a deep sigh, as if to say that the night has not been nearly long enough and that it is agony to leave. Once up, he does not instantly pull on his trousers. Instead he comes close to the lady and whispers whatever was left unsaid during the night. Even when he is dressed, he still lingers, vaguely pretending to be fastening his sash.

Presently he raises the lattice, and the two lovers stand together by the side door while he tells her how he dreads the coming day, which will keep them apart; then he slips away. The lady watches him go, and this moment of parting will remain among her most charming memories.

IN SPRING IT IS THE DAWN

In spring it is the dawn that is most beautiful. As the light creeps over the hills, their outlines are dyed a faint red and wisps of purplish cloud trail over them.

In summer the nights. Not only when the moon shines, but on dark nights too, as the fireflies flit to and fro, and even when it rains, how beautiful it is!

In autumn the evenings, when the glittering sun sinks close to the edge of the hills and the crows fly back to their nests in threes and fours and twos; more charming still is a file of wild geese, like specks in the distant sky. When the sun has set, one's heart is moved by the sound of the wind and the hum of the insects.

In winter the early mornings. It is beautiful indeed when snow has fallen during the night, but splendid too when the ground is white with frost; or even when there is no snow or frost, but it is simply very cold and the attendants hurry from room to room stirring up the fires and bringing charcoal, how well this fits the season's mood! But as noon approaches and the cold wears off, no one bothers to keep the braziers alight, and soon nothing remains but piles of white ashes.

THINGS THAT HAVE LOST THEIR POWER

A large tree that has been blown down in a gale and lies on its side with its roots in the air.

The retreating figure of a sumo wrestler who has been defeated in a match.

A woman, who is angry with her husband about some trifling matter, leaves home and goes somewhere to hide. She is certain that he will rush about looking for her; but he does nothing of the kind and shows the most infuriating indifference. Since she cannot stay away for ever, she swallows her pride and returns.

I. Morris, trans., *The Pillow Book of Sei Shōnagon* (New York: Columbia University Press, 1967), Vol. 1, pp. 49, 216–217, 29–30, 1, 132, respectively.

The Hōryūji Temple, built by Prince Shōtoku in 607, contains the oldest wooden buildings in the world. They are the best surviving examples of Chinese Buddhist architecture. Note the groups of visiting students in the foreground. [Reuters/Bettmann]

Nara and Heian Buddhism

The Six Sects of the Nara period each represented a separate philosophical doctrine within Mahayana Buddhism. Their monks trained as religious specialists in monastic communities set apart from the larger society. They studied, read sutras, copied texts, meditated, and joined in rituals. The typical monastery was a self-contained community with a Golden Hall for worship, a pagoda that housed a relic or sutra, a belfry that rang the hours of the monastic regimen, a lecture hall, a refectory, and dormitories with monks' cells.

As in China, monasteries and temples were involved with the state. Tax revenues were assigned for their support. Monks prayed for rain in time of drought. In 741, temples were established in every province to protect the state by reading sutras. Monks prayed for the health of the emperor. The Temple of the Healing Buddha (Yakushiji) was built by an emperor when his consort fell ill. In China, in order to protect tax revenues and the family, laws were enacted to limit the number of monks and nuns. In Nara Japan, where Buddhism spread only slowly outside the capital area, the same laws took on a prescriptive force. The figure that had been a limit in China became a goal in Japan. Thus the involvement of the state was the same as in China, but its role was far more supportive.

Japan in the seventh and eighth centuries was also much less culturally developed than China. The Japanese came to Buddhism not from the philosophical perspectives of Confucianism or Taoism but from the magic and mystery of Shinto. The appeal of Buddhism to the early Japanese was, consequently, in its colorful and elaborate rituals; in the gods, demons, and angels of the Mahayana pantheon; and, above all, in the beauty of Buddhist art. The philosophy took longer to establish itself. The speed with which the Japanese mastered the construction of temples with elaborate wooden brackets and gracefully arching tile roofs, as well as the loveliness of Nara Buddhist sculpture, wall paintings, and lacquer temple altars, was no less an achievement than their establishment of a political system based on the T'ang codes.

Japan's cultural identity was also different. In China, Buddhism was always viewed as Indian and alien. Its earliest Buddha statues, like those of northwestern India, looked Greek. That Buddhism was part of a non-Chinese culture was one factor leading to the Chinese persecution of Buddhists during the ninth century. In contrast, Japan's cultural identity or cultural self-consciousness took shape only during the Nara and early Heian periods. One element in that identity was the imperial cult derived from Shinto. But as a religion, Shinto was no match for Buddhism. The Japanese were aware that Buddhism was foreign, but it was no more so than Confucianism and all the rest of the T'ang culture that had helped shape the major portion of the Japanese identity, so there was no particular bias against it. Consequently, Buddhism entered deeply into Japanese culture and retained its vitality longer. It was not until the seventeenth or eighteenth centuries that Japanese elites became so Confucian as to be anti-Buddhist.

In 794, the court moved to Heian. Buddhist temples soon became as entrenched in the new capital as they had been in Nara. The two great new Buddhist sects of the Heian era were Tendai and Shingon.

Saichō (767–822) had founded a temple on Mount Hiei to the northwest of Kyoto in 785. He went to China as a student monk in 804 and returned the following year with the teachings of the Tendai sect (*T'ien T'ai* in Chinese). He spread in Japan the doctrine that salvation was not solely for monastic specialists but could be attained by all who led a life of contemplation and moral purity. He was a religious reformer who instituted strict monastic rules and a twelve-year training curriculum for novice monks at his mountain monastery. Over the next few centuries, the sect grew until thousands of temples had been built on Mount Hiei, and it remained a center of Japanese Buddhism until it was destroyed in the wars of the sixteenth century. Many later Japanese sects emerged from within the Tendai fold, stressing one or another doctrine of its syncretic teachings.

The Shingon sect was begun by Kūkai (774–835). He studied Confucianism, Taoism, and Buddhism at the court university. Deciding that Buddhism was superior, he became a monk at the age of eighteen. In 804, he went to China with Saichō. He returned two years later bearing the Shingon doctrines and founded a monastery on Mount Koya to the south of the Nara plain and far from the new capital. Kūkai was an extraordinary figure. He was a bridge builder, a poet, an artist, and one of the three great calligraphers of his age. He is sometimes credited with inventing the *kana* syllabary and with introducing tea into Japan. Shingon doctrines center on an eternal and cosmic Buddha, of whom all other Buddhas are manifestations. *Shingon* means "true word" or "mantra," a verbal formula with mystical powers. It is sometimes called *esoteric Buddhism* because it had secret teachings that were passed from master to disciple. In China, Shingon had died out as a sect in the persecutions of the mid-ninth century, but it was tremendously successful in Japan. Its doctrines even spread to the Tendai center on Mount Hiei. Part of the appeal was in its air of mystery and its complex rituals involving signs, the manipulation of religious objects, and mandalas—maps of the cosmic Buddhist universe.

During the later Heian period, Buddhism began to be assimilated. At the village level, the folk religion of Shinto took in many Buddhist elements. In the high culture of the capital, Shinto was almost absorbed by Buddhism. Shinto deities came to be seen as the local manifestations of universal Buddhas. The cosmic or "Great Sun Buddha" of the Shingon sect, for example, was easily identified with the sun goddess. Often, great Buddhist temples had smaller Shinto shrines on their grounds. The job of the Buddha was to watch over Japan, whereas the shrine deity had the lesser task of guarding the temple itself. Not until the mid-nineteenth century was Shinto disentangled from Buddhism, and then for political ends.

Japan's Early Feudal Age

The year 1185, or 1160 if we include Taira rule in Kyoto, marked another major turning point in Japanese history. It began the shift from centuries of rule by a civil aristocracy to centuries of rule by one that was military. It saw the formation of the *bakufu* (tent government), a completely non-Chinese type of government. It saw the emergence of the *shōgun* as the de facto ruler of Japan, although in theory he was a military official of the emperor. It marked the beginning of new cultural forms and initiated changes in family and social organization.

Rise of Minamoto Yoritomo

The seizure of Kyoto by Taira Kiyomori's military band in 1160 fell far short of being a national military hegemony, for other bands still flourished elsewhere in Japan. In the decades after Kiyomori's victory, the Taira embraced the elegant life-style of the Kyoto court while ties to their base area along the Inland Sea weakened. They assumed that their tutelage over the court would be as enduring as had been that of the Fujiwara. In the meantime, the Minamoto were rebuilding their strength in eastern Japan. In 1180, Minamoto Yoritomo responded to a call to arms by a disaffected prince, seized control of eastern Japan (the rich Kanto plain), and began the war that ended in 1185 with the downfall of the Taira.

Yoritomo's victory in 1185 was national, for his

armies had ranged over most of Japan. After his victory, warriors from every area vied to become his vassals. Wary of the blandishments of Kyoto that had weakened the Taira forces, Yoritomo set up his headquarters at Kamakura. It was thirty miles south of present-day Tokyo, at the edge of his base of power in eastern Japan (see Map 11-2). He called his govern-

MAP 11-2 MEDIEVAL JAPAN AND THE MONGOL INVASIONS *Kamakura and Kyoto were the two centers of power during the Namakura period, 1185–1333. The* bakufu *was in one and the court in the other. After 1336 the Ashikaga* bakufu *was established in Kyoto, absorbing the powers of the court.*

GOVERNMENT BY MILITARY HOUSES	
1160–1180	Taira rule in Kyoto
1185–1333	Kamakura *bakufu*
1185	Founded by Minamoto Yoritomo
1219	Usurped by Hōjō
1221	Armed uprising by Kyoto court
1232	Formation of Jōei Legal Code
1274 and 1281	Invasion by Mongols
1336–1467	Ashikaga *bakufu*
1336	Begun by Ashikaga Takauji
1392	End of Southern Court
1467	Start of warring states

ment the *bakufu* in contrast to the civil government in Kyoto. Like the house government of the Fujiwara or the "cloister government" of the retired emperors, the offices he established were few and practical: one to deal with his samurai retainers, one to administer and execute his policies, and one to hear legal suits. Each office was staffed by vassals. The decisions of these offices, built up into a body of customary law, were codified in 1232 as the Jōei Code. Yoritomo also appointed military governors in each province and military stewards on the former estates of the Taira and others who had fought against him. These appointments carried the right to some of the income from the land. The rest of the income, as earlier, went to Kyoto as taxes or as revenues to the noble owners of the estates.

The Question of Feudalism

Scholars often contend that Yoritomo's rule marks the start of feudalism in Japan. Feudalism may be defined in terms of three criteria: lord–vassal relationships, fiefs given in return for military service, and a warrior ethic. Do these apply to Kamakura Japan?

Certainly, the mounted warriors who made up the armies of Yoritomo were predominantly his vassals, not his kin. The Minamoto and Taira houses had originally been extended families, very much like the Fujiwara or the earlier Yamato nobility. Yoritomo's brothers were among his generals. But after he came to power, he favored his vassals over his kin, and the lateral blood ties gave way to the vertical and political

lord–vassal bond. On the question of fiefs, the answer is ambiguous. Kamakura vassals received rights to income from land in exchange for military service. But the income was usually a slice of the surplus from the estates of Kyoto nonmilitary aristocrats. Fiefs, as such, did not appear until the late fifteenth century.

However, there is no ambiguity regarding the warrior ethic, which had been developing among regional military bands for several centuries before 1185. The samurai prized martial qualities such as bravery, cunning, physical strength, and endurance. They gave their swords names. Their sports were hunting, hawking, and archery—loosing their arrows at the target while riding at full tilt. If the military tales of the period are to be believed, their combat was often individual, and before engaging in battle warriors would call out their pedigrees. That is to say, warriors thought of themselves as a military aristocracy that practiced "the way of the bow and arrow," "the way of the bow and horse," "the way of the warriors," and so on. In the Buddhism-tinged *Tale of Heike,* a military romance recounting the struggle between the Taira and the Minamoto, a Taira general asks a vassal from eastern Japan

"Sanemori, in the eight eastern provinces are there many men who are as mighty archers as you are?"

"Do you then consider me a mighty archer?" asked Sanemori with a scornful smile. "I can only draw an arrow thirteen handbreadths long. In the eastern provinces there are any number of warriors who can do so. There is one famed archer who never draws a shaft less than fifteen handbreadths long. So mighty is his bow that four or five ordinary men must pull together to bend it. When he shoots, his arrow can easily pierce two or three suits of armor at once. Even a warrior from a small estate has at least five hundred soldiers. They are bold horsemen who never fall, nor do they let their horses stumble on the roughest road. When they fight, they do not care if even their parents or children are killed; they ride on over their bodies and continue the battle.

"The warriors of the western province are quite different. If their parents are killed, they retire from the battle and perform Buddhist rites to console the souls of the dead. Only after the mourning is over will they fight again. If their children are slain, their grief is so deep that they cease fighting altogether. When their rations have given out, they plant rice in the fields and go out to fight only after reaping it. They dislike the heat of summer. They grumble at the severe cold of winter. This is not the way of the soldiers of the eastern provinces."[5]

[5] H. Kitagawa and B. Tsuchida, trans., *The Tale of Heike* (Tokyo: Tokyo University Press, 1975), p. 330.

The Taira soldiers, according to the story, "heard his words and trembled."

The Kamakura military band thus pretty well fits our definition of feudalism. Nonetheless, qualifications are in order, as warrior bands were only one part of the whole society. One qualification is that Kamakura Japan still had two political centers. The *bakufu* had military authority, but the Kyoto court continued the late Heian pattern of civil rule. It appointed civil governors; it received tax revenues; and it controlled the region about Kyoto. Noble families, retired emperors, and the great Buddhist temples—in control of vast estates—also contributed to Kyoto's ongoing power. It also remained the fount of rank and honors. After his victory in 1185, Yoritomo asked the emperor for the title of "barbarian-quelling generalissimo" *(Sei i tai shōgun,* conventionally shortened to *shōgun).* He was refused, and only after the retired emperor died in 1192 did Yoritomo get the title to match his power. Even then, the award of the title was justified by the fact that Yoritomo was a Minamoto offshoot of the imperial line.

The small size of Yoritomo's vassal band is an even more telling argument against viewing Japan as fully feudal at this time. Numbering about two thousand before 1221 and three thousand thereafter, most of the band were concentrated in eastern Japan. But even if as many as half were distributed about the rest of the country as military governors and stewards, there would have been only one hundred in a region the size of Massachusetts, because Japan in 1180 was about fifteen times larger than that state. Given the difficulties of transportation and communications, how could so few control such a large area? The answer is that they did not have to.

The local social order of the late Heian era continued into the Kamakura period. Governors, district magistrates, and local notables—including many warriors who were not members of Yoritomo's band—were in place and continued to function more or less as they had earlier. To gain an influence on the local scene, the newly appointed Kamakura vassals had to win the cooperation of these local figures. In short, even if the Kamakura vassals themselves could be called feudal, they were no more than a thin skim on the surface of a society constructed according to older principles.

Kamakura Rule After Yoritomo

As soon as Yoritomo died in 1199, his widow and her Hōjō kinsmen moved to usurp the power of the Minamoto house. The widow, having taken holy orders after her husband's death, was known as the Nun Shōgun. One of her sons was pushed aside. The other became shōgun but was murdered in 1219. After that, the Hōjō ruled as regents for a puppet shōgun, just as the Fujiwara had been regents for figurehead emperors. The Kyoto court tried to take advantage of the usurpation to lead an armed uprising against Kamakura in 1221, but the rebellion was quickly suppressed. New military stewards were then placed on the lands of those who had joined in the uprising. Any society based on personal bonds faces the problem of how to transfer loyalty from one generation to another. That the Kamakura vassals fought for the Hōjō in 1221, despite the Hōjō usurpation of the Minamoto rule, suggests that loyalty had become institutional. They were loyal to the *bakufu,* which guaranteed their income from land. Their personal loyalty to the Minamoto had ended with the death of Yoritomo.

In 1266, Kublai Khan (see Chapter 10) sent envoys demanding that Japan submit to his rule. He had subjugated Korea in 1258, and his army looked outward across the Tsushima Straits. The Kyoto court was terrified, but the Hōjō at Kamakura refused. The first Mongol invasion fleet arrived with thirty thousand troops in 1274, but was destroyed by a typhoon. The Mongols again sent envoys. This time, they were beheaded. A second invasion force arrived in 1281, two years after Kublai had completed his conquest of southern China. Carrying one hundred forty thousand troops, it was an amphibious operation on a scale new to world history. With gunpowder bombs and phalanxes of archers protected by a forward wall of soldiers carrying overlapping shields, the Mongol forces were formidable.

The Japanese tactics of fierce individual combat were not appropriate to their foe. But a wall of stone had been erected along the curved shoreline of Hakata Bay in northwestern Kyushu, and the Mongols were held off for two months until again *kamikaze,* or "divine winds," sank a portion of their fleet and forced the rest to withdraw. Preparations for a third expedition ended with Kublai's death in 1294.

The burden of repelling the Mongols fell on Kamakura's vassals in Kyushu. Non-Kamakura warriors of Kyushu also were mobilized to fight under the command of military governors. But as no land was taken, unlike in 1221, there were few rewards for those who had fought, and dissatisfaction was rife. Even temples and shrines demanded rewards, claiming that their prayers had brought about the divine winds.

Mongol invaders battling with an intrepid samurai horseman. Note the bomb bursting in the air at the upper right of this late thirteenth-century Japanese scroll painting. [Tokyo National Museum]

Women in Warrior Society

The Nun Shōgun was one of a long line of important women in Japan. Although historians no longer speak of an early matriarchal age, there is no denying that the central figure of Japanese mythology was the sun goddess, who ruled the Plain of High Heaven. In the late Yayoi age, the shaman ruler Pimiko was probably not an exceptional figure; she was followed by the empresses of the Yamato and Nara courts, and they in turn by the great women writers of the Heian period. During the era of the Kamakura *bakufu,* there was only one Nun Shōgun, but the daughters of warrior families, as well as the sons, often trained in archery and other military arts. Women also occasionally inherited the position of military steward. As long as society was stable, women fared relatively well. But as fighting became more common in the fourteenth century, their position began to decline, and as warfare became endemic in the fifteenth, their status plummeted. To protect the integrity of the military fief—the warrior's reward for serving his lord in battle and the lord's guarantee that his warriors would continue their service—multigeniture, in which daughters as well as sons inherited property, gave way from this time to unigeniture, inheritance by the most able son.

The Ashikaga Era

At times, formal political institutions seem rocklike in their stability, and history unfolds within the framework that they provide. Then, almost as if a kaleidoscope had been shaken, the old institutions collapse and are swept away. In their place appear new institutions and new patterns of personal relations that, often enough, had begun to take shape within the confines of the old. It is not easy to explain the timing of such upheavals, but they are easy to recognize. One occurred in Japan between 1331 and 1336.

Various tensions had developed within late Kamakura society. The patrimony of a warrior was divided among his children. Over several generations, vassals became poorer, often falling into debt. High-ranking vassals of Kamakura were dissatisfied with the Hōjō monopolization of key *bakufu* posts. In the meantime, the ties of vassals to Kamakura were weakening, while the ties to other warriors within their region were growing stronger. New regional bands were ready to emerge. The precipitating event was a revolt in 1331 by an emperor who thought emperors should actually rule. Kamakura sent Ashikaga Takauji (1305–1358), the head of a branch family of the Minamoto line, to put down the revolt. Instead, he joined it, giving a clear signal to other regional lords, who threw off Kamakura's control and destroyed the Hōjō *bakufu* in Kamakura.

What emerged from the dust and confusion of the period from 1331 to 1336 was a regional multistate system centering on Kyoto. Each region was based on a warrior band about the size of the band that had brought Yorimoto to power a century-and-a-half earlier. In the central Kyoto region, Ashikaga Takauji established his *bakufu.* Its offices were simple and functional: a samurai office for police and military matters, an administrative office for financial matters, a documents office for land records, and a judicial board to settle disputes. The offices were staffed by Takauji's vassals, with the most trusted vassals holding the highest posts. They were lords (now called *daimyo*) in their own right who also usually held appointments as military governors in the provinces surrounding Kyoto. The *bakufu* also appointed vassals to watch over its interests in the far north, in eastern Japan, and in Kyushu.

Government in the outlying regions was more diverse. Some lords held several provinces, some only one. Some had integrated most of the warriors in their areas into their bands. Others had several unassimilated military bands in their territories, forcing them to rely more on the authority of Kyoto. Formally, all regional lords or *daimyo* were the vassals of the shōgun. But the relationship was often nominal. Sometimes the regional lords lived on their lands; sometimes they lived in Kyoto.

The relationship between the Kyoto *bakufu* and the regional lords fluctuated during the period from 1336 to 1467. At times, able lords made their regions into virtually independent states. At other times, the Kyoto *bakufu* became stronger. The third shōgun, for example, tightened his grip on the Kyoto court. He even relinquished the military post of shōgun—giving it to his son in 1394—in order to take the highest civil post of grand minister of state. He improved relations with the great Buddhist temples and Shinto shrines and established ties with Ming China. Most significant were his military campaigns, which dented the autonomy of regional lords outside of the inner Kyoto circle.

But the institution of vassalage in Japan's early feudal society contained a contradiction that even the third shōgun could not overcome. He had to rely on his vassals. To strengthen them for his campaigns, he gave them the authority to levy taxes; to unify in their own hands all judicial, administrative, and military authority in their regions; and to take on unaffiliated warriors as their direct vassals. But in doing so, he left problems for his successors. As ties of personal loyalty wore thin, new local warrior bands began to form in the interstices of the Ashikaga regional states.

Agriculture, Commerce, and Medieval Guilds

Population figures for medieval Japan are rough estimates at best, but recent scholarship suggests six mil-
lion for the year 1200 and twelve million for 1600. Much of the increase occurred during the Kamakura and Ashikaga periods, when the country was fairly peaceful. The increase was brought about by land reclamation and improvements in agricultural technology: Iron-edged tools became available to all. New strains of rice were developed. Irrigation and diking improved. Double cropping began with vegetables planted during the fall and winter in dry fields, which were flooded and planted in rice during the spring and summer.

In the Nara and early Heian periods, the economy was almost exclusively agricultural. Japan had no money, no commerce, and no cities—apart from Nara, which developed into a temple town living on assigned revenues, and Kyoto, where taxes were consumed. Following the example of China, the government had established a mint, but little money actually circulated. Taxes were paid in grain and labor. Commercial transactions were largely barter, with silk or grain as the medium of exchange. Artisans produced for the noble households or temples to which they were attached. Peasants were economically self-sufficient.

From the late Heian period, partly as a side effect of fixed tax quotas, more of the growing agricultural surplus stayed in local hands. This trend accelerated during the Kamakura and Ashikaga periods, when there was a transfer of income from the court aristocrats to the warrior class. As this transfer occurred, artisans detached themselves from noble households and began to produce for the market. Military equipment was an early staple of commerce, but gradually *sake*, lumber, paper, vegetable oils, salt, and products of the sea also became commercialized. A demand for copper coins appeared, and as they were no longer minted in Japan, they were imported in increasingly huge quantities from China.

During the Kamakura period, independent merchants handling the products of artisans appeared as well. Some trade networks spread over all Japan. More often, artisan and merchant guilds, not unlike those of medieval Europe, paid a fee in exchange for monopoly rights in a given area. Early Kyoto guilds paid fees to powerful nobles or temples, and later to the Ashikaga *bakufu*. In outlying areas, guild privileges were obtained from the regional feudal lords. From the Kamakura period onward, markets were held periodically in many parts of Japan, by a river or at a crossroads. Some place names in Japan today reveal such an origin. Yokkaichi, today an industrial city, means "fourth-day market." It began as a place where markets were held on the fourth, fourteenth, and twenty-fourth days of each month. During the fourteenth and fifteenth centuries, such markets were held with increasing frequency until, eventually, permanent towns were established.

Buddhism and Medieval Culture

The Nara and Heian periods are often referred to as Japan's classical age. The period that followed—say, from 1200 to 1600—is often called medieval. It was medieval in the root sense of the word in that it lay between the other two major spans of premodern Japanese history. It was also medieval in that it shared some characteristics that we label medieval in Europe and China. However, there is an important difference. Medieval Japan was a direct outgrowth of classical Japan; one can even say that there was some overlap during the early Kamakura. In contrast, Europe was torn by barbarian invasions, and a millennium separated the classical culture of Rome and high medieval culture. Even to have a Charlemagne, Europe had to wait for half a millennium. In China, too, the era of political disunity and barbarian invasions lasted four hundred years, and it was during these years that its medieval Buddhist culture blossomed.

The results of the historical continuity in Japan are visible in every branch of its culture. The earlier poetic tradition continued with great vigor. In 1205, the compilation of the *New Collection from Ancient and Modern Times (Shinkokinshū)* was ordered by the same emperor who began the 1221 rebellion against Kamakura. The flat *Yamato-e* style of painting that had reached a peak in the *Genji Scrolls* continued into the medieval era with scrolls on historical and religious themes or fairy-tale adventures. Artisanal production continued without a break. The same techniques of lacquerwork with inlaid mother-of-pearl that had been employed, say, to make a cosmetic box for a Heian court lady were now applied to produce saddles for Kamakura warriors. In short, just as Heian estates continued on into the Kamakura era, and just as the authority of the court continued, so did Heian culture extend into medieval Japan.

Nonetheless, medieval Japanese culture had some distinctly new characteristics. First, as the leadership of the society shifted from court aristocrats to military aristocrats, new forms of literature appeared. The medieval military tales were as different from the *Tale of Genji* as the armor of the mounted warrior was from the no less colorful silken robes of the court nobility. Second, a new wave of culture entered from China. If the Nara and Heian had been shaped by T'ang culture, medieval Japan—although not its institutions—was shaped by Sung culture. This link is immediately apparent in the ink paintings of medieval Japan. Third, and most important, the medieval centuries were Japan's age of Buddhist faith. A religious revolution occurred during the Kamakura period and deepened during the Ashikaga. It fundamentally influenced the arts of Japan.

Japanese Pietism: Pure Land and Nichiren Buddhism

Among the doctrines of the Heian Tendai sect was the belief that the true teachings of the historical Buddha had been lost and that salvation could be had only by calling on the name of Amida, the Buddha who ruled over the Western Paradise (or Pure Land). During the tenth and eleventh centuries, itinerant preachers

The mid-Heian monk Kūya (903–972) preached Pure Land doctrines in Kyoto and throughout Japan. Little Buddhas emerge from his mouth. [Sekai Bunka photo]

Nobles in ox-drawn carriages and commoners on foot attend a sermon by the Pure Land monk Ippen (1239–1289). [Tokyo National Museum]

began to spread Pure Land doctrines and practices beyond the narrow circles of Kyoto. Kūya (903–972), the "saint of the marketplace," for example, preached not only in Kyoto and throughout the provinces, but even to the aboriginal Ainu in northernmost Japan. The doctrine that the world had fallen on evil times and that only faith would suffice was given credence by earthquakes, epidemics, fires, and banditry in the capital, as well as wars throughout the land. The deepening Buddhist coloration of the age can be read in the opening lines of the thirteenth-century *Tale of Heiki,* written just two centuries after the *Tale of Genji* and the *Pillow Book:*

The sound of the bell of Jetavana echoes the impermanence of all things. The hue of the flowers of the teaktree declares that they who flourish must be brought low. Yea, the proud ones are but for a moment, like an evening dream in springtime. The mighty are destroyed at the last, they are but as the dust before the wind.[6]

In the early Kamakura era, two figures stand out as religious geniuses who experienced the truth of Pure Land Buddhism within themselves. Hōnen (1133–1212) was perhaps the first to say that the invocation of the name of Amida alone was enough for salvation and that only faith rather than works or rituals counted. These claims brought Hōnen into conflict with the older Buddhist establishment and marked the emergence of Pure Land as a separate sect. Hōnen was followed by Shinran (1173–1262), who taught that even a single invocation in praise of Amida, if done with perfect faith, was sufficient for salvation. But perfect faith was not the result of human effort: It was a gift from Amida. Shinran taught that pride was an obstacle to purity of heart. One of his most famous sayings is "If even a good man can be reborn in the Pure Land, how much more so a wicked man."[7] Shinran is saying that the evil man is less inclined to assume that he is the source of his own salvation and therefore more inclined to place his complete trust in Amida.

Shinran's emphasis on faith alone led him to break many of the monastic rules of earlier Buddhism: He

[6]A. L. Sadler, trans., *The Tenfoot Square Hut and Tales of the Heike* (Rutland, VT, and Tokyo: Charles E. Tuttle, 1972), p. 22.

[7]Tsunoda, deBary, and Keene, p. 217.

ate meat; he married a nun, and thereafter the Pure Land sect had a married clergy; and he taught that all occupations were equally "heavenly" if performed with a pure heart. Exiled from Kyoto, he traveled about Japan establishing "True Pure Land" congregations. (When the Jesuits arrived in Japan in the sixteenth century, they called this sect "the devil's Christianity.")

As a result of a line of distinguished teachers after Shinran, its doctrinal simplicity, and its reliance on the practice of piety, Pure Land Buddhism became the dominant form of Buddhism in Japan and remains so today. It was also the only sect in medieval Japan—apart from the Tendai sect on Mount Hiei— to develop political and military power. As a religion of faith, it developed a strong church as a protection for the saved while they were still in this world. As peasants became militarized during the fifteenth century, some Pure Land village congregations created self-defense forces. At times, they rebelled against feudal lords. In one instance, Pure Land armies ruled the province of Kaga for over a century. These congregations were smashed during the late sixteenth century, and the sect was depoliticized.

A second devotional sect was founded by Nichiren (1222–1282), who believed that the Lotus Sutra perfectly embodied the teachings of the Buddha. He instructed his adherents to chant, over and over, "Praise to the Lotus Sutra of the Wondrous Law," usually to the accompaniment of rapid drumbeats. Like the repetition of "Praise to the Amida Buddha" in the Pure Land sect or comparable verbal formulas in other religions around the world, the chanting optimally induced a state of religious rapture. The concern with an internal spiritual transformation was common to both the devotional and the meditative sects of Buddhism. Nichiren was remarkable for a Buddhist in being both intolerant and nationalistic.

He blamed the ills of his age on rival sects and asserted that only his sect could protect Japan. He predicted the Mongol invasions, and his sect claimed credit for the "divine winds" that sank the Mongol fleets. Even his adopted Buddhist name, the Sun Lotus, combined the term for the rising sun of Japan with that of the flower that had become the symbol of Buddhism.

Zen Buddhism

Meditation had long been a part of Japanese monastic practice. Zen meditation and doctrines were introduced by monks returning from study in Sung China. Eisai (1141–1215) transposed to Japan the Rinzai sect in 1191 and Dōgen (1200–1253) the Sōtō sect in 1227. Eisai's sect was patronized by the Hōjō rulers in Kamakura and the Ashikaga in Kyoto. Dōgen established his sect on Japan's western coast, far from centers of political power.

Zen in Japan was a religion of paradox. Its monks were learned, yet it stressed a return to ignorance, to the uncluttered "original mind," attained in a flash of intuitive understanding. Zen was punctiliously traditional, the most Chinese of Japanese medieval sects. The authority of the Zen master over his pupil-monks was absolute. Yet Zen was also iconoclastic. Its sages were depicted in paintings as tearing up sutras to make the point that it is religious experience and not words that count. Within a rigidly structured monastic regimen, a vital give-and-take occurred as monks tested their understanding, gained through long hours of meditation, in encounters with their master. Buddhism stressed compassion for all sentient beings, yet in Japan, the Zen sect included many samurai whose duty it was to fight and kill. A few military leaders encouraged the practice of Zen among their retainers in the hope of instilling a single-minded attention to duty; a handful of Hōjō and Ashikaga rulers

An austere fifteenth-century Zen garden of rock and raked gravel-like mountains rising from the "ocean waves" formed from gravel. This garden is part of the Ryōanji temple in northwest Kyoto along the mountains' fringe. [Japan National Tourist Office]

PORTFOLIO III

Buddhism

Buddhism, along with Jainism and Upanishadic Hinduism, arose out of the spiritual ferment of Vedic India during the centuries after 700 B.C. Buddhism shares a kinship with these other religions much like the relationship found further west between Judaism, Christianity, and Islam.

Siddhartha Gautama was born about 566 B.C., a prince in a petty kingdom near what is now the border of India and Nepal. He was reared amid luxury and comforts, married at sixteen, and had a child. According to legend, when at age twenty-nine he saw an old man, a sick man, and a corpse, he suddenly realized that all humans would suffer the same fate. Gautama renounced his wealth and family and entered the life of a wandering ascetic. He visited famous teachers, practiced extremes of ascetic self-deprivation, and finally discovered the "middle path." At the age of thirty-five, he attained *nirvana,* becoming the *Buddha,* or the "enlightened one." In early Buddhism all of the cosmic drama of religious self-transformation was compressed into the human figure of Gautama meditating under the Bodhi tree. The rest of his eighty years the Buddha spent teaching others the truths he had learned. Even during his lifetime, communities of Buddhist monks and nuns (the *sangha*) developed, with a tradition of support for the monks by lay adherents.

Basic to the Buddha's understanding of the human condition were the "four noble truths": (1) that all life is suffering—an endless karmic chain of births and rebirths; (2) that the cause of the suffering is desire—it is desire that binds humans to the wheel of *karma;* (3) that escape from the suffering and endless rebirths can come only by the cessation of desire and the attainment of nirvana; and (4) that the path to nirvana is eightfold. The eightfold path requires right views, thought, speech, actions, living, efforts, mindfulness, and meditation.

Ethical living combined with long periods of meditation may lead to an inner spiritual awakening or realization. Progress in the inner spiritual life may lead, eventually, to enlightenment, to liberation or release from the trammels of karmic causation. Because the goal of Buddhism is for all humans to become buddhas, some have called Buddhism the most otherworldly of the great world religions. Even for the historical Buddha the way was not easy and one lifetime was not enough. (While meditating before achieving enlightenment, he recalled events from his former lives. The stories of these earlier lives are told in the Jataka tales.) For others, even with the Buddha's teachings in hand, the way was hard. Monks and nuns might meditate for years and attain an inner spiritual awakening, but only a few would gain the complete release required for Buddhahood. Most could hope only for a rebirth in a higher spiritual state, to begin again closer, as it were, to the goal. For lay people the stress was on ethical living in human society. The Buddha condemned the caste system that flourished in the India of his day. He held that poverty was a cause of immorality, and that it was futile to attempt to suppress crime with punishments. He identified with all humanity, saying "He who attends on the sick attends on me."

Buddhism spread rapidly along the Ganges River and through northern India. In the time of King Ashoka (272–232 B.C.) of the Mauryas, it spread to southern India and Ceylon. This was its great missionary age. Eventually, however, Buddhism in India was re-Hinduized: It developed schools of metaphysics and a pantheon of gods and cosmic Buddhas. It developed devotional sects. Buddhism's meditative techniques helped shape Hindu yogic exercises. As these changes occurred, Buddhism in India lost its character as a reform movement, its *raison d'être,* and was reabsorbed into Hinduism between A.D. 500 and 1500.

India apart, two major currents of Buddhism spread out over Asia. One known as the "Way of the Elders" *(Theravada)* swept through Southeast Asia. Its teachings were close to early Indian Buddhism, and it was influenced as well by other strands of Indian culture. Scenes from the great Indian epic, the *Mahabharata,* adorn the inner walls of Thai temples. Buddhism remains today the predominant religion in Burma, Thailand, Cambodia, Laos, and Vietnam, although it must contend with more recent secular ideologies. In Thailand alone it remains the state religion: Thai kings rule as Buddhist monarchs, Thai boys spend short periods as Buddhist monks, and temples *(wats)* continue as centers of village life. Before the spread of Islam, Buddhism also flourished in what is today Malaysia and Indonesia. The temple of Borobudur in central Java remains one of the great monuments of world Buddhism; it represents in stone the Buddhist spiritual universe.

The second major current, known to its adherents as the "Greater Vehicle" *(Mahayana)* spread through northwestern India to Afghanistan and Central Asia, and then to China, Korea, and Japan. This current carried with it many doctrines. One key doctrine contained the ideal of the *bodhisattva,* a being who had gone all the way to the final goal of nirvana, but held off in order to help others attain salvation. One such bodhisattva, who became elevated to the status of a cosmic Buddha ruling over the Western Paradise (or Pure Land), was Amitabha (or Amida). Devotion to this Buddha and to others figured prominently in East Asian Buddhism.

Another doctrine, that of the Ch'an (in China) or Zen (in Japan) sect, stressed meditation and perhaps was closer to the teachings of the historical Buddha. Buddhism in Afghanistan and Central Asia eventually gave way to Islam. In China, Buddhism was weakened by the great persecution of 845. In all of East Asia there were tensions between Buddhism and the more worldly teachings of Confucius. During the modern century, the struggle has been between religion and modern secular doctrines, as it has in other parts of the world.

III-1   Siddhartha Gautama at Age Twenty-nine. *Gautama, having renounced all worldly attachments, cuts his hair in the forest before setting off on his spiritual quest. Scenes from the life of the Buddha are as common in Buddhist art as those of Jesus in Christian art. This is an early nineteenth-century Bangkok temple mural. [Luca Invernizzi Tettoni/Art Resource]*

III-2   Fasting Buddha. *Before Gautama arrived at the "middle path," he practiced severe austerities for six years. According to a description in an ancient text: "My limbs became like some withered creepers with knotted joints;" my buttocks like a buffalo's hoof . . . my ribs like rafters of a dilapidated shed; the pupils of my eyes appeared sunk deep in their sockets as water appears shining at the bottom of a deep well. . . ." This (fourth-to-second-century-*B.C.*) statue of the Buddha from Gandhara (in present-day Pakistan) reflects the Greek influence on early Buddhist sculpture. [Borromeo, EPA/Art Resource]*

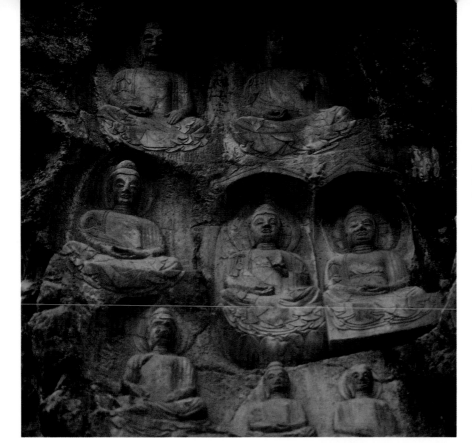

III-3   Stone Sculpture from the Valley of the Thousand Buddhas *(Sung dynasty (960–1279)). The position of the Buddha's hands in each niche signifies an aspect of his activities, including, for example, meditation and preaching. [Bildarchiv Preussischer Kulturbesitz]*

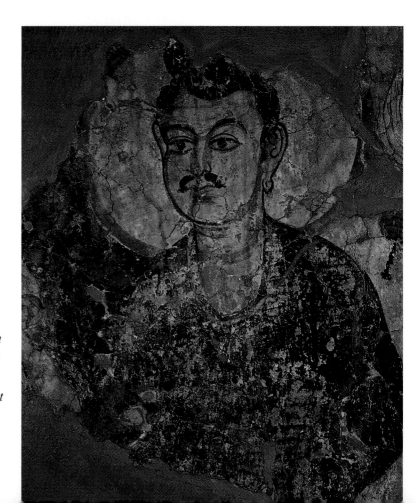

III-4   Buddha with Aureole. *This Buddhist sanctuary mural at Miran on the Silk Road through Central Asia shows both Indian and Greek influences. [Borromeo, EPA/Art Resource]*

III-5   Buddha on a Throne. *This fifth-to-sixth-century painting (left) is on the walls of a cave in Ajanta, India. The Buddha, seated on a lotus throne, teaches his disciples. The lotus, like the Buddha, emerges from the floating world of mud and water but is not defiled by it.* [Borromeo, EPA/Art Resource]

III-6   Thai Buddha in Bronze. *This walking Buddha (right) is from the fourteenth century. Buddhism remains the predominant religion in present-day Thailand.* [Luca Invernizzi Tettoni/Art Resource]

III-7 Barbarian Royalty Worshiping the Buddha. *This Sung or Yuan dynasty Chinese painting depicts the peoples known to China in the thirteenth century. That all came from afar to worship suggests the universality of the Buddha's teachings. [Cleveland Museum of Art, Gift of Mr. and Mrs. Severance A. Millikin, 57.358]*

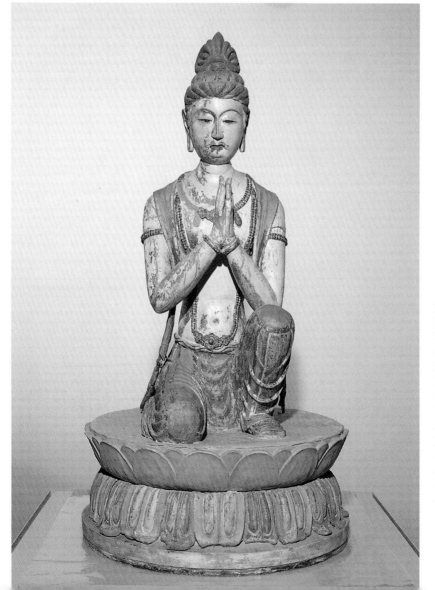

III-8 *Bodhisattva* Kneeling in Attitude of Worship. *This polychrome bodhisattva is from a cave temple at Tunhuang in western China. An example of T'ang dynasty sculpture, it expresses Buddhist piety. [Arthur M. Sackler Museum, Harvard University, Cambridge, Massachusetts, First Fogg China Expedition, 1923]*

III-9   Zen Patriarch.
*The Indian Bodhidharma,
the first patriarch of the
Zen sect, as depicted by
Itō Jakuchū (1716–1800).
Bodhidharma's face re-
flects the fierce insight
gained by years of medi-
tation. The strong brush-
strokes in his robe, how-
ever, are the focus of the
painting.* [Reproduced by
Courtesy of the Trustees
of the British Museum]

III-10   Zen Monks in Japan. *These Zen monks in a meditation hall are in training to become priests. Many people in postwar Japan have tried Zen meditation; few have been able to integrate it with the demands of modern life. [Elliott Erwitt/Magnum]*

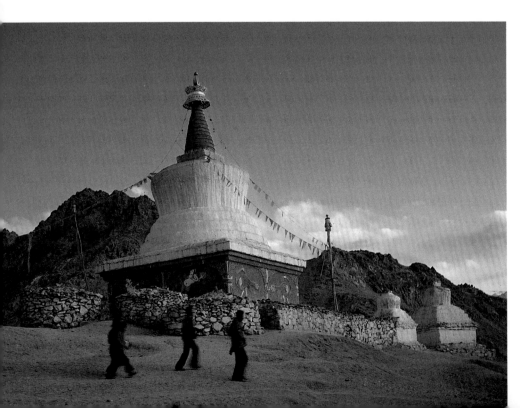

III-11   A Buddhist Stupa in Ladakh. *A stupa contains a relic of the Buddha or a sutra containing his teachings. In Ladakh, Nepal, and Tibet, the stupa takes this form. In China, Korea, and Japan, it takes the form of a pagoda. [Dale Williams]*

Hakuin's Enlightenment

Hakuin (1686–1769) was a poet, a painter, and a Zen master. He wrote in colloquial Japanese as well as in Chinese. He illustrated the continuing power of the Zen tradition in postmedieval times. In an autobiographical account of his spiritual quest, he first told of his disappointments and failures, but then wrote

In the spring of my twenty-fourth year, I was painfully struggling at the Eiganji in the province of Echigo. I slept neither day nor night, forgetting either to eat or sleep. A great doubt suddenly possessed me, and I felt as if frozen to death in the midst of an icy field extending thousands of *li*. A sense of an extraordinary purity permeated my bosom. I could not move. I was virtually senseless. What remained was only "*Mu*." Although I heard the master's lectures in the Lecture Hall, it was as though I were listening to his disclosure from some sixty or seventy steps outside the Hall, or as if I were floating in the air. This condition lasted for several days until one night I heard the striking of a temple bell. All at once a transformation came over me, as though a layer of ice were smashed or a tower of jade pulled down. Instantly I came to my senses. Former doubts were completely dissolved, like ice which had melted away. "How marvelous! How marvelous!" I cried out aloud. There was no cycle of birth and death from which I had to escape, no enlightenment for which I had to seek.

But Hakuin's teacher did not accept this as adequate. Hakuin's quest continued. Eight years later:

At the age of thirty-two I settled in this dilapidated temple [Shōinji]. In a dream one night my mother handed me a purple silk robe. When I lifted it I felt great weights in both sleeves. Examining it, I found in each sleeve an old mirror about five or six inches in diameter. The reflection of the right-hand mirror penetrated deep into my heart. My own mind, as well as mountains and rivers, the entire earth, became serene and bottomless. The left-hand mirror had no luster on its entire surface. Its face was like that of a new iron pan not yet touched by fire. Suddenly I became aware that the luster on the left-hand mirror surpassed that of the right by a million times. After this incident, the vision of all things was like looking at my own face. For the first time I realized the meaning of the words, "The eyes of the Tatha-gata behold the Buddha-nature."

▶ *Compare these passages to the passage from the Lotus Sutra in the document box entitled "The True Nature of the Buddha According to the Lotus Sutra" in Chapter 12.*

W. T. de Bary, ed., *The Buddhist Tradition in India, China, and Japan* (New York: Modern Library, 1972), pp. 384, 387–388.

even went so far as to practice Zen themselves.

The most remarkable aspect of Zen was its influence on the arts of medieval Japan. The most beautiful gardens, for example, were in Zen temples. Many were designed by Zen masters. The most famous, at Ryōanji, consists of fifteen rocks set in white sand. Others only slightly less austere contain moss, shrubs, trees, ponds, and streams. With these elements and within a small compass, rocks become cliffs, raked sand becomes rivers or the sea, and a little world of nature emerges. If a garden may be said to possess philosophic stillness, the Zen gardens of Daitokuji and other Kyoto temples have it.

Zen monks such as Josetsu, Shūbun, and Sesshū certainly number among the masters of ink painting in East Asia. One painting by Josetsu shows a man trying to catch a catfish with a gourd. Like the sound of one hand clapping, the impossibility of catching a catfish with a gourd presents as art the kind of logical conundrum used to expound Zen teachings. Sesshū painted in both the broken-ink style, in which splash-like brush strokes represent an entire mountain landscape, and a more usual calligraphic style. Because the artist's creativity itself was seen as grounded in his experience of meditation, a painting of a waterfall or a crow on a leafless branch in winter was viewed

A landscape by the Zen monk Sesshū (1420–1506). [Tokyo National Museum]

as no less religious than a painting of the mythic Zen founder Bodhidharma.

Nō Plays

Another fascinating product of Ashikaga culture was the Nō play, a kind of mystery drama without parallels elsewhere in East Asia. The play was performed on an almost square, bare wooden stage (often outdoors) by male actors wearing robes of great beauty and carved, painted masks of enigmatic expressions. Many such masks and robes number among Japan's national treasures. The chorus was chanted to the accompaniment of flute and drums. The language was poetic. The action was slow and highly stylized:

Circling about the stage could represent a journey, and a motion of the hand, the reading of a letter. At a critical juncture in most plays, the protagonist was possessed by the spirit of another and performed a dance. Spirit possession was a commonplace in Japanese folk religion and also occurred in the *Tale of Genji*. Several plays were shown in a single performance; comic skits called "Crazy Words" were usually interspersed between them to break the tension.

Nō plays reveal a medley of themes present in medieval Japanese culture. Some pivot on incidents in the struggle between the Taira and the Minamoto.

"Broken ink"–style painting by the Zen monk Sesshū (1420–1506). [Tokyo National Museum]

The Arts and Zen Buddhism

Zen Buddhism in Japan developed a theory of art that influenced every department of high medieval culture. Put simply, the theory is that intuitive action is better than conscious, purposive action. The best painter is one so skilled that he no longer needs to think of technique but paints as a natural act. Substitute a sword for a brush, and the same theory applies: A warrior who has to stop to consider his next move is at a disadvantage in battle. To this concern with direct, intuitive action is added the Zen distinction between the deluded mind and the "original mind." The latter is also referred to as the "no mind," or the mind in the enlightened state. The highest intuitive action proceeds from such a state of being. This theory was applied, in time, to the performance of the actor, to the skill of the potter, to archery, to flower arrangement, and to the tea ceremony. Compare the following two passages, one by Seami (1363–1443), the author of many Nō plays, and the other by Takuan Sōhō (1573–1645), a famous Zen master of the early Tokugawa era (see Chapter 20).

Sometimes spectators of the Nō say, "The moments of 'no-action' are the most enjoyable." This is an art which the actor keeps secret. Dancing and singing, movements and the different types of miming are all acts performed by the body. Moments of "no-action" occur in between. When we examine why such moments without actions are enjoyable, we find that it is due to the underlying spiritual strength of the actor which unremittingly holds the attention. He does not relax the tension when the dancing or singing come to an end or at intervals between the dialogue and the different types of miming, but maintains an unwavering inner strength. This feeling of inner strength will faintly reveal itself and bring enjoyment. However, it is undesirable for the actor to permit this inner strength to become obvious to the audience. If it is obvious, it becomes an act, and is no longer "no-action." The actions before and after an interval of "no-action" must be linked by entering the state of mindlessness in which one conceals even from oneself one's intent. This, then, is the faculty of moving audiences, by linking all the artistic powers with one mind.

Where should a swordsman fix his mind? If he puts his mind on the physical movement of his opponent, it will be seized by the movement; if he places it on the sword of his opponent, it will be arrested by the sword; if he focuses his mind on the thought of striking his opponent, it will be carried away by the very thought; if the mind stays on his own sword, it will be captured by his sword; if he centers it on the thought of not being killed by his opponent, his mind will be overtaken by this very thought; if he keeps his mind firmly on his own or on his opponent's posture, likewise, it will be blocked by them. Thus the mind should not be fixed anywhere.

R. Tsunoda, W. T. de Bary, and D. Keene, *Sources of Japanese Tradition* (New York: Columbia University Press, 1958), p. 291 (Selection 1); W. T. de Bary, ed., *The Buddhist Tradition* (New York: Modern Library, 1972), p. 377 (Selection 2).

Some are religious: A cormorant fisher is saved from the king of hell for having given lodging to a priest. Some plays pick up incidents from the *Tale of Genji* or the Heian court: The famous Heian beauty and poet Ono no Komachi is possessed by the spirit of a lover she has spurned; their conflict is left to be resolved in a Buddhist afterlife. The Buddhist idea of impermanence, of this world as a place of suffering, and of the need to relinquish worldly attachments are found in many plays. Some plays are close to fairy tales: A fisherman takes the feather robe of an angel, but when she begins to sicken and grow wan, he returns the robe and she dances for him a dance that is performed only in heaven. Some plays are based on stories from China: A traveler dreams an entire lifetime on a magical pillow while waiting for a bowl of millet to cook. Another play reflects the constant Japanese ambivalence toward Chinese culture from which Japan had borrowed so much: Po Chu-i, the T'ang poet most famous in Japan, rows a boat over the seas and comes to the shores of Japan, where he is met by fishermen who turn him back in the name of Japanese poetry. One fisherman speaks:

You in China make your poems and odes out of the Scriptures of India; and we have made our "uta" out of the poems and odes of China. Since then our poetry is a blend of three lands, we have named it Yamato, the great blend, and all our songs "Yamato uta."[8]

At the end, the fisherman is transformed into the Shinto god of Japanese poetry and performs the "Sea Green Dance."

Early Japanese History in World Perspective

During the first millennium A.D., the major development in world history was the spread of the civilizations that had risen out of the earlier philosophical and religious revolutions. In the West, the process began with the spread of civilization from Greece to Rome, continued with the rise of Christianity and its diffusion within the late Roman Empire, and entered a third phase when the countries of northern Europe became civilized by borrowing Mediterranean culture. The spread was slow because Rome was no longer a vital center. By contrast, in East Asia the spread of civilization from its Chinese heartland was more rapid because in the early seventh century, the T'ang empire had been reestablished—more vital, more exuberant, and more powerful than ever before. Within the East Asian culture zone, and apart from post-T'ang China itself, there were three major developing areas: Vietnam, Korea, and Japan.

All three used Chinese writing for most of their history, combined indigenous and Chinese elements to create distinctive cultures and national identities, and in premodern times built independent states. The contrast between these countries and other areas around China is interesting. Vietnam, Korea, and Japan were more Chinese in their culture than Tibet, Mongolia, or Manchuria. Yet during the modern era, the latter areas have been swallowed up by China, whereas Korea, Vietnam, and Japan have preserved their independence. These three nations used Chinese culture to forge self-identities that could resist Chinese domination, just as present-day Third World

nations borrow Western systems and ideas to build states that are politically anti-Western.

For all their political independence and unique social institutions, Vietnam and Korea would absorb increasingly large amounts of Chinese culture as the centuries passed. By the eighteenth century, Korea, some say, was more Confucian than China itself, although this is open to question. Vietnamese law codes in the same era were essentially Chinese codes with a few minor variations. Japan, too, was powerfully influenced by successive waves of Chinese culture; but because it was bigger, more populous, and more distant, it became the major variant to the Chinese pattern within East Asian civilization. It reflected, often brilliantly, the potentials of East Asian culture in a non-Chinese milieu.

Of particular interest to Western students are the striking parallels that developed between Japan and northwestern Europe. Both had centuries of feudalism: serfs on the estates of nobles; castles and mounted warriors who wore armor and fought in the service of their lords, cultures in which the glorification of valor and military prowess conflicted with the gentler virtues of their religions; merchant guilds and decentralized political economies. These parallels should not be surprising because both Japan and northwestern Europe began as backward tribal or post-tribal societies onto which heartland cultures were grafted during the first millennium A.D.

Suggested Readings

C. BLACKER, *The Catalpa Bow* (1975). A fascinating study of folk Shinto.

R. BORGEN, *Sugawara no Michizane and the Early Heian Court* (1986). A study of a famous courtier and poet.

D. BROWN and E. ISHIDA, eds., *The Future and the Past* (1979). A translation of a history of Japan written in 1219.

M. COLLCUTT, *Five Mountains* (1980). A study of the monastic organization of medieval Zen.

P. DUUS, *Feudalism in Japan* (1969). An easy survey of the subject.

W. W. FARRIS, *Heavenly Warriors: The Evolution of Japan's Military, 500–1300* (1992).

W. W. FARRIS, *Population, Disease, and Land in Early Japan, 645–900* (1985). An innovative reinterpretation of early history.

K. F. FRIDAY, *Hired Swords: The Rise of Private Warrior Power in Early Japan* (1991). The interpretation

---

[8]A. Waley, trans., *The Nō Plays of Japan* (New York: Grove Press, 1957), p. 252.

in this book may be compared to that in Farris's *Heavenly Warriors.*

J. W. HALL, *Government and Local Power in Japan, 500–1700: A Study Based on Bizen Province* (1966). The best book on Japanese history to 1700.

J. W. HALL and J. P. MASS, eds., *Medieval Japan* (1974). A collection of topical essays on medieval history.

J. W. HALL and T. TOYODA, *Japan in the Muromachi Age* (1977). Another collection of essays.

D. KEENE, ed., *Anthology of Japanese Literature from the Earliest Era to the Mid-Nineteenth Century* (1955).

D. KEENE, ed., *Twenty Plays of the Nō Theatre* (1970).

J. M. KITAGAWA, *Religion in Japanese History* (1966). A survey of religion in premodern Japan.

I. H. LEVY, *The Ten Thousand Leaves* (1981). A fine translation of Japan's earliest collection of poetry.

J. P. MASS, *The Development of Kamakura Rule, 1180–1250* (1979).

J. P. MASS and W. HAUSER, eds., *The Bakufu in Japanese History* (1985). Topics in *bakufu* history from the twelfth to the nineteenth centuries.

I. MORRIS, *The World of the Shining Prince: Court Life in Ancient Japan* (1964). A study of the court during the age in which *The Tale of Genji* was written.

I. MORRIS, trans., *The Pillow Book of Sei Shōnagon* (1967). Observations about the Heian court life by the Jane Austen of ancient Japan.

S. MURASAKI, *The Tale of Genji,* trans. by E. G. Seidensticker (1976). The world's first novel and the greatest work of Japanese fiction.

S. MURASAKI, *The Tale of Genji,* trans. by A. Waley (1952). A comparison of this translation with that of Seidensticker is instructive.

R. J. PEARSON et al., eds., *Windows on the Japanese Past: Studies in Archaeology and Prehistory* (1986).

D. L. PHILIPPI, trans., *Kojiki* (1968). Japan's ancient myths.

E. O. REISCHAUER and A. M. CRAIG, *Japan: Tradition and Transformation* (1989). A widely used text covering the total sweep of Japanese history from the early beginnings to the present day.

D. T. SUZUKI, *Zen and Japanese Culture* (1959).

R. TSUNODA, W. T. DEBARY, and D. KEENE, comps., *Sources of the Japanese Tradition* (1958). A collection of original religious, political, and philosophical writings from each period of Japanese history. The best reader.

H. P. VARLEY, *Imperial Restoration in Medieval Japan* (1971). A study of the 1331 attempt by an emperor to restore imperial power.

A. WALEY, trans., *The Nō Plays of Japan* (1957). Medieval dramas.

K. YAMAMURA, ed., *Medieval Japan* (1990), Vol. 5 of the Cambridge History of Japan.

The Sasanid King Ardashir II (r. A.D. 379–383) as depicted on a stone relief carving of his investiture. The carving is at Taq i Bustan in Iran. [Bildarchiv Preussischer Kulturbesitz]

Iran and India Before Islam

In this chapter, we look at South and southwestern Asia before the spread of the Muslim faith and Islamic rule ushered in new eras that brought cultural and religious change to major portions of both regions and linked them in new ways.

In Iran, the period from the breakdown of Parthian rule at the beginning of the third century A.D. to the coming of Islam in the seventh was one of relative political stability under a single long-lived dynasty of Persian imperial rulers known as the Sasanids. Although Zoroastrian traditions recovered their vitality in this period, the social and political system became heavily balanced in favor of a small ruling nobility and foreign policy centered in constant competition with the Byzantine Empire. This competition finally exhausted the resources of the Sasanids, much as it did those of Byzantium. Both empires were ripe for defeat at the hands of the unleashed energies of the Arabs, whose armies, flying the banner of Islam, moved out of the Arabian peninsula in the second third of the seventh century.

India experienced a similarly spectacular revival of empire under the Gupta kings, who presided also over a cultural efflorescence of unprecedented magnificence. Then incursions of new waves of steppe peoples from about 500 A.D. brought an era of political fragmentation. Nevertheless, regional empires emerged that lasted until the thirteenth century, when Muslim power in the north under the Delhi sultans began to forge new patterns of power and culture north and south.

The coming of Islamic civilization—with Muslim conquerors or, much more often, with Muslim traders and religious brotherhoods—took place at very different times and with differing consequences in each of these two major cultural areas.

In Iran, the Islamic presence was a significant factor in government and public life from the early years of the Arab conquests in the mid-seventh century, although religious conversion of the populace in the various regions of the traditional Iranian cultural and political sphere took considerably longer.

In northwestern India, Arab armies penetrated the Indus region as early as 711, and Muslim rulers of Central Asian extraction controlled the Panjab from around 1000. The establishment of the so-called Delhi Sultanate in 1205 marked the entrenchment of Muslim ruling dynasties in the Indian heartlands. Similarly, Sufi brotherhoods made significant converts in India from about the thirteenth century onward. However, in earlier trading communities on the coasts of Gujarat and South India, Muslim settlers and converts provided the nuclei of smaller, often scattered Muslim communities that grew up within the larger Hindu society and flourished.

IRAN

The Parthians

Parthian Arsacid rule (ca. 247 B.C.–A.D. 223) began in the eastern Iranian province of Parthia in Seleucid times, soon extended to the southeastern shores of the Caspian, and eventually came to dominate the Iranian heartlands of the Achaemenids before them (see Chapter 7). The Parthian dynasty even managed by 129 B.C. to bring a permanent end to Seleucid power east of the Euphrates. The Parthians also continued the Iranian imperial as well as cultural traditions begun by the Achaemenids. The relative Parthian tolerance of religious diversity was paralleled by the growth of regionalism in political and cultural affairs. A growing nobility built strong local power bases and became the backbone of the military power of the realm. Aramaic, the common language of the empire, gradually lost ground to regional Iranian tongues after the second century B.C. The Parthian dialect and Greek became widely influential but could not replace Aramaic.

Despite their general religious tolerance, the Parthians still upheld such Zoroastrian traditions as the maintenance of a royal sacred fire at a shrine in their Parthian homeland and the inclusion of priestly advisers on the emperor's council. The last century or so of their rule saw increased emphasis on Iranian as opposed to foreign traditions in religious and cultural affairs. This emphasis was perhaps in reaction to the almost constant warfare with the Romans on their west flank and the Greco-Bactrian Kushan threat to the east. By this time, Christianity and Buddhism were making sufficient converts in western and eastern border areas to threaten Zoroastrian tradition directly for the first time. This threat may have stimulated Parthian attempts to collect the largely oral Zoroastrian textual heritage. In this and other ways, Parthian rule laid the groundwork for the nationalistic emphases of the next few centuries, despite later Sasanid efforts to portray this era as one of weakness and decline in native Iranian traditions.

The Sasanid Empire (A.D. 224–651)

The Sasanids were, like the Achaemenid founders of the earliest Iranian empire, a Persian dynasty. Claiming to be the rightful heirs of the Achaemenids, the Sasanids put themselves forward as champions of Iranian legitimacy and tried to brand the Parthians as outside invaders from the northeast who followed Greek and other foreign ways. Much of the lasting bad reputation of the Parthians stems from the fact that they are still known only through hostile Sasanid or Roman sources.

The first Sasanid king, Ardashir (reigned A.D. 224–ca. 239), was a Persian warrior noble who had a priestly family background. The Sasanid name came from his grandfather, Sasan. Ardashir and his son, Shapur I (r. ca. 239–272), built a strong internal administration in Persia (Fars) and extended their sway to Ctesiphon and abroad. While still his father's field general, Shapur took Bactria from the Kushans, thereby greatly expanding the Sasanid realm. Under his long rule, the empire grew significantly, not only in the east, but also beyond the Caucasus in the north and into Syria, Armenia, and parts of Anatolia in the west. Shapur inflicted humiliating defeats on three Roman emperors, even capturing one of them, Valerian. Thus he could justifiably claim to be a restorer of Iranian glory and a "king of kings," or *shahanshah*.

The palace of the Sasanid Shahanshahs at Ctesiphon. Built by Shapur I in the capital that the Sasanids inherited from the Arsacids, the imperial palace is only partially preserved. The gigantic four-story structure is said to have greatly impressed the Arab invaders in the seventh century. The massive open-vaulted hall or bay was a feature of Persian architecture that would be used later in Iranian mosques. [Bettmann Archive]

He also centralized and rationalized taxation, the civil ministries, and the military, although neither he nor his successors could fully counterbalance the growing power of the nobility.

With the shift of the Roman Empire east to Byzantium at the beginning of the fourth century A.D., the stage of imperial conflict for the next 350 years was set: Byzantium (Constantinople) on the Bosporus and Ctesiphon on the Tigris were to be the seats of the two mightiest thrones of Eurasia until the coming of the Arabs. Each from time to time won victories over the other, and each championed a different religious orthodoxy, but neither could ever completely conquer the other. In the sixth century, each produced their greatest emperors: the Byzantine Justinian (r. 527–565) and the Sasanid Chosroes Anosharvan ("Chosroes of the Immortal Soul," r. 531–579). Yet, less than a century after their deaths, the new Arab power reduced one empire dramatically and destroyed the other. Byzantium survived with the loss of most of its imperial domains for another eight hundred years, but the Sasanid imperial order was swept away with the last of its rulers in 651. Memory of the Sasanids did not, however, entirely die. Chosroes, for example, became a legendary model of greatness for Persians and a symbol of imperial splendor even among the Arabs.

Society and Economy

Sasanid society was largely like that of earlier times. At all levels, the extended family was (as it is even today in Iran) the basic social unit. Zoroastrian orthodoxy recognized four classes: priests, warriors, scribes, and peasants. The great divide was between the royal house, the priesthood, and the warrior nobility on the one hand, and the common people of the cities (artisans, traders, and so on) and the rural peasantry on the other.

The basis of the economy remained agriculture. The long-term trend was toward the concentration of land ownership among an ever-richer minority of the royalty, the nobility, and the priesthood. The growth of great estates was similar to that in Roman domains and was no less responsible for an increased imbalance between the rich few and the impoverished many. More and more small farmers were reduced to serfdom in the latter half of this era. The burden of land taxation, like that of conscript labor work and army duty, hit hardest those least able to afford it. It was not without eventual popular reaction, as the Mazdakite movement, which is discussed later, shows.

The Sasanids also closely oversaw and heavily taxed the lucrative caravan trade that traversed their

The luxury art of the Sasanids was the culmination of the long development of earlier Iranian traditions. It was consciously Iranian and oriental rather than Greco-Roman, although Western influence was inevitable. A popular motif was the hunt, always a favorite pastime of Persian aristocrats. The stylized figures shown at the bottom of this silver bowl are typical of the Sasanid style. [Bettmann Archive]

mathematics were particularly well received. Hellenistic culture also was revived in the academy at Jundishapur in Khuzistan, where refugee scholars from Byzantium came to teach medicine and philosophy after Justinian closed the Greek academies in the west.

Religion

ZOROASTRIAN REVIVAL. Religion played a significant role in Sasanid life not only at the popular level but even in affairs of state. The Sasanids institutionalized Zoroastrian ritual and theology as state orthodoxy. Although they were simply continuing the Arsacid patronage of Zoroastrian worship, the Sasanids claimed to be restoring the true faith after centuries of neglect. The initial architect of this propaganda and the Zoroastrian revival was the first chief priest of the empire, Tosar (or Tansar). Under Ardashir, Tosar instituted a state church organization and began the fixation of an authoritative, written canon of the Avesta, the scriptural texts that include the hymns of Zarathushtra. He may also have instituted a calendar reform and banned all images in the temples of the land, replacing them with the sacred altar fires of Zoroastrian tradition.

The greatest figure in Sasanid religious history was Tosar's successor, Kartir, or Kirdir, who served as chief priest to Shapur I and his three successors (ca. 239–293). Although his zealotry was at first kept in check by the religiously tolerant and eclectic Shapur, Kirdir gained greater power and influence after Shapur's death. He is the one figure other than a Sasanid king for whom we have personal inscriptions in the rock reliefs of the dynasty. He seems to have made numerous efforts to convert not only pagans, but also Christians, Buddhists, and other followers of foreign traditions. His chief opponents were, however, the Manichaeans, whom he considered Zoroastrian heretics, much as they were regarded by Christian groups as Christian heretics.

MANICHAEISM. Mani (A.D. 216–277) was born of a noble Parthian family but was raised in Babylonia. A cosmopolitan who spoke Aramaic, Persian, and Greek and had traveled to India, Mani preached a message similar to, but at crucial points radically divergent from, its Zoroastrian, Judaic, and Christian forerunners. It centered on a radically dualistic and moralistic view of reality in which good and evil, spirit and matter, always warred. His preaching was avowedly missionary, presenting itself as the culmi-

territory, as well as export and import trade by sea. Silk and glass production increased under government monopoly, and the state controlled mining as well. The many urban centers of the empire and the foreign trade relied on a money system. It was from Jewish bankers in Babylonia and their Persian counterparts that Europe and the rest of the world got the use of bills of exchange (the very word *check* comes from a Pahlavi word).[1]

Sasanid aristocratic culture drew on diverse traditions, from Roman, Hellenistic, and Bactrian-Indian to Achaemenid and other native Iranian ones. Its heyday was the reign of Chosroes. Iranian legendary history and courtly literature were popular, as were translations of Indian narrative literature. Indian influences—not only religious ones, as in the case of Buddhist ideas, but also artistic and especially scientific ones—were especially strong. Indian medicine and

[1] R. Girshman, *Iran* (Harmondsworth, U.K.: Penguin Books, 1954), pp. 341–346. "Pahlavi" is the name of the middle Persian language that gradually replaced Aramaic as the Iranian *lingua franca* in Sasanid times.

A Report of Mani's Words About His Mission

The following excerpt is from The Cologne Mani Codex, *a Greek biographical work on Mani's early life that was unknown until the past two decades since its discovery in a damaged but largely intact manuscript codex. The tiny parchment "pocketbook" on which it was written dates from around* A.D. 400, *and so it is not long removed from Mani's lifetime. In it, the Manichaean author cities one of Mani's "gospels."*

He wrote [thus again and] said in the Gospel of his most holy hope: "I, Mani, an apostle of Jesus Christ through the will of God, the Father of Truth, from whom I also was born, who lives and abides forever, existing before all and also abiding after all. All things which are and will be subsist through his power. For from this very one I was begotten; and I am from his will. From him all that is true was revealed to me; and I am from [his] truth. [The truth of ages which he revealed] I have seen, and [that] truth I have disclosed to my fellow travelers; peace I have announced to the children of peace, hope I have pro- claimed to the immortal race. The Elect I have cho- sen and a path to the height I have shown to those who ascend according to this truth. Hope I have pro- claimed and this revelation I have revealed. This immortal Gospel I have written, including in it these eminent mysteries, and disclosing in it the greatest works, the greatest and most august forms of the most eminently powerful works. These things which he [revealed], I have shown [to those who live from] the truest vision, which I have beheld, and the most glorious revelation revealed to me."

From *The Cologne Mani Codex,* trans. from the Greek by Ron Cameron and A. J. Dewey (Missoula, MT: Scholars Press, 1979), p. 53.

nation and restoration of the original unity of Zoroas- trian, Christian, and Buddhist teachings. Mani may have been the first person in history consciously to

An angel from a Manichaean mural of Central Asia (ca. eighth–ninth century A.D.*). Paintings such as this are an important source for our knowledge of Manichaean communities.*

"found" a new religious tradition or to seek to create a "scripture" for his followers. He called his new sys- tem "Justice," although it has been known to outsid- ers as Manichaeism. Mani's movement proved a pop- ular one; its popularity probably contributed to Kirdir's and later attempts to establish a Zoroastrian "orthodoxy" and scriptural canon.[2]

Kirdir eventually won his struggle against Mani and had him executed as a heretic in 277. But Mani's movement was destined to have great consequences. It spread westward to challenge the young Christian church (Saint Augustine was once a Manichaean) and eastward along the silk route to coexist in Central Asia with Nestorian Christian and Mahayana Buddhist communities as a third major universalistic tradition until after the coming of Islam. Its ideas figured even centuries later in both Christian and Islamic heresies that challenged the mainstream theologies of both traditions. Its adherents probably carried the Western planetary calendar to China, where in some areas it was used for centuries.

[2] W. C. Smith, *The Meaning and End of Religion* (New York: Harper & Row, 1962), pp. 92–98.

ZOROASTRIAN ORTHODOXY. Kartir had firmly grounded Zoroastrian orthodoxy despite the persistence of such challenges to it as that of Mani. This orthodoxy became the backbone of Sasanid culture. Soon the Sasanids' Persian dialect, *Pahlavi*, became the official imperial language, displacing Parthian (although many Parthian words entered the later Persian language). Eventually, the Zoroastrian sacred texts were set down in Pahlavi. In later Sasanid times, the priests produced many new writings, ranging from commentaries to myth, theology, and wisdom literature. Throughout Sasanid times, the priesthood grew in power as the jurists and legal interpreters as well as the liturgists and scholars of the land. With increasing endowments of new fire temples, the church establishment eventually controlled much of the wealth of Iran.

Later Sasanid Developments

Despite the high Zoroastrian moral intent of many of their rulers, the Sasanid ideal of justice did not include equal distribution of the empire's bounty. The

---

On the Propagation of Mazda-Worship

The following excerpts are from an inscription of Kirdir, the second high priest to serve under the Sasanids. Here he proclaims his successful efforts to consolidate and spread the worship of Ahura Mazda. The time of the inscription is the reign of Vahram II, 276–293. A.D. *The* yazads *are beneficent divine beings, the* devs *the evil minions of the "Evil Spirit," Ahriman.*

And I was made Mobad and Judge of the whole empire, and I was made Master of Ceremonials and Warden of the Fires of Anahid-Ardashir and Anahid the Lady at Istakhr. And I was styled "Kirder by whom Vahram's soul is saved, Mobad of Ohrmazd." And in every province and place of the whole empire the service of Ohrmazd and the yazads was exalted, and the Mazda-worshipping religion and its priests received much honour in the land. And the yazads, and water and fire and cattle, were greatly contented, and Ahriman and the devs suffered great blows and harm. And the creed of Ahriman and the devs was driven out of the land and deprived of credence. And Jews and Buddhists and Brahmans and Aramaic and Greek-speaking Christians and Baptisers and Manichaeans were assailed in the land. And images were overthrown, and the dens of demons were (thus) destroyed, and the places and abodes of the yazads [i.e., fire temples] were established. . . . And from the first I, Kirder, underwent much toil and trouble for the yazads and the rulers, and for my own soul's sake. And I caused many fires and priestly colleges to flourish in Iran, and also in non-Iranian lands. . . . And I made the Mazda-worshipping religion and its good priests esteemed and honoured in the land. . . .

Mary Boyce, ed. and trans., *Textual Sources for the Study of Zoroastrianism* (Manchester, U.K.: University Press, 1984), pp. 112–113.

radical inequalities between the aristocracy and the common folk in Sasanid lands erupted in conflict in one instance: the Mazdakite movement at the end of the fifth century. Its leader, Mazdak, seems to have drawn his ideas ultimately from Manichaeism. Those ideas included similar ascetic tendencies; they were pessimistic about the evil state of the material world; and they urged vegetarianism, tolerance, and brotherly love. Mazdak's egalitarian preaching, which included a demand for a more equal distribution of society's goods, was attractive especially to the oppressed classes, and one Sasanid ruler, Kavad I (r. 488–531), was even sympathetic for a time to Mazdak's ideas of social justice. However, in 528, Kavad's third son, the later Chosroes Anosharvan, carried out an official massacre of Mazdak and his most important followers. Although this finished the Mazdakites, the name was still used later, in Islamic times, for various Iranian popular revolts.

INDIA

Golden Age of the Guptas

The Gupta era has always marked for Indians a special high point of their civilization. Historians have seen in it the source of "classical" norms for both Hindu religion and Indian culture, the symbolic equivalent of Periclean Athens, Augustan Rome, or Han China. The Guptas ruled at a time when the various facets of Indian life took on the recognizable patterns of a single civilization that, however diverse the many cultural-linguistic parts it comprised, extended its influence over all the subcontinent. A major contributing factor in this development was the relative peace and stability that marked most of the Gupta reign.

Gupta Rule

The first Gupta king was Chandragupta (r. A.D. 320–ca. 330; not to be confused with Chandragupta Maurya: see Chapter 7). He came to prominence first in Magadha and then the rest of the Ganges basin largely through his marriage to princess Kumaradevi, daughter of the leader of a powerful tribe north of the Ganges. Although their reign inaugurated Gupta power, it was their son, Samudragupta, and especially their grandson, Chandragupta II (r. ca. 375–415), who turned kingdom into empire and presided over the Gupta "golden age."

The Gupta realm became the greatest in the subcontinent, extending from the borders of the Panjab and Kashmir south to the Narbada River in the western Deccan and east to modern Assam (see Map 12-1). The Gupta sphere of influence was still larger, including some of the Kushan and Saka kingdoms of the northwest as well as much of the eastern coast of India and possibly Ceylon (Sri Lanka). More than the Mauryans, the Guptas were usually ready to accept a defeated ruler as a vassal prince rather than to try to place his kingdom under direct central administrative control. Seated at the old Mauryan capital of Pataliputra, Gupta splendor and power had no rival. Under Chandragupta II, India was arguably the most civilized and peaceful country in the world.

Two further Gupta kings sustained this prosperity for another half century, despite invasions by a new wave of steppe nomads, the Huns, from about 440 onward. Various weaker kings followed until the empire collapsed around 550, but repeated Hun incursions had already overrun western India by about 500. When another Indian ruler did manage to break Hun control in northwestern India (530), the Guptas were too weak to reestablish their sovereignty in the north.

Harsha, a descendant of the Guptas through his grandmother, managed to revive some of the Gupta splendor between 616 and 657. He ruled long and well over a loose empire that stretched across North India. When he died without heirs, the empire broke up again, and the final echo of Gupta grandeur was gone. The succeeding centuries before the arrival of Muslim invaders in about A.D. 1000 saw several dynasties share power in North India but no unified rule of any duration. Outside the north, the main centers of regional empires were in the western Deccan and in Tamilnad (the extreme south), where several long-lived dynasties shared control after Gupta times. The cultural impetus of Indian civilization now shifted visibly to the Deccan and South.

Gupta Culture

With the decline of Rome in the West, from Gupta until Muslim times Indian culture experienced little

MAP 12-1 INTERNATIONAL TRADE ROUTES IN GUPTA AND SASANID TIMES *This map shows the Gupta and Sasanid empires and the trade routes that linked them to each other and to other areas of the world.*

The Bodhisattva Avalokiteshvara from Ajanta. This is one of the magnificent murals from the Ajanta Buddhist cave shrines and surely one of the masterpieces of world religious art. The colossal figure is that of the bodhisattva *of infinite compassion. Even through the damage of centuries, this Gupta masterpiece projects an aura of serene majesty. The inclined head of Avalokiteshvara, his tranquil face, and his gesturing hands all convey compassion. [University of Michigan/Dr. Spink]*

new influence from outside. India's chief contacts were now with Southeast Asia and China, and most of the cultural transmission was from India eastward, not vice versa.

The Gupta period and later centuries saw massive

A Chinese Traveler's Report on the Gupta Realm

Fa-Hsien, a Chinese Buddhist monk, was the first of several Chinese known for traveling to India to study and bring back Buddhist scriptures from the intellectual centers of Buddhist thought there. He, like later travelers of whom we know, wrote an account of his travels, first through Central Asia, then all over India, then through Ceylon and Indonesia again to China (A.D. 399–414).

▶ *For other traveler's reports, see "Marco Polo Describes the City of Hangchow" (Ch. 10) and "Ibn Battuta Visits Mogadishu and Kilwa (1331)" (Ch. 19).*

On the sides of the river, both right and left, are twenty *sanghârâmas* [monasteries], with perhaps 3000 priests. The law of the Buddha is progressing and flourishing. Beyond the deserts are the countries of Western India. The kings of these countries are all firm believers in the law of Buddha. They remove their caps of state when they make offerings to the priests. The members of the royal household and the chief ministers personally direct the food-giving; when the distribution of food is over, they spread a carpet on the ground opposite the chief seat (the president's seat) and sit down before it. They dare not sit on couches in the presence of the priests. The rules relating to the almsgiving of kings have been handed down from the time of Buddha till now. Southward from this is the so-called middle-country (Mâdhyadeśa). The climate of this country is warm and equable, without frost or snow. The people are very well off, without poll tax or official restrictions. Only those who till the royal lands return a portion of profit of the land. If they desire to go, they go; if they like to stop, they stop. The kings govern without corporal punishment; criminals are fined, according to circumstances, lightly or heavily. Even in cases of repeated rebellion they only cut off the right hand. The king's personal attendants, who guard him on the right and left, have fixed salaries. Throughout the country the people kill no living thing nor drink wine, nor do they eat garlic or onions, with the exception of Chandâlas [outcasts] only. The Chandâlas are named "evil men" and dwell apart from others; if they enter a town or market, they sound a piece of wood in order to separate themselves; then men, knowing who they are, avoid coming in contact with them. In this country they do not keep swine nor fowls, and do not deal in cattle; they have no shambles or wine-shops in their marketplaces. In selling they use cowrie shells. The Chandâlas only hunt and sell flesh. Down from the time of Buddha's Nirvâna, the kings of these countries, the chief men and householders, have raised vihâras [monasteries] for the priests, and provided for their support by bestowing on them fields, houses, and gardens, with men and oxen. Engraved title-deeds were prepared and handed down from one reign to another; no one has ventured to withdraw them, so that till now there has been no interruption. All the resident priests having chambers (in these vihâras) have their beds, mats, food, drink, and clothes provided without stint; in all places this is the case. The priests ever engage themselves in doing meritorious works for the purpose of religious advancement (karma—building up their religious character), or in reciting the scriptures, or in meditation.

From "Buddhist Country Records," in *Si-Yu-Ki: Buddhist Records of the Western World*, trans. Samuel Beal (London, 1884: Reprint, Delhi: Oriental Books Reprint Corporation, 1969), pp. xxxvii–xxxviii.

---

literary and artistic productivity, of which only a few outstanding examples can be mentioned. The claim of the Gupta era to being India's golden age of culture could be sustained solely on the basis of its magnificent architecture and sculpture, the wall paintings of the Ajanta caves, and the matchless drama and verse of Kalidasa. The "Shakespeare" of Sanskrit letters, Kalidasa flourished in the time of Chandragupta II and Kumaragupta. Poetry, painting, sculpture, dance, drama, and music were popularly practiced as well as patronized in the aristocratic households of the cities that set the cultural standards in each region.

One index of the culture was its emphasis on education, which was available in Jain and Buddhist

A Lyric Poem of Kalidasa

Perhaps the greatest lyric poet as well as dramatist of Sanskrit letters, Kalidasa repre-
sents all that was refined and aesthetically sophisticated about Gupta culture. In the
following poem, he paints a picture in words from an epic tale about Kumāra, the divine
offspring of Shiva, and his consort, the goddess Parvati.

KUMĀRA'S FIGHT AGAINST THE DEMON
TĀRAKA

A fearful flock of evil birds, ready for the joy of eating
   the army of demons,
flew over the host of the gods, and clouded the sun.

A wind continually fluttered their umbrellas and banners,
and troubled their eyes with clouds of whirling dust,
so that the trembling horses and elephants
and the great chariots could not be seen.

Suddenly monstrous serpents, as black as powdered
   soot,
scattering poison from their upraised heads,
frightful in form,
appeared in the army's path.

The sun put on a ghastly robe
of great and terrible snakes, curling together,
as if to mark his joy
at the death of the enemy demon.

And before the very disc of the sun
jackals bayed harshly together,
as though eager fiercely to lap the blood
of the king of the foes of the gods, fallen in battle.

Lighting heaven from end to end,
with flames flashing all around,
with an awful crash, rending the heart with terror,
a thunderbolt fell from a cloudless sky.

The sky poured down torrents of red-hot ashes,
with which were mixed blood and human bones,
till the flaming ends of heaven were filled with smoke
and bore the dull hue of the neck of an ass.

Like the thundered threat of the angry death-god
a great crash broke the walls of the ears,
a shattering sound, tearing the tops of the mountains,
   and wholly filling the belly of heaven.

The host of the foe was jostled together.
The great elephants stumbled, the horses fell,
and all the footmen clung together in fear,
as the earth trembled and the ocean rose to shake the
   mountains.

And, before the host of the foes of the gods,
dogs lifted their muzzles to gaze on the sun,
then, howling together with cries that rent the ear-
   drums,
they wretchedly slunk away.

                  —*Kumara-sambhava,* 15.14

From Louis Renou, ed., *Hinduism* (New York: G. Braziller, 1962), pp. 181–182.

monasteries and in Brahmanical schools. Religious texts were not the only focus: Rhetoric, prose and poetic composition, grammar, logic, medicine, and metaphysics were typical subjects. Based on the still older Indian number system that came later via the Arabs to the West as the "Arabic numerals," mathematics was cultivated for theoretical as well as practical purposes.

In sculpture, the superb technique and expressive serenity of Gupta style grew out of the native Mathura and Greco-Roman schools. Hindu, Jain, and Buddhist works all shared the same style and conven-tions. The monastic complex at Sarnath was a great center for sculpture. Even in handwork and luxury crafts, Gupta products achieved new levels of quality and were in great demand abroad: silks, muslin, linen, ivory and other carvings, bronze metalwork, gold and silver work, and cut stones, among others. In architecture, Gupta splendor is less evident, except in the culmination of cave-shrine (Chaitya-hall) development at Ajanta and in the earliest surviving free-standing temples in India. The Hindu temple underwent its important development in post-Gupta times, during the eighth century and afterward.

The Durga Temple at Aihole. This Hindu temple in the southern Deccan shows how the older Chaitya-hall of the rock-cut or cave variety, such as at Ajanta, influenced the shape of free-standing temples in Gupta times. Note the small spire that became a fixture of later Indian temple architecture. [University of Michigan/Dr. Spink]

Consolidation of Indian Civilization (ca. A.D. 300–1000)

The Guptas' support of Brahmanic traditions and Vaishnava[3] devotionalism reflected the ascendancy of Hindu over Buddhist traditions as the mainstream of Indian religious life. In Gupta and subsequent times down to the advent of Muslim rule, Indian civilization assumed its classical shape, its enduring "Hindu" forms of social, religious, and cultural life.

Society

In these centuries, the fundamentally hierarchical character of Hindu/Indian society solidified in practice and theory. The oldest manual of legal and ethical theory, the *Dharmashastra* of Manu, dates from about A.D. 200. Based on Vedic tradition, it treats the *dharma* appropriate to one's class and stage of life, rules for rites and study of the Veda, pollution and purification measures, dietary restrictions, royal duties and prerogatives, and other legal and moral questions.

In it, we find the classic statement of the four-class theory of social hierarchy, This ideal construct rests on the basic principle that every person is born into a particular station in life (as a result of *karma* from

earlier lives), and every station has its particular *dharma,* or appropriate duties and responsibilities, from the lowest servant to the highest prince of Brahman. The basic framework is the Brahmans' ancient division of Aryans into the four *varnas,* or classes, of *Brahman* (priest), *Kshatriya* (noble/warrior), *Vaishya* (tradesperson), *Shudra* (servant). These divisions reflect an ancient attempt to fix the status and power of the upper three groups, especially the Brahmans, at the expense of the Shudras and the "fifth estate" of non-Aryan "outcasts," who performed the most polluting jobs in society. Although class distinctions had already hardened before 500 B.C., the classes were, in practice, somewhat fluid. When the traditional occupation of a *varna* was closed to a member, he could often take up another, all theory to the contrary. When Brahmans, Vaishyas, or even Shudras gained political power as rulers (as was evidently the case with the Mauryas, for example), their family gradually became recognized as *Kshatriyas,* the appropriate class for princes.

Although the four classes, or *varnas,* provide the theoretical basis for caste relations, much smaller and far more numerous subgroups, or *jatis,* are the units to which our English term *caste* best refers, if only rather clumsily. (*Caste* comes from *casta,* the word the Portuguese used for *jati.*) These basic and lasting divisions (most of which represent occupational groups) were already the primary units of social distinction in Gupta times. *Jati* groupings are hereditarily determined and distinguished essentially on principles of purity and pollution, which are expressed in three kinds of regulation: (1) commensality (one may take food only from or with persons of the same or a higher caste group); (2) endogamy (one may marry only within the group); and (3) trade or craft limitation (one must practice only the trade of one's group).[4]

As much as the caste system has been criticized, it has been the functional principle of Indian social organization for at least two millennia. It enabled Hindus to accommodate foreign cultural, racial, and religious communities within Indian society by treating them simply as new caste groups. As a result of it, everyone could tell by dress and other marks how to relate to a given person or group, giving great stability and security to the individual and to society. It represented also the logical extension of the doctrine of *karma*—whether as justification, product or partial

[3] *Vaishnava* or *Vaishnavite* means "related to Vishnu"; similarly, *Shaiva* or *Shaivite* refers to Shiva worship (compare with *Jaina/Jain* for devotees of the way of the *Jinas* such as Mahavira).

[4] A. L. Basham, *The Wonder That Was India* (New York: 1963), pp. 148–149.

cause of the caste system itself—into society (see Chapter 2).

Religion

HINDU RELIGIOUS LIFE. The growth of devotional cults of Vishnu, Shiva, Kali, and other deities unknown or unimportant in Vedic religion went on apace in Gupta and later times. The temple worship of a particular deity has ever since remained a basic form of Hindu piety. After Vishnu (especially in his form as the hero-savior Krishna) and Shiva (originally a fertility god identified with the Vedic deity Rudra), the chief focus of devotion came to be the goddess in one of her many forms, such as Parvati, Shakti, Durga, or Kali. Vishnu and Shiva, like Parvati, have many forms and names and have always been easily identified with other deities, who are then worshiped as one form of the Supreme Lord or Goddess. Older animal or nature deities were always part of popular Indian piety, presumably since Indus Valley days. Indian reverence for all forms of life and stress on *ahimsa,* or "noninjury" to living beings (see Chapter 2), is most vivid in the sacredness of the cow, which has always been both symbolically and economically a mainstay of life in India.

In the development of Hindu piety and practice, a major strand was the tradition of ardent theism known as *bhakti,* or "loving devotion." *Bhakti* was already evident, at the latest by A.D. 200, in the Bhagavad Gita's treatment of Krishna. Gupta and later times saw the rise, especially in the Tamil-speaking south, of schools of *bhakti* poetry and worship. The central *bhakti* strand in Hindu life derives in good part from the Tamil and other vernacular poets who first sang the praises of Shiva or Vishnu as Supreme Lord. Here, pre-Aryan religious sensibilities apparently reasserted themselves through the non-Aryan Dravidian peoples of the south. The great theologian of devotional Hinduism, Ramanuja (d. ca. 1137), would later come from this same Dravidian tradition. Of major importance also to devotional piety was the development in this era of the Puranas—epic, mythological, and devotional texts. They are still today the functional sacred scriptures of grassroots Hindu religious life (the Vedic texts remaining the special preserve of the Brahmans).

Whichever god or goddess a Hindu worships, there has never been any objection to paying homage on the proper occasion to other appropriate deities. Most Hindus view one deity as Supreme Lord but see others as manifestations of the Ultimate at lower levels. Hindu polytheism is not "idolatry" but a vivid affirmation of the infinite forms that transcendence takes in the created world. The sense of the presence of the divine in everything is evident at the popular level in the immense importance attached to sacred places in India. It is the land of religious pilgrimage *par excellence.* Sacred mountains, rivers, trees, and groves are all *tirtha*s, or "river fords" to the divine.

The philosophical or theological articulation of Hindu polytheism and relativism found its finest form in post-Gupta formulations of Vedanta ("the end of the Veda"). This is one of the six major Hindu systems of thought based on the Vedas, especially the Upanishads. The major Vedantic thinker was Shankara (d. 820). He stressed a strict "nonduality" of the Ultimate, teaching that Brahman was the only Reality behind the "illusion" *(maya)* of the world of sense experience. Yet he accepted the worship of a single lesser god or goddess as appropriate for those who could not follow his extraordinary norm—the intellectual realization of the formless Absolute beyond all "name and form" (see Chapter 2).

BUDDHIST RELIGIOUS LIFE. The major developments of these centuries were (1) the solidification of what would later become the two main strands of Buddhist tradition, the Mahayana and the Theravada, and (2) the spread of Buddhism abroad from its Indian homeland. The Mahayana ("Great Vehicle [of salvation]") arose in the first century B.C., although Mahayana ideas had been foreshadowed in divergent schools of Buddhist thought as early as the fourth century B.C. Its proponents differentiated it sharply from the older, more conservative traditions of monk-oriented piety and thought, which they called the Hinayana ("Little Vehicle"). Mahayana speculation developed in the style of Upanishadic monism: Buddhas were viewed as manifestations of a single principle of "Ultimate" Reality, and the Buddha Sidhartha Gautama was held to be but one Buddha among many. In the Mahayana, the model of the Buddha's infinite compassion for all beings was paramount. The highest goal was not a *nirvana* of "selfish" extinction but the enlightened status of a *bodhisattva,* or "Buddha-to-be." The *bodhisattva* postpones individual enlightenment and vows to remain in the round of existence until he has helped all other beings achieve nirvana.

What makes it possible for the *bodhisattva* to offer this aid is the infinite merit gained through a long career of self-sacrifice. Salvation becomes possible not only through one's individual efforts, but also

A

B

through devotion to the great Buddhas and *bodhisatt-vas*. At the popular level, this idea translated into devotional cults of the transcendent Buddha and many other Buddhas and *bodhisattvas* similarly conceived of as divine beings. Of such cults, one of the most important was that of the Buddha Amitabha, the personification of infinite compassion. Amitabha pre-

Vishnu, Durga, and Shiva. Images of three of India's most important Hindu deities, seventh to eleventh centuries A.D. *Figure A shows Vishnu seated upon the conquered Naga, or serpent deity. Figure B shows the goddess Durga standing on a defeated bull-headed demon. Her six arms hold weapons lent to her by Shiva and Vishnu for the battle. Figure C is a magnificent South Indian bronze of Shiva. The fluid, balanced image depicts the so-called "dancing Shiva" engaged in his dance of simultaneous destruction and creation of the universe, an artistic-mythical rendering of the eternal flux of all worldly existence. [(A) Diana L. Eck; (B) Museum of Fine Arts, Boston— Denman W. Ross Collection; (C) W. R. Nelson Gallery of Art]*

C

sides over the Western Paradise, or Pure Land, to which (through his infinite compassion) all who have faith in him have access. (See Chapter 12 for a discussion of the influence of Pure Land Buddhism in Japan.)

The older, more conservative "way of the elders" (Theravada) was never the totally selfish elite tradition of the few that its Mahayana critics claimed it to be. Its focus was always the monastic community, but lay devotees were needed to support this community; moreover, their service and gifts to the monks were a major source of merit for the laity. The emphasis on gaining merit for a better rebirth through high stan-

Relinquishing the Fruits of Action and Devoting Oneself to Krishna

The Bhagavad Gita is the most widely revered and often quoted of all Hindu religious texts. In these verses (Bhagavad Gita 12.6–19), Krishna (Vishnu) tells his friend and disciple, the young warrior Arjuna, of the highest path to salvation, which involves both abandoning one's attachment to human goals and desires and devoting oneself in pure faith to the Supreme Lord Krishna.

▶ *Compare this view of a life of religious faith and devotion to those expressed in "Saint Francis of Assisi Sets Out His Religious Ideals" (Ch. 15) and "Guru Arjun's Faith" (Ch. 24).*

. . . men intent on me renounce all actions to me and worship me, meditating with singular discipline.

When they entrust reason to me, Arjuna, I soon arise to rescue them from the ocean of death and rebirth.

Focus your mind on me, let your understanding enter me;
then you will dwell in me without doubt.

If you cannot concentrate your thought firmly on me, then seek to reach me, Arjuna, by discipline in practice.

Even if you fail in practice, dedicate yourself to action;
performing actions for my sake, you will achieve success.

If you are powerless to do even this, rely on my discipline,
be self-controlled, and reject all fruit of action.

Knowledge is better than practice, meditation better than knowledge,
rejecting fruits of action is better still—it brings peace.

One who bears hate for no creature is friendly, compassionate, unselfish,
free of individuality, patient, the same in suffering and joy.

Content always, disciplined, self-controlled, firm in his resolve,
his mind and understanding dedicated to me, devoted to me, he is dear to me.

The world does not flee from him, nor does he flee from the world;
free of delight, rage, fear, and disgust, he is dear to me.

Disinterested, pure, skilled, indifferent, untroubled,
relinquishing all involvements, devoted to me, he is dear to me.
He does not rejoice of hate, grieve or feel desire;
relinquishing fortune and misfortune, the man of devotion is dear to me.

Impartial to foe and friend, honor and contempt,
cold and heat, joy and suffering, he is free from attachment.

Neutral to blame and praise, silent, content with his fate,
unsheltered, firm in thought, the man of devotion is dear to me.

From Barbara Stoller Miller, trans., *The Bhagavad-Gita: Krishna's Counsel in Time of War* (Toronto: Bantam Books, 1986), pp. 112–113.

dards of conduct was strong for monks and laity alike. Popular lay devotion to the Buddha and pilgrimage to his relics at various *stupas* also became prominent in Theravada practice. Conversely, although the Mahayana also held up monastic life as the ideal, one of its greatest attractions was its strong devotionalism and virtually polytheistic delight in divine Buddhas and *bodhisattvas* to whom the average person could pray for mercy, help, and rebirth in paradise. The basis of Theravada piety and practice was the scriptural collection of the traditional teachings ascribed to the Buddha, as reported by his disciples. Theravadins rejected the Mahayana claim that later texts (e.g., the Lotus Sutra) contained the highest teachings of the Buddha.

The Theravada was the form of Buddhism that India gave to Ceylon, Burma, and parts of Southeast Asia. The Mahayana was the dominant form carried into Central Asia and China, where it became the

The Buddha preaching his first sermon. This seated, high-relief figure of the Buddha, found in the ruins of Sarnath, is one of the finest pieces of Gupta sculpture. Both the hand gesture, which signifies the setting in motion of the eternal dharma, *and the etherealized body and head suggest the new concept of the Buddha that emerged with the Mahayana. In Gupta times, Sarnath was a thriving monastic center as well as one of the major schools for the best sculpture of the day. [Diana L. Eck]*

INDIA FROM THE GUPTA AGE TO CA. A.D. 1000	
A.D. 320–ca. 467	Gupta period
320–330	Reign of Chandragupta, first Gupta king
376–454	Reigns of Chandragupta II and Kumaragupta: Kalidasa flourishes; heyday of Gupta culture
ca. 440	Beginning of Hun invasions from Central Asia
ca. 455–467	Reign of last strong Gupta monarch, Skandagupta
399–414	Chinese Buddhist monk, Fa-Hsien, travels in India
616–657	Reign of Harsha; revival of Gupta splendor and power
820	Death of Vedantin philosopher-theologian, Shankara
550–ca. 1000	Regional Indian kingdoms in north and south; major Puranas composed; age of first great Vaishnava and Shaivite devotional poets in southern India

major form of religious practice until the ninth century. Tantric Buddhism, an esoteric Mahayana tradition heavily influenced by Hindu Tantric speculation and ritual, entered Tibet from North India in the seventh century and became the dominant tradition there. From China, Mahayana teachings spread in the fifth to eighth centuries to fertile new fields in Korea and then Japan.

Pre-Islamic Iran and India in World Perspective

From a European or American perspective, the center of the world in the early centuries of the Christian era is typically seen as having been the late Roman and Near Eastern world of late antiquity in the Mediterranean basin. Such a perspective fails to recognize that in global perspective the loci of major political power, cultural creativity, and religious vitality throughout most of the early centuries A.D. included, alongside the Roman world, also Iran, India, and China. Even in the Roman "West," Africa and south-

The True Nature of the Buddha, According to the Lotus Sutra

The Lotus Sutra (Saddharmapundarikasutra, "Lotus of the True Dharma") is one of the best-loved sacred texts of Mahayana Buddhism. Its original Sanskrit text was translated many times into Chinese (the earliest being in A.D. 225), as well as into Tibetan and other languages. The following passage is a key one for the development of the idea of the cosmic form of the Buddha. Note that Tathagata, *"thus gone" (i.e., having achieved release, or* nirvana*) is one of the names used for a Buddha.*

▶ *Compare this passage to the reflections of the Japanese Zen Buddhist master Hakuin on his own spiritual quest in the box entitled "Hakuin's Enlightenment" in Chapter 11.*

Fully enlightened for ever so long, the Tathagata has an endless span of life, he lasts for ever. Although the Tathagata has not entered Nirvana, he makes a show of entering Nirvana, for the sake of those who have to be educated. And even today my ancient course as a Bodhisattva is still incomplete, and my life span is not yet ended. From today onwards still twice as many hundreds of thousands of Nayutas of Kotis of aeons must elapse before my life span is complete. Although therefore I do not at present enter into Nirvana (or extinction), nevertheless I announce my Nirvana. For by this method I bring beings to maturity. Because it might be that, if I stayed here too long and could be seen too often, beings who have performed no meritorious actions, who are without merit, a poorly lot, eager for sensuous pleasures, blind, and wrapped in the net of false views, would, in the knowledge that the Tathagata stays (here all the time), get the notion that life is a mere sport, and would not conceive the notion that the (sight of the) Tathagata is hard to obtain. In the conviction that the Tathagata is always at hand they would not exert their vigour for the purpose of escaping from the triple world, and they would not conceive of the Tathagata as hard to obtain.

Hence the Tathagata, in his skill in means, has uttered to those beings the saying that "Rarely, O monks, do Tathagatas appear in the world." Because, during many hundreds of thousands of Nayutas of Kotis of aeons those beings may have the sight of a Tathagata, or they may not. And therefore, basing my statement on this fact, I say that "Rarely, O monks, do Tathagatas appear in the world." To the extent that they understand the rarity of a Tathagata's appearance, to that extent they will wonder (at his appearance), and sorrow (at his disappearance), and when they do not see the Tathagata, they will long for the sight of him. The wholesome roots, which result from their turning their attention towards the Tathagata as towards an objective basis, will for a long time tend to their weal, benefit and happiness. Considering this, the Tathagata, although he does not actually enter Nirvana, announces his entering into Nirvana, for the sake of those to be educated. And that is a discourse on Dharma by the Tathagata himself. When he utters it, there is in it no false speech on the part of the Tathagata.

—15, 268–272

From Edward Conze, ed., *Buddhist Texts Through the Ages* (New York: Harper Torchbooks, 1964), pp. 142–143.

---

western Asia were prominent both politically and culturally. Roman imperial strength rapidly shifted east to Byzantium; Alexandria was the great center of Hellenism for several centuries; and the major doctrinal councils of the Christian church were held in Asia and Africa. Our perspective must necessarily change when we give proper recognition to historical realities still further east down to the rise of Islam in the seventh century: the Sasanid imperial cultural of Iran, the Zoroastrian revival, the Manichaean movement, the compilation of the Babylonian and Palestinian Tamuds, the completion of the *Mahabharata* and *Ramayana,* Gupta imperial power, Gupta imperial power, Gupta art and literature, Indian religious thought, and the spread of Mahayana Buddhism across Central Asia into China and thence to Japan.

Portions of Asia and Africa were thus the settings for impressive and often momentous historical developments. Consequently, simplistic notions of the progressive "rise of the West" from classical antiquity to modern times do not hold very well for the first millennium A.D., especially when we take into view the coming of Islam in its last third. To any impartial observer, the Western world in these centuries does not appear to have held much promise as a future center of globally important political or cultural life. Instead, progressiveness and culture seemed to be best embodied in either Sasanid or Gupta culture, or in East Asia. The majesty and unity of Chinese imperial power and cultural under the Han dynasty (221 B.C.–A.D. 220) and its reestablishment under the Sui (589–618) and T'ang (618–907) dynasties, or the cultural, political, and religious vibrancy of the heavily Chinese-influenced Nara (710–794) and Heian (794–1180) periods in Japan, cannot be underestimated.

A revised perspective would thus see a number of important centers of cultural, religious, and political traditions around the globe, both in the Asian kingdoms and also notably in the Mediterranean imperial domain of Byzantium and in Aksumite Ethiopia. Hindu tradition and Indian culture were undergoing important developments, while Buddhism was waning in its Indian homeland even as it found new and rich fields for conquest in Central Asia, China, and Japan, as well as Southeast Asia. Zoroastrian Iran appeared well on its way into a second millennium of Iranian imperial splendor under the Sasanids.

Yet Iran would soon face the most cataclysmic changes of all the major centers of world culture in this age, and these changes would later overtake much of India and other parts of South Asia. Who could have suspected in the time of Chosroes Anoshirvan how radically Persian culture would be shaken, recast, and given new life in Islamic forms within three or four centuries? The imminent coming of this last major world religious and cultural tradition would fundamentally transform many early centers of civilization.

Suggested Readings

IRAN

M. BOYCE, ed. and trans., *Textual Sources for the Study of Zoroastrianism* (1984). An extremely valuable anthology with an important introduction that includes Boyce's arguments for a revision (to sometime between 1400 and 1200 B.C.) of the dates of Zoroaster's life.

M. BOYCE, *Zoroastrians: Their Religious Beliefs and Practices* (1979). A detailed survey by the current authority on Zoroastrian religious history. See Chapters 7–9.

R. N. FRYE, *The Heritage of Persia* (1963). Still one of the best surveys. Chapter 6 deals with the Sasanid era.

R. GHIRSHMAN, *Iran* (1954 [orig. ed. 1951]). An introductory survey—simpler and less detailed than Frye's.

R. GHIRSHMAN, *Persian Art: The Parthian and Sasanid Dynasties* (1962). Superb photographs, and a very helpful glossary of places and names. The text is minimal and less useful.

GEO WIDENGRAN, *Mani and Manichaeism* (1965). Still the standard introductory survey of Mani's life and the later spread and development of Manichaeism.

INDIA

A. L. BASHAM, *The Wonder That Was India* (1963). Still the best accessible general survey of classical Indian religion, society, literature, art, and political organization.

W. T. DE BARY et. al., comp. *Sources of Indian Tradition*, 2nd ed. (1958). Vol. I, *From the Beginning to 1800*, ed. and rev. by Ainslie T. Embree (1988). Excellent selections from a wide variety of Indian texts, with good introductions to chapters and individual selections.

S. DUTT, *Buddhist Monks and Monasteries of India* (1962). The standard work. See especially Chapters 3 ("Bhakti") and 4 ("Monasteries Under the Gupta Kings").

D. G. MANDELBAUM, *Society in India* (1972). 2 vols. The first two chapters in Volume I of this large and interesting study of caste, family, and village relations are a good introduction to the caste system.

B. ROWLAND, *The Art and Architecture of India: Buddhist/Hindu/Jain*, 3rd rev. ed. (1970). See the excellent chapters on Sungan, Andhran, and other early Buddhist art (6–8, 14), the Gupta period (15), and the Hindu Renaissance (17–19).

V. A. SMITH, *The Oxford History of India*, 4th rev. ed. (1981). See especially pages 164–229 (the Gupta period and following era to the Muslim invasions).

R. THAPAR, *A History of India*, Part I (1966), pp. 109–193. Three chapters covering the rise of mercantilism, the Gupta "classical pattern," and the southern dynasties to ca. A.D. 900.

P. YOUNGER, *Introduction to Indian Religious Thought* (1972). A sensitive attempt to delineate classical concerns of Indian religious thought and culture.

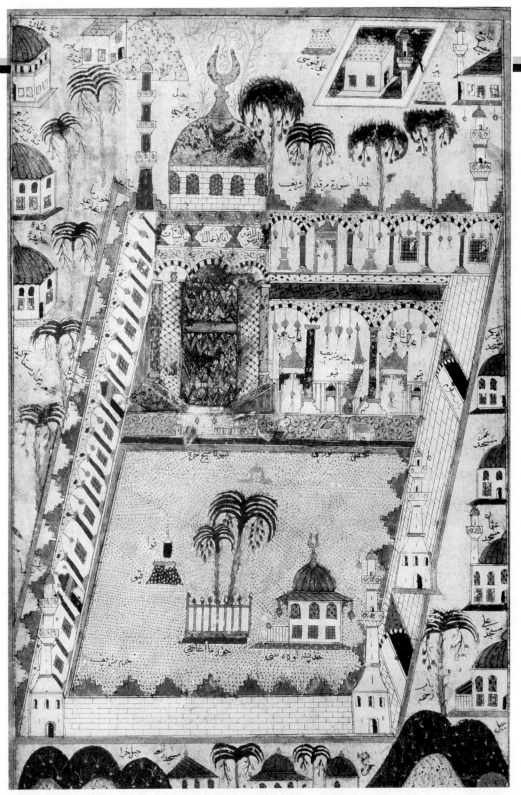

A miniature painting of the Prophet's Mosque in Medina (dated Shawwal 27, 1121, or December 27, 1709 in the Christian calendar). The mosque contains the tomb of Muhammad. [Bildarchiv Preussischer Kulturbesitz]

The Formation of Islamic Civilization (622–945)

I slamic civilization arose as the last great world civilization up to now, if one excepts the post-Enlightenment modern West. On the one hand, its rise is the story of the creation, spread, and elaboration of distinctive Islamic religious, social, and political institutions within an initially Arab-dominated empire. On the other, it is the story of how, in older cultural environments, Islamic ideas and institutions evolved from their Arabian beginnings into a cosmopolitan array of cultures. Each was a different, new creation of a particular place and particular circumstances, yet each was identifiably part of a larger, international Islamic civilization.

The basic ideas and ideals of the Islamic worldview derived from a single, prophetic-revelatory event, Muhammad's proclamation of the Qur'an.[1] This event galvanized the Arabs into a new kind of unity—that of the community of *Muslims,* or "submitters" to God. This community subsequently spread far beyond Arabia, and Persians, Indians, and others raised it to new heights. Arab military prowess and cultural consciousness joined with a new religious orientation to effect one of the most permanent revolutions in history. But it was the peoples of the older cultural heartlands who sustained this revolution and built a new civilization. It was their acceptance of a new vision of society (and, indeed, of reality) as more compelling than any older vision—Jewish, Greek, Iranian, Christian, Buddhist—that allowed an Islamic civilization to come into being.

[1] The common English transliteration of this Arabic word, *Koran,* is today being replaced by the more accurate *Qur'an;* similarly, *Muhammad* is preferable to *Mohammed, Muslim* to *Moslem, amir* to *emir,* and *ulama* to *ulema.*

361

Origins and Early Development

Setting

At the beginning of the seventh century A.D., the dominant Eurasian political powers, Christian Byzantium and Zoroastrian Iran, or Persia, had confronted one another for over four centuries. This rivalry did not, however, continue much longer. In the wake of one final, mutually exhausting conflict (608–627), a new Arab power broke in from the southern deserts to humble the one and destroy the other.

Pre-Islamic Arabia was not just the home of desert camel nomads. In the Fertile Crescent, Byzantium and Iran had managed to keep the nomads of the Syrian and northern Arabian steppe at bay with the help of small Arab client kingdoms that served as buffer states on the edge of the desert (a major one of which was Christian in faith). Settled Arab kingdoms had long existed in the agriculturally rich highlands of southern Arabia, which had direct access to the international trade that moved by land and sea along its coasts (see Chapter 8). Some of these kingdoms, including a Jewish one in the sixth century, had been independent; others had been under Persian or Abyssinian domination. Farther north, astride the major trade route through the western Arabian highland of the Hijaz, the town of Mecca was a center of the caravan trade. It was also a pilgrimage center because of its famous sanctuary, the Ka'ba (or Kaaba), where many pagan Arab tribes had their gods enshrined. The settled Arabs of Mecca formed a thriving merchant republic in which older tribal values were breaking down under the strains of urban and com-

The Ka'ba in Mecca. The Ka'ba is viewed in Muslim tradition as the site of the first "house of God" built by Abraham and his son Ishmael at God's command. It is held to have fallen later into idolatrous use until Muhammad's victory over the Meccans and his cleansing of the holy cubical structure (ka'ba means cube). The Ka'ba is the geographical point toward which all Muslims face when performing ritual prayer. It and the plain of Arafat outside Mecca are the two foci of the pilgrimage of Hajj that each Muslim aspires to make at least once in a lifetime.

Imru l-Qais, the Wandering Poet-Hero

With little written or visual artistic tradition, the ancient Arabs focused on the perfection of the oral word. Each tribe had a poet who in his verse extolled the greatness and prowess of his people and their ancestry and humiliated tribal enemies with satire and polemic. Such verse reinforced the cultural ideals that sprang from the life of the camel nomads of the desert: generosity and hospitality to a fault, family pride and honor, fearless audacity in love and battle, and delight in the animals and other natural beauties of the marginal desert world. In this excerpt from a famous poem of Imru l-Qais (d. ca. 540?), we see a standard beginning of the Arabic lyric ode, or qasida: the sight of an abandoned camp that recalls some past event to the poet. There follow here boastful memories of amorous adventure and a brief segment from later in the poem about the poet's hard existence (which fell to him after his father, ruler of one of the northern desert kingdoms, banished him because he refused to give up poetry—an occupation his father felt was improper for a prince).

Here halt, and weep, for one long-remembered love, for an old
Camp at the edge of the sands that stretch from the Brakes to Floodhead,
From Clearward to the Heights. The marks are not gone yet,
For all that's blown and blown back over them, northward, southward.
Look at the white-deer's droppings scattered in the old yards
And penfolds of the place, like black pepperseeds.
. . . .
I suffered so for love, so fast the tears ran down
Over my breast, the sword-belt there was soaked with weeping.
And yet—the happy days I had of them, of women
. . . .
One day on a sandhill back she would not do my will,
And swore an oath, and swore she meant to keep her oath.
. . . .
That night I passed the wardens who watched their tents, the men
Who would have welcomed me, for the glory of murdering me,
In an hour when Pleiades glittered in the night-heaven
Like a jewelled girdle, gem and pearl and gem;
In such an hour I came; she was all doffed for sleep
But for a shift; close by the screen of the tent she lay.
God's oath on me! she whispered, but thou hast no excuse!

And now I know that thou wilt be wild for ever.
Forth we went together; I led; she trailed behind us
A robe's embroidered hem, that tracks might tell no tales.
When we were past the fenced folkyards, then we made straight
For the heart of the waste, the waves and tumbled hillocks of sand.
I pulled her head to mine by the lovelocks, and she pressed
Against me, slender, but soft even at the ankle.
Thin-waisted she was, and white, sweetly moulded about the belly,
And the skin above her breasts shone like a polished mirror,
Or a pearl of the first water, whiteness a little gilded,
Fed of a pure pool unstirred by the feet of men
. . . .
And taking a water-skin from the house, I would strap it close
Over my shoulder—how often!—and meek to such a saddle
Crossing some hollow place like the flats of Starverib Waste
Have I heard the wolf, like a spendthrift who's gambled his darlings away,
Howl! He would howl. I would answer: It's a poor trade we follow
For profit, if thou hast kept as little as I have kept;
Whatever we get, thou and I, we bolt it; and it's gone.
A man will never be fat who thrives as we two thrive.

From Eric Schroeder, trans., *Muhammad's People* (Portland, ME: Bond Wheelwright, 1955), pp. 3–5.

mercial life. But neither the Meccans nor other settled Arabs were wholly cut off from the nomads, who lived on herding and sporadic raids on settlements and caravans.

The Arabic language, a Semitic tongue of the Afro-Asiatic family (see Chapter 8), defined and linked the Arab peoples, however divided they were by religion, blood feuds, rivalry, and open conflict. From the Yemen north to Syria–Palestine and the Euphrates, the major element of culture that the Arabs shared was their highly developed poetic idiom. Traditionally, every tribe had a poet to exhort its warriors and challenge its enemies with insults before battle. Poetry contests were also held, often in conjunction with the annual trade fairs that brought diverse tribes together under a general truce.

The popular notion of Islam as a "religion of the desert" is largely untrue. Islam began in a commercial center and first flourished in an agricultural oasis. Its first converts were settled Meccan townsfolk and date farmers of Yathrib (Medina). Before becoming Muslims, most of these Arabs had been pagans, but some had been Jews or Christians, or had been influenced by Jews or Christians. Caravans passed north and south through Mecca, and no merchant who engaged in this traffic, as Muhammad himself did, could have been ignorant of different cultures. Early Muslim leaders used the Arabs as warriors and looked to Arab cultural ideals for roots long after the locus of Islamic power had left Arabia. But the empire and culture that they built were centered in the heartlands of Eurasian urban culture and based on settled communal existence rather than desert tribal anarchy.

Muhammad and the Qur'an

Muhammad (ca. 570–632) was raised an orphan in one of the less well-to-do commercial families of the venerable Meccan tribe of Quraysh. Later, in the midst of a successful business career made possible by his marriage to Khadija, a wealthy Meccan widow, he grew increasingly troubled by the idolatry, worldliness, and lack of social conscience around him. These traits would have been equally offensive to sensitive Jewish or Christian piety and morality, about which he certainly knew something. Yet Muhammad did not find his answers in these traditions; they remained somehow foreign to mainstream Arab culture, even though some Arab tribes were Jewish or Christian.

ORIGINS AND EARLY DEVELOPMENT OF ISLAM	
ca. 570	Birth of Muhammad
622	The Hijra ("emigration") of Muslims to Yathrib (henceforward *al-Madina*, "The City [of the Prophet]"); beginning of Muslim calendar
632	Death of Muhammad; Abu Bakr becomes first "successor" (*Khalifa*, caliph) to leadership, reigns 632–634
634–644	Caliphate of Umar; rapid conquests in Egypt and Iran
644–656	Caliphate of Uthman (member of Umayyad clan); more conquests; Qur'an text established; growth of sea power
656–661	Contested Caliphate of Ali; first civil war
661–680	Caliphate of Mu'āwiya; founding of Umayyad dynasty (661–750); capital moved to Damascus; more expansion
680	Second civil war (680–692) begins with death of al-Husayn at Karbala

Muhammad's discontent with the moral status quo and older religious solutions prepared the way for a sudden religious experience that changed his life when he was about forty years old. He felt himself called by the one true God to "rise and warn" his fellow Arabs about their frivolous disregard for morality and the worship and service due their creator. On repeated occasions, revelation came to him through a figure who was gradually identified as God's messenger angel, Gabriel. It took the form of a "reciting" (*qur'an*) of God's word—now rendered in "clear Arabic" for the Arabs, just as it had been given to previous prophets in Hebrew or other languages for their peoples.

The message of the Qur'an was clear: The Prophet is to warn his people against idolatrous worship of false gods and against all immorality, especially injustice to the weak and less fortunate—the poor, orphans, widows, and women in general. A judgment day at the end of time will see everyone bodily resurrected to stand alone and face eternal punishment in hellfire or eternal joy in paradise, according to how one has lived. The way to paradise lies in proper gratitude to God for the bounties of His created world, His prophetic and revelatory guidance, and His readiness

A   B

Qur'anic pages. With the Muslim aversion to images, calligraphy became a major art form in the early centuries of Islam and has continued to flourish. The Arabic script developed primarily to render the Qur'anic text as exactly as possible, and the calligraphic are developed along with it. The earliest script widely used for the Qur'an was the horizontally elongated Kufic script, which dominated qur'anic calligraphy for three centuries. Figure A shows a page from an eighth-century Qur'an written in Kufic script. After the tenth century, other scripts began to predominate. An example of one regional script, the so-called Magribi, or North African, is shown in Figure B. [Freer Gallery of Art]

to forgive the penitent. Social justice and obedient worship and service of the one Lord are demanded of every human. Everyone is to recognize his or her creatureliness and God's transcendence. The proper response is "submission" *(islam)* to God's will, becoming *muslim ("submissive"* or *"surrendering")* in one's worship and morality. All of creation praises and serves God by its very nature; only humans have been given a choice, either to obey or to reject Him.

In this Qur'anic message, the moral monotheism of Judaic and Christian tradition (very likely reinforced by Zoroastrian and Manichaean ideas) reached its logical conclusion in a radically theocentric vision; it demanded absolute obedience to the one Lord of the Universe. The Qur'anic revelations explicitly state that Muhammad is only the last in a long line of prophets chosen to bring God's word: Noah, Abraham, Moses, Jesus, and nonbiblical Arabian figures like Salih had been sent before on similar missions. Because the communities of these earlier prophets had strayed from the teachings of their

scriptures or had altered them, Muhammad was given one final reiteration of God's message. Jews and Christians, like pagans, were summoned to respond to the moral imperatives of the Qur'an he recited to them.

The Prophet's preaching fell largely on deaf ears in the first years after his calling. However, a small number gradually followed the lead of his wife, Khadija, in recognizing him as a divinely chosen reformer of individual and communal life. Some prominent Meccans did join him, but the merchant aristocracy as a whole resisted. His preaching against their traditional gods and goddesses threatened not only their ancestral ways but also their Meccan pilgrimage shrine and the lucrative trade it attracted. The Meccans began to persecute Muhammad's followers. After the deaths of Khadija and Muhammad's uncle and protector Abu Talib, the situation worsened, and the Prophet even had to send a small band of Muslims to seek refuge in Abyssinia for a time. Then, as a result of his growing reputation as a moral and holy man, Muhammad was

The Qur'an, or "Recitation," of God's Word

The Qur'an has many themes, ranging from moral admonition, social justice, the eternal punishment that awaits the ungodly, and exemplary stories of past peoples and their prophets, to God's majesty and uniqueness, His bountiful natural world and compassion for humankind, and the joys of paradise. The following short selections touch on (1) God's mercies in His creation and their importance as signs of God's bounty and mercy; (2) praise of God the Almighty, the Creator; (3) Abraham as one of the previous prophets who testified to God and brought His revelations to their people, and (4) the final Judgment Day.

God created the heavens and the earth—a real creation. Let Him be exalted above all false worship. . . .

The night and the day He has made to serve your ends. Sun, moon and stars are all recruited to His command and here, too, are signs for those who use their minds. There is a sign, too, for mindful folk, in the colours of rich diversity in the manifold things He has arrayed for you. . . .

He has also set the mountains firm on the earth that it may be solid under you.

There are rivers and tracks for you so that you may find your way, landmarks too, and the stars by which men are piloted. Shall He, then, who created, be on a par with that which does not? Will you not realise?

Were you set to count up the mercies of God you would not be able to number them. God is truly forgiving and merciful.

—Sura 16.3,12,15–18

He is God. There is no god but He. He knows the hidden and the evident. He is the merciful Lord of mercy.

He is God, there is no god but He. He is the King, the holy One, the Lord of peace, the Keeper of faith, the watch-Keeper, the all-strong, the ever-powerful, the Self-aware in His greatness. Glory be to God above all that idolators conceive.

—Sura 59.22–23

You people of the Book, why are you so argumentative about Abraham, seeing that the Torah and the Gospel were only sent down after his time? Will you not use your reason? You are people much given to disputing about things within your comprehension: why insist on disputing about things of which you have no knowledge? Knowledge belongs to God and you lack it!

Abraham was not a Jew, nor was he a Christian. He was a man of pure worship (a *hanif*) and a Muslim: he was not one of those pagan idolaters. . . .

—Sura 3.65–67

But what, when the earth is crushed and crumbled into dust and your Lord comes, and the angels rank on rank, and *Jahannam* is brought into view on that Day? On that Day man will recall what he has been. But what will the realisation avail him? He will say: "Would that for my very life I had reckoned earlier for this Day!" None requites as God does on that Day: none can bind as He binds.

"O soul at rest, return to your Lord, welcomed in His welcoming. Enter among My servants, enter My Paradise."

—Sura 89.21–30

From Kenneth Cragg, trans., *Readings in the Qur'an* (London: Collins, 1988), pp. 102, 86–87, 121, 166.

called to Yathrib (an agricultural oasis about 240 miles north of Mecca) as a neutral arbitrator among its five quarrelsome tribes, three of which were Jewish. Having sent his Meccan followers ahead, Muhammad fled Mecca in July 622 for Yathrib, afterward to be known as Medina (al-Madina, "the City [of the Prophet]"). Some dozen years later, this "emigration," or Hegira, became the starting point for the Islamic calendar. This event marked the creation of a distinctive Islamic community, or *Umma*.[2]

[2] The twelve-month Muslim lunar year is shorter than the Christian solar year by about eleven days, giving a difference of about three years per century. Muslim dates are reckoned from the month in 622 in which Muhammad began his Hegira (Arabic: *Hijra*). Thus Muslims celebrated the start of their lunar year 1401 in November 1980 (A.D. 1979–1980 a.h. [Anno Hegirae] 1400), whereas it was only 1,358 solar years from 622 to 1980.

Muhammad quickly cemented ties between the Meccan emigrants and the Medinans, many of whom became converts. Raids on the caravans of his Meccan enemies established his leadership. They point also to the economic as well as religious dimension of the Medinan-Meccan struggle. The Arab Jews of Medina by and large rejected his message and authority. They even had contacts with his Meccan enemies, moving Muhammad to turn on the Jews, kill or enslave some, banish others, and take their lands. Many of the continuing revelations of the Qur'an from this period pertain to communal order or to the Jews and Christians who rejected Islam.

The basic Muslim norms took shape in Medina: allegiance to the *Umma;* honesty in public and personal affairs; modesty in personal habits; abstention from alcohol and pork; fair division of inheritances; improved treatment of women, especially as to their property and other rights within marriage; careful regulation of marriage and divorce; ritual ablution before any act of worship, be it Qur'an-reciting or prayer; three (later five) daily rites of worship, facing the Meccan Ka'ba; payment of a kind of tithe to support less fortunate Muslims; daytime fasting for one month each year; and, eventually, pilgrimage to Mecca *(Hajj)* at least once in a lifetime, if one were able.

Acceptance of Islamic political authority brought a kind of tolerance. A Jewish oasis yielded to Muhammad's authority and was allowed, unlike the resistant Medinan Jews, to keep its lands, practice its faith, and receive protection in return for the payment of a head tax. This practice was followed ever after for Jews, Christians, and other "people of Scripture" who accepted Islamic rule. After long conflict, the Meccans surrendered to Muhammad, and his generosity in accepting them into the *Umma* set the pattern for the later Islamic conquests. Following an age-old practice, Muhammad cemented many of his alliances with marriage (although as long as Khadija was alive, he did not take a second wife). In the last years of the Prophet's life, the once tiny band of Muslims became the heart of an all-Arabian tribal confederation, bound together by personal allegiance to Muhammad, submission *(islam)* to God, and membership in the *Umma* of "submitters."

Early Islamic Conquests

In 632, Muhammad died after an illness, leaving neither a son nor a named successor. The new *Umma* faced its first major crisis. A political struggle be-

The Omar Mosque, or Dome of the Rock, in Jerusalem. An early example of Islamic architecture (but not a "mosque"), it dates from the seventh century, during the first wave of Arab expansion. It is built on the rock from which Muslims believe Muhammad ascended into heaven and on which Jews believe Abraham prepared to sacrifice Isaac. The lower right of the picture shows the western "wailing" wall of the second temple, a site sacred to Jews. [David H. Wells, 1990]

tween Meccan and Medinan factions ended in a pledge of allegiance to Abu Bakr, the most senior of the early Meccan converts. Many of the naturally independent Arab tribes renounced their allegiance to the Prophet upon his death. Nevertheless, Abu Bakr's rule (632–634) as Muhammad's successor, or "caliph" (Arabic: *khalifa*), reestablished Medinan hegemony and at least nominal religious conformity over the whole of Arabia. The Arabs were forced to recognize in the *Umma* a new kind of supratribal community that demanded more than allegiance to a particular leader.

Course of Conquest

Under the next two caliphs, Umar (634–644) and Uthman (644–656), Arab armies burst out of the peninsula, intent on more than traditional bedouin booty raids. In one of the most astonishing sets of military operations ever, they conquered the Byzantine and Sasanid territories of the Fertile Crescent (by 640), Egypt (by 642), and most of Iran (by 643). For the first time in centuries, the lands from Egypt to Iran were united under one rule. Finally, Arab armies swept west over the Byzantine-controlled Libyan coast and,

in the east, pushed to the Oxus, defeating the last Sasanid ruler by 651.

An interlude of civil war during the contested caliphate of Ali (656–661) slowed the expansion briefly. Then, under the fifth caliph, Mu'āwiya (661–680), expansion and consolidation of the new empire progressed. By 680, control of greater Iran was solidified by permanent Arab garrisoning of Khorasan, much of Anatolia was raided, Constantinople was besieged (but not taken), and Armenia was brought under Islamic rule. In the Mediterranean, an Islamic fleet conquered Cyprus, plundered Sicily and Rhodes, and crippled Byzantine sea power.

Succeeding decades saw the eastern Berbers of Libyan North Africa defeated and converted in substantial numbers, if often superficially or nominally, to Islam. With their help, "the West" (*al-Maghrib,*

MAP 13-1   MUSLIM CONQUESTS AND DOMINATION OF THE MEDITERRANEAN TO ABOUT 750   *The rapid spread of Islam (both religion and political-military power) is shown here. From the West's viewpoint, the important fact was that in the 125 years after Muhammad's rise Muslims came to dominate Spain and all areas south and east of the Mediterranean.*

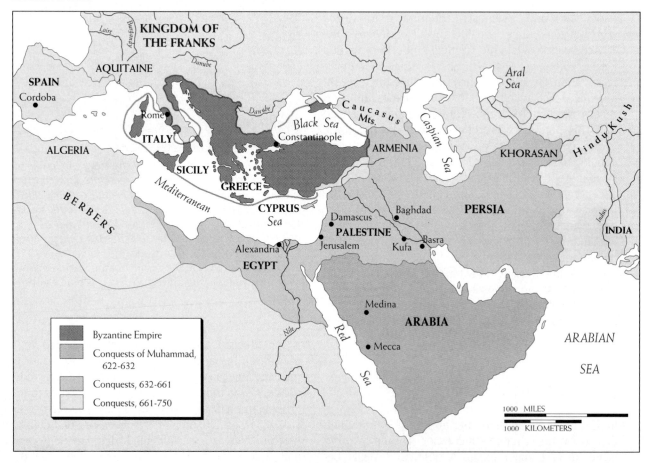

modern Morocco and Algeria), fell quickly. In 711, raids into Spain began (the name of the Berber Muslim leader of the first invaders, Tariq, lives on in *Gibraltar,* a corruption of *Jabal Tariq,* "Mount Tariq"). By 716, the disunited Spanish Visigoth kingdoms had fallen, and much of Iberia was under Islamic control. Pushing farther north into France, the Arabs were finally checked by a defeat at the hands of Charles Martel south of Tours (732). At the opposite end of the empire, buoyed by large-scale Arab immigration, Islamic forces consolidated their holdings as far as the Oxus River basin. In 710, Arab armies reached the Indus region of Sind. The Muslim Arabs now controlled the former Sasanid Empire and beyond. The Byzantine realm was reduced by half and Islamic power was supreme from the Atlantic to central Asia (see Map 13-1).

Factors of Success

A combination of factors contributed to this rapid expansion. The basic factor was surely the weakened military and economic condition of the Byzantine and Sasanid states—the result of their repeated warfare with one another over many decades. Also basic was the capacity of the new Islamic vision of society and life to unite the Arabs and to attract others as well. Its corollary was the commitment among the Islamic leadership to extend "the abode of submission" *(Dar al-Islam)* abroad. However, too much has been made of the general Muslim zeal for martyrdom. Assurance of paradise for those engaged in *jihad,* or "struggle (in the path of God)," is less likely to have motivated the average Arab tribesman—who, at least at the beginning, was usually only nominally a Muslim—as much as promise of the booty of war. The marginal life in the peninsula was such that the hope of greater prosperity must have been very compelling.

Yet religious zeal cannot be wholly discounted, especially as time went on. The early policy of sending Qur'an-reciters among the armies' pagan tribesmen to teach the essentials of Muslim faith and practice had its effects. A major factor was certainly the leadership of the first caliphs and field generals. This leadership combined with the economic and military exhaustion of Byzantium and Iran to give Arab armies a distinct advantage. Another element was the readiness of subject populations in many areas to accept, even to welcome, Islamic rule as a relief from Byzantine or Persian oppression. Important here was the Muslim willingness to allow Christian, Jewish, and even Zoroastrian groups to continue as minorities

(with their own legal systems and no military obligations) under the protection of Islamic rule. In return, they had to recognize Islamic political authority, pay a non-Muslim head tax *(jizya),* and refrain from proselytizing or interfering with Muslim religious practice. (Ironically, as time went on, the economic and social realities of the head tax and other strictures on non-Muslims impelled many Christians and Jews to convert.)

Finally, what gave the conquests overall permanence, besides the vitality of the new faith, were the astute policies followed by the early leaders: relatively little bloodshed or destruction of property or economies in conquest; the adoption, with minimal change, of existing administrative systems (and personnel); the adjustment of unequal taxation; the appointment of capable governors; and the strategic siting of new Islamic garrison towns like Basra, Kufa, and Fustat (later Cairo).

The New Islamic Order

Unlike rulers who take over an empire and continue the existing religious and cultural traditions, the Muslims brought with them a new worldview that demanded a new political, social, and cultural reality, however long it might take to effect it. Beyond their military and administrative problems loomed the ultimately more important question of the nature of the Islamic state and society. Under the Prophet, a new kind of community, the *Umma,* had replaced, at least in theory and basic organization, the tribal, blood-based social and political order in Arabia. Yet, once the Arabs (most of whom became Muslims) had to rule non-Arabs and non-Muslims, new problems arose that tested the ideal of an Islamic polity. Chief among these problems were leadership and membership qualifications, social order, and religious and cultural identity.

The Caliphate

Allegiance to Muhammad had rested on his authority as a divine spokesperson and as a gifted leader. His first successors were chosen much as were Arab *shaykhs* ("sheiks"), or tribal chieftains, by agreement of the leaders, or elders, of the new religious "tribe" of Muslims, on the basis of superior personal qualities. Added to these qualities was now the precedence in faith conferred by piety and association with the Prophet. Their titles were "successor" *(khalifa,* or caliph), "leader" *(imam*—used also for the Muslim

A   B

C   D

Early Islamic coins. The development of early Islamic coinage reflects the evolution of Muslim self-awareness. The earliest Arabic kingdom had no coinage of its own. The first Islamic caliphs and governors took over the Byzantine and Sasanid coinage (Figure A: a Sasanid silver dirham with the head of the emperor), adding brief Arabic inscriptions (Figure B), and then slightly altering previous imagery on the coins (Figure C: "standing caliph" with sword and Arab headdress rather than Byzantine crown). It was only under Abd al-Malik, caliph from 685–705, that reform of the coinage led to the abandonment of all imagery depicting the human form in favor of Arabic inscriptions proclaiming the basic Muslim faith (Figure D: The inscription reads "There is no god but God, One, without partner"). [American Numismatic Society of New York]

who stands in front of Muslim worshipers to lead them in ritual prayer), and "commander *(amir)* of the faithful." These names underscored political and religious authority, both of which most Muslims were willing to recognize in the caliphs Abu Bakr and Umar, and potentially in Uthman and Ali. Unfortunately, by the time of Uthman and Ali, various dissensions led to internal strife, then civil war. Yet the first four caliphs had all been close to Muhammad, and this closeness gave their reigns a nostalgic aura of pristine purity, especially as the later caliphal institution was based largely on sheer power and/or hereditary succession.

The nature of Islamic leadership became an issue with the first civil war (656–661) and the recognition of Mu'awiya, a kinsman of Uthman, as caliph. He founded the first dynastic caliphate, that of his Meccan clan of Umayya (661–750). Hereditary Umayyads held power until they were ousted by the Abbasid clan in 750, which based its legitimacy on descent from an uncle of the Prophet (Abbas—hence, "Abbasid"). The Umayyads had the prestige of the office held by the first four, "rightly guided" caliphs. But

they also suffered by the comparison, as they were judged by many to be worldly kings where the earlier four had been true Muslim successors to Muhammad.

The Abbasids won the caliphate by open rebellion in 750, aided by their exploitation of pious dissatisfaction with Umayyad worldliness, non-Arab Muslim resentment of Arab preference (primarily in Iran), and ongoing dissension among Arab tribal factions in the garrison towns. For all their stress on the Muslim character of their caliphate, they were scarcely less worldly and continued the hereditary rule begun by the Umayyads. This they did well enough to retain control of most of the far-flung Islamic territories until 945. Thereafter, although their line continued until 1258, the caliphate was primarily a titular office representing an Islamic unity that existed politically in name only.

The Ulama

Although the caliph could exert his power, as the Abbasids did occasionally, to influence religious matters, he was never "emperor and pope rolled into one," as many Western writers have claimed. Religious leadership in the *Umma* devolved instead on another group. The functional successors of the Prophet in society at large were those Muslims recognized for piety and learning and sought as informal or even formal (as with state-appointed judges) authorities. Initially, they were the "Companions" (male and female) of Muhammad, with the greatest stature in the original Medinan *Umma*—including the first four caliphs. As this generation died out, they were replaced by those younger followers most concerned with preserving, interpreting, and applying the Qur'an, and with maintaining the norms of the Prophet's original *Umma*. Because the Qur'an contained very little actual legislative material, they had to draw on precedents from the practice of Medina and Mecca, as well as on oral traditions about the Prophet and Companions. They also had to standardize and develop grammatical rules for a common learned Arabic language, based on the Qur'an and pre-Islamic poetry. Furthermore, they had to develop and perfect the phonetic, cursive Arabic script, a task done so well that the script was gradually applied as the standard written form for languages wherever Islamic religion and culture became dominant: among Turks, Iranians, Indians, Indonesians, Malays, East Africans, and others. In these and other religious, intellectual, and cultural achievements, they developed an endur-

ing pattern of education based on study under those persons highest in the unbroken temporal chain of trustworthy Muslims linking the current age with that of the earliest *Umma*.

As an unofficial but generally recognized infrastructure in Islamic society, these scholars came to be known as *ulama* ("persons of right knowledge," the Anglicized Arabic plural of *'alim*). Some of the most pious *ulama* refused to be judges for the Umayyads. However, their personal legal opinions and collective discussions of issues, ranging from theological doctrine to criminal punishments, established a general basis for religious and social order. By the ninth century, they had largely defined the understanding of the divine Law, or *Shari'a*, that Muslims ever after have held to be definitive for legal, social, commercial, political, ritual, and moral concerns. This understanding and the methods by which it was derived form the Muslim science of jurisprudence, the core discipline of Islamic learning.

The centers of *ulama* activity were Medina, Mecca, and especially Iraq (primarily Basra and Kufa, later Baghdad), then Khorasan, Syria, North Africa and Spain, and Egypt. In Umayyad times, the *ulama* had already become the guardians of the Muslim conscience, often serving as the chief critics of caliphal rule when it departed too far from Muslim norms. In time, they became a new elite, one eventually identi-

The ritual worship, or prayer. These illustrations show the sequence of movement prescribed for the ritual prayers that each Muslim should perform five times a day. Various words of praise, prayer, and recitation from the Qur'an accompany each position and movement. The ritual symbolizes the Muslim's complete obedience to God and recognition of God as the one, eternal, omnipotent Lord of the universe.

fied with the upper class of each regional society under Islamic rule. Caliphs and their governors regularly sought their advice but often only for moral sanction (or legal sanction—the two are, in the Muslim view, the same) of a contemplated or accomplished action. Some *ulama* acquiesced in dubious sanctions and compromised themselves. Yet incorruptible *ulama* were seldom persecuted for their opinions (except when they supported sectarian rebellions), mostly because of their status and influence among rank-and-file Muslims.

Thus, without building a formal clergy, the Muslims developed a workable legal-moral system based on a formally trained if informally recognized scholarly elite and a tradition of concern with religious ideals in matters of public affairs and social order. If the caliphs and their deputies were seldom paragons of piety and often ruthless, they had at least to act with some circumspection and give compensating support for Muslim pious standards in public. Thus, the *ulama* shared the *de facto* leadership in Muslim societies with the rulers, even if unequally—a pattern that has endured in Islamic states.

The Umma

A great strength of the Qur'anic message was its universalism. Although Muhammad may have conceived of his community first as an Arab one, the logical extension of the Qur'anic preaching was the acceptance into the *Umma* of anyone, of whatever race or nationality, who would submit to God and follow Muslim precepts. By the time of the first conquests, the new state was already so rooted in Muslim ideals that non-Arab converts had to be accepted, even if it meant loss of tax revenue. The social and political status of new converts was, however, clearly second to that of Arabs. Umar had organized the army register, or *diwan,* according to tribal precedence in conversion to, or (in the unique case of Christian Arab tribes) fighting for, Islam. The *diwan* served as the basis for the distribution and taxation of the new wealth, which perpetuated Arab precedence. The new garrisons, which rapidly became urban centers of Islamic rule and culture, kept the Arabs enough apart so that they were not simply absorbed into the cultural patterns or the traditions of the foreign territories. The Qur'an's centrality in Muslim life and the notion of its perfect Arabic form ensured the dominance of the Arabic language. So did the gradual implementation of Arabic in administration, where it replaced Aramaic, Greek, Middle Persian, or Coptic.

Non-Arab converts routinely attached themselves to Arab tribes as "clients," which assured protection and a place in the *diwan.* Still, this attachment also meant acceptance of a permanent second-class citizenship alongside the Arabs. Although many non-Arabs, especially Persians, mastered Arabic and prospered, dissatisfaction among client Muslims was widespread and led to their participation in uprisings against caliphal authority. Persian-Arab tensions were especially strong in Umayyad and early Abbasid times. Nevertheless, a Persian cultural renaissance eventually raised the Islamicized modern Persian language to high status in Islamic culture. Consequently, it profoundly affected religion, art, and literature in much of the Islamic world.

Caliphal administration joined with the evolution of legal theory and practice and the consolidation of religious norms to give stability to the emerging Islamic society. So strong was the power of the Muslim vision of society, that when a caliph, or even a dynasty like the Umayyads, was superseded, the *Umma* and the caliphal office went on. There were, however, conflicting notions of that vision. In the course of the first three Islamic centuries, two major interpretations crystallized that reflected idealistic interpretations of the *Umma,* its leadership and membership. When neither proved viable in the practical world of society and politics, they became minority visions that continued to fire the imaginations of some but failed to win broad-based support. The third, "centrist," vision found favor with the majority; it could speak to a wide spectrum and accommodate inevitable compromises in the higher cause of Islamic unity.

THE KHARIJITES. The most radical idealists traced their political origin to the first civil war (656–661). They were the Kharijites, or "seceders"—so named because they seceded from Ali's camp when, in their view, he compromised with his enemies. The Kharijite position was that the Muslim polity must be based on strict Qur'anic principles. The Kharijites espoused a total egalitarianism among the faithful and held that the leadership of the *Umma* belonged to the best Muslim, whoever that might be. They took a moralistic, rigorist view of who the true members of the *Umma* were: Anyone who committed a major sin was no longer a Muslim. Extreme Kharijites called on true Muslims to join them in rebellion against the morally compromised authority of the reigning caliph. The extremist groups were constant rallying points for opposition to the Umayyads and, to a lesser degree, the Abbasids. More moderate Kharijites tem-

Scenes of Husayn's martyrdom from a Shi'ite passion play in Iran. The role of the martyrdom of al-Husayn, son of Ali and grandson of Muhammad, in Shi'ite piety can hardly be exaggerated. Husayn's martyrdom and that of the imams *after him form the basis for the Shi'ite interpretation of history, which stresses the suffering of the* imams *and of true Muslims who follow them in this world, and promises a reward beyond the grave for the faithful. The performance of passion plays about Husayn's death is unique to Shi'ite Muslim practice. [Peter Chelkowski]*

pered their aversion to tolerating less-than-pious Muslims and the rule of less-than-ideal caliphs, yet they retained a strong sense of the moral imperatives of Muslim personal and collective duty.

Kharijite ideals proved very attractive and influenced wider Muslim pietism in the long run. Although the movement declined in Abbasid times, even today moderate Kharijite groups survive in Muscat, Oman, and North Africa.

THE SHI'A. A second position was defined largely in terms of leadership in the *Umma*. Muhammad had no surviving sons, and his son-in-law and cousin Ali claimed the caliphate in 656, partly on the basis of his familial ties to the Prophet. His claim was contested by Mu'āwiya in the first Islamic civil war. When Mu'āwiya took over by default after a Kharijite murdered Ali in 661, many of Ali's followers felt that Islamic affairs had gone awry. Although it is difficult to

date the crystallization of the developed ideology of the "partisans of Ali" (*Shi'at Ali*, or simply the *Shi'a*, or *Shi'ites*), their roots go back to Ali's murder and especially to that of his son Husayn at Karbala, in Iraq (680).

Whereas most Muslims esteemed Ali for his closeness to Muhammad, the Shi'ites believed that he was the Prophet's appointed successor. Ali's blood tie with Muhammad was augmented in Shi'ite thinking by belief in the Prophet's designation of him as the true *imam,* or Muslim leader, after him. Numerous rebellions in Umayyad times rallied around various figures claiming descent from such a designated and related successor, whether Ali or merely any member of Muhammad's clan of Hashim. Even the Abbasids based their right to the caliphate on their Hashimite blood. The major Shi'ite pretenders who emerged in the ninth and tenth centuries based their claims on both the Prophet's designation and their descent from

Ali and Fatima, Muhammad's daughter. They also stressed the idea of a divinely inspired knowledge passed on by Muhammad to his designated heirs. The true Muslim was the faithful follower of the *imam*s, who carried both Muhammad's blood and his mantle of spiritual authority.

When Shi'ites failed to establish a true *imam* as head of the imperial state, they interpreted this failure theologically. They saw Ali's assassination by a Kharijite, and especially the brutal massacre of Husayn and his family by Umayyad troops, as proofs of the evil nature of the rulers of this world, and as rallying points for true Muslims. The martyrdom of Ali and Husayn was extended to a line of Alid *imam*s that varied among different groups of Shi'ites. True Muslims, like their *imam*s, must suffer. But they would be vindicated in the end by an expected *mahdi,* or "guided one," who would usher in a messianic age and a judgment day that would see the faithful rewarded. (In the Sunni tradition, which we discuss next, similar "mahdist" movements also played a role throughout Islamic history.)

On several occasions in later history, Shi'ite rulers did gain control of some Islamic states. But only after 1500, in Iran, did Shi'ite tradition prevail as the majority faith in a major Muslim state. The Shi'ite vision of the true *Umma* has been a powerful one, but not one that has been able to muster sufficient consensus to dominate the larger Islamic world.

THE CENTRISTS.   Kharijite and Shi'ite causes were repeatedly taken up by disaffected groups in the early and later Islamic empire. But it was a third, less sharply defined position on the nature of leadership and membership in the *Umma* that ultimately gained acceptance from most Muslims. In some ways a compromise, it proved acceptable not only to lukewarm Muslims or simple pragmatists, but also to persons of piety as intense as that of any Kharijite or Shi'ite. We may term the proponents of this position *centrists.* To emphasize the correctness of their views, they eventually called themselves *Sunnis*—followers of the tradition *(sunna)* established by the Prophet and the Qur'an. Neither they, nor the Shi'ites, nor the Kharijites, have ever been a single sect or group; they have always encompassed a wide range of reconcilable, if not always truly compatible, ideas and groups. They have comprised the broad middle spectrum of Muslims who have tended to put communal solidarity and maintenance of the Islamic polity above purist adherence to certain theological positions. They have been inclusivist rather than exclusivist, a trait that has typified the Islamic (unlike the Christian) community through most of history.

The centrist position was simply the most workable general framework for the new Islamic state. Its basic ideas were

1. The *Umma* is a theocratic entity, a state under divine authority; this translates into a nomocracy, or *Umma* under the authority of God's law, the Shari'a. The sources of guidance are, first, the Qur'an; second, the precedent of the Prophet; and, third and fourth, the interpretive efforts and consensus of the Muslims (in practice, the *ulama*).
2. The caliph is the absolute temporal ruler, charged with administering and defending the Abode of Islam and protecting Muslim norms and practice; he possesses no greater authority than other Muslims in matters of faith.
3. A person who professes to be Muslim by witnessing that "There is no god but God, and Muhammad is His Messenger" should be considered a Muslim (because "only God knows what is in the heart"), and not even a mortal sin excludes such a person automatically from the *Umma.*

Under increasingly influential *ulama* leadership, these and other basic premises of Muslim community came to serve as the theological underpinnings of both the caliphal state and the emerging international Islamic social order.

The High Caliphate

The consolidation of the caliphal institution began with the victory of the Umayyad caliph Abd al-Malik in 692 in the second civil war. The succeeding century and a half marks the era of the "high caliphate," the politically strong, culturally vibrant, wealthy, and centralized institution that flourished first under the Umayyads in Damascus and then in the Abbasid capital at Baghdad.[3] The height of caliphal power and splendor came only after the final Umayyad decline, in the first century of Abbasid rule, largely during the caliphates of the fabled Harun al-Rashid (786–809) and his third son, al-Ma'mun (813–833).

---

[3]This periodization of early Islamic government follows that of M. G. S. Hodgson, *The Venture of Islam*, Vol. 1 (Chicago: University of Chicago Press, 1984), pp. 217–236.

EARLY PERIOD OF THE HIGH CALIPHATE	
680–694	Second civil war
685–705	Caliphate of Abd al-Malik; second civil war (680–694); consolidation, arabization of administration
705–715	Caliphate of al-Walid; Morocco conquered, Spain invaded; Arab armies reach the Indus
ca. 750	Introduction of paper manufacture from China through Samarqand to Islamic world
750	Abbasids seize Caliphate from Umayyads, begin new dynasty (750–1258)
756	Some Umayyads escape to Spain, found new dynasty (756–1030)
762–766	New Abbasid capital built at Baghdad

The Abbasid State

The Abbasids' revolution was based on non-Arab disaffection, Khorasanian regionalism, and Shi'ite religio-political hopes. Their victory effectively ended Arab dominance of the empire along with Umayyad ascendancy (except in Spain). The shift of the imperial capital from Damascus to the new "city of peace" built at Baghdad on the Tigris (762–766) symbolized the eastward shift in cultural and political orientation under the new regime. In line with this shift, more and more Persians (albeit arabicized Persians—at least in language) entered the bureaucracy. In the Abbasid heyday under Harun, the highest caliphal advisory office, that of the vizier (Arabic: *wazir*), was dominated by the Khorasanian family of the Barmakids. Religiously, the Abbasids' disavowal of Shi'ite hopes for a divinely inspired imamate reflected their determination to gain the support of a broad spectrum of Muslims, even if they still stressed their descent from al-Abbas, uncle of both Muhammad and Ali.

Whereas the Umayyads had relied on their Syrian Arab forces, for their main troops the Abbasids used principally Khorasanian Arabs and Iranians and, in the provinces, regional mercenaries. Beginning in the ninth century, however, they enlisted large numbers of slave soldiers *(mamluks),* mostly Turks from the northern steppes, as their personal troops. The officers of these forces, themselves military slaves, soon seized the positions of power in the central and pro-

vincial bureaucracies and the army. In a matter of years, the caliphs were dominated by their *mamluk* officers. This domination led to an increasing alienation of the Muslim populace from their own rulers. This alienation was evident in Iraq itself, where unrest with this overbearing Turkish guard led the Abbasid caliph to remove the government from Baghdad to the newly built city of Samarra sixty miles up the Tigris, where it remained from 836 to 892.

Society

The deep division between rulers and populace—the functionally secular state and its Muslim subjects—was ever after typical of Islamic society. However, even while the independence of more and more provincial rulers reduced the power of the Abbasid state after the mid-ninth century, such rulers generally chose to recognize caliphal authority at least in name. They thereby secured legitimacy for their rule and put themselves forward as guardians of the Islamic polity, which found its actual cohesiveness in the Muslim ideals being standardized by the *ulama.*

We must remember, however, that full conversion of the diverse populace of the Islamic Empire lagged far behind the centralization of political power and the development of Islamic socio-religious institutions. It appears that Iraq and Iran (especially Khorasan, which saw early large-scale Arab Muslim immigration) were the two most important areas of the early Islamization of local elites until well into the twelfth century. They were followed by Spain, North Africa, and Syria. Conversion and fuller Islamization, when it came, meant the development of a self-confident Muslim polity no longer threatened by other religious communities or political forces and a correspondingly diminished need for centralized caliphal power.[4]

Decline

The eclipse of the caliphal state was foreshadowed at the very outset of Abbasid rule, when one of the last Umayyads escaped the general slaughter of his family by fleeing west to Muslim Spain. Supported by Syrian, Yemenite, and some Berber tribes, he founded a Spanish Islamic state that stood for nearly three hun-

[4]Richard W. Bullet, *Conversion to Islam in the Medieval Period* (Cambridge, MA: Harvard University Press, 1979), especially pp. 7–15, 128–138.

dred years (756–1030), producing the spectacular Moorish culture of Spain. Protected by sheer distance from Abbasid control, the Spanish Umayyads even assumed the title of caliph in 929, so strong were they and so weak were the Abbasids by this time. In all the Abbasid provinces, regional governments were always potential bases for independent states. Besides various Kharijite states among the Berbers, the earliest separate state in North Africa was set up in 801 by the governor of Harun al-Rashid in the area of modern Tunisia. A later North African regional dynasty, the Fatimids, even conquered Egypt and set up Shi'ite rule in 969 that claimed to be the only true caliphate.

In the East, Iran grew ever harder for Baghdad to control. Beginning in 821 in Khorasan, Abbasid governors or rebel groups set up independent dynasties repeatedly for two centuries. As a result of weakness, the caliph had usually to recognize their *de facto* sway over various parts of the Iranian plateau. Among the longest-lived of these regional Iranian dynasties were the Samanids of Khorasan and Transoxiana, who held power at Bukhara as nominal vassals of the caliph from 875 until 999. The Samanids gave northeastern Iran a long period of economic and political security from Turkish steppe invaders. Under them, Persian poetry and Arabic scientific studies started what was to become over the next centuries a Persian

Islamic cultural renaissance of substantial proportions.

Of greatest consequence for the caliphal state was, however, the rise in the mountains south of the Caspian of a Shi'ite clan, the Buyids, who took over Abbasid rule in 945. Although they kept the caliph himself "in office," he and his descendants were henceforth largely puppets in the hands of Buyid "commanders" (*amirs* or *emirs*); later, *sultans*). In 1055, the Buyids were replaced by the more famous Seljuk rulers, or *sultans*. Thus, the caliphal state broke up, even though Abbasid caliphs continued as figureheads of Muslim unity until the Mongol invaders killed the last of them in 1258.

"Classical" Culture of Abbasid Times

The pomp and splendor of the Abbasid court were grand enough to become the stuff of Islamic legend such as we find preserved much later in the tales of *The Thousand and One Nights.* Their rich cultural legacy similarly outlived the Abbasids themselves. Their power and glory were made possible by a strong army and central government and vigorous internal and external trade. The latter may have been stimulated by the prosperous T'ang Empire of China, with which the Islamic world had much overland and sea contact. It was, for example, in the mid-eighth century that paper manufacture was introduced from China to the Islamic world through Transoxiana, at Samarkand.

Intellectual Traditions

The Abbasid heyday was marked by sophisticated tastes and an insatiable thirst for knowledge—not simply religious, but *any* knowledge. An Arab historian called Baghdad "the market to which the wares of the sciences and arts were brought, where wisdom was sought as a man seeks after his stray camels, and whose judgment of values was accepted by the whole world."[5] Older traditions continued and flourished. Contacts (primarily among intellectuals) between Muslims and Christian, Jewish, Zoroastrian, and other "protected" religious communities contributed to the cosmopolitanism of the age. Some older intel-

[5] See Oleg Grabar, *The Formation of Islamic Art* (New Haven, CT: Yale University Press, 1973), especially pp. 1–103, 206–213.

The mosaic floor from the bath and pleasure hall of an Umayyad palace or hunting lodge in the desert of Khirbat al-Mafjar in modern Israel. Both the Umayyad and Abbasid caliphs built splendid palaces in the tradition of their imperial Byzantine, Roman, and Persian predecessors. [Department of Antiquities, State of Israel]

lectual traditions experienced a revival in early Abbasid times, as in the case of Hellenistic learning. Philosophy, astronomy, mathematics, medicine, and other natural sciences enjoyed strong interest and support. In Islamic usage, philosophy and the sciences were subsumed under *falsafa* (from Greek *philosophia*). Islamic culture took over the tradition of rational inquiry from the Hellenistic world and de-

Bowl and Kufic inscription. This tenth-century Iranian ceramic bowl was likely a product of the Samanid pottery workshops of northeastern Iran. The use of block lettering with red highlighting on a white background provides dramatic contrast. The lettering is unusual in that the Arabic cursive letters are written individually, not joined to one another. The inscription can thus be read in different ways, but the most likely reading is ya huwa *or "O He (God)", words of praise in common litanies of worship and prayer. [Seattle Art Museum, Eugene Fuller Memorial Collection 57.18, Paul Macapia, photographer]* veloped as well as preserved it at a time when Europe was by comparison a cultural wasteland.

Arabic translations of Greek and Sanskrit works laid the basis for progress in astronomy and medicine. Translation reached its peak in al-Ma'mun's new academy under the guidance of a Nestorian Christian, Hunayn ibn Ishaq (d. 873), noted for his medical and Greek learning. Before, during, and after his time, there were Arabic translations of everything from Galen, Ptolemy, Euclid, Aristotle, Plato, and the Neo-Platonists to the fables that had been translated from Sanskrit originals into Middle Persian under the Sasanids. Such translations stimulated not only Arabic learning, but also that of the less advanced Western European world, especially in the twelfth and thirteenth centuries.

Language and Literature

Arabic language and literature developed greatly in the wider cultural sphere of the new empire. On the secular side, there developed, largely among the secretarial class of the Abbasid bureaucracy, a significant genre of Arabic writing known as *adab,* or "manners." This genre included essays and didactic literature influenced by earlier Persian letters. As

---

The Splendor of the Abbasid Court

The following excerpts from al-Khatib's description of a visit by Byzantine ambassadors to Baghdad in 917 give some glimmer of the extravagant magnificence of the Islamic capital at the height of its opulence and power.

Then it was commanded that the ambassadors should be taken round the palace. Now there were no soldiers here, but only the eunuchs and the chamberlains and the black pages. The number of the eunuchs was seven thousand in all, four thousand of them white and three thousand black; the number of the chamberlains was also seven thousand, and the number of the black pages, other than the eunuchs, was four thousand; the flat roofs of all the palace being occupied by them, as also of the banqueting-halls. Further, the store-chambers had been opened, and the treasures therein had been set out as is customary for a bride's array; the jewels of the Caliph being arranged in trays, on steps, and covered with cloths of black brocade. When the ambassadors entered the Palace of the Tree and gazed upon the Tree, their astonishment was great. For there they saw birds fashioned out of silver and whistling with every motion, while perched on a tree of silver weighing 500 *dirhams.* Now the wonder of the ambassadors was greater at seeing these than at any of the other sights that they saw.

. . . Then at length, after the ambassadors had thus been taken round twenty-three various palaces, they were brought forth to the Court of the Ninety. Here were the pages of the Privy Chamber, full-armed, sumptuously dressed, each of admirable stature. In their hands they carried swords, small battle-axes, and maces. The ambassadors next passed down the lines formed by the black slaves; the deputy chamberlains, the soldiers, the footmen, and the sons of the chieftains, until they again came to the Presence Hall. Now there were a great number of the Slavic eunuchs in all these palaces, who during the visit were occupied in offering to all present water, cooled with snow, to drink; also sherbets and beer and some of these slaves went round with the ambassadors, to whom, as they walked or sat to take rest in some seven different places, water was thus offered, and they drank.

. . . Finally, they came again to the presence of the Caliph Muktadir, whom they found in the Palace of the Crown upon the bank of the Tigris. He was arrayed in clothes of Dabik-stuff embroidered in gold, being seated on an ebony throne overlaid with Dabik-stuff embroidered in gold likewise, and on his head was the tall bonnet called *galansuwah.* Suspended on the right of the throne were nine necklaces, like prayer beads and to the left were seven others, all of famous jewels, the largest of which was of such a size that its sheen eclipsed the daylight. Before the Caliph stood five of his sons, three to the right and two to the left. Then the ambassadors, with their interpreter, halted before Muktadir, and stood in the posture of humility, with their arms crossed.

Oleg Grabar, *The Formation of Islamic Art* (New Haven, CT: Yale University Press, 1973), pp. 168, 170–171.

The Wit and Wisdom of al-Jahiz

One of the great masters of Arabic prose, al-Jahiz (d. 869) left a number of works behind, among them his Book of Proof. *The following excerpts from this book of essays and clever sayings reflect his talent for the succinct and vivid.*

Ghailān son of Kharasha said to Ahnaf, "What will preserve the Arabs from decline?" He replied, "All will go well if they keep their swords on their shoulders and their turbans on their heads and ride horseback and do not fall a prey to the fools' sense of honour." "And what is the fools' sense of honour?" "That they regard forgiving one another as a wrong."

'Umar said, "Turbans are the crowns of the Arabs."

An Arab of the desert was asked why he did not lay aside his turban. "Surely," said he, "a thing which contains the hearing and the sight ought to be prized."

'Ali said—God be well pleased with him!—"The elegance of a man is in his bonnet, and the elegance of a woman is her boots." And Ahnaf said, "Let your shoes be fine, for shoes are to men what anklets are to women."

'Abdullah son of Ja'far said to his daughter, "O little daughter, beware of jealousy, for it is the key of divorce; and beware of chiding, for it breeds hate. Always adorn and perfume thyself, and know that the most becoming adornment is antimony and the sweetest perfume is water."

'Abdullah son of Ja'far bestowed largesse of every kind on Nusaib Abu'l-Hajinā, who had made an ode in praise of him. "Why," they asked, "do you treat a fellow like this so handsomely—a negro and a slave?" "By God," he answered, "if his skin is black, yet his praise is white and his poem is truly Arabian. He deserves for it a greater reward than he has gotten. All he received was only some lean saddle-camels and clothes which wear out and money which is soon spent, whereas he gave an ode fresh and brilliant and praise that will never die."

Mu'āwiyah held an assembly at Kūfa to receive the oath of allegiance as Caliph. Those who swore loyalty to him were required to abjure allegiance to [the House of] 'Ali son of Abū Tālib—may God honour him! A man of the Banū Tamīm came to Mu'āwiyah, who demanded that he should repudiate 'Ali. "O Prince of the Faithful," he replied, "we will obey those of you that are living, but we will not renounce those of you that are dead." Mu'āwiyah turned to Mughīa and said, "Now, this is a man! Look after him well!"

. . . .

'Auf said on the authority of Hasan: "The feet of a son of Adam will not stir [from the place of judgment] until he be asked of three things—his youth, how he wore it away; his life, how he passed it; and his wealth, whence he got it and on what he spent it."

Yūnus son of 'Ubaid said: "I heard three sayings more wonderful than any I have ever heard. The first is the saying of Hassān son of Abū Sinān—'Nothing is easier than abstinence from things unlawful: if aught make thee doubt, leave it alone.' The second is the saying of Ibn Sīrīn—'I have never envied any one any thing.' The third is the saying of Muwarrik al-'Ijlī—'Forty years ago I asked of God a boon which He has not granted, and I have not despaired of obtaining it.' They said to Muwarrik, 'What is it?' He replied, 'Not to meddle with that which does not concern me.'"

From James Kritzeck, ed., *Anthology of Islamic Literature* (New York: New American Library, Meridian Books, 1964), pp. 91–92.

translations of different genres of writings increased the range of the original bedouin idiom, poetry was able to build on the sophisticated tradition of the Arabic ode, or *qasida*.

Grammar was central to the interpretation of the Qur'an that occupied the *ulama* and provided the core of an emerging curriculum of Muslim learning. A major form of Arabic writing was historical and bio-graphical literature. It owed much to the ancient bedouin accounts of "the battle days of the Arabs." But it arose primarily to supply information about, first, the lives of the Prophet and the earliest Companions, then those of subsequent generations of Muslims. This information was crucial to judging the reliability of the "chains" of transmitters included with each traditional report, or *hadith*. The *hadith* contained

Traditions from and About the Prophet

The following are the texts of three hadiths, *or traditions about the words and actions of Muhammad and his companions. Such reports were transmitted from the early days of Islam after Muhammad's death, in order to instruct or regulate Muslims in the practice of their new faith. Many such reports were forged by persons who wished to lend prophetic authority to particular practices or ideas that seemed good to them, and the* ulama *developed elaborate methods of* Hadith *criticism to identify falsified or inaccurately transmitted traditions. These examples are drawn from major* Hadith *collections compiled largely in the third century of the Hijra.*

The Apostle of God passed by a pile of grain. He put his hand into the midst of it, and his fingers encountered moisture.

He exclaimed, "O merchant, what is this?"

The owner of the grain said. "It has been damaged by the rain, O Apostle of God."

Then he replied, "If that is the case, why not put the damaged grain on top of the pile so that people can see it?"

Then he concluded, "Whoever practices fraud is not one of us."

Ibn 'Umar heard a man swear, saying, "No, I swear by the Ka'bah!" Ibn 'Umar said, "Swear by none other than God. I heard the Apostle of God say, 'Whoever swears by other than God commits blasphemy and makes someone or something an associate with God.' "

When the Prophet awoke he would say, "O God, it is you who enables us to wake up in the morning and it is you who brings us into the evening. You enable us to live. You cause us to die, and at the Resurrection we go to you." When evening came he would say, "O God, it is you who brings us into the evening, and it is you who enables us to wake up in the morning. You enable us to live. You cause us to die, and with you is the issue of our life."

Ibn 'Abbas addressed the people of Al-Basrah [a city in Iraq, founded by the Muslims in 638 A.D.] at the end of Ramadān [the month of fasting], saying, "O people of Al-Basrah, do your duty and give alms after fasting." The people looked at each other.

He said, "Who is here from Medina? Come forth and teach your brothers. Should they not know that the Apostle of God prescribed as alms to be given at the end of Ramadān, a half *sā* [a cubic measure] of wheat, or a *sā* of barley, or a *sā* of dates, to be given by every person, slave and free, man and woman?"

From Kenneth Cragg and Marston Speight, eds., *Islam from Within: Anthology of a Religion* (Belmont, CA: Wadsworth, 1980), pp. 84, 89, 92–93.

---

words and/or deeds ascribed to Muhammad and the Companions; it became the chief source of Muslim legal and religious norms alongside the Qur'an, as well as the basic unit of history and biography. The *Hadith,* a collection of these reports, existed also as a separate genre that was mined by preachers and by the developing schools of legal interpretation, whose crowning glory was the work of al Shafi'i (d. 820) on the theory of legal reasoning.

Art and Architecture

In art and architecture, the Abbasid era saw the crystallization of a "classical" Islamic style by about A.D. 1000. Except for ceramics and Arabic calligraphy, there was nothing radically new about the discrete elements of Islamic art and architecture; most had clear antecedents in Greco-Roman, Byzantine, or Iranian art. What was new was the deployment of older forms and motifs to new ends and in new combinations, and also the spread of such elements to new locales, generally in a movement from east (especially the Fertile Crescent) to west (Syria, Egypt, North Africa, and Spain). Sasanid stucco decoration techniques and designs turned up, for example, in Egypt and North Africa. Chronologically, urban Iraq developed an Islamic art first, then made its influence felt east and west, whether in Bukhara or in Syria and

A

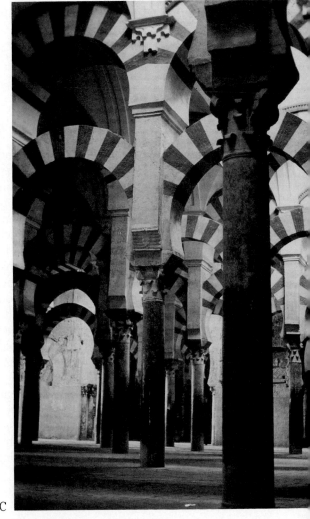

The congregational mosque. Three examples of the finest great mosques of the classical Islamic world. Such buildings were designed not only for worship; their large courtyards and pillared halls were intended to hold the population of a given city and could be used for governmental purposes or for mustering troops in time of war. Their splendor also announced the power and wealth of Islamic rule. Figure A shows the mosque of Ibn Tulun, in Cairo from 876 to 879. Figure B is the great mosque at Qayrawan in modern Tunisia, built between the eighth and ninth centuries. Figure C shows the Spanish Ummayad mosque as Cordoba, built and added to from the eighth to the tenth centuries, in a series of roofed extensions—unlike the other two, which are only partially covered. [Robert Nowitz/William Graham/Peter Greenberg]

C

Qayrawan. Also new was the combination of discrete forms, as in the case of the colonnade (or hypostyle) mosque or the minaret tower.

The Muslims had good reason to be self-confident about their faith and culture and to want to distinguish them from others. Most monuments of the age express the distinctiveness they felt. Particular formal items, such as calligraphic motifs and inscriptions on buildings, became characteristic of Islamic architecture and defined its functions. Most striking in many ways was the avoidance of pictures or icons and overt symbols in public art. This was, of course, in line with the strong Muslim aversion both to any hint of idolatry and to the strongly iconographic traditions of Christian art. Although this iconoclasm was later eased in various strands of Islamic culture, it was a telling expression of the thrust of Muslim faith and the culture it animated. Overall, the artistic achievements of the Islamic world before the year 1000 impress us with an identifiable quality that is both distinctively and "classically" Islamic, whatever the details of a particular example.[6]

Formation of Islamic Civilization in World Perspective

The rise of Islam as both a world religious tradition and an international civilization is by any standard one of the great watershed events of world history. The new traditions forged first in the Arabian peninsula and then in Syria, Iraq, North Africa, Iran, and beyond were to change much of Asia and Africa and parts of Europe in major ways. Religiously, the Islamic movement was destined to become, along with the Buddhist and Christian movements, one of the three major universalist, missionary traditions of world religious history. Politically and socially, the Islamic order for government and society spread and developed in new environments to an extent far beyond even the imagination of Muhammad and his companions.

The Islamic polity was in its first three centuries the most dynamic and expansive imperial state of its day. During the same time, Chinese emperors of the T'ang were rebuilding and improving on the previous Han *imperium;* Charlemagne and the Carolingians

[6] Ibid.

were struggling to hammer out a much smaller, more homogeneous empire and a cultural renaissance in the relatively backward world of Western Europe; Byzantium was fighting to survive against Islamic arms and turning inward to conserve its traditions; and post-Gupta India was divided under diverse regional kings and still subject to new forces (including those of Islam) moving into northwestern India.

As different as the two were, only China compared favorably with or surpassed the Islamic world during this period in terms of political and military power, cultural unity and creativity, and cultural self-consciousness. The T'ang empire and that of the Abbasids wielded commensurate power in their heydays, although over time the Chinese held together as a centralized state much better than the Islamic empire. Certainly, they were the two greatest political and cultural units in the world in their age. They each had one cultural language, although Chinese was the language of more of the masses of China's empire than was Arabic of the Islamic dominions. They also shared the central military use of nomadic cavalry as well as the adaptive ability to incorporate new peoples into their larger culture—although Islamic cultures proved more flexible on this count. Indeed, the great elasticity and adaptability of Islam as a religious tradition and as a social order were striking in ways that clearly belie its present-day reputation in the West as inherently a rigid and inflexible system of values and practices.

Nevertheless, the bases of Islamic empire were clearly different, spread as the empire was over vastly more culturally heterogeneous and widely dispersed geographical areas than that of China. Conquest initially fueled the economy of the new Islamic state, but, in the long run, trade and urban commercial centers proved to be the backbone of Islamic prosperity, as well as the chief means of dissemination of the Muslim faith to new lands. The Islamic empire was agrarian-based, yet the overall climate, soil, and water conditions for food production were not as good as those in China or Western Europe. The key element that the majority of Islamic lands were (and are) lacking was abundant water, so that supporting dense populations well was difficult. This hindrance did not stop the development of impressive Islamic states, societies, and cultures, but it did set limits to such development.

The Islamic achievement was different from any other in this period primarily in that it resulted from an effort to build something new rather than to recapture or resuscitate previous traditions, whether of religion, society, or government. In later centuries, the early Arabic impress of Islamic culture and religion was tempered and changed by the vast numbers of Persian- and Turkish-speaking Muslims and also the many regional groups, from Urdu- or Swahili-speakers in India or Africa to Malay and Indonesian Muslims of Southeast Asia. Nevertheless, Arabic went abroad with the holy Qur'an as the sacred language of God's final revelation. Since that emergence from the Arabian peninsula, Muslims of all the world have learned little or much of Arabic and the sacred Book, but always something.

This achievement was a new historical phenomenon, at least in terms of the scale of its occurrence. Although Muslim faith can be seen as largely a reformation of Semitic monotheism, it was more fundamentally an effort to do something new. It was an attempt to subsume older traditions of Jews or Christians in a more comprehensive vision of God's plan on earth rather than an attempt to reform these earlier traditions. This is not to say that Muslims did not build on previous traditions; they adopted and adapted the traditions of the many older centers of Afro-Eurasian cultures. Yet, as both a civilization and a religious tradition, Islam developed its own strikingly recognizable stamp that persisted wherever Muslims extended the *Umma.*

Suggested Readings

J. ASHTIANI, T. M. JOHNSTONE, J. D. LATHAM, R. B. SERGEANT, and G. R. SMITH, eds., *'Abbasid Belles Lettres* (1990). A wide-ranging survey of Arabic letters between A.D. 750 and 1258, arranged by genres and major writers.

A. F. L. BEESTON, T. M. JOHNSTONE, R. B. SERGEANT, and G. R. SMITH, eds., *Arabic Literature to the End of the Umayyad Period* (1983). The most comprehensive survey of the early Arabic historical, religious, poetic, and other literary sources.

K. CRAGG and R. MARSTON SPEIGHT, eds., *Islam from Within: Anthology of a Religion* (1980). One of the best and most sensitive collections of selections from Islamic primary sources.

F. M. DONNER, *The Early Islamic Conquests* (1981). The introduction and first chapter are especially good for an introduction to many important issues in the origin and spread of Islam.

H. A. R. GIBB, *Mohammedanism: An Historical Survey* (1970). Despite the offensive title, still the best brief introduction to Islam as a religious tradition.

H. A. R. GIBB, *Studies on the Civilization of Islam,* ed. by S. J. Shaw and W. R. Polk (1962). This volume of selected essays by Gibb has some very helpful general studies on Islamic political order and religion.

O. GRABAR, *The Formation of Islamic Art* (1973). A critical and creative interpretation of major themes in the development of distinctively Islamic forms of art and architecture.

G. E. VON GRUNEBAUM, *Classical Islam: A History 600–1258,* trans. by K. Watson (1970), pp. 1–140. A competent, culturally oriented introductory survey of formative developments.

M. G. S. HODGSON, *The Classical Age of Islam* (1974). 3 vols. Vol. I, *The Venture of Islam.* The most thoughtful and comprehensive attempt to deal with classical Islamic civilization as a whole and in relation to contemporaneous non-Islamic cultures.

A. HOURANI, *A History of the Arab Peoples* (1991). A masterly survey of the Arabs down through the centuries and a clear picture of many aspects of Islamic history and culture that extend beyond the Arab world.

B. LEWIS, ed., *Islam and the Arab World* (1976). A large-format, heavily illustrated volume with many excellent articles on diverse aspects of Islamic (not simply Arab, as the misleading title suggests) civilization through the premodern period.

F. RAHMAN, *Major Themes of the Qur'an* (1980). The best introduction to the basic ideas of the Qur'an and Islam, seen through the eyes of a perceptive Muslim modernist scholar.

M. A. SHABAN, *Islamic History: A New Interpretation* (1971–76). 2 vols. An Influential reassessment of the course of Islamic history to A.D. 1055.

D. SOURDEL, *Medieval Islam* (1979). Eng. trans. by W. M. Watt (1983). A brief but excellent survey of the world of medieval Islam with emphasis on social, religious, and political institutions.

The bejeweled cover of the "Golden Manuscript" of Echternach, a gift given by King Otto III (r. 983–1002) and his mother to the abbey of Echternach, produced in Trier, Germany between 985 and 991. The crucified Christ hangs over a personification of the earth. [Germanisches Nationalmuseum, Nürnberg]

14

The Early Middle Ages in the West to 1000: The Birth of Europe

The early Middle Ages were the period in which a distinctive Western European culture began to emerge and in this sense mark the birth of Europe. In geography, government, religion, and language, Western Europe became a land distinct from both the eastern or Byzantine world and the Arab or Muslim world. This was a period of recovery from the collapse of Roman civilization, a time of forced experimentation with new ideas and institutions. Western European culture, as we know it today, was born of a unique, inventive mix of surviving Greco-Roman, new Germanic, and evolving Christian traditions.

The early Middle Ages have been called, not with complete fairness, a "dark age" because during these centuries the people of Europe lost touch with classical, especially Greek, learning and science. In this period, there were fierce invasions from the north and the east by peoples that the Romans somewhat arrogantly called barbarians. To the south, the Mediterranean was transformed by Arab dominance into an inhospitable "Muslim lake." Although Western trade with the East was by no means completely cut off, Western people became more isolated than they had been before. A Europe thus surrounded and assailed from the north, east, and south understandably became somewhat insular and even stagnant. On the other hand, being forced to manage by themselves, Western Europeans also learned to develop their native resources. The reign of Charlemagne saw a modest renaissance of antiquity. And the peculiar social and political forms that emerged during this period—manorialism and feudalism—not only were successful for coping with unprecedented chaos on local levels, but also proved to be fertile seedbeds for the growth of distinctive Western institutions.

On the Eve of the Frankish Ascendancy

Germanic Migrations and Arab Invasions

As we have already seen, by the late third century A.D., the Roman Empire had become too large for a single sovereign to govern. For this reason, Emperor Diocletian (r. 284–305) divided the empire into an eastern and a western half, each with its own emperor and, eventually, imperial bureaucracy. Emperor Constantine the Great (r. 306–337) briefly reunited the empire by conquest (it was redivided within thirty years of his death) and was sole emperor of the east and the west after 324. In 330, Constantine created the city of Constantinople as the new administrative center of the empire and the imperial residence. Constantinople gradually became a "new Rome," replacing the old, whose internal political quarrels and geographic distance from new military fronts in Syria and along the Danube River made it less appealing. Rome and the western empire were actually on the wane in the late third and fourth centuries, well before the barbarian invasions in the west began. In 286, Milan had already replaced Rome as the imperial residence in the west; in 402, the seat of western government was moved yet again, to Ravenna. When the barbarian invasions began in the late fourth century, the west was in political disarray, and imperial power and prestige had shifted decisively to Constantinople and the east.

GERMANIC TRIBES AND THE WEST. The German tribes did not burst on the west all of a sudden. They were at first a token and benign presence. Before the great invasions from the north and the east, there had been a period of peaceful commingling of the Germanic and the Roman cultures. The Romans "imported" barbarians as domestics and soldiers before the German tribes came as conquerors. Barbarian soldiers rose to positions of high leadership and fame in Roman legions. In the late fourth century, however, this peaceful coexistence came to an end due to a great influx of Visigoths ("western Goths") into the empire. The Visigoths themselves had been pushed into the empire in 376 by a violent people, the Huns, who migrated from the area of modern Mongolia. The

Visigoths, a Christianized (albeit unorthodox) Germanic tribe, won from the eastern emperor Valens rights of settlement and material assistance within the empire in exchange for their defense of the frontier as *foederati*, special allies of the emperor. When in place of promised assistance the Visigoths received harsh treatment from their new allies, they rebelled, handily defeating Roman armies under Valens at the battle of Adrianople in 378.

After Adrianople, the Romans passively permitted the settlement of barbarians within the very heart of Western Europe. There was little resistance in the western empire because it was badly overextended, physically weakened by decades of famine, pestilence, and overtaxation, and politically divided by ambitious military commanders. By the second half of the fourth century, the Roman will to resist had simply been sapped. The root cause of the Roman Empire's fall lay not in unprecedented moral decay and materialism, but in a combination of political mismanagement, military weakness and physical impoverishment and disease.

The late fourth and early fifth centuries saw the invasion of still other tribes: the Vandals, the Burgundians, and the Franks. In 410, Visigoths revolted under Alaric (ca. 370–410) and sacked the "eternal city" of Rome. From 451 to 453, Italy suffered the invasions of Attila the Hun (r. 433–453), known to contemporaries as the "scourge of God." In 455, the Vandals overran Rome.

By the mid-fifth century, power in Western Europe had passed decisively from the hands of the Roman emperors to those of barbarian chieftains. In 476, the traditional date for the fall of the Roman Empire, the barbarian Odoacer (ca. 434–493) deposed and replaced the western emperor Romulus Augustulus and ruled as "king of the Romans." By the end of the fifth century, the western empire was thoroughly overrun by barbarians. The Ostrogoths settled in Italy, the Franks in northern Gaul, the Burgundians in Provence, the Visigoths in southern Gaul and Spain, the Vandals in North Africa and the Mediterranean, and the Angles and Saxons in England (see Map 14-1). Barbarians were now masters of the west—but masters who were willing to learn from the people they had conquered.

Western Europe was not transformed into a savage land. The military victories of the barbarians did not result in a great cultural defeat of the Roman Empire. The barbarians were militarily superior, but the Romans retained their cultural strength. In all but Britain and northern Gaul, Roman language, law, and gov-

MAP 14-1 BARBARIAN MIGRATIONS INTO THE WEST IN THE FOURTH AND FIFTH CENTURIES *The forceful intrusion of Germanic and non-Germanic barbarians into the Empire from the last quarter of the fourth century through the fifth century made for a constantly changing pattern of movement and relations. The map shows the major routes taken by the usually unwelcome newcomers and the areas most deeply affected by the main groups.*

ernment coexisted with new Germanic institutions. In Italy under Theodoric, Roman law gradually replaced tribal custom. Only the Vandals and the Anglo-Saxons refused to profess at least titular obedience to the emperor in Constantinople.

Behind this accommodation of cultures was the fact that the Visigoths, the Ostrogoths, and the Vandals entered the west as Christianized people. They professed, however, a religious creed—Arianism—that was considered heretical in the west. Arian Christians believed that Jesus Christ was not one identical being with God the Father—a point of view that had been condemned in 325 by the Council of Nicea (see Chapter 6). Later, around 500, the Franks, under their

strong king, Clovis, converted to the orthodox or "Catholic" form of Christianity supported by the bishops of Rome, and they helped conquer and convert the Goths and other barbarians in Western Europe.

All things considered, rapprochement and a gradual interpenetration of two strong cultures—a creative tension—marked the period of the Germanic migrations. The stronger culture was the Roman, and it became dominant in a later fusion. Despite western military defeat, it can still be said that the Goths and the Franks became far more romanized than the Romans were germanized. Latin language, Nicene Christianity, and eventually Roman law and government were to triumph in the west during the Middle Ages.

Salvian the Priest Compares the Romans and the Barbarians

Salvian, a Christian priest writing around 440, found the barbarians morally superior to the Romans—indeed, truer to Roman virtues than the Romans themselves, whose failing were all the more serious because they, unlike the barbarians, had knowledge of Christianity.

▶ *Compare this response to the barbarians to the response of an earlier Roman to the Huns in the box entitled "Ammianus Marcellinus Describes the People Called Huns" in Chapter 6. For another response to a clash of cultures, see "How the Hindus Differ from the Muslims" in Chapter 16.*

In what respects can our customs be preferred to those of the Goths and Vandals, or even compared with them? And first, to speak of affection and mutual charity, almost all barbarians, at least those who are of one race and kin, love each other, while the Romans persecute each other. . . . The many are oppressed by the few, who regard public exactions as their own peculiar right, who carry on private traffic under the guise of collecting the taxes. . . . So the poor are despoiled, the widows sigh, the orphans are oppressed, until many of them, born of families not obscure, and liberally educated, flee to our enemies that they may no longer suffer the oppression of public persecution. They doubtless seek Roman humanity among the barbarians, because they cannot bear barbarian inhumanity among the Romans. And although they differ from the people to whom they flee in manner and in language; although they are unlike as regards the fetid odor of the barbarians' bodies and garments, yet they would rather endure a foreign civilization among the barbarians than cruel injustice among the Romans.

It is urged that if we Romans are wicked and corrupt, that the barbarians commit the same sins. . . . There is, however, this difference, that if the barbarians commit the same crimes as we, yet we sin more grievously. . . . All the barbarians . . . are pagans or heretics. The Saxon race is cruel, the Franks are faithless . . . the Huns are unchaste—in short there is vice in the life of all the barbarian peoples. But are their offenses as serious as [those of Christians]? Is the unchastity of the Hun so criminal as ours? Is the faithlessness of the Frank so blameworthy as ours?

"Of God's Government," in James Harvey Robinson, ed., *Readings in European History,* Vol. 1 (Boston: Athenaeum, 1904), pp. 28–30.

The Byzantine Empire

As Western Europe succumbed to the Germanic invasions, imperial power shifted to the Byzantine Empire, that is, to the eastern part of the Roman Empire. Emperor Constantine the Great began the rebuilding of Byzantium in 324, renaming the city Constantinople in 330. Constantinople became the sole capital of the empire and remained so until the successful revival of the western empire in the eighth century by Charlemagne. Between 324 and 1453 the Byzantine empire passed from an early golden age of expansion and splendor to a time of contraction and splintering and finally to a period of catastrophic defeat by the Ottoman Turks.

REIGN OF JUSTINIAN. In terms of territory, political power, and culture, the first period of Byzantine history (324–632) was far and away its greatest. At the height of this period, the emperor Justinian (r. 527–565) ruled with the assistance of his wife and co-empress, the brilliant and beautiful Theodora. The daughter of a bear trainer in the circus, her activities may have included prostitution, if the controversial *Secret History* of Justinian's court historian, Procopius, is to be believed. An influential counselor, Theodora became a major figure in imperial government. When in 532 Justinian contemplated abdication following riots that left much of the city in ruins and thousands dead, Theodora stiffened his resolve and saved his rule.

The imperial goal in the east—as reflected in the policy "one God, one empire, one religion"—was to centralize government and impose legal and doctrinal conformity. To this end Justinian collated and revised Roman law. This codification had become a pressing matter because of the accumulation of an enormous number of often contradictory legal decrees. Justinian's *Corpus Juris Civilis* (body of civil law) was a fourfold compilation undertaken by a learned committee of lawyers. These works had little immediate effect on medieval common law, but beginning with the Renaissance, they provided the foundation for most subsequent European law down to the nineteenth century, and they were especially helpful to rulers who aspired to centralize their states.

Portrayals of Justinian (above) and Theodora (below) prepared for the consecration of the church of St. Vitale in Ravenna. Justinian is surrounded by an apostolic twelve attendants: soldiers, government officials, and clergy. Theodora, idealized, is flanked by government officials, clergy, and ladies-in-waiting. On the hem of her robe is a portrayal of the Magi bearing gifts to the infant Jesus, a royal effort, characteristic of Eastern emperors, to infuse political power with spiritual authority. [Art Resource]

MAP 14-2 THE BYZANTINE EMPIRE UNDER JUSTINIAN *The inset shows the empire in 1025, before its losses to the Seljuq Turks.*

Religion also served imperial centralization. Since the fifth century, the patriarch of Constantinople had crowned emperors in Constantinople. This practice reflected the close ties between rulers and the Church. In 380 Christianity became the official religion of the eastern empire. The patriarchs of Constantinople, Alexandria, Antioch, and Jerusalem became very rich and powerful between the fourth and sixth centuries. As clerical ranks grew, the Church in turn served the state as a welfare agency for the poor and needy.

During Justinian's reign the empire's strength was its more than fifteen hundred cities. Of these, the largest, with perhaps 350,000 inhabitants, was the imperial capital, Constantinople, the cultural crossroads of the Asian and European civilizations (see Map 14-2). The large provincial cities had populations of 50,000. During the fourth and fifth centuries, councils composed of wealthy landowners known as decurions governed these cities. Decurions were the economic and intellectual elite of the empire. They were also heavily taxed and for this reason were not the emper-

A portrayal of David and Goliath, an example of early Byzantine silverwork. [Metropolitan Museum of Art, Gift of J. Pierpont Morgan, 1917, (17.190.396)]

or's most loyal servants. In the sixth century Justinian replaced the decurion councils with special governors and bishops on whom he could better rely.

EASTERN INFLUENCES.   During the reign of Heraclius (610–641), the empire took an eastern, as opposed to a Roman, direction. Heraclius spoke Greek, not Latin. He spent his entire reign resisting Persian and Islamic invasions, which began in earnest in the seventh century. Islamic armies proved initially invincible; after 632, they progressively overran the empire and directly attacked Constantinople for the first time in 677. Not until the reign of Leo III (717–741) were they repulsed and most of Asia Minor regained by the empire.

Leo, however, offended western Christians when he forbade the use of images in eastern churches and tried to enforce the ban in the west. His efforts insulted the western Church, which had carefully nurtured the adoration of Jesus, Mary, and the saints in images and icons. Historians have speculated that

Byzantine church decoration consisted predominantly of rigidly stylized mosaics. A theme repeated endlessly in these church mosaics is that of Christ the Ruler of All. The stern, bearded judge is quite different from the gentle figure of Christ as the good shepherd. This example, from the church of St. Savior in Istanbul, dates to about 1100. [American History Museum]

One of the most influential achievements of Byzantine art and architecture was the great church of Hagia Sophia (Holy Wisdom) built by the emperor Justinian between 532 and 537 in Istanbul (formerly Constantinople), Turkey. This interior view shows its great dome, 107 feet in diameter, and rich decoration of marbles and mosaics. After the Turkish conquest of Constantinople in 1453, the building became a mosque for nearly five hundred years. It has been a museum since 1935. [Wim Swaan]

Another great surviving example of Byzantine architecture—from a much later period than Hagia Sophia—is St. Mark's in Venice (below). Most of the building dates to the eleventh century and was built to house the remains of the apostle Mark, said to have been taken from Alexandria in Egypt. The building carries the characteristic rounded arches, numerous domes, and mosaics of the Byzantine style. The ornamental pointed arches and pinnacles of the facade's upper story are later additions. [Italian Government Travel Office, New York]

Leo and his immediate successors pursued this unfortunate policy under the influence of Islam, which condemned image veneration, perhaps hoping to placate the Muslims by joining them on this point of doctrine. Be that as it may, the banning of images became a major expression of eastern Caesaro-papism, the direct imperial involvement in Church dogma that, as we will see, the western Church always resisted. In addition to creating a new division within Christendom, the ban on images led to the destruction of much religious art until it was reversed in the late eighth century.

In 1071, the Byzantine Empire suffered a major defeat at the hands of the Muslim Seljuq Turks. Successful over Byzantine armies at Manzikert, the Turks rapidly overran the eastern provinces of the empire. This defeat marked the beginning of the end of the empire, although the actual end—at the hands of the Seljuqs' cousins, the Ottoman Turks—still lay centuries ahead. After two decades of steady Turkish advance, the eastern emperor invoked western aid in 1092. Three years later the west launched the first of the Crusades (see Chapter 15). A century later (1204) the Crusaders would inflict more damage on Constantinople and eastern Christendom than all previous non-Christian invaders had done.

Throughout the early Middle Ages, the Byzantine Empire remained a protective barrier between Western Europe and hostile Persian, Arab, and Turkish armies. The Byzantines were also a major conduit of classical learning and science into the west down to the Renaissance. While Western Europeans were fumbling to create a culture of their own, the cities of the Byzantine Empire provided them a model of a civilized society.

Islam and Its Effects on East and West

As our review of the history of the Byzantine Empire indicates, a new drama began to unfold in the sixth century with the rise of a rival far more dangerous to the west than the German tribes: the new faith of Islam. During the lifetime of the prophet Muhammad (570–632) and thereafter, invading Arab armies claimed the attention and resources of the emperors in Constantinople, who found themselves in a life-and-death struggle. Unlike the Germanic invaders, who absorbed and adopted the culture and religion of Rome, the Arabs, although generally tolerant of Christian and Jewish minorities, ultimately imposed their own culture and religion on the lands they conquered (see Chapter 13.)

By the middle of the eighth century, Arabs had conquered the southern and eastern Mediterranean coastline (territories currently held, for the most part, by Islamic states) and occupied parts of Spain, which they controlled or strongly influenced until the fifteenth century. In addition, their armies pushed north and east through Mesopotamia and Persia and beyond. These conquests would not have been so rapid and thorough had the contemporary Byzantine and Persian empires not been exhausted by a long period of war. The Arabs struck at the conclusion of the successful campaign of Byzantine emperor Heraclius (d. 641) against the Persian king Chosroes II. Most of the population in the conquered area spoke Semitic languages and was more easily fired by hatred of the Byzantine Greek army of occupation than it was inspired to unity by a common Christian tradition. The Christian community was itself badly divided. The Egyptian (also known as *Coptic*) and Syrian churches were Monophysitic. Heraclius's efforts to impose Greek orthodox beliefs on these churches only increased the enmity between Greek and Semitic Christians, many of whom leaned toward Monophysitism. Many Egyptian and Syrian Christians may have looked on Arabs as deliverers from the Byzantine conquerors.

Muslims tolerated conquered Christians and Jews, whether orthodox or Monophysite, provided they paid taxes, kept their distance, and made no efforts to proselytize Muslim communities. Always anxious to maintain the purity of their religion and culture, the Arabs forbade mixed marriages and any conscious cultural interchange. Special taxes on conquered peoples encouraged them to convert to Islam.

Assaulted on both their eastern and their western frontiers and everywhere challenged in the Mediterranean, the Europeans developed a lasting fear and suspicion of the Muslims. They found a welcome buffer in the east, however, during the reign of the Byzantine Leo III (717–740), who stopped Arab armies at Constantinople after a year's siege (717–718). Leo and his successors in the Isaurian dynasty of Byzantine rulers maintained a successful defensive organization against the Arabs, so effective that it permitted the rulers of the following Macedonian dynasty (867–1057) to expand militarily and commercially into Muslim lands.

As for the west's immediate dangers, the ruler of the Franks, Charles Martel, defeated a raiding party of Arabs on the western frontier of the Frankish kingdom near Tours (today in central France) in 732, a victory that ended any possible Arab effort to expand into Western Europe by way of Spain. From the end of the seventh century to the middle of the eleventh, the Mediterranean remained something of a Muslim lake, and while western trade with East Asia was not cut off during these centuries, it was significantly decreased and carried on in keen awareness of Muslim dominance.

When trade wanes, cities decline, and with them those centers for the exchange of goods and ideas that prevent a society from becoming insular. The Arab invasions and presence in the Mediterranean area during a crucial part of the early Middle Ages created the essential conditions for the birth of Western Europe as a distinctive cultural entity. Arab belligerency forced Western Europeans to fall back on their own distinctive resources and to develop their own peculiar Germanic and Greco-Roman heritage into a unique culture. The Arabs accomplished this by diverting the attention and energies of the eastern empire at a time of Frankish and Lombard ascendancy (thereby preventing Byzantine expansion into the west) and by greatly reducing western navigation of the Mediterranean (thereby closing off much eastern trade and cultural influence).

The Developing Roman Church

One institution remained firmly entrenched within the cities during the Arab invasions: the Christian Church. The Church had long modeled its own structure on that of the imperial Roman administration. Like the latter, it aspired to be a centralized, hierarchical government with strategically placed "viceroys" (bishops) in European cities who looked for spiritual direction to their leader, the bishop of Rome. This was not immediately realized, however, because many bishops at this time still thought of themselves as the supreme Church authority within their own sees or cathedral towns.

As the western empire crumbled and populations emigrated to the countryside after the barbarian and Arab invasions, local bishops and cathedral chapters (ruling bodies of clergy) filled the vacuum of authority left by the removal of Roman governors. The local cathedral became the center of urban life and the local bishop the highest authority for those who remained in the cities—just as in Rome, on a larger and more fateful scale, the pope took control of the city as the western emperors gradually departed and

died out. Left to its own devices, Western Europe soon discovered that the Christian Church was a rich repository of Roman administrative skills and classical culture.

The Christian Church had been graced with special privileges, great lands, and wealth by Emperor Constantine and his successors. In 313, Constantine issued the Edict of Milan, giving Christians legal standing and a favored status within the empire. In 391, Emperor Theodosius I (r. ca. 379–395), after whose death the empire would again be divided into eastern and western parts, raised Christianity to the official religion of the empire. Both Theodosius and his predecessors acted as much for political effect as out of religious conviction; in 313, Christians composed about one-fifth of the population of the empire and unquestionably composed the strongest group among the competing religions. Mithraism, the religion popular among army officers and restricted to males, was its main rival.

Challenged to become a major political force, the Church survived the period of Germanic and Arab invasions as a somewhat spiritually weakened and compromised institution, yet it was still a potent civilizing and unifying force. It had a religious message of providential purpose and individual worth that could give solace and meaning to life at its worst. The western Church also had a ritual of baptism and a creedal confession that united people beyond the traditional barriers of social class, education, and sex. After the Germanic and Arab invasions, the Church alone possessed an effective hierarchical administration, scattered throughout the old empire, staffed by the best-educated minds in Europe and centered in emperorless Rome. The Church also enjoyed the services of growing numbers of monks, who were not only loyal to its mission but also objects of great popular respect. Monastic culture proved again and again to be the peculiar strength of the Church during the Middle Ages.

MONASTIC CULTURE. The first monks were hermits who withdrew from society to pursue a more perfect way of life. They were inspired by the Christian ideal of a life of complete self-denial in imitation of Christ. The popularity of monasticism began to grow as Roman persecution of Christians waned in the mid-third century. Embracing the biblical "counsels of perfection" (chastity, poverty, and obedience), the monastic life became the purest form of religious practice.

Anthony of Egypt (ca. 251–356), the father of her-

The rule of St. Benedict, followed by most medieval monasteries required that the monks spend a third of their day doing manual labor. This served to make the monastery self-sufficient and self-contained. Here monks are shown doing a variety of agricultural tasks. [Vincent Varga Archives]

mit monasticism, was inspired by Jesus' command to the rich young man: "If you will be perfect, sell all that you have, give it to the poor, and follow me" (Matthew 19:21). Anthony went into the desert to pray and work, setting an example followed by hundreds in Egypt, Syria, and Palestine in the fourth and fifth centuries. This hermit monasticism was soon joined by the development of communal monasticism. In southern Egypt in the first quarter of the fourth century, Pachomius (ca. 286–346) organized monks into a highly regimented common life. Such monastic communities grew to contain a thousand or more inhabitants, little "cities of God," separated from the collapsing Roman and the nominal Christian world. Basil the Great (329–379) popularized communal monasticism throughout the east, providing a rule that lessened the asceticism of Pachomius and directed monks beyond their enclaves of perfection into such social services as caring for orphans, widows, and the infirm in surrounding communities.

Athanasius (ca. 293–373) and Martin of Tours (ca. 315–ca. 397) introduced monasticism into the west, where the teaching of John Cassian (ca. 360–435) and Jerome (ca. 340–420) helped shape its basic values and practices. The great organizer of western monasticism was Benedict of Nursia (ca. 480–547). In 529, Benedict founded the mother monastery of the Benedictines at Monte Cassino in Italy, the founda-

tion on which all western monasticism has been built. Benedict also wrote a sophisticated *Rule for Monasteries,* a comprehensive plan that both regimented and enriched monastic life. According to the Benedictine *Rule,* the monastery was hierarchically organized and directed by an abbot, whose command was beyond question. Periods of devotion (about four hours each day were set aside for the "work of God," that is, regular prayers and liturgical activities) and study alternated with manual labor—a program that permitted not a moment's idleness and carefully promoted the religious, intellectual, and physical well-being of the monks.

DOCTRINE OF PAPAL PRIMACY. Constantine and his successors, especially the eastern emperors, ruled religious life with an iron hand and consistently looked on the Church as little more than a department of the state. Such "Caesaro-papism"—Caesar acting as pope—involved the emperor directly in the Church's affairs, even to the point of enabling him to play the theologian and allowing him to impose conciliar solutions on doctrinal quarrels. State control of religion was the original Church–State relation in the west.

The bishops of Rome, however, never accepted such intervention and opposed it in every way they could. In the fifth and sixth centuries, taking advantage of imperial weakness and distraction, they developed for their own defense the weaponry of the doctrine of "papal primacy." This doctrine raised the Roman pontiff to an unassailable supremacy within the Church when it came to defining Church doctrine and maintaining clerical allegiance. It also put him in a position to make important secular claims and was destined to occasion repeated conflicts between Church and State, pope and emperor, throughout the Middle Ages.

DIVISION OF CHRISTENDOM. The Christian Church began to divide into independent eastern (Byzantine) and western (Roman Catholic) churches during the early Middle Ages. This was due in part to linguistic and cultural differences between east and west. A novel combination of Greek, Roman, and East Asian elements shaped Byzantine culture, and a strong mystical orientation to the next world also led eastern Christians to submit more passively than western popes could ever submit to Caesaro-papism.

As in the west, eastern Church organization closely followed that of the secular state. A "patriarch" ruled

Pope Gelasius I Declares the "Weightiness" of Priestly Authority

Some see this famous letter of Pope Gelasius to Emperor Anastasius I in 494 as an extreme statement of papal supremacy. Others believe it is a balanced, moderate statement that recognizes the independence of both temporal and spiritual power and seeks their close cooperation, not the domination of Church over State.

There are two powers, august Emperor, by which this world is chiefly ruled, named, the sacred authority of the priests and the royal power. Of these, that of the priests is the more weighty, since they have to render an account for even the kings of men in the divine judgment. You are also aware, dear son [emperor], that while you are permitted honorably to rule over humankind, yet in things divine you bow your head humbly before the leaders of the clergy and await from their hands the means of your salvation. In the reception and proper disposition of the heavenly mysteries you recognize that you should be subordinate rather than superior to the religious order, and that in these matters you depend on their judgment rather than wish to force them to follow your will. [And] if the ministers of religion, recognizing the supremacy granted you from heaven in matters affecting the public order, obey your laws, lest otherwise they obstruct the course of secular affairs, with what readiness should you not yield them obedience to whom is assigned the dispensing of the sacred mysteries of religion?

James Harvey Robinson, ed., *Readings in European History,* Vol. 1 (Boston: Athenaeum, 1904), pp. 72–73.

---

over "metropolitans" and "archbishops" in the cities and provinces, and they, in turn, ruled over bishops, who stood as authorities over the local clergy.

Contrary to the evolving western tradition of universal clerical celibacy, which western monastic culture encouraged, the eastern Church permitted the marriage of parish priests (but not monks), while strictly forbidding bishops to marry. The eastern Church also used leavened bread in the Eucharist, contrary to the western custom of using unleavened bread. Also unliked in the west was the tendency of the eastern Church, which was constantly beset with doctrinal controversy, to accommodate the politically powerful Arian and Monophysite Christians. Moreover, there were conflicting political claims to jurisdiction over newly converted areas in the northern Balkans.

Beyond these issues, the major factors in the religious break between east and west revolved around questions of doctrinal authority. The eastern Church put more stress on the authority of the Bible and the ecumenical councils of the Church in the definition of Christian doctrine than on the counsel and decrees of the bishop of Rome. The claims of Roman popes to a special primacy of authority on the basis of the apostle Peter's commission from Jesus in Matthew 16:18 ("Thou art Peter, and upon this rock I will build my church") were completely unacceptable to the east, where the independence and autonomy of regional churches held sway. This basic issue of ultimate authority in matters of faith culminated in the mutual excommunication of Pope Nicholas I and Patriarch Photius in the ninth century and that of Pope Leo IX and Patriarch Michael Cerularius in 1054.

A second major issue in the separation of the two churches was the western addition of the *filioque* clause to the Nicene-Constantinopolitan Creed. According to this anti-Arian clause, the Holy Spirit proceeds "also from the Son" *(filioque)* as well as from the Father, making clear the western belief that Christ was fully one essence with God the Father and not a lesser being.

The final and most direct issue in the religious division of Christendom was the iconoclastic controversy of the first half of the eighth century. As noted earlier, after 725, the Byzantine emperor, Leo III (r. 717–741), attempted to force western popes to abolish the use of images in their churches. This stand met fierce official and popular resistance in the west, where images were greatly cherished, and in the east as well.

Leo's direct challenge of the pope came almost simultaneously with still another aggressive act against the western Church: attacks by the heretofore docile Lombards of northern Italy. Assailed by both the emperor and the Lombards, the pope in Rome seemed surely doomed. But there has not been a more resilient and enterprising institution in Western history than the Roman papacy. Since the pontificate of Gregory the Great, Roman popes had eyed the Franks of northern Gaul as Europe's ascendant power and their surest protector. Imperial and Lombard aggression against the Roman pope in the first half of the eighth century provided the occasion for the most fruitful political alliance of the Middle Ages. In 754, Pope Stephen II (752–757) enlisted Pepin III and his Franks as defenders of the Church against the Lombards and as a western counterweight to the eastern emperor. This marriage of religion and politics created a new western church and empire; it also influenced much of the course of Western history into modern times.

MAJOR POLITICAL AND RELIGIOUS DEVELOPMENTS OF THE EARLY MIDDLE AGES	
313	Emperor Constantine issues the Edict of Milan
325	Council of Nicea defines Christian doctrine
410	Rome invaded by Visigoths under Alaric
413–426	St. Augustine writes *The City of God*
451	Council of Chalcedon further defines Christian doctrine
451–453	Europe invaded by the Huns under Attila
476	Barbarian Odoacer deposes western emperor and rules as king of the Romans
488	Theodoric establishes kingdom of Ostrogoths in Italy
529	St. Benedict founds monastery at Monte Cassino
533	Justinian codifies Roman law
732	Charles Martel defeats Arabs at Tours
754	Pope Stephen II and Pepin III ally

The Kingdom of the Franks

Merovingians and Carolingians: From Clovis to Charlemagne

A warrior chieftain, Clovis (ca. 466–511), who converted to orthodox Christianity around 496, founded the first Frankish dynasty, the Merovingians, named for Merovich, an early leader of one branch of the Franks. Clovis and his successors subdued the pagan Burgundians and the Arian Visigoths and established the kingdom of the Franks within ancient Gaul, making the Franks and the Merovingian kings a significant force in Western Europe. The Franks themselves occupied a broad belt of territory that extended throughout modern France, Belgium, The Netherlands, and western Germany, and their loyalties remained strictly tribal and local. In attempting to govern this sprawling kingdom, the Merovingians encountered what proved to be the most persistent problem of medieval political history—the competing claims of the "one" and the "many." On the one hand, the king struggled for a centralized government and transregional loyalty, and on the other, powerful local magnates strove to preserve their regional autonomy and traditions.

The Merovingian kings addressed this problem by making pacts with the landed nobility and by creating the royal office of count. The counts were men without possessions to whom the king gave great lands in the expectation that they would be, as the landed aristocrats often were not, loyal officers of the kingdom. But like local aristocrats, the Merovingian counts also let their immediate self-interests gain the upper hand. Once established in office for a period of time, they too became territorial rulers in their own right, with the result that the Frankish kingdom progressively fragmented into independent regions and tiny principalities. This centrifugal tendency was further assisted by the Frankish custom of dividing the kingdom equally among the king's legitimate male heirs.

Rather than purchasing allegiance and unity within the kingdom, the Merovingian largess simply occasioned the rise of competing magnates and petty tyrants, who became laws unto themselves within their regions. By the seventh century, the Frankish king was king in title only and had no effective executive power. Real power came to be concentrated in the office of the *mayor of the palace*, who was the spokesman at the king's court for the great landowners of the three regions into which the Frankish king-dom was divided: Neustria (roughly western France), Austrasia (roughly central Germany), and Burgundy. Through this office, the Carolingian dynasty rose to power.

The Carolingians (from Carolus, or Charles, after-ward Charlemagne, or Charles the Great) controlled the office of the mayor of the palace from the ascent to that post of Pepin I of Austrasia (d. 639) until 751, when, with the enterprising connivance of the pope, they simply expropriated the Frankish crown. Pepin II (d. 714) ruled in fact if not in title over the Frankish kingdom. His illegitimate son, Charles Martel ("the Hammer"; d. 741), created a great cavalry by bestow-ing lands known as *benefices* or *fiefs* on powerful nobles, who, in return, agreed to be ready to serve as the king's army. It was such an army that checked the Arab probings on the western front at Tours in 732—an important battle that helped to secure the borders of Western Europe.

The fiefs so generously bestowed by Charles Mar-tel to create his army came in large part from landed property that he usurped from the Church. His alli-ance with the landed aristocracy in this grand manner permitted the Carolingians to have some measure of political success where the Merovingians had failed. The Carolingians created counts almost entirely out of the landed nobility from which the Carolingians themselves had risen. The Merovingians, in contrast, had tried to compete directly with these great aristo-crats by raising the landless to power. By playing to strength rather than challenging it, the Carolingians strengthened themselves, at least for the short term. Because the papacy was by this time completely de-pendent on the protection of the Franks against the Eastern emperor and the Lombards, it gave little thought to the fact that its savior had been created in part with lands to which it held claim. Later, the Franks partially compensated the Church for these lands.

FRANKISH CHURCH. The Church came to play a large and enterprising role in the Frankish govern-ment. By Carolingian times, monasteries were a dom-inant force. Their intellectual achievements made them respected repositories of culture. Their religious teaching and example imposed order on surrounding populations. Their relics and rituals made them magi-cal shrines to which pilgrims came in great numbers. Thanks to their donated lands and serf labor, many had become very profitable farms and landed estates, their abbots rich and powerful magnates. By Merovin-

gian times, the higher clergy were already employed in tandem with counts as royal agents. It was the pol-icy of the Carolingians, perfected by Charles Martel and his successor, Pepin III ("the Short"; d. 768), to use the Church to pacify conquered neighboring tribes—Frisians; Thuringians; Bavarians; and espe-cially the Franks' archenemies, the Saxons.

Conversion to Nicene Christianity became an inte-gral part of the successful annexation of conquered lands and people; the cavalry broke their bodies, while the clergy won their hearts and minds. The Anglo-Saxon missionary Saint Boniface (born Wynfrith; ca. 680–754) was the most important of the German clergy who served Carolingian kings in this way. Christian bishops in missionary districts and elsewhere became lords, appointed by and subject to the king—an ominous integration of secular and reli-gious policy in which lay the seeds of the later Investi-ture Controversy of the eleventh and twelfth centuries.

The Church served more than Carolingian territo-rial expansion. Pope Zacharias (741–752) also sanc-tioned Pepin the Short's termination of the vestigial Merovingian dynasty and the Carolingian accession to outright kingship of the Franks. With the pope's public blessing, Pepin was proclaimed king by the nobility in council in 751, and the last of the Merovin-gians, the puppet king Childeric III, was hustled off to a monastery and dynastic oblivion. According to leg-end, Saint Boniface anointed Pepin, thereby investing Frankish rule from the very start with a certain sacral character.

Zacharias's successor, Pope Stephen II (752–757), did not let Pepin forget the favor of his predecessor. Driven from Rome in 753 by the Lombards, Pope Ste-phen appealed directly to Pepin to cast out the invad-ers and to guarantee papal claims to central Italy, which was dominated at this time by the eastern em-peror. In 754, the Franks and the Church formed an alliance against the Lombards and the eastern em-peror. Carolingian kings became the protectors of the Catholic church and thereby "kings by the grace of God." Pepin gained the title *patricius Romanorum*, "father-protector of the Romans," a title heretofore borne only by the representative of the eastern em-peror. In 755, the Franks defeated the Lombards and gave the pope the lands surrounding Rome, an event that created what came to be known as the *Papal States*. The lands earlier appropriated by Charles Mar-tel and parceled out to the Frankish nobility were never returned to the Church, despite the appearance in this period of a most enterprising fraudulent docu-ment designed to win their return, the *Donation of*

Constantine (written between 750 and 800), which, however, was never universally accepted in the west. This imperial parchment alleged that the Emperor Constantine had personally conveyed to the Church his palace and "all provinces and districts of the city of Rome and Italy and of the regions of the west" as permanent possessions. It was believed by many to be a genuine document until definitely exposed as a forgery in the fifteenth century by the humanist Lorenzo Valla.

The papacy had looked to the Franks for an ally strong enough to protect it from the eastern emperors. It is an irony of history that the Church found in the Carolingian dynasty a western imperial government that drew almost as slight a boundary between State and Church, secular and religious policy, as did eastern emperors. Although eminently preferable for the popes to eastern domination, Carolingian patronage of the Church proved in its own way to be no less Caesaro-papist.

Reign of Charlemagne (768–814)

Charlemagne, the son of Pepin the Short, continued the role of his father as papal protector in Italy and his policy of territorial conquest in the north. After King Desiderius and the Lombards of northern Italy were decisively defeated in 774, Charlemagne took the title "King of the Lombards" in Pavia. He widened the frontiers of his kingdom further by subjugating surrounding pagan tribes, foremost among them the Saxons, whom the Franks brutally Christianized and dispersed in small groups throughout Frankish lands.

The False *Donation of Constantine*

Among the ways in which Roman ecclesiasts fought to free the western church from political domination was to assert its own sovereign territorial and political rights. One of the most ambitious of such assertions was the so-called Donation of Constantine *(eighth century), a fraudulent document claiming papal succession to much of the old Roman Empire.*

The Emperor Caesar Flavius Constantinus in Christ Jesus to the most Holy and blessed Father of fathers, Silvester, Bishop of the Roman city and Pope; and to all his successors, the pontiffs, who shall sit in the chair of blessed Peter to the end of time. . . . Grace, peace, love, joy, long-suffering, mercy . . . be with you all. . . . For we wish you to know . . . that we have forsaken the worship of idols . . . and have come to the pure Christian faith. . . .

To the holy apostles, my lords the most blessed Peter and Paul, and through them also to blessed Silvester, our father, supreme pontiff and universal pope of the city of Rome, and to the pontiffs, his successors, who to the end of the world shall sit in the seat of blessed Peter, we grant and by this present we convey our imperial Lateran palace, which is superior to and excels all palaces in the whole world; and further the diadem, which is the crown of our head; and the miter; as also the super-humeral, that is, the stole which usually surrounds our imperial neck; and the purple cloak and the scarlet tunic and all the imperial robes. . . .

And we decree that those most reverend men, the clergy of various orders serving the same most holy Roman Church, shall have that eminence, distinction, power and precedence, with which our illustrious senate is gloriously adorned; that is, they shall be made patricians and consuls. And we ordain that they shall also be adorned with other imperial dignities. Also we decree that the clergy of the sacred Roman Church shall be adorned as are the imperial officers. . . .

We convey to the oft-mentioned and most blessed Silvester, universal pope, both our palace, as preferment, and likewise all provinces, palaces and districts of the city of Rome and Italy and of the regions of the West; and, bequeathing them to the power and sway of him and the pontiffs, his successors, we do determine and decree that the same be placed at his disposal, and do lawfully grant it as a permanent possession to the holy Roman Church.

Henry Bettenson, ed., *Documents of the Christian Church* (New York: Oxford University Press, 1961), pp. 137–141.

MAP 14-3   THE EMPIRE OF CHARLEMAGNE TO 814   *Building on the successes of his prede-cessors, Charlemagne greatly increased the Frankish domains. Such traditional ene-mies as the Saxons and the Lombards fell under his sway.*

The Danubian plains were brought into the Frankish orbit by the virtual annihilation of the Avars, a tribe related to the Huns. The Arabs were chased beyond the Pyrenees. By the time of his death on January 28, 814, Charlemagne's kingdom embraced modern France, Belgium, Holland, Switzerland, almost the whole of Germany, much of Italy, a portion of Spain, and the island of Corsica (see Map 14-3).

THE NEW EMPIRE.   Encouraged by his ambitious advisers, Charlemagne came to harbor imperial de-signs. He desired to be not only king of all the Franks

Carolingian architecture. The cathedral church at Aachen (in modern Germany) containing the chapel of Charlemagne. The original parts were constructed between 792 and 805. [Bildarchiv Foto Marburg]

but a universal emperor as well. He had his sacred palace city, Aachen (in French, Aix-la-Chapelle), constructed in conscious imitation of the courts of the ancient Roman and of the contemporary eastern emperors. Although he permitted the Church its independence, he looked after it with a paternalism almost as great as that of any eastern emperor. He used the Church above all to promote social stability and hierarchical order throughout the kingdom—as an aid in the creation of a great Frankish Christian empire. Frankish Christians were ceremoniously baptized, professed the Nicene Creed (with the *filioque* clause), and learned in church to revere Charlemagne.

Charlemagne fulfilled his imperial pretensions on Christmas Day, 800, when Pope Leo III (795–816) crowned him emperor. If the coronation benefited the Church, as it certainly did, it also served Charlemagne's designs. Before his coronation, Charlemagne had been a minor western potentate in the eyes of eastern emperors. After the coronation, eastern emperors reluctantly recognized his new imperial dignity, and Charlemagne even found it necessary to disclaim ambitions to rule as emperor over the east. Here began what would come to be known as the Holy Roman Empire, a revival, based in Germany, of the old Roman Empire in the west.

THE NEW EMPEROR.   Charlemagne stood a majestic six feet, three-and-one-half inches tall—a fact secured when his tomb was opened and exact measurements of his remains were taken in 1861. He was nomadic, ever ready for a hunt. Informal and gregarious, he insisted on the presence of friends even when he bathed and was widely known for his practical jokes, lusty good humor, and warm hospitality. Aachen was a festive palace city to which people and gifts came from all over the world. In 802, Charlemagne even received from the caliph of Baghdad, Harun-al-Rashid, a white elephant, the transport of which across the Alps was as great a wonder as the creature itself.

Charlemagne had five official wives in succession, possessed many mistresses and concubines, and sired numerous children. This connubial variety created special problems. His oldest son by his first marriage, Pepin, jealous of the attention shown by his father to the sons of his second wife and fearing the loss of paternal favor, joined with noble enemies in a conspiracy against his father. Pepin spent the rest of his life in confinement in a monastery after the plot was exposed.

PROBLEMS OF GOVERNMENT.   Charlemagne governed his kingdom through counts, of whom there were perhaps as many as 250. They were strategically located within the administrative districts into which the kingdom was divided. In Carolingian practice, the count tended to be a local magnate, one who already possessed the armed might and the self-interest to enforce the will of a generous king. He had three main duties: to maintain a local army loyal to the king, to collect tribute and dues, and to administer justice throughout his district.

This last responsibility he undertook through a district law court known as the *mallus*. The *mallus* assessed *wergeld,* or the compensation to be paid to an injured party in a feud, the most popular way of settling grievances and ending hostilities. In very difficult cases, where guilt or innocence was unclear, recourse was often taken to judicial duels or to such "divine" judgments as the length of time a defendant's hand took to heal after immersion in boiling water. In the ordeal by water, another divine test applied when human judgment was stymied, a defendant was thrown with his hands and feet bound into a river or pond that was first blessed by a priest; if he floated, he was pronounced guilty, because the pure water had obviously rejected him; if, however, the water received him and he sank, he was deemed innocent.

As in Merovingian times, many counts used their official position and new judicial powers to their own advantage, becoming little despots within their districts. As the strong were made stronger, they became more independent. They looked on the land grants with which they were paid as hereditary positions rather than generous royal donations—a development that began to fragment Charlemagne's kingdom. Charlemagne tried to supervise his overseers and improve local justice by creating special royal envoys known as *missi dominici,* lay and clerical agents (counts and archbishops and bishops) who made annual visits to districts other than their own. But their impact was only marginal. Permanent provincial governors, bearing the title of prefect, duke, or margrave, were created in what was still another attempt to manage the counts and to organize the outlying regions of the kingdom. But as these governors became established in their areas, they proved no less corruptible than the others.

Charlemagne never solved the problem of a loyal bureaucracy. Ecclesiastical agents proved no better than secular ones in this regard. Land-owning bishops had not only the same responsibilities but also the same secular life-styles and aspirations as the royal counts. Except for their attendance to the liturgy and to church prayers, they were largely indistinguishable from the lay nobility. Capitularies, or royal decrees, discouraged the more outrageous behavior of the clergy. But Charlemagne also sensed, rightly as the Gregorian reform of the eleventh century would prove, a danger to royal government in the emergence of a distinctive and reform-minded class of ecclesias-

During the Carolingian Renaissance scholars made editions of the works of Gregory the Great, shown here in a monastic scriptorium receiving the divine word from a dove perched on his shoulder. Below St. Gregory three monks-are shown writing. Note the inkwell held by the middle monk. Before the invention of the printing press in about 1450, manuscripts could only be duplicated by laborious hand copying. Much of this painstaking work was done by monks. [Kunsthistorisches Museum, Vienna]

tical landowners. Charlemagne purposefully treated his bishops as he treated his counts, that is, as vassals who served at the king's pleasure.

ALCUIN AND THE CAROLINGIAN RENAISSANCE. Charlemagne accumulated a great deal of wealth in the form of loot and land from conquered tribes. He used a substantial part of this booty to attract Europe's best scholars to Aachen, where they developed court culture and education. By making scholarship materially as well as intellectually rewarding, Charlemagne attracted such scholars as Theodulf of Orleans,

Peasants plowing and tilling in an early-eleventh-century illustration. The moldboard plow shown here came into use in Carolingian times. It had a heavier blade than the earlier "scratch" plow and could plow and could cut deep furrows in the soil, greatly improving crop yields. [Bildarchiv Preussischer Kulturbesitz, Alfredo Degli Orti, 1991]

Angilbert, his own biographer Einhard, and the renowned Anglo-Saxon master Alcuin of York (735–804), who, at almost fifty, became director of the king's palace school in 782. Alcuin brought classical and Christian learning to Aachen and was handsomely rewarded for his efforts with several monastic estates, including that of Saint Martin of Tours, the wealthiest in the kingdom.

Although Charlemagne also appreciated learning for its own sake, this grand palace school was not created simply for love of antiquity. Charlemagne intended it to upgrade the administrative skills of the clerics and officials who staffed the royal bureaucracy. By preparing the sons of nobles to run the religious and secular offices of the realm, court scholarship served kingdom building. The school provided basic instruction in the seven liberal arts, with special concentration on grammar, logic, and mathematics, that is, training in reading, writing, speaking, and sound reasoning—the basic tools of bureaucracy. A clearer style of handwriting—the Carolingian minuscule—and accurate Latin appeared in the official documents. Lay literacy increased. Through personal correspondence and visitations, Alcuin created a genuine, if limited, community of scholars and clerics at court and did much to infuse the highest administrative levels with a sense of comradeship and common purpose.

A modest renaissance or rebirth of antiquity occurred in the palace school as scholars collected and preserved ancient manuscripts for a more curious posterity. Alcuin worked on a correct text of the Bible and made editions of the works of Gregory the Great and the monastic *Rule* of Saint Benedict. These scholarly activities aimed at concrete reforms and served official efforts to bring uniformity to Church law and liturgy, to educate the clergy, and to improve moral life within the monasteries.

THE MANOR AND SERFDOM. The agrarian economy of the Middle Ages was organized and controlled through village farms known as *manors*. Here peasants labored as farmers in subordination to a lord, that is, a more powerful landowner who gave them land and a dwelling in exchange for their services and a portion of their crops. That part of the land farmed by the peasants for the lord was the *demense*, on average about one-quarter to one-third of the arable land. All crops grown there were harvested for the lord.

A social hierarchy based on personal status and the size of their property existed among the peasantry, and by custom peasants were treated differently according to their position within it. When a *freeman*, that is, a peasant with his own modest allodial or hereditary property (property free from the claims of a feudal overlord) became a serf by surrendering this property to a greater landowner in exchange for his protection and assistance, the freeman received it back from the lord with a clear definition of economic and legal rights that protected the freeman's self-interest. Although the land was no longer his property, he had full possession and use of it, and the number of services and the amount of goods to be supplied the lord were often carefully spelled out. On the other hand, peasants who entered the service of a lord without any real property to bargain with (perhaps some farm implements and a few animals) ended up as *unfree* serfs and were much more vulnerable to the lord's demands, often spending up to three days a week working the lord's fields. Truly impoverished peasants who lived and worked on the manor as serfs had the lowest status and were the least protected.

By the time of Charlemagne, the moldboard plow, which was especially needed in northern Europe where the soil was heavy, and the three-field system of land cultivation were coming into use. These developments improved agricultural productivity. Unlike the older "scratch" plow, which crisscrossed the field with only slight penetration, the moldboard cut deep into the soil and turned it to form a ridge, providing a natural drainage system for the field as well as permitting the deep planting of seeds. Unlike the earlier two-field system of crop rotation, which simply alternated fallow with planted fields each year, the three-field system increased the amount of cultivated land by leaving only one-third fallow in a given year. It also better adjusted crops to seasons. In winter, one field was planted with winter crops of wheat or rye; in the summer, a second field was planted with summer crops of oats, barley, and lentils; and the third field was left fallow, to be planted in its turn with winter and summer crops.

Serfs were subject to so-called dues in kind: firewood for cutting the lord's wood, sheep for grazing their sheep on the lord's land, and the like. In this way, the lord, by furnishing shacks and small plots of land from his vast domain, created an army of servants who provided him with everything from eggs to boots. The frequent discontent of the commoners with that system is reflected in the high number of recorded escapes. An astrological calendar from the period marks the days most favorable for escaping. Escaped serfs roamed the land as beggars and vagabonds, searching for new and better masters.

RELIGION AND THE CLERGY. As owners of the churches on their lands, the lords had the right to raise chosen serfs to the post of parish priest, placing them in charge of the churches on the lords' estates. Although Church law directed the lord to set a serf free before the serf entered the clergy, lords were reluctant to do this and risk thereby a possible later challenge to their jurisdiction over the ecclesiastical

property with which the serf, as priest, was invested. Lords rather preferred a "serf priest," one who not only said the mass on Sundays and holidays but also continued to serve his lord during the week, waiting on the lord's table and tending his steeds. Like Charlemagne with his bishops, Frankish lords cultivated a docile parish clergy.

The ordinary people looked to religion for comfort and consolation. They considered baptism and confession of the Creed a surety of future salvation. They baptized their children, attended mass, tried to learn the Lord's Prayer, and received extreme unction from the priest as death approached. This was all probably done with more awe and simple faith than understanding. Instruction in the meaning of Christian doctrine and practice remained at a bare minimum, and the local priests on the manors were no better educated than their congregations. People understandably became particularly attached in this period to the more tangible veneration of relics and saints.

Charlemagne shared many of the religious beliefs of his ordinary subjects. He collected and venerated relics, made pilgrimages to Rome, frequented the church of Saint Mary in Aachen several times a day, and directed in his last will and testament that all but a fraction of his great treasure be spent to endow masses and prayers for his departed soul.

Breakup of the Carolingian Kingdom

In the last years of his life, an ailing Charlemagne knew that his empire was ungovernable. The seeds of dissolution lay in regionalism, that is, the determination of each locality, no matter how small, to look first—and often only—to its own self-interest. Despite his considerable skill and resolution, Charlemagne's realm became too fragmented among powerful regional magnates. Although they were his vassals, these same men were also landholders and lords in their own right. They knew that their sovereignty lessened as Charlemagne's increased and accordingly became reluctant royal servants. In feudal society, a direct relationship existed between physical proximity to authority and loyalty to authority. Local people obeyed local lords more readily than they obeyed a glorious but distant king. Charlemagne had been forced to recognize and even to enhance the power of regional magnates in order to win needed financial and military support. But as in the Merovingian kingdom, so also in the Carolingian the tail came increasingly to wag the dog. Charlemagne's major attempt to enforce subordination to royal dictates and a transregional discipline—through the institution of the *missi dominici*—proved ultimately unsuccessful.

LOUIS THE PIOUS. The Carolingian kings did not give up easily, however. Charlemagne's only surviving son and successor was Louis the Pious (r. 814–840), so-called because of his close alliance with the Church and his promotion of puritanical reforms. Louis had three sons by his first wife. According to Salic or Germanic law, a ruler partitioned his kingdom equally among his surviving sons. Louis, who saw himself as an emperor and no mere German king, recognized that a tripartite kingdom would hardly be an empire and acted early in his reign, in the year 817, to break this legal tradition. This he did by making his eldest son, Lothar (d. 855), coregent and sole imperial heir. To Lothar's brothers, he gave important but much lesser appanages, or assigned hereditary lands: Pepin (d. 838) became king of Aquitaine, and Louis "the German" (d. 876) became king of Bavaria, over the eastern Franks.

In 823, Louis's second wife, Judith of Bavaria, bore him still a fourth son, Charles, later called "the Bald" (d. 877). Mindful of Frankish law and custom and determined that her son should receive more than just a nominal inheritance, the queen incited the brothers Pepin and Louis to war against Lothar, who fled for refuge to the pope. More important, Judith was instrumental in persuading Louis to reverse his earlier decision and to divide the kingdom equally among his four living sons. As their stepmother and the young Charles rose in their father's favor, the three older brothers feared still further reversals, so they decided to act against their father. Supported by the pope, they joined forces and defeated him in a battle near Colmar (833).

As the bestower of crowns upon emperors, the pope had an important stake in the preservation of the revived western empire and the imperial title, both of which Louis's belated agreement to an equal partition of his kingdom threatened to undo. The pope condemned Louis and restored Lothar to his original inheritance. But Lothar's regained imperial dignity only stirred anew the resentments of his brothers, including his stepbrother, Charles, who resumed their war against him.

THE TREATY OF VERDUN AND ITS AFTERMATH. When Louis the Pious died in 840, the empire was thrown into civil war. In 843, with the treaty of Verdun, peace finally came to Louis's surviving heirs (Pepin had

CAROLINGIAN DYNASTY (751–987)	
751	Pepin III "the Short" becomes king of the Franks
755	Franks drive Lombards out of central Italy; creation of Papal States
768–814	Charlemagne rules as king of the Franks
774	Charlemagne defeats Lombards in northern Italy
750–800	*Donation of Constantine* protests Frankish domination of Church
800	Pope Leo III crowns Charlemagne
814–840	Louis the Pious succeeds Charlemagne as "Emperor"
843	Treaty of Verdun partitions the Carolingian Empire
870	Treaty of Mersen further divides Carolingian Empire
875–950	New invasions by Vikings, Muslims, and Magyars
962	Ottonian dynasty succeeds Carolingian in Germany
987	Capetian dynasty succeeds Carolingian in France

died in 838). But this agreement also brought about the disaster that Louis had originally feared: The great Carolingian empire was partitioned according to Frankish law into three equal parts. Lothar received a middle section, which came to be known as Lotharingia, that embraced roughly modern Holland, Belgium, Switzerland, Alsace-Lorraine, and Italy. Charles the Bald received the western part of the kingdom, or roughly modern France. And Louis the German came into the eastern part, or roughly modern Germany (see Map 14-4). Although Lothar retained the imperial title, the universal empire of Charlemagne and Louis the Pious ceased to exist after Verdun. Not until the sixteenth century, with the election in 1519 of Charles I of Spain as the Holy Roman Emperor Charles V, would the western world again see a kingdom as vast as Charlemagne's.

The Treaty of Verdun, the oldest written document in French, proved to be only the beginning of Carolingian fragmentation. When Lothar died in 855, his middle kingdom was divided equally among his three surviving sons. This partition of the partition left the middle, or imperial, kingdom much smaller and weaker than those of Louis the German and Charles

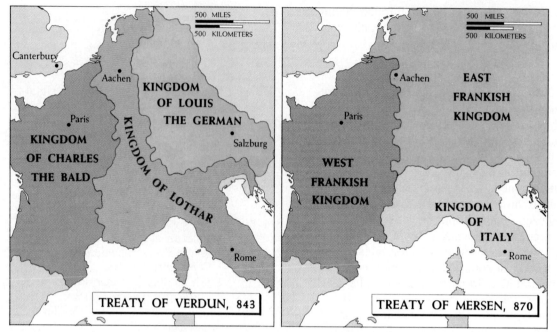

MAP 14-4 THE TREATY OF VERDUN (843) AND THE TREATY OF MERSEN (870) *The Treaty of Verdun divided the kingdom of Louis the Pious among his three feuding children: Charles the Bald, Lothar, and Louis the German. After Lothar's death in 855 the middle kingdom was so weakened by division among his three sons that Charles the Bald and Louis the German divided it between themselves in the Treaty of Mersen.*

the Bald. Henceforth, Western Europe saw an eastern and a western Frankish kingdom—roughly Germany versus France—at war over the fractionalized middle kingdom, a contest that has continued into modern times.

When Charles the Bald died in 877, both the papal and the imperial thrones fell on especially hard times. Each became a pawn in the hands of powerful Italian and German magnates, respectively. Neither pope nor emperor knew dignity and power again until a new western imperial dynasty in Germany—the Ottonians—attained dominance during the reign of Otto I (962–973). It is especially with reference to this juncture in European history—the last quarter of the ninth and the first half of the tenth century—that one may speak with some justification of a "dark age."

Simultaneously with the internal political breakdown of the empire and the papacy came new barbarian attacks, set off probably by overpopulation and famine in northern Europe. The late ninth and tenth centuries saw successive waves of Normans (North men), better known as Vikings, from Scandinavia; Magyars, or Hungarians, the great horsemen from the eastern plains; and Muslims from the south (see Map

14-5). In the 880s, the Vikings penetrated to the imperial residence of Aachen and to Paris. Moving rapidly in ships and raiding coastal towns, they were almost impossible to defend against and kept Western Europe on edge. The Franks built fortified towns and castles in strategic locations, which served as refuges. When they could, they bought off the invaders with outright grants of land (for example, Normandy) and payments of silver. During this period, local populations became more dependent than ever before on local strongmen for life, limb, and livelihood. This brute fact of life provided the essential precondition for the maturation of feudal society.

Feudal Society

The Middle Ages were characterized by a chronic absence of effective central government and the constant threat of famine, disease, and foreign invasion. In this state of affairs the weaker sought the protection of the stronger, and the true lords and masters became those who could guarantee immediate protection from rapine and starvation. The term *feudal*

MAP 14-5 VIKING, MUSLIM, AND MAGYAR INVASIONS TO THE ELEVENTH CENTURY *Western Europe was sorely beset by new waves of outsiders from the ninth to the eleventh century. From north, east, and south a stream of invading Vikings, Magyars, and Muslims brought the west at times to near collapse and of course gravely affected institutions within Europe.*

society refers to the social, political, military, and economic system that emerged.

A feudal society is a social order in which a regional prince or a local lord is dominant, and the highest virtues are those of mutual trust and fidelity. In a feudal society, what people require most is the firm assurance that others can be depended on in time of dire need. It is above all a system of mutual rights and responsibilities.

During the early Middle Ages, the landed nobility became great lords who ruled over their domains as miniature kingdoms. They maintained their own armies and courts, regulated their area's tolls, and even minted their own coins. Large warrior groups of vassals were created by extensive bestowals of land, and they developed into a prominent professional military class with its own code of knightly conduct. In feudal society, most serfs docilely worked the land, the

clergy prayed and gave counsel, and the nobility— both landed and vassal—maintained law and order by swift steed and sword.

Origins

The origins of feudal government can be found in the divisions and conflicts of Merovingian society. In the sixth and seventh centuries, there evolved the custom of individual freemen placing themselves under the protection of more powerful freemen. In this way, the latter built up armies and became local magnates, and the former solved the problem of simple survival. Freemen who so entrusted themselves to others were known as *ingenui in obsequio* ("freemen in a contractual relation of dependence"). Those who so gave themselves to the king were called *antrustiones*. All men of this type came to be described collectively as *vassi* ("those who serve"), from which evolved the term *vassalage,* meaning the placement of oneself in the personal service of another who promises protection in return.

Landed nobles, like kings, tried to acquire as many such vassals as they could, because military strength in the early Middle Ages lay in numbers. Because it proved impossible to maintain these growing armies within the lord's own household, which was the original custom, or to support them by special monetary payments, the practice evolved of simply granting them land as a "tenement." such land came to be known as a *benefice,* or a *fief,* and vassals were expected to dwell on it and maintain their steeds and other accoutrements of war in good order. Originally vassals, therefore, were little more than gangs-in-waiting.

Vassalage and the Fief

Vassalage involved "fealty" to the lord. To swear fealty was to promise to refrain from any action that might in any way threaten the lord's well-being and to perform personal services for him on his request. Chief among the expected services was military duty as a mounted knight. This could involve a variety of activities: a short or long military expedition, escort duty, standing castle guard, and/or the placement of one's own fortress at the lord's disposal, if the vassal was of such stature as to have one. Continuous bargaining and bickering occurred over the terms of service. Limitations were placed on the number of days a lord could require services from a vassal. In France in the eleventh century, about forty days of service per year were considered sufficient. It also became possible for vassals to buy their way out of military service by a monetary payment known as *scutage.* The lord, in turn, applied this payment to the hiring of mercenaries, who often proved more efficient than contract-conscious vassals. Beyond his military duty, the vassal was also expected to give the lord advice when he requested it and to sit as a member of his court when it was in session.

Beginning with the reign of Louis the Pious (814–840), bishops and abbots swore fealty and received their offices from the king as a benefice. The king formally "invested" these clerics in their offices during a special ceremony in which he presented them

---

Bishop Fulbert Describes the Obligations of Vassal and Lord

Trust held the lord and vassal together. Their duties in this regard were carefully defined. Here are six general rules for vassal and lord, laid down by Bishop Fulbert of Chartres in a letter to William, Duke of Aquitaine, in 1020.

He who swears fealty to his lord ought always to have these six things in memory: what is harmless, safe, honorable, useful, easy, practicable. *Harmless,* that is to say, that he should not injure his lord in his body; *safe,* that he should not injure him by betraying his secrets or the defenses upon which he relies for safety; *honorable,* that he should not injure him in his justice or in other matters that pertain to his honor; *useful,* that he should not injure him in his possessions; *easy* and *practicable,* that that good which his lord is able to do easily he make not difficult, nor that which is practicable he make not impossible to him.

That the faithful vassal should avoid these injuries is certainly proper, but not for this alone does he de-serve his holding; for it is not sufficient to abstain from evil, unless what is good is done also. It remains, therefore, that in the same six things mentioned above he should faithfully counsel and aid his lord, if he wishes to be looked upon as worthy of his benefice and to be safe concerning the fealty which he has sworn.

The lord also ought to act toward his faithful vassal reciprocally in all these things. And if he does not do this, he will be justly considered guilty of bad faith, just as the former, if he should be detected in avoiding or consenting to the avoidance of his duties, would be perfidious and perjured.

James Harvey Robinson, ed., *Readings in European History,* Vol. 1 (Boston: Athenaeum, 1904), p. 184.

with a ring and a staff, the symbols of high spiritual office. Louis's predecessors had earlier confiscated Church lands with only modest and belated compensation to the Church in the form of a tithe required of all Frankish inhabitants. Long a sore point for the Church, the presumptuous practice of the lay investiture of the clergy provoked a momentous confrontation between Church and State in the eleventh and twelfth centuries, when reform-minded clergy rebelled against what they then believed to be involuntary clerical vassalage.

The lord's obligations to his vassals were very specific. He was, first of all, obligated to protect the vassal from physical harm and to stand as his advocate in public court. After fealty was sworn and homage paid, the lord provided for the vassal's physical maintenance by the bestowal of a benefice, or fief. The fief was simply the physical or material wherewithal to meet the vassal's military and other obligations. It could take the form of liquid wealth as well as the more common grant of real property. There were so-called money fiefs, which empowered a vassal to receive regular payments from the lord's treasury. Such fiefs created potential conflicts because they made it possible for one country to acquire vassals among the nobility of another. Normally, the fief consisted of a landed estate of anywhere from a few to several thousand acres. But it could also take the form of a castle.

In Carolingian times, a benefice, or fief, varied in size from one or more small villas to several *mansi,* which were agricultural holdings of twenty-five to forty-eight acres. The king's vassals are known to have received benefices of at least thirty and as many as two hundred such mansi, truly a vast estate. Royal vassalage with a benefice understandably came to be widely sought by the highest classes of Carolingian society. As a royal policy, however, it proved deadly to the king in the long run. Although Carolingian kings jealously guarded their rights over property granted in benefice to vassals, resident vassals were still free to dispose of their benefices as they pleased. Vassals of the king, strengthened by his donations, in turn created their own vassals. These vassals, in turn, created still further vassals of their own—vassals of vassals of vassals—in a reverse pyramiding effect that had fragmented land and authority from the highest to the lowest levels by the late ninth century.

Fragmentation and Divided Loyalty

In addition to the fragmentation brought about by the multiplication of vassalage, effective occupation of the land led gradually to claims of hereditary possession. Hereditary possession became a legally recognized principle in the ninth century and laid the basis for claims to real ownership. Fiefs given as royal donations became hereditary possessions and, with the passage of time, in some instances even the real property of the possessor. Further, vassal engagements came to be multiplied in still another way as enterprising freemen sought to accumulate as much land as possible. One man could actually become a vassal to several different lords. This development led in the ninth century to the concept of a "liege lord"— one master whom the vassal must obey even to the harm of the others, should a direct conflict among them arise.

The problem of loyalty was reflected not only in the literature of the period, with its praise of the virtues of honor and fidelity, but also in the ceremonial development of the very act of "commendation" by which a freeman became a vassal. In the mid-eighth century, an "oath of fealty" highlighted the ceremony. A vassal reinforced his promise of fidelity to the lord by swearing a special oath with his hand on a sacred relic or the Bible. In the tenth and eleventh centuries, paying homage to the lord involved not only the swearing of such an oath but also the placement of the vassal's hands between the lord's and the sealing of the ceremony with a kiss.

As the centuries passed, personal loyalty and service became quite secondary to the acquisition of property. The fief overshadowed fealty; the benefice became more important than vassalage; and freemen proved themselves prepared to swear allegiance to the highest bidder.

The Early Middle Ages in World Perspective

In Western Europe, the centuries between 400 and 1000 witnessed both the decline of European classical civilization and the birth of a new European civilization. Beginning with the fifth century, the barbarian invasions separated Western Europe culturally from its classical age. No other world culture experienced such a separation, which was centuries long in the west. Although some important works and concepts survived from antiquity due largely to the Christian Church, Western civilization would for centuries be recovering its rich classical past in "renaissances" stretching into the sixteenth century. Out of the mixture of barbarian and surviving (or recovered) classical culture, Western civilization, as we know it today, was born. Aided and abetted by the Christian Church, the Carolingians created a new imperial tradition. But the early medieval society of the west remained highly fragmented, probably more so than anywhere else in the world, despite a certain common religious culture. Regions were organized into institutions designed primarily to ensure that all would be fed and cared for (manorialism) and that outside predators would be successfully repulsed (feudalism). It was not a time of great cultural ambition.

In China, particularly in the seventh and eighth centuries, the T'ang dynasty rulers also searched for ways to secure Chinese borders against foreign expansion from Turkey and Tibet. As in Western Europe, religion and philosophy served and did not compete with the state (although this would change in the West after the twelfth century). Early medieval China was, however, far more cosmopolitan and politically unified than Western Europe. China was also centuries ahead in technology. Printing with movable type existed there by the tenth century, an invention the West did not see until the fifteenth century. Chinese rulers governed effectively far beyond their immediate centers of government. The T'ang dynasty held sway over their empire in a way Carolingian rulers could only imagine.

In Japan, the Yamato court (300–680), much like that of the Merovingians and Carolingians, struggled to unify and control the countryside. It was also aided by a religion friendly to royalty, Shinto. As in the West, a Japanese identity evolved through struggle and accommodation with outside cultures, especially with the Chinese, the dominant influence on Japan between the seventh and twelfth centuries. But foreign cultural influence, again as in the West, never managed to eradicate the indigenous culture. By the ninth century, a distinctive Sino-Japanese culture existed. But Japan, again like Western Europe, remained a fragmented land during these centuries, despite a certain allegiance and willingness to pay taxes to an imperial court. Throughout Japan, the basic unit of political control consisted of those same highly self-conscious and specially devoted armed knights we saw in Western Europe. A system of lordship and vassalage evolved around bands of local mounted warriors who were known as *samurai*. Through this system, local order was maintained in Japan until the fifteenth century. Like the Merovingian and Carolingian courts, the Japanese court had to tolerate strong and independent regional rulers.

In the seventh century, Islam gave birth to still another powerful new international civilization, one that reached from India to Spain by 710. Consolidated by a line of successful caliphates between 750 and 945, Islam had divided by the tenth century into more exclusive (Kharijite and Shi'ite) and more inclusive (Sunni) factions. Again as in Western Europe, its central government had broken down. But the politically strong and culturally vibrant period of the high caliphate under the Umayyads and Abbasids (Islam's "classical" period) overlapped in time the Carolingian heyday, when Western Europe witnessed the birth of a new political empire and a little cultural Renaissance of its own.

Finally, in the centuries just before the awakening of Western European civilization, India enjoyed the high point of its civilization, the Gupta Age (320–467). While Western Europeans struggled for some degree of political and social order, a vocationally and socially limiting caste system neatly imposed order on Indian society from Brahmans to outcasts. Culture, religion, and politics flourished amid this unity.

All things considered, one may say that most of the world's great civilizations were reaching a peak when that of the West was just coming to life. This may be attributed to the fact that the other world civilizations never experienced disruptions in their cultures by foreign invaders on the magnitude known in the West during the early Middle Ages.

Suggested Readings

M. BLOCH, *Feudal Society,* Vols. 1 and 2, trans. by L. A. Manyon (1971). A classic on the topic and as an example of historical study.

P. BROWN, *Augustine of Hippo: A Biography* (1967). Late antiquity seen through the biography of its greatest Christian thinker.

H. CHADWICK, *The Early Church* (1967). Among the best treatments of early Christianity.

B. CUNLIFFE, *Greeks, Romans and Barbarians* (1988). A quantitative account.

R. H. C. DAVIS, *A History of Medieval Europe: From Constantine to St. Louis* (1972). Unsurpassed in clarity.

K. F. DREW, ed., *The Barbarian Invasions: Catalyst of a New Order* (1970). Collection of essays that focuses the issues.

F. DVORNIK, *Byzantium and the Roman Primacy* (1966).

H. Fichtenau, *The Carolingian Empire: The Age of Charlemagne,* trans. by Peter Munz (1964). Strongest on the political history of the era.

John V. A. Fine, *The Early Medieval Balkans: Sixth–Twelfth Centuries* (1983). The formation of multiculturalism in the region.

F. L. Ganshof, *Feudalism,* trans. by Philip Grierson (1964). The most profound brief analysis of the subject.

P. Geary, *Before France and Germany* (1988). The medieval evolution of these territories.

A. F. Havighurst, ed., *The Pirenne Thesis: Analysis, Criticism, and Revision* (1958). Excerpts from the scholarly debate over the extent of Western trade in the East during the early Middle Ages.

Richard Hodges et al., *Mohammed, Charlemagne, and the Origins of Europe* (1982). Good on the society and economy of early medieval Europe.

D. Knowles, *Christian Monasticism* (1969). Sweeping survey with helpful photographs.

R. Krautheimer, *Early Christian and Byzantine Architecture* (1965). Makes the developments clear and interesting.

M. L. W. Laistner, *Thought and Letters in Western Europe, 500 to 900* (1957). Among the best surveys of early medieval intellectual history.

C. H. Lawrence, *Medieval Monasticism* (1989). Comprehensive survey.

J. Leclercq, *The Love of Learning and the Desire for God: A Study of Monastic Culture,* trans. by Catherine Misrahi (1962). Lucid, delightful, absorbing account of the ideals of monks.

J. Leclercq, F. Vandenbroucke, and L. Bouyer, *The Spirituality of the Middle Ages* (1968). Perhaps the best survey of medieval Christianity, East and West, to the eve of the Protestant Reformation.

R. McKitternick, *The Frankish Kingdoms Under the Carolingians, 751–987* (1983).

C. Mango, *Byzantium: The Empire of New Rome* (1980).

P. Munz, *The Age of Charlemagne* (1971). Penetrating social history of the period.

T. Noble, *The Republic of St. Peter* (1988). How the Church became an empire.

H. Pirenne, *A History of Europe, I: From the End of the Roman World in the West to the Beginnings of the Western States,* trans. by Bernhard Maill (1958). Comprehensive survey, with now controversial views on the demise of Western trade and cities in the early Middle Ages.

S. Runciman, *Byzantine Civilization* (1970). Succinct, comprehensive account by a master.

P. Sawyer, *The Age of the Vikings* (1962). The best account.

O. von Simson, *Sacred Fortress: Byzantine Art and Statecraft in Ravenna* (1948).

R. W. Southern, *The Making of the Middle Ages* (1973). Originally published in 1953, but still a fresh account by an imaginative historian.

C. Stephenson, *Medieval Feudalism* (1969). Excellent short summary and introduction.

A. A. Vasiliev, *History of the Byzantine Empire 324–1453* (1952). The most comprehensive treatment in English.

H. Waddell, ed., *The Desert Fortress* (1957).

S. F. Wemple, *Women in Frankish Society: Marriage and the Cloister 500–900* (1981). The impact of Christian marriage customs on the Franks.

L. White, Jr., *Medieval Technology and Social Change* (1962). Often fascinating account of how primitive technology changed life.

The famous four horsemen of the Apocalypse, who, according to the book of Revelation in the New Testament, will bring devastation and death upon the world at the end of time. This lavish depiction was made by Spanish Cistercian monks in the early thirteenth century. [The Pierpont Morgan Library, New York M.429.f.94]

412

The High Middle Ages (1000–1300)

The high Middle Ages mark a period of political expansion and consolidation and of intellectual flowering and synthesis. The noted medievalist Joseph Strayer has called this period the age that saw "the full development of all the potentialities of medieval civilization."[1] Some even argue that as far as the development of western institutions is concerned, it was a more creative period than the later Italian Renaissance and the German Reformation.

The high Middle Ages saw the borders of Western Europe largely secured against foreign invaders. Although there was intermittent Muslim aggression well into the sixteenth century, fear of assault from without diminished. A striking change occurred in the late eleventh and twelfth centuries. Western Europe, which had for so long been the prey of foreign powers, became through the Crusades and foreign trade the feared hunter within both the Eastern and the Arab worlds.

During the high Middle Ages, "national" monarchies emerged in France, England, and Germany. Parliaments and popular assemblies representing the interests of the nobility, the clergy, and the townspeople also appeared at this time to secure local rights and customs against the claims of the developing dynasties. The foundations of modern representative institutions can be found in this period.

The high Middle Ages saw a revolution in agriculture that increased both food supplies and populations. This period witnessed a great revival of trade and commerce, the rise of towns, the development of banking and credit, and the emergence of a "new rich" merchant class, the ancestors of modern capi-

[1] *Western History in the Middle Ages—A Short History* (New York: Appleton-Century-Crofts, 1955), pp. 9, 127.

413

talists. Universities came into being at this time, and vernacular and romance literatures emerged. With the recovery of the writings of the ancient Greek philosophers, made possible by the revival of Eastern trade and by contacts with Muslim intellectuals particularly through Spain, urban culture and education received a new stimulus. Unlike the dabbling in antiquity in Carolingian times, the twelfth century enjoyed a true renaissance of classical learning.

The high Middle Ages were also the time when the Latin or Western church established itself as an authority independent of monarchical secular government, thereby indirectly sowing the seeds of the distinctive Western separation of Church and State. This occurred during the Investiture Struggle of the late eleventh and twelfth centuries. In this confrontation between popes and emperors, a reformed papacy overcame its long subservience to the Carolingian and Ottonian kings. The papacy won out, however, by becoming itself a monarchy among the world's emerging monarchies, thereby preparing the way for still more dangerous confrontations between popes and emperors in the later Middle Ages.

Revival of Empire, Church, and Towns

Otto I and the Revival of the Empire

The fortunes of both the old empire and the papacy began to revive when the Saxon Henry I ("the Fowler"; d. 936), the strongest of the German dukes, became the first non-Frankish king of Germany in 918. Henry rebuilt royal power by forcibly consolidating the duchies of Swabia, Bavaria, Saxony, Franconia, and Lotharingia. He secured imperial borders by checking the invasions of the Hungarians and the Danes. Although greatly reduced in size by comparison with Charlemagne's empire, Henry's German kingdom still placed his son and successor Otto I (936–973) in a strong territorial position.

The very able Otto maneuvered his own kin into positions of power in Bavaria, Swabia, and Franconia. He refused to treat each duchy as an independent hereditary dukedom, as was the trend among the nobility. He rather dealt with each as a subordinate member of a unified kingdom. In a truly imperial gesture in 951, Otto invaded Italy and proclaimed himself its king. In 955, he won his most magnificent victory when he defeated the Hungarians at Lechfeld, a feat comparable to Charles Martel's earlier victory over the

Saracens near Tours in 732. The victory of Lechfeld secured German borders against new barbarian attack, further unified the German duchies, and earned Otto the well-deserved title "the Great."

As part of a careful rebuilding program, Otto, following the example of his predecessors, enlisted the Church. Bishops and abbots, men who possessed a sense of universal empire yet did not marry and found competitive dynasties, were made royal princes and agents of the king. Because these clergy, as royal bureaucrats, received great landholdings and immunity from local counts and dukes, they also found such vassalage to the king very attractive.

In 961, Otto, who had long aspired to the imperial crown, responded to a call for help from Pope John

Otto I (912–973) was Holy Roman emperor from 936–973. The four tribute-bearing maidens symbolize his dominion over all of Western Europe. [Alinari/Art Resource]

XII (955–964). In recompense, Pope John crowned Otto emperor in February 2, 962. At this time, Otto also recognized the existence of the Papal States and proclaimed himself their special protector. The Church was now more than ever under royal control. Its bishops and abbots were Otto's appointees and bureaucrats, and the pope reigned in Rome only by the power of the emperor's sword. Pope John belatedly recognized the royal web in which the Church had become entangled. As a countermeasure, he joined Italian opposition to the new emperor. This turnabout brought Otto's swift revenge. An ecclesiastical synod over which Otto personally presided deposed Pope John and proclaimed that henceforth no pope could take office without first swearing an oath of allegiance to the emperor. Under Otto I—with popes ruling at the emperor's pleasure—western Caesaro-papism reached a peak.

Otto had shifted the royal focus from Germany to Italy. His successors became so preoccupied with running the affairs of Italy that their German base began to disintegrate, sacrificed to imperial dreams. They might have learned a lesson from the contemporary Capetian kings, the successor dynasty to the Carolingians in France, who wisely mended local fences and concentrated their limited resources on securing a tight grip on their immediate royal domain, which was never neglected for the sake of foreign adventure. The Ottonians, in contrast, reached far beyond their grasp when they tried to subdue Italy. As the briefly revived empire began to crumble in the first quarter of the eleventh century, the Church, long unhappy with Carolingian and Ottonian domination, prepared to declare its independence and exact its own vengeance.

The Reviving Catholic Church

CLUNY REFORM MOVEMENT. During the late ninth and early tenth centuries, the clergy had become tools of kings and magnates, and the papacy a toy of Italian nobles. The Ottonians made bishops their servile princes, and popes also served at their pleasure. A new day dawned for the Church, however, thanks not only to the failing fortunes of the empire but also to a new force for reform within the Church itself. In a great monastery in Cluny in east-central France, a reform movement appeared.

Since the fall of the Roman Empire, popular support for the Church had been especially inspired by the example of the monks. Monasteries provided an important alternative style of life for the religiously earnest in an age when most people had very few options. The tenth and eleventh centuries saw an unprecedented boom in their construction. Monks remained the least secularized and most spiritual of the Church's clergy. Their cultural achievements were widely admired, and their relics and rituals were considered magical.

Cluny, the main source of the reform movement, was founded in 910 by William the Pious, duke of Aquitaine. A Benedictine monastery, Cluny modified Saint Benedict's *Rule for Monasteries* by placing a special emphasis on liturgical purity and deemphasizing manual labor. Intensely loyal to their monasteries, Cluny monks were intent on maintaining a spiritual church. The reformers among them rejected the subservience of the clergy, especially that of the German bishops, to royal authority and viewed the pope in Rome as a more appropriate higher authority after their abbots than any king or emperor. The Cluny reformers further resented the transgression of ascetic piety by "secular" parish clergy, who maintained concubines in a relationship akin to marriage. (Later, a distinction would be formalized between the secular clergy who lived and ministered in the world [*saeculum*] and the regular clergy, monks and nuns withdrawn from the world and living according to a special rule [*regula*].)

The Cluny reformers resolved to free the clergy from both kings and "wives," to create an independent and chaste clergy. The Church alone was to be the clergy's lord and spouse. Although part of a general movement for church reform across Europe at this time, the Cluny reformers made a definite contribution to the Western separation of Church and State and to the creation of a celibate clergy.

Cluny rapidly became a center from which reformers were dispatched to monasteries throughout France and Italy. It grew to embrace almost fifteen hundred dependent cloisters, each devoted to monastic and Church reform. In the last half of the eleventh century, the Cluny reformers reached the summit when the papacy embraced their reforms.

In the late ninth and early tenth centuries, the movement inspired the "Peace of God," a series of Church decrees that attempted to lessen the endemic warfare of medieval society by threatening excommunication for all who, at any time, harmed such vulnerable groups as women, peasants, merchants, and clergy. The Peace of God was subsequently reinforced by proclamations of the "Truce of God," a Church order that everyone must abstain from every

A drawing of the famous Romanesque third abbey church of St. Peter of the monastery of Cluny, France, built between 1080 and 1225, and ultimately destroyed by war and demolished between 1806 and 1823 except for one tower. When built in the twelfth century it was the largest church in Europe (555 feet long). [Giraudon/Art Resource]

form of violence and warfare during a certain part of each week (eventually from Wednesday night to Monday morning) and in all holy seasons.

Popes devoted to reforms like those urged by Cluny came to power during the reign of Emperor Henry III (1039–1056). Pope Leo IX (1049–1054) promoted regional synods in opposition to simony (that is, the selling of spiritual things, such as Church offices) and clerical concubinage. He also placed Cluniacs in key administrative posts in Rome. During the turbulent minority of Henry III's successor, Henry IV (r. 1056–1106), reform popes began to assert themselves more openly. Pope Stephen IX (1057–1058) reigned without imperial ratification, contrary to the earlier declaration of Otto I. Pope Nicholas II (1059–

1061) took the unprecedented step of establishing a College of Cardinals in 1059, and henceforth this body alone elected the pope.

INVESTITURE STRUGGLE: GREGORY VII AND HENRY IV. It was Pope Gregory VII (1073–1085), a fierce advocate of Church reform who had entered the papal bureaucracy a quarter century earlier during the pontificate of Leo IX, who put the Church's declaration of independence to the test. Cluniacs had repeatedly inveighed against simony. In 1075, Pope Gregory condemned under penalty of excommunication the lay investiture of clergy at any level. He had primarily in mind the emperor's well-established custom of installing bishops by presenting them with the ring and

Pope Gregory VII Asserts the Power of the Pope

Church reformers of the high Middle Ages vigorously asserted the power of the pope within the Church and his rights against emperors and all others who might encroach on the papal sphere of jurisdiction. Here is a statement of the basic principles of the Gregorian reformers, known as the Ditatus Papae *("Sayings of the Pope"), which is attributed to Pope Gregory VII (1073–1085).*

That the Roman Church was founded by God alone.

That the Roman Pontiff alone is rightly to be called universal.

That the Pope may depose the absent.

That for him alone it is lawful to enact new laws according to the needs of the time, to assemble together new congregations, to make an abbey of a canonry; and to divide a rich bishopric and unite the poor ones.

That he alone may use the imperial insignia.

That the Pope is the only one whose feet are to be kissed by all princes.

That his name alone is to be recited in churches.

That his title is unique in the world.

That he may depose emperors.

That he may transfer bishops, if necessary, from one See to another.

That no synod may be called a general one without his order.

That no chapter or book may be regarded as canonical without his authority.

That no sentence of his may be retracted by any one; and that he, alone of all, can retract it.

That he himself may be judged by no one.

That the Roman Church has never erred, nor ever, by the witness of Scripture, shall err to all eternity.

That the Pope may absolve subjects of unjust men from their fealty.

Church and State through the Centuries: A Collection of Historic Documents, trans. and ed. by S. Z. Ehler and John B. Morrall (New York: Biblo and Tannen, 1967), pp. 43–44.

---

staff that symbolized episcopal office. After Gregory's ruling, bishops no more than popes were to be the creations of emperors. As popes were elected by the College of Cardinals and were not raised up by kings or nobles, so bishops would henceforth be installed in their offices by high ecclesiastical authority as empowered by the pope and none other.

Gregory's prohibition came as a jolt to royal authority. Since the days of Otto I, emperors had routinely passed out bishoprics to favored clergy. Bishops, who received royal estates, were the emperors' appointees and servants of the state. Henry IV's Carolingian and Ottonian predecessors had carefully nurtured the theocratic character of the empire in both concept and administrative bureaucracy. The Church and religion were integral parts of government. Henry considered Gregory's action a direct challenge to his authority. The territorial princes, on the other hand, ever tending away from the center and eager to see the emperor weakened, were quick to see the advan-

tages of Gregory's ruling: If the emperor did not have a bishop's ear, then a territorial prince might. In the hope of gaining an advantage over both the emperor and the clergy in their territory, the princes fully supported Gregory's edict.

The lines of battle were quickly drawn. Henry assembled his loyal German bishops at Worms in January 1076 and had them proclaim their independence from Gregory. Gregory promptly responded with the Church's heavy artillery; he excommunicated Henry and absolved all Henry's subjects from loyalty to him. The German princes were delighted by this turn of events, and Henry found himself facing a general revolt led by the duchy of Saxony. He had no recourse but to come to terms with Gregory. In a famous scene, Henry prostrated himself outside Gregory's castle retreat at Canossa on January 25, 1077. There he reportedly stood barefoot in the snow off and on for three days before the pope absolved his royal penitent. Papal power had, at this moment, reached its

A twelfth-century manuscript illustrating the struggle between Emperor Henry IV and Pope Gregory VII. In the top panel, Henry installs his puppet pope, Clement III, and drives Gregory from Rome. Below, Gregory dies in exile. As can be seen, the sympathies of the artist, a monk, were with Gregory, not Henry. [University of Jena]

pinnacle. But Gregory's grandeur, as he must surely have known when he pardoned Henry and restored him to power, was very soon to fade. In 1084, Henry forced Gregory into exile and installed his own anti-pope—Clement III—in his place.

The settlement of the investiture controversy came in 1122 with the Concordat of Worms. Emperor Henry V (r. 1106–1125) formally renounced his power to invest bishops with ring and staff. In exchange, Pope Calixtus II (1119–1124) recognized the emperor's right to be present and to invest bishops with fiefs before or after their investment with ring and staff by the Church. The emperor also effectively retained the right to nominate or veto a candidate. The old Church–State "back scratching" in this way continued, but now on very different terms. The clergy received their offices and attendant religious powers solely from ecclesiastical authority and no longer from kings and emperors. Rulers continued to bestow lands and worldly goods on high clergy in the hope of influencing them; the Concordat of Worms made the clergy more independent but not necessarily less worldly.

The Gregorian party won the independence of the clergy at the price of encouraging the divisiveness of the political forces within the empire. The pope made himself strong by making imperial authority weak. In the end, those who profited most from the investiture controversy were the local princes.

The First Crusades

If an index of popular piety and support for the pope in the high Middle Ages is needed, the Crusades

A symbolic portrayal of Melchizedek, biblical high priest and king of Salem, blessing Abraham, the father of the Hebrew people. Christian priests viewed this biblical event as prefiguring the blessings they bestowed on the kings of Europe as they went forth on crusades to the Holy Land. [Giraudon/Art Resource]

amply provide it. What the Cluny reform was to the clergy, the First Crusade to the Holy Land, proclaimed by Pope Urban II at the Council of Clermont in France in 1095, was to the laity: an outlet for the heightened religious zeal of what was Europe's most religious century before the Protestant Reformation. Actually, there had been an earlier Crusade of French knights, who, inspired by Pope Alexander II, had attacked Muslims in Spain in 1064. Unlike later Crusades, which were undertaken for patently mercenary as well as religious motives, the early Crusades were to a very high degree inspired by genuine religious piety and were carefully orchestrated by the revived papacy. Participants in the First Crusade to the Holy Land were promised a plenary indulgence should they die in battle, that is, a complete remission of the penance required of them for their mortal sins and hence release from suffering for them in purgatory. But this spiritual reward was only part of the crusading impulse. Other factors were the widespread popular respect for the reformed papacy and the existence of a nobility newly strengthened by the breakdown of imperial power and eager for military adventure. These elements combined to make the First Crusade a rousing success.

The eastern emperor had petitioned both Pope Gregory VII and Pope Urban II for aid against advancing Muslim armies. The western Crusaders did not, however, assemble for the purpose of defending Europe's borders against aggression. They freely took the offensive to rescue the holy city of Jerusalem—which had been in non-Christian hands since the seventh century—from the Seljuq Turks. To this end three great armies—tens of thousands of Crusaders—gathered in France, Germany, and Italy. Following different routes, they reassembled in Constantinople in 1097 (see Map 15-1). The convergence of these spirited soldiers on the eastern capital was a cultural shock that only deepened eastern antipathy toward the west. The weakened eastern emperor, Alexis I, suspected their motives, and the common people, who were forced to give them room and board, hardly considered them Christian brothers in a common cause—especially after Rome and Constantinople

had separated in 1054. Nonetheless, these fanatical Crusaders accomplished what no eastern army had ever been able to do. They soundly defeated one Seljuq army after another in a steady advance toward Jerusalem, which fell to them on July 15, 1099.

The victorious Crusaders divided the conquered territory into the feudal states of Jerusalem, Edessa, and Antioch, which they allegedly held as fiefs from the pope. Godfrey of Bouillon, leader of the French-German army (and after him his brother Baldwin), ruled over the kingdom of Jerusalem. However, the Crusaders remained only small islands within a great sea of Muslims, who looked on the western invaders as hardly more than savages. Native persistence finally broke the Crusaders around mid-century, and the forty-odd-year Latin presence in the east began to crumble. Edessa fell to Muslim armies in 1144. A Second Crusade, preached by the eminent Bernard of Clairvaux (1091–1153), Christendom's most powerful monastic leader, attempted a rescue, but it met with dismal failure. In October 1187, Jerusalem itself was reconquered by Saladin (1138–1193), king of Egypt and Syria, and, save for a brief interlude in the thirteenth century, it remained thereafter in Islamic hands until modern times.

A Third Crusade in the twelfth century (1189–1192) attempted yet another rescue, enlisting as its leaders the most powerful western rulers: Emperor Frederick Barbarossa; Richard the Lion-Hearted, king of England; and Philip Augustus, king of France. But the Third Crusade proved a tragicomic commentary on the passing of the original crusading spirit. Frederick Barbarossa accidentally drowned in the Saleph River while en route to the Holy Land. Richard the Lion-Hearted and Philip Augustus reached the outskirts of Jerusalem, but their intense personal rivalry shattered the Crusaders' unity and chances of victory. Philip Augustus returned to France and made war on English continental territories, and Richard fell captive to the Emperor Henry VI as he was returning to England. (Henry VI suspected Richard of plotting against him with Henry's mortal enemy, Henry the Lion, the duke of Saxony, who happened also to be Richard's brother-in-law.) The English were forced to pay a handsome ransom for their king's release. Popular resentment of taxes for this ransom became part of the background of the revolt against the English monarchy that led to the royal recognition of the Magna Carta in 1215.

The long-term achievement of the first three Crusades had little to do with their original purpose. Politically and religiously, they were a failure, and the

MAP 15-1   THE EARLY CRUSADES   *Routes and several leaders of the Crusades during the first century of the movement (opposite page). Indicated names of the great nobles of the First Crusade do not exhaust the list. The even showier array of monarchs of the Second and Third still left the Crusades, on balance, ineffective in achieving their ostensible goals.*

The "Castle of the Knights" (Krak-des-Chevaliers), the most magnificent of the many crusader castles built in the Holy Land in the twelfth and thirteenth centuries whose ruins can still be found in Syria, Lebanon, and Jordan. Situated in northern Syria a few miles from the Lebanese border, its defense consisted of two massive walls, one rising above the other, divided by a great moat. The Muslims of the same period used very similar military architecture. [Arab Information Center, New York]

Holy Land reverted as firmly as ever to Muslim hands. These Crusades were more important for the way they stimulated western trade with the east. The merchants of Venice, Pisa, and Genoa followed the Crusaders' cross to lucrative new markets. The need to resupply the new Christian settlements in the Near East not only reopened old trade routes that had long been closed by Arab domination of the Mediterranean but also established new ones. It is a commentary on both the degeneration of the original intent of the Crusades and their true historical importance that the Fourth Crusade (1202–1204) became an enterprising commercial venture manipulated by the Venetians.

Trade and the Growth of Towns (1100–1300)

During the centuries following the collapse of the Roman Empire, Western Europe became a closed and predominantly agricultural society, with small international commerce and even less urban culture. The great seaports of Italy were the exceptions. Venice, Pisa, and Genoa continued to trade actively with Constantinople and throughout the eastern Mediterranean, including Palestine, Syria, and Egypt, during the Middle Ages. The Venetians, Europe's most sober businessmen, jealously guarded their eastern trade, attacking western Christian competitors as quickly as Muslim predators. The latter were largely subdued by the success of the First Crusade, which proved a trade bonanza for Italian cities as the Mediterranean was

opened to greater western shipping. Venice, Pisa, and Genoa maintained major trading posts throughout the Mediterranean by the twelfth century (see Map 15-2).

THE NEW MERCHANT CLASS. The western commercial revival attendant on these events repopulated the urban centers of the old Roman Empire and gave birth to new industries. Trade put both money and ideas into circulation. New riches, or the prospect of them, improved living conditions, raised hopes, and increased populations. In the twelfth century, Western Europe became a "boom-town." Among the most interesting creations were the traders themselves, who formed a new, distinctive social class. These prosperous merchants did not, as might first be suspected, spring from the landed nobility. They were, to the contrary, poor, landless adventurers who had absolutely nothing to lose and everything to gain by the risks of foreign trade. For mutual protection, they traveled together in great armed caravans, buying their products as cheaply as possible at the source and selling them as dearly as possible in western marketplaces. They have been called the first western capitalists, inspired by profit and devoted to little more than amassing fortunes. But their very greed and daring laid the foundations for Western urban life as we have come to know it today.

Although in power, wealth, and privilege the great merchants were destined to join and eventually eclipse the landed aristocracy, they were initially misfits in traditional medieval society. They were free-

MAP 15-2 MEDIEVAL TRADE ROUTES AND REGIONAL PRODUCTS *Medieval trade in the west was not of the same intensity nor of the same geographical breadth in all periods. The map shows some of the channels that came to be used in interregional commerce. Labels tell part of what was carried in that commerce.*

men, often possessed of great wealth, yet they neither owned land nor tilled the soil. They did not value land and farming but were persons of liquid wealth constantly on the move. Aristocrats and clergy looked down on them as degenerates, and the commoners viewed them with suspicion. They were intruders within medieval society, a new breed who did not fit into the neat hierarchy of clergy, nobility, and serfs.

Merchants fanned out from the great Flemish and Italian trading centers: Bruges, Ghent, Venice, Pisa, Genoa, Florence. Wherever they settled in large numbers, they lobbied for the degree of freedom necessary for successful commerce, opposing tolls, tariffs, and other petty restrictions that discouraged the flow of trade. This activity brought them into initial conflict with the norms of static agricultural society. But as they demonstrated the many advantages of vigorous trade, the merchants progressively won their case. They not only remodeled city government to favor their new industries and the free flow of trade, but also imparted to the cities an aura of importance unknown during previous centuries. By the late Middle Ages, cities commonly saw themselves as miniature states, even self-contained Christendoms.

The Rue de Matelas, a street in Rouen, Normandy, was preserved intact from the Middle Ages to World War II. Note the narrowness of the street and the open sewer running down its center. The houses were built of rough cast stone, mud, and timber. [Roger-Viollet]

As they grew and became prosperous, medieval cities also became very jealous of their good fortune. They took every measure to protect skilled industries, to expand trade, and to prevent competition from the surrounding countryside. Government remained in the hands of the rich and the few—patricians, *grandi*, the "old rich"—although wealthy merchants, aspiring to the noble style of life, increasingly found their way into the inner circles of government, as money proved early that it could talk. By the thirteenth century, city councils, operating on the basis of aristocratic constitutions and composed of patricians and wealthy merchants—the old rich *and* the new rich—internally controlled city life. These oligarchies were increasingly confronted by small artisans, who demanded improved living conditions and a role in policymaking. Skilled artisans formed the far greater part of the new burgher class and organized to express their will through powerful corporations or craft guilds. Exclusive organizations for the various skilled trades, these guilds set standards, certified craftsmen, and worked to enhance the economic well-being and political influence of their members. The high and late Middle Ages also saw a deepening conflict between craft masters, who were determined to keep their numbers at an absolute minimum, and journeymen, who found themselves frozen at the lower levels of their trades. The self-protectiveness and internal conflicts of medieval cities did not, however, prevent them from forming larger trade associations, such as the famous German Hanseatic League, or Hansa, which kept Baltic trade a German monopoly well into the fifteenth century.

CHANGES IN SOCIETY. The rise of a merchant class caused an important crack in the old social order.

New-rich merchants, a class originally sprung from ordinary, landless people, broke into the aristocracy, and in doing so, they drew behind them the leadership of the new artisan class created by the urban industries that had grown up in the wake of trade growth. In the late Middle Ages, the "middle classes" would firmly establish themselves.

Although from one perspective medieval towns were overly self-protective and "egoistic," they also became a force for innovation and change beyond their walls. This fact is all the more remarkable when it is remembered that towns at this time contained hardly more than 5 percent of the populations. Townspeople became a major force in the breakup of feudal society, aiding both kings and the peasantry at the expense of the landed nobility. Generally speaking, towns and kings tended to ally themselves against the great feudal lords. A notable exception may be seen in England, where the towns joined the barons against the oppressive monarchy of King John (r. 1199–1216) and became a part of the parliamentary opposition. Townspeople generally, however, found their autonomy better preserved by having one distant master rather than several nearer and factious overlords. Kings, in turn, counted on the liquid wealth and administrative skills of the town-dwellers, who began to replace the clergy and the nobility in the royal bureaucracy. Urban money made it possible for kings to hire mercenary armies and thereby to decrease their dependence on the noble cavalry—

The English Nobility Imposes Restraints on King John

The gradual building of a sound English constitutional system in the Middle Ages was in danger of going awry if a monarch overstepped the fine line dividing necessary strength from outright despotism. The danger became acute under the rule of King John. The English nobility, therefore, forced the king's recognition of the Magna Carta (1215), which reaffirmed the traditional rights and personal liberties of free men against royal authority. The document has remained enshrined in English law.

A free man shall not be fined for a small offense, except in proportion to the gravity of the offense: and for a great offense he shall be fined in proportion to the magnitude of the offense, saving his freehold; and a merchant in the same way, saving his merchandise; and the villein shall be fined in the same way, saving his wainage, if he shall be at our [i.e., the king's] mercy; and none of the above fines shall be imposed except by the oaths of honest men of the neighborhood. . . .

No constable or other bailiff of ours [i.e., the king] shall take anyone's grain or other chattels without immediately paying for them in money, unless he is able to obtain a postponement at the good will of the seller.

No constable shall require any knight to give money in place of his ward of a castle [i.e., standing guard] if he is willing to furnish that ward in his own person, or through another honest man if he himself is not able to do it for a reasonable cause; and if we shall lead or send him into the army he shall be free from ward in proportion to the amount of time which he has been in the army through us.

No sheriff or bailiff of ours [i.e., the king], or any one else, shall take horses or wagons of any free man, for carrying purposes, except on the permission of that free man.

Neither we nor our bailiffs will take the wood of another man for castles, or for anything else which we are doing, except by the permission of him to whom the wood belongs. . . .

No free man shall be taken, or imprisoned, or dispossessed, or outlawed, or banished, or in any way injured, nor will we go upon him, nor send upon him, except by the legal judgment of his peers, or by the law of the land.

To no one will we sell, to no one will we deny or delay, right or justice.

James Harvey Robinson, ed., *Readings in European History*, Vol. 1 (Boston: Atheneaum, 1904), pp. 236–237.

an important step in the consolidation of territories divided for centuries by feudal allegiances and customs.

From the burgher ranks, kings drew the skilled lawyers who began the long process of replacing feudal custom with centralized Roman law, and towns also often had powerful militias that could be enlisted in royal service. Kings, in return, gave towns political recognition and guaranteed their constitutions (in formal charters) against territorial magnates. This was more easily done in the stronger coastal towns than in interior areas, where urban life remained less vigorous and territorial power was on the rise. In France, towns became integrated into the royal government. In Germany and Austria, by contrast, towns fell under ever tighter control by territorial princes. In Italy, towns uniquely grew to absorb their surrounding territory, becoming city-states.

Towns also aided the peasantry, to the detriment of the landed nobility. A popular maxim of the time in German cities was: *Stadtluft macht frei*—"City air sets one free." Cities passed legislation making serfs who spent a year and a day within their walls freemen. New urban industries provided lucky peasants vocations alternative to farming. The new money economy made it possible for serfs or their urban patrons to buy their freedom from feudal services and rents as the latter became translatable into direct money payments. A serf or his patron could simply buy up the "contract." The growth of a free peasantry became especially evident in the thirteenth century.

All of this worked against the landed nobility. As urban trade and industries put more money into circulation, its value decreased (inflation). The great landowners, whose wealth was static, found themselves confronted, on the one hand, by serfs who longed to flee to the city and, on the other, by rising prices. They were losing their cheap labor supply and facing diminished productivity; at the same time, they had to pay more for their accustomed style of life. The nobility were not disciplined people, and many fell prey to money-wise urban merchants, who beat them out of their landed wealth.

The new urban economy worked, then, to free both kings and peasants from dependence on feudal lords, although it was a long and complex process. As royal authority became centralized and kings were able to hire mercenary soldiers, the noble cavalry became militarily obsolescent, at most a minor part of the king's armed forces. In addition, as towns and urban industries grew, attracting serfs from the farms, the nobility gradually lost its once all-powerful economic base. The long-term consequence: a strengthening of monarchy.

Medieval Universities and Scholasticism

Thanks to Spanish Muslim and Jewish scholars, the logical works of Aristotle, the writings of Euclid and Ptolemy, the basic works of Greek physicians and Arab mathematicians, and the larger texts of Roman law became available to Western scholars in the early twelfth century. Muslim scholars preserved these works, translated portions of the Greek ones into Latin, and wrote extensive, thought-provoking commentaries on ancient texts. This renaissance of ancient knowledge, in turn, provided the occasion for the rise of universities.

BOLOGNA AND PARIS. The first important Western university was in Bologna. It received its formal grant of rights and privileges from the emperor Frederick Barbarossa in 1158. University members, like clergy, were granted royal immunity from local jurisdiction and were viewed by local townspeople as a group apart. In Bologna, we find the first formal organizations of students and professors and the first degree programs—the institutional foundations of the modern university.

The "university" was at first simply a program of study that gave the student a license to teach others. Originally, the term *university* meant no more than a group or corporation of individuals who were united by common self-interest and for mutual protection. As the local townspeople viewed both masters and students as foreigners without civil rights, such a union was necessary. It followed the model of a medieval trade guild. Bolognese students formed such a bloc in order to guarantee fair rents and prices from the townspeople and regular and high-quality teaching from their professors. Price gouging by townspeople was met with the threat to move the university to another town—a threat that could easily be carried out because the university at that time was not a great, fixed physical plant. Professors who failed to meet students' expectations were boycotted. The mobility of the first universities gave them a unique independence.

Professors also formed protective associations and established procedures and standards for certification to teach within their ranks. The first academic degree was a certificate *(licentia docendi)* given by the chancellor, which granted graduates in the liberal

The seven liberal arts of the medieval university curriculum are here depicted as seven women before whom sit the great authorities of antiquity: arithmetic (authority unclear), geometry (Euclid), astronomy (Ptolemy), music (Pythagoras), grammar (Donatus or Priscian), rhetoric (Cicero or Quintilian), and dialectic or logic (Aristotle). [Art Resource]

arts program or in the higher professional sciences of medicine, theology, and the law "the right to teach anywhere" *(ius ubique docendi)*.

Bologna was distinguished as the center for the revival of Roman law. From the seventh to the eleventh centuries, only the most rudimentary manuals of Roman law were available to be circulated. With the growth of trade and towns in the late eleventh century, Western scholars came into contact with the larger and more important parts of the Roman *Corpus Juris Civilis* of Justinian. The study and dissemination of this new material was directed by Irnerius (b. ca. 1060). He and his students made authoritative commentaries or glosses on individual laws following their broad knowledge of the *Corpus Juris.* Around 1140, a monk named Gratian, also a resident of Bologna, created the standard legal text in church or canon law, the *Concordance of Discordant Canons,* known more commonly as Gratian's *Decretum.*

As Bologna provided the model for southern European universities and the study of law, Paris became the model for northern Europe and the study of theology. Oxford, Cambridge, and, much later, Heidelberg were among Paris's imitators. All these universities required a foundation in the liberal arts for further study in the higher sciences of medicine, theology, and law. The arts program consisted of the *trivium* (grammar, rhetoric, and logic) and the *quadrivium* (arithmetic, geometry, astronomy, and music). Before the emergence of the universities, the liberal arts had been taught in the cathedral and monastery schools, that is, schools attached to cathedrals or monasteries for the purpose of training clergy. The most famous of the cathedral schools were those of Rheims and Chartres.

The University of Paris grew institutionally out of the cathedral school of Nôtre Dame, receiving its charter in 1200 from King Philip Augustus and Pope

Innocent III. Papal sanction and regulations, among them the right of the faculty to strike, were issued in 1231 in the bull *Parens scientiarum* and gave the university freedom from local church control. At this time, the University of Paris consisted of independent faculties of arts, canon law, medicine, and theology, with the masters of arts, who were grouped together in four national factions (French, Norman, English-German, and Picard), the dominant faculty.

At Paris, the college system originated. At first, colleges were no more than hospices providing room and board for poor students. But the educational life of the university rapidly expanded into these fixed buildings and began to thrive on their sure endowments. In Paris, the most famous college was the Sorbonne, founded around 1257 by Robert de Sorbon,

chaplain to the king, for the purpose of educating advanced theological students. In Oxford and Cambridge, the colleges became the basic unit of student life, indistinguishable from the university. By the fifteenth and sixteenth centuries, colleges had tied the universities to physical plants and fixed foundations, restricting their previous autonomy and freedom of movement.

CURRICULUM. Before the twelfth century, the education available within the cathedral and monastic schools was quite limited. Students learned grammar, rhetoric, and elementary geometry and astronomy. They used the Latin grammars of Donatus and Priscian and studied Saint Augustine's *On Christian Doctrine,* Cassiodorus's *On Divine and Secular Learning,*

Bishop Stephen Complains About the New Scholastic Learning

Scholasticism involved an intellectual, learned approach to religion and its doctrines rather than simple, uncritical piety. Many saw in it a threat to the study of the Bible and the Church Fathers, as doctrines that should simply be believed and revered were rationally dissected for their logical meaning by allegedly presumptuous and none-too-well-trained youths. Here is a particularly graphic description of the threat, replete with classical allusion, as perceived by Stephen, Bishop of Tournai, in a letter to the pope written between 1192 and 1203.

The studies of sacred letters among us are fallen into the workshop of confusion, while both disciples applaud novelties alone and masters watch out for glory rather than learning. They everywhere compose new and recent *summulae* [little summaries] and commentaries, by which they attract, detain, and deceive their hearers, as if the works of the holy fathers were not still sufficient, who, we read, expounded Holy Scripture in the same spirit in which we believe the apostles and prophets composed it. They prepare strange and exotic courses for their banquet, when at the nuptials of the son of the king of Taurus his own flesh and blood are killed and all prepared, and the wedding guests have only to take and eat what is set before them. Contrary to the sacred canons there is public disputation over the incomprehensible deity; concerning the incarnation of the Word, verbose flesh and blood irreverently litigate. The indivisible Trinity is cut up and wrangled overso that now there

are as many errors as doctors, as many scandals as classrooms, as many blasphemies as squares. . . . Faculties called liberal having lost their pristine liberty are sunk in such servitude that adolescents with long hair impudently usurp their professorships, and beardless youths sit in the seat of their seniors, and those who don't yet know how to be disciples strive to be named masters. And they write their *summulae* moistened with drool and dribble but unseasoned with the salt of philosophers. Omitting the rules of the arts and discarding the authentic books of the artificers, they seize the flies of empty words in their sophisms like the claws of spiders. Philosophy cries out that her garments are torn and disordered and, modestly concealing her nudity by a few specific tatters, neither is consulted nor consoles as of old. All these things, father, call for the hand of apostolic correction. . . .

Lynn Thorndike, *University Records and Life in the Middle Ages* (New York: Octagon Books, 1971), pp. 22–24.

and the various writings of Boethius (d. 524). Boethius was important for instruction in arithmetic and music and especially for the transmission of the small body of Aristotle's logical works known before the twelfth century. After the textual finds of the early twelfth century, western scholars had the whole of Aristotle's logic, the astronomy of Ptolemy, the writings of Euclid, and many Latin classics. By the mid-thirteenth century the ethical, physical, and metaphysical writings of Aristotle were in circulation in the west.

In the high Middle Ages the learning process was very basic. The student wrote commentaries on authoritative texts, especially those of Aristotle. The teachers encouraged their students not to strive independently for undiscovered truth, but to organize and harmonize the accepted truths of tradition. The basic assumption was that truth already existed and it had only to be organized and elucidated. Such conviction made logic and dialectic supreme within the liberal arts.

The Scholastic program of study, based on logic and dialectic, reigned supreme in all the faculties—in law and medicine as well as in philosophy and theology. Scholasticism was a peculiar method of study. The student read the traditional authorities in his field, formed short summaries of their teaching, disputed it by elaborating arguments pro and con, and then drew his own modest conclusions. The twelfth century saw the rise of the "summa," a summary of all that was known about a topic and a work whose sole purpose was to conciliate traditional authorities.

Society

Order of Life

Four basic social groups were distinguished in the Middle Ages: those who fought (the landed nobility); those who prayed (the clergy); those who labored (the peasantry); and, after the revival of towns in the eleventh century, those who traded and manufactured (the townspeople). It would be false to view each of these groups as closed and homogeneous. Throughout medieval society, like tended to be attracted to like regardless of social grouping. Barons, archbishops, rich farmers, and successful merchants had far more in common with each other than they did with the middle and lower strata of their various professions.

NOBLES. As a distinctive social group, all noblemen did not begin simply as great men with large hereditary lands. Many rose from the ranks of feudal vassals or warrior knights. The successful vassal attained a special social and legal status based on his landed wealth (accumulated fiefs), his exercise of authority over others, and his distinctive social customs, all of which set him apart from others in medieval society. By the late Middle Ages there had evolved a distinguishable higher and lower nobility living in both town and country. The higher were the great landowners and territorial magnates; the lower were petty landlords, descendants from minor knights, new-rich merchants who could buy country estates, and wealthy farmers patiently risen from ancestral serfdom.

It was a special mark of the nobility that they lived on the labor of others. Basically lords of manors, the nobility of the early and high Middle Ages neither tilled the soil like the peasantry nor engaged in the commerce of merchants—activities considered beneath their dignity. The nobleman resided in a country mansion or, if he were particularly wealthy, a castle. He was drawn to the countryside as much by personal preference as by the fact that his fiefs were usually rural manors. Arms were his profession; the nobleman's main occupation and reason for living was waging war, although he also spent a great deal of time managing his estate and governing those under his jurisdiction. His fief provided the means to acquire the expensive military equipment that his rank required, and he maintained his enviable position as he had gained it, by fighting for his chief.

The nobility accordingly celebrated the physical strength, courage, and constant activity of warfare. Warring gave them both new riches and an opportunity to gain honor and glory. Knights were paid a share in the plunder of victory, and in time of war everything became fair game. Special war wagons, designed for the collection and transport of booty, followed them into battle. Before the twelfth century, many knights greeted periods of peace with sadness, as such lulls could mean economic stagnation and boredom. Whereas the peasants and the townspeople counted on peace as the condition of their occupational success, the nobility despised it as unnatural to their profession. They looked down on the peasantry as cowards who ran and hid in time of war. Urban merchants, who amassed wealth by business methods strange to feudal society, were held in equal contempt, which increased as the affluence and political power of the townspeople grew. The nobility possessed as strong a sense of superiority over these "unwarlike" people as the clergy did over the general run of laity. After the twelfth century, the glamour of knighthood began to fade; increasing numbers of nobility then sought to buy out their military service and devote their lives to safer if less adventurous and lucrative pursuits.

The nobleman nurtured his sense of distinctiveness within medieval society by the chivalric ritual of dubbing to knighthood, a ceremonial entrance into the noble class that became almost a religious sacrament. The ceremony was preceded by a bath of purification, confession, communion, and a prayer vigil. Thereafter the priest blessed the knight's standard, lance, and sword. As prayers were chanted, the priest girded the knight with his sword and presented him his shield, enlisting him as much in the defense of the church as in the service of his lord. Dubbing raised the nobleman to a state as sacred in his sphere as clerical ordination made the priest in his. This comparison is quite legitimate. The clergy and the nobility were medieval society's privileged estates. The appointment of noblemen to high ecclesiastical office and their eager participation in the Church's Crusades had strong ideological and social underpinnings as well as economic and political motives.

In peacetime, the nobility had two favorite amusements: hunting and tournaments. As a result of the threat to towns and villages posed by wild animals, the great hunts actually aided the physical security of the ordinary people, while occupying the restless noblemen. However, where they could, noblemen progressively monopolized the rights to game, forbidding the commoners from hunting in the "lords' " forests. This practice built resentment among the common people to the level of revolt. Free game, fishing, and access to wood were basic demands in the petitions of grievance and the revolts of the peasantry throughout the high and later Middle Ages.

From the repeated assemblies in the courts of barons and kings, set codes of social conduct or "courtesy" developed in noble circles. With the French leading the way, mannered behavior and court etiquette became almost as important as battlefield expertise. Knights became literate gentlemen, and lyric poets sang and moralized at court. The cultivation of a code of behavior and a special literature to eulogize if was not unrelated to problems within the social life of the nobility. Noblemen were notorious philanderers; their illegitimate children mingled openly with their legitimate offspring in their houses. The advent of courtesy was, in part, an effort to reform this situation. Although the poetry of courtly love was sprinkled with frank eroticism and the beloved in these epics were married women pursued by those to whom they were not married, the love recommended by the poet was usually love at a distance, unconsummated by sexual intercourse. It was love without touching, a kind of sex without physical sex, and only as such was it considered ennobling. Court poets depicted those who did carnally consummate their illicit love as reaping at least as much suffering as joy from it.

By the fourteenth century, several factors forced the landed nobility into a steep economic and political decline from which it never recovered. These were the great population losses of the fourteenth century brought on by the Great Plague; the changes in military tactics occasioned by the use of infantry and heavy artillery during the Hundred Years' War; and the alliance of the wealthy towns with the king. Generally, one can speak of a waning of the landed nobility after the fourteenth century. Thereafter, the effective possession of land and wealth counted far more than parentage and family tree as qualification for entrance into the highest social class.

CLERGY. Unlike the nobility and the peasantry, the clergy was an open estate. Although clerical ranks reflected the social classes from which the clergy came and a definite clerical hierarchy formed, one was still a cleric by religious training and ordination, not by the circumstances of birth or military prowess. There were two basic types of clerical vocation: the regular and the secular clergy. The former were the orders of monks, who lived according to a special ascetic rule (regula), some in cloisters separated from the world, others performing their acts of charity and religious services in the world. They were the spiritual elite among the clergy, and theirs was not a way of life lightly entered. Canon law required that one be at least twenty-one years of age before making a final profession of the monastic vows of poverty, chastity, and obedience. Their personal sacrifices and high religious ideals made the monks much respected in high medieval society.

Although many monks (and also nuns, who increasingly embraced the vows of poverty, obedience, and chastity without a clerical rank) secluded themselves altogether, the regular clergy were never completely cut off from the secular world. They maintained frequent contact with the laity through such charitable activities as feeding the destitute and tending the sick, through liberal arts instruction in monas-

For noblewomen, the cloistered life became an increasingly important alternative to both spinsterhood and loveless marriages, and cloisters increased in variety and numbers during the high Middle Ages. [Alinari/Art Resource]

tic schools, through special pastoral commissions from the pope, and as supplemental preachers and confessors in parish churches during Lent and other peak religious seasons. It became the special mark of the Dominican and Franciscan friars to live a common life according to a special rule, and still to be active in worldly ministry. Some monks, because of their learning and rhetorical skills, even rose to prom-

inence as secretaries and private confessors to kings and queens.

The secular clergy were those who lived and worked directly among the laity in the world *(saeculum)*. They formed a vast hierarchy. There were the high prelates—the wealthy cardinals, archbishops, and bishops, who were drawn almost exclusively from the nobility—the urban priests, the cathedral canons, the court clerks; and, finally, the great mass of poor parish priests, who were neither financially nor intellectually very far above the common people they served (the basic educational requirement was an ability to say the Mass). Until the Gregorian reform in the eleventh century began to reverse the trend, many parish priests lived with women in a relationship akin to marriage, and their concubines and children were accepted within the communities they served. As a result of their relative poverty, it was not unusual for priests to "moonlight" as teachers, artisans, or farmers, a practice also accepted and even admired by their parishioners.

During the greater part of the Middle Ages, the clergy were the "first estate," and theology was the queen of the sciences. How did the clergy come into such prominence? It was basically popular reverence for the clergy's role as mediator between God and humanity that made this superiority possible. The priest brought the very Son of God down to earth when he celebrated the sacrament of the Eucharist; his absolution released penitents from eternal punishment for mortal sin. Theologians elaborated the distinction between the clergy and the laity very much to the clergy's benefit. The belief in the superior status of the clergy underlay the evolution of clerical privileges and immunities in both person and property. As holy persons, the clergy could not be taxed by secular rulers without special permission from the proper ecclesiastical authorities. Clerical crimes fell under the jurisdiction of special ecclesiastical courts, not the secular courts. Because churches and monasteries were deemed holy places, they too were free from secular taxation and legal jurisdiction.

By the fourteenth century, townspeople came increasingly to resent the special immunities of the clergy. They complained that it was not proper for the clergy to have greater privileges yet far fewer responsibilities than all others who lived within the town walls. Although the separation of Church and State and the distinction between the clergy and the laity have persisted into modern times, after the fifteenth century the clergy ceased to be the superior class that they had been during most of the Middle Ages.

Saint Francis of Assisi Sets Out His Religious Ideals

Saint Francis of Assisi (1182–1226) was the founder of the Franciscan Order of friars. Here are some of his religious principles as stated in the definitive Rule of the Order, approved by the pope in 1223; the rule especially stresses the ideal of living in poverty.
▶ *Compare this view of a life of religious faith and devotion to those expressed in "The Lord Krishna Speaks of True Devotion" (Ch. 12) and "Guru Arjun's Faith" (Ch. 24).*

This is the rule and way of living of the Minorite brothers, namely, to observe the holy Gospel of our Lord Jesus Christ, living in obedience, without personal possessions, and in chastity. Brother Francis promises obedience and reverence to our lord Pope Honorius, and to his successors who canonically enter upon their office, and to the Roman Church. And the other brothers shall be bound to obey Brother Francis and his successors.

I firmly command all the brothers by no means to receive coin or money, of themselves or through an intervening person. But for the needs of the sick and for clothing the other brothers, the ministers alone and the guardians shall provide through spiritual friends, as it may seem to them that necessity demands, according to time, place, and the coldness of the temperature. This one thing being always borne in mind, that, as has been said, they receive neither coin nor money.

Those brothers to whom God has given the ability to labor shall do so faithfully and devoutly, but in such manner that idleness, the enemy of the soul, being averted, they may not extinguish the spirit of holy prayer and devotion, to which other temporal things should be subservient. As a reward, moreover, for their labor, they may receive for themselves and their brothers the necessities of life, but not coin or money; and this humbly, as becomes the servants of God and the followers of most holy poverty.

The brothers shall appropriate nothing to themselves, neither a house, nor a place, nor anything; but as pilgrims and strangers in this world, in poverty and humility serving God, they shall confidently go seeking for alms. Nor need they be ashamed, for the Lord made Himself poor for us in this world.

A Source Book of Medieval History, ed. by Frederic Austin Ogg (New York: Cooper Square, 1972), pp. 375–376.

PEASANTS.   The largest and lowest social group in medieval society was the one on whose labor the welfare of all the others depended: the agrarian peasantry. They lived on and worked the manors of the nobility, the primitive cells of rural social life, and all were to one degree or another dependent on their lords and considered their property. The manor had originally been a plot of land within a village, ranging from twelve to seventy-five acres in size, assigned to a certain member by a settled tribe or clan. This member and his family became lords of the land, and those who came to dwell there formed a smaller self-sufficient community within a larger village community. In the early Middle Ages, such a manor consisted of the dwellings of the lord and his family, the cottages of the peasant workers, agricultural sheds, and fields. The landowner or lord of the manor required a

certain amount of produce (grain, eggs, and the like) and a certain number of services from the peasant families who came to dwell on and farm his land. The tenants were free to divide the labor as they wished, and what goods remained after the lord's levies were met were their own. A powerful lord might own many such manors, and kings later based their military and tax assessments on the number of manors owned by a vassal landlord.

There were both servile and free manors. The tenants of the latter had originally been freemen known as *coloni,* original inhabitants and petty landowners who swapped their small possessions for a guarantee of security from a more powerful lord, who came in this way to possess their land. Unlike the pure serfdom of the servile manors, whose tenants had no original claim to a part of the land, the tenancy obli-

For hundreds of years and over a great part of Europe the manor was basic for much of the population. Despite regional variation and changes that came with the revival of trade and growth of towns, manors in the West had enough common features to justify this modern reconstruction of a characteristic example. Note the lord's hall and lands (demesne), *the peasant village with common grounds and services for the nine families* (a–j) *dwelling on this manor, the church and its lands* (glebe), *peasant holdings in open fields, and areas for woodcutting and hunting. [The Granger Collection]*

gations on free manors tended to be limited and their rights more carefully defined. Tenants of servile manors were by comparison far more vulnerable to the whims of their landlords. These two types of manors tended, however, to merge; the most common situation was the manor on which tenants of greater and lesser degrees of servitude dwelt together, their services to the lord defined by their personal status and local custom.

Marc Bloch, the modern authority on manorial society, has vividly depicted the duties of tenancy:

On certain days the tenant brings the lord's steward perhaps a few small silver coins or, more often, sheaves of grain harvested on his fields, chickens from his farm yard, cakes of wax from his beehives or from the swarms of the neighboring forest. At other times he works on the arable or the meadows of the demesne [the lord's plot of land in the manoral fields, between one third and one half of that available]. Or else we find him carting casks of wine or sacks of grain on behalf of the master to distant residences. His is the labour which repairs the walls or moats of the castle. If the master has guests the peasant strips his own bed to provide the necessary extra bedclothes. When the hunting season comes round he feeds the pack. If war breaks out he does duty as a foot-soldier or orderly, under the leadership of the reeve of the village.[2]

The lord also had the right to subject his tenants to exactions known as *banalities.* He could, for example, force them to breed their cows with his bull, and to pay for the privilege, as well as to grind their corn in his mill, bake their bread in his oven, make their wine in his wine press, buy their beer from his brewery, and even surrender to him the tongues or other choice parts of all animals slaughtered on his lands. He had the right to levy small taxes at will.

Exploited as the serfs may appear to have been from a modern point of view, their status was far from outright chattel slavery. It was to the lord's advantage to keep his serfs healthy and happy; his welfare, like theirs, depended on a successful harvest. Serfs had their own dwellings and modest strips of land and lived by the produce of their own labor and organization. They were permitted to market for their own profit what surpluses might remain after the harvest. They were free to choose their spouses within the local village, although the lord's permission was required if a wife or husband was sought from another village. And serfs were able to pass a goodly portion of their property (their dwellings and field strips) and worldly goods on to their children.

Two basic changes occurred in the evolution of the manor from the early to the later Middle Ages. The first was the fragmentation of the manor and the rise to dominance of the single-family unit. As the lords parceled out their land to new tenants, their own plots became progressively smaller. The increase in the number of tenants and the decrease in the lord's fields brought about a corresponding reduction in the labor services exacted from the tenants. In France, by the reign of Louis IX (1226–1270), only a few days a year were required, whereas in the time of Charlemagne, peasants had worked the lord's fields several days a week. By the twelfth century, the manor was hopelessly fragmented. As the single-family unit replaced the clan as the basic nuclear group, assess-

[2] *Feudal Society,* trans. by L. A. Manyon (Chicago: University of Chicago Press, 1968), p. 250.

ments of goods and services fell on individual fields and households, no longer on manors as a whole. Family farms replaced manorial units. Children continued to live with their parents after marriage, and several generations of one family could be found within a single household, although nuclear families were also commonplace. The peasants' carefully nurtured communal life made possible a family's retention of its land and dwelling after the death of the head of the household. In this way, land and property remained in the possession of a single family from generation to generation.

The second change in the evolution of the manor was the translation of feudal dues into money payments, a change made possible by the revival of trade and the rise of the towns. This development, which was completed by the thirteenth century, permitted

A medieval shoemaker. Guilds of shoemakers date back to ancient Rome. In the Middle Ages most people wore homemade clogs or wooden shoes. Leather shoes made to order by skilled craftsmen could be quite costly and elaborate in style and were mostly for the upper classes. [Vincent Varga Archives]

serfs to hold their land as rent-paying tenants and to overcome their servile status. Although tenants thereby gained greater freedom, they were not necessarily better off materially. Whereas servile workers had been able to count on the benevolent assistance of their landlords in hard times, rent-paying workers were left by and large to their own devices; their independence caused some landlords to treat them with indifference and even resentment.

Lands and properties that had been occupied by generations of peasants and recognized as their own were always under the threat of the lord's claim to a prior right of inheritance and even outright usurpation. As their demesnes declined, the lords were increasingly tempted to encroach on such traditionally common lands. The peasantry fiercely resisted such efforts, instinctively clinging to the little they had. In many regions, they successfully organized to win a role in the choice of petty rural officials. By the mid-fourteenth century, a declining nobility in England and France, faced with the ravages of the Great Plague and the Hundred Years' War, attempted to turn back the historical clock by increasing taxes on the peasantry and passing laws to restrict their migration into the cities. The peasantry responded with armed revolts in the countryside. These revolts were rural equivalents of the organization of late medieval cities in sworn communes to protect their self-interests against rulers. The revolts of the agrarian peasantry, like those of the urban proletariat, were brutally crushed. They stand out at the end of the Middle Ages as violent testimony to the breakup of medieval society. As growing national sentiment would break its political unity and heretical movements would end its nominal religious oneness, the revolts of the peasantry revealed the absence of medieval social unity.

TOWNSPEOPLE.   In the eleventh century, towns and cities held only about 5 percent of Western Europe's population. Nonetheless, one could find there the whole of medieval society: nobles visiting their townhouses, peasants living or working within the walls, resident monks and priests, university scholars, great merchants and poor journeymen, pilgrims en route to shrines, and beggars passing through. By modern comparison, the great majority of medieval towns were merely small villages. Of some three thousand late medieval German towns, for example, twenty-eight hundred had populations under one thousand, and only fifteen had in excess of ten thousand inhabitants. Only London, Paris, and the great merchant capitals of Italy—Florence, Venice, and Naples—

approached one hundred thousand by the fifteenth century.

Women appear to have slightly outnumbered men. War, the perils of long-distance travel, and illness resulting from immoderation in food and drink combined to reduce male ranks. The frequent remarriage of widows, whose inheritances made them attractive mates, and the Church's siphoning of an already short supply of eligible bachelors into religious life, contributed to the large number of unmarried women. Those from the upper classes entered nunneries and Beguine convents, and the very poor might join wandering bands of prostitutes. The great mass of lower and middle-strata married women worked as virtual partners in their husbands' trades or crafts. It has been speculated that the fact that unmarried women formed a large, unproductive surplus contributed to the prejudice of late medieval society against them and made them the more vulnerable targets of the great witch hunts of the fifteenth and sixteenth centuries.

The term *bourgeois* first appeared in the eleventh century to describe a new addition to the three traditional social ranks of knight (noble), cleric, and serf. The term initially designated the merchant groups, who formed new communities or "bourgs" as bases of operation in or around the old Roman towns that were governed by the landed nobility. These men, whose business was long-distance trade and commerce, were at first highly suspect within traditional medieval society. Clerics condemned the profits they gained from lending money as immoral usury, and noblemen viewed their fluid wealth and mobility as politically disruptive. The merchants in turn resented the laws and customs of feudal society that gave the nobility and the clergy special privileges. Town life was often disrupted because regional laws permitted the nobility and the clergy to live beyond the rules that governed the activities of everyone else.

Merchants especially wanted an end to the arbitrary tolls and tariffs imposed by regional magnates over the surrounding countryside. Such regulations hampered and could even bring to a standstill the flow of commerce on which both merchants and craftsmen in the growing urban export industries depended. The townspeople needed simple, uniform laws and a government sympathetic to their business interests; they wanted a government in which merchants and craftsmen had a major voice. That need created internal and external struggles with the old landed nobility. This basic conflict led towns in the high and late Middle Ages to form their own independent communes and to ally themselves with kings against the nobility—developments that created a powerful challenge to feudal society.

Despite unified resistance to external domination, the medieval town was not an internally harmonious social unit. It was a collection of many selfish, competitive communities. Only families of long standing and those who owned property had the full rights of citizenship and a say in the town's government. Workers in the same trade lived together on streets that bore their name, apparently doing so as much to monitor one another's business practices as to dwell among peers. Sumptuary laws regulated not only the dress but even the architecture of the residences of the various social groups. Merchant guilds appeared in the eleventh century and were followed in the twelfth by the craft guilds (organizations of drapers, haberdashers, furriers, hosiers, goldsmiths, and so on). These organizations existed solely to advance the business interests of their members and to advance their personal well-being. They won favorable government policies and served as collection agencies for the unpaid accounts of individual members. The guilds also formed distinctive religious confraternities, close-knit associations that ministered to the needs of member families in both life and death.

The merchants and the stronger craft guilds quickly won a role in town government. New-rich patricians married into the old nobility and aped their social customs. Sharing the power of government in the city councils, the craft guilds used their position in the most selfish way to limit their membership, to regulate their own wages favorably, and to establish exacting standards of workmanship so that their products could not be copied by others. Trademarks first appeared in the twelfth century. So rigid and exclusive did the dominant guilds become that they stifled their own creativity and inflamed the journeymen who were excluded from joining their ranks. In the fourteenth century, unrepresented artisans and craftsmen, a true urban proletariat prevented by law from either forming their own guilds or entering the existing guilds, revolted in a number of places: Florence, Paris, and the cities of Flanders. Their main opponents were the merchant and craft guilds, which had themselves risen to prominence by opposing the antiquated laws and privileges of the old nobility.

Medieval Women

The literary image and the social reality of medieval women are two very different things. The image, both for contemporaries and for us today, was strongly influenced by male Christian clergy, whose ideal was the celibate life of chastity, poverty, and obedience. Drawing on classical, medical, philosophical, and legal traditions that predated Christianity, as well as on ancient biblical theology, Christian theologians depicted women as physically, mentally, and morally weaker than men. On the basis of such assumptions, the medieval Church and society sanctioned the coercive treatment of women, including corrective wife-beating. Christian clergy generally considered marriage a debased state by comparison with the religious life, and in their writings they praised virgins and celibate widows over wives. Women, as the Bible clearly taught, were the "weaker vessel." In marriage, their role was to be subject and obedient to their husbands, who, as the stronger partners, had a duty to protect and discipline them.

This image of the medieval woman suggests that she had two basic options in life: to become either a subjugated housewife or a confined nun. In reality, the vast majority of medieval women were neither.

Both within and outside Christianity the image of women—not yet to speak of the reality of their lives—was contradicted. In chivalric romances and courtly love literature of the twelfth and thirteenth centuries, as in the contemporaneous cult of the Virgin Mary, women were presented as objects of service and devotion to be praised and admired, even put on pedestals and treated as superior to men. If the Church shared traditional misogynist sentiments, it also condemned them, as in the case of the *Romance of the Rose* (late thirteenth century) and other popular "bawdy" literature. The learned churchman Peter Lombard (1100–1169) sanctioned an image of women that was often invoked in didactic Christian literature. In his widely influential *Book of Sentences,* the standard textbook in theological faculties from the thirteenth to the sixteenth centuries, he asked why Eve was created from Adam's rib and not instead taken from his head or his feet. The answer was clear. God took Eve from Adam's side because he wanted woman neither to rule over nor to be enslaved by man, but to stand squarely at his side, as his companion and partner in mutual aid and trust. By so insisting on the spiritual equality of men and women and their shared responsibility to one another within marriage, the Church also helped to raise the dignity of women.

Women also had basic rights under secular law that prevented them from being treated as mere chattel. All the major Germanic law codes recognized the economic freedom of women, that is, their right to inherit, administer, dispose of, and confer on their children family property and wealth. They could press charges in court against men for bodily injury and rape. Depending on the country in question, punishments for rape ranged from fines, flogging, and banishment to blinding, castration, and death.

The nunnery was an option for only a very small number of unmarried women from the uppermost classes. Entrance required a dowry *(dos)* and could be almost as expensive as a wedding, although usually it was less. Within the nunnery, a woman could rise to a position of leadership as abbess or mother superior and could exercise an organizational and administrative authority denied her in much of secular life. However, the nunneries of the established religious orders were also under male supervision, so that even abbesses had finally to answer to higher male authority.

Nunneries also provided women an escape from the debilitating effects of multiple pregnancies. When, in the ninth century, under the influence of Christianity, the Carolingians made monogamous marriage their official policy (heretofore they had practice polygyny and concubinage and had permitted divorce), it was both a boon and a burden to women. On the one hand, the selection of a wife now became a very special event. Wives gained greater dignity and legal security. On the other hand, a woman's labor as household manager and the bearer of children greatly increased. The aristocratic wife not only ran a large household but also was the agent of her husband during his absence. In addition to these responsibilities, one wife now had sole responsibility for the propagation of heirs. Such demands clearly took their toll. The mortality rates of Frankish women increased and their lifespans decreased after the ninth century. The Carolingian wife also became the sole object of her husband's wrath and displeasure. Under such conditions, the cloister could serve as a welcome refuge to women. However, the number of women in cloisters was never very great. In late medieval England, for example, there are estimated to have been no more than thirty-five hundred.

The vast majority of medieval women were neither aristocratic housewives nor nuns, but working women in trades and businesses. Every evidence suggests that they were respected and loved by their husbands, perhaps because they worked shoulder by shoulder and hour by hour with them. Between the ages of ten and fifteen, girls were apprenticed in a trade much as were boys, and they learned to be

Three scenes of women planting and harvesting from a late twelfth century "Maiden's Mirror" (a young woman's guide to good conduct). The vast majority of medieval women were working peasants and townswomen. [Bildarchiv Preussischer Kulturbesitz]

later Middle Ages, townswomen increasingly had the opportunity to go to school and to gain vernacular literacy.

It is also true that women did not have as wide a range of vocations as men. They were excluded from the learned professions of scholarship, medicine, and law. They often found their freedom of movement within a profession more carefully regulated than a man's. Usually women performed the same work as men for a wage 25 percent lower. And, as is still true today, they filled the ranks of domestic servants in disproportionate numbers. Still, women were as prominent and as creative a part of workaday medieval society as men.

Medieval Children

Some historians have found evidence to suggest that medieval parents remained emotionally distant from their children, showing them little interest and affection. Evidence of low parental regard for children comes from a variety of sources. First, the art and sculpture of the Middle Ages rarely portray children as distinct from adults; pictorially, children and adults look alike. Moreover, high infant and child mortality could only have made emotional investment in children risky. How could a medieval parent, knowing that a child had a 30–50 percent chance of dying before age five, dare become too emotionally attached?

skilled workers. If they married, they either continued their particular trade, operating their bakeshops or dress shops next to their husbands' businesses, or they became assistants and partners in the shops of their husbands. Women appeared in virtually every "blue-collar" trade, from butchers to goldsmiths, although they were especially active in the food and clothing industries. Women belonged to guilds, just like men, and they became craftmasters. In the

Children watching a puppet show. [Bodleian Library]

Also, during the Middle Ages, children directly assumed adult responsibilities. The children of peasants became laborers in the fields alongside their parents as soon as they could physically manage the work. Urban artisans and burghers sent their children out of their homes to apprentice in various crafts and trades between the ages of eight and twelve. In many and perhaps most instances a child was placed in the home of a known relative or friend, but often he or she ended up with a mere acquaintance, even a complete stranger. That children were expected to grow up fast in the Middle Ages is also suggested by the canonical ages for marriage: twelve for girls and fourteen for boys.

Infanticide is an even more striking indication of low esteem for children. The ancient Romans abandoned unwanted children at birth. In this way they regulated family size, although the surviving children appear to have been given both attention and affection. The Germanic tribes of medieval Europe, by contrast, had large families but tended to neglect their children. Infanticide appears to have been directed primarily against girls. Early medieval penance books and church synods condemned the practice outright and also forbade parents to sleep with infants and small children, as it became an occasion and an excuse (alleged accidental suffocation) for killing them.

Also, among the German tribes one paid a much lower *wergild,* or fine, for injury to a child than for injury to an adult. The *wergild* for injuring a child was only one-fifth that for injuring an adult. That paid for injury to a female child under fifteen was one-half the *wergild* for injury to a male child—a strong indication that female children were the least esteemed members of German tribal society. Mothers appear also to have nursed boys longer than they did girls, which favored boys' health and survival. However, a woman's *wergild* increased a full eightfold between infancy and her childbearing years, at which time she had obviously become highly prized.[3]

Despite such varied evidence of parental neglect of children, there is another side to the story. Since the early Middle Ages, physicians and theologians, at least, have clearly understood childhood to be a distinct and special stage of life. Isidore of Seville (560–636), the metropolitan of Seville and a leading intellectual authority throughout the Middle Ages, carefully distinguished six ages of life, the first four of which were infancy (between one and seven years of age), childhood (seven to fourteen), adolescence, and youth.

According to the medical authorities, infancy proper extended from birth to anywhere between six months and two years (depending on the authority) and covered the period of speechlessness and suckling. The period thereafter, until age seven, was considered a higher level of infancy, marked by the beginning of a child's ability to speak and his or her weaning. At age seven, when a child could think and act decisively and speak clearly, childhood proper began. After this point, a child could be reasoned with, could profit from regular discipline, and could begin to train for a lifelong vocation. At seven a child was ready for schooling, private tutoring, or an apprenticeship in a chosen craft or trade. Until physical growth was completed, however—and that could extend to twenty-one years of age—a child or youth was legally under the guardianship of parents or a surrogate authority.

There is evidence that high infant and child mortality, rather than distancing parents from children, actually made parents look on them as all the more precious. The medical authorities of the Middle Ages were those of antiquity—Hippocrates, Galen, and Soranus of Ephesus. They dealt at length with postnatal care and childhood diseases. Both in learned and popular medicine, sensible as well as fanciful cures can be found for the leading killers of children (diarrhea, worms, pneumonia, and fever). When infants and children died, medieval parents grieved as pitiably as modern parents do. In the art and literature of the Middle Ages, we find mothers baptizing dead infants and children or carrying them to pilgrim shrines in the hope of reviving them. There are also examples of mental illness and suicide brought on by the death of a child.[4]

We also find a variety of children's toys, even devices like walkers and potty chairs, clear evidence of special attention being paid to children. The medieval authorities on child rearing widely condemned child abuse and urged moderation in the disciplining of children. In church art and drama, parents were urged to love their children as many loved Jesus. By the high Middle Ages, if not earlier, children were widely viewed as special creatures having their own needs and possessed of their own rights.

[3] David Herlihy, "Medieval Children," in *Essays on Medieval Civilization,* ed. by B. K. Lackner and K. R. Phelp (Austin: University of Texas Press, 1978), pp. 109–131.

[4] Klaus Arnold, *Kind und Gesellschaft im Mittelalter und Renaissance* (Paderborn, 1980), pp. 31, 37.

Politics

England and France: Hastings (1066) to Bouvines (1214)

WILLIAM THE CONQUEROR. The most important change in English political life was occasioned in 1066 by the death of the childless Anglo-Saxon ruler Edward the Confessor, so named because of his reputation of piety. Edward's mother was a Norman princess, and this fact gave the duke of Normandy a hereditary claim to the English throne. Before his death, Edward, who was not a strong ruler, acknowledged this claim and even directed that his throne be given to William of Normandy (d. 1087). But the Anglo-Saxon assembly, which customarily bestowed the royal power, had a mind of its own and vetoed Edward's last wishes. It chose instead Harold Godwinsson. This defiant action brought the swift conquest of England by the powerful Normans. William's forces defeated Harold's army at Hastings on October 14, 1066. Within weeks of the invasion, William was crowned king of England in Westminster Abbey, both by right of heredity and by right of conquest.

The Norman king thoroughly subjected his noble vassals to the crown, yet he also consulted with them regularly about decisions affecting the royal realm. The result was a unique blending of the "one" and the "many," a balance between monarchical and parliamentary elements that was ever since characterized English government.

For the purposes of administration and taxation, William commissioned a county-by-county survey of his new realm, a detailed accounting known as the *Domesday Book* (1080–1086). The title of the book reflects the thoroughness of the survey: Just as none would escape the doomsday judgment of God, so none was overlooked by William's assessors.

HENRY II. William's son, Henry I (r. 1100–1135), died without a male heir, throwing England into virtual anarchy until Henry II (r. 1154–1189) mounted the throne as head of the new Plantagenet dynasty. Henry brought to the throne greatly expanded French holdings, partly by inheritance from his father (Burgundy and Anjou) and partly by his marriage to Eleanor of Aquitaine (1122–1204), a union that created the so-called Angevin or English-French empire. Eleanor married Henry while he was still the count of Anjou and not yet king of England. The marriage oc-

curred only eight weeks after the annulment of Eleanor's fifteen-year marriage to the ascetic French king Louis VII in March 1152. Although the annulment was granted on grounds of consanguinity (blood relationship), the true reason for the dissolution of the marriage was Louis's suspicion of infidelity (according to rumor, Eleanor had been intimate with her cousin). The annulment was very costly to Louis, who lost Aquitaine together with his wife. Eleanor bore Henry eight children, five of them sons, among them the future kings Richard the Lion-Hearted and John. Not only did England, under Henry, come to control most of the coast of France, but Henry also conquered a part of Ireland and made the king of Scotland his vassal.

The French king, Louis VII, who had lost both his wife and considerable French land to Henry, saw a mortal threat to France in this English expansion. He responded by adopting what came to be a permanent French policy of containment and expulsion of the English from their continental holdings in France—a policy that did not finally succeed until the mid-fifteenth century, when English power on the Continent collapsed at the conclusion of the Hundred Years' War.

POPULAR REBELLION AND MAGNA CARTA. As Henry II acquired new lands abroad, he became more autocratic at home. He forced his will on the clergy in the Constitutions of Clarendon (1164), measures that placed limitations on judicial appeals to Rome, subjected the clergy to the civil courts, and gave the king control over the election of bishops. The result was strong political resistance from both the nobility and the clergy. The archbishop of Canterbury, Thomas á Becket (ca. 1118–1170), once Henry's compliant chancellor, broke openly with the king and fled to Louis VII. Becket's subsequent assassination in 1170 and his canonization by Pope Alexander III at the altar in 1172 forced the king to retreat from his heavy-handed tactics, as popular resentment grew.

English resistance to the king became outright rebellion under Henry's successors, the brothers Richard the Lion-Hearted (r. 1189–1199) and John (r. 1199–1216). Their burdensome taxation in support of unpopular foreign Crusades and a failing war with France left the English people little alternative. In 1209, Pope Innocent III excommunicated King John and placed England under interdict because the English king had tried to make an unworthy crony the archbishop of Canterbury against the wishes of the English clergy. This humiliating experience saw King

Although Gothic architecture was adopted throughout medieval Europe, it originated in France and enjoyed immense popularity there. Gothic was, in fact, often known in the Middle Ages as the "French style." Among the earliest examples of French Gothic architecture was the abbey church of Saint Denis near Paris, built by Abbot Suger between 1137–1144. This photograph shows the ribbed vaulting and pointed arches in the interior of the church. [Jean Roubier]

John declare his country a fief of the pope. But it was the defeat of the English by the French at Bouvines in 1214 that proved the last straw. With the full support of the clergy and the townspeople, the English barons revolted against John. The popular rebellion ended with the king's grudging recognition of the Magna Carta ("Great Charter") in 1215.

This monumental document was a victory of feudal over monarchical power in the sense that it secured the rights of the many—the nobility, the clergy, and the townspeople—over the autocratic king; it restored the internal balance of power that had been the English political experience since the Norman Conquest. The English people—at least the privileged English people—thereby preserved their right to be represented at the highest levels of government, especially in matters of taxation. The monarchy remained intact, however, and its legitimate powers and rights were duly recognized and preserved. This outcome contrasted with the experience on the

Continent, where victorious nobility tended to humiliate kings and emperors and undo all efforts at centralization.

With a peculiar political genius, the English consistently refused to tolerate either the absorption of the power of the monarchy by the nobility or the abridgment of the rights of the nobility by the monarchy. Although King John continued to resist the Great Charter in every way he could, his son Henry III formally ratified it, and it has ever since remained a cornerstone of English law.

PHILIP II AUGUSTUS.   During the century-and-a-half between the Norman Conquest (1066) and the Magna Carta (1215), a strong monarchy was never in question in England. The English struggle in the high Middle Ages was to secure the rights of the many, not the authority of the king. The French faced the reverse problem during this period. Powerful feudal princes dominated France for two centuries, from the beginning of the Capetian dynasty (987) until the reign of Philip II Augustus (1180–1223). During this period, the Capetian kings wisely concentrated their limited resources on securing the royal domain, their uncontested territory surrounding Paris known as the Île-de-France. They did not rashly challenge the more powerful nobility. Aggressively exercising their feudal rights in this area, they secured absolute obedience and a solid base of power. By the time of Philip II, Paris had become the center of French government and culture, and the Capetian dynasty a secure hereditary monarchy. Thereafter, the kings of France were in a position to impose their will on the French nobles, who were always in law, if not in political fact, the king's sworn vassals.

The Norman conquest of England helped stir France to unity and make it possible for the Capetian kings to establish a truly national monarchy. The duke of Normandy, who after 1066 was master of the whole of England, was also among the vassals of the French king in Paris. Capetian kings understandably watched with alarm as the power of their Norman vassal grew.

Philip Augustus faced, at the same time, an internal and an international struggle, and he was successful in both. His armies occupied all the English territories on the French coast, with the exception of Aquitaine. As the showdown with the English neared on the Continent, however, the Holy Roman Emperor Otto IV (r. 1198–1215) entered the fray on the side of the English, and the French found themselves assailed from both east and west. But when the international armies finally clashed at Bouvines on July 27, 1214, in what became the first great European battle in history, the French won handily over the English and the Germans. This victory unified France around the monarchy and thereby laid the foundation for French ascendancy in the later Middle Ages. Philip Augustus also gained control of the lucrative urban industries of Flanders. The defeat so weakened Otto IV that he fell from power in Germany.

The Hohenstaufen Empire (1152–1272)

During the twelfth and thirteenth centuries, stable governments developed in both England and France. In England, the Magna Carta balanced the rights of the nobility against the authority of the king, and in France, the reign of Philip II Augustus secured the authority of the king over the competitive claims of the nobility. The experience within the Holy Roman Empire, which embraced Germany, Burgundy, and northern Italy by the mid-thirteenth century, was a very different story (see Map 15-3). There, primarily as a result of the efforts of the Hohenstaufen dynasty to extend imperial power into southern Italy, disunity and blood feuding remained the order of the day for two centuries and left as a legacy the fragmentation of Germany until modern times.

FREDERICK I BARBAROSSA.   The investiture struggle had earlier weakened imperial authority. A new day seemed to dawn for imperial power with the accession to the throne of Frederick I Barbarossa (1152–1190), the first of the Hohenstaufens, the successor dynasty within the empire to the Franks and the Ottonians. The Hohenstaufens not only reestablished imperial authority but also initiated a new phase in the contest between popes and emperors, one that was to prove even more deadly than the investiture struggle had been. Never have kings and popes despised and persecuted one another more than they did during the Hohenstaufen dynasty.

As Frederick I surveyed his empire, he saw powerful feudal princes in Germany and Lombardy and a pope in Rome who believed that the emperor was his creature. There existed, however, widespread disaffection with the incessant feudal strife of the princes and the turmoil caused by the theocratic pretensions of the papacy. Popular opinion was on the emperor's side. Thus, Frederick had a foundation on which to rebuild imperial authority, and he shrewdly took ad-

MAP 15-3   GERMANY AND ITALY IN THE MIDDLE AGES
Medieval Germany and Italy were divided lands. The Holy Roman Empire (Germany) embraced hundreds of independent territories that the emperor ruled only in name. The papacy controlled the Rome area and tried to enforce its will in Romagna. Under the Hohenstaufens (mid-twelfth to mid-thirteenth centuries), internal German divisions and papal conflict reached new heights; German rulers sought to extend their power to southern Italy and Sicily.

vantage of it. Switzerland became Frederick's base of operation. From there he attempted to hold the empire together by stressing feudal bonds.

HENRY VI AND THE SICILIAN CONNECTION.   Frederick's reign ended with stalemate in Germany and defeat in Italy. Before his death in 1190, an opportunity had opened to form a new territorial base of power for future emperors when the Norman ruler of the kingdom of Sicily, William II (r. 1166–1189) sought an alliance with Frederick that would free him to pursue a scheme to conquer Constantinople. The alliance was sealed in 1186 by a most fateful marriage between Frederick's son—the future Henry VI (r. 1190–1197)—and Constance, heiress to the kingdom of Sicily. This alliance proved, however, to be only another well-laid political plan that went astray. The Sicilian connection became a fatal distraction for Hohenstaufen kings, leading them repeatedly to sacrifice their traditional territorial base in northern Europe to the temptation of imperialism. Equally ominous, this union of the empire with Sicily left Rome encircled, thereby ensuring the undying hostility of a papacy already thoroughly distrustful of the emperor. The marriage alliance with Sicily proved to be the first step in what soon became a fight to the death between pope and emperor.

Henry VI died in September 1197, with chaos his immediate heir. Between English intervention in its politics and the pope's deliberate efforts to sabotage the Hohenstaufen dynasty, Germany was thrown into anarchy and civil war. England gave financial support to anti-Hohenstaufen factions. Its candidate for the imperial throne, Otto of Brunswick of the rival Welf dynasty, was crowned Otto IV by his supporters in Aachen in 1198 and later won general recognition in Germany. With England supporting Otto, the French rushed in on the side of the fallen Hohenstaufen—the beginning of periodic French fishing in troubled German waters. Meanwhile, Henry VI's four-year-old son, Frederick, was safely, and ominously, tucked away as a ward of Pope Innocent III.

POPE INNOCENT III (1198–1215).   Pope Innocent III was a papal monarch in the Gregorian tradition of papal independence from secular domination. He proclaimed and practiced as none before him the doctrine of the plenitude of papal power. In a famous statement he likened the relationship of the pope to the emperor—or the Church to the State—to that of the sun to the moon. As the moon received its light from the sun, so the emperor received his brilliance (that is, his crown) from the hand of the pope—an allusion to the famous precedent set on Christmas Day, 800, when Pope Leo III crowned Charlemagne.

Although this pretentious theory greatly exceeded Innocent's ability to practice it, he and his successors did not hesitate to act on their ambitions. When Philip II tried unlawfully to annul his marriage, Inno-

Pope Innocent III (1198–1215) made the papacy a great power with financial resources and a bureaucracy equal to those of secular monarchies. Innocent III began the papal challenge of the Hohenstaufen dynasty that ended with its demise in the mid-thirteenth century. [SCALA/Art Resource]

cent placed France under interdict, suspending all Church services save baptism and the last rites; the same punishment befell England when King John presumed to appoint an unworthy archbishop of Canterbury.

Innocent made the papacy a great secular power, with financial resources and a bureaucracy equal to those of contemporary monarchs. It was during his reign that the papacy transformed itself into the efficient ecclesio-commercial complex that was attacked by reformers throughout the later Middle Ages. He reserved to the pope the absolution of many sins and religious crimes, forcing those desirous of pardons or exemptions to bargain directly with Rome. It was a measure of the degree to which the papacy had embraced the new money economy that it employed Lombard merchants and bankers to collect the growing papal revenues.

FREDERICK II. Hohenstaufen support remained alive in Germany despite the dynasty's fall, and Otto IV reigned over a very divided kingdom. In October 1209, Pope Innocent crowned him emperor; but the pope quickly changed from benefactor to mortal enemy when, after his coronation, Otto proceeded to reconquer Sicily and once again to pursue an imperial policy that left Rome encircled. Within four months of his papal coronation, Otto received a papal excommunication.

Pope Innocent, casting about for a counterweight to the treacherous Otto, joined the French, who had remained loyal to the Hohenstaufens against the English-Welf alliance. It was now that his new ally, Philip Augustus, impressed on the pope the fact that a solution to their problems with Otto IV lay near at hand in Innocent's ward, Frederick of Sicily. Frederick, the son of the late Hohenstaufen Emperor Henry VI, was now of age and, unlike Otto, had an immediate hereditary claim to the imperial throne. In December 1212, the young Frederick, with papal, French, and German support, was crowned king of the Romans in Mainz, as Frederick II. Within a year-and-a-half, Philip Augustus ended the Welf interregnum of Otto IV on the battlefield of Bouvines. Philip sent Frederick II Otto's fallen imperial banner from the battlefield, a bold gesture that suggested the extent to which Frederick's ascent to the throne was intended to be that of a French-papal puppet.

He soon disappointed any such hopes. Frederick was Sicilian and dreaded travel beyond the Alps. Only nine of his thirty-eight years as emperor were spent in Germany. Although Frederick continued to pursue royal policies in Germany through his representatives, he desired only one thing from the German princes, the imperial title for himself and his sons, and he was willing to give them what they wanted to secure it. His eager compliance with their demands laid the foundation for six centuries of German division. In 1220 he recognized the jurisdictional claims of the ecclesiastical princes of Germany, and in 1232 he extended the same recognition to the secular princes. The German princes were undisputed lords over their territories. Frederick's concessions have been characterized as a German equivalent to the Magna Carta in the sense that they secured the rights of the German nobility. Unlike the Magna Carta, however, they did so without at the same time securing the rights of monarchy. The Magna Carta placed the king and the nobility (parliament) in England in a creative tension; the reign of Frederick II simply made the German nobility petty kings.

Frederick had an equally disastrous relationship with the pope, who excommunicated him no fewer than four times. The pope won the long struggle that ensued, although his victory proved in time to be a Pyrrhic one. In the contest with Frederick II, Pope Innocent IV (1243–1254) launched the Church into European politics on a massive scale, and his wholesale secularization of the papacy made the Church highly vulnerable to the criticism of religious reformers and royal apologists. Innocent organized and led the German princes against Frederick. These princes—thanks to Frederick's grand concessions to them—had become a superior force and were in full control of Germany by the 1240s.

When Frederick died in 1250, the German monarchy died with him. The princes established an informal electoral college in 1257, which thereafter reigned supreme (it was formally recognized by the emperor in 1356). The "king of the Romans" became their puppet, this time with firmly attached strings; he was elected and did not rule by hereditary right. Between 1250 and 1272, the Hohenstaufen dynasty slowly faded into oblivion.

Independent princes now controlled Germany. Italy fell to local magnates. The connection between Germany and Sicily, established by Frederick I, was broken. The papal monarchy emerged as one of Europe's most formidable powers, soon to enter its most costly conflict with the French and the English.

Medieval Russia

In the late tenth century, Prince Vladimir of Kiev (r. 972–1015), then Russia's dominant city, received delegations of Muslims, Roman Catholics, Jews, and Greek Orthodox Christians. Each group hoped to see Russians embrace its religion. Vladimir chose Greek Orthodoxy, which became the religion of Russia, adding cultural bonds to the commercial ties that had long linked Russia to the Byzantine Empire.

POLITICS AND SOCIETY.   Vladimir's successor, Yaroslav the Wise (r. 1016–1054), developed Kiev into a magnificent political and cultural center, with architecture rivaling that of Constantinople. He also sought contacts with the West in an unsuccessful effort to counter the political influence of the Byzantine emperors. After his death, Russians were slowly divided by rivalry among their princes into three cultural groups: the Great Russians, the White Russians, and the Little Russians (Ukrainians). Autonomous principalities also challenged Kiev's dominance, and it became just one of several national centers.

Government in the principalities combined monarchy (the prince), aristocracy (the prince's council of noblemen), and democracy (a popular assembly of all adult males). The broadest social division was between freemen and slaves. Freemen included the clergy, army officers, boyars (wealthy landowners), townsmen, and peasants. Slaves were mostly prisoners of war. Debtors working off their debts made up a large, semi-free, intermediate group.

MONGOL RULE (1243–1480).   In the thirteenth century, Mongol (or Tatar) armies swept over China, much of the Islamic world, and Russia (see Chapters 9 and 16). Ghengis Khan (1155–1227) invaded Russia in 1223 and Kiev fell to Batu Khan in 1240. Russian cities became tribute-paying principalities of the segment of the Mongol Empire called the *Golden Horde* (a phrase derived from the Tatar words for the color of Batu Khan's tent), which had its capital at Sarai, on the lower Volga. The *Golden Horde* stationed officials in Russian towns to oversee taxation and the conscription of soldiers into Tatar armies.

Mongol rule further divided Russia from the west. The Mongols intermarried with the Russians and also created harems filled with Russian women. Russians who resisted were sold into slavery in foreign lands. Russian women—under the influence of Islam, which had become the religion of the Golden Horde—began to wear veils and to lead more secluded lives. The Mongols, however, left Russian political institutions and religion largely intact and, thanks to their far-flung trade, brought most Russians greater peace and prosperity than they had enjoyed before.

RUSSIAN LIBERATION.   The princes of Moscow cooperated with their overlords in the collection of tribute and grew wealthy under the Mongols. As Mongol rule weakened, the princes took control of the territory surrounding the city. In a process that has come to be known as "the gathering of the Russian land," they then gradually expanded the principality of Moscow through land purchases, colonization, and conquest.

In 1380, Grand Duke Dimitri of Moscow (1350–1389) defeated Tatar forces at Kulikov Meadow in a victory that marked the beginning of the decline of Mongolian hegemony. Another century would pass before Ivan III, called Ivan the Great (d. 1505), would bring all of northern Russia under Moscow's control and end Mongolian rule in 1480. By the last quarter of the fourteenth century Moscow had replaced Kiev as the political and religious center of Russia. In Russian eyes it was destined to become the "third Rome" after the fall of Constantinople to the Turks in 1453.

France in the Thirteenth Century: Reign of Louis IX

If Innocent III realized the fondest ambitions of medieval popes, Louis IX (r. 1226–1270), the grandson of Philip Augustus, embodied the medieval view of the perfect ruler. His reign was a striking contrast to that of his contemporary, Frederick II of Germany. Coming to power in the wake of the French victory at Bouvines (1214), Louis inherited a unified and secure kingdom. Although he was endowed with a moral character that far excelled that of his royal and papal contemporaries, he was also at times prey to naiveté. Not beset by the problems of sheer survival, and a reformer at heart, Louis found himself free to concentrate on what medieval people believed to be the business of civilization.

Magnanimity in politics is not always a sign of strength, and Louis could be very magnanimous. Although in a position to drive the English from their French possessions during negotiations for the Treaty of Paris (1259), he refused to take such advantage. Had he done so and ruthlessly confiscated English territories on the French coast, he might have lessened, if not averted altogether, the conflict of the Hundred Years' War (ca. 1337–1453). Although he occasionally chastised popes for their crude ambitions, Louis remained neutral during the long struggle between Frederick II and the papacy, and his neutrality redounded very much to the pope's advantage. For their assistance, both by action and by inaction, the Capetian kings of the thirteenth century became the objects of many papal favors.

Louis's greatest achievements lay at home. The efficient French bureaucracy, which his predecessors had used to exploit their subjects, became under Louis an instrument of order and fair play in local government. He sent forth royal commissioners (enquêteurs), reminiscent of Charlemagne's far less successful *missi dominici*, to monitor the royal officials responsible for local governmental administration. These royal ambassadors were received as genuine tributes of the people. Louis further abolished private wars and serfdom within his royal domain, gave his subjects the judicial right of appeal from local to higher courts, and made the tax system, by medieval standards, more equitable. The French people came to associate their king with justice, and national feeling, the glue of nationhood, grew very strong during his reign.

Respected by the kings of Europe, Louis became an arbiter among the world's powers, having far greater moral authority than the pope. During his reign, French society and culture became an example to all of Europe, a pattern that would continue into the modern period. Northern France became the showcase of monastic reform, chivalry, and Gothic art and architecture. Louis's reign also coincided with the golden age of Scholasticism, which saw the convergence of Europe's greatest thinkers on Paris, among them Saint Thomas Aquinas and Saint Bonaventure.

Louis's perfection remained, however, that of a medieval king. Like his father, Louis VIII (r. 1223–1226), Louis was something of a religious fanatic. He sponsored the French Inquisition. He led two French Crusades against the Arabs, which were inspired by the purest religious motives but proved to be personal disasters. During the first (1248–1254), Louis was captured and had to be ransomed out of Egypt. He died of a fever during the second in 1270. It was especially for this selfless, but also quite useless, service on behalf of the Church that Louis IX later received the rare honor of sainthood.

The High Middle Ages in World Perspective

With its borders finally secured, Western Europe concentrated during the high Middle Ages on its political institutions and cultural development, something denied it during the early Middle Ages. In England and France, modern Western nations can be seen in formation. Within the empire, imperial rule both revived (under Otto I) and totally collapsed (during the Hohenstaufen dynasty). Everywhere, society successfully organized itself from noble to serf. With the flourishing of trade and the expansion of towns, a new wealthy class patronized education. Western Europe's first universities appeared, and a movement called Scholasticism brought a new, and often forbidding, order to knowledge. The major disruption of the period, however, was an unprecedented conflict between former allies. The Roman Catholic Church had become a monarchy in its own right, able to compete with secular states and even to dethrone (by excommunication and interdict) kings and princes. The foundation was thereby laid both for perpetual conflict between popes and rulers, which lasted well into early modern times, and for the creation of the peculiar Western separation of Church and State.

For Western Europe, the high Middle Ages were a

period of clearer self-definition during which the West gained much of the shape we have come to recognize today. Other world civilizations had already become established and were beginning to depart their "classical" or "golden" periods. For them, the best lay behind rather than ahead.

Under the Sung dynasty (960–1279) before Mongolian rule, China continued its technological advance. In addition to printing, the Chinese invested the abacus and gunpowder. They also enjoyed a money economy unknown in the West. But culturally, these centuries between 1000 and 1300 were closed and narrow by comparison with those of the T'ang dynasty. Politically, the Sung was far more autocratic. In China (as in Western European lands like England and France, although not in Italy and the empire), regional aristocracies ceased to be serious obstacles to a strong centralized government.

Chinese women generally held a lower status and had fewer vocational options than Western women, as the practice of footbinding dramatically attests. As in the West, a higher degree of freedom and self-government developed in the countryside, especially by the fourteenth century, as peasants gained the right to buy and sell land and to fulfill traditional labor obligations by money payments. Intellectually, China, like the West, had a Scholastic movement within its dominant philosophy; Confucianism made religious and philosophical thought more elaborate, systematic, and orthodox. Whereas Western Scholasticism had the effect of making Christianity aloof, elitist, and ridiculed by its lay critics, Confucianism remained a philosophy highly adaptable and popular among laypeople.

In the late twelfth century, Japan shifted from civilian to military rule; the Kamakura *bakufu* governed by mounted warriors who were paid with rights to income from land in exchange for their military services. This rise of a military aristocracy marked the beginning of Japan's "medieval," as distinct from its "classical," period. Three Mongol invasions in the thirteenth century also required a strong military. With a civilian court also in existence, Japan actually had a dual government (that is, two emperors and two courts) until the fourteenth century. However, this situation differed greatly from the deep and permanent national divisions developing at this time among the emerging states and autonomous principalities of Western Europe.

Japanese women, more like those in Western Europe than in China, traditionally played a prominent role in royal government and court culture. Nun Shō-gun, for example, succeeded her husband for a brief period of Kamakura rule in the late twelfth century. But the prominence of women in government would also change in Japan by the fourteenth century.

Within the many developing autonomous Islamic lands at this time, the teaching of Muhammad created an international culture. The regular practice of religious fundamentals made it possible for Muslims to transcend their new and often very deep regional divisions. Similarly, Christianity made it possible for Englishmen, Frenchmen, Germans, and Italians to think of themselves as one people and unit in Crusades to the Holy Land. As these Crusades began in the late eleventh century, Islam too was on the march, penetrating Turkey and Afghanistan, and impinging upon India, where it gained a new challenge in Hinduism.

Suggested Readings

EMILIE AMT, ed., *Women's Lives in Medieval Europe: A Sourcebook* (1992). Outstanding collection of sources.

P. ARIÈS, *Centuries of Childhood: A Social History of Family Life*, trans. by Robert Baldick (1962). Controversial pioneer effort on the subject.

J. W. BALDWIN, *The Government of Philip Augustus* (1986). A scholarly feat.

J. W. BALDWIN, *The Scholastic Culture of the Middle Ages: 1000–1300* (1971). Best brief synthesis available.

M. W. BALDWIN, ed., *History of the Crusades, I: The First Hundred Years* (1955). Basic historical narrative.

G. BARRACLOUGH, *The Medieval Papacy* (1968). Brief, comprehensive survey, with pictures.

G. BARRACLOUGH, *The Origins of Modern Germany* (1963). Penetrating political narrative.

ROBERT BARTLETT, *Trial by Fire and Water: The Medieval Judicial Ordeal* (1986).

M. BLOCH, French Rural Society, trans. by J. Sondheimer (1966). A classic by a great modern historian.

J. BONY, *French Gothic Architecture of the Twelfth and Thirteenth Centuries* (1983).

J. BRUNDAGE, *Law, Sex, and Christian Society in Medieval Europe* (1987). Everything about the topic of sex in all its scholastic subtlety.

C. BYNAM, *Holy Feast, Holy Fast: The Religious Significance of Food to Medieval Women* (1987). An analysis of the mind-set of cloistered women through their attitudes toward food.

A. CAPELLANUS, *The Art of Courtly Love*, trans. by J. J. Parry (1941). Translation of this classic along with other documents from the court of Marie de Champagne.

M. CLAGETT, G. POST, and R. REYNOLDS, eds.,

Twelfth-Century Europe and the Foundations of Modern Society (1966). Demanding but stimulating collection of essays.

F. COPLESTON, *A History of Philosophy, III/1: Ockham to the Speculative Mystics* (1963). The best introduction to Ockham and his movement.

F. C. COPLESTON, *Aquinas* (1965). Best introduction to Aquinas's philosophy.

R. H. C. DAVIS, *A History of Medieval Europe: From Constantine to St. Louis, Part 2* (1972).

G. DUBY, *Rural Economy and Country Life in the Medieval West* (1968). Slice-of-life analysis.

G. DUBY, *The Three Orders: Feudal Society Imagined,* trans. by Arthur Goldhammer (1981). Large, comprehensive, and authoritative.

R. and J. GIES, *Marriage and Family in the Middle Ages* (1983).

E. GILSON, *Heloise and Abelard* (1968). An analysis and defense of medieval scholarly values.

J. GOODY, *The Development of the Family and Marriage in Europe* (1983). Bold interpretation of the Church's marital legislation, ascribing unflattering, materialistic motives to the Church.

ELIZABETH M. HALAM, *Capetian France 987–1328* (1980). Especially good on politics and heretics.

B. HANAWALT, *The Ties That Bound: Peasant Families in Medieval England* (1986). Analysis of family structure and relationships.

C. H. HASKINS, *The Renaissance of the Twelfth Century* (1927). Still the standard account.

C. H. HASKINS, *The Rise of Universities* (1972). A short, minor classic.

D. HERLIHY, *Medieval Households* (1985). Sweeping survey of Middle Ages that defends the medieval family against modern caricatures.

D. HERLIHY, *Opera Muliebria* (1990). Brief, pioneer effort to describe the many vocational and employment opportunities of medieval women.

J. C. HOLT, *Magna Carta,* 2nd ed. (1992). The famous document and its interpretation by succeeding generations.

E. H. KANTOROWICZ, *The King's Two Bodies* (1957). Controversial analysis of political concepts in the high Middle Ages.

G. LEFF, *Paris and Oxford Universities in the Thirteenth and Fourteenth Centuries: An Institutional and Intellectual History* (1968). Very good on debates on Scholasticism.

J. LE GOFF, *The Birth of Purgatory* (1981).

R. S. LOOMIS, ed., *The Development of Arthurian Romance* (1963). A basic study.

R. S. LOPEZ and I. W. RAYMOND, eds., *Medieval Trade in the Mediterranean World* (1955). An illuminating collection of sources, concentrated on southern Europe.

E. MÂLE, *The Gothic Image: Religious Art in France in the Thirteenth Century* (1913). A classic.

P. MANDONNET, *St. Dominic and His Work* (1944). For the origins of the Dominican Order.

H. E. MAYER, *The Crusades,* trans. by John Gilligham (1972). Extremely detailed, and the best one-volume account.

J. MOORMAN, *A History of the Franciscan Order* (1968). The best survey.

J. B. MORRALL, *Political Thought in Medieval Times* (1962). A readable and illuminating account.

J. T. NOONAN, *Contraception: A History of Its Treatment by the Catholic Theologians and Canonists* (1967). A fascinating account of medieval theological attitudes toward sexuality and sex-related problems.

E. PANOFSKY, *Gothic Architecture and Scholasticism* (1951). A controversial classic.

C. PETIT-DUTAILLIS, *The Feudal Monarchy in France and England from the Tenth to the Thirteenth Century,* trans. by E. D. Hunt (1964). A political narrative.

H. PIRENNE, *Medieval Cities: Their Origins and the Revival of Trade,* trans. by Frank D. Halsey (1970). A minor classic.

J. M. POWELL, *Innocent III: Vicar of Christ or Lord of the World* (1963). Excerpts from the scholarly debate over Innocent's reign.

F. W. POWICKE, *The Thirteenth Century* (1962). An outstanding treatment of English political history.

H. RASHDALL, *The Universities of Europe in the Middle Ages,* Vols. 1–3 (1936). Dated but still a standard comprehensive work.

F. RÖRIG, *The Medieval Town,* trans. by D. J. A. Matthew (1971). Excellent on northern Europe.

S. SHAHAR, *The Fourth Estate: A History of Women in the Middle Ages* (1983). Readable survey.

O. VON SIMSON, *The Gothic Cathedral* (1956).

R. W. SOUTHERN, *Medieval Humanism and Other Studies* (1970). Provocative and far-ranging essays on topics in the intellectual history of the high Middle Ages.

B. TIERNEY, *The Crisis of Church and State 1050–1300* (1964). A very useful collection of primary sources on key Church–State conflicts.

W. L. WAKEFIELD and A. P. EVANS, eds., *Heresies of the High Middle Ages* (1969). A major document collection.

J. WEISHEIPL, *Friar Thomas* (1980). Biography of Thomas Aquinas that attempts to do justice to the human side of the story as well as to the theological.

S. WILLIAMS, ed., *The Gregorian Epoch: Reformation, Revolution, Reaction* (1964). Variety of scholarly opinion on the significance of Pope Gregory's reign presented in debate form.

R. L. WOLFF and H. W. HAZARD, eds., *History of the Crusades 1189–1311* (1962).

South Indian bronze figure of Krishna dancing on the head of the serpent Kaliya, from Vijayanagar, ca. fifteenth century. Kaliya, according to a legend, was infesting the waters of the Jumna River until Krishna leaped in and emerged dancing on the vanquished snake. [Asian Art Museum of San Francisco, The Avery Brundage Collection B65B72]

The Islamic Heartlands and India (ca. 1000–1500)

By the mid-tenth century in the Islamic world, centralized caliphal power had broken down. Regional Islamic states with distinctive political and cultural configurations now dominated—a pattern that would endure to modern times (see Map 16-1). Yet Islamic lands remained part of a single larger civilization. Muslims from Córdoba in Spain could (and did) travel to Bukhara in Transoxiana or Zanzibar on the East African coast and feel much at home. Both regionalism and cosmopolitanism, diversity and unity, have characterized Islamic civilization ever since the tenth century.

In the social and religious spheres, the five hundred years between 1000 and 1500 saw the growth of a truly international Islamic community, united by shared norms of social, religious, and political order represented and maintained by the Muslim religious scholars (*ulama*). Sufism, that strand of Islam stressing personal piety and allegiance to a spiritual master, gained widespread popularity in this period, especially after 1200, through the growth of Sufi affiliations or brotherhoods. These popular organizations deeply influenced Muslim life everywhere, often countering the more limiting aspects of *ulama* conformity. Shi'ite ideas also offered an alternative vision of society for many. Shi'ite movements loyal to Ali and his heirs repeatedly challenged but ultimately failed to displace centrist, Sunni demographic dominance of most of the Islamic world, even though Shi'ite dynasties exercised political control over major parts of the Islamic heartlands in the tenth and eleventh centuries, from Iran to Egypt and North Africa.

MAP 16-1 THE ISLAMIC HEARTLANDS, 1000–1500 *Shown are the major ruling dynasties.*

Culturally, the rise of the New Persian language in the tenth century culminated thereafter in a rich new Islamic literature. A Persian renaissance fueled the spread of Persian as the major language of Islam alongside (or, in the Islamic East, even above) Arabic. The Persian-dominated Iranian and Indian Islamic world became more and more distinct from the western Islamic lands.

Two Asian steppe peoples, the Mongols and the Turks, rose to political dominance in these centuries, but with different results. The spread of the Turks added a substantial Turkish linguistic and cultural tinge to the Islamic world, especially through their presence as ruling dynasties such as the Saljuqs, the Mamluks of Egypt, and the "slave-kings" of Delhi. The Mongols, on the other hand, conquered a major part of the Islamic heartlands during the thirteenth century. Their culture and religion, however, although not without considerable influence (chiefly in the persistence of elements of their legal code, the *Yasa*), did not become dominant in the Islamic any more than the Chinese or the Eastern Christian lands they conquered. Islam impinged more and more in this age on civilization in the Indian subcontinent, Southeast Asia, and sub-Saharan Africa. Although it had not yet converted a majority in these regions, it became the major new influence in all of them.

THE ISLAMIC HEARTLANDS

Religion and Society

The notable developments of this period for the shape of Islamic society were the consolidation and institutionalization of Sunni legal and religious norms, Sufi mystical piety, and Shi'ite sectarianism.

Consolidation of Sunni Orthopraxy

The *ulama* (both Sunni and Shi'ite) gradually became an entrenched religious, social, and political elite throughout the Islamic world, especially after the breakdown of centralized power in the tenth century. Their integration into local merchant, land-owning, and bureaucratic classes led to stronger identification of these groups with Islam.

From the eleventh century onward the *ulama*'s power and fixity as a class were expressed in the institution of the *madrasa*, or college of higher learning. On the one hand, the *madrasa* had grown up naturally as individual experts frequented a given mosque or private house and attracted students seeking to learn the Qur'an, the *Hadith* ("Tradition"), jurisprudence, Arabic grammar, and the like. On the other hand, the *madrasa*'s formal fixation through the endowment of buildings, scholarships, and salaried chairs was a device employed by rulers for their own as well as for pious ends. It gave them a measure of control over the *ulama* through their influence on the appointment of teachers and thus on the legal or theological slant of the curriculum. At least in theory, such control might serve to combat unwelcome sectarianism as well. In notable contrast to the Western university, with its corporate organization and granting of institutional degrees, the *madrasa* was rather a support institution for individual teachers, who gave personal certification to students for the mastery of particular subjects. It served, in other words, to give an institutional base (often providing not only teaching space but stipends and living quarters for students) to the long-developed system in the Islamic world of students seeking the best teachers in the various religious disciplines and studying texts with them until they received the teachers' "permission" to transmit and teach those same texts themselves. The absence of diplomas or degrees in the *madrasa*s for completion of a particular course of study indicates the personalist rather than (as in Europe) the corporate nature of Muslim education.[1]

Largely outside *ulama* control, popular, "unofficial" piety flourished in local pilgrimages to saints' tombs, in folk celebrations of Muhammad's birthday and veneration of him in song and poetry, and in the ecstatic worship in song and dance of some Sufi groups. But the shared traditions that directed family and civil law, the daily prayer-rituals, fasting in the month of Ramadan, and the yearly Meccan pilgrimage remained the public bond among virtually all Muslims, even most Kharijites or Shi'ites. In the Christian world, dogmatic theological positions determined sectarian identity. In contrast, the tendency in the Islamic world, for all its many theological disputes and schools of thought, was to define Islam in terms of the things that Muslims do—hence by ortho*praxy* (practice) rather than by ortho*doxy* (beliefs). The chief arbiters of normative Sunni Islam were four mutually tolerant schools of Muslim legal interpretation (*fiqh*), not the various schools of theological interpretation.

A basic Sunni orthopraxy, discouraging further religious or social innovation, was well established by the year 1000 as the dominant Muslim tradition, even though Shi'ite aspirations often made themselves felt either politically or theologically. The emergence of a conservative theological orientation tied to one of the four main Sunni legal schools, the Hanbalites (after Ibn Hanbal, d. 969), narrowed the scope for creative doctrinal change. The Hanbalites stressed reliance only on the Qur'an and the *Hadith* and a literalist reading of both. Thus, a certain orthodoxy was joined

[1] G. Makdisi, "Madrasa and University in the Middle Ages," *Studia Islamica* 31 (1970): 255–264.

The Sultan Hasan Madrasa and Tomb-Mosque. This imposing Mamluk building (1356–1363) was built to house teachers and students studying all four of the major traditions or "schools" of Islamic law. Living and teaching spaces are combined here in a building with a mosque and the Sultan's tomb enclosure. [William A. Graham]

with the orthopraxy of the *Umma*, although there was no "church" to enforce either. Also, a growing social conservatism among the *ulama* reflected their places in regional social aristocracies. As often as not, the *ulama* were as committed to the status quo as were the rulers.

Sufi Piety and Organization

Sufi piety stresses the spiritual and mystical dimensions of Islam. The term *Sufi* apparently came from the Arabic *suf* ("wool") as a result of the old ascetic practice of wearing only a coarse woolen garment. Sufi simplicity and humility had roots with the Prophet and the Companions but developed as a distinctive tendency when, after about A.D. 700, various male and female pietists emphasized a godly life that went beyond the mere observance of Muslim duties. Some stressed the ascetic avoidance of temptations, others loving devotion to God. Psychologically, Sufi piety bridged the abyss between the human and the divine that is implied in the exalted Muslim concept of an omnipotent Creator. Socially, Sufi piety merged

with folk piety, including such popular practices as saint veneration, shrine pilgrimage, ecstatic worship, and seasonal festivals. Sufi writers collected stories of the earlier saints, wrote treatises on the Sufi way, and composed some of the world's finest mystical poetry.

Some Sufis were revered as spiritual masters and saints. Their disciples formed brotherhoods that, from about the eleventh century, became both regional and international organizations. Each had its distinctive mystical teaching, Qur'anic interpretations, and devotional practice. These fraternal orders proved to be the chief instruments of the further spread of Muslim faith, as well as a locus of popular piety in almost all Islamic societies. Organized Sufism has always attracted members from the populace at large (in this, it differs from most monasticism), as well as those dedicated to poverty or other radical disciplines. Indeed, Sufi orders became in this age one of the typical social institutions of everyday Muslim life in Islamic lands. Whether Sunni or Shi'ite, casually or seriously pious, large numbers of Muslims have ever since identified in some degree with one or another Sufi order.

A Muslim Description of Sufism

Writing at the end of the fourteenth century, the great historian and sociological commentator Ibn Khaldun prepared a massive "introduction" to history, the Muqaddima. *In it he described all aspects of Islamic civilization, including the various sectarian groups and schools of thought in the Islamic community. The following excerpts are taken from his long discussion of the Sufis.*

. . . The Sufi approach is based upon constant application to divine worship, complete devotion to God, aversion to the false splendour of the world, abstinence from the pleasure, property, and position to which the great mass aspire, and retirement from the world into solitude for divine worship. These things were general among the men around Muhammad and the early Muslims.

Then, worldly aspirations increased in the second [eighth] century and after. At that time, the special name of Sufis was given to those who aspired to divine worship.

Very few people share the self-scrutiny of the Sufis, for negligence in this respect is almost universal. Pious people who do not get that far perform, at best, acts of obedience. The Sufis, however, investigate the results of acts of obedience with the help of mystical and ecstatic experience, in order to learn whether they are free from deficiency or not. Thus, it is evident that the Sufis' path in its entirety depends upon self-scrutiny with regard to what they do or do not do, and upon discussion of the various kinds of mystical and ecstatic experience that result from their exertions. This, then, crystallizes for the Sufi novice in a "station." From that station, he can progress to another, higher one.

. . . .

Thus, the Sufis had their special discipline, which is not discussed by other representatives of the religious law. As a consequence, the science of the religious law came to consist of two kinds. One is the special field of jurists and muftis. It is concerned with the general laws governing the acts of divine worship, customary actions, and mutual dealings. The other is the special field of the Sufis. It is concerned with pious exertion, self-scrutiny with regard to it, discussion of the different kinds of mystical experience to another, and the interpretation of the technical terminology of mysticism in use among them.

From Ibn Khaldun, *The Muqaddimah*, trans. by Franz Rosenthal, ed. and abridged by N. J. Dawood (Princeton, NJ: Princeton University Press, 1967), pp. 358–360.

Consolidation of Shi'ite Traditions

Shi'ite traditions crystallized between the tenth and twelfth centuries. Numerous states now came under Shi'ite rulers, some even before the Shi'ite Buyids took Baghdad in 945 (see Chapter 13). Yet the differences separating the diverse Shi'ite groups precluded a unified Shi'ism. Only the strongest Shi'ite state, that of the North African Fatimids, was able to establish an important empire in Egypt. And a substantial Shi'ite populace developed only in Iran, Iraq, and the lower Indus (Sind).

Two Shi'ite groups emerged as the most influential. The "Seveners," or "Isma'ilis," were those who recognized Isma'il (d. ca. 760), first son of the sixth Alid *imam*, as the seventh *imam* (rather than his brother). The Isma'ilis were esoterics and for that reason often referred to as "Batinis" ("interiorists," "esoterics"). Their thought drew on Gnostic and Neo-Platonic philosophy, knowledge of which they reserved for a spiritual elite. Isma'ili groups were often revolutionary, and three of them founded states that had substantial impact on the Islamic world. The other group, the Qarmatians of eastern Arabia, ruled or disrupted Iraq, Syria, and Arabia through much of the tenth century; the Fatimids conquered North Africa (909) and Egypt (969) and ruled as Shi'ite caliphs until 1171. The Nizari Isma'ili "Assassins" formed a radical theocracy in the Elburz mountains south of the Caspian Sea; they were at daggers drawn with other Shi'ite and Sunni states from 1090 to 1258.

By the eleventh century, however, most Shi'ites accepted a line of twelve *imam*s (descended through another son of the sixth *imam*), the last of whom is said to have disappeared in Samarra (Iraq), in 873, into a concealment from which he will emerge as the Mahdi, or "Guided One," who ushers in the messianic age and final judgment. Still today, the Shi'ite majority, the "Twelvers," focus on the martyrdom of the twelve *imams* and look for their intercession on the Day of Judgment. They have flourished best in Iran, the home of most Shi'ite thought, whatever the sect. The Buyids who took control of the Abbasid caliphate in 945 were Twelvers. So were the later Iranian Safavids, who made Twelver doctrine the "state religion" of Iran in the sixteenth century (see Chapter 24).

Unity and Diversity

The western half of the Islamic world after the tenth century developed two regional foci: (1) in Spain, Moroccan North Africa, and to a lesser extent, west Africa; and (2) in Egypt, Syria–Palestine, Anatolia, and, to a lesser extent, Arabia and Libyan North Africa. The history of the eastern half of the Islamic world in the period between 1000 and 1500 was marked by the dramatic impact of the Mongols' expansion into the region in the thirteenth century.

The Islamic West: Spain and North Africa

The grandeur of Moorish Islamic culture in Spain is visible still in Córdoba's great mosque and the ruins of the legendary Alhambra castle. In European lore and literature, the *Chanson de Roland* preserves the echo of Charlemagne's retreat through the Pyrenees after he failed to check the first Umayyad ruler's growing power. That ruler, Abd al-Rahman I (r. 756–788), is less well known in the modern West, but it was he who founded the cosmopolitan tradition of Umayyad Spanish culture at Córdoba, which over the next two centuries was the cultural hub of the western world. Renowned for its medicine, science, literature, intellectual life, commercial activity, public baths and gardens, and courtly elegance, Córdoba reached its zenith under Abd al-Rahman III (r. 912–961). He even assumed the title of caliph in 929. His absolutist but benevolent rule saw a largely unified and peaceful Islamic Spain. The mosque-university of Córdoba that he founded was the earliest institution of its kind; it attracted students from Europe as well as from the Islamic world.

An irony of this cosmopolitan world was the rigorist conservatism that dominated both Muslim and Christian thought in Spain. From time to time, it sparked Muslim-Christian conflict—a product perhaps of the uniquely close and threatening contact of the two communities. Externally, Abd al-Rahman III checked both the new Fatimid Islamic power in the Mediterranean and the Christian kingdoms in the Spanish north, making possible this golden era of Moorish power and culture. But fragmentation into warring Muslim principalities allowed a resurgence of Spain's Christian states between about 1000 and 1085, when Toledo fell permanently back into Christian hands.

There were brief Islamic revivals in Spain and North Africa under the African reform movements of the Almoravids and Almohads. The Almoravids originated as a religious-warrior brotherhood among Ber-

Stretching up one hundred meters, the Giralda bell tower of the Seville cathedral was originally built as a Muslim minaret ca. 1190. Its upper portion was rebuilt in late-Renaissance style by a Spanish Christian architect in the 1560s. [Art Resource]

A Muslim Biographer's Account of Maimonides

The following are excerpts from the section on Maimonides (Arabic: Musa ibn Maymun) in the biographical dictionary of learned men compiled by Ibn al-Qifti (d. 1248). In the first section, omitted here, Ibn al-Qifti describes how the Spanish Jewish savant at first dissembled conversion to Islam when a new Berber ruler demanded the expulsion of Christians and Jews from Spain and North Africa in about 1133. He goes on to tell how Maimonides then made preparations and moved his family to the more tolerant Islamic world of Cairo, where he eventually became the court physician. The final section (omitted) concludes with mention of his marriage, death, and accomplishments. It was not at all unusual for Jews or Christians to hold high office under Muslim rulers in many places.

. . . This man was one of the people of Andalus, a Jew by religion. He studied philosophy in Andalus, was expert in mathematics, and devoted attention to some of the logical sciences. He studied medicine there and excelled in it. . . .

. . . After assembling his possessions in the time that was needed for this, he left Andalus and went to Egypt, accompanied by his family. He settled in the town of Fusṭāṭ, among its Jews, and practiced his religion openly. He lived in a district called al-Maṣīṣa and made a living by trading in jewels and suchlike. Some people studied philosophy under him. . . .

He married in Cairo the sister of a Jewish scribe called Abu'l-Ma'ālī, the secretary of the mother of Nūr al-Dīn 'Alī, known as al-Afdal, the son of Ṣalāḥ al-Dīn Yūsuf ibn Ayyūb, and he had a son by her who today is a physician in Cairo after his father. . . .

Mūsā ibn Maymūn died in Cairo in the year 605 [1208–9].[1] He ordered his heirs to carry his body, when the smell had ceased, to Lake Tiberias and bury him there, seeking to be among the graves of the ancient Israelites and their great jurists, which are there. This was done.

He was learned in the law and secrets of the Jews and compiled a commentary on the Talmud, which is a commentary and explanation of the Torah; some of the Jews approve of it. Philosophic doctrines overcame him, and he compiled a treatise denying the canonical resurrection. The leaders of the Jews held this against him, so he concealed it except from those who shared his opinion in this. He compiled an abridgement of twenty-one books of Galen, with many additions, in sixteen books. It came out very abridged and quite useless; nothing can be done with it. He edited the Kitāb al-Istikmāl [Book of Perfection] of Ibn Aflah al-Andalusī, on astronomy, and improved it, for there was some confusion in the original. He also edited the Kitāb al-Istikmāl of Ibn Hūd, on mathematics. This is a fine, comprehensive book, needing some correction. He corrected and improved it. . . .

Reading the Torah in a Spanish synagogue. A picture from a Hebrew Haggada, Spain, fourteenth century. Until their expulsion by Christian rulers at the end of the fifteenth century, Jews formed a significant minority in Spain. [The British Library]

In the latter part of his life he was troubled by a man from Andalus, a jurist called Abu'l-'Arab ibn Ma'īsha, who came to Fusṭāṭ and met him. He charged him with having been a Muslim in Andalus, accused him [of apostasy] and wanted to have him punished.[2] 'Abd al-Raḥīm ibn 'Alī al-Fāḍil prevented this, and said to him, "If a man is converted by force, his Islam is not legally valid."

[1] In fact, he died in 1204.

[2] The penalty for apostasy was death.

From Bernard Lewis, ed. and trans., *Islam from the Prophet Muhammad to the Capture of Constantinople*, Vol. 2 (New York: Harper and Row, 1974), pp. 189–192.

ber nomads in West Africa. Having subdued virtually all of northwestern Africa, in 1086 they carried their zealotry from their new capital of Marrakesh into Spain and reunited its Islamic kingdoms. Under their rule, the arabized Christians (Mozarabs) were persecuted and many were driven out, as were some Moorish Jews. The subsequent wars began the last extended phase of the "Reconquest" (*Reconquista*) in Spain. These conflicts, in which Christian rulers sought to regain and Christianize the peninsula, are best known in the West for the exploits of El Cid (d. 1099), the adventurer and mercenary who became the Spanish national hero.

A new reform movement, the Almohads, ended Almoravid rule in Morocco in 1147 and then conquered much of southern Spain. Before their demise (1225 in Spain; 1275 in Africa), they stimulated a brilliant revival of Spanish Islamic culture. During this era, paper manufacture reached Spain and then the rest of Western Europe. The long westward odyssey of Indian fable literature through Iran and the Arab world ended with Spanish and Latin translations in thirteenth-century Spain. The most illustrious products of this Spanish Islamic intellectual world were

a major philosopher and physician, Ibn Rushd (Averroës, d. 1198); perhaps the greatest Muslim mystical thinker, Ibn al-Arabi (d. 1240); and the famous Arab-Jewish philosopher, Maimonides (d. 1204), who was forced to spend much of his life abroad in Cairo.

The Islamic West: Egypt and the Eastern Mediterranean World

THE FATIMIDS.   The major Islamic presence in the Mediterranean from the tenth to the twelfth century was that of the Shi'ite Fatimids. They began as a Tunisian dynasty, then conquered Morocco, Sicily, and Egypt (969). In Egypt, they built their new capital, Cairo (*al-Qahira*, "the Victorious"), near the original garrison town of the earliest Arab conquest. They took their name from their claim to descent from Muhammad's daughter, Fatima. Their rule as Shi'ite caliphs meant that, for a time, there were three "caliphates"—in Baghdad, Córdoba, and Cairo. The Fatimids were Isma'ilis (see the earlier discussion of "Religion and Society"). Content to rule a Sunni majority in Egypt, they sought recognition as true *imams*

The Alhambra, Patio of the Lions, viewed from the Hall of Justice. Built largely in the fourteenth century by the Nasrid dynasty, the magnificent, sprawling palace buildings of the Alhambra marked the twilight of Islamic culture in Spain. [Bettmann Archive]

An Egyptian bronze incense burner of Copto-Arabic origin (eighth–ninth century). This nearly intact piece of fine metalwork is a reminder of the constant presence of the Coptic Christian community in Egypt throughout the Islamic times and down to the present day. [Freer Gallery of Art]

well as they did their Sunni majority. Many Copts held high offices, even that of vizier. Jews, like Copts, usually fared well under the Fatimids, except for the general persecution of Jews and Christians under the apparently deranged caliph al-Hakim (d. 1021).

After 1100, the Fatimids declined, falling in 1171 to Salah al-Din (Saladin), a military leader and administrator under the Turkish ruler of Syria, Nur al-Din. Saladin, a Sunni Kurd with considerable leadership talent, is well known in the West for his battles (including the retaking of Jerusalem in 1187) and eventual compromise truce with the invading Crusaders. After Nur al-Din's death, Saladin managed not only to rule Egypt but also to bring Syria–Palestine and Mesopotamia under his sway. In doing so, he founded the short-lived Ayyubid dynasty that, under

by other Isma'ili groups. They did win the allegiance of a Shi'ite state in Yemen and were able, for a time, to take western Arabia and most of Syria from the Buyid "guardians" of the Abbasid caliphate (see Chapter 13).

The Fatimid reign spawned two splinter groups that have played visible, if minor, roles at certain points in history. The Druze of modern Lebanon and Syria originated around 1020 with a few members of the Fatimid court who professed belief in the divinity of one of the Fatimid caliphs. The tradition they founded is too far from Islam to be considered a Muslim sect. The Isma'ili Assassins, on the other hand, were a radical movement founded by a Fatimid defector in the Elburz mountains of Iran at the beginning of the twelfth century. The name "Assassins" comes not from the political assassinations that made them infamous but from a European corruption of the Arabic *Hashishiyyin* ("users of hashish"). A local Syrian name, it was possibly connected with the story that the Assassins were manipulated with drugs to undertake their usually suicidal missions. The Assassins were defeated and their mountain redoubt destroyed by the Mongols in the thirteenth century.

The Fatimids built the Azhar mosque in Cairo as a center of learning, a role it maintains today, although for Sunni, not (as then) Shi'ite, scholarship. Fatimid rulers treated Egypt's Coptic Christians generally as

WESTERN ISLAMIC LANDS	
756–1021	Spanish Umayyad dynasty
912–961	Rule of Abd al-Rahman III; height of Umayyad power and civilization
969–1171	Fatimid Shi'ite dynasty in Egypt
ca. 1020	Origin of Druze community (Egypt/Syria)
1171	Fatimids fall to Salah al-Din (Saladin), Ayyubid lieutenant of the ruler of Aleppo
1056–1275	Almoravid and Almohad dynasties in North Africa, West Africa, and Spain
1096–1291	Major European Christian crusades into Islamic lands; some European presence in Syria–Palestine
1189	Death of Ibn Rushd (Averroës), philosopher
1204	Death of Musa ibn Maymun (Maimonides), philosopher and Jewish savant
1240	Death of Ibn al-Arabi, theosophical mystic
1250–1517	Mamluk sultanate in Egypt and (from late 1200s) Syria; claim laid to Abbasid Caliphate
1260	Mamluk victory at Ain Jalut halts Mongol advance into Syria
1406	Death of Ibn Khaldun, historian and social philosopher
ca. 1300	Rise of Ottoman state in western Anatolia

various successors, controlled all three areas until Egypt fell to the Mamluks in 1250 and most of Syria and Mesopotamia to the Mongols by 1260.

Like Nur al-Din, and on the model of the Saljuqs (see pp. 459–461), Saladin founded *madrasas* to teach and promote Sunni law. His and his Ayyubid successors' reigns in Egypt saw the entrenchment of a self-conscious Sunnism under a program of mutual recognition and the teaching of all four Sunni schools of law. Henceforward Shi'ite Islam disappeared from Egypt.

THE MAMLUKS.   The heirs of the Fatimids and Saladin in the eastern Mediterranean were the redoubtable Mamluk *sultan*s ("[those with] authority"). As rulers of Egypt, they styled themselves after the example of the Saljuqs (see pp. 459–461). The Mamluks alone among major Islamic dynasties withstood the Mongol invasions that closely followed their accession. Their victory at Ain Jalut in Palestine in 1260 marked the end of the Mongols' westward movement. The first Mamluk sultan (r. 1250–1257), Aybak, and his successors were elite Turkish and Mongol slave officers, mostly Kipchak Turks, drawn originally from the bodyguard of Saladin's dynasty. Whereas the early Mamluks were often succeeded by sons or brothers, after the 1390s succession was more often a survival of the fittest; no sultan reigned more than a few years. The Mamluk state was based on a military fief system and total control by the slave-officer elite.

The Mamluk sultan Baybars (r. 1260–1277), who took the last Crusader fortresses, has lived on in Arab legend as a larger-than-life figure. To legitimize his rule, he revived the Abbasid caliphate at least in name after its demise in the fall of Baghdad (1258; discussed later) by installing an uncle of Baghdad's last Abbasid at Cairo. He made treaties with Constantinople and Western European sovereigns, as well as with the newly converted Muslim ruler—or *khan*, of the Golden Horde—of the Mongol Tatars of southern Russia. He was the first Egyptian sultan to appoint judges from each of the four law schools to administer justice, and his public works in Cairo were numerous. He extended Mamluk rule south to Nubia and west among the Berbers.

As trade relations with the Mongol domains improved gradually after 1300 (they were restored formally after 1322), the Mamluks enjoyed substantial prosperity. At their zenith, theirs was the only true empire to occupy the central Islamic lands between the time of the early Abbasids and the later Ottomans. Although in general the Mamluks' decline set in from about 1300, the prosperity and peace achieved during the reign of Ibn Qala'un (1310–1340) were notable. The Black Death epidemic of 1347–1348 in the Arab Middle East hurt the Mamluk and other regional states badly. Yet the Mamluks went on, despite decline, and effectively survived even the Ottoman conquest of Egypt in 1517, because Mamluks continued to rule as Ottoman governors into the nineteenth century.

The architecture of the Mamluks, especially that of the reigns of Baybars and the extravagant Nasir (r. 1293–1340), much of which still graces Cairo, remains their most magnificent bequest to posterity. Calligraphy, metalwork, and mosaics were among the arts and crafts of special note. The Mamluks patronized outstanding scholars, the most important of whom was the greatest Islamic social historian and philosopher, Ibn Khaldun (d. 1406). He was born of a Spanish Muslim family in Tunis and settled in Cairo as an adult. Mamluk scholarship excelled in several areas, notably history, biography, and the sciences of astronomy, mathematics, and medicine.

The tomb of Qa'it Bey, Cairo (built 1472 to 1474), the finest example of Mamluk architecture in Cairo. [Egyptian Tourist Authority]

The Pre-Mongol Islamic East

We noted in Chapter 13 that the Iranian dynasties of the Samanids at Bukhara (875–999) and the Buyids at Baghdad (945–1055) were the major eastern usurpers of the previously unified Abbasid rule. Their take-overs epitomized the rise of regional states that had begun to undermine the caliphate in its eastern and western reaches by the ninth century. Similarly, the demise of each of these dynasties reflected a second important pattern already emerging before them: namely, the ascendancy of Turkish slave-rulers (like the Mamluks later in the west) and of Oghuz Turkish peoples, or Turkomans. With the successors of the Samanids and the Buyids, the process begun by the use of Turkish slave troops in ninth-century Baghdad ended in the permanent presence in the Islamic world of Turks. As late converts, they became typically the most zealous of Sunni Muslims.

THE GHAZNAVIDS.   The rule of the Samanids in Transoxiana was finally wiped out by a Turkoman group. But they had already lost all of eastern Iran south of the Oxus in 994 to one of their own slave governors, Subuktigin (r. 976–997). He set up his own state in modern Afghanistan, at Ghazna, whence he and his son and successor, Mahmud of Ghazna (r. 998–1030), launched successful campaigns against his former masters. The Ghaznavids are notable for their patronage of Persian literature and culture and their conquests in northwestern India, which began a lasting Muslim presence in India. Mahmud was their greatest ruler. His name is still known in South Asia for his booty raids and his destruction of temples in western India. His empire at its peak stretched from western Iran to the Oxus and the Indus.

The great scientist and mathematician al-Biruni (d. 1048) and the epic poet Firdawsi (d. ca. 1020) were among the scholars and artists whom Mahmud attracted to Ghazna. Firdawsi's *Shahnama* ("The Book of Kings") is the masterpiece of Persian literature, an epic of sixty thousand verses that helped fix the new Persian language and revive the pre-Islamic Iranian cultural tradition. After Mahmud, the empire began to break up, although Ghaznavids ruled at Lahore until 1186.

THE SALJUQS.   The Saljuqs were the first major Turkish dynasty of Islam. They were a steppe clan who settled in Transoxiana, became avid Sunnis, and extended their sway over Khorasan in the 1030s. In 1055, they took Baghdad, where the nominal Abbasid

*"Friday Mosque," Isfahan. Begun in the tenth century, it was rebuilt in classic four-*iwan *form by the Saljuq Malik Shah from 1088 to 1089 and remodeled by the Safavids in the fifteenth and seventeenth centuries. The huge, half-dome facade, or* iwan, *is characteristic of Iranian mosque architecture. This view shows the large open courtyard with its ablution-pools in the center and the southern* iwan, *behind which is the original covered area built by Malik Shah. [Diane Rawson, Photo Researchers]*

caliph was happy to greet them as his deliverers from the Shi'ite Buyids. As a new guardian of the caliphate and master of an Islamic empire, the Saljuq leader Tughril Beg (r. 1037–1063) took the title of sultan to signify his temporal power and control. He was accordingly invested by the caliph as "king of east and west." He and his first successors made various Iranian cities their capitals instead of Baghdad.

New Turkish tribes joined their ranks, and Saljuq arms extended Islamic control for the first time into the central Anatolian plateau at Byzantine expense.

EASTERN ISLAMIC LANDS	
875–999	Samanid dynasty, centered at Bukhara
945–1055	Buyid Shi'ite dynasty in Baghdad, controls caliphs
994–1186	Ghaznavid dynasty in Ghazna (modern Afghanistan) and Lahore (modern Pakistan), founded by Subuktigin (r. 976–997) and his son, Mahmud of Ghazna (r. 998–1030)
1020	Death of Firdawsi, compiler of *Shahnama*
ca. 1050	Death of al-Biruni, scientist and polyglot
1055–1194	Saljuq rule in Baghdad
1063–1092	Viziership of Nizam al-Mulk
1111	Death of al-Ghazzali, theologian and scholar
1219–1222	Gengis Khan plunders eastern Iran to Indus region
1258	Hulegu Khan conquers Baghdad
1261	Mamluk–Mongol treaty halts westward Mongol movement
1260–1335	Hulegu and his Il-Khanid successors rule Iran
1379–1405	Campaigns of Timur-i Lang (Tamerlane) devastate entire Islamic East
1405–1494	Timurids, successors of Tamerlane, rule in Transoxiana and Iran
1405–1447	Shahrukh, Timurid ruler at Herat; great patronage of the arts and philosophy

They even captured the Byzantine emperor in a victory in Armenia in 1071. They also conquered much of Syria and wrested Mecca and Medina from the Shi'ite Fatimids. The first Turkish rule in Asia Minor (Anatolia) dates from 1077, when the Saljuq governor there set up a separate sultanate of the Saljuqs of Rum ("Rome," i.e., Byzantium). These latter Saljuqs were not displaced until after 1300 by the Ottomans, another, still greater Turkish dynasty who would transform all of Asia Minor into Turkish territory (see Chapter 24).

The most notable figure of Saljuq rule was the vizier Nizam al-Mulk, who was the real power behind two sultans (r. 1063–1092). In his era, new roads and inns (caravanserais) for trade and pilgrimage were built, canals were dug, mosques and other public buildings were founded (including the first great Sunni *madrasas*, the personal projects of Nizam al-Mulk), and science and culture were patronized. He supported an extremely accurate calendar reform and himself wrote a major work on the art of governing, the *Siyasatnamah*. Before his murder by an Isma'ili Assassin in 1092, he appointed as professor in his Baghdad *madrasa* Muhammad al-Ghazzali (d. 1111), probably the greatest Muslim religious thinker of all time. He also patronized the mathematician and astronomer Umar Khayyam (d. 1123), whose Western fame rests on the poetry of his "quatrains," or *Ruba'iyat*.

After declining fortunes in the early twelfth century, Iranian Saljuq rule crumbled and by 1194 was wholly wiped away by another Turkish slave dynasty from Khwarizm in the lower Oxus basin. By 1200, these Khwarizm Shahs had built a large if shaky empire and sphere of influence covering Iran and Transoxiana. In the same era, the Abbasid caliph at Baghdad, Nasir (r. 1180–1225), tried to establish an independent caliphal state in Iraq. But neither his heirs nor the Khwarizm Shahs were long to survive in the face of events already unfolding on the Asian steppes.

The Mongol Age

MONGOLS AND ILKHANIDS. The building of a vast Mongol empire spanning Asia from China to Poland in the early thirteenth century proved to be momentous not only for Eastern Europe and China (see Chapter 10), but also for Islamic Eurasia and India. A Khwarizm Shah massacre of Mongol ambassadors brought down the full wrath of the Great Khan, Genghis, on the hapless Islamic east. He plundered mercilessly (1219–1222) from Transoxiana and Khorasan to the Indus, razing entire cities. The death of Genghis Khan (1227) and the division of his empire into four khanates under his four sons gave the Islamic world some respite. In 1255, Hulagu Khan, a grandson of Genghis, again led a massive army across the Oxus. Constantly adding Turkish troops to his forces (Mongol armies normally included many Turks), he went from victory to victory, destroying the Assassins of northwestern Iran along with every other Iranian state. In 1258, when the Abbasid caliph foolishly refused to surrender, Hulagu's troops smashed Baghdad's defenses and plundered it, killing at least eighty thousand men, women and children, including the caliph and his sons.

Quatrains (*Ruba'iyat*) from the Pen of Umar Khayyam (d. 1123)

Although Edward Fitzgerald's very beautiful and very free translation of Khayyam's Persian Ruba'iyat *is justly famous, the following more literal translation of three quatrains from the famous astronomer-poet also gives a good sense of the rather cynical but wry reflection evident in many of the ruba'iyat.*

As the stars have no increase but sorrow,
They restore nothing without taking away again;
If the unborn could know what we
Suffer from the universe, they would not come at all.

There was a water-drop, it joined the sea,
A speck of dust, it was fused with earth;

What of your entering and leaving this world?
A fly appeared, and disappeared.

Khayyam, if you are drunk on wine, enjoy it,
If you are with the tulip-cheeked, enjoy her:
Since the world's business ends in nothing,
Think that you are not and, while you are, enjoy it.

From Peter Avery and John Heath-Stubbs, *The Ruba'iyat of Omar Khayyam* (Harmondsworth, U.K.: Penguin, 1981), pp. 53, 56, 82.

Under the influence of his wife and many of his inner circle who were Nestorian Christians or Buddhists, Hulagu spared the Christians of Baghdad. He followed this policy in his other conquests, including the later sack of Aleppo, which, like Baghdad, resisted. When Damascus surrendered, Christians had what proved to be a vain hope of the impending fall of Mamluk Cairo and the consequent collapse of Islamic power. Hulagu's further drive west was slowed by rivalry with his kinsman Berke. A Muslim convert, Berke ruled the khanate of the Golden Horde, the Mongol state centered in southern Russia north of the Caucasus. He was in contact with the Mamluks, and some of his Mongol troops even fought with them in their major victory over Hulagu in Palestine (1260), which prevented Mongol penetration to Egypt. A treaty in 1261 between the Mamluk sultan and Berke established a formal alliance that confirmed the breakup of Mongol unity and of the autonomy of the four khanates: in China (the Yuan dynasty), in Iran (the Ilkhans), in Russia (the Golden Horde), and in Transoxiana (the Chagatays).

For his part, Hulagu gave allegiance to the new

Genghis Khan holding an audience. This Persian miniature shows the great conqueror and founder of the Mongol empire with members of his army and entourage as well as an apparent supplicant (right, center). [Bildarchiv Preussischer Kulturbesitz]

The Mongol Catastrophe

For the Muslim east, the sudden blitzkrieg of the Mongol hordes was an indescribable calamity. Something of the shock and despair of their reaction can be seen in the history of Ibn al-Athir (d. 1233), who lived during the time of their first onslaught. He writes in this selection about the year 1220–1221, when the Mongols ("Tartars") burst in on the eastern lands.

I say, therefore, that this thing involves the description of the greatest catastrophe and the most dire calamity (of the like of which days and nights are innocent) which befell all men generally, and the Muslims in particular; so that, should one say that the world, since God Almighty created Adam until now, hath not been afflicted with the like thereof, he would but speak the truth. For indeed history doth not contain aught which approaches or comes nigh unto it.

. . . .

. . . Now this is a thing the like of which ear hath not heard; for Alexander, concerning whom historians agree that he conquered the world, did not do so with such swiftness, but only in the space of about ten years; neither did he slay, but was satisfied that men should be subject to him. But these Tartars conquered most of the habitable globe and the best, the most flourishing and most populous part thereof, and that whereof the inhabitants were the most advanced in character and conduct, in about year; nor did any country escape their devastations which did not fearfully expect them and dread their arrival.

Moreover they need no commissariat, nor the conveyance of supplies, for they have with them sheep, cows, horses, and the like quadrupeds, the flesh of which they eat, [needing[naught else. As for their beasts which they ride, these dig into the earth with their hoofs and eat the roots of plants, knowing naught of barley. And so, when they alight anywhere, they have need of nothing from without. As for their religion, they worship the sun when it arises, and regard nothing as unlawful, for they eat all beasts, even dogs, pigs, and the like; nor do they recognise the marriage-tie, for several men are in marital relations with one woman, and if a child is born, it knows not who is its father.

Therefore Islâm and the Muslims have been afflicted during this period with calamities wherewith no people hath been visited. These Tartars (may God confound them!) came from the East, and wrought deeds which horrify all who hear of them, and which thou shalt, please God, see set forth in full detail in their proper connection. . . .

From Edward G. Browne, *A Literary History of Persia*, Vol. 2 (Cambridge, U.K.: Cambridge University Press, 1902), pp. 427–430, *passim*.

Great Khan of China. He and his heirs ruled the old Persian Empire from Azerbaijan for some seventy-five years as the Great Khan's viceroys (*Il-Khans*; from which Hulagu's line is named *Ilkhanid*). Here, as elsewhere, the rule of the Mongols did not eradicate the society that they inherited. Unlike the Arabs before them, they did not convert Muslim subject populations to their own faith. Instead, both their native paganism and their Buddhist and Christian leanings yielded to Muslim faith and practice, although religious tolerance remained the norm under their rule. After 1335, Ilkhanid rule fell prey to the familiar pattern of a gradual breaking away of provinces, and for fifty years, Iran was again fragmented.

TIMURIDS AND TURKOMANS. This situation prepared the way for a Turko-Mongol conquest from Trans-oxiana, under Timur-i Lang ("Timur the Lame," or "Tamerlane"). If Genghis Khan's much earlier invasions had been devastating, they could not match Timur's savage campaigns between 1379 and his death in 1405. These raids were not aimed at building a new, centralized empire so much as at sheer conquest. Timur was a Muslim convert evidently possessed of a strong sense of his role as the protector of commerce and the punisher of the injustices of regional petty tyrants and populist—often Shi'ite—extremist groups alike. Still, whatever his ends, they hardly justified his means. In successive campaigns, he swept everything before him: all of eastern Iran (1379–1385); western Iran, Armenia, the Caucasus, and upper Mesopotamia (1385–1387); Central Asia from Transoxiana to the Volga and as far as Moscow (1391–1395); southwestern Iran, Mesopotamia, and

The Gur-i-mir, the tomb of Timur in Samarkand. Built from 1490 to 1501 by Timur's grandson, this tile-covered structure houses the tombs of Shahrukh, Ulug Beg, and other Timurid heirs, as well as that of Timur himself. [Bettmann Archive]

Syria (1391–1393); North India (1398); and northern Syria and Anatolia (1400–1402). Timur's sole positive contributions seem to have been the buildings he sponsored at Samarkand, his capital. He left behind him death, disease, destruction, and political chaos over the entire eastern Islamic world, which did not soon recover. His was, however, the last great steppe invasion, for firearms soon took the steppe horsemen's advantage away forever.

Timur's sons shared his conquests with varying results in Transoxiana and Iran (1405–1494). The most successful Timurid was Shahrukh (r. 1405–1447), who ruled a united western and eastern Iran for a time. His capital, Herat, became an important center of Persian Islamic culture and Sunni piety. He patronized the famous Herat school of miniature painting as well as Persian literature and philosophy. The Timurids had to share the control of Iran with Turkoman dynasties in western Iran, once even losing Herat to one of them. They and the Turkomans were the last Sunnis to rule Iran. Both were eclipsed at the end of the fifteenth century by the rise of the militant Shi'ite dynasty of the Safavids, who ushered in a new era in the Iranian world (see Chapter 24).

Spread of Islam Beyond the Heartlands

The period from roughly 1000 to 1500 saw the spread of Islam as a lasting religious, cultural, and political force into new areas (see Map 16-2). Not only Eurasia

Building the castle of Khawarnaq, ca. 1494. This is one of the magnificent illustrations of the Khamsa, *or "Fire Poems" of Nizami, painted by the head of the great art academy of Herat, Bihzad (died ca. 1515). It was Shahrukh's patronage that led to this flourishing school of painting. [The British Library]*

MAP 16-2   ISLAMIC POLITICAL SOVEREIGNTY IN 1500   *Areas with either Islamic political control or majority Muslim populations. Southern Spain had been under Islamic control until 1492.*

from the Caspian and Black Seas north to Moscow (under the Golden Horde), but also Greece and the Balkans, through the Ottoman Turks, came under the control of Islamic governments (see Chapter 24). In the African and Asian worlds, India, Southeast Asia (Malaysia and Indonesia), inland West Africa, and coastal East Africa all became major spheres of Islamic political or commercial power, or both. In all these areas, conversion to Islam and the absorption of Islamic cultural influences came most often at the hands of Sufi orders. Merchants, too, were major agents of Islamization in these regions.

Conquest was a third (and demographically less important) means to the eventual conversion to Islam

of significant groups in the areas in question. Conversion reached sometimes only ruling elites and sometimes wider circles of a population. In India, Southeast Asia, and sub-Saharan Africa, significant numbers of the populace (often the majority) retained their inherited religious practices and faith. Therefore, if we treat these regions, specifically India, from the standpoint of the spread of Islam, it is not because Islam was the only, or even the major, element in Indian civilization during this period. It is rather that the coming of Islam signaled truly epochal changes in the history of important parts of South Asia.

INDIA

Establishment of Islam

Islamic civilization in India, like earlier Indian civilization, was formed by the creative interaction of in-

vading foreigners with indigenous peoples. Whereas the early Arab and Turkish invaders were a foreign Muslim minority, later Indian Muslims were as much Indian as Muslim. A new dimension was added thereby both to Indian and to Islamic civilization.

Early Spread of Islam into India

Well before the Ghaznavids came to the Panjab, Muslims were to be found even outside the original Arab conquest areas in Sind (see Map 16-3). Muslim merchants had settled in the port cities of Gujarat and southern India to profit from internal Indian trade as well as from trade with the Indies and China. Wherever Muslim traders went, converts to Islam were attracted by business advantages as well as by the straightforward ideology and practice of Islam and its egalitarian, supposedly "classless" ethic. Sufi orders had also gained a foothold in the south, giving today's southern Indian Muslims very old roots. Sufi piety

MAP 16-3   THE INDIAN SUBCONTINENT, 1000–1500   *Shown are major kingdoms and regions.*

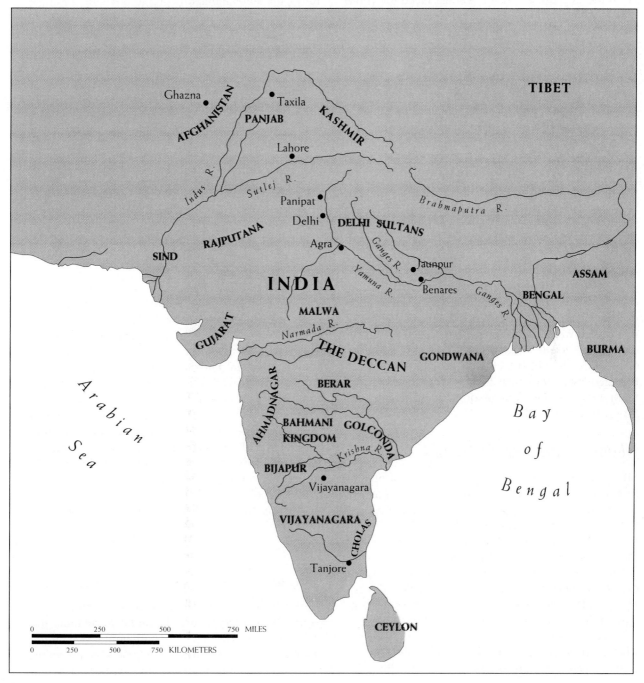

also drew converts in the north, especially when the Mongol devastation of Iran in the thirteenth century sent refugees streaming over the mountains into North India. Many of these refugee converts strengthened Islamic armies and administration as well as Muslim cultural and religious life in the subcontinent.

Muslim-Hindu Encounter

From the beginning, Muslim leaders faced the problem of ruling a country dominated by an utterly different culture and religion. Much as early Muslim rulers in Iran had given the Zoroastrians legal status as "People of the Book" (like Christians and Jews; see Chapter 13), the first Arab conquerors in Sind (711) had treated Hindus not as pagans but as "protected peoples" under Muslim sovereignty. These precedents gave the Ghaznavids and later Muslim rulers in India a pragmatic basis for coexistence with their Hindu subjects. These precedents did not, of course, remove Hindu resistance to Muslim rule.

The chief obstacle to Islamic expansion in India was the military prowess and tradition of a Hindu warrior class that emerged after the Hun and other Asian tribal invasions of the fifth and sixth centuries. Apparently descended from such invaders and the native warrior (Kshatriya) class of Hindus, this class was known from about the mid-seventh century as *Rajputs*. Rulers and fighters of northern Hindu society, they were a large group of clans bound together by a fierce warrior ethic and a patriotism evident in their adherence to Hindu culture and strong traditionalism. They fought the Muslim invaders with great tenacity, but their inability to unite eventually brought them under Muslim domination in the sixteenth century (see Chapter 24).

Islamic States and Dynasties

After the Ghaznavids and a brief interlude of Afghan rule, a series of Turkish-Afghan rulers known as the "Slave Sultans of Delhi" extended and maintained Islamic power over North India for nearly a century (1206–1290). Although after the first major figure of this dynasty, Iltutmish (r. 1211–1236), only one other sultan actually was a military slave, such slaves, or *mamluks*, figured prominently in the elites and leadership of the new regime. Five of Iltutmish's descendants ruled after him until 1266. The most independent and virogous of these was his daughter Raziyya, who ruled the sultanate for four years from 1337.

Four later Muslim dynasties—the Khaljis, the Tughluqs, the Sayyids, and the Lodis—carried on the Delhi sultanate through the fifteenth century. This series of Islamic reigns was interrupted only by several years of chaos following the Mongol-Turkish invasion and infamous devastation of Delhi by Timur in 1398, from which the city took decades to recover. Even before this devastating invasion, however, roughly from the latter part of the reign of the controversial Tughluqid ruler, Muhammad Ibn Tughluq (1324–1351), the sultanate had begun to break up. Over the next two centuries, until the advent of the Mughals in the sixteenth century, many smaller principalities split off from the Delhi sultanate and become partially or wholly independent sultanates, Rajput kingdoms, or small Hindu or Muslim principalities.

In fact, to some degree throughout its history, the sultanate's authority over its provincial governors—and especially the regional Hindu leaders and elites such as the Rajput princes—was a variable affair, even in the heartlands of its North Indian territory. Especially in the fourteenth and fifteenth centuries, the sultanate was often only the most prominent among many other sultanates and kingdoms of North India and the Deccan. Regional rule was the predominant reality across the length and breadth of the subcontinent, much as it had been before the Ghaznavids or the slave-sultans.

The most important of the independent Islamic states was that of the Bahmanids in the Deccan (1347–1527). These rulers were famous for the intellectual life of their court and for their architecture, as well as for their role in containing the powerful southern Indian Hindu state of Vijayanagar (1336–1565). (A Bahmani battle with the raja of Vijayanagar in 1366 had the first documented use of firearms and gunpowder in the subcontinent.) Most of the regional capitals provided fertile ground for cultural life. Jaunpur, to the north of Banaras, became, for example, an asylum for artists and intellectuals after Timur's sack of Delhi and boasted an impressive tradition of Islamic architecture. Kashmir was an independent sultanate from 1346 to 1589 and a center of literary activity where Indian works were also translated into Persian.

Religious and Cultural Accommodation

Despite the enduring division of the subcontinent into large and small political and administrative units, the first five hundred years after Mahmud of Ghazna proved to be an era in which Islam became an enduring and important, if still a minority, part of Indian

How the Hindus Differ from the Muslims

Al-Biruni (d. ca. 1050), probably the greatest scholar-scientist of medieval Islam, was born in Khwarizm in northeastern Iran. Much of his later life was spent at the court of Sultan Mahmud of Ghazna, and he accompanied Mahmud on various expeditions into northwestern India. Alongside his natural scientific work, he learned Sanskrit, made a deep study of India and the Hindus, and wrote a "History of India." The following selections from the first pages of this work show something of the reach and sophistication of his mind.

▶ *Compare this response to a clash of cultures to "Ammianus Marcellinus Describes the People Called Huns" in Chapter 6 and "Salvian the Priest Compares the Romans and the Barbarians" in Chapter 14.*

. . . The barriers which separate Muslims and Hindus rest on different causes.

First, they differ from us in everything which other nations have in common. And here we first mention the language, although the difference of language also exists between other nations. If you want to conquer this difficulty (i.e., to learn Sanskrit), you will not find it easy, because the language is of an enormous range, both in words and inflections, something like the Arabic, calling one and the same thing by various names, both original and derived, and using one and the same word for a variety of subjects, which, in order to be properly understood, must be distinguished from each other by various qualifying epithets.

. . . .

Secondly, they totally differ from us in religion, as we believe in nothing in which they believe, and *vice versá*. On the whole, there is very little disputing about theological topics among themselves; at the utmost, they fight with words, but they will never stake their soul or body or their property on religious controversy. On the contrary, all their fanaticism is directed against those who do not belong to them—against all foreigners. They call them *mleecha*, i.e.,

impure, and forbid having any connection with them, be it by intermarriage or any other kind of relationship, or by sitting, eating, and drinking with them, because thereby, they think, they would be polluted. They consider as impure anything which touches the fire and the water of a foreigner; and no household can exist without these two elements. Besides, they never desire that a thing which once has been polluted should be purified and thus recovered, as, under ordinary circumstances, if anybody or anything has become unclean, he or it would strive to regain the state of purity. They are not allowed to receive anybody who does not belong to them, even if he wished it, or was inclined to their religion. This, too, renders any connection with them quite impossible, and constitutes the widest gulf between us and them.

In the third place, in all manners and usages they differ from us to such a degree as to frighten their children with us, with our dress, and our ways and customs, and as to declare us to be devil's breed, and our doings as the very opposite of all that is good and proper. By the by, we must confess, in order to be just, that a similar depreciation of foreigners not only prevails among us and the Hindus, but is common to all nations towards each other.

From Edward C. Sachau, *Alberuni's India*, Vol. 1 (London: Kegan Paul, Trench, Truebner, 1910), pp. 17, 19, 20.

culture, most fully in the north, but also in the Deccan. The Delhi sultans, by virtue of good fortune and at least sometimes strength, were able, except for Timur's invasion, to fend off the Mongol danger, much as the Mamluks had in Egypt. They thereby provided a basic political and social framework within which Islam could take root. Although the ruling class remained a Muslim minority of Persianized Turks and Afghans set over a Hindu majority, conversion went on at various levels of society. Some Hindu converts came from the ruling classes who served the Muslim overlords. *Ghazis* ("warriors" for Islam), like the Turks of the same era in Anatolia, carried Islam by force of arms to pagan groups in eastern Bengal and Assam. Perhaps most significant, Sufi orders converted numerous Hindus among the lower classes.

A dervish ritual dance in which several adepts have been overcome and have swooned. Used as a technique of ecstasy, such dances and the dhikr, *or ritual chanting, have always been popular—and for some Muslims, always controversial. This seventeenth-century Mughal miniature shows the dancing adepts as well as spectators, among whom are two Europeans on the far left. [Victoria and Albert Museum, London]*

The Muslim aristocracy, at first mostly foreigners, were usually treated in Indian society as a separate caste group or groups. Similarly, when lower class or other Hindus converted, they were assimilated into "Muslim castes," usually identified by occupation.

Sanskrit had long been the Indian scholarly language and its lingua franca, but in this period its use as a lingua franca diminished. Some regional languages, such as Tamil in the south, began to gain status as literary and administrative languages, and Persian became the language of intellectual and cultural life for the ruling elites of North India until the collapse of Muslim power in the nineteenth century. However, the coming of substantial numbers of Muslims to the subcontinent led to the development of a new language composed of both Perso-Arabic Muslim elements and indigenous Indian elements that would ultimately gain wide use and influence in the subcontinent in modern times. This language, Urdu-Hindi, was a derivative form of the Sanskrit-related Prakrit dialects of the eastern Panjab and western Uttar Pradesh. It began to take shape not long after the initial influx of Muslims in the eleventh century (its first literary use goes back to the fourteenth century A.D.) and developed in response to the increasing need of Hindus and Muslims for a shared medium of communication. It became the lingua franca of the Delhi region and began to become a literary language of North Indian and Deccan Muslims in the seventeenth and eighteenth centuries. Indo-European in grammatical structure, it used Perso-Arabic forms, vocabulary, and script and was at first called *Hindi* ("Indian") or *Dakani* ("southern"), then in British times, often *Hindustani*. The name "Urdu" came into use also in the late seventeenth or eighteenth century and, in the course of the nineteenth century, with the growing problem of communalist tensions between Hindus and Muslims, came to serve as the name for one of two branches into which the language split. *Urdu* designated the branch both associated with Muslim culture and oriented toward its Perso-Arabic heritage in its further development, whereas *Hindi* was used for the branch associated with Hindu culture and oriented in its further development toward its Hindu Sanskritic heritage. Each would later become an official national language, Urdu for modern Pakistan and Hindi for modern India.

Indian Muslims—Arabs, Turks, Iranians, Mongols, Afghans, indigenous converts, or whatever—were always susceptible to Hindu influence (in language, marriage customs, and caste consciousness). However, they were never utterly absorbed into the varied

INDIA	
ca. 900–1300	Chola dynasty in southern India
1137	Death of Ramanuja
1206–1290	Slave-kings of Delhi
1290–1320	Khalji sultans of Delhi
1320–1413	Tughluqid sultans of Delhi
1414–1526	Sayyid sultans of Delhi
1336–1565	Hindu dynasty of Vijayanagar
1347–1527	Muslim Bahmanid dynasty in the Deccan
1398	Timur's sack of Delhi

but identifiable Hindu culture that predominated in the subcontinent, as earlier invaders had been. Their religious commitment and their identification of themselves culturally as Muslims seemed key to ensuring that they remained in some measure a group apart, conscious of their uniqueness in the Hindu world and proud to be distinct. The Muslim ruling classes saw themselves as the protectors and propagators of Islam in India. It is a measure of their sense of belonging to a larger Muslim community, the *Umma* (see Chapter 13), that despite their independence of the rest of the Islamic world, most of the sultans of Delhi sought recognition for their rule in India from the nominal Abbasid caliphs in Baghdad or, in Mamluk times, in Cairo.

Nevertheless, reciprocal influence of Muslims and Hindus was inevitable, especially in the sphere of popular piety. Sufi devotion had an appeal similar to that of Hindu *bhakti* movements (see Chapter 12), and each at times influenced the other. Some of India's most revered Sufi and *bhakti* saints date from the fourteenth and fifteenth centuries. During this period, various theistic mystics strove to transcend the mutual antagonism and exclusivism of the more rigorous Muslims and Hindus. They typically preached devotion to a God who saves His worshipers without regard either to Hindu caste obligations or to legalistic observance of Muslim orthopraxy. The poet-saints Ramananda (d. after 1400) and Kabir (d. ca. 1518) were the two most famous such reformers.

Other Traditions

These developments remind us that the history of India from 1000 to 1500 was far from being principally

that of the Muslims, although that is our focus here. This period was also important for the other religious and cultural communities of India that as a whole vastly outnumbered the Muslims. The Jain tradition continued to flourish, notably in Gujarat; Rajasthan; and, to the south, Karnataka. In the north, the Muslim conquests effectively ended by the eleventh century the already greatly diminished Indian Buddhist monastic and lay traditions. The role of the Muslim destruction of temples and monasteries in the virtual disappearance of Buddhism during this period has, however, been unduly emphasized. Buddhism was already waning in the seventh century as a major presence in Indian life, long before Islam became a factor in Indian history. On the other hand, the attraction to Islam of the merchant classes, which had traditionally supported Buddhism, may have been underestimated until now by modern scholarship. Still,

A bronze likeness of Ganesha from Vijayanagar (fifteenth or sixteenth century). This magnificent South Indian bronze figure is that of the elephant-headed god of learning and writing, who symbolizes the identity of the microcosm (the human) and the macrocosm (the elephant), a basic concept of Hindu thought. [Asian Art Museum of San Francisco, The Avery Brundage Collection B64B18]

the coming of Islam either dealt the *coup de grace* to Buddhism in India or coincided with the final stage of its reduction to the status of a small minority tradition.

Hindu religion and culture continued to flourish, even in areas of Muslim control, as the continuing social and religious importance of the Brahmans and the popularity of *bhakti* (devotional) movements throughout India attest. In Brahmanic religious learning, this was an age of scholasticism that produced many commentaries and manuals, but few seminal works. *Bhakti* creativity was much greater. The great Hindu Vaishnava Brahman, Ramanuja (d. 1137), provided a theological basis for *bhakti* devotion, reconciling its ideas with the classical Upanishadic Hindu worldview in the Vedantin tradition. He rejected, however, Upanishadic and Vedantin monism in favor of a qualified dualism that gave great scope to the theistic devotionalism that characterizes Vaishnavite piety. Important examples of *bhakti* movements are the Shaivite and Vaishnavite traditions associated, respectively, with the *bhakti* poets of the *nayanars* and *alvars* in Tamilnad. *Bhakti* piety underlies the masterpiece of Hindu mystical love poetry, Jayadeva's *Gita Govinda* (twelfth century), which is devoted to Krishna, the most important of Vishnu's incarnations.

The south continued to be the center of Hindu cultural, political, and religious activity. Of several important dynastic states in the south during this age, the foremost was that of the Cholas (fl. ca. 900–1300). Aside from their military exploits and long political ascendancy, this dynasty can claim lasting fame purely for the school of bronze sculpture that they patronized at their capital of Tanjore. Their mightiest successor, the kingdom of Vijayanagar (1336–1565), subjugated the entire south in the fourteenth century and held out against its Muslim foes longer than had any other kingdom. Vijayanagar itself was one of India's most lavishly developed cities and a center of the cult of Shiva before its destruction by the Bahmanid sultan of the Deccan.

The Islamic Heartlands and India, 1000–1500, in World Perspective

This period in both Islamic and other Asian territories is difficult to characterize simply. The spread of Islam to new peoples or their ruling elites has been taken as a theme of this chapter. However, we have also seen that the history of Islam in India is hardly the history of the whole. The vast conquests and movements of the Mongols and Central Asian Turks across inner Asia were among the most striking developments in world history in this period; they often had cataclysmic effects on Chinese, South Asian, West Asian, and Eastern European societies and states. These conquests and migrations did not build lasting major states or civilizations, but they did bring destruction of existing orders and forced the further migration of many people who fled their advance. They also contributed, however unintentionally, new and often significant human resources to existing civilizations like those of China and the Islamic heartlands.

During this age, Islam became a truly international tradition of religious, political, and social values and institutions. It did so by being highly adaptable and open to "indigenization" in the seemingly hostile contexts of polytheistic Hindu and African societies (see Chapter 19). Also during this age very distinct traditions of art, language, and literature, for all their local, regional, or national diversity, became intelligible and identifiable parts of a larger whole defined by a Muslim identity. Islamic civilization had nothing of the territorial contiguity or homogeneous linguistic and cultural traditions of either Chinese or Japanese civilization. Nevertheless, the Islamic world was an international reality in which a Muslim could travel and meet other Muslims of radically diverse backgrounds with much common ground for understanding.

Indian traditional culture was not, like the Islamic, bound up with an expanding, missionary religious tradition. Yet in this age, Hindu kingdoms developed and throve in Indonesia. Buddhism, even while dwindling into a small minority tradition in its Indian homeland, was expanding across much of Central and eastern Asia, thereby solidifying its place as an international missionary tradition. Christianity, by contrast, was not rapidly expanding in Africa, Asia, or Europe; but by 1500 its western European branch was poised on the brink of internal revolution and international proselytism that would begin with or soon after the voyages of discovery of the late fifteenth and early sixteenth centuries.

At the beginning of this period (1000–1500), Europe was almost a backwater of culture and power by comparison with major Islamic or Hindu states, let alone those of China and Japan. At its close, however, European civilization was riding the crest of a cultural renaissance, enjoying economic and political growth, and starting the global exploration that would turn into a flood of imperial expansion and affect most of the rest of the globe. Neither Islamic, Indian, African, Chinese, nor Japanese culture and society were so radically changed or changing in their basic ideas and institutions as were those of Western Europe over these five hundred years.

Suggested Reading

THE ISLAMIC HEARTLANDS

C. E. Bosworth, *The Islamic Dynasties: A Chronological and Genealogical Handbook* (1967). A handy reference work for dynasties and families important to Islamic history in all periods and places.

J. A. Boyle, ed., *The Cambridge History of Iran*, Vol. 5, *The Saljuq and Mongol Periods* (1968). Useful and reasonably detailed articles on political, social, religious, and cultural developments.

P. K. Hitti, *History of the Arabs*, 8th ed. (1964). Still a useful English resource, largely for factual detail. See especially Part IV, "The Arabs in Europe: Spain and Sicily."

M. G. S. Hodgson, *The Expansion of Islam in the Middle Periods*, Vol. 2 of *The Venture of Islam*. 3 vols. (1964). The strongest of Hodgson's monumental three-volume survey of Islamic civilization and the only English work of its kind to give the period 945–1500 such broad and unified coverage.

A. Hourani, *A History of the Arab Peoples* (1991). The newest survey history and the best, at least for the Arab Islamic world.

B. Lewis, ed., *Islam and the Arab World* (1976). A large-format, heavily illustrated volume with many excellent articles on diverse aspects of Islamic (not simply Arab, as the misleading title indicates) civilization through the premodern period.

D. Morgan, *The Mongols* (1986). A recent and readable survey history.

J. J. Saunders, *A History of Medieval Islam* (1965). A brief and simple, if sketchy introductory survey of Islamic history to the Mongol invasions.

D. Sourdel, *Medieval Islam*, trans. by W. M. Watt (1983). The synthetic, interpretive chapters on Islam and the political and social orders (4, 5), and on towns and art (6), are especially helpful.

B. Spuler, *The Mongols in History*, trans. by Geoffrey Wheeler (1971). A short introductory survey of Mongol history, of which Chapters 2–5 are most relevant.

B. Spuler, *The Muslim World: A Historical Survey*, trans. by F. R. C. Bagley (1960). 3 vols. Volumes I and II are handy references offering a highly condensed chronicle of Islamic history from Muhammad through the fifteenth century.

INDIA

W. T. de Bary et al., comp., *Sources of Indian Tradition*, 2nd ed. (1958). Vol. I, *From the Beginning to 1800*, ed. and rev. by Ainslie T. Embree (1988). Excellent selections from a wide variety of Indian texts, with good introductions to chapters and individual selections.

S. M. Ikram, *Muslim Civilization in India* (1964). The best short survey history, covering the period 711 to 1857.

R. C. Majumdar, gen. ed., *The History and Culture of the Indian People*, Vol. VI, *The Delhi Sultanate*, 3rd ed. (1980). A comprehensive political and cultural account of the period in India.

M. Mujeeb, *The Indian Muslims* (1967). The best cultural study of Islamic civilization in India as a whole, from its origins onward.

F. Robinson, ed., *The Cambridge History of India, Pakistan, Bangladesh, Sri Lanka, Nepal, Bhutan, and the Maldives* (1989). A recent and very helpful quick reference source with brief but well-done survey essays on a wide range of topics relevant to South Asian history down to the present.

A. Wink, *Al-Hind: The Making of the Indo-Islamic World*, Vol. 1 (1991). The first of five promising volumes to be devoted to the Indo-Islamic world's history. This volume treats the seventh to eleventh century.

The World in Transition

etween 1500 and 1800, the major centers of world civilization achieved political organization and stability that in some cases endured into the present century. This period also witnessed a shift in the balance of world political and economic power toward Europe. That shift was anything but inevitable. It was the result of paths taken by Europeans and not taken by the peoples and governments of other areas of the world.

Sixteenth-century Japan was torn by feudal wars among its various small states and regions. This civil conflict eroded the manorial social structure. The adoption of the spear and then the musket in place of the sword allowed the development of foot-soldier armies that displaced the mounted samurai. By approximately 1600, however, a new political regime was establishing itself on the basis of a "feudal" society involving complex vassal–lord relationships in many, although not all, ways similar to those in medieval Europe. Tokugawa Ieyasu established his government in Edo (now Tokyo). Through a series of land transfers and confiscations, he surrounded himself with unquestionably loyal retainers and placed those of less certain loyalty at a far geographical remove from his capital. He and his successors required their vassals to send their families to live as virtual hostages near the court in Edo. Finally, Tokugawa Japan adopted a policy of isolation from the rest of the world. Although stable and relatively prosperous, Japan remained separated from the larger world from the 1630s until the middle of the nineteenth century.

Spared comparable civil strife, China entered on an epoch of remarkable strength, expansion, and cultural achievement. The Ming and Ch'ing dynasties ruled for more than five centuries, and only a short period of strife accompanied the transfer of power from one to the other in 1644. The emperors of both dynasties governed in an absolute manner. The bureaucracy—referred to as *mandarins* by the Jesuits, who came to China in the sixteenth century—was chosen meritocratically through a complex series of examinations, and it governed efficiently. The population of China expanded steadily. China experienced a third commercial revolution. Chinese shipping expanded. Although a truly national economy did not emerge, China possessed several regional economies, each as large as that of a major European national state. A banking system spread through the country to foster commerce. What did not occur in China, for all its commercial enterprise, was the development of industrialism. Nonetheless, at the end of this era, China appeared to be a very strong, stable nation. As in Japan, Confucian teachings had become ever more influential.

In 1550, over a century of continued political and military strength lay before the Islamic world. The Ottoman Empire was at the time perhaps the most powerful military state in the world. The Safavids securely governed Iran as would the

Mughals India a few years later. However, by the middle of the seventeenth century, the power of all three empires was on the wane even as their cultural vitality was still immense. The growing military and naval strength of Europe defeated the Ottoman Turks at the sea battle of Lepanto in 1571 and in numerous land engagements during the seventeenth century. The final Turkish siege of Vienna failed in 1683. In Iran, the intense religiosity of the Shi'ite Safavids led to the neglect of political and military structures and, consequently, to difficulty in halting aggression from the Turks. At the same time, a distinctive mode of Shi'ite pietism arose among the populace in Iran. The Mughal Empire in India experienced a slow but steady decline after the late seventeenth century. By the battle of Plassey in 1757, the British East India Company had established a position of strength from which, within less than a century, Britain would come to govern the entire Indian subcontinent.

Early in the sixteenth century, Western Europe began to be divided between Protestantism and Roman Catholicism. The sectarian splintering that has resulted in hundreds of modern Protestant denominations also began at this time. Even within Catholicism, deep divisions developed between Catholics who favored traditional practices and those who championed the reforms of the Counter-Reformation and the Jesuits. A century-and-a-half of religious war and theological conflict followed. Rulers made the most of these divisions to consolidate their territories politically. Confessionalization (that is, strict enforcement of a particular "orthodox" religious belief and practice) went hand in hand with the creation of modern Western states.

Four factors account largely for this momentous shift in the cultural balance of the Western world. First, the new monarchies that had arisen in the late Middle Ages, particularly in France, England, and Spain, now successfully unified their realms. Between 1500 and the middle of the eighteenth century, those monarchs learned to tame their aristocracies, to collect taxes efficiently, and to build effective armies and navies. Second, in league with the commercial sectors of their national economies, the monarchs and their bureaucrats encouraged voyages of commercial expansion and discovery. Through those voyages, Europeans penetrated markets across the globe. They also conquered and colonized the American continents and thereby Europeanized two vast, rich land masses much larger than Europe itself. Third, during the seventeenth century, European thinkers carried out new intellectual explorations that culminated in the Scientific Revolution. The new knowledge and methods of rational investigation of physical nature permitted them to develop their technological skills more fully. As a consequence, the fourth factor came into play, as Europeans, and most particularly the British, achieved an early foundation of industrial manufacturing that would permit further domination of world markets with inexpensive consumer goods.

	EUROPE	NEAR EAST/INDIA
1500	*1517–1555* Protestant Reformation *1533–1584* Ivan the Terrible of Russia reigns *1540* Jesuit Order founded by Ignatius Loyola *1543–1727* Scientific Revolution *1556–1598* Philip II of Spain reigns *1558–1603* Elizabeth I of England reigns *1562–1598* French wars of religion *1581* The Netherlands declares its independence from the Spanish Habsburgs *1588* Defeat of the Spanish Armada *1589–1610* Henry IV, Navarre, founds Bourbon dynasty of France	*1500–1722* Safavid Shi'ite rule in Iran *1512–1520* Ottoman ruler Selim I *1520–1566* Ottoman ruler Suleiman the Magnificent *1525–1527* Babur founds Mughal dynasty in India *1540* Hungary under Ottoman rule *1556–1605* Akbar the Great of India reigns *1571* Battle of Lepanto; Ottomans defeated *ca. 1571–1640* Safavid philosopher-writer Mullah Sadra *1588–1629* Shah Abbas I of Iran reigns
1600	*1618–1648* Thirty Years' War *1640–1688* Frederick William, the Great Elector, reigns in Brandenburg–Prussia *1642–1646* Puritan Revolution in England *1643–1715* Louis XIV of France reigns *1682–1725* Peter the Great of Russia reigns *1688* Glorious Revolution in England *1690* "Second Treatise of Civil Government," by John Locke	*1605–1657* Period of religious toleration in Mughal Empire, India *1628–1657* Shah Jahan reigns; builds Taj Mahal as mausoleum for his beloved wife *1646* Founding of Maratha empire *1648* Delhi becomes capital of Mughal Empire *1658–1707* Shah Aurangzeb, the "World Conqueror," reigns in India; end of religious toleration toward Hindus; beginning Mughal decline *1669–1683* Last military expansion by Ottomans: 1669, seize Crete; 1670s, the Ukraine; 1683, Vienna
1700	*1701* Act of Settlement provides for Protestant succession to English throne *1702–1713* War of Spanish Succession *1740–1748* War of Austrian Succession *1756–1763* Seven Years' War *ca. 1750* Industrial Revolution begins in England *1772* First partition of Poland *1793* and *1795* Last two partitions of Poland	*1700* Sikhs and Marathas bring down Mughal Empire *1708* British East India Company and New East India Company merge *1722* Last Safavid ruler forced to abdicate *1724* Rise in the Deccan of the Islamic state of Hyderabad *1725* Nadir Shah of Afghanistan becomes ruler of Persia *1739* Persian invasion of northern India, by Nadir Shah *1748–1761* Ahmad Shah Durrani of Afghanistan invades India *1757* British victory at Plassey, in Bengal

1500–1800 Commercial revolution in Ming-Ch'ing China; trade with Europe; flourishing of the novel *1543* Portuguese arrive in Japan *1568–1600* Era of unification follows end of Warring States Era in Japan *1587* Spanish arrive in Japan *1588* Hideyoshi's sword hunt in Japan *1592–1598* Ming´ troops battle Hideyoshi's army in Korea	*1506* East coast of Africa under Portuguese domination *1507* Mozambique founded by Portuguese *1517* Spanish crown authorizes slave trade to its South American colonies; rapid increase in importation of slaves to the New World *1554–1659* Sa'did Sultanate in Morocco *1575* Union of Bornu and Kanem by Idris Alawma (r. 1575–1610); Kanem-Bornu state the most fully Islamic in West Africa *1591* Moroccan army defeats Songhai army; Songhai Empire collapses	*1519* Conquest of the Aztecs by Cortes; Aztec ruler, Montezuma (r. 1502–1519) killed; Tenochtitlán destroyed *1529* Mexico City becomes capital of the Viceroyalty of New Spain *1533* Pizarro begins his conquest of the Incas *1536* Spanish under Mendoza arrive in Argentina *1544* Lima becomes capital of the Viceroyalty of Peru *1584* Sir Walter Raleigh sends expedition to Roanoke Island (North Carolina)
1600 Tokugawa Ieyasu wins battle of Sekigahara, completes unification of Japan *1600–1868* Tokugawa shogunate in Edo *1630s* Seclusion adopted as national policy in Japan *1644–1694* Bashō, Japanese poet *1644–1911* Ch'ing (Manchu) dynasty in China *1661–1722* K'ang Hsi reign in China *1673–1681* Revolt of southern generals in China *1699* British East India Company arrives in China	*1600s* English, Dutch, and French enter the slave trade; slaves imported to sugar plantations in the Caribbean *1619* First African slaves in North America land in Virginia *1652* First Cape Colony settlement of Dutch East India Company *1660–1856* Omani domination of East Africa; Omani state centered in Zanzibar; 1698, takes Mozambique from Portuguese	*1607* The London Company establishes Jamestown Colony (Virginia) *1608* Champlain founds Quebec
1701 Forty-seven rōnin incident in Japan *1716–1733* Reforms of Tokugawa Yoshimune in Japan *1737–1795* Reign of Ch'ien Lung in China *1742* Christianity banned in China *1784* American traders arrive in China *1787–1793* Matsudaira Sadanobu reforms in Japan *1798* White Lotus Rebellion in China	*1702* Asiento Guinea Trade Company founded for slave trade between Africa and the Americas *1700s* Transatlantic slave trade at its height *1741–1856* United Sultanate of Oman and Zanzibar *1754–1817* Usman Dan Fodio, founder of sultanate in northern and central Nigeria; the Fulani become the ruling class in the region *1762* End of Funj Sultanate in eastern Sudanic region	*1776–1781* American Revolution *1783–1830* Simón Bolívar, Latin American soldier, statesman *1791* First ten amendments to U.S. Constitution (Bill of Rights) ratified *1791* Negro slave revolt in French Santo Domingo *1791* Canada Constitution Act divides the country into Upper and Lower Canada

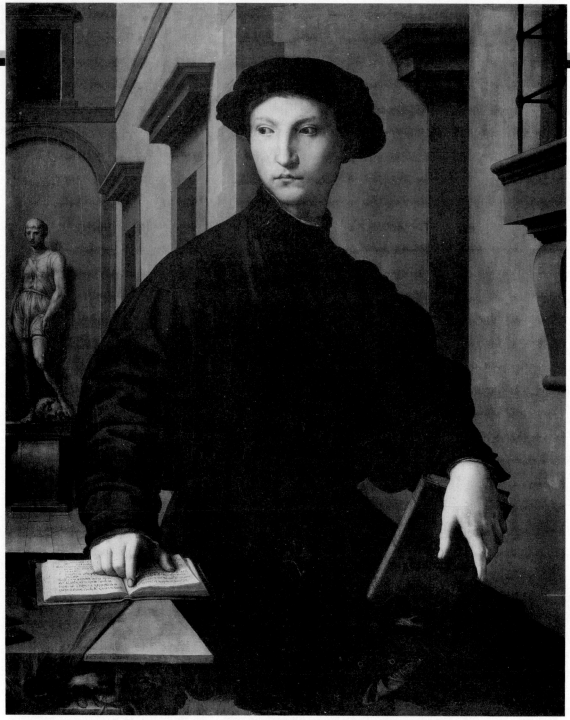

Portrait of the young Ugolino Martelli by Agnolo di Cosimo di Mariano, called Bronzino (1503–1572). Martelli was a prominent humanist scholar. Bronzino, court artist and sculptor for Cosimo I de' Medici, Duke of Florence, was an exemplar of Florentine mannerism. [Staatliche Museen zu Berlin, Preussischer Kulturbesitz, Gemäldegalerie. Photo: Jorg P. Anders]

The Late Middle Ages and the Renaissance in the West (1300–1527)

17

The late Middle Ages and the Renaissance mark a time of unprecedented calamity and of bold new beginnings in Europe. There was the Hundred Years' War between England and France (1337–1453), an exercise in seemingly willful self-destruction, made even more terrible in its later stages by the introduction of gunpowder and the invention of heavy artillery. There was almost universal bubonic plague, known to contemporaries as the Black Death. Between 1348 and 1350, waves of plague killed as much as one-third of the population in many regions and transformed many pious Christians into believers in the omnipotence of death. There was a great schism within the Catholic Church that lasted thirty-seven years (1378–1415) and saw by 1409 the election of no fewer than three competing popes and colleges of cardinals. Furthermore, there was the onslaught of the Turks, who in 1453 marched seemingly invincibly through Constantinople and toward the west. As their political and religious institutions buckled; as disease, bandits, and wolves ravaged their cities in the wake of war; and as Muslim armies gathered at their borders, Europeans beheld what seemed to be the imminent total collapse of Western civilization.

But if the late Middle Ages saw unprecedented chaos, it also witnessed a rebirth that would continue into the seventeenth century. Two modern Dutch scholars have employed the same word (*Herfsttij,* "harvesttide") with different connotations to describe the period, one interpreting the word as a "waning" or "decline" (Johan Huizinga), the other as a true "harvest" (Heiko Oberman). If something was dying away, some ripe fruit and seed grain were also being gathered. The late Middle Ages were a creative breaking up.

It was during this period that such scholars as Marsilius of Padua, William of Ockham, and Lorenzo Valla produced lasting criticisms of medieval assumptions about the nature of God, humankind, and

MAP 17-1 THE HUNDRED YEARS' WAR *The Hundred Years' War went on intermittently from the late 1330s to 1453. These maps show the remarkable English territorial gains up to the sudden and decisive turning of the tide of battle in favor of the French by the forces of Joan of Arc in 1429.*

society. It was a period in which kings worked through parliaments and clergy through councils to place lasting limits on the pope's temporal power. The principle that sovereigns (in this case, the pope) are accountable to the bodies of which they are the head was established. The arguments used by conciliarists (advocates of the judicial superiority of a Church council over a pope) to establish papal accountability to the body of the faithful provided an example for the secular sphere. National sovereigns, who also had an independent tradition of ruler accountability in Roman law, were reminded of their responsibility to the body politic.

The late Middle Ages also saw an unprecedented scholarly renaissance. Italian Humanists made a full recovery of classical knowledge and languages and set in motion educational reforms and cultural changes that would spread throughout Europe in the fifteenth and sixteenth centuries. In the process, the Italian Humanists invented, for all practical purposes, critical historical scholarship and exploited a new fifteenth-century invention, the "divine art" of printing with movable type. It was during this period that the vernacular, the local language, began to take its place alongside Latin, the international language, as a widely used literary and political language. The independent nation-states of Europe progressively superseded the universal Church as the community of highest allegiance, as patriotism and incipient nationalism became a major force. Nations henceforth "transcended" themselves not by journeys to Rome but by competitive voyages to the Far East and the Americas, as the age of global exploration opened.

A time of both waning and harvest, constriction (in the form of nationalism) and expansion (in the sense of world exploration), the late Middle Ages saw medieval culture grudgingly give way to the ages of the Renaissance and the Reformation.

Political and Social Breakdown

Hundred Years' War and Rise of National Sentiment

From May 1337 to October 1453, England and France periodically engaged in what was for both a futile and devastating war (see Map 17-1).

CAUSES OF THE WAR. The conflict was initiated by the English king Edward III (r. 1327–1377), who held a strong claim to the French throne as the grandson of Philip the Fair (r. 1285–1314). When Charles VI (r. 1322–1328), the last of Philip the Fair's surviving sons, died, Edward, who was only fifteen at the time, asserted his right to Capetian succession. The French barons, however, were not willing to place an English king on the French throne. They chose instead Philip VI of Valois (r. 1328–1350), the first of a new French dynasty that was to rule into the sixteenth century.

In the background were other equally important causes. For one thing, the English king held certain French territories as fiefs from the French king. Thus he was, in law, a vassal of the French king. As Philip's vassal, Edward was theoretically if not in fact committed to support policies detrimental to England, if his French lord so commanded.

Still another factor that fueled the conflict was French support of the Bruces of Scotland, strong opponents of the English overlordship of Scotland who had won a victory over the English in 1314. The French and the English were also at this time quarreling over Flanders, a French fief, yet also a country whose towns were completely dependent for their livelihood on imported English wool.

Finally, there were decades of prejudice and animosity between the French and the English people, who constantly confronted one another on the high seas and in port towns. Taken together, these various factors made the Hundred Years' War a struggle to the death for national control and identity.

FRENCH WEAKNESS.   Throughout the conflict, France was statistically the stronger: It had three times the population of England, was far the wealthier, and fought on its own soil. Yet for the greater part of the conflict, until after 1415, the major battles ended in often stunning English victories. France was not as strong as it appeared. It was internally disunited by social conflict and the absence of a centralized system of taxation to fund the war. As a tool to provide him money, the king raised a representative council of towns and nobles that came to be known in subsequent years as the *Estates General.* It convened in 1355, and although it levied taxes at the king's request, its members also used the king's plight to enhance their own regional rights and privileges. France, unlike England, still struggled in the fourteenth century to make the transition from a fragmented feudal society to a more centralized "modern" state. Beyond this lay the clear fact of English military superiority, due to the greater discipline of its infantry and the rapid-fire and long-range capability of that ingeniously simple weapon, the English longbow, which could shoot six arrows a minute with a force sufficient to pierce an inch of wood or the armor of a knight at two hundred yards. Finally, French weakness was related in no small degree to the comparative mediocrity of its royal leadership during the Hundred Years' War.

Progress of the War

The war had three major stages of development, each ending with a seemingly decisive victory by one or the other side.

CONFLICT DURING THE REIGN OF EDWARD III.   By slapping an embargo on English wool to Flanders, Edward sparked urban rebellions by the merchants and the trade guilds. The Flemish cities, led by Ghent, revolted against the French. Having at first taken as neutral a stand as possible in the conflict, these cities, whose economies faced total collapse without imported English wool, signed a half-hearted alliance with England in January 1340, acknowledging Edward as king of France.

Edward defeated the French fleet in the first great battle of the war in the Bay of Sluys on June 23, 1340. But his subsequent effort to invade France by way of Flanders failed, largely because his allies proved undependable. As a stalemate developed, a truce was struck that was more or less observed until 1346. In that year, Edward attacked Normandy and won a series of easy victories that were capped by that at Crécy in August. This victory was quickly followed by the seizure of Calais, which the English held thereafter for over two hundred years. Both sides employed scorched-earth tactics and completely devastated the areas of conflict.

Exhaustion and the onset of the Black Death forced a second truce in late 1347, and the war entered a lull until 1355. On September 19, 1356, the English won their greatest victory near Poitiers, routing the noble cavalry and even taking the French king, John II the Good (r. 1350–1364), captive back to England. After the English victory at Poitiers, there was a complete breakdown of political order in France. Disbanded soldiers from both sides became professional bandits, roaming the land, pillaging areas untouched by the war, and bringing disaster almost as great as the war itself.

Power in France lay with the privileged classes, which expressed their will through the representative assembly of the Estates General. Unlike the English

Parliament, which represented the interests of a comparatively unified English nobility, the French Estates General was a many-tongued lobby, a forum for the diverse interests of the new-rich urban commercial and industrial classes, the territorial princes, and the clergy. Such a diverse body was no instrument for effective government.

On May 9, 1360, another milestone of the war was reached when England forced the Peace of Bretigny on the French. This agreement declared Edward's vassalage to the king of France ended and affirmed Edward's sovereignty over English territories in France. France also pledged to pay a ransom of three million gold crowns to win King John's release. In return, Edward renounced his claim to the French throne. Such a partition of French territorial control was completely unrealistic, and sober observers on both sides knew that it could not long continue.

FRENCH DEFEAT AND THE TREATY OF TROYES. After Edward's death, the English war effort lessened considerably, partly as a result of domestic problems within England. In 1396, France and England signed still another truce, this time backed up by the marriage of Richard II to the daughter of the French king, Charles VI (r. 1380–1422). This truce lasted through the reign of Richard's successor, Henry IV of Lancaster (r. 1399–1413). His successor, Henry V (r. 1413–1422), reheated the war with France by taking advantage of the internal French turmoil created by the rise

This painting of Joan of Arc (1412–1431) in the National Archives of Paris is believed to be a contemporary portrait. [Service Photographique des Archives Nationales]

THE HUNDRED YEARS' WAR (1337–1443)	
1340	English victory at Bay of Sluys
1346	English victory at Crécy and seizure of Calais
1347	Black Death strikes
1356	English victory at Poitiers
1358	*Jacquerie* disrupts France
1360	Peace of Bretigny recognizes English holdings in France
1381	English Peasants' Revolt
1415	English victory at Agincourt
1422	Treaty of Troyes proclaims Henry VI ruler of both England and France
1429	Joan of Arc leads French to victory at Orléans
1431	Joan of Arc executed as a heretic
1453	War ends; English retain only the coastal town of Calais

to power of the duchy of Burgundy under John the Fearless (r. 1404–1419).

Henry V struck hard in Normandy, and his army routed the numerically stronger but tactically less shrewd French royal forces at Agincourt on October 25, 1415. By 1419, the Burgundians had allied with the English. With Burgundian support, France became Henry V's for the taking, at least in the short run. The Treaty of Troyes in 1420 disinherited the legitimate heir to the French throne, the dauphin (a title used by the king's oldest son), the future Charles VII, and made Henry V successor to the mad Charles VI. When Henry V and Charles VI died within months of one another in 1422, the infant Henry VI of England was proclaimed in Paris to be king of both France and England under the regency of the duke of Bedford. The dream of Edward III, the pretext for continuing the great war, was now, for the moment, realized: In

1422, an English king was the proclaimed ruler of France. The dauphin went into retreat in Bourges, where, on the death of his father, he became Charles VII to most Frenchmen, who ignored the Treaty of Troyes.

JOAN OF ARC AND THE WAR'S CONCLUSION.   Joan of Arc (1412–1431), a peasant from Domremy, presented herself to Charles VII in March 1429. When she declared that the King of Heaven had called her to deliver besieged Orléans from the English, Charles was understandably skeptical. But the dauphin and his advisers, in retreat from what seemed to be a completely hopeless war, were desperate and were willing to try anything to reverse French fortunes on the battlefield. Certainly the deliverance of Orléans, a city strategic to the control of the territory south of the Loire, would be a godsend. Charles's desperation overcame his skepticism, and he gave Joan his leave to try and rescue the city.

Circumstances worked perfectly to Joan's advantage. The English force was already exhausted by its six-month siege of Orléans and actually at the point of withdrawal when Joan arrived with fresh French troops. After the English were repulsed at Orléans, there followed a succession of French victories that were popularly attributed to Joan. Joan truly deserved much of the credit, but not, however, because she was a military genius. She gave the French people and armies something that military experts could not: a unique inspiration and an almost mystical confidence in themselves as a nation. Within a few months of the liberation of Orléans, Charles VII received his crown in Rheims and ended the nine-year "disinheritance" prescribed by the Treaty of Troyes.

Charles forgot his liberator as quickly as he had embraced her. Joan was captured by the Burgundians in May 1430, and although the French king was in a position to secure her release, he did little to help her. She was turned over to the Inquisition in English-

Joan of Arc Refuses to Recant Her Beliefs

Joan of Arc, threatened with torture, refused to recant her beliefs and instead defended the instructions she received from the voices that spoke to her. Here is a part of her self-defense from the contemporary trial record.

On Wednesday, May 9th of the same year [1431], Joan was brought into the great tower of the castle of Rouen before us the said judges and in the presence of the reverend father, lord abbot of St. Cormeille de Compiegne, of masters Jean de Châtillon and Guillaume Erart, doctors of sacred theology, of André Marguerie and Nicolas de Venderes, archdeacons of the church of Rouen, of William Haiton, bachelor of theology, Aubert Morel, licentiate in canon law; Nicolas Loiseleur, canon of the cathedral of Rouen, and master Jean Massieu.

And Joan was required and admonished to speak the truth on many different points contained in her trial which she had denied or to which she had given false replies, whereas we possessed certain information, proofs, and vehement presumptions upon them. Many of the points were read and explained to her, and she was told that if she did not confess them truthfully she would be put to the torture, the instruments of which were shown to her all ready in the tower. There were also present by our instruction

men ready to put her to the torture in order to restore her to the way and knowledge of truth, and by this means to procure the salvation of her body and soul which by her lying inventions she exposed to such grave perils.

To which the said Joan answered in this manner: "Truly if you were to tear me limb from limb and separate my soul from my body, I would not tell you anything more: and if I did say anything, I should afterwards declare that you had compelled me to say it by force." Then she said that on Holy Cross Day last she received comfort from St. Gabriel; she firmly believes it was St. Gabriel. She knew by her voices whether she should submit to the Church, since the clergy were pressing her hard to submit. Her voices told her that if she desired Our Lord to aid her she must wait upon Him in all her doings. She said that Our Lord has always been the master of her doings, and the Enemy never had power over them. She asked her voices if she would be burned and they answered that she must wait upon God, and He would aid her.

The Trial of Jeanne D'Arc, trans. by W. P. Barrett (New York: Gotham House, 1932), pp. 303–304.

held Rouen. The Burgundians and the English wanted Joan publicly discredited, believing this would also discredit her patron, Charles VII, and might demoralize French resistance. The skilled inquisitors broke the courageous "Maid of Orléans" in ten weeks of merciless interrogation, and she was executed as a relapsed heretic on May 30, 1431. Charles reopened Joan's trial at a later date, and she was finally declared innocent of all the charges against her on July 7, 1456, twenty-five years after her execution. In 1920, the Church declared her a saint.

Charles VII and Philip the Good made peace in 1435, and a unified France, now at peace with Burgundy, progressively forced the English back. By 1453, the date of the war's end, the English held only the coastal enclave of Calais.

During the Hundred Years' War, there were sixty-eight years of at least nominal peace and forty-four of hot war. The political and social consequences were lasting. Although the war devastated France, it also awakened the giant of French nationalism and hastened the transition in France from a feudal monarchy to a centralized state.

The Black Death

PRECONDITIONS AND CAUSES.   In the late Middle Ages, nine-tenths of the population were still farmers. The three-field system, in use in most areas since well before the fourteenth century, had increased the amount of arable land and thereby the food supply. The growth of cities and trade had also stimulated

---

Boccaccio Describes the Ravages of the Black Death in Florence

The Black Death occasioned the poet, Humanist, and storyteller Giovanni Boccaccio (1313–1375) to assemble his great collection of tales, the Decameron. *In it, ten congenial men and women flee Florence to escape the plague and wile away the time telling stories. In one of the stories, Boccaccio embedded a fine clinical description of plague symptoms as seen in Florence in 1348 and of the powerlessness of physicians and the lack of remedies.*

In Florence, despite all that human wisdom and forethought could devise to avert it, even as the cleansing of the city from many impurities by officials appointed for the purpose, the refusal of entrance to all sick folk, and the adoption of many precautions for the preservation of health; despite also humble supplications addressed to God, and often repeated both in public procession and otherwise, by the devout; towards the beginning of the spring of the said year (1348) the doleful effects of the pestilence began to be horribly apparent by symptoms that shewed as if miraculous.

Not such were these symptoms as in the East, where an issue of blood from the nose was a manifest sign of inevitable death; but in men and women alike it first betrayed itself by the emergence of certain tumours in the groin or the armpits, some of which grew as large as a common apple, others as an egg, some more, some less, which the common folk called gavoccioli. From the two said parts of the body this deadly gavocciolo soon began to propagate and spread itself in all directions indifferently; after which the form of malady began to change, black spots or livid making their appearance in many cases on the arm or the thigh or elsewhere, now few and large, now minute and numerous. And as the gavocciolo had been and still was an infallible token of approaching death, such also were these spots on whomsoever they shewed themselves. Which maladies seemed to set entirely at naught both the art of the physician and the virtues of physic; indeed, whether it was that the disorder was of a nature to defy such treatment, or that the physicians were at fault and, being in ignorance of its source, failed to apply the proper remedies; in either case, not merely were those that recovered few, but almost all died within three days of the appearance of the said symptoms, sooner or later, and in most cases without any fever or other attendant malady.

The Decameron of Giovanni Boccaccio, trans. by J. M. Rigg (New York: Dutton, 1930), p. 5.

---

agricultural science and productivity. But as the food supply grew, so also did the population. It is estimated that Europe's population doubled between the years 1000 and 1300. By 1300, the balance between food supply and population was decisively tipped in favor of the latter. There were now more people than food to feed them or jobs to employ them, and the average European faced the probability of extreme hunger at least once during his or her expected thirty-five-year life span.

Famines followed the population explosion in the first half of the fourteenth century. Between 1315 and 1317, crop failures produced the greatest famine of the Middle Ages. Great suffering was inflicted on densely populated urban areas like the industrial towns of The Netherlands. Decades of overpopulation, economic depression, famine, and bad health progressively weakened Europe's population and made it highly vulnerable to the virulent bubonic plague (named the "buboes," or swollen lymphatic glands, it caused) that struck with full force in 1348. This Black Death followed the trade routes into Europe. Appearing in Sicily in late 1347, it entered Europe through the port cities of Venice, Genoa, and Pisa in 1348, and from there, it swept rapidly through Spain and southern France and into northern Europe. Areas that lay outside the major trade routes, like Bohemia, appear to have remained virtually unaffected. By the end of the fourteenth century, it is estimated that Western Europe as a whole had lost as much as two-fifths of its population, and a full recovery was not made until the sixteenth century (see Map 17-2 on p. 484).

POPULAR REMEDIES. In the Black Death, people confronted a catastrophe against which they had neither understanding nor defense. Never have Western people stood so helpless against the inexplicable and the uncontrollable. Contemporary physicians did not know that the disease was transmitted by rat- or human-transported fleas, and hence the most rudimentary prophylaxis was lacking. Popular wisdom held that a corruption in the atmosphere caused the disease. Some blamed poisonous fumes released by earthquakes, and many adopted aromatic amulets as a remedy. According to the contemporary observations of Boccaccio, who recorded the varied reactions to the plague in the *Decameron* (1353), some sought a remedy in moderation and a temperate life; others gave themselves over entirely to their passions (sexual promiscuity among the stricken apparently ran high); and still others, "the most sound, perhaps,

in judgment," chose flight and seclusion as the best medicine.[1]

Among the most extreme social reactions were processions of flagellants, religious fanatics who beat their bodies in ritual penance until they bled, believing that such action would bring divine intervention. The Jews, who were hated by many because of centuries of Christian propaganda against them and the fact that they had become society's money lenders (a disreputable and resented profession), became scapegoats. Pogroms occurred in several cities, sometimes incited by the advent of flagellants. The terror created by the flagellants, whose dirty bodies may have actually served to transport the disease, became so socially disruptive and threatening even to established authority that the Church finally outlawed such processions.

SOCIAL AND ECONOMIC CONSEQUENCES. Among the social and economic consequences of the plague were a shrunken labor supply and the devaluation of the estates of the nobility. Villages vanished in the wake of the plague. As the number of farm laborers decreased, their wages increased and those of skilled artisans soared. Many serfs now chose to commute their labor services by money payments, to abandon the farm altogether, and to pursue more interesting and rewarding jobs in skilled craft industries in the cities, an important new vocational option opened by the Black Death. Agricultural prices fell as a result of lowered demand, and the price of luxury and manufactured goods—the work of skilled artisans—rose. The noble landholders suffered the greatest decline in power from this new state of affairs. They were forced to pay more for finished products and for farm labor, and they received a smaller return on their agricultural produce. Everywhere their rents were in steady decline after the plague.

To recoup their losses, some landowners converted arable land to sheep pasture, substituting more profitable wool production for labor-intensive grain crops. Others abandoned the effort to farm their land and simply leased it to the highest bidder. Most ominously, legislation was sought to force peasants to stay on their farms and to freeze their wages at low levels, that is, to close off immediately the new economic opportunities opened for the peasantry by the demographic crisis. In France, the direct tax on the

[1] *The Decameron of Giovanni Boccaccio,* trans. by J. M. Rigg (New York: Dutton, 1930), p. 5.

MAP 17-2 SPREAD OF THE BLACK DEATH *Apparently introduced by seaborne rats from Black Sea areas where plague-infested rodents have long been known, the Black Death brought huge human, social, and economic consequences. According to one of the lower estimates, it killed twenty-five million in Europe. The map charts the spread of the plague in the mid-fourteenth century. Generally following trade routes, it reached Scandinavia by 1350, and some believe it then went on to Iceland and even Greenland. Areas off the main trade routes were largely spared.*

peasantry, the *taille,* was increased, and opposition to it was prominent among the grievances behind the *Jacquerie,* a great revolt of French peasants against the nobility in 1358. A Statute of Laborers was passed by the English Parliament in 1351 that limited wages

to preplague levels and restricted the ability of peasants to leave the land of their traditional masters. Opposition to such legislation was also a prominent factor in the English Peasants' Revolt of 1381.

Although the plague hit urban populations especially hard, the cities and their skilled industries came, in time, to prosper from it. Cities had always been careful to protect their interests; as they grew, they passed legislation to regulate competition from rural areas and to control immigration. After the plague, their laws were progressively extended over

Portrayal of the last days of the plague in Rome, from the Belles Heures *of Jean, Duke of Berry (fifteenth century). That the plague is now over is made clear by the angel hovering above the city, a symbol that God's wrath has come to an end. [Metropolitan Museum of Art, The Cloisters Collection, Purchase, 1954]*

the surrounding lands of nobles and feudal landlords, many of whom were peacefully integrated into urban life on terms very favorable to the cities.

The basic unit of urban industry was the master and his apprentices (usually one or two). Their numbers were purposely kept low and jealously guarded. As the craft of the skilled artisan was passed from master to apprentice only very slowly, the first wave of plague created a short supply of skilled labor almost overnight. But this short supply also raised the prices of available manufactured and luxury items to new heights. Ironically, the omnipresence of death whetted the appetite for the things that only skilled urban industries could produce. Expensive cloths and jewelry, furs from the north, and silks from the south were in great demand in the second half of the fourteenth century. Faced with life at its worst, people insisted on having the very best. The townspeople profited coming and going: As wealth poured into the cities and per capita income rose, the cost to urban dwellers of agricultural products from the countryside, which were now less in demand, actually declined.

The Church also profited from the plague as gifts and bequests multiplied. Although the Church, as a great landholder, also suffered losses, it had offsetting revenues from the vastly increased demand for religious services for the dead and the dying.

New Conflicts and Opportunities. By increasing the importance of skilled artisans, the plague contributed to new conflicts within the cities. The economic and political power of local artisans and trade guilds grew steadily in the late Middle Ages along with the demand for their goods and services. The merchant and patrician classes found it increasingly difficult to maintain their traditional dominance and grudgingly gave guild masters a voice in city government. As the guilds won political power, they encouraged restrictive legislation to protect local industries. These restrictions, in turn, brought confrontations between master artisans, who wanted to keep their numbers low and to expand their industries at a snail's pace, and the many journeymen, who were eager to rise to the rank of master. To the long-existing conflict between the guilds and the urban patriciate was now added a conflict within the guilds themselves.

Another indirect effect of the Great Plague was assistance to monarchies in the development of centralized states. The plague caused the landed nobility to lose much of their economic power during the same period in which the military superiority of paid professional armies over the traditional noble cavalry was being demonstrated by the Hundred Years' War. The plague also killed large numbers of clergy—perhaps one-third of the German clergy fell victim to it as they heroically ministered to the sick and dying. This reduction in clerical ranks occurred in the same century in which the residence of the pope in Avignon (1309–1377) and the Great Schism (1378–1415; discussed later) were undermining the Church's popular support. After 1350, the two traditional "containers" of monarchy—the landed nobility and the Church— were on the defensive, and to no small degree as a consequence of the plague. Kings took full advantage of the new situation, as they drew on growing national sentiment to centralize their governments and economies.

Ecclesiastical Breakdown and Revival: The Late Medieval Church

During the reign of Pope Innocent III (1198–1216), papal power reached its height. Innocent elaborated the doctrine of papal plenitude of power and on that authority declared saints, disposed of benefices, and created a centralized papal monarchy with a clearly political mission.

What Innocent began, his successors perfected. The thirteenth-century papacy became a powerful political institution governed by its own law and courts, serviced by an efficient international bureaucracy, and preoccupied with secular goals.

Boniface VIII and Philip the Fair

Pope Boniface VIII (1294–1303) came to rule when England and France were maturing as nation-states. In England, a long tradition of consultation between the king and powerful members of English society evolved into formal "parliaments" during the reigns of Henry III (1216–1272) and Edward I (1272–1307), and these parliaments helped to create a unified kingdom. During the reign of the French king Philip IV the Fair (1285–1314) France was an efficient, centralized monarchy. Boniface had the further misfortune of bringing to the papal throne memories of the way earlier popes had brought kings and emperors to their knees. He was to discover that the papal monarchy of the early thirteenth century was no match for the new political powers of the late thirteenth century.

Pope Boniface VIII (1294–1303) who opposed the taxation of the clergy by the kings of France and England and issued one of the strongest declarations of papal authority, the bull Unam Sanctam. The statue is in the Museo Civico, Bologna, Italy. [Alinari/Art Resource]

France and England were on the brink of all-out war when Boniface became pope (1294). As both countries mobilized for war, they used the pretext of preparing for a crusade to tax the clergy heavily. Viewing English and French taxation of the clergy as an assault on traditional clerical rights, Boniface issued a bull, *Clericis Laicos,* which forbade lay taxation of the clergy without prior papal approval.

In England, Edward I retaliated by denying the clergy the right to be heard in the royal court, in effect removing from them the protection of the king. But it was Philip the Fair who struck back with a vengeance. In August 1296, he forbade the exportation of money from France to Rome, thereby denying the papacy revenues without which it could not operate. Boniface had no choice but to concede Philip the right to tax the French clergy "during an emergency."

In the year 1300, Boniface's fortunes appeared to revive. Tens of thousands of pilgrims flocked to Rome in that year for the Jubilee celebration. In a Jubilee year, all Catholics who visited Rome and there fulfilled certain conditions received a special indulgence, or remission of their sins. Heady with this display of popular religiosity, Boniface reinserted himself into international politics. Philip, seemingly spoiling for another fight with the pope, arrested Boniface's Parisian legate, Bernard Saisset, the bishop of Pamiers. Boniface demanded Saisset's unconditional release. A bull, *Ausculta Fili* ("Listen, My Son"), was sent to Philip in December 1301, pointedly informing him that "God has set popes over kings and kingdoms."

UNAM SANCTAM (1302).   Philip unleashed a ruthless antipapal campaign. Boniface made a last-ditch stand against state control of national churches when on November 18, 1302, he issued the bull *Unam Sanctam.* This famous statement of papal power declared that temporal authority was "subject" to the spiritual power of the Church.

After *Unam Sanctam,* the French moved against Boniface with force. An army of the king surprised the pope in mid-August 1303 at his retreat in Anagni. Boniface was badly beaten and almost executed before an aroused populace liberated him and returned him safely to Rome.

Marsilius of Padua Denies Coercive Power to the Clergy

According to Marsilius (ca. 1290–1342), a pamphleteer for the royal cause, the Bible gave the pope no right to pronounce and execute sentences on any person. The clergy held a strictly moral and spiritual rule, their judgments to be executed only in the afterlife, not in the present one. Here, on earth, they should be obedient to secular authority. Marsilius argued this point by appealing to the example of Jesus.

We now wish . . . to adduce the truths of the holy Scripture . . . which explicitly command or counsel that neither the Roman bishop called pope, nor any other bishop or priest, or deacon, has or ought to have any rulership or coercive judgment or jurisdiction over any priest or nonpriest, ruler, community, group, or individual of whatever condition. . . . Christ himself came into the world not to dominate men, nor to judge them [coercively] . . . not to wield temporal rule, but rather to be subject as regards the . . . present life; and moreover, he wanted to and did exclude himself, his apostles and disciples, and their successors, the bishops or priests, from all coercive authority or worldly rule, both by his example and by his word of counsel or command. . . . When he was brought before Pontius Pilate . . . and accused of having called himself king of the Jews, and [Pilate] asked him whether he had said this . . . [his] reply included these words . . . "My kingdom is not of this world," that is, I have not come to reign by temporal rule or dominion, in the way . . . worldly kings reign. . . . This, then, is the kingdom concerning which he came to teach and order, a kingdom which consists in the acts whereby the eternal kingdom is attained, that is, the acts of faith and the other theological virtues; not however, by coercing anyone thereto.

Marsilius of Padua: The Defender of Peace: The Defensor Pacis, trans. by Alan Gewirth (New York: Harper, 1967), pp. 113–116.

There was to be no papal retaliation by Boniface or his successors. Indeed, Pope Clement V (1305–1314), a former archbishop of Bordeaux, declared that *Unam Sanctam* should not be understood as in any way diminishing French royal authority. Clement established the papal court at Avignon, on the southeastern border of France, in 1309. There the papacy would remain until 1377.

After Boniface's humiliation, popes never again so seriously threatened kings and emperors, despite continuing papal excommunications and political intrigue. In the future, the relation between Church and State would tilt toward state control of religion within particular monarchies and the subordination of ecclesiastical to larger secular political purposes.

The Great Schism (1378–1417) and the Conciliar Movement to 1449

Pope Gregory XI (1370–1378) reestablished the papacy in Rome in January 1377, ending what had come to be known as the "Babylonian Captivity" of the Church in Avignon, the reference being to the biblical bondage of the Israelites. The return to Rome proved to be short lived, however. On Gregory's death on March 27, 1378, the cardinals, in Rome, elected an Italian archbishop as Pope Urban VI (1378–1389), who immediately proclaimed his intention to reform the Curia. This announcement came as an unexpected challenge to the cardinals, most of whom were French, and made them amenable to royal pressures to return the papacy to Avignon. The French king, Charles V, not wanting to surrender the benefits of a papacy located within the sphere of French influence, lent his support to a schism.

Five months after Urban's election, on September 20, 1378, thirteen cardinals, all but one of whom was French, formed their own conclave and elected a cousin of the French king as Pope Clement VII (1378–1397). They insisted, probably with some truth, that they had voted for Urban in fear of their lives, surrounded by a Roman mob that demanded the election of an Italian pope. Be that as it may, thereafter the papacy became a "two-headed thing" and a scandal to Christendom. Allegiance to the two papal courts divided along political lines: England and its allies (the Holy Roman Empire, Hungary, Bohemia, and Poland) acknowledged Urban VI, whereas France and its orbit (Naples, Scotland, Castile, and Aragon) supported Clement VII. Only the Roman line of popes, however, came to be recognized as official in subsequent Church history.

THE COUNCIL OF CONSTANCE (1414–1417). In 1409, a council was convened in Pisa that deposed both the Roman and the Avignon popes and elected in their stead its own new pope. But to the council's consternation, neither of these accepted its action, so after 1409, Christendom confronted the spectacle of three contending popes. This intolerable situation ended when the emperor Sigismund prevailed on the Pisan pope John XXIII to summon a "legal" council of the Church in Constance in 1414, a council also recognized by the reigning Roman pope Gregory XII. Gregory, however, soon resigned his office, raising grave doubts forevermore about whether the council was truly convened with Rome's blessing and hence valid. In a famous declaration entitled *Haec Sancta,* the council fathers asserted their supremacy and proceeded to conduct the business of the Church.

They also executed the Bohemian reformer Jan Hus on July 6, 1415. Hus was the rector of the University of Prague, and he had been strongly influenced in his teaching by the English reformer John Wycliffe (d. 1384). Hus advocated communion for laity with both wine and bread (traditionally only the priest had received both; the laity had received only bread, indicating the clergy's spiritual superiority over them); denied the dogma of transubstantiation (that wine and bread become the true body and blood of Christ by priestly consecration); and questioned the validity of sacraments performed by priests who led immoral lives.

In November 1417, the council successfully accomplished its main business when it elected a new pope, Martin V (1417–1431), after the three contending popes either had resigned (Gregory XIII) or were deposed (Benedict XIII and John XXIII). The council made provisions for regular meetings of Church councils, scheduling a general council of the Church for purposes of reform within five, then seven, and thereafter every ten years. Constance has remained, however, an illegitimate Church council in official eyes; nor are the schismatic popes of Avignon and

A German portrayal of the burning of Jan Hus for heresy and the dumping of his ashes into the Rhine to prevent their becoming relics. [Vincent Varga Archives]

Pisa recognized as legitimate (for this reason another pope could take the name John XXIII in 1958).

THE COUNCIL OF BASEL (1431–1449). Conciliar government of the Church both peaked and declined during the Council of Basel. This council curtailed papal powers of appointment and taxation and directly negotiated peace with the Hussites of Bohemia, conceding the latter's demands for communion with cup as well as bread, free preaching by their ordained clergy, and like punishment of clergy and laity for the same mortal sins. The council also recognized the right of the Bohemian church to govern its own internal affairs, much as the church in France and England had long since done.

During the pontificate of Pope Eugenius IV (1431–1447), the papacy regained much of its prestige and authority and successfully challenged the Council of Basel. The notion of conciliar superiority over popes died with the collapse of the Council of Basel in 1449. A decade later, the papal bull *Execrabilis* (1460) condemned appeals to councils as "erroneous and abominable" and "completely null and void."

But the conciliar movement was not a total failure. It planted deep within the conscience of all Western peoples the conviction that the leader of an institution must be responsive to its members and that the head exists to lead and serve, not to bring disaster on, the body.

Revival of Monarchy: Nation Building in the Fifteenth Century

After 1450, there was a progressive shift from divided feudal to unified national monarchies as "sovereign" rulers emerged. This is not to say that the dynastic and chivalric ideals of feudal monarchy did not continue. Territorial princes did not pass from the scene, and representative bodies persisted and in some areas even grew in influence. But in the late fifteenth and early sixteenth centuries, the old problem of the one and the many was decided clearly in favor of the interests of monarchy.

The feudal monarchy of the high Middle Ages was characterized by the division of the basic powers of government between the king and his semiautonomous vassals. The nobility and the towns acted with varying degrees of unity and success through such evolving representative assemblies as the English Parliament, the French Estates General, and the Spanish Cortes to thwart the centralization of royal power. As a result of the Hundred Years' War and the schism in the Church, the nobility and the clergy were in decline in the late Middle Ages. The increasingly important towns began to ally with the king. Loyal, businesswise townspeople, not the nobility and the clergy, staffed the royal offices and became the king's lawyers, bookkeepers, military tacticians, and foreign diplomats. It was this new alliance between king and town that finally broke the bonds of feudal society and made possible the rise of sovereign states.

In a sovereign state, the power of taxation, war making, and law enforcement is no longer the local right of semiautonomous vassals but is concentrated in the monarch and is exercised by his chosen agents. Taxes, wars, and laws become national rather than merely regional matters. Only as monarchs were able to act independently of the nobility and the representative assemblies could they overcome the decentralization that had been the basic obstacle to nation building.

Monarchies also began to create standing national armies in the fifteenth century. As the noble cavalry receded and the infantry and the artillery became the backbone of armies, mercenary soldiers were recruited from Switzerland and Germany to form the major part of the "king's army."

The more expensive warfare of the fifteenth and sixteenth centuries increased the need to develop new national sources of royal income. The expansion of royal revenues was especially hampered by the stubborn belief among the highest classes that they were immune from government taxation. The nobility guarded their properties and traditional rights and despised taxation as an insult and a humiliation. Royal revenues accordingly grew at the expense of those least able to resist and least able to pay. The king had several options. As a feudal lord he could collect rents from his royal domain. He could also levy national taxes on basic food and clothing, such as the *gabelle* or salt tax in France and the *alcabala* or 10 percent sales tax on commercial transactions in Spain. The king could also levy direct taxes on the peasantry and on commercial transactions in towns under royal protection. This he did through agreeable representative assemblies of the privileged classes in which the peasantry did not sit. The French *taille* was such a tax. Sale of public offices and issuance of high-interest government bonds appeared in the fifteenth century as innovative fund-raising devices. But kings did not levy taxes on the powerful nobility. They turned to rich nobles, as they did to the great bankers of Italy and Germany, for loans, bargaining with the privileged classes, who in many instances remained as much the kings' creditors and competitors as their subjects.

France

There were two cornerstones of French nation building in the fifteenth century. The first was the collapse of the English holdings in France following the Hundred Years' War. The second was the defeat of Charles the Bold and the duchy of Burgundy. Perhaps Europe's strongest political power in the mid-fifteenth century, Burgundy aspired to dwarf both France and the Holy Roman Empire as the leader of a dominant middle kingdom. It might have succeeded in doing so had not the continental powers joined together in opposition. When Charles the Bold died in defeat in a battle at Nancy in 1477, the dream of Burgundian empire died with him.

The dissolution of Burgundy ended its constant intrigue against the French king and left Louis XI (r. 1461–1483) free to secure the monarchy. The newly acquired Burgundian lands and his own Angevin inheritance permitted the king to end his reign with a kingdom almost twice the size of that with which he had started. Louis successfully harnessed the nobility, expanded the trade and industry, created a national postal system, and even established a lucrative silk industry at Lyons (later transferred to Tours).

A strong nation is a two-edged sword. It was because Louis's successors inherited such a secure and efficient government that France was able to pursue Italian conquests in the 1490s and to fight a long series of losing wars with the Habsburgs in the first half of the sixteenth century. By the mid-sixteenth century, France was again a defeated nation and almost as divided internally as it had been during the Hundred Years' War.

Spain

Spain, too, became a strong country in the late fifteenth century. Both Castile and Aragon had been poorly ruled and divided kingdoms in the mid-fifteenth century. The marriage of Isabella of Castile (r. 1474–1504) and Ferdinand of Aragon (r. 1479–1516) changed that situation. The two future sovereigns married in 1469, despite strong protests from neighboring Portugal and France, both of which foresaw the formidable European power such a union would create. Castile was by far the richer and more populous of the two, having an estimated five million inhabitants to Aragon's population of under one million. Castile was also distinguished by its lucrative sheep-farming industry, which was run by a government-backed organization called the *Mesta*, another example of developing centralized economic planning. Although the two kingdoms were dynastically united by the marriage of Ferdinand and Isabella in 1469, they remained constitutionally separated, as each retained its respective government agencies—

These sculptures of Ferdinand (r. 1479–1516) and Isabella (r. 1474–1504) are from the royal chapel in the Cathedral of Granada. Their marriage in 1469, which joined the kingdoms of Aragon and Castile, united Spain. [Robert Frerck]

separate laws, armies, coinage, and taxation—and cultural traditions.

Ferdinand and Isabella could do together what neither was able to accomplish alone: subdue their realms, secure their borders, and venture abroad militarily. Townspeople allied themselves with the crown and progressively replaced the nobility within the royal administration. The crown also extended its authority over the wealthy chivalric orders, a further circumscription of the power of the nobility.

Spain had long been remarkable among European lands as a place where three religions—Islam, Judaism, and Christianity—coexisted with a certain degree of toleration. This toleration ended dramatically under Ferdinand and Isabella, who made Spain the prime example of state-controlled religion. Ferdinand and Isabella exercised almost total control over the Spanish church as they placed religion in the service of national unity. They appointed the higher clergy and the officers of the Inquisition. The Inquisition, run by Tomás de Torquemada (d. 1498), Isabella's confessor, was a key national agency established in 1479 to monitor the activity of converted Jews (conversos) and Muslims (Moriscos) in Spain. In 1492, the Jews were exiled and their properties were confiscated. In 1502, nonconverting Moors in Granada were drive into exile. Spanish spiritual life remained largely uniform and successfully controlled, a major reason for Spain's remaining a loyal Catholic country throughout the sixteenth century and providing a base of operation for the European Counter-Reformation.

Ferdinand and Isabella were rulers with wide horizons. They contracted anti-French marriage alliances that came to determine a large part of European history in the sixteenth century. In 1496, their eldest daughter, Joanna, later known as "the Mad," married Archduke Philip, the son of Emperor Maximilian I. The fruit of this union, Charles I of Spain, the first ruler over a united Spain, came by his inheritance and election as Emperor Charles V in 1519 to rule over a European kingdom almost equal in size to that of Charlemagne. A second daughter, Catherine of Aragon, wed Arthur, the son of the English King Henry VII, and after Arthur's premature death, she married his brother, the future King Henry VIII. The failure of this latter marriage became the key factor in the emergence of the Anglican Church and the English Reformation.

The new Spanish power was also revealed in Ferdinand and Isabella's promotion of overseas exploration. Their patronage of the Genoese adventurer Christopher Columbus (1451–1506), who discovered the islands of the Caribbean while sailing west in search of a shorter route to the spice markets of the Far East, led to the creation of the Spanish empire in Mexico and Peru, whose gold and silver mines helped to make Spain Europe's dominant power in the sixteenth century.

England

The last half of the fifteenth century was a period of especially difficult political trial for the English. Following the Hundred Years' War, a defeated England was subjected to internal warfare between two rival branches of the royal family, the House of York and the House of Lancaster. This conflict, known to us today as the War of the Roses (as York's symbol, according to legend, was a white rose, and Lancaster's a red rose), kept England in turmoil from 1455 to 1485.

The Lancastrian monarchy of Henry VI (r. 1422–1461) was consistently challenged by the duke of York and his supporters in the prosperous southern towns. In 1461, Edward IV (r. 1461–1483), son of the duke of York, successfully seized power and instituted a strong-arm rule that lasted over twenty years. Edward, assisted by loyal and able ministers, effectively bent Parliament to his will. His brother and successor was Richard III (r. 1483–1485). During the reign of the Tudors, a tradition arose that painted Richard III as an unprincipled villain who murdered Edward's sons in the Tower of London to secure the throne. The best-known version of this characterization—unjust according to some—is found in Shakespeare's *Richard III.* Be that as it may, Richard's reign saw the growth of support for the exiled Lancastrian Henry Tudor. Henry returned to England to defeat Richard on Bosworth Field in August 1485.

Henry Tudor ruled as Henry VII (r. 1485–1509), the first of the new Tudor dynasty that would dominate England throughout the sixteenth century. In order to bring the rival royal families together and to make the hereditary claim of his offspring to the throne uncontestable, Henry married Edward IV's daughter, Elizabeth of York. He succeeded in disciplining the English nobility through a special and much feared instrument of the royal will known as the *Court of Star Chamber.* Henry shrewdly construed legal precedents to the advantage of the crown, using English law to further his own ends. He managed to confiscate noble lands and fortunes with such success that he governed without dependence on Parliament for royal funds, always a cornerstone of strong monarchy. In these ways, Henry began to shape a monarchy that became one of early modern Europe's most exemplary governments during the reign of his granddaughter, Elizabeth I.

The Holy Roman Empire

Germany and Italy are the striking exceptions to the steady development of centralized nation-states in the last half of the fifteenth century. Unlike France, Spain, and England, the Holy Roman Empire saw the many thoroughly repulse the one. In Germany, territorial rulers and cities resisted every effort at national consolidation and unity. As in Carolingian times, rulers continued to partition their kingdoms, however small, among their sons, and by the late fifteenth century, Germany was hopelessly divided into some three hundred autonomous political entities.

The princes and the cities did work together to create the machinery of law and order, if not of union, within the divided empire. An agreement reached between the emperor Charles IV and the major German territorial rulers in 1356, known as the *Golden Bull,* established a seven-member electoral college consisting of the archbishops of Mainz, Trier, and Cologne; the duke of Saxony; the margrave of Brandenburg; the count Palatine; and the king of Bohemia. This group also functioned as an administrative body. They elected the emperor and, in cooperation with him, provided what transregional unity and administration existed. The figure of the emperor gave the empire a single ruler in law, if not in actual fact.

In the sixteenth and seventeenth centuries, German territorial princes became virtually sovereign rulers within their various domains. The resulting disunity aided religious dissent and conflict. It was in the cities and territories of still feudal, fractionalized, backward Germany that the Protestant Reformation broke out in the sixteenth century.

The Renaissance in Italy (1375–1527)

In his famous study, *Civilization of the Renaissance in Italy* (1867), Jacob Burckhardt described the Renaissance as the prototype of the modern world. He believed that it was in fourteenth- and fifteenth-century Italy, through the revival of ancient learning, that new secular and scientific values first began to supplant traditional religious beliefs. This was the period in which people began to adopt a rational, objective, and statistical approach to reality and to rediscover the importance of the individual. The result, in Burckhardt's words, was a release of the "full, whole nature of man."

Other scholars have found Burckhardt's description too modernizing an interpretation of the Renaissance and have accused him of overlooking the continuity with the Middle Ages. His critics especially stress the strongly Christian character of Humanism and the fact that earlier "renaissances" also revived the ancient classics, professed interest in Latin language and Greek science, and appreciated the worth and creativity of individuals.

Most scholars nonetheless agree that the Renaissance was a time of real transition from the medieval to the modern world. Medieval Europe, especially before the twelfth century, had been a fragmented feudal society with an agriculturally based economy, its thought and culture largely dominated by the Church. Renaissance Europe, especially after the fourteenth century, was characterized by growing national consciousness and political centralization, an urban economy based on organized commerce and capitalism, and ever greater lay and secular control of thought and culture.

It was especially in Italy between the late fourteenth and the early sixteenth centuries, from roughly 1375 to 1527, the year of the sack of Rome by imperial soldiers, that the distinctive features and achievements of the Renaissance, which also deeply influenced northern Europe, are most strikingly revealed.

The Italian City-State: Social Conflict and Despotism

Italy had always had a cultural advantage over the rest of Europe because its geography made it the natural gateway between East and West. Venice, Genoa, and Pisa traded uninterruptedly with the Near East throughout the Middle Ages and maintained vibrant urban societies. During the thirteenth and fourteenth centuries, trade-rich cities expanded to become powerful city-states, dominating the political and economic life of the surrounding countryside. By the fifteenth century, the great Italian cities had become the bankers of much of Europe.

The growth of Italian cities and urban culture was also assisted by the endemic warfare between the emperor and the pope. Either might have successfully challenged the cities. They chose instead to weaken one another and thus strengthened the merchant oligarchies of the cities. Unlike in northern Europe, where the cities tended to be dominated by kings and princes, Italian cities were left free to expand into states. They absorbed the surrounding countryside and assimilated the area nobility in a unique urban meld of old and new rich. There were five such major, competitive states in Italy: the duchy of Milan; the republics of Florence and Venice; the Papal States; and the kingdom of Naples (see Map 17-3).

MAP 17-3 RENAISSANCE ITALY *The city-states of Renaissance Italy were self-contained principalities whose internal strife was monitored by their despots and whose external aggression was long successfully controlled by treaty.*

Florentine women worked at needlework, spinning, and weaving. These activities took up much of a woman's time and contributed to the elegance of dress for which both male and female Florentines were famed. [Alinari/Art Resource]

Social strife and competition for political power were so intense within the cities that for survival's sake, most had evolved into despotisms by the fifteenth century. Venice was the notable exception. It was ruled by a successful merchant oligarchy with power located in a patrician senate of three hundred members and a ruthless judicial body, the Council of Ten, that anticipated and suppressed rival groups. Elsewhere, the new social classes and divisions within society produced by rapid urban growth fueled chronic, near-anarchic conflict.

Florence was the most striking example. There were four distinguishable social groups within the city. The first was the old rich, or *grandi,* the nobles and merchants who had traditionally ruled the city. The second group was the emergent new-rich merchant class, capitalists and bankers known as the *popolo grasso,* or "fat people." They began to challenge the old rich for political power in the late thirteenth and early fourteenth centuries. Then there were the middle-burgher ranks of guild masters, shopkeepers, and professionals, those small businessmen who, in Florence as elsewhere, tended to take the side of the new rich against the conservative policies of the old rich. Finally, there was the omnipresent *popolo minuto,* the poor masses who lived from hand to mouth: In 1457, one-third of the population of Florence, about thirty thousand people, were officially listed as paupers.

These social divisions produced conflict at every level of society. In 1378, a great revolt by the poor, known as the Ciompi Revolt, established a chaotic four-year reign of power by the lower Florentine classes. True stability did not return to Florence until the ascent to power in 1434 of Cosimo de' Medici (1389–1464).

The wealthiest Florentine and an astute statesman, Cosimo controlled the city internally from behind the scenes, skillfully manipulating the constitution and influencing elections. His grandson, Lorenzo the Magnificent (1449–1492), ruled Florence in almost totalitarian fashion during the last quarter of the fifteenth century.

Despotism was less subtle elsewhere. In order to prevent internal social conflict and foreign intrigue from paralyzing their cities, the dominant groups cooperated to install a hired strongman, known as a *podestá,* for the purpose of maintaining law and order. He held executive, military, and judicial authority, and his mandate was simple: to permit, by whatever means required, the normal flow of business. Because these despots could not depend on the divided populace, they operated through mercenary armies.

Political turbulence and warfare gave birth to diplomacy, by means of which the various city-states stayed abreast of foreign military developments and, if shrewd enough, gained power and advantage short of actually going to war. Most city-states established resident embassies during the fifteenth century. Their ambassadors not only represented them in ceremonies and as negotiators but also became their watchful eyes and ears at rival courts.

Whether within the comparatively tranquil republic of Venice, the strong-arm democracy of Florence, or the undisguised despotism of Milan, the wealthy Italian city proved a most congenial climate for an unprecedented flowering of thought and culture. Renaissance culture was promoted as vigorously by despots as by republicans and by secularized popes as enthusiastically as by the more spiritually minded.

Humanism

Some scholars describe Humanism as an unchristian philosophy that stressed the dignity of humankind and championed individualism and secular values. Others argue that the Humanists were true champions of authentic Catholic Christianity. Still others see Humanism as a form of scholarship consciously designed to promote a sense of civic responsibility and political liberty. One of the most authoritative modern commentators, Paul O. Kristeller, has accused all these views of dealing more with the secondary effects of Humanism than with its essence, which he believes was no particular philosophy or value system but simply an educational program concentrated on rhetoric and sound scholarship for their own sake.

A terra-cotta bust of Lorenzo de' Medici by the sculptor Andrea del Verrocchio (ca. 1435–1488). [National Gallery of Art, Washington; Samuel H. Kress Collection]

There is truth in each of these definitions. Humanism was the scholarly study of the Latin and Greek classics and the ancient Church Fathers both for their own sake and in the hope of a rebirth of ancient norms and values. Humanists were advocates of the *studia humanitatis,* a liberal arts program of study that embraced grammar, rhetoric, poetry, history, politics, and moral philosophy. The Florentine Leonardo Bruni (1374–1444) first gave the name *humanitas* ("humanity") to the learning that resulted from such scholarly pursuits. Bruni was a student of Manuel Chrysoloras, a Byzantine scholar who opened the

Italian Renaissance of the late Middle Ages. The latter was more secular and lay dominated, had broader interests, recovered more manuscripts, and possessed far superior technical skills than earlier "rebirths" of antiquity. Unlike their Scholastic rivals, Humanists were not content only to summarize and compare the views of recognized authorities on a question but went directly to the original source itself and drew their own conclusions. Avidly searching out manuscript collections, Italian Humanists made the full sources of Greek and Latin antiquity available to scholars during the fourteenth and fifteenth centuries. Mastery of Latin and Greek was the surgeon's tool of the Humanist. There is a kernel of truth—but only a kernel—in the arrogant boast of the Humanists that the period between themselves and classical civilization was a "dark middle age."

PETRARCH, DANTE, AND BOCCACCIO. Francesco Petrarch (1304–1374) was the father of Humanism. He left the legal profession to pursue his love of letters and poetry. Although most of his life was spent in and around Avignon, he became caught up in Cola di Rienzo's popular revolt and two-year reign (1347–1349) in Rome as "tribune" of the Roman people. He served the Visconti family in Milan in his later years. Petrarch celebrated ancient Rome in his *Letters to the Ancient Dead,* fancied personal letters to Cicero, Livy, Vergil, and Horace. He also wrote a Latin epic poem (*Africa,* a poetic historical tribute to the Roman general Scipio Africanus) and a set of biographies of famous Romans *(Lives of Illustrious Men).* He tirelessly collected ancient manuscripts; among his finds were some letters by Cicero. His critical textual studies, elitism, and contempt for the allegedly useless learning of the Scholastics were features that many later Humanists also shared. Petrarch's most famous contemporary work was a collection of highly introspective love sonnets to a certain Laura, a married woman whom he romantically admired from a safe distance. Medieval Christian values can be seen in his imagined dialogues with Saint Augustine and in tracts written to defend the personal immortality of the soul against the Aristotelians.

Petrarch was, however, far more secular in orientation than his famous near-contemporary Dante Alighieri (1265–1321), whose *Vita Nuova* and *Divine Comedy* form, with Petrarch's sonnets, the cornerstones of Italian vernacular literature. Petrarch's student and friend Giovanni Boccaccio (1313–1375), author of the *Decameron,* one hundred bawdy tales

world of Greek scholarship to a generation of young Italian Humanists when he taught at Florence between 1397 and 1403.

The first Humanists were orators and poets. They wrote original literature, in both the classical and the vernacular languages, inspired by the newly discovered works of the ancients, and they taught rhetoric within the universities. When Humanists were not employed as teachers of rhetoric, their talents were sought as secretaries, speech writers, and diplomats in princely and papal courts.

The study of classical and Christian antiquity existed before the Italian Renaissance. There were recoveries of ancient civilization during the Carolingian renaissance of the ninth century, within the cathedral school of Chartres in the twelfth century, during the great Aristotelian revival in Paris in the thirteenth century, and among the Augustinians in the early fourteenth century. However, these precedents only partially compare with the grand achievements of the

Petrarch's Letter to Posterity

In old age, Petrarch wrote a highly personal letter to posterity in which he summarized the lessons he had learned during his lifetime. The letter also summarizes the original values of Renaissance Humanists: their suspicion of purely materialistic pleasure, the importance they attached to friendship, and their utter devotion to and love of antiquity.

I have always possessed extreme contempt for wealth; not that riches are not desirable in themselves, but because I hate the anxiety and care which are invariably associated with them . . . I have, on the contrary, led a happier existence with plain living and ordinary fare. . . .

The pleasure of dining with one's friends is so great that nothing has ever given me more delight than their unexpected arrival, nor have I ever willingly sat down to table without a companion. . . .

The greatest kings of this age have loved and courted me. . . . I have fled, however, from many . . . to whom I was greatly attached; and such was my innate longing for liberty that I studiously avoided those whose very name seemed incompatible with the freedom I loved.

I possess a well-balanced rather than a keen intellect—one prone to all kinds of good and wholesome study, but especially to moral philosophy and the art of poetry. The latter I neglected as time went on, and took delight in sacred literature. . . . Among the many subjects that interested me, I dwelt especially upon antiquity, for our own age has always repelled me, so that, had it not been for the love of those dear to me, I should have preferred to have been born in any other period than our own. In order to forget my own time, I have constantly striven to place myself in spirit in other ages, and consequently I delighted in history. . . .

If only I have lived well, it matters little to me how I have talked. Mere elegance of language can produce at best but an empty fame.

Frederic A. Ogg, ed., *A Source Book of Mediaeval History* (New York: American Book Company, 1908), pp. 470–473.

---

told by three men and seven women in a country retreat from the plague that ravaged Florence in 1348, also pioneered Humanist studies. An avid collector of manuscripts, Boccaccio also assembled an encyclopedia of Greek and Roman mythology.

EDUCATIONAL REFORMS AND GOALS.   Pietro Paolo Vergerio (1349–1420) left a classic summary of the Humanist concept of a liberal education:

We call those studies liberal which are worthy of a free man; those studies by which we attain and practice virtue and wisdom; that education which calls forth, trains, and develops those highest gifts of body and mind which ennoble men and which are rightly judged to rank next in dignity to virtue only, for to a vulgar temper, gain and pleasure are the one aim in existence, to a lofty nature, moral worth and fame.[2]

[2] Cited by De Lamar Jensen, *Renaissance Europe: Age of Recovery and Reconciliation* (Lexington, MA: D. C. Heath, 1981), p. 111.

The ideal of a useful education and well-rounded people inspired far-reaching reforms in traditional education. Quintilian's *Education of the Orator*, the full text of which was discovered by Poggio Bracciolini (d. 1459) in 1416, became the basic classical guide for the Humanist revision of the traditional curriculum. The most influential Renaissance tract on education, Vergerio's *On the Morals that Befit a Free Man*, was written directly from classical models. Vittorino da Feltre (d. 1446) was a teacher who not only directed his students to a highly disciplined reading of Pliny, Ptolemy, Terence, Plautus, Livy, and Plutarch but also combined vigorous physical exercise and games with intellectual pursuits. Another educator, Guarino da Verona (d. 1460), rector of the new University of Ferrara and a student of the Greek scholar Manuel Chrysoloras, streamlined the study of classical languages and gave it systematic form. Baldassare Castiglione's famous *Book of the Courtier,* written for the cultured nobility at the court of Urbino, stressed the importance of integrating knowledge of language and history with athletic, military, and musical skills, as well as good manners and moral character.

THE FLORENTINE ACADEMY AND REVIVAL OF PLATONISM. Of all the important recoveries of the past made during the Italian Renaissance, none stands out more than the revival of Greek studies, especially the works of Plato, in fifteenth-century Florence. Many factors combined to bring this revival about. An important foundation was laid in 1397 when the city invited Manuel Chrysoloras to come from Constantinople and promote Greek learning. A half-century later (1439), the ecumenical Council of Ferrara-Florence, having convened to negotiate the reunion of the eastern and western churches, opened the door for many Greek scholars and manuscripts to enter the west. After the fall of Constantinople to the Turks in 1453, Greek scholars fled to Florence for refuge. This was the background against which Platonic scholarship developed under the patronage of Cosimo de' Medici and the supervision of Marsilio Ficino (1433–1499) and Pico della Mirandola (1463–1494).

Although the thinkers of the Renaissance were interested in every variety of ancient wisdom, they seemed to be especially attracted to Platonism and those Church Fathers who had tried to synthesize Platonic philosophy and Christian teaching. In private residences, Ficino and other humanists met to discuss the works of Plato and the Neoplatonists: Plotinus, Proclus, Porphyry, and Dionysius the [Pseudo-] Areopagite. Historians have romanticized these meetings into the so-called "Florentine Academy." Ficino also edited and published the complete works of Plato.

The appeal of Platonism lay in its flattering view of human nature. Platonism distinguished between an eternal sphere of being and the perishable world in

---

Pico della Mirandola States the Renaissance Image of Man

One of the most eloquent descriptions of the Renaissance image of humankind comes from the Italian Humanist Pico della Mirandola (1463–1494). In his famed Oration on the Dignity of Man *(ca. 1486), Pico describes humans as free to become whatever they choose.*

The best of artisans [God] ordained that that creature [man] to whom He had been able to give nothing proper to himself should have joint possession of whatever had been peculiar to each of the different kinds of being. He therefore took man as a creature of indeterminate nature and, assigning him a place in the middle of the world, addressing him thus: "Neither a fixed abode nor a form that is thine alone nor any function peculiar to thyself have we given thee, Adam, to the end that according to thy longing and according to thy judgment thou mayest have and possess what abode, what form, and what functions thou thyself shalt desire. The nature of all other beings is limited and constrained within the bounds of laws prescribed by Us. Thou, constrained by no limits, in accordance with thine own free will, in whose hand We have placed thee, shall ordain for thyself the limits of thy nature. We have set thee at the world's center that thou mayest from thence more easily observe whatever is in the world. We have made thee neither of heaven nor of earth, neither mortal nor immortal, so that with freedom of choice and with honor, as though the maker and molder of thyself, thou mayest fashion thyself in whatever shape thou shalt prefer. Thou shalt have the power to degenerate into the lower forms of life, which are brutish. Thou shalt have the power, out of thy soul's judgment, to be reborn into the higher forms, which are divine." O supreme generosity of God the Father, O highest and most marvelous felicity of man! To him it is granted to have whatever he chooses, to be whatever he wills.

Giovanni Pico della Mirandola, *Oration on the Dignity of Man,* in *The Renaissance Philosophy of Man,* ed. by E. Cassirer et al. (Chicago: Phoenix Books, 1961), pp. 224–225.

which humans actually lived. Human reason was believed to belong to the former, indeed, to have preexisted in this pristine world and to continue to commune with it, as their knowledge of mathematical and moral truth bore witness.

CRITICAL WORK OF THE HUMANISTS: LORENZO VALLA. Because they were guided by a scholarly ideal of philological accuracy and historical truthfulness, the Humanists could become critics of tradition even when that was not their intention. Dispassionate critical scholarship shook long-standing foundations, not the least of which were those of the medieval Church.

The work of Lorenzo Valla (1406–1457), author of the standard Renaissance text on Latin philology, the *Elegance of the Latin Language* (1444), reveals the explosive character of the new learning. Although a good Catholic, Valla became a hero to later Protestants as a result of his defense of predestination against the advocates of free will and his exposé of the *Donation of Constantine* (see Chapter 14). The exposé of the *Donation* was not intended by Valla to have the devastating force that Protestants attributed to it. He only demonstrated in a careful, scholarly way what others had long suspected. Using the most rudimentary textual analysis and historical logic, Valla proved that the document contained such anachronistic terms as *fief* and made references that would have been meaningless in the fourth century. In the same dispassionate way, Valla also pointed out errors in the Latin Vulgate, then the authorized version of the Bible for the Roman Catholic Church.

Such discoveries did not make Valla any less loyal to the Church, nor did they prevent his faithful fulfillment of the office of Apostolic Secretary in Rome under Pope Nicholas V. Nonetheless, historical criticism of this type served those less loyal to the medieval Church, and it was no accident that young Humanists formed the first identifiable group of Martin Luther's supporters (see Chapter 18).

Renaissance Art

In Renaissance Italy, as in Reformation Europe, the values and interests of the laity were no longer subordinated to those of the clergy. In education, culture, and religion, the laity assumed a leading role and established models for the clergy to imitate. This resulted in part from the Church's loss of its international power during the great crises of the late Middle Ages. But it was also encouraged by the rise of national sentiment, the creation of competent national bureaucracies staffed by laity rather than clerics, and the rapid growth of lay education during the fourteenth and fifteenth centuries. Medieval Christian values adjusted to a more this-worldly spirit. Men and women began again to appreciate and even glorify the secular world, secular learning, and purely human pursuits as ends in themselves.

This perspective on life is prominent in the painting and sculpture of the High Renaissance, the late fifteenth and early sixteenth centuries, when the art of the period reached its full maturity. In imitation of Greek and Roman art, painters and sculptors attempted to create harmonious, symmetrical, and properly proportioned figures and to portray the human form with a glorified realism. Whereas Byzantine and Gothic art had been religious and idealized in the extreme, Renaissance art, especially in the fifteenth century, became a realistic reproduction of nature and of human beings as a part of nature. Giotto (1266–1336), the father of Renaissance painting, signaled the new direction. An admirer of Saint Francis of Assisi, whose love of nature he shared, Giotto painted a more natural world than his Byzantine and Gothic predecessors. Although still filled with religious seriousness, his work was no longer quite so abstract and unnatural a depiction of the world.

Renaissance artists had the considerable advantage of new technical skills developed during the fifteenth century. In addition to the availability of oil paints, the techniques of using shading to enhance realism *(chiaroscuro)* and adjusting the size of figures so as to give the viewer a feeling of continuity with the painting *(linear perspective)* were perfected. Compared with their flat Byzantine and Gothic counterparts, Renaissance paintings seem filled with energy and life and stand out from the canvas in three dimensions.

LEONARDO DA VINCI (1452–1519). More than any other person in the period, Leonardo exhibited the Renaissance ideal of the universal person, one who is not only a jack-of-all-trades but also a true master of many. One of the greatest painters of all time, Leonardo was also a military engineer for Ludovico il Moro in Milan, Cesare Borgia in Romagna, and the French king Francis I. Leonardo advocated scientific experimentation, dissected corpses to learn anatomy, and was an accomplished, self-taught botanist. His inventive mind foresaw such modern machines as airplanes and submarines. Indeed, the variety of his

A

C

B

D

The School of Athens, fresco by Raphael in the Vatican in Rome, painted ca. 1510–1511. The symmetry and organic unity of the painting, as well as its theme of antiquity, make it one of the most telling examples of Renaissance classicism. [Bettmann Archive]

The developing knowledge of human anatomy and physiology, opposite page. Figure A, from a manuscript of about 1292, shows the venous system and a few abstract internal organs. Since postmortems were forbidden, medieval renderings of the human body were based only on speculation and animal dissection. Figure B, from the Guidebook of Barber Surgeons of York *(fifteenth century), now in the British Museum, shows points for blood-letting, long an accepted medical practice. The drawings of the human fetus in Figure C are by Leonardo da Vinci. Renaissance artists and scientists began to base their portrayal of the human body on actual study. Figure D is a woodcut illustration of John of Carcar from* De Humanis Corporis Fabrica (Structure of the Human Body) *by the great Flemish anatomist, Andreas Vesalius (1514–1565). This work, published in Basel in 1543, was the foundation for the modern knowledge of anatomy. [A: The Bodleian Library, Oxford; B: Egerton MS. 2572, f. 50, reproduced by permission of the British Library Board; C and D: Bettmann Archive]*

interests was so great that it tended to shorten his attention span, so that he was constantly moving from one activity to another. His great skill lay in conveying inner moods through complex facial features, such as that seen in the most famous of his paintings, the *Mona Lisa.*

RAPHAEL (1483–1520). Raphael, an unusually sensitive man whose artistic career was cut short by his premature death at thirty-seven, was apparently loved by contemporaries as much for his person as for his work. He is famous for his tender madonnas, the best known of which graces the monastery of San Sisto in Piacenza. Art historians praise his fresco *The School of Athens,* an involved portrayal of the great masters of Western philosophy, as one of the most perfect examples of Renaissance artistic theory and technique. It depicts Plato and Aristotle surrounded by the great philosophers and scientists of antiquity, who are portrayed with the features of Raphael's

David, by Michelangelo. One of the most famous—and popular—of all the world's sculptures, it was carved from 1501 to 1504 and now stands in the Galleria dell' Accademia in Florence. [Alinari/SCALA/Art Resource]

famous contemporaries, including Leonardo and Michelangelo.

MICHELANGELO (1475–1564). The melancholy genius Michelangelo also excelled in a variety of arts and crafts. His eighteen-foot godlike sculpture *David*, which long stood majestically in the great square of Florence, is a perfect example of the Renaissance artist's devotion to harmony, symmetry, and proportion, as well as his extreme glorification of the human form. Four different popes commissioned works by Michelangelo, the most famous of which are the frescoes for the Sistine Chapel, painted during the pontificate of Pope Julius II (1503–1513), who also set Michelangelo to work on the pope's own magnificent tomb. The Sistine frescoes originally covered ten thousand square feet and involved 343 figures, over half of which exceeded ten feet in height. This labor of love and piety, painted while Michelangelo was lying on his back or stooping, took four years to complete and left Michelangelo partially crippled. A man who lived to be almost ninety, Michelangelo insisted on doing nearly everything himself and permitted his assistants only a few of the many involved chores.

His later works mark, artistically and philosophically, the passing of High Renaissance painting and the advent of a new, experimental style known as *mannerism*, which reached its peak in the late sixteenth and early seventeenth centuries. A reaction against the simplicity and symmetry of High Renaissance art, which also found expression in music and literature, mannerism made room for the strange and even the abnormal and gave freer reign to the subjectivity of the artist. It derived its name from the fact that it permitted the artist to express his own individual perceptions and feelings, to paint, compose, or write in a "mannered" or "affected" way. Tintoretto (d. 1594) and especially El Greco (d. 1614) became its supreme representatives.

Slavery in the Renaissance

Throughout Renaissance Italy, slavery flourished as extravagantly as art and culture. A thriving western slave market existed as early as the twelfth century. At

Black slavery existed in Europe during the sixteenth century. Katharina, portrayed in this drawing by the German painter Albrecht Dürer, was a slave in the service of Joa Bradao, a friend of Dürer and an economics minister from Portugal living in Antwerp, then the financial center of Europe. [Marburg, Art Resource, New York]

tients in lieu of fees—and it was not unusual to find them even in the service of a priest."[3]

In addition to widespread household or domestic slavery, collective plantation slavery following East Asian models developed in the west. In the savanas of Sudan and on Venetian estates on the islands of Cyprus and Crete in the eastern Mediterranean, sugar cane plantations were worked by gangs of slaves—an anticipation of later west Mediterranean and New World slavery.

Owners had complete dominion over their slaves; in Italian law, this meant the "[power] to have, hold, sell, alienate, exchange, enjoy, rent or unrent, dispose of in [their] will[s], judge soul and body, and do with in perpetuity whatsoever may please [them] and [their] heirs and no man may gainsay [them]."[4]

A strong, young, healthy slave cost the equivalent of the wages paid a free servant over several years. But taking into account a lifetime of free service thereafter, such slaves were very good bargains. The Tartars and Africans appear to have been the worst treated. But as in ancient Greece and Rome, slaves at this time were generally accepted as family members and were integrated into households. Not a few women slaves became mothers of their masters' children, and there is plenty of evidence that wives resisted their husbands' acquisition of young female slaves. Quite a few children of such unions were adopted and raised as legitimate heirs of their fathers. It was clearly in the interest of their owners to keep slaves healthy and happy; otherwise they were of little use and could even become a threat. Still, slaves remained a foreign and suspected presence in Italian society; they were, as all knew, uprooted and resentful people.

Italy's Political Decline: The French Invasions (1494–1527)

Treaty of Lodi

As a land of autonomous city-states, Italy had always preserved its peace and safety from foreign invasion, especially from invasion by the Turks, by depending on internal cooperation. Such cooperation had been maintained during the last half of the fifteenth century, thanks to a carefully constructed political alli-

this time the Spanish sold Muslim slaves captured in raids and war to wealthy Italians and other interested buyers. After the Black Death (1348–1350) had reduced the supply of laborers everywhere in Western Europe, the demand for slaves soared. They began to be imported from Africa, the Balkans, Constantinople, Cyprus, Crete, and the lands surrounding the Black Sea. At this time slavery was multicultural; slaves were taken randomly from conquered people and represented many races: whites and Asians as well as Africans; Tartars, Circassians, Greeks, Russians, Georgians, and Iranians. "By the end of the fourteenth century, there was hardly a well-to-do household in Tuscany without at least one slave: brides brought them [to their marriages] as part of their dowry, doctors accepted them from their pa-

[3] Iris Origo, *The Merchant of Prato: Francesco di Marco Datini 1335–1410* (New York: Godine, 1957), pp. 90–91.
[4] Ibid., p. 209.

ance known as the Treaty of Lodi (1454–1455). The terms of the treaty brought Milan and Naples, long traditional enemies, into alliance with Florence. These three stood together for decades against Venice, which was frequently joined by the Papal States to create an internal balance of power that also made possible a unified front against Italy's external enemies.

The peace made possible by the Treaty of Lodi ended in 1494, when Naples, supported by Florence and the Borgia pope Alexander VI (1492–1503), prepared to attack Milan. At this point, the Milanese despot Ludovico il Moro made what proved to be a fatal response to these new political alignments: He appealed for aid to the French.

Charles VIII's March Through Italy

The French king, Louis XI, had resisted the temptation to invade Italy, while nonetheless keeping French dynastic claims in Italy alive. His successor, Charles VIII (r. 1483–1498), an eager youth in his twenties, responded to Ludovico's call with lightning speed. Within five months, he had crossed the Alps (August 1495) and raced as conqueror through Florence and the Papal States into Naples.

Charles's lightning march through Italy also struck terror in non-Italian hearts. Ferdinand of Aragon, whose native land and self-interests as king of Sicily now became vulnerable to a French-Italian axis, took the initiative to create a counteralliance: the League of Venice, formed in March 1495, with Venice, the Papal States, and the Emperor Maximilian I joining Ferdinand against the French. The stage was set for a conflict between France and Spain that would not end until 1559.

Ludovico il Moro meanwhile recognized that he had sown the wind; having desired a French invasion only so long as it weakened his enemies, he now saw Milan threatened by the whirlwind of events that he had himself created. In reaction, he joined the League of Venice, and this alliance was able to send Charles into retreat by May. Charles remained thereafter on the defensive until his death in April 1498.

Pope Alexander VI and the Borgia Family

The French returned to Italy under Charles's successor, Louis XII (r. 1498–1515), this time assisted by a new Italian ally, the Borgia pope Alexander VI (1492–1503). Alexander, probably the most corrupt pope who ever sat on the papal throne, openly promoted the political careers of the children he had had before he became pope, Cesare and Lucrezia, as he placed the efforts of the powerful Borgia family to secure a political base in Romagna in tandem with papal policy there.

In Romagna, several principalities had fallen away from the Church during the Avignon papacy, and Venice, the pope's ally within the League of Venice, continued to contest the Papal States for their loyalty. Seeing that a French alliance could give him the opportunity to reestablish control over the region, Alexander agreed to abandon the League of Venice, a withdrawal of support that made the league too weak to resist a French reconquest of Milan. In exchange, Cesare Borgia received the sister of the king of Navarre, Charlotte d' Albret, in marriage, a union that greatly enhanced Borgia military strength. Cesare also received land grants from Louis XII and the promise of French military aid in Romagna. His cunning and determination would make him the model for Machiavelli's *The Prince*.

All in all, it was a scandalous trade-off, but one that made it possible for both the French king and the pope to realize their ambitions within Italy. Louis successfully invaded Milan in August 1499. In 1500, Louis and Ferdinand of Aragon divided Naples between them, while the pope and Cesare Borgia conquered the cities of Romagna without opposition.

Pope Julius II

Cardinal Giuliano della Rovere, a strong opponent of the Borgia family, became Pope Julius II (1503–1513). He suppressed the Borgias and placed their newly conquered lands in Romagna under papal jurisdiction. Julius came to be known as the "warrior pope" because he brought the Renaissance papacy to a peak of military prowess and diplomatic intrigue. Shocked as were other contemporaries by this thoroughly secular papacy, the Humanist Erasmus (ca. 1466–1536), who had witnessed in disbelief a bullfight in the papal palace during a visit to Rome, wrote a popular anonymous satire entitled *Julius Excluded from Heaven*. This humorous account purported to describe the pope's unsuccessful efforts to convince Saint Peter that he was worthy of admission to heaven.

Assisted by his powerful French allies, Pope Julius drove the Venetians out of Romagna in 1509, thereby ending Venetian claims in the region and fully securing the Papal States. Having realized this long-sought papal goal, Julius turned to the second major undertaking of his pontificate: ridding Italy of his former ally, the French invaders. Julius, Ferdinand of Aragon, and Venice formed a second Holy League in October 1511, and within a short period, Emperor Maximilian I and the Swiss joined them. By 1512, the league had the French in full retreat, and Swiss armies soundly defeated them in 1513 at Novara.

The French invaded Italy still a third time under Louis's successor, Francis I (r. 1515–1547). French armies massacred Swiss soldiers of the Holy League at Marignano in September 1515, revenging the earlier defeat at Novara. The victory won from the Medici pope, Leo X, was the Concordat of Bologna in August 1516, an agreement that gave the French king control over the French clergy in exchange for French recognition of the pope's superiority over Church councils and his right to collect taxes from the French clergy. This was an important compromise that helped keep France Catholic after the outbreak of the Protestant Reformation. But the new French entry into Italy also led to the first of four major wars with Spain in the first half of the sixteenth century: the Habsburg-Valois wars, none of which France won.

Niccolò Machiavelli

The period of foreign invasions made a shambles of Italy. The same period that saw Italy's cultural peak in the work of Leonardo, Raphael, and Michelangelo also witnessed Italy's political tragedy. One who watched as French, Spanish, and German armies wreaked havoc on his country was Niccolò Machiavelli (1469–1527). The more he saw, the more convinced he became that Italian political unity and independence were ends that justified any means. A Humanist and a careful student of ancient Rome, Machiavelli admired the heroic acts of ancient Roman rulers, what Renaissance people called their *Virtu*. Romanticizing the old Roman citizenry, he lamented the absence of heroism among his compatriots. Such a perspective caused his interpretation of both ancient and contemporary history to be somewhat exaggerated. His Florentine contemporary,

Machiavelli Discusses the Most Important Trait for a Ruler

Machiavelli believed that the most important personality trait of a successful ruler was the ability to instill fear in his subjects.

▶ *For other perspectives on law, leadership, and government, see the following document boxes: "Hammurabi Creates a Code of Law in Mesopotamia" (Ch. 1), "Legalism" (Ch. 2), "Thucydides Reports Pericles on Athenian Democracy" (Ch. 4), "Polybius Summarizes the Roman Constitution" (Ch. 5), "The Edicts of Ashoka" (Ch. 7), and "Some Reforms of Akbar" (Ch. 24).*

Here the question arises; whether it is better to be loved than feared or feared than loved. The answer is that it would be desirable to be both but, since that is difficult, it is much safer to be feared than to be loved, if one must choose. For on men in general this observation may be made: they are ungrateful, fickle, and deceitful, eager to avoid dangers, and avid for gain, and while you are useful to them they are all with you, offering you their blood, their property, their lives, and their sons so long as danger is remote, as we noted above, but when it approaches they turn on you. Any prince, trusting only in their words and having no other preparations made, will fall to his ruin, for friendships that are bought at a price and not by greatness and nobility of soul are paid for indeed, but they are not owned and cannot be called upon in time of need. Men have less hesitation in offending a man who is loved than one who is feared, for love is held by a bond of obligation which, as men are wicked, is broken whenever personal advantage suggests it, but fear is accompanied by the dread of punishment which never relaxes.

Niccolò Machiavelli, *The Prince* (1513), trans. and ed. by Thomas G. Bergin (New York: Appleton-Century-Crofts, 1947), p. 48.

Guicciardini, a more sober historian less given to idealizing antiquity, wrote truer chronicles of Florentine and Italian history.

The juxtaposition of what Machiavelli believed the ancient Romans had been with the failure of contemporary Romans to realize such high ideals made him the famous cynic we know in the popular epithet *Machiavellian*. Only an unscrupulous strongman, he concluded, using duplicity and terror, could impose order on so divided and selfish a people.

It has been argued that Machiavelli wrote *The Prince* in 1513 as a cynical satire, not as a serious recommendation of unprincipled despotic rule. To take his advocacy of tyranny literally, it is argued, contradicts both his earlier works and his own strong family tradition of republican service. But Machiavelli seems to have been in earnest when he advised rulers to discover the advantages of fraud and brutality. He apparently hoped to see a strong ruler emerge from the restored powerful Medici family.

Whatever Machiavelli's hopes may have been, the Medicis were not destined to be Italy's deliverers. The second Medici pope, Clement VII (1523–1534), watched helplessly as Rome was sacked by the army of Emperor Charles V in 1527, also the year of Machiavelli's death.[5]

Suggested Readings

M. ASTON, *The Fifteenth Century: The Prospect of Europe* (1968). Crisp social history, with pictures.

H. BARON, *The Crisis of the Early Italian Renaissance*, Vols. 1 and 2 (1966). A major work, setting forth the civic dimension of Italian Humanism.

B. BERENSON, *Italian Painters of the Renaissance* (1901). Still incisive.

G. BRUCKER, *Giovanna and Lusanna: Love and Marriage in Renaissance Florence* (1986). A tale of unhappy marriage and extramarital love, more in the spirit of Bergman than of Fellini, and apparently typical of much of Renaissance Italy.

G. BRUCKER, *Renaissance Florence* (1983). Considered the best introduction to the subject.

J. BURCKHARDT, *The Civilization of the Renaissance in Italy* (1867). The old classic that still has as many defenders as detractors.

C. CIPOLLA, *Before the Industrial Revolution: European Society and Economy, 1000–1700* (1976). Readable sweeping account.

W. K. FERGUSON, *Europe in Transition 1300–1520* (1962). A major survey that deals with the transition from medieval to Renaissance society.

W. K. FERGUSON, *The Renaissance* (1940). A brief, stimulating summary of the Renaissance in both Italy and northern Europe.

F. GILBERT, *Machiavelli and Guicciardini* (1984). The two great Renaissance historians compared.

M. GILMORE, *The World of Humanism 1453–1517* (1952). A comprehensive survey, especially strong in intellectual and cultural history.

J. R. HALE, *Renaissance Europe: The Individual and Society, 1480–1520* (1971). A many-sided treatment of social history.

D. HAY, *Europe in the Fourteenth and Fifteenth Centuries* (1966). A many-sided treatment of political history.

D. HAY, *The Italian Renaissance* (1977). For those who want the subject in a nutshell.

A. HUDSON, *The Premature Reformation: Wycliffite Texts and Lollard History* (1988). The teaching of John Wycliffe and the movement it stimulated.

J. HUIZINGA, *The Waning of the Middle Ages: A Study of the Forms of Life, Thought, and Art in France and The Netherlands in the Dawn of the Renaissance* (1924). A classic study of "mentality" at the end of the Middle Ages.

G. HUPPERT, *After the Black Death* (1986). A social historian's perspective on the transition from the Renaissance to modern times.

D. JENSEN, *Renaissance Europe: Age of Recovery and Reconciliation* (1981). Up-to-date textbook.

R. KIECKHEFER, *Unquiet Souls* (1984). Penetrating and sympathetic study of fourteenth-century religious life.

C. KLAPISCH-ZUBER, *Women, Family, and Ritual in Renaissance Italy* (1985). Sober essays, stressing the negative status of women and unfairness of male treatment of them.

R. J. KNECHT, *Francis I* (1982). Up-to-date biography of the French king.

P. O. KRISTELLER, *Renaissance Thought: The Classic, Scholastic, and Humanist Strains* (1961). A master shows the many sides of Renaissance thought.

I. MACLEAN, *The Renaissance Notion of Women* (1980). A study of largely unflattering theories about women found in learned tracts on theology, philosophy, law, and medicine.

L. MARTINES, *Power and Imagination: City States in Renaissance Italy* (1980). Stimulating account of cultural and political history.

H. A. MISKIMIN, *The Economy of Early Renaissance Europe 1300–1460* (1969). Shows the interaction of social, political, and economic change.

[5]For placement of the western Renaissance in world perspective, see the conclusion of Chapter 18.

E. Muir, *Civic Ritual in Renaissance Venice* (1981). A study of the use of pageantry for political purposes.

F. Oakley, *The Western Church in the Later Middle Ages* (1979). Vigorous defense of the integrity of late medieval religion.

H. A. Oberman, *The Harvest of Medieval Theology* (1963). A demanding synthesis and revision.

N. Orme, *English Schools in the Middle Ages* (1973). Introduction to elementary education.

E. Perroy, *The Hundred Years' War,* trans. by W. B. Wells (1965). The most comprehensive one-volume account.

Y. Renovard, *The Avignon Papacy 1305–1403,* trans. by D. Bethell (1970). Standard narrative.

Q. Skinner, *The Foundations of Modern Political Thought I: The Renaissance* (1978). A broad survey, very comprehensive.

M. Spinka, *John Hus's Concept of the Church* (1966).

J. W. Thompson, *Economic and Social History of Europe in the Later Middle Ages 1300–1530* (1958). A bread-and-butter account.

B. Tierney, *The Crisis of Church and State 1050–1300* (1964). Part 4 provides the major documents in the clash between Boniface VIII and Philip the Fair.

B. Tierney, *Foundations of the Conciliar Theory* (1955). An important study showing the origins of conciliar theory in canon law.

W. Ullmann, *Origins of the Great Schism* (1948). A basic study by a controversial interpreter of medieval political thought.

C. T. Wood, *Philip the Fair and Boniface VIII* (1967). Excerpts from the scholarly debate over the significance of this confrontation.

P. Ziegler, *The Black Death* (1969). A highly readable journalistic account.

Family Life West and East in the Premodern Era

A family has a certain force and logic of its own, regardless of the time and place in which it exists. The routine of family life conspires with basic instincts to establish characteristic patterns of behavior, reinforcing natural feelings and building expectations among family members. Time, place, and culture, however, are important. A person raised in a twelfth-century family would be different from one raised in a twentieth-century family, and growing up in Europe is not the same as growing up in China. But the differences do not lie in the ability of husbands and wives to love one another or of parents to make sacrifices for their children. They lie, rather, in the ways different cultures and religions infuse family life with values and influence the way individuals perceive relationships and the behavior of family members.

THE WESTERN EUROPEAN FAMILY

Later Marriages Between 1500 and 1800, men and women in Western Europe and England married at later ages than they had in previous centuries. Men tended to be in their mid- to late twenties rather than in their late teens and early twenties, and women in their early to mid-twenties rather than in their teens. The canonical, or Church-sanctioned, age for marriage remained fourteen for men and twelve for women, and engagements might occur at these young ages, especially among royalty and nobility. As it had done throughout the high and later Middle Ages, the Church also recognized as valid the free, private exchange of vows between a man and a woman at these minimal ages. However, after the Reformation, which condemned such clandestine unions, the Church increasingly required both parental agreement and public vows in church before a marriage could be recognized as fully licit—procedures it had always actually preferred.

Late marriage in the West reflected the difficulty couples had supporting themselves independently. The difficulty arose because of the population growth that occurred during the late fifteenth and early sixteenth centuries, when Western Europe recovered much of the population loss incurred during the Great Plague. Larger families meant more heirs and hence a greater division of resources. In Germanic and Scandinavian countries, the custom of a fair sharing of inheritance among all male children worked to delay marriages, for divided inheritances often meant small incomes for the recipients. It simply took the average cou-

ple a longer time than previously to prepare themselves materially for marriage. In the sixteenth century, one in five women never married, and these, combined with the estimated 15 percent who were unmarried widows, constituted a sizable unmarried female population.

A later marriage meant a marriage of shorter duration because couples who married in their thirties would not spend as much time together as couples who married in their twenties. Such marriages also contributed to more frequent remarriage for men because women who bore children for the first time at advanced ages had higher mortality rates than younger mothers. Moreover, as growing Church condemnation and the rapid growth of orphanages and foundling homes between 1600 and 1800 confirm, delayed marriage increased premarital sex and raised the number of illegitimate children.

Arranged Marriages Marriage tended to be "arranged" in the sense that the parents customarily met and discussed the terms of the marriage before the prospective bride and bridegroom became party to the discussions. But the wealth and social standing of the bride and the bridegroom were not the only things considered when parents arranged a marriage. By the fifteenth century, it was not unusual for the two involved people to have known each other in advance and even to have had some prior relationship. Also, emotional feeling for one another was increasingly respected by parents. Parents did not force total strangers to live together, and children had a legal right to protest and resist an unwanted marriage. A forced marriage was by definition invalid, and parents understood that unwanted marriages could fail. The best marriage was one desired by both parties and supported by their families.

Family Size The Western European family was conjugal, or nuclear; that is, it consisted of a father and a mother and two to four children who survived into adulthood. This nuclear family lived within a larger household, consisting of in-laws, servants, laborers, and boarders. The average husband and wife had seven or eight children, a birth about every two years. Of these, however, an estimated one-third died by age five, and one-half by their teens. Rare is the family, at any social level, that did not experience infant mortality and child death.

Birth Control Artificial birth control has existed since antiquity. The ancient Egyptians used alligator dung and other acidic sperm killers, and sponges were also popular. In the West, the Church's condemnation of *coitus interruptus* (male withdrawal before ejaculation) during the thirteenth and fourteenth centuries suggests that a contraceptive mentality—that is, a conscious and regular effort at birth control—may have been developing at this time. But early birth control measures, when applied, were not very effective, and for both historical and moral reasons the Church firmly opposed them. During the eleventh century it suppressed an extreme ascetic sect, the Cathars, whom it accused of practicing birth control. The Church also opposed (and still opposes) contraception on moral grounds. According to Saint Thomas Aquinas, a moral act must always aid and abet, never frustrate, the natural end of the being or thing in question, and he believed that the natural end of sex could be only the birth of children and their godly rearing within the bounds of holy matrimony and the community of the Church.

Wet Nursing The Church allied with the physicians of early modern Europe on another intimate family matter: the condemnation of women who hired nurses to suckle their newborn children, sometimes for as long as a year and a half. The practice was popular among upper-class women, who looked on it as a symbol of their high rank. Wet nurses were women who had recently had a baby or were suckling a child of their own, and who, for a fee, agreed also to suckle another child. The practice appears to have increased the risk of infant mortality, exposing infants to a strange and shared milk supply from women who were usually not as healthy as the infants' own mothers and who often lived under less sanitary conditions. But nursing an infant was a chore some upper-class women found distasteful, and their husbands also preferred that they not do it. Among women, vanity and convenience appear to have been motives for turning to wet nurses. For husbands, more was at stake in the practice. Because the Church forbade sexual intercourse while a woman was lactating, and sexual intercourse was also believed to spoil a lactating woman's milk (pregnancy, of course, eventually ended her milk supply), a nursing wife often became a reluctant lover. In addition, nursing had a contraceptive effect (about 75 per-

cent effective). Some women prolonged nursing their children precisely to delay a new pregnancy, and some husbands understood and cooperated in this form of family planning. For other husbands, however, especially noblemen and royalty who desired an abundance of male heirs, nursing seemed to rob them of offspring and to jeopardize the patrimony; hence, their support of wet nursing.

Loving Families? The traditional Western European family had features that may seem cold and unloving. When children were between the ages of eight and thirteen, parents routinely sent them out of their homes into apprenticeships, off to school, or into employment in the homes and businesses of relatives, friends, and even strangers. In addition, the emotional ties between spouses seem to have been as tenuous as those between parents and children. Widowers and widows often married again within a few months of their spouses' deaths, and marriages with extreme disparity in age—between older men and younger women and between older women and younger men—also suggest limited affection.

In response to such modern-day criticism, an early modern parent would surely have asked, "What greater love can parents have for their children than to equip them to make their way vocationally in the world?" An apprenticed child was a self-supporting child, and hence a child with a future. Considering primitive living conditions, contemporaries could also appreciate the purely utilitarian and humane side of marriage and understand when widowers and widows quickly married again. On the other hand, marriages with extreme disparity in age were no more the norm in early modern Europe than the practice of wet nursing, and they received just as much criticism and ridicule.

THE TRADITIONAL CHINESE FAMILY[1]

The Meaning of Family In Chinese the word for "family" and "home" is the same; all who live together under one

[1] The sources for the following are Maurice Freedman, *The Study of Chinese Society: Essays by Maurice Freedman* (Stanford, CA: Stanford University Press, 1979); Martin C. Yang, *A Chinese Village: Taitou, Shantung Province* (New York: Columbia University Press, 1965); and Margery Wolf, "Child Training and the Chinese Family," in Maurice Freedman, ed., *Family and Kinship in Chinese Society* (Stanford, CA: Stanford University Press, 1970), pp. 37–62.

A Chinese Merchant's Family, ca. 1865. *In a pose reflecting the gender divisions within the traditional Chinese family, the father sits with his sons on the right, his wife and daughter sit on the left. [Courtesy Peabody & Essex Museum, Salem, MA/Collections of the Essex Institute)*

roof are "family." As in premodern Europe, the traditional Chinese family or home was society's fundamental unit. But, more so than in the West, its members were also very conscious of belonging to larger and different social groups. These groups included, for example, all one's living kin, people to whom one was related by blood or by marriage. Duties and obligations to kin did not have the same importance as those to one's immediate family, and relations with kin usually lacked the intimacy and charity of those within the family. But kin formed a permanent and prominent part of one's social world.

In addition to family and kin, people also had a sense of belonging to the ruling regime or "state." Rulers tried to nurture such a sense of group identity with the state beyond family and clan by stressing the broadest possible relationships. These rulers especially exalted patrilineage, or membership in a group that traced its history through untold generations of males. Patrilineage also won out in the West in the later Middle Ages, but only after a long period in which matrilineal lines had been recognized and the mother's side of the family had been genealogically preserved. Despite efforts by Chinese rulers to exalt the state, the Chinese never felt the closeness to the state that they did to their immediate family and kin. In the West, by contrast, a state consciousness was more successfully inculcated, as the formation of scores of national cultures after the fourteenth century attests.

Finally, the traditional Chinese family looked on its uncounted deceased ancestors as intimate family members. People believed that the spirits of their ancestors roamed the earth and scrutinized their every action. Such belief became a spur to good behavior and achievement. As in Western Christendom, the Chinese people believed that the world of the living communed with that of the dead. The living were admonished to act in ways that would please and bring honor to their dead ancestors, lest the spirits of their ancestors bring misfortune upon them. It was believed that ancestor spirits could bring success or failure, depending on how one behaved. In Western Europe, by contrast, the living were thought to be of more help to the dead than the dead to the living. By special prayers and masses, people believed they could help their deceased relatives pass through purgatory and into heaven.

Family Size The average Chinese family had five or six members, slightly smaller than the average European family of seven or eight, although in both East and West families varied greatly in size. Like Western religious teaching, Confucianism exalted the authority of the father as a patriarch over the family and stressed the virtues of order and obedience within it, and it deemed no religious virtue to be greater than loyalty to one's family.

Family Relationships A marriage was costly to the bride's family and thus arranged with great care. During negotiations, mothers played the dominant role in finding husbands for their daughters (in Western Europe, fathers took the lead). This actually worked in the bride's favor, as the mother better understood what marriage involved and probably got her the best possible mate. However, the mother also got the credit or blame for a marriage's success or failure. The prospective bride and bridegroom played a far lesser role in marital arrangements than they did in Western Europe.

The traditional Chinese family discriminated against women, and against none more so than a daughter-in-law. This was because a daughter-in-law was not a natural family member, but an alien person artificially incorporated into the family unit by marriage. Brides often found the transition from their own to their husbands' family to be traumatic. After the wedding, the bride became the sole responsibility of her husband's family, legally and economically, breaking ties with her own family to a degree unheard of in Western Europe. No longer able to count on the security and affection of her own family, she often found the reception within her husband's household to be demanding and stressful, especially in the first few years, when she was carefully watched and grudgingly integrated into her new family's routine. Confucianism may have contributed to this state of affairs; it stressed family solidarity against foreign influence and advised families to isolate daughters-in-law.

A new wife came immediately under the authority of her mother-in-law, who scrupulously regulated her every activity within the new household. Such regulation was more exaggerated in well-ordered, high-status families than in more informal, low-status families. Always the bride's husband had to defer to his mother's decisions about his wife's role within the household. A daughter-in-law could not protest this situation because of her total dependence on her mother-in-law's good will. Whether in the way she bore and reared her children or in the way she related to the members of the household, a daughter-in-law who found herself at odds with her mother-in-law faced great difficulty; in the end, it often became a choice between capitulation or misery.

In addition, a daughter-in-law found herself competing with her mother-in-law for the loyalty and affection of her husband. Both women depended almost entirely on him for their well-being, and because he too had a deep and unbreakable commitment to each, he was put to the test to treat each in a way that did not offend the other. But with the passage of time, and especially after she had given birth, a daughter-in-law gained greater respect and freedom within the household.

Child Rearing Chinese parents' chief aim was to create loyal and obedient children who would support them in their old age. This was true in European rural society as well, but among the European burgher classes rearing a strong and independent child whose success brought honor to the family was an equally important goal. As in Western Europe, Chinese parental treatment of children, especially boys, changed dramatically after age six or seven. Children at that age came under the strict discipline of their father, who henceforth dealt with them in an aloof and formal manner—the best way, it was thought, to render them subservient. The father believed that his children would likely become the adults he wished them to be if they feared him and counted displeasing him a shameful act. As among Europeans, Chinese parents resisted overly generous displays of affection and indulgence, lest children be spoiled and rendered undependable in later life, when their parents' welfare would hang totally on their loyalty.

Mothers took a different approach to child rearing than fathers. Bearing children made a woman important within the family, and her children were also the key to her future well-being and security. Whereas the father sought to retain his children's loyalty by inculcating fear, the mother cultivated a more affectionate relationship, often assuming the role of quiet advocate and mediator for her children with their father. Both parents beat disobedient children, but as a child matured, corporal punishment became increasingly the responsibility of the father, another feature shared with European society. The mother became the parent in whom a child might confide and with whom a child might joke.

On the whole, daughters were treated less harshly and more affectionately than sons, because parents knew that their daughters would soon leave them to become members of their husbands' households, and once gone, they would never be theirs again. Inasmuch as parents were not dependent on their daughters for their future well-being, they found themselves in a position to treat them with greater informality and affection and with less need to drill respect and obedience into them. The result was happier relationships between daughters and both fathers and mothers.

Erasmus of Rotterdam in a 1526 engraving by Albrecht Dürer. Erasmus influenced all of the reform movements of the sixteenth century. He was commonly said to have "laid the egg that Luther hatched." [National Gallery of Art, Washington, D.C.]

18

The Age of Reformation and Religious Wars

In the second decade of the sixteenth century, there began in Saxony in Germany a powerful religious movement that rapidly spread throughout northern Europe, deeply affecting society and politics as well as the spiritual lives of men and women. Attacking what they believed to be burdensome superstitions that robbed people of both their money and their peace of mind, Protestant reformers led a broad revolt against the medieval Church. In a relatively short span of time, hundreds of thousands of people from all social classes set aside the beliefs of centuries and adopted a more simplified religious practice.

The Protestant Reformation challenged aspects of the Renaissance, especially its tendency to follow classical sources in glorifying human nature and its loyalty to traditional religion. Protestants were more impressed by the human potential for evil than by the inclination to do good and encouraged parents, teachers, and magistrates to be firm disciplinarians. On the other hand, Protestants also embraced many Renaissance values, especially in the sphere of educational reform and particularly with regard to training in ancient languages. Like the Italian Humanists, the Protestant reformers studied ancient languages and went directly to the original sources; only for them this meant the study of the Hebrew and Greek scriptures and the consequent challenge of traditional institutions founded on the authority of the Bible.

The road to the Reformation was long in preparation. As the Protestant ethic influenced an entire age, it was also itself born out of changes in European society beyond those within the purely religious and ecclesiastical spheres.

For Europe, the late fifteenth and the sixteenth centuries were a period of unprecedented territorial ex-

513

pansion and ideological experimentation. Permanent colonies were established within the Americas, and the exploitation of the New World's human and seemingly endless mineral resources was begun. The American gold and silver imported into Europe spurred scientific invention and a weapons industry and touched off an inflationary spiral that produced a revolution in prices by the end of the sixteenth century. The new bullion also helped to create international traffic in African slaves, who were used in ever increasing numbers to work the mines and the plantations of the New World as replacements for American natives. This period further saw social engineering and political planning on a large scale as newly centralized governments developed long-range economic policies, a practice that came to be known as *mercantilism.*

The late fifteenth and the sixteenth centuries also marked the first wide-scale use of the printing press, an invention greatly assisted by the development of a process of cheap paper manufacture and publishers eager to exploit a fascinating new technology. Printing with movable type was invented by Johann Gutenberg (d. 1468) in the mid-fifteenth century in the German city of Mainz. Residential colleges and universities had greatly expanded in northern Europe during the fourteenth and fifteenth centuries, creating a literate public in the cities eager to possess and read books. The new technology also made propaganda possible on a massive scale, as pamphlets could now be rapidly and inexpensively produced.

On the Eve of the Reformation

External Expansion and the Emergence of Capitalism

On the eve of the Reformation, the geographical and intellectual horizons of Western people were broadening. The trade routes opened by Portugal to Africa and Asia and by Spain to its emerging empire in the Americas shifted the center of commerce in Europe from the Mediterranean and Baltic to the Atlantic seaboard. (As we describe in more detail in Chapter 23, the voyages of discovery that began in the fifteenth and sixteenth centuries, particularly those of Christopher Columbus that began in 1492, set in motion the economic and colonial expansion that eventually brought European dominance to much of the globe.) The flood of spices and precious metals that flowed

back into Europe over these new routes was a mixed blessing. It contributed to a steady rise in prices during the sixteenth century that created an inflation rate estimated at 2 percent a year. The new supply of bullion from the Americas joined with enlarged European production to increase greatly the amount of coinage in circulation, and this increase in turn fed inflation. Fortunately, the increase in prices was by and large spread over a long period and was not sudden. Prices doubled in Spain by mid-century and quadrupled by 1600. In Luther's Wittenberg, the cost of basic food and clothing increased almost 100 percent between 1519 and 1540. Generally, wages and rents remained well behind the rise in prices.

The new wealth enabled governments and private entrepreneurs to sponsor basic research and expansion in the printing, shipping, mining, textile, and weapons industries—the growth industries of the Age of Reformation. There is also evidence of mercantilism or large-scale government planning in such ventures as the French silk industry and the Hapsburg–Fugger development of mines in Austria and Hungary.

During the thirteenth and fourteenth centuries, capitalist institutions and practices had already begun to develop in the rich Italian cities. Those who owned the means of production, either privately or corporately, were clearly distinguished from the workers who operated them. Wherever possible, monopolies were created in basic goods. High interest was charged on loans—actual, if not legal, usury. And the capitalist "virtues" of thrift, industry, and orderly planning were evident everywhere—all intended to permit the free and efficient accumulation of wealth.

The late fifteenth and sixteenth centuries saw the maturation of such capitalism together with its peculiar social problems. The new wealth and industrial expansion raised the expectations of the poor and the ambitious and heightened the reactionary tendencies within the established and wealthy classes. This effect, in turn, greatly aggravated the traditional social divisions between the clergy and the laity, the higher and the lower clergy, the urban patriciate and the guilds, masters and journeymen, and the landed nobility and the agrarian peasantry.

The Northern Renaissance

The scholarly works of northern Humanists created a climate favorable to religious and educational reforms immediately preceding the Reformation. Northern Humanism was initially stimulated by the impor-

Erasmus Describes the "Philosophy of Christ"

Although Erasmus called his ideal of the way people should live the "philosophy of Christ," he found it taught by classical authors as well. In this selection, he comments on its main features, with obvious polemic against the philosophy of the Scholastics.

This kind of philosophy [the philosophy of Christ] is located more truly in the disposition of the mind than in syllogisms. Here life means more than debate, inspiration is preferable to erudition, transformation [of life] a more important matter than intellectual comprehension. Only a very few can be learned, but all can be Christian, all can be devout, and—I shall boldly add—all can be theologians. Indeed, this philosophy easily penetrates into the minds of all; it is an action in special accord with human nature. What else is the philosophy of Christ, which he himself calls a rebirth, than the restoration of human nature . . . ? Although no one has taught this more perfectly than Christ, nevertheless one may find in the books of the pagans very much which does agree with it. There was never so coarse a school of philosophy that taught that money rendered a man happy. Nor has there ever been one so shameless that fixed the chief good in vulgar honors and pleasures. The Stoics understood that no one was wise unless he was good. . . . According to Plato, Socrates teaches . . . that a wrong must not be repaid with a wrong, and also that since the soul is immortal, those should not be lamented who depart this life for a happier one with the assurance of having led an upright life. . . . And Aristotle has written in the *Politics* that nothing can be a delight to us . . . except virtue alone. . . . If there are things that belong particularly to Christianity in these ancient writers, let us follow them.

John C. Olin, ed. and trans., *Christian Humanism and the Reformation: Desiderius Erasmus.* (New York: Harper, 1965), pp. 100–101.

---

tation of Italian learning through such varied intermediaries as students who had studied in Italy, merchants, and the Brothers of the Common Life (an influential lay religious movement that began in The Netherlands). The northern Humanists tended to come from more diverse social backgrounds and to be more devoted to religious reforms than their Italian counterparts. They were also more willing to write for lay audiences.

The most famous of the northern Humanists was Desiderius Erasmus (1466–1536), the reputed "prince of the Humanists." Erasmus gained fame as both an educational and a religious reformer. He aspired to unite the classical ideals of humanity and civic virtue with the Christian ideals of love and piety. He believed that disciplined study of the classics and the Bible, if begun early enough, was the best way to reform both individuals and society. He summarized his own beliefs with the phrase *philosophia Christi*, a simple, ethical piety in imitation of Christ. He set this ideal in starkest contrast to what he believed to be the dogmatic, ceremonial, and factious religious practice of the later Middle Ages. To promote his own religious beliefs, Erasmus edited the works of the Church Fathers and made a Greek edition of the New Testament (1516), which became the basis for his new, more accurate Latin translation (1519), later used by Martin Luther.

These various enterprises did not please Church authorities. At one point in the mid-sixteenth century, all of Erasmus's works were placed on the *Index of Forbidden Books.* Erasmus also received Luther's unqualified condemnation for his views on the freedom of human will. Still, Erasmus's didactic and scholarly works became basic tools of reform in the hands of both Protestant and Catholic reformers.

The best known of early English Humanists was Sir Thomas More (1478–1535), a close friend of Erasmus. It was while visiting More that Erasmus wrote his most famous work, *The Praise of Folly* (1511), an amusing and profound exposé of human self-deception that was quickly translated from the original Latin into many vernacular languages. More's *Utopia* (1516), a criticism of contemporary society, still rivals

Portrait of Thomas More by Hans Holbein ca. 1490. More was executed in 1535 by order of King Henry VIII. [Bildarchiv Preussischer Kulturbesitz]

the plays of Shakespeare as the most read sixteenth-century English work. *Utopia* depicts an imaginary society based on reason and tolerance that has overcome social and political injustice by holding all property and goods in common and by requiring all to earn their bread by the sweat of their own brow.

Although More remained staunchly Catholic, Humanism in England, as in Germany, played an important role in preparing the way for the English Reformation. A circle of English Humanists, under the direction of Henry VIII's minister Thomas Cromwell, translated and disseminated late medieval criticisms of the papacy and many of Erasmus's satirical writings.

Whereas in Germany, England, and France Humanism prepared the way for Protestant reforms, in Spain it entered the service of the Catholic Church. Here the key figure was Francisco Jiménez de Cisneros (1437–1517), a confessor to Queen Isabella, and after 1508 Grand Inquisitor—a position from which he was able to enforce the strictest religious orthodoxy. Jiménez was a conduit for Humanist scholarship and learning. He founded the University of Alcalá near Madrid in 1509, printed a Greek edition

of the New Testament, and translated many religious tracts that aided clerical reform and control of lay religious life. His greatest achievement, taking fifteen years to complete, was the *Complutensian Polyglot Bible,* a six-volume work that placed the Hebrew, Greek, and Latin versions of the Bible in parallel columns. Such scholarly projects and internal Church reforms joined with the repressive measures of Ferdinand and Isabella to keep Spain strictly Catholic throughout the Age of Reformation.

Religion and Society

The Protestant Reformation occurred at a time of sharp conflict between two very old foes: the emerging nation-states of Europe, which were bent on conforming and centralizing their realms, and the many self-governing towns and regions, which had long run their own affairs. Since the fourteenth century, the king's law threatened to displace local law and custom almost everywhere, creating in many towns and territories a keen sense of the loss of traditional rights and freedoms. As a protest against arbitrary, self-aggrandizing, hierarchical authority in the person of the pope, the Reformation came to be closely identified in the minds of its supporters with what we today might call states' rights or local control. For many, the religious revolt became also part of a struggle to remain politically free.

The Reformation broke out first in the free imperial cities of Germany and Switzerland. There were about sixty-five such cities, and each was in a certain sense a little kingdom unto itself. The great majority had Protestant movements, but with mixed success and duration. Some quickly turned Protestant and remained so. Some were Protestant only for a short time. Still others (by far the minority) tolerated both Protestant and Catholic practice, with the followers of the majority practice conceding the minority some qualified rights of worship, normally in private homes or outside the city limits.

Conflict between cities and higher princely or royal authority over political rights was not the only source of tension affecting cities as the Reformation began. They were also torn by deep internal social and political divisions. Certain groups favored the Reformation more than others. In many places guilds whose members were prospering and rising socially—printers are a prominent example—led the Reformation. Guilds with a history of opposition to reigning governmental authority also stand out among early Protestant supporters. There is plenty of evidence to suggest that people who felt pushed around and bullied by either local or distant authority—whether it was a guild by an autocratic local government or an entire city or region by a powerful prince or king—tended to perceive in the Protestant movement an ally.

Both in town and in countryside social and political experience coalesced with larger religious issues. The townspeople of German and Swiss towns, for example, found themselves facing incorporation into the territory of a powerful local prince and being transformed from free citizens into obedient subjects. Under such circumstances the Protestant sermon or tract seemed directly relevant to their lives. When Luther and his comrades preached about a priesthood of all believers, scorned the authority of ecclesiastical landlords, and ridiculed papal laws as arbitrary human inventions, political as well as religious nerves were touched, as much in the villages as in the towns. Like city-dwellers, the peasants on the land also heard in the Protestant sermon and pamphlet a promise of political liberation and even of a degree of social betterment. More than the townspeople, the peasants found their traditional liberties, from fishing and hunting to representation at local diets, progressively being chipped away by the great secular and ecclesiastical landlords who ruled over them.

The Protestant Reformation also could not have occurred without the monumental crises of the medieval Church during the "exile" in Avignon, the Great Schism, the conciliar period, and the Renaissance papacy. On the eve of the Reformation, Rome's international network of Church offices, which had brought religious unity to Europe during the Middle Ages, was falling apart in many areas. This collapse was hurried along by a growing sense of regional identity—incipient nationalism—and local secular administrative competence. The long-entrenched benefice system of the medieval Church, which permitted important ecclesiastical posts to be sold to the highest bidders and left parishes without active, resident pastors, had proved detrimental to local religious life. The substitutes hired by nonresident holders of benefices, who lived elsewhere (mostly in Rome) and milked the revenues of their offices, performed their chores mechanically and had neither first-hand knowledge of nor much sympathy with local needs and problems. Rare was the late medieval German town that did not have complaints about the maladministration, concubinage, and/or fiscalism of their clergy, especially among the higher clergy (i.e., bishops, abbots, and prelates).

Communities loudly protested the financial abuses of the medieval Church long before Luther published his famous summary of economic grievances in the *Address to the Christian Nobility of the German Nation* (1520). The sale of indulgences, a practice greatly expanded on the eve of the Reformation, had also been repeatedly attacked before Luther.

City governments attempted to improve local religious life just before the Reformation by endowing special preacherships. These beneficed positions provided for well-trained and dedicated pastors and regular preaching and pastoral care, which went beyond the routine performance of the Mass and traditional religious functions. In many instances, these preacherships became platforms for Protestant preachers.

Magistrates also restricted the growth of ecclesiastical properties and clerical privileges. During the Middle Ages, special clerical rights in both property and person had come to be recognized by canon and civil law. Because they were holy places, churches and monasteries had been exempted from the taxes and laws that affected others. They were treated as special places of "sacral peace" and asylum. It was considered inappropriate for holy persons (clergy) to be burdened with such "dirty jobs" as military service, compulsory labor, standing watch at city gates, and other obligations of citizenship. Nor was it thought right that the laity, of whatever rank, should sit in judgment on those who were their shepherds and intermediaries with God. Churches were accordingly exempted from taxes and recognized as inviolable places of asylum, and the clergy were exempted from the jurisdiction of the civil courts. On the eve of the Reformation, measures were passed to restrict such privileges, end the abuses associated with them, and bring the clergy under the local tax code.

The Reformation

Martin Luther and the German Reformation to 1525

Unlike France and England, late medieval Germany lacked the political unity to enforce "national" religious reforms during the late Middle Ages. There were no lasting Statutes of Provisors (1351) and *praemunire* (1353, 1365), as in England, nor a Pragmatic Sanction of Bourges (1385), as in France, limiting papal jurisdiction and taxation on a national scale. What happened on a unified national level in England and France occurred only locally and piecemeal within German territories and towns. As popular resentment of clerical immunities and ecclesiastical abuses, especially regarding the selling of indulgences, spread among German cities and towns, an unorganized "national" opposition to Rome formed. German Humanists had long given voice to such criticism, and by 1517, it was pervasive enough to provide a solid foundation for Martin Luther's reform.

Luther (1483–1546) was the son of a successful Thuringian miner. He was educated in Mansfeld, Magdeburg, where the Brothers of the Common Life were his teachers, and in Eisenach. Between 1501 and 1505, he attended the University of Erfurt. After receiving his master of arts degree in 1505, Luther registered with the Law Faculty in accordance with his parents' wishes. But he never began the study of law. To the shock and disappointment of his family, he instead entered the Order of the Hermits of Saint Augustine in Erfurt on July 17, 1505. This decision had apparently been building for some time and was resolved during a lightning storm in which a terrified Luther, crying out to Saint Anne for assistance (Saint Anne was the patron saint of travelers in distress), promised to enter a monastery if he escaped death.

Ordained in 1507, Luther pursued a traditional course of study, becoming in 1509 a *baccalaureus biblicus* and *sententiarius,* that is, one thoroughly trained in the Bible and the *Sentences* of Peter Lombard. In 1510, he journeyed to Rome on the business of his order, finding there justification for the many criticisms of the Church he had heard in Germany. In 1511, he was transferred to the Augustinian monas-

Martin Luther Discovers Justification by Faith Alone

Many years after the fact, Martin Luther described his discovery that God's righteousness was not an active, punishing righteousness but a passive, transforming righteousness, which made those who believed in him righteous as God Himself is righteous.

Though I lived as a monk without reproach, I felt that I was a sinner before God with an extremely disturbed conscience. I could not believe that he was placated by my satisfaction. I did not love, yes, I hated the righteous God who punishes sinners, and secretly, if not blasphemously, certainly murmuring greatly, I was angry with God, and said, "As if, indeed, it is not enough, that miserable sinners, eternally lost through original sin, are crushed by every kind of calamity by the law of the decalogue, without having God add pain to pain by the gospel and also by the gospel threatening us with his righteousness and wrath!" Thus I raged with a fierce and troubled conscience. Nevertheless, I beat importunately upon Paul at that place, most ardently desiring to know what St. Paul wanted.

At last, by the mercy of God, meditating day and night, I gave heed to the context of the words, namely, "In it the righteousness of God is revealed, as it is written, 'He who through faith is righteous shall live'" [Romans 1:17]. There I began to understand that the righteousness of God is that by which the righteous lives by a gift of God, namely by faith. And this is the meaning: the righteousness of God is revealed by the gospel, namely, the passive righteousness with which merciful God justifies us by faith, as it is written, "He who through faith is righteous shall live." Here I felt that I was altogether born again and had entered paradise itself through open gates. There a totally other face of the entire Scripture showed itself to me. Thereupon I ran through the Scriptures from memory. I also found in other terms an analogy, as, the work of God, that is, what God does in us, the power of God, with which he makes us strong, the wisdom of God, with which he makes us wise, the strength of God, the salvation of God, the glory of God.

And I extolled my sweetest word with a love as great as the hatred with which I had before hated the word "righteousness of God." Thus that place in Paul was for me truly the gate to paradise.

Preface to the Complete Edition of Luther's Latin Writings (1545), in *Luther's Works,* Vol. 34, ed. by Lewis W. Spitz (Philadelphia: Muhlenberg Press, 1960), pp. 336–337.

Luther and the Wittenberg reformers with Elector John Frederick of Saxony (1532–1547), painted about 1543 by Lucas Cranach the Younger (1515–1586). Luther is on the far left, Philip Melanchthon in the front row on the far right. [Toledo Museum of Art, Toledo, Ohio; gift of Edward Drummond Libbey]

tery in Wittenberg, where he earned his doctorate in theology in 1512, thereafter becoming a leader within the monastery, the new university, and the spiritual life of the city.

THE ATTACK ON INDULGENCES. Reformation theology grew out of a problem common to many clergy and laity at this time: the failure of traditional medieval religion to provide full personal or intellectual satisfaction. Luther was especially plagued by the disproportion between his own sense of sinfulness and the perfect righteousness that medieval theology taught that God required for salvation. Traditional Church teaching and the sacrament of penance proved to be of no consolation. Luther wrote that he came to despise the phrase "righteousness of God," for it seemed to demand of him a perfection he knew neither he nor any other human being could ever achieve. His insight into the meaning of "justification by faith alone" was a gradual process that extended over several years, between 1513 and 1518. The righteousness God demands, he concluded, was not one that came from many religious works and ceremonies but was present in full measure in those who simply believed and trusted in the work of Jesus Christ, who alone was the perfect righteousness satisfying to God. To believe in Christ was to stand before God clothed in Christ's sure righteousness.

This new theology made indulgences unacceptable. An indulgence was a remission of the temporal penalty imposed by the priest on penitents as a "work of satisfaction" for their committed mortal sins. According to medieval theology, after the priest had absolved penitents of guilt for their sins, they still remained under an eternal penalty, a punishment God justly imposed on them for their sins. After absolution, however, this eternal penalty had been transformed into a temporal penalty, a manageable "work of satisfaction" that the penitent could perform here and now (for example, through prayers, fasting, almsgiving, retreats, and pilgrimages). Penitents who defaulted on such prescribed works of satisfaction could expect to suffer for them in purgatory.

At this point, indulgences came into play as an aid to a laity made genuinely anxious by the belief in a future suffering in purgatory for neglected penances or unrepented sins. In 1343, Pope Clement VI (1342–1352) had proclaimed the existence of a "treasury of merit," an infinite reservoir of good works in the Church's possession that could be dispensed at the pope's discretion. It was on the basis of this declared treasury that the Church sold "letters of indulgence," which covered the works of satisfaction owed by penitents. In 1476, Pope Sixtus IV (1471–1484) extended indulgences also to purgatory. Originally, indulgences had been given only for the true self-sacrifice of going on a crusade to the Holy Land. By Luther's time, they were regularly dispensed for small cash payments (very modest sums that were regarded as a good work of almsgiving) and were presented to the laity as remitting not only their own future punishments, but also those of their dead relatives presumed to be suffering in purgatory.

O ihr deutschen mercket mich recht/
    Des heiligen Vaters Papstes Knecht/
Bin ich/vnd br ing euch ist allein/
    Zehn tausent vnd neun hundert car ein/
Gnad vnd Ablaß von einer Sünd/
    Vor euch/ewer Eltern/Weib vnd Kind/
Sol ein jeder geweeret sein
    So viel ihr legt ins Kästelein/
So bald der Gülden im Becken klingt/
    Im hup die Seel im Himel springt/

A contemporary caricature depicts John Tetzel, the famous indulgence preacher. The last lines of the jingle read: "As soon as gold in the basin rings, right then the soul to heaven springs." It was Tetzel's preaching that spurred Luther to publish his ninety-five theses. [Staatliche Lutherhalle, Wittenberg]

In 1517, a Jubilee indulgence, proclaimed during the pontificate of Pope Julius II (1503–1513) to raise funds for the rebuilding of Saint Peter's in Rome, was revived and preached on the borders of Saxony in the territories of Archbishop Albrecht of Mainz. Albrecht was much in need of revenues as a result of the large debts he had incurred in order to hold, contrary to Church law, three ecclesiastical appointments. The selling of the indulgence was a joint venture by Albrecht, the Augsburg banking house of Fugger, and Pope Leo X (1513–1521), half the proceeds going to the pope and half to Albrecht and his creditors. The famous indulgence preacher John Tetzel (d. 1519) was enlisted to preach the indulgence in Albrecht's territories because he was a seasoned professional who knew how to stir ordinary people to action. As he exhorted on one occasion:

Don't you hear the voices of your dead parents and other relatives crying out, "Have mercy on us, for we suffer great punishment and pain. From this you could release us with a few alms. . . . We have created you, fed you, cared for you, and left you our temporal goods. Why do you treat us so cruelly and leave us to suffer in the flames, when it takes only a little to save us?"[1]

When on October 31, 1517, Luther posted his ninety-five theses against indulgences, according to tradition, on the door of Castle Church in Wittenberg,

he protested especially against the impression created by Tetzel that indulgences actually remitted sins and released the dead from punishment in purgatory—claims he believed went far beyond the traditional practice and seemed to make salvation something that could be bought and sold.

ELECTION OF CHARLES V AND THE DIET OF WORMS. The ninety-five theses were embraced by Humanists and other proponents of reform. They made Luther famous overnight and prompted official proceedings against him. As sanctions were being prepared against Luther, Emperor Maximilian I died (January 12, 1519), and this event, fortunate for the Reformation, turned all attention from heresy in Saxony to the contest for a new emperor.

The pope backed the French king, Francis I. However, Charles I of Spain, a youth of nineteen, succeeded his grandfather and became Emperor Charles V (see Map 18-1). Charles was assisted by both a long tradition of Habsburg imperial rule and a massive Fugger campaign chest, which secured the votes of the seven electors.

During the same month in which Charles was elected emperor, Luther entered a debate in Leipzig (June 27, 1519) with the Ingolstadt professor John Eck. During this contest, Luther challenged the infallibility of the pope and the inerrancy of Church councils, appealing, for the first time, to the sovereign authority of Scripture alone. All his bridges to the old Church were burned when he further defended cer-

[1]*Die Reformation in Augenzeugen Berichten,* ed. by Helmar Junghans (Dusseldorf: Karl Rauch Verlag, 1967), p. 44.

MAP 18-1 THE EMPIRE OF CHARLES V *Charles's rule over the lands shown here, plus Spain's overseas possessions, came about through dynastic marriages and simple chance. Many crowns and titles were bestowed on him; in 1519 he was elected emperor, giving him new burdens and responsibilities.*

A Lutheran broadsheet by Sebald Behaim (ca. 1524) depicts Martin Luther, Bible in hand, confronting the pope. Behind Luther stand poor artisans and simple folk, symbolized by the proud peasant with torn trousers and a flail. Behind the pope stand high clergy and representatives of well-to-do professions, who had an interest in preserving the old faith; bellmakers, goldsmiths, candlemakers, and fishermen can be discerned. [Lutherhalle Wittenberg]

tain teachings of Jan Hus that had been condemned by the Council of Constance. In 1520, Luther signaled his new direction with three famous pamphlets: the *Address to the Christian Nobility of the German Nation,* which urged the German princes to force reforms on the Roman Church, especially to curtail its political and economic power in Germany; the *Babylonian Captivity of the Church,* which attacked the traditional seven sacraments, arguing that only two were proper, and which exalted the authority of Scripture, Church councils, and secular princes over that of the pope; and the eloquent *Freedom of a Christian,* which summarized the new teaching of salvation by faith alone. On June 15, 1520, the papal bull *Exsurge Domine* condemned Luther for heresy and gave him sixty days to retract. The final bull of excommunication, *Decet Pontificem Romanum,* was issued on January 3, 1521.

In April 1521, Luther presented his views before a diet of the empire in Worms, over which the newly elected Emperor Charles V presided. Ordered to recant, Luther declared that to do so would be to act against Scripture, reason, and his own conscience. On May 26, 1521, he was placed under the imperial ban and thereafter became an "outlaw" to secular as well as to religious authority. For his own protection, friends hid him in Wartburg Castle, where he spent almost a year in seclusion, from April 1521 to March 1522. During his stay, he translated the New Testament into German, using Erasmus's new Greek text, and he attempted by correspondence to oversee the first stages of the Reformation in Wittenberg.

The Reformation was greatly assisted in these early years by the emperor's war with France and the advance of the Ottoman Turks into Eastern Europe. Against both adversaries Charles V who also re-

Peasants plunder a German monastery in 1525. The peasant revolt of 1524–1525 frightened both Protestant and Catholic rulers, who united to suppress the rising. [Bildarchiv Preussischer Kulturbesitz]

mained a Spanish king with dynastic responsibilities outside the empire, needed German troops, and to that end, he promoted friendly relations with the German princes. Between 1521 and 1559, Spain (the Habsburg dynasty) and France (the Valois dynasty) fought four major wars over disputed territories in Italy and along their borders. In 1526, the Turks overran Hungary at the Battle of Mohacs, while in Western Europe the French-led League of Cognac formed against Charles for the second Habsburg–Valois war. Thus preoccupied, the emperor agreed through his representatives at the German Diet of Speyer in 1526 that each German territory was free to enforce the Edict of Worms (1521) against Luther "so as to be able to answer in good conscience to God and the emperor." That concession, in effect, gave the German princes territorial sovereignty in religious matters and the Reformation time to put down deep roots. Later (in 1555), such local princely control over religion would be enshrined in imperial law by the Peace of Augsburg.

THE PEASANTS' REVOLT.   In its first decade, the Protestant movement suffered more from internal division than from imperial interference. By 1525, Luther had become as much an object of protest within Germany as was the pope. Original allies, sympathizers, and fellow travelers declared their independence from him.

Like the German Humanists, the German peasantry also had at first believed Luther to be an ally. The peasantry had been organized since the late fifteenth century against efforts by territorial princes to override their traditional laws and customs and to subject them to new regulations and taxes. Peasant leaders, several of whom were convinced Lutherans, saw in Luther's teaching about Christian freedom and his criticism of monastic landowners a point of view close to their own, and they openly solicited Luther's support of their political and economic rights, including their revolutionary request for release from serfdom. Luther and his followers sympathized with the peasants; indeed, for several years, Lutheran pamphleteers made *Karsthans,* the burly, honest peasant with his flail or hoe, a symbol of the simple life that God desired all people to live. The Lutherans, however, were not social revolutionaries, and when the peasants revolted against their masters in 1524–1525, Luther not surprisingly condemned them in the strongest possible terms as "unchristian" and urged the princes to crush their revolt without mercy. Tens of thousands of peasants (estimates run between seventy thousand and one hundred thousand) had died by the time the revolt was put down.

For Luther, the freedom of the Christian was an inner release from guilt and anxiety, not a right to restructure society by violent revolution. Had Luther supported the Peasants' Revolt, he would have not only contradicted his own teaching and belief but also ended any chance of the survival of his reform beyond the 1520s.

Zwingli and the Swiss Reformation

Switzerland was a loose confederacy of thirteen autonomous cantons or states and allied areas (see Map 18-2). Some cantons (e.g., Zürich, Bern, Basel, and Schaffhausen) became Protestant, some (especially around the Lucerne heartland) remained Catholic, and a few other cantons and regions managed to effect a compromise. Among the preconditions of the Swiss Reformation were the growth of national sentiment occasioned by opposition to foreign mercenary service (providing mercenaries for Europe's warring nations was a major source of Switzerland's livelihood) and a desire for Church reform that had persisted in Switzerland since the councils of Constance (1414–1417) and Basel (1431–1449).

THE REFORMATION IN ZURICH.   Ulrich Zwingli (1484–1531), the leader of the Swiss Reformation, had been humanistically educated in Bern, Vienna, and Basel. He was strongly influenced by Erasmus, whom he credited with having set him on the path to reform. An eloquent critic of mercenary service, Zwingli believed such service threatened both the political sovereignty and the moral well-being of the Swiss confederacy. By 1518, Zwingli was also widely known for opposition to the sale of indulgences and religious superstition.

In 1519, Zwingli gained the position of people's priest in Zurich, the base from which he engineered the Swiss Reformation. In March 1522, he was part of a group who defied the Lenten fast—an act of protest analogous to burning one's national flag today. Zwingli's reform guideline was very simple and very effective: Whatever lacked literal support in Scripture was to be neither believed nor practiced. A disputation held on January 29, 1523, concluded with the city government's sanction of Zwingli's Scripture test. Thereafter Zürich became, to all intents and purposes, a Protestant city and the center of the Swiss Reformation. A harsh discipline was imposed by the new Protestant regime, making Zürich one of the first examples of a puritanical Protestant city.

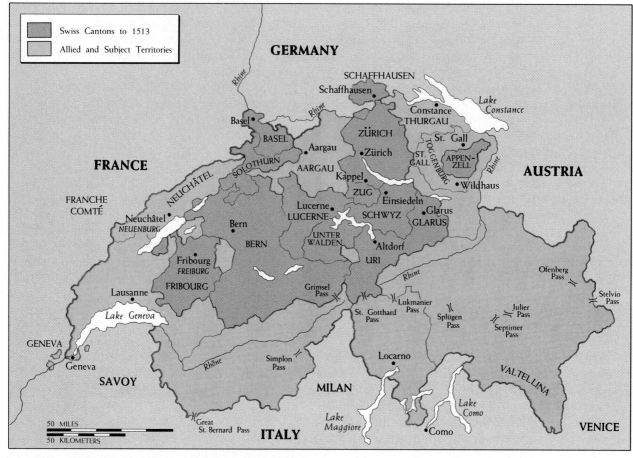

MAP 18-2 THE SWISS CONFEDERATION *While nominally still a part of the Holy Roman Empire, Switzerland grew from a loose defensive union of the central "forest cantons" in the thirteenth century to a fiercely independent association of regions with different languages, histories, and finally, religions.*

THE MARBURG COLLOQUY. Landgrave Philip of Hesse (1504–1567) sought to unite Swiss and German Protestants in a mutual defense pact, a potentially significant political alliance. His efforts were spoiled, however, by theological disagreements between Luther and Zwingli over the nature of Christ's presence in the Eucharist. Zwingli maintained a symbolic interpretation of Christ's words, "This is my body"; Christ, he argued, was only spiritually, not bodily, present in the bread and wine of the Eucharist. Luther, to the contrary, insisted that Christ's human nature could share the properties of his divine nature; hence, where Christ was spiritually present, He could also be bodily present, for His was a special nature.

Philip of Hesse brought the two Protestant leaders together in his castle in Marburg in early October 1529, but they were unable to work out their differ-

ences on this issue. Luther left thinking Zwingli a dangerous fanatic. Although cooperation between the two sides did not cease, the disagreement splintered the Protestant movement theologically and politically.

Anabaptists and Radical Protestants

The moderate pace and seemingly small ethical results of the Lutheran and Zwinglian reformations discontented many people, among them some of the original co-workers of Luther and Zwingli. Many desired a more rapid and thorough implementation of primitive Christianity and accused the major reformers of going only halfway. The most important of these radical groups were the Anabaptists, the sixteenth-century ancestors of the modern Mennonites and Amish. The Anabaptists were especially distinguished by their rejection of infant baptism and their insistence on only adult baptism (*anabaptism* derives from the Greek word meaning "to rebaptize"), believing that baptism as a consenting adult conformed to Scripture and was more respectful of human freedom. An early statement of Anabaptist belief was the Schleitheim Confession (1527).

Anabaptists physically separated from society to form a more perfect community in imitation of what they believed to be the example of the first Christians. Due to the close connection between religious and civic life in this period, such separatism was viewed by the political authorities as a threat to basic social bonds.

At first, Anabaptism drew its adherents from all social classes. But as Lutherans and Zwinglians joined with Catholics in opposition to the Anabaptists, a more rural, agrarian class came to make up the great majority. In 1529, rebaptism became a capital offense throughout the Holy Roman Empire. It has been estimated that between 1525 and 1618 at least one thousand and perhaps as many as five thousand men and women were executed for rebaptising themselves as adults.

Political Consolidation of the Lutheran Reformation

DIET OF AUGSBURG.   Charles V returned to the empire in 1530 to direct the Diet of Augsburg, a meeting of Protestant and Catholic representatives assembled for the purpose of ending the religious divisions. With its terms dictated by the Catholic emperor, the diet adjourned with a blunt order to all Lutherans to revert to Catholicism. The Reformation was by this time too firmly established for that to occur, and in February 1531, the Lutherans responded with the formation of their own defensive alliance, the Schmalkaldic League, which achieved a stalemate with the emperor, who was again distracted by renewed war with France and the Turks.

EXPANSION OF THE REFORMATION.   In the 1530s, German Lutherans formed regional consistories, judicial bodies composed of theologians and lawyers, which oversaw and administered the new Protestant churches. These consistories replaced the old Catholic episcopates. Under the leadership of Philip Melanchthon, Luther's most admired colleague, educational reforms were enacted that provided for compulsory primary education, schools for girls, a Hu-

manist revision of the traditional curriculum, and catechetical instruction of the laity in the new religion. These accomplishments earned Melanchthon the title "praeceptor of Germany."

The Reformation also dug in elsewhere. Introduced into Denmark by Christian II (r. 1513–1523), Danish Lutheranism throve under Frederick I (r. 1523–1533), who joined the Schmalkaldic League. Under Christian III (r. 1536–1559) Lutheranism became the state religion. In Sweden, Gustavus Vasa (r. 1523–1560), supported by a Swedish nobility greedy for Church lands, confiscated Church property and subjected the clergy to royal authority at the Diet of Vesteras (1527).

In politically splintered Poland, Lutherans, Anabaptists, Calvinists, and even Antitrinitarians found room to practice their beliefs, as Poland, primarily as a result of the absence of a central political authority, became a model of religious pluralism and toleration in the second half of the sixteenth century.

REACTION AGAINST PROTESTANTS: THE INTERIM. Charles V made abortive efforts in 1540–1541 to enforce a compromise agreement between Protestants and Catholics. As these and other conciliar efforts failed, he turned to a military solution. In 1547, imperial armies crushed the Protestant Schmalkaldic League.

The emperor established puppet rulers in Saxony and Hesse and issued as imperial law the *Augsburg Interim,* a new order that Protestants everywhere must readopt old Catholic beliefs and practices. But the Reformation was too entrenched by 1547 to be ended even by brute force. Confronted by fierce Protestant resistance and weary from three decades of war, the emperor was forced to relent.

The Peace of Augsburg in September 1555 made the division of Christendom permanent. This agreement recognized in law what had already been well established in practice: *cuius regio, eius religio,* meaning that the ruler of a land would determine the religion of the land. Lutherans were permitted to retain all Church lands forcibly seized before 1552. Those discontented with the religion of their region were permitted to migrate to another.

Calvinism and Anabaptism were not recognized as legal forms of Christian belief and practice by the Peace of Augsburg. Anabaptists had long adjusted to such exclusion by forming their own separatist communities. Calvinists, however, were not separatists and could not choose this route; they remained determined not only to secure the right to worship publicly as they pleased but also to shape society according to their own religious convictions. While Anabaptists retreated and Lutherans enjoyed the security of an established religion, Calvinists organized to lead national revolutions throughout northern Europe in the second half of the sixteenth and the first half of the seventeenth century.

John Calvin and the Genevan Reformation

Calvinism was the religious ideology that inspired or accompanied massive political resistance in France, The Netherlands, and Scotland. It established itself within the Palatinate during the reign of Elector Frederick III (1559–1576). Believing strongly in both divine predestination and the individual's responsibility to reorder society according to God's plan, Calvinists became zealous reformers determined to transform and order society according to their religious beliefs. In a famous and controversial study, *The Protestant Ethic and the Spirit of Capitalism* (1904), the German sociologist Max Weber argued that this peculiar combination of religious confidence and self-disciplined activism produced an ethic that stimulated and reinforced emergent capitalism, bringing Calvinism and later Puritanism into close association with the development of modern capitalist societies.

Political Revolt and Religious Reform in Geneva. Whereas in Saxony religious reform paved the way for a political revolution against the emperor, in Geneva a political revolution against the local prince-bishop laid the foundation for religious change. Genevans successfully revolted against the House of Savoy and their resident prince-bishop in the late 1520s. In late 1533, Bern dispatched Protestant reformers to Geneva. In the summer of 1535, after much internal turmoil, the Protestants triumphed, and the traditional Mass and other religious practices were removed. On May 21, 1536, the city voted officially to adopt the Reformation: "to live according to the Gospel and the Word of God . . . without . . . any more masses, statues, idols, or other papal abuses."

John Calvin (1509–1564), a reform-minded Humanist and lawyer, arrived in Geneva after these events, in July 1536. Guillaume Farel (1489–1565), the local Protestant reformer, successfully pleaded with him to stay and assist the Reformation.

Before a year had passed, Calvin had drawn up articles for the governance of the new church, as well

The French reformer and theologian John Calvin (1509–1564). [Musée Historique de la Réformation et Bibliothèque Calvinienne, Geneva. H. Pattusch]

as a catechism to guide and discipline the people, both of which were presented for approval to the city councils in early 1537. As a result of the strong measures proposed to govern Geneva's moral life, the reformers were suspected by many of desiring to create a "new papacy." Both within and outside Geneva, Calvin and Farel were perceived as going too far too fast. In February 1538, the reformers were exiled from the city.

Calvin went to Strasbourg, a model Protestant city, where he became pastor to the French exiles there. During his two-year stay in Strasbourg, Calvin wrote biblical commentaries and a second edition of his masterful *Institutes of the Christian Religion,* which many consider the definitive theological statement of the Protestant faith. Calvin also married and participated in the ecumenical discussions urged on Protestants and Catholics by Charles V. Most important, he learned from the Strasbourg reformer Martin Bucer how to implement the Protestant Reformation successfully.

Calvin's Geneva. In 1540, Geneva elected officials who were favorable to Calvin and invited him to return. This he did in September 1540, never to leave the city again. Within months of his arrival, new ecclesiastical ordinances were implemented that provided for cooperation between the magistrates and the clergy in matters of internal discipline. Following the Strasbourg model, the Genevan church was organized into four offices: (1) pastors, of whom there were five; (2) teachers or doctors to instruct the populace in and to defend true doctrine; (3) elders, a group of twelve laymen chosen by and from the Genevan councils and empowered to "oversee the life of everybody"; and (4) deacons to dispense church goods and services to the poor and the sick.

Calvin and his followers were motivated above all by a desire to transform society morally. Faith, Calvin taught, did not sit idly in the mind but conformed one's every action to God's law. The "elect" should live in a manifestly God-pleasing way, if they were truly God's elect. The majesty of God demanded nothing less. In the attempt to realize this goal, Calvin spared no effort. The consistory became his instrument of power. This body was composed of the elders and the pastors and was presided over by one of the city's four syndics, or civil magistrates. It enforced the strictest moral discipline, meting out punishments for a broad range of moral and religious transgressions—from missing church services (a fine of three sous) to fornication (six days on bread and water and a fine of sixty sous) and, as time passed, increasingly for criticism of Calvin.

After 1555, the city's syndics were all devout Calvinists, and Geneva became home to thousands of exiled Protestants who had been driven out of France, England, and Scotland. Refugees (more than five thousand), most of them utterly loyal to Calvin, came to make up over one-third of the population of Geneva. From this time until his death in 1564, Calvin's position in the city was greatly strengthened and the syndics were very cooperative.

Catholic Reform and the Counter-Reformation

SOURCES OF CATHOLIC REFORM. The Protestant Reformation did not take the medieval church completely by surprise. Much internal criticism and many efforts at internal reform preceded the Counter-Reformation in reaction to Protestant successes. Before the Reformation, ambitious proposals had been set forth to bring about the long-demanded reform of the Church in head and members.

Catholic reformers were found within a variety of self-motivated lay and clerical movements. Two important organizations that brought reform-minded clergy and laity together were the Modern Devotion and the Oratory of Divine Love. The former, also

known as the Brothers of the Common Life, was an organized group of laity and clergy who fostered the religious life outside formal ecclesiastical offices and apart from formal religious vows. The Oratory of Divine Love, founded in Rome in 1517, was an exclusive informal organization of earnest laity and clergy who were both learned and deeply committed to traditional religious devotion. Like Erasmus, whose reli-

PROGRESS OF PROTESTANT REFORMATION ON THE CONTINENT	
1513–1517	Fifth Lateran Council fails to bring about reform in the Catholic Church
1517	Luther posts ninety-five theses against indulgences
1519	Charles I of Spain elected Holy Roman Emperor (as Charles V)
1519	Luther challenges infallibility of pope and inerrancy of Church councils at Leipzig Debate
1521	Papal bull excommunicates Luther for heresy
1521	Diet of Worms condemns Luther
1521–1522	Luther translates the New Testament into German
1524–1525	Peasants' Revolt in Germany
1527	*Schleitheim Confession* of the Anabaptists
1529	Marburg Colloquy between Luther and Zwingli
1530	Diet of Augsburg fails to settle religious differences
1531	Formation of Protestant Schmalkaldic League
1534–1535	Anabaptists assume political power in city of Munster
1536	Calvin arrives in Geneva
1540	Jesuits, founded by Ignatius of Loyola, recognized as order by pope
1546	Luther dies
1547	Armies of Charles V crush Schmalkaldic League
1548	Augsburg *Interim* outlaws Protestant practices
1555	Peace of Augsburg recognizes rights of Lutherans to worship as they please
1545–1563	Council of Trent institutes reforms and responds to the Reformation

Ignatius of Loyola's "Rules for Thinking with the Church"

As leaders of the Counter-Reformation, the Jesuits attempted to live by and instill in others the strictest obedience to Church authority. The following are some of the eighteen rules included by Ignatius in his Spiritual Exercises *to give both Jesuits and lay Catholics positive direction. These rules also indicate the Catholic reformers' refusal to compromise with Protestantism.*

In order to have the proper attitude of mind in the Church Militant we should observe the following rules:

1. Putting aside all private judgment, we should keep our minds prepared and ready to obey promptly and in all things the true spouse of Christ our Lord, our Holy Mother, the hierarchical Church.
2. To praise sacramental confession and the reception of the Most Holy Sacrament once a year, and much better once a month, and better still every week. . . .
3. To praise the frequent hearing of Mass.
4. To praise highly the religious life, virginity, and continence; and also matrimony, but not as highly. . . .
5. To praise the vows of religion, obedience, poverty, chastity, and other works of perfection and supererogation. . . .
6. To praise the relics of the saints . . . [and] the stations, pilgrimages, indulgences, jubilees, Crusade indulgences, and the lighting of candles in the churches.

7. To praise the precepts concerning fasts and abstinences . . . and acts of penance. . . .
8. To praise the adornments and buildings of churches as well as sacred images. . . .
9. To praise all the precepts of the church. . . .
10. To approve and praise the directions and recommendations of our superiors as well as their personal behavior. . . .
11. To praise both positive and scholastic theology. . . .
12. We must be on our guard against making comparisons between the living and those who have already gone to their reward, for it is no small error to say, for example: "This man knows more than St. Augustine," "He is another Saint Francis, or even greater." . . .
13. If we wish to be sure that we are right in all things; we should always be ready to accept this principle: I will believe that the white that I see is black, if the hierarchical Church so defines it. For I believe that between . . . Christ our Lord and . . . His Church, there is but one spirit, which governs and directs us for the salvation of our souls.

The Spiritual Exercises of St. Ignatius, trans. by Anthony Mottola (Garden City, NY: Doubleday, 1964), pp. 139–141.

gious writings the members admired, they taught that inner piety and good Christian living, not theological arguments and disputations, were the surest way to reform the Church.

IGNATIUS OF LOYOLA AND THE JESUITS. Of the various reform groups, none was more instrumental in the success of the Counter-Reformation than the Society of Jesus, the new order of Jesuits, organized by Ignatius of Loyola in the 1530s and officially recognized by the Catholic Church in 1540. The society grew within the space of a century from its original ten members to more than fifteen thousand scattered throughout the world, with thriving missions in India, Japan, and the Americas.

The founder of the Jesuits, Ignatius of Loyola (1491–1556), had been a dashing Basque courtier and caballero in his youth. He began his spiritual pilgrimage in 1521 after he had been seriously wounded during a battle with the French. During a lengthy and painful convalescence, he passed the time by reading Christian classics. So impressed was he with the heroic self-sacrifice of the Church's saints and their methods of overcoming mental anguish and pain that

PORTFOLIO IV

Christianity

The teaching of Jesus gave birth to Christianity. His simple message of faith in God and self-sacrificial love of one's neighbor attracted many people whose religious needs were not adequately met by the philosophies and religions of the ancient world. After Jesus' crucifixion and resurrection, his devout followers expected him to return in glory, defeat sin and evil, and take them away with him to heaven—a radical eschatological vision that also heightened Christianity's initial appeal. In the writings of St. Paul and the teachings of the early Church, Jesus became the Christ, the son of God, the long-awaited Messiah of Jewish prophecy. According to John's gospel, Jesus was also the *logos,* the eternal principle of all being, after which the thinkers of antiquity had quested. Christianity thus offered people something more than philosophy, law, and ritual.

Christianity proclaimed the very Incarnation of God in a man, the visible presence of eternity in time. According to early Christian teaching, the power of God's Incarnation in Jesus lived on in the preaching and sacraments of the Church under the guidance of the Holy Spirit. Christian thinkers here borrowed from the popular Asian cults of the Roman world, which had also offered their followers a sacramental participation in deity and spiritual redemption from sin. But Christianity went beyond them all when it declared the source of all being to be no longer transcendent and proclaimed the Messiah to have arrived. The Christian message was that, in Jesus, eternity had made itself accessible to every person here and now and forevermore.

The first Christians were drawn from among the rich and poor alike. People flocked to the new religion for both materialistic and deeply religious reasons. For some believers, Christianity promised a better material life. But its appeal also lay in its unique ability to impart to people a sense of spiritual self-worth regardless of their place or prospects in society. The gospel of Jesus appealed to the hopelessly poor and powerless as readily as to the socially rising and well-to-do.

In the late second century, the Romans began persecuting Christians both as "heretics" (because of their rejection of the traditional Roman gods) and as social revolutionaries. At the same time, dissenting Christians, particularly sects claiming a direct spiritual knowledge of God apart from Scripture, brought new internal divisions to the young Church by advocating Christian heresies of their own. Such challenges had to be met, and by the fourth century effective weapons against both state terrorism and Christian heresy were in place: an ordained official clergy; a hierarchical Church organization; orthodox creeds; and a biblical canon, the New Testament. Christianity not only gained legal status within the Roman Empire, but, by the fourth century, was the favored religion of the emperor as well.

The fortune of Christianity after the fall of Rome (A.D. 476) is one of history's great success stories. Aided by the enterprise of its popes and the example of its monks, the Church cultivated an appealing lay piety centered on the Lord's Prayer, the Apostles' Creed, veneration of the Virgin, and the sacrament of the Eucharist. Clergy became both royal teachers and bureaucrats within the kingdom of the Franks. Despite a growing schism between the Eastern (Byzantine) and Western churches, and a final split in 1054, by 1000 the Church held real economic and political power. In the eleventh century, reform-minded prelates ended secular interference in its spiritual affairs; the traditional lay practice of investing clergy in their offices was condemned under penalty of excommunication. For several centuries thereafter the Church would remain a formidable international force, successfully challenging kings and emperors and inspiring crusades against the non-Christian world.

By the fifteenth century, the new states of Europe had stripped the Church of much of this political power. It would henceforth be progressively confined to its present role of spiritual and moral authority. Christianity's greatest struggles ever since then have been not with kings and emperors over political power, but with materialistic philosophies and worldly ideologies, over spiritual and moral hegemony within an increasingly pluralistic and secular world. Since the sixteenth century, a succession of Humanists, Skeptics, Deists, Rationalists, Marxists, Freudians, Darwinians, and atheists have attempted to explain away some of traditional Christianity's most basic teachings.

In addition, the Church has endured major internal upheaval. After the Protestant Reformation (1517–1555) made the Bible widely available to the laity, the possibilities for internal criticism of Christianity multiplied geometrically. Beginning with the split between Lutherans and Zwinglians in the 1520s, Protestant Christians have fragmented themselves into hundreds of sects, each claiming the true interpretation of Scripture. The Roman Catholic Church, by contrast, has maintained its unity through these perilous times. However, present-day discontent with papal authority threatens the modern Catholic church almost as seriously as the Protestant Reformation once did.

But Christianity is nothing if not resilient. It continues to possess the simple, almost magically appealing, gospel of Jesus. It finds itself within a world whose religious needs and passions still remain deep and basic.

IV-2   The Birth of Christ by Albrecht Dürer *(1471–1528). Mary and Joseph (below) are portrayed with the infant Jesus, who is surrounded by playful admiring angels. The miniaturized figures surrounding the scene are local patrons and dignitaries bearing their family coats of arms. [Bildarchiv Preussischer Kulturbesitz]*

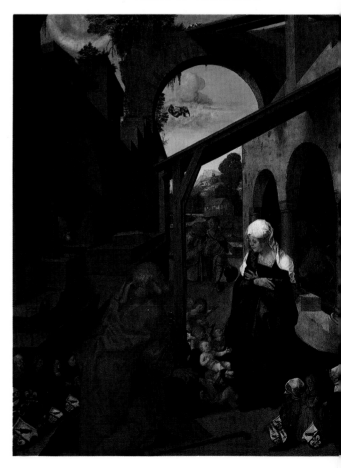

IV-1   The Annunciation. *This scene (above), painted in 1430 by Fra Angelico, illustrates a passage from the Gospel of Luke (1:26 ff.): "The angel Gabriel was sent from God" to Mary "and said unto her, the Holy Ghost shall come upon thee, and the power of the Highest shall overshadow thee: therefore also that holy thing which shall be born of thee shall be called the Son of God." The impending redemption of humanity through Mary, the new Eve, and Christ, the new Adam, is juxtaposed with the fall of Adam and Eve and their expulsion from paradise (shown on the left). The beam of light represents the Holy Spirit. The small panels at the bottom illustrate scenes from the life of Mary. [Bildarchiv Preussischer Kulturbesitz]*

IV-3   The Crucifixion of Christ by Velázquez de Silva *(ca. 1630). Christ is portrayed as radiant and triumphant even in death, his resurrection seeming to be imminent in his crucifixion—a scene intended to invoke quiet meditation. [Bildarchiv Preussischer Kulturbesitz]*

IV-4   Heaven and Hell. *According to Christian teaching, man and woman were created nearly perfect by their Maker and lived in harmony with both God and nature. After the Fall, however, those unredeemed by God's grace were condemned to suffer eternally in hell, whereas the redeemed would return to a state of harmony in heaven. Here are imaginative portrayals of paradise and hell by the Dutch painter, Hieronymus Bosch (ca. 1450–1516). These are the two side panels from Bosch's triptych known as the "Garden of Delights." [Giraudon/Art Resource]*

IV-5   Early Christian Art. *The catacombs were underground tunnels where Christians buried their dead. This painting is on the wall of the catacomb of Priscilla in Rome. [Scala/Art Resource]*

IV-6   The Latin Bible. *This tenth-century miniature shows St. Jerome (ca. A.D. 340–420), seated in the center, handing out copies of his Latin translation of the Bible (the Vulgate) for the monks' distribution to the world. The Vulgate became Christendom's authoritative Bible until new translations from the Greek and Hebrew were adopted by Protestant Christians in the sixteenth century. [Bibliothèque Nationale, Paris]*

IV-7   Popes and the Papacy. *The power of the popes in the Western Church derives from Matthew 16:19, in which Jesus describes Peter, or Peter's faith, as the "rock" on which his church is to be built. This passage was interpreted as setting Peter above the other apostles, and, by extension, Rome and its bishops above the other episcopal sees of Christendom. This fourth-century mosaic from the apse of Santa Costanza, Rome, shows Jesus giving Peter the key to Heaven. [Scala/Art Resource]*

IV-8   Popes and the Papacy. *The efforts of Pope Boniface VIII (1294–1303) to stem the rising tide of secular political power, particularly in England and France, failed. A few years after his reign, in 1309, the papacy moved to Avignon on the southeastern border of France and was never again the powerful political force it had been in the twelfth and thirteenth centuries. [Scala/Art Resource]*

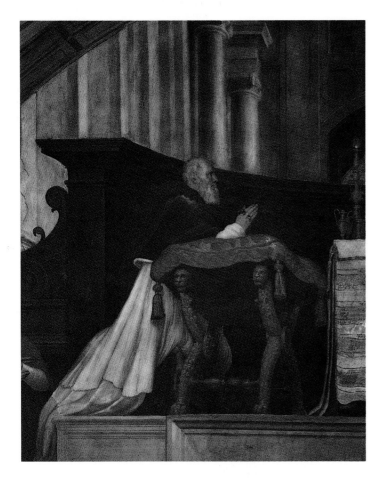

IV-9   Popes and the Papacy. *Raphael's portrait of the great military pope Julius II (1503–1512) at Mass. Julius secured the papal states by successfully driving the Venetians out of Romagna in 1509 and, with the help of powerful allies, the French out of Italy in 1512. His notorious worldliness and militarism led Erasmus to make him the object of a famous satire in which Pope Julius, clad in his papal robes, is refused entrance to heaven by St. Peter, who failed to recognize him as a Christian. [Scala/Art Resource]*

IV-10   A Christian View of the Crusades. *Christians briefly recaptured the Holy Land in the late-eleventh and early-twelfth centuries. This painting shows the Crusaders besieging Antioch in 1097 en route to Jerusalem, which fell to them in 1099. The artist, evidently unfamiliar with the architecture of the region, shows a European rather than a Middle Eastern city. [Scala/Art Resource]*

IV-11   A Gothic Cathedral. *The interior of the Gothic Cathedral at Reims (right) is a space designed to impress upon the worshiper the smallness of man and the soaring majesty of God.* [Scala/Art Resource]

IV-12   A Baroque Church. *Baroque art and architecture is a grandiose three-dimensional display of life and energy and very congenial to post-Reformation Catholicism, as it set forth to reclaim the lands and people lost to the Protestant Reformation. The style is the reverse of the new Protestant churches, which were, by comparison, remarkably subdued. At left is the Baroque altar of the chapel of St. Ignatius in Rome.* [Scala/Art Resource]

IV-13   An Early Church in Rome. *The old basilica of St. Peter was built during the reign of Constantine the Great (306–337). The financing of the rebuilding of this church by the selling of indulgences occasioned Martin Luther's famous protest and the eventual division of Christendom by the Protestant Reformation. [Scala/Art Resource]*

IV-14   A Reformation Protestant Church. *Protestant churches were generally designed so that nothing might distract the eye from the preaching of God's word. This Calvinist church in Lyon has no decorations, paintings, statuary, or elaborate stained glass, and the preacher is absolutely at center stage. In Zwinglian churches the walls were even white-washed and no music or singing was permitted. Such simplicity contrasts starkly with the Baroque style of contemporary Catholic churches. [Bibliothèque Publique et Universitaire de Genève]*

he underwent a profound religious conversion; henceforth he, too, would serve the Church as a soldier of Christ.

After recuperating, Ignatius applied the lessons he had learned during his convalescence to a program of religious and moral self-discipline that came to be embodied in the *Spiritual Exercises.* This psychologically perceptive devotional guide contained mental and emotional exercises designed to teach one absolute spiritual self-mastery over one's feelings. It taught that a person could shape his or her own behavior, even create a new religious self, through disciplined study and regular practice.

Whereas in Jesuit eyes Protestants had distin-

MAP 18-3   THE RELIGIOUS SITUATION ABOUT 1560   *By 1560, Luther, Zwingli, and Loyola were dead, Calvin near the end of his life, the English break from Rome fully accomplished, and the last session of the Council of Trent about to assemble. The map shows the religious geography of Western Europe at this time.*

guished themselves by disobedience to Church authority and religious innovation, the exercises of Ignatius were intended to teach good Catholics to deny themselves and submit without question to higher Church authority and spiritual direction. Perfect discipline and self-control were the essential conditions of such obedience. To them was added the enthusiasm of traditional spirituality and mysticism—a potent combination that helped counter the Reformation and win many Protestants back to the Catholic fold, especially in Austria and Bavaria and along the Rhine.

COUNCIL OF TRENT (1545–1563). The broad success of the Reformation and the insistence of the Emperor Charles V forced Pope Paul III (1534–1549) to call a general council of the Church to define religious doctrine. The long-delayed council met in 1545 in the city of Trent in northern Italy. There were three sessions, spread over eighteen years, from 1545 to 1563, with long interruptions due to war, plague, and imperial and papal politics. The council's most important reforms concerned internal Church discipline. Steps were taken to curtail the selling of Church offices and other religious goods. Many bishops who resided in Rome rather than within their dioceses were forced to move to their appointed seats of authority. The Council of Trent strengthened the authority of local bishops so that they could effectively discipline popular religious practice. The Council of Trent also sought to give the parish priest a brighter image by requiring him to be neatly dressed, better educated, strictly celibate, and active among his parishioners. To this end, the council also called for the construction of a seminary in every diocese.

The English Reformation to 1553

THE KING'S AFFAIR. Native religious dissent along Wycliffite lines (known as *Lollardy*, a term of abuse) and Humanism may be said to have prepared the soil for the seeds of Protestant reform in England. But it was King Henry VIII's unhappy marriage that furnished the plough that truly broke the soil. Henry had married Catherine of Aragon (d. 1536), a daughter of Ferdinand and Isabella of Spain, and the aunt of Emperor Charles V. By 1527, the union had produced no male heir to the throne and only one surviving child, a daughter, Mary Tudor. Henry was justifiably concerned about the political consequences of leaving only a female heir. People in this period believed it unnatural for women to rule over men. At best, a

woman ruler meant a contested reign; at worst, turmoil and revolution. Henry even came to believe that his union with Catherine, who had numerous miscarriages and stillbirths, had been cursed by God, because before their marriage, Catherine had been the wife of his late brother, Arthur.

By 1527, Henry, thoroughly enamored of Anne Boleyn, one of Catherine's ladies in waiting, decided to put Catherine aside and marry Anne. This he could not do in Catholic England without papal annulment of the marriage to Catherine. And therein lay a problem. The year 1527 was also the year when soldiers of the Holy Roman Empire mutinied and sacked Rome, and the reigning pope, Clement VII, was at the time a prisoner of Charles V, Catherine's nephew. Even if this had not been the case, it would have been virtually impossible for the pope to grant an annulment of the marriage. Not only had it survived for eighteen years but it had been made possible in the first place by a special papal dispensation required because Queen Catherine had previously been the wife of Henry's brother, Arthur.

After Cardinal Wolsey, Lord Chancellor of England since 1515, failed to secure the annulment, Thomas Cranmer (1489–1556) and Thomas Cromwell (1485–1540), both of whom harbored Lutheran sympathies, became the king's closest advisers. Finding the way to a papal annulment closed, Henry's new advisers struck a different course: Why not simply declare the king supreme in English spiritual affairs as he was in English temporal affairs? Then the king himself could settle the king's affair.

REFORMATION PARLIAMENT. In 1529, Parliament convened for what would be a seven-year session that earned it the title of "Reformation Parliament." During this period, it passed a flood of legislation that harassed and finally placed royal reins on the clergy. In January 1531, the clergy in Convocation (a legislative assembly representing the English clergy) publicly recognized Henry as head of the Church in England "as far as the law of Christ allows." In 1533, Parliament passed the Submission of the Clergy, effectively placing canon law under royal control and thereby the clergy under royal jurisdiction.

In January 1533, Henry wed the pregnant Anne Boleyn, with Thomas Cranmer officiating. In 1534, Parliament ended all payments by the English clergy and laity to Rome and gave Henry sole jurisdiction over high ecclesiastical appointments. The Act of Succession in the same year made Anne Boleyn's children legitimate heirs to the throne, and the Act of

Thomas More Stands by His Conscience

More (introduced earlier in this chapter on pp. 515–516), loyal Catholic to the end, repudiated the Act of Supremacy as unlawful; he believed that it contradicted both the laws of England and the king's own coronation oath. More important, he believed that the act transgressed centuries of European tradition, by which he felt bound by conscience to stand, even if it meant certain death. In the following excerpt, More defended himself in a final interrogation, as reported by his prosecutors.

▶ *For a comparative perspective on victims of conscience, see "The Castration of Ssu-Ma Ch'ien" (Ch. 9).*

"Seeing that . . . ye are determined to condemn me [More said] . . . I will now in discharge of my conscience speak my mind plainly and freely. . . . Forasmuch as this indictment is grounded upon an Act of Parliament directly repugnant to the laws of God and his holy Church, the supreme government of which . . . may no temporal prince presume by any law to take upon him it is insufficient to charge any Christian man [who refuses to recognize this Act]."

For proof thereof, he [More] declared that this realm, being but one member and small part of the Church, might not make a particular law disagreeable with the general law of Christ's universal Catholic Church, no more than the city of London, being but one poor member in respect of the whole realm, might make a law against an Act of Parliament to bind the whole realm. So further showed he that it was contrary both to the laws and statutes of our own land . . . and also contrary to the sacred oath which the King's Highness himself and every Christian prince always with great solemnity received at their coronations. . . .

Then . . . the Lord Chancellor . . . answered that seeing that all the bishops, universities, and best learned men of the realm had to this Act agreed, it was much marvel that he [More] alone against them all would so stiffly stick thereat. . . .

To this Sir Thomas replied . . . : "Neither as yet have I chanced upon any ancient writer or doctor that so advanceth, as your Statute doth, the supremacy of any secular and temporal prince . . . and therefore am I not bounde, my Lord, to conform my conscience to the Council of one realm against the general Council of [the whole of] Christendom. For of the foresaid holy bishops I have, for every bishop of yours, above one hundred. And for one Council or Parliament of yours (God knoweth what manner of one), I have all the Councils made these thousand years. And for this one Kingdom [of England], I have all other Christian realms."

The Reformation in England: To the Accession of Elizabeth I, ed. by A. G. Dickens and Dorothy Carr (New York: St. Martin's Press, 1968), pp. 71–72.

Supremacy declared Henry "the only supreme head in earth of the church of England."

THE PROTESTANT REFORMATION UNDER EDWARD VI. Henry's political and domestic boldness was not carried over to the religious front, although the pope did cease to be the head of the English Church and English Bibles were placed in English churches. Despite his political break with Rome, the king remained decidedly conservative in his religious beliefs, and Catholic doctrine remained prominent in a country seething with Protestant sentiment. Henry absolutely forbade the English clergy to marry and threatened any clergy who were twice caught in concubinage with execution. The Six Articles of 1539 reaffirmed transubstantiation, denied the Eucharistic cup to the laity, declared celibate vows inviolable, provided for private masses, and ordered the continuation of auricular confession.

Edward VI (r. 1547–1553), Henry's son by his third wife Jane Seymour, gained the throne when he was only ten years old. Anne Boleyn had been executed in 1536 for adultery and her daughter Elizabeth declared illegitimate and thus ineligible to succeed to the English throne.

Under Edward, England fully enacted the Protestant Reformation. Henry's Six Articles and laws against heresy were repealed, and clerical marriage and communion with cup were sanctioned. In 1549, the Act of Uniformity imposed Thomas Cranmer's

MAIN EVENTS OF THE ENGLISH REFORMATION	
1529	Reformation Parliament convenes
1532	Parliament passes the Submission of the Clergy, an act placing canon law and the English clergy under royal jurisdiction
1533	Henry VIII weds Anne Boleyn; Convocation proclaims marriage to Catherine of Aragon invalid
1534	Act of Succession makes Anne Boleyn's children legitimate heirs to the English throne
1534	Act of Supremacy declares Henry VIII "the only supreme head of the church of England"
1535	Thomas More executed for opposition to Acts of Succession and Supremacy
1535	Publication of Coverdale Bible
1539	Henry VIII imposes the Six Articles, condemning Protestantism and reasserting traditional doctrine
1547	Edward VI succeeds to the throne under protectorships of Somerset and Northumberland
1549	First Act of Uniformity imposes *Book of Common Prayer* on English churches
1553–1558	Mary Tudor restores Catholic doctrine
1558–1603	Elizabeth I fashions an Anglican religious settlement

Book of Common Prayer on all English churches. Images and altars were removed from the churches in 1550. The Second Act of Uniformity, passed in 1552, imposed a revised edition of the *Book of Common Prayer* on all English churches. A forty-two-article confession of faith, also written by Thomas Cranmer, was adopted, setting forth a moderate Protestant doctrine.

All these changes were short lived, however. In 1553, Catherine of Aragon's daughter, Mary Tudor, succeeded Edward (who had died in his teens) to the English throne and proceeded to restore Catholic doctrine and practice with a single-mindedness that rivaled that of her father. It was not until the reign of Anne Boleyn's daughter, Elizabeth (1558–1603), that a lasting religious settlement was worked out in England (to be discussed later).

Wars of Religion

The late sixteenth century and the first half of the seventeenth century are described as an "age of religious wars" because of the bloody opposition of Protestants and Catholics across the length and breadth of Europe. In France, The Netherlands, England, and Scotland in the second half of the sixteenth century, Calvinists fought Catholic rulers for the right to form their own communities, to practice their chosen religion openly, and to exclude from their lands those they deemed heretical. In the first half of the seventeenth century, international armies of varying religious persuasions marched against one another in central and northern Europe during the Thirty Years' War. By the middle of the seventeenth century, English Puritans had successfully revolted against the Stuart monarchy and the Anglican Church. In the second half of the sixteenth century, the political conflict, which had previously been confined to central Europe and a struggle for Lutheran rights and freedoms, shifted to Western Europe—to France, The Netherlands, England, and Scotland—and became a struggle for Calvinist recognition.

Genevan Calvinism and Tridentine Catholicism were two equally dogmatic, aggressive, and irreconcilable church systems. Calvinism adopted a presbyterian organization that magnified regional and local religious authority: Broads of presbyters, or elders, representing the many individual congregations of Calvinists, directly shaped the policy of the Church at large. By contrast, the Counter-Reformation sponsored a centralized episcopal church system, hierarchically arranged from pope to parish priest, that stressed absolute obedience to the person at the top. The high clergy—the pope and his bishops—not the synods of local churches, ruled supreme. Calvinism proved attractive to proponents of political decentralization in contest with totalitarian rulers, whereas Catholicism remained congenial to the proponents of absolute monarchy determined to maintain "one king, one church, one law" throughout the land.

French Wars of Religion (1562–1598)

Henry II died accidentally during a tournament in 1559. His sickly fifteen-year-old son, Francis II, came to the throne under the regency of the queen mother, Catherine de Médicis. With the monarchy so weakened, three powerful families saw their chance to control France and began to compete for the young king's ear. They were the Bourbons, whose power lay in the south and west; the Montmorency-Châtillons, who controlled the center of France; and the Guises, who were dominant in eastern France. The Guises were by far the strongest, and the name of Guise was interchangeable with militant, ultra-Catholicism. The Bourbon and Montmorency-Châtillon families, in contrast, developed strong Huguenot (as the French Protestants were called) sympathies, largely for political reasons. The Bourbon Louis I, prince of Condé (d. 1569), and the Montmorency-Châtillon Admiral Gaspard de Coligny (1519–1572) became the political leaders of the French Protestant resistance.

Often for quite different reasons, ambitious aristocrats and discontented townspeople joined Calvinist churches in opposition to the Guise-dominated French monarchy. In 1561, over two thousand Huguenot congregations existed throughout France, although Huguenots were a majority of the population in only two regions: Dauphine and Languedoc. Although they made up only about one-fifteenth of the population, Huguenots were in important geographic areas and were heavily represented among the more powerful segments of French society. Over two-fifths of the French aristocracy became Huguenots. Many apparently hoped to establish within France a principle of territorial sovereignty akin to that secured within the Holy Roman Empire by the Peace of Augsburg (1555). In this way, Calvinism indirectly served the forces of political decentralization.

CATHERINE DE MÉDICIS AND THE GUISES. Following Francis II's death in 1560, Catherine de Médicis continued as regent for her minor son, Charles IX (r. 1560–1574). Fearing the power and guile of the Guises, Catherine, whose first concern was always to preserve the monarchy, sought allies among the Protestants. In 1562, she granted Protestants freedom to worship publicly outside towns—although only privately within them—and to hold synods or church assemblies. In March, this royal toleration came to an abrupt end when the duke of Guise surprised a Protestant congregation at Vassy in Champagne and proceeded to massacre several score—an event that marked the beginning of the French wars of religion (March 1562).

Perpetually caught between fanatical Huguenot and Guise extremes, Queen Catherine always sought to balance the one side against the other. Like the Guises, she wanted a Catholic France; she did not, however, desire a Guise-dominated monarchy.

On August 22, 1572, four days after the Huguenot

Catherine de Médicis (1519–1589) exercised enormous power in France during the reign of her three sons Francis II (1559–1560), Charles IX (1560–1574), and Henry III (1574–1589). [Roger-Viollet]

Henry of Navarre had married King Charles IX's sister, Marguerite of Valois—a sign of growing Protestant power—Coligny was struck down, although not killed, by an assassin's bullet. Catherine had apparently been a part to this Guise plot to eliminate Coligny. After its failure, she feared both the king's reaction to her complicity and the Huguenot response under a recovered Coligny. Summoning all her motherly charm and fury, Catherine convinced Charles that a Huguenot coup was afoot, inspired by Coligny, and that only the swift execution of Protestant leaders could save the crown from a Protestant attack on Paris. On the eve of Saint Bartholomew's Day, August 24, 1572, Coligny and three thousand fellow Huguenots were butchered in Paris. Within three days, an estimated twenty thousand Huguenots were executed in coordinated attacks throughout France. The event changed the nature of the struggle between Protestants and Catholics both within and beyond the borders of France. It was thereafter no longer an internal contest between Guise and Bourbon factions for French political influence, nor was it simply a Huguenot campaign to win basic religious freedoms. Henceforth, in Protestant eyes, it became an international struggle to the death for sheer survival against an adversary whose cruelty now justified any means of resistance.

RISE TO POWER OF HENRY OF NAVARRE. Henry III (r. 1574–1589), who was Henry II's third son and the last to wear the French crown, found the monarchy wedged between a radical Catholic League, formed in 1576 by Henry of Guise, and vengeful Huguenots. Like the queen mother, Henry III sought to steer a middle course, and in this effort he received support from a growing body of neutral Catholics and Huguenots who put the political survival of France above its religious unity. Such *politiques,* as they were called, were prepared to compromise religious creeds as might be required to save the nation.

In the mid-1580s the Catholic League, supported by the Spanish, became completely dominant in Paris. In what came to be known as the Day of the Barricades, Henry III attempted to rout the league with a surprise attack in 1588. The effort failed badly and the king had to flee Paris. Forced by his weakened position into guerrilla tactics, Henry successfully plotted the assassination of both the duke and the cardinal of Guise. The Catholic League reacted with a fury that matched the earlier Huguenot response to the Massacre of Saint Bartholomew's Day. The king now had only one course of action: He struck an alliance with his Protestant cousin, Henry of Navarre, in April 1589.

As the two Henry's prepared to attack the Guise stronghold of Paris, however, a fanatical Dominican friar stabbed Henry III to death. Thereupon the Bourbon Huguenot Henry of Navarre succeeded the childless Valois king to the French throne as Henry IV (r. 1589–1610).

Henry IV came to the throne as a *politique,* weary of religious strife and prepared to place political peace above absolute religious unity. He believed that a royal policy of tolerant Catholicism would be the best way to achieve such peace. On July 25, 1593, he publicly abjured the Protestant faith and embraced the traditional and majority religion of his country. "Paris is worth a Mass," he is reported to have said.

The massacre of Huguenots in Paris on Saint Bartholomew's Day, August 24, 1572, as remembered by François Dubois, a Huguenot eyewitness. [Museum of Lausanne, Switzerland]

Philip II of Spain (1556–1598) at age twenty-four, by Titian. Philip was the dominant ruler of the second half of the sixteenth century. However, he was finally denied victory over the two areas in which he most sought to impose his will, The Netherlands and England. [Museo del Prado, Madrid]

On April 13, 1598, a formal religious settlement was proclaimed in Henry IV's famous Edict of Nantes. This religious truce—and it was never more than that—granted the Huguenots, who by this time numbered well over one million, freedom of public worship, the right of assembly, admission to public offices and universities, and permission to maintain fortified towns. Most of the new freedoms, however, were to be exercised within their own towns and territories. As significant as it was, the edict only transformed a long hot war between irreconcilable enemies into a long cold war. To its critics, it had only created a state within a state.

Imperial Spain and the Reign of Philip II (1556–1598)

Until the English defeated his mighty Armada in 1588, no one person stood larger in the second half of the sixteenth century than Philip II of Spain. During the first half of Philip's reign, attention focused on the Mediterranean and Turkish expansion. In May 1571, a Holy League of Spain, Venice, and the pope defeated the Turks in the largest naval battle of the sixteenth century. A fleet under the command of Philip's half-brother, Don John of Austria, engaged the Ottoman navy under Ali Pasha off Lepanto in the Gulf of Corinth on October 7, 1571. Before the engagement ended, thirty thousand Turks had died and over one-third of the Turkish fleet was sunk or captured.

REVOLT IN THE NETHERLANDS. The spectacular Spanish military success in southern Europe was not repeated in northern Europe when Philip attempted to impose his will within The Netherlands and on England and France. The resistance of The Netherlands especially proved the undoing of Spanish dreams of world empire.

The Netherlands were the richest area not only of Philip's Habsburg kingdom, but of Europe as well (see Map 18-4). The merchant towns of The Netherlands were also, however, Europe's most independent; many, like magnificent Antwerp, were also Calvinist strongholds. A stubborn opposition to the Spanish overlords formed under William of Nassau, the Prince of Orange (r. 1533–1584). Like other successful rulers in this period, William of Orange was a *politique* who placed The Netherlands' political autonomy and well-being above religious creeds. He personally passed through successive Catholic, Lutheran, and Calvinist stages.

The year 1564 saw the first fusion of political and religious opposition to Spanish rule, the result of Philip II's unwise insistence that the decrees of the Council of Trent be enforced throughout The Netherlands. A national covenant was drawn up called the *Compromise,* a solemn pledge to resist the decrees of Trent and the Inquisition.

Philip dispatched the duke of Alba to suppress the revolt. His army of ten thousand men journeyed northward from Milan in 1567 in a show of combined Spanish and papal might. A special tribunal, known

MAP 18-4   THE NETHERLANDS DURING THE REFORMATION   *The northern provinces of The Netherlands—the United Provinces—were mostly Protestant in the second half of the sixteenth century. The southern provinces—the Spanish Netherlands—made peace with Spain and remained largely Catholic.*

to the Spanish as the Council of Troubles and among The Netherlanders as the Council of Blood, reigned over the land. Several thousand suspected heretics were publicly executed before Alba's reign of terror ended.

William of Orange had been an exile in Germany during these turbulent years. He now emerged as the leader of a broad movement for The Netherlands' independence from Spain.

After a decade of persecution and warfare, the ten largely Catholic southern provinces (what is roughly modern Belgium) came together in 1576 with the seven largely Protestant northern provinces (what is roughly the modern Netherlands) in unified opposi-

This sixteenth-century satirical painting depicts The Netherlands as a milk cow. Elizabeth of England—which had long-standing commercial ties with Flanders—feeds the cow; Philip II of Spain—which was trying to reassert control over the country—attempts to ride her; William of Orange—who headed the anti-Spanish rebellion—tries to milk the animal; and the King of France—which sought to profit from the rebellion at Spain's expense—holds the tail. [Rijksmuseum, Amsterdam]

tion to Spain. This union, known as the Pacification of Ghent, was accomplished on November 8, 1576. It declared internal regional sovereignty in matters of religion. It was a Netherlands version of the territorial settlement of religious differences brought about in the Holy Roman Empire in 1555 by the Peace of Augsburg.

In January 1579, the southern provinces formed the Union of Arras and made peace with Spain. The northern provinces responded with the formation of the Union of Utrecht. Spanish preoccupation with France and England in the 1580s permitted the northern provinces to drive out all Spanish soldiers by 1593. In 1596, France and England formally recognized the independence of these provinces. Peace was not, however, concluded with Spain until 1609, when the Twelve Years' Truce gave the northern provinces their virtual independence. Full recognition came finally in the Peace of Westphalia in 1648.

England and Spain (1553–1603)

Mary I and Elizabeth I. Before Edward VI died in 1553, he had agreed to make the Protestant Lady Jane Grey—the teen-aged daughter of a powerful Protestant nobleman and, more important, the granddaugh-

ter on her mother's side of Henry VIII's *younger* sister Mary—his successor in place of the Catholic Mary Tudor (r. 1553–1558). But popular support for the principle of hereditary monarchy was too strong. Popular uprisings in London and elsewhere led to Jane Grey's removal from the throne within days of her crowning. She was eventually beheaded. Once enthroned, Mary proceeded to repeal the Protestant statutes of Edward and return England to the strict Catholic religious practice of her father, Henry VIII.

Mary's half-sister and successor, Elizabeth I (r. 1558–1603), the daughter of Henry VIII and Anne Boleyn, was perhaps the most astute politician of the sixteenth century in both domestic and foreign policy. She repealed the anti-Protestant legislation of Mary and guided a religious settlement through Parliament that prevented England from being torn asunder by religious differences in the sixteenth century, as the Continent was.

Catholic extremists hoped to replace Elizabeth with the Catholic Mary Stuart, Queen of Scots. But Elizabeth acted swiftly against Catholic assassination plots and rarely let emotion override her political instincts.

Elizabeth dealt cautiously with the Puritans, who were Protestants working within the national Church to "purify" it of every vestige of "popery" and to make

Elizabeth I of England, painted in 1592 by Marcus Gheeraerts. Note that she is standing on a map of her kingdom. Elizabeth is considered by many to be the most successful ruler of the sixteenth century. [National Portrait Gallery, London]

tionalists. Elizabeth refused to tolerate this group, whose views on independence seemed to her to be patently subversive.

DETERIORATION OF RELATIONS WITH SPAIN. A series of events led inexorably to war between England and Spain, despite the sincerest desires on the part of both Philip II and Elizabeth to avoid a direct confrontation. Following Don John's demonstration of Spain's seapower at the famous naval battle of Lepanto in 1571, England signed a mutual defense pact with France. Also in the 1570s, Elizabeth's famous seamen, John Hawkins (1532–1595) and Sir Francis Drake (?1545–1596), began to prey regularly on Spanish shipping in the Americas. Drake's circumnavigation of the globe between 1577 and 1580 was one in a series of dramatic demonstrations of English ascendancy on the high seas. In 1585, Elizabeth signed a treaty that committed English soldiers to The Netherlands. These events made a tinderbox of English-Spanish relations. The spark that finally touched it off was Elizabeth's reluctant execution of Mary, Queen of Scots (1542–1587) on February 18, 1587, for complicity in a plot to assassinate Elizabeth. Philip II ordered his Armada to make ready.

On May 30, 1588, a mighty fleet of 130 ships bearing twenty-five thousand sailors and soldiers under the command of the duke of Medina-Sidonia set sail for England. But the day belonged completely to the English. The invasion barges that were to transport Spanish soldiers from the galleons onto English shores were prevented from leaving Calais and Dunkirk. The swifter English and Netherlands ships, assisted by an "English wind," dispersed the waiting Spanish fleet, over one-third of which never returned to Spain.

The news of the Armada's defeat gave heart to Protestant resistance everywhere. Although Spain continued to win impressive victories in the 1590s, it never fully recovered from this defeat. Spanish soldiers faced unified and inspired French, English, and Dutch armies. By the time of Philip's death on September 13, 1598, his forces had been successfully rebuffed on all fronts.

The Thirty Years' War (1618–1648)

During the second half of the sixteenth century, Germany was an almost ungovernable land of 360 autonomous political entities. The Peace of Augsburg (1555) had given each a significant degree of sovereignty within its own borders. Each levied its own

its Protestant doctrine more precise. The Puritans had two special grievances: (1) the retention of Catholic ceremony and vestments within the Church of England, and (2) the continuation of the episcopal system of Church governance.

Sixteenth-century Puritans were not separatists, however. They worked through Parliament to create an alternative national Church of semiautonomous congregations governed by representative presbyteries (hence, Presbyterians), following the model of Calvin and Geneva. The more extreme Puritans wanted every congregation to be autonomous, a law unto itself, with neither higher episcopal nor presbyterian control. They came to be known as *Congrega-*

MAP 18-5   RELIGIOUS DIVISION ABOUT 1600   *By 1600 few could seriously expect Christians to return to a uniform religious allegiance. In Spain and southern Italy Catholicism remained relatively unchallenged, but note the existence of large minorities, both Catholic and Protestant, elsewhere.*

tolls and tariffs and coined its own money, practices that made land travel and trade between the various regions difficult, where not impossible. In addition, many of these little "states" were filled with great power pretensions. Political decentralization and fragmentation characterized Germany as the seventeenth century opened; it was not a unified nation like Spain, England, or even strife-filled France.

Religious conflict accentuated the international and internal political divisions (see Map 18-6). During this period, the population within the Holy Roman Empire was about equally divided between Catholics and Protestants, the latter having perhaps a slight numerical edge by 1600. The terms of the Peace of Augsburg (1555) had attempted to freeze the territorial holdings of the Lutherans and the Catholics. In the intervening years, however, the Lutherans had gained political control in some Catholic areas, as had the Catholics in a few previously Lutheran areas. There was religious strife in the empire not only between Protestants and Catholics but also between liberal and conservative Lutherans and between Lutherans and the growing numbers of Calvinists.

As elsewhere in Europe, Calvinism was the political and religious leaven within the Holy Roman Empire. Unrecognized as a legal religion by the Peace of

MAP 18-6   THE HOLY ROMAN EMPIRE ABOUT 1618   *On the eve of the Thirty Years' War the Empire was politically and religiously fragmented, as revealed by this somewhat simplified map. Lutherans dominated the north and Catholics the south, while Calvinists controlled the United Provinces and the Palatinate and were important in Switzerland and Brandenburg.*

Augsburg, Calvinism established a strong foothold within the empire when Frederick III (r. 1559–1576), a devout convert to Calvinism, made it the official religion of his land on becoming Elector Palatine (ruler within the Palatinate) in 1559. By 1609, Palatine Calvinists headed a Protestant defensive alliance supported by Spain's sixteenth-century enemies: England, France, and The Netherlands.

If the Calvinists were active within the Holy Roman Empire, so also were their Catholic counterparts, the Jesuits. Staunchly Catholic Bavaria, supported by Spain, became militarily and ideologically for the Counter-Reformation what the Palatinate was for Protestantism. From there, the Jesuits launched successful missions throughout the empire. In 1609, Maximilian, duke of Bavaria, organized a Catholic League to counter a new Protestant alliance that had been formed in the same year under the leadership of the Calvinist Elector Palatine, Frederick IV (r. 1583–1610). When the league fielded a great army under the command of Count Johann von Tilly, the stage was set, both internally and internationally, for the worst of the religious wars, the Thirty Years' War.

During its course, the war drew in every major Western European nation—at least diplomatically and financially if not in terms of direct military involvement. It was the worst European catastrophe since the Black Death of the fourteenth century.

The Treaty of Westphalia in 1648 brought all hostilities within the Holy Roman Empire to an end. It firmly reasserted the major feature of the religious settlement of the Peace of Augsburg (1555), as the ruler of each land was again permitted to determine the religion of his land. The treaty also gave the Calvinists their long-sought legal recognition. The independence of the Swiss Confederacy and the United Provinces of Holland, long recognized in fact, was now proclaimed in law.

By confirming the territorial sovereignty of Germany's many political entities, the Treaty of Westphalia perpetuated German division and political weakness into the modern period. Only two German state attained any international significance during the seventeenth century: Austria and Brandenburg-Prussia. The petty regionalism within the empire also reflected on a small scale the drift of larger European politics. During the seventeenth century, distinctive nation-states, each with its own political, cultural, and religious identity, reached maturity and firmly established the competitive nationalism of the modern world.

Change and Conflict in Early Modern Society

The religious conflicts of the sixteenth and seventeenth centuries changed Western religious institutions permanently in many lands, spurred the witch hunts of the later Middle Ages to new heights almost everywhere, and set intellectuals to thinking more profoundly about human nature and society.

Revolution in Religious Practices and Institutions

A comparison of religious life between the fifteenth and sixteenth centuries illustrates the dimensions of the religious revolution wrought by the Reformation. In the fifteenth century, in many of the great cities of central Europe that would later turn Protestant, the clergy and the religious made up 6 to 8 percent of the total urban population. They also legislated and taxed, tried cases in special Church courts, and enforced their laws with threats of excommunication.

The Church calendar regulated the daily life of the city, making about one-third of the year a time of religious observance or celebration. There were frequent periods of fasting; on almost one hundred days out of the year a pious Christian could not, without special dispensation, eat eggs, butter, fat, and/or meat.

Monasteries and especially nunneries were among society's most prominent and influential institutions. The children of the most powerful citizens resided there. Local aristocrats closely identified with particular churches and chapels. On the streets friars came and went begging. In the churches priests read the Mass and liturgy entirely in Latin. Images of the saints were regularly displayed, and on certain holidays their relics were paraded about and venerated.

A booming business flourished at local religious shrines, where pilgrims gathered by the thousands. Several times during the year, special preachers arrived to sell letters of indulgence, which promised their bearers release from punishment in purgatory for unrepented sins.

When one looks at these same cities a century later, after the Reformation, one finds few changes in politics and society; the same aristocratic families govern as before and the rich have generally grown richer. But where are the clergy? Overall numbers of clergy have fallen by two-thirds and religious holidays have shrunk by one-third. Monasteries and nunneries are nearly absent. Many of those not confiscated outright by secular authorities and turned to purely secular purposes have been transformed into hospices for the sick and poor or into public educational institutions, their endowments also directed to these new purposes.

In the churches, which have been reduced in number by at least one-third, worship is conducted almost completely in the vernacular. In some, particularly those in Zwinglian cities, the walls are stripped bare and whitewashed to make sure the congregation meditates only on God's word. The laity observe no obligatory fasts. Indulgence preachers no longer appear. Local shrines have been closed; anyone now openly venerating saints, relics, and images is subject to fine and punishment.

Copies of Luther's translation of the New Testament or excerpts from it can be found in private homes, and meditation on them is encouraged by the new Protestant clergy. The latter have married, rapidly and in large numbers. They now pay taxes and are punished for their crimes by civil courts. In the committees that now regulate domestic moral life, the laity are more prominent than the clergy.

Not all Protestant clergy remained enthusiastic about this new state of affairs. Many desired to regain the old clerical power and strict control over the lives of the laity (called "new papists" by the laity). Moreover, many laity were just as ambivalent about the Reformation's success. Over half of the original converts returned to the Catholic fold before the end of the sixteenth century. Still, Protestantism brought about permanent changes in a great part of the European religious world.[2]

Witchcraft and Witch Hunts

Between 1400 and 1700, courts sentenced an estimated seventy to one hundred thousand people to death for harmful magic *(malificium)* and diabolical witchcraft. In addition to supposedly inflicting harm on their neighbors, these witches were said to attend mass meetings known as *sabbats,* to which they were believed to fly. They were also accused of indulging in sexual orgies with the Devil, who appeared at such gatherings in animal form, most often as a he-goat. Still other charges against them were cannibalism (they were alleged to be especially fond of small

[2] S. Ozment, *Protestants: The Birth of a Revolution* (New York: Doubleday, 1992), pp. 24–28.

Depicted here are four witches who were burned at the stake at Wittenberg in 1540. The four were accused of commerce with the devil and of directing magic against their neighbors. [Hacker Art Books]

Christian children) and a variety of ritual acts and practices designed to insult every Christian belief and value. Where did such beliefs come from? Their roots were in both popular and elite cultures, especially clerical culture.

In village societies, so-called cunning folk played a positive role in helping people cope with calamity. People turned to them for help when such natural disasters as plague and famine struck or when such physical disabilities as lameness or inability to conceive offspring befell either them or their animals. The cunning folk provided consolation and gave people hope that such natural calamities might be averted or reversed by magical means.

Possession of magical powers, for good or ill, made one an important person within village society. Not surprisingly, claims to such powers seem most often to have been made by the people most in need of security and influence, namely, the old and the impoverished, especially single or widowed women. But witch beliefs in village society might also have been a way of defying urban Christian society's attempts to impose its laws and institutions on the countryside. From this perspective, village Satanism became a fanciful substitute for an impossible social revolt, a way of spurning the values of one's new masters. It is also possible, although unlikely, that witch beliefs in rural society had a foundation in local fertility cults, whose semipagan practices, designed to

A Confession of Witchcraft

This confession of witchcraft is exacted from a burgomaster during a witch panic in seventeenth-century Bamberg in central Germany. The account, an official transcript, accurately describes the process by which an innocent victim was brought, step by step, to confession—from the confrontation with his accusers to the application of increasingly painful tortures. By at last concurring in the accusation (albeit reluctantly and only after torture), the victims were believed by their executioners to be saving their souls as they lost their bodies. Having the victims' own confession may also have helped allay the executioners' consciences.

On Wednesday, June 28, 1628, was examined without torture Johannes Junius, Burgomaster at Bamberg, on the charge of witchcraft: how and in what fashion he had fallen into that vice. Is fifty-five years old, and was born at Niederwaysich in the Wetterau. Says he is wholly innocent, knows nothing of the crime, has never in his life renounced God; says that he is wronged before God and the world, would like to hear of a single human being who has seen him at such gatherings [as the witch sabbats].

Confrontation of Dr. Georg Adam Haan. Tells him to his face that he will stake his life on it, that he saw him, Junius, a year and a half ago at a witch-gathering in the electoral council-room, where they ate and drank. Accused denies the same wholly.

Confronted with Hopffens Elsse. Tells him likewise that he was on Haupts-moor at a witch-dance; but first the holy wafer was desecrated. Junius denies. Hereupon he was told that his accomplices had confessed against him and he was given time for thought.

On Friday, June 30, 1628, the aforesaid Junius was again without torture exhorted to confess, but again confessed nothing, whereupon, . . . since he would confess nothing, he was put to the torture, and first the

Thumb-screws were applied [both hands bound together, so that the blood ran out at the nails and everywhere]. Says he has never denied God his Saviour nor suffered himself to be otherwise baptized [i.e., initiated into devilish rites]. Will again stake his life on it; feels no pain in the thumb-screws.

Leg-screws. Will confess absolutely nothing; knows nothing about it. He has never renounced God; will never do such a thing; has never been guilty of this vice; feels likewise no pain. Is stripped and examined; on his right side is found a bluish mark, like a clover leaf, is thrice pricked therein, but feels no pain and no blood flows out.

Strappado [the binding of the prisoner's hands behind the back, and pulling them up by a rope attached to a pulley, resulting in the slow dislocation of the shoulders]. Says he never renounced God; God will not forsake him; if he were such a wretch he would not let himself be so tortured; God must show some token of his innocence. He knows nothing about witchcraft. . . .

On July 5, the above named Junius is without torture, but with urgent persuasions, exhorted to confess, and at last he . . . confesses.

Translations and Reprints from the Original Sources of European History, Vol. 3 (Philadelphia: University of Pennsylvania, 1912), pp. 23–24.

---

ensure good harvests, acquired the features of diabolical witchcraft under Church persecution.

Popular belief in magic was the essential foundation of the great witch hunts of the sixteenth and seventeenth centuries. Had ordinary people not believed that certain gifted individuals could aid or harm others by magical means, and had they not been willing to make accusations, the hunts could never have occurred. But the contribution of learned society was equally great. The Christian clergy also practiced a kind of magic, that of the holy sacraments, and the

exorcism of demons had been one of their traditional functions within society. Fear of demons and the Devil, which the clergy actively encouraged, allowed them to assert their moral authority over people and to enforce religious discipline and conformity.

In the late thirteenth century, the Church declared that only its priests possessed legitimate magical power. Inasmuch as such power was not human, theologians reasoned, it had to come either from God or from the Devil. If it came from God, then it was obediently confined to and exercised only on behalf of the

Church. Those who practiced magic outside the Church evidently derived their power from the Devil. From such reasoning grew accusations of "pacts" between non-Christian magicians and Satan. This made the witch hunts a life-and-death struggle against Christian society's worst heretics and foes, those who had directly sworn allegiance to the Devil himself.

The Church based its intolerance of magic outside its walls on sincere belief in and fear of the Devil. But attacking witches was also a way for established Christian society to extend its power and influence into new areas. To accuse, try, and execute witches was also a declaration of moral and political authority over a village or territory. As the cunning folk were local spiritual authorities, revered and feared by people, their removal became a major step in the establishment of a Christian beachhead in village society.

About 80 percent of the victims of witch hunts were women, the vast majority between forty-five and sixty years of age and widowed. This fact has suggested to some that misogyny fueled the witch hunts. Based in male hatred and sexual fear of women, and occurring at a time when women threatened to break out from under male control, witch hunts, it is argued, were simply woman hunts. Older women may, however, have been vulnerable for more basic social reasons. As a largely nonproductive and dependent social group, ever in need of public assistance, older and widowed women became natural targets for the peculiar "social engineering" of the witch hunts.

It may, however, be the case that gender played a purely circumstantial role. Because of their economic straits, more women than men claimed the supernatural powers that made them influential in village society. This put them on the front lines in disproportionate numbers when the Church declared war against all who practiced magic without its blessing. Also, the involvement of many of these women in midwifery associated them with the deaths of beloved wives and infants and thus made them targets of local resentment and accusations. Both the Church and their neighbors were prepared to think and say the worst about these women. It was a deadly combination.

Why did the witch hunts come to an end in the seventeenth century? Many factors played a role. The emergence of a new, more scientific worldview made it difficult to believe in the powers of witches. When, in the seventeenth century, mind and matter came to be viewed as two independent realities, words and thoughts lost the ability to affect things. A witch's curse was merely words. With advances in medicine and the beginning of insurance companies, people learned to rely on themselves when faced with natural calamity and physical affliction and no longer searched for supernatural causes and solutions.

Witch hunts also tended to get out of hand. Accused witches sometimes alleged that important townspeople had attended sabbats; even the judges could be so accused. At this point, the trials ceased to serve the purposes of those who were conducting them. They not only became dysfunctional but also threatened anarchy.

Finally, although Protestants also hunted witches, the Reformation may have contributed to an attitude of mind that put the Devil in a more manageable perspective. Protestants ridiculed the sacramental magic of the old Church as superstition and directed their faith to a sovereign God absolutely supreme over time and eternity. Even the Devil served God's purposes and acted only with His permission. Ultimately, God was the only significant spiritual force in the universe. This belief made the Devil a less fearsome creature. "One little word can slay him," Luther wrote of the Devil in the great hymn of the Reformation.

Writers and Philosophers

The end of the sixteenth century saw much weariness with religious strife and incipient unbelief as many could no longer embrace either old Catholic or new Protestant absolutes. Intellectually as well as politically, the seventeenth century would be a period of transition, one already well prepared for by the thinkers of the Renaissance, who had reacted strongly against medieval intellectual traditions.

The writers and philosophers of the late sixteenth and seventeenth centuries were aware that they lived in a period of transition. Some embraced the emerging new science wholeheartedly (Hobbes and Locke), some tried to straddle the two ages (Cervantes and Shakespeare), and still others ignored or opposed the new developments that seemed mortally to threaten traditional values (Pascal).

MIGUEL DE CERVANTES SAAVEDRA. Spanish literature of the sixteenth and seventeenth centuries was influenced by the peculiar religious and political history of Spain in this period. Spain was dominated by the Catholic Church, whose piety was strongly promoted by the Spanish rulers Charles I—who became the Holy Roman Emperor as Charles V (r. 1516–1556)—and his son, Philip II (r. 1556–1598). The intertwining of Catholic piety and Spanish political power underlay literary preoccupation with medieval chivalric virtues, in particular, honor and loyalty.

Generally acknowledged to be the greatest Spanish writer of all time, Cervantes (1547–1616) was preoccupied in his work with the strengths and weaknesses of religious idealism. Cervantes was the son of a nomadic physician. Having received only a smattering of formal education, he educated himself by insatiable reading in vernacular literature and immersion in the "school of life." As a young man, he worked in Rome for a Spanish cardinal. In 1570, he became a soldier and was decorated for gallantry in the Battle of Lepanto (1571). He conceived and began to write his most famous work, *Don Quixote,* in 1603, while languishing in prison after conviction for theft.

The first part of *Don Quixote* appeared in 1605, and a second part followed in 1615. If, as many argue, the intent of this work was to satirize the chivalric romances so popular in Spain, Cervantes failed to conceal his deep affection for the character he had created as an object of ridicule, Don Quixote. Don Quixote, a none-too-stable middle-aged man, is driven mad by reading too many chivalric romances. He comes to believe that he is an aspirant to knighthood and must prove his worthiness. To this end, he acquires a rusty suit of armor, mounts an aged horse, and chooses for his inspiration a quite unworthy peasant girl whom he fancies to be a noble lady to whom he can, with honor, dedicate his life.

Don Quixote's foil in the story—Sancho Panza, a clever, worldly-wise peasant who serves as Don Quixote's squire—watches with bemused skepticism, but also with genuine sympathy, as his lord does battle with a windmill (which he mistakes for a dragon) and repeatedly makes a fool of himself as he gallops across the countryside. The story ends tragically with Don Quixote's humiliating defeat by a well-meaning friend, who, disguised as a knight, bests Don Quixote in combat and forces him to renounce his quest for knighthood. The humiliated Don Quixote does not, however, come to his senses as a result. He returns sadly to his village to die a shamed and broken-hearted old man.

Throughout *Don Quixote,* Cervantes juxtaposed the down-to-earth realism of Sancho Panza with the old-fashioned religious idealism of Don Quixote. The reader perceives that Cervantes really admired the one as much as the other and meant to portray both as attitudes necessary for a happy life. Cervantes wanted his readers to remember that if they are to be truly happy, men and women need dreams, even impossible ones, just as much as they need a sense of reality.

WILLIAM SHAKESPEARE. There is much less factual knowledge about William Shakespeare (1564–1616), the greatest playwright in the English language, than one would expect of such an important figure. He apparently worked as a schoolteacher for a time and in this capacity acquired his broad knowledge of Renaissance learning and literature. There is none of the Puritan distress over worldliness in his work. He took the new commercialism and the bawdy pleasures of the Elizabethan Age in stride and with amusement. In matters of politics, as in those of religion, he was very much a man of his time and not inclined to offend his queen.

That Shakespeare was interested in politics is apparent from his history plays and the references to contemporary political events that fill all his plays. He seems to have viewed government simply, however, through the character of the individual ruler, whether Richard III or Elizabeth Tudor, not in terms of ideal

The English dramatist and poet, William Shakespeare. This engraving by Martin Droeshout appears on the title page of the collected edition of his plays published in 1623 and is probably as close as we shall come to knowing what he looked like.

systems or social goals. By modern standards, he was a political conservative, accepting the social rankings and the power structure of his day and demonstrating unquestioned patriotism.

Shakespeare knew the theater as one who participated in every phase of its life—as a playwright, actor, and part owner of a theater. He was a member and principal dramatist of a famous company of actors known as the King's Men.

Shakespeare's work was an original synthesis of the best past and current achievements. He mastered the psychology of human motivation and passion and had a unique talent for psychological penetration.

Shakespeare wrote histories, comedies, and tragedies. The tragedies are considered his unique achievement. Four of these were written within a three-year period: *Hamlet* (1603), *Othello* (1604), *King Lear* (1605), and *Macbeth* (1606). The most original of the tragedies, *Romeo and Juliet* (1597), transformed an old popular story into a moving drama of "star-cross'd lovers." Both Romeo and Juliet, denied a marriage by their factious families, die tragic deaths. Romeo, finding Juliet and thinking her dead after she has taken a sleeping potion, poisons himself. Juliet, awakening to find Romeo dead, stabs herself to death with his dagger.

Throughout his lifetime and ever since, Shakespeare has been immensely popular with both the playgoer and the play reader. As Ben Jonson, a contemporary classical dramatist who created his own school of poets, put it in a tribute affixed to the First Folio edition of Shakespeare's plays (1623): "He was not of an age, but for all time."

BLAISE PASCAL. Pascal (1623–1662) was a French mathematician and a physical scientist widely acclaimed by his contemporaries. Torn between the continuing dogmatism and the new skepticism of the seventeenth century, he aspired to write a work that would refute both the Jesuits, whose casuistry (i.e., confessional tactics designed to minimize and even excuse sinful acts) he considered a distortion of Christian teaching, and the skeptics, who either denied religion altogether (atheists) or accepted it only as it conformed to reason (deists). Pascal never realized such a definitive work, and his views on these matters exist only in piecemeal form. He wrote against the Jesuits in his *Provincial Letters* (1656–1657), and he left behind a provocative collection of reflections on humankind and religion that was published posthumously under the title *Pensées*.

Pascal was early influenced by the Jansenists, sev-enteenth-century Catholic opponents of the Jesuits. Although good Catholics, the Jansenists shared with the Calvinists St. Augustine's belief in the total sinfulness of human beings, their eternal predestination by God, and their complete dependence on faith and grace for knowledge of God and salvation.

Pascal believed that reason and science, although attesting to human dignity, remained of no avail in matters of religion. Here only the reasons of the heart and a "leap of faith" could prevail. Pascal saw two essential truths in the Christian religion: that a loving God, worthy of human attainment, exists, and that human beings, because they are corrupted in nature, are utterly unworthy of God. Pascal believed that the atheists and deists of the age had spurned the lesson of reason. For him, rational analysis of the human condition attested to humankind's utter mortality and corruption and exposed the weakness of reason itself in resolving the problems of human nature and destiny. Reason should rather drive those who truly heed it to faith and dependence on divine grace.

Pascal made a famous wager with the skeptics. It is a better bet, he argued, to believe that God exists and to stake everything on his promised mercy than not to do so, because if God does exist, everything will be gained by the believer, whereas the loss incurred by having believed in God should He prove not to exist is by comparison very slight.

Pascal was convinced that belief in God measurably improved earthly life psychologically and disciplined it morally, regardless of whether God proved in the end to exist. He thought that great danger lay in the surrender of traditional religious values. Pascal urged his contemporaries to seek self-understanding by "learned ignorance" and to discover humankind's greatness by recognizing its misery. Thereby he hoped to counter what he believed to be the false optimism of the new rationalism and science.

BARUCH SPINOZA. The most controversial thinker of the seventeenth century was Baruch Spinoza (1632–1677), the son of a Jewish merchant of Amsterdam. Spinoza's philosophy caused his excommunication by his own synagogue in 1656. In 1670, he published his *Treatise on Religious and Political Philosophy,* a work that criticized the dogmatism of Dutch Calvinists and championed freedom of thought. During his lifetime, both Jews and Protestants attacked him as an atheist.

Spinoza's most influential writing, the *Ethics,* appeared after his death in 1677. Religious leaders universally condemned it for its apparent espousal of pantheism. God and nature were so closely identified by Spinoza that little room seemed left either for divine revelation in Scripture or for the personal immortality of the soul, denials equally repugnant to Jews and to Christians. The *Ethics* is a very complicated work, written, in the spirit of the new science, as a geometrical system of definitions, axioms, and propositions.

The most controversial part of the *Ethics* deals with the nature of substance and of God. According to Spinoza, there is only one substance, which is self-caused, free, and infinite, and God is that substance. From this definition, it follows that everything that exists is in God and cannot even be conceived of apart from Him. Such a doctrine is not literally pantheistic, because God is still seen to be more than the created world that He, as primal substance, embraces. Nonetheless, in Spinoza's view, statements about the natural world are also statements about divine nature. Mind and matter are seen to be extensions of the infinite substance of God; what transpires in the world of humankind and nature is a necessary outpouring of the divine.

Such teaching clearly ran the danger of portraying the world as eternal and human actions as unfree and inevitable, the expression of a divine fatalism. Such points of view had been considered heresies by Jews and Christians because the views deny the creation of the world by God in time and destroy any voluntary basis for personal reward and punishment.

THOMAS HOBBES. Thomas Hobbes (1588–1679) was the most original political philosopher of the seventeenth century. Although he never broke with the Church of England, he came to share basic Calvinist beliefs, especially the low view of human nature and the ideal of a commonwealth based on a covenant, both of which find eloquent expression in Hobbes's political philosophy.

Hobbes was an urbane and much-traveled man and one of the most enthusiastic supporters of the new scientific movement. During the 1630s, he visited Paris, where he came to know Descartes, and after the outbreak of the Puritan Revolution (see Chapter 21) in 1640, he lived as an exile in Paris until 1651. Hobbes also spent time with Galileo in Italy and took a special interest in the works of William Harvey (1578–1657) (see Chapter 25). Harvey was a physiologist famed for the discovery of how blood circulated through the body; his scientific writings influenced Hobbes's own tracts on bodily motions.

Hobbes was driven to the vocation of political philosophy by the English Civil War (see Chapter 21). In 1651, his *Leviathan* appeared. Its subject was the political consequences of human passions, and its originality lay in (1) its making natural law, rather than common law (i.e., custom or precedent), the basis of all positive law, and (2) its defense of a representative theory of absolute authority against the theory of the divine right of kings. Hobbes maintained that statute law found its justification only as an expression of the law of nature and that political authority came to rulers by way of the consent of the people.

Hobbes viewed humankind and society in a thoroughly materialistic and mechanical way. Human beings are defined as a collection of material particles in motion. All their psychological processes begin with and are derived from bare sensation, and all their motivations are egoistical, intended to increase pleasure and minimize pain.

Despite this seemingly low estimate of human beings, Hobbes believed much could be accomplished by the reasoned use of science. All was contingent, however, on the correct use of that greatest of all human powers, one compounded of the powers of most people: the commonwealth, in which people are united by their consent in one all-powerful person.

The key to Hobbes's political philosophy is a brilliant myth of the original state of humankind. According to this myth, human beings in the natural state are generally inclined to a "perpetual and restless desire of power after power that ceases only in death."[3] As all people desire, and in the state of nature have a natural right to, everything, their equality breeds enmity, competition, and diffidence, and the desire for glory begets perpetual quarreling—"a war of every man against every man."[4]

Whereas earlier and later philosophers saw the original human state as a paradise from which humankind had fallen, Hobbes saw it as a corruption from which only society had delivered people. Contrary to the views of Aristotle and of Christian thinkers like Thomas Aquinas, in the view of Hobbes human beings are not by nature sociable, political animals; they are self-centered beasts, laws unto themselves, utterly without a master unless one is imposed by force.

According to Hobbes, people escape the impossible state of nature only by entering a social contract

[3]*Leviathan Parts I and II*, ed. by H. W. Schneider (Indianapolis: Bobbs-Merrill, 1958), p. 86.
[4]Ibid., p. 106.

that creates a commonwealth tightly ruled by law and order. The social contract obliges every person, for the sake of peace and self-defense, to agree to set aside personal rights to all things and to be content with as much liberty against others as he or she would allow others against himself or herself.

Because words and promises are insufficient to guarantee this state, the social contract also establishes the coercive force necessary to compel compliance with the covenant. Hobbes believed that the dangers of anarchy were far greater than those of tyranny, and he conceived of the ruler as absolute and unlimited in power, once established in office. There is no room in Hobbes's political philosophy for political protest in the name of individual conscience, nor for resistance to legitimate authority by private individuals—features of the *Leviathan* criticized by his contemporary Catholics and Puritans alike.

JOHN LOCKE.   Locke (1632–1704) has proved to be the most influential political thinker[5] of the seventeenth century. His political philosophy came to be embodied in the Glorious Revolution of 1688–1689. Although he was not as original as Hobbes, his political writings were a major source of the later Enlightenment criticism of absolutism, and they gave inspiration to both the American and the French revolutions.

Locke read deeply in the works of Francis Bacon, René Descartes, and Isaac Newton and was a close friend of the English physicist and chemist Robert Boyle (1627–1691). Some argue that he was the first philosopher to be successful in synthesizing the rationalism of Descartes and the experimental science of Bacon, Newton, and Boyle.

Locke's two most famous works are the *Essay Concerning Human Understanding* (1690) (discussed in Chapter 25) and the *Two Treatises of Government* (1690). Locke wrote *Two Treatises of Government* against the argument that rulers were absolute in their power. Rulers, Locke argued, remain bound to the law of nature, which is the voice of reason, teaching that "all mankind [are] equal and independent, [and] no one ought to harm another in his life, health, liberty, or possessions,"[6] inasmuch as all human beings are the images and property of God. According to Locke, people enter social contracts, empowering legislatures and monarchs to "umpire" their disputes,

precisely in order to preserve their natural rights, and not to give rulers an absolute power over them.

Whenever that end [namely, the preservation of life, liberty, and property for which power is given to rulers by a commonwealth] is manifestly neglected or opposed, the trust must necessarily be forfeited and the power devolved into the hands of those that gave it, who may place it anew where they think best for their safety and security.[7]

From Locke's point of view, absolute monarchy was "inconsistent" with civil society and could be "no form of civil government at all."[8]

Locke's main differences with Hobbes stemmed from the latter's views on the state of nature. Locke believed that the natural human state was one of perfect freedom and equality in which the natural rights of life, liberty, and property were enjoyed, in unregulated fashion, by all. The only thing lacking in the state of nature was a single authority to give judgment when disputes inevitably arose as a result of the natural freedom and equality possessed by all. Contrary to the view of Hobbes, human beings in their natural state were not creatures of monomaniacal passion but were possessed of extreme goodwill and rationality. They did not surrender their natural rights unconditionally when they entered the social contract; rather, they established a means whereby these rights could be better preserved. The warfare that Hobbes believed characterized the state of nature emerged for Locke only when rulers failed in their responsibility to preserve the freedoms of the state of nature and attempted to enslave people by absolute rule, that is, to remove them from their "natural" condition. Only then were the peace, goodwill, mutual assistance, and preservation in which human beings naturally live and socially ought to live undermined, and a state of war was created.

The Renaissance and Reformation in World Perspective

During the Renaissance, Western Europe recovered its classical cultural heritage, from which it had been separated for almost eight centuries. No other world civilization had known such disjunction from its cul-

---

[5] Locke's scientific writings are discussed in Chapter 25.

[6] *The Second Treatise of Government*, ed. by T. P. Peardon (Indianapolis: Bobbs-Merrill, 1952), chap. 2, sects. 4–6, pp. 4–6.

[7] Ibid., chap. 13, sect. 149, p. 84.

[8] Ibid.

tural past. It was due to the work of Byzantine and Islamic scholars that ancient Greek science and scholarship were rediscovered in the West. During this period, Western Europe also recovered from national wars to establish permanent centralized states and regional governments. Even the great population losses of the fourteenth century were recovered by 1500. By the late fifteenth and sixteenth centuries, Europeans were in a position to venture far afield to the shores of Africa, southern and eastern Asia, and the new world of the Americas, directly confronting for the first time the different civilizations of the world from Japan to Brazil.

But Western history between 1500 and 1650 was especially shaped by an unprecedented schism in Christianity, as Lutherans and other Protestant groups broke with Rome. The religious divisions contributed to both national and international warfare, which by the seventeenth century devastated the empire on a scale unseen since the Black Death.

The other world civilizations moved more slowly, maintained greater social and political unity, and remained unquestionably more tolerant of religious belief than the West. Under Mongol rule (1279–1368), China tolerated all indigenous religions as well as Islam and Eastern Christianity. No crises on the scale of those that rocked the West struck China, although plagues from 1586 to 1589 and from 1639 to 1644 killed 20–30 percent of the inhabitants in populous regions. China moved steadily from Mongol to Ming (1368–1644) to Ching (1644–1911) rule without major social and political upheaval. By comparison to the West, its society was socially static, and its rulers maintained unified, even despotic, control. Whereas the West also had highly centralized and authoritarian governments between 1350 and 1650, unlike China, it also managed more successfully to balance the interests of the one with those of the many. In the West, parliaments and estates general, representing the nobility, and lesser representative political bodies gained a permanent right to express their views forcefully to higher authority.

Although parallels may be drawn between the court culture of the Forbidden Palace in Peking and that of King Louis XIV in seventeenth-century France, Chinese government and religious philosophy (Confucianism) remained more unified and patriarchal than their counterparts in the West. There was never the degree of political dissent and readiness to fragment Chinese society in the name of religion that characterized Western society, even in the West's own "age of absolutism." On the other hand, the Chinese readily tolerated other religions, as their warm embrace of Jesuit missionaries attests. There is no similar Western demonstration of tolerance for Asian religious philosophy.

Voyages of exploration also set forth from Ming China, especially between 1405 and 1433, reaching India, the Arabian Gulf, and East Africa. These voyages did not, however, prove to be commercially profitable as those of the West would be, nor did they spark any notable commercial development in China. It is an open question whether this was because the Chinese were less greedy, curious, or belligerent than the Portuguese and Spanish.

Like the West in the later Middle Ages, Japan experienced its own political and social breakdown after 1467, when the *bakufu* government began to collapse. Japan's old manorial society progressively fell apart, and a new military class of vassalized foot soldiers, armed with spears and muskets, replaced the mounted samurai as the new military force. In 1590, Hideyoshi (r. 1536–1598) disarmed the peasantry and froze the social classes, thereby laying the foundation for a new social and political order in Japan. Building on this achievement, Tokugawa rule (1600–1850) managed to stabilize and centralize the government by 1650. Much as Western kings had to "domesticate" their powerful noblemen to succeed, Japanese rulers learned to integrate the many regional daimyo lords into government. Like Louis XIV, Tokugawa shōguns required these lords to live for long periods of time at court, where their wives and children also remained. As in most Western countries, the shōguns of Japan thus avoided both fragmented and absolutist government.

Like the Chinese, the Japanese were also admirers of the Jesuits, who arrived in Japan with the Portuguese in 1543. The admiration was mutual, leading to three hundred thousand Christian converts by 1600. As in China, the Jesuits treated native religion as a handmaiden and prelude to superior Christian teaching. But the tolerance of Christianity did not last as long in Japan as in China. Christianity was banned in the late sixteenth century as part of Hideyoshi's internal unification program. With the ascent of more tolerant Confucianism over Buddhism among the Japanese ruling classes, Christianity and Western culture would again be welcomed in the nineteenth century.

During the age of Reformation in the West, absolutist Islamic military regimes formed in the Ottoman empire, among the Safavids in Iran, and among the Mughals in India. In all three cultures, religion became tightly integrated into government, so that they never knew the divisiveness and political challenge periodically prompted in the West by Christianity. In opposition to the expansive Ottomans, Shah Abbas I (r. 1588–1629) allied with the Europeans and welcomed Dutch and English traders. Embracing Shi'ite religion and the Persian language (the rest of the Islamic world was mostly Sunni and spoke Arabic or different regional languages), Iran progressively isolated itself. Unlike the West, the Timurid empire of the Indian Mughals, particularly under Akbar the Great (r. 1556–1605), and extending into the late seventeenth century, encouraged religious toleration even to the point of holding discussions among different faiths at the royal court. As in China and Japan, India too was prepared to live with and learn from the West.

Suggested Readings

R. H. BAINTON, *Erasmus of Christendom* (1960). Charming presentation.

C. BOXER, *Four Centuries of Portuguese Expansion 1415–1825* (1961). A comprehensive survey by a leading authority.

F. BRAUDEL, *The Mediterranean and the Mediterranean World in the Age of Philip the Second,* Vols. 1 and 2 (1976). The widely acclaimed work of a French master historian.

E. CAMERON, *The European Reformation* (1990). Large synthesis of recent studies, with most attention given to the German Reformation.

O. CHADWICK, *The Reformation* (1964). Among the best short histories and especially strong on theological and ecclesiastical issues.

N. COHN, *The Pursuit of the Millennium* (1957). Traces millennial speculation and activity from the Old Testament to the sixteenth century.

A. G. DICKENS, *The Counter Reformation* (1969). A brief narrative with pictures.

A. G. DICKENS, *The English Reformation* (1974). The best one-volume account.

B. DIEFENDORF. *Beneath the Cross: Catholics and Huguenots in Sixteenth Century Paris* (1991).

G. DONALDSON, *The Scottish Reformation* (1960). A dependable, comprehensive narrative.

R. DUNN, *The Age of Religious Wars 1559–1689* (1979). An excellent brief survey of every major conflict.

M. DURAN, *Cervantes* (1974). Detailed biography.

J. H. ELLIOTT, *Europe Divided 1559–1598* (1968). A direct, lucid narrative account.

G. R. ELTON, *England Under the Tudors* (1955). A masterly account.

G. R. ELTON, *Reformation Europe 1517–1559* (1966). Among the best short treatments and espically strong on political issues.

E. ERIKSON, *Young Man Luther: A Study in Psychoanalysis and History* (1962). A controversial study that has opened a new field of historiography.

H. O. EVENNETT, *The Spirit of the Counter Reformation* (1968). An essay on the continuity of Catholic reform and its independence from the Protestant Reformation.

J. H. FRANKLIN, ed. and trans., *Constitutionalism and Resistance in the Sixteenth Century: Three Treatises by Hotman, Beza, and Mornay* (1969). Three defenders of the right of people to resist tyranny.

R. FULOP-MILLER, *The Jesuits: A History of the Society of Jesus,* trans. by F. S. Flint and D. F. Tait (1963). A critical survey, given to psychological analysis.

P. GEYL, *The Revolt of The Netherlands, 1555–1609* (1958). The authoritative survey.

M. GREENGRASS, *The French Reformation* (1987). Summary account, pulling everything together succinctly.

H. GRIMM, *The Reformation Era: 1500–1650* (1973). Very good on later Lutheran developments.

C. HAIGH, *The English Reformation Revised* (1988). Argues that the English Reformation was less revolutionary than historians have traditionally argued.

R. HSIA, *The German People and the Reformation* (1989). Collection illustrative of the new social history of the German Reformation.

J. L. IRWIN, ed., *Womanhood in Radical Protestantism, 1525–1675* (1979). A rich collection of sources.

H. JEDIN, *A History of the Council of Trent,* Vols. 1 and 2 (1957–1961). Comprehensive, detailed, and authoritative.

D. JENSEN, *Reformation Europe, Age of Reform and Revolution* (1981). An excellent, up-to-date survey.

T. F. JESSOP, *Thomas Hobbes* (1960). A brief biographical sketch.

W. K. JORDAN, *Edward VI: The Young King* (1968). The basic biography.

R. KIECKHEFER, *European Witch Trials: Their Foundations in Popular and Learned Culture 1300–1500* (1976). One of the very best treatments of the subject.

R. M. KINGDON, *Transition and Revolution: Problems and Issues of European Renaissance and Reformation History* (1974). Covers politics, printing, theology, and witchcraft.

R. J. KNECHT, *The French Wars of Religion, 1559–1598* (1989).

A. KORS and E. PETERS, eds., *European Witchcraft, 1100–1700* (1972).

C. LARNER, *Enemies of God: The Witchhunt in Scotland* (1981). One of the more detailed and authoritative accounts of witch hunting.

P. LASLETT, *Locke's Two Treatises of Government,* 2nd ed. (1970). Definitive texts with very important introductions.

A. MACFARLANE, *The Family Life of Ralph Josselin: A Seventeenth Century Clergyman* (1970). Exemplary family history.

J. McNEILL, *The History and Character of Calvinism* (1954). The most comprehensive account, very readable.

J. R. MAJOR, *Representative Institutions in Renaissance France* (1960). An essay in French constitutional history.

G. MATTINGLY, *The Armada* (1959). A masterpiece, novel-like in style.

K. MOXLEY, *Peasants, Warriors, and Wives* (1989). The English Reformation through popular art.

J. E. NEALE, *The Age of Catherine de Medici* (1962). A short, concise summary.

J. NEALE, *Queen Elizabeth I* (1934). A superb biography.

D. NUGENT, *Ecumenism in the Age of Reformation: The Colloquy of Poissy* (1974). A study of the last ecumenical council of the sixteenth century.

S. OZMENT, *The Age of Reform 1250–1550: An Intellectual and Religious History of Late Medieval and Reformation Europe* (1980).

S. OZMENT, *Protestants: The Birth of a Revolution* (1992).

S. OZMENT, *When Fathers Ruled: Family Life in Reformation Europe* (1983).

J. H. PARRY, *The Age of Reconnaissance* (1964). A comprehensive account of explorations from 1450 to 1650.

T. K. RABB, ed., *The Thirty Years' War* (1972). Excerpts from the scholarly debate over the war's significance.

E. F. RICE, JR., *The Foundations of Early Modern Europe 1460–1559* (1970). A broad, succinct narrative.

J. H. M. SALMON, ed., *The French Wars of Religion: How Important Were the Religious Factors?* (1967). Scholarly debate over the relation between politics and religion.

J. J. SCARISBRICK, *Henry VIII* (1968). The best account of Henry's reign.

J. J. SCARISBRICK, *The Reformation and the English People* (1991). Very readable, but controversial argument that the most striking thing about the English Reformation was the vigor of Catholicism at century's end.

A. SOMAN, ed., *The Massacre of St. Bartholomew's Day: Reappraisals and Documents* (1974). The results of an international symposium on the anniversary of the massacre.

L. SPITZ, *The Religious Renaissance of the German Humanists* (1963). Comprehensive and entertaining.

J. STAYER, *Anabaptists and the Sword* (1972). One of the most lucid and sympathetic accounts.

G. STRAUSS, ed. and trans., *Manifestations of Discontent in Germany on the Eve of the Reformation* (1971). A rich collection of sources for both rural and urban scenes.

R. H. TAWNEY, *Religion and the Rise of Capitalism* (1947). Advances beyond Weber's arguments relating Protestantism and capitalist economic behavior.

K. THOMAS, *Religion and the Decline of Magic* (1971). Something of a classic on the subject.

E. TROELTSCH, *The Social Teaching of the Christian Churches,* Vols. 1 and 2, trans. by Olive Wyon (1960).

M. WEBER, *The Protestant Ethic and the Spirit of Capitalism,* trans. by Talcott Parsons (1958). First appeared in 1904–1905 and has continued to stimulate debate over the relationship between religion and society.

C. V. WEDGWOOD, *The Thirty Years' War* (1939). The authoritative account.

C. V. WEDGWOOD, *William the Silent* (1944). An excellent political biography.

F. WENDEL, *Calvin: The Origins and Development of His Religious Thought,* trans. by Philip Mairet (1963). The best treatment of Calvin's theology.

MERRY WIESNER, *Working Women in Renaissance Germany* (1986). Looking at women outside the family in the workaday world.

G. H. WILLIAMS, *The Radical Reformation* (1962). A broad survey of the varieties of dissent within Protestantism.

A bronze plaque showing three warriors from Benin, West Africa. The famous Benin bronze sculptures are among the finest artistic works of all African cultures. Note that the two small figures in the background apparently depict Portuguese or other European soldiers. [Peabody Museum, Harvard University]

Africa (ca. 1000–1800)

19

Even a cursory look at the history of Africa in the period beginning around A.D. 1000 reveals widely diverse experiences for different parts of this vast continent. For example, while North Africa and Egypt after 1000 were involved in the major power struggles of the Islamic heartlands, sub-Saharan Africa developed much more according to internal African dynamics and other external influences. Similarly, by 1500, although many parts of the continent were little influenced by outsiders or their affairs, others were caught up in the repercussions of new developments in Europe and the Islamic worlds and the changing power balance between the two.

In this chapter, we explore, region by region, some of the salient developments in Africa over the long period from 1000 to 1800. Our initial focus is Africa above the equator, where the Islamic tradition played an increasing role during this period and where a series of substantial empires and kingdoms developed and flourished. We then turn to the coming of the Europeans and specifically to the development of the massive Atlantic slave trade that, between the fifteenth and nineteenth centuries, far outstripped the older, "oriental" slave trade. Finally, we discuss East and southern Africa and the effect first of Arab-Islamic and then of European influence there.

North Africa and Egypt

As we glimpsed in Chapter 16, Egypt and the other North African states played a central role in Islamic and Mediterranean history in the first half of the second millennium. From Tunisia to Egypt, a prominent aspect of this period was the struggle for the minds of the masses between Sunni religious and political leaders and their Shi'ite, especially Isma'ili, counterparts. By the thirteenth century, however, the Shi'ites had become a small minority of the Muslim population of Mediterranean Africa. In Egypt, a Sunni revival confirmed the Sunni character of Egyptian piety and religious practice and established the Shafi'ite tradition of Sunni legal interpretation. In the rest of North Africa, the Maliki legal school of Sunni thought carried the day.

On the political stage, this period witnessed the relatively powerful and long-lived dynasties of the Fatimids (909–969 in Tunisia; 969–1171 in Egypt), the Almoravids (1056–1147 in Senegal and the western Sudan; 1062–1118 in Marrakesh and western North Africa; 1086–1147 in Spain), the Almohads (1130–1269 in western North Africa; 1145–1212 in Spain), the Ayyubids (1169–1250 in Egypt), and the Mamluks (1250–1517 in Egypt and the eastern Mediterranean). In general, a feisty regionalism was characteristic of the states, city-states, and tribal groups in the lands north of the Sahara and along the lower Nile, especially vis-à-vis external power centers such as Baghdad and Spain. No single power proved capable of controlling them for long. This regionalism even persisted from the sixteenth century onward, after most of North Africa came within the influence—and often direct control—of the Ottoman Empire centered in Istanbul and felt the pressure of the Ottoman-European naval rivalry in the the Mediterranean.

By 1800 the nominally Ottoman domains from Egypt to Algeria were effectively independent. In Egypt, Istanbul had established direct rule after the Ottoman defeat of the Mamluks in 1517, but by the seventeenth and eighteenth centuries this direct rule had already passed to Egyptian governors descended from the former ruling Mamluks. Even though very weak in the eighteenth century, the Mamluk gover-

nors survived for another hundred years until the rise of Muhammad Ali in the wake of the French invasion of 1800 (see Chapter 33). The Mediterranean coastlands between Egypt and Morocco were officially Ottoman provinces, or regencies, whether under local governors or Ottoman military deputies drawn from the ranks of the Janissaries (see Chapter 24). By the eighteenth century, however, the Regency of Algiers to the east of Morocco was a separate, locally run principality existing primarily on piracy. The Regency of Tripoli was in the hands of a family of hereditary, effectively independent rulers. In Tunisia, a Janissary state operated with virtual independence of its nominal Ottoman overlords.

Morocco, ruled by a long series of *Sharif*s (leaders claiming descent from the family of the prophet Muhammad), was the only North African sultanate to remain fully independent after the sixteenth century. The most important *Sharifian* dynasty was that of the Sa'dis (1554–1659). At least one major reason for Morocco's success in maintaining its independence was that the country's Arab and Berber populations united in face of the threat posed after 1500 by marauding Portuguese and Spaniards.

Spread of Islam in Africa South of the Sahara

Islamic influence in sub-Saharan Africa began as early as the eighth century and by 1800 affected most of the Sudan and the coast of East Africa as far south as modern Zimbabwe. All in all, the process was peaceful, gradual, and partial. Typically, Islam never

Feluccas on the Nile. These lateen-rigged sailing vessels are the traditional river boats of Egypt and are still in use today. [Photograph by Eliot Elisofon, National Museum of African Art, Eliot Elisofon Archives, Smithsonian Institution]

penetrated beyond the ruling or commercial classes of a region. Even among these classes, it tended to coexist or blend with indigenous ideas and practices. Nevertheless, Islam and its carriers were momentous for the regions they affected. Agents of Islam brought, on the one hand, military and commercial developments and, on the other, the Qur'an and Arabic scholarship and literate culture. In West as in East Africa, the arrival of literate culture proved to be as important an event for the subsequent history of those areas as any other development. Many innovations, in fields ranging from architecture and technology to intellectual life and administrative practice, depended on writing and literacy, which are among the most important supports of the development of large-scale societies and cultures.

Comparison of the spread of Islam in West and central Africa with that in East Africa is instructive. In East Africa, Muslim traders moving down the coastline with the time-honored monsoon trade routes had begun the "Islamization" of port towns and coastal regions even before A.D. 800. From the thirteenth century onward in particular, the growth of not only Islamic trading communities but also Islamic city-states along the coast from Mogadishu to Kilwa became a major factor in the history of this region.

By contrast, in the western and central parts of the continent, Islam penetrated south of the Sahara and north of the rain forests not by sea, but by overland routes, primarily south from North Africa and Egypt across the Sahara, but also west and southwest from the Nilotic regions south of the Sahara. Nevertheless, as in East Africa, the agents of Islamization (where it occurred) were also traders, chiefly Berbers who traveled the desert routes (see Chapter 8) to trading towns like Awdaghast on the edge of the Sahel as early as the eighth century. From there Islam spread south to centers such as Kumbi and finally farther, southeast to the Niger and beyond and west into Senegambia. Another source for the gradual spread of Islam into the central and western Sudan was Egypt and the Nilotic Sudan. The agents there were sometimes traders, but primarily emigrants from the east seeking new land farther west. From these eastern Islamic areas, migrating Arab tribal groups in particular came to settle in the central sub-Saharan Sahel. Although many more Arab migrants moving west followed the Mediterranean coast from Egypt to North Africa, substantial numbers sifted westward to Lake Chad and the Niger regions from the ninth to the sixteenth centuries and later.

Some Muslim conversion in the western and cen-

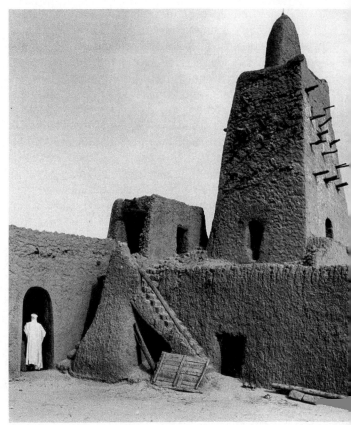

The Djinguereber mosque in Timbuktu. This mud and wood building is typical of western Sudanese mosques. The distinctive tower of the mosque was a symbol of the presence of Islam, which came to places like Timbuktu in central and West Africa by way of overland trade routes. [Photograph by Eliot Eliosofon, National Museum of African Art, Eliot Eliosofon Archives, Smithsonian Institution]

tral Sudan came quite early, virtually always through the medium of Muslim traders. The year 985 marks the first time that a royal court of West Africa—that of the kingdom of Gao, east of the Niger bend—officially became Muslim (see Chapter 8 and below). The Gao rulers did not, however, try to convert their subjects. By contrast, as we discuss later in the chapter, the rulers of the later kingdom of Ghana, who themselves long maintained their indigenous traditions, kept a separate township near their capital of Kumbi for the Muslim merchants with whom they dealt extensively and the Muslim advisers who helped them govern.

From the 1030s, zealous militants known as Almoravids (Arabic *al-Murabitun,* after their fortified retreat centers, or *ribats*) began an overt conversion campaign in coastal Mauritania and Senegal and extended it to the western Sahel and Sahara. This movement eventually swept into Ghana's territory, taking first Awdaghast and finally Kumbi in 1076. Thereafter, the forcibly converted Soninke ruling group of Ghana spread Islam among their own populace and farther south in the savannah. Here they converted Mande-speaking traders, who spread it in time south into the forests as well. Farther west, the Fulbe rulers of Takrur along the Senegal became Muslim in the 1030s and propagated their new faith among their subjects. The Fulbe, or Fulani, would remain important agents of the spread of Islam as they migrated gradually into new regions as far south and east as Lake Chad over the next eight centuries. Some rulers in the lake Chad region were Muslim as early as 1100.

Some major groups in West Africa, especially in the sub-Niger region, strongly resisted Islamization altogether. Notable among them were the Mossi kingdoms founded in the Volta region at Wagadugu around 1050 and Yatenga about 1170.

Sahelian Empires of the Western and Central Sudan

It is not the case, as was once believed, that urbanization and state formation in sub-Saharan Africa occurred only after the beginning of, and in response to, trans-Saharan trade with the Islamic world (the fabled "golden trade of the Moors"), which dates largely from the end of the first millennium.[1] As we noted in Chapter 8, a series of substantial states had risen in the first millennium A.D. in the Sahel regions just south of the Sahara proper. In the period from about 1000 to 1600, four of these kingdoms developed into notable and relatively long-lived empires: Ghana, Mali, and Songhai in the western Sudan, and Kanem-Bornu in the central Sudan.

Ghana

Ghana was the state that established the model for later empires of the Sahel region of the western Sudan, even though those that succeeded it were larger. Essentially a regional empire noted and esteemed by Arab Islamic writers far away, Ghana was located well north of modern Ghana (and unrelated to it except by name) in the region between and north of the inland Niger delta and the upper Senegal. A Ghanaian kingdom originated as early as A.D. 400–

600, but Ghana emerged as a regional power only near the end of the first millennium and flourished for about two centuries thereafter. Its capital of Kumbi (or Kumbi Saleh) was on the desert's edge and thus well sited for the Saharan and the Sahelian trade networks. Ghana's central population group were the Soninke, a northern Mande-speaking people of Awkar, or Wagadu, as the natives called the region. *Ghana,* the Soninke term for "ruler," was the name by which Berbers and Arabs knew the region and hence the name that was passed on in our earliest written sources.

The Ghanaian rulers were matrilineally descended (through the previous king's sister). They exercised their power through a council of ministers. The reports that we have, above all from the eleventh-century Muslim writer, al-Bakri (see the box on p. 557), indicate that the king was supreme judge and held court regularly to hear grievances. The royal ceremonies reported to have been held in Kumbi Saleh were embellished with the full trappings of regal wealth and power appropriate to a king who was considered to be divinely blessed or possibly even semi-divine.

Ghana's power was built on a solid economic base. Tribute from the empire's many chieftaincies and taxes on royal lands and crops (primarily grown in the southern part of the region, near the Niger and Senegal) supplemented the major source of income: duties levied on all incoming and outgoing trade. This trade, both north-south between the Sahara and the savannah and especially east-west through the Sahel between the Senegambia regions and more easterly trading towns like Gao on the Niger Bend, involved a variety of goods, notably imported salt, copper, cloth, and metal goods such as copper, likely in exchange for gold and perhaps kola nuts from the south. The regime apparently also profited from control of the gold (and, presumably, the slave) trade that originated in the savannah to the south and west, in the tributary regions of the Bambuk and Galam regions of the middle Senegal and its southern tributary, the Faleme; and in the Boure region of the upper Niger and its tributaries.

Although the king and court of Ghana did not convert to Islam, they made elaborate arrangements to accommodate Muslim specialists and, presumably, traders, who even had their own settlement a few miles from the royal preserve in Kumbi Saleh. Literate Muslims were employed to organize and administer the government, and Muslim legists served as advisers to the ruler. In Ghana's stratified society, slaves

[1] S. K. and R. J. McIntosh, *Prehistoric Investigations at Jenne, Mali* (1980), pp. 41–59, 434–461; R. Oliver, *The African Experience* (New York: HarperCollins, 1991), p. 90–101.

Ghana and Its People in the Mid-Eleventh Century

The following excerpt is from the geographical work of the Spanish Muslim geographer al-Bakri (d. 1094). In it, he describes with great precision some customs of the ruler and the people of the capital of Ghana as he carefully gleaned them from other Arabic sources and travelers (he never visited West Africa himself, it seems).

Ghāna is a title given to their kings; the name of the region is Awkār, and their king today, namely in the year 460/1067–8, is Tankā Manīn. . . . This Tankā Manīn is powerful, rules an enormous kingdom, and possesses great authority.

The city of Ghāna consists of two towns situated on a plain. One of these towns, which is inhabited by Muslims, is large and possesses twelve mosques, in one of which they assemble for the Friday prayer. There are salaried imams and muezzins, as well as jurists and scholars. In the environs are wells with sweet water, from which they drink and with which they grow vegetables. The king's town is six miles distant from this one and bears the name of Al-Ghāba. Between these two towns there are continuous habitations. The houses of the inhabitants are of stone and acacia *(sunt)* wood. The king has a palace and a number of domed dwellings all surrounded with an enclosure like a city wall *(sūr)*. In the king's town, and not far from his court of justice, is a mosque where the Muslims who arrive at his court *(yafid 'alayh)* pray. Around the king's town are domed buildings and groves and thickets where the sorcerers of these people, men in charge of the religious cult, live. In them too are their idols and the tombs of their kings. . . .

All of them shave their beards, and women shave their heads. The king adorns himself like a woman [wearing necklaces] round his neck and [bracelets] on his forearms, and he puts on a high cap *(tartūr)* decorated with gold and wrapped in a turban of fine cotton. He sits in audience or to hear grievances against officials *(mazālim)* in a domed pavilion around which stand ten horses covered with gold-embroidered materials. Behind the king stand ten pages holding shields and swords decorated with gold, and on his right are the sons of the [vassal] kings of his country wearing splendid garments and their hair plaited with gold. The governor of the city sits on the ground before the king and around him are ministers seated likewise. . . . When the people who profess the same religion as the king approach him they fall on their knees and sprinkle dust on their heads, for this is their way of greeting him. As for the Muslims, they greet him only by clapping their hands.

Their religion is paganism and the worship of idols *(dakākīr)*. When their king dies they construct over the place where his tomb will be an enormous dome of *sāj* wood. Then they bring him on a bed covered with a few carpets and cushions and place him beside the dome. At his side they place his ornaments, his weapons, and the vessels from which he used to eat and drink, filled with various kinds of food and beverages.

From J. F. P. Hopkins, trans.; N. Levtzion and J. F. P. Hopkins, eds., *Corpus of Early Arabic Sources for West African History* (Cambridge, UK: Cambridge University Press, 1981). pp. 79–80.

were at the bottom of the hierarchy; farmers and draftsmen above them; merchants above them; and the king, his court and the nobility on top.

A huge, well-trained army secured the king's control of his dominions and enabled him to extend his sway during the late tenth century to the Atlantic shore and to the south as well (see Map 19-1). Ghanaian troops were strong enough to capture the town of Awdaghast, the important southern terminus of the trans-Saharan trade route to Morocco, from the Berbers in 992. The empire was, however, vulnerable to attack from the desert fringe, as the Berber forces of the Almoravids proved in 1054, when they swept down on Awdaghast and took it in a single raid. Some traditions seem to claim that further Berber raids brought down the Ghanaian state in 1076, but these accounts have been questioned by recent historians. In the final analysis, we cannot be certain that ancient Ghana actually met its demise by 1100. Rather, there are reports of its continued existence and involvement in trade late in the twelfth century. Even more, there are indications that Ghana's rulers may have

MAP 19-1 AFRICA CA. 900–1500 *Shown are major cities and states referred to in the text. The main map shows the region of West Africa occupied by the empire of Ghana from ca. 990 to ca. 1180. The inset shows the region occupied by Mali between 1230 and 1450.*

been converted to Islam soon after 1100 and that throughout the twelfth century they joined the Almoravids in proselytizing for Islam and cooperated with them on military and economic matters. What appears likely is that Ghana's regional empire was destroyed in the last quarter of the twelfth century by the actively anti-Muslim Soso people, a Malinke clan from the mountainous region southeast of Kumbi

Saleh and west of Jenne who had long been a part of the Ghanaian empire. Their brief ascendancy between 1180 and 1230 spelled the end of the once great transregional power centered at Kumbi.[2]

[2]D. Conrad and H. Fisher, "The Conquest That Never Was: Ghana and the Almoravids, 1076," *History in Africa* 9 (1982): 1–59; 10 (1983): 53–78.

Mali

After the Almoravid Muslim reform movement began to make itself felt in the western Sahel at the end of the eleventh century, the proselytizing zeal of these reformers led to the conversion of many of the ruling classes of the region to Islam. It was, however, over a half-century after the breakup of Ghana's empire before anyone in the western Sahel, Muslim or non-Muslim, could reestablish an empire of comparable extent. With Ghana's collapse and the Almoravids' failure to build a new empire below the Sahara (largely as a result of their greater interest in North Africa), the western Sudan broke up into various smaller kingdoms. The former Ghanaian provinces of Mande and Takrur had already become independent before 1076, and in the early twelfth century Takrur's control of the Senegal valley and the gold-producing region of Galam made it briefly the strongest state in the western Sudan. It was, however, soon eclipsed by developments to the east, along the upper Niger: first the brief Soso ascendancy and then the growing power of Mali.

In the mid-thirteenth century, the Keita ruling clan of one of the Ghanaian successor kingdoms, Mali, was able to forge a new and lasting empire. This empire arose in all likelihood on the same economic base as that of Ghana and Takrur earlier: monopolization of the lucrative north-south gold trade. The Keita kings dominated enough of the Sahel to control the flow of West African gold from the Senegal regions and the forestlands south of the Niger to the trans-Saharan trade routes, and the flow of copper and especially salt that returned in exchange. Because they were centered farther south, in the fertile land along the Niger, than their Ghanaian predecessors had been, they were better placed to control all trade on the upper Niger and to add to it that on the Gambia and Senegal to the west. They were also able to use war captives for plantation labor in the Niger inland delta and thereby to produce surplus food for trade.

Agriculture and cattle farming were the primary occupations of the population and were, together with control of the gold trade, the mainstays of the economy. Farming and hunting were closely tied and were practiced by the nobility as well as lower ranking classes. Rice was grown in the riverine regions and millet in the drier parts of the Sahel. These crops, as well as beans, yams, and other agricultural products, made for a plentiful food supply that outside visitors found noteworthy. Fishing was strong among specialized smaller groups along the Niger and else-

SAHELIAN EMPIRES OF THE WESTERN SUDAN	
ca. 990–ca. 1180?	Empire of Ghana
1076	Ghana loses Awdaghast to Almoravids
1180–1230	Soso clan briefly controls the old Ghanaian territories
ca. 1230–1450	Empire of Mali, founded by Sundiata
1230–1255	Reign of Sundiata
1312–1337	Reign of Mansa Musa
1374	Independent Songhai state emerges in Gao after throwing off Malian rule
ca. 1450–1600	Songhai empire at Gao
1464–1591	Askia dynasty
1464–1492	Reign of Sonni Ali
1493–1528	Reign of Askia Muhammad al-Turi
1549–1583	Reign of Askia Dawud
1590s	Collapse of the Songhai empire

where. Animal husbandry was strongest among the pastoralists of the Sahel, such as the Fulani (or Fulbe), but cattle, sheep, and goats were also plentiful in the Niger region by the fourteenth century. Many of the Fulani seem to have been attracted by excellent pasturages to the riverine regions. The chief craft specialties were metal working—of iron and gold—and weaving—of cotton grown within the empire.

The Malinke, a southern-Mande-speaking people of the upper Niger region, formed the core population of the new state. They appear to have lived in walled urban settlements typical of the western savannah region. Each such walled town was surrounded by its own agricultural land and held perhaps one to fifteen thousand people and enough arable land within its walls to deal, presumably, with an emergency siege. Each was linked to its neighboring cities by trade connections and possibly intermarriage.

The Keita dynasty had converted very early to Islam (ca. 1100) and even claimed descent from the Prophet's famous first muezzin (the person who voices the call to worship), Bilal, a former black slave from Abyssinia whose son was said to have settled in the Mande-speaking region. During its heyday in the thirteenth and fourteenth centuries, the kings of Mali often made the pilgrimage to Mecca. They brought back with them not only such important instruments of power as large Barbary war horses, but also new ideas about political and military organization as practiced in the central Islamic lands. Through Muslim traders' networks, Islam also connected Mali to other areas of Africa, especially those to the east, from Kano and Hausaland in the Sahel to the forests in the south.

Mali's imperial power was built largely by the efforts of one leader, the Keita King Sundiata (or Sunjaata; r. 1230–1255). Sundiata and his successors, helped by significant population growth in the western savannah, exploited their region's wealth of agricultural resources and the commercial skills of the Malinke people to produce an empire even more powerful than its Ghanaian predecessor. Sundiata extended his control well beyond the former domains of Ghana, west to the Atlantic coast and beyond Timbuktu in the east. By controlling the commercial centers of Gao, Walata, and Jenne, he was able to take the Saharan as well as the Niger trade fully in hand. He built his capital, Niani, into a major city. Niani was located on the Sankarani River in the savannah plain at the edge of the forest in the gold and iron-rich land of Mani, well away from the lands of the Sahel nomads and well south of Ghana's capital of Kumbi. It had access to the forest trade products of gold, kola nuts, and palm oil, it was easily defended by virtue of its surrounding small hills, and it was easily reached by water by way of the Sankarani.

The empire that Sundiata and his successors built ultimately encompassed three major historical regions and language groups of Sudanic West Africa: (1) the Senegal region (including Takrur), occupied by speakers of the West Atlantic group of related Niger-Kongo languages (such as Fulbe, Tukulor, Wolof, Serer); (2) the central Mande states between Senegal and Niger, occupied by the Niger-Kongo-speaking Soninke and Mandinke peoples; and (3) the peoples of the Niger in the region of Gao who spoke Songhai, the only Nilo-Saharan language isolated to the west of the Lake Chad basin. The power of Mali was always less that of a centralized bureaucratic state than that of the center of a vast sphere of influence that included provinces and tribute-paying kingdoms. Many individual chieftaincies and dependencies retained much of their independence, but recognized the sovereignty of the supreme, sacred *mansa,* or "emperor," of the Malian realms.

The greatest Keita king proved to be Mansa Musa (r. 1312–1337), whose pilgrimage through Mamluk Cairo to Mecca in 1324 became famous in Egypt and elsewhere abroad. He paid out or gave away so much gold in Cairo alone that he started a massive inflation that lasted over a decade. He returned from his pilgrimage with many Muslim scholars, artists, and ar-

The great mosque at Jenne, one of the important commercial centers controlled by the empire of Mali in the thirteenth and fourteenth centuries. [ARAMCO]

Mansa Musa in Cairo

The following account is by a Damascene scholar, al-Umari (d. 1349), who spent much of his life in Cairo. Here he describes what he learned of Mansa Musa's reception by the Mamluk sultan. The report reflects the respect commanded by Musa among the Cairenes, both for his piety and for his wealth and obvious power (he had a massive entourage with him).

From the beginning of my coming to stay in Egypt I heard talk of the arrival of this sultan Mūsā on his Pilgrimage and found the Cairenes eager to recount what they had seen of the Africans' prodigal spending. I asked the emir Abū 'l-'Abbās Aḥmad b. al-Ḥāk the *mihmandar* and he told me of the opulence, manly virtues, and piety of this sultan. "When I went out to meet him (he said), that is, on behalf of the mighty sultan al-Malik al-Nāṣir, he did me extreme honour and treated me with the greatest courtesy. He addressed me, however, only through an interpreter despite his perfect ability to speak in the Arabic tongue. Then he forwarded to the royal treasury many loads of unworked native gold and other valuables. I tried to persuade him to go up to the Citadel to meet the sultan, but he refused persistently, saying: 'I came for the Pilgrimage and nothing else. I do not wish to mix anything else with my Pilgrimage.' He had begun to use this argument but I realized that the audience was repugnant to him because he would be obliged to kiss the ground and the sultan's hand. I continued to cajole him and he continued to make excuses but the sultan's protocol demanded that I should bring him into the royal presence, so I kept on at him till he agreed.

"When we came in the sultan's presence we said to him: 'Kiss the ground!' but he refused outright saying: 'How may this be?' Then an intelligent man who was with him whispered to him something we could not understand and he said: 'I make obeisance to God who created me!' then he prostrated himself and went forward to the sultan. The sultan half rose to greet him and sat him by his side. They conversed together for a long time, then sultan Mūsā went out. The sultan sent to him several complete suits of honour for himself, his courtiers, and all those who had come with him, and saddled and bridled horses for himself and his chief courtiers. He also furnished him with accommodation and abundant supplies during his stay.

"When the time to leave for the Pilgrimage came round the sultan sent to him a large sum of money with ordinary and thoroughbred camels complete with saddles and equipment to serve as mounts for him, and purchased abundant supplies for his entourage and others who had come with him. He arranged for deposits of fodder to be placed along the road and ordered the caravan commanders to treat him with honour and respect. . . ."

From J. F. P. Hopkins, trans.; N. Levtzion and J. F. P. Hopkins, eds., *Corpus of Early Arabic Sources for West African History* (Cambridge, UK: Cambridge University Press, 1981), pp. 269–270.

chitects in tow to grace his court. At home, he consolidated Mali's power, securing peace for most of his reign throughout his vast dominions. Musa's claimed devoutness as a Muslim translated into a positive environment for the further spread of Islam in the empire and beyond; but not all conversions of his and later reigns survived Mali's decline in the next century. Under his rule, Timbuktu became known far and wide for its *madrasas* and libraries, and its poets, scientists, and architects, making the city the leading intellectual center of sub-Saharan Islamic religion and culture as well as one of the major trading cities of the Sahel. It would retain these roles far past the period of Mali's imperial dominance.

Mali's dominance waned after Musa's time, most sharply in the fifteenth century. A chief cause seems to have been destructive rivalries for the succession to the *mansa*'s throne. As time went on, more and more subject dependencies became independent, and the empire shrank in extent and power. In the 1430s, Berber Tuaregs wrested control from Mali of much of its Sahelian dominions, including Timbuktu and Walata. The non-Muslim Mossi kingdom in the savanna and tropical forestlands to the south made large inroads on Malian territory in the middle of the century, and after 1450 the rise of a new Songhai power in Gao to the east signaled the end of Mali's imperial authority.

Songhai

Evidence suggests that as early as the eleventh or twelfth century there was a Songhai kingdom in the region of Gao, on the eastern arc of the Great Bend of the Niger. This kingdom and the region of Gao came under the control of Mali and its Malinke rulers in 1325, at the hands of Mansa Musa. With the rise of a dynasty in Gao known as the Sunni or Sonni in the late fourteenth century, around 1375, Mali's domination ended. For the next century, the kingdom flourished, but not until the reign of the greatest Sunni ruler, Sonni Ali (1464–1492), did it develop into an imperial power. Beginning with Sonni Ali's reign, the Songhai empire became so powerful in the entire upper Niger region and beyond that it dominated the political history of the western Sudan for more than a century and was arguably the most powerful state of the age in Africa (see Map 19-2). With a powerful military built around a river flotilla of boats and a horse cavalry of great mobility, Sonni Ali took Jenne and Timbuktu. He went on to push the Tuareg Berbers back into the northern Sahel and Sahara—extending his control as far as Taghaza and Walata—and to stifle any southern forestland threat with victories over the Mossi and Dogon kingdoms.

After Sonni Ali's accidental death in 1492, rule passed to the Askia, an Islamic Soninke dynasty. Askia Muhammad al-Turi (r. 1493–1528) succeeded Sonni Ali and continued his expansionist policies. Between them, Sonni Ali and Askia Muhammad al-Turi built an empire that stretched west nearly to the Atlantic, northwest into the Sahara, and east into the central Sudan. Taking advantage of their control of

access to the gold and other desirable commodities of West Africa, they emulated their Ghanaian predecessors in cultivating and expanding the ancient caravan trade across the Sahara to the North African coasts of Libya and Tunisia. This provided their major source of wealth.

Sonni Ali, who held to the traditional African religious practices and faith of his people, was never a good Muslim and was at odds with the *ulama* of Timbuktu, particularly, during his entire reign. Muhammad al-Turi, in contrast, was an active and enthusiastic Muslim. He used the Islamic empire of Mali as his model for building up the Songhai state. In Muhammad's reign, Muslim scholars from the Arab world came in substantial numbers to the Songhai cities of Gao, Timbuktu, and Jenne. He appointed Muslim judges *(qadis)* in towns throughout the empire and made Timbuktu into a major intellectual and legal training center for the whole Sudan. He also replaced native Songhais with Arab Muslim immigrants as government officials in an apparently successful effort to strengthen his centralized power. Taking his Islam seriously, Muhammad made a triumphal pilgrimage to Mecca much like Mansa Musa before him. At Mecca, he was hailed as "Caliph of the western Sahara." He also supported from his vast royal treasury both the poor and the great sufi leaders, or *marabouts,* as well as the construction of mosques throughout the realm. Nevertheless, in the end his reforms were not sufficient to Islamize the majority of the various peoples of the empire or to ensure a strong central state under the less able successors who followed him.

The last powerful Askia leader was Askia Dawud

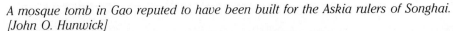

A mosque tomb in Gao reputed to have been built for the Askia rulers of Songhai.
[John O. Hunwick]

MAP 19-2 AFRICA CA. 1500–1800 *Important towns, regions, peoples, and states. The inset shows the empire of Songhai at its greatest extent in the early sixteenth century.*

(r. 1549–1583), under whom Songhai economic prosperity and intellectual life reached its apogee. The trans-Saharan trade reached new heights, and royal patronage of the arts rose correspondingly to new levels. The Askia had to fight battles with the Mossi to the south and with Berber forces from as far away as the Sultanate of Morocco in the north (Taghaza was taken by Moroccan forces just after Askia Dawud's death). Civil war broke out over succession to the throne in 1586, and the empire was divided thereafter. In a battle in 1591, a motley but well-armed military force sent by the Sa'dis of Morocco used superior gunpowder weapons and the aid of disaffected Songhai princes to inflict a defeat on the last Askia of Gao at Tondibi. This battle was as much an index of the weakness of the empire as a measure of Moroccan power but proved the decisive event in the collapse of the Gao empire. Rapidly thereafter, the once great imperial state was reduced to its original holdings in the Niger valley and became only one among many regional competitors in the western Sudan.

Kanem and Kanem-Bornu

A fourth sizable Sahelian empire—this one in the central Sudan—arose some time after 1100. This state, called Kanem, began in the region of the same

Muslim Reform in Songhai

Around 1500, Askia Muhammad al-Turi, the first Muslim among the rulers of Songhai, wrote to the North African Muslim theologian Muhammad al-Maghili (d. 1504) with a series of questions about proper Muslim practices. These excerpts are from the seventh question of al-Turi and the answers given by al-Maghili. Here one sees something of the zeal of the new convert to conform to traditional religious norms, as well as the rather strict and puritanical "official line" of the conservative Maliki ulama *on "pagan" mores. Also evident is the king's desire for bettering social order and his concern for justice in the market and elsewhere. However, also manifest is that many of the more strongly Shari'a-minded* ulama *did not want to compromise at all, let alone allow syncretism to emerge among formerly pagan, newly converted groups.*

FROM AL-TURI'S SEVENTH QUESTION:

Among the people [of the Songhay Empire said Askia Muhammad], there are some who claim knowledge of the supernatural through sand divining and the like, or through the disposition of the stars . . . [while] some assert that they can write (talismans) to bring good fortune . . . or to ward off bad fortune. . . . Some defraud in weights and measures. . . .

One of their evil practices [continued Askia Muhammad] is the free mixing of men and women in the markets and streets and the failure of women to veil themselves . . . [while] among the people of Djenné [Jenne] it is an established custom for a girl not to cover any part of her body as long as she remains a virgin . . . and all the most beautiful girls walk about naked among people. . . .

So give us legal ruling concerning these people and their ilk, and may God Most High reward you!

FROM AL-MAGHILI'S ANSWER:

The answer—and God it is who directs to the right course—is that everything you have mentioned concerning people's behavior in some parts of this country is gross error. It is the bounden duty of the commander of the Muslims and all other believers who have the power [replied al-Maghili] to change every one of these evil practices.

As for any who claims knowledge of the supernat-ural in the ways you have mentioned . . . he is a liar and an unbeliever. . . . Such people must be forced to renounce it by the sword. Then whoever renounces such deeds should be left in peace, but whoever persists should be killed with the sword as an unbeliever; his body should not be washed or shrouded, and he should not be buried in a Muslim graveyard. . . .

As for defrauding in weights and measures [continued al-Maghili] it is forbidden *(haram)* according to the Qur'an, the Sunna and the concensus of opinion of the learned men of the Muslim community. It is the bounden duty of the commander of the Muslims to appoint a trustworthy man in charge of the markets, and to safeguard people's means of subsistence. He should standardize all the scales in each province. . . . Similarly, all measures both large and small must be rectified so that they conform to a uniform standard. . . .

Now, what you mentioned about the free mixing of men and women and leaving the pudenda uncovered is one of the greatest abominations. The commander of the Muslims must exert himself to prevent all these things. . . . He should appoint trustworthy men to watch over this by day and night, in secret and in the open. This is not to be considered as spying on the Muslims; it is only a way of caring for them and curbing evildoers, especially when corruption becomes widespread in the land as it has done in Timbuktu and Djenné [Jenne] and so on.

Translated by J. O. Hunwick (1963); reprinted in Basil Davidson, *The African Past* (New York: Grosset and Dunlap, The Universal Library, 1967), pp. 86–88.

name—Kanem—which stretches over the Sahel into the Sahara northeast of Lake Chad. Roughly contemporaneous with the Malian empire to the west, Kanem began as a southern Saharan confederation of the black nomadic tribes known as Zaghawah. These tribes were spread over much of the south-central and southeastern Sahara. By the twelfth century, a Zaghawah group known as the Kanuri had apparently settled in Kanem, and from there they set out on a campaign of military expansion during the thirteenth century. Their key leader in this effort, Mai Dunama Dibbalemi (r. ca. 1221–1259), was a contemporary of Sundiata in Mali. Like Sundiata, Dibbalemi was a Muslim—indeed, probably the first Kanuri leader to embrace Islam, although there are traditions recalling a Muslim ruler in the Kanem region as early as 1085. In any case, Islam appears to have entrenched itself among the Kanuri ruling class during Dibbalemi's reign. Dibbalemi used it as a sanction for his rule, which otherwise had the familiar African trappings of sacred kingship. It also provided a rationale for expansion through *jihad,* or holy "struggle" against pagans.

Dibbalemi and his successors expanded Kanuri power north into the desert far enough to include the Fezzan in modern Libya and northeast along the Sahel-Sahara fringe toward Nilotic Africa. In both directions, the Kanuri controlled important trade routes—north to Libya and east to the Nile and Egypt. The next two centuries saw the mixing of Kanuri and local Kanembu peoples, primarily those known as the So. There was a corresponding transformation of the Kanuri leader from a nomadic *shaykh* to a Sudanic king and a change of the Kanem state from a nomadic to a largely sedentary kingdom replete with quasi-feudal institutions. Like Mali to the west, Kanem's authority over its dominions was of two kinds: direct rule over, and taxation of, core territories and groups and indirect control over and the collection of tribute from a wider region of local vassal chieftaincies. Linguistic and (Muslim) religious acculturation progressed most rapidly in the core territories under direct Kanuri rule.

Civil strife, largely over the succession to the kingship, weakened the Kanuri state in the later fourteenth and especially the fifteenth centuries. Kanuri control of Kanem weakened, and in the fifteenth century the locus of power shifted from Kanem proper westward, to the land of Bornu, southwest of Lake Chad. Here, at the end of the fifteenth century, a new Kanuri empire arose almost simultaneously with the collapse of the Askia dynasty of the Songhai empire at

CENTRAL SUDANIC EMPIRES	
ca. 1100–1500	Kanuri empire of Kanem
ca. 1220s–1400	Height of empire of Kanem
1221–1259	Reign of Mai Dunama Dibbalemi
1575–1846	Kanuri empire of Kanem-Bornu
1575–1619	Reign of Idris Alawma, major architect of the state

Gao. Near the end of the sixteenth century, the acquisition of firearms and the assistance of Turkish military instructors enabled the Kanuri leader Idris Alawma (r. ca. 1575–1610) to form a renewed union of Kanem and Bornu. He set up an avowedly Islamic state and extended his rule even into Hausaland, the territory to the west, between Bornu and the Niger River. The center of trading activity as well as political power and security now shifted from the Niger Bend region east to the territory controlled by the Kanuri.

Deriving its prosperity from the trans-Saharan trade, Idris Alawma's regional empire survived for nearly a century. It was finally broken up by a long famine, repeated Tuareg attacks, lack of strong leadership, and loss of trade control to smaller, better organized Hausa states. The ruling dynasty held out until 1846, but by the end of the seventeenth century, its power had been sharply reduced by the growing Hausa states to the west. These states, in what is now northern Nigeria, had first become important in the late fifteenth century. Their real power was to come only in the nineteenth century with their unification under the Fulani sultanate of Sokoto (see Chapter 33).

The Eastern Sudan

The Christian states of Maqurra and Alwa in the Nilotic Sudan, or Nubia, survived for more than six hundred years from their early seventh-century beginnings. Often thought of as isolated, Christian Nubia in fact maintained political, religious, and commercial contact with Egypt, the Red Sea world, and the east-central and even central Sudan. Architectural influence in the form of Nubian red brick construction has been traced as far west as Chadic Bornu and even modern northeastern Nigeria.

After A.D. 1000, both Maqurra and Alwa continued treaty relations with their more powerful northern neighbors: first the Fatimids and then the Ayyubids and Mamluks who succeeded to power in Egypt. Mamluk times saw many new pressures put on the old relations, however. The Mamluks intervened repeatedly in the affairs of their Nubian neighbors, and Arab nomads constantly threatened not only the Mamluk state but even more the Nubian states. From late Fatimid times onward, both Maqurra and Alwa were more and more subject to immigrating Arab Muslim tribesmen as well as the influence of Arab Muslim traders (especially in the coastal trading towns on the Red Sea) and growing Muslim minorities. The result was a long-term intermingling of Arabic and Nubian cultures and the creation of a new Nilotic Sudanese people and culture.

Islam spread slowly with the Arab immigrants into the upper Nile region as time went on. A significant factor in the gradual disappearance of Christianity in the Nubian region was the apparently elite character of Christianity there to begin with and its association with the northern and foreign Egyptian world of Coptic Christianity. In any case, Maqurra became officially Muslim at the beginning of the fourteenth century with a change in rulers orchestrated by the Mamluks; although Christianity survived until late in the same century, its days were numbered. The Islamization of the Alwa region came somewhat later, carried out in part by Muslim religious teachers, often trained in Cairo, who combined Sufi teachings with the legal training and expertise of the *ulama.* Their work went on most markedly under the long-lived Funj sultanate that replaced the Alwa state.

The Funj state flourished in the region between the Blue and White Niles and to the north along the main Nile from just after 1500 until 1762. The Funj were originally cattle nomads who apparently adopted Islam in the first decades after setting up their kingdom. In the course of the late sixteenth and the seventeenth centuries, with the influx of Arabic-speaking Nubians from the north, the Funj developed an Islamic society whose Arabized character was unique in sub-Saharan Africa. A much reduced Funj state held out until an Ottoman-Egyptian invasion in 1821.

BENIN	
ca. 1100–1897	Benin state
ca. 1300	First Ife king of Benin state
1440–1475	Reign of Ewuare

The Forestlands—Coastal West and Central Africa

West African Forest Kingdoms: The Example of Benin

We have little or no written evidence before the sixteenth century of the many states and smaller societies that flourished in the southern forested reaches of the Sudanic savannahs and in the tropical forests to their south. However, other kinds of evidence reveal that many states, some with distinct political, religious, and cultural traditions, had developed in the southern and coastal regions of West Africa several centuries before the first Portuguese reports in 1485. Even those states like Asante or the Yoruba kingdoms of Oyo and Ife, which reached their height only after 1500, had much earlier origins. Benin, the best known of these forest kingdoms, reflects, especially in its art, the great sophistication of West African culture before 1500.

BENIN STATE AND SOCIETY. According to linguistic evidence, the Edo speakers of Benin have occupied the southern Nigerian region between Yorubaland and the Ibo peoples east of the lower Niger for several thousand years. Traditional Edo society is organized according to a lineage system with a strong patrilineal bias and an emphasis on primogeniture. The village is the fundamental political unit, and within the village, authority is built around the organization of males into age-grade units.[3]

According to archaeological evidence, the local traditions of the Edo culture of Benin were closely linked to those of Ife, one of the two most prominent Yoruba states to the northwest of Benin. Some kind of distinct kingdom of Benin likely existed as early as the twelfth century, and traditional accounts of both Ife and Edo agree that a scion of the Ife ruling family was sent to rule in Benin around 1300. There are indications that the power of the king, or *oba,* at this time was sharply limited by the Edo leaders who invited the foreign ruler. These leaders were known as the *uzama,* an order of hereditary indigenous chiefs. According to tradition, the fourth Benin *oba* managed to take more control from these chiefs for himself and to institute something of the ceremonial of absolute

[3] A. F. C. Ryder, *Benin and the Europeans, 1485–1897* (New York: Longman, 1969), p. 1. Ryder's work has also served as a basic reference for the following brief summary about Benin.

monarchy. However, only in the fifteenth century, with King Ewuare, did this small monarchy become a royal autocracy and develop into a large state of major regional importance.

Ewuare rebuilt the capital—known today as Benin City—and named it and his kingdom Edo. He apparently established a government in which he had sweeping authority, although this authority was exercised in light of the deliberations of a royal council. Ewuare formed this council not only from the *uzama* of the palace but also from the towns. He gave each of the chiefs specific administrative responsibilities and ranks in the government hierarchy. Ewuare and his successors developed a tradition of military kingship and engaged in major wars of expansion, both into Yorubaland to the west and Ibo country across the Niger River to the east. They also claimed for the office of *oba* an increasing ritual authority that presaged more radical developments in the king's role.

In the seventeenth century, the *oba* would virtually withdraw into the palace, becoming much less active, transformed from a military leader into a religious figure with supernatural powers. Human sacrifice, specifically of slaves, seems to have been part of the cult of deceased kings, and actually became more frequent later, in the nineteenth century. Succession by primogeniture, which Ewuare had established, was discontinued. Instead, the new *oba* came to be chosen by the *uzama* from any branch of the royal family.

BENIN ART. The lasting significance of Benin, however, lies not in its political history but in its court art, which reached its zenith in its famous brass sculptural work. An ancient Benin tradition suggests that an Ife craftsman came to Benin at the behest of the ruler to teach the brass- and bronze-casting techniques developed first in Ife. Certainly the splendid terra-cotta, ivory, and brass statuary sculpture of the Ife-Benin civilization are among the glories of human creativity. These magnificent sculptures, initially fully realistic or naturalistic and later sometimes highly stylized, are by all indications wholly indigenous African products. Their artistic and technical lineage is today often traced by scholars to the sculptures of the Nok culture of ancient West Africa (see Chapter 8), although this linkage is yet to be proven.

The best of the sculptures before the sixteenth century and the coming of the Portuguese (who themselves figure in later representations) are cast brass plaques depicting legendary and historical scenes, which were mounted on the walls and columns of the royal palace in Benin City (cf. p. 552). There are also

A sixteenth-century Nigerian sculpture enclosing a salt-cellar. The central figure is in Portuguese dress. [Metropolitan Museum of Art, Bell and Rogers Fund, 1972.63]

brass heads, apparently of royalty, that seem to parallel the many life-size terra-cotta and brass heads found at Ife. The heads at Ife are held to represent the Oni, or religious chief of ancient Ife, or particular ancestors, who are thereby reverently remembered by their descendants.

These artistic traditions were not limited only to Ife and Benin; similar sculptures have been found both well to the north and in the Niger delta. Most spectacularly, recent excavations east of the Niger at Igbo-Ukwu have unearthed many stunning terra-cottas and bronzes that, although quite distinct, belong to the same general artistic culture, which appears now to date as early as the ninth century. These artifacts stand as a reminder of the high cultural level attained in many traditional African societies that had little or no contact with the extra-African world.

European Arrivals on the Coastlands

Along the coasts of West and central Africa, many changes portentous for African history as a whole occurred between 1500 and 1800. Those wrought by the burgeoning Atlantic slave trade are the most famous (see the following subsections). Of comparable importance are changes connected with trade in West African gold and other commodities and the effects associated with the importation and spread in West and central Africa of food crops such as maize, peanuts, squash, sweet potatoes, cocoa, and cassava (manioc) from the Americas. In general, the gradual involvement of Africa in the emerging global economic system was the key development that laid the groundwork for eventual colonial domination of the continent, especially its coastal regions, by the Europeans. The names given by Europeans to segments of the coastline—the Grain (or Pepper) Coast, the Ivory Coast, the Gold Coast, and the Slave Coast—identify the main exports that could be extracted by ship and vividly indicate the nature of the emerging relationship.

SENEGAMBIA.   In West Africa, Senegambia—which takes its name from the Senegal and Gambia rivers—was one of the earliest regions affected by European trade. The interior parts of this region had long been involved in both trans-Saharan trade and east–west trade in the Sahel and savannah, especially in the heydays of the empires of Ghana, Mali, and Songhai. Senegambia's trade with the maritime European powers, as in the older overland trade, was primarily in gold and in products such as salt, cotton goods, hides, and copper. For roughly a century, the Wolof and other Senegambian states also provided slaves to the coast for European purchase; indeed, of all African slaves exported during the sixteenth century, as much as a third came from Senegambia. Thereafter, however, the focus of the slave trade shifted south and east along the coast, and although the number of slaves taken from Senegambia remained steady, the importance of slaving relative to other forms of trade declined. Over time, Portuguese-African mulattos and the British came to control the Gambia River trade, whereas the French won the Senegal River markets. These developments presaged the long-term division of the region into spheres of influence among European powers, particularly the British and French, in colonial times.

THE GOLD COAST.   The Gold Coast, like Senegambia, was one of the West African coastal districts most affected by the arrival of international maritime trade. The name derives from the region's rise to importance in the period after 1500 as the outlet for the more southern of West Africa's gold fields in the forestland of Akan. Here, beginning with the Portu-

guese at Elmina in 1481, but primarily after 1600, European states and companies built numerous coastal forts to protect their trade from each other's predations and from pirates' raids and to serve as depots for inland goods. The trade in gold, kola nuts, and other commodities seems to have encouraged the growth of larger states in the region, perhaps because larger units could better handle and control the overland commerce. The growth of Akan forest states near the coast and the Gonja state just north of the forest provides an instance of this phenomenon.

The intensive contact of the Gold Coast with Europeans also led to the importation and spread of American crops, notably maize and cassava, into the tropical forests of this region. The success of these crops here as elsewhere in West and central Africa brought change. It likely contributed to substantial population growth in the sixteenth and seventeenth centuries, especially in the Akan region.

The Gold Coast escaped the ravages of the slave trade for some decades; it was even an importer of slaves until long after 1500. However, slaves finally came to be big business in the late seventeenth century, especially in the Accra region, when the economy was so disrupted by the slave trade that gold mining declined sharply. Eventually more gold came into the Gold Coast from the sale of slaves than that going out from its own resources.

Central Africa

Before 1500, the vast central area of the subcontinent had been to some degree cut off from long-distance international trade and contact by its own geographical barriers: swamps in the north, coastal rain forests to the west, highlands to the east, and deserts in the south. These barriers shaped the two-pronged route by which Bantu peoples and their languages had, over many centuries, moved from western and west-central Africa south into the Zaïre basin and east around the equatorial forest into the lakes of highland East Africa. In the tropical central region, throughout history, regional interaction in movements of peoples and in trade and culture had been the norm. Here as in other parts of Africa, however, both large and small political, economic, and social units could be found. Peoples such as the Lunda and Luba, on the southern savannah below the tropical rain forest, were able to carve out sizable kingdoms by about the fifteenth century and to expand their control over neighboring areas into the eighteenth century.

The coming of the Portuguese and their maritime

trade to the western coastal regions began to change the regional isolation of the central African lands, albeit only very slowly. The Portuguese came looking for a new source of gold and silver but found none. Instead, they exported such goods as ivory and palm cloth. Ultimately, their main business came to be exporting human beings for foreign slavery. These slaves were taken first for gang labor to the Portuguese sugar plantation venture on São Thomé island in the Gulf of Guinea. Then, in vast numbers, people were sent as slaves to perform similar plantation labor in Brazil. In the 1640s, the Dutch briefly succeeded the Portuguese as the major suppliers of African slaves to English and French plantations in the Caribbean. Until then, however, the Portuguese were the European presence in central Africa.

THE KONGO KINGDOM.   The major African state with which the Portuguese dealt after coming to central Africa in 1483 was that of Kongo. Dating from probably the fourteenth century, the Kongo kingdom was located on a fertile, well-watered plateau in the region south of the lower Zaïre River valley between the coast and the Kwango River in the east. Here, astride the border between forest and grassland, the Kongo kings had built a central government based on a pyramid structure of tax or tribute collection balanced by rewards given to those who were faithful in paying their taxes. Kongo society was dominated by the king, whose authority was tied to acceptance of him as a kind of spiritual spokesman of the gods or ancestors. By 1600, the Kongo state was half the size of England and alongside farming boasted a rather high state of craft specialization in weaving and pottery, salt production, fishing, and metal working.

The Portuguese brought Mediterranean goods, preeminently luxury textiles from North Africa, to use in the Kongo tribute-reward system and to trade for African goods. Amidst the rather hard agrarian life of most of the Kongo peoples, such luxury goods helped raise the prestige and wealth of the ruler and his elites. However, because the greatest central African resource turned out to be its peoples, rather than gold or minerals, slaves became the primary form of export commodity that could be used for obtaining foreign luxury goods. Meanwhile, imports such as fine clothing, tobacco, and alcohol did nothing to replace the labor pool lost to slavery.

At first, the Portuguese put time and effort into education and Christian proselytizing, but later the need for more slaves led to a focus on exploiting the human resources of central Africa. Regional rulers

CENTRAL AFRICA	
1300s	Kongo kingdom founded
1483	Portuguese come to central African coast
ca. 1506–1543	Reign of Affonso I as king of Kongo
1571	Angola becomes Portuguese proprietary colony

sought to procure slaves from neighboring kingdoms, as did Portuguese traders who went inland themselves. As the demand grew, more and more local rulers used attacks on neighboring groups to garner slaves for the Portuguese traders.

The Kongo ruler Affonso I (r. ca. 1506–1543), a convinced Christian convert, began by welcoming Jesuit missionaries and supporting conversion. But in time he broke with the Jesuits and began to stress traditional practices, even though he himself remained a Christian. Affonso did much to consolidate the government, but he had constant difficulty in curbing the more exploitative slaving practices as well as the more independent-minded provincial governors. The latter often dealt directly with the Portuguese, undermining royal authority. Affonso's successor, Diogo, moved finally to restrict Portuguese activity to Mpinda harbor and the Kongo capital of Mbanza Kongo (São Salvador). A few years later, Portuguese attempts to designate the Kongo royal successor led to a bloody uprising against the foreigners that in turn led to a Portuguese boycott on trade with the kingdom.

A short while later, a series of disastrous internal wars waged by rebellious warriors known as the Jaga effectively shattered the power of the Kongo state. Slavery apparently contributed significantly to the factionalism in the provinces and the unrest that fueled the Jaga wars. Their aftermath saw increased roles for Portuguese independent traders and adventurers, who subsequently carried on trading outside of government channels and tried to control and manipulate the Kongo kings. A period of renewed strong leadership after the 1570s still did not stop the processes of fragmentation that led to the breakup of the kingdom a century later.

Kongo did, however, enjoy renewed vigor in the seventeenth century. Maize and then cassava were introduced and began slowly to become part of the

Affonso I of Kongo Writes to the King of Portugal

Affonso, the Christian African king of Kongo, wrote a number of letters to the Portuguese monarch about the Portuguese presence in his dominions. The one reproduced here was written in 1526. It complains ostensibly of the effects of slaving on the Kongo people and economy, but behind this masterly diplomatic lament lies the real issue: that the Portuguese were circumventing his own royal monopoly on the inland slave trade. One of the insidious effects of the massive demand of the Atlantic trade for slaves was the ever increasing engagement of African monarchs and chieftains as well as merchants in one or another aspect of slaving.

▶ *For another response to the intrusions of a European power, see the box entitled "Commissioner Lin Urges Morality on Queen Victoria" in Chapter 34.*

Sir, Your Highness [of Portugal] should know how our Kingdom is being lost in so many ways that it is convenient to provide for the necessary remedy, since this is caused by the excessive freedom given by your factors and officials to the men and merchants who are allowed to come to this Kingdom to set up shops with goods and many things which have been prohibited by us, and which they spread throughout our Kingdoms and Domains in such an abundance that many of our vassals, whom we had in obedience, do not comply because they have the things in greater abundance than we ourselves; and it was with these things that we had them content and subjected under our vassalage and jurisdiction, so it is doing a great harm not only to the service of God, but the security and peace of our Kingdoms and State as well.

And we cannot reckon how great the damage is, since the mentioned merchants are taking every day our natives, sons of the land and the sons of our noblemen and vassals and our relatives, because the thieves and men of bad conscience grab them wishing to have the things and wares of this Kingdom which they are ambitious of; they grab them and get them to be sold; and so great, Sir, is the corruption and licentiousness that our country is being completely depopulated, and Your Highness should not agree with this nor accept it as in your service. And to avoid it we need from those [your] Kingdoms no more than some priests and a few people to teach in schools, and no other goods except wine and flour for the holy sacrament. That is why we beg of Your Highness to help and assist us in this matter, commanding your factors that they should not send here either merchants or wares, because it is *our will that in these Kingdoms there should not be any trade of slaves nor outlet for them.** Concerning what is referred above, again we beg of Your Highness to agree with it, since otherwise we cannot remedy such an obvious damage. Pray Our Lord in His mercy to have Your Highness under His guard and let you do for ever the things of His service. I kiss your hands many times. . . .

*Emphasis in the original.

Basil Davidson, *The African Past* (New York: Grosset and Dunlap, The Universal Library, 1967), pp. 191–193.

---

staple diet of the populace. The Kongo kings, all descended from Affonso, ruled as divine-right monarchs set at the apex of a complex social and political pyramid that rose from district headmen through provincial governors to the court nobility and the king. Royal power came to depend on a royal guard of musket-armed hired soldiers from tribes of the Stanley Pool area. The financial base of the kingdom rested on tribute from officials holding positions at the king's pleasure and on taxes and tolls on commerce. Christianity, the state religion, was accommodated to traditional religion in areas involving the ancestor cult, talismanic magic, and sorcery. Kongo sculpture, iron and copper technology, and dance and music flourished.

ANGOLA. To the south, in Portuguese Angola, the experience was still worse than in Kongo. The Ndongo kingdom flourished among the Mbundu people during the sixteenth century. In 1571, a Portuguese decision to turn Angola into a proprietary colony (the first white colonial enterprise in black Africa) set in motion colonizing and "civilizing" efforts that ended in failure. By the end of the century, Angola was exporting thousands of slaves yearly through the port of Luanda. In less than a century, the hinterland had been plundered and depopulated. New internal trade in salt and the eventual spread of American food crops such as maize and cassava did produce some positive changes in the interior, but in the coastal region among the western Mbundu, the Portuguese arrival led to economic and social catastrophe.

The Slave Trade

Slavery seems to have been one of the unhappy facts of human societies as far back as we can trace its history. Although linked to warfare and the age-old practice of taking war captives, it cannot be fully explained by military necessity any more than by economic necessity. Virtually every premodern state around the globe depended on slavery to some extent. The Mediterranean and African worlds were no exception, in both the pre-Islamic and the Islamic periods. Slave institutions in sub-Saharan Africa were very ancient and included traffic with the ancient Mediterranean world. The Islamic states of southwestern Asia and North Africa continued and even increased this traffic, importing slaves from both the Sudan and Horn of Africa as well as the East African coast, although they took fewer slaves from Africa than from Eastern Europe and central Asia. Central Asia, for example, was the source of most of the (largely Turkish) slave-soldier dynasties that came to rule many Islamic states from India to North Africa. (Hence it is not surprising that our word *slave* derives from the Arabic word for *Slav*.) Both Mediterranean Christian and Islamic peoples were using slaves— mostly Greeks, Bulgarians, Turkish prisoners of war, and Black Sea Tartars, but also Africans—well before the voyages of discovery opened sub-Saharan sources of slaves for the new European colonies overseas.

Not all forms of slavery were as dehumanizing as the chattel slavery that came to predominate (with the sanction of Christian authorities) during the colonization of the Americas. Islamic law, for example, although permitting slavery, also ameliorated it. All slavery, however, involves the forceful exploitation and degradation of some human beings for the profit of others, the denial of basic freedoms, and some-

times the sundering of even the closest family ties, often violently. Africa suffered immense social devastation during the centuries it was the chief supplier of slaves to the world. The societies that were built to a great extent on the exploitation of African slavery also suffered enduring consequences, not the least of which, many believe, is racism.

Slavery and Slaving in Africa

The trade that supplied African slaves, long before the fifteenth century, to the Islamic lands of the Mediterranean and to southwestern and southern Asia has been termed conventionally the "oriental" slave trade. The savannahs of the Sudan and the Horn of Africa were the two prime sources of slaves for this trade. The trade managed by Europeans, conventionally called the "occidental" slave trade, can be traced at least to the thirteenth century, when Europeans established sugarcane plantations on Cyprus soon after Muslim forces had driven them out of the Holy Land. Slaves proved an especially profitable work force for the labor-intensive process of sugar production. This industry subsequently spread westward to Crete and Sicily, and in the fifteenth century, to the Portuguese Atlantic islands of Madeira, then São Thomé. The Portuguese in particular developed the plantation system of slave labor as they began their expansion into the Atlantic and beyond. Although the savannah and Horn regions were the earliest sources for this trade, voyages beginning in the fifteenth century by first the Portuguese and then other Europeans opened the western coasts of Africa as far south as Angola, making them the prime slaving areas. A third but less important source region for both occidental and oriental trades was the eastern coast of Africa below the Horn.

The history of slaving in Africa can be roughly summarized as follows.[4] Before the full development of the Atlantic slave trade by about 1650, slavery and slave trading were no more significant in Africa than anywhere else in the world. Indigenous African slavery was practiced much as in other premodern societies. It was apparently most common, if still limited, in the areas of the savannah and Horn, presumably as a result of the involvement of these areas in external slave trading. In the western and central Sudan, slavery came largely to be regulated by Islamic norms, but in the Horn, specifically in Ethiopia, slavery was practiced in both Christian and Muslim communities.

[4]The summary follows closely that of P. Manning, *Slavery and African Life: Occidental, Oriental, and African Slave Trades* (Cambridge: Cambridge University Press, 1990), pp. 127–140.

Slave dealing in the streets of Zanzibar. Slaving was a part of East African trade for centuries. [Bettmann Archive]

Estimates suggest that about ten thousand slaves per year, most of them female, were taken from sub-Saharan Africa through the oriental trade.

By about 1650, the newer occidental slave trade of the Europeans had grown even in size with the oriental trade and for the ensuing two centuries far surpassed it. Its effects dominated all of Africa, disrupting especially western and central African society. As a result of the demand for young male slaves on the plantations of the Americas, West Africa experienced a sharp drain on its productive male population. Between 1640 and 1690, although the price of a slave at the coast remained constant, the number of slaves sold to European carriers doubled, indicating the increasing participation of Africans in the expanding trade. With the growing demand for slaves came an increase in warfare in western and central Africa. Moreover, as the external trade destroyed the regional male-female population balance, an internal market for female slaves in particular arose.

These developments accelerated during the eighteenth century—at the height of the occidental trade. It was also during this period that African states and slave traders were most heavily involved as regulators of the trade and suppliers for it. Slave prices at times accelerated accordingly. Owing to population depletion and regional migrations, however, the actual number of sold slaves declined in some areas. The population decline in the coastal and inland areas hardest hit by the ravages of the trade became sharp in the later eighteenth century but continued in places even until 1850.

As European states slowly began to outlaw slaving and slavery in the nineteenth century, occidental demand slowed and prices for slaves sank. The result was that the oriental and internal trades increased. Slave exports from East Africa and the Sudan and Horn increased significantly after about 1780, and indigenous African slavery, predominantly of women, also expanded. Indeed, in the mid-nineteenth century the internal African trade increased sufficiently to surpass the combined oriental and (now outlawed and decreasing) occidental trade by about 1850. This traffic was dominated by the same figures—merchants, warlords, and rulers—who had previously profited from external trade. Indigenous slavery began a real decline only at the end of the nineteenth century, in part because of the dominance of European colonial regimes and in part because of internal changes. The formal end of African indigenous slavery occurred over a long period, beginning in 1874 in the Gold Coast and ending only in 1928 in Sierra Leone.

The Atlantic System

The occidental slave trade was part of a larger system of Atlantic trade that linked Europe, Africa, and the European colonies in South America, the Caribbean, and North America. In this system the Americas supplied labor-intensive products like tobacco, sugar, coffee, precious metals, cotton, and indigo. Europe supplied products like textiles, liquor, guns, metal goods, and beads, not to mention various forms of cash, including even gold. And Africa supplied gold, ivory, wood, palm oil, gum, and other products, as well as the slaves who provided the labor to create the American products. By the eighteenth century, slaves were the predominant African export.

Native American peoples provided the first source of labor for the exploitation of American resources by European colonials, particularly in South America and Mexico. Native Americans, however, were decimated by conquest and European diseases, or proved unsatisfactory as plantation laborers, and entrepreneurs began to look elsewhere. First the Portuguese, and then the Spanish, Dutch, French, and English (others would follow, including Americans), turned to West, central, and, to a lesser degree, southeastern Africa, where they found an ample supply of slaves. Thus the Atlantic slave trade was not the result of racist principles—although they developed once the trade began and were used to justify it—but the economic needs of the colonial powers and their willingness to exploit weaker peoples to satisfy them.

The Portuguese, who were the principal carriers throughout most of the history of the trade, had a virtual monopoly until the Dutch broke it in the 1640s and briefly became the chief carriers. The French and English came into the trade only in the late seventeenth century; yet over the course of the eighteenth, the period that saw the greatest shipments, they carried almost half the total traffic. Americans, too, were latecomers but avid slavers who managed to make considerable profits before and even after Britain and the United States outlawed slaving in 1807.

If gold and the search for a sea route to Asia brought the first European ships to Africa, slaves were the main commodity for which they returned for a very long time. Slaving was an important part of the massive new overseas trade that largely financed European and American economic development and the industrial revolutions that dramatically changed the west during the nineteenth century. The success of this trade, bought at the price of immense human suffering, was a major factor in propelling Europe and some of its colonial offshoots in the Americas into world dominance by the twentieth century.

The African Side of the Atlantic Trade

With the exception of the Portuguese in central Africa, European slave traders generally obtained their human cargoes from private or government-sponsored African middlemen at coastal forts or simply at anchorages along the coast. A system of forts built by Europeans mostly between 1640 and 1750, for exam-

ple, dominated the Gold Coast. This situation was the result of both the desire and ability of Africans to control inland trade and the vulnerability of Europeans to disease in the equatorial regions (a new European arrival stood a less than 50 percent chance of surviving a year on the tropical African coast). Thus it was largely African middlemen who undertook the actual capture or procurement of slaves and the often difficult and dangerous task of marching them to the coast. These middlemen were generally either wealthy merchants who could mount slaving expeditions inland or the agents of African chieftaincies or kingdoms that sought to profit from the trade.

The media of exchange were varied. At first they usually involved mixed barter for goods that ranged from gold dust or firearms to beads and spirits. As time went on, they came increasingly to involve some form of monetary payment. The effect of this exchange was to drain productive resources (human beings) in return for nonproductive wealth.

The chief West and central African slaving regions provided different numbers of slaves at different times, and the total number of exported slaves varied sharply between periods. When one area was unable to produce sufficient numbers to meet demand (whether as a result of depopulation of choice areas, local warfare, or changing state policies), the European traders shifted their buying to other points. Thus, between 1526 and 1550 the major sources of the slaves for the Atlantic trade were the Kongo-Angola region (34 percent), the Guinea coast of Cape Verde (25.6 percent), and Senegambia (23.5 percent).[5] By contrast, between 1761 and 1810, the French drew some 52 percent of their slaves from Angola and 24 percent from the Bight of Benin but only 4.8 percent from Senegambia, whereas the British relied most heavily on the Bight of Biafra and central Africa.[6] Traders naturally went where population density and the presence of active African merchant or state suppliers promised the best numbers and prices, although prices do not seem to have varied radically in a given period.

The Extent of the Trade

Taken as a whole, the slave trade varied in extent quite sharply from period to period. Only about 3 per-

[5] Philip Curtin, *The Atlantic Slave Trade: A Census* (Madison: University of Wisconsin Press, 1969), p. 101.

[6] Curtin, pp. 101; 129; James A. Rawley, *The Transatlantic Slave Trade: A History* (New York: W. W. Norton, 1981), p. 129.

cent of the total occidental trade came before 1600, and only about 14 percent between 1600 and 1700. The period of greatest activity, 1701–1810, accounted for over 60 percent of the total, and even the final half-century of slaving until 1870 accounted for over 20 percent of the total. Despite moves by European nations to abolish slaving in the early 1800s, the Portuguese still transported more than a million slaves to Brazil between 1811 and 1870. In fact, the total number of slaves landed in the Americas in these final years of the trade exceeded that for the entire seventeenth century.[7] We would do well to remember how long it actually took the "modern" occidental world to abolish the trade in African slaves.

The overall number of African slaves exported in the course of the occidental trade—effectively, between 1451 and 1870—is still debated and must be seen in the larger context of all types of slaving in Africa in the same period. A major unknown—for both the occidental and the oriental trades—is the number of slaves who died under the brutal conditions to which they were subjected when captured and transported overland and by sea. The most reliable estimates pertain only to those slaves who actually landed abroad, and these estimates are more reliable for the occidental trade than for the older, smaller, and more dispersed oriental trade. As the table on this page shows, just those who actually reached an American or Old World destination in the occidental trade totaled more than eleven million souls.

Estimates based on recent scholarship that attempts to account for slaves who died "in transport" suggest that at a minimum, Africa lost some thirteen million people to the Atlantic trade alone during its four centuries of existence. In the same period, another five million or more were lost to the oriental trade. Finally, the occidental trade spurred an apparently huge increase in internal slavery, and according to the estimate of one expert, an additional fifteen million additional people were enslaved within African societies themselves.[8]

Impact of the Slave Trade

AFRICAN CONSEQUENCES. The statistics in the previous section hint at the impact slave trading had on African life and history. Still, the question of the actual effects remains difficult and disputed. The tendency of modern scholarship has been to emphasize the importance for African history of the coming of the maritime European powers in general and the Atlantic slave trade in particular. Regarding the slave trade, it is safe to say that the impact was considerable, however much that general conclusion must be qualified in the light of particular cases. Consider some examples.

We do not know for certain if the Atlantic trade brought net population loss or gain to specific areas of West Africa; the wide and rapid spread of maize and cassava cultivation in forest regions after these plants had been imported from the Americas may have fueled African population increases that offset regional human loss through slaving. We know, however, that slaving took away large numbers of the strongest young men in many areas; or, in the oriental-trade zones, a majority of the young women.

Similarly, we do not know if more slaves were captured as by-products of local wars or as the result of pure slave raiding, but we do know they were captured and removed from their societies.

Nor do we know if slaving always inhibited development of trade or perhaps often stimulated it, because commerce in a range of African products—from ivory to wood and hides—often accompanied that in slaves. Still, we do know that in general, the exchange of productive human beings for money or goods that were generally not used to build a productive economy was a great loss for African society as a whole.

Finally, because we do not yet have accurate estimates of the total population of Africa at different

ESTIMATED SLAVE IMPORTS INTO THE AMERICAS AND OLD WORLD BY REGION, 1451–1870	
British North America	523,000
Spanish America	1,687,000
British Caribbean	2,443,000
French Caribbean	1,655,000
Dutch Caribbean	500,000
Danish Caribbean	50,000
Brazil (Portuguese)	4,190,000
Old World	297,000
Total	11,345,000

Figures as calculated by James A. Rawley, *The Transatlantic Slave Trade: A History* (New York: W. W. Norton, 1981), p. 428, based on his and other more recent revisions of the careful but older estimates of Philip D. Curtin, *The Atlantic Slave Trade: A Census* (Madison: University of Wisconsin Press, 1969), especially pp. 266, 268.

[7] Rawley, p. 429; Curtin, p. 268.
[8] Manning, pp. 37, 170–171.

Loading plan for the main decks of the 320-ton slave ship Brookes. *The* Brookes *was only 25 feet wide and 100 feet long, but as many as 609 slaves could be crammed on board for the nightmarish passage to the Americas. The average space allowed each person was only about 78 inches by 16 inches. [Photographs and Prints Division, Schomburg Center for Research in Black Culture, The New York Public Library, Astor, Lenox, and Tilder Foundations]*

times over the four centuries of the Atlantic slave trade, we cannot determine with certainty its demographic impact. We can, however, make some educated guesses. If, for example, tropical Africa had possibly fifty million inhabitants in 1600, it would then have had 30 percent of the combined population of the Americas, the Middle East, Europe, and Africa. If in 1900, after the depredations of the slave trade, it had seventy million inhabitants, its population would have dropped to only slightly more than 10 percent of the combined population of the same world regions. Accordingly, current best estimates indicate that overall African population growth suffered significantly as a result of the devastating numbers of citizens lost to enslavement or to the warfare and birth-rate declines inevitably tied to the slave trade. Figures like these also give some idea of slavery's probable impact on Africa's ability to keep up in the modern industrializing world around it.[9]

It is important to remember that even in West and

central Africa, which bore the brunt of the Atlantic trade, its impact and the response to it were so varied in different places and times that even accurate overall statistics could be misleading for particular cases. In a few cases, kingdoms such as Dahomey (the present Republic of Benin) seem to have sought and derived immense economic profit for a time by making slaving a state monopoly. In other cases, kingdoms such as Benin sought to stay almost completely out of slaving and derived no gain from it. In many instances, including the rise of Asante power or the fall of the Yoruba Oyo empire, it now appears that increased slaving was in part a result as well as a cause of regional instability and change. Increased warfare meant increased prisoners to be enslaved and a surplus to be sold off; however, the question as to whether slaving gave good cause for war is still a major one in each regional context.

Similarly, if one can establish, as seems evident, a major increase in indigenous slavery as a result of the external trade to occident and orient during the centuries in question, we have to assume major social consequences for African society as a whole, but the

[9]On all of the preceding points regarding probable impact of the trade, see Manning, pp. 126–148, 168–176.

specific consequences would differ according to the specifics of regional situations. For example, in West Africa relatively more males were taken as slaves than females, whereas in the Sahelian Sudanic regions relatively more females than males were taken. In the west, the loss of so many males increased the pressures for polygyny and possibly the regional use of female slaves as well, whereas in the Sahelian Sudanic regions, the loss of women may have stimulated polyandry and reduced the birthrate significantly.

No one can escape the fact that even if slavery existed previously in Africa, the scale of the Atlantic trade demand for slaves was unprecedented and hence had an unprecedented impact on indigenous social, political, and economic realities. In general, the slave trade measurably changed patterns of life and balances of power in the main affected areas, whether by stimulating trade or warfare (or at least raiding for new supplies), by disrupting previous market and political structures, by increasing slavery inside Africa substantially, or by disturbing the male-female ratio (and hence the work-force balance and eventual birth-rate patterns) and consequently the basic social institution of monogamous marriage. If the overseas slave trade did not substantially and irrevocably change every region it touched, at the least it encouraged a siphoning of much indigenous energy into ultimately counterproductive or destructive directions. This, in turn, meant the inhibition of true economic development, especially in central and coastal West Africa. The Atlantic slave trade must by any standard be described as one of the major tragic results of European involvement in the African continents.

CONSEQUENCES ABROAD. The impact of the slave trade was certainly not limited to Africa. Whites in the New World numbered about twelve million in 1820, compared to some six million blacks. However, up to that time only about two million whites had migrated there, compared to some eleven million or more Africans forcibly imported as slaves. In such numbers we glimpse the effects of brutal slave-work conditions and the high mortality and sharply reduced birth rates of slave populations relative to those of the white free populations. Two-fifths of all slaves taken by Europeans were landed in Portuguese Brazil, and the consequent impact on the population of that country has certainly been great. None of these statistics, however, enable us to assess adequately the role that slavery has played in the Americas or, in particular, the United States. The United States actually received only a bit more than a quarter as many slaves as did Brazil alone or the British and French Caribbean regions together, yet the consequences of the forced migration of just over a half-million Africans have been and remain massive. Consider just the American Civil War and the endurance of societal racism and inequality or, more positively, the African impact on our industrial development; our language; and our musical, literary, and artistic culture. The Atlantic slave trade's impact has been and continues to be felt at both ends of the original "trade."

East Africa

Swahili Culture and Commerce

The participation of East African port towns in the lucrative southern seas trade was ancient. Arabs, Indonesians and, at times, Indians had trafficked there for centuries. Many of them had been absorbed into what had become, sometime during the first millennium A.D., from Somalia south, a predominantly Bantu-speaking population. From the eighth century onward, Islam traveled along with Arab and Persian sailors and merchants to these southerly trading centers of what the Arabs called the land of al-Zanj, or "the Blacks" (hence the name "Zanzibar"). Conversion to Islam, however, went on slowly and only along the coastal perimeter. In the thirteenth century, Muslim traders from Arabia and Iran began to come in increased numbers and to dominate the coastal cities. From this time forward, Islamic faith and culture were influential and often predominant along the sea coast, from the port of Mogadishu south to that of Kilwa. By 1331, the traveler Ibn Battuta writes of Mogadishu as a thoroughly Islamic port and speaks of the ruler and inhabitants of Kilwa as Muslims. He also notes that there were now mosques for the faithful in these towns.[10]

By this time, a common language had developed out of the interaction of Bantu and Arabic speakers along the coast. This tongue is called Swahili, or Kiswahili, from the Arabic sawahil, "coastlands," a word used from ancient times for the East African coast. Its structure is Bantu and its vocabulary is Bantu with a strong admixture of Arabic. It is written traditionally in the Arabic script, like Persian, Ottoman Turkish,

[10] Travels in Asia and Africa, 1325–1354, trans. and selected by H. A. R. Gibb (New York: Robert M. McBride, 1929), pp. 110–113.

Ibn Battuta Visits Mogadishu
and Kilwa (1331)

Ibn Battuta (d. 1369 or 1377), *a native of Tangier, became one of history's most famous travelers through his voluminous and entertaining writings about his long years of relentless journeying from Africa to India and China. In the following two excerpts from his description of his trip down the East African coast in 1331, he describes first the reception of visitors at Mogadishu and then the Sultan of Kilwa.*

▶ *For other traveler's reports, see "Marco Polo Describes the City of Hangchow" (Ch. 10) and "A Chinese Traveler's Report on the Gupta Realm" (Ch. 12).*

MOGADISHU

From there [Somalia] we sailed fifteen nights and arrived at Mogadishu, which is a very large town. The people have very many camels, and slaughter many hundreds every day. They have also many sheep. The merchants are wealthy, and manufacture a material which takes its name from the town and which is exported to Egypt and elsewhere.

Among the customs of the people of this town is the following: when a ship comes into port, it is boarded from *sanbuqs*, that is to say, little boats. Each *sanbuq* carries a crowd of young men, each carrying a covered dish, containing food. Each one of them presents his dish to a merchant on board, and calls out: "This man is my guest." And his fellows do the same. Not one of the merchants disembarks except to go to the house of his host among the young men, save frequent visitors to the country. In such a case they go where they like. When a merchant has settled in his host's house, the latter sells for him what he has brought and makes his purchases for him. Buying anything from a merchant below its market price or selling him anything except in his host's presence is disapproved of by the people of Mogadishu. They find it of advantage to keep to this rule.

THE SULTAN OF KILWA

When I arrived, the Sultan was Abu al-Muzaffar Hasan surnamed Abu al-Mawahib [the Father of Gifts] on account of his numerous charitable gifts. He frequently makes raids into the Zanj country, attacks them and carries off booty, of which he reserves a fifth, using it in the manner prescribed by the Koran. That reserved for the kinsfolk of the Prophet is kept separate in the Treasury, and, when Sharifs come to visit him, he gives it them. They come to him from Iraq, the Hijaz, and other countries. I found several Sharifs from the Hijaz at his court, among them Muhammad ibn Jammaz, Mansur ibn Labida ibn Abi Nami and Muhamma ibn Shumaila ibn Abi Nami. At Mogadishu I saw Tabl ibn Kubaish ibn Jammaz, who also wished to visit him. This Sultan is very humble: he sits and eats with beggars, and venerates holy men and descendants of the Prophet.

G. S. P. Freeman-Grenville, *The East African Coast: Select Documents*, 2nd ed. (London: Rex Collings, 1975), pp. 27–28, 31–32.

Urdu, and many other languages of Islamic peoples that are totally unrelated to Arabic or even the Semitic language family.

The hybrid nature of the Swahili language mirrors the hybrid character of Swahili culture, with its distinctive combination of African and Islamic features. Current historical theory suggests that like the language, the origin of Swahili culture is basically African with a large contribution by Arab, Persian, and other extra-African elements. It is nonetheless not wrong to suggest that this admixture created a new consciousness and identity. Today, the many coastal peoples who share the Swahili language and culture are of mixed ethnic character, joining African to Persian, Indian, Arab, and other ancestry, and it has ever been a source of pride for many older Swahili families to claim descent from illustrious Persian or Arab lineages of importance in Islamic history.

Swahili language and culture may have developed first and most influentially in the northern towns of Manda, Lamu, and Mombasa, then further south along the coast to Kilwa. They remained localized

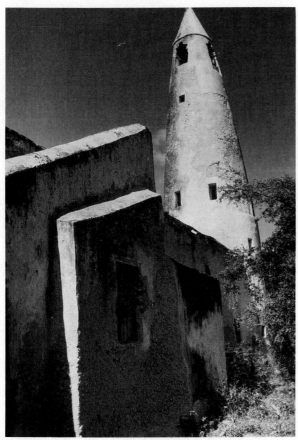

The Friday mosque at Shela on the southeastern coast of Lamu Island, Kenya. This fine example of late Swahili architecture dates to the early nineteenth century. It is the only surviving pre-twentieth century mosque in the region with a minaret. Swahili settlements on Lamu Island date to about the fifteenth century and enjoyed a period of substantial wealth that reached its zenith in the nineteenth century. [Peter Greenberg]

were impressive. Beginning in the twelfth century, we can trace the development of stone-building techniques (first using coral blocks on red clay, later lime mortar). These techniques were used for mosques, fortress-palaces, harbor fortifications, fancy private homes, and commercial buildings alike; all have their own distinctive cast that bespeaks a creative joining of African and Arabo-Persian elements.

Local states had their administrative centers in these trading towns. Today, historians are recognizing that their ruling dynasties were probably African in origin, with an admixture of Arab or Persian blood from immigrants. In these coastal centers, an advanced and cosmopolitan level of culture reigned; by comparison, the majority of the populace in the small villages lived in mud and sometimes stone houses. Most of the latter earned their living by either farming or fishing, the two basic occupations of the coastal peoples besides trade. Society seems to have consisted of three principal groups: the local nobility, the commoners, and resident foreigners engaged in local commerce. Slaves constituted a fourth class of people, although the extent of their local use (as opposed to their sale) is disputed.

The flourishing trade of the coastal centers was fed mainly by the export of inland ivory. Other exports included gold, slaves, turtle shells, ambergris, leopard skins, pearls, fish, sandalwood, ebony, and local cotton cloth. The chief imports were cloth, porcelain, glassware, china, glass beads, and glazed pottery. Certain exports tended to dominate particular ports: cloth, sandalwood, ebony, and ivory at Mogadishu; ivory at Manda; or gold at Kilwa (brought up the coast from still farther south, at the port of Sofala). Cowrie shells were a common medium of payment in the inland trade, but coins minted at Mogadishu and Kilwa from the fourteenth century were increasingly used in the major trading centers. The gold trade seems to have become important only in the fifteenth century.

East Africa and the Omanis of Zanzibar

The decline of the original Swahili civilization in the sixteenth century can be attributed primarily to the loss of much of the trade that had originally made everything possible. The arrival of the Portuguese, and their subsequent destruction of both the old oceanic trade patterns (in particular, the Islamic commercial monopoly) and the main Islamic city-states along the eastern coast, seems to be the chief cause.

largely along the coast until very recent times. Likewise, the spread of Islam was largely limited to the coastal civilization and did not reach inland. The one possible exception is the Zambezi valley, where Muslim traders did penetrate some distance upriver (in contrast to the lands farther north, in the Horn of Africa, where Islamic kingdoms developed in the Somali hinterland as well as on the coast).

The height of Swahili civilization came during the fourteenth and fifteenth centuries. Its centers were the harbor trading towns, most of which were on coastal islands or easily defended peninsulas. To these ports came merchants from abroad and from the African hinterlands, some to settle and stay. These towns

However, some scholars point also to decreases in rainfall or invasions of Zimba peoples from inland regions as contributing factors in the decline.

Be that as it may, there is no question that the Portuguese intended to gain control of the southern-seas trade for their own purposes (see Chapter 24). In Africa, as everywhere, they saw the "Moors" as their implacable enemies. Many Portuguese viewed the struggle to wrest the commerce and the seaport commercial centers of Africa and Asia from Islamic control not only in terms of commercial and nationalist warfare but also as a Christian crusade.

The initial Portuguese victories along the African coast led to the submission of many small Islamic coastal ports and states. However, there was no concerted effort to spread Christianity beyond the fortified settlements established in places like Sofala, Zanzibar, Mozambique, and Mombasa. Thus, the long-term cultural and religious consequences of the Portuguese presence were slight.

What the Portuguese did bring to the east coast, however, was widespread economic decline. When the inland Africans refused to cooperate with them, the formerly heavy gold trade up the Zambezi from Sofala dried up. The militant Portuguese presence also sharply reduced Muslim coastal shipping from India and Arabia. Ottoman efforts in the late sixteenth century failed to defeat the Portuguese, but after 1660, the strong eastern Arabian state of Oman raided the African coast with impunity. In 1698, the Omanis took Mombasa and ejected the Portuguese everywhere north of Mozambique.

The Omanis rapidly shifted their home base to Zanzibar, which became a new and major power center in East Africa. Their control of the ivory and slave trade along the coast seems to have fueled a substantial recovery of east coast prosperity by the later eighteenth century. Zanzibar itself benefited from the introduction of clove cultivation from Mauritius in the 1830s. Cloves became its staple export thereafter. (The clove plantations would become also the chief market of a new, devastating slave trade, interior to East Africa, that flourished into the late nineteenth century even as the external trade in slaves was crushed.) The domination of the east coast by Omani African sultans, descendants of the earlier invaders, continued with some lapses until 1856. Thereafter, Zanzibar and its holdings on the coast became independent under a separate branch of the same family that ruled in Oman. Zanzibar passed eventually to the British when they, the Germans, and the Italians divided East Africa in the late 1880s. Still, the Islamic imprint on the whole coast has survived until the present.

Southern Africa

Southeastern Africa: "Great Zimbabwe"

At about the same time that the trading centers of the east coast were beginning to flourish, a very different kind of African civilization was enjoying its heyday inland and farther south, in the rocky, savannah-woodland watershed between the Limpopo and Zambezi rivers, in modern southern Zimbabwe. This civilization was a purely African one sited far enough inland never to have felt the impact of Islam. It was founded in the tenth or eleventh century by the ancestors of the Bantu-speaking Shona people, who still inhabit the same general area of southeastern Africa. It seems to have developed into a large and prosperous state between the late thirteenth and the late fifteenth centuries. We know it only through the archaeological remains of an estimated one hundred and fifty settlements in the Zambezi–Limpopo region.

By far the most impressive of these ruins, and the apparent capital of this ancient Shona state, is that known today as "Great Zimbabwe"—a huge, sixty-odd-acre site encompassing two different major building complexes. One—the so-called acropolis—is a series of stone enclosures on a high hill. It overlooks the other, much larger, enclosure, which contains numerous ruins and a large circular tower, all surrounded by a massive wall some thirty-two feet high and in places as much as seventeen feet thick. The acropolis complex may have contained a shrine, whereas the larger enclosure was apparently the royal

EAST AND SOUTHEAST AFRICA	
900–1500	"Great Zimbabwe" civilization
ca. 1200–1400	Development of Bantu Kiswahili language
ca. 1300–1600	Height of Swahili culture
1698	Omani forces take Mombasa, oust Portuguese from East Africa north of the port of Mozambique
1741–1856	Long-lived united sultanate of Oman and Zanzibar

palace and fort. The impressive stonework reflects a wealthy and sophisticated society. The artifacts found at the site include gold and copper ornaments, soapstone carvings, and imported beads, as well as china, glass, and porcelain of Chinese, Syrian, and Persian origins.

The state itself seems to have had some degree of control of the increasing gold trade between more inland areas and the east-coast port of Sofala. Its territory lay to the east and south of substantial gold-mining enterprises that tapped both the alluvial gold of the Zambezi tributaries and the gold-ore deposits that stretched southwest in a broad band below the middle Zambezi. We can speculate that this large settlement must have been the capital city of a prosperous empire and the residence of a ruling elite. Its wider domain was made up mostly of smaller settlements of common folk who lived by subsistence agriculture and cattle raising and whose culture was considerably different from that of the capital.

The reasons for the flowering of the Great Zimbabwe civilization are speculative. Available evidence suggests first a general population growth and increasing economic prosperity in the Zambezi–Limpopo region before A.D. 1500. Even earlier sites further south, such as Mapungubwe, suggest that other large-state entities may have preceded the heyday of Great Zimbabwe proper. The specific impetus for Great Zimbabwe may have been a significant immigration around A.D. 1000 of late-Iron-Age Shona speakers who brought with them mining techniques and/or farming innovations, along with their ancestor cults. Improved farming and animal husbandry could have led to substantial population growth. Another material cause may have been an increase in the gold trade between Sofala and the inland gold mining areas. Great Zimbabwe, functioning as intermediary, could have been the chief beneficiary of this trade. This hypothesis links the flourishing of Zimbabwe to the general flourishing of the East African coast from about the thirteenth century.

These theories are not mutually exclusive, however. Without written or new archaeological sources, we shall likely never know exactly what allowed this impressive civilization to develop and to dominate its region for nearly two hundred years. The reasons for its demise are also obscure. It appears that the northern and southern sectors of the state split up and major populations moved away from the environs of Great Zimbabwe, likely as a result of exhaustion of the farming and grazing land there. The southern successor kingdom was that known as Changamire, a state that survived to become very powerful from the late 1600s until about 1830. The northern successor state, which stretched along the middle and lower course of the Zambezi, was known to the first Portuguese sources as the kingdom ruled by the Mwene Mutapa, or "Master Pillager," the title of its sixteenth-century ruler, Mutota, and his successors.

The Portuguese in Southeastern Africa

As just mentioned, the Portuguese arrival in the first years of the sixteenth century was catastrophic for the

"Great Zimbabwe," so called because it is the most impressive of three hundred such stone ruins in modern Zimbabwe and neighboring countries. These sites give clear evidence of the advanced iron-age mining and cattle-raising culture that flourished in this region between about A.D. 1000 and 1500. The people, thought to have been of Bantu origins, apparently had a highly developed trade in gold and copper with outsiders, including Arabs on the east coast. As yet, all too little is known about this impressive society. [Bettmann Archive]

Fort Jesus at Mombasa, built by the Portuguese as a major stronghold for their domination of the East African coast. [Peter Greenberg]

East African coastal economy. With determination, they destroyed Swahili control of both the inland gold trade and the multifaceted overseas trade. Their chief object was to obtain gold from interior southeastern Africa in the Zambezi region. However, because the gold production of the entire region was small and because they encountered repeated difficulties in trying to control it, the Portuguese derived little lasting profit from the enterprise. When they had problems sustaining the Zambezi gold trade by trying simply to take the place of the Swahili merchants on the coast, the Portuguese established fortified posts up the Zambezi and eventually got involved in the regional politics of the Shona peoples who controlled the region. This tactic proved disastrous for stability in the area and led to ongoing strife between the invaders and the Shona kingdoms. In the 1690s, the Changamire Shona dynasty conquered the northern Shona territory and permanently pushed the Portuguese out of the gold country.

All along the Zambezi, however, a lasting and de-

stabilizing consequence of Portuguese intrusion was the creation of quasi-tribal chiefdoms. These were led by mixed-blood Portuguese landholders, or *prazeros*, who were descended from the first Portuguese estate holders along the Zambezi. These estate holders had obtained and built up huge estate communities. Their descendants eventually formed a few clanlike groups of mixed-blood members (from unions with Africans, Indian immigrants, or other estate families). By the end of the eighteenth century, they controlled vast land holdings, commanded military troops (often made up largely of slaves), and were a disruptive force in the region, because they were too strong for either the Portuguese or the regional African rulers to control. They serve, however, as a reminder of how diverse the peoples of modern Africa are.

South Africa: The Cape Colony

In South Africa, the Dutch planted the first European colonials almost inadvertently. Yet, the consequences of their action were to be far graver and farther reaching than almost any other European incursion onto African soil. The first Cape settlement was built in 1652 by the Dutch East India Company simply to provide a resupply point and way station for Dutch vessels on their way back and forth between Holland and the East Indies. Despite original Company intentions, the support station grew gradually into what became by century's end a settler community larger than the Company station itself (the population of the colony in 1662, including slaves, was 392; by 1714, it had reached 3,878).[11] These settlers were the forebears of the Afrikaners of modern South Africa.

Once the Company station became a settlers' colony as well, many of the less powerful Khoikhoi people of the region were gradually incorporated into the new colonial economy. The local Khoikhoi (see Chapter 8) were almost exclusively pastoralists; they had neither traditions of strong political organization nor an economic base beyond their herds. At first, they bartered livestock freely to Dutch ships and then to the Company settlement for iron, copper, and tobacco. However, as Company employees were released from service, they sought to establish farms and become suppliers of the Cape station. Initially, they looked to the rich soils of the southwestern Cape and soon began to displace the Khoikhoi there. Conflicts and even armed struggle ensued; the results

[11] R. Elphick and H. Giliomee, *The Shaping of South African Society, 1652–1820* (Cape Town: Longman, 1979), p. 4.

were the consolidation of European landholdings and a breakdown of Khoikhoi unity and, eventually, society itself. Dutch military success led to even greater Dutch control of the Khoikhoi by the 1670s. Treated as free persons, many Khoikhoi drifted into the service of the Company and individual Europeans, so that as a group they became the chief source of wage labor for the colonials—labor in increasingly greater demand as the colony's size and economy grew.

The other way that the colony met its labor need was through the importation of large numbers of slaves to the colony. Coming from all along the southern-seas trade routes, including India, East Africa, and Madagascar, these slaves made possible a profitable agricultural industry as well as a comfortable domestic existence for the European colonists. The slave institution set the tone for relations between the emergent, and ostensibly "white," Afrikaner population and the "coloreds" of any race, free or not (all of whom could eventually be easily identified with slave peoples in the colony).

After the first settlers spread out around the Company station, nomadic white livestock farmers, or *Trekboers*, moved more widely afield, leaving the richer, but limited, farming lands of the coastal peninsula for the drier tableland farther inland. There they contested still wider groups of Khoikhoi cattle herders for the best grazing lands. To this end, they developed military techniques—most notably the "commando," a collective civilian punitive raid—to secure their way of life by force where necessary. Again, the Khoikhoi were the losers. By the end of the seventeenth century, they were stripped almost completely of their own pasturages; most of their chiefdoms were shattered in the warfare; and their way of life was destroyed. More and more Khoikhoi took up employment in the colonial economy, now among the Trekboers as well as the settled colonists. Others moved north to join with other refugees from the Cape society (e.g., slaves, mixed-bloods, and some freedmen) to form raiding bands operating along the frontiers of Trekboer territory close to the Orange River. The dis-

integration of Khoikhoi society continued apace in the eighteenth century, fueled most sharply by three devastating epidemics of smallpox, a European import against which this previously isolated group had virtually no immunity.

The Cape society in this period was thus a diverse one. The Dutch officials of the Company (including imported Dutch Reformed ministers), the emerging Afrikaners (both settled colonists and Trekboers), the Khoikhoi, and the slaves of diverse nationality played differing roles in the emerging new society radiating from Capetown. Intermarriage and cohabitation of masters and slaves added to the complexity of the emerging society, despite laws designed to keep such mixing in check. Accommodation of the nonwhite minority groups within the Cape society went on apace; the slow emergence of *Afrikaans*, a new vernacular language of the colonial society, shows that the Dutch immigrants themselves were also subject to acculturation processes. By the time of English domination after 1795, the social and political foundations—and the bases of the *Apartheid* doctrine—of modern South Africa were firmly laid.

Africa, 1000–1800, in World Perspective

Developments in African history from 1000 to 1800 varied markedly by region. Along the southern shores of the Mediterranean, the key new factor was the Ottoman Turks' imperial expansion into Egypt and North Africa and their long hegemony in the Mediterranean. The influence of Islam reached across the Sahara from North Africa and the Middle East to the Sudan, where Muslim conversion played a growing social and political role, especially among the ruling elites. The Islamic tradition provided a common thread of experience and a shared arena of expression for at least some classes and groups in societies spread over a vast area from Egypt to Senegambia. At the same time, most Africans from the Sahara south clung largely to their older traditions. In central and southern Africa, except along the east coast, and in the West African forests there was little or no evidence of an Islamic presence beyond individual Muslims involved in trade. On the east coast, however, the Muslim religion played an important role in the development of the distinctive Swahili culture and language, and Islamic traders linked the region to India, China, and the Indies.

Along the Atlantic and Indian Ocean coasts of Africa, the key new development of the fifteenth century was the appearance of ships of the newly potent nations of Christian Europe and the traders and missionaries they carried. First the Portuguese, and later the Dutch, Spaniards, and other Europeans, came by sea in search of commerce and eventually spheres of influence. If the European voyages of discovery of the fifteenth and sixteenth centuries were portentous for the world in general, they were especially so for Africa, presaging the continent's involvement in a new and expanding global trading system dominated by Europeans. This system generally exploited rather than profited African development, as the infamous Atlantic slave trade and the South African experience most vividly illustrate.

Suggested Readings

J. ABUN-NASR, *A History of the Maghrib in the Islamic Period* (1987). The most recent North African survey. Pages 59–247 are relevant to this chapter.

D. BIRMINGHAM, *Central Africa to 1870* (1981). Chapters from the *Cambridge History of Africa* that give a brief and lucid overview of developments in this region.

P. BOHANNAN and P. CURTIN, *Africa and Africans,* rev. ed. (1971). Very accessible, topical approach to diverse aspects of African history, culture, society, politics, and economic institutions.

M. CRATON, ed., *Roots and Branches: Current Directions in Slave Studies* (1979). Diverse articles by scholars such as Curtin and Lovejoy; note especially those on the European plantation system by S. M. Greenfield.

P. D. CURTIN, *The Atlantic Slave Trade: A Census* (1969). Still a basic work, and useful for an overview of the trade, even though figures in many areas have since been refined or amended by other work.

P. D. CURTIN, *Economic Change in Precolonial Africa: Senegambia on the Eve of the Slave Trade* (1975). The chapter on slave trading is an illuminating treatment of the topic with respect to one area of Africa.

P. D. CURTIN, S. FEIERMANN, L. THOMPSON, and J. VANSINA, *African History* (1978). An older, but masterly survey. The relevant portions are chaps. 6–9.

R. ELPHICK, *Kraal and Castle: Khoikhoi and the Founding of White South Africa* (1977). An incisive, informative interpretation of the history of the Khoikhoi and their fateful interaction with European colonization.

R. ELPHICK and H. GILIOMEE, *The Shaping of South African Society, 1652–1820* (1979). A superb, synthetic history of this crucial period.

J. D. FAGE, *A History of Africa* (1978). Still a readable survey history.

H. A. GEMERY and J. S. HOGENDORN, eds., *The Uncommon Market: Essays in the Economic History of the Atlantic Slave Trade* (1979). Useful statistics on trans-Saharan and particular African regions of the Atlantic slave trade.

M. HISKETT, *The Development of Islam in West Africa* (1984). The standard survey study of the subject. Of the relevant sections (chaps. 1–10, 12, 15), that on Hausaland, which is treated only in passing in this text, is noteworthy.

R. W. JULY, *A History of the African People,* 3rd ed. (1980). Chapters 3–6 treat Africa before about 1800 area by area; chap. 7 deals with "The Coming of Europe."

R. W. JULY, *Precolonial Africa: An Economic and Social History* (1975). Chapter 10 gives an interesting overall picture of slaving in African history.

I. M. LEWIS, ed., *Islam in Tropical Africa* (1966), pp. 4–96. Lewis's introduction to this volume is one of the best brief summaries of the role of Islam in West Africa and the Sudan.

P. MANNING, *Slavery and African Life: Occidental, Oriental, and African Slave Trades* (1990). An admirably concise yet probing and careful economic-historical synthesis of the evidence, with multiple tables and statistics to supplement the magisterial analysis. An indispensable attempt at presenting the "big picture" of African slavery.

D. T. NIANI, ed. *Africa from the Twelfth to the Sixteenth Century,* UNESCO General History of Africa, vol. IV (1984). Many survey articles cover the various regions and major states of Africa in the centuries noted in the title.

R. OLIVER, *The African Experience* (1991). A masterly, balanced, and engaging sweep through African history, offering outstanding syntheses and summaries of the results and implications of recent research.

J. A. RAWLEY, *The Transatlantic Slave Trade: A History* (1981). Impressively documented, detailed, and well-presented survey history of the Atlantic trade; little focus on African dimensions.

A. F. C. RYDER, *Benin and the Europeans: 1485–1897* (1969). A basic study.

JOHN K. THORNTON, *The Kingdom of Kongo: Civil War and Transition, 1641–1718* (1983). A detailed and perceptive analysis for those who wish to delve into Kongo state and society in the seventeenth century.

M. WILSON and L. THOMPSON, eds., *The Oxford History of South Africa,* Vol. I., *South Africa to 1870* (1969). Relatively detailed, if occasionally dated, treatment of the region.

Chinese general. One of the guardian figures along the road to the Ming tombs near Nanking. [Bettmann Archive]

Index

Awdaghast, 248, 557
Awrangzeb, 735, 737, 738–739
Ayacucho, Battle of, 817
Ayala, Plan of, 972, 973
Aybak, 458
Ayodhya, 218
Ayyubids, 457, 554
Azerbaijan, 462, 727, 728, 729, 1186
Azhar mosque, 457
Aztecs, 38, 686, 693, 695, 696–697

Babur, 729, 739
Babylon, 6, 7–8, 11, 17, 18, 66, 68, 131, 133, 209, 211, 346
Babylonian captivity, 68, 488
Babylonian Captivity of the Church (Luther), 522
Babylonian Exile, 211
Bacchus, 157
Bacon, Francis, 754–755, 904
Bactria, 140, 222, 225, 344
Baden, Max of, 1088
Badoglio, Pietro, 1144
Baganda, 1006
Baghdad, 308, 371, 374, 375, 378, 453, 456, 458, 459, 460, 903
Bahmanids, 466, 735
Bahrain, 22, 729
Bakri, al-, 556, 557
Bakufu, 329, 330, 549
  Ashikaga, 332–333, 601
  Kamakura, 329, 331–332, 333, 446
  Tokugawa, 607, 609, 610, 612–614, 1037–1039, 1041
Baldwin, Stanley, 1100
Balearic Islands, 152
Balfour Declaration, 1089, 1202
Balkans, 190, 196, 464, 724
  annexation of Bosnia, 1076
  outbreak of World War I, 1079–1080
  Russia and, 1073
  Wars, 1073, 1077, 1078
  and World War II settlement, 1153
Baltic states, 1090, 1092, 1094, 1135, 1137, 1185–1186
Baltimore, Lord, 712
Baluchistan Mountains, 18, 19
Bambuhu, 248
Banalities, 433, 666
Bangladesh, 1208, 1219
Banna, al-, Hasan, 1003
Bantu, 250–251, 253, 568, 576, 1004, 1009
Baptism, 188
Barbarians, Rome and, 163, 181, 190–191, 196, 201, 203
Basel
  Council of, 489–490, 523
  Treaty of, 793
Bashŏ, 615–616
Basil the Great, 395
Basra, 369, 371
Bastille, Fall of, 781–783
Baths, Roman, 184
Batista, Fulgencio, 1212
Battles. *See under specific battles, e.g.* Bulge, Battle of
Batu Khan, 444
Bavaria, 398, 414, 637
Baybars, 458
Bay of Bengal, 19
Beaverbrook, Lord, 1149
Becquerel, Henri, 945
Belgian Congo. *See* Zaire
Belgium, 397, 400, 405, 536, 635n, 789, 793, 805, 923, 1071
  Common Market, 1172
  NATO, 1163

in World War I, 1081
in World War II, 1137, 1145
Belgrade, 727
Bell, The, 859
Bell, Alexander Graham, 904
Bello, Muhammad, 1006
Benedict, Saint, 395, 403, 415
Benedictines, 395, 415
Benedict XIII, Pope, 489
Benefices, 398, 408, 409
Benelux countries, 1172
Beneš, Eduard, 1162
Bengal, 737, 988
Benin, 552, 566–567, 575, 1006
Benin City, 567
Bentinck, William, 987
Benue River, 250
Berbers, 375, 376, 456, 458
  Almoravids and, 454, 557
  Islam and, 368–369, 555
  in Morocco, 554, 563
  Taureg, 562, 565
Berchtold, Leopold, 1079
Bergson, Henri, 948
Beria, Lavrenty, 1179
Bering Sea, 4, 37, 690
Berke, 461
Berlin, 1090, 1145, 1166
  Blockade, 1162–1163
  Congress of, 1073
  Decrees, 798, 799
  Wall, 1158, 1167, 1181, 1189
Bern, 526
Bernard of Clairvaux, 421
Bernstein, Eduard, 926–927
Berry, Jean, Duke of, 485
Bessarabia, 1092, 1135
Bessus, 132
Bethmann-Hollweg, Theobald von, 1079, 1080, 1081
Beyond Good and Evil (Nietzsche), 947
Bhagavad Gita, 221, 354, 356
Bhakti, 354, 469, 470, 738
Bharhut, 220
Bhutto, Benazir, 1209
Bible
  Complutension Polygot, 516
  Copernican theory and, 753
  Erasmus' translation, 515
  Hebrew, 67–68, 71–72
  historical scholarship and, 939
  Luther's translation, 522
  Vulgate, 499
Bihzad, 731
Bilal, 559
Bill of Rights
  England, 632
  United States, 717, 866, 868
Bimbisara, 214
Bindusara, 215, 217
Birth control, 509
Birth of Tragedy (Nietzsche), 947
Biruni, al-, 459, 467
Bishop of Rome, 395, 396
Bishops, 394, 402, 408–409, 416–417
Bismarck, Otto von, 844, 851, 852–853, 926, 940–941, 1011, 1066, 1071, 1073, 1074, 1075
Black Death, 430, 434, 458, 477, 479, 482–486, 503
Black Hand, 1079
Black Sea, 94, 193, 464, 772, 997
"Bleeding Kansas," 878
Blenheim, Battle of, 638
Blitzkrieg, 1140, 1147
Bloch, Marc, 433
Blücher, Field Marshal von, 807
Boccaccio, Giovanni, 482, 483, 496–497
Bodhidharma, 238, 302

Bodhisattvas, 219–220, 354–355, 357
Boeotia, 109, 115, 122, 128
Boers, Great Trek of, 1005–1006, 1009
Boer War, 898
Boethius, 429
Bogotá, 817
Bohemia, 645, 667, 767, 836, 858
Boleyn, Anne, 530, 531, 532
Bolivar, Simón, 816–817
Bolivia, 38, 695, 813, 817, 966
Bologna
  Concordat of, 505
  university in, 426–427
Bolsheviks, 889, 927–929, 1086–1087
Bonaparte, Jerome, 799
Bonaparte, Joseph, 800
Bonaparte, Louis Napoleon. *See* Napoleon III
Bonaparte, Napoleon. *See* Napoleon I
Boniface, Saint, 398
Boniface VIII, Pope, 486–487
Book of Changes, The (Confucian), 51
Book of Common Prayer, 532, 628
Book of History, The (Confucian), 51
Book of Poetry, The (Confucian), 51–52
Book of Rites, The (Confucian), 52
Book of Sentences, 436
Book of the Courtier (Castiglione), 497–498
Book of the Dead, 17
Bordeaux, 853
Borgia, Cesare, 504
Borgia family, 504
Bornu, 250, 565
Borodin, Michael, 1032
Borodino, Battle of, 803
Bosnia, 1073
  Austrian annexation of, 1076
  in civil war, 1191
Bosnians, in Habsburg Empire, 858
Bosphorus, 192–193, 345, 772
Bossuet, Jacques Benigne, 633–634
Boston Massacre, 715–716
Bosworth Field, Battle of, 492
Botha, President, 1201
Botswana, 250, 1201
Boulton, Matthew, 675
Bourbons, 533, 534–535, 632–638, 803, 813, 824, 854. *See also specific names*
Bourgeoisie, 435, 679
Bouvines, Battle of, 440, 441, 443, 445
Boxer Rebellion, 1026–1027
Boyars, 650, 651
Boyle, Robert, 548
Brahe, Tycho, 751–752
Brahman, 58, 59–60, 354, 470
Brahmanas, 27, 29
Brahman class, 26, 27, 29–30, 221, 353
Brahmanic age, 27, 28, 29
Brainwashing, 1220
Bramho Samaj, 990
Brandenburg-Prussia, 541, 646
Brandt, Willy, 1167
Brasilia, 981
Brazil, 963, 965
  colonial, 699–700, 814
  democratization in, 1237
  economic development in, 980–981
  independence of, 818–819
  monarchical government in, 975–976, 977
  Paraguayan War, 976
  political instability in, 981
  postwar, 1217
  Republic of, 978–979
  slavery in, 574, 576, 706, 960, 976–977
  under Vargas, 979–981
Brest-Litovsk, Treaty of, 1088, 1094
Bretigny, Peace of, 480
Brezhnev Doctrine, 1188–1189
Brezhnev, Leonid, 1181, 1182

Cyrus I, 209
Cyrus the Great, 209, 213
Czechoslovakia
  democratic revolution in, 1190
  division of, 1192–1193
  formation of, 1092, 1094
  Germany and, 1107, 1132–1133
  Soviet Union and, 1162, 1167
  Warsaw Pact, 1163
Czech Republic, 1193
Czechs, 858

Dacia, 181
Dadu, 738
Dadu Panth, 738
Dahomey, 1006, 1011–1012
Daimyo, 333, 601–602, 607, 611, 612–613, 1037, 1039
Daladier, 1133
D'Alembert, Jean de Rond, 758
Dalton, John, 935
Damascus, 374, 375
Dan Fodio, Usman, 996, 1006, 1007
D'Annunzio, Gabriele, 1101
Dante Alighieri, 496, 750
Danton, Jacques, 789, 791
Danube River, 181, 190, 193, 196, 386, 724, 772, 798
Danzig, 1134
Dar al-Islam, 369
Dardanelles, 723, 1073, 1084, 1162
Darius I, 107, 211, 212, 213
Darius II, 122, 130, 131, 132
Darwin, Charles, 934, 936–937, 938, 952
David, King, 68
David (Michelangelo), 502
Dawes Plan of 1924, 1099, 1106
D-Day, 1145
Debs, Eugene, 888
Debt peonage, 960
Decameron (Boccaccio), 483, 496–497
Deccan, 215, 217, 349, 466, 467, 468, 470, 735, 737
Decembrist Revolt, 820–822, 823
Decet Pontificem Romanum, 522
Decius, 198
Declaration of Independence, 717
Declaration of Indulgence, 631
Declaration of Pillnitz, 786
Declaration of the Rights of Man and Citizen, 783–784, 820
Decolonization, 1169, 1171, 1197, 1198, 1236–1237
De Gaulle, Charles, 1137, 1149, 1169, 1172–1173
Deism, 760
DeKlerk, F.W., 1201–1202, 1238
Delacroix, Eugene, 824
De Legibus (Cicero), 175
Delhi, 468, 989
  slave sultans of, 466, 467
Delian League, 113–114, 115
Delos, 114
Delphi, 96, 99, 100, 105
Demesne, 403, 434
Demeter, 99
Demetrius, 222
Democracy
  Athenian, 106–107, 117–119, 138, 140
  in nineteenth century, 923–924
  postwar, 1236–1239
  in Sumer, 8
Democratic Party, in United States, 890, 896, 1077, 1174, 1176
Democratic Republicans, 869
Democritus of Abdera, 74–75, 80
Demosthenes, 73, 128

Denmark
  Common Market, 1173
  NATO, 1163
  Protestant Reformation in, 525
  Prussia and, 851
  World War II, 1137
Deputies on mission, 790, 791
Derby, Lord, 861
De Rerum Natura (Lucretius), 175
Dervish, 468
Descartes, René, 547, 548
Descent of Man, The (Darwin), 934, 937
Description of the World, A (Polo), 308
Desiderius, King, 399
Dessalines, Jean-Jacques, 814
Developing countries, 1169
Devi, 23
Devolution, War of, 635
Devshirme, 726, 727
Dharma, 61, 64, 66, 217, 220–221, 353
Dharmashastra, 353
Dialogues on the Two Chief Systems of the World (Galileo), 752
Dias, Bartholomew, 689
Diaz, Porfirio, 971–972
Dibbalemi, Mai Dunama, 565
Dictator, in Rome, 148
Diderot, Denis, 748, 758, 759, 766
Diem Ngo Dinh, 1231
Dien Bien Phu, Battle of, 1231
Dingiswayo, 1004
Diocletian, 183, 192, 194, 198, 386
Diodorus of Sicily, 241
Diogenes of Sinope, 77
Dionysian festival, 105, 123, 126
Dionysius I, 77
Dionysius II, 77
Dionysus, 157
Discourse on the Moral Effects of the Arts and Sciences (Rousseau), 764–765
Discourse on the Origin of Inequality (Rousseau), 764–765
Discovery of India, The (Nehru), 1208
Disraeli, Benjamin, 861–862, 896, 1070, 1073
Divine Comedy (Dante), 496, 750
Divine right of kings, 633–634
Diwan, 372
Dmitri, Grand Duke, 444
Dodecanese Islands, 1077
Dögen, 336
Dollar Diplomacy, 964
Domesday Book, 439
Domesticity, cult of, 919
Dominicans, 431, 698, 699
Domitian, 180
Domus, 186
Donation of Constantine, 398–399, 499
Donatus, 428
Don Juan of Austria, 535, 538
Don Quixote (Cervantes), 545
Don River, 1140
Dorians, 89–90
Doryphoros (Polycleitus), 126
Douglas, Stephen A., 878, 879
Dover, Treaty of, 631
Drake, Francis, 538
Dravidian language, 19, 354
Dream of the Red Chamber, The, 601
Dred Scott decision, 878
Dresden, Battle of, 803
Dreyfus Affair, 855–856, 925, 940, 952
Dreyfus, Alfred, 855–856
Druze, 457
Dr. Zhivago (Pasternak), 1179
Dual Alliance, 1074, 1076
Dubček, Alexander, 1167, 1190
DuBois, W.E.B., 884
Dukkha, 64, 66

Duma, in Russia, 931
Dumouriez, General, 789
Dunkirk (Dunkerque), 538
  evacuation of, 1137, 1150
Dürer, Albrecht, 512
Durga, 23, 354
Durham, Earl of, 897
Durkheim, Émile, 951
Durrani, Ahmad Shah, 997
Dutch East India Company, 581–582
Dutch studies, in Japan, 620–621
Dyaus, 28
Dying Gaul, 136

Eannatum, 8
Earth, age of, 3
East Africa, 231, 232, 233, 238, 251–253, 1011
  agricultural revolution, 237
  Islam in, 555, 741
  Omanis in, 579
  Portuguese impact on, 578–579, 580–581
  state-building in, 1006
  Swahili culture in, 576–578
  See also Africa; *specific countries*
East Asia
  languages of, 33
  See also specific countries
Eastern Europe
  agriculture in, 670
  democratization of, 1188–1191, 1238–1239
  preindustrial family in, 660, 661
  Soviet Union and, 1162, 1163, 1165–1166, 1185, 1187–1189, 1236
  See also specific states
East Germany, 1163
  democratic revolution in, 1189
  refugees from, 1167
East India Company, 598, 711, 716, 737, 987–988, 989, 990, 1018
East Prussia, 646, 773, 798
Ebert, Friedrich, 1106
Ebro River, 153
Ecclesiastical History (Eusebius), 200
Eck, John, 520
Eclogues (Vergil), 175
Economic Consequences of the Peace, The (Keynes), 1093
Ecuador, 38, 695, 813, 817
Edessa, 421
Edgerton, Franklin, 61
Edict of Maximum Prices, 194
Edirne, 724
Edison, Thomas, 904
Edo (Africa), 566, 567
Edo (Japan), 607, 609, 611, 612–613, 1037, 1041. *See also* Tokyo
Education, secular versus religious, 939–941
Education Acts, in Britain, 940
Education of the Orator (Quintilian), 497
Edward I of England, 486
Edward III of England, 478–479, 480
Edward IV of England, 492
Edward VI of England, 531–532, 537
Edward the Confessor, 439
Ego, 950
Egypt, 67, 88, 89, 110, 115, 121, 134, 191, 231, 232, 233, 235, 246, 248, 565, 1202, 1203
  ancient
    Alexander the Great, 130
    Cleopatra, 166
    Hellenistic culture in, 135, 140
    Neolithic societies in, 5
    Nile River civilizations in, 12–17
    Persia and, 211
    religion in, 12–13, 15, 16, 66
    See also Kush *below*
  Britain and, 998, 1010, 1070, 1165

Muzzaffar Ali, 720
Mycale, 109
Mycenae, 88
Mycenaeans, 88–90, 91, 109
Mysore, 987
Myths, Sumerian, 11

Nacionalismo, 968
Nadir Shah, 730–731, 737
Naevius, 175
Nagasaki, atomic bombing of, 1058, 1145
Nagy, Imre, 1166, 1189
Nakae Tōju, 618
Namibia, 1199, 1200
  independence of, 1198
Nanak, 735, 737–738
Nan Chao, 289, 290
Nancy, Battle of, 491
Nandas, 214, 215
Nanking, 265, 1021, 1022, 1033, 1034
  Treaty of, 1018
Nantes, Edict of, 535, 636, 637
Napata, 239, 240
Naples, 145, 434, 494, 504, 645, 679
  Revolution of 1820, 812, 813
  unification of Italy, 850
Napoleon I (Napoleon Bonaparte), 793–807, 806–
    807, 815, 997
Napoleon III (Louis Napoleon), 834–835, 849,
    853, 911, 923
Napoleonic code, 796
Napoleonic wars, 794, 796–799, 800–803, 806–
    807, 997
Naqshbandiya, 738
Nara Japan. *See* Japan, Nara/Heian
Narbada River, 349
Narrow Road of Oku, The (Basho), 615–616
Naruhito of Japan, 1225
Naseby, Battle of, 629
Nasir, 458, 460
Nassau, 851–852
Nasser, Gamal Abdel, 1165, 1204
Nathan the Wise (Lessing), 761
National Assembly, France, 781, 782, 834, 854–
    855
National Association for the Advancement of
    Colored People, 884
National Constituent Assembly, France, 781,
    782, 783, 784, 785, 786
National Council of French Women (CNFF), 921
National Farmers Alliance and Industrial Union,
    890
National Industrial Recovery Act (NIRA), 1122–
    1123
Nationalism
  in Africa, 1012–1013, 1199
  in Argentina, 968–969
  French Revolution and, 745
  in nineteenth century, 820, 838
Nationalist China (Kuomintang), 1028, 1031–
    1037, 1056, 1060
National Labor Union, 887
National Studies, in Japan, 619–620
National Union of Women's Suffrage Societies,
    920
Native Americans
  Christianity and, 698–699
  forced removals of, 884
  labor servitude of, 703–704
  population decline, 705–706
  precolonial, 38, 690–696
  wars and warfare, 884–885
Natsume Sōseki, 1051
Natural law, 757
Natural selection, 936–937
Natural Theology, 939
Naxos, 107

Nazca, 39, 695
Nazi Party
  in *Reichstag* elections, 1108, 1109, 1111
  Stormtroopers (SA), 1105, 1108, 1111
  Twenty-Five Points, 1105
  in war years, 1148
  See also Germany, Nazi
Ndongo, 570
Nearchus, 135
Near East
  early civilizations in, 5–18, 38, 48
  Neolithic societies in, 5
  religons of. *See* Christianity; Islam; Judaism
Nebuchadnezzar II, 68
Nefertiti, 15
Nehru, Jawaharlal, 993, 995, 1208, 1209
Nelson, Horatio, 794, 797, 798
Nemea, 96, 99
Neocolonial economy, 965
Neolithic Age, 4–5, 902
  in Africa, 236–237, 246
  in Americas, 37
  in China, 30–31
  in India, 18–19
Neolocalism, 659
Neoplatonists, 752
Neo-Taoism, 264, 267, 269
Nerchinsk, Treaty of, 597
Nero, 180, 188–189
Nerva, 180
Nestorian Christianity, 291, 308, 347, 378, 461
Netherlands, 538, 923, 1137, 1142
  agricultural revolution in, 669, 670
  Calvinism in, 526
  China and, 620–621
  Common Market, 1172
  Congress of Vienna, 805
  decolonization, 1169
  Habsburgs and, 645
  Napoleon and, 803
  NATO, 1163
  political divisions of, 635n
  in slave trade, 573, 574
  in South Africa, 581–582
  in southern-seas trade, 742
  wars and warfare
    England, 631
    France, 635–636, 637, 638, 789
    Spain, 535–537
  See also Holland
Neustria, 398
New Amsterdam, 712
New Atlantis, The, 754–755
Newburn, Battle of, 628
New Carthage, 154
New Deal, 888, 1122–1124
New Economic Policy (NEP), 1115, 1117
New Freedom, 896
New Granada, Viceroyalty of, 813
New Kingdom of Egypt, 14–16
New Life Movement, 1034
New Mexico, 971
Newton, Isaac, 548, 752, 755–756, 760
New York, 712, 868
New Youth, 1030, 1031
New Zealand, 897
Nguni, 1004–1005
Niani, 560
Nicaragua, 1178
  Sandinistas in, 1215–1216, 1238
Nicea, Council of, 199–200, 387
Nicene Creed, 200, 387, 396, 398, 401
Nichiren Buddhism, 336
Nicholas I, Pope, 396
Nicholas I of Russia, 821–822, 858
Nicholas II, Pope, 416
Nicholas II of Russia, 861, 927, 930–931, 1077
Nicholas V, Pope, 499

Nicias, Peace of, 121
Nien Rebellion, 1021–1022
Nietzsche, Friedrich, 939, 946–947
Nigeria, 238, 250, 1006, 1169
Niger-Kongo language, 234, 235, 236, 560
Niger River, 230, 231, 235, 237–238, 246, 248,
    555, 556, 559, 562, 567, 1008
Nightmare (Hsu Hui), 1222
Nikon, Patriarch, 652
Nile River, 5, 12, 230, 231, 232, 233, 234, 238–
    239, 240, 241, 565, 566, 1008
  early civilizations of, 12–17, 48, 89
Nile Valley, 236, 252
Nilo-Saharan language, 234–235, 238, 560
Nimwegen, Peace of, 636, 637
Ninety-five theses, 520
Nineveh, 17, 131
Nine Years' War, 637
Ningpo, 1018
Nirvana, 66, 269, 271, 354
Nixon, Richard, 1168, 1176–1177, 1182, 1215,
    1221, 1222, 1233
Nizam al-Mulk, 460
Nizari Isma'ili "Assassins," 453
Nkrumah, Kwame, 1199
Nobility
  Charter of (Russia), 771
  in eighteenth century, 676–678
  in Middle Ages, 429–430, 490
Nobunaga, Oda, 602–603, 605, 610
Nok, 238, 567
Nō plays, 338–340, 617
Noriega, Manuel, 1178
Normandy, 479, 480
Normans, 406
  Conquest of England, 439, 440, 441
North Africa, 232, 233, 234, 235, 236, 237, 248
  France and, 823, 1009, 1011, 1071
  Islam in, 368–369, 371, 373, 375, 376, 380,
      453, 454, 456, 553–554
  Ottoman rule in, 724
  Vandals in, 386
  in World War II, 1138–1139, 1143
  See also Africa; *specific countries*
North America
  British colonies of, 708, 712, 896–897
  French and Indian War, 710–711
  See also America; Canada; United States
North American Free Trade Agreement, 1218
North Atlantic Treaty Organization (NATO),
    1163, 1171, 1172, 1178, 1194
Northern Society, 821
North, Lord, 716
Norway, 922, 923, 1137, 1163, 1173
Novara, Battle of, 505
Novgorod, 308
Novum Organum (Bacon), 754–755
Nubia, 231, 237, 238–239, 243, 458, 565–566
Nuclear Test Ban Treaty, 1167
Nujoma, Sam, 1198
Nullification Crisis, 870
Numantia, 157
Numidia, 163
Nunneries, 436, 541, 542
Nun Shogun, 331, 332
Nur al-Din, 457, 458
Nuremberg Laws, 1113
Nyamwezi, 1006

Oba, 567
Oberman, Heiko, 477
O'Connell, Daniel, 825
Octavian. *See* Augustus
October Manifesto, 930
Odes (Horace), 176
Odoacer, 386
Odysseus, 91, 92

Sepoy Mutiny (Revolt of 1857), 988, 989, 992
September Massacres, 787, 791
Septimius Severus, 190–191
Serbia, 858
  assassination of Francis Ferdinand, 1079
  Austria and, 1079–1080
  in Balkan Wars, 1073, 1077
  in civil war, 1191–1192
  Slav union and, 1076
Serbo-Croatians, in Habsburg empire, 858
Serfs
  emancipation of, 836, 845, 858–859
  in Middle Ages, 403–404, 407, 426, 432, 433
  in Prussia, 647, 666
  in Russia, 660, 666–667, 858–859
  See also Peasants
Sesshū, 337
Seven Weeks' War, 851
Seven Years' War, 710–712, 718, 766
Seville, 701, 813
Sewer systems, 912, 913
Seymour, Jane, 531
Shafi'i, 380
Shahnama (Firdawsi), 459
Shah-namah, 720
Shahrukh, 463
Shaka, 1004–1005
Shakespeare, William, 166, 492, 545–546
Shakti, 354
Shamans, 303
Shamash, 66
Shang dynasty, 31–34, 49, 51, 255
Shanghai, 1018, 1022
Shangtu, 306, 309
Shankara, 354
Shantung, 1029
Shapur I, 344
Sharif, Nawaz, 1209
Sharifs, 554, 739
Shaw, George Bernard, 925
Shaybani, Muhammad, 739
Shaykhs, 369
Shcharansky, Anatoly, 1182
Shensi, 1034
Shi'a Islam, 373–374, 375, 376, 449, 451, 453–
   454, 456–458, 553, 997, 1207
Shibusawa Eiichi, 1044
Shih K'o, 302
Shingon Buddhism, 328
Shinran, 335–336
Shinto, 274, 317–319, 320, 323, 328, 410, 620,
   1224
Shirakawa, Emperor, 322
Shiva, 23, 221, 354, 470
Shivaji, 737
Shōgun, 328, 333
Shona, 579, 581
Shōwakai Party, 1055
Shūbun, 337
Shudras, 26, 28, 353
Siberia, 302, 1071, 1183
Sicily, 77, 94, 121, 368, 456, 571, 1143
  Hohenstauffens and, 442, 444
  Rome and, 152, 154, 157
  unification of Italy, 850
Siddhartha Gautama. *See* Buddha
Sieyès, Emmanuel, Abbé, 779
Sigismund, Emperor, 489
Sikhs, 735–738, 987, 988, 1208, 1209
Silesia, 645, 646, 649, 709
Silk Road, 260, 347, 1025
Silla, 316, 1025
Simonides of Cous, 100
Sinai Desert, 67, 70
Sinan, 726–727
Sind, 465, 466
Sind Mountains, 19
Sinkiang, 1025

Sioux, 885
Sirhindi, 738
Sistan, 225
Sistine Chapel, 502
Six Articles of 1539, 531
Six Dynasties era, 265, 309
Sixteen Kingdoms, 265
Sixtus IV, Pope, 519
Siyasatnamah (Nizam al-Mulk), 460
Skeptics, 134
Slater, Samuel, 871
Slavery and slave trade
  African, 252, 514, 571–576, 683
    abolition of, 573, 574
    Atlantic passage, 707
    Atlantic system and, 572–573
    in Cape colony, 582
    in Central Africa, 569, 570
    extent of, 573–574
    impact on Africa, 574–576
    internal, 556–557, 571, 574, 575–576, 579
    origins of, 571–572
    sources for, 571, 573
    in West Africa, 567–568
  ancient, 274–276
  in Brazil, 699, 960, 976–977
  Greece and, 92, 104
  Kush and, 243
  in Latin America, 706–709
  Mesopotamia and, 11–12
  in North America, 707, 708–709
  oriental, 571, 572
  plantation system and, 706–709, 717
  prevalence in premodern states, 571
  religious conversion and, 708
  in Renaissance, 502–503
  revolts and, 814
  slave-soldiers, 466, 467, 571, 726, 727
  in United States, 576, 706, 708–709, 899
    abolitionists and, 875, 876, 879
    Emancipation Proclamation, 879
    extension of, 870, 875–876, 878–879
    life of slaves, 874–875
    Southern economy and, 874
Slave Sultans of Delhi, 466, 467
Slepak, Vladimir, 1182
Slovakia, 1193
Slovenia, 1076, 1191
Sluys, Battle of, 479
Smith, Adam, 761–762, 765, 820
Smith, W. H., 908
Smith, William Robertson, 939
Snow, C. P., 946
So, 565
Social contract, 547–548
Social Contract, The (Rousseau), 765
Social Darwinism, 937, 938
Social Democratic party (SPD), in Germany,
   922, 926–927, 1088, 1093, 1108
Social Gospel movement, 891
Socialism, 832
  in Britain, 889, 924, 925
  First International and, 924
  in France, 925–926
  in Germany, 924, 926–927
  in Russia, 927–929
  in United States, 888–889
  See also Marxism
Socialist party, in France, 926
Social Revolutionary Party, in Russia, 927, 930,
   1086, 1087
Social Security Administration, 1123
Society of Jesus. *See* Jesuits
Society of Missionaries of Africa (White
   Fathers), 942
Socrates, 47, 76–77, 126
Sofala, 578, 579, 580
Sogdiana, 225

Sokoto, 565, 1006
Solano López, Francisco, 976
Solferino, Battle of, 849
Solidarity movement, 1188
Solomon, King, 68
Solon, 104–105, 106, 107
Solzhenitsyn, Aleksandr, 1179
Soma, 29
Somalia, 1200
Somaliland, 1012
Somme, Battle of, 1085
Songhai, 561, 562–565
Soninke, 248, 249, 560
Sonni Ali, 562
Sons of Liberty, 713
Sophists, 75–76, 78, 125
Sophocles, 126
Soranus of Ephesus, 438
Sorbon, Robert de, 428
Sorbonne, 428
Sorel, Georges, 951
Soso people, 558
Sōtō sect, of Zen Buddhism, 336
South Africa, 897, 1199
  apartheid in, 582, 1200–1201, 1236
  creation of, 1005–1006
  Dutch East India Company in, 581–582
  end of *apartheid,* 1201–1202, 1238
South America. *See* Latin America
South Carolina, 870, 879
Southern-seas trade, Islam and, 741–742
Southern Society, 821
Soviets, 930, 1087
Soviet Union
  Baltic states and, 1137
  Brezhnev years in, 1182
  collapse of, 1178, 1185–1187, 1207, 1239
  collective leadership in, 1179
  collectivization, 1117–1118, 1180
  Communist Party, 1114, 1116, 1118–1120,
    1179, 1183, 1185, 1186
  democratization of, 1182–1185, 1238, 1239
  dissident movement in, 1182
  Eastern Europe and, 1162, 1163, 1165–1166,
    1185, 1187–1189, 1236
  foreign relations
    Afghanistan, 1207
    Atlantic Charter, 1153
    Britain, 1134–1135
    China, 1032, 1219, 1220, 1222
    Cuba, 1213
    France, 1134–1135
    Germany, 1056, 1135–1136, 1185
    Japan, 1056, 1142, 1145
    Spain, 1132
    United States, 1160–1163, 1166–1169, 1177–
     1178, 1181, 1182
    Vietnam, 1182, 1233
    Warsaw Pact, 1163
    West Germany, 1167
  industrialization of, 1116–1118
  Khrushchev years in, 1179–1181
  New Economic Policy (NEP), 1115, 1117
  purges, 1118–1120, 1179
  religion in, 1152, 1182
    Islam, 1207
  Stalin–Trotsky factions, 1115–1116
  war communism, 1114–1115
  wars and warfare
    Afghanistan, 1168, 1182
    Japan, 1056
    World War II, 1058, 1137, 1138, 1140, 1143,
     1144, 1151–1152, 1153–1155
  See also Russia
Spaak, Paul-Henri, 1172
Spain, 400, 923, 1071
  Carthage and, 152, 153
  Common Market, 1173

Witch hunts, 542–544
Wittenberg, 514, 519, 520
Witte, Sergei, 930
Wolfe, James, 710–711
Wollstonecraft, Mary, 920
Wolof, 568
Wolsey, Cardinal, 530
Women
  in Athens, 119–120
  in China, 260, 262, 286–287, 446
  employment patterns, 915–916
  goddess worship, 23
  industrial workers, 829–832, 872, 916
  Islam and, 367
  in Japan, 332, 1016
  literacy of, 44
  in Middle Ages, 435–437
  middle class, 917–919
  in Nazi Germany, 1113–1114, 1147
  in Paleolithic Age, 4
  preindustrial family economy and, 661–663
  prostitution and, 916–917
  in Rome, 145, 159
  in Sparta, 103
  witch hunts and, 544
  women's rights movement, 877, 906, 919–922
Women's Social and Political Union, 921
Working class, in nineteenth century, 826–828, 912, 916, 922–924
Works and Days (Hesiod), 97, 176
World War I, 898, 1076–1094
  events leading to, 1076–1077
  Japan in, 1052
  outbreak of, 1077–1081
  outcome of, 1088–1089
  peace settlement of, 1089–1094
  Russian Revolution and, 1086
  United States and, 896, 899, 1085
  war strategies in, 1081–1085
World War II, 898, 969, 1136–1147
  bombing raids in, 1144–1145
  Brazil in, 980
  cost of, 1145, 1147
  domestic fronts, 1147–1152
  end of, 1145
  in Europe, 1136–1138, 1143–1144, 1145, 1150
  events leading to, 1127–1136, 1156
  Japan in, 1056, 1058, 1059, 1142–1143
  in North Africa, 1138–1139, 1143

  in Pacific, 1058, 1142–1143, 1145
  peace conferences, 1152–1155
  in Russia, 1138, 1140, 1143, 1144, 1151–1152
Worms, 417
  Concordat of, 418
  Diet of, 522
  Edict of, 523
Wounded Knee, Battle of, 885
Writing
  alphabetic, 43
  Chinese, 32, 340
  cuneiform, 8, 9–10
  development of, 5, 42
  Greek alphabet and, 94
  hieroglyphics, 13
  Japanese, 325
  literacy and, 42–45
Wu, Empress, 284–285
Wu Ti, 259–260, 263, 267, 269
Wycliffe, John, 489

Xenophanes of Colophon, 72
Xenophon, 76
Xerxes, 108, 109, 123, 124

Yahweh, 68, 70, 71
Yalta Conference, 1153–1154
Yama, 29
Yamagata Aritomo, 1042, 1043, 1047, 1050
Yamagata Bantŏ, 621
Yamato court, 274, 410
Yamato state, 315–319
Yamuna River, 27
Yang Kuei Fei, 289
Yangtze Basin, 296, 587
Yangtze River, 30, 36, 257, 284, 587
Yaroslav the Wise, 444
Yathrib, 364, 366. *See also* Medina
Yayoi culture, 314, 315
Yellow River, 5, 30, 35, 255, 256, 263, 284, 295, 296, 306, 309, 594
Yellow River Valley, 30–31
Yellow Turbansm, 264, 269
Yeltsin, Boris, 1185, 1186, 1239
Yemen, 244, 245, 364, 457, 1202
Yenan, 1036
Yi dynasty, 1025

Yin and *yang,* 50, 266, 294
Yokkaichi, 333–334
Yoruba, 566
Yoruba Oyo, 575
Yoshida Shigeru, 1225
Young Plan of 1929, 1099, 1108
"Young Turk" revolution, 999, 1076
Yuan dynasty, 302–309, 461
Yuan Shih-k'ai, 1028, 1029, 1031
Yucatán, 38, 691, 692
Yueh Chih, 225
Yugoslavia, 162
  civil war in, 1191–1192
  ethnic differences in, 1191
  formation of, 1092, 1094, 1191
  in World War II, 1139, 1153
Yunnan, 288, 289, 588, 595

Zacharias, Pope, 398
Zaghawah, 565
Zaibatsu, 1044, 1054, 1060
Zaire, 250, 1169, 1200, 1201
Zaire River, 569
Zama, Battle of, 154
Zambesi River, 230, 231, 232, 238, 579, 580, 581, 1008
Zambesi Valley, 578
Zambia, 1004, 1200
Zanzibar, 251, 576, 579, 1006, 1010–1011
Zapata, Emiliano, 956, 972, 973, 975
Zarathustra (Zoroaster), 82, 207, 208
Zasulich, Vera, 859
Zemstvos, 930
Zen Buddhism, 293, 299, 302, 336–338, 339, 615
Zeno, 74, 135
Zeus, 28, 99, 126
Zia ul-Haqq, 1209
Ziggurat, 11
Zimbabwe, 579–580, 1004, 1071, 1201, 1219
  independence of, 1198
Zimbezi-Limpopo region, 579–580
Zionism, 910, 952–953, 1089, 1202
Zola, Émile, 856
Zoroaster (Zarathustra), 207, 208
Zoroastrianism, 207–209, 213, 222, 226, 279, 291, 343, 344, 346, 349, 365, 376, 466
Zulu, 1005, 1201
Zurich, Reformation in, 523
Zwingli, Ulrich, 523–524